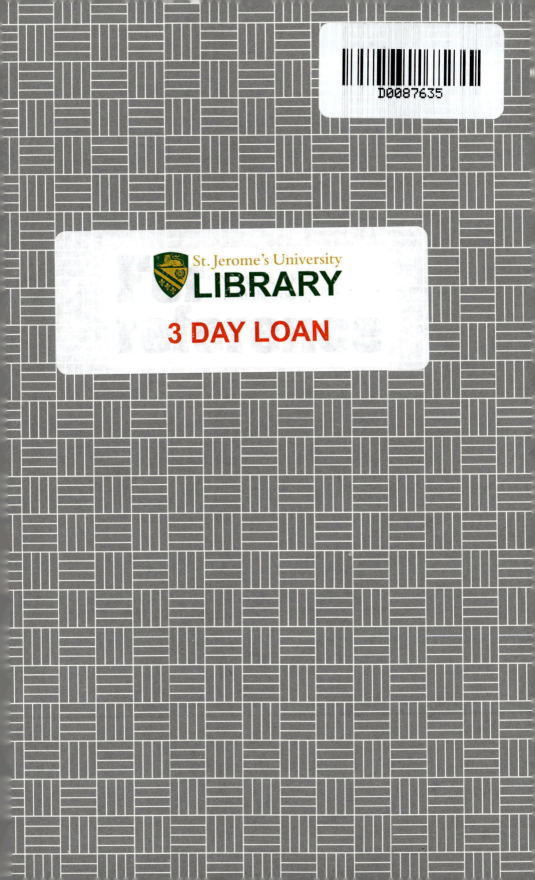

ENCYCLOPEDIA OF LITERATURE AND CRITICISM

ENCYCLOPEDIA OF LITERATURE AND CRITICISM

EDITED BY

Martin Coyle
Peter Garside
Malcolm Kelsall
and
John Peck

 Gale Research Inc. · DETROIT · NEW YORK

First published 1990
by Routledge
11 New Fetter Lane, London EC4P 4EE

Simultaneously published in the USA and Canada by
Gale Research Inc.
835 Penobscot Bldg.,
Detroit, MI 48226–4094

© 1991 Routledge

Phototypeset in 10/12½ Ehrhardt, Linotron 300 by
Input Typesetting Ltd, London
Printed in England by Richard Clays Ltd, St Ives plc

British Library Cataloguing in Publication Data
Encyclopedia of Literature and Criticism
I. Coyle, Martin
801.95

ISBN 0–8103–8331–4

CONTENTS

III. POETRY

IV. DRAMA

V. THE NOVEL

VI. CRITICISM

VII. PRODUCTION AND RECEPTION

VIII. CONTEXTS

IX. PERSPECTIVES

X. AFTERWORD

ACKNOWLEDGEMENTS

PERMISSIONS

1. John Williams: British Poetry Since 1945

'From the Frontier of Writing' in *Haw lantern*
© Seamus Heaney
Published by Faber and Faber, 1987
Used by permission in the US of Farrar, Straus and Giroux, Inc.

'The Badger' in *Fieldwork*
© Seamus Heaney
Published by Faber and Faber, 1979
Used by permission in the US of Farrar, Straus and Giroux, Inc.

'Dockery and Son' and 'Love Again' in *Collected Poems*
© Phillip Larkin
Published by Faber and Faber, 1988

'Saint's Island' in *Flowers and Insects*
© Ted Hughes
Published by Faber and Faber, 1986
Reprinted in the US by permission of Harper and Row

'The Clever Garden'
© George Macbeth
Published by Martin Secker and Warburg

'Rage for Order' in *Poems 1962–1978*
by Derek Mahon
OUP 1979

'Christophorus' by Mary Casey
© Gerard Casey
Enitharnon Press, 1981

'The Welsh Hill Country' in *Selected Poems*
by R. S. Thomas
© Gwydion Thomas
Published by Bloodaxe Books, 1986

Selected Poems by Tony Harrison
© Tony Harrison
Published by Penguin, 1987

Selected Poems by Carol Rumens
© Carol Rumens
Published by Chatto and Windus, 1987

The Memory of War
by James Fenton
Reprinted by permission of Peters Fraser and Dunlop Group Ltd
Published by Penguin Books

Collected Poems by Geoffrey Hill
Reprinted by permission of Andre Deutsch

Ariel by Sylvia Plath
© Ted Hughes
Reprinted by permission
Reprinted in the US by permission of Harper and Row
Published by Faber and Faber, London

2. Thomas Gardner: Contemporary American Poetry

'North American Sequence', 'Meditation at Oyster Bay' and 'The Rose' in
Collected Poems 1966 by Theodore Roetke
Used by permission of Doubleday, a division of Bantam, Doubleday, Dell
Publishing Group Inc.
© 1962 by Beatrice Roetke, Administratrix of the estate
© 1960 (as above)
© 1963 (as above)
respectively.
Published in the US by permission of Faber and Faber

'To a Friend Going Blind' and 'Patience' in *Erosion* by Jorie Graham.
© Princetown University Press, 1983

'At the Fishouses' in *The Complete Poems 1927–1979* by Elizabeth Bishop.
© 1947 by Elizabeth Bishop.
Renewal copyright © by Elisabeth Bishop 1974.

3. Jan Montefiore: Women and the Poetic Tradition

Permissions have been sought for all extracts. However, certain copyright
details had not been made available to Routledge at time of going to press.

PREFACE

The aims and intentions of *Literature and Criticism* are probably best described by an account of the project's history. Our brief from the publisher was for a work of reference, covering the field of literary and critical activity now usually described as 'English' or 'English Literature'. From the earliest stages of planning, however, we felt that what was needed went beyond a descriptive guide to authors and texts on conventional lines. The idea began to take shape of a work that acknowledged both the existence of texts and the surrounding structure of critical debate. We moved towards a notion of a reference work which not only covered English literature, but also dealt with how it has been discussed and how it is being discussed now.

Such a work could not, and should not, aim to be an objective guide. On the contrary, it was agreed that we should consciously set out to engage scholars and critics of different persuasions, with the prospect that their varying perspectives would be reflected in the essays. While subject areas were specified in general outline, authors were invited to question divisions and propose their own modifications. Attention was drawn to some of the implications of our scope (for instance, that essays would need to achieve a balance appropriate to their subject between 'literature' and 'criticism'). We encouraged writers to address recent critical and scholarly issues in their field and to indicate where they felt new ground might be broken.

The Encyclopedia's sections and an approximate order of subjects were drafted at an early stage, so that most contributors wrote with an awareness of the particular context in which their essays would be placed. As new ideas (and some gaps) came to our attention, a few additional titles were commissioned; some local changes in order were also made as opportunities for creating fresh currents and tensions between neighbouring essays became available. The rationale behind the structure, nevertheless, remains largely unchanged. The introductory 'keynote' essays in Section I, lay out the parameters of the debate, and propose issues which reverberate throughout the volume: what do we mean by literature now? is there a present role for criticism? how can we describe the complex and ever-changing relationship between these terms? Sections II–V, in external organization at least, reflect more traditional ways of thinking about 'English' as a subject. The essays in

Section II are patterned according to established ideas of 'period' and literary 'movement', though standard assumptions – including the lines of demarcation dividing cultural eras – are always open to challenge. In the third, fourth and fifth sections topics are assembled under the 'genre' headings of poetry, drama and the novel. Authors, on the other hand, were by no means bound by conventional categorizations, which are often questioned from within sections and at their margins.

Much in the later sections is less familiar to a 'literary guide'. The essays grouped under 'Criticism' (Section VI) show a strong commitment to methodologies which in the last twenty-five years have had a dramatic effect on English studies, transforming critical approaches to literature. Our dedication of a whole section to 'Production and Reception' (Section VII) gives recognition to a fresh academic concern for the material and cultural conditions of writing and reading, an area of activity which has significantly altered conceptions of literary history and, indeed, of the institution of 'English' itself. The following section (VIII) examines literature in the context of the history of ideas and in terms of its relations with the other arts, from painting and music to film. It is in keeping with the idea of debate which informs the Encyclopedia that the 'high seriousness' of the opening essay here should be matched at the end by an essay on pop culture.

A similar sense of challenge is found in Section IX ('Perspectives'), which steps outside the limits generally set by the tradition of Anglo-American criticism and surveys literature in English from the viewpoint of the wider world. The final essay – 'W(h)ither English?' – is in one sense the volume's journey's end, but also provides a new starting-point by questioning the very assumptions on which the Encyclopedia is based. In its punning title the essay seems to sum up not only the vitality of contemporary criticism but also its diverse uncertainties and readiness to find new ways of reading literature.

Different readers will, of course, use this book in different ways. Some will be browsing, others will want to read a specific essay. To assist readers wishing to pursue a field of study in greater detail, authors were asked to add to their essay a list of about twelve books or articles for 'Further Reading'. The reference system used throughout the volume is a version of the 'Harvard' method, modified to suit our requirements. Reference keys within the essays normally give author's name and date of publication in parenthesis – for instance (Kermode, 1979) – which is then expanded into a full citation in 'Further Reading' or (when absent there) in 'Additional Works Cited'. When the date of the first publication is felt to be significant, it is either worked into the text or included within brackets in the key thus: (Burckhardt, [1860] 1944). This means that the edition of Burckhardt cited was published in 1944, but that the title itself first appeared in 1860. Page and volume numbers are given in the normal way within keys.

Many people have contributed to the making of *Literature and Criticism*, not least Jonathan Price of Routledge who first conceived the project. To him, as to our authors, our thanks and gratitude. Thanks are also due to friends who guided us on our way, including our colleagues at Cardiff, Catherine Belsey and Stephen Copley. Finally, we are indebted to Sheila Morgan for her tireless secretarial and administrative assistance.

Martin Coyle, Peter Garside, Malcolm Kelsall, John Peck
University of Wales, Cardiff

I. INTRODUCTION

I

LITERATURE

ROGER FOWLER

1. PRELIMINARY CONSIDERATIONS

In the field of literary studies, about which and within which I am writing, there are many general books with titles such as *What is Literature?* (Jean-Paul Sartre, [1949] 1967), *Theory of Literature* (René Wellek and Austin Warren, [1948] 1963), *Théorie de la littérature* (Tzvetan Todorov, 1965), *Literary Theory: An Introduction* (Terry Eagleton, 1983), *Modern Literary Theory: A Comparative Introduction* (Ann Jefferson and David Robey, 1982). All of these are plain, straightforward, casually worded titles, cast in the unquestioned ordinary discourse of the field. The books themselves may interrogate such expressions (Eagleton's study is in a sense devoted to this critique); however, people in this field know what the phrases mean, have an idea what kind of books such titles indicate when they are encountered on the PN shelves of a university library. But what are the implications of these unobtrusive phrases? The rhetorical question 'What is literature?' takes it for granted that there is such an entity as 'Literature', but implies that its identification or definition is not entirely unproblematic; and Sartre seems to undertake to sort out some of the problems on behalf of his reader. 'Theory of Literature' again presupposes the existence of an entity 'Literature' and promises the possibility of an abstract, systematic account of that entity, as scientists offer theories of similarly abstract, difficult and important matters such as magnetism and photosynthesis. The titles based on the phrase 'literary theory' do not necessarily commit themselves to the existence of 'Literature', but they do imply an activity of theorizing within what I have called, in my own equally casual and ordinary opening expression, 'the field of literary studies'. Theorizing within this area may have various objectives, as we shall see; but the main aim has been to answer the question 'What is Literature?' Discourses addressing this question have traditionally been called 'poetics', more recently 'theory of literature'.

>*Note that in this essay, to designate the idea of 'high, imaginative, creative litera-*

3

ture', the 'honorific' or 'aesthetic' idea of literature, I will always use the following style of reference: 'Literature'. The capital L is to signal that its proponents regard it as something valued and special; the quotation marks are to signal that I do not commit myself to the idea.

I do not think we can take for granted the implications extracted above: namely that there exists an entity 'Literature'; that 'Literature' exists but is difficult to define; that 'Literature' can be pinned down by a theory which will then remove the current problems and make future literary studies plain sailing; that it is only a question of finding the correct theory, the correct set of defining criteria. That is not how theory works, anyway. It is not the case that theory recognizes a pre-existing object or concept and proceeds to formulate the correct (or, at least, a coherent) description of that object. On the contrary, the object or concept is in a very real sense *constructed* by the theory. So 'Literature' is a different entity depending on what theory constructs the concept, whether 'it' is theorized by Roman Jakobson, by Northrop Frye, by Wolfgang Iser, and so on. The books by Eagleton, and by Jefferson and Robey, and the present volume display exactly this process of different theories constructing different entities with the same name 'Literature'. This relativity is entirely healthy: it shows the vitality, creativity and intellectual importance of literary studies.

The mood of quest is poignantly reflected in the title of one modern collection of essays, *In Search of Literary Theory* (Bloomfield, 1972). But the first, and most substantial, contribution to the book, by M. H. Abrams (1972), is a very sensible and positive treatment of theoretical pluralism. Abrams starts with an account of the attack on literary theorizing by philosophers such as Morris Weitz in the 1950s and 1960s (e.g. Weitz, 1964). According to Abrams, theory's critics maintain that questions such as 'What is tragedy?', 'What is poetry?' are 'bogus questions'. They fallaciously presuppose some single essence waiting to be defined. Here Wittgenstein's notion of 'family resemblances' is invoked. If we look at a corpus of poems, we see that some resemble others in some features, others are related by different features, and so on; just as some members of a family may have pointed noses, others may have red hair, others large hands: no one need have all three characteristics for the whole set to be perceived as a family. The generalization 'family' or 'poetry' is not defined by a feature or set of features possessed by all members, but by a complex set of criss-crossing and only partly shared criteria. Abrams parts company with the philosophers by refusing to conclude from this (doubtless correct) position that theory is useless. He shows that different theoreticians have asked different kinds of questions concerning the texts about which they have generalized, and have achieved different, and permanently valuable, insights, constructing between them a set of operative analytic tools. What is

4

wrong with theory is simply the delusion that there exists, waiting to be discovered, some single essence to 'Literature'.

What, then, can we take for granted? What facts and premises are there which will advance theoretical work in literary studies? The answers to these questions will still be relative to one's own approach, and the initial propositions I offer reflect my interests in linguistic criticism, text and discourse analysis, and sociolinguistics.

2. INITIAL PREMISES

(i) Criteria and values of 'Literature' in modern critical discourse

In English criticism, the aesthetic sense of 'Literature' was firmly established only in the nineteenth century, and was closely linked with the nationalistic sense of 'English literature'. In the twentieth century, there have been innumerable aesthetic and critical theories devoted to explaining and developing this sense of the term, applying it to the description of texts, authors, periods, movements. There are also theories which dispute the concept of 'Literature' or which treat 'Literature' as a socio-cultural or political construct, to be described and analysed as such. However, for most students of literature, the concept of 'Literature' is a given idea, something agreed by common sense. In section 5 of this essay I will examine some typical discourses of two major critical schools, New Criticism and Formalism/Structuralism, bringing to the surface some of the usual values and criteria which modern critics attach to the concept of 'Literature'.

(ii) Critical procedures and topics

Like the concept 'Literature', the procedures and interests of critics are open for inspection and for development. Critics are concerned with such matters as myth, genre, metaphor, point of view, language and consciousness, verisimilitude, coherence, which are not necessarily dependent on assumptions about an entity 'Literature'. All of the topics I have just instanced are also of importance to students of texts which would not normally be included in 'Literature'. It is highly likely that progress in understanding these matters would be facilitated if we removed the complication of 'literary' status.

(iii) A literature as a corpus

If we speak of 'English literature' or 'Spanish literature', there is no difficulty about knowing what these expressions refer to, no mystery about the term. English literature is a corpus of past and contemporary texts which can be enumerated: *Caedmon's Hymn* . . . *Piers Plowman* . . . *King Lear* . . . *Absalom and Achitophel* . . . *Tristram Shandy* . . . *In Memoriam* . . . *The Rainbow* . . . *Lucky Jim* . . . *Under Milk Wood* . . . *Midnight's Children* . . . *Whale Nation.* . . . Note that English or Spanish literature is not only a corpus, it is also a canon: a normative set of texts embodying and exemplifying certain values (cf. (v), (vi), below).

(iv) 'Text'

Whatever else some item from the literature might be, or might be categorized as, it is essentially a text. There is a loose sense of 'text' in literary criticism, where it means little more than 'the words on the page' with contextual, historical and other aspects supposedly filtered out. In linguistics, 'text' can be given a specific, and rich, technical definition; and a linguistic definition gives the critic access to a range of clear concepts and tried working procedures which can be fed back into critical practice. A main feature of my treatment of 'text' is that I stress its origin and role in discourses present in society.

(v) Social positioning of a literature

A corpus such as English literature has objective and describable social, cultural, economic and institutional positionings and links. For example, a literature has determinate relationships with the publishing industry, with other media, with education. To expand somewhat on the latter point, people are employed in schools and colleges to teach English literature, and what is taught is publicly examined by inviting comment on a canon of 'set texts'. The teaching of a national literature is a social practice which presumably has some conscious or unconscious ideological function. It is beyond my scope to pursue this analysis, but it is clear that the social and ideological function of 'Literature' could be accessed by analysing the institutions which are involved in its use (see, for example, Eagleton, 1976; Widdowson, 1982; Williams, 1981).

(vi) Ideology in a literature and the ideology of 'Literature'

Because a corpus of texts is handled in relation to social institutions, it is intersubjectively valid for the people in the relevant society, and the most important consequence of this intersubjective validity is that the literature is experienced in terms of the beliefs and values of the society; it is ideologically impregnated by its social positioning. The meanings of texts are constructed by the discourses of critics and teachers who, as we have seen, are socially positioned. Similarly with the abstract category 'Literature' for which theory searches. The need to have a privileged category 'Literature' is probably a condition of modern society, and this need is supplied by the discourses of critics and theoreticians, continuously articulating norms and values which create the imagined general concept.

(vii) 'Literature' as a word

Although 'Literature' as a concept has not been theorized to everyone's agreement, it is a fact that *literature* is an English word with a known etymology, with cognates in most European languages, and with a well documented semantic history. So, below, I will begin my analysis with a synopsis of the changing usage of the term. This analysis leads to some comments on the use of the term in modern critical discourse.

3. THE HISTORY OF THE WORD 'LITERATURE' IN ENGLISH

'Poetics' or 'theory of Literature' is documented as far back as the Greek philosopher Plato (*c.* 427–347 BC). The basic terms to which, for over two thousand years, theoretical discussion was attached, were 'poet' and 'poetry', irrespective of genre or metrical form. The words 'literature', 'littérature', 'letteratura' and 'Literatur' have come to occupy the space of 'poetry' only within the last two centuries (see Wellek, 1970; Williams, 1976). The following two sets of dictionary definitions show to some extent, first, modern usage, and second, the route to that usage:

> **literature.** 1. written material such as poetry, novels, essays, etc., esp. works of imagination characterized by excellence of style and expression and by themes of general or enduring interest. 2. the body of written work of a particular culture or people: *Scandinavian literature.* 3. written or printed matter of a particular type or on a particular subject: *scientific literature; the literature of the violin.* 4. printed material giving a particular type of information: *sales literature.* 5. the art or profession of a writer. 6. *Obsolete.* Learning.
>
> (*Collins Dictionary of the English Language*, 1986)

> **literature.** 1. Acquaintance with 'letters' *or* books; polite or humane learning; literary culture. Now *rare* and *obsolescent*. 2. Literary work or production; the activity or profession of a man of letters; the realm of letters. 3a. Literary productions as a whole; the body of writings produced in a particular country or period, or in the world in general. Now also in a more restricted sense, applied to writing which has claim to consideration on the ground of beauty of form or emotional effect. b. The body of books and writings that treat of a particular subject. c. *colloq.* Printed matter of any kind.
>
> (*Oxford English Dictionary*, Compact Edition, 1971)

In English, the word 'literature' goes back to the fourteenth century; but the aesthetic sense of 'Literature' is basically a usage of the nineteenth and twentieth centuries. From the late Middle ages to the eighteenth century, 'literature' was predominantly an intellectual property of a person: knowledge of letters, books and languages; a property usually applauded (Collins sense 6, OED 1). The OED's quotations include Skelton (1529) 'I know your vertu and your lytterature', Johnson (*Life of Milton*, 1780) 'His literature was unquestionably great. He read all the languages which are considered either as learned or polite.' The early usages of the term refer broadly to all book-learning, without the modern specialization to 'imaginative, creative "Literature"'. But the 'literate' or 'literary' person was privileged, uncommon: necessarily so, since the ability to read, and access to books, were restricted to social and economic élites. And of course the new printed book was itself an élite object. Many of the OED's quotations show the terms 'literature', 'literate' and 'literary' being used as compliments. There is an element of social judgement, explicit in a striking comment by Bradshaw (1513): 'The comyn people . . . whiche without lytterature and good informacyon Ben lyke to brute beestes'. By the eighteenth century, the evaluative overtone was established: Goldsmith (1759) 'literary merit', Johnson (1773) 'literary reputation'.

In the later eighteenth century there developed a second meaning of 'literature': it became not only the man-of-letters' *knowledge* of books, but also the professional writer's occupation, the *production* of books (Collins 5, OED 2). OED quotes Isaac Disraeli (1803): 'Literature, with us, exists independent of patronage or association.' 'Literature' in this sense of the profession of writing was not specialized to the production of any particular kind of book, certainly not necessarily 'high' or 'imaginative' 'Literature'. But the idea of a professional, paid, activity implies some status for the individual's skill, so this usage again has a potential for favourable connotation. This is clear if we quote more fully from Johnson. The opening paragraph of his *Life of Cowley* (1779; one of OED's sources) refers to 'an author whose pregnancy of imagination and elegance of language have deservedly set him high in the ranks of literature'. This author is not in fact the poet Abraham Cowley, but his previous biographer Bishop Thomas Sprat. So here Johnson speaks of 'literature' in the sense of 'writing', not of the modern 'Literature'. But the context of Johnson's own language is suggestive: 'elegance', 'imagination', 'ranks' connote for the modern reader the style of literary criticism or reviewing, and this sort of linguistic context would be receptive to the modern notion of 'Literature', which was to emerge in the next century.

A further semantic shift paved the way. The original sense, book-learning, the knowledge of the literate or polite reader, faded. 'Literature' as profession remained, though 'writer', 'author' and 'writing' became common terms within the area of production in the eighteenth century, and especially in the period of Romanticism with its stress on the activity of the poet. The major change was that the word 'literature' also came to mean a body of writings produced in a particular culture or a particular period, as defined in the first sentence of OED 3. René Wellek has shown how this sense of a national literature became current in Italian, French, German and English in the eighteenth century; he claims that the term 'literature' and its cognates underwent a simultaneous 'nationalization' and 'aesthetization' from about 1760 (Wellek, 1970, pp. 5–8). His quotations do show that the term was beginning to appear in English in the sense of a corpus: George Colman (1761), 'Shakespeare and Milton seem to stand alone, like first rate authors, amid the general wreck of old English Literature'; Johnson (1774), 'what is undeservedly forgotten of our antiquated literature might be revived'. Wordsworth ('Preface to *Lyrical Ballads*', 1800) has the new sense: 'different eras of literature', 'literature and theatrical exhibitions'; Coleridge ('Shakespeare's Judgment Equal to his Genius', ?1808) speaks of 'polite literature'. Peacock (1820) refers straightforwardly to 'Greek and Roman literature' and, more complex, '[Poetry] still exists without rivals in any other department of literature' and 'The history of Herodotus is half a poem: it was written while the whole field of literature belonged to the Muses' (in Adams, 1971, p. 493).

The usages 'national' and 'period' literature are very important for the development towards the aesthetic sense of 'Literature'; from the nineteenth century the national and the aesthetic senses co-exist as if naturally. The point is that a concept of 'national literature' is not value-free; in fact it symbolizes sets of ideas valued or desired (alternatively, but less frequently, disliked): the 'spirit' of a nation or of an age. The grafting of the aesthetic on to the nationalistic in the semantic development of the word 'literature' provides a second level of justification for claims of value.

In the period of English Romanticism, the central aesthetic terms were still 'poetry', 'poem', 'poet' (Wordsworth, Coleridge, Peacock, Shelley). English literature at that time was dominated by the lyric poem, and that was the model the theorists had in mind. But there was occasionally a sense of terminological awkwardness, the realization that 'poetry' was being used in two senses – 'imaginative or creative "Literature"' and 'metrical composition'. The need to distinguish, to treat 'poetry' as a sub-part of some more inclusive category of creative writing, can be sensed in the two last quotations from Peacock. Wordsworth and Coleridge are at times very conscious of the problem: see Coleridge's *Biographia Literaria*, chapter 14, and Wordsworth's grudging footnote to the 'Preface': 'I here use the word *poetry* (though against my own judgement) as opposed to the word *prose*, and synonymous with metrical composition' (in Adams, 1971, p. 437). Both Wordsworth and Coleridge would prefer to use 'poetry' as the general term, opposing it to 'science'; but they are very aware of the problem offered by new non-metrical imaginative writings – Coleridge refers to 'novels and romances' as candidates for poetic status,

9

and adjusts his definition so as to exclude them. Neither theorist uses the word 'literature' in the sense of 'Literature'.

That move comes very late in England, much later than in France. The first English critic of major stature and influence to give the term 'literature' its full modern meaning of 'imaginative Literature' was Matthew Arnold. The concept is clear in 'The Function of Criticism at the Present Time' (1864): as well as collectives such as 'the literature of France and Germany' and 'English literature', we find a free use of phrases such as 'great works of literature or art', 'creative literary genius', 'the creation of a masterwork of literature', which show that a full transition to the aesthetic sense has been made (in Adams, 1971, pp. 582–95). The Platonic and romantic ancestry of Arnold's ideas could be shown, but the discourse is that of modern criticism, enabled by the full 'aesthetization' of the term 'literature'. What remained to be done were the construction of a canon, a list of works which counted as 'Literature'; the formation of a 'common-sense' set of assumptions about those of their characteristics which qualified them as 'art'; and the construction of a technical descriptive terminology.

4. TOWARDS MODERN ENGLISH CRITICISM

The fact that I have explored the semantic history of the *English* word 'literature' in detail, and with reference to writers who are prominent in the canon of eighteenth- and nineteenth-century English literature and criticism, indicates that I am concentrating on a particular tradition of theory and criticism. It is an English tradition, frankly a parochial one; for France, or Germany, or Russia, the history and the possible theoretical positions would be different. A comparative approach might have given the impression that 'Literature' exists universally but is regarded, or realized, differently in different cultures. My position is that 'Literature' cannot be assumed to exist; however, the word 'literature' does (with cognates in other European languages), and this word has been one instrument in a specific theorizing of the category 'Literature' in our culture. If 'Literature' is a cultural category, one has to concentrate on a particular cultural context, and describing it from within is bound to seem parochial. By 'our' culture I mean English-speaking Britain and America, where there is a common economic organization, an integrated publishing and reviewing industry, and very similar educational systems.

Among students and critics of literature in this culture, there is a shared core of assumptions and procedures clustering around the idea of 'Literature': for instance, that literary texts are coherent, are fictional, are of high value; that the text itself should be studied, that the author's intentions are irrelevant, and so on. Such assumptions, I believe, form a basis of taken-for-granted 'common sense' about 'Literature' for most people who have received a literary education in this society. They may sound old-fashioned at the end of the twentieth century, particularly in the context of contemporary approaches described elsewhere in this and other volumes. However, on the evidence of publishers' catalogues, university library stocks, course reading lists, and run-of-the-mill reviewing and academic criticism, such assumptions are still widely current. Even practitioners of alternative approaches (e.g., linguistic, feminist, psychoanalytic, Marxist) have constantly to take notice of more conservative assumptions, so such writing is usually dialectical or argumentative in procedure (for example MacCabe, 1988; Widdowson, 1982). In the next section I will attempt to identify some of the major 'common-sense' ideas about 'Literature' which are current.

This core of common sense was fully formed by about 1940. A full historical account of its development and its cultural context would contain analysis of at least four areas: (1) the incorporation of 'English' in the education system both at university level and in courses for workers; (2) the argument that English literature had an important national and spiritual role for the population, developing Arnold's ideas in the contexts of pessimism about religion and of international war; (3) the fixation of English literature as a normative canon or 'Great Tradition', a canonization in which F. R. Leavis and his followers took the initiative; and (4) the growth and later dominance of the related critical practices known as 'Practical Criticism' and 'New Criticism' under the leadership of I. A. Richards and William Empson in England, and R. P. Warren, Cleanth Brooks, Allen Tate and other conservatives of the American South. These developments have been well discussed and documented by others (see Tillyard, 1958; Palmer, 1965; Eagleton, 1983; Baldick, 1983).

5. CHARACTERISTICS OF 'LITERATURE' IN MODERN CRITICAL DISCOURSE

At the outset I indicated that we cannot assume that there exists some entity 'Literature' waiting for the proper definition. In fact, the plethora of supposed defining criteria, often conflicting, that have been offered over the past two centuries and are still in circulation today suggests that the definition of 'Literature' is a fruitless quest. Many writers have demonstrated the futility of the project (see, for example, Eagleton, 1983, chap. 1; Ellis, 1974, chap. 2; A. Fowler, 1982, chap. 1). 'Literature' is not a single entity which can be defined by listing a fixed set of criteria; it is, rather, a cultural category to which a whole range of characteristics has been attributed. It might be better to make the category 'literary texts' rather than 'Literature', as John M. Ellis does:

> The category of literary texts is not distinguished by defining characteristics but by the characteristic use to which those texts are put by the community.
>
> (1974, p. 50)

and:

> texts are made into literature by the community, not by their authors.
>
> (p. 47)

Alastair Fowler makes a similar point, with a greater precision about terminology:

> Literature should not be regarded as a class at all, but as an aggregate. It is not what literary works have in common, but constitutes, rather, the cultural object of which they are parts.
>
> (1982, p. 3)

The point is that an 'aggregate' is a loose category, not implying any particular internal structure, and an open category, admitting new entrants as the culture determines. Within the culture, writers and readers have a good idea of which are and are not the literary texts, existing and potential; and they know that they have diverse characteristics and are regarded in a multiplicity of different ways by the critics. This knowledge might be called 'literary competence': but it is not a knowledge of some universal property of 'Literature', as the structuralists claim (Culler, 1975, chap. 6); it is a highly complex and relative cultural knowledge, acquired through experience of modes of discourse within 'literary' institutional settings.

Around this aggregate of texts 'Literature', critics weave their own discourse of description, interpretation, evaluation. Critical discourse is again an aggregate, containing a wide diversity of interests and of key terms. It is from the key terms that, in the past, theoreticians have attempted to distil an essence of 'Literature'. It is, however, more logical simply to extract a list of characteristics that have been predicated of texts in the aggregate 'Literature', and understand how their diversity arises.

Depending on their interests, critics emphasize different sets of characteristics in the texts they study, and these emphases are reflected in the characteristic terms of critical discourse. Those critics who are more concerned with narrative genres will foreground 'fiction', those specializing in verse will stress 'expression' or 'verbal patterning'; some will value 'realism', 'particularity', 'verisimilitude', others prefer to think of 'Literature' as conveying abstract, 'universal' 'truths'. Such differences are not surprising, given the complex history of literary theory and of the cultural institution of 'Literature', not to mention the wide spectrum of genres and modes of discourse that 'Literature' is supposed to include. There are even contradictory characteristics alleged of 'Literature'. For example, 'Literature' is by some supposed to promote changes in readers, purging or integrating their emotions, whereas other critics assume that the reader's engagement with a text is a contemplative, dispassionate state which leaves him or her unchanged in practical terms. The latter critic might say that the former is concerned with 'rhetoric', not 'Literature', if it came to the issue. Such contradiction would be damaging if literary theory were a science with some prospect of, in Saussure's expression, defining and delimiting itself. In actuality literary theory is not a science but a field of social activity devoted to discourse about certain canons of texts (plays, novels, sonnets, etc., but not graffiti, shopping lists, newspapers, etc.); criticism is discourse carried on in relation to particular institutional contexts (schools and universities, reviews, publishing houses, but not hospitals, Parliament, sports magazines). Differences of the kinds mentioned, even contradictions, are not theoretically resolvable oppositions so much as divergences of personal experience, cultural and political leaning, as might be expected in an activity which is social rather than scientific.

In this climate of pluralism, a number of characteristics have been recurrently attributed to texts through the long history of theorizing about 'Poetry' or 'Literature'; they still constantly crop up in modern criticism and theory, and have often been invoked as defining criteria. Considered as defining criteria, every one of these features can be rejected as not being necessary-and-sufficient. A characteristic such as 'tight formal organization' may be found in some texts (e.g. sonnets) and not others (novels) among the category 'Literature'; and the same characteristic may be found in texts which are not treated as 'Literature' (menus, lists of football scores). But the refutability of the criteria is of no concern if we regard the quest for a definition of 'Literature' as misplaced effort. As 'attributed characteristics' of texts, rather than as 'criteria for "Literature"', they are of great interest for illuminating the culture's use of certain kinds of texts.

Wellek and Warren (1963, chap. 2) and Abrams (1965) contain accessible reviews of attributed 'literary' properties. Wellek and Warren's survey is comprehensive, although it is sometimes difficult to distinguish between what the authors are claiming and what they are reporting. Despite the existence of newer theoretical works which attack the 'New Critical' approach, Wellek and Warren is still an important textbook on Literature courses, and a rich source of terminology and taken-for-granted distinctions (e.g. between 'intrinsic' and 'extrinsic' criticism). Abrams's encyclopedia article is about theories of poetry, but it is readily applied to 'Literature', since general literary theory has been dominated by poetic theory, and the source authors, from Plato to the romantics, are the same. Abrams has the convenience of arranging theories within a handy framework of classification; he distinguishes (pp. 640–7) four types of 'theory of poetry':

1. mimetic or imitative theories, which pay attention to the relationship between the text and the world it represents;
2. pragmatic theories, which regard the text as 'instrumental toward achieving certain effects in the reader';
3. expressive theories, in which 'the poet moves into the center of the scheme and himself becomes the prime generator of the subject matter, attributes, and values of a poem';
4. objective theories, which focus attention on 'the text itself', minimizing or excluding the other three dimensions.

This was drawn up as a historical scheme, the four types of theory succeeding one another, from Greek antiquity through to the eighteenth century (mimetic yielding to pragmatic), from Romanticism (expressive) through to the twentieth century (objective). In fact, traces of all four theories remain in modern criticism and theory: modern criticism, even 'practical criticism', is by no means just 'objective'. In order to show this modern heterogeneity, the scheme can be adapted to work synchronically. Abrams's scheme isolates four components of 'poetic' communication – in his terms, (1) 'external world'; (2) 'audience'; (3) 'poet'; and (4) 'poem' – and classifies theories according to which component is given most attention (it is of course a matter of degree). The scheme is similar to Jakobson's famous analysis of the six 'constitutive factors in any speech event' designed to identify six functions of language, including the 'poetic function' (1960, p. 353). It will be convenient to substitute some more neutral terms and to change the sequence of exposition: (i) 'world'; (ii) 'writer'; (iii) 'reader'; and (iv) 'text'. We can then group modern critics' proposed or presupposed characteristics of 'Literature' according as they make reference to the four components.

>*I have chosen to use Abrams's scheme, based on very traditional and simple literary categories, because these categories facilitate the linking of my account with its sources. Any attempt at a proper theoretical elucidation of the concepts involved would require a much more sophisticated framework, and one drawn from some other field than existing literary theory so that the metalanguage would not tautologously duplicate the object language. There are a number of promising frameworks available in linguistics, sociolinguistics and text grammar, e.g. Jakobson (1960); Hymes (1972); Halliday (1978); de Beaugrande and Dressler (1981). My own preference is for a developed Hallidayan model.*

A particular 'critical position' is likely to be defined by a cluster of features drawn from more than one of the four areas, but let us consider each separately.

(i) World

Since classical times, it has been held that 'Literature' is a form of discourse which has a special and important relationship with the world, although the nature of that relationship has shifted in different periods of theory. 'Mimetic' theories foreground the notion of 'imitation' of a world, and seem to presuppose a belief in an already existing world. Such a belief is overt only rarely, for example in defence of documentary or naturalist preferences in the novel. More generally, theorists and critics have tended to interpret mimesis as a constructive process in which an appearance of reality is created or a universal interpretation of reality is formed. A typical move is to contrast 'poetic' or 'literary' language with 'scientific' or 'referential' language in regard to the kind of reference the text makes:

> The centre of literary art is obviously to be found in the traditional genres of the lyric, the epic, the drama. In all of them, the reference is to a world of fiction, of imagination. The statements in a novel, in a poem, or in a drama are not literally true; they are not logical propositions. There is a central and important difference between a statement, even in a historical novel or a novel by Balzac which seems to convey 'information' about actual happenings, and the same information appearing in a book of history or sociology.
>
> (Wellek and Warren, 1963, p. 125)

The key terms are 'fiction' and 'imagination', apparently used synonymously. This is only one sense of the term 'imagination', and means the exercise of an inventive or creative power to give the illusion of a possible but not actual world, a world which may even be an enhancement of the 'real world'. This view of poetic invention received its classic formulation in Sir Philip Sidney's *Apologie for Poetrie* (1595): even Wellek and Warren's semantic distinction between fictional and historical statements harks back to Sidney's 'the poet . . . nothing affirmeth, and therefore never lieth'.

If a fictional text does not represent an actual world, it may construct an illusion of one with exceptional vividness, particularity, detail – qualities that are much admired by critics and reviewers today. For example, in the *Sunday Times* 'Books' section, 9 October 1988, apropos three novelists and a poet (Larkin), we find: 'Her descriptive powers alone mark her as a novelist of outstanding ability', 'sparkling powers of description', 'the novel evokes well 1950s social detail', 'a sure and detailed reality'. The illusion of particularity is 'verisimilitude', and most critics are aware that it needs cautious handling. If a text is perceived to cling to a particular social or historical milieu, it becomes difficult to square with the claim of permanence or universality which is often made for literary texts. The usual way out is to modify the argument in the direction of 'typicality': that which is vividly evoked is an exemplar of a species, and therefore amenable to the illustration of universal laws or general truths. This, according to the apologists for 'Literature', is how 'Literature' conveys 'Truth' even though its texts supposedly do not consist of logical propositions with truth-values. The source for this argument is Dr Johnson, and the dialectic of general-in-particular is still a preoccupation of modern critics.

>*The traditional insistence on a sharp distinction between 'fictional' and 'non-fictional' texts as a criterion for 'literary' versus 'non-literary' is one of the most troublesome claims of literary theory. To say that a literary text is 'fictional'. i.e. non-referential, conveying no separately evidenced reality, is to render the text inaccessible to rational analysis (the problem of inaccessibility is compounded by the claim of 'autonomy' – see (iv) below). From the point of view of text-linguistics, the distinction is unnecessary. It would generally be held that all texts are 'constructive' or 'constitu-tive': that representation through language is a constructive process in which a version of a possible world is shaped by the structure and the semiotic properties of the medium. There is of course a philosophical distinction, a distinction of reference, to be drawn between the world created in a novel and the world reported in a newspaper; but as far as textual semantics is concerned, 'create' and 'report' are the same. A news story is just as much a creation of discourse as is a 'literary' short story with imagined characters and narrative etc. (I am referring to news stories about real events, not the fantasies indulged by the tabloids!) Three areas of linguistics are currently being developed which help us understand the constructive nature of discourse in represen-tation. First, there is an approach drawing on cognitive psychology and cognitive semantics which seeks to explain the building of a textual world, an intersubjective structure of concepts and relationships, in terms of 'schemata' ('frames', 'scripts', 'prototypes', etc.) which are fields of knowledge shared by producers and consumers of texts and which are made accessible to the reader through linguistic cues (de Beaugrande and Dressler, 1981, chap. 5). Second, related to the analysis of schemata is the study of 'inferencing': the interpretation of texts in terms of world-knowledge, systems of beliefs about the world (Downes, 1984, chap. 9; Brown and Yule, 1983). Third, functional linguistics (Halliday, 1985) provides analytic tools for studying how the perspective from which a textual world is regarded is shaped by linguistic choices in what Halliday calls the 'ideational' function of language (see Halliday, 1971, 1978; Fowler, 1977, 1986 on 'mind-style').*

(ii) Writer

For literary theory and criticism up to the era of structuralism and post-structuralism, it was of overwhelming importance that the text was written by, or originated with, an identifiable individual. Despite denials in contemporary theory, this preoccupation is still popular today. Where such an individual is not recoverable, we still speak as if he or she existed: 'the *Beowulf* poet'. The writer is accorded great status, and designated with the special term 'author' or 'poet' – the latter used in general theoretical discussions or apologias for 'Literature', regardless of genre or metrical form. The author is an authority, having something permanently valuable to say (cf. 'Truth' above): 'literary' authors have been regarded as philosophers, seers, sages; the strongest claims in this line were made by Shelley (*Defence of Poetry*, 1821):

> But poets ... are not only the authors of language and of music, of the dance, and architecture, and statuary, and painting; they are the institutors of laws, and the founders of civil society, and the inventors of the arts of life, and the teachers who draw into a certain propinquity with the beautiful and the true that partial apprehension of the agencies of the invisible world which is called religion. ... Poets are the unacknowledged legislators of the world.
>
> (in Adams, 1971, p. 500)

They derive these powers either from divine inspiration ('Muses') which transforms their nature, putting them in a 'frenzy' (Shakespeare), a superhuman state in which they perceive and interpret the world with a clarity beyond 'our' powers; or by special gifts or skills. Authors and poets may be credited with unusual quantities of wisdom, insight, or personal qualities such as compassion, generosity, leadership – see Wordsworth, 'a man ... endowed with more lively sensibility, more enthusiasm and tenderness, who has a greater knowledge of human nature, and a more comprehensive soul, than are supposed to be common among mankind' (in Adams, 1971, p. 437). They may be said to be 'creative' or 'imaginative' in the sense of 'inventive', able to think up new possible worlds or fictions. Or there is Coleridge's definition of 'imagination', 'that synthetic and magical power ... [which] reveals itself in the balance or reconciliation of opposite and discordant qualities ... blends and harmonises the natural and the artificial' (in Adams, 1971, p. 471). This idea has had a great influence in directing the New Critics' attention to properties of unity and tension in texts.

As Abrams notes, Romanticism brought the subjectivity of the poet to the centre of critical and theoretical attention. Personal expression became the goal, not only for content, Wordsworth's 'spontaneous overflow of powerful feelings', but also for style, the achievement of a recognizable 'personal voice', a quality still stressed by reviewers and by stylistic analysts though generally played down by academic critics. A review of Philip Larkin's *Collected Poems* gives a typical formulation: 'a poetry of dry, occasionally sour, utterly distinctive plain-speaking, a voice neither simple nor great' (*Sunday Times*, 9 October 1988).

Among poets, T. S. Eliot (1917) dissented from the 'expressive' theory, affirming rather the impersonality of poetic composition: 'The progress of an artist is a continual self-sacrifice, a continual extinction of personality' (in

17

Adams, 1971, p. 785). 'New Criticism' argued that no attention should be given to the person of the author; by the act of writing, writers write themselves out of the texts and neither their personality nor their intentions are relevant to criticism (see Wimsatt, 1954). Attention should rather be given to craftsman-ship at the level of the text, 'the work itself'; and an even more radical banishment of the author is effected in the post-structuralist theory of Barthes and of Foucault (1979). However, a need for, and a high regard for, the 'author' persists in popular thinking about 'Literature' and in reviewing.

>The displacement of the author in post-structuralism is an attack on an ideology of higher knowledge and power, and on the notion of individual ownership of texts and meanings. Granting those arguments, it seems still to be desirable to retain the term 'writer' for someone who engages in the practice of textual production. Writers can then be described in terms of their various cultural, institutional and economic situations: what publishers publish them, what media they use, what associations they belong to, how they are paid and/or otherwise employed. (Similar questions can be asked about readers.) The circumstances of linguistic practice determine the modes of discourse, and therefore the ranges of meaning, available to speakers and writers; this is a commonplace assumption in the ethnography of communication (see, for example, Bauman and Sherzer, 1974; Gumperz and Hymes, 1972), and is implicit in materialist analyses of textual production and consumption (see Eagleton, 1976). A radical claim of linguistics which may help us understand the situation of writer, text and context is that discourses and their significances pre-exist the act of writing; the writer may choose the words and structures, but communication takes place only because they are already impregnated with social meanings. It is in this sense that we can say that writers, like any communicating subjects, are semiotically constituted by their texts, and it is in this way that textual illusions such as the 'implied author' (Booth, 1961) are constructed for the reader.

(iii) Reader

An awareness of and respect for an 'author' who controls the text of the 'work' correlatively implies an inferior and inactive reader, a passive reader who is acted upon by the work. Apologists for 'Literature' take their cue from Horace's dictum that poetry is 'dulce et utile', sweet and useful; 'Literature' has the dual goal to 'delight' and 'instruct' the reader. The key term for the first half of the conjunction is 'pleasure', defined variously: it could be a feeling of the sublime, the relief of a cathartic purging of violent feelings, a harmonization of impulses (Richards, 1924), even just an agreeable feeling of admiration for the poet's skill: in the review of Larkin mentioned above, 'pleasure' is used four times in that sense in quick succession – 'the pleasure of alliteration' and so on. In more 'aesthetic' theories, pleasure is more distanced, contemplative, static: Wellek and Warren call it 'non-acquisitive contemplation' (1963, p. 32).

According to the second half of the Horatian stipulation, 'Literature' has the useful function of instructing the reader; Wellek and Warren express it thus: 'literary language . . . wants to influence the attitudes of the reader, persuade him, and ultimately change him' (1963, p. 23). The problem with this is that 'Literature' becomes hard to distinguish from propaganda and rhetoric. Wellek and Warren struggle with this difficulty for two or three pages; and their qualification that 'Genuine poetry affects us more subtly' (p. 24) hardly solves it, though it does, interestingly, give a feeling of a *covert* ideological purpose in 'Literature'. Not that such a purpose is necessarily covert. There is a quite open, confident, didactic tradition in English and American claims for the moral and the cultivating powers of 'Literature', what I would call a genteel anti-materialist tradition. Its origins lie in Victorian pessimism about religion, science, and 'the progressive vulgarization of English middle-class culture' (Wimsatt and Brooks, 1967, p. 440). The epigram for believers in the moral and civilizing qualities of 'Literature' was provided by Arnold in 1880:

> More and more mankind will discover that we have to turn to poetry to interpret life for us, to console us, to sustain us. Without poetry, our science will appear incomplete; and most of what now passes with us for religion and philosophy will be replaced by poetry.
>
> (in Adams, 1971, p. 596)

'Literature', with other 'art' forms, came to be treated as a cultural and moral force in the twentieth century, institutionalized as canons of books whose textual worlds were to be emulated, teaching humane and dignified values, a counter-balance to philistinism.

A different view of the relationship between 'Literature' and readers is argued by Russian Formalism. In formalism the text is the central focus, but the theory of 'defamiliarization' can be regarded as a psychological theory about reading and perception. Viktor Shklovsky ([1917] 1965) argued that in ordinary life perception is dulled, habituated; art, by making language strange, making reading difficult, forces the reader to discard the veil of common sense and see the world in a new light. The theory of defamiliarization treats the reader as an active and responsible percipient, not as a passive absorber of values or a mere reactor.

>One of the most important moves in recent theory and criticism has been to attribute to the reader a much more prominent and active role than was traditionally allowed: there is for example a school of 'reception theory' giving the reader a central place in the construction of the text (see Holub, 1984). Roland Barthes provides a typically provocative epigram for the belief of a whole range of contemporary approaches: 'in the text, only the reader speaks' (1975, p. 151). The meanings of the text are realized

or constituted by readers, on the basis of their knowledge of the semiotic codes which the culture makes available for texts to signify, and on the basis of their background knowledge of the world, and their beliefs, which allow the realization of references, and inferencing. Now, as with any communication, there is never a complete matching of codes and knowledge between participants; in the case of literary texts, the gap between writer and reader may be very wide because of the practice of preserving and valuing highly texts which are historically and culturally distant from the situation of the modern reader. Literary education provides tutored experience of a range of modes of discourse within a canon, with guidance on the cues (topoi, figures, techniques, conventions) which make significances accessible. (This is not essentially different from the ordinary processes of socialization into varieties of discourse which we experience and learn from through school, work and institutional pressures as we grow up.) If the product is 'literary competence', this is a resource of historically and culturally variable knowledge, and of modes of reading; not an abstract universal knowledge of 'properties of "Literature"' as claimed in structuralist poetics (Culler, 1975).

No amount of literary education, or indeed textual specificity, will completely close the gap between writer and reader, but then, that is a condition of all communication. De Beaugrande and Dressler's treatment of 'informativity' may be relevant here. A text in which everything is transparent to the reader is uninformative and ineffective; but when readers have to bridge a gap, have to work to supply meanings, the text is, paradoxically, informative and effective (de Beaugrande and Dressler, 1981, chap. 7 and passim). This account may have some bearing on the effect of 'defamiliarization'.

(iv) Text

It should be realized that the modern period's theorization of 'Literature' as 'text' took place in the context of the exclusion of mimetic, pragmatic and expressive factors, or at least of their falling into disfavour. Thus the basic strategy of modern textual theory is the drawing of a boundary around the text. The literary text is said to be 'autonomous', existing independently of its origins in history and in the life of an individual writer, not directed to any practical purpose nor indeed affecting the reader in any flesh-and-blood way. Wimsatt and Beardsley's stipulations against intention and effect (Wimsatt, 1954, pp. 3–39) express the modern theorists' desire to limit and exclude, and have been a powerful influence on American and English theory and criticism from the 1950s. Similarly 'the world' is excluded: 'Literature' does not depict a pre-existing reality, but autonomously creates a world of its own – hence the insistence in such textbooks as Wellek and Warren's (1963) on 'fiction', 'imagination', 'invention'. Nor does the literary text have the logical responsibility of science, respect for the truth or falsehood of reference (Richards, 1924). The doctrine of autonomy rejects the relevance of world, writer and reader. The text is self-sufficient, 'has its own life', in Eliot's words: the

metaphor of an organism, following Coleridge, is often appealed to, an integrated structure of parts working to sustain its own life. More generally, the
theory of autonomy is expressed in an inward-looking, centripetal, almost
narcissistic vocabulary: 'the poem itself', 'intrinsic structure', 'intrinsic criticism', 'inherent', 'immanent', 'essential'; also a reflexive rather than transitive
terminology: 'autotelic', 'self-reflexive', 'self-focusing', 'self-referential'.

Saying that a literary text is 'autonomous' does not solve the ontological
puzzle of what kind of entity it is. But the ease with which the pronoun 'it'
can be deployed makes it clear that the literary text is regarded as an *object* of
some kind. In modern criticism the original etymology of the word 'poesis' is
revived: the text is regarded as a made or crafted thing, a *work* of art, an
'artefact'; some metaphorical designations apply to the literary text the concreteness of traditional plastic arts: 'icon', 'urn', 'monument'. It is not surprising that several approaches to poetics stress the materiality of the literary text,
the significance of the medium, generally recognized to be language. Such
approaches may be called 'formalist'; the most self-aware and articulate of
such approaches find their ancestry in the Russian Formalism of the 1920s
(see Hawkes, 1977; Bennett, 1979; Lemon and Reis, 1965), their fulfilment
in the structuralism of the 1960s (Hawkes, 1977; Culler, 1975) and their most
authoritative spokesmen in Viktor Shklovsky ([1917] 1965) Jan Mukařovský
([1932] 1965) and Roman Jakobson (1960). Jakobson pronounced that the
'poetic function of language' (i.e. that property which makes 'Literature' 'literary') consists in 'The set (*Einstellung*) toward the MESSAGE as such, focus
on the message for its own sake. . . . This function, by promoting the palpability
of signs, deepens the fundamental dichotomy of signs and objects' (1960, p.
356). By 'message' Jakobson means the form of the language of the text,
phonological and graphological, syntactic and semantic, rather than the communicated content. The focus on textual form is achieved by a high level of
structuration, parallelism, a concentration of rhetorical techniques thickening
the texture of language, 'promoting the palpability of signs'; in Shklovsky's
terms, 'increasing the difficulty and length of perception' ([1917] 1965, p. 12).
Derek Attridge, analysing the language of Jakobson's own analyses, has shown
that the theory amounts basically to an intense admiration for complexity and
minuteness of structural patterning (Attridge, 1987, p. 24). Linguistic formalism therefore has much in common with the New Criticism's preoccupation
with complexity of rhetorical structure. A related definition of art is provided
by Umberto Eco who draws attention to 'overcoding', the loading of the text
with a maximum of significant adornment (Eco, 1976, pp. 264ff.). Formalism
is a baroque conception of 'Literature' that is bound to privilege the lyric poem
as the supreme exemplar of 'verbal art'.

A further major feature of both formalist and New Critical conceptions of
'Literature' is its hypothesis of a special 'literary language' or 'poetic language'

distinct from 'ordinary language' or 'scientific language'. Wellek and Warren (1963, pp. 22–6) run through the criteria in terms of which Anglo-American theory (largely drawing on the semantic theory of I. A. Richards) distinguishes a literary or poetic use of language: it is non-referential, non-practical, non-casual, and so on. One of Wellek and Warren's reported criteria recalls European or linguistic formalism: 'Poetic language organizes, tightens, the resources of everyday language, and sometimes does even violence to them, in an effort to force us into awareness and attention' (p. 24). Poetic language is deviant from language at large, breaks the phonological, syntactic, semantic and pragmatic rules, by devices aimed to estrange, dehabitualize, our relation to our lives in the way proposed by Shklovsky. The textual devices involved in estrangement have been extensively studied in linguistic stylistics. (For example, Leech, 1969; Cluysenaar, 1976. For further discussion of 'literary language' and 'defamiliarization', see Fowler, 1981 and 1986.)

>*The partnership of formalism and linguistics has shown in what sense texts are objective formal structures, and how we may give substance to the New Critics' idea of 'the words on the page'. Texts are verbal constructs, and may be defined as such, and described, in terms of the categories which have been given sophisticated formulation in twentieth-century linguistics. They are sequences of sentences, sequences which are not random but well-formed by virtue of what Halliday and Hasan (1976) call 'cohesive' relationships tying sentence to sentence. Then each sentence is a syntactic formation which is minutely describable in terms of clauses, phrases, word-classes and morphemes, transformations, etc. Texts are lexical structures, patterns of words drawn from the vocabulary resource of the language. They are also semantic constructs, sequences of propositions exhibiting relationships such as paraphrase, tautology, contradiction, negation, entailment, presupposition, antonymy, hyponymy, and so on. Finally, at their most material level, texts are made of sounds or letters, and may be described by phonological or graphological analysis. All these statements about the levels of linguistic structure, and their describability in terms of modern linguistic analysis, apply equally to any text, whether it be 'conversation', 'advertisement', 'poem', 'football commentary', or 'novella'. Often, characteristic patterns in the objective linguistic structure of the text will mark it as belonging to a particular text type or genre: for instance there is a typical metrical and rhyme scheme for Shakespearian sonnets, and a typical vocabulary and modality for weather forecasts. But although individual genres may be stylistically distinguished, there is no single linguistic criterion, or set of criteria, which distinguish(es) all the 'literary' genres from all the 'non-literary' genres; those linguists who, following Jakobson, have claimed that there are empirical linguistic criteria for 'Literature', have done a disservice to text theory and textual description. However, if that futile search is abandoned, description of the formal structure of texts is a fundamental part of most branches of literary studies.*

The immediate caveat to be entered is that texts are not simply formal structures of language. My comments on 'world', 'writer' and 'reader' suggest an alternative concept of texts as 'social discourse' (Fowler, 1981) or 'communicative occurrences' (de Beaugrande and Dressler, 1981). Text in the strictly linguistic sense of formal patterning indicated in the previous paragraph is only the medium of discourse; it has force and significance only when it makes accessible to a reader knowledge, representations, beliefs and values which the culture tacitly agrees to associate with the linguistic structures in a given communicative context. In terms of linguistics more broadly considered, this means that formal linguistics must be supplemented by pragmatic analysis (Brown and Yule, 1983; Levinson, 1983). Pragmatics is usually defined as 'the relationship between texts and their users', a somewhat misleadingly dichotomous distinction, since 'use' ought to be integral to 'being a text'. Roughly, pragmatics returns to the text the notions of source and addressee, writer or speaker, and reader or listener, each party socially situated and therefore constituted of and constituting social significances; the parties both active in various ways, e.g. performing speech acts, turn-taking, inferencing; the text signifying against a rich context of background knowledge, shared information, beliefs, commonplaces. I have no space, and no brief, to elaborate this theory here. In any case, it is a theory of text and discourse, not a theory of 'Literature'.

6. FINAL REMARKS

'Literature' is classically regarded as a distinct and highly valuable entity, but no literary theorist or aesthetician has succeeded in defining 'it' satisfactorily; in my view the pursuit of 'Literature' into innumerable dead ends is a waste of intellectual energy. This is not to reject the importance of the notion, or of the social values assigned to it. On the contrary, 'Literature' is a major social force. I would like to refer to just one example. As I write this piece, the British government is busy standardizing the content of school education by establishing a compulsory range of core curriculum subjects, including English. The consultative document *English for Ages 5 to 11* (Cox, 1988) has a chapter 'Literature' arguing various reasons for the importance of literary texts in children's lives, and for the importance of literary studies from the earliest stages of schooling. Of course, I would heartily agree. My point is not to be destructive, but simply to observe that a document such as *English for Ages 5 to 11* provides wonderful evidence for the use of the term 'literature' in contemporary discourse. You may know a term by the company it keeps. Phrases such as 'the best imaginative literature' and 'the value of literature in personal life and development' (Cox, 1988, p. 27) show the persistence of the traditional values; and the instrumentality, the social role envisaged by the committee which produced the report, is quite evident to anyone who cares to analyse the context of educational/political practice.

The processes and values involved are easier to understand if one drops

'Literature' and simply talks about literary texts, their structures and their many roles in social practice. Such a simplification would surely also help literary education in schools, and advanced literary studies among specialists, by replacing mysterious notions like 'imagination' and 'art' with operable analytic concepts and tools. I have recommended technical tools drawn from text linguistics; other ranges of analytic and theoretical ideas will be characterized elsewhere in this book, hopefully leading to an overall demystification of literary studies.

FURTHER READING

Abrams, M. H. (1965) 'Theories of Poetry'. In Alex Preminger (ed.), *Princeton Encyclopedia of Poetry and Poetics*, Princeton University Press, Princeton, pp. 639–49

——(1972) 'What's the Use of Theorising about the Arts?' In M. W. Bloomfield (ed.), *In Search of Literary Theory*, Cornell University Press, Ithaca, pp. 3–54

Adams, Hazard (ed.) (1971) *Critical Theory Since Plato*, Harcourt Brace Jovanovich, New York

Culler, Jonathan (1975) *Structuralist Poetics*, Routledge & Kegan Paul, London

Eagleton, Terry (1983) *Literary Theory: An Introduction*, Basil Blackwell, Oxford

Ellis, John M. (1974) *The Theory of Literary Criticism*, University of California Press, Berkeley

Fowler, Alastair (1982) *Kinds of Literature: An Introduction to the Theory of Genres and Modes*, Clarendon Press, Oxford

Fowler, Roger (1986) *Linguistic Criticism*, Oxford University Press, Oxford

——(ed.) (1987) *A Dictionary of Modern Critical Terms*, revised and enlarged edition, Routledge & Kegan Paul, London

Harari, Josué V. (ed.) (1979) *Textual Strategies: Perspectives in Post-Structuralist Criticism*, Methuen, London

Hawkes, Terence (1977) *Structuralism and Semiotics*, Methuen, London

Jakobson, Roman (1960) 'Concluding Statement: Linguistics and Poetics'. In T. A. Sebeok (ed.), *Style in Language*, Massachusetts Institute of Technology Press, Cambridge, pp. 350–77

Jefferson, Ann and Robey, David (eds) (1982) *Modern Literary Theory: A Comparative Introduction*, Batsford Academic, London

Lodge, David (ed.) (1972) *Twentieth Century Literary Criticism: A Reader*, Longman, London

——(ed.) (1988) *Modern Criticism and Theory: A Reader*, Longman, London

Newton, K. M. (ed.) (1988) *Twentieth-Century Literary Theory: A Reader*, Macmillan, London

Wellek, René (1970) 'The Name and Nature of Comparative Literature'. In René Wellek, *Discriminations*, Yale University Press, New Haven, pp. 3–36

Wellek, René and Warren, Austin (1963) *Theory of Literature*, Penguin, Harmondsworth [first published 1948]

Wimsatt, W. K. and Brooks, Cleanth (1967) *Literary Criticism: A Short History*, Vintage, New York [first published 1957]

ADDITIONAL WORKS CITED

Attridge, Derek (1987) 'Closing Statement: Linguistics and Poetics in Perspective'. In Nigel Fabb, Derek Attridge, Alan Durant and Colin MacCabe (eds), *The Linguistics of Writing: Arguments between Language and Literature*, Manchester University Press, Manchester, pp. 15–32

Baldick, Chris (1983) *The Social Mission of English Criticism, 1848–1932*, Clarendon Press, Oxford

Barthes, Roland (1975) *S/Z*, translated by Richard Miller, Jonathan Cape, London

——(1979) 'From Work to Text'. In Josué V. Harari (ed.), *Textual Strategies: Perspectives in Post-Structuralist Criticism*, Methuen, London, pp. 73–81

Bauman, R. and Sherzer, J. (eds) (1974) *Explorations in the Ethnography of Speaking*, Cambridge University Press, Cambridge

Beaugrande, Robert de and Dressler, Wolfgang (1981) *Introduction to Text Linguistics*, Longman, London

Bennett, Tony (1979) *Formalism and Marxism*, Methuen, London

Booth, Wayne C. (1961) *The Rhetoric of Fiction*, University of Chicago Press, Chicago

Brown, Gillian and Yule, George (1983) *Discourse Analysis*, Cambridge University Press, Cambridge

Cluysenaar, Anne (1976) *Introduction to Literary Stylistics*, Batsford, London

Cox, C. B. (1988) *English for Ages 5 to 11*, Department of Education and Science, London

Downes, William (1984) *Language and Society*, Fontana, London

Eagleton, Terry (1976) *Criticism and Ideology*, Verso, London

Eco, Umberto (1976) *A Theory of Semiotics*, Macmillan, London

Foucault, Michel (1979) 'What is an Author?'. In Josué V. Harari (ed.), *Textual Strategies: Perspectives in Post-Structuralist Criticism*, Methuen, London, pp. 141–60

Fowler, Roger (1977) *Linguistics and the Novel*, Methuen, London

——(1981) *Literature as Social Discourse*, Batsford, London

Gumperz, John J. and Hymes, Dell (eds) (1972) *Directions in Sociolinguistics*, Holt, Rinehart & Winston, New York

Halliday, M. A. K. (1971) 'Linguistic Function and Literary Style: An Inquiry into the Language of William Golding's *The Inheritors*'. In Seymour Chatman (ed.), *Literary Style: A Symposium*, Oxford University Press, New York, pp. 330–65

——(1978) *Language as Social Semiotic*, Edward Arnold, London

——(1985) *Introduction to Functional Grammar*, Edward Arnold, London

Halliday, M. A. K. and Hasan, Ruqaiya (1976) *Cohesion in English*, Longman, London

Holub, Robert C. (1984) *Reception Theory*, Methuen, London

Hymes, Dell (1972) 'Models of the Interaction of Language and Social Life'. In John J. Gumperz and Dell Hymes (eds), *Directions in Sociolinguistics*, Holt, Rinehart & Winston, New York, pp. 38–71

Leech, Geoffrey N. (1969) *A Linguistic Guide to English Poetry*, Longman, London

Lemon, Lee T. and Reis, Marion J. (eds and trans.) (1965) *Russian Formalist Criticism: Four Essays*, University of Nebraska Press, Lincoln

Levinson, S. C. (1983) *Pragmatics*, Cambridge University Press, Cambridge

MacCabe, Colin (ed.) (1988) *Futures for English*, Manchester University Press, Manchester

Mukařovský, Jan (1965) 'Standard Language and Poetic Language'. In Paul L. Garvin (ed. and trans.), *A Prague School Reader on Esthetics, Literary Structure and Style*, Georgetown University Press, Washington, pp. 17–30 [essay first published 1932]

Palmer, D. J. (1965) *The Rise of English Studies*, Oxford University Press, London

Richards, I. A. (1924) *Principles of Literary Criticism*, Kegan Paul, Trench, Trubner, London

Sartre, Jean-Paul (1967) *What is Literature?*, Methuen, London [first published 1949]

Shklovsky, Viktor (1965) 'Art as Technique'. In Lee T. Lemon and Marion J. Reis (eds), *Russian Formalist Criticism: Four Essays*, University of Nebraska Press, Lincoln, pp. 5–24 [essay first published 1917]

Tillyard, E. M. W. (1958) *The Muse Unchained: An Intimate Account of the Revolution in English Studies at Cambridge*, Bowes, London

Todorov, Tzvetan (1965) *Théorie de la littérature*, Editions du Seuil, Paris

Weitz, Morris (1964) *Hamlet and the Philosophy of Language*, Chicago University Press, Chicago

Widdowson, Peter (ed.) (1982) *Re-reading English*, Methuen, London

Williams, Raymond (1976) *Keywords*, Fontana, London

——(1981) *Culture*, Fontana, London

Wimsatt, W. K. (1954) *The Verbal Icon*, University of Kentucky Press, Lexington

2

CRITICISM

CHRISTOPHER NORRIS

INTRODUCTION

It seems to me that a good way of grasping what is involved in recent literary-critical debates is to go right back to one of their major sources in Spinoza's *Theologico-Political Treatise* (1670). This work raises all the relevant issues and does so, moreover, in a context of highly charged political and ideological argument which resembles our own at numerous points. These include (1) the question of interpretative truth, or whether literature provides any kind of veridical knowledge, as distinct from its purely aesthetic or imaginative yield; (2) the relation between scriptural exegesis and secular literary criticism, a theme taken up from Spinoza by Matthew Arnold ([1865] 1973) and Frank Kermode (1979), among others; (3) the status of narrative understanding *vis-à-vis* philosophy, history and political theory; and (4) the extent to which these other disciplines may themselves be affected by bringing them into contact with certain techniques of rhetorical close-reading, techniques most familiar to students of literature. I shall also – towards the end – have something to say about the case of Salman Rushdie's novel *The Satanic Verses* (1988), since the attack on Rushdie by religious fundamentalists bears a striking resemblance to Spinoza's treatment at the hands of orthodox thinkers, Christian and Jewish alike. (For the record: he was excommunicated by the Synagogue at Amsterdam in 1656 and his writings thereafter condemned and vilified as atheist impostures, 'forged in Hell by a renegade Jew and the devil'.)

It is one main argument of this essay that literary criticism has developed historically alongside the efforts of Enlightenment thought to combat the forces of religious prejudice, unreason and dogma. Critical theory – the handiest cover-term for a range of competing schools and ideas – could scarcely have emerged in anything like its current form without this background history of brave endeavour on the part of Spinoza and other such liberalizing thinkers. And it is all the more important to bear these facts in mind at a time when

Enlightenment values are again under attack, not only from the religious-fundamentalist quarter but also from various 'postmodernist' gurus who reject the whole legacy of critical reason as just another species of what Nietzsche diagnosed as the will-to-power masquerading as pure, disinterested truth (see Norris, 1988). Since space is limited I shall often cross-refer to other topics discussed in this volume (e.g. hermeneutics, New Historicism, deconstruction, post-structuralism, Marxist criticism etc.) in the hope that readers will have time and inclination to follow them up. This chapter is – as should be evident enough by now – no dispassionate survey of the current literary-critical scene but a polemical piece which interprets that scene to its own argumentative ends. Nevertheless I would also want to claim that these are the most important issues in present-day criticism and that they are best understood by way of a jointly historical and theoretical approach inspired by Spinoza's pioneering work.

SCRIPTURAL HERMENEUTICS AND SECULAR CRITIQUE

Frank Kermode offers a lead for such reflections in his book *The Genesis of Secrecy* (1979), a study of the various hermeneutic methods brought to bear upon religious and secular texts. What chiefly interests Kermode – writing from the standpoint of a professed 'outsider', one for whom the sense of scripture cannot be a matter of revealed or self-evident truth – is the constant dialogue between orthodox readings and those that admit some degree of interpretative licence, some novel understanding more keenly responsive to the pressures of social or doctrinal change. At such moments there occurs a kind of paradigm-shift, a swerve from the 'literal' (i.e. the received or canonical) reading of a text to one that more knowingly accommodates scripture to the needs of present understanding. And the result of this process is to generate narrative 'secrets', or meanings of an occult, arcane or specialized nature that reveal themselves only to readers in possession of the requisite hermeneutic skills. It is precisely through this interplay of literal and figurative readings that the texts of tradition (whether sacred or secular) continue to provoke debate among adherents to various creeds and ideologies. Such is indeed the character of the 'classic', as Kermode defines it: a work whose meaning is perpetually open to acts of interpretative revision, so that no single reading – orthodox or otherwise – can possibly exhaust its manifold signifying potential (see Kermode, 1975). If the orthodox version lays claim to *truth* through divine inspiration or self-authorizing warrant, the rival account can always challenge that authority by affording the pleasure of a privileged access to *meanings* (or subtleties of hermeneutic insight) that necessarily elude the self-appointed guardians of mainstream orthodox tradition.

And so it has come about, according to Kermode, that techniques originally devised by biblical scholars – often with the purpose of reconciling variant truth-claims – have now migrated into the field of secular literary studies, giving rise to the numerous competing schools of present-day critical theory. These parallels are perhaps most striking in the discourse of French post-structuralism, a poetics that attaches maximum value to the notions of plural meaning, creative misprision, 'intertextuality', or reading as a process of trans-formative engagement with codes and conventions beyond the grasp of any orthodox interpretative method (see especially Barthes, 1975, 1976). For Ker-mode, such ideas are best understood as a secularized version of the approach adopted by biblical scholars when they read some passage from the Gospels as 'fulfilling' an obscure Old Testament prophecy, or when they treat the latter as in some sense prefiguring the advent of revealed Christian truth. What occurs in these transactions is a complex process of typological adjustment where reading is at once constrained by the codes of some existing 'interpret-ative community', and allowed sufficient scope to negotiate the gap between past and present modes of understanding (see Charity, 1966). In periods of relative stability there will emerge a prevailing doctrinal consensus which sets the basic terms for debate and effectively excludes any marginal or deviant reading. At other times – epochs of religious or political upheaval – this consensus will often break down to the point where all manner of novel interpretations arise and the ground-rules are changed to accommodate the readings, rather than the other way around.

Kermode's main point is that we cannot understand the dynamics of tradition (or canon-formation) without taking stock of these constant shifts in the balance of power between orthodox and unorthodox modes of understanding. Thus 'the story of modern biblical exegesis', he writes, 'tends to confirm the view that it takes a powerful mind to attend to what is written at the expense of what it is written about' (Kermode, 1979, p. 119). Spinoza's contribution was to make this possible by severing the hitherto sacrosanct tie between textual meaning and revealed truth, thus leaving criticism free to pursue its enquiries without interference from the authorized custodians of scriptural tradition:

> The Bible, he held . . . is of divine origin, but it is accommodated to human understanding, which may ascertain its meanings, but must not confound them with truths. 'It is one thing to understand the meaning of Scripture, and quite another to understand the actual truth.' Five centuries of Jewish interpretative rationalism stood behind Spinoza; but he was addressing the problems of his own day, and saw that the confusion of meaning and truth might result in the suppression of religious liberty. His pious book seemed blasphemous in 1670, so powerful is the atavistic preference for truth over meaning.
>
> (p. 119)

This is certainly one reason for Spinoza's notoriety among Christian and Jewish believers alike. But when Kermode equates 'truth' with revealed *religious* truth – God's word vouchsafed to the elect through a species of privileged hermeneutic insight – he overlooks that other kind of truth that Spinoza regards as the highest object of all philosophical enquiry, and which offers the only reliable means to criticize erroneous habits of belief. Thus in the sentence that he cites from Spinoza in the passage above Kermode seems not to recognize the crucial ambivalence that inhabits this term. On the one hand 'truth' is the presumptive warrant that authorizes mainstream exegetes (clerics and commentators) to impose their own interpretation of scripture as possessing divine warrant. On the other, it signifies the capacity of reason to examine such claims, whatever their source, and determine whether or not they meet the required standard of truthful (adequate) ideas. For otherwise there could be no grounds of appeal against those various forms of prejudice, dogmatism or unthinking doctrinal adherence that all too often result – in Spinoza's view – from the confusion between meaning and truth.

This helps to explain what several commentators have noted about Kermode's work since *The Genesis of Secrecy*: namely, his tendency to vacillate on the question of just how far readings are determined by the pressures of institutional control, or the resistance to change exerted by prevalent modes of consensus thinking. Very often this criticism is couched in ideological terms, as a doubt concerning Kermode's even-handedness – his studied ambivalence, as some would have it – between an interest in the more advanced or radical forms of post-structuralist theory and a lingering attachment to tradition, continuity and the status of 'the classic' as a means of transcending these otherwise awkward antinomies (see Arac, 1987). One could just as well argue – from a sympathetic standpoint – that Kermode is engaged in a project of revisionist theory that values texts for their plurality of meaning, or their openness to radically new interpretations. My concern is not to adjudicate this issue but to ask what bearing it might have on his account of Spinoza, as summarized above. And it is significant here that Kermode's re-statement of the truth/meaning distinction is one that puts 'truth' very firmly on the side of authority, tradition and vested institutional power, while 'meaning' is aligned with the interpreter's freedom to challenge or transform those values, to read texts always in light of changing historical or cultural concerns, hence to save the 'classic' – or the idea of 'tradition' – from becoming a mere slogan in the service of some closed or monological system of beliefs. Thus 'truth' figures mainly as a kind of sacred preserve, a repository of values inherently resistant to time and change. 'Meaning', on the other hand, is that which denies all forms of canonical closure, all attempts to identify the interpreter's role with the faithful handing-down of unquestioned, self-authorizing truths.

To this extent Kermode might be thought to approximate the stance of a 'strong revisionist' critic such as Harold Bloom, one for whom the best, most productive readings are those that engage – like the poets before them – in an agonistic struggle with their source-texts (or Oedipal precursors), and which thus lay claim to an order of imaginative insight unglimpsed by more orthodox interpreters (see Bloom, 1973, 1976, 1982). But Kermode clearly differs with Bloom in believing that there do exist powerful constraints upon any such revisionist programme, among them those forms of 'institutional control' that provide at least a background of consensual understanding against which to judge these novel departures. On this point he agrees with Stanley Fish: that criticism is a communal sense-making enterprise, one that requires some measure of continuity (or deference to established norms), even in periods like the present when it appears that just about every such convention is subject to doubt and disagreement (Fish, 1979, 1989). What emerges in the end from Kermode's treatment of this question is a refusal – a deliberate and principled refusal – to decide between these seeming alternatives, since both play a necessary role in every act of commentary or criticism. And indeed, there is no escaping this conclusion if one accepts, like Kermode, that meaning is entirely a product of interpretative codes and conventions, a matter of perpetual adjustment (as hermeneutic theorists would have it) between the 'pre-understanding' that constitutes tradition and the needs of some present community of readers engaged in making sense of that same tradition (see Gadamer, 1975, 1979). For it then becomes clear that any new interpretation – any challenge to the current institutional *status quo* – will have to make terms with the existing consensus of qualified opinion, at least if it wants to gain a hearing among readers deemed competent to judge on such questions.

Of course this predicament is by no means unique to Kermode's way of stating the issue. In fact it is a version of the 'hermeneutic circle', as described by philosophers like Heidegger and Gadamer: the argument that all interpretation takes place within a given cultural context of beliefs, values and knowledge-constitutive interests which can never be fully articulated – let alone subjected to radical critique – since they operate at a level of tacit presupposition which alone makes it possible to exchange ideas on a basis of shared understanding (cf. Palmer, 1969; Hoy, 1979). On this view it is strictly inconceivable that a text could put up the kind of stubborn resistance to consensus values – or provoke the kind of stubbornly resistant reading – that would constitute a genuine challenge to prevailing institutional norms. There could thus be no question of criticizing consensus-values from an alternative (more rational or enlightened) standpoint, since this would entail the impossible claim that thinking can achieve an order of knowledge ideally independent of the beliefs, meanings or presuppositions that make up a given cultural 'form of life'. And from this line of argument it can readily be deduced – as happens with the more conservative applications of such doctrine – that there is simply no point in offering criticisms which will either be altogether lacking in persuasive force (in so far as they flout all the relevant conventions), or otherwise be obliged to make tolerable sense on terms that have always been decided in advance by some given interpretative community. For if thinkers like Gadamer are right – if understanding is always and inevitably confined to the 'hermeneutic circle' of tacit foreknowledge – then it is hard to conceive how reading could break with the currency of accepted ideas or commonsense belief.

In short, this philosophy ends up in a prison-house of its own elaborate devising where there is no longer any role for the values of truth and falsehood, since everything is decided by pre-emptive appeal to beliefs that hold good for us, and which therefore operate to screen out any evidence that fails to fit in with the prevalent consensus-view. We can now go back to that passage from Kermode and see just what is wrong with the idea of Spinoza as having more or less invented modern hermeneutics by severing the link between meaning and truth. In fact Kermode himself gives reason to doubt this claim when he recalls (midway through the same passage) that Spinoza 'expressed a particular dislike for the practice of distorting meaning "in order to make it conform with some meaning already entertained" ', and furthermore that 'he neatly convicts his illustrious predecessor Maimonides of this offence, which he thinks intellectually disreputable and liable to favour political authoritarianism' (Kermode, 1979, p. 119). For one then has to ask by what standard precisely readings may judged as 'distorting' the text in accordance with 'some meaning already entertained'. What Spinoza has in mind when he criticizes Maimonides (in the *Theologico-Political Treatise*) is the habit, among biblical commentators, of starting out from a position of assumed authority – an orthodox stance with regard to questions of doctrinal truth – and then finding ever more elaborate and ingenious ways of bringing the text into line with that initial prejudice. Hence his objection to those 'Kabbalistic triflers' whose stock-in-trade it is – so Spinoza argues – to produce all manner of hermeneutic subtleties or swerves from the literal meaning of scripture while failing to respect the most elementary rules of historical and textual scholarship. By such means they are enabled to pass clean over any signs of resistance in the text, any obstacles, inconsistencies or disruptions of narrative coherence (as between the various Old and New Testament sources), that would call their whole approach into doubt.

For Spinoza, on the contrary, the proper business of scriptural exegesis is to apply its best efforts to the task of rational reconstruction, that is, to explaining just how it came about – under what precise historical conditions, what pressures of circumstance, doctrinal adherence, and so forth – that the texts in question should so often have resorted to inadequate (i.e. 'imaginary') techniques for enforcing their message. And this requires in turn that reason be allowed full scope for the exercise of a critical hermeneutics that distances itself equally from both major schools of interpretative thought. On the one hand it is a matter (as Kermode well sees) of liberating commentary from those pre-emptive truth-claims that mistake their own *de facto* authority – their orthodox standing or purely institutional warrant – for some privileged mode of access to truth as revealed by divine inspiration to a priestly elect. To this extent, certainly, Spinoza's great achievement lay in his having dissociated questions of 'truth' from questions of interpretative method. But he is equally insistent – as against Kermode – that criticism cannot make a start in challenging these false claims to truth unless it acknowledges the existence of alternative, more enlightened or rational forms of interpretative procedure. For otherwise thinking will indeed be trapped in an endless process of specular self-confirmation, a 'hermeneutic circle' which allows texts to mean only what they *must* be construed as meaning in accordance with the dictates of this or that readerly prejudice. Such prejudice may take the form of an adherence to orthodox canons of interpretative response which derive their authority from law, tradition or respect for 'truth' as identified (mistakenly) with the sacred word of scripture. But it can also be seen in those counter-canonical or 'strong revisionist' readings which reject all appeals to authority and truth in the name of a new-found hermeneutic freedom. For here also there is nothing to prevent mere prejudice from making what it will of the text, this time in the guise of a liberation-movement which merely reproduces an alternative set of prejudicial truth-claims, meanings and values.

Spinoza is very firm in maintaining the contrary position: that truth is what resists such encroachments of unreason by offering good argumentative grounds for not taking scripture (or anything else) on trust, but subjecting its claims to the tribunal of critical reason. This conviction is manifest at every level and in every aspect of his work. It informs his writings on scriptural exegesis through Spinoza's insistence, first, that the texts be read with an eye to their internal contradictions and downright absurdities – claims that are simply unacceptable to reason – and second, that these problems should not be set aside by appealing to divine inspiration (or the paradoxical nature of revealed religious truth), but should rather be traced back to their source in the socio-political conditions prevailing at the time when they were first set down. In short, Spinoza sees absolutely no virtue in the kind of hermeneutic subtlety that developed in the reading of biblical texts, and whose influence has undoubtedly carried across into the practice of present-day secular literary criticism. For there is no denying Kermode's central claim: that this influence may be traced in many of the privileged key-terms (ambiguity, paradox, intertextuality, 'revisionary ratios' and so forth) which have characterized the discourse of advanced critical thinking over the past fifty years and more. But to see Spinoza as a signal precursor of these and related developments (e.g. modern hermeneutic philosophy) is to read him with a mind more closely attuned to such modern ideas than to anything in his own work. For it is precisely his aim to prevent interpretation from working its sophistical mischief, that is to say, its capacity for inventing new pretexts, new varieties of ingenious reader-response, in order to avoid the problems involved in making rational sense of the scriptures.

Hence Spinoza's sceptical attitude with regard to miracles, prophecies, divine interventions and other such dubious items of faith, adopted – as he argues – solely with the purpose of persuading ignorant and credulous minds, and lacking all semblance of rational truth. Where the subtle-minded exegetes go wrong is in attempting to reconcile these passages with the requirements of a latter-day 'interpretative community', one whose members cannot (or at any rate should not) be so easily imposed upon by suchlike persuasive techniques. In short, 'we may explain the words of Scripture according to our preconceived opinions, twisting them about, reversing or completely changing their literal sense, however plain it may be' (Spinoza, [1670] 1884a, vol. i, p. 117). But this approach is misguided – a source of manifold errors and delusions – in so far as it substitutes mere ingenuity (or interpretative flair) for the much more difficult business of analysing texts in relation to their socio-historical conditions of production. What makes it especially dangerous (and seductive) is the scope this method offers for new ways of reading which appear to contest the orthodox account, but which in fact just involve some accommodating 'twist' – some convenient swerve from the literal sense – by which to head off any real question as to the nature of scriptural 'truth' and the interests of those who purport to expound it.

So Spinoza is quite definitely *not* saying – as Kermode would have him say – that new readings must always 'accommodate' the old through a harmonizing process of interpretative revision which aims to reconcile discrepant details by shedding all illusions of ultimate validity or truth. Certainly he seeks to liberate commentary from the kind of pre-emptive doctrinal truth-claim that would treat scripture as a timeless repository of divinely sanctioned commands. Interpreters who take this line are merely demonstrating their own inability to resist the kinds of partial and self-interested reading that have propped up various forms of priestly or institutional control down through the ages. To be sure, Spinoza seeks to challenge this authoritarian regime of truth by removing scripture from the custody of those who would claim some unique, self-validating access to the Word of God as revealed through various arcane techniques of divinatory reading or hermeneutic exegesis. But it is precisely on account of his desire to resist such unwarranted impositions – such manipulative strategies designed to place power in the hands of a privileged interpretative élite – that Spinoza argues the case for a different order of truth-claim, one that goes by way of philological scholarship, historical criticism, the detailed comparison of biblical source-texts, along with an analysis of social institutions, the politics of religious belief, and what amounts to a genealogical critique of all such value-systems. For he sees very clearly that scriptural hermeneutics, if pursued in isolation from these other kinds of study, must always lead back to a self-enclosed realm of pre-emptive institutional constraints. Any resistance to received ways of reading and thinking will therefore involve something other and more than a 'strong revisionist' approach to questions of scriptural meaning. It will have to take account of material factors – history, circumstance, prejudice, error, contradictions in the scriptural record, and so forth – which find no place in the hermeneutic model of textual understanding as a circular exchange between tradition (the realm of pre-established meanings and values) and modernity (the point where those values are harmonized with latter-day interpretative interests).

CRITICISM, THEORY, AND THE CLAIM OF REASON

So Spinoza's example is immensely significant in the present context of debate, though not in quite the way that Kermode suggests. His influence has been greatest on those thinkers (critical theorists of various persuasion) whose work is aimed squarely 'against interpretation', or at any rate against the view – widely held among literary critics – that the object of reading is somehow to release the largest possible range of meanings from a given text or passage. This idea can of course be traced back to Coleridge and his set-piece examples of 'practical criticism' as applied to Shakespeare, Wordsworth and others (Coleridge, [1817] 1983). But its real apotheosis comes at the point when T. S. Eliot – in a series of canonical essays (in particular 'Tradition and the Individual Talent' and 'The Metaphysical Poets') – effectively equates the proper interests of criticism with those of close-reading or rhetorical exegesis (see Eliot, 1964a, b). The subsequent story is familiar enough, from William Empson's *Seven Types Of Ambiguity* (1930) – where multiple meaning is taken as the hallmark or touchstone of poetic value – to the American New Criticism, French post-structuralism, and at least one variety of deconstruction, as practised by literary critics for whom it offers a degree of hermeneutic freedom denied by other, more orthodox schools (e.g. Hartman, 1980, 1981; Miller, 1985; also Leitch, 1983).

Of course it might be argued, in support of Kermode's central claim, that this whole complex chapter of developments grows out of – and at various points returns to – its origin in the practice of scriptural interpretation. Thus Eliot wrote an essay on Lancelot Andrewes, the seventeenth-century Anglican bishop, drawing attention not only to his historical importance as a defender of orthodox (High Church) interests, but also to the highly distinctive prose-style of Andrewes's sermons, in particular his technique of 'dividing the word of God', or practising a form of minute textual exegesis which closely resembled certain aspects of Eliot's own criticism (Eliot, 1928). And at the opposite extreme – 'opposite' at least in terms of doctrinal persuasion – one finds Geoffrey Hartman, in his recent essays, offering the example of Jewish Midrash as a model for the kind of commentary that breaks with orthodox interpretative constraints and ranges freely over a multitude of source-texts, analogues and rival commentaries (see Hartman, 1980). So to this extent at least Kermode has good warrant for his view that modern criticism derives in large part from techniques first invented for the purpose of scriptural exegesis.

But he errs – as I have argued – in counting Spinoza among the adepts of that same tradition. Spinoza belongs much more in company of those critics and theorists who have held out against the dominant idea of *interpretation* as the normal mode of literary-critical activity, and of multiple meaning (or the 'plural text') as its most rewarding object of study. This alternative tradition goes right back to Aristotle, with his stress in *The Poetics* on the virtues of an orderly, disciplined method of approach that starts out from observed regularities of structure in various types of text, and then proceeds inductively to specify the rules or conventions governing that genre. The most obvious heirs of Aristotelian thinking are those modern formalist or structuralist movements which likewise see no virtue in producing ever more sophisticated interpretations of individual texts, but concentrate rather on the various poetic devices (or modes of narrative employment) that characterize literary discourse in general (Todorov, 1977; Genette, 1979; Rimmon-Kenan, 1983). However, there are other reasons – more germane to my argument here – why critics should have come to view interpretation with a certain principled mistrust, a sense that it falls in all too readily with conformist or institutionalized habits of thought (see Culler, 1975). And I think that Kermode indicates one source of these misgivings when he locates the point of departure for modern hermeneutics in the severance of that link between truth and meaning which had previously governed the practice of scriptural commentary. For it now became possible for interpreters to claim that theirs was a wholly autonomous activity, a practice of reading ideally unconstrained by any obligation to respect the imperatives of reason, logic, historical scholarship, or other such 'non-literary' standards of cognitive accountability. That is to say, there developed a specialized discourse of literary-critical debate where those standards were perceived as strictly extraneous to the structures of inwrought meaning – ambiguity, paradox, irony and so forth – which set poetry apart from all forms of everyday communicative language.

For the New Critics especially this became a high point of principle, a dogma connected with the orthodox ban on readings that failed to pay close enough attention to 'the words on the page', and which thus fell back into the bad habit of invoking historical, biographical or suchlike strictly irrelevant kinds of knowledge. Where these readings offend most gravely is in failing to respect the difference between the mode of *sui generis* imaginative 'truth' that poetry is uniquely able to provide, and those other sorts of truth that involve the application of factual or logical criteria. Hence the various 'heresies' anathematized by W. K. Wimsatt, the high priest and guardian of 'old' New Critical orthodoxy (Wimsatt, 1954). Worst of all was the heresy of paraphrase, since this involved the notion – an affront to their every last precept and principle – that poetic meaning could be somehow re-stated in the simplified form of a rational prose discourse that would have no need of devices like irony and paradox. And behind this there loomed the yet more threatening prospect of a criticism that would take poems seriously *in the wrong way*; that would treat them as offering arguments, advancing truth-claims, or engaging with issues beyond their proper realm of self-enclosed meaning and value. Indeed, one could view this whole modern enterprise – in the wake of Eliot's pioneering essays – as a kind of elaborate *cordon sanitaire*, a system of self-authorizing checks and interdictions designed to insulate poetry (or the criticism of poetry) from any contact with history, politics, or questions of a wider socio-cultural import.

This project discovers its best, most satisfying form in a work like Cleanth Brooks's *The Well Wrought Urn* (1947), a sequence of neatly turned interpretative essays on poets from Donne and Marvell to Wordsworth and Keats, each chapter leading up to the same (wholly circular) conclusion: that all good poetry is paradoxical through and through, since paradox or its kindred rhetorical tropes (ambiguity, irony etc.) are of the essence of poetry, and can therefore provide an indubitable index of aesthetic worth. Very often such judgements emerge from a reading that is by no means innocent of its own historical bias or ideological *parti pris*. The most obvious example is his chapter on Marvell's 'Horatian Ode: to Cromwell on his return from Ireland', a set-piece essay in rhetorical close-reading which takes its cue from Eliot's well-known remarks about the poem's eminently 'graceful' and 'civilized' demeanour. Thus when Brooks praises the 'Horatian Ode' for its qualities of ironic equipoise – its managing to sustain a finely-held balance between Royalist and Cromwellian sympathies – one can see that he has not only contrived to smuggle in a sizeable amount of 'extraneous' historical baggage, but has also signalled his own strong preference for Marvell's tactful way of handling (or evading) the issue, as compared, say, with Milton's unambiguous commitment to a politics of radical change. It is no coincidence that Brooks's aesthetic criteria have this effect of valuing poetry in proportion as its rhetoric negates, resists or disowns any kind of overt political standpoint. In fact one could argue that this entire New Critical lexicon – 'paradox', 'irony', 'wit', 'balance', 'impersonality' and so forth – was invented for the purpose of elevating poets (like Donne or Marvell) whose work displayed a fine indifference to politics, and devaluing others (like Milton or Shelley) who espoused any kind of republican or left-wing stance. At least this would go some way towards explaining why Eliot, for one, mounts his case against Milton and Shelley on technical grounds that scarcely account for the sheer vehemence of his attack (see Eliot, 1957a, b). So when Leavis later wrote that Milton's 'dislodgement' from the canon had been accomplished with 'remarkably little fuss', he was speaking in the name of a critical movement – a confidently orthodox movement – whose aversion to left-wing politics could now be passed off as involving nothing more than a respect for poetry itself, or the imperatives of textual close-reading (Leavis, 1952).

More recently, critics have become very aware of this alignment between the idea of poetry as an autonomous, self-enclosed realm of meaning, and the covert presence of a certain 'aesthetic ideology' that discovers its elective home ground in precisely such a mystified rhetoric of form and value (see Graff, 1970, 1979; de Man, 1986; Sprinker, 1987). One of the earliest to make this connection was William Empson in his book *The Structure of Complex Words* (1951). By this time Empson had developed deep misgivings, not only with regard to the American New Criticism – which he saw as promoting an irrationalist doctrine in league with a widespread 'Neo-Christian' revival – but also in respect of his own early work, since *Seven Types of Ambiguity* (1930) could be taken as a virtual manifesto for just the kind of reading that Empson now deplored. It seemed to many readers of the earlier book – especially the passages on Donne, Herbert, Hopkins and other religious poets – that Empson was drawing a straightforward equation between literary value and the sheer multiplicity of meaning to be found in this or that instance. And furthermore, his method appeared to work best with poems where 'ambiguity' shaded into 'paradox', or where the mere possibility of 'alternative reactions to the same piece of language' – a description roughly covering Types One to Three – gave way to 'full-blown states of psychological conflict', states which very often resulted (in Empson's view) from a neurotic struggle with the more sinister implications of Christian theology (Empson, [1930] 1961, pp. 192–233). Thus if the book has any ordering principle, Empson writes, it is the progress through stages of 'increasing logical and psychological complication', to the point where 'ambiguity' is a term hardly adequate to convey the clash of contradictory beliefs or value-systems (p. 184).

The most striking example is Empson's treatment of Herbert's 'The Sacrifice' (pp. 226–33), a passage that has also given maximum offence to critics of an orthodox (Christian or scholarly) mind. But what Empson found so disturbing in retrospect was the way that *Seven Types* had been taken up as a primer or source-text for the kind of rhetorical close-reading that identified 'paradox' as the chief value and distinguishing mark of poetic language in general. For interpreters could then go on to claim – as did the New Critics, some of them explicitly, others through various forms of analogical transfer – that poetry and religion were deeply akin, since both gave access to imaginative truths beyond the reach of mere analysis or plain-prose reason. Thus for Cleanth Brooks it is a matter of principle – inevitably borne out in the reading – that 'what Wordsworth wanted to say demanded his use of paradox . . . [and] could only be said powerfully through paradox' (Brooks, 1947, p. 198). Hence the great danger, as Empson saw it, that this powerful new mode of rhetorical exegesis would indeed take the path that Eliot had signalled in his essay on Lancelot Andrewes. That is to say, it showed all the signs of developing into a form of surrogate religious orthodoxy, one that came equipped with the full apparatus of doctrinal rules and prohibitions. And then there would be nothing to prevent it from reverting – as Eliot and some of his disciples clearly wished – to that stage of pre-critical consensus belief when religious doctrine was the only measure of interpretative truth, and when meaning (as revealed through scriptural exegesis) placed absolute limits on the exercise of rational thought.

In fact the New Critics had problems with Empson, not least on account of his anti-Christian crusade, his attitude of sturdy common-sense rationalism, and – very much in keeping with this – his flat refusal, in *Seven Types*, to treat poetic language as a privileged mode of utterance, exempt from the usual standards of sense-making logic and consistency. One sign of his recalcitrance in this regard was Empson's habit of paraphrasing poems, most often by recording multiple attempts to tease out the sense of some particular passage, and then leaving the reader to sort them all into some kind of working synthesis. What this method implied – in stark opposition to New Critical doctrine – was that poetry could and should be made accountable to reason; that its interests were continuous with those of our practical, everyday understanding; and therefore that interpreters were merely practising a form of high-priestly mystification when they made it such a point of principle that poetry should not be paraphrased. All the same Empson had to recognize that there were passages in *Seven Types* – notably the treatment of Herbert – which lent themselves to a reading totally at odds with his tough-minded rationalist stance. This was why he set out, with *The Structure of Complex Words*, to develop a theory of multiple meaning that could not be annexed to any form of religious or quasi-religious exegetical technique.

There is no room here for a detailed account of this brilliant, quirky, at times problematic, but often superbly convincing and original book. Sufficient to say that it develops the following theses: (1) that 'complex words' can best be understood as containing verbal 'equations' (or structures of logico-semantic entailment) which condense whole arguments into a single key-word, or a sequence of such words in context: (2) that the best, most rewarding instances – like 'wit' and 'sense' in Pope's *Essay on Criticism*, or 'sense' in a whole range of literary works, from *Measure for Measure* to *The Prelude* and *Sense and Sensibility* – will display an especially rich, complex, or problematical use of these semantic resources; and (3) that where the method comes up against resistance – where the key-word in question proves wholly unamenable to any kind of logico-semantic analysis – then here we have a case of some irrational doctrine, some attempt to short-circuit the structures of intelligible sense and impose what amounts to a species of irrationalist (or merely 'rhetorical') truth-claim. The approach tends to work best with a poem like the *Essay on Criticism*, where Pope is clearly running through a whole gamut of witty variations on the possible meanings of 'wit' and 'sense', a virtuoso performance that responds ideally to Empson's analytical technique. Elsewhere, as in the chapters on Wordsworth and Milton, he is obliged to admit that the method has failed, at least to the extent that something in the poetry – some structure of deviant equations, alogical entailment or downright 'paradox' – has proved resistant to any kind of truth-functional analysis. But even here, Empson urges, it is important to see just *why* the analysis fails; to understand how the poets (Wordsworth in particular) are exploiting rhetorical devices which do, undeniably, have great persuasive force, but whose effect is none the less dependent on our not enquiring too closely into their modes of semantic operation.

In this respect he takes something like the line of argument adopted by Jürgen Habermas, conceding the existence of forces – social and linguistic – that operate to block or frustrate the desire for rational communication, but also holding out the redemptive prospect of an 'ideal speech-situation' where these obstacles would no longer work their mischief and language would achieve at least the possibility of a working rational consensus (Habermas, 1979, 1984, 1987). However, Empson differs in maintaining that this principle extends to poetry – or literary language in general – rather than applying only to those discourses where truth is more obviously in question. For it is Empson's belief, as we have seen, that any too-willing acquiescence in poetry's power to insinuate paradoxes, straightforward falsehoods or 'profound' pseudo-truths may itself give rise to serious distortions in our dealing with language in its everyday uses. Thus for Empson – unlike Habermas – there is no question of fencing poetry off in some privileged domain of 'aesthetic' truth where the standard requirements simply do not apply. On the contrary, he argues, any adequate reading of a poem will make every effort to explicate its sense in rationally accountable terms. Only then – at the point of ultimate resistance – will the critic have to recognize that there may indeed be structures of meaning that elude her or his logical grasp, though not because they somehow embody a wisdom (or an order of 'paradoxical' truth) that shows up the inherent limitations of rational thought as applied to poetic language. For if this were the case then one would have no choice but to regard poetry – and the best poetry at that – as belonging to a realm of 'aesthetic' value where questions of truth and falsehood were simply irrelevant. And it is no exaggeration to say that Empson's criticism after *Seven Types* was devoted almost entirely to the task of rebutting what he saw as the pernicious effects of this aestheticizing creed.

Other commentators – Gerald Graff among them – have likewise perceived how the move to cut poetry off from any appeal to the rational prose virtues may lead toward a wholesale mystification of social and political thought. In his earliest book (*Poetic Statement and Critical Dogma*, 1970) Graff took issue with the New Critics on precisely this ground: that their approach came down to an expert technique for disregarding truth-values in literature, or for treating any 'statements' that a poem might make as hedged about with so many qualifying attitudes – ambiguity, irony, paradox and so forth – that it became simply impertinent to ask whether such statements possessed any kind of validity or truth. And in the sequel (*Literature Against Itself*, 1979) he extended this critique to post-structuralist, postmodernist and other such forms of fashionable anti-mimetic doctrine which, according to Graff, continued the 'old' New Critical drive to dissociate literature from cognitive interests of any kind, or from what was now thought of as the 'repressive' regime of Enlighten-ment rationality and truth. On the contrary, he argues: 'what compels the theory that literary works make no statements is not the nature of literary works but the cultural constraints upon our theorizing about literary works' (Graff, 1979, p. 163). Thus it has more to do with the prevailing conditions of late twentieth-century cultural politics than with anything so radical as a wholesale attack on the codes and conventions of classic 'bourgeois' realism.

The effect of such ideas is all the more disabling, as Graff sees it, on account of that pervasive sense of unreality that has come to characterize our conditions of existence in a world given over to mass-media techniques, fictive appearances masquerading as truth, and the wholesale distortion of consensus interests in the name of political 'realism'. For at this point the difference between fact and fiction becomes so impossibly blurred that a curious reversal begins to take place, with theorists proclaiming that the real is unknowable except by analogy with the literary text, and moreover with the kind of postmod-ern text that constantly adverts to its own fictive character, thus working to undo the old mimetic illusion that held us in thrall to false ideas of objectivity and truth. Thus 'one of the defining aspects of the current situation is the penetration of literary ideologies and paradigms into areas heretofore imper-vious to them – with a consequent loss of oppositional tension between literary culture and general society' (Graff, 1979, pp. 1–2). In support of this conten-tion one could point to various disciplines (notably philosophy and histori-ography) where the claim is now made, by 'advanced' thinkers in the field, that any notion of truth must henceforth be abandoned since the only knowl-edge worth having is one that accepts the self-interested nature of all such values and the fact that 'truth' is what presently counts according to this or that language-game, narrative schema or consensus of informed opinion.

Richard Rorty puts this case in respect of philosophy as just another 'kind of writing' on a level with poetry, literary criticism and the human sciences at large (see Rorty, 1982, 1989). And Hayden White (1978) has argued to similar effect: that historians had better catch up with developments in the area of narrative poetics – or study of the various tropes or figures involved in the production of historical texts – if they want to avoid the kind of old-fashioned positivist thinking bound up with the claim to tell it like it really was ('*wie es eigentlich gewesen*').

What these proposals have in common is a turn toward literary models – and models of a distinctly postmodern or post-structuralist provenance – with a view to subverting received ideas of rational or truth-telling discourse. This is why Graff (like Habermas) diagnoses the advent of postmodernist thinking as a loss of that productive 'oppositional tension' that previously marked the relationship between literature and the other humanistic disciplines. It has led to what he sees as a widespread failure of intellectual nerve, not only among literary critics but also – and perhaps more disturbingly – among those who have invoked literary theory as a source of new procedures or interpretative paradigms for the human sciences at large. Graff makes a closely related point when he discusses Kermode's argument (in *The Sense of an Ending*, 1969) that 'fictions' are the only means we possess of interpreting experience, explaining events, or imposing some provisional order of sense upon the otherwise chaotic and disparate mass of historical data. The trouble with this argument, he suggests, is that it collapses the difference between story-telling interests – which may indeed articulate our deep desire for narrative consistency and shape – and those other kinds of interest (cognitive or critical) which allow us to hold out against delusory or mystified forms of understanding. In other words, it is hard to see what could count as an objection to some existing narrative paradigm – maybe some potent myth of origins adopted in the interest of a dominant power-group – if there is no ground of appeal outside the conditions of intelligibility created by this or that fictive economy of truth.

This applies not only to Kermode's treatment of the issue but also to those various competing schools of post-structuralist, reader-response or hermeneutic theory that elevate the notion of multiple meaning – or the 'plural' text – into a touchstone of aesthetic value. What these theories have in common is a kind of utopian mystification, a belief that any talk of interpretative 'truth' is *per se* an imposition of unwarranted authority and power, so that only by opening texts to all the multitude of possible senses and meanings can criticism work to challenge or subvert this closed economy of truth. This attitude finds its most seductive expression in a work like Roland Barthes's *S/Z* (1975), a virtuoso demonstration of what commentary can achieve when released from all the irksome rules and constraints of a reading compliant with traditional interpretative norms. It is likewise manifest in the writings of 'American deconstructionists' like Geoffrey Hartman, those for whom the line between 'creative' and 'critical' texts is at best a mere product of scholarly convention, an attempt to delegitimize any form of commentary that makes a point of 'crossing over' from the one to the other domain, and which thus constitutes a standing challenge to the orthodox division of realms (Hartman, 1980). To this way of thinking the most radical gesture available to critics is one that breaks down all the commonplace (institutional) distinctions between meaning and truth, text and commentary, 'literature' and 'criticism', or – in Kermode's case – narrative fiction and the various (equally fictive) methodologies that attempt to theorize the workings of narrative.

TRUTH AND CRITICISM

Spinoza's point was exactly the reverse of what these present-day critics are arguing. That is to say, he saw nothing but multiplied error and confusion in the habit of 'accommodating' reason to faith, or adapting the requirements of rational critique to a sense of what the passage in question *ought* to mean according to some present (orthodox or other) interpretative consensus. This is where he differs most sharply with critics like Kermode, those for whom the single most important distinction is that between 'closed' and 'open' readings, or degrees of liberty along a scale of hermeneutic options running from the sheerly conformist to the downright heterodox. But no matter how extreme these localized points of disagreement, they are still conceived as taking place against a background of communal values and beliefs, an ongoing dialogue that sets the terms for meaningful interpretative debate. For Spinoza, on the contrary, truth was what resisted all such attempts to make sense of scripture through a sequence of endless hermeneutical revisions, a process of adjustment by which problematic passages could be brought into line with the needs of present understanding. The result of this practice, as Spinoza sees it, is to leave the field open to interpreters – orthodox or otherwise – whose readings will be based on nothing more than mere prejudice, either through their habit of passive compliance with existing codes and conventions, or conversely through their zeal to revise the established, canonical sense of things in order to save doctrinal appearances. What is lacking in both cases is any ground for the critique of scriptural truth-claims – or orthodox beliefs of whatever kind – that would not in the end come down to some version of the hermeneutic circle, or the appeal to readerly 'foreknowledge' as an ultimate horizon of interpretative method.

For it is at this point that reading becomes a genuinely critical activity, an active engagement with the meanings of scripture that treats them not as tokens of God's revealed truth, but as fallible signs adapted to the limits of human understanding under this or that set of contingent historical circumstances. In which case criticism cannot be confined – as it was for Maimonides and other more traditional exegetes – to the business of 'reconciling' reason and faith by requiring of the former a due subservience to the dictates of orthodox belief, and allowing only for such innovative turns in the reading of scripture as would prevent reason from getting into conflict with those same imperative truths. It is against this doctrine – one whose aim and effect are to subjugate reason to revelation – that Spinoza presents his whole battery of arguments in the *Theologico-Political Treatise* (for a more detailed treatment, see Strauss, 1965). For present purposes it is enough to point out that Spinoza rejects any curbs or limits placed upon the exercise of critical reason; that he is willing to acknowledge the truth-claims of religion only in so far as they concern matters of faith (as distinct from the interests of free rational enquiry); and that he is deeply suspicious of those super-subtle exegetes who attempt to reconcile these different modes of knowledge by abandoning the literal signification of scripture and offering their own ingenious glosses (or tropological 'swerves' from the manifest sense) by way of avoiding any clash between reason and faith. For it is reason's prerogative to raise questions about scripture which can and should be raised even where they constitute an argument for regarding scriptural truth-claims as in no way binding on the activity of rational thought.

For Spinoza, these questions extend into the areas of comparative philology, textual criticism, political history and what would nowadays be called the sociology of belief. They also involve a close attention to issues in the field of narrative poetics in so far as that discipline serves to indicate those problematic points where the 'truth' of scripture turns out to be a matter of fictive or 'imaginary' knowledge. But it can only fulfil such a purpose by respecting the distinction between meaning and truth, or those aspects of scripture that have to be interpreted in order to produce any kind of coherent sense, and those passages that are capable of reasoned exposition in light of 'adequate ideas'. Thus Spinoza very firmly rejects the kind of levelling pan-textualist view that regards all truths as products of interpretation, or all attempts to theorize narrative as reducing in the end to yet another form of narrative fiction. In fact this viewpoint is more closely related to the tradition of scriptural exegesis that Spinoza attacks in Maimonides and other proponents of a more 'hermeneutical' approach. That is to say, it starts out from the foregone conclusion that truth is what emerges from the ongoing dialogue of variant readings or interpretations, a dialogue that allows for new departures in the interest of maintaining narrative coherence, but which excludes any appeal to rational criteria outside its own privileged sphere of understanding.

Spinoza has three main objections to bring against this mainstream philosophy of textual exegesis. First, it leaves no room for the *criticism* of scriptural texts, taking 'criticism' to mean something other – and more – than an endless production of ingenious new readings that never touch upon basic issues of validity and truth. Second, it places the interpreter beyond reach of effective counter-argument, since his or her reading can always claim access to a 'truth' that reveals itself only to those with the wisdom (or the requisite hermeneutic skills) to draw out the authentic meaning of scripture, a meaning necessarily opaque or invisible from the standpoint of mere human reason. And third – in consequence – it works to promote a mystified state of understanding where readings acquire a certain spurious authority through the absence of enlightened critical reflection on their historically contingent origins. This is why Spinoza's critique of revelation (i.e. his attack on the idea of scripture as a source of divinely-sanctioned meaning and truth) goes along with a deep scepticism with regard to miracles, prophecy, supernatural interventions and other such ruses adopted in compliance with the demands of popular prejudice. 'Wherefore so far as our understanding goes, those phenomena which we clearly and distinctly understand have a much better right to be called works of God, and to be referred to the will of God than those about which we are entirely ignorant, although they appeal powerfully to the imagination, and compel men's admiration' (Spinoza, [1670] 1884a, vol. 1, p. 86). From which it follows that the belief in miracles, prophecy and suchlike superstitious items of faith can only be encouraged – or protected from rational criticism – by an attitude to scripture that disarms reason by subjecting it to the dictates of revealed religious truth.

These arguments of Spinoza may help to show what is wrong with the postmodern turn against 'Enlightenment' values across various disciplines and currently fashionable schools of thought. They are characterized chiefly by a failure to distinguish between two very different kinds or orders of truth-claim. On the one hand 'truth' may be conceived in the traditional (Platonic or Christian) sense, as resulting from an inward revelation vouchsafed to some few elect minds or spirits. It is Spinoza's main argument against excessive reliance on the witness of scriptural narrative that it tends to promote just such a mystified version of truth, since the scriptures (including the New Testament parables) are often couched in obscure, cryptic or allegorical terms which give little hold for rational understanding. (For Kermode, by contrast, it is these passages that present interpretation with its greatest challenge, and which thus give rise to the subtlest, most rewarding forms of revisionist commentary.) This is why Spinoza perceives a close relation between belief in the authenticity of biblical narrative – in the truth of those events supposedly set down under guidance of divine inspiration – and belief in miracles, proph- ecies and other such happenings that run directly counter to natural law and reason alike. In other words, the inability to distinguish true ideas from fictive, inadequate or 'imaginary' notions is one that gives rise to all manner of credulous or downright superstitious attitudes. Spinoza allows that there may have been times – periods of crisis, civil discord, threats to the sense of Jewish national identity – when the Old Testament prophets were justified in exploiting such beliefs with the object of enforcing obedience to the law. But this could only be a matter of short-term strategic necessity, and surely not in any sense a model for subsequent (more enlightened or rational) communities of knowledge.

Hence Spinoza's first rule of adequate understanding: 'to distinguish and separate the true idea from other perceptions, and to keep the mind from confusing with true ideas those which are false, fictitious, and doubtful' (Spinoza, [1677] 1884b, vol. 2, p. 18). And from this precept it follows that the knowledge attained directly or naïvely through narrative representation is not to be confused with the knowledge that derives from a reasoned critique of such first-order narrative beliefs. It can thus be argued that Spinoza's philosophy amounts to a point-for-point reversal of the programme announced by postmodern sceptics (and, less stridently, by thinkers like Kermode) who see no exit from the hermeneutic hall of mirrors. Pierre Macherey makes the point with specific reference to Spinoza, and by way of arguing against those critics who fail to perceive the essential distinction between narrative and critical discourse:

> Fiction is not *truer* than illusion; indeed, it cannot usurp the place of knowledge. But it can set illusion in motion by penetrating its insufficiency, by transforming our relationship to ideology. . . . Fiction deceives us in so far as it is feigned; but this is not a primary act of deception because it aimed at one even more profound, exposing it, helping to release us from it.
>
> (Macherey, 1978, p. 64)

This is why it is wrong – a determinate misreading – to treat Spinoza as belonging to the line of hermeneutic thinkers for whom epistemological questions of truth and falsehood were banished altogether from the realm of textual or narrative understanding. He adopts this standpoint only in regard to that particular form of confusion which mistakes the unwarranted truth-claims of scripture – prophecies, miracles and the like – for items of veridical belief. Here indeed, as Kermode argues, Spinoza holds it necessary to give imagination its due and not follow the line of those (like Maimonides) who create all kinds of sophistical error by striving to accommodate faith to reason. But this applies only to passages that resist the best efforts of enlightened commentary, or which cannot be construed in accordance with the standards of rational consistency and truth. And even here, Spinoza thinks, it is the commentator's task not to treat such passages as bearing a mystical, allegorical or revelatory import beyond reach of further analysis, but – on the contrary – to ask what precisely were the socio-historical conditions that caused them to be couched in a manner so resistant to the interests of rational comprehension.

One major source of confusion here is the belief that prevails among post-structuralists, postmodernists, and others of a kindred (anti-Enlightenment) persuasion: namely, that any talk of 'truth' – in whatever disciplinary or cultural context – must always involve a covert appeal to some ultimate, transcendent source of meaning and value, an appeal whose authority can only derive from a mystified ('metaphysical') ground of all knowledge. To some extent, no doubt, this confusion has been reinforced by a simplified misreading of what Derrida has to say about 'logocentrism' or the so-called Western 'metaphysics of presence', terms which are commonly taken to signify a repressive regime of old-fashioned ideas about language, truth and reality which can now be 'deconstructed' – once and for all – by pointing up their blind-spots of rhetorical implication (see Derrida, 1976). That this is a travesty of Derrida's arguments should be clear to anyone who has read his work and not relied on the usual handful of slogans taken out of context. In fact he makes a point of insisting *first* that standards of truth and right reading are integral to the deconstructive enterprise, and *second* that any notion of escaping logocentrism – of jumping outside it, so to speak, 'with both feet' – is yet another form of inverted metaphysical thinking, and one that is destined to fall straight back into the most naïve of pre-critical assumptions (Derrida, 1981).

So it is not just a matter of unmasking all truth-claims as complicitous with a sovereign 'metaphysics of presence' that runs all the way, as Terry Eagleton (1986) puts it, 'from Plato to Nato'. If this were the only message of Derrida's work – as it is for many of his literary-critical disciples – then deconstruction would amount to little more than a series of elegant (though rather tedious) variations on a well-worn theme. What is distinctive about Derrida's writing is the extreme analytical rigour with which he draws out the elements of textual resistance – the antinomies or unstable binary oppositions – that tend to undermine this classical (ultimately Christian and Platonist) economy of truth. And in order to do so he operates always with a strict regard for those other kinds of truth-claim that regulate the critical reading of texts and which are simply indispensable to any project whose aim is to question that otherwise seamless metaphysical enclosure. For the alternative, as we have seen, is to introduce a radical split or disjunction between questions of meaning and questions of truth, such that criticism becomes in the end a kind of brooding on textual mysteries, and none the less so for maintaining an outlook of 'postmodern' scepticism that professes to oppose all forms of orthodox doctrinal adherence. It is for this reason that Derrida insists – and more emphatically in his recent writings – that deconstruction is far from abandoning the standards of 'serious' philosophical debate (see Derrida, 1989). These standards are those of argumentative rigour, fidelity to the text in hand, and a willingness not to let one's own prejudices – or the dictates of consensual wisdom – prevent one from perceiving problematic details that go strongly against the interpretative grain. In short, deconstruction derives all its critical force from the way that it questions certain kinds of mystified truth-claim while yet subscribing to the highest standards of argumentative rigour and respect for the protocols of textual close-reading. If this fact goes unnoticed by many opponents it is equally lost upon those who embrace deconstruction as a licence for dispensing with every last principle of truth, validity and reason.

The point is best made in a passage by Paul de Man, responding to the widespread mistaken belief that a deconstructive reading can find no room for epistemological questions (or values of truth and falsehood). It all depends, de Man writes,

> on how one 'understands' the relationship between truth and understanding. Understanding is not a version of one single and universal Truth that would exist as an essence, a hypostasis. The truth of a text is a much more empirical and literal event. What makes a reading more or less true is simply the predict-ability, the necessity of its occurrence, regardless of the reader or of the author's wishes. . . . It depends, in other words, on the rigor of the reading as an argument. Reading is an argument (which is not necessarily the same as a polemic) because it has to go against the grain of what one would want to happen in the name of what has to happen: this is the same as saying that understanding is an epistemo-logical event prior to being an ethical or aesthetic value. This does not mean that there can be a true reading, but that no reading is conceivable in which the question of its truth or falsehood is not primarily involved.
>
> (de Man, 1978, p. xi)

My point is that Spinoza not only raises these questions but raises them in a sharply insistent form which as yet finds no room for the convenient escape-route represented by the discourse of aesthetic values. And this is nowhere more apparent than in Spinoza's dealing with fiction as a determinate mode of knowledge, a mode that stands (so to speak) half-way between truth and falsehood, since it involves untruths that are knowingly entertained as such, rather than mistaken for adequate ideas. It is precisely this aspect of Spinoza's thinking that has led thinkers like Macherey to propose a new point of depar-ture for Marxist 'theoretical practice', an approach that would respect the relative autonomy attained by various levels of cultural production, and thus avoid the reductionist error that treated them indifferently as so many forms of ideological 'false consciousness' (Macherey, 1978). What is crucial is the insistence that questions of truth and falsehood not be overriden by a mystified appeal to some alternative realm of aesthetic understanding where such ques-tions are effectively ruled out of court.

It is here that Macherey's approach to these questions converges with de Man's on a number of crucial points. Both see nothing but error and delusion in the idea that literature must somehow be exempt from all rational sense-making standards (or values of truth and falsehood). Both make this point in direct opposition to an idealist (or metaphysical) philosophy of art which locates the highest values of aesthetic experience in a realm of self-confirming aesthetic values – 'organic form', the poem as 'verbal icon', 'concrete universal' and so forth – which then serve as a pretext for avoiding any question as to the social and material factors bound up with the work of literary production. And finally, they both – though de Man more emphatically – equate this powerful mystifying drive with a tendency to ignore the ontological difference between language (as a realm of signifying structures irreducible to the order of intuitive or phenomenal self-evidence) and reality (or the naturalized, 'commonsense' view of reality) as that which presents itself directly to the senses without any intervening process of linguistic mediation. This is why, in de Man's words, although 'it is by no means an established fact that aesthetic values and literary structures are incompatible', nevertheless 'their compatibility, or lack of it, has to remain an open question', so that 'the manner in which the teaching of literature, since its beginning in the later nineteenth century, has foreclosed the question is unsound, even if motivated by the best of intentions' (de Man, 1986, p. 25). For the effect of this premature conflation of realms is to exclude the possibility that language itself – or language as the unstable force-field of relations between logic, grammar and rhetoric – might offer resistance to the various forms of uncritical or naturalized perception that derive their considerable power from precisely such delusive totalizing metaphors.

At this stage it is worth recalling a passage from Althusser and Balibar's *Reading Capital* (1970), since they offer what amounts to a point-for-point endorsement of the case I have presented thus far. Spinoza was the first thinker

> to have raised the problem of *reading* and, in consequence, of *writing* . . . also the first to have proposed both a theory of history and a philosophy of the opacity of the immediate. With him, for the first time ever, a man held together in this way the essence of reading and the essence of history in a theory of the difference between the imaginary and the true.
>
> (p. 16)

It was on the basis of these Spinozist categories, they argue, that Marx was able to achieve his most significant theoretical advance, a distinction between 'science' and 'ideology' which avoided the errors of reductionist thought while maintaining the material specificity of discourse at its various levels of production. And this break was in turn made possible by what they describe as 'the dissipation of the *religious* myth of reading', that is to say, the move against hermeneutic models which located the truth of the text in some realm of occult, allegorical or figural sense, a realm to which readers could only have access through divine revelation, intuitive foreknowledge or other such privileged modes of entry. This is why – as I have argued – Spinoza stands firmly apart from the long tradition of exegetical thought which began with the attempt to 'accommodate' Old and New Testament scriptural texts, and whose latest (hermeneutic and post-structuralist) variants still bear the mark of that seemingly remote prehistory.

Hence the connection that Althusser and Balibar make between Spinoza's theory of language (or 'writing and reading') and his signal contribution to Marxist debate about the nature and modalities of historical knowledge. This connection has to do with his threefold argument: (1) that our grasp of historical events is necessarily partial and timebound (i.e. that it belongs to the realm of *experientia vaga*, or inadequate and confused ideas); (2) that this condition also applies to any knowledge attained through language, since verbal signs – written or spoken – are likewise subject to all manner of chance collocations or random associative linkage, and are thus inherently suspect from the standpoint of reason; and (3) that the mind's only recourse against these sources of error is to theorize the conditions that brought them about – the historical, causal or linguistic factors – and thereby achieve the kind of rational grasp that converts 'passive' into 'active' understanding. And it is here that questions of writing and reading acquire a special salience in Spinoza's work, along with the related topic of fictive or 'feigned' utterances, those that occupy a third domain of knowledge situated (so to speak) *between* truth and falsehood, and which therefore – as Althusser and Macherey argue – cannot be assigned to some separate realm of non-cognitive or purely 'aesthetic' values. Thus fiction gives access to 'adequate ideas' in so far as it reworks, deconstructs or estranges the materials of common-sense (ideological) perception, or the forms under which experience presents itself to a mind held captive by 'knowledge of imagination'. The most important point here is that Spinoza – like Althusser and Macherey – insists on treating fiction as a determinate mode of knowledge, admittedly a partial or 'mutilated' mode, but one that has its own distinctive role to play in the process of arriving at adequate ideas.

THE CRITIQUE OF REVELATION REVISITED

The case of Salman Rushdie's novel *The Satanic Verses* (1988) is one that raises a number of pertinent questions about fictional truth and the status of literary texts in relation to forms of religious and political power. Like Spinoza, Rushdie has had the courage to stand up against a resurgent fundamentalist movement whose authority rests on the appeal to scriptural warrant, and whose reading of scripture is clearly dictated by the struggle between rival claimants to the 'truth' as revealed through divine inspiration to a self-proclaimed pious elect. Like Spinoza again, he sets out to show how such movements come about; how the mystagogues are able to maintain their power by exploiting a range of 'imaginary' devices – prophecy, miracles, divine interventions, all manner of occult or supernatural 'proofs' – in order to win assent for doctrines that could scarcely withstand critical scrutiny. 'In despotic statecraft', Spinoza writes, 'the supreme and essential mystery [is] to hoodwink the subjects, and to mask the fear, which keeps them down, with the specious garb of religion' (Spinoza, [1670] 1884a, vol. 1, p. 5). As we have seen, Spinoza goes various ways around to break the hold of such delusive beliefs, or – what he thinks should be sufficient for the purpose – to show how they arise from errors of understanding which in turn have their cause in some particular context of socio-political existence. On balance he considers the New Testament superior to the Old since (for instance) 'the long deductions and arguments of Paul . . . are in nowise written from supernatural revelation' (p. 159). But there can be little doubt that Spinoza maintained a deep mistrust of all religious truth-claims, especially where these took the form of an appeal to scriptural authority backed up – as so often – by the threat of dire punishments (real or imaginary) for anyone who challenged their presumptive self-evidence.

One line of response in the Rushdie affair has been to point out that this is after all a work of fiction – 'postmodernist' fiction at that – and should therefore not be judged (much less condemned) as if it were claiming any kind of factual, historical or truth-telling warrant. Or again, to adopt an alternative idiom: *The Satanic Verses* belongs to the genre of so-called 'magical realism', a mode that typically mixes up the orders of verisimilitude and fantasy-projection to a stage where the reader loses all sense of where the one shades off into the other. From this point of view the whole controversy would seem just an absurd category-mistake, a confusion brought about by the failure to recognize that literary works are not in the business of arguing a case, reinterpreting history or engaging in matters of doctrinal dispute. The Ayatollah and his fundamentalist disciples would then be seen as literal-minded readers – non-readers more often – who attacked Rushdie's novel on the mistaken grounds first, that it was a travesty of actual events in the life of the Prophet and the history of Islam, and second that it was preaching a set of irreligious or wickedly heterodox ideas at variance with everything their faith held sacred. So the best defence of Rushdie's book would be to point out its elaborately fictive construction – its not belonging to the 'language-game' of presenting truths, offering arguments, challenging scriptural witness, etc. – and thus make it clear that the charges of apostasy were based on a gross misunderstanding.

This argument of course had the virtue of promising to soothe fundamentalist passions and afford at least the basis of a working truce in an enflamed situation. Rushdie himself made the point in an open letter to Rajiv Gandhi protesting against the fact that his novel had been banned by an act of government in India:

The section of the book in question (and let's remember that the book isn't actually about Islam, but about migration, metamorphosis, divided selves, love, death, London and Bombay) deals with a prophet who is not called Muhammad living in a highly fantasticated city – made of sand, it dissolves when water falls upon it – in which he is surrounded by fictional followers, one of whom happens to bear my own first name. Moreover, this entire sequence happens in dream, the fictional dream of a fictional character, an Indian movie-star, and one who is losing his mind, at that. How much further from history could one get?

(in Appignanesi and Maitland, 1989, p. 44)

Clearly it is vital – not only for Rushdie but for many writers working under oppressive religious or political regimes – that this distinction be respected and that novels not be read as if they were straightforward statements of authorial belief. And yet there is a sense in which one begs the whole question by adopting this standpoint, since it rests on principles that enjoy wide support in our own (relatively secularized) societies, but which would count for nothing with Rushdie's fundamentalist opponents. At their broadest these principles have to do with the separation of powers between Church and State, the 'self-evident' democratic freedoms of thought and speech, and – closely related to these – the (again relative) autonomy of art as a form of expression exempt from certain otherwise normative juridical constraints. And it could further be argued that literary criticism has developed a more specialized version of the same basic attitude, one that progressively elaborates a whole range of concepts (aesthetic disinterest, the 'suspension of disbelief', ambiguity, paradox, the 'implied author', intertextuality and so forth) by way of backing up this claim for literature as a mode of utterance with its own *sui generis* standards of imaginative truth (see Hohendahl, 1982; Eagleton, 1984).

These are some of the values invoked by Rushdie in the above-cited passage. It is a stance whose history begins in the English Renaissance period with Sir Philip Sidney's defence of poetry as a 'feigned' or fictive mode of utterance, one that could not be held to account – as Plato or the latter-day puritans would have it – as if poets were engaged in the same kind of language-game as philosophers, moralists or historians. This issue was confronted over again when the novel emerged as a distinctive genre in the mid- to late eighteenth century. The main problem here was that prose-fiction, unlike poetry, lacked the more obvious formal markers of 'literary' status, and could thus all too easily be mistaken for factual or truth-telling discourse. Hence the various efforts – in the legislative sphere as well as among critics and commentators on the novel – to explain just how this distinction might be upheld and where exactly the line should be drawn between novels on the one hand and news reports, historical narratives, political tracts or theological arguments on the other (Davis, 1983). This can best be understood in Habermasian terms as an aspect of the progressive separating out or specialization of discursive regimes that gave rise to the modern 'public sphere' of differential validity-claims, with literature enjoying a large measure of autonomy *vis-à-vis* those other forms of knowledge (Habermas, 1962). And there is, as we have seen, some reason for regarding Spinoza as the first philosopher to have worked out this distinction in detail, thus resisting the tendency to confuse matters of revealed or authoritative truth with fictive or imaginary modes of representation. This is why one can take it as Spinoza's chief contribution to the history of secular interpretative thought that he managed to liberate the practice of textual hermeneutics from its erstwhile bondage to the dictates of orthodox belief. It is important to remember that the very possibility of open debate on such questions is a freedom that was won in large part through the efforts – very often the reviled and persecuted efforts – of writers who claimed an imaginative licence to satirize the truth-claims of religion.

Graham Swift makes this point – echoing Rushdie's own position – when he writes of *The Satanic Verses* that 'a work of literature is *more* than free expression. It is creative expression, which does not argue, state, or assert, so much as make. A novel exists, *lives* in the minds of its readers, as no statement or assertion can' (in Appignanesi and Maitland, 1989, p. 219). And Carlos Fuentes offers what is perhaps the most eloquent defence of this kind by invoking the example of Mikhail Bakhtin, 'probably the greatest theorist of the novel in our century', and 'one whose life, in a way, is as exemplary as his books'. It is worth citing his remarks at some length since they state the case for imaginative freedom – and for the novel as our last, best hope for such freedom – while following Bakhtin in his pinpoint diagnosis of the pressures that make for conformity, dogmatism, and other forms of oppressive 'monological' discourse (see Bakhtin, 1981). Thus, according to Fuentes,

> Rushdie's work perfectly fits the Bakhtinian contention that ours is an age of competitive languages. The novel is the privileged arena where languages in conflict can meet, bringing together, in tension and dialogue, not only opposing characters, but also different historical ages, social levels, civilizations and other dawning realities of human life. . . . But this is precisely what the Ayatollahs of this world cannot suffer. For the Ayatollahs reality is dogmatically defined once and for all in a sacred text. But a sacred text is, by definition, a completed and exclusive text. You can add nothing to it. It does not converse with anyone. . . . It offers a perfect refuge for the insecure who then, having the protection of a dogmatic text over their heads, proceed to excommunicate those whose security lies in the search for truth. . . . When we all understood everything, the epic was possible. But not fiction. The novel is born from the fact that we do not understand one another any longer, because unitary, orthodox language has broken down. Impose a unitary language: you kill the novel, but you also kill society.
>
> (in Appignanesi and Maitland, 1989, pp. 245–6)

It is no coincidence that this coupling of Rushdie and Bakhtin goes by way of several interconnected themes – persecution, liberty of thought, the closed or 'monological' character of religious discourse – that were first brought together in Spinoza's critique of revelation. In fact one could argue that Spinoza belongs very much in the company of those novelists, poets, satirists and other such 'literary' figures whose work had the effect – at least in the long run – of securing vital new freedoms, at first for their own (henceforth recognizably distinctive) kind of writing, then in the realms of philosophy, politics, theology and other such contested domains. To this extent Kermode would be justified in his claim that Spinoza more or less invented the practice of secular hermeneutics, a practice which could only come into being with the challenge to canonical, self-authorized versions of scriptural truth.

But one must also recall Spinoza's argument – taken up by theorists like Althusser and Macherey – that fictions cannot be treated on a level with falsehoods or consigned to a realm of non-cognitive 'aesthetic' value where questions of truth and error simply do not arise. For it is precisely by virtue of what Spinoza terms the mixed or 'multiplex' character of fictive discourse – its power to clarify confused ideas by subjecting them to a different, more rigorous or undeceiving order of narrative representation – that criticism is enabled to perceive the blind-spots, the errors of 'common-sense' belief or ideology, that would otherwise pass for truth. This is simply a more 'philosophical' way of making the point that novels can effectively argue a case and, what is more, give rise to counter-arguments which take fiction seriously for just that reason. And this applies not only to obvious instances – the *roman à thèse*, political novels, conversion narratives or other such overtly didactic works – but also to writing whose design on the reader is much less palpable, but which none the less provokes a whole range of attitudinal responses, from straightforward endorsement to downright angry rejection. The latter alternative is one that rarely figures in the discourse of academic criticism, since here – as we have seen – there is a countervailing tendency to elevate issues of aesthetic worth above questions of argumentative warrant. But one still finds notable exceptions to this rule, among them Macherey, de Man, Empson, and others (like Gerald Graff) who have held out against the widespread aestheticizing drift. What unites these thinkers across otherwise considerable differences of view is the conviction, first, that fictive works make statements (or involve propositional attitudes); second, that criticism should not seek refuge in a realm of sacrosanct 'literary' values; and third, that one can indeed argue with texts on a range of issues – philosophical, political or socio-historical – which do inescapably lead on to questions of truth and falsehood.

The move to dissociate literature from truth-claims of any kind is one that can only trivialize fiction, or reduce it to the level of a pure, self-occupied play with narrative codes and conventions that could have no possible bearing on matters of real-world practical concern. Significantly, it is a move that is made more often by theorists of the postmodern – by literary critics, sympathetic or hostile – than by novelists (for instance Kurt Vonnegut, Angela Carter, E. L. Doctorow and Rushdie himself) who apparently see no problem about combining on the one hand a commitment to various forms of experimental, postmodern or defamiliarizing technique, and on the other a continuing (if intermittent) use of the documentary-realist mode (Hutcheon, 1987). What characterizes their work – and Rushdie's in particular – is a constant intertwining of fictive and factual (or imaginary and truth-conditional) discourse which deliberately eschews such ready-made distinctions and asks us to conceive of alternative realities perceptibly akin to our own, but differing from it in certain crucial respects. To this extent they are working in the same area as modal logicians and 'possible worlds' theorists, those who seek to establish the rules or constraints that regulate the transfer of properties, individuals and events from one such world to another. It would then be a question for the literary critic just how far 'realism' – or the realist effect – is a product of the 'trans-world identity' that holds between certain crucial features that turn out to be invariant across these otherwise disparate realms (Pavel, 1987). One of them (the world we do in fact inhabit) would enjoy a greater or lesser degree of ontological privilege depending on the analytic framework adopted, or on the analyst's willingness to accept some version of 'modal realism' that treated all worlds as equally compossible, and therefore as *actually existing* so far as we can tell from our own (common-sense or this-worldly) standpoint (Lewis, 1986).

My purpose in these last few paragraphs has been, once again, to challenge the idea that fictional texts have nothing to do with values of truth and falsehood, or with issues that arise more obviously in relation to other kinds of writing (historical, political, philosophical and so forth). It may also help to explain what is less than satisfactory about that line of defence in the Rushdie case which takes it for granted that fictions are somehow exempt from the commonplace requirements of truth-telling discourse. Of course this idea has a long prehistory, from Plato (who considered it a downright scandal) to those subsequent apologists for poetry and fiction, from Sir Philip Sidney to Shelley, Arnold, I. A Richards and the New Critics, all of whom took the view that literature offered a different sort of 'truth', one that involved an appeal to values – of imagination, creativity, 'emotive' meaning, ambiguity, paradox, etc. – which were simply irreducible to cognitive standards of veridical utterance. In which case clearly the Islamic fundamentalists have got it wrong, not to mention a long succession of priests and commissars who have likewise ignored the essential difference between fictive and other modes of discourse.

Returning to Spinoza is one way of grasping what has been at stake in the controversy over *The Satanic Verses*. For Spinoza, it is unthinkable that fiction should be treated as belonging to a realm quite apart from the interests of reason and truth, a realm of 'pseudo-statements' (in Richards's phrase) where

55

the only operative standard of value is the pragmatist appeal to what is 'good in the way of belief' (Richards, 1924). On the contrary: fiction is a contested zone *between* truth and falsehood where 'adequate ideas' are mixed (but not inextricably mixed) with imaginary, erroneous, metaphorical, analogical and other such illusory knowledge-effects. Thus, according to Macherey: 'fiction, not to be confused with illusion, is the substitute for, if not the equivalent of, knowledge. A theory of literary production must show us what the text "knows", how it "knows"' (Macherey, 1978, p. 64). It is therefore the task of criticism to explain just how – by what structural mechanisms specific to the nature of narrative form – fiction is enabled to reveal the limits of its own 'imaginary' presuppositions. And this follows directly from the Spinozist principle that errors of understanding (or 'ideas of imagination') are not mere mistakes to be put down to some localized aberration on the part of this or that individual thinker. Rather, they always take rise from the chain of 'multiplex' concatenated causes and effects which reason is presently unable to perceive owing to the limits placed upon it by prevailing forms of consensus belief, whether religious or socio-political in origin.

For Spinoza, the distinction between truth and error is one that can and must be maintained despite all the melancholy evidence to date that error has a hold upon human minds that may resist the best efforts of enlightened critique. And it is especially in the realm of fiction – the border-zone where 'inadequate ideas' are reworked into a different, more complex and articulated form – that theory is best placed to understand the effects of imaginary misrecognition. This is why a novel like *The Satanic Verses* has a power to convince – and also to antagonize – beyond what might be expected according to the current postmodernist wisdom. Rushdie himself takes exactly this line in an interview conducted at a time (mid-September 1988) when the hate-campaign had begun to build up but had not yet assumed lethal proportions:

> I guess some people might get upset because it is not reverent, but the point is a serious attempt to write about religion and revelation from the point of view of a secular person. I think that's a perfectly legitimate exercise. Besides, Moham-mad is a very interesting figure. He's the only prophet who exists even remotely within history. He is the only one about whom there is some half-established more-or-less factual historical information. That makes him a human being and doubly interesting.
>
> (in Appignanesi and Maitland, 1989, p. 41)

In the reading of fiction we are constantly engaged in that process of adjudicating different orders of truth-claim which Spinoza presents as the only means toward a better, more enlightened understanding. That is to say, the chief interest of critical thought is to see where the text reveals more than it can say, or where the need to make sense of recalcitrant details imposes a reading counter to received or canonical ideas of what the text ought to mean. This argument receives its strongest theoretical elaboration at the hands of those critics (like Macherey) who have adopted an overtly Spinozist approach in the reading of literary works. But it is also presupposed by any methodology – whether Marxist, deconstructionist, feminist, sociological or New Historicist – which operates on the principle that criticism can produce a knowledge of the text beyond what is given at the level of straightforward self-evidence or 'common-sense' belief. And to this extent one could claim that all the most significant developments in modern critical theory have their origin (knowingly or not) in Spinoza's way of treating the co-implicated orders of truth, falsehood, error and fiction. Above all, they take for granted his basic premise with regard to the latter: that fictive ideas (or imaginary representations) are potentially a source of genuine knowledge in so far as they allow for a critical undertaking that seeks to distinguish those various orders and articulate the structural relations between them.

This is why the Rushdie affair raises issues that cannot be conveniently shunted aside by protesting that fiction has nothing to do with matters of doctrinal import or the truth-claims of revealed religion. Critics who take this accommodating line – no doubt with the best of placatory intentions – are ignoring the close relationship that exists between the critique of scriptural authority advanced by secularizing thinkers like Spinoza and the undeceiving virtues of fictive representation when directed against the forces of bigotry, superstition, and religious or political intolerance. Marina Warner makes this point most effectively in the following rejoinder to Rushdie's fundamentalist opponents. What has chiefly aroused their indignation, she writes,

> is the idea that the Devil managed to interpolate verses into the Koran. Erasmus came into conflict with the Church because he found that the original canonical translations of the New Testament had not been accurate. . . . Of course Salman Rushdie never cast himself in any way as a learned commentator on the authenticity of the Koran, in the Erasmian sense, but the crisis has given his levity, his satire, a new, momentous seriousness, and its lessons should be built on, to make an appeal to moderate thinkers within Islam, who are able to entertain the possibility of historicist and textual analysis of the Koran.
>
> (in Appignanesi and Maitland, 1989, p. 210)

In this respect *The Satanic Verses* asks to be read in much the same way as works like Voltaire's *Candide* or Shelley's *Prometheus Unbound*, writings whose sheer argumentative force – and whose power to provoke extreme forms of hostile response – was scarcely the less for the fact of their adopting a fictive, poetic or 'imaginary' form. Shelley provides the most interesting case for comparison here since he read and admired (and even translated) Spinoza, as well as publishing his own, much reviled essay 'The Necessity of Atheism' (1811) and also, in his poetry, presenting what amounted to a full-scale Spinozist attack on the values of institutionalized Christian belief, albeit in the guise of a counter-mythology decked out with various arcane – mostly neo-Platonist – allegorical devices. These latter did nothing to obscure the central message: that religion had lent itself all too easily to the interests of an orthodox élite whose power derived partly from the joint machinations of church and state, and partly from the sway of superstitious belief over minds held captive by 'confused' or 'imaginary' ideas. Certainly few readers – sympathetic or otherwise – would have failed to perceive that the prose-tract and the poetry were equally a part of Shelley's campaign against the truth-claims of revealed religion.

CONCLUSION: LITERARY THEORY AND THE GROUNDS OF DISSENT

This essay has argued that current debates in literary theory are one major forum where Spinoza's ideas are still very actively at work, though not without continued opposition from various quarters. The most important point on which these critics divide is the question whether literary works can be construed as advancing propositions, arguing a case, or involving knowledge-constitutive interests that are capable of reasoned assessment and critique. Empson's later writings are perhaps the most striking example of a project that concerns itself both with questions in the realm of literary theory – giving rise to his arguments in *The Structure of Complex Words* – and with broader issues of a moral, historical and (above all) religious import. But it is wrong to suggest that these are separate interests since, as we have seen, Empson's defence of a truth-functional semantics applied to the language of poetry and fiction goes along with his aversion to Christian belief and his resolute attempts to make sense of literature on rationally accountable terms. In fact his entire critical production after *Milton's God* (1961) was devoted to arguing the case for various authors – Marlowe, Donne, Marvell, Coleridge, Joyce, Eliot, Yeats and others – as either the victims of neurotic guilt and conflict brought on by their accepting the full implications of Christian theology, or as having bravely resisted that doctrine, only to be kidnapped by neo-Christian interpreters in pursuit of some pious message or other (Empson, 1984, 1987a, b). My point is not to claim that these essays are all of them equally convincing, or that they represent a full-scale project of radically secularized hermeneutic thought growing directly out of Empson's historico-semantic researches in *Complex Words*. What they do help to show is the close relation that exists between a rationalist desire to demystify the sources of erroneous or confused belief, and an attitude to questions of literary meaning that refuses to fall back upon ideas of ambiguity, paradox, 'pseudo-statement', fictive licence or other such handy escape-routes.

It is no coincidence, therefore, that Empson's reading of Milton stands squarely in the line of left-romantic or radical revisionist accounts which begins with Blake's famous dictum (that Milton was 'of the Devil's party without knowing it'), and continues with Shelley's more elaborated version of the same antinomian thesis in his *Defence of Poetry* (1821)). Where Empson most emphatically rejoins this tradition is in arguing first, that Milton's poetry has to do with doctrinal issues at the heart of Christian belief, and thus cannot be treated – as critics like C. S. Lewis would have it – as 'great literature' but wildly heretical, and hence no problem from an orthodox theological stand-point; second, that the poem runs into all manner of difficulty in its effort to make good sense of the story and thereby justify God's ways to man; and third, that we should at least give Milton due credit for the evidence that his feelings revolted – at whatever 'unconscious' level – against the demands of his official religious creed. In short, Empson comes out steadfastly against the kind of reading that treats literary works as belonging to a realm of 'imaginative' truths unaccountable to plain-prose reason or the standards of commonplace human decency. This was why the New Critics found problems with Empson's work, admiring his extreme sophistication in the business of close-reading or verbal exegesis, but warning against his tendency to think that poems offered arguments, or grounds for taking issue with their (supposed) argumentative claims. John Crowe Ransom articulates this feeling of unease when he writes that Empson takes poetry 'too seriously', and thus threatens to violate 'the law of its kind'. This habit went back to Empson's reading of Herbert in *Seven Types of Ambiguity*, a reading that not only teased out the paradoxes of Herbert's 'The Sacrifice', but which pushed them to the point of extracting a series of antinomies – logical contradictions – that seemed to impugn the very bases of Christian faith. For Ransom, in short, 'the metaphysical procedure was singu-larly like the theological, with a rather important difference: the poet was playful, while the theologian was in dead earnest.' And again: metaphysical poetry had to 'suggest theologies . . . to suggest them, or to imitate them; not to *be* them' (Ransom, 1938, pp. 328–9). Nothing could capture more precisely the distance that separates Empson's thinking from the currency, not only of the old New Criticism (with its marked 'neo-Christian' ethos), but also from those subsequent movements of thought which likewise drive a wedge between questions of meaning and values of truth and falsehood.

Jonathan Culler makes this point with admirable force in his book *Framing the Sign* (1988). Like Empson, he thinks it an alarming fact about recent (post-war) Anglo-American criticism that so much of this work is given over to a religious – or crypto-religious – set of doctrines and values, a tendency that is then passed off as just an aspect of our Christian 'cultural heritage', so that any serious attempt to question them is viewed as subversive, misguided, or somehow in bad taste. 'That this idea should be possible indicates just how far education has abandoned its historic tasks, of combating superstition, encouraging sceptical debate about competing religions and their claims or their myths, and fighting religious dogmatism and its political consequences' (Culler, 1988, p. 78). What is more, this falling-back into postures of religious conformism on the part of literary critics goes along with a widespread popular resurgence of fundamentalist belief among various creeds and denominations, a development that is all too clearly visible in the current Christian and Islamic revivalist campaigns. As Culler points out, this situation is doubly ironic in so far as the critique of dogmatic religion was a process initiated and carried through very largely on principles that derived from comparative philology, textual criticism, narrative poetics and other such fields of study. 'At the beginning of the eighteenth century, one might say without greatly oversimplifying, Protestants took the Bible to be the word of God; by the beginning of the twentieth century this belief was untenable in intellectual circles' (p. 79). Culler makes no mention of Spinoza's role in this history of thought, but it is reasonable to suppose – on all the evidence we have seen so far – that it would scarcely have taken the shape it did, or exerted such a powerful influence, had Spinoza not written the *Theologico-Political Treatise*.

Culler goes on to deplore the way that this critical tradition has been kept from view by the orthodox (or not-so-orthodox) pieties of present-day academic scholarship. Thus he notes that there has lately been a 'striking revival of interest in the sacred', not only on the part of those conformist 'Neo-Christians' whom Empson singled out for attack, but also among the votaries of myth-criticism, psychoanalysis, narrative theory, hermeneutics, and even deconstruction (thus 'Geoffrey Hartman . . . jokingly proposes that literature departments should be rechristened "Departments of Mystery Management" ', p. 81). In each case, so Culler argues, 'instead of leading the critique of dogmatic mythologies, literary criticism is contributing to the legitimation of religious discourse' (p. 79). To which he might have added the further observation that this process can only be helped along – or at any rate encounters no effective resistance – from those schools of postmodern neo-pragmatist thought that come out 'against theory', or against the whole tradition of enlightened rational critique. For here also it is no great distance from moderate, historically-informed versions of the relativist argument (i.e. that ideas of reason and truth are always in some degree culture-specific) to the adoption of a wholesale irrationalist creed that denounces such ideas as chimerical at best, and at worst as mere instruments of the will-to-power masquerading as pure, disinterested knowledge. And at this point – where Nietzsche is most often invoked – there is nothing to prevent the further slide into a form of mystical or mythopoeic thought whose strongest affinities (as Habermas argues) are with doctrines evolved among right-wing opponents of Enlightenment thinking in the immediate post-Kantian period.

It seems to me that Culler gets the emphasis right when he argues that 'respect for religious values' – whether Christian, Jewish, Islamic or whatever – should not be interpreted as granting those values a total exemption from critical scrutiny, or restoring them to the kind of sacrosanct status that they once enjoyed as matters of revealed truth. And he is likewise persuasive when he treats current issues in the field of literary theory as variants of the characteristic liberal dilemma: how to make allowance for the sheer variety of creeds, ideologies and belief-systems while reserving the right to criticize any manifest failures on their part with respect to these same (no doubt culture-specific) values of uncoerced rational debate. What is crucial here is the distinction established by Spinoza (and developed by Kant) between *matters of faith* where each individual is at liberty to believe and profess as they wish, and *matters of reason* or intellectual conscience where again there is (or should be) no constraint under law, but where the rule is that this freedom not be curtailed by any imposition of dogmatic beliefs. From this point of view the liberal dilemma comes about through a basic confusion of realms, a failure to grasp that one can indeed criticize ideologies or religions for promoting narrow, intolerant or prejudicial behaviour without thereby setting up to judge them from one's own (equally prejudiced and intolerant) standpoint. For this objection would apply only if one's grounds for thus judging were a matter of unargued belief or passive compliance with the dictates of an absolute creed. But the whole point of the liberal distinction between private and public realms is to prevent such unwarranted intrusions of faith upon the freedoms of thought, conscience and expression.

Now of course it may be argued – as it has been by various parties to the debate over Rushdie's book – that liberalism itself has a political agenda, a core-set of values and beliefs, and hence should not pose as some kind of neutral adjudicative discourse devoid of such partisan interests. But, once again, this ignores what is distinctive about liberal ideology: the fact that it can indeed be put to such self-interested, partial or prejudiced uses, yet still provide a yardstick by which to measure these distortions of its own legitimizing claims. Thus – to take what is perhaps the most familiar example – a document may be framed which has a good deal to say (in good liberal fashion) about the 'rights of man', but which the framers – and interpreters for a good while thereafter – choose to understand as specifically excluding women and slaves. But one should also remark the other side: that the blind-spots of prejudice do come to light in the end, albeit (most often) against considerable odds of entrenched self-interest and selective interpretation. And the reason why liberalism exhibits this self-correcting tendency – unlike more dogmatic ideologies and creeds – is the fact that its central terms (freedom, justice, equality) are themselves subject to critical reassessment in the light of changing social ideas and not tied down to some stipulative meaning in accordance with scriptural warrant, revealed truth, the natural order of society, or other such potent immobilizing myths. This difference is basically what separates the parties in the dispute over Rushdie's novel. On the one side are assembled those who advocate an allegiance to truths beyond reach of critical assessment or reasoned debate. On the other gathered are those – admittedly in a state of some confusion at present – whose appeal (or whose best possible ground of appeal) is to the interests of open discussion and enquiry into the values that sustain both their own and their opponents' argumentative positions. Any hint of ethnocentric smugness here should be amply dispelled by the occasional reminder – such as Empson provides – of just how long it took for courageous free-thinkers like Erasmus, Montaigne, Spinoza or Voltaire to knock Christianity into some kind of civilized shape.

This is where literary theory comes in, as a discourse specialized in the adjudication of different orders of truth-claim. 'Above all', Culler writes,

> we should work to keep alive the critical, demythologizing force of contemporary theory – a force which a considerable number of critics are striving to capture and to divert to pious ends. *Down with the priests!* is an unlikely motto for literary studies these days, but we ought to ask why this is so and turn some of our analytical energies on our own relation to religious discourse and ideology – not as a theoretical investigation asking whether literary studies could ever free itself from the theological weight of the hermeneutic tradition or the idea of authority invested in a special text, but as a practical, political way of challenging the authority of a potentially repressive religious discourse and ensuring that we do not encourage respect for it.
>
> (1988, p. 80)

My only quarrel with this concerns Culler's suggestion that the two kinds of knowledge – 'theoretical' and 'practical' – are somehow at odds, or that the former involves an expense of intellectual effort that might better be directed to 'practical' ends. In fact his book gives clear indications to the opposite effect, as for instance by including a chapter on Empson – and specifically on *Complex Words* – where Culler argues that issues of interpretative theory bear directly on questions in the wider (socio-historical) realm of understanding. It seems to me that this has been the central issue in recent debates about the 'function of criticism' – or the purpose of literary studies – at a time when such debates are unignorably affected by the pressures of real-world political circumstance. One point where those pressures can be felt to impinge is precisely on the question – as Culler puts it – whether literary criticism 'could ever free itself from the theological weight of the hermeneutic tradition or the idea of authority invested in a special text' (p. 80). And this question is by no means confined to the academy, as can be seen all too plainly in the reaction to Rushdie's novel.

FURTHER READING

Althusser, L. and Balibar, E. (1970) *Reading Capital*, translated by Ben Brewster, New Left Books, London

Appignanesi, L. and Maitland, S. (eds) (1989) *The Rushdie File*, Fourth Estate Books, London

Bakhtin, M. M. (1981) *The Dialogic Imagination*, translated and edited by Michael Holquist and Caryl Emerson, University of Texas Press, Austin

Culler, Jonathan (1988) *Framing the Sign*, Basil Blackwell, Oxford

de Man, Paul (1986) *The Resistance to Theory*, University of Minnesota Press, Minneapolis

Derrida, Jacques (1976) *Of Grammatology*, translated by G. C. Spivak, Johns Hopkins University Press, Baltimore

Eagleton, Terry (1984) *The Function of Criticism*, Verso, London

Empson, William (1951) *The Structure of Complex Words*, Chatto & Windus, London

——(1961) *Seven Types of Ambiguity*, Penguin, Harmondsworth [first published 1930]

Fish, Stanley (1979) *Is There A Text In This Class? The Authority of Interpretive Communities*, Harvard University Press, Cambridge

Kermode, Frank (1979) *The Genesis of Secrecy*, Harvard University Press, Cambridge

Norris, Christopher (1988) *Deconstruction and the Interests of Theory*, Frances Pinter, London; University of Oklahoma Press, Norman

ADDITIONAL WORKS CITED

Arac, Jonathan (1987) *Critical Genealogies: Historical Situations for Postmodern Literary Studies*, Columbia University Press, New York

Arnold, Matthew (1973) 'Tractatus Theologico-Politicus', 'Spinoza and the Bible' and 'The Bishop and the Philosopher'. In R. H. Super (ed.), *Lectures and Essays in Criticism*, University of Michigan Press, Ann Arbor, pp. 56–64, 158–82, 40–55 [essays first published 1865]

Barthes, Roland (1975) *S/Z*, translated by Richard Miller, Jonathan Cape, London

——(1976) *Image-Music-Text*, translated by Stephen Heath, Fontana, London

Bloom, Harold (1973) *The Anxiety of Influence*, Oxford University Press, New York

——(1976) *Poetry and Repression: Revisionism from Blake to Stevens*, Yale University Press, New Haven

——(1982) *Agon: Towards a Theory of Revisionism*, Oxford University Press, New York

Brooks, Cleanth (1947) *The Well Wrought Urn*, Harcourt Brace, New York

Charity, A. C. (1976) *Events and Their Afterlife*, Cambridge University Press, Cambridge

Coleridge, S. T. (1983) *Biographia Literaria*, edited by James Edgell and W. Jackson Bate, Routledge & Kegan Paul, London [first published 1817]

Culler, Jonathan (1975) *Structuralist Poetics: Structuralism, Linguistics, and the Study of Literature*, Routledge & Kegan Paul, London

Davis, Lennard J. (1983) *Factual Fictions: Origins of the English Novel*, Columbia University Press, New York

de Man, Paul (1978) 'Preface' to Carol Jacobs, *The Dissimulating Harmony*, Johns Hopkins University Press, Baltimore

Derrida, Jacques (1981) 'The Double Session'. In Jacques Derrida, *Dissemination*, translated by Barbara Johnson, Athlone Press, London, pp. 173–285

——(1989) 'Afterword: toward an ethic of discussion'. In Jacques Derrida, *Limited Inc*, 2nd edn, Northwestern University Press, Evanston, pp. 111–60

Eagleton, Terry (1986) 'Frère Jacques, or the Politics of Deconstruction'. In Terry Eagleton, *Against the Grain: Selected Essays*, Verso, London, pp. 79–87

Eliot, T. S. (1928) *For Lancelot Andrewes*, Faber & Faber, London

——(1957a) 'Milton I'. In T. S. Eliot, *On Poetry and Poets*, Faber & Faber, London [essay first published 1936]

——(1957b) 'Milton II'. In T. S. Eliot, *On Poetry and Poets*, Faber & Faber, London [essay first published 1947]

——(1964a) 'Tradition and the Individual Talent'. In T. S. Eliot, *Selected Essays*, Faber & Faber, London [essay first published 1919]

——(1964b) 'The Metaphysical Poets'. In T. S. Eliot, *Selected Essays*, Faber & Faber, London [essay first published 1921]

Empson, William (1961) *Milton's God*, Chatto & Windus, London

——(1984) *Using Biography*, Chatto & Windus, London

——(1987a) *Argufying*, edited by John Haffenden, Chatto & Windus, London

——(1987b) *Faustus and The Censor*, Basil Blackwell, Oxford

Fish, Stanley (1989) *Doing What Comes Naturally: Change, Rhetoric, and the Practice of Theory in Literary and Legal Studies*, Oxford University Press, New York

Gadamer, H.-G. (1975) *Truth and Method*, translated by Garrett Barden and John Cumming, Sheed & Ward, London

——(1979) *Philosophical Hermeneutics*, translated by David E. Linge, University of California Press, Berkeley and Los Angeles

Genette, G. (1979) *Narrative Discourse: An Essay in Method*, translated by Jane E. Lewin, Cornell University Press, Ithaca

Graff, Gerald (1970) *Poetic Statement and Critical Dogma*, Northwestern University Press, Evanston

——(1979) *Literature Against Itself: Literary Ideas in Modern Society*, University of Chicago Press, Chicago

Habermas, Jürgen (1962) *Strukturwändel der Offentlichkeit*, Luchterhand, Neuwied

——(1979) *Communication and the Evolution of Society*, translated by Thomas McCarthy, Heinemann, London

——(1984) *The Theory of Communicative Action*, vol. 1, translated by Thomas McCarthy, Heinemann, London

——(1987) *The Philosophical Discourse of Modernity: Twelve Lectures*, translated by Frederick Lawrence, Polity Press, Cambridge

Hartman, Geoffrey (1980) *Criticism in the Wilderness*, Yale University Press, New Haven

——(1981) *Saving the Text: Literature/Derrida/Philosophy*, Johns Hopkins University Press, Baltimore

Hohendahl, Peter Uwe (1982) *The Institution of Criticism*, Cornell University Press, Ithaca

Hoy, David C. (1979) *The Critical Circle*, University of California Press, Berkeley and Los Angeles

Hutcheon, Linda (1987) *A Poetics of Postmodernism*, Routledge, London

Kermode, Frank (1969) *The Sense of an Ending*, Oxford University Press, New York

___(1975) *The Classic*, Faber & Faber, London

Leavis, F. R. (1952) 'Mr Eliot and Milton'. In F. R. Leavis, *The Common Pursuit*, Chatto & Windus, London, pp. 39–65

Leitch, Vincent (1983) *Deconstructive Criticism: An Advanced Introduction*, Columbia University Press, New York

Lewis, David (1986) *On the Plurality of Worlds*, Basil Blackwell, Oxford

Macherey, Pierre (1978) *A Theory of Literary Production*, translated by Geoffrey Wall, Routledge & Kegan Paul, London

Miller, J. Hillis (1985) *The Linguistic Moment: Wordsworth to Stevens*, Princeton University Press, Princeton

Palmer, Richard (1969) *Hermeneutics: Interpretation Theory in Schleiermacher, Dilthey, Heidegger, and Gadamer*, Northwestern University Press, Evanston

Pavel, Thomas A. (1987) *Fictional Worlds*, Harvard University Press, Cambridge

Ransom, John C. (1938) 'Mr Empson's Muddles', *Southern Review*, 4, 322–39

Richards, I. A. (1924) *Principles of Literary Criticism*, Kegan Paul, Trench, Trubner, London

Rimmon-Kenan, S. (1983) *Narrative Fiction: Contemporary Poetics*, Methuen, London

Rorty, Richard (1982) *Consequences of Pragmatism*, University of Minnesota Press, Minneapolis

___(1989) *Contingency, Irony, and Solidarity*, Cambridge University Press, Cambridge

Rushdie, Salman (1988) *The Satanic Verses*, Viking/Penguin, New York and London

Spinoza, Benedict de (1884a) *Theologico-Political Treatise*. In R. H. M. Elwes (trans.), *The Chief Works of Benedict de Spinoza*, vol. 1, George Bell, London [first published 1670]

___(1884b) *On the Improvement of Understanding*. In R. H. M. Elwes (trans.), *The Chief Works of Benedict de Spinoza*, vol. 2, George Bell, London [first published 1677]

Sprinker, Michael (1987) *Imaginary Relations: Aesthetics and Ideology in the Theory of Historical Materialism*, Verso, London

Strauss, Leo (1965) *Spinoza's Critique of Religion*, Schocken Books, New York

Todorov, T. (1977) *The Poetics of Prose*, translated by Richard Howard, Basil Blackwell, Oxford

White, Hayden (1978) *Tropics Of Discourse*, Johns Hopkins University Press, Baltimore

Wimsatt, W. K. (1954) *The Verbal Icon: Studies in the Meaning of Poetry*, University of Kentucky Press, Lexington

II. LITERATURE AND HISTORY

3

MEDIEVAL LITERATURE
AND THE MEDIEVAL
WORLD

DOUGLAS GRAY

In Cicero's *Somnium Scipionis* the younger Scipio in a dream meets his famous grandfather, Scipio Africanus Major, and is carried up by him to the heavens; he looks down upon Carthage 'from an exalted place, bright and shining, filled with stars':

> As I looked out from this spot, everything appeared splendid and wonderful. Some stars were visible which we never see from this region, and all were of a magnitude far greater than we had imagined. . . . And, indeed, the starry spheres easily surpassed the earth in size. From here the earth appeared so small that I was ashamed of our empire which is, so to speak, but a point on its surface.
>
> (trans. Stahl, 1952, p. 72)

His grandfather shows him the nine spheres which make up the universe – the celestial sphere, 'embracing all the rest . . . confining and containing all the other spheres', in which 'are fixed the eternally revolving movements of the stars', and beneath it, revolving in an opposite direction, those of the seven planets down to the moon ('below the moon all is mortal and transitory, with the exception of the souls bestowed upon the human race by the benevolence of the gods. Above the moon all things are eternal'), and beneath it the earth, never moving. He is amazed by the great and pleasing sound of the music of the spheres:

> That . . . is a concord of tones separated by unequal but nevertheless carefully proportioned intervals, caused by the rapid motion of the spheres themselves. The high and low tones blended together produce different harmonies. . . . Gifted men, imitating this harmony on stringed instruments and in singing, have gained for themselves a return to this region, as have those who have devoted their exceptional abilities to a search for divine truths. The ears of mortals are filled with this sound, but they are unable to hear it.
>
> (pp. 73–4)

This profoundly influential and highly poetic passage (which was admired by medieval readers and was echoed by some of the greatest medieval writers), besides being a fine statement of the dominant view of the cosmos, and of the nature of music, may suggest to the historian of medieval literature a number of other important patterns and ideas – as, for instance, a yearning (if not a rage) for order (note however that the ideal harmony is a balance of *movement*, not as is sometimes thought, a hierarchy that is fixed and rigid), as well as the sad realization of the gulf between eternal harmony and the life of man in this world.

But an obvious point which should be made first is that this scene comes from a classical text, and it may justly be taken to highlight the importance of the legacy of the ancient world in medieval culture, and of the very remarkable continuities between the two cultures. The words 'medieval' and 'the Middle Ages' perpetuate an old and a misleading view which comes from Renaissance humanism and from the Enlightenment, that of a radical break with a lost and glorious classical past, followed at the end of the period by another radical break, the rediscovery of the ancient world and its culture, called, significantly, a 'rebirth' or a 'renaissance'. Some sense of how oversimplified this view is can be seen in an episode early in the *Inferno* (*c.* 1307–21), where Dante, terrified by strange beasts, meets a shade, who identifies himself as the poet who 'sang of that just son of Anchises who came from Troy after proud Ilium was burned'. Amazement turns to reverence – '*tu se' lo mio maestro e 'l mio autore*', 'thou art my master and my author' – and Virgil is to be his guide through hell. Later, Dante is introduced to another four great 'authors' – Homer 'the sovereign poet', Horace the satirist and moralist, Ovid and Lucan. These are venerated and, in varying degrees, used by medieval writers. The 'authors' form part of the school curriculum, with an introductory set of 'minor authors', including Donatus the grammarian, 'Cato' the moralist, and 'Aesop' the fabulist (in Latin), for beginners. Much was lost – a number of Roman authors and, since a knowledge of Greek became rare in the West, the first-hand experience of Greek literature. The story of the *Iliad* was known through an epitome, and Homer's fame as a great poet survived, but since he was a Greek, his version was deemed to be a partial one by those who liked to think that their ancestors had been Trojans. Even more important were the historical effects of the chaos at the end of the empire, notably the ending of pagan culture and the disappearance of the old, educated pagan élite; what was often lost in consequence was an urbanity, learning lightly worn and elegantly expressed, a tolerance of differing points of view.

Because of the great changes in the cultural and social context, it is not surprising to find some strange transformations and misunderstandings of ancient stories and myths. What is important is that these stories and myths do live on, in hundreds of re-tellings, paraphrases or translations, made often into new and excellent works of art (so that in one English romance the story of Orpheus and Eurydice is transformed into a story of a rescue from fairyland, and the Greek and Trojan heroes in the so-called '*romans d'antiquité*', although they worship 'gods', are in outward appearance, and in many of their inner problems, very similar to the chivalrous heroes of the twelfth century). There are two points of significance here: first, that there is no question of a passive 'acceptance' of the 'legacy' of the ancient world, but rather an imaginative recasting or reinterpretation of the old stories, and second, that though some of the results of this may seem to a rigorously 'classical' viewpoint decidedly odd, it is evidence of an extraordinary closeness to and a familiarity with the stories of antiquity which implies a continuity with the past rather than any sort of 'break'. The authors of the past were being used to serve the needs of the present. At the same time, there was throughout the Middle Ages a series of 'classical revivals' or *renovationes*, usually marked not only by a new enthusiasm but also by a desire to improve latinity and style – notably in the Carolingian period, in the twelfth century, as well as in the late medieval Italy of Petrarch and his successors. *Humanitas* is a quality that can be found in many medieval writers, 'religious' as well as 'secular'; and one may distinguish various forms of 'medieval humanism'.

In terms of the life of the intellect and of the spirit there is no doubt that the most revolutionary change was the triumph of Christianity. It endorsed that ancient view of the universe as the ordered and harmonious creation of God, and it offered its own vision of harmony in the vision of eternal life for the blessed. But it also made extreme demands, and sometimes brought extreme tensions as well as hope. Two conversions which had far-reaching effects may be taken as examples – those of an emperor and of a professor of rhetoric. In 312, before a battle, the emperor Constantine is said to have seen a vision of a cross of light, with the words '*hoc signo vinces*': 'by this sign you shall conquer'; he was ordered to place the sign on his helmet and on those of his men, which he did – and conquered. The great vision of the shining cross is one which impressed itself on medieval mystical piety. But its connection with victory and with war was no less influential. Although the 'justness' of a war had to be demonstrated, the way was opened for military campaigns in support of a militant faith, and for a great deal of bloodshed in the name of the Cross. Another result was that a persecuted minority religion became an 'official' and a 'state' religion, which was to affect the lives of people both pious and negligent. It also developed a complex bureaucracy (which could be a 'way to the top' for talented young men of humble origins). And it became one of the strongest centres of power, even though the claims of the papacy were not always eagerly accepted by secular rulers or by political theorists. The conversion of Augustine in Milan in 386 was no less significant. He was only one among the number of the great 'Fathers' of the Church, but his influence was profound and pervasive – most obviously on theology, but not exclusively so. The *Confessions* (397–8), with its interest in the inner life of the soul and in the process of conversion and of self-knowledge, is echoed, whether strongly or faintly, in later works of spiritual instruction and of autobiography. His *City of God* (413–26), with its powerful images of the two opposing cities of Jerusalem and Babylon, and of the Christian man as an exile from his true home and as a pilgrim journeying through a hostile, deceitful and transitory world, is reflected in various kinds of medieval literature. The pilgrimage and the quest become dominant images, and the blend of faith and anxiety a characteristic one.

The one safe generalization that can be made about medieval Christianity is that it was complex and various. At one intellectual extreme, in the 'schools', one could find highly sophisticated philosophical arguments attempting to establish the tenets of the faith on rational and provable foundations; at another, much evidence of ignorance and indifference, or an intense popular piety that is often indistinguishable from magic. But this contrast was not simply one between the 'clerks' and the 'lewed' or the lay folk. There were ignorant and indifferent clerics, and lay men and women with a deep interest in theology and the life of the spirit. Nor was it a case of the 'higher' ecclesiastical strata simply handing down an official doctrine and spirituality to the people; the evidence suggests that the demands of popular piety were both intense and influential (in the establishment of the cults of saints, for instance). The parish clergy were often very close to their flocks in modes of life and of thought, and the parish church was a social as well as a religious focus. There was a strongly ascetic element in medieval Christianity – most people at one point or another thought of (or were reminded of) the great gulf between the omnipotence of God and the littleness of man, of the inevitability of death which would bring an end to worldly pomp and pretensions, of the wiles of the devil and of the spiritual dangers of indulging the flesh. People were taught – though very many seem to have taken little heed of the doctrine – that the demands of the spiritual world were of more consequence than those of the temporal. It was the monastery above all which symbolized the ideal of a total commitment to the life of the spirit and the contempt of the world. Like all ideals in all periods of history, it was not always easy to maintain, but throughout the Middle Ages the monastery, as a centre of both spirituality and learning, made an important contribution to culture. Asceticism could be, and was, carried to extremes, but it is important to remember that alongside the contempt of the world expressing itself in a horror of sinful flesh, 'the food of worms', there is, in the mainstream of medieval Christianity, a firm belief in the dignity of man as the child of God.

There is also much change and development, both in doctrine (as in the changing views of Purgatory) and in spirituality (as is often pointed out, it becomes the 'fashion' in the high and later Middle Ages to stress the human and the pathetic aspects of the story of the Incarnation). Popular piety made urgent demands, and beside the traditional and institutionalized spiritual 'vehicles' of the Church, as symbolized by cathedral, parish church and monastery, new spiritual movements developed, sometimes persecuted, sometimes eventually accepted (as in the case of the Franciscans). These movements often begin with the urge to cure the corruptions and worldliness of the church by a return to the ideal of apostolic poverty. The medieval centuries saw the arrival of the friars (at first, significantly, often greeted with hostility by the monks, and by the parish clergy; later, accused of slipping into worldliness), and the establishment of béguinages and various kinds of lay communities. There were many and various movements for reform; there was constant argument and criticism; the church faced challenges from without and from within. Medieval religion was far from being monolithic, or static; it was marked rather by vitality and by tension, with the church attempting to 'harmonize' these enthusiastic and sometimes potentially disruptive movements. There were tensions also in the spiritual life of individuals: preachers and teachers stirred the hope of eternal life in the heavenly Jerusalem (memorably expressed in some of the great hymns – 'O quanta qualia sunt illa sabbata'), but also stirred anxiety about that great day of accounting at the end of time – 'Dies irae, dies illa . . .'.

It would be wrong to dwell so long on medieval Christianity that it might seem to be somehow separate from the rest of medieval culture. It was part of the whole texture of life. The sacred and the secular often seem to have overlapped completely, sometimes with astonishing results – in the fifteenth-century English *Second Shepherds' Play* there is a comic scene with a stolen sheep which clearly and boldly parodies the sacred scene of the adoration of the Christ-child that follows. Perhaps more than any other practice, that of the pilgrimage illustrates the way in which the life of the world and the life of the spirit could collide or coalesce. Pilgrimage was the literal expression of that ancient idea of the Christian's pilgrimage through life towards the heavenly Jerusalem; it was a solemn penitential act, a symbolic journey to death (a will had to be made, and one's affairs put in order); it was also a spiritually efficacious practice drawing virtue and heavenly reward from the power of the shrine visited, whether at Jerusalem, Rome, Compostela, Walsingham, Canterbury (the shrine of the 'holy blisful martyr' Saint Thomas, who was reputed to help folk 'whan that they were seke'), or at a host of others; it was also a way of seeing the world (as Chaucer remarks, when spring comes people start to long to go on pilgrimage) and in some of its aspects not altogether unlike modern tourist travel (one fifteenth-century German pilgrim rebukes the noblemen who carve their names and their coats of arms on the holy shrines; and Venetian galley-owners seem to have done very well from the pilgrim-trade to the Holy Land); it was also a way of meeting people and making new acquaintances. Moralists sometimes spoke severely about this, and about people like the Wife of Bath, who 'koude muchel of wandrynge by the weye', but the greatest poet of medieval England made a pilgrimage his central image of the jostling and often inharmonious world of different classes and human types, where, as might be expected, 'diverse folk diversely they said'.

It would also be wrong to think only in terms of intellectual changes and movements. Medieval literature was the product of the new societies that emerged from the break-up of the late Roman empire, and continued to develop, as the predominantly rural, agricultural world of the early Middle Ages slowly and fitfully became the uneasy and relatively urbanized world of the fifteenth century. The patterns of rural life continued (in literature the voice of the peasant is rarely heard, unless he has been graced with a miracle or vision like Cædmon (*fl.* 670), and his way of life is rarely described), but towns grew in number and in size from the eleventh century, in a period of relative peace and renewal. To these crowded, noisy, and often violent and demanding centres people were attracted by the hope of wealth and the relative freedom offered by town life. Some became cities, and many developed considerable political power. The wealth of the great merchants and burgesses could be used for the building of civic churches and cathedrals and for the patronage of the arts. The towns were the cradle of the medieval universities (although the subsequent relationship between 'town' and 'gown' was often a violent one). Guilds and fraternities could provide education, welfare services, processions and pageants (and in the north, the great cycles of mystery plays). Towns were the setting for ceremonies in honour of patron saints and for fairs. They were centres to which travelling entertainers, minstrels and story-tellers brought their wares. The considerable influence of the towns on literature does not always show itself in an obvious way – but it is obvious enough that Dante's turbulent relationship with his native Florence is central to his inspiration, as are town life and mercantile values to Boccaccio's *Decameron* (1349–51), while Chaucer is pre-eminently a London poet.

The castle, which is to most modern readers a more characteristic 'image' of the Middle Ages, is, if we think of a crusader castle or an English castle in Wales, a remarkable example of advanced military technology, but it could also be a symbol of oppression (a monk-chronicler of Peterborough records that in Stephen's reign, evil and rapacious men 'filled the land with castles'). It could also be the splendid setting for the social life of the aristocracy (often described in lively scenes in literature, as in *Sir Gawain and the Green Knight*, *c.* 1375–1400). That idealization of the mores of the knightly classes, the large and very long-lived concept of 'chivalry', was played out on the battlefield but also in pageant and tournament, and was celebrated by writers, especially in

74

the genre of 'romance' through heroes like Arthur, Gawain, Lancelot. In this fictional world youth and love reign. From the twelfth century, there develops an extensive vernacular literature of love in the lyrics of the troubadours and the trouvères, and in the immensely fashionable stories of Tristan and Iseult or Lancelot and Guinevere. In the formation and the dissemination of this, women (who, although their role in society was normally highly circumscribed, could sometimes wield considerable political power and, like the later Joan of Arc, change the course of history) seem to have played an important role, sometimes as authors (e.g. Marie de France, or the women troubadours), often as patrons, and always as a dominant and influential part of the audience.

In the early and high Middle Ages, the traditional bonds of society were a series of complex ties and obligations between a lord and his liegemen or vassals, loosely described as 'feudalism'. The giving of service, aid and counsel was reciprocated by the granting of a gift, a *beneficium* (a fief, a grant of land; support and protection). This produced strains, conflicts of homage, aristocratic land-hunger and restlessness, as well as providing an apparent pattern for stability. But its influence is felt throughout medieval literature. In fiction at least, a lover might see himself as the vassal of his lady. And in both fiction and life, a Christian knight could see himself as the vassal of God, an idea which finds its finest expression in the hero's death-scene in the *Chanson de Roland* (? *c.* 1100), where Roland, like a good liegeman, lifts up his glove to God as the angels bear his soul to Paradise. The immense stress on the necessity of personal loyalty meant that 'breaking faith' became almost the worst of sins, and the words for 'traitor' (as well as those for loyalty, faith or 'troth') became profoundly charged with emotion. It is significant that Dante, who is hardly a 'feudal' writer, reserves the deepest places in Hell for the great traitors – Ganelon (the betrayer of Roland) and Judas.

For most people, and for much of the time, life in the Middle Ages was far from being an ideal 'mirror' of the divine harmony. Invasions, wars, rebellions (like the Jacquerie in France in 1358, or the Peasants' Revolt in England in 1381), and plagues (especially the terrible Black Death of 1348–9) all took their toll. Both the great and the humble could easily fall victim to violence. There were robbers and outlaws, who found refuge in the forests (in medieval literature typically the setting for magical events, and the haunts of madmen and fugitives from justice – and injustice). In sharp contrast to the orderly harmony of the heavens, the life of man in the unstable and transitory world below the moon seemed to moralists disorderly, sinful and without spiritual purpose. Langland begins his *Piers Plowman* (*c.* 1367–86) with a description of a 'field full of folk' all going about their business with little thought for God. In this vision of the world as it is rather than as it should be, society is full of corruption (memorably personified as Lady Meed). Many moralists, surveying the life around them, echoed the question, 'How can one not be a satirist?' Certainly, there was a rich and various tradition of satire, not all of it tending straightforwardly to the improvement of the world. And there were reformers, revolutionaries, and prophetic millenarian visionaries who proclaimed that the end of the world was foretold by the coming of an Antichrist or by the dawning of the third and final Age of the Spirit.

In order to maintain his faith in the immanent justice of God a medieval person must have needed all the fortitude extolled by the moralists and all the consolation offered by the church. But it would be misleading to exaggerate the 'disharmony' of medieval life. Most of Europe at various periods enjoyed times of peace and prosperity. Nor should one underestimate the capacity of human beings to endure and to carry on. And as in all traditional societies, a round of rituals and ceremonies and festivals – religious, agrarian, civic – maintained and ensured continuity. The desire for stability and order is reflected in the 'mirrors for princes', the books of instruction for rulers on how to govern a realm justly and in peace. Royal pageantry – coronations, marriages, progresses, solemn funerals – celebrated and by implication urged the stable continuity of the kingdom.

There were also intellectual patterns of harmony. The ideal merging of rest and action was to be found in heaven, but some mystics attempted to glimpse it on earth through contemplation. A characteristic emphasis on reason can be seen not only in the intricate and compendious *Summae* of the philosophers, but in the way Reason appears as a personified character in some philosophical poems. These patterns could also be found in the contemplation and study of the orderly universe. There was much discussion of the numerological mysteries, and of the numerological basis of music (Boethius distinguished *musica mundana*, the music of the universe, expressing the principle of concord through numerical ratios, *musica humana*, the harmony of the microcosm of man, the concord of body and soul, and the equilibrium of man's 'temperament' (a word which still reflects these ancient views), and *musica instrumentalis*, the music made by man, which should imitate the harmony of the spheres and follow its laws of proportion). In his *Parliament of Fowls* (*c.* 1380), Chaucer shows Nature – the viceregent of God – maintaining the order and continuity of life in the diversity of species. The Middle Ages saw considerable progress in many areas of scientific thought (thanks to the Arabs, much of Greek science had been rediscovered). And this interest in science was shared by creative writers. Here the most notable example is Chaucer, the most scientifically minded of the great English poets. He wrote *A Treatise on the Astrolabe* and possibly *The Equatorie of the Planetis*, and, although he self-deprecatingly remarks in his *House of Fame* (*c.* 1374–85) that he is too old to 'learn of stars', he seems to have had a knowledge of quite up-to-date astronomy. Dante, too, had scientific interests; and from our point of view, it is of interest that at the end of *Paradiso*, when he describes '*la dolce sinfonia dell'altro Paradiso*', his vision of the wheel of the blessed is one of harmonious movement ('but now my desire and will, like a wheel that spins with even motion, were revolved by the Love that moves the sun and the other stars').

Medieval literature is the product of a 'traditional' society, one that prized the handing on of beliefs, mores and stories. 'Old books' is a term of approval – as against 'novelty'. There is in fact much innovation and individuality, but it is often carefully disguised (the story, we will be told, really comes from an old book, or the experience occurred in a dream – as if our easy modern acceptance of the 'truth' of fiction did not come so easily then). The art of the medieval writer consisted largely in the playing of delicate variations (rather in the manner of a musical composer) on traditional forms, matter and formulas. It is important, too, to remember that the central 'literary' tradition, with its connections with classical antiquity, its 'authors' and its 'books' and its manuals of rhetoric, is far from being the only, or indeed the most important one. Although literacy seems to have increased during the course of the Middle Ages, it was never widespread, and 'literacy' in the narrower sense of an ability to read and write Latin was even more limited. But there was a very important non-literary culture. As in many traditional societies, beliefs and examples were handed on very often by word of mouth, by parents, nurses, older people. What is now called 'oral literature' was of great importance. There are many references to the 'singing' or 'telling' or 'hearing' of stories; and it seems likely that there was a variety of ways of performing such works. Even the more 'literary' authors seem to have had a very close (and to a modern author, an enviably close) relationship with their audience. It is important not to think of 'oral/popular' and 'literate/learned/courtly' cultures as quite opposed and separate entities. There was constant interaction – a folk-tale or a motif from a popular story or song would be taken up and used and changed by a more literary writer; stories and forms from the 'higher' culture would find their way into the oral tradition. And literature, whether 'written' or 'oral', was only one of the 'media' by which instruction and entertainment came. There were the visual images of drama and pageantry. Pictures (used by the church in windows and wall-paintings as 'laymen's books') were also important. The poet Villon (c. 1431–63) imagines his old mother saying: 'I am a poor old woman who knows nothing and has never read a letter. In my parish church I see Paradise painted, where there are harps and lutes, and a Hell where the damned are boiled. The one frightens me, the other gladdens and rejoices me' (*Testament*, 893–8).

Much of medieval literature has been lost, and much no doubt was never written down, but what has survived shows an extraordinary variety of forms and genres. Some are continuations or developments of those of the literature of antiquity; others (like some of the specifically Christian genres, such as the miracle play) have no connection with classical antiquity. And there is a similar linguistic variety. Medieval Latin was the language of the 'clerks', and used as a still living language; it produced a fine literature, by no means limited to works of doctrine and devotion, but including plays (secular as well as religious), sharp satires, and many very secular lyrics (like those in the famous twelfth-century *Carmina Burana*) as well as hymns and sacred songs. But even its greatest achievements were matched and often overshadowed by those of the vernacular literatures. In the twelfth and thirteenth centuries the courtly culture of France was dominant and influential: the fashionable romances (often with stories coming from Celtic sources – Geoffrey of Monmouth's account of the history of the Britons, and especially of the rise and fall of the great king Arthur seems to have started something of a 'Celtic revival') spread to Italy, to Scandinavia, to Germany.

The development of English literature in this period has some distinctive features. It is a remarkable and a fortunate fact of history that a large and varied body of early writing in Old English or 'Anglo-Saxon' has survived – including some impressive poetry written in a form of alliterative verse. This literary tradition was not an entirely isolated one: there was a thriving tradition of 'Anglo-Latin' writing with which it had connections, as it did with the 'central' (and predominantly religious) European Latin tradition. However, with the Norman Conquest of 1066, English was no longer the language of the new upper classes, whose literature was in French – and in the character-istic local variety that developed, Anglo-Norman (the literature in Anglo-Norman is diverse and by no means 'provincial': it produces, for instance, one of the great *Tristan* romances). Writings in Latin continue throughout the period. The scattered remains of English writing from the late twelfth century on are usually humble, and in a language which, not surprisingly, has under-gone some deep changes. But in the fourteenth century, the status of English improves (and gradually Anglo-Norman fades away), and from the second half of this century we have a dazzling array of works – *Sir Gawain and the Green Knight, Pearl, Piers Plowman*, and other poems written in a form of the old alliterative metre; the writings of Chaucer and Gower show an easy elegance and a familiarity with French and Latin literature, and in the case of Chaucer, England's first vernacular poet of European stature, a remarkable knowledge of Italian. Two results of this curious cultural history deserve mention: there is, firstly, compared with continental literatures, often a kind of 'time-lag' – prose romances, for instance, which appear in French in the thirteenth century, are not found in English until the fifteenth. On the other hand, literature of a 'popular' kind is well represented in the surviving remains.

No one can fix a date on which the 'Middle Ages' ended and the 'Renais-sance' began. The best that can be done is to isolate some changes and developments (many of which certainly have 'medieval' roots) which gradually spread alongside older traditional patterns. These changes are economic and social, and intellectual. The invention and spread of printing in the second half of the fifteenth century, for instance, eventually produced something of a cultural 'revolution', but it is easy to exaggerate both its effects and the speed at which it occurred (in Northern Europe for a long time, printed books looked like, and were usually treated as if they were, manuscript books; and the tastes of both printers and readers seems to have been generally conservative). It is possible to argue that much of the impetus for the Reformation came from within late medieval religion itself. And alongside the older kinds of 'medieval humanism' there developed the so-called 'New Learning', the last and the most influential of the medieval *renovationes* of classical antiquity. The intense devotion to the authors of antiquity that pervades the life of Chaucer's older contemporary Petrarch, who played such an influential role in this, takes us back to our starting-point. His imitation of Virgil, the *Africa* (conceived in 1333, abandoned in the 1350s), celebrates Scipio and the history of the struggle between Rome and Carthage ('my Cicero' was one of his favourite authors, and Scipio, whom he takes to exemplify both Roman and Christian virtues, one of his heroes). It is incomplete, and in one way is a lament for the glories of the past. Petrarch's view of the present and of the future also tended to be a melancholy one, but in his successors the idea of the break with the classical past became a real and a rigid one.

But there are continuities at the end of the period as well as at its beginning. If the schoolchildren of the Renaissance were brought up on 'chaste' Latin, and if they were instilled with religious views that were in dogmatic content either different from those of earlier times, or stricter, much about their world view remained very similar. The old scientific view of the cosmos that we saw in the *Somnium Scipionis* lived on for a very long time. Men who were prepared to kill each other for the sake of doctrine often expressed their personal devotion in very similar ways, which are the direct or the indirect descendants of the emphases and the practices of medieval 'affective' piety (examples may be found in *The Book of Common Prayer*, or in the Lutheran chorales so movingly set by Bach). And there are continuities in literature, both sophisticated (as in *The Faerie Queene*) and popular (as in the ballads). Antiquarian and historical interest in the period and its culture continued and was joined in the late eighteenth and the nineteenth centuries by a Romantic rediscovery of the middle Ages, which produced some fine as well as some extraordinary works of art.

These two strands have continued to interweave in our more modern attempts to understand the literature of the medieval past. The first good 'edition' of the text of *The Canterbury Tales* by Tyrwhitt in 1775 was a premonition of a long series. Much more has been discovered about the elusive 'context' of medieval literature – about the history and development of the vernacular languages and their varieties, for instance. Here the historical research of the nineteenth and twentieth centuries has made vital contributions: in our understanding of philosophical concepts and modes of argument, of ideological concepts such as 'chivalry', of the structures of medieval society (as in the work of Marc Bloch, 1961, and others); literary students have been able to draw on the work of historians of art to illuminate images and iconographic patterns in their texts, on the work of historians of music – and on the twentieth-century movement to restore 'authentic' performances and instruments – and on the work of anthropologists in understanding 'traditional society' and oral literature. Some medieval authors early established a 'canonical' position – notably, Dante in Italy, and in England Chaucer, who is acclaimed as a leading poet from the early fifteenth century (and who provokes the first distinguished criticism of an English medieval author, in Dryden's splendid seventeenth-century appreciation). Other writers and works slip out of sight, and are rediscovered by enthusiastic later critics. Thomas Warton's *History of English Poetry* (1774–81) treats a wide range of the earlier literature: it is remarkable for the breadth of its knowledge and for the sympathy of its judgements. From the end of the nineteenth century, medieval literature became a subject for academic university criticism, and the products of this in general reflect the changing emphases and fashions of that discipline. However, the particular characteristics of the literature have meant that the criticism has usually been more attentive to the historical contexts, and more wholeheartedly comparativist in scope (as in the work of W. P. Ker, 1897) than that of later periods has been. Distinctive too has been a tension (often a creative one) between a 'Romantic' enthusiasm for early literature, leading, for instance, to a stress on the quality of individuality, and a firmly nonromantic approach, which would stress the importance of tradition and convention (seen, for instance, in the work of E. R. Curtius, 1953, on rhetorical topics). More recently, structuralist, post-structuralist, feminist and neohistoricist studies have appeared. Rather interestingly, medieval literary works have always presented some of the problems that these later theories have had to address: the frequent absence of the 'author', the instability of the 'text', the fragmentary context, the sense of difference or 'alterity' alongside the flash of recognition, and so on. In the end, however, it is the quality of the best medieval literature that is its true memorial – as Edwin Muir in his *Autobiography* says of his discovery of medieval art in Italy: 'things truly made preserve themselves through time in the first freshness of their nature.'

FURTHER READING

Auerbach, Erich (1953) *Mimesis*, translated by W. R. Trask, Princeton University Press, Princeton

Burrow, J. A. (1982) *Medieval Writers and their Work*, Oxford University Press, Oxford

Chaytor, H. J. (1945) *From Script to Print*, Heffer, Cambridge
Clanchy, M. T. (1979) *From Memory to Written Record*, Edward Arnold, London
Crombie, Alastair Cameron (1957) *Augustine to Galileo: the History of Science A.D. 400–1650*, 2nd edn, 2 vols, Heinemann, London
Heer, Friedrich (1962) *The Medieval World, Europe 1100–1300*, translated by J. Sondheimer, Weidenfeld, London
Keen, Maurice Hugh (1984) *Chivalry*, Yale University Press, New Haven
Ker, W. P. (1897) *Epic and Romance*, Macmillan, London
Leclercq, Jean (1961) *The Love of Learning and the Desire for God*, translated by C. Misrahi, Fordham University Press, New York
Leff, Gordon (1958) *Medieval Thought: St Augustine to Ockham*, Penguin, Harmondsworth
Lewis, C. S. (1964) *The Discarded Image*, Cambridge University Press, Cambridge
Murray, Alexander (1978) *Reason and Society in the Middle Ages*, Clarendon Press, Oxford
Southern, R. W. (1953) *The Making of the Middle Ages*, Hutchinson, London
——(1961) *Western Society and the Church in the Middle Ages*, Penguin, Harmondsworth
Vinaver, Eugène (1971) *The Rise of Romance*, Clarendon Press, Oxford
Zumthor, Paul (1972) *Essai de poétique médiévale*, Editions du Seuil, Paris

ADDITIONAL WORKS CITED

Bloch, Marc (1961) *Feudal Society*, translated by L. A. Manyon, Routledge, London
Curtius, Ernst Robert (1953) *European Literature and the Latin Middle Ages*, translated by W. R. Trask, Routledge, London
Stahl, William Harris (trans.) (1952) *Macrobius: Commentary on the Dream of Scipio*, Columbia University Press, New York

4

THE RENAISSANCE

GEORGE PARFITT

This essay is being written in the twentieth century, at a time when (at least in some academies) long-held views about the nature of literature and literary criticism are being overhauled or displaced. In considering what the term 'the Renaissance' means, I am aware that prevailing definitions have their origins in times before my own, and that I am inevitably influenced both by these definitions and by a process of redefinition which is continuing as I write.

Collins English Dictionary (1979) defines 'renaissance' simply as 'revival' or 'rebirth', but it describes 'the Renaissance' in epochal language as 'the period of European history marking the waning of the Middle Ages and the rise of the modern world; usually considered as beginning in Italy in the 14th century'. If this period definition is applied only to England, it needs to be added that the English Renaissance is usually understood to begin no sooner than the start of the sixteenth century. If we link 'the Renaissance', as description of a period, with 'renaissance', defined as 'rebirth/revival', however, we clearly have an evaluative description. This much is perhaps intimated even in Collins's phrase about 'the waning of the Middle Ages', which certainly suggests that medievalism in the period is something enervated and in process of being replaced by a new dynamic: Death is giving way to (new) Birth. So far as England is concerned, there is also perhaps the sense that until 'the Renaissance' reached these shores from Italy this was a barbaric province in Europe's cultural empire.

So it is misleading to consider 'the Renaissance' as merely a period term. To use it in a purportedly neutral way (in the sense, say, of 'the reign of Victoria') is to suppress recognition of the term's value-laden basis. How judgemental 'the Renaissance' is becomes clearer when we notice that the basic meaning 'rebirth' requires the question 'rebirth of what?'; to which the stock answer for the historical period is 'classicism'. That which is born again must have been dead, and in so far as we think of rebirths as good events, we must presumably consider deaths as bad. So the Middle Ages are to be seen as a period which lacked the good which is classicism. Moreover, if we develop the valuation involved in the idea of 'the Renaissance' as classicism reborn and go on to seek out this valuation in sixteenth-century England, we shall find ourselves noticing and valuing some phenomena (say, Surrey's translation of Virgil into blank verse) while deprecating or ignoring others (perhaps the last gasps of the native alliterative tradition). The organic nature of the image of birth/death/rebirth will also encourage us to think cyclically, tracing development and decline in a way which unites period and evaluation: as the Middle Ages wane and the modern world rises, we move into a period of vitality and juvenescence.

This account might suggest that 'the Renaissance' is less useful as a term for a period *in toto* than as a description of a tendency within a period; a tendency to be regarded with approval because associated with a rebirth of classicism. But it is also obvious that, in so far as 'the Renaissance' can be defined in value terms, it can be detached from any single period, along lines familiar in uses of expressions such as 'romanticism' or 'classicism' itself. All that is needed is to remove the capital letter. Even the capital may be retained where 'Renaissance' is qualified or used metaphorically. Thus, if 'the Renaissance' is equated with fourteenth-century Italy's alleged rediscovery of the classics, it must be either paradox or metaphor to speak of a *Twelfth Century Renaissance* (the title of a book by Christopher Brooke, 1969). When we speak of 'a Renaissance man', we are likely to mean one with virtues we associate with the period of 'the Renaissance'. But if we reunite period and valuation to describe a tendency within an epoch it follows that we need other terms for whatever in the period ignores or resists this tendency. So we may use 'medieval' in the sense of old-fashioned or downright bad, or we may toy with the word 'Reformation'. But the latter dazzles rather than clarifies: is 'Reformation' part of 'the Renaissance' or in opposition to it? How far is it useful as a parallel term, signifying the reformation of religion, as distinct from a secular reformation ('Renaissance')?

Keeping these uncertainties in mind, and accepting that 'the Renaissance' is fundamentally an evaluative term descriptive of a tendency within a period, we can turn to fleshing out the word. Collins refers to 'intensified classical scholarship' and to 'the assertion of the active and secular over the religious and contemplative life', while adding associations with 'scientific and geographical discovery' and 'a sense of individual human potentialities'. It is hardly difficult to set these against versions of medievalism, seen as incorporating a Christianity hostile to the classics; scholasticism; advocacy of the contemplative life; deprecation of individualism and physicality. But (leaving aside that this travesties the Middle Ages) it is easy to argue that such antitheses are too crude to be of much use, or that they are most useful as a rough guide to battles *within* the period of 'the Renaissance'. So we might consider the idea of a battle between 'waning' medievalism and 'rising' Renaissance; yet the contest was less unbalanced than this may suggest. Struggles between New Learning and Old ('old' Aristotle and 'new' Plato) remain lively in England to the end of the sixteenth century and beyond. And if Columbus's discovery of the Americas in 1492 is symptomatic of Renaissance discovery, what do we call Galileo's troubles of more than a century later? A 'sense of human potentialities' never really triumphs in sixteenth-century England. Marlowe's *Faustus* and Shakespeare's *Hamlet* are classics of a struggle to realize potential, but hardly signifiers of success in such a struggle, while the idea of human fulfilment is pretty decisively swamped in early seventeenth-century drama (has 'the Renaissance' ended by the time of *Sejanus* and *The Revenger's Tragedy*?). Spirituality remains strong throughout the sixteenth century, both as an inheritance from the Middle Ages and in such phenomena as the theologies of Reform and Neoplatonism. Indeed, the history of the century in England could be written as a conflict between religious and secular impulses, and it would be absurd to speak of such a conflict as one of the waning of the former and rising of the latter: absurd because grossly over-simple.

There is yet another dimension which should inform our sense of 'the Renaissance', this being a social one. Castiglione's *Il Cortegiano* (published 1528) is a classic of the European Renaissance, while Thomas Hoby's translation (1561) is a classic of the English Renaissance. Castiglione's concerns include the fashioning of the Renaissance courtier or gentleman. These two terms are not synonymous, for a gentleman need not belong to a court, but they overlap (a courtier will be a gentleman, and a gentleman should be courteous) and they help to define a socio-cultural nexus which relates 'the Renaissance' to the ideas of the courtly and genteel; and thus to the possession of, or aspiration to, wealth, power and an ostensibly cultured lifestyle. 'Gentleman', because of the elasticity and relatively open nature of the category in England, should warn us from too heavy a stress on exclusivity. A Sidney may be marked as genteel by birth, but a mere Shakespeare may end his life armigerous. There is, however, a clear link between the values associated with 'the Renaissance' and the concept of gentility; and this link may be seen materially. Most specifically, you need to have money to possess or even visit art objects and to claim the leisure to develop your human potentiality; most generally, you need both education and self-consciousness to participate in 'the Renaissance', at least as defined above.

We are now saying that 'the Renaissance' indicates a minority or élite tendency within a period, from which it follows that most people in the period did not participate in 'the Renaissance' – and could not. There is little in 'the Renaissance' for peasants of either sex, and probably not much for artisans either. The emphasis on the idea of the gentle*man* and the fact that so many of the products of 'the Renaissance' are male-made means that 'the

Renaissance' continues to use women rather than freeing them or encouraging any sense of individual female potentiality. It can be argued that sixteenth-century England saw increased opportunities for some on the fringes of gentility (and for a very few beyond the fringes), but the objective remains participation in the genteel or, more exactly, the acquisition of a culture which has a strong genteel focus. In either case the hegemony of gentility remains.

Defining 'the Renaissance' has fascinated academics of the twentieth century, and there has been sturdy resistance, amounting almost to an academic Counter-Reformation, to the equating of 'medieval' with waning or bad. (To make matters still more complicated, it should be remembered that such a key figure of the English Renaissance as Edmund Spenser also rejected this equation.) But discussions have tended to accept the perspectives, valuings and social focus of 'the Renaissance' as defined above. Humanism is good; classicism is desirable; gentility is to be endorsed. So Sir Philip Sidney remains a role-model for men, and, in some quarters, females are still expected to aspire to be Stella, as defined/made by the male poet of *Astrophil and Stella* (1591). If we recall the enormous influence of Jacob Burckhardt's *The Civilization of the Renaissance in Italy* ([1860] 1944) we shall notice that such views are mainly orthodoxies of the nineteenth century, contributing to a Whiggish, progressive construct, as in Collins's 'waning' and 'rising'. We might then wonder just how valuable such a 'Renaissance' is in our own time. But before this is considered further, it is necessary to look briefly at two shifts of perspective in literary studies of the sixteenth century in England which took place earlier in our century, and which are intimately associated with each other.

These shifts both involve a reaction against a view of the English Renaissance which sees the court of Elizabeth I as central to a body of achievement in poetry, music and drama (and, to a lesser extent, in the plastic arts) which made England a Renaissance state comparable with France and Spain. Such an account virtually reduces 'the Renaissance' in England to a High Renaissance of some twenty-five years, positing a false dawn early in the century, a period of 'drabness' (medievalism) and then, with, say, the publication of Spenser's *Shepheardes Calender* in 1579, the true rebirth. One reaction against this account (to concentrate on verse) has involved the upgrading of Wyatt (as against the more 'Elizabethan' Surrey), some favourable reassessment of George Gascoigne, and attention to the poetry associated with Ralegh and Greville; all this at the expense of Sidney and Spenser. The second shift, which can be said to have prompted the first, has worked either by virtually ignoring the English High Renaissance or by contrasting it unfavourably with another 'renaissance', which occurs after 1600 and is best known, in poetry, by the labels 'The School of Donne' and 'The Tribe of Ben'.

One of the things which Spenser's *The Faerie Queene* (1590, 1596) signifies is the quintessence of the English Renaissance epic. As such, it stands as a monument to its author's awareness of the classics, his understanding of the importance of the idea of the gentleman and his sense of the potential of both the individual and the nation. Aesthetically, although incomplete, it can (with some effort) be considered High Renaissance art in its organization of parts into a harmonious, unified whole and in its decorative elaboration and refinement. The reaction against such verse as Spenser's has involved a turning away from epic to lyric (as happened also to Milton) and specifically to a type of lyric which is strong-lined rather than mellifluous, rhythmically various, syntactically compressed and, in its imagery, recherché rather than conventional and relatively accessible: from Spenser to Donne. And although the great early markers of this shift are H. J. C. Grierson's edition of Donne (1912), and his anthology of metaphysical poets (1921), it is more useful here to link the shift with the precepts and practice of T. S. Eliot, because this underlines the historicity of the shift itself, associating it with Eliot's interest in the modernism of some nineteenth-century French poets and of his own creative writing. What survives of Spenserianism in *The Waste Land* (1922) are fragments, ripe for parody, and questioning the relevance of such a Renaissance for Eliot's time.

For some years Eliot was much admired by F. R. Leavis, by *Scrutiny* (the periodical with which Leavis was so closely associated) and by the New Criticism. Leavis resented the suggestion that he and his followers understressed the sixteenth century, and it is true that Leavisian attitudes led to serious attention to Wyatt and to efforts to revive the reputation of such as Gascoigne. But Leavis's own practice makes his resentment seem faintly absurd, for in his *Revaluation* (1936) English poetry of the sixteenth century scarcely exists. In effect, the story begins with Donne (although there have to be frequent nervous reminders of Shakespeare). It is the seventeenth century which matters, and its heroes are Donne, Jonson and Marvell, who are to be seen in a native tradition rather than a classical one. The key words are now 'maturity' and 'civilized', rather than 'courtly' and 'genteel'. The method of *Scrutiny* and New Criticism, moreover, was Practical Criticism, democratic in its deprecation of prior knowledge and therefore of the need for libraries. Some, noting the social origins of such as F. R. and Q. D. Leavis and L. C. Knights, have been tempted to see this shift in terms of the bourgeoisie revolting against genteel hegemony. Part of the revenge would be to subvert the great models of the traditional account of the English Renaissance, replacing these with the urban (rather than courtly) Donne, Jonson and Marvell. However, the *Scrutiny* movement was itself, in the final analysis, élitist and, being ahistoricist, could scarcely be expected to spend much time defining 'the Renaissance'. Spenser's court may have been decentred and its place taken by Donne's Inns of Court. Leavis may have hoped that the editor of the *Times Literary Supplement* and the Director-General of the BBC would lose their cultural places to Downing College, Cambridge. But the Inns of Court were genteel institutions and Downing is part of an exclusive academy.

Leavis and *Scrutiny* constituted the most important movement in English literary criticism from the early 1940s into the 1970s, but the movement did not lack opponents, among whom were F. W. Bateson, E. M. W. Tillyard and C. S. Lewis. The relevant controversies concerned both methodology and valuings, including views of 'the Renaissance'. Lewis, a champion of the medieval, nevertheless upholds 'the Renaissance' (Elizabethan) against the 'drabness' of sixteenth-century medievalism. Both he and Tillyard stand by Spenser, while Bateson (at odds with Leavis over method) has something of his opponent's apparent lack of interest in the Elizabethan Renaissance. But even these disagreements seem to accept a paradigm while arguing over personnel. The cast may be changed, but the play remains much the same – the harmonious world of Tillyard's *The Elizabethan World Picture* (1943).

What is lacking in both the orthodoxy and the reaction is any real questioning of the acceptance of genteel hegemony. The effort of *Scrutiny* included a rewriting of the canon of great English literature, and the effort was, in part, salutary. But *Scrutiny*'s essays into social history make it clear that the rewriting was based on a sentimental view of a rural past of hierarchic contentment. The gentry remain in place. But a view of 'the Renaissance' is now slowly being developed which marks a potentially radical departure from almost everything so far outlined. A central statement (perhaps better described as an adumbration) comes in Raymond Williams's *The Country and the City* (1973).

Formally speaking, Williams's book neither attempts an account of 'the Renaissance' nor concerns itself much with the sixteenth century. Williams makes it clear in his introductory chapter that he is writing an account of the country-and-city theme from the conscious perspective of his own roots in the England-Wales borderlands. The subjectivity which Williams acknowledges is important in itself, since it marks a break with the essentialism of the Arnoldian tradition, but it is perhaps more significant that Williams identifies himself with the native radical tradition, for it is this, imparting a class dimension to his book, which informs the attack on Country House poetry that is central to its Renaissance section.

Williams's approach to poems like Jonson's 'To Penshurst' is by way of a critique of pastoral, in which he argues that the history of pastoral is marked by the progressive widening of a gap between Nature and Art. Crudely put, Williams sees 'To Penshurst' as excluding that in Nature which is manifest in labour and the peasant, in the interests of showing solidarity with the gentry. Although Williams's account is inadequate (involving a misunderstanding of the generic nature of such poems as 'To Penshurst') and although it is highly specific in its concentration upon one type of early seventeenth-century poem, his writing has important implications for our sense of 'the Renaissance'. The view exemplified by the 'Age of Shakespeare' volume of the *Pelican Guide to English Literature* (ed. Ford, 1955) sees the strength of the period as inhering in the union of classical and popular, but this endorsement of the popular is literary rather than socio-political, and does not of itself seriously question the gentility principle of orthodox views. Williams, however, implies a critical perspective which is mainly interested in the viewpoints of the marginalized elements in society, a perspective which may be associated with those of such Marxist historians as Rodney Hilton (1977) and Christopher Hill (1958). If Country House poetry is to be viewed with suspicion as propaganda for the gentry (and if we remember that such verse functions within monarchic views of the responsibility of the gentry), it follows that the strong tendency in orthodox views of 'the Renaissance' to identify with courtly and genteel values may itself be questioned. Sir Philip Sidney may cease to be our role-model and we may prefer to remember that Sir Robert Sidney, occasional dweller at Penshurst, showed tendencies to boorishness and alcoholism.

The radical critique of an aspect of gentryism makes Williams's book an important introduction to that which is distinctive in contemporary thinking about 'the Renaissance', even though the changes we are concerned with are as yet far from decisive.

It was suggested above that Williams offers a perspective to set against one which, in effect, offers Sidney and Stella as models. In this sense, Williams is hinting at the possibility of alternatives to the orthodoxy and to the revision of it which can be found earlier in our century. Among these alternatives is a new (or renewed) historicism and the acceptance of the idea that 'the Renaissance' might be seen as plural rather than monolithic. Williams's class politics have not been followed up to any great extent and the emphasized texts in standard accounts of the period of the English Renaissance have remained much the same as in the orthodox versions. How true the latter point is can be seen by a glance at the index to Gary Waller's *English Poetry in the Sixteenth Century* (1986). But even slight shifts of emphasis are important, cumulatively representing quite major changes. This is partly a matter of giving more prominence to such satirists as Marston and Hall in the late sixteenth century, and to a prose writer like Thomas Nashe. But rather more important is the rewriting of standard figures. To emphasize the Protestantism of Sidney, for example, is to reduce concern with his poetics as purely aesthetic; to study patronage in socio-economic terms reduces essentialism; and to attend to the satirists of the Inns of Court is to stare at the face of cynicism and social unease, instead of at that of a Hilliard miniature. Wyatt, Gascoigne, Ralegh and Donne, among others, can be read in terms of suspicion, struggle and failure – the world of Lacey Baldwin Smith's account of Tudor paranoia (*Treason in Tudor England*, 1986). The change can be summed up by a view of Spenser which regards his effort to articulate orthodox Elizabethan attitudes to Justice – in Book Five of *The Faerie Queene* – as of interest *because* it fails. Another symbol would be finding Rafe's silence at the end of Thomas Dekker's *The Shoemaker's Holiday* (*c.* 1600) as important as the play's statement of accord between monarch and people.

Deconstruction of orthodox views of what is of prime importance in the English literary Renaissance may be connected with the revisionism of recent work in Tudor history (see, for instance, *The Reign of Elizabeth I*, ed. Haigh, 1984) and with the revival of historicism in literary studies, with its emphasis on particularity at the expense of essentialism. At the same time, concepts of the singularity of the text come into question when we notice, for instance, pressures from modern feminism. So far as 'the Renaissance' is concerned, this is of particular interest since the English High Renaissance is headed by a woman – Elizabeth I. The cult of Elizabeth is essentially a male construct (with whatever willing compliance by the queen herself). It is an elaborate definition of what women should be, as seen by men. There is, so far as I know, as yet no full-scale analysis of the myth by a feminist historian, but there are signs that the male-dominated view of Renaissance women which the myth enshrines is beginning to be called into question. This is partly through interest in writings of the period actually by women and partly through re-examination of how women are represented by male authors. Stella is looking unsteady on her pedestal, and the witches in *Macbeth* are being rethought and revalued.

Potentially, this adds up to a fundamental shift, from 'genteel' to 'marginalized' and from the acceptance of the orthodox ideal of 'the Renaissance' to a critique of that ideal which identifies 'genteel' as the enemy, doubts the efficacy of humanism and wonders about the respect traditionally given to classicism. What then begins to seem of most interest is what is suggested by such words as 'flaw', 'tension', 'subversion' and 'resistance' (to dominant ideologies). Some of this was foreshadowed in New Criticism, but the latter's emphasis on the School of Donne was almost wholly without historical context, remaining idealist and lacking the materiality which is a feature of contemporary thinking about 'the Renaissance'.

This is not to suggest that revision of 'the Renaissance' has yet gone very far. If we ask what 'the Renaissance' means even to undergraduates today, the answers are likely to be dispiriting, suggesting that the term has little if any meaning to them. Given how few English undergraduates have looked at sixteenth-century texts or studied sixteenth-century history in school, this is hardly surprising. Even if there is some notion of the English Renaissance, the continental version will almost certainly be an unknown area. Such purchase as there is for 'new thinking' is almost wholly within higher education, and very patchy even there. So far as many teachers are concerned in England 'the

Renaissance' poses no problems: it exists and must, with acquiescence, be learnt.

Depressing as such thoughts are, they provide a good reason why the shift described should be welcomed, for it provides the possibility of reviving 'the Renaissance'. It is proper that awareness of orthodoxies and literary canons should be accompanied by alertness to the value systems which have gone into the construction of the orthodoxies and canons. Certainly, any socialist (at least) who permits either of these to become anaesthetized from a socio-political dimension is a traitor, or a neuter. For many, in higher education as outside it, consciousness of such orthodoxies and canons must be accompanied by a sense of being outsiders in relation to them. Typically, outsiders are only admitted to participation in orthodoxies and canons on the latter's terms (a process which may be largely unconscious on both sides). Here again, a socialist should be particularly alert to the situation, for to take on trust anything in a social organization which you want to change fundamentally is to volunteer for the handcuffs. The result of such alertness should not be to ignore the cultural products of such an organization, denying that there is anything to be learnt from studying such phenomena and the materials which are their constituents. To hate the formations of power articulated by the court of Elizabeth I is proper, and may entail a final rejection of most of the literature generated by that court, but to ignore or write out that court and its products as topics for study is to handicap yourself hopelessly. To become aware of the cracks in such monoliths as *The Faerie Queene* is to begin to see that other formulations are possible but it is also to see how implicated we are in dominant, even if manifestly imperfect, systems. Few have denied that Book Five of that poem suggests a poet struggling to shape his material into coherence, and some have posited that this was so because Spenser had allowed his idealist 'poetic' impulse to become coarsened (complicated?) by too much reality. Another way of putting this would be to say that the view of justice this book seems anxious to endorse is admirable, but that the dramatization of this view is unsatisfactory because the contemporary figures and situations in the allegory do not comfortably enact the basic view. All would have been well if Lord Grey had been better at governing Ireland and if the Irish would only have seen where their true interest lay.

Which gives the game away. If only slaves would see the beneficence of the institution; if only Hindus would understand how absurd their devotion to cows is; if only women would realize how they provoke men ... The real importance of Book Five of *The Faerie Queene* is not that Spenser has chosen poor illustrations of a good case, but that he seeks to endorse a case which is itself bad. The oppressive enactment of authoritarian 'justice' is evil, whatever the particular manifestation. But there is a further point, which is that to encounter Book Five is to recognize how powerful its Justice is and to see (when the mask drops) how shameful are its operations. A traditional view of 'the Renaissance' sees humanism as a good, and must see the expressed objectives of *The Faerie Queene* as participating in this version of Good. It must therefore try to defend Spenser's Justice, if necessary by drawing on essentialist philosophies. If, however, we adopt the position of the critical outsider, we are, if not liberated, at least in contact with the possibility of becoming liberated.

As the last few paragraphs have perhaps suggested, much of the 'new thinking' we are concerned with has come from writers on the political left, while a fuller account would stress also the contributions of feminists and gays. If the time comes when such a critique of orthodoxies amounts to real pressure on those who endorse them, the supporters of such orthodoxies will do well to examine for themselves the values on which the relevant ideology is based; but that will be their concern, not mine. The sense of 'the Renaissance' which I regard as valuable in contemporary discussions is one which is critical of humanist emphases (which is not the same as suggesting that all such emphases are to be rejected out of hand) and also critical of the structures which encouraged and endorsed them. It will seek to draw attention to what is involved in the sort of orthodox view of 'the Renaissance' which was sketched earlier in this essay and it will wish to stress the valuings which go to make up the orthodoxy. It will be concerned with the weaknesses and evils in the artefacts of this Renaissance. It will (or should) do these things because its standpoint will (or should) be that of the oppressed and silenced. But it will only have some chance of establishing its case if the viewpoint is an informed one. So long as the 'rabble' in Spenser's fifth book remains ignorant it will fall in swathes to the flail of Talus. Autodidacts of the nineteenth century knew this, and studied their Milton and their Shelley.

FURTHER READING

Burke, Peter (1964) *The Renaissance*, Longman, London

Davies, Stevie (ed.) (1978) *Renaissance Views of Man*, Manchester University Press, Manchester

Dollimore, Jonathan and Sinfield, Alan (eds) (1985) *Political Shakespeare*, Manchester University Press, Manchester

Goldberg, Jonathan (1983) *James I and the Politics of Literature*, Johns Hopkins University Press, Baltimore

Greenblatt, Stephen J. (1980) *Renaissance Self-Fashioning*, Chicago University Press, Chicago

Kinney, A. and Collins, D. (eds) (1987) *Renaissance Historicism*, Massachusetts University Press, Amherst

Kristeller, Paul Oskar (1961) *Renaissance Thought*, Harper, New York

Lytle, G. and Orgel, S. (eds) (1981) *Patronage in the Renaissance*, Princeton University Press, Princeton

Martines, Lauro (1985) *Society and History in English Renaissance Verse*, Basil Blackwell, Oxford

Mandrou, Robert (1978) *From Humanism to Science*, Penguin, Harmondsworth

Sinfield, Alan (1983) *Literature in Protestant England*, Harvester, Brighton

Woodbridge, Linda (1984) *Women and the English Renaissance*, Harvester, Brighton

ADDITIONAL WORKS CITED

Brooke, Christopher (1969) *The Twelfth Century Renaissance*, Thames & Hudson, London

Burckhardt, Jacob (1944) *The Civilization of the Renaissance in Italy*, translated by S. G. C. Middlemorse, Phaidon Press, London [first published 1860]

Ford, Boris (ed.) (1955) *The Pelican Guide to English Literature*, vol. 2, Penguin, Harmondsworth

Grierson, H. J. C. (1912) *Donne: Poetical Works*, Oxford University Press, Oxford

――(1921) *Metaphysical Lyrics and Poems*, Oxford University Press, Oxford

Haigh, Christopher (ed.) (1984) *The Reign of Elizabeth I*, Macmillan, London

Hill, Christopher (1958) *Puritanism and Revolution*, Secker & Warburg, London

Hilton, Rodney (1977) *Bond Men Made Free*, Methuen, London

Leavis, F. R. (1936) *Revaluation*, Chatto & Windus, London

Smith, Lacey Baldwin (1986) *Treason in Tudor England*, Cape, London

Tillyard, E. M. W. (1943) *The Elizabethan World Picture*, Chatto & Windus, London

Waller, Gary F. (1986) *English Poetry of the Sixteenth Century*, Longman, London

Williams, Raymond (1973) *The Country and the City*, Chatto & Windus, London

5

AUGUSTANISM

DAVID NOKES

In recent years the term 'Augustan' has been treated to a good deal of critical knockabout. According to Donald Greene (1967–76), the early eighteenth century was more Augustinian than Augustan, and we might with equal logic and greater euphony describe its literature as Mesopotamian. Maximillian E. Novak has suggested that 'perhaps the Brutan Age would be a more accurate appellation since the appeal to English liberty might call on both the Brutus who invented Roman liberty and the Brutus who was the last to defend it' (1984, p. 2). In 1916 George Saintsbury gave his own spin to the term 'Augustan' in the subtitle to his book *The Peace of the Augustans*; 'A Survey of Eighteenth Century Literature as a Place of Rest and Refreshment'. Almost sixty years later, Pat Rogers' *Augustan Vision* presented the same period less as *fête-champêtre* than as freak-show. 'Eighteenth century England', he wrote, 'has a Janus-like capacity to exhibit poverty and plenty, cultivation and ignorance, refinement and brutality' (1974, p. 9). As Claude Rawson has observed, ' "Augustan" remains serviceable largely because of its near-meaninglessness' (1985, p. 243).

Defined in its most traditional terms, the word Augustan makes an important ideological assumption. The OED expresses it thus: 'Augustan: connected with the reign of Augustus Caesar, the palmy period of Latin literature (1704). 2. Hence, of the palmy period of purity and refinement of any national literature.' This explicit correlation between imperial authority and literary refinement lies at the root of critical uneasiness with the term. Used as a shorthand label, 'Augustan' would seem to beg a number of political questions. Hence the desire to hit upon a term which might more accurately represent the complexities of an age which used the imagery of imperial Rome sometimes to dignify, but often to stigmatize political ambitions and cultural stereotypes. Dryden, among the first to make a systematic use of the Augustan parallel, willingly embraced its ideological implications. As Novak writes, Dryden was 'not merely comfortable with the notion of a new Augustan age, but . . .

93

consciously attempted to develop an Augustan myth' (1984, p. 2). His poem *Astraea Redux*, modelled in part on Virgil's fourth eclogue, compares the return of Charles II to England with Octavian's victory over Mark Antony at Actium, and goes on to prophesy a new golden age of peace, prosperity and poetry:

> O Happy Age! Oh times like those alone
> By fate reserved for great Augustus Throne!
> When the joint growth of Arms and Arts foreshow
> The world a Monarch, and that Monarch you!
>
> (ll. 320–3)

Yet, as literary critics have recognized, the era of Augustus Caesar was as notable for tyranny and vice as for tolerance and verse. 'The most memorable characteristic of Augustus's Rome,' writes Donald Greene, 'is that it was a totalitarian empire ruled by a powerful and competent despot, who, in the realm of literature, kept a stable of highly skilled writers, such as Horace and Virgil, to write some of the most exquisite government propaganda ever composed' (1967–76: 1975, p. 128). Is Augustanism then merely a euphemism for imperialism? Yes, according to Laura Brown, who sees Pope's *Windsor Forest* as 'an encoding of the aesthetic of imperialism' (1985, p. 37). For Brown, 'Pope's major works stand as documents of the ideological structures of the period' (p. 3): structures which borrow the imagery of the classical past to mystify capitalist and imperialist impulses. Certainly, among the more enthusiastic celebrants of a neo-Augustan culture were several, Dryden included, who employed their literary talents to produce government propaganda. For most twentieth-century critics, however, the significance of such panegyric exercises is overshadowed by the volume of satires in which the language of the Augustan myth is exaggerated into self-parody. These academic defenders of the notion of a self-critical 'Augustanism' detect in the numerous re-workings of Augustan motifs by eulogists as well as ironists, a desire to separate iconography from ideology. Such a separation was often best achieved by substituting a Horatian for an Augustan label, since Horace's refusal of high political office under Augustus offered a model of cultural independence, placing the integrity of the artist above the inducements of the state.

Rawson has argued that for those writers most successful in naturalizing the Augustan idiom, the intrinsic ambiguity of the parallel could itself provide a source of imaginative independence. 'The discreditable elements of Augustus's traditional reputation, so far from being mainly fuel for anti-Augustan sentiments, were themselves a positive strength where panegyric needed to carry a latent reservation or monitory note, or where a high political idealism needed to be checked by a recognition of harsher realities' (1985, p. 247). For satirists like Pope and Swift, whose works betray a restless oscillation between ideals of libertarianism and authoritarianism, the imagery of Augustanism was valuable precisely because of its capacity to function as a double standard. It provided them with a mosaic of allusions in which the moral imperatives of art and nature were constantly juxtaposed with the social exigencies of politics and the state.

Recent critical attempts either to rehabilitate the term Augustan by underpinning its ideological assumptions, or to replace it altogether by some more liberal designation ('Horatian', 'Brutan') less coloured by imperialist connotations, suggest apparent dissatisfaction with Rawson's notion of the 'positive strength' of ambiguity. For Laura Brown, the question of authorial intentions is irrelevant; the ideology of imperialism is inseparable from the iconography of Augustanism. Thus, despite the explicit critique of capitalism offered in Pope's *Epistle to Bathurst*, she has no hesitation in classifying the poem as an 'Imperialist Work' whose rhetoric of 'consumer-fetishism . . . accepts and even celebrates the system that the poem locally satirizes' (1985, p. 111).

Unhappiness with the totalitarian connotations of the 'Augustan' label has influenced discussion not only of the themes, but also of the forms of the literature so designated. Johnson confirmed that it was Dryden whose poetry, both in style and subject-matter, first embodied the Augustan ethos: 'What was said of Rome, adorn'd by Augustus, may be applied by an easy metaphor to English poetry embellish'd by Dryden; *lateritiam invenit; marmoream reliquit*, he found it brick and left it marble' (ed. 1952, vol. 1, p. 332). It is worth pausing to consider the exact term of Johnson's 'easy metaphor'. The words 'adorn'd' and 'embellish'd' suggest not some fundamental reconstruction, but rather a classical face-lift. Such marmoreal embellishments of Augustan verse as the regularized iambic line and 'heroic' couplet provide poetry with the dignity of a public institution. Yet beneath the classical cladding the original foundations remain intact. This notion was enthusiastically endorsed by twentieth-century critics anxious to discern the lineaments of a vernacular tradition beneath the classical façade of Augustan poetry. In a series of influential essays, F. R. Leavis ([1936] 1964), T. S. Eliot ([1921] 1932) and Maynard Mack ([1949] 1959) endeavoured to trace back the 'line of wit' in Pope's poetry, via Dryden, to native origins in the work of Donne. What is particularly interesting about these attempts to present Dryden and Pope as latter-day Metaphysicals, is the way in which their terminology reproduces political concerns characteristic of critical debate in the eighteenth century itself. At root the issue turns upon an assumed dichotomy between a native quality of the imagination, usually associated with Shakespeare and Donne, and a form of alien cultural imperialism, represented by the 'rules' of neo-classicism, which is arbitrary, doctrinaire, but above all, foreign. 'Dryden's genius', wrote Leavis, 'comes out in a certain native English strength; the strength that led Hopkins to say of him: "He is the most masculine of our poets; his style and his rhythms lay the strongest stress of all our literature on the naked thew and sinew of the

English language" ' ([1936] 1964, p. 33). For Leavis, the 'line of wit' which came to an end with Pope, produced a poetry of English muscle, not of Italian marble. Similarly, in the eighteenth century, Pope's *Essay on Criticism* was attacked by John Dennis for betraying the literary rights of free-born Englishmen in favour of a slavish idolatry to classical icons. As a Catholic, Pope's 'servile deference' to authority smacked of the prescriptiveness of the French academicians whose acceptance of papal infallibility and Bourbon absolutism made them willing slaves of the Stagyrite. Dennis regarded Pope 'as an Enemy not so much to me as to my KING, to my COUNTRY, to my RELIGION and to that LIBERTY which has been the sole Felicity of my Life' (ed. Hooker, 1939, vol. 2, p. 115).

In 1936 Leavis began his celebrated revaluation of Pope with the phrase 'Pope has had bad luck'. In the thirty years which followed the appearance of that study, Pope's luck, like that of all the other major Augustan writers, changed decisively. No longer dismissed as the 'little monster of Twit'nam', Pope was transformed into the master of mock-heroics, and custodian of humanist values. Dryden was no longer pilloried as a political time-server, but hailed as the exponent of a healthy and intellectually respectable scepticism. Swift was rescued from the baleful influence of Thackeray's denunciation, ('filthy in word, filthy in thought, furious, raging, obscene') and promoted to the status of a moral guerrilla. Johnson was brought out from the shadow of Macaulay's condescension and celebrated for the lucidity, integrity and intellectual force of his Christian stoicism.

Clearly, for the generation of the New Critics, something in the notion of Augustanism corresponded closely with their own cultural priorities. The Augustan writers, with their allusive blend of art and nature, tradition and the individual talent, represented a paradigm for a culture whose accommodation with the idioms of social and political life did not preclude, but rather proclaimed the centrality of a humanist concern for moral values. In particular, the New Critics celebrated a quality of doubleness, ambiguity or irony in eighteenth-century literature; an ambiguity which offered the promise of aesthetic order, admitting yet restraining the heterogeneity of human experience through the precise modulations of literary tone. As one later critic has observed: 'The New Critics saw the world in pieces and they wanted to put it back together again. Hence the significance of their critical vocabulary . . . Brooks's passion for paradox in which two contradictory concepts are catapulted into coherence; Warren's impure poetry which earns its vision by incorporating its opposite; and their joint dedication to the superfusion of form and content' (Fetterley, 1985, p. 16). The rhythms of balanced opposition so characteristic of Augustan prosody were presented not as a monotonous and superficial striving for symmetry, but as the imaginative embodiment of the complexities of human nature. In Pope the *concordia discors* and in Swift the use of ironic masks, were analysed to reveal a view of the world at once urbane and yet subversive. Their fondness for rhetorical patterns of confrontation based upon puns, paradoxes and antitheses was seen as the expression of a rage for order *not* (*pace* Saintsbury) complacent and restful, but combative and challenging. Their evocation of an ideal of Horatian retirement was regarded as neither acquiescent nor solipsistic, but as a declaration of cultural independence which, while drawing its sustenance from social idioms, succeeded in transforming the social world into an extended metaphor for moral concerns.

Maynard Mack's essay 'Wit and Poetry and Pope' is characteristic of this approach. Analysing the portrait of Narcissa ('Odious! in woollen! 'twould a saint provoke!') from Pope's *Epistle to Cobham*, he writes:

> This, to the extent that it illustrates anything, illustrates the poem's prose argument that our ruling passion continues to our last breath. But as a metaphor it explores, not without considerable profundity, through the character of one type of woman, the character of the human predicament itself. Here we have, as her name implies, the foolish self-lover; but also – in a wider, more inevitable and uncensorable sense – the self-lover who inhabits each of us by virtue of our moral situation, the very principle of identity refusing to be erased. Here too we have the foolish concern for appearances, vastly magnified by the incongruity of its occasion; but also the fundamental human clutching at the familiar and the known. And embracing it all is the central paradox of human feelings about death and life. Cold limbs don't need wrapping (the conjunction of terms suggests that death can be apprehended but not comprehended), nor dead faces shading; and yet, as our own death rituals show, somehow they do. The levels of feeling and experience startled into activity in this short passage can hardly be more than pointed at in the clumsiness of paraphrase.
>
> (Mack, [1949] 1959, pp. 34–5)

Starting from a desire to prove that Pope's poetry is not merely a 'poetry of statement', Mack's close reading of this passage insists upon a poetic depth of association whose imaginative effect is profoundly moral. A similar tendency to identify moral complexity with literary ambiguity can be found in the postwar revaluations of Swift's satires which elevated irony into a measure of the discriminating conscience. Martin Price concludes his analysis of *A Modest Proposal* with these words:

> The Modest Proposer implicates more and more of us in his own madness. His obtuseness becomes the ironic counterpart of a much more terrible moral degradation. The device is frequent in Swift. His patient fools are not always less terrible than the knaves they betray. The surface of the irony is a comedy of irresponsible folly, of the moral obliviousness of a dedicated pedant or theorist. Beneath the surface lies the guilt of most men, who are less naive and transparent but all the more responsible.
>
> (1953, p. 74)

Common to both analyses, and to many others like them, is the implication of inclusiveness and universality in the moral views expressed through a subtle blending of literary tones. Irony is represented not as a simple didactic or censorious device, neatly dividing the world into two antithetical camps, the fallen and the chosen; rather its alternating current of moral oppositions creates a series of reverberations that touch upon a world of infinite complexity.

This notion of moral inclusiveness is fundamental to the liberal humanist defence of Augustan literature. The enemies of Augustanism, variously labelled in the satires of Pope and Swift as moderns, dunces, enthusiasts and fanatics, have in common a dedication to a single, visionary, utopian view of the world. Represented as projectors and theorists, they share a desire to refine away the complexities of human nature in pursuit of a millennialist goal as seductive and irrational as that of the scientist of Lagado to obtain sunbeams from cucumbers. Sympathetic commentators, like Walter Jackson Bate on Johnson or Maynard Mack on Pope, seek to embody in the presentation of their subjects similar qualities of humanist conviction, appearing often less as critics than disciples in the heroic struggle against the forces of doctrinaire conformity. Bate describes Johnson as a 'heroic, intensely honest and articulate pilgrim in the strange adventure of human life' (1975, p. xx), adding that 'one of the first effects he has on us is that we find ourselves catching, by contagion, something of his courage' (p. 4). Rejecting the theoretician's *idée fixe*, whether represented in the works of Rousseau or of Derrida, such humanist defenders of Augustan literature detect within its structure of balanced oppositions not the encoding of some formalist or imperialist myth, but a quality of moral struggle. The characteristic patterns of antithesis and paradox, juxtaposing art and nature, past and present, reason and passion, create an art of order from the equipoise of polarized extremes:

> Where Order in Variety we see,
> And where, tho' all things differ, all agree.
> (*Windsor Forest*, ll. 15–16)

The triumph of civilization is thus represented above all in the centripetal tensions of the literary work itself. Writing of *The Dunciad*, Emrys Jones sees the poem's visionary apocalypse as the formal embodiment of Pope's victory over anarchy: 'The poet at once succumbs to and defies the power of Dulness; and what destroys the world completes the poem' (1968, p. 260). The more tessellated the fragments which are shored against ruin, the greater the force of moral and imaginative synthesis which turns chaos into art. Hence the historical studies which followed in the wake of the New Critical revaluation of Augustan literature served to confirm and strengthen the prevailing tone of liberal humanist approbation. Detailed scholarly analyses of the classical and Christian sources of Pope's allusions by such figures as Reuben Brower (1959) and Earl Wasserman (1959) reinforced the notion of cultural inclusiveness.

These analyses were offered not as specimens of literary archaeology, but as vital clues to the processes of the creative imagination. What they revealed was a poetry which had the multi-layered detail of an orchestral score; a poetry which functioned as a living palimpsest, re-investing the literature of the past with a new mythopoeic potency. Thus Mack comments on the pervasive literary echoes and allusions that characterize Pope's translations of Homer: 'Through a sensitivity to analogy that has probably never been surpassed, Pope's two translations at their best become echo-chambers wherein . . . one may hear reverberations from the whole literary culture of the West' (ed. 1967, vol. 7, p. lviii).

One of the earliest challenges to this critical tendency of valorizing allusiveness as a form of humanist mythopoeia, came from an unlikely source. In a lively monograph, *Literary Meaning and Augustan Values* (1974), Irvin Ehrenpreis questioned some of Mack's assumptions:

> In his studies of Pope's poetry, Maynard Mack sometimes implies that he is enhancing the literary value of a work when he is in a most rewarding way disclosing its origins. Professor Mack observes that Pope in a few lines of the *Epistle to Cobham* may echo Cowley's paraphrase of a famous passage from Virgil's Georgics, celebrating the farmer's life. 'If so,' says Professor Mack, 'the Virgilian passage masses behind Pope's contrast of court and country the most authoritative of all literary precedents.' Now I am puzzled what to make of this. The lines in Pope's poem –
>
> > In life's low vale the soil the virtues like,
> > They please as beauties, here as wonders strike –
> > (ll. 143–4)
>
> are deeply ironical and are framed in an elaborate conceit of Pope's own workmanship. Nothing in the lines invites us to look for literary allusions. Professor Mack observes meticulously that Pope was not deliberately alluding to Virgil or Cowley. Such a passage, he says, shows 'at the most reminiscence, not allusion'. But the fact remains that the passage is less enriched than confused if one brings in Virgil.
>
> (p. 9)

Ehrenpreis concludes, from this and similar examples, that 'allusion as such may decorate, handsomely; it cannot deepen'. This courteous reproof signalled an important departure from the tendency of identifying the Augustan use of classical allusions with a cultural tradition of humanism. Ehrenpreis's puzzlement was quickly followed by the more polemical analyses of feminist and deconstructionist critics who viewed allusiveness as a symbol not of inclusiveness but of exclusivity. Homeric echoes and imitations of Horace were regarded at best as forms of ideological disguise. Thus Laura Brown writes that: 'The more we know about Pope's use of the classics, the more we can understand about the system of beliefs that justified English imperial expansion' (1985, p. 27). At worst, the scholarly fetishization of such allusions by modern critics was seen as a form of cultural snobbery designed to turn Augustan studies into a kind of élitist club. In *The New Eighteenth Century* (1987), Felicity Nussbaum and Laura Brown vigorously reject the extension of this club ethos which, they argue, has resulted from the institutionalization of Augustan studies in America under the aegis of the American Society for Eighteenth Century Studies. Echoing William H. Epstein (1985), they describe the Yale Boswell 'industry' as an editorial project 'on the model of American corporate enterprise' funded by the Mellon banking fortune. Trading under the banner of liberal humanism, they present this corporate enterprise as a bastion of conservative critical complacency:

> [It] has continued to support the stereotype of pervasive and long-term stability in the period, a political stability linked to an image of equivalent social and cultural coherence, to a sense of an unchallenged class hierarchy, represented and perpetuated in a literary culture where aesthetics, ethics, and politics perfectly mesh. Thus the eighteenth century has fostered a criticism whose ultimate concern is the preservation and elucidation of canonical masterpieces of cultural stability.
>
> (1987, p. 5)

Nussbaum and Brown cite Howard Weinbrot as a paid-up member of the Augustan club whose commitment to the defence of a notion of cultural stability results in a rejection of all forms of modern critical theory. Weinbrot writes: 'the balkanisation of literary studies continues. As scholars take the time to learn more about the history of women, sexuality, or the latest version of some derivative critical theory, they take less time to learn about literary texts themselves, and the dominant cultures that produced them. Consequently, the periphery becomes the center' (1985, p. 709). For Nussbaum and Brown, however, the periphery *is* the centre. Their critical energies are directed towards re-examining those figures whose experiences, whether as writers, readers or fictional characters, have been marginalized or neglected by the assumed inclusiveness of the liberal humanist definition of Augustan culture. 'The most important work, we would argue, always insists on the relations between ideology, gender, race and class, and on the functions of the oppressed and excluded in texts and cultural formations' (p. 20).

In much the same spirit, Ellen Pollak argues that Belinda, supposedly the central character in *The Rape of the Lock*, is in fact marginalized by the poem's ideological structure:

> Ideologically, however, it is Belinda who is situated on the margins of this text. For her visibility in the poem not only signals her nonexistence as a subject, but finally points to the latent, and more powerful, masculine presence of which she has been figured as the sign.
>
> (1985, p. 79)

For Pollak, Pope's 'aesthetic flawlessness' represents not the triumph of a morally inclusive art, but the word-perfect contrivance of a deception. Thus his 'privileging of the female voice' in *Eloisa to Abelard* indicates not an identification with female emotion, but 'a voyeuristic male appropriation of female eroticism in the service of a phallocentric ordering of desire in which both excess and lack are figured as female' (pp. 182–6).

Such polarized divisions between the defenders of Augustan humanism and those for whom both Augustanism and Augustan studies represent forms of cultural oppression, would seem to depend upon a shared conviction that individual literary works have a representative or paradigmatic status. Both Leavis and Laura Brown insist on seeing Pope as the voice of his age, though their descriptions of the values of that age are very different. Commenting on Pope's assertion that "Tis Use alone that sanctifies Expense', Leavis writes: 'Pope is at one with a society to which these were obvious but important truths.' He adds that the 'correctness' of Pope's style 'derives its strength from a social code and a civilization' ([1936] 1964, pp. 72, 68). Yet it is perfectly possible to view both Pope and Swift not as members of a dominant culture, but as marginalized outsiders. In his satires Pope frequently presents himself not as a man 'at one' with his society, but as isolated and excluded, not merely by his Catholicism, but by his moral integrity. The authority of his judgemental tone depends in large part upon a sense of cultural alienation. Detached from the mundane compromises of the social and political milieux, he appears as a lone crusader for truth in a world of corruption, vice and venality:

> Yes, the last Pen for Freedom let me draw,
> When truth stands trembling on the edge of Law.
> (*Epilogue to the Satires*, Dialogue II, ll. 248–9)

For Swift, too, the Augustan model served not to confer some general approbation on the values of a dominant culture, but as a standard of integrity, legitimizing and compelling the intellectual endeavours of an élite band of cultural revolutionaries. He wrote to Pope in September 1723:

> I have often endeavoured to establish a Friendship among all Men of Genius, and would fain have it done. They are seldom above three or four Cotemporaries and if they could be united would drive the world before them; I think it was so among the poets in the time of Augustus.
> (ed. Williams, 1963–5, vol. 2, p. 465)

The critical tendency to regard Pope and Swift as representative voices of a dominant Augustan culture – whether that culture be defined in terms of refinement or imperialism – ignores the powerful sense of social and psychological displacement which energizes their satires. Recent scholarship has drawn increased attention to such feelings of alienation. Brean Hammond (1986) has suggested that Pope's physical deformity resulted in an ambiguous quality of 'marginalized sexuality' which separated him from the 'masculinist confidence' of much of his society (p. 154). Howard Erskine-Hill (1975) and Douglas Brooks-Davies (1985), detecting numerous Jacobite allusions in his poetry, have argued that Pope's Catholicism gave him the instincts of a member of an oppressed minority. Swift's life demonstrates insistent patterns of both political and psychological displacement. Forced into virtual exile in Ireland after 1713 he described himself in a letter to Bolingbroke as one 'banished to a country of slaves and beggars' where he was left to die 'in a rage, like a poisoned rat in a hole' (ed. Williams, 1963–5, vol. 3, p. 382). When these men use the language of Augustanism it represents not an 'encoding of imperialism' but an appeal to an ideal of independence. The moral indignation which sounds throughout their works assumes the tones of the dispossessed. It is of course possible to represent such protestations of exclusion as forms of ideological mystification and false consciousness which merely hijack the moral vocabulary of dispossession in order to reinforce cultural formations of control. Yet the kind of literary criticism which insists on discounting surface meanings, identifying Pope with an imperialist ethic which his poetry, explicitly at least, rejects, would seem to reduce rather than expand our understanding of the diversity of Augustan political attitudes.

Undoubtedly there are weaknesses in the New Critical tendency to subsume all questions of ideology and intention into a discussion of form. The imagination, however subtle, is not an inevitable guarantor of moral wisdom. In my own writings on Swift I have tried to suggest some contextual limitations to the moral inclusiveness of his irony. Comparing the language of his sermons with that of *A Modest Proposal*, one finds disturbing similarities of both tone and sentiment between Swift and his ironic persona. In his sermon 'On the Poor Man's Contentment' Swift writes:

> Perhaps there is not a word more abused than that of the poor, or wherein the world is more generally mistaken. Among the number of those who beg in our streets, or are half-starved at home, or languish in prison for debt, there is hardly one in a hundred who doth not owe his misfortune to his own laziness or drunkenness or worse vices. To these he owes those very diseases which often disable him from getting his bread. Such wretches are deservedly unhappy; they can only blame themselves; and when we are commanded to have pity on the poor, these are not understood to be of their number.
>
> (ed. Davis et al., 1939–74, vol. 9, p. 191)

'There is something unpleasantly pharisaical about the smug formula "deservedly unhappy" which Swift applies to the ninety-nine in every hundred of the beggars he meets' (Nokes, 1985, p. 275). Such harsh and unironic sentiments which find expression in several of Swift's sermons and pamphlets might lead us to question Martin Price's morally comfortable reading of *A Modest Proposal*. We should be careful of celebrating as irony, or dignifying as paradox, sentiments which, more simply expressed, would prove unacceptable to modern tastes. As Ehrenpreis writes:

> What one finds in many re-interpretations of Augustan literature is really a flight from explicit meaning. . . . Some friends of Augustan writing have tried over the past thirty years to interest modern readers in that literature by showing how it can satisfy modern taste. They have dwelled on the allusiveness, the indirection, the subversiveness of the authors. In poems that sound conventional they have found iconoclasm.
>
> (1974, p. 7)

It is perhaps hardly surprising that these sustained attempts to identify in irony and allusion the complex imaginative expression of a morally congenial art should have been countered by the deconstructivist efforts of Marxists, feminists and others to decode the iconography of Augustanism as a form of cultural oppression.

Increasingly, the 'new' eighteenth century of 1980s literary scholarship appears as a period of diversity, contradiction and experimentation which stubbornly defies categorization under the Augustan label. Ideological critics like Nussbaum and Brown direct their attention to the margins of society, to the 'functions of the oppressed and excluded in texts and cultural formations' (1987, p. 20). Meanwhile a historicist like Pat Rogers who declares that 'events fascinate me more than ideology' (1985, p. 76) is concerned to investigate the factual particularity of literary references which resist any simple metaphorical or methodological synthesis. Roger Lonsdale's edition of *The New Oxford Book of Eighteenth Century Verse* (1984) is characteristic of this recent tendency to stress not the coherence of a dominant culture but the diversity and eclecticism of literary styles and voices. Noting the 'hypnotically influential way in which the eighteenth century succeeded in anthologising itself', he argues that traditional accounts of Augustan verse, which emphasize its 'lucidity, elegance and refinement', have depended upon an exclusive process of selection by editors and scholars who 'with some honourable exceptions . . . have in fact returned again and again to the same familiar material':

> It is commonly assumed that the restraints imposed by polite taste were so pervasive that it never occurred to eighteenth-century poets to write in certain ways or on certain subjects, as if for several decades they simply failed to experience various basic human interests or emotions. In fact, throughout the century there were poets oblivious of, or indifferent to, the inhibitions of polite taste.
>
> (p. xxxvi)

The patient explorer, Lonsdale suggests, who cares to venture beyond the prescribed boundaries of Augustan Good Taste and Decorum, will find 'the vigorous, humorous, idiosyncratic verse of authors, many of them anonymous, who felt impelled at least to try to describe with some immediacy and colloquial directness the changing world they lived in, often for anything but a polite readership' (p. xxxvii). Margaret Doody takes up a similar strain in her book *The Daring Muse* (1985) which, while retaining the word Augustan in its subtitle, 'Augustan Poetry Reconsidered', stretches the term to cover a variety of authors previously excluded from the classical pantheon. 'Too much talk about "decorum" and "correctness" can only depress the uninitiated', she writes, casting aside the customary identification of Augustanism with refinement. Instead, in her studies of provincial and 'uneducated' writers, women poets and Dissenters, she emphasizes the excitement, the diversity and the strangeness of eighteenth-century poetry.

It would seem, in such works as these, as if 'Augustanism' has finally been deconstructed as a myth of literary history; the critical expression of a notion of coherence in which irony asserted the freedom of the imagination to explore, challenge and subvert the social iconography of an age. Excluded, exuberant and daring, the writers of the eighteenth century now stand as individualists, separated rather than joined by the social idioms of their works.

FURTHER READING

Brower, Reuben (1959) *Alexander Pope: The Poetry of Allusion*, Clarendon Press, Oxford

Doody, Margaret Anne (1985) *The Daring Muse: Augustan Poetry Reconsidered*, Cambridge University Press, Cambridge

Ehrenpreis, Irvin (1974) *Literary Meaning and Augustan Values*, University Press of Virginia, Charlottesville

Erskine-Hill, Howard (1975) *The Social Milieu of Alexander Pope*, Yale University Press, New Haven

Fussell, Paul (1965) *The Rhetorical World of Augustan Humanism*, Clarendon Press, Oxford

Greene, Donald (1970) *The Age of Exuberance: Backgrounds to Eighteenth-Century English Literature*, Random House, New York

Lonsdale, Roger (ed.) (1984) *The New Oxford Book of Eighteenth Century Verse*, Oxford University Press, Oxford

Nokes, David (1987) *Raillery and Rage, A Study of Eighteenth-Century Satire*, Harvester Press, Brighton

Nussbaum, Felicity and Brown, Laura (eds) (1987) *The New Eighteenth Century*, Methuen, New York

Rogers, Pat (1974) *The Augustan Vision*, Weidenfeld & Nicolson, London

Weinbrot, Howard D. (1978) *Augustus Caesar in 'Augustan' England: The Decline of a Classical Norm*, Princeton University Press, Princeton

ADDITIONAL WORKS CITED

Bate, Walter Jackson (1975) *Samuel Johnson*, Harcourt Brace Jovanovich, New York

Brooks-Davies, Douglas (1985) *Pope's 'Dunciad' and the Queen of Night*, Manchester University Press, Manchester

Brown, Laura (1985) *Alexander Pope*, Basil Blackwell, Oxford

Davis, H. *et al.* (eds) (1939–74) *Prose Works of Jonathan Swift*, 16 vols, Basil Blackwell, Oxford

Eliot, T. S. (1932) 'John Dryden'. In T. S. Eliot, *Selected Essays*, Faber & Faber, London [essay first published 1921]

Epstein, William H. (1985) 'Professing the Eighteenth Century', *ADE Bulletin*, 81, 20–5

Fetterley, Judith (1985) Unpublished paper delivered to the Modern Language Association, quoted in Ellen Pollak, *The Poetics of Sexual Myth, Gender and Ideology in the Verse of Swift and Pope*, University of Chicago Press, Chicago

Greene, Donald (1967–76) 'Augustinianism and Empiricism: A Note on Eighteenth-Century Intellectual History', *Eighteenth Century Studies*, I (1967–8), 33–68; see also rejoinders and review articles in *ECS* (1968–9), 293–300; (1971–2), 456–63; (1975–6), 128–33

Hammond, Brean S. (1986) *Pope*, Harvester Press, Brighton

Hooker, E. N. (ed.) (1939) *The Critical Works of John Dennis*, 2 vols, Johns Hopkins University Press, Baltimore

Johnson, Samuel (1952) *The Lives of the English Poets*, 2 vols, Oxford University Press, Oxford [first published 1779–81]

Jones, Emrys (1968) *Pope and Dulness*, British Academy Chatterton Lecture, London

Leavis, F. R. (1964) *Revaluation*, Penguin Books, Harmondsworth [first published 1936]

Mack, Maynard (1959) 'Wit and Poetry and Pope'. In J. L. Clifford (ed.), *Eighteenth-Century English Literature, Modern Essays in Criticism*, Oxford University Press, New York, pp. 21–41 [essay first published 1949]

——(ed.) (1967) *The Twickenham Edition of the Works of Alexander Pope*, vol. 7, Methuen, London

Nokes, David (1985) *Jonathan Swift, A Hypocrite Reversed*, Oxford University Press, Oxford

Novak, Maximillian E. (1984) 'Shaping the Augustan Myth'. In P. J. Korshin and R. R. Allen (eds), *Greene Centennial Studies*, University Press of Virginia, Charlottesville, pp. 1–21

Pollak, Ellen (1985) *The Poetics of Sexual Myth, Gender and Ideology in the Verses of Swift and Pope*, University of Chicago Press, Chicago

Price, Martin (1953) *Swift's Rhetorical Art*, Yale University Press, New Haven

Rawson, Claude (1985) 'The Augustan Idea'. In Claude Rawson, *Order from Confusion Sprung*, Allen & Unwin, London, pp. 242–52

Rogers, Pat (1985) *Eighteenth Century Encounters*, Harvester Press, Brighton

Wasserman, Earl (1959) *The Subtler Language*, Johns Hopkins University Press, Baltimore

Weinbrot, Howard D. (1985) 'Recent Studies in the Restoration and Eighteenth Century', *Studies in English Literature, 1500–1900*, 25, 671–710

Williams, Sir Harold (ed.) (1963–5) *The Correspondence of Jonathan Swift*, 5 vols, Clarendon Press, Oxford

6

ROMANTICISM

DAVID PUNTER

The notion of joining, or even of rehearsing, the many arguments concerning the meaning of the term 'Romanticism' is one calculated to strike fear into the heart of the most hardened scholar. Perhaps, though, it is worth stating the three most obvious difficulties which accompany the use of the term. First, it is used in a variety of Western cultural contexts, having a bearing on many European literatures and arts as well as on American culture. Second, the various language-based movements associated with the term cover a wide time-scale, with German, English and French romanticisms occupying different periods of literary history. And third, although our concern here is with literature, romanticism is a notion, a tide of feeling, a set of expressive attitudes and devices with application in almost every art; again, the movements in the visual arts and in music coincide only imprecisely with those in the literary field.

To these we may add another important but more hidden problem. Although it is perhaps not impossible to date the beginnings of Romanticism within the eighteenth century and in a widespread set of reactions to Enlightenment thinking on epistemology, aesthetics and human behaviour, it is extremely difficult to date its end; and in many respects – in, for example, popular notions of the creative practice and social role of the artist or poet – romanticism is still very much with us. Certainly the root term 'romance', which had a long and distinguished literary history, has continued to move through a constantly modifying pattern of usage to the present day, and neither in its pop forms (the 'romance magazine') nor in its more technical applications (for example, the Freudian concept of the 'family romance') does it show any signs of dying out.

What is easier, however, is to name the most significant figures in British Romanticism. For the most part, they are primarily poets: Blake (problematically), Wordsworth, Coleridge, Keats, Shelley, Byron, perhaps Burns. On the sidelines stand the essayists, Hazlitt, Lamb and De Quincey. The question of the romantic novel, the subject of a heroic but methodologically dubious study by Robert Kiely (1972), is altogether more vexed: the gothic novel of Ann Radcliffe, Matthew Lewis and Mary Shelley clearly has strong romantic affinities, as does the sentimental fiction of Fanny Burney and the later high romanticism of the Brontës; but the most important fiction writer of the period was, after all, Jane Austen, and here the argument about Romanticism waxes loud and long (see Butler, 1975). It cannot fail to be noticed, of course, that the poets are men; the novelists, with few exceptions, are women. The dramatists are best not mentioned, except in so far as they provide some of the ancestry for that highly significant Victorian genre, the stage melodrama.

We may, for the most part, see romanticism in Britain as occurring between the years 1770 and 1840; and many critics would agree that we can identify certain historical determinants. The rejection of the canons of reason established by the eighteenth-century philosophers surely did not occur arbitrarily: reason ceased to be a trusted guide at least in part because a rapidly industrializing and urbanizing world, in which old patterns of work and relationship were breaking down, no longer seemed amenable to reason. Wordsworth's longing for solitude and condemnation of city amusements did not take place in a social vacuum; and neither did Blake's acid rejection of commerce as the keynote of all things. Romanticism is redolent of a sustained societal threat to privacy and to the valued life of the individual; it also shows a very varied but always engaged set of attitudes towards politics, and here the context of the French Revolution and turn-of-the-century English radicalism is crucial.

We do not need to be sociologists of literature to see that these events and tendencies conduced to a particular psychological complexion. It includes the nostalgia of gothic fiction, of historical genre painting, of Cobbett's rural fury, of John Martin's later Miltonic apocalypticism. It includes also an intense dwelling on the peculiarities of the relationship between the intensities of the inner self and the beauties of the natural world. It includes a strong focus on the continuity of the personality and the factors which threaten that continuity, and thus it is hardly surprising to find the romantics speculating on the origins and nature of human consciousness. It entails an acknowledgment of the power of passion for good or ill; and in contemporary criticism, as we shall see, we have to deal with this concentration on passion and perhaps on the embarrassment which comes with trying to account for it or comment on it in a systematic way.

We can be more precise about the genre basis of British romanticism. In fiction, the typical form is expressionistic: dealing more with the insides of minds and feelings than with the temporal coherences of narrative. In poetry, we can parallel this in such long autobiographical poems as Wordsworth's *The Prelude*; but the more frequent form is the brief, intensely meditative ode, most famously in Keats's work. Behind this there lies one of the many romantic paradoxes: that the evident longing for rich, continuing life emerges frequently as short lyric burst or even as impassioned fragment, as emblematically with Coleridge's 'Kubla Khan'.

The great founding fathers of recent criticism of Romanticism to some extent reflect this paradox. M. H. Abrams's *The Mirror and the Lamp* (1953), a magisterial attempt to reconstruct a coherent romantic theory of art, shows both an impassioned engagement with its subject and an urge towards systematization which throws romantic inconsistency into high relief. Northrop Frye, in *Fearful Symmetry* (1947) – ostensibly a book on Blake but really an attempt at constructing a mythic theory of poetry on the basis of romantic concepts – finds pattern everywhere but leaves us with unanswered questions about why these patterns required to be hidden so excellently by the writers themselves. Mario Praz's older *The Romantic Agony* (trans. 1933), which deals in exhaustive detail with romantic attitudes to sexuality, has been regarded by some as hardly a work of criticism at all; yet in its obsessive tone and endless fascination with the perversity of detail it can be seen as itself standing squarely in a European romantic tradition.

The tendency to produce enormous synthesizing books on Romanticism has waned somewhat over the last two decades, partly because of the difficulties of the subject-matter and partly because of changes in critical theory which place in question the urge towards systemic domination in general. It has continued however, as in Thomas McFarland's colossal *Coleridge and the Pantheist Tradition* (1969) and his later *Romanticism and the Forms of Ruin* (1981), whose title calls to mind the Ozymandias-like fate of those who attempt to include all they survey. The rather different enterprise of John Beer (1968, 1977, 1978) has produced a long series of works on Blake, Coleridge and Wordsworth characterized by both meticulous scholarship and a ceaseless attempt to work not at the periphery of Romanticism but in terms of great central concepts which have now come to seem so commonplace that they suffer from a slippage of focus – Wordsworth's attitudes to humanity, for example. Peter Thorslev, in *Romantic Contraries* (1984), essays again the difficult question of what a romantic poem *is*, while ending by betraying a forgiveable Promethean impatience.

But when one tries to survey the field of recent criticism of Romanticism as a whole, the image which comes irresistibly to mind is Arnoldian; it is of mighty armies clashing by night, albeit armies well-equipped with sophistication and formidable in their terminologies. For while a great deal of quiet and traditional textual work and work in the history of ideas proceeds – mostly focused on individual writers – Romanticism has simultaneously become a site on which battle has been joined between the most important tendencies in literary theory.

Interestingly, structuralism cannot be included among these tendencies.

Although structuralists and formalists of differing quality have paid attention to individual romantic poems, and although lyrics of the complexity of Blake's and Coleridge's invite repeated structuralist re-reading, on the whole the structuralists have tended to dismiss Romanticism as woolly, preferring classical order and modernist slyness of meaning.

This rested, I think, partly on a misunderstanding of Romanticism; which is that passion is inconsistent with irony. Fortunately recent studies have begun to redress the balance (see Simpson, 1979), and this is as it should be bearing in mind, at the very least, Blake's thinly veiled sarcasms and Byron's single-handed elevation of a genre of romantic satire. For the passion, the inwardness on which so many romantic poems depend is intimately associated with self-reflexiveness, a restlessness of consciousness which is constantly uncovering the inadequacy of former positions and thus necessarily undermining its own self-confidence with a mixture of annoyance and wry humour.

This renewed attention to romantic irony is thus of a piece again with tendencies in recent criticism, and particularly with post-structuralist ones. For the whole deconstructionist exercise is founded on a premise which was highly congenial to the romantics, namely the built-in limitations of human reason which result in every use of the *logos* simultaneously displaying, as it were, its own underside. The 'Ode on a Grecian Urn' ends in a paradox of endless productivity not because Keats could not think of any other way of ending the poem, but because such paradox seemed to him of the essence of creativity, that mysterious process whereby the most intimate disclosure of the soul simultaneously entails the 'chameleon-like' process of dissolving personality into a range of fictional Others. The highest romantic skill is 'negative capability', because as we approach the essence of our individuality what we find is that individuality showing its irreducible connections, outward to the contexts of the world, back in time to invisible origins. It is surely no accident that much of Blake's and Shelley's work consisted of the *rewriting* of myth, for the knowledge that writing is, as Derrida would put it, 'trace' is essential to the romantic agon.

The connections here pass from Rousseau through Nietzsche, the great founding father of deconstruction, for whom order dissolved before the power of the will. This will is a thing of illusion, yet it produces fictions which actually control our being in the world, as Shelley also said in *Prometheus Unbound*. And these controlling fictions do not control merely our individual lives; they are also and inseparably the originating material of our social orderings. Small wonder, then, that we can see much of the most interesting criticism of Romanticism under two heads: deconstructive criticism, which attempts to close up the individual circles we have just described; and historical criticism of various kinds, which attempts to reassert the reality status of these fictions and their effects.

> To read is to understand, to question, to know, to forget, to erase, to deface, to
> repeat – that is to say, the endless prosopopoeia by which the dead are made to
> have a face and a voice which tells the allegory of their demise and allows us to
> apostrophise them in our turn. No degree of knowledge can ever stop this
> madness, for it is the madness of words.
>
> (de Man, 1979, p. 68)

Paul de Man's words, from his essay 'Shelley Disfigured', alert us to the
endemic difficulty of assessing the contribution of deconstruction to knowledge; perhaps the only sensible question which can be put is to ask what
deconstructionists *do*, or what they have done and are doing in relation to
Romanticism. And a short answer, if an evasive one, is that what the deconstructionists – principally de Man, Harold Bloom and Geoffrey Hartman –
are doing is re-encountering romantic poems and participating in a mutual
reshaping.

We cannot say clearly that this process of reflexive reshaping sheds any
extra light specifically on Romanticism; what we can say is that the depth and
extent of their engagement with Romanticism – in de Man's *The Rhetoric of
Romanticism* (1984), for example, or in Hartman's essays on the romantics in
Beyond Formalism (1970) – demonstrates something further about the *life* which
romantic poems continue to have, and something about the loop of literary
history by which they now come to figure as the preferred site of the most
complex and convoluted forms of criticism. In speaking of Blake, Wordsworth
and others, these critics do not make any attempt on the comprehensive or
the definitive; we could say instead that their movement is Yeatsian, a turning
around in space which smacks both of a feeling for room and of an endless
puzzling over the productivity of the human consciousness.

As this is the preferred movement, so the preferred subgenre of the deconstructionists is the fragment, as both subject-matter and critical product. What
is at worst avoided and at best transcended in this form of criticism is any
question of the poet's self-consciousness; what is paradoxical is the way in
which, certainly in the writings of de Man, an intense if hidden reconjuring
of the personality of the poet is coupled with a theoretical insistence on the
very impossibility of such a reconjuring. We have the strange spectacle of a
sublimated meeting of consciousness paraded as a chance encounter between
un-authored texts. Certainly thus the problem of intentionality disappears from
the agenda; the danger is that the problem of meaning in its essential connections with value disappears with it, leaving us watching the deconstructionists
pondering why they are interested in the romantics at all.

There is no doubting, however, the intelligence and indeed the excitement
of such essays as Hartman's 'Wordsworth, Inscriptions, and Romantic Nature
Poetry' (1970, pp. 206–30), or the way in which such essays extend the range
of possible insights into the poems; what can be doubted is whether methods

– or anti-methods – which have borne great fruit in the hands of the masters are transferable, or whether instead they are the latest form of an age-old critical élitism – not unknown to the romantics themselves – revolving around issues of genius.

An example of the better kind of deconstruction occurs in Nelson Hilton's *The Literal Imagination: Blake's Vision of Words* (1983), undoubtedly a strenuous attempt to enter Blake's world if, as it were, by the back door and when there are no personalities around to observe. An example of the worse kind would be Tilottama Rajan's *Dark Intrepreter: The Discourse of Romanticism* (1980), wherein is conjured up a web of words so abstractly intricate that we feel returned to the world of the romantics' alchemical and cabbalistic forefathers. Somewhere in between, in my judgement, lies David Simpson's *Irony and Authority in Romantic Poetry* (1979); but this is a book which demonstrates the perils of in-betweenness in an unfortunate way, by slipping and sliding between a deconstructionist discourse and one where more old-fashioned questions of value still have a place.

The variability within deconstruction is not merely one of quality; it is more importantly one of purpose and focus. For deconstruction, as practised in connection with romantic poetry – for prose offers considerable resistance to the deconstructionist project – tends towards two opposite conclusions. One is nihilism, the total instability of the object which leaves its existence only in the (unknowable) mind of the critic; the other is a kind of transcendence, an involuted worship of textual complexity which seems in the end a curious amalgam of New Critical over-valuation of textual organization and neo-romantic 'appreciation' not readily different in its claims to evidence and valuation from the criticism of such generally reviled figures as Pater and Swinburne.

At all events, the deconstructionist criticism of romantic texts is committed to the unknowability of the past, and to the inadvisability of value judgements. On both of these counts it has been challenged over recent years by critics whom we might loosely call historicist, but who are actually of quite different persuasions. First there are the American New Historicists, perhaps most notably Jerome J. McGann (1983) and Clifford Siskin (1988), although Michael G. Cooke (1976, 1979) could conceivably be classed in this category as well; and then there are the largely British critics, such as Marilyn Butler (1981) or John Barrell (1972, 1980, 1983) to whom I suppose one must reluctantly attach the label Old Historicist.

The difference between them could in fact hardly be more fundamental, since it is a difference about the nature of history itself. For the New Historicists, the influence of Foucault among others entails seeing history as a series of discursive practices or interlocking ideologies: history is a struggle for power, certainly, but the power sought is over discursive space, and the fate of the underling is to be robbed of his or her language. For Butler and Barrell, as for the older Marxist historians of Romanticism rooted in the world of E. P. Thompson, history consists of such old-fashioned things as actions, movements and events, and a type of political judgement is possible which relates these past events to the present and permits value judgements upon them. Not so for the New Historicists, for whom the struggle of discourses is ineluctable, and who at their most extreme represent a variety of determinism which would have shaken the good Victorian Marx to his social foundation.

It has to be said, however, that the practice of New Historicism in connection with Romanticism is far better than its underpinnings. McGann's *The Romantic Ideology* (1983) is an intelligent and penetrating book, while Siskin in *The Historicity of Romantic Discourse* (1988) confronts us, albeit at rather too great a length, with an enormously important question: why is it that, whatever our critical persuasion, we continue to treat the romantics as though they were the discoverers of uncharted realms of the human psyche when in fact it could more usefully be said that the problems they discuss were in fact their own historical products? Siskin is perfectly right to claim that this extremely non-deconstructive fallacy underlies the work of Bloom and de Man, although it is not made clear enough how the critic should work this insight through in detail.

Butler's book *Romantics, Rebels and Reactionaries* (1981) has made a surprising impact: surprising not because there is a problem with the book, which is an excellent piece of literary-historical scholarship, but because the approach she uses has been common currency in British criticism for some twenty years. My own suspicion is that the impact is partly due to the transition across the Atlantic; on the whole, it is fair to say that despite the labours of David Erdman (1954) American criticism of the romantics has not touched historical base for a long time, and the possibilities of this type of criticism – political criticism is a better term than Old Historicism – clearly took the theorists and speculators aback.

Barrell's work on Clare and other romantic writers and painters demonstrates the same sound historical sense, but across a broader spectrum; and indeed his work points to a surprising lack in the whole area of cross-genre criticism of the romantic arts. In this context it is also worth mentioning two writers, Donald Low (1977) and Roger Sales (1983), who have recently done much to reassert a historical connection, that between Romanticism and the Regency as a historical moment, which had shown signs of disappearing. As the work of the deconstructors tends to concentrate on the work of the transcendentalists (Shelley), the soliloquizers (Wordsworth) and the aesthetes (Keats), so the emphasis on historical conditions tends towards the reaffirmation of the poets of the poor (Clare) and of the aristocracy (Byron) in their actual setting.

It appears to me that if we are looking for brilliant textual criticism, it is to de Man, Hartman and one or two of their followers that we must turn; but if we are looking for insights which will get us further with what Romanticism actually *was* – and, perhaps, still is – it is to the political critics and those knowledgeable about the social environment that we have to resort. The problem with criticism of Romanticism at the moment, as I see it, is that the gap between these areas is impassably wide, but this is surely unavoidable, for two reasons: first, because what we see here are different versions of the actual building blocks of history and the self, and second, because the nature of the investment made by these different critics in their objects of attention is quite different. What is sad is that this does an injustice to the romantics, those writers who, above all, were tremblingly aware of the inseparability of discourse and the self, politics and the inward, poetry and all those external forces which were ranged against poetry and, of course, against criticism too.

Thus the battleground; what of the shadows? In my opinion, feminist criticism has not yet made many inroads into Romanticism, and what it has done has been interestingly split along a line rather analogous to the battle zone itself. On the one hand, there has been a considerable amount of feminist reading which has fallen into what I would call the trap of enlightened biographism. It is, of course, vitally important to recall to mind the dire facts of women's lives in the late eighteenth and early nineteenth centuries; on the other hand, if intentionalism is a problem for masculinist criticism, I am not clear why it should be free from fault for feminists. What can be said about this line of enquiry is that it has shown that there were a great number of women writers at the time, and that some of them have been unjustly disregarded; what might be more interesting would be whether it could be shown, for example, that there is a feminine version of Romanticism – or even that there is not – but this is not a line of questioning which has been pursued, partly because the other side of feminist work has demonstrated an allegiance to the problematic insights of Lacan so intense as to fall into the category of hero-worship. The best work done has in any case not fallen directly into the field of Romanticism, and this may be quite proper if we accept that these demarcations are in any case masculinist; Mary Poovey's *The Proper Lady and the Woman Writer* (1984) is an excellent and wide-ranging study, although its bearing on Romanticism as such is not clear, and Ellen Moers on the female Gothic (1976, 1979) gives us one of the most important general insights into the construction of the imagination during the period.

A surprising absence is of psychological and psychoanalytic readings of Romanticism, for which books on individual authors, like Diana Hume George's (1980) on Blake, can be no substitute. There is much work here to be done, and much of it need not fall into the trap of over-explanation; Freud himself was deeply indebted to Romanticism and constantly used a romantic model of the artist as a touchstone for the breadth of human creativity, and there are direct connections between his case histories and a number of romantic texts such as James Hogg's *Confessions of a Justified Sinner* (1824). One can readily imagine deconstructive work of this kind, along the lines of Samuel Weber's *Freud Legende* (1979), which might serve an important purpose in bridging the severed worlds of discursive determination and historical choice.

An analogous gap occurs in the study of the genesis of Romanticism, and specifically in the contemporary account of 'pre-Romanticism'. Book after book pays lip-service to the precursive roles of Chatterton, Smart, Cowper; yet this very notion of 'precursive role' not only should be the site of substantive challenge, but also raises important theoretical questions both in the deconstructionist camp (what is this myth of unstable origins?) and the historicist (what real conditions are here being ignored/sublated?). These, after all, are writers of the slipped text; and/or they are writers from an alienation so endemic as to prevent full emergence into the public realm. At the very least, they are partial and problematic excisions from the canon, and apt for re-reading.

There is a similar problem about what might thus be called 'post-Romanticism'. Tennyson, Browning, Swinburne, Rossetti – these are the names of the survival of romantic textuality. But perhaps this is merely to carp; the question is, I think, about how Romanticism 'comes into view', what our horizon of expectation is in relation to it, especially in generations where the old copies of Wordsworth, Scott, Byron are disappearing from family bookshelves. This touches again, I think, on the problem that Romanticism, in our own age and in much of its criticism, figures as an assumed universality in a way that, for example, neo-classicism does not. In so far as the canon is changing at all, and that is slight, it is to the exclusion of those writers seen as representative of non-universal experience, typically Burns, who is now much more ill-thought-of than previously, and to the inclusion of expressionistic representatives – the gothic novelists – of what are taken to be enduring problems of, for example, power and sexuality.

Yet Siskin is surely correct to assert that Romanticism should be seen less as discovery than as construction, a construction amply with us in the twentieth century in the work of poets like Berryman and Hughes. Part of this construction revolved around the supreme value of the inaccessible, in which respect the writers were the heirs, not of Chaucer, Donne, Pope, but of the theologians, whether we think of Blake on radical Christianity or Coleridge's rather dusty religiosity. Thus we might say that in the romantics the moment of worship, or meditation, goes inside and reconstructs its own narcissistic root. In this respect, it reads often less like a record of revelation than an account of thwarting as social pressure reduces the value accorded to this process.

To go a little further with the analysis of this construction, we might say that Romanticism is alive with gods: not only the gods of the established church, of course, but a whole pantheon of Greek and other deities, and one of the most important principles to grasp here is the way in which romantic discourse continually reaches out for ways of 'housing' these gods within the psyche; which is itself an attempt to transcend a specific form of alienation. Narcissus thus becomes one of the great archetypes of the age; what is reflected is the self, whether heroized, ironized or even apprehended, as Wordsworth so often does, in its quotidian narratives. What has also to be said, though, is that this narcissism is inextricably bound up with a certain version of patriarchy, whether overt in Gothic fiction or in the subtler and disguised forms to be found in Blake and Coleridge. It is as though, with the passing of a particular conjuncture in which writers could graft themselves seamlessly on to the conventional modes of social domination, there emerges instead a need to invent new mythologies about the relation between masculinity and creativity, mythologies which now have a clear place for women, but as with Blake's Enitharmon, Coleridge's Sara, Keats's Moneta, a place which mainly embraces stimulus and frustration; women appear in a greater variety of adjunct positions but not as prime movers.

What may also be said is that some of these gods are not the safe gods of the city but the risky deities of the wilderness; Gothic, of course, is a term intimately bound up with the notion of barbarism, and Blake and Shelley are particularly concerned with the gods and forgotten emperors who inhabit the realms where the writ of convention does not run. At the same time, however, this tendency towards the wilderness is contained; these are not the cultural barbarities of Leavisite demonology, but apprehensions of forces which might in fact contribute to cultural renewal if they can be properly harnessed, as even Orc fits in to an assigned place in Parnassus.

These reflections on the gods and the wilderness lead inevitably, I think, to speculations on death; and it can be said that Romanticism encompasses death in a way which classicism did not. Wordsworth's preoccupation with epitaphs was no accident; right through Romanticism there runs a fascination with individual annihilation which is a clear refraction of a sense of the passing away of stability. Emblematically, we have Keats's dual attitude to healing and obliteration; on the American side, the deathly fiction of Edgar Allan Poe as the culmination of the long sequence of horrors which serve to add piquancy to the romantic message about the intensification of everyday life.

Turning back to 'Kubla Khan', we can find there one of the most resonant apprehensions of what the romantic commitment to art might require; and it is a perhaps over-neat critical paradox to place this agonized cry for a transcending authenticity in the face of death over against Norman Fruman's long indictment of Coleridge's plagiarisms (1971). But this is perhaps important: that what appals the romantics is the impossibility of the authentic, the sense that, whatever voice one speaks in, that voice turns out to have its own less than conscious imperatives.

And these problems of authenticity and rebellion perhaps remind us of a final point; which is that Romanticism is, in a specific way, a defining moment of Western literature. There has been little evidence of a comparable movement in Chinese or Japanese literature until, in fact, very recently; and one might argue that this recent phenomenon has been precisely due to the possibilities of the unconventional opening up in previously rigidly stratified societies. There too one finds the sense of the awesome risks run when trying to move counter to societal pressure; and yet one is led to speculate, in the case of Western Romanticism, on the extent to which these pressures were themselves part of the constructed world which the romantics inhabited.

The enduring problem for criticism of the romantics, it seems to me, might also be put in terms of that vexed word 'authenticity'; does the best criticism seek, in some sense, to 'take the romantics on their own terms', to construct a critical discourse which might obey some of the romantic imperatives; or do we serve the purposes of criticism better by trying to open up a gap between the romantic moment and our own? Certainly it is easy to find ways in which Romanticism appears to prefigure many of our own preoccupations – in, for example, its apprehensions of the unconscious, in its disconcerted dealings with the power of language – but in the end the question remains: do we see these prefigurings because we are now able to view Romanticism clearly, or because we are ourselves, in the West in the late twentieth century, still bound into ways of seeing the world which, in their emphasis on the frustrations of alienation and the devaluations implied by certain kinds of social and technological change, are effects of romantic reconstructions of self and world?

FURTHER READING

Abrams, M. H. (1953) *The Mirror and the Lamp: Romantic Theory and the Critical Tradition*, Oxford University Press, New York

Bloom, Harold (1973) *The Anxiety of Influence: A Theory of Poetry*, Oxford University Press, New York

——*et al.* (1979) *Deconstruction and Criticism*, Seabury Press, New York

Butler, Marilyn (1981) *Romantics, Rebels and Reactionaries: English Literature and its Background 1760–1830*, Oxford University Press, Oxford

Cooke, Michael G. (1979) *Acts of Inclusion: Studies Bearing on an Elementary Theory of Romanticism*, Yale University Press, New Haven

de Man, Paul (1984) *The Rhetoric of Romanticism*, Columbia University Press, New York

Hartman, Geoffrey (1970) *Beyond Formalism: Literary Essays 1958–1970*, Yale University Press, New Haven

Kiely, Robert (1972) *The Romantic Novel in England*, Harvard University Press, Cambridge

McGann, Jerome J. (1983) *The Romantic Ideology: A Critical Investigation*, Chicago University Press, Chicago

Praz, Mario (1933) *The Romantic Agony*, translated by Angus Davidson, Oxford University Press, London

Simpson, David (1979) *Irony and Authority in Romantic Poetry*, Macmillan, London

Siskin, Clifford (1988) *The Historicity of Romantic Discourse*, Oxford University Press, New York

ADDITIONAL WORKS CITED

Barrell, John (1972) *The Idea of Landscape and the Sense of Place 1730–1840: An Approach to the Poetry of John Clare*, Cambridge University Press, London

——(1980) *The Dark Side of the Landscape: The Rural Poor in English Paintings 1730–1840*, Cambridge University Press, Cambridge

——(1983) *English Literature in History 1730–80: An Equal, Wide Survey*, Hutchinson, London

Beer, John (1968) *Blake's Humanism*, Manchester University Press, Manchester

——(1977) *Coleridge's Poetic Intelligence*, Macmillan, London

——(1978) *Wordsworth and the Human Heart*, Macmillan, London

Butler, Marilyn (1975) *Jane Austen and the War of Ideas*, Clarendon Press, Oxford

Cooke, Michael G. (1976) *The Romantic Will*, Yale University Press, New Haven and London

de Man, Paul (1979) 'Shelley Disfigured'. In Harold Bloom *et al.*, *Deconstruction and Criticism*, Seabury Press, New York, pp. 39–73

Erdman, David (1954) *Blake, Prophet against Empire: A Poet's Interpretation of the History of his own Times*, Princeton University Press, Princeton

Fruman, Norman (1971) *Coleridge: The Damaged Archangel*, Braziller, New York

Frye, Northrop (1947) *Fearful Symmetry: A Study of William Blake*, Princeton University Press, Princeton

George, Diana Hume (1980) *Blake and Freud*, Cornell University Press, Ithaca

Hilton, Nelson (1983) *The Literal Imagination: Blake's Vision of Words*, California University Press, Berkeley

Low, Donald (1977) *That Sunny Dome: A Portrait of Regency Britain*, Dent, London

McFarland, Thomas (1969) *Coleridge and the Pantheist Tradition*, Clarendon Press, Oxford

——(1981) *Romanticism and the Forms of Ruin: Wordsworth, Coleridge and Modalities of Fragmentation*, Princeton University Press, Princeton

Moers, Ellen (1976) *Literary Women: The Great Writers*, Doubleday, New York

——(1979) 'Female Gothic'. In George Levine and U. C. Knoepflmacher (eds), *The Endurance of 'Frankenstein'*, University of California Press, Berkeley

Poovey, Mary (1984) *The Proper Lady and the Woman Writer: Ideology as Style in the Works of Mary Wollstonecraft, Mary Shelley and Jane Austen*, Chicago University Press, Chicago

Rajan, Tilottama (1980) *Dark Interpreter: The Discourse of Romanticism*, Cornell University Press, Ithaca

Sales, Roger (1983) *English Literature in History 1780–1830: Pastoral and Politics*, Hutchinson, London

Thorslev, Peter L., Jr. (1984) *Romantic Contraries: Freedom versus Destiny*, Yale University Press, New Haven

Weber, Samuel (1979) *Freud Legende: Drei Studien zum Psychoanalytischen Denken*, Walter Verlag AG, Olten, Switzerland

7

MODERNISM

DAVID BROOKS

Literary criticism is not an exact science. Attempts at precise definition often say as much about the time in which they are made as they do about the thing defined. A significant difficulty in the definition of modernism is that there are, in effect, two principal schools of thought concerning the term. Modernism can be seen on the one hand as applying to a particular group of writers and artists in a particular period, and on the other as describing a certain artistic posture, an attitude toward the Modern, as viable today as it was seventy years ago, and just as possible long before that.

The first of these schools, moreover, is itself subdivided, some suggesting that modernism functions as a grab-bag into which a number of other and perhaps lesser developments (realism, naturalism, symbolism, impressionism, expressionism, imagism, vorticism, futurism, dadaism, surrealism, etc.) might be stuffed, and others that it is in fact a school among such schools, or that there is a High Modernism quite strictly limited to certain figures significant or emerging in the period immediately surrounding the First World War and so, as a literary phenomenon, to a small group (Ezra Pound, T. S. Eliot, Wyndham Lewis, James Joyce principal amongst them) who share some particular formal and conceptual characteristics. The situation is further complicated by two other major factors: that modernism was pantechnical – as much a phenomenon of music, painting, sculpture and their influence as it was of literature – and emphatically international, an upheaval not just in English, but in Western art generally.

Even this early, however, one must take care not to distort the discussion. While one of the principal ways in which modernist writers achieved their desired severance from the immediate and largely domestic tradition was through the use of exotic models, and one undeniable origin of English modernism might thus be located in the first concerted attempts to imitate forms and styles recently developed in France and elsewhere, an over-emphasis upon exotic injection should not be seen to suggest that there were no coeval

attempts at severance or development within more exclusively English parameters, although in some ways these – the muted modernisms of Thomas
Hardy, Edward Thomas or D. H. Lawrence, for example – found their task
harder and their profile less dramatic.

There is, also, a third factor to be kept in mind. Modernism's critique of
the established poetic is in many ways homologous with a contemporaneous
and as yet ill-documented feminist critique of patriarchal poetics. An appropriate consideration of the role of women writers in the period may eventually
alter significantly the received history of the movement. As Rachel Blau Du
Plessis argues,

> The confluence of modernist literary history with the self-presentation of male
> poets certainly compromises one's ability to discern the intertextualities of mod-
> ernism, even the possible primogeniture of the female, not the male, writer.
> Modernist diction may, in ways still to be fully elucidated, be indebted to female
> gender stances (in Stein, in Loy, in Moore). Marianne DeKoven, assimilating
> Kristeva, sees modernist 'experimental writing as anti-patriarchal', a stance
> necessary to rupture dominant culture by a focus on the signifier, not the
> signified, and interestingly initiated by a woman, Gertrude Stein. Jeanne Kammer
> suggests that the modernist style in Dickinson, [Marianne] Moore and H. D.
> was born from the pressures of silence – 'habits of privacy, camouflage, and
> indirection' – which resulted in 'linguistic compression' and 'juxtaposition'.
>
> (1986, p. 7)

One widespread but problematic view of modernism is outlined by M. H.
Abrams in his *Glossary of Literary Terms* (1981). Most critics, he suggests,
agree that modernism 'involves a deliberate and radical break with the traditional bases both of Western culture and of Western art', and that the
precursors of this break 'are thinkers who questioned the certainties that had
hitherto provided a support to social organization, religion, morality, and the
conception of the human self – thinkers such as Friedrich Nietzsche
(1844–1900), Marx, Freud, and James Frazer, whose *The Golden Bough*
(1890–1915) stressed the correspondence between central Christian tenets
and barbaric myths and rituals'. He then suggests that the principal activity of
literary modernism takes place 'after World War I shook men's faith in the
foundations and continuity of Western civilization and culture' (p. 109).

As a potted definition this is perhaps acceptable, but it needs clarification.
The roots of literary modernism are undoubtedly in attempts by writers to
come to terms with a new view of human beings emerging through the deeply
interrelated, if apparently very different ideas of Darwin, Marx, Nietzsche and
others. If (to summarize these most crudely) the popular conception of the
human being before Darwin had been as a fallen angel, it became, after *The
Origin of Species* (1859), far more likely as but a risen ape; if the popular
conception of history, before Marx, had been of something in which individual

effort could sometimes play a crucial part, it had to contend, after *Das Kapital* (first volume 1867), with the possibility that a great deal of it had been responding instead to economic imperatives; if the popular conception of human action, before Freud, had been based upon a possibility of self-knowledge, of presence of mind, *The Interpretation of Dreams* (1900), *The Psychopathology of Everyday Life* (1901) and other works established the disturbing possibility that one could never really know more than the ostensible reasons for such action; if the popular conception of morality, before Nietzsche, was of something in essence indisputable, anchored by a concept of a god outside the human machine, and so not subject to the vagaries of mortality, it became, after *Thus Spake Zarathustra* (1883–5) or *The Gay Science* (1882), but a necessary and effective human fiction, subject to human readjustment.

Crude as so brief a summary must be, the sense is perhaps clear that one by one from about the middle of the nineteenth century – and even this date is arbitrary – the foundations of an earlier understanding of the nature and place of humanity were so shaken that, by the end of the century, a great many artists and writers throughout the Western world had developed a kind of future-shock, a sense that one view of the world and the meaning and place of human existence had been taken from them, and that a replacement had not yet arrived, or that a sometimes bewildering array of possible replacements were contending for sovereignty. The broadest view of modernism is that, unconsciously as well as consciously, technically as well as thematically, it encompasses not only comprehensions and accommodations, but also the initial apprehensions of this change, and that the range of its works extends from George Moore and George Gissing to Joyce and Wyndham Lewis, from Browning and Arnold to Eliot and Pound.

But already this restricts it severely. The emergence of the new view of human being covers a lengthy period, and the attempts to come to terms with it begin early. One must either allow literary modernism to start with the likes of Flaubert, Whitman, Poe (to the translation of whom Baudelaire devoted so much of his life), and chart through a large number of other writers its rather slow progress toward England (the drama out of Scandinavia – the influence, for example, of Ibsen on Shaw or Joyce – the novel out of France and Russia, the poetry from the United States or, through Pound's work on the translations of Ernest Fenollosa, from as far away as Japan or China), or one must speak disjunctively of a pre-modernism that covers a number of the aforementioned movements, representing the first stages of what might ultimately be seen as an epistemological shift beginning some time before *The Origin of Species* and arguably still not over.

Whether this might still leave us with a High Modernism or Modernism Proper starting at some point in or around 1914 is another question. There is no doubt that, for many of the writers whom we might now consider to be pre-eminent amongst the modernists, there was a particular point at which everything changed, but even these differ significantly as to the specific event or date concerned. D. H. Lawrence has claimed (*Kangaroo*, 1923) that 'It was in 1915 the old world ended', Virginia Woolf ('Mr Bennett and Mrs Brown', 1924) that 'On or about December 1910 human character changed' (1966, p. 321), while Ezra Pound might instead have chosen the debut of Imagism in the tearoom of the British Museum in April 1912, and H. G. Wells the Moroccan crisis of 1905. Even the established commentators on modernism do not readily agree: Harry Levin (1966), for example, would seem to see the years 1922–4 as a climax of the movement, Richard Ellmann (1960) would prefer 1900.

Differ as such accounts may do, they clearly identify an era, and it should not surprise us to find something of a consensus amongst anthologies of works of modernism that the four decades from 1890 to 1930 adequately mark its period. The very long Age of Victoria had come to an end in 1901, the transitional reign of Edward VII in 1910, and, as had the death of Elizabeth three centuries earlier, this brought about a widespread thawing of mores. With the death of Edward, suggests Virginia Woolf, 'All human relations shifted – those between masters and servants, husbands and wives, parents and children. And when human relations change there is at the same time a change in religion, conduct, politics, and literature' (1966, p. 321). The First World War subsequently brought to many the conviction, already asserted by an *avant garde*, that something had gone very wrong with Western civilization, that writers and artists had been somehow delinquent, and that the established modes of art and thought were not only ill-equipped to remedy the situation, but might have severely inhibited one's ability to assess it in the first place. The central, if not the definitive feature of modernism becomes accordingly a re-evaluation of literary tradition and a dislocation from immediate formal models, differing from previous revolutions of this kind in its breadth, its intensity, and the rapidity – even synchronicity – with which it produced its major works (the appearance of Joyce's *Ulysses*, Eliot's *The Waste Land*, Rilke's *Duino Elegies* and many other significant works in the one year, 1922, might in this sense mark a modernist climax).

From the midst of things, however, there can be much confusion of efficient and sufficient causes: cataclysmic events may seem to bring about cataclysmic changes, but in many particular instances the ground has long been in preparation. Even should we choose, with Abrams, to single out Pound, Joyce, Eliot, Lewis and others as a modernist core, we still have to come to terms not only with the fact that a number of their own key works and corresponding developments pre-date the war (Joyce's *Dubliners* 1905, Eliot's 'Prufrock' 1909, Pound's 'The Seafarer' 1910, 'Liu Ch'ê' and 'In a Station of the Metro' 1913), and that their major post-war works are made possible in large part by their earlier experiments, but also with their own, often emphatically-acknowledged indebtedness to such as Conrad, James, Ibsen, Hulme, Browning, or the French *Symbolistes*, in the work of many of whom a number of the technical advances of High Modernism are foreshadowed or can be first glimpsed.

To confine modernism, no less than most other literary 'movements', to a strict period obviously has its dangers. Subjected to the kind of careful reading that Nietzsche recommends in the Preface to *Daybreak* ('slowly, deeply, looking cautiously before and aft, with reservations, with doors left open, with delicate eyes and fingers', [1881] 1982, p. 5), almost any text will be found to qualify itself, to divulge antecedents, to share as much of the past as it does of its own moment, and so seem to support the assertion of Paul de Man and others that much of what at first seems to distinguish a work of one period from a work of another can in fact be found in both, and that the apparent demarcations of literary history may owe less to radical distinctions than to failures of close reading.

De Man, indeed, chooses to speak not so much of modernism itself as of a 'Modernity' that denotes not the one, isolable historical period but a series of 'incandescent' moments of a desire 'to wipe out whatever came earlier, in the hope of reaching at last a point that could be called a true present, a point of origin that marks a new departure' (1971, p. 148). Terry Eagleton would seem to elaborate the particular quality of such points when he writes of

> a sense of one's particular historical conjuncture as being somehow peculiarly pregnant with crisis and change . . . [A] portentous, confused yet curiously heightened self-consciousness of one's own historical moment, at once self-doubting and self-congratulatory, anxious and triumphalistic together . . . [A]t one and the same time an arresting and denial of history in the violent shock of the immediate present, from which vantage point all previous developments may be complacently consigned to the ashcan of 'tradition'.
>
> (1986, p. 139)

'Modernism', accordingly, might be seen not as the only, but as merely the most recent and perhaps most salient of such moments, and 'modernity' a term applicable to several periods in our literary history, as useful in describing certain Jacobean writers, or writers of the Restoration and early eighteenth century as those of the late nineteenth and early twentieth.

Instead of the one period of modernism, it might be more accurate to speak of a number in which there have been preoccupations with modernity, and even, through or beneath these (as de Man argues), of a doomed and paradoxical need to reject the past that is an aspect of all writing. Whether or not that need itself becomes a preoccupation of a particular period, however, we need not take this to suggest that, if the intended application is specified, the term modernism cannot be a useful one, or that there is not a number of factors pertinent to all applications and a useful story to encompass them. If it might be said that modernity, as a broader literary-historical phenomenon, represents the various stages of the apprehension, comprehension and assimilation of more than the one significant shift in the order and structure of human knowledge and belief, it might also be said that the previous occurrences of such shifts have other names already, and that that which occurred in the late nineteenth and early twentieth centuries has its own distinguishing features, its own particular intellectual and historical circumstances.

Without doubt the most central of these is the need to respond in some manner to the various apparent determinisms of the late nineteenth century. The response in some cases takes the form of an attempt to assimilate, and in others of attempts to escape or to transcend such determinisms, and this can help to explain some of the very different forms, subjects and strategies of modernism. That in almost all cases these responses entail an attitude to the immediate past and, accordingly, to time itself, however, can be seen to bring to these different forms, subjects and strategies a strong unifying factor, an ambivalence towards the past that is the result at once of the desire for a radical forgetting and the sense of loss that this entails. There is a need to reject the immediate past and a desire to re-present or reinterpret history in a way undetermined by the inherited discourse.

The origin of this popular conception of modernism – of its desire to awaken from 'the nightmare of history' and to achieve an immediacy of contact with a hypothetical 'reality' uninhibited by accumulated and often obsolete techniques and cultural assumptions – de Man (1971, pp. 146–7) locates in Nietzsche's claim that the inability to forget the past not only distinguishes the human from the animal, but can also mask the true nature of human being. It is, for Nietzsche, only upon moments of a radical forgetting, when life can be experienced in a nonhistorical way, that anything 'truly great and human' can be erected' ('The Use and Abuse of History', [1874] 1910, p. 11).

De Man, however, goes a step further. 'As soon as modernism becomes conscious of its own strategies', he writes,

> – and it cannot fail to do so if it is justified . . . in the name of a concern for the future – it discovers itself to be a generative power that not only engenders history, but is part of a generative scheme that extends far back into the past. . . . Considered as a principle of life, modernity becomes a principle of origination and turns at once into a generative power that is itself historical. It becomes impossible to overcome history in the name of life or to forget the past in the name of modernity, because both are linked by a temporal chain that gives them a common destiny.

> (1971, p. 150)

For de Man, as for Nietzsche himself, the 'ruthless forgetting' that can be seen as one of modernism's centrepins becomes not only paradoxical and ultimately impossible, but may itself represent one of the most effective moments of all creativity. Literature may be 'nothing less than this constantly doomed, ironically self-undoing attempt to make it new, this ceaseless incapacity ever quite to awaken from the nightmare of history' (Eagleton, 1986, p. 136).

Many of the central works of modernism – *The Waste Land*, the *Cantos*, *Ulysses* – bear this out strongly. Although each may in some way endeavour to awaken from a nightmare of history, the past, and particularly the literary past, has a high and complex profile within them. Far from ignoring or defying tradition, they attempt to redefine it, to see beyond the formal imperatives of the immediate past and to re-select from the vast body, domestic and otherwise, of the literature which preceded them. Finding their impulse in a creativity highly conscious of its own departure, they must also, as a consequence, constantly remind us of, and so paradoxically sustain, the very things which they seek to jettison or modify. Whether or not we see such a phenomenon as definitive of modernism itself or simply as marking an essential or climactic stage in its development, it would seem that de Man's points must be accommodated, and that it might be better to see the identity of modernism as inhering in the nature, range and profile of its dialogue with history than in a clear severance from it.

But to see such dilemmas in theoretical terms alone – to see, for example, their centrality to modernism as but the momentary intensification of a perpetual aspect of modernity *per se* – would be itself somewhat paradoxical in its neglect of an immediate, momentous and (at the time) unique historical circumstance. The First World War was an event so devastating that it created rapidly a set of demands upon artists and writers that most would have found inconceivable before it, and that might therefore be said, if not actually to introduce modernism proper, to divide it into two major moments, the second of which, for many, condemned dramatically a historical innocence or ignorance in the first.

In the decades before the war, many works of literature seem governed by a sense of loss, of personal and cultural displacement, that might best be described as Faustian. The pursuit of knowledge has overreached itself and resulted in a radical discomfort, an alienation of the human from its former image of itself, clearly registered in works as diverse as Conrad's *Heart of Darkness* (1899), Wilde's *The Picture of Dorian Gray* (1890), Moore's *Esther Waters* (1894), Wells's *Tono Bungay* (1909) and Ford Madox Ford's *The Good Soldier* (1915), at the end of each of which the central characters, having explored beneath the surface of or otherwise significantly expanded their prior knowledge and experience, find themselves isolated, somehow deprived by their own efforts of the very world they had sought to know or save.

This element in early modernist literature need not always be conscious or readily apparent. An intriguing variant is found in a popular fiction of imprisonment and wronged identity, the doubled characters and labyrinthine dungeons of which embody the discomfort of a movement from a metaphysical to a relative morality, from a univocal to a dialogic story of reality. Foreshadowed in Alexandre Dumas' *The Count of Monte Cristo* (1844) this line may be traced through such works as Marcus Clarke's *For the Term of His Natural Life* (1872) and Anthony Hope's *The Prisoner of Zenda* (1894) to a climax in Kafka's *The Castle* in 1926.

While the Faustian myth is in no way eradicated by the Great War, several of the major works thereafter – those most often said to characterize High Modernism – are dominated by something quite different. Experience and investigation are seen not as agencies of alienation, but, for those who can withstand the initial disorientation, as the most likely means of restitution or accommodation. *The Waste Land, Ulysses* and the *Cantos* in particular are dominated not by a myth of unwitting destruction, but by one of quest for which, having its origins likewise in the end of a cataclysmic conflict, the story of Odysseus is particularly suited. The artist, hitherto alienated by investigation, now becomes its agent. Punished for irreverence, he or she now learns or re-learns, through arduous experience, lessons which had somehow been disastrously forgotten.

The investigation, moreover, takes a particular turn, at once a reaction to and culmination of the kinds of knowledge which had cast a shadow over so much of the pre-war literature. In each instance, the major theoretical advances of that period had laid bare, within or beneath the subjects of their examination, systems or structures hitherto largely unsuspected. To many, these were 'impersonal', 'unnatural', in that it was an aspect of the known person, the known nature that they contradicted. In this sense the English 'decadent' poets of the 1890s (Dowson, Johnson, Yeats himself for a time) may have but concentrated a wider feeling in their frequent expression of the alienation of the artist and the futility of individual action that Wilde had so strikingly foreshadowed in his 'Taedium Vitae' (1881).

Certain writers – the Imagist poets in particular – had already, before the war, embarked upon attempts to close this apparent rift between Art and Life, and the war but brought home to a larger number what these few had been arguing for some time. Pound, for example, had been asserting since 1912 what Wilfred Owen subsequently discovered in the trenches and so eloquently registered in his famous Preface ('This book is not about heroes. English Poetry is not yet fit to speak of them'): that the conventions and decorums of English poetry as this generation had inherited them – its established forms and metres, its proprieties of tone, diction and subject – curtailed severely its ability to present the real world with any accuracy and immediacy.

When writers after the First World War came to reassess their cultural function, it was therefore upon ways of knowing, ways of seeing that they concentrated. As a glance at Pound's 'three principles' of Imagism (1912) might suggest –

1 Direct treatment of the 'thing' whether subjective or objective.
2 To use absolutely no word that does not contribute to the presentation.
3 As regarding rhythm: to compose in the sequence of the musical phrase, not in sequence of a metronome.

(ed. 1960, p. 3)

– such writers attempted not only to confront some hypothetical reality beneath the apparent irrealities that, perpetuated at once in the minds and techniques of writers of the earlier period, had so marginalized or alienated them, but to do so with a set of tools appropriate to the task. The systems of writing, of literature, had to be reassessed in order to ensure that they were not in themselves inhibiting the ability to confront the real, and they had to be reassessed in the light of the kind of new understandings of language and of thought which are now seen to have pointed to language itself as the system of systems.

This, then, is the period of the High Modernism of Joyce, Pound, Eliot, Stein and others, marked by texts of an increasing self-consciousness – texts which, conveying 'a radical dissatisfaction with the commonsense view of the real' (Munton, 1984), break up or dislocate conventional narrative or presentational procedures, sometimes even the sentence and the word, and in so doing not only draw attention to and undermine conventional notions of what a novel or poem or play should be, but attempt to circumvent the intrusion of established discourse upon their presentations, whether or not these are seen by their writers to be presentations of the 'real'. So each of the chapters of *Ulysses*, for example, employs a different narrative mode and invites the reader to compare the ways in which the material therein is inflected. So the ideogrammatic method of the *Cantos* endeavours to avoid the connective tissue of conventional discourse and invites the reader to arrange and explain its imagistic fragments in accordance with his or her understanding and ability.

Too great a focus upon the textual self-consciousness of such works, however, is in danger of forgetting that this is but one part – albeit a central one – of a greater denaturalization. It is perhaps inevitable that the widespread detection and analysis of the systems underlying or even comprising human being should come down to language itself as the system at the heart of these systems – at about the same time, incidentally, that in Geneva Ferdinand de Saussure was formulating, in his *Course in General Linguistics* (1916), a theory which would underpin and consolidate this very perception. While we should not see it as modernism itself, the 'High' Modernism of Pound, Joyce and Eliot, in its textual self-consciousness, becomes thus a logical consummation of an extended process, a consummation in a sense inherent in that process from the start.

Acknowledgement of a measure of proto-structuralism in the work of the high modernists, in any case, can help to qualify some of the principal criticisms levelled against them – the suggestion (such as we find in Lukács, 1963, or Jameson, 1979) of a tendency towards immersion within the world of individual character and consequent neglect of wider social contexts which meant that their works exemplify, rather than counteract, the deterioration of their times, or the concomitant accusation, occasioned by the notorious 'difficulty' of many modernist works, of an intellectual élitism and even a predisposition toward authoritarian politics.

The proto-structuralist account, for example, can show the work of Joyce, Pound, Lewis and others as de-naturalizing character itself, pointing less to any purported integrity it may possess than to the systems of which it is composed or which operate through and control it, and so to the way in which it is in fact contiguous with a world that had hitherto been regarded as outside or beyond it. Ultimately this is no more nor less a Fascist than a Marxist gambit. Pointing the way to the destabilization of the *status quo* by showing what had been thought natural to be instead a construct, a product of human systems, might be said to have been a prerequisite of both, as even Eagleton seems to admit when he acknowledges the modernism of Berthold Brecht (1986, p. 140).

The notorious 'difficulty' of so many modernist texts has doubtless a number of sources. It may spring from a predisposition toward the *writerly* rather than the *readerly* text, or from a desire rather to stimulate the faculty of thought itself than to dictate the particular nature of things thought. It may spring from a concern on the writers' part to maintain in the texture of their work an evident presence of the past, or from a post-Nietzschean insistence on the role of the will in overcoming eternal recurrence. Whatever its origins, however, it is perhaps best seen not as a conscious arrogance toward the reader, but in the light of that *ostranenie* – the *estrangement* that might prepare the way for a fresh seeing – for which, unbeknown to most of the English modernists, the Russian Formalist Viktor Shklovsky and others were arguing at the time (see Shklovsky, 1965). There are exceptions, of course. The support of Pound, Lewis and others for authoritarian regimes is well known. But theirs is an intellectual position common enough in the period – arguably little different in kind from those of Yeats, Eliot or D. H. Lawrence – and is perhaps easier to condemn in hindsight than it was to resist at the time. It might, ultimately, index less an inherent disposition in the strategies and subjects of the texts themselves than the very crisis in Western civilization and urgency of the felt need for intellectual and social solutions that are the root and explanation of so much of the modernist endeavour.

FURTHER READING

Bradbury, M. and McFarlane, J. (eds) (1976) *Modernism*, Penguin, Harmondsworth

de Man, Paul (1971) 'Literary History and Literary Modernity'. In Paul de Man, *Blindness and Insight*, Oxford University Press, London

Eagleton, Terry (1986) 'Capitalism, Modernism and Postmodernism'. In Terry Eagleton, *Against the Grain: Selected Essays*, Verso, London

Ellmann, Richard and Feidelson, Charles (eds) (1965) *The Modern Tradition: Backgrounds of Modern Literature*, Oxford University Press, New York

Ford, Boris (ed.) (1963) *The Modern Age*, (vol. 7 of *The Pelican Guide to English Literature*), Penguin, Harmondsworth

Kenner, Hugh (1971) *The Pound Era*, University of California Press, Berkeley

Kristeva, Julia (1980) 'The Ethics of Linguistics', 'Word, Dialogue, and Novel' and 'From One Identity to an Other'. In Julia Kristeva, *Desire in Language*, edited by Leon S. Roudiez, Basil Blackwell, Oxford

Levenson, M. H. (1984) *A Genealogy of Modernism: A Study in English Literary Doctrine 1908–1922*, Cambridge University Press, Cambridge

Lukács, Georg (1963) 'The Ideology of Modernism'. In Georg Lukács, *The Meaning of Contemporary Realism*, translated by J. and N. Mander, Merlin Press, London [essay first published 1955]

Pound, Ezra (1960) *Literary Essays*, edited by T. S. Eliot, Faber & Faber, London

Schwartz, S. (1985) *The Matrix of Modernism: Pound, Eliot and Early Twentieth Century Thought*, Princeton University Press, Princeton

Wilson, Edmund (1931) *Axel's Castle: A Study in the Imaginative Literature of 1870 to 1930*, Charles Scribner's Sons, New York

ADDITIONAL WORKS CITED

Abrams, M. H. (1981) *A Glossary of Literary Terms*, 4th edn, Holt, Rinehart & Winston, London

Du Plessis, Rachel Blau (1986) *H.D.: The Career of that Struggle*, Harvester Press, Brighton

Ellmann, Richard (1960) 'Two Faces of Edward'. In Richard Ellmann (ed.), *Edwardians and Late Victorians*, Columbia University Press, New York, pp. 188–210

Jameson, Fredric (1979) *Fables of Aggression: Wyndham Lewis, the Modernist as Fascist*, University of California Press, Berkeley

Levin, Harry (1966) 'What Was Modernism?'. In Harry Levin, *Refractions: Essays in Comparative Literature*, Oxford University Press, New York, pp. 271–95

Munton, Alan (1984) 'Fredric Jameson: Fables of Aggression'. In Seamus Cooney (ed.), *Blast 3*, Black Sparrow Press, Santa Barbara

Nietzsche, Friedrich (1982) *Daybreak*, translated by R. J. Hollingdale, Cambridge University Press, Cambridge [first published 1881]

——(1910) 'The Use and Abuse of History'. In Friedrich Nietzsche, *Thoughts Out of Season: part II*, translated by Adrian Collins, T. N. Foulis, Edinburgh [essay first published 1874]

Shklovsky, Viktor (1965) 'Art as Technique'. In Lee T. Lemon and Marion J. Reis (eds and trans), *Russian Formalist Criticism: Four Essays*, University of Nebraska Press, Lincoln [essay first published 1917]

Woolf, Virginia (1966) *Collected Essays*, vol. 1, edited by Leonard Woolf, The Hogarth Press, London

8

POSTMODERNISM

ROBERT B. RAY

Because in common usage the word 'modern' simply means 'contemporary', the term 'postmodernism' has seemed, from the start, like the vocabulary of science fiction. How, after all, can something which exists now be said to come *after* the present? The word's apocalyptic tone, its connotations of nihilistic rejection, issue from this oxymoronic aspect which seems to provide a way of speaking about the impossible. To say 'I am postmodern' would be, for most people, something like saying 'I am asleep' – it can be done, but what does it mean? Of course, the confusion vanishes when we replace 'modern' with 'modernism' and explain that the latter refers less to historical time than to a specific movement in the arts. Even with this refinement, however, the words 'postmodern' and 'postmodernism' have not yet lost their fundamental strangeness – a strangeness corresponding perhaps to the radical break with traditional assumptions about meaning which the postmodern situation has effected. As we grow used to the word 'postmodernism', we may also get used to its implications.

In 1924, two years after the *annus mirabilis* of *Ulysses* and *The Waste Land*, Virginia Woolf suggested that modernism, or at least 'the modern world', had begun 'on or about December 1910' when 'human character changed' (Woolf, [1924] 1950, p. 96). In 1977, with a mock seriousness typical of *post*modernism, Charles Jencks, offered that modernism had *ended* on 15 July 1972 at 3.32 p.m. (Jencks, 1984, p. 9). For Jencks, the symbolism of this moment derived from a specific architectural event, the demolition of modernist Minouru Yamasaki's Pruitt-Igoe housing project, deemed obsolete by St Louis city planners. The term 'postmodernism' did indeed find its first widespread circulation in architecture, but it migrated rapidly until it now seems to designate simultaneously an aesthetic style, a cultural situation, a critical practice, an economic condition, and a political attitude. Thus, depending on one's definition, different dates present themselves as the start of what counts as 'post':

Did, for example, postmodernism begin in 1984 when the US Supreme Court ruled that copyright laws did not prohibit home off-the-air video taping?

In 1972, when the percentage of Americans employed in service industries reached twice that in manufacturing?

In 1971, when Barry Commoner's *The Closing Circle* formulated the First Two Laws of Ecology, 'Everything is connected to everything else', and 'Everything must go somewhere'?

In 1968, when European and American student strikes demonstrated the wide appeal of the anti-war, feminist and minority rights movements?

In 1962, when Andy Warhol, taking his friends' advice to suppress all traces of abstract expressionism, produced his first Campbell Soup Cans?

In 1954, when for the first time, more than half of American homes had television?

In 1952, when the Lettrist International (the prototype of the Situationists) disrupted Charlie Chaplin's Ritz Hotel press conference, explaining that 'We believe that the most urgent expression of freedom is the destruction of idols, especially when they present themselves in the name of freedom' (Marcus, 1982, p. 15)?

In 1946, when Arnold Toynbee referred to a 'Post-Modern' historical age (Toynbee, 1965), and Randall Jarrell described Robert Lowell as 'post- or anti-modernist' (Calinescu, 1987, p. 267)?

In 1913, when Marcel Duchamp mounted an upside-down bicycle wheel to a kitchen stool, thereby 'producing' the first 'readymade' (Duchamp's own term for an everyday object, named, signed and offered as 'art')?

In 1863, when the dandies that Baudelaire described strolled in Haussmann's rebuilt Paris, using their clothes as an emblem of ambivalent revolt?

In 1855, when the Parisian World Exhibition became the first to have an exhibit called 'Photography'?

In 1852, when the Bon Marché, the first department store, opened in Paris, one year after the Crystal Palace and three years before the Louvre (Williams, 1982, p. 66)?

In 1850, when Flaubert began his *Dictionary of Received Ideas*, a dead-pan citation of everyday life?

In 1836, when the Parisian *La Presse* became the first commercial daily newspaper, 'arguably the first consumer commodity: made to be perishable, purchased to be thrown away' (Terdiman, 1985, p. 120)?

That any of these dates (and a dozen others) could legitimately mark the decisive break suggests the single most important thing about postmodernism: unlike impressionism, cubism, expressionism, and even modernism, it cannot best be understood as simply another movement in the arts. Thus, the standard typological moves of literary criticism do not work very well to distinguish postmodernism from its predecessors. When cataloguing 'postmodernist devices' (self-reflexivity, parody, etc.) identifies Beckett and Nabokov (previously claimed for modernism) as the great *post*modernist writers, we know something is wrong. Here, then, are six different attempts to explain the postmodern.

REDEMPTION

postmodern . . . the term has lately been losing its luster.
(Thomas Crow, in Foster, 1987, p. 1)

Any person, any object, any relationship can mean absolutely anything else.
(Walter Benjamin, [1928] 1977, p. 175)

The best way to understand postmodernism is to think about the story of Douglas Sirk. Of Danish extraction, Sirk settled in Germany, working in the theatre until 1934 when he began making films at UFA, the largest German studio. He left three years later, by which time his vaguely leftist credentials had begun to cause him trouble. Settling in the United States in 1939, he languished at Warner Brothers and Columbia before catching on with Universal where he made the five movies on which his reputation rests: *Magnificent Obsession* (1952), *All That Heaven Allows* (1955), *Written on the Wind* (1956), *Tarnished Angels* (1957) and *Imitation of Life* (1959). This work is of a piece: big-budget, commercially successful (except for *Tarnished Angels*) melodramas, starring Rock Hudson (except for *Imitation*). At their release, they received no critical attention; like most Hollywood products, they entertained, made money and vanished.

In the late 1960s, however, then retired to Switzerland, Sirk began giving a series of interviews to film scholars. He now claimed that his movies (remarkably dated in just 10–15 years) had, in fact, been subversive, critical parodies of American 'bourgeois values' and Hollywood's taste for melodrama. Intentionally or not, Sirk had perfectly timed his play. It was eagerly received by an Anglo-American film studies community aflush with two incompatible enthusiasms: *auteurism* (which focused on a movie's director) and leftist ideology. Sirk provided a bridge between the two, as an *auteur* hero whose struggle against Hollywood's 'repressive studio system' had involved sly criticisms of capitalist values. That these values rested above all on exactly the kind of individualism *auteurism* assumed bothered no one. The Sirk boom was on, and analyses of his films flowered in journals and at conferences. By 1978, one film scholar could matter-of-factly refer to Sirk's 'famous ironic subtext'.

As a parable, what does this story tell us about postmodernism? To start with, Sirk's interviews involved a *remotivation* of his own films: by commenting on them, he changed their meaning, redeeming an otherwise valueless cur-

rency. Such remotivation, far from being unusual, has become the late twentieth century's paradigmatic cultural practice. In high culture, this move
descends from Duchamp's readymades, passing through Ives's musical
allusions, cubism's collages, surrealism's 'headline poetry', pop art's image
appropriations, and ending, for the moment at least, with Sherrie Levine's
overt piracies of images by Edward Weston, Egon Schiele and Joan Miró.
Sirk's case, in effect, amounts to an extension of Duchamp's readymades
tactic, for Sirk remotivated found objects *that were his own work* without
modifying or 'correcting' them in any way. (The closest comparison would be
to Duchamp's remotivated *Mona Lisa* ('Shaved') which leaves the original
untouched, but depends on his own previous modification, the goateed
'L.H.O.O.Q.'.)

Such remotivations occur even more often in mass culture where they go
by the name 'recuperation'. Those who use this word have in mind the co-
option of once-radical techniques for commercial purposes, the assimilation,
say, of surrealism's discontinuities by advertising. Often, of course, the remotivations run in the opposite direction: witness 'recuperation' itself, whose benign
medical meaning has been made over into a pejorative by leftist cultural critics.
Similarly, Dick Hebdige (1979) has shown how, to mark their opposition to
dominant values, British youth cultures have inevitably relied on re-contextual-
izing existing fashions. Thus, among the mods, 'the conventional insignia of
the business world – the suit, collar and tie, short hair, etc. – were stripped
of their original connotations – efficiency, ambition, compliance with authority'
(pp. 104–5).

Before such phenomena of remotivation, the formalist methodologies of
modernism (with their belief in art's autonomy) reach their explanatory limits.
As an example of postmodernism, the Sirk case represents the shift from work
to textuality. Postmodernism retains the notion of the art object, but redefines
it as a *site*, a crossroads traversed by communicative highways continuously re-
routed by external, extra-textual circumstances – the conditions of publicity.
Any method which attends *only* to the object will prove inadequate. Could we,
for example, itemize the properties of that class of texts most susceptible to
Sirkian-styled remotivations? In 1964, Susan Sontag still thought we could,
ironically saying of camp (the prototype of all drastic re-readings) that 'not
everything can be seen as Camp. It's not *all* in the eye of the beholder' (1966,
p. 277). But of course it *is*. What class of texts or events cannot be made over?
High art? – see Duchamp's *Mona Lisa*. Real historical tragedy? – see Mel
Brooks's send-up of Nazism in *The Producers*.

Although Sirk claimed for himself the critical perspective of modernism,
the Sirkian phenomenon (a different entity) represents the new situation we
call postmodernism: semiotic volatility and necessary complicity. (1) Sirk
opportunistically seized on the instability of his own signs to make his movies

mean something else; (2) his ideological critique, if it existed, worked within dominant, even ideologically contaminated, forms – melodrama, classical narrative, star vehicles, the commercial cinema, misogyny. This is the lesson: in postmodernism, modernism's commitment to the sanctity of art and the politics of confrontation give way to what Brecht (1966) called 'refunctioning' and 'cunning': the tradition is revived, but rewritten; the battle is fought, but not on grounds that will alert the enemy.

Why has remotivation become so common in the late twentieth century? To what specific circumstances does it correspond? Over fifty years ago, in what could be called the founding essay of postmodernism, Walter Benjamin ([1935] 1969) identified the crucial fact as mechanical reproduction and the historical juncture as mid-nineteenth-century Paris, when new forms (photography, cheap books, lithography) and their attendant mass culture first challenged the supremacy of traditional aesthetic practice. By now, the effects of mechanical reproduction have become far more evident: an immense increase in the number of signs, an uncontrollable multiplication of their possible contextualizations. By itself, photography is the perfect collage machine (Ulmer, 1985), isolating fragments of the world and making them available for endless reframings. As I write, I have before me a page from *Tennis Week* which reproduces a previous *Newsweek* cover of a homeless American family, now recaptioned:

> Although *TW* likes to claim star photographer Melchior DiGiacomo as its own, we must admit that from time to time he does stray into loftier quarters. Above is featured his January 2nd *Newsweek* cover, headlining the magazine's in-depth report on the country's homeless. Our congratulations!

By referring to such remotivations as 'hijacking', one writer (Ball, 1987, p. 34) suggests the homology between cultural practice and everyday life in the postmodern world. For just as modern transportation exposes passengers to the threat of unscheduled detours, mechanical reproduction, by disseminating signs, leaves them open to unpredictable re-routings of their own. Artists since Duchamp have recognized this condition. In the 1960s, the Situationists exploited it for political polemics, practising what they called *détournement*, a 'reterritorialization' of objects through appropriations like recaptioned comic strips. Jacques Derrida has described this historical situation in a famous passage whose urgency could only have occurred in a media age:

> And this is the possibility on which I want to insist. . . . Every sign, linguistic or non-linguistic, spoken or written . . . in a small or large unit, can be *cited*, put between quotation marks: in so doing it can break with every given context, engendering an infinity of new contexts in a manner which is absolutely illimitable. This does not imply that the mark is valid outside of a context, but on the contrary that there are only contexts without any center or absolute anchoring.
>
> (1977, pp. 185–6)

Mechanical reproduction has other effects as well. By indiscriminately preserving and distributing even the most disposable cultural productions (think how television revives everything), it stimulates an aesthetic whose appropriative basis is ecological. Andy Warhol made this connection explicit:

> I always like to work on leftovers, doing the leftover things. Things that were discarded, that everyone knew were no good. . . . if you can take it and make it good or at least interesting, then you're not wasting as much as you would otherwise. You're recycling work and you're recycling people, and you're running your business as a byproduct of other businesses. Of other *directly competitive* businesses, as a matter of fact. So that's a very economical operating procedure.
>
> (1975, p. 93)

The biological metaphor ('recycling') accurately describes the eco-systems of contemporary culture, where the division between text and paratext (e.g. blurbs, book jackets, criticism) seems increasingly uncertain. Of enormous importance to these eco-systems are the institutions of learning, art and publicity which have arisen in response to mechanical reproduction's commodification of information. Such institutions work ceaselessly to negotiate, influence, delimit the meanings of the cultural objects which they produce or distribute, subjecting any text's network to a continuous re-routing, to 'switching' in railroad parlance. Thus, the Hollywood studio system, a prime example, uses press releases, ads, posters, studio-sponsored fanzines, the star system, star bios, interviews, press leaks and plants, the Academy Awards – all to de-emphasize a film's role in determining its own reading. Aberrant decoding (Eco, 1972, p. 121), like Sirk's, enables individual readers or groups (such as feminist critics) to play this game as well, to read against the grain of intentions, thereby profitably remotivating Hollywood's product for other, typically political, purposes. Postmodernism recognizes that meaning becomes an apparatus matter: production, distribution and consumption all influence meaning, and the 'encrustations' (reviews, gossip, synopses, etc.) surrounding the text almost always dominate it (Bennett, 1982). In these circumstances, all meaning is a form of propaganda.

We might say, for example, that the Sirk phenomenon depended less on Sirk's movies than on an anxious academic community's deference to 'European intellectuals' and need for publishing *Lebensraum*: here, after all, was a new topic. The information apparatuses are voracious; mechanical reproduction accelerates their assimilative powers to the point that, by 1987, postmodernism as a topic had already become old hat. From the start, the modernists feared this situation, which threatened both to remove works from artists' control and to use them up through overexposure. If the modernist response was to retreat from this scene by using difficulty to protect works from mass appropriation (see Mallarmé), the postmodernist one was to settle within it, experimenting with the possibilities afforded by mechanical reproduction in a dead-pan, complicitous merger of criticism and profiteering for which dandyism (a critique of consumerism dependent on shopping) is the prototype (see Warhol, 1975). By playing this ambiguous game, Sirk demonstrated postmodernism's characteristic fact: the limitless possibilities for *reading differently*, for practising 'a semiotic guerrilla warfare' (Eco, 1972, p. 121), on the very art objects that modernism had thought were invulnerable.

TELEVISION

Everything in the world exists to end in a book.

(Mallarmé, [1862] 1968)

What Was Literature?

(Leslie Fiedler, 1982)

Everything wants to be television.

(Gregory L. Ulmer, 1989)

The best way to understand postmodernism is to think about a pun: in French, *poste* means 'television set' (Ulmer, 1985). Postmodernism is really *poste*modernism, what happened when modernism met TV. That wordplay may start to explain why in a literary encyclopaedia, I seem studiously to be avoiding written fiction, poetry and drama. These are the familiar, but still shocking facts: 99 per cent of American households have television (more than have refrigerators or indoor plumbing), and in those households, the television runs nearly eight hours a day (more than most people work or sleep). The formal story-telling function, once the property of literature, has been taken over by film and television, which have also appropriated nineteenth-century fiction's realistic mode. As one writer has remarked, TV is not simply a part of modern life, 'TV virtually *is* modern life' (Steinberg, 1980, p. 141). We have begun to realize, as George Steiner wrote in 1952, 'that the "book as we have known it" has been a significant phenomenon only in certain areas and cultures, and only during a relatively short span of history' (Steiner, 1972, p. 187).

If Mallarmé's remark suggests that modernism was the high point of the book, then postmodernism is what comes after. In another sense, however, postmodernism also represents the *beginning* of something, the second decisive shift in human history affecting the way we store, retrieve and communicate information. Postmodernism is the moment when the alphabetic tradition, which had succeeded the oral, yields its dominance to the electronic – when television, tape recorders and computers take over roles previously played by writing, books and libraries. We do not yet know the consequences of this shift. We do know that the first, from orality to literacy, profoundly changed human memory, reasoning and imagination. In an alphabetic culture, even the illiterate think in ways unfamiliar to a completely oral civilization.

Walter Ong (1982) has proposed that the electronic age amounts to a 'secondary orality' in which conceptualization, as in oral cultures, depends less on literacy's abstractions than on stories, images, heroes; less on the power of argument than on audio-visual mnemonics. The result is not so much the loss of the common cultural tradition, as television's critics have maintained, as its *replacement* by the most massive, pervasive intertext the world has ever known. Mickey Mouse, Elvis, *Star Wars*, The Beatles – who (in the West, at least) does not recognize these names? Amidst this swarm, the experimental arts try out different kinds of electronic thinking, seeking conceptual correspondences for television's ceaseless discontinuity.

While postmodernist fiction's penchant for abrupt transitions, comic-book characters and melodramatic plotting (see Pynchon's *V* and *The Crying of Lot 49*) obviously issues from mass culture, the real question posed by the electronic paradigm is whether thinking, as we have defined it, is possible at all without the distance which television obliterates (Jameson, 1984). We cannot yet know the answer; 'the postmodern', our name for the beginning of Ong's 'electronic age', is too new. We may suspect, however, that thinking (much less literature) will no more go unmarked by this shift than it did by the first one. Perhaps the pun is the model for thinking in a television age, for the pun (beloved by Duchamp, Joyce, Cage, Derrida, Lacan) reproduces TV's own unmotivated, but consequential leaps, linking areas of knowledge and experience previously kept discrete. In postmodernism, the pun complements the metaphor, vehicles between points in our knowledge, allowing an electronic thinking: neither induction nor deduction, but *con*duction (Ulmer, 1989).

THE RETURN

The making of superior art is arduous, usually. But under modernism, the appreciation, even more than the making, of it has become more taxing, the satisfaction and exhilaration to be gotten from the best new art more hard-won. . . . Yet the urge to relax is there, as it's always been. It threatens and keeps on threatening standards of quality.

(Clement Greenberg, 1980, p. 14)

Q: Is that what Pop Art is all about?
A: Yes. It's liking things.

(Andy Warhol, in Swenson, 1963)

The best way to understand postmodernism is to think about pleasure. From Manet to the *nouveau roman*, modernism's austerity expressed itself in terms of standards: functionalism without ornamentation, expression without sentimentality, 'a purer meaning for the words of the tribe' (Mallarmé). In practice, this stance translated into a gradual retreat from figurative painting, melodic composition, narrative fiction and autobiographical lyric – moves which can be summed up as 'the hushing of anecdote' (Schneider, 1971, p. 104). Leftist modernism, in particular, always suspected that pleasure followed the route of ideology; thus, in the surgical metaphor Flaubert so often borrowed from his father, elements allowing for easy gratification had to be cut out. With a very different politics, another branch of modernism simply regarded mass taste as degrading and used difficulty to defend against accessibility. The most naked statement of this stance is Mallarmé's:

> The hour is a serious one: the people are being educated, great doctrines are going to spread. Make sure that if there is vulgarization it is of morality, not art, and that your efforts do not tend toward making you . . . that grotesque and pitiful thing, a *working-class poet*.
> Let the masses read works on morality, but for heaven's sake do not give them our poetry to spoil.
> O poets, you have always been proud; now, even more, become disdainful.
>
> ([1862] 1968, p. 202)

Like any repressed term, however, pleasure always shadowed even the most rigorous modernism, often appearing as an ambivalence about the official poetic. Mallarmé himself could joke about his own methods, putting off a publisher impatient for 'Tombeau (de Verlaine)' with the remark, 'Wait . . . at least until I add a little obscurity' (in Gibson, 1979, p. 92). Brecht is the transitional figure. In 1926, having arrived at his famous alienation effect, he spoke as a modernist: 'I aim at an extremely classical, cold, highly intellectual style of performance. I'm not writing for the scum who want to have the cockles of their hearts warmed.' Twenty-two years later, he had changed his mind: 'From the start it has been the theatre's business to entertain people, as it has all of the other arts. It is this business which always gives it its particular dignity; it needs no other passport than fun, but this it has got to have' (Brecht, ed. 1964, pp. 14, 180).

Brecht, of course, had already recognized that for alienation purposes, modernism's emigration from 'the realm of the merely enjoyable' (p. 179) had gone as far as it could, and that for an avant-garde audience, inured by transgression, 'the only really shocking things', as a later artist would admit, 'are delicacy and beauty' (Eno, 1981, p. 52). Certainly postmodernism's return to representational painting, strong plots and simpler musical structures derives, in part at least, from the exhaustion of modernism's repertoire. Amidst the high seriousness of modernism, as Roland Barthes often pointed out, *sentimentality* could be a scandal.

From abstract expressionism to pop art, from Robbe-Grillet to Borges, from bop to rock and roll, the transition to postmodernism represents the return of things easier to like. It would be naïve, of course, to see in this change the workings of a cultural pleasure principle. In Freudian terms, it is, however, the return of the repressed other of modernism, mass culture and popular taste – cartoons and soup cans, detective stories and science fiction, songs and beat. As Freud predicted, this return has typically deployed itself along the very lines of the original repression. The camp sensibility, enormously important to postmodernism, began as a way of enjoying what had previously been censored on political or aesthetic grounds: things deemed 'bad' by the 'best standards' returned as 'good' (because funny) – Carmen Miranda, art deco, *Reefer Madness* (the US Government's 1936 anti-marijuana propaganda film). At its most radical, the camp disposition (another strategy for reading against the grain) challenged postmodernism's characteristic imbalance: democratic consumption undid oligopolistic production, as interpreting differently enabled readers to resist the messages sent by those with all the equipment.

THE HYBRID

There were not always novels in the past, and there will not always have to be; not always tragedies, not always great epics; not always were the forms of commentary, translation, indeed, even so-called plagiarism, playthings in the margins of literature; they had a place not only in the philosophical but also in the literary writings of Arabia and China. Rhetoric has not always been a minor form, but set its stamp in antiquity on large provinces of literature. All this to accustom you to the thought that we are in the midst of a mighty recasting of literary forms, a melting down in which many of the opposites in which we have been used to think may lose their force.

(Walter Benjamin, [1934] 1979, p. 224)

What is clear is that Barthes and Derrida are the *writers*, not the critics, that students now read.

(Rosalind Krauss, 1980, p. 40)

The best way to understand postmodernism is to think about Julian Barnes's *Flaubert's Parrot* (1985) and Roland Barthes's *S/Z* (1974). *Flaubert's Parrot*, nominally a novel (and a modest best-seller), tells the fictional story of narrator Geoffrey Braithwaite's obsession with Flaubert. The book's principal interest, however, lies in its digressions from this slight *donnée*. Woven into the narrative of Braithwaite's search for 'A Simple Heart's' original parrot are brief, playful, compelling forays into biography and criticism, conducted in a variety of forms: alternative chronologies (one on the good, one on the bad events in Flaubert's life, one in Flaubert's own words), an annotated collection of Flaubert's animal metaphors (bears being preferred), eleven connections between Flaubert and trains (he hated them but needed them for his affairs), a dictionary of received ideas on Flaubert (he hated mankind!), a mock exam, etc. The decisive point concerning this medley is less its formal inventiveness than its capacity to make knowledge appear, as Roland Barthes called for, 'where it is not expected' (1986, p. 242). Officially neither biography nor criticism, *Flaubert's Parrot* achieves the effect of both: a knowledge effect enhanced by erudition's passage through the novelesque.

S/Z, nominally a critical study (and an academic best-seller), pursues a line-by-line examination of Balzac's novella *Sarrasine*. The book's principal interest, however, lies in its 'divagations', brief, numbered, titled passages in which the rigour of the *explication du texte* is loosened by 'a number of fictive elements' (Barthes, 1986, p. 289), specifically the *other stories* which *Sarrasine's* literal meaning engenders, and which the reader begins to imagine in the concentrated idleness that 'makes sense' of narrative. Balzac's hero arrives at a terrible moment: having just made a first rendezvous with his beloved, he is accosted by a stranger and warned of the terrible dangers that threaten him should he keep it. He hesitates, and in a passage called 'The Story's Interest', Barthes supposes what will happen should Sarrasine turn away (the story will be over).

Even *S/Z*'s analytical sections depart from critical protocol, studded as they are with distinctively whimsical punctuation (both arabic *and* roman numerals, abbreviations, asterisks, italics, entirely capitalized words) and multiple metaphors (the text is 'a braid', 'a network', 'a telephone system', 'a contract', 'a musical score'). *S/Z*, in fact, issues from a camp disposition that dislocates its readymade (Balzac's novella) from its prescribed place in 'traditional fiction', remotivating it (*à la* Sirk) for the avant-garde.

Flaubert's Parrot interrupts its story with commentary, *S/Z* its analysis with fiction – the process in both cases resembling contemporary recording, where 'straight' musical signals are 'treated' (with reverberation, delay, compression, chorusing, etc.) on their way to the final mix; Barnes's 'compressed' biographical speculations 'echo' off the Braithwaite fiction, which like the wall causing reverberation, can be set more or less far away; Barthes's doubling of Balzac's plot lines 'choruses' Sarrasine's adventures with other stories and other possibilities for their understanding.

At stake in these books, and in postmodernism as a whole, is the founding segregation mandated by Plato: the discourses responsible for discovering and communicating knowledge were not to mix with the irresponsible ones of art. Thus, while the conventions of clarity, consistency and reason attached to the former, the latter assumed the benefits of its second-class citizenship: fiction, imagery and decoration. Postmodernism represents the miscegenation of the two modes – aesthetic thinking, conceptual art. The resulting hybrid text reproduces in itself the basic cultural principle which only postmodernism has acknowledged as a working heuristic, that the meaning of events depends entirely on the commentary gathering to them.

The desire for the hybrid text has come from both artist and critic. 'I wanted to put painting once again at the service of the mind', Duchamp said early in the century, explaining his wish to escape the French expression, *bête comme un peintre* (see Tomkins, 1968, p. 13). From the other direction comes the longing for 'the pleasure of the text', the voluptuousness of art. Hence this remark of Derrida's, appearing after only the first page-and-a-half of a 108-page essay: 'Since we have already said everything, the reader must bear with us if we continue on awhile. If we extend ourselves by force of play. If we then *write* a bit' (1981, p. 65).

This impulse has prompted the unclassifiable texts of postmodernism: Borges' *Labyrinths*, Calvino's *If on a Winter's Night a Traveller*, Derrida's *Glas*, Barthes's *Roland Barthes* and *A Lover's Discourse*, Lévi-Strauss's *Tristes Tropiques*, Godard's films, Cage's writings, Syberberg's *Our Hitler*, Lacan's seminars. As a group, these works stage at the level of representation the collapse of modernism's privileged oppositions: avant-garde and mass culture, private and public spheres, theoretical and practical activity. Contemporary life everywhere witnesses the mutual implication of previously discrete domains: a public event, the Super Bowl, impinges on the private, as several million television viewers simultaneously flush their toilets during a time-out, clogging New York's sewers. How can we represent this circular determination? The vocabulary of 'deconstruction', 'dissolution', 'undoing' overemphasizes postmodernism's reactionary preoccupation with modernism. At its best, postmodernism corresponds to a culture's instinct for a *via nova*, a new way to write and think about our situation that will go beyond the novel and the essay, perhaps by combining them.

THE IDEAL WORK

The composition of vast books is a laborious and impoverishing extravagance. To go on for five hundred pages developing an idea whose perfect oral expression is possible in a few minutes! A better course of procedure is to pretend that these books already exist, and then to offer a résumé, a commentary. Thus proceeded Carlyle in *Sartor Resartus*. Thus Butler in *The Fair Heaven*. These are works which suffer the imperfection of being themselves books, and of being no less tautological than the others. More reasonable, more inept, more indolent, I have preferred to write notes upon imaginary books.

(Jorge Luis Borges, 1962, pp. 15–16)

The best way to understand postmodernism is to think about a book that Walter Benjamin never wrote. Benjamin's original plan for his study of mid-nineteenth-century Paris (the *Arcades Project*) has become one of the most famous and suggestive ideas in contemporary thought. Impressed by the cinematic technique of montage (where meaning results from the juxtaposition of discrete images and sounds) and the surrealists' interest in the fragment, Benjamin wanted to compose a book made up entirely of quotations: lines from Baudelaire, photographs, objective data, eyewitness accounts, cartoons, newspaper stories, historical documents, passages from fiction. He intended to add the barest minimum of his own commentary, perhaps no more than captions under pictures and a few connecting lines between citations. As he put it in his journal, 'Method of this work: literary montage. I need say nothing. Only show' (1983–4, p. 5).

Since Benjamin was forswearing the powers of explicit analysis for the potential of emblematic images (whether pictorial or written), everything depended on his choices and their arrangement. The idea would be for the pregnant detail to 'shimmer before the reader like the flash thoughts of a memory' so that the material history of mid-nineteenth-century Paris might appear. An example: in arguing that Parisian revolutionary movements repeatedly sought to deny and interrupt history's apparent inevitability, Benjamin observed that 'On the night of the first evening of fighting (in the July Revolution [of 1830]) it turned out that the clocks in towers were being fired on simultaneously and independently from several places in Paris' (in Buck-Morss, 1981, p. 56).

'History', Benjamin wrote, 'breaks down into images, not into stories' (1983–4, p. 25), and arranging those images so as to make understandable the world they represented became for him like analysing the images of dreams. In his notebook, he quoted another writer:

> The past has left behind in literary texts images of itself that are comparable to the images which light imprints on a photosensitive plate. Only the future possesses developers active enough to bring these plates out perfectly.
>
> (p. 32)

Four suggestions why the *Arcades Project* is the ideal work of postmodernism:

1. By choosing mid-nineteenth-century Paris, Benjamin identified the time and place of postmodernism's origins. In the Paris arcades (the first shopping malls), mass consumer culture begins. While England perfected industrial production France anticipated post-industrial marketing, fostering desire through its inventions: the department store, the commercial daily press, the photograph. Only this site could occasion modernism, a reactionary movement, founded on a nervous hostility to the democratization of taste. Similarly, only this movement could spawn *post*modernism, an opportunistic movement, premised on a sense of the possibilities scattered by mass culture and mechanical reproduction.

2. By proposing to select material from every cultural level, Benjamin implicitly challenged modernism's absolutist faith in high culture. 'I won't steal anything valuable or appropriate any witty turns of phrase', Benjamin promised. 'But the trivia, the trash'. This gathering of scraps was not to be criticized

for its ideological contamination (à la Adorno), but allowed to speak for itself: 'this, I don't want to take stock of, but let come into its own in the only way possible: use it' (Benjamin, 1983–4, p. 5). Benjamin anticipates postmodernism's insight that the route to the *episteme* (science, knowledge) is through a culture's *doxa*, its received ideas, opinions and stories.

3. Limiting himself to found materials, readymades, Benjamin could only work by appropriation and remotivation, an ecological scavenging. Significantly, while rationally justified as a 'dialectical' strategy in tune with Benjamin's genuine (yet willed) Marxism, this method solicited him with the reward of pleasure. Delighted by surrealism, overcome by Aragon's novel/memoir *Le Paysan de Paris* (itself a collage text) (Buck-Morss, 1981, p. 65), he could not turn his back on the devices of art. His text would have been a hybrid – an 'exact fantasy', Adorno called it, rejecting the plan (Buck-Morss, 1977, p. 129).

4. The book was never written. We are free to imagine it and to develop its commentary.

THE LIST

The value of alphabetic listings is that each word is automatically assigned a specific but logically arbitrary place in the system, a space that only that item can fill. It is thus of immense value in retrieval systems dealing with masses of disordered information, such as subscriptions for the telephone or students in class.

(Jack Goody, 1977, p. 110)

Temptation of the alphabet: to adopt the succession of letters in order to link fragments is to fall back on what constitutes the glory of language. . . . an unmotivated order . . . which is not arbitrary (since everyone knows it, recognizes it, and agrees on it). The alphabet is euphoric: no more anguish of 'schema', no more rhetoric of 'development', no more twisted logic, no more dissertations!

(Roland Barthes, 1977, p. 147)

The best way to understand postmodernism is with a list.

A: allegory, appropriation, aberrant decoding, *Arcades Project*, Ashbery
B: banality, *bricolage*, biographeme, Benjamin, Barthes, Baudrillard, Borges, Barthelme
C: collage, co-option, complicity, camp, conceptual art, consumption, computer, compact disc, chance, Cage, Calvino
D: displacement, dandyism, dead-pan, *détournement*, deconstruction, difference, desire, democratization, *Dictionary of Received Ideas*, Derrida, Duchamp
E: exchange value, everyday life, ecology, entropy (Pynchon)

F: feminism, film, fashion, fetish, *Finnegans Wake*

G: graffiti, Godard

H: heterogeneity, heteroglossia (Bakhtin)

I: image, iterability (Derrida), intertextuality, implosion (Baudrillard)

J: *jouissance*

K: knell (*Glas*), knowledge

L: lateness, levelling, Lacan

M: mechanical reproduction, media, MTV, multi-national corporations, montage, mass culture, mime (Derrida), margins

N: nuclear, neo, nostalgia

O: overdetermination, OULIPO (Workshop for Potential Literature)

P: pop art, pun, parody, pastiche, *poste*, plagiarism, photography, popularization, performance

Q: quotation

R: readymade, recuperation, remotivation, repetition, Rauschenberg

S: Situationists, spectacle, speed, sign, signature, site-specific art, Sirk

T: television, tape recorders, textuality

U: urinal (Duchamp), uniformity (Warhol)

V: volatility (semiotic), video, vernacular, voyeuristic, *V* (Pynchon)

W: word-processor, Walkman, Warhol

X: Xerox

Y: yuppies

Z: *[S]/Z*

FURTHER READING

Benjamin, Walter (1969) 'The Work of Art in the Age of Mechanical Reproduction'. In Walter Benjamin, *Illuminations*, translated by Harry Zohn, Schocken, New York [essay first published 1935]

Buck-Morss, Susan (1981) 'Walter Benjamin – Revolutionary Writer (I) and (II)', *New Left Review*, 128 and 129, 50–75 and 77–95

Calinescu, Matei (1987) *Five Faces of Modernity: Modernism, Avant-Garde, Decadence, Kitsch, Postmodernism*, Duke University Press, Durham

Foster, Hal (ed.) (1983) *The Anti-Aesthetic: Essays on Postmodern Culture*, Bay Press, Port Townsend

Huyssen, Andreas (1986) *After the Great Divide: Modernism, Mass Culture, Postmodernism*, Indiana University Press, Bloomington

Jameson, Fredric (1984) 'Postmodernism, or The Cultural Logic of Late Capitalism', *New Left Review*, 146, 53–92

Lyotard, Jean-François (1984) *The Postmodern Condition: Report on Knowledge*, translated by Geoff Bennington and Brian Massumi, University of Minnesota, Minneapolis

Screen (1987) *Postmodern*, vol. 28, no. 2, London

Sontag, Susan (1966) 'Notes on "Camp"'. In Susan Sontag, *Against Interpretation*, Delta, New York

Ulmer, Gregory L. (1985) *Applied Grammatology*, Johns Hopkins University Press, Baltimore

Wallis, Brian (ed.) (1984) *Art after Modernism: Rethinking Representation*, Godine, Boston

Warhol, Andy (1975) *The Philosophy of Andy Warhol*, Harcourt Brace Jovanovich, New York

ADDITIONAL WORKS CITED

Ball, Edward (1987) 'The Great Sideshow of the Situationist International', *Yale French Studies*, 73, 21–37

Barnes, Julian (1985) *Flaubert's Parrot*, Knopf, New York

Barthes, Roland (1974) *S/Z*, translated by Richard Howard, Hill & Wang, New York

——(1977) *Roland Barthes*, translated by Richard Howard, Hill & Wang, New York

——(1986) *The Rustle of Language*, translated by Richard Howard, Hill & Wang, New York

Benjamin, Walter (1977) *The Origin of German Tragic Drama*, translated by John Osborne, New Left Books, London [first published 1928]

——(1979) 'The Author as Producer'. In Walter Benjamin, *Reflections*, translated by Edmund Jephcott, Harcourt Brace Jovanovich, New York, pp. 220–38 [first published 1934]

——(1983–4) 'N [Theoretics of Knowledge; Theory of Progress]', translated by Leigh Hafrey and Richard Sieburth, *The Philosophical Forum*, 15, Nos. 1–2, 1–40

Bennett, Tony (1982) 'Text and Social Process: The Case of James Bond', *Screen Education*, 41, 3–14

Borges, J. L. (1962) *Ficciones*, Grove, New York

Brecht, Bertolt (1964) *Brecht on Theatre*, edited by John Willett, Hill & Wang, New York

——(1966) 'Writing the Truth; Five Difficulties'. In Bertolt Brecht, *Galileo*, translated by Richard Winston, Grove, New York

Buck-Morss, Susan (1977) *The Origin of Negative Dialectics*, Free Press, New York

Derrida, Jacques (1977) 'Signature Event Context', *Glyph*, 1, 172–97

——(1981) *Dissemination*, translated by Barbara Johnson, University of Chicago Press, Chicago

Eco, Umberto (1972) 'Towards a Semiotic Enquiry into the Television Message', *Working Papers in Cultural Studies*, 3, 103–26

Eno, Brian (1981) 'Interview' (conducted by Mikal Gilmore and Spottswood Erving), *Musician*, 32 (April-May), 48–52

Fiedler, Leslie (1982) *What Was Literature?: Class Culture and Mass Society*, Simon & Schuster, New York

Foster, Hal (ed.) (1987) *Discussions in Contemporary Culture*, 1, Bay Press, Seattle

Gibson, Robert (ed.) (1979) *Modern French Poets on Poetry*, Cambridge University Press, Cambridge

Goody, Jack (1977) *The Domestication of the Savage Mind*, Cambridge University Press, Cambridge

Greenberg, Clement (1980) *The Notion of Post-Modern*, Sir William Dobell Art Foundation, Sydney

Hebdige, Dick (1979) *Subculture: The Meaning of Style*, Methuen, London

Jencks, Charles A. (1984) *The Language of Postmodern Architecture*, Rizzoli, New York

Krauss, Rosalind (1980) 'Poststructuralism and the "Paraliterary" ', *October*, 13, 16–40

Mallarmé, Stéphane (1968) 'Art for All'. In Roland N. Stromberg (ed.), *Realism, Naturalism, and Symbolism: Modes of Thought and Expression in Europe, 1848–1914*, Harper & Row, New York, 200–2 [essay first published 1862]

Marcus, Greil (1982) 'The Long Walk of the Situationist International', *The Village Voice*, May: Voice Literary Supplement, 13–19

Ong, Walter J. (1982) *Orality and Literacy*, Methuen, London

Schneider, Pierre (1971) *The World of Manet 1832–1883*, Time-Life Books, New York

Steinberg, Cobbett (1980) *TV Facts*, Facts on File, New York

Steiner, George (1972) 'After the Book'. In George Steiner, *On Difficulty and Other Essays*, Oxford University Press, New York [essay first published 1952]

Swenson, Gene R. (1963) 'What is Pop Art? Interview with Andy Warhol', *Art News*, 62 (November), 24, 60

Terdiman, Richard (1985) *Discourse/Counter-Discourse: The Theory and Practice of Symbolic Resistance in Nineteenth-Century France*, Cornell Univeristy Press, Ithaca

Tomkins, Calvin (1968) *The Bride and the Bachelors*, Penguin, New York

Toynbee, Arnold (1965) *A Study of History*, abridged by D. C. Somervell, Dell, New York

Ulmer, Gregory L. (1989) *Teletheory*, Routledge, London

Williams, Rosalind (1982) *Dream Worlds: Mass Consumption in Late Nineteenth-Century Paris*, University of California Press, Berkeley

Woolf, Virginia (1950) 'Mr Bennett and Mrs Brown'. In Virginia Woolf, *The Captain's Death Bed and Other Essays*, Harcourt Brace Jovanovich, New York [essay first published 1924]

III. POETRY

9

GENRE

ALASTAIR FOWLER

Literature has always been organized in genres, that is, in groups of works –
tragedies, comedies, epigrams and the like – that belong together because they
stand in the same tradition. Each genre is characterized by certain features,
certain constellations of formal qualities; so that its members share many
resemblances. How, exactly, do individual works relate to other similar works?
Various answers to this question have been given, and have seemed for a time
to hold the secret of literary originality. In consequence, genre has come to
be one of the most compelling concepts in the whole of literary theory. It
occupies a central position, beset with elusive issues. How do generic conventions change? Is this the same as asking how literature itself changes? Is
classification by genre possible? Or is genre an accumulation of constantly
changing codes? Are there rules of genre that condition aesthetic judgements?
Such questions may appear abstract and general; yet they are involved in every
act of criticism. This essay will glance at how they have been answered during
the last century.

From the point of view of genre, the nineteenth century was an intensely
creative period. It gave itself over to innovation and generic mixture with an
almost medieval boldness. This was not achieved, however, against a background of adequate genre theory, for after the decay of neo-classical rhetoric
a chasm had opened between practice and theory.

Three seeds of generic thinking, at most, proved fertile in the Victorian
period. One was the idea of evolution of literary forms, on the biological
model. Schiller had proposed that genres develop from 'primitive' or 'naïve'
to 'artificial' or 'sentimental' versions. This valuable idea was taken up by
many others, and eventually developed by C. S. Lewis (1942) into a distinction
between a fresh 'primary' stage (exemplified by Homer's epics) and a 'secondary', self-consciously imitative stage (represented by Virgil's *Aeneid*), more
concerned with considerations of generic purity.

Another idealized mixture: original writers had to make sure that pure forms of genre were blurred, mixed, or if possible evaded altogether. The third seed took root, contradictorily, in the hypothesis of a 'natural' division of all literature into dramatic, lyric and narrative. Its fertility, however, even in good critics like the mid-nineteenth-century Eneas Sweetland Dallas, produced a blighted, metaphysical luxuriance; burgeoning in meditations on hypostatized entities such as 'the lyric'. In a famous Festschrift article of 1967, René Wellek (1970) showed how unedifyingly vague such meditations mostly were (and, one might add, still are). Nevertheless, Wellek's salutary destructive work may have been taken a little too far. There is substance in Susanne K. Langer's neo-Kantian account of 'the great literary forms' in *Feeling and Form* (1953): her discussion of the use of tenses in lyric, for example, still retains interest. It is possible that the triple division, which after all goes back to Plato, may at least correspond to logical alternatives in the conscious construction of literary elements.

Romantic repudiation of the categories of genre was carried to a logical conclusion by Benedetto Croce, an anti-rhetorical theorist of very considerable influence. To Croce generic categories were simply 'false distinctions', showing 'of what dialectic pirouettes and sublime trivialities even philosophers are capable, when they begin to treat of the Aesthetic, of the tragic, comic, and humorous' (1909, p. 361). He conceded the existence of a 'bond of likeness' such as is observed among individuals, but denied, precociously, that such 'family likeness' had anything to do with definable classes (p. 119). Thus, each literary work approached is the subject of a unique aesthetic encounter, to which general ideas have no relevance. It is easy but facile to dismiss Croce's theory as relativistic, or as a mere *riscaldamento* of the doctrines of German Romanticism. He was a hero of modernism, and made a courageous attempt to penetrate beyond customary abstractions to the actual mental phenomena of criticism, and may be regarded as anticipating not only Wittgensteinian themes but also those of phenomenology – to say nothing of American New Criticism. More specifically, a Crocean approach was to underlie certain aspects of E. D. Hirsch's theory of intrinsic genre, discussed below. It recognizes, indeed, an enduring truth: namely, that genuine aesthetic responses are to individual works, not merely to representatives of classes.

However important Croce's ideas may now seem, in the early decades of this century they were almost totally ignored by literary scholars, who calmly went about their business of chronicling the 'fixed historical kinds'. Studies such as W. W. Greg's important *Pastoral Poetry and Pastoral Drama* (1906), James Hutton's learned *The Influence of the Greek Anthology* (1922), and Dwight L. Durling's *Georgic Tradition in English Poetry* (1935) consisted for the most part of empirical lists of works, debts and 'influences'; if any theoretical impulse informed them, it was a quasi-Darwinian desire to trace formal evolution. Such work has continued through more recent decades, although now with a more sophisticated method: among several excellent examples one might mention John Chalker's *The English Georgic* (1969) and Helen Cooper's *Pastoral: Medieval into Renaissance* (1977). Because of its diachronic approach, this sort of genre study has recently been out of critical fashion. But undeservedly – when most theoretically interesting criticism has long gone, it will remain of enduring value for its well-ordered information. Indeed, Greg's book, and others like it, laid the foundation for modern comparative literature studies. And the early chronicle histories of pastoral and georgic provided grist for the finer historiographic mills of a theorist like Ralph Cohen in *The Art of Discrimination* (1964), as well as for political applications like Anthony Low's *The Georgic Revolution* (1987).

The claims of traditional genre were asserted more theoretically by the Chicago Aristotelians – the philosopher Richard McKeon, the critics Elder Olson and R. W. Keast, the literary historian Bernard Weinberg, and above all the historian of ideas R. S. Crane. Committed to the teaching of critical method as an academic subject, the Chicago school was in theory pluralistically tolerant; but in practice its classicism was narrowly prescriptive – as in the way it dismissed German romantic ideas out of hand. The Chicagoans' approach was rhetorical, in the sense that they insisted criticism should be appropriate to the original historical genres – should treat, in a proportionate way, such rhetorical features of a work as plot, imitated action, character and diction (Aristotle's 'parts' of tragedy). Thus plot, a cardinal feature, is the focus in Crane's 'Concept of Plot and the Plot of *Tom Jones*' (1952). The Chicagoans' return to rhetorical detail may be considered a sort of progress. But their insistence on rigid genre boundaries, between classes with defining characteristics, vitiated all they achieved. They had put on blinkers excluding literature's true complexity and untidiness. In any case, the criticism performed under their aegis was not, in the event, very impressive. Perhaps their reaffirmation of neglected rhetorical ideas, perhaps only Crane's authority of intellect and personality, makes the Chicago school seem at all important.

The Chicago school explicitly assumed, just as the non-theoretical chroniclers assumed implicitly, that the historical kinds had each a peculiar 'external' form, a distinctive structure (like the octave and sestet of Petrarchan sonnets), definite and identifiable in much the same way as the features of biological species. The kinds evolved, to be sure; yet, contradictorily, they ran true to type and were invariable. Not surprisingly, the more minute literary history became, the shorter the lives of these invariable fixed kinds. They had, indeed, precise common characteristics; but these were so many and so arbitrary as to defy rationalization.

Understandably, critics who wanted a more explanatory concept of grouping turned to a broader approach, and examined what it was that similar genres had in common, and especially genres in different historical periods. These have tended to paint with a rather loose brush. They may be described as modal critics; although, particularly after Northrop Frye, the terms 'mode', 'genre' and 'kind' have all been used with a bewildering variety of applications. Modal studies have a great exemplar in Frye's *Anatomy of Criticism* (1957), a book that has inspired countless others; they include works like T. R. Henn, *The Harvest of Tragedy* (1966), Abbie Findlay Potts, *The Elegiac Mode* (1967), Renato Poggioli, *The Oaten Flute* (1975) and Mikhail Bakhtin, *Rabelais and His World* (1968) on the carnival or comic mode.

Modal critics tend to ignore historical development. Indeed, many of them adopt a synchronic method, treating literature as if it were all written in the present – the domain of assumptions they privilege. Necessarily they must ignore many distinctions, and make do with a small number of shared features. This simpler, more malleable material enables them to achieve explanatory facility, if not exactly explanatory force. And the modal critics can claim a certain adventitious half-validity, in that many nineteenth-century and modern writers, at least, themselves adopted a modal view.

As one might almost expect, if it were not so paradoxical, the best of the synchronic modal critics are those, like Frye and Angus Fletcher, who know a great deal of literary history. The reader of Fletcher's *Allegory: The Theory of a Symbolic Mode* (1964) finds a keen excitement in his brilliant development of such ideas as the generation of subcharacters. This, one feels, is how literature really works. And one might say the same of William Empson's *Some Versions of Pastoral* (1935), so far as its investigation of thematic interaction of plot and subplot is concerned. Even Empson's treatment of *Alice in Wonderland* as pastoral, although hardly defensible historically, overextends the mode in an interesting way. Such criticism serves to put literary works beside unaccustomed neighbours in an illuminating way. Often this is done to make a contentious point; for modal critics are given to moral synthesis, and tend to be impatient moralists.

Frye's *Anatomy of Criticism* is a marvellous, maddening book, which draws, in a way unusual among 'powerful' theoretical works, on a wide range of deeply considered reading. Frye addresses himself to the understanding not of literary works, but of generic ingredients of literature at large. He sets out several highly original ideas about how genres might be compared: as, for example, by their 'mimetic mode' or height – their heroes' powers on a scale of human possibility. (For example, epic heroes are above average, but do not have the same supernatural involvements as those of romance.) Unfortunately, Frye's bold insights are a little clouded by his free use of terms like 'mode' in new and not adequately defined senses. Nor does he develop them to the point at which they might persuade or challenge verification. Moreover, he often distinguishes modes (in the sense, this time, of genres) by poetical rather than critical procedures – distributing them among scalar compartments of mental space, perhaps, or among the seasons of a notional year. Such schematizing, however pedagogically suggestive it may be, is too arbitrarily imposed: it points to an unsatisfactory resolution of the historical problem. Frye's genre theory has been associated with structuralism, a connection he rightly disclaims; nevertheless, it would seem to be limited, in some ways, by a similarly synchronic disposition.

The next phase, that of the 1960s, needs to be seen in distant perspective, taking in the nature of meaning itself. Since Aristotle, this had been understood in terms of two complementary models: namely, the coding-decoding model, and the common-sense model of inferred intentions. Now, however, New Critics like William K. Wimsatt, Monroe Beardsley and Cleanth Brooks introduced a method of interpretation whereby intention was disregarded, even flouted; they preferred to select interpretations that maximized richness. Not surprisingly, they had little interest in genre, with its constraining indications of the kind of work and meanings the writer intended. (Indeed, Wimsatt rejected the Chicago approach quite vigorously.) In any case, the New Critics limited their attention to a small number of closely related 'lyric' genres, all of short length. Other genres they ignored, or even despised (as did the contemporary Cambridge critics), but without developing theoretical reasons for doing so.

New Criticism focused its attention, albeit not very systematically, on unobvious or inadvertent meanings. This practice was taken to a theoretical extreme by the French structuralists, who did not regard writing as having any interesting, or indeed accessible, connection with writers. (Structuralism is a school of thought that attends to relations between things to the virtual exclusion of their substance and historical functions.) The structuralists thought of interpretation as exclusively an affair of decoding and analysing the results. Neither intention to mean nor biographical and immediate historical contexts of writing had the slightest value for them. Roland Barthes and other structuralists even spoke of the 'death' of the author. All that existed was 'Text'. Eventually, literature came to be seen, especially by the deconstructionists, as a series of intertextualities in which texts generated texts within a synchronic stasis.

The structuralists differed from the New Critics, however, in having no objection to genre abstractions, or to thinking in terms of classes – although of course they dismissed traditional genre theory out of hand. Indeed, genre was a congenial subject to them, being a coding system, on which they might be expected to excel. And, in the event, they succeeded in bringing out how far generic features were precisely codings, and not merely arbitrary marks of identification. Structuralist successes were mostly in theorizing about the novel (previously neglected, as a form that only developed after traditional genre theory). Gérard Genette (1980), in particular, deserves mention. One or two structuralist studies of other modes are also of interest, such as Tzvetan

Todorov's *The Fantastic: A Structural Approach to a Literary Genre* (trans. 1973). Todorov's work is fresh and interesting, and less blinkered than usual by synchronism, since it studies a group of works mostly produced within a short historical period. For the most part, the structuralists ignored context, not to speak of historical change; Fredric Jameson's fine article 'Magical Narratives: Romance as Genre', developed in *The Political Unconscious* (1981), was a notable exception – if, indeed, he counts at all as one of their number. Structuralism invariably treated genres as definable classes: hence one of the points of Jacques Derrida's attempt (1980) to subvert it deconstructively, by showing that indications of genre, by not themselves being within the genre, introduce inevitable 'contamination'. Such 'problems' only arise when genres are thought of as classes.

At the opposite extreme from structuralism, E. D. Hirsch's *Validity in Interpretation* (1967) reasserted authorial intention as the criterion of meaning. Hirsch reacted against the irresponsibilities of the New Critics; yet he shared certain of their emphases, notably that on the free-standing uniqueness of individual works. In this, he could even be regarded as a Crocean. Hirschian intentionalism is of no direct concern here; but there are far-reaching implications for genre theory in his analysis of the communication of meaning. For Hirsch, this is invariably communication of types. Broad genres in the traditional sense, however, he discounts as inevitably 'extrinsic'. They are of no more than transitory value, as a scaffolding of temporary use in constructing the intrinsic type; distant horizons which at best help to arrive at the far more narrowly circumscribed type that is of real interest. Hirsch's main concern is to develop a concept of this 'intrinsic genre', the type that 'lies somewhere between the vague, heuristic genre idea with which an interpreter always starts and the individual, determinate meaning with which he ends' (1967, p. 81). Much of the central contention of *Validity in Interpretation* have never been rebutted. Yet it was denied by those who found easy New-Critical or structuralist habits hard to break. And its emphasis on validity has been by-passed by an increasingly pragmatist theory. Nevertheless, his insistence that interpretation calls for inferences about intended meaning has been justified by recent developments in psycholinguistics and in the philosophy of meaning. It remains to be seen whether his theory can be adjusted to allow for local indeterminacies, and whether his concept of 'intrinsic genre' – a type distinct from full linguistic realization – will come to be accepted.

Another work of fundamental theoretical importance appeared about the same time: Roman Ingarden's *The Literary Work of Art* (1965). Ingarden's clear exposition of the stratified structures whereby literary works exist, although in itself generalized to a point fairly close to boredom, had considerable explanatory power, and stimulated many detailed accounts of genre, by critics now better informed theoretically than the early annalists. For analysis of point of view, various narrational modes and the like, the work of the structuralist Genette has already been mentioned. Drier, but subtler and more penetrating is the phenomenological account in Félix Martínez-Bonati's *Fictive Discourse and the Structures of Literature* (trans. 1981). And a comprehensive account of narrative, enriched with many valuable examples, may be found in F. K. Stanzel, *A Theory of Narrative* (trans. 1984).

As regards poetry, Ralph Cohen's monograph (1964) on Thomson's *Seasons* draws on prolonged theoretical considerations of the georgic mode; and some of the implications of this work are well brought out in his 'Innovation and Variation: Literary Change and Georgic Poetry' (1974). Cohen here comes to grips with the fundamental yet widely avoided problem of generic innovation. In passing, he makes the important point that genres change at a different rate from other literary conventions, so that they can be of great assistance in breaking into the hermeneutic circle. Other work of significant general import in this phase includes essays by W. D. Stempel (1970) and Hans Robert Jauss (1977), discussing the part played by genre in reception of a work.

Meanwhile the ideas of the philosopher Ludwig Wittgenstein were being brought to bear on genre theory. Wittgenstein had shown that many groupings, such as games, are not hard-edged classes susceptible to rigid definition, but have a coherence which more resembles that of a family. Rather than defining characteristics, their members share family resemblances. By these a family is easily recognized; yet not all of them need be exhibited by any single individual member. This approach began to be applied to literature in a tentative way by several critics in the 1960s: for example Robert C. Elliott (1962), Maurice Mandelbaum (1965) and Graham Hough (1966). A sense of the impossibility of definition may also underlie Richmond Alexander Lattimore's *Story Patterns in Greek Tragedy* (1964). Lattimore was unable to treat even Attic tragedy as a single class, and posited a less logically tidy arrangement distributing features among various subgenres or variant types (discovery tragedy, revenge tragedy and the like). Once the concept of family resemblance was introduced, its further application had a natural inevitability. All subsequent genre theory, it seems, must take account of the Wittgensteinian insight.

Thoroughgoing application of family resemblance theory came with Alastair Fowler's *Kinds of Literature* (1982), an attempt to construct, if not a comprehensive theory of genre, at least a speculative description of the entire field. Considering genres as families made it possible, even obligatory, to adopt a diachronic approach, and so offered a fresh approach to the problem of historical change. For Fowler, the so-called fixed historical kinds are not at all fixed, but mutable, continually renewed repertoires of characteristic features (external structure, rhetoric, topics and the like). Such repertoires are not a means of classification so much as a resource of signs in a language or coding system that allows economical yet intelligible communication. Change of the repertoires is continual, for new works signify precisely by their modulating of specific previous states of the genre. Hence their own addition to it modifies the existing state, and a series of such successive changes may alter it almost out of recognition. From these changing kinds, however, less volatile 'modes' may be abstracted, consisting not of complete repertoires, but only of a few representative features, mostly rhetorical. These modes can be applied in the deliberate mixture of genres, whether local or pervasive, that most literary events consist of. Throughout, *Kinds of Literature* represents genre as a continually dynamic metamorphosis whereby, in the course of history, kinds are assembled, become more consciously practised (Lewis's 'secondary genre'), form the basis of modes, enter into temporary mixtures, hybrids or modulations, and combine to form new kinds. By this diachronic approach, Fowler attempted at once to overthrow the basis of traditional genre theory, and at the same time to argue that many ancient ideas of genre only need recasting and new application for them to be relevant to modern literature.

Philosophically, Fowler's ideas represented an unsatisfactory amalgam of Wittgenstein, Carnap and the non-structuralist element in Saussure; and he overestimated the part played in interpretation by coding. But he addressed a clear need, and made some contributions, such as the distinction between generic labels and actual genres (which change independently), or the idea of multiple stages in formation (particularly his 'tertiary genre', that is, symbolic transformation of a secondary genre). Perhaps, too, the frequency of his examples may encourage theorists to come to grips with more of the complexity of genre in actual literary history.

The same need to review traditional genre theory was addressed by others in very different ways. Heather Dubrow's *Genre* (1982) is an introductory essay without pretensions to original theorizing. But in fact it clears a great deal of ground economically, and its sensitive treatment of the part played by genre in interpretation (heuristic, rather than determinative) breaks new paths. Adena Rosmarin's *The Power of Genre* (1986), by contrast, attempts an ambitious general theory of genre from a structuralist standpoint. Rosmarin rejects all notions of inductive procedure and descriptive validity; her criterion of good genre criticism is simply explanatory power. Only by virtue of this power, indeed, do genres themselves exist; and when better 'explanations' or genres come along, they replace the former. Many critics doubtless think in such terms of definitions and classes; and deductive inferences almost certainly form part of our automatic mental processing. But only the absence of examples from Rosmarin's highly abstract book enables her to identify such processes with an adequate critical response. (Even reading – let alone criticism – continually enriches logical procedures by imagination.) Rosmarin is almost always extremely clear, and clearly discloses how much the synchronic structuralist approach is bound up with nineteenth-century metaphysical concepts of generic classes.

Others have turned to the question of how different genres are related in groups, or to the idea of systems of genres. Paul Hernadi's *Beyond Genre: New Directions of Literary Classification* (1972) offers a useful survey of genre theories, but tends to take up a rather uncritical stance towards various 'maps' or diagrams purporting to set out the true geography of genre in some unspecified mental space. Ernst Robert Curtius adopted a more factual, diachronic method in *European Literature and the Latin Middle Ages* (1948), a classic study tracing many historical schemes of genres. This approach is developed in greater detail, and a good deal more subtly, by Claudio Guillén. Guillén's *Literature as System* (1971) analyses many different versions of the tripartite division of literature, and could be interpreted as demonstrating the invalidity of such imposed schemes.

From the work of these and other learned comparatists, a better understanding has emerged of the way in which each literary period privileges certain genres, and erects what amount to revised generic hierarchies – as in seventeenth-century England, for example, epigram, georgic and satire were revalued; or in the nineteenth century, lyric and novel. This line of thought has recently been elaborated into extended studies of the literary canon, some of them with narrowly political motivations. But can literature and its genres properly be said to operate as a system? The most rigorous contemporary theorizing seems to call this into question, while suggesting that, in the heuristic processing of assumptions of genre, neighbouring and contrasting relations have a useful function.

The most interesting recent work on genre, however, is found less often in these very theoretical studies than in descriptions of individual kinds or modes. Here one might instance Guillén's accounts of picaresque, summarized in *Literature as System* (1971), or of the epistle (Guillén, 1986). Rosalie Colie's brilliant evocation of Renaissance genres in *The Resources of Kind* (1973) has stimulated many other genre studies, as has Barbara Lewalski's *Brief Epic: The Genre, Meaning and Art of 'Paradise Regained'* (1966). To mention only monographs, Ian Donaldson's *The World Upside-Down* (1970), Colie's *Shakespeare's 'Living Art'* (1974), Lewalski's *'Paradise Lost' and the Rhetoric of Literary Forms* (1985) and Gordon Braden's *Renaissance Tragedy and the Senecan Tradition: Anger's Privilege* (1985) are some of the best of these. Descriptions of Renaissance genres naturally predominate; but there has also been outstanding medieval work, such as John Stevens's *Medieval Romance* (1973) and A. C. Spearing's *Medieval Dream Poetry* (1976). So far as modes are concerned, an influential account of pastoral is Thomas G. Rosenmeyer's *The Green Cabinet: Theocritus and the European Pastoral Lyric* (1969). And on comedy, particularly the carnival element, Mikhail Bakhtin's *Rabelais and His World* (1968) and his interesting but loosely argued *The Dialogic Imagination: Four Essays* (trans. 1981) have had comparable influence. Hybrid kinds have attracted some of the most interesting studies: notably Madeleine Doran's *Endeavours of Art* (1954) and Cyrus Hoy's *The Hyacinth Room* (1964), both largely concerned with tragi-comedy (which is treated by the latter as a mode revived by Samuel Beckett).

For periods more recent than the eighteenth century, there is very little genre theory to go on; so that critics are obliged to engage in the primary task of labelling appropriate groupings and perhaps describing them for the first time. From E. M. Forster (*Aspects of the Novel*, 1927) and Robert Liddell (*A Treatise on the Novel*, 1947) onwards, an army of critics has attempted to describe 'the novel' or to distinguish its subgenres. (Among the latter, Peter Garrett has identified an unusually distinct form in *The Victorian Multiplot Novel*, 1980.) With modernism, if not earlier, groupings become often highly conjectural, and tend to have too little consensus even for useful debate. An example is the grouping proposed in Martin Esslin's *The Theatre of the Absurd* (1961), which may be felt to have something less than unitary force. On the other hand, there is fairly wide agreement on a narrative genre often called metafiction, which is characterized by features, such as damaged verisimilitude, that draw attention to the work's artefactual status. Linda Hutcheon's *Narcissistic Narrative: The Metafictional Paradox* (1981) and Patricia Waugh's *Metafiction* (1984) are discernibly concerned with more or less the same grouping.

And, even within this, many would agree on another, still more specific, group of narratives, in which a character may be engaged in writing, and there are inset texts or works of art, displaced symbols of creativity, or talk of papers and writing materials. Fowler may label this the *poioumenon* (work making itself) or work-in-progress novel; Steven Kellman (1980) may label it 'the self-begetting novel' but they largely agree on the extent and characteristics of the grouping. With so much agreement, it is hard to believe that the accounts do not have some descriptive validity, at least of a temporary character. Other modern generic identifications include subgenres of the short story. And, in one of the most exciting recent developments, several scholars have proposed an alternative form of epic (the Callimachean epic: short, complex, discontinuous) largely excluded from traditional genre theory. A good introduction to this topic is John Kevin Newman *The Classical Epic Tradition* (1986). It would also be true to say that divine comedy is a mode now beginning to be better understood than at any time since the Middle Ages.

But much remains to be done, particularly in identifying contemporary poetical genres and relating them to their tradition. Such is the deficiency of genre theory in this area that when, against the odds, a modern kind is identified – such as 'the poem on a picture' – the response in terms of emulative output is almost overwhelming. Thus, there have been three recent anthologies of picture poems, a Gale bibliography listing thousands of exemplars, a national competition and two exhibitions at the Tate. When contemporary literature is more fully studied in this way, it may not look so very different from the literature of traditional genre theory, with its lists of familiar kinds.

The more general of the genre theories described so far are comparatively external and superficial, consisting in the main, as they do, of empirical enumeration of generic features, with only desultory attempts to explain their interconnection. Clearly we now need more focus on the actual functions of these characteristics. In recent decades, fortunately, the functioning of individual literary elements has been the topic of many quite detailed studies, particularly within the freer environment of narratology, untrammelled by traditional theory. Good examples of this trend are Michael Irwin, *Picturing: Description and Illusion in the Nineteenth Century Novel* (1979), and Mary Ann Caws, *Reading Frames in Modern Fiction* (1985). So far, most of these studies – pursued, as they were, within the unreal world of 'the novel' – have been innocent of generic considerations. But similar methods could be applied to features differentiated by genre. How does this descriptive device actually function, one might enquire, in works exemplifying a particular genre, as distinct from how it works in others? How does novelistic framing differ from romantic, say, or dramatic, or elegiac? Such an approach may prove to be a valuable avenue for future genre criticism.

On a broader front, genre critics like all others will have to come to grips with modern concepts of meaning, such as Dan Sperber and Deirdre Wilson's theory of relevance (1986). As Sperber and Wilson have made very clear, coding and decoding – and that must include generic codes – play only a limited part in communication and interpretation, which are largely a matter of small-scale inferences guided by relevance. The principle of relevance operates at every stage. In the case of literary interpretation, relevance must necessarily be to readers' own cognitive environments – even to their own interests. But, whether they know it or not, they are also continually guided by relevance to what they assume to be the writer's intentions. (These promise, after all, the pleasure of recognizing intended harmonies.) Generic organization may be conjectured to facilitate interpretative inferences at almost every level of structure.

If it is true that readers do not so much decode as select the most accessible relevant inferences, then those of them who are familiar with appropriate genres will access the topics and formal conventions of these first, and so form assumptions of intended meaning more easily. Organization according to genre offers a rich encyclopedia of mutually related words, formal patterns, ideas, emotions and shared assumptions, on which readers automatically draw for relevant items. Subsequently, of course, good readers further enrich this relatively crude communication of meaning with many inferences – doubtless including some based on the individual writer's relation to his generic group, or on his known eccentricities, originality and the like. Thus, the idea that genres constitute horizons of meaning may not be wrong, so much as lacking in explanatory detail. To determine just how relevance theory applies to the generic element in communication must surely be an early objective for genre theory.

FURTHER READING

Cohen, Ralph (1974) 'Innovation and Variation: Literary Change and Georgic Poetry'. In Ralph Cohen and Murray Krieger, *Literature and History*, University of California Press, Berkeley

Colie, Rosalie (1973) *The Resources of Kind*, edited by Barbara Keifer Lewalski, University of California Press, Berkeley

Dubrow, Heather (1982) *Genre*, Methuen, London

Fletcher, Angus (1964) *Allegory: The Theory of a Symbolic Mode*, Cornell University Press, Ithaca

Fowler, Alastair (1982) *Kinds of Literature*, Harvard University Press, Cambridge; Oxford University Press, Oxford

Frye, Northrop (1957) *Anatomy of Criticism*, Princeton University Press, Princeton

Guillén, Claudio (1971) *Literature as System*, Princeton University Press, Princeton

Hernadi, Paul (1972) *Beyond Genre: New Directions in Literary Classification*, Cornell University Press, Ithaca

Hirsch, E. D. (1967) *Validity in Interpretation*, Yale University Press, New Haven

Langer, Susanne K. (1953) *Feeling and Form: A Theory of Art*, Routledge & Kegan Paul, London; Scribner, New York

Rosenmeyer, Thomas G. (1969) *The Green Cabinet: Theocritus and the European Pastoral Lyric*, University of California Press, Berkeley

Rosmarin, Adena (1986) *The Power of Genre*, University of Minnesota Press, Minneapolis

ADDITIONAL WORKS CITED

Cohen, Ralph (1964) *The Art of Discrimination*, Routledge & Kegan Paul, London; University of California Press, Berkeley

Crane, R. S. (1952) 'The Concept of Plot and the Plot of *Tom Jones*'. In R. S. Crane (ed.), *Critics and Criticism*, University of Chicago Press, Chicago

Croce, Benedetto (1909) *Aesthetic as Science of Expression and General Linguistic*, translated by Douglas Ainslie, Macmillan, London

Derrida, Jacques (1980) 'The Law of Genre', *Glyph*, 7, 176–201, 202–229

Elliott, Robert C. (1962) 'The Definition of Satire', *Yearbook of Comparative and General Literature*, 11, 199–23

Genette, Gérard (1980) *Figures I, II, III*, translated by J. E. Lewin as *Narrative Discourse*, Basil Blackwell, Oxford

Guillén, Claudio (1986) 'Notes toward the Study of the Renaissance Letter'. In Barbara Keifer Lewalski (ed.), *Renaissance Genres*, Harvard English Studies, 14

Hough, Graham (1966) *An Essay on Criticism*, Duckworth, London

Jameson, Fredric (1975) 'Magical Narratives: Romance as Genre', *New Literary History*, 7, 135–63

——(1981) *The Political Unconscious: Narrative as a Socially Symbolic Act*, Methuen, London

Jauss, Hans Robert (1977) 'Littérature médiévale et expérience esthétique', *Poétique*, 8, 322–36

Kellman, Steven (1980) *The Self-Begetting Novel*, Columbia University Press, New York

Lewis, C. S. (1942) *Preface to 'Paradise Lost'*, Oxford University Press, London

Mandelbaum, Maurice (1965) 'Family Resemblances and Generalization Concerning the Arts', *American Philosophical Quarterly*, 2, 219–28

Sperber, Dan and Wilson, Deirdre (1986) *Relevance: Communication and Cognition*, Harvard University Press, Cambridge

Stempel, W. D. (1970) 'Pour une description des genres littéraires'. In W. D. Stempel, *Beiträge zur Textlinguistik*, W. Fink, Munich

Wellek, René (1970) 'Genre Theory, the Lyric, and *Erlebnis*'. In René Wellek, *Discriminations*, Yale University Press, New Haven, pp. 225–52

10

POETRY

C. K. STEAD

The *Concise Oxford Dictionary*'s first definition of 'poetry' is 'Art or work of the poet'. Its first definition of a poet is 'Writer of poems'. Two pages back a plumber is 'Workman who fits and repairs water pipes'; and plumbing is 'Plumber's work'.

The differences between the two ways of defining are subtle but important. It's clear 'plumber's work' is usually done by a plumber, but may be done by a home handyman. On the other hand 'poetry' can only be produced by a poet. Poetry is evidence of the condition of being a poet. But more, there is that definite article: not 'a poet' but 'the poet', which suggests a more special and singular identity. The capacity to be 'poet' is something in-born. In this sense it is almost possible to imagine a 'poet' who has never written a poem.

The *Concise Oxford*'s second definition of poetry is 'elevated expression of elevated thought or feeling in metrical or rhythmical form'; and its second definition of poet is 'writer in verse, esp. one possessing high powers of imagination, expression, etc.' 'Elevated . . . elevated . . . high': the poet clearly belongs on some kind of pinnacle or pedestal. He and his work are lifted above the common. In earlier times he has been credited with mystical or magical powers, capable of making crops grow or rain to fall. He has been charged with celebrating weddings and victories, with lamenting defeats and deaths, and with committing to memorable form the history of family, clan or kingdom. He has been the channel of collective feeling, the packager of myth, wisdom and history. He has had about him something of the priest and something of the oracle. He has had commerce with the Muse and been receiver and transmitter of the divine breath. His symbols have included the Aeolian harp, played upon by the winds of inspiration, and the winged horse Pegasus, whose hoof striking the ground on Mount Olympus brought forth the Hippocrene fountain.

Not much of all this remains clearly present in modern notions of the poet; yet, faintly, it all remains. The words 'poet' and 'poetry' may appear neutral until you turn out the light when they will be seen still to glow in the dark like hot coals. When the fashion in twentieth-century literature turned against the more extravagant claims for the poet's art inherited from the romantic movement, the words 'poet' and 'poetry' were given a rest. 'Poetry' became 'verse', and 'poets' 'practitioners'. This was the period when anthologies had titles like *The Faber Book of Modern Verse* (1936), *The Oxford Book of Modern Verse* (1936), *The Penguin Book of English Romantic Verse* (1968), and so on. And in the writings of F. R. Leavis and the *Scrutiny* group especially, but also in the work of many other critics during the 1930s, 1940s and 1950s, authors of poems were almost always 'practitioners', seldom 'poets'. The words 'poet' and 'poetry' could not be neutralized simply by giving them a neutral context. They brought with them grand claims and magical associations. If literature was to be rid of that baggage, the words had to be set aside. But as the words have come back, so have the associations, which were probably in any case never effectively shed.

There are a number of reasons for this curious power that resides in the idea of poetry, and hence in the word. One is that language more than anything else is what distinguishes us as a species, and poetry has been generally conceded to the most comprehensive and demanding use, or manifestation, of language. Language represents power in society. There are other forms power can take, from brute force through to the most modern operations of science and technology. But populations are still influenced and ultimately controlled by the word. Not by poems, true; but in language resides the ordering of human affairs; and though the poet is no longer the rhetorician and public bard, the sense that he has special understanding of that source of power earns a deference which you may choose to see as superstitious, but which is none the less real. It must surely be some sense of this fact which led Shelley to claim in his *Defence of Poetry* (1821) that poets were the unacknowledged legislators of the world.

Of course, it has to be acknowledged that for any and every function which is practical and specific, poetry is unsatisfactory. Messages and information are best conveyed in prose; plans for buildings, roads, bridges, in design sketches and specifications. Science and mathematics have their own languages. So has modern philosophy. As human skills have become more specialized, the function of poetry has contracted, and so it, too, has become more specialized. One no longer looks to a poet to teach history, or ethics, or the management of crops – all of which in the past have been conveyed 'in metrical or rhythmical form'. As these purposes have vanished from poetry, what has been left has not been a weakened brew but rather a stronger and more arcane spirit. The object of the poem, as T. S. Eliot saw it, was to be 'poetry, and not another thing' (1928, p. viii). The object of all those other kinds of language which have a specific function is to serve that function. When it is served –

the message understood, the information conveyed, the alarm sounded, the reward delivered – that is the end of the matter. Such language is there to be used – and, Paul Valéry suggests, *used up*. The purpose of literary language in general, and most particularly of that kind of literary language we call poetry, is to survive any particular use. In fact language becomes poetry when it is comprehensive enough to attain to a life of its own beyond any single function.

There used to be an argument between aesthetes and moralists about what was the proper aim and object of poetry. Traditionally, poetry was enjoyed. It gave pleasure. It represented beautiful things and was itself beautiful. This was the decorative aspect of the art of poetry. On the other hand there was always the feeling that when this side became overemphasized, poetry lost some of its power, its weight, its, in Matthew Arnold's phrase, 'high serious-ness' ([1888] 1938, p. 20). Against its aesthetic function was, therefore, its moral one. Poetry had to delight but also to instruct. In fact its aesthetic function, from this point of view, was hardly more than a sugar coating so that the pill of morality would be effortlessly swallowed.

The argument has swung back and forth, with now one side now the other seeming to have the upper hand. Since the time of the romantic movement Keats has been held up as the great exemplar of the poetry of aestheticism – though even then it was not quite beauty for beauty's sake but beauty for the sake of the truth it bodied forth. The great public poets of the nineteenth century, on the other hand, and especially Tennyson, were read as moralists. This may not have been quite fair to them; but along with the pleasures and profits of a large audience, which Tennyson enjoyed, went disadvantages not suffered by those poets who have had 'fit audience though few'. Chief among those disadvantages was that a large audience, when there is one, asks that poetry should speak for causes beyond itself. It is not permitted to be 'poetry, and not another thing'.

So in the late years of the nineteenth century there was a reaction against poetry-as-morality – the Art for Art's Sake movement, which had a brief heyday and then died in the cold blast of scandal emanating from the trial of Oscar Wilde.

All such arguments are inevitably crude, since the antagonists tend to answer one another rather than to look clearly at the object of dispute which lies between them. Those who argue for morality are invariably arguing for a particular morality; while the 'aesthete' is often arguing against that morality rather than for poetry. Poetry becomes like the child in a custody case between warring parents – not permitted to have its own identity, but claimed by each as a possession.

Wordsworth said the poet was 'a man speaking to men' (ed. 1974, p. 138). That does not at first sight seem to match the exalted notion of the poet we have been considering. But Wordsworth goes on to make clear that those

166

human qualities which are general, as distinct from those which make a person a professional, or a specialist, will be unusually highly developed in the poet; and that the person to whom the poet speaks will be addressed 'not as a lawyer, a physician, a mariner, an astronomer, or a natural philosopher, but as a Man' (ed. 1974, p. 139). Here we have the notion of the Common Reader in a form which I think answers the objections of modern literary theorists who have argued that no such animal exists – that we are all 'specialist' readers, with special interests, commitments, and (whether recognized or not) ideological bases. Wordsworth's statement does not deny that we are none of us innocent readers. What it insists on is that beneath our special interests and ideological or theoretical commitments lies the innocent ground of our humanity. It is not that the Common Reader is one person and the specialist another. It is that in every specialist there is also a Common Reader, and this is the 'Man' to whom the poetry addresses itself. This seems to me unarguably true. There is a special kind of neutrality about poetic language. As soon as it begins to argue, to cajole, to insist, the sense that we are reading a poem diminishes. Of course poets can write political or 'committed' verses, and these will sometimes (not always) survive as poems. But when they do, that is because their statement seems to exist in inverted commas. They dramatize the passion of commitment. As soon as reasoning replaces passion and dramatization in such writing, the sense that this is a poem vanishes. It is this latter kind of writing that twentieth-century criticism has tended to call 'rhetoric', using the word not in its older sense of a set of learnable skills with language, but pejoratively. 'We make of the quarrel with others rhetoric', says W. B. Yeats; 'of the quarrel with ourselves, poetry' ([1918] 1959, p. 331).

There are elements of craft skill with poetry as with all the arts; but what seems to be implied when we distinguish between an art and a craft is that learned skills will not be enough – there must be that in-born potential as well. And because poetry is an art with a long history, the poet must inherit the tradition through the medium of those who have gone before. Not that poets must have read assiduously back through the ages (though it will be none the worse for them if they have); but rather that there is a flow-on effect – a kind of apostolic succession. All past poetry is present in the poetry of the present. The poet (especially the young poet) reads rather in the way the body breathes, drawing life from what has gone before as from an atmosphere. The poet's individual talent is not sufficient to account for poetry. Only those who have acquired, by however selective a method, that sense of a living tradition flowing through poetry from age to age into the present, will carry the tradition forward.

It is true that the history of poetry is full of schools, wars, and youthful rebellions. The romantic poets rebelled against the Augustans; modernists rebelled against the great figures of the nineteenth century. In France rebellion is almost required – romantics against classicists, Parnassians against romantics, symbolists against Parnassians, modernists against symbolists, and so on. But where rebellion occurs the flow-on effect is never less marked, and sometimes more. There is no need for rebellion where what has gone before has had no effect. It is because, in literature as in society at large, the French are such traditionalists that they have such need of rebellion.

So far I have moved around my subject in general without attempting to say what is and what is not poetry. In the popular mind – that is to say, among people who do not normally read poetry – a poem is distinguishable by the fact that it is broken up into lines which usually rhyme and have some metrical pattern. Poetry is manifest in its form. Even before modern poets began to abandon regular forms, this notion was less than satisfactory. It must always have been apparent that you could write out a statement that would satisfy the formal requirements of a sonnet, or of any other verse form, without achieving poetry; while, conversely, passages of prose – in the King James Bible, or *Moby Dick*, or *Wuthering Heights*, to take only three very obvious examples – were so heightened, and so powerful in their effect, that no reader would want to quarrel with the suggestion that they were poetry. Poetry then, almost by definition, is a quality, not a form; though of this you may add, if your disposition is strongly conservative, that the quality 'poetry' does not alone make a poem, and that a poem occurs only when that quality finds itself in conjunction with one or another of the traditional forms.

But there seems little point in insisting upon limits which poets themselves have set aside. 'Free verse', 'open form', 'field' poems, poems in prose, 'open' sonnets – though these developments certainly do not rule out the use of traditional forms, rhyme schemes and metres, they do tend to make any rigorous observance of old measures seem like an exercise in literary pastiche – just as a modern musician writing in the style of Mozart, however brilliantly, would seem to be engaged more in a stylistic exercise than in the composition of new and original music.

What I think we have to say is that a poem will have form, but that *the form which matters* (and this will be true even of, say, a traditional sonnet) is the one which is unique to that poem; and that a poem is a piece of writing in any form which manifests throughout, and in its unity, the quality of poetry. We have to say further, that the quality of poetry will be achieved from time to time in compositions which by intention (a novel) or failure (some of Ezra Pound's *Cantos*), do not amount as a whole to poems. And we have to recognize that often in the present day, readers and critics find the fragmentary but brilliant flashes of gold in the seam of rock of greater human and even semantic interest than the extracted and crafted ore. This is neither to be regretted nor applauded; it is simply a fact – an important fact – of literary life in our time.

Of course that begs the question of what is the quality of poetry. But we can (once again) walk around it, attempting to describe if not to define. That something is to be seen as 'poetry' will depend on a consensus of readers over a period of time.

Poems exhibit in their writing some quality – force, intensity, density, texture, incandescence – which makes them exceptional. The language seems to have a life beyond its most obvious function, which is to 'mean'. Reading it is an experience demanding and receiving more of the reader than is the case with a non-poetic text. But all of that is true of most texts which are literary as distinct from those texts which are not. So we have, really, a spectrum of literary texts from the least to the most intense, from the least to the most densely textured, from the least to the most semantically active and alive with a talent for composition, and somewhere along that spectrum we pass into the realm of 'poetry'. Traditional forms have given an illusion of marking a clear dividing line between the one and the other, but all they signal really is an intention on the part of the writer. The distinction of poetry, as already observed, resides more in a quality of language than in a measurable form.

One of its commonest features is said to be imagery – and I will come back to that, in part to agree, in part to question. But I think perhaps less challenge-able as an inevitable feature of poetic language is economy, and this is so even in a writer like Shakespeare, where at a glance what we appear to have is linguistic opulence, words in excess of the needs of the statement. We are told frequently that economy is a stylistic virtue; that 'brevity is the soul of wit' – and so on. If that is the case (and I think it is), it must be for a better reason than that generations of teachers and critics have said so. And the reason is probably relatively simple. If all of whatever was intended in twelve words – evocation, meaning, emotion, aural and visual effect – can be conveyed in eight, then those eight words, because they are working harder, doing more, will seem more active, energetic, muscular, radioactive (any one of a number of metaphors will make the point) than the twelve doing the same work. And this has the paradoxical effect of making us more rather than less aware of language as language. The language does its work; but it exists also for its own sake and in its own right. When that happens we begin to feel the action of poetry.

Many of the most obvious and exhilarating examples of this in English are found in Shakespeare. In *Antony and Cleopatra*, Caesar reflects on the fickleness of the populace who want a leader only before they have him and after they lose him:

> It hath been taught us from the primal state
> That he which is was wish'd until he were;
> And the ebb'd man, ne'er lov'd till ne'er worth love,
> Comes dear'd, by being lack'd.
>
> (I. iv. 41-4)

The lines say what the dramatic moment requires them to say, but in a way so peculiar and compacted that to anyone sensitive to language the words have a life much more memorable than their meaning alone will account for. But then, as if to double up on the effect, the speech offers an image of the fickleness of the crowd ('this common body') moving with the 'tide' like a 'flag' (said by the Shakespeare commentaries to be an iris, as indeed it is – but can we not equally read it as a flag in the more obvious sense?) in a stream –

> This common body
> Like to a vagabond flag upon a stream
> Goes to and back, lackeying the varying tide
> To rot itself with motion.
>
> (I. iv. 44–7)

Here again it is not simply the 'meaning' that accounts for the 'poetry'; but neither alone does the image, though the image is beautiful and succinctly apposite. Again there is a sense of energy springing out of economy; and also a music in the way the words echo and half-imitate one another's sounds – 'vagabond flag upon'; 'back, lackeying'; 'lackeying the varying'. The life of the language is so intense it not only serves meaning, it also stands apart from meaning.

One of the most interesting examples, or series of examples, illustrating a failure by later poets to recognize what it is in Shakespeare's poetry that accounts for its linguistic richness is to be found in the many nineteenth-century poetic dramas which attempt to imitate him. Most make the mistake of adding 'imagery' more and more lavishly to the basic statement. That imagery is decoration laid on, rather than something growing inevitably out of the drama. The language is static and the effect artificial. The lines seem to call attention to themselves rather than to express a character or a situation. They are 'poetic' in the bad sense.

In the present century, although a great deal of thought has been given to the nature, status and function of the poetic image, the emphasis of modernist and postmodern poets on spoken language – an emphasis made more than ever possible by the freeing-up of poetic forms – has reduced the predominance of imagery as a prime element in poetic language. It used to be said (citing Aristotle) that the use of metaphor was a measure of genius, and that a simile was only a weak metaphor, lacking the courage of its convictions. Today it is at least as plausible to reverse the proposition and argue that a metaphor is only a simile laying claim to an exactness it does not possess; and that poetic imagery can too easily become a short-cut. When in doubt that you are achieving 'poetry', lay on some images! In such cases imagery becomes only another artificiality, a form of 'poetic diction' – what Wordsworth called, in a withering phrase, a 'family language of poets' (ed. 1974, p. 131).

I do not mean to suggest that metaphor, with all its subtle variations that are usually gathered under the general heading of 'the poetic image', has had its day. But for the moment, current stylistic practice seems more often than not to suggest that the uniquely 'poetic' element in language lies elsewhere.

Much, perhaps most, poetry works by one or another form of analogy. There is almost always an air of mysteriousness or obscurity at some level. But imagery is not the only way by which language can be made to mean more than it says, or say more than it means. Sometimes the whole poem may seem to suggest, or stand for, a subject nowhere stated in the text, as in William Carlos Williams's famous

> so much depends
> upon
>
> a red wheel
> barrow
>
> glazed with rain
> water
>
> beside the white
> chickens.
>   (ed. 1976, p. 57)

No imagery there; and *why* so much depends upon the wheel barrow, *what* depends upon it, the poet has not permitted himself to say. What he has ensured is that we have experienced it; and over that primary experience he has in effect hung a sign saying 'This is important'. The colour, the shapes, the shine, the contrasts – these are prior to thought and outlast it. Williams's 'The Red Wheelbarrow' is probably a poem against intellect – or one that puts the intellect in its place; but if it is, we as readers must not merely assent – we must make it so.

Then there are times when the whole poem may seem to contain its opposite, as in Wordsworth's strange lines about the death of Lucy:

> No motion has she now, no force;
>   She neither hears nor sees;
> Rolled round in earth's diurnal course,
>   With rocks, and stones, and trees.
>   (ed. 1977, p. 364)

where the 'force' and 'motion' of the second pair of lines seem at least in part to belong to Lucy, who is said to lack them, but for whom the whole natural world has become a single eternally revolving vault.

Ever since the French Symbolists enunciated it as a principle, there has been a recognition among modern poets that, whether by accident or design, some of the best effects in poetry are achieved by a kind of openness which suggests more than it says, leaving the reader free to engage with the language and discover, or impose, 'meaning'. Poems mean many different things to different readers. Some readings may be wrong because they are perverse, silly, or ignore something of prime importance; but many different readings may be right, because one half of any reading is the reader. If one reading alone is unambiguously and unchallengeably right, we may say we are not dealing with a poetic text. It is this fact which renders so many 'definitive' academic readings, dismissive of all others, inevitably absurd.

The romantic poets quarrelled with their Augustan predecessors about what was called 'poetic diction' – whether there was or was not a restricted language appropriate to poetry. The attempt was to get rid of literary conventions and get back closer to the living language. As romantic poetry itself became, through the nineteenth century, a set of conventions there was yet another rebellion in the name of spoken language – that of the twentieth-century modernists.

Throughout this period there has also been an ever greater insistence upon particularity, concretion, in poetic language. For Dr Johnson, as for most literary theorists and poets of the eighteenth century, the purpose of poetry was to offer, in verse as near to impeccable as could be, general truths. As the faith in general truths has diminished, so the insistence upon the mysteriousness and at the same time the particularity of poetry has increased. Poetry deals in the concrete, not in abstract ideas, which belong to philosophy and other forms of prose discourse. 'No ideas but in things', William Carlos Williams insists (1983, p. 6) – a statement nicely matched by his wheelbarrow poem. And even poets like W. H. Auden and Philip Larkin who were, or became, relatively conservative in their attitude to poetic form, and who seem at times to versify abstract ideas, are really dramatizers of a position rather than its proponents. Along with the 'idea' in their poems goes the dramatized persona, its upholder, to whom various readers are free variously to respond.

Language refers, 'means', denotes, points to what exists outside and beyond itself. On the other hand language has a texture of its own. It has sound, literally; and metaphorically it has colour, taste, smell and feel. It also evokes sense impressions through meaning. It forms itself – or is formed – into grammatical structures which have symmetry and can have beauty independent of the meanings and references which they also create. In the breaking or unusual compression of the normal decorums of syntax, language can enact personality, muscularity, restlessness, anxiety. By imposing itself upon the breathing of the reader it can have a direct physical effect matching that upon mind and imagination. There is in fact such complex potential in the operations of language that it is almost impossible to be simultaneously conscious of all the things a rich poetic text is doing at any one moment. We may receive the whole operation in a single experience; and we may go back and take it apart, making ourselves conscious of all that it contained. What I think is not possible is to receive the full impression and be fully conscious of it at the same time – any more than it is possible to watch a movie and at the same time be aware of it frame by frame.

How then is such a complex operation achieved by the poet? It happens, it seems, most often by a kind of speeding up of mental processes, and it is this, I suppose, which poets have traditionally called 'inspiration'. Because in this kind of writing something is achieved that could not be produced by means of fully conscious and controlled effort, poets have tended to describe the experience magically – the feeling, for example, of being 'breathed through' by the divine spirit, or possessed by the Muse. T. S. Eliot once called it demonic possession, describing his experience in completing the final section of *The Waste Land* (see Eliot, 1957). Of course, not all poetry is 'inspired'. Among twentieth-century poets, both W. B. Yeats and Dylan Thomas laboured their poems through many painful drafts. But one way or another an exceptional text seems to require an exceptional state of being. It is not something to be achieved simply by acts of will; and poets develop ways with themselves of achieving the necessary condition. This means in turn that poetry is a highly personal art, and one that calls not merely for invention but for that higher faculty which the romantics called imagination.

Yet it has been traditionally thought of as a mimetic art – an art which 'imitates', or holds a mirror up to nature. Both these views – the personal and the mimetic – are surely correct. When the sense of a particular viewer disappears – when, as Yeats says, the poet vanishes into the quicksilver at the back of the mirror – our desire that the view should be particular, peculiar, per onal, in fact unique, may go unsatisfied. On the other hand (and this may happen if poetry goes too far in the direction of a surreal or fantastic vision, or in the case of a poet like John Ashbery whose grammar parodies many meanings but denies all of them any warrant), when the poet insists so much upon the uniqueness if his vision that we begin to lose all sense of a common world shared by reader and writer, then equally, if the poetry is not sustained by some quirk of fashion, or as that fashion passes, the call will be for more mirror and less imagining. These are poles between which the poetic pendulum inevitably and always swings.

From these opposite and necessary ends of the argument come the two seeming contradictory but really reconcilable truisms about poetry: that it deals in truth ('The true poets must be truthful', Wilfred Owen said – ed. 1955, p. 41), and that it deals in falsity ('the truest poetry is the most feigning', Shakespeare has the Clown say in *As You Like It*, III, iii). Plato's position, at least in the *Republic*, is rather odd, in that he castigates – in fact casts out – the poets, not for excesses of imagination but because their mimesis is of the real world which is necessarily itself only an image of the Ideal. Poetry is a copy of a copy and the poet is punished for his fidelity to, in Wallace Stevens's phrase, 'things as they are' ('The Man with the Blue Guitar', ed. 1955, p. 165).

Matthew Arnold's view was that poetry would gradually take over a large part of the ground occupied by religion. T. S. Eliot mocked Arnold for this ([1930] 1951, p. 434); but if we can broaden the term 'poetry' and include all the arts, then it could be said that Arnold's prediction has been proved right. The practice of formal religion in Western society has declined in the past hundred years, while for a sizeable section of the population (though still perhaps a minority) the arts – music, literature, painting, theatre, one or all of these – represent man's highest intellectual and spiritual achievements and are the source of anything from relaxation and superior entertainment through to enlightenment and exaltation.

On the other hand, since Arnold's time the public for poetry has seemed to decline markedly, and its dissemination has in a significant degree become part of the function of university English Departments. Though it might be argued that no one who cares about poetry could do other than welcome this development, and even that English studies have saved poetry from extinction, there is room for a good deal of doubt. Academics have more and more seemed to be the possessors of the necessary keys of entry to a mysterious and difficult art; and at the same time, by 'teaching' poetry and examining students on their reading of it, they have invaded, and in many cases laid waste to, what perhaps ought to be an inviolable private domain. Poetry has become an area of specialist knowledge, like physics or higher mathematics, and teachers in schools seem less and less willing to treat it as a natural part of a general curriculum. So where it appears university studies have helped poetry, they may also have done it harm.

There must also be a question as to whether the decline in a potential audience for poetry since the nineteenth century is as absolute as it appears. Dylan Thomas, much of whose work was so obscure it seemed unimaginable that it could ever be popular, had a huge following on both sides of the Atlantic in the early 1950s. T. S. Eliot, in a different, more decorous way, must have achieved very considerable sales over a lifetime. In America, Allen Ginsberg in the 1960s and 1970s revived the figure of the popular public bard. In London in 1965 a poetry reading which included Ginsberg on the programme filled the Albert Hall and many were turned away. Yet that was also the period when John Betjeman, a totally different kind of poet, was becoming a household name. More recently in Britain, Craig Raine, poet and poetry editor at Eliot's old firm Faber & Faber, has again given poetry a public face. In fact it is probably wrong to think of 'the public' for poetry. There are a number of publics for it, different and overlapping.

Meanwhile current critical theory has made what might be seen as the latest attempt to deprive those words 'poet' and 'poetry' of the power we began by discussing. It tells us that the poet is irrelevant – indeed in some sense non-existent; and that there is not a 'poem' but a 'text'. When reader and text are joined, the poem comes into being, uniquely. Thus the text itself in its unread state is less important than what is made of it when it is read – and there is no hierarchy of texts.

This view, which within its limits makes perfectly good sense, is usually presented as a kind of liberation – a rebellion against the authority of all the academic criticism and commentary which stands in the way of every fresh new reading. So it may be; but it is also a rebellion of the academic against the authority of literature. If both poet and poem are denied primary importance then the critic has written himself into the position of primacy. The significant creative skill passes from poet to reader, and is demonstrated in what the critic makes of the text.

Poetry, however, is so intrinsic and inevitable an upshot of linguistic life and consciousness, it will surely survive in one form or another, whatever happens to it in the marketplace, and in the minds and writings of those who are its critics and theorists.

FURTHER READING

Fowler, Alastair (1982) *Kinds of Literature*, Clarendon Press, Oxford

Fussell, Paul (1965) *Poetic Meter and Poetic Form*, Random House, New York

Hardy, Barbara (1977) *The Advantage of Lyric*, Athlone Press, London

Leech, Geoffrey (1969) *A Linguistic Guide to English Poetry*, Longman, London

Nowottny, Winifred (1962) *The Language Poets Use*, Athlone Press, London

Preminger, Alex (1975) *The Princeton Encyclopedia of Poetry and Poetics*, enlarged edn, Macmillan, London

Rosenthal, M. L. (1987) *The Poet's Art*, Norton, New York

Scully, J. (ed.) (1966) *Modern Poets on Modern Poetry*, Collins, London

Shelley, Percy Bysshe (1954) *Defence of Poetry*. In *Shelley's Prose*, edited by David Lee Clark, University of New Mexico Press, Albuquerque, pp. 275–97 [essay first published 1821]

Stead, C. K. (1964) *The New Poetic*, Hutchinson, London

Valéry, Paul (1958) *The Art of Poetry*, translated by Denise Folliot (vol. 7 of *The Collected Works of Paul Valéry*, edited by Jackson Matthews), Pantheon Books, New York

Wordsworth, William (1974) 'Preface to the *Lyrical Ballads*'. In *The Prose Works of William Wordsworth*, vol. 1, edited by W. J. B. Owen and Jane Worthington Smyser, Clarendon Press, Oxford, pp. 118–59 [essay first published 1800]

Yeats, W. B. (1959) 'Per Amica Silentia Lunae'. In W. B. Yeats, *Mythologies*, Macmillan, London [essay first published 1918]

ADDITIONAL WORKS CITED

Arnold, Matthew (1938) 'The Study of Poetry'. In Matthew Arnold, *Essays in Criticism: Second Series*, edited by S. R. Littlewood, Macmillan, London, pp. 1–40 [essay first published 1888]

Eliot, T. S. (1928) 'Preface'. In T. S. Eliot, *The Sacred Wood*, 2nd edn, Faber & Faber, London, pp. vii–x

——(1951) 'Arnold and Pater'. In T. S. Eliot, *Selected Essays*, 3rd edn, Faber & Faber, London, pp. 431–43 [essay first published 1930]

——(1957) 'The Three Voices of Poetry'. In T. S. Eliot, *On Poetry and Poets*, Faber & Faber, London, pp. 89–102 [essay first published 1953]

Owen, Wilfred (1955) *The Poems of Wilfred Owen*, edited by Edmund Blunden, Chatto & Windus, London

Stevens, Wallace (1955) *The Collected Poems of Wallace Stevens*, Faber & Faber, London

Williams, William Carlos (1976) 'The Red Wheelbarrow'. In *William Carlos Williams: Selected Poems*, edited by Charles Tomlinson, Penguin, Harmondsworth [poem first published 1923]

——(1983) *Paterson*, Penguin, Harmondsworth [first published 1946–58]

Wordsworth, William (1977) *Poems*, vol. 1, edited by John O. Hayden, Penguin, Harmondsworth

11

EPIC AND ROMANCE

MICHAEL O'CONNELL

Throughout most of Western literary history, until the rise of the novel, epic and romance were the dominant forms of extended narrative. Epic, represented supremely by the *Iliad* and the *Odyssey* of Homer and the *Aeneid* of Virgil, held pride of place both in terms of its antiquity and a general sense of its seriousness in conveying the values of a civilization. The accomplishment represented by the classical epics meant that the genre itself was understood as the most ambitious to be undertaken by a poet, that a successful epic would be the artistic culmination of a civilization. Romance, on the other hand, has been the Proteus, the great shape-shifter, of narrative. If epic has been defined by its subject-matter and, to a certain extent, by the form of the three classical examples, romance has proved much harder to pin down. No one subject-matter can be said to characterize it, no 'classic' text gave it shape, no prestigious critical discussion considered its elements and form, as Aristotle's *Poetics* did for epic and tragedy. Northrop Frye, in *The Secular Scripture* (1976), believes romance to be the very ground of narrative, but he cannot be said so much to have finally bound this Proteus as to have relished its many tricks. It might be argued on the basis of etymology that for the past three centuries romance has turned itself into the novel; in using a single word for both, Italian (*il romanzo*), French (*le roman*), and German (*der Roman*) all identify the romance with the novel. English, of course, insists on the distinction, and when the term 'romance' is used in the context of discussions of the novel, it generally implies a narrative less tied to the realism of incident, plot or character thought proper to that genre. But recent discussion of the origins of the novel, especially that by Michael McKeon (1987), suggests its inextricable ties to romance and the naïveté of any simple distinction between the two.

Aristotle defined epic as a representation in dignified verse of serious actions (*Poetics* 5). Typically these serious actions have concerned war; a synonym for epic has been heroic poetry, the heroism defined by a martial ethos. This is obviously true of the Homeric poems, and while military heroism is problematized in the *Aeneid*, it is clear there, too, that valour and might are the ground upon which more complex values are developed. Twentieth-century critics have made a distinction between 'primary' epics and those they have termed 'secondary'. Primary epics are poems that have come more or less directly out of a culture in which the heroic military ethos is still dominant, the eighth-century BC world of Homer, the Anglo-Saxon England of *Beowulf*, and the twelfth-century Spain and France of the *Poema de mio Cid* and the *Chanson de Roland*. This does not mean that the poet is contemporary with the events and heroes he sings of; in all these examples (with the exception of the Spanish poem), the wars and exploits predate the poet by at least two centuries. In fact there is good reason to believe that the poets were memorializing cultures that were passing away even as they celebrated them. The *Beowulf* poet, for example, portrays Scandinavian culture some two centuries earlier (in so far as it can be dated), but most scholars believe him to have been a Christian. Still, the poet of primary epic cultivates a sense of anonymity about himself and the world he inhabits and asks his listeners to accept the values of the heroes of his song. Such a poet typically is anonymous, even Homer being nothing more than a name and a set of legends. The poems may not necessarily come from a pre-literate culture, but most elements of them suggest that they were meant for oral delivery.

Secondary epics are composed by poets of highly literate cultures with developed literary traditions in which primary epic stands in a venerated position. The social and political world of these poets has become too complex for a martial ethos to be accepted simply and uncritically; typically, too, the aristocratic class in which the ethos inhered has either ceased to exist or ceased to be functional. The great original of secondary epic is the *Aeneid*, which takes as its model the two Homeric poems but uses them to establish a story of Roman origins. The world in which Virgil was writing had just emerged from the civil wars attendant on the collapse of the Roman republic and the establishment of Augustus' regime. Twentieth-century criticism has emphasized the ambiguity of Virgil's portrayal of military power; on the one hand it appears necessary for the founding of Rome and the conquest of Latium, but on the other it is the violence that has destroyed Troy and sweeps before it the ancient Italic culture that existed before the Trojans' arrival. Throughout one senses that Virgil intends the reader to understand a relation to his contemporary world, that the martial violence of civil war has also had its terrible costs, that the present order rests upon a bloodstained foundation. If Milton's *Paradise Lost* (1667) is the final epic that establishes its generic status unambiguously, it is scarcely less unambiguous in its overturning of the military ethos bound up with the genre. Milton's 'Iliad' is the parodic War in Heaven of Books V and VI in which the battles between the good and the fallen angels escalate into the absurdity of cosmic violence which cannot kill any of the participants. In the Proem to Book IX, as he asserts that his own argument is 'Not less but more heroic than the wrath/ Of stern Achilles', Milton rejects war as a subject, 'hitherto the only argument Heroic deemed', and laments that 'the better fortitude/ Of patience and heroic martyrdom' has remained unsung. In doing so he grandly brushes aside the traditional topoi of epic in favour of his own 'higher argument' of humanity's fall and redemption. After Milton all narrative that asserts some continuity with the epic tradition, whether Pope's *Dunciad* (1743), Wordsworth's *Prelude* (1805, 1850) or Joyce's *Ulysses* (1922), will assume an ironic relation to the martial ethos of primary epic.

Epic has most frequently been labelled a *genre* of narrative poetry by twentieth-century criticism. By genre theorists have meant to imply both a particular kind of literary structure and a historical relation to the social and cultural conditions which gave it birth. As extended narratives on heroic themes, however, epics of widely separated times and places have seemed to share many characteristics; they derive from similar aristocratic ideologies and express, in some measure, a martial ethos. Moreover the cultural potency of the Homeric poems in antiquity and the *Aeneid* from antiquity through the Renaissance gave them a normative status in European literature; for secondary epic the literary tradition inhering in these poems became a powerful cultural determinant supplementing political and historical conditions. For these reasons epic has appeared sufficiently stable and influential as a narrative kind to be considered a genre.

For romance, as the term is currently used, there appears no such stable identity; no common ideology, subject-matter or normative text can be seen to define it as a genre. Only when romance is paired with an adjective, as in 'chivalric' or 'Arthurian romance', 'Greek romance', 'pastoral romance', or 'gothic romance', is it generally considered a genre, for in these cases groups of texts with historical connections are associated. In its original usage, however, as it defined a group of texts that arose in the context of twelfth-century French feudalism, the term did indeed define a specific genre of narrative. The word was first applied to works written in Old French, which was itself called 'Romans' to distinguish it as a derived language from Latin proper, and hence the term came to denote stories of chivalry in that language. Chrétien de Troyes' five poems (late twelfth century) and Gottfried von Strassburg's German *Tristan und Iseult* (*c.* 1210) are the literary centrepieces of the genre of chivalric romance. The genre came late to England, but it has been estimated that over a hundred examples exist, the best of which is *Sir Gawain and the Green Knight* (*c.* 1375). Malory's late fifteenth-century translation, collection and extension of the romances, the *Morte d'Arthur*, may be considered as the last version of the genre properly understood. By the late seventeenth century the term came to be applied more generally to long works of fiction whose narrative and characterization resembled the chivalric tales in evading the realism of other prose fiction. This latter usage in turn has led twentieth-century critics, somewhat anachronistically, to label as romances the prose fiction of the second and third centuries AD, the *Aethiopica* of Heliodurus, the *Leucippe and Cleitophon* of Achilles Tatius, the *Daphnis and Chloe* of Longus in Greek and even *The Golden Ass* of Apuleius in Latin. The ultimate source for Shakespeare's *Pericles*, the anonymous *History of Apollonius, King of Tyre* (in Latin but possibly derived from a Greek original), is another example of this genre of 'Greek romance'. In the sixteenth century Jorge de Montemayor would write his Spanish *Diana* and Sir Philip Sidney the *Arcadia* under the influences of these ancient romances. The final period of Shakespeare's dramatic activity also falls under the spell of this type of narrative; twentieth-century criticism has chosen to designate the tragi-comedies he wrote between 1608 and 1611, *Pericles, Cymbeline, The Winter's Tale* and *The Tempest*, his 'late romances'. In addition, the Renaissance saw the revival of the tradition of the chivalric romance, what might be termed 'secondary romance', in Boiardo's *Orlando Innamorato* (1483) and its great successor, the *Orlando Furioso* (1516, 1521, 1532) of Ariosto. Following extended critical discussion of the competing claims of epic and romance in the middle of the sixteenth century, Tasso self-consciously melded this type of literary romance to epic in his *Gerusalemme Liberata* (1581). Spenser produced the supreme example in English of this kind of 'secondary romance' in *The Faerie Queene* (1590, 1596), a poem which combines romance structure and subject-matter with epic intentions of engaging history and the political moment.

Although romance has been much discussed in late twentieth-century criticism, a comprehensive account of its nature is yet to be written. Handbook descriptions of romance have spoken most frequently of a narrative defined by marvels, magic, strange or exotic settings, and characterization that tends toward the ideal rather than the realistic. The complexity, indeed the unpredictability, of the romance plot is often noted as well. Northrop Frye, in *Anatomy of Criticism* (1957), termed romance a *mode*, a word implying a broader category than genre, one abstracted from the question of historicity. Mode, in fact, may be understood as roughly the equivalent of genre but with the significant omission of its relation to actual social and cultural conditions. In twentieth-century critical practice 'romance' has most often been used not so much to define a work as to describe elements in a narrative, motifs, mood, types of characters, plot situations and the like. The two most influential theoretical treatments, by Frye and by Fredric Jameson, have reached antithetical conclusions on its nature and its appeal. For Frye romance is 'the structural core of all fiction'; a direct descendant of folk-tale, romance 'brings us closer than any other aspect of literature to the sense of fiction, considered as a whole, as the epic of the creature, man's vision of his own life as a quest' (1976, p. 15). Frye's sense of romance is essentially ahistorical; the context of a particular romance is other romances, and a critic of romance is 'very quickly led from what the individual work says to what the entire convention it belongs to is saying through the work' (1976, p. 60). He sees the structure of romance as a cyclical movement that involves descent into a night world, a place symbolic of death, alienation or psychic paralysis, then a return to an idyllic world of restored life and reintegration, expressed frequently in a marriage. What is at issue is human identity, confusion or loss of it in the descent and a recovery of true identity in the ascent and return. It is this pattern that leads Frye to identify ancient romances with the medieval and in turn to identify both with novelistic 'romances' of the past three centuries. To Frye romance differs from epic and tragedy in that heroism is most frequently understood in terms of suffering; a suffering, enduring heroine will often have more active power in romance than the hero, or the male hero must allow himself to be acted upon. Frye notes how close this is to the Christian ethos, whose ascendancy largely parallels that of romance. But in spite of close connections between 'the imaginative universe' of romance and Christianity, he does not believe there is a causal connection. Rather romance is the 'secular scripture', analogous to the biblical scriptures which convey Christian myth, but antedating it, fabulous and not tied to belief, and able to supersede it, he believes, in a humanistic 'recovery of myth'.

Jameson's Marxist analysis of romance responds directly to the ahistoricism of Frye's construction of the mode, but is tied to a larger project of understanding the operation of genre historically as a complex of elements at work in the sign system of a literary text. Jameson agrees with Frye in seeing romance as projecting a particular kind of world, but it is the projection itself that he sees as having significance:

> Romance is that form in which the *world-ness* of *world* reveals itself. . . . for romance as a literary form is that event in which world in the technical sense of the transcendental horizon of my experience becomes precisely visible as something like an innerworldly object in its own right, taking on the shape of *world* in the popular sense of nature, landscape, and so forth.
>
> (1975, p. 142)

Within the 'world' projected by romance Jameson calls attention to the binary division of good and evil, which he wants to historicize as a division between the self and the Other; he understands evil as that which is radically different from one's self, the stranger, the barbarian, whatever is 'alien, different, strange, unclean, unfamiliar' (1981, p. 115). Hence the division between good and evil, which he believes (perhaps mistakenly) is transcended in other genres (e.g. tragedy and comedy), represents a survival of a 'magical thought mode' in romance, 'one which springs from a precapitalist, essentially agricultural way of life' (1975, p. 141). Outside a purely Marxist structure of analysis, this understanding of evil as derived simply from Otherness may seem curiously naïve to many readers. But Jameson uses it to derive romance 'in its original strong form' from the needs of the feudal nobility in the twelfth century to define itself against what opposes it and yet recognize its resemblance to that opposition. Its persistence as a mode comes from 'substitutions, adaptations, and appropriations' which it makes in altered historical circumstances of the 'raw materials of magic and Otherness' that had come from its original socio-economic context (1981, p. 131). His penetrating discussion of these 'substitutions, adaptations, and appropriations' in nineteenth- and twentieth-century novels (including *I Promessi Sposi*, 1827, and *La Chartreuse de Parme*, 1839) fills in the missing historicity of Frye's construction of romance and serves to underscore the persistence of romance, even if the ultimate question *why* it should persist remains resistant to historicist analysis. Still, Jameson's main purpose is to create a more flexible understanding of genre in which a text is seen not as given meaning by participation in a single genre but as composed of 'structurally contradictory or heterogeneous elements, generic patterns and discourses' (1981, p. 141). In this way genre theory projects a model of the coexistence or tension between several generic modes or strands in a text, and analysis aims to comprehend generic categories not as defining absolutes but as *ad hoc* constructs.

Making use of this sense of genre, one can understand epic and romance not as distinct narrative possibilities but as inextricably bound up in one another. If we follow Frye in abstracting romance from the social conditions of twelfth-century feudalism that gave rise to a specific genre of chivalric romance and treat it instead as narrative mode, even the *Odyssey* can appear to have as much in common with romance structures as it does with epic. At the level of plot it is a poem defined by adventures and the marvellous; moreover, its action is a double quest, a son's quest for his father and the father's quest for son and wife. The poem presupposes the heroic military ethos of the *Iliad*, but its encounters are more frequently ones involving individual cunning and endurance; in a sense the virtues of the warriors at Troy begin to seem obsolescent in the struggle of Odysseus. The focus of the poem on individual identity, particularly in the return to an identity that had been obscured by the warrior ethos, seems also characteristic of the concerns of romance. In short, though we lack knowledge of the specific non-epic genres that surrounded the Homeric poems, we can hypothesize narratives analogous to what we understand as romance that countered epic values or rendered them problematic.

The coalescence of epic and romance in the great narrative poems of the sixteenth century, *Orlando Furioso*, *Gerusalemme Liberata*, *Os Lusiadas* and *The Faerie Queene*, and the struggle of the theorists of the period over the distinction between epic and romance also point to the need to conceptualize competing narrative possibilities rather than a rigid separation between them. Giovambattista Giraldi-Cintio, in his *Discorsi intorno al comporre dei romanzi* (1554), the first of the Renaissance theorists to distinguish romance from the ancient epics, was well aware of the separate origins of romance in French and Spanish chivalric narratives. He is everywhere attentive to the formal distinctions between romance as practised by Boiardo and Ariosto and the epics of Homer and Virgil, not only the use of a rhymed stanzas and the divisions into cantos but the multiplicity of plots and the interwoven narrative structure of romance. For him the *romanzi* are modern poems which derive their characteristics from the Italian language and the differing customs of contemporary court society. But he assumes throughout an essential similarity between ancient epic and modern romance. Both are types of the heroic poem and make use of similar heroes, similar plot material, poetic devices, ornamentation, and so forth. In practice he moves freely back and forth between ancient narrative and the romances to illustrate his directives for the composition of romance. Such differences as he finds are formal: multiplicity of heroes and plot in romance over against the unity of ancient epic. But in its greater variety of plot incident and in its mixing of 'high' and 'low' characters he, like other theorists of the period, posits the similarity of the *Odyssey* to modern romance. Tasso, in his *Discorsi dell'arte poetica* (1587, but written in the 1560s, before publication of the *Gerusalemme Liberata*), goes even further in asserting the essential unity of romance and epic. He acknowledges that some have seen multiplicity of plot as suggesting that the *romanzo* is a different genre (*specie*) from epic. But because both imitate the magnanimous deeds of heroic figures and both use the same means of narrative (as opposed to scenic representation), they are essentially the same. Unity of action, moreover, is important to both. Tasso does not praise the multiplicity of Ariosto's romance; in so far as Ariosto fails to achieve unity, his poem is lacking, but this is not because romance is a different genre following different internal rules from epic. He argues as he does in part to establish his own practice in the *Gerusalemme Liberata*, in which epic and romance elements have been melded together with more theoretical self-consciousness than Ariosto attempted.

The greater cultural prestige of epic is implicit throughout the critical discussions of the sixteenth century, so that critics either reject romance elements as less worthy or attempt, as Giraldi-Cintio and Tasso do, to subsume romance within epic in a more general sense of the 'heroic poem'. The prestige of epic rested in part on the half-recognized way Virgil was understood to have encompassed the national and political in the *Aeneid*. The Roman poet had adapted the elements of Homeric epic to a historical design that not only tied a contemporary patron to a fictional ancestor but did so within a myth that purports to underlie the structures of political power. Virgil thus founded and elaborated the myth upon which the Augustan order could rest; in doing so he gave body to traditions, perhaps Etruscan, of origins from Asia Minor. But even more significantly he related these traditions to contemporary need and created an imaginative structure that answered the needs of a political world torn by civil war and an absolutism clothed in republican structures. No work of literature, perhaps no other imaginative work of the Western tradition, has ever responded so fully to a historical and political moment. In doing so Virgil was confirming epic in its central role as a narrative that engages the central values and political concerns of a society. By contrast, romance, in its feudal origins, is preoccupied by the individual and status relations within a fragmented political world. In a discussion of the ideology of medieval English romance Stephen Knight (1986) has recently noted that 'the absence of centralized state power is the overarching political factor that typifies the world of feudal relations'. In its focus on the solitary knight, romance appears unable or unwilling to conceptualize a larger political world. This difference of concentration, epic on a larger political context and romance on the individual psyche, suggests why the two became bound up with one another in the early modern period.

The rise of nation states extended to poets the challenge of celebrating national and historical experience. Ariosto's position as court poet in a culturally distinguished but politically insignificant duchy explains to some extent the circumscribed and largely ironic character of the epic elements within the *Orlando Furioso*. The main epic element of Ariosto's design rests in the fiction that he was singing the ancestry of his Ferrarese patrons, the Este, as Virgil had established in Aeneas the ancestry of the Julian dynasty. But he surrounds this fiction with an element of amused irony and in so doing allows us to see why he writes 'secondary romance' rather than epic, indeed why the mix of romance and epic motifs is an unequal one in the *Orlando Furioso*. Given the political character of Italy in the sixteenth century, any serious epic intentions would appear to have been doomed to either formalism or ironic expression. Patricia Parker (1979) has suggested that Ariosto self-consciously thematizes the concerns of romance through a narrative that defers closure and celebrates the wanderings (*errori*) of its knights. He thus appears to set his poem against the purposefulness, and perhaps the nationalism, of epic and to create an aesthetic space that seeks to avoid deep commitment to the relations of power. Tasso, also patronized by the Este at the court of Ferrara, attempted to contain romance within the confines of epic in the *Gerusalemme Liberata*, in a sense to reverse the positions they had held in the *Orlando Furioso*. To do so he chose a historical subject, the First Crusade, and in Goffredo created a hero who would express the fervour and commitment of Counter-Reformation Catholicism. In the poem the romance elements, centred primarily in Rinaldo (also the fictional ancestor of the Este), express the *errori*, in both senses, that keep him from achieving the epic goals. The poem is undeniably successful in its formal integration of romance within an epic structure. And yet as epic its political dimension remains imperfectly realized, even puzzling. In its subject-matter the poem appears to want to gesture out toward the contemporary victory at Lepanto, but if it does so, it is with such reticence that the meaning of such gesture remains obscure, unrealized. Instead it is the romance element that for most readers has remained most memorable in the poem.

To find a narrative poem in the sixteenth century that celebrates historical accomplishment in unambiguously epic terms, one would need to turn to the Portuguese epic, *Os Lusiadas* (1572), of Luis de Camoëns. Here the subject matter of Vasco da Gama's voyage to the East becomes a vehicle of national celebration on a scale that, if not Virgilian, at least has sufficient amplitude to have become the centrepiece of a language and a literature. But like other 'heroic' narrative in the Renaissance, it too must be understood as admitting romance into epic intentions. 'Romance' becomes a digressive element within the epic narrative that deflects both hero and poet from the accomplishment of the heroic work of imperial conquest and imperial celebration. Recently David Quint (1985) has argued that romance represents a mercantile ethos that runs implicitly counter to the dominant aristocratic ethos expressed through the epic narrative. However one characterizes these romance elements, it is clear they conflict with the national dimension of the poem expressed in its epic character.

Spenser's *Faerie Queene* is the most prominent example in English in which romance and epic have been drawn together in a 'heroic' narrative. And yet unlike the Italian poems that were his primary models (and, of them, principally Ariosto's), he does not for the most part derive meaning from the relation, or competition, of romance and epic. Instead he can give significance to the elements of romance through the highly flexible symbolic system, the allegory, that emerges from them. At the same time Spenser intends a political and nationalist dimension for his poem that would appear the proper end of epic; unlike the Italian poets he writes in a political context in which such a dimen-sion was possible, indeed almost inevitable. Given his desire to celebrate Elizabeth and the nation, it may appear strange that he did not choose to write in a more insistently epic vein, in, say, the manner of Camoëns. But in this the fact that the sovereign was a woman no doubt complicated the choice of historical subject and made the structural and narrative multiplicity of romance seem more able to accommodate the kind of refracted political dimension the age seemed to require. Beginning with pastoral eclogues in *The Shepheardes Calender* (1579) and imitating the opening of the *Aeneid* in *The Faerie Queene*, Spenser clearly wished to be understood as imitating Virgilian epic, particularly in its engagement with contemporary history. In the 'Letter to Ralegh' which prefaced the first edition of the poem, he says he intends to portray the Queen allegorically in the figure of the Faery Queen and her kingdom in Faeryland, adding: 'And yet in some places els, I doe otherwise shadow her.' In practice he refracts the figure of Elizabeth into Una, Belphoebe, Britomart and Mercilla as well as the unrealized Gloriana, some of them active heroines, some passive foci of particular royal virtues. The epic element of his allegorical romance resides in allusion to the historical from within the fiction, much as Virgil was understood to allude to his contemporary world. In Book V ('The Legend of Justice') this motif of epic engagement with power becomes particularly intense, even though Spenser maintains a romance structure and manner. Jameson's suggestion of seeing genre as a flexible index of the concerns of a narrative is particularly useful with *The Faerie Queene*, where romance and epic mingle throughout and in which a growing personalism in the final completed book of the poem is signalled by a turn from epic toward pastoral romance.

Although Milton's specific discussions of the 'heroic poem' do not distinguish between epic and romance – Homer, Virgil, Ariosto, Tasso and Spenser and the subject-matter of their poems are all conflated – it is obvious that *Paradise Lost* represents in every way a conscious turn away from romance and toward the generic specification of epic. He rejects rhyme, stanzas and cantos in favour of the blank verse that he calls an 'ancient liberty recover'd to Heroic Poem from the troublesome and modern bondage of Riming'. He begins *in medias res* and uses narrative flashbacks to structure a narrative that consists of a unified rather than a multiple action. But the most significant – and in some sense paradoxical – choice consists in the subject-matter he selected. When he had asserted his ambitions in heroic poetry in the 1640s, he favoured Arthurian material, a subject that would seem more proper to romance treatment. But his opposition to monarchy and his desire for a 'true' subject, instead of the merely legendary, led him away from Arthur and toward biblical history. Given the tradition of epic, the fall of Adam and Eve would not seem the obvious choice to engage its traditional concerns. And yet by grafting the account of the rebellion of Satan on to the story of the Fall, Milton managed both to give the poem amplitude and, in ways that sometimes sort oddly with his own republicanism, to engage history and the character of human politics. The paradox of *Paradise Lost* as an epic lies not only in its rejection of militarism and an aristocratic ethos but in its movement toward an individual 'paradise within' that expresses Milton's own late estrangement from power. Milton somehow manages to accomplish the thematics of romance within epic form. Nor is the poem without specific feints towards romance. In Book II, for example, the epic encounter between Satan and Death is interrupted by the intervention of Sin that brings on a parodic romance allegory in the manner of Spenser. Later Adam's idealization of Eve and his own rationalizations for joining Eve in the Fall suggest a generic swerve toward romance designed, within the epic context, to evoke suspicion. Even in its overall rejection, romance has a place within the complex generic mix of *Paradise Lost*.

Meanwhile protean romance had transformed itself into prose fiction, where, as McKeon (1987) has recently argued, it is deeply involved in the origins of the novel. In *Don Quixote* (1605, 1615) the specific forms and concerns of romance may be made to appear impermeable to the realism of that new genre. But as romance is naturalized in the next two centuries, it can be found leading a comfortable afterlife not only in the novels of Fielding and Richardson but in eighteenth- and nineteenth-century subgenres of the novel where its existence is acknowledged in terms like gothic romance and historical romance. In the twentieth century science fiction, which has been dubbed 'scientific romance', substitutes future for past and becomes one of its characteristic modern transmutations.

FURTHER READING

Auerbach, Erich (1953) *Mimesis*, Princeton University Press, Princeton

Bakhtin, M. M. (1981) 'Epic and Novel'. In M. M. Bakhtin, *The Dialogic Imagination*, University of Texas Press, Austin

Bowra, C. M. (1945) *From Virgil to Milton*, Macmillan, London

Frye, Northrop (1957) *Anatomy of Criticism*, Princeton University Press, Princeton

——(1976) *The Secular Scripture: A Study of the Structure of Romance*, Harvard University Press, Cambridge

Jameson, Fredric (1975) 'Magical Narratives: Romance as Genre', *New Literary History*, 7, 135–63

——(1981) *The Political Unconscious: Narrative as a Socially Symbolic Act*, Cornell University Press, Ithaca, chap. 2

Knight, Stephen (1986) 'The Social Function of the Middle English Romances'. In David Aers (ed.), *Medieval Literature: Criticism, Ideology, and History*, Harvester, Brighton

McKeon, Michael (1987) *The Origins of the English Novel, 1600–1740*, Johns Hopkins University Press, Baltimore

Parker, Patricia (1979) *Inescapable Romance: Studies in the Poetics of a Mode*, Princeton University Press, Princeton

Quint, David (1985) 'The Boat of Romance and Renaissance Epic'. In Kevin Brownlee and Marina Scordilis Brownlee (eds), *Romance: Generic Transformation from Chrétien de Troyes to Cervantes*, University Press of New England, Hanover

12

LYRIC

DAVID LINDLEY

When Barbara Hardy begins her book *The Advantage of Lyric* with the claim that 'lyric poetry isolates feeling in small compass and so renders it at its most intense' (1977, p. 2), she offers a definition of the lyric genre with which many contemporary readers would feel comfortable, and one which can be paralleled in many places. This definition suggests that lyric is necessarily brief, a record of a momentary experience distilled and compressed to reveal feeling and emotion. But there are other frequently encountered formulations. Northrop Frye, for example, takes up Mill's definition of lyric as an utterance that is 'overheard', and defines it by its 'radical of presentation', where 'the poet, so to speak, turns his back on his listeners, though he may speak for them, and though they may repeat some of his words after him' (1957, p. 250). For Susanne Langer, however, lyric is defined as 'the literary form that depends most directly on pure verbal resources – the sound and evocative power of words, metre, alliteration, rhyme, and other rhythmic devices, associated images, repetitions, archaisms, and grammatical twists. It is the most obviously linguistic creation, and therefore the readiest instance of poesis' (1953, p. 159). Andrew Welsh takes a similar line when he observes that lyric is 'finally less a particular genre of poetry than a distinctive way of organizing language' in which 'there are basic conflicts between the traditional demands of a long poem and the very different organization of a lyric-centred language' (1978, p. 21). Jonathan Culler, from a different critical perspective, concentrates on the rhetorical figure of apostrophe (direct address, as in 'O Rose, thou art sick'). He suggests that we should 'distinguish two forces in poetry, the narrative and apostrophic', and 'that the lyric is characteristically the triumph of the apostrophic' (1981, p. 149).

While these definitions are significantly different in the qualities they see as central to the lyric, they are alike in their attempt to isolate 'lyric' as a category of very general applicability, a mode of utterance or a poetic stance that can be used to bring together poems from different periods and different cultures.

'Lyric' in categorizations of this kind is being used as a 'universal' term. Behind them all, albeit at some distance, lies Aristotle's division of literature into three major kinds. But Sidney's *An Apology for Poetry* offers a very different kind of definition. The lyric poet, in his view, 'with his tuned lyre and well-accorded voice, giveth praise, the reward of virtue, to virtuous acts; ... gives moral precepts, and natural problems; ... sometimes raiseth up his voice to the height of the heavens, in singing the lauds of the immortal God' ([1595] 1965, p. 118). Joshua Poole in 1657 offered an anatomy of the lyric genre as encompassing 'Madrigals, Sonnets, Hymns, Ballets, Odes, whereof some are amorous, some rural, some military, some jovial, made for drollery and drinking' (quoted in Curran, 1986, pp. 24–5). For both these writers lyric is defined and categorized by its aims, its subject-matter or form, and in the later writer particularly an attempt is made to produce both a taxonomy and a hierarchy of the subspecies of the genre.

The variousness of modern statements, and their difference from those of the past, focus clearly the problems that face anyone attempting to write about lyric in general terms or using the term in discussion of individual poems. The most obvious clash is that between attempts to isolate a universal, trans-historical lyric principle, and a conviction that such a search is inherently futile in the face of historical change. On the one side W. R. Johnson states quite firmly: 'I regard this genre as immutable and universal. Its accidents may and always do show extraordinary variations as it unfolds in time, but its substance abides' (1982, p. 2). René Wellek, however, argues that 'one must abandon attempts to define the general nature of the lyric or the lyrical. Nothing beyond generalities of the tritest kind can result from it' (1970, p. 252). But even if one were to accept a historically contingent view of genre it would still leave many problems, for during its history the term 'lyric' has acted on the one hand as a general generic term covering a variety of different sub-genres – pastoral, hymn, ode and the like – but on the other has itself been used as a sub-generic term for a specifically song-like poem, to be differentiated from sonnet or elegy, for example. The assertion of a necessary link between lyric and music (a connection embodied in the most frequent contemporary use of the term to describe words for songs) itself brings complications, since attitudes towards the relationship of the two arts have themselves changed a great deal over the centuries.

Faced with these layers of confusion one might at this point be tempted simply to abandon the term entirely. But yet one finds in much contemporary literary criticism a casual use of the words 'lyric' and 'lyrical' which suggests that some kind of clarification of terms is still necessary. It is an axiom for any act of writing or reading that generic considerations affect both what can be written and how, and also what kinds of response readers can make to different texts. The importance of generic assumptions, whether made explicit or not, can be illustrated by Annabel Patterson's remarks on the critical fortunes of Ben Jonson's poetry. She argues:

> the [lyric] genre continues to be defined normatively, in ways that exclude dozens of poems that their authors once thought of as lyric. The reason for this is clear. The modernist view of lyric as an intense, imaginative form of self-expression or self-consciousness, the most private of all genres, is, of course, a belief derived from Romanticism. As a belief, it is inevitably inhospitable to poems like Jonson's, which derive from a classical tradition, inchoate but powerful, that sanctioned lyric with a social or political content.
>
> (in Hosek and Parker, 1985, p. 151)

Faulty generic assumptions can render literature of the past at worst invisible, at best imperfectly understood. Readers, therefore, must always attempt to render explicit the preconceptions they bring to lyric poetry. For though generic labels seem to aspire to a quasi-scientific objectivity, laying out a map of literature which enables the reader to draw firm boundaries and clear distinctions, they are always terms produced within a particular matrix of discriminations, recording the distinctions particular to culturally produced and historically determined needs. Generic assumptions dictate the nature of the contract between reader and poem, and it is the historical gap between the conditions of a poem's production and its present reception which ensure that the nature of the contract can never be fixed. Furthermore, the generic map is itself never absolute; its terms and categories are always relative. The boundaries between genres are permeable, with one literary kind affecting and modifying another, and so creating a need for different distinctions. Lyric, then, must always be defined in relationship to the other literary kinds which impinge upon it. At the same time definitions that critics offer have to be understood in the context of their more general assumptions about literature.

The category of lyric is best regarded as a construct made within a nexus of a number of possible determinants not all of which have been equally important at every historical moment. These co-ordinates are of different kinds, among them those of form, subject-matter, social function, self-presentation and linguistic character.

In describing many literary genres the match of a given kind of subject to a particular form is a straightforward starting-point. In the case of lyric, even this is difficult, for it has always embraced a variety of subject-matter. In classical times lyric was the name both for substantial, public poems, usually termed 'odes', and for poems of love or sociable songs. In the last two hundred years or so the public ode has been transformed, interiorized into what Abrams (1970) calls the 'greater Romantic lyric'. In the process the realm of public poetry has contracted markedly (to the point that the office of Poet Laureate is now often regarded as an institutionalized joke). At the same time, however, the range of subject permitted to the shorter lyric has widened immeasurably from the fairly rigidly constrained repertory of the classical writers, so that a classification such as that proposed by Poole can no longer serve to delimit lyric's territory. This does not mean that recognition of the relationship of individual poems one to another in terms of their subject is unimportant; paradoxically perhaps, such affiliations become increasingly significant to the reader's experience even as it becomes less and less possible to produce a comprehensive list of permitted subjects. But such links no longer distinguish lyric from other kinds. As Alastair Fowler has remarked:

> In modern poetry, the collapse of many kinds into 'lyric' has given subgenre an enlarged function. Most short poems of our time belong to well-defined subgenres. But these modern subgenres are so numerous that, being mostly unlabelled, they are unrecognized in the main, and hard to describe.
>
> (1982, p. 114)

But in earlier periods the comparatively strictly delimited lyric repertoire of subject had a more important function in demarcating larger generic boundaries, and it is important that modern readers are able to respond to the witty, playful delight with which earlier poets deploy, test and challenge the conventional topoi that a subject-defined genre made available.

If subject is not now crucial to the definition of the genre, the lyric forms – the sonnet, the common-measure of hymnody, the villanelle and so on – also do no more than distinguish various lyric sub-genres. (They are, of course, none the less important for that, and repay critical attention.) But perhaps it is still true that a vestigial connection with music, with the idea of a repeated tune enacted in a repeated stanza form, has some force in creating our sense of a poem as a 'lyric'. What was once a major determinant of poetic genre, distinguishing lyric from elegy, for example, has come to seem much less significant, partly because of the absorption of continuous elegiac meditation under the lyric umbrella, partly through the rise of free verse; but the musical connection of lyric is still felt to be significant, and is traced in the disposition of words in stanza forms.

To most modern readers any attempt to make form or subject the determinant of lyric as a genre will seem self-evidently inadequate. We have become accustomed to attempting to define the genres of poetry not by their subject-matter, but by the way they offer a particular relationship between the poet's voice and the ostensible subject of the poem. We need to recognize, however, that the privileging of the subjectivity or objectivity of the poem's voice is itself the product of the culture of the last two hundred years or so. We need also to understand how hopelessly inadequate such criteria are when brought to bear on poetry of earlier periods. The medieval lyricist, for example, wrote poems for a whole variety of reasons, but rarely if ever to stake out a personal and originally conceived territory. The poet who wrote 'I sing of a maiden that is makeless' (i.e. 'matchless', 'without a mate') uses the first-person pronoun not as an assertion of individual perception, but to stand, as it were, as spokesman for the devotional community who might read or hear the poem. As Douglas Gray says, medieval lyrics were

> sometimes put to what we might recognise as 'literary' uses (e.g. in plays), but more often than not the impulse behind them is quite functional and practical. . . . The lyrics were meant to be, and were, used, sometimes in private devotion and prayer, sometimes for public devotional display, sometimes to emphasize and drive home points in sermons.
>
> (1972, p. 37)

This statement is true of much religious verse throughout the centuries, and is as applicable to the hymns of Watts or Wesley as to the medieval lyric. But it also applies to the secular lyrics of the Middle Ages. The voice of medieval poetry is determined by its functional purpose or the social situation of its composition and performance.

Such factors are significant also in the Renaissance, when poetry was not necessarily destined for a large, anonymous audience in print. It might circulate in manuscript as communication initially between groups of friends; whether printed or not, it could serve as tribute of praise from poet to patron, and be an instrument in self-advancement. Poets, therefore, had a clear sense of their audience, and their readers often had a sharp awareness of the relationship between text and poet. It is this, for example, that enables the playfulness with which Sidney both is and is not the Astrophil of his sonnet sequence. But this does not imply a simple, direct relationship between a poem and 'the poet's own feelings'. It has become something of a cliché to declare that it is during the period of the Renaissance that modern notions of the individual self were in the process of formation. It is commonplace to see in the poetry first of Wyatt and then of Donne the emergence of particular, individualized voices escaping from the anonymity of medieval conventions. But such views are true only in part. Renaissance writers were trained within the disciplines of rhetoric. This was not only an external discipline, which predisposed authors to be aware of generic decorum or made them sensitive to the games words could be made to play – although it was also both of those things. Rhetorical education was built upon the foundation of imitation, of learning from approved models, working and reworking the topoi or commonplaces. It dictated a habit of mind which saw language as an instrument of persuasion, and poetry as a branch of epideictic rhetoric, a means of instruction through praise or blame. Poems are therefore always addressed to someone; they do not 'turn their back' on the reader. In almost all Renaissance poetry there is a self-conscious, public dimension.

This, of course, is not to deny that Renaissance poetry does express 'feeling', nor to ignore the ways in which that poetry figures the negotiation between public and private selves. But it is to insist that a poet like Donne would have looked on M. L. Rosenthal's recent assertion that 'we should not confuse poetry with rhetoric' (1987, p. 96) with blank amazement. It is to suggest that reading Donne as if he were primarily expressing feeling is largely to miss the point and pleasure of his poetry. Finally, it is to assert that neither Donne's poetry, nor that of his contemporaries can be defined as lyric on the basis of its presumed truth to personal feeling. Indeed, the genres of Renaissance poetry were distinguished by criteria of form, appropriate language and subject rather than those of personal stance or feeling. Songs in stanza form on love are lyrics, as are longer, public odes or epithalamia, and they are to be distinguished from verse epistles, love-elegies, epigrams, satires and the rest. It was certainly possible to blend different genres, particularly the lyric and the epigram, as Rosalie Colie (1973) demonstrates, but for their effects such blendings relied upon a generic awareness largely given through the disciplines of rhetoric.

Critics have for half a century been drawing attention to the essentially rhetorical nature of Donne's poetry – and, indeed, one reason for his reinstatement in the canon in the earlier part of this century was precisely that he seemed to provide a model for the modernist attempt to escape from a romantic tyranny of personal feeling. The persistence, however, among school and university students, of the wish to find 'real feeling' in Donne's poetry is a mark of the enormous power that a romantic and post-romantic aesthetic still possesses to condition what is generally understood to be the business of lyric poetry.

The notion of lyric as essentially the personal utterance of a poet's feelings only takes root in the early nineteenth century. Most modern readers derive their assumptions about poetry in general, and lyric in particular, from the attitude seemingly embodied in Wordsworth's famous dictum about poetry as 'the spontaneous overflow of powerful feeling'. Many qualifications are needed to this picture, even as it applies to the romantics. They were not so simply obsessed with private utterance, and Wordsworth's 'egotistical sublime' has to be taken alongside Keats's assertion of the 'chameleon poet'. The association of lyric with the expression of personal emotion was not entirely new, and it is really only later in the nineteenth century that criteria of intensity of feeling and brevity of expression were allied to subjectivity as the essential conditions of lyric poetry. But none the less it is manifestly true that the generic map, for the previous 250 years largely determined by neo-classical rhetorical criteria, underwent a radical shift.

MacLean defines the shift thus:

The principles which had long served to divide poetry into kinds and to arrange them in a hierarchy... were not first principles to the Romantics. By the principles fundamental to the Romantics, poetry in the highest sense was one as the soul is; it was constituted, as is the soul, of the elements of thought and feeling; if divisible into important kinds, it was divisible by some such system as Wordsworth used in arranging his poems according to the psychological faculty predominant in the composition of each.

(1952, p. 459)

As a consequence, it is during this period that significant boundaries are drawn between lyric and narrative (a division that neither medieval nor Renaissance poets would have seen as important), and between poetry spoken in the voice of the poet, and poetry spoken through a dramatic persona (a distinction that most Renaissance poets would have found difficult to comprehend). It is in romantic and post-romantic poetry that the sense of a lyric as a poem recording a moment of perception, an encounter that leads to a fusion of perceiver and perceived expressed in the symbolic language of poetry, becomes firmly entrenched.

Any number of different explanations can be offered to account for this shift, not least a very different perception of the role of the poet in society, but what matters most is to take the basic point that lyric becomes perhaps the most privileged of poetic kinds, absorbing into itself the elegy, or poem of introspective meditation. At the same time it tends to modulate other literary kinds, so that epic and narrative are 'lyricized' by being presented under the control of personal reflection.

At first sight it might seem that the increasing monopoly of poetry by the lyric tends to undermine the possibility of any useful generic distinction. But it can be argued that, precisely as a consequence, new combinations and distinctions are forced into being. Avrom Fleishman records that 'to convey the stages of personal experience – especially during periods of alienation or recovery from it – a new form emerged: the lyric sequence' (1985, p. 368). This was not perhaps entirely new, but the lyric sequence has persisted as a significant genre to the present day. It might also be suggested that the insistence on lyric being defined as a personal mode of expression necessitated the emergence as a distinct genre of the consciously entertained dramatic monologue of which Browning is the most celebrated exponent. Subsequently, the distinction between dramatic and personal utterance has become less significant, and lyrics spoken through clearly signalled 'personae' have an important place among current poetic kinds. As Curran (1986) has argued, generic distinctions are no less important to romantic and subsequent poetry, however different is the basis upon which they are made.

In our own century the modernist reaction against the romantic emphasis upon the subjective led to a search for an impersonal voice, an objective poetic mode. Eliot's oft-quoted remark that 'poetry is not the expression of personality but an escape from personality' (1951, p. 21) may conveniently be taken to typify the reaction, but it is one which finds echoes with variation throughout the century – Pound's 'objectivity and again objectivity', William Carlos Williams's 'no poetry but in things', or Olson's projectivist manifesto urging poets to get rid 'of the interference of the individual as ego' are typical expressions. In its turn this aesthetic has been modified, extended or denied. One direction has been to turn the symbolic inwards to produce the private 'confessional' poetry of the 1960s. Another has been to take further the destruction of presence of the poet in the elusive, indeterminable poetry of John Ashbery or J. H. Prynne. At the same time other poets have sought to recreate a poetry which deals directly with the personal situation and experience of the poet, but does so in a way that is not occluded and private.

Paradoxically the outcome for the lyric as genre has been to produce two simultaneous but ultimately incompatible understandings of what the term might imply. On the one hand the romantic and post-romantic notion of lyric as essentially concerned with the poet's expression of personal feeling is still alive and well – it is what informs most of the 'creative writing' taught in schools, for example. But at the same time the modernist legacy has been to reserve lyric as term for a poem in which the formal resources of language are deployed to achieve an objectivity and impersonality of utterance. Particularly important has been the sense that concentration on form, or what might be termed the 'musical' in language, is central. As David Trotter puts it, talking of the poetry of Geoffrey Hill:

> Formal discipline is once more the only guarantee that poetry resembles unfallen speech, a speech which can awaken echoes of the lost kingdom of innocence and original justice.
>
> (1984, p. 216)

(The sense of belatedness here remarked can be paralleled in a number of contemporary poets, so that 'lyric' itself as a label may seem to carry a nostalgic charge.) The uneasy coexistence of these two imperatives as primary definitions of the lyric tends to render much casual use of the term in critical writing vague and unhelpful.

Part of the problem of using the term 'lyric' at all is that criticism for at least the last fifty years has not been particularly concerned with generic discrimination. For while one can chart the progress from a romantic, subjective definition of lyric through Eliot's view of poetry in general as an escape from subjectivity, to a later reaction in the work of poets such as Larkin, Harrison or Heaney, each in their own different ways establishing a clear sense of the origin of their poems in an individual geographical and personal situation, the question of what constitutes a specifically 'lyric' genre has been largely ignored by the academic voices who increasingly dominate the study of poetry. For all their differences from one another neither the New Criticism nor its unruly child deconstruction, which between them have dominated the discussion of lyric poetry in recent years, has made a fundamental dent in romantic and post-romantic notions of what defines the lyric genre. Responding successively to modernist and postmodernist writing they have tended to focus first upon the poem as verbal icon, then upon the play of language and deferral of meaning. They have considered the problems of subjectivity as central, though their approach to the question has been significantly different. Indeed, Jonathan Arac, providing an 'Afterword' to an important collection of essays entitled *Lyric Poetry: Beyond New Criticism*, draws attention to the continuity between New Criticism and the 'new new criticism', and concludes:

> Few of these papers work hard on actually addressing what is at stake in the notion of 'lyric poetry'. Most notions of lyric offered here are tactical, set up only to be devalued or rejected. The most common sense among those who have used the notion is that lyric expresses pure subjectivity.
>
> (in Hosek and Parker, 1985, pp. 352–3)

There are two problems which derive from the lack of attention to generic theory in much recent criticism. First, the fact that a post-romantic notion of what constitutes the lyric still dominates academic criticism serves to highlight the way in which neither New Criticism, nor its successors in the business of close-reading of poems are much interested in history. For though it is possible to read pre-romantic poetry from a deconstructive perspective – and though such an enterprise is not, of itself, unjustifiable – there is always the danger of partiality and blindness that can result. Any notion of genre must be deployed with historical sensitivity if it is to be a tool to unlock the difference of ourselves from the past. It is exciting to deconstruct Donne or Milton, and much can be revealed in the process about the ways in which their poetry may be made to speak to our present concerns – but it is at least as important to uncover the ways in which their language is alien and different, and generic self-consciousness can aid in the understanding of that difference. The second problem is rather different. For if subjective notions of the lyric have blanked off some literature of the past they also threaten to render invisible some of the things that are happening currently. Particularly in song lyric and in the expressly politicized poetry of Black communities we find that there is a lyric practice which is public rather than private, in which the speaker defines not so much a self as a community. In many respects this poetry, often tied to performance, looks back to a broader understanding of the nature and function of lyric than the voices of the academy often entertain.

'Lyric', then, is a desperately slippery term for the critic to handle. It is called upon to stand for some universal impulse; it needs to serve the needs of historical awareness, and yet has to function as a way of distinguishing

certain kinds of poem within the range of contemporary poetry. Today, perhaps, it is best seen as a sub-generic term, at least in 'high' literature, marking
off poetry which privileges the musical resources of language and what Denise
Levertov calls an 'uncommon speech of paradise' (1983, p. 5). The other
common contemporary use of the term specifically for words actually written
for musical setting allows rather different possibilities. When used for poetry
of the past it has to be used with a self-conscious sense of historical distance
and difference. The critic must always attempt to use the label as clearly as
possible, with a precise sense of the particular function appropriate to different
analytic tasks.

FURTHER READING

Brower, Reuben A. (ed.) (1970) *Forms of Lyric*, Columbia University Press, New York
Culler, Jonathan (1981) 'Apostrophe'. In Jonathan Culler, *The Pursuit of Signs*, Rout-
    ledge & Kegan Paul, London, pp. 135–54
Frye, Northrop (1957) *Anatomy of Criticism*, Princeton University Press, Princeton
Hardy, Barbara (1977) *The Advantage of Lyric*, Athlone Press, London
Hollander, John (1975) *Vision and Resonance*, Oxford University Press, New York
Hosek, Chaviva and Parker, Patricia (eds) (1985) *Lyric Poetry: Beyond New Criticism*,
    Cornell University Press, Ithaca
Johnson, W. R. (1982) *The Idea of Lyric: Lyric Modes in Ancient and Modern Poetry*,
    University of California Press, Berkeley
Lindley, David (1985) *Lyric*, Methuen, London
MacLean, Norman (1952) 'From Action to Image: Theories of the Lyric in the
    Eighteenth Century'. In R. S. Crane (ed.), *Critics and Criticism*, University of
    Chicago Press, Chicago
Rogers, William Elford (1983) *The Three Genres and the Interpretation of Lyric*, Princeton
    University Press, Princeton
Wellek, René (1970) 'Genre Theory, the Lyric and *Erlebnis*'. In René Wellek, *Discrimin-
    ations*, Yale University Press, New Haven, pp. 225–52
Welsh, Andrew (1978) *Roots of Lyric*, Princeton University Press, Princeton

ADDITIONAL WORKS CITED

Abrams, M. H. (1970) 'Structure and Style in the Greater Romantic Lyric'. In
    H. Bloom (ed.), *Romanticism and Consciousness*, Norton, New York
Colie, Rosalie L. (1973) *The Resources of Kind*, edited by Barbara K. Lewalski, University
    of California Press, Berkeley
Curran, Stuart (1986) *Poetic Form and British Romanticism*, Oxford University Press,
    New York
Eliot, T. S. (1951) *Selected Essays*, 3rd edn, Faber & Faber, London
Fleishman, Avrom (1985) 'Notes for a History of Victorian Poetic Genres', *Genre*, 18,
    363–74
Fowler, Alastair (1982) *Kinds of Literature*, Clarendon Press, Oxford

Gray, Douglas (1972) *Themes and Images in the Medieval English Religious Lyric*, Routledge & Kegan Paul, London

Langer, Susanne K. (1953) *Feeling and Form*, Routledge & Kegan Paul, London

Levertov, Denise (1983) *Poems 1960–1967*, New Directions, New York

Rosenthal, M. L. (1987) *The Poet's Art*, Norton, New York

Sidney, Sir Philip (1965) *An Apology for Poetry*, edited by Geoffrey Shepherd, Nelson, London [first published 1595]

Trotter, David (1984) *The Making of the Reader*, Macmillan, London

13

NARRATIVE VERSE

JOSEPH BRISTOW

Every poem tells a story. Every poem does so because narrative is a condition not just of poetry, but of textuality itself. Whether producing or consuming literary texts, writers and readers are bound to a process of structuring relations between units of meaning into sequences shaped by generic expectations. Within these terms, narrative defines the particular order a textual sequence may take up from start to finish. This question of textual order – its theorization in relation to a multiplicity of technicalities: genre, temporality, point of view, and so on – has found a space within literary studies known as 'narratology' or 'narrative theory'. Books on this topic abound. But their focus of interest is not poetry or even, more specifically, 'narrative verse'. Rather, narrative is usually considered to be the province of prose fiction. There are historical reasons for this restricted association between narrative and novels, short stories and related forms in prose. When English was established as a legitimate object of study in higher education at the end of the nineteenth century it was the novel that first attracted formalist criticism (Henry James's 'The Art of Fiction', 1884, is especially significant in determining the early debate). Thereafter, the issues of 'narrative technique' and 'narrative structure' became key preoccupations in what is now loosely referred to as traditional literary criticism. To this day, it is generally assumed that when discussing the most dominant literary form in prose, the novel, the critic is obliged to analyse aspects of narrative. Novels, it seems, are about their status as narratives. Poems, by generic contrast, appear to concern something other than the telling of stories – even though, by virtue of being texts, poems ineluctably *narrate*. Again, the complex register of terms built up by narratology – Mikhail Bakhtin's 'chronotope' (Bakhtin, 1981) or Genette's influential 'histoire/récit/narration' (Genette, 1982) – are rarely translated into the criticism of poetry. (For a full discussion of recent theories of narrative, see Martin, 1986.) Literary criticism instead gives priority to the rhetorical features of poetry: imagery –

frequently the fetish of 'close-readings' of this type of writing – provides the often exclusive focus of much criticism of poetry.

If poetry is infrequently looked at through a narratological terminology, this may be because lyric, rather than 'narrative verse', holds sway as the genre above all others in critical writings on poetry. And one of the most conspicuous features of lyric is its *resistance* to narrative. Lyric is characterized by an impulse to transcend the conditions of its articulation. Hence its frequent appeals to apostrophe ('O!' and 'Ah!') where apparently (since mimetically) spontaneous sounds, ones that have no referential effects in their own right, provide the illusion of immediacy (see Culler, 1981, pp. 135–54). Moreover, lyric is central to the criticism of poetry for at least two further reasons. First, there exists a consensus that lyric is, by and large, more convenient to teach to students. The formal features of lyric can be grasped quite promptly in the classroom, and traditional criticism has found lyric to suit particular critical needs – for example, the identification of ambiguity, paradox and unity, much favoured by the once very influential American New Critics. Narrative poems have, of course, existed in great numbers on the syllabus, but instead of being thought of primarily in terms of their narrativity they have been allocated to different generic formations – ballad, epic and romance are the obvious ones. On occasions, critics have thought it fit to speak of 'verse novels' – Elizabeth Barrett Browning's *Aurora Leigh* ([1857] 1978) is one example. The second reason for the critical dominance of lyric concerns its hegemony as *the* poetic form in the twentieth century. For as long as English Studies has been established, lyric has served as the form for most poems produced within the period. The development of 'free verse' after the First World War has much to do with the ascendancy of lyric. Even in the final decades of the twentieth century, those few journals such as *New Statesman and Society* and *The Listener* that publish poetry alongside other cultural materials (journalism, essays, reviews), reserve what marginal space they have for poetry to lyrics. In terms of the layout of such weekly publications, poetry has roughly the same signifi- cance as the crossword puzzle – a *minority* of readers is committed to it. As the institutional interest in lyric has become more and more specialized and theoretically complex, poetry has – in inverse proportions – taken on an increasingly unimportant cultural position so that it now stands as a 'higher' (and, to many people, inaccessible) form of 'art' that speaks neither to nor for the *Zeitgeist*. Rather, it continues as a form in the tellingly labelled 'little' magazines to provide for a tiny audience which is largely made up of poets and academics. Most contemporary readers of poetry are – if not producers of the stuff – students of English Literature.

It may be thought, then, that poetry has few readers outside the academy, and that those small numbers of readers it does have are interested less in its narrative than its lyric features. But at this point there emerges a new distinction that literary criticism, old and new, nearly always ignores. This is the distinction between academically recognized and non-academically enjoyed and very popular poetry. It is a distinction that exists to separate Shakespeare from folk-songs, Milton from Ranter writings, Tennyson from the music-hall, and Philip Larkin from Pam Ayres. Although, on inspection, it can be seen that each member of each of the pairs listed here has historical affinities with the other's writing, poetry officially assigned to the canon of 'great' English literature is all too often dissociated from the popular forms it relates to, and from which much of its meaning is generated. (To observe that Tennyson could be most vulgarly jingoistic may, in the eyes of more conservative critics, appear to 'degrade' the poet's 'art'.) In Britain, the pantheon of contemporary poets is supposed to include such figures as Seamus Heaney, Ted Hughes and Thom Gunn. Certainly, academic sales – in schools, colleges and higher education – keeps these writers in the public eye, and, largely because of this success, one of them has been crowned Poet Laureate (a delightfully antiquated office). But such poets are enjoyed to a far lesser degree than more 'popular' writers of sentimental 'verse' (like Patience Strong and Helen Steiner Rice); than Pam Ayres, who won a prize in a TV talent contest (*Opportunity Knocks*) in the early 1970s and went on to sell thousands of her book, *Some of Me Poetry* (1972); than the punk writings of John Cooper Clark and Jools; than the Black activist poetry of Linton Kwesi Johnson; and most recently, than the Black street culture narratives of hip-hop and rap, whose sales – on vinyl, cassette and compact disc, along with video – run into millions world-wide. Poetry (if one can *dare* to call it that, and I will) of highly consumable kinds, written and performed in English, is global. But it is not, as many examination syllabuses presume, 'art'. In other words, it cannot be taken seriously because it is *popular*. And it has been up to a newly-thriving discipline like Communication Studies to find reasons and methods for studying this kind of popular culture.

Poetry that enjoyed considerable popularity in previous eras – like the medieval ballad, the nursery rhyme, the Victorian parlour poem, and the music-hall song – has held a conspicuously peripheral place in English Studies. Even in those fields where myths and legends provide the substance of popular poetry – notably in Old English and Middle English Studies – the critical approach to such texts has traditionally been philological, providing illuminating knowledge about dialect and the history of the language. Popular poems, ones that reach out and speak *for* the people, go back to *Beowulf* and come right up to date, with an equally appealing rhythmical insistence, in rap. That is certainly not to say there is an uninterrupted passage from one distant historical moment to the 1990s. It is, instead, simply to argue that ruling class prejudice based on an élitist notion of 'culture' reigns supreme by disfavouring popular forms. 'Narrative verse', which subsumes many popular poems, such as those medieval ballads belonging to an oral tradition, marks out one of the few areas of traditional literary studies where 'high' and 'low' art are brought together in a self-conscious manner. Yet what legitimately constitutes 'narrative verse' is unclear. English Studies may be eager to exclude Pam Ayres, William MacGonagall (the Scottish poet infamous for his hilariously clumsy handling of metre and rhyme) and even John Betjeman from the canon of works deemed worthy of serious reflection. But the academic discipline of English is uncertain about a category that contains popular writings which also have a claim on 'great' literature. What, then, might prove acceptable to the institution as 'narrative verse'?

To begin with, there are several key problems with the naming of this far from coherent category. Not only does literary criticism tend to play down the narrativity of poetry, it also holds in lesser esteem the notion of 'verse'. *Poetry* has always been more highly regarded than *verse*. In his *Apologie for Poetrie* (1595), Sir Philip Sidney points out that 'it is not rhyming and versing that maketh a Poet'; but rather that the distinguished 'Senate of Poets hath chosen verse as their fittest raiment'. Verse, therefore, is a medium distinct from prose, while poetry is the remarkable verbal product poets make which need not (but usually does) appear in verse. More than 400 years later, verse has descended from its former Parnassian heights to the commercial level of the greetings card. In a similarly commercial but much more culturally respectable manner, verse is now also recognized as the substance of poetry anthologies. Practically all of the numerous Oxford University Press anthologies have titles pertaining to different (and ever-mutable) types of verse – *Christian Verse, Light Verse, Victorian Verse*, or whatever. *Verse* is an appropriate term in this publishing context because it provides a label for books which represent the 'popular' face of academic study in English. Such anthologies are often bought as gifts for friends and family, and book clubs buy them up in large quantities for their readers. Here, then, verse has the status of a type of writing that both academics and non-academics can enjoy between the same covers. The editors of each anthology are academics – their expertise is to be respected. The non-academic readership is likely to be predominantly middle-class with something of a passing interest in the literary 'heritage'.

These books obviously contain works that would elsewhere be classified as poetry. This point could not be borne out more clearly than by *The Oxford Book of Narrative Verse*, edited by Iona and Peter Opie in 1983. (Its predecessor, edited by Vere Collins, came out in 1930.) The anthology opens with Chaucer and concludes with W. H. Auden. A large proportion of its contents is devoted to the nineteenth century. And most of its inclusions are 'long' poems of more than two hundred lines. Again, many of these examples of narrative verse could be grouped under other headings – epic, ballad and so on. But all the 'verses' here have one thing in common, and that is, very plainly, that they tell stories. Their voice is a narrative one that moves purposefully from the beginning through the middle to the end of the tale, although deviations in linear sequence can and do occur. The exemplary lesson to be learned from these not particularly remarkable findings is that story-telling – explicit narration – is rarely equated with 'poetry'. Once a *poem* tells a story, however, and once it goes into a 'popular' anthology from a respectable university press, it becomes a *verse*.

The Opies' editorial responsibility for this anthology should not pass without notice since it says much about their publisher's assumptions of what constitutes 'narrative verse'. Iona and Peter Opie do not stand in the mainstream of English Studies. Their highly-regarded scholarship ranges across other disciplinary fields – such as folk studies, local history, education and anthropology. This crossing of disciplines occurs because their work is centred on texts – mostly rhymes and songs – for and by children. The Opies are best known for their archival work on children's oral culture (see Opie and Opie, 1967). In the academic world, they are associated with pre-literate forms. The fact that their names appear on the cover of an OUP anthology brings 'narrative verse' into close alignment with writings that may be considered profoundly unliterary. Words such as 'undeveloped', 'primitive' and 'naïve' – often possessing repressively tolerant rather than pejorative connotations here – form part of a limited vocabulary used by English Studies to cope with works, even ones written by 'great' poets, that can all too easily appear clumsy, simplistic and, above all, childish. But rather than offer to the literary-minded non-academic public a book packed with folk-songs, ballads and good old Victorian favourites like George R. Sims's 'Christmas Day in the Workhouse', the Opies present 'narrative verse' by canonical authors.

Sifting through the contents, something of a pattern begins to emerge. In the Victorian period, for example, Matthew Arnold's early poem 'The Forsaken Merman' (*c.* 1847–8) sits comfortably next to Robert Browning's 'The Pied Piper of Hamelin' (1842). Arnold's poem is based on a story in the recently translated tales of Hans Christian Andersen that gained instant popularity with children. Browning's poem, which is uncharacteristic of his oeuvre, adopts a tale recorded in Nathaniel Wanley's *Wonders of the Little World* (1678) (a title held in the poet's childhood library). Two decades later, Christina Rossetti published 'Goblin Market' (1862), which is also represented here. Her poem draws on folk narratives and nursery rhymes, using biblical types in the name of firm Christian instruction, to produce a poem which places a cautionary tale for children within a framework aimed at an adult readership. Other poems, either learned in school or written with a children's audience in mind, turn up: Henry Wadsworth Longfellow's 'Paul Revere's Ride' (1861) and Lewis Carroll's 'The Hunting of the Snark' (1876) are prominent examples. These 'verses', it needs to be borne in mind, are the ones a non-academic audience is likely to remember these poets by. Here are Arnold, Browning and Christina Rossetti at their most 'popular', and, in many respects, their most unrepresentative. 'The Forsaken Merman', 'The Pied Piper of Hamelin' and 'Goblin Market' may well remind many readers of their first encounter with 'great' poetry. The pleasure – often a childish pleasure – of such poems relates to three overdetermined features that characterize not only the vigour of much 'verse' but also the style of contemporary popular cultural forms like rock 'n' roll – namely, repetition, rhythm and rhyme. 'I'm a poet/but don't know it' is a well-known joke learnt at an early age that pokes fun at the perceived pretensions of 'great' poetry. But the mutually reinforcing rhythm and rhyme of this tidy piece of epigrammatic wit are regularly enjoyed in the kinds of celebratory verses found, for example, in birthday cards and the classified columns of local newspapers.

Many of the poems selected by the Opies entreat their readers to return to worlds previously inhabited in childhood – places located in fairy-tale, legend and ancient history that seem entirely removed from the circumstances in which the poems are read. Tennyson's chiming-rhyming and suspensefully lovelorn story of 'The Lady of Shalott' (1832, revised 1842) appeals to a medieval feudal order. Likewise, Dante Gabriel Rossetti's 'The White Ship' (1881) invokes the voice of the medieval balladeer. In 'The White Ship', the butcher of Rouen tells the story of how he was the sole survivor of a shipwreck that took the lives of Prince William (heir to Henri I), the Prince's half-brother and half-sister, and several other aristocrats in 1120: 'By none but me can the tale be told,/The Butcher of Rouen, poor Berold' (ll. 1–2). The syntax is noticeably inverted to foreground the rhymes, and this inversion archaizes the style to evoke an ordinary man's speech from a bygone era. The poem uses a largely monosyllabic register to produce an illusion of naïveté. A butcher, representing the voice of the people, reports his tragedy in similarly structured couplets that possess an antiquated but, by virtue of that, permissible clumsiness. Since Berold is a mere mortal, and not a symbol of divine aristocratic blood, he turns an ordinary man's phrase, rather than poeticizing in the tropes of courtly rhetoric. The illusion of archaism and simplicity is compounded by the use of one device common to many ballads: paratactic syntax (or parataxis). Not only is the word order inverted, it is situated in a syntax that mostly organizes its clauses side by side, often through the use of the conjunction 'and': 'King Henry of England's realm was he,/And Henry Duke of Normandy' (ll. 11–12). (Tennyson's poem adheres to the same principle.) Parataxis is often viewed as the 'simplest' form of sentence construction since it puts together catalogues of clauses in a manner that makes any of them appear interchangeable. Its opposite, hypotactic syntax (or hypotaxis), depends on structures of main and subordinate clauses that insist on irreversible syntactic orders. Hypotaxis may be regarded as more 'complex', particularly when it guides the structure of much intellectual writing. Yet such associations between types of syntax and relative values of 'simplicity' and 'complexity' can be misleading, and contribute to prejudicial distinctions between 'good' and 'bad' literature.

Antony Easthope's helpful analysis of a feudal ballad, 'Three Ravens', in his innovative study *Poetry as Discourse* (1983, pp. 78–95), points out that parataxis destabilizes the position from which the narrative voice of the poem is to be understood. In hypotaxis, by contrast, the subject of the main clause is clearly in place, and so a hierarchy of syntactic relations is subordinated around that subject. The challenge of parataxis – one might even argue, its complexity – is that it places its clauses in an arbitrary (because largely interchangeable) order. For example, the following four lines could to some extent be reordered without disturbing the meaning of the sentence:

> The sails were set, and the oars kept tune
> To the double flight of the ship and the moon:
>
> Swifter and swifter the White Ship sped
> Till she flew as the spirit flies from the dead.
>   (ll. 74–5)

In one respect, at least, parataxis might be thought of as more 'open', even democratic, than the potentially authoritarian (because hierarchical) organization of hypotaxis. This inference about 'democratic' syntax suggests that parataxis is not exactly 'simple' since its ordering points to issues of power – the equalizing distribution of meaning between and within clauses. A final observation relates to the narrative properties of parataxis. If a catalogue of similarly conjoined clauses can be arbitrarily reordered, it is worth asking how this type of syntax enables stories to progress, particularly when relating a sequence of events. In the passage from 'The White Ship', there is only one marker of time (or deictic) present: 'Till'. However, the line beginning with this deictic could be placed at either the start, middle or end of the excerpt. The point to be made here is an obvious one: the temporal features of the text do not foreground linear progression even though linear progression is something we might expect in narrative verse. Rather, the ship itself becomes an icon of the text's arbitrary movement where there is no authoritarian voice articulating a forceful logic – of cause and effect, of singular direction – within the poem. Indeed, the ship's movement appears to be independent of the voice that tells of her journey. The narrator's power to narrate, therefore, is put into the background. In conclusion, it might be argued that parataxis, taken together with the related structures of repetition and choice of vocabulary, renders this poem accessible to a wider non-academic audience because it does not summon up the imposing authority of, say, Milton's 'Grand Style' – an impressively hypotactic style.

Attention to syntactic and linguistic features plays a major part in the grouping of texts into generic formations. Yet it must not be forgotten that different genres are used for different aesthetic and political purposes at different historical moments in relation to broader cultural issues. Dante Gabriel Rossetti's medievalism reaches out to a number of radical and reactionary Victorian claims on the chivalric past – from A. W. Pugin's conservative interest in the 'Gothic Revival' to William Morris's utopian socialist novel *News from Nowhere* (1891). Such claims – which are too detailed to be dealt with here – were made on behalf of opposing sections of Victorian culture. To comprehend the balladic invocations of 'The White Ship' still further, by making historical sense of its language and style, connections must be realized with Dante Gabriel Rossetti's particular milieu (the Pre-Raphaelite Brotherhood) and his work as a cultural practitioner in a number of fields. The conditions in which his work was produced, the verbal and visual transactions that define his oeuvre, and questions about the late Victorian readership for his poetry, need to be taken into account. Finally, to add to an already demanding list of considerations, the reprinting of this poem in an anthology of narrative verse likewise needs to be assessed since it makes a statement on behalf of contemporary British culture.

This essay, then, has come round full circle. Yet one question for it remains. What is the purpose of an essay in the present *Encyclopaedia* that looks at a variety of poems, with some shared generic features, through the lens of 'narrative verse'? The answer needs reiterating. The category of 'narrative verse' serves to focus on kinds of poetry which, because of their presumed naïvety, simplicity and even childishness, would otherwise be removed from the canon of English literature were it not for the inconvenient fact that poems regarded as belonging to this type have come from the pens of authors who have written far more 'serious' works. As it stands, this category does not lead very far, only, in fact, towards the blurred boundaries of those preconceptions that pigeonhole these poems into a genre, rather than to more challenging questions about history and culture. One poem, already mentioned, in the Opies' collection, that has received a great deal of critical attention recently, is Christina Rossetti's 'Goblin Market' (see Edmond, 1988, pp. 170–203). This poem has not been rediscovered for its qualities as an item of 'narrative verse'. It has instead come to notice because of the recent emergence of new kinds of feminist knowledge alerting contemporary readers to late Victorian social issues surrounding femininity: prostitution; anorexia nervosa; lesbianism and sisterly love; the role of the single woman; and ideologies of motherhood and childcare. It is misleading when the author of a major study of genre asserts that the longest poem of the Victorian period, *Aurora Leigh*, has received renewed critical interest 'not because it is a good poem, or a good poem by a woman, but because it is a *long* poem' (Fowler, 1982, p. 248). Were it not for

Cora Kaplan's 1978 edition from The Women's Press, Elizabeth Barrett Browning's *magnum opus*, so popular in its own day, would not be valued as it is now as a triumphant example of mid-Victorian *women's* writing. To the more orthodox critical mind, genre serves as an unbending evaluative index of literary works – whether they successfully or unsuccessfully apply themselves to their chosen form. The field is, then, laid open for critics to pontificate on how to 'judge' the work in question. And such 'judgement' is still frequently passed off as 'discrimination'. Barely a genre, problematically popular, familiar among non-academics and children alike, 'narrative verse' has only been tolerated as a rag-bag of well-worn favourites that allows poetry a place where it can be tolerably *enjoyable*. But now, as drastic changes make their mark on English Studies, there are altogether newer methods for reading these stories in poetry. Such methods interrelate the poem with other discursive contexts to set about breaking up so-called 'discriminations' between 'high' and 'low' forms of cultural production.

FURTHER READING

Bakhtin, M. M. (1981) *The Dialogic Imagination*, translated by Caryl Emerson and Michael Holquist, University of Texas Press, Austin

Browning, Elizabeth Barrett (1978) *Aurora Leigh and Other Poems*, edited by Cora Kaplan, The Women's Press, London [first published 1857]

Culler, Jonathan (1981) *The Pursuit of Signs*, Routledge & Kegan Paul, London

Easthope, Antony (1983) *Poetry as Discourse*, Methuen, London

Edmond, Rod (1988) *Affairs of the Hearth: Victorian Poetry and Domestic Narrative*, Routledge, London

Fowler, Alastair (1982) *Kinds of Literature*, Clarendon Press, Oxford

Genette, Gérard (1982) *Figures of Literary Discourse*, Basil Blackwell, Oxford

Hawthorn, Jeremy (ed.) (1985) *Narrative: From Malory to Motion Pictures*, Edward Arnold, London

Martin, Wallace (1986) *Recent Theories of Narrative*, Cornell University Press, Ithaca

Opie, Iona and Peter (1967) *The Lore and Language of School Children*, Oxford University Press, London

____(eds) (1983) *The Oxford Book of Narrative Verse*, Oxford University Press, London

Scholes, Robert and Kellogg, Robert (1966) *The Nature of Narrative*, Oxford University Press, New York

14

WOMEN AND THE POETIC TRADITION: THE OPPRESSOR'S LANGUAGE

JAN MONTEFIORE

knowledge of the oppressor
this is the oppressor's language

yet I need it to talk to you
(Adrienne Rich, *The Fact of a Doorframe*, 1986 (b) p. 117)

The history of women's poetry in the English language is long, contentious and partly obscure. It is also constantly changing, thanks partly to the efforts of editors and publishers who have made and are making much previously unknown material widely available, and to feminist scholars' increasingly wide and detailed examination of women poets and their relation both to one another and to the poetic culture of their day. This enlarging and clarifying of the map of women's poetry is one of the major achievements of academic feminism. The new discoveries and rediscoveries, some very recent indeed, have begun to percolate to a wider readership, but the process is slow; there is still little general awareness of how many women poets there have been, or how much and how well they wrote. Although anyone who studies women's poetry soon realizes that much of it has been ignored, undervalued or forgotten by the creators and endorsers of the canon of English Literature, the extent of the forgotten material, particularly in the seventeenth and eighteenth centuries, has been hard to grasp because it is continually in the process of being revealed.

For example, fifteen years ago the feminist critic Cora Kaplan remarked on 'the dearth of good women poets in the eighteenth and early nineteenth century' (1975, p. 16); yet in 1984 the publication of Roger Lonsdale's edition of *The New Oxford Book of Eighteenth-Century Verse*, including poems by women, nearly all of which had been out of print for 200 years, showed that the real dearth had been of *published* 'good women poets'; Lonsdale's recent collection,

Eighteenth-Century Women Poets (1989) shows this even more emphatically, and alters the previous all-male picture of eighteenth-century verse out of all recognition. Understanding of the traditions of seventeenth-century women's poetry is also undergoing revision: the editors of *Kissing the Rod: An Anthology of Seventeenth Century Women's Verse* (Greer *et al.*, 1988), who like Lonsdale have both unearthed new poets and republished known ones, insist that their work is not definitive but pioneering and introductory: 'We are at the beginning of a long process of literary archaeology' (p. 31). While the efforts of these editors (and of Cora Kaplan herself, whose anthology *Salt and Bitter and Good: Three Centuries of English and American Women's Verse*, 1975, remains a classic), is crucially important in introducing readers to unknown territory, full editions of the resurrected poets are also needed. Clearly, until this work of editing is really advanced, and readers have had time to ponder the poems and think through their implications, no generalizations about pre-1800 women's poetry can be definitive. This does not mean, however, that I shall avoid making them, since it is impossible to understand a subject without defining it; others will, necessarily, dispute and deconstruct my definitions.

To begin, then, with a rough chronology: the tradition of English women's poetry begins, so far as we know, in the late sixteenth century. If there were ladies at the English court who wrote poems in English comparable to the innovating *lais* of Marie de France (*c.* 1140–1200), or if women composed any of the traditional songs, lyrics and ballads, these poets are forgotten and totally anonymous. The example of the Saxon nun Hrotsvita of Gandersheim (*c.* 935–72), poet and dramatist, shows that women in religious houses did produce distinguished poetry, but I do not know of any English poems written by pre-Reformation nuns. The first verses known to be by women were produced by highly educated Tudor noblewomen such as Mary Herbert, Countess of Pembroke (1561–1621), who, together with her brother Philip Sidney, versified the Psalms. There was a first flowering of women's poetry in the seventeenth century, inaugurated by Aemilia Lanier's brilliant *Salve Deus Rex Iudaeorum* (1611). Lanier's poems combine religious meditation with courtly elegance; these qualities separate out in her successors, roughly according to the political-religious divisions of English society in the Civil War. On the one side there is religious poetry, both personal and discursive, mainly associated with radical Protestantism: Anne Bradstreet (1613–72), who emigrated to New England and became one of the first American poets, is the best known exemplar of this tradition; on the other, there is courtly verse, often but not always secular, whose best-known practitioners are mostly associated with the Royalist party: Aphra Behn, Katherine Philips ('Orinda'), Anne Killigrew and the unknown 'Ephelia'.

The following century used to look less interesting than we now know it was since the publication of Lonsdale's anthologies. Anne Finch, Countess of

Winchelsea (1661–1720), is an important poet, witty, intelligent, angry and sensitive, whose oeuvre includes satire, meditation, and some of the earliest nature poetry. The Black American poet Phyllis Wheatley (*c.* 1735–84) is deservedly well known; so are the early romantics Anna Seward (1742–1809) and Charlotte Smith (1749–1809); others who look promising are Mary Leapor, Jean Adams, Anna Barbauld and Anna Plumptre, author of a denunciatory 'Ode to Moderation' (all in Lonsdale, 1984). But women's poetry really comes of age in the mid-nineteenth century with the advent of two crucially important women writers. The first of these, Elizabeth Barrett Browning (1806–61), a poet of immense ambition, energy and achievement, celebrated in her lifetime, eclipsed and then rediscovered by feminists in the 1970s, was a strongly enabling influence on the other, Emily Dickinson (1832–86), the story of whose reputation has been the inverse of Barrett Browning's: virtually unknown and unpublished until her death, after which fame and recognition steadily increased. These are not the only important women poets in this period: Emily Brontë (1818–48) and Christina Rossetti (1830–94) produced work of distinction.

In the twentieth century, there are two main identifiable 'moments' of creative energy in women's poetry (and, as with the history of men's poems, the greatest range, ambition and achievement have been shown by American rather than English poets). In the first third of the century, Gertrude Stein (1874–1946), Amy Lowell (1874–1925), Marianne Moore (1887–1964) and, in particular, H.D. (Hilda Doolittle, 1886–1961), all contributed in important and specifically feminine (or female) ways to the origins and development of Modernist poetry. Alongside these flourished more traditionally skilled writers such as Elinor Wylie (1885–1928), Edna St Vincent Millay (1892–1950) and Louise Bogan (1897–1928). And from the 1970s on, the advent of the women's movement and an accompanying growth in women's consciousness of themselves, has stimulated the creative energies of a great many women poets, of whom Adrienne Rich (b. 1929) is the best known. Much feminist poetry was strongly influenced by the work of Sylvia Plath (1932–63). Though Plath was not a feminist, her creation of a poetry of domestic or personal, specifically female experience, transformed by rage and imaginative energy into a poetry of mocking or agonized intensity, has made her work a model for political women poets. The past twenty years have also been a fine period for poetry by Black women; the work of Gwendolyn Brooks (b. 1917) has been joined by that of Audre Lorde (b. 1934), Michelle Cliff (b. 1948), Grace Nichols (b. 1950) and June Jordan (b. 1936). With the exception of these poets and of Phyllis Wheatley, the poets mentioned in this brief history are all bourgeois (or, occasionally, aristocrats), sometimes wealthy, invariably white.

This is, inevitably, a deeply inadequate account of women's poetry over 400 years. More consciously than most historians, I have distorted by omission, especially in my summary of twentieth-century poetry, which ignores the poems of all English women since Christina Rossetti and leaves unmentioned several important poets – no Charlotte Mew, no Stevie Smith, no Edith Sitwell, no Anne Sexton, no Elizabeth Bishop, no Denise Levertov, no Margaret Atwood. I have also, as the last name indicates, said nothing about women poets writing in English in countries other than Britain and the United States. The intention of this brief chronicle is, simply, to be a sketch map which should enable the reader to get her bearings on the geography of women's poetry.

The word 'tradition' is itself difficult and contentious in this area. Because women poets have traditionally been excluded from the canon of English poetry, it is tempting to imagine them as existing outside tradition, or as forming a separate poetic tradition of their own: an idea which, as I have argued elsewhere (Montefiore, 1987, pp. 11–13), owes much to a still widespread romantic ideology of poetry as transcendence. To read women's poems only for their articulation of female experience, and only in relation to one another, is to disregard that engagement with their cultural and historical context which produces much of their meaning; and while reading women's poems with this narrowly essentialist focus is much better than not reading them at all, it still makes for tunnel vision. I would argue, conversely, that no one can write poems without being enabled, however contradictorily, by knowledge of a tradition, even if their relation to that tradition is marginal and awkward. To produce even straightforward forms like ballads, and to do it well, a poet must learn the skill of narrating a story by stanzas (and to leave gaps in the right places so as not to bore her audience by telling them too much), the art of metrical competence and, probably, an ear for refrains. All these things must be learned from the examples which tradition makes available. Equally, ambitious discursive poems like Aemilia Lanier's 'Description of Cookeham' or Katherine Philips's metaphysical lyrics imply a considerable intellectual as well as technical apprenticeship. Really ambitious poetry cannot be produced unless the poet is highly educated, as well as having access to that minimum of literacy, leisure, privacy and economic advantage which, as Virginia Woolf insisted in *A Room of One's Own* (1928), are essential for the production of serious imaginative writing. It was the opening of higher education to women a hundred years ago that enabled the flowering of women's poetry in the twentieth century; and women poets have been almost exclusively white and middle class because higher education has been available almost exclusively to the socially and racially privileged. In a class society, which Britain was and is, few working-class boys and virtually no working-class girls, however brilliant, get to college, whereas bourgeois women have a strong chance of a good education. In so far as bourgeois women were allowed to cultivate their minds – 'to write, or read, or think, or to enquire', as Anne Finch wrote in 'The Introduction' (in Kaplan, 1975, p. 62) – they participated, though always marginally and always with a difference, in the poetic conventions and the literary rhetoric, not to mention the religious-political debates of their day. Traditional themes and conventions could be enabling as well as constraining: and the 'oppressor's language' need not necessarily be felt as oppressive.

The ambiguous ways in which women poets connect with the traditions which they have, however problematically, inherited, can best be seen by examining some women poets in detail. The following lines by Aemilia Lanier, the first important woman poet of whom we know, shows how the conventions of Jacobean poetry could be so receptive to feminine transformation as to be, at first sight, unnoticeable. In 'The Description of Cookeham' (1611), the poet recalls her patron, Anne Clifford, walking in her garden:

> How often did you visite this faire tree,
> Which seeming joyfull in receiving thee,
> Would like a Palme tree spread his armes abroad,
> Desirous that you there should make abode:
> Whose faire greene leaves much like a comely vaile,
> Defended *Phebus* when he would assaile:
> Whose pleasing boughes did yeeld a coole fresh ayre,
> Joying his happinesse when you were there.
> Where beeing seated, you might plainely see,
> Hills, vales, and woods, as if on bended knee
> They had appeard, your honour to salute,
> Or to preferre some strange unlook'd for sute:
> All interlac'd with brookes and christall springs,
> A Prospect fit to please the eyes of Kings:
> And thirteene shires appear'd all in your sight,
> Europe could not affoard much more delight.
>
> (in Greer *et al.*, 1988, p. 47)

This evocation of a natural landscape instinct with female presence can be read as a utopian vision of a woman-centred paradise, comparable to Christina Rossetti's much later visionary forest, 'Where every mother-bird brought up its brood/ Safe in some leafy niche/ Of oak or ash, of cypress or of beech' ('An Old-World Thicket', in Kaplan, 1975, p. 139). But Lanier's poem is not, any more than Rossetti's, a straightforward feminist idyll. In her exploitation of such familiar hyperbolic tropes as hills that abase themselves before a powerful presence, and in the representations of personified Nature that dominate the poem, she is using the Elizabethan conventions of deferential poetry addressed to noble patrons, and more particularly the tradition of courtly celebration of aristocratic ladies, most notably of course Queen Elizabeth herself. (Lanier's magnum opus *Salve Deus Rex Iudaeorum* significantly begins with an invocation of the dead Elizabeth as 'Cynthia', the name by which both

Ralegh and Jonson had deified her.) Her celebration of her patron's home as an earthly paradise parallels Jonson's 'To Penshurst' (which her poem may have anticipated), and her use of the pathetic fallacy resembles the Mutability Cantos of *The Faerie Queene*. The poet's skill and confidence efface any tension between her feminism and her deference to the aristocracy, so that her poem is at once a site of female meanings associated with nurturing and maternity (the feminized fertile landscape, the semi-divine presence of the Countess, the tree which shelters from an oppressively masculine sun), and an exploitation of rhetoric and topoi developed by male poets to flatter powerful women, the connecting link being the myth of female divinity (see Greer *et al.*, 1988, pp. 51–2).

It is notable in this poem, as in all of Aemilia Lanier's work, that the poet represents herself as a woman, addressing the mind of another woman, with no sense at all that her femininity constitutes any poetic disadvantage. This is even more apparent in her long poem *Salve Deus Rex Iudaeorum*, a feminist retelling of the crucifixion of Christ which explicitly argues that power and cruelty are the prerogatives of men:

> First went the Crier with open mouth proclayming
> The heavy sentence of Iniquitie,
> The Hangman next, by his base office clayming
> His right in Hell, where sinners never die,
> Carrying the nayles, the people still blaspheming
> Their maker, using all impiety;
> The Thieves attending him on either side,
> The Serjeants watching, while the women cri'd.
>
> (in Rowse, 1978, p. 109)

It is astonishing to find the poet using the techniques of stanzaic narration developed by Spenser, not simply to transform the gospel account of the journey to Golgotha into the Jacobean ritual of public execution, but to parallel Christ's innocence and powerlessness with that of the women who witness and protest against this legal slaughter – as, the poet implies, they still do.

Aemilia Lanier's apparently effortless control and transformation of poetic conventions is matched, though never again with such feminist confidence and anger, in the work of some of her seventeenth-century successors, particularly in the courtly tradition. Aphra Behn's profane and erotic poems show a similar ease with their lyric-narrative conventions, while Katherine Philips exploits the courtly tradition of celebrating the beauty and virtue of ladies, as for example in her poem 'To the Excellent Mrs A.O.' (1664):

> Her mind is so entirely bright,
> The splendour would but wound our sight,
> And must to some disguise submit,
> Or we could never worship it.

And we by this relation are allow'd
Lustre enough to be Lucasia's cloud.
(in Greer *et al.*, 1988, p. 192)

But for many, indeed for most other women poets of the seventeenth century, the traditions in which they write are much more problematic: the prevalent assumptions about what poetry was, and who wrote it, denied women access to powerful language. The Protestant Anne Bradstreet wrote in 1650, famously, 'I am obnoxious to each carping tongue/ That says, my hand a needle better fits' (in Kaplan, 1975, p. 29), and Anne Finch is roused to bitter and still pertinent eloquence on the same theme in 'The Introduction' (1714):

Alas! a woman that attempts the pen,
Such an intruder on the rights of men,
Such a presumptuous Creature, is esteem'd,
The fault, can by no vertue be redeem'd.
They tell us, we mistake our sex and way;
Good breeding, fassion, dancing, dressing, play
Are the accomplishments we shou'd desire;
To write, or read, or think, or to enquire
Wou'd cloud our beauty, and exaust our time,
And interrupt the Conquests of our prime;
Whilst the dull mannage, of a servile house
Is held by some, our utmost art, and use.
(in Kaplan, 1975, p. 62)

Fine poet though Anne Finch is, it is evidently not possible for her to define herself as great in the way that Elizabeth Barrett Browning or Emily Dickinson were to do in the nineteenth century – or, nearer our own time, H.D. and Gertrude Stein. Her combativeness becomes defensive hesitancy in the work of many of her successors, none of whom show anything like Lanier's bold appropriation of biblical material and courtly poetic convention to her own ends.

The main obstacle to female poetic achievement in the eighteenth century is, I would suggest, the hypnotizing authority of the canon of classical literature, which by the eighteenth century had become unquestionable. The epics of Virgil and Homer, the odes and satires of Horace, had for educated men the authority both of acknowledged greatness and of familiarity: they constituted the accepted models of what poetry ought to be, and what a gentleman ought to know. Education in English (and European) schools and universities meant studying the canonical classical texts and becoming sufficiently fluent in Latin and Greek to imitate them. Milton's *Paradise Lost*, which takes its narrative structure and its style from Virgil's *Aeneid* and beyond that from the *Iliad* and the *Odyssey*, is the obvious instance of the great poem which itself becomes canonical, modelled on the classical epic; but all the major male poets from

1600 on go to classical originals for discursive, satiric, or (of course) pastoral poetry; thus, Donne's *Elegies* look back to Ovid, and his *Satires*, like Marvell's, to Roman origins. By the eighteenth century, literary culture becomes even more relentlessly neoclassical: in Pope, its greatest poet, classical epic is a constant presence, both as norm and as subject for parody, and Horace's satires are nearly as important.

The cultural hegemony of the classical canon was disabling for women, as for males who were not gentlemen, not only because its forms were or might be alien to their preoccupations, but because they had little or no opportunity to know the canonical texts. The male monopoly of the universities where Homer and Virgil were taught meant that the 'singing school' of the monuments of classical magnificence was closed to them. Even if by luck or perseverance a woman did become fluent in Latin or Greek, she could never inherit this culture as by right, in the way that a boy schooled in Virgil and versifying would do. There was no obvious alternative to the strict Augustan conventions of poetry; and when one reads eighteenth-century women's poetry, it does seem – at least to this reader – that the available poetic forms and language seriously limited the ways in which it was possible for women to understand and represent their lives. It is disconcerting, for example, to find the able poet Mary Leapor in 'An Essay on Woman' (1745) representing different aspects of women's experience in the form of personified stereotypes and invocation of conventional wisdom, both clearly drawn from Pope's misogynist poem 'On the Characters of Women':

> Pamphilia's wit who does not strive to shun,
> Like death's infection or a dog-day's sun?
> The damsels view her with malignant eyes,
> The men are vexed to find a nymph so wise:
> And wisdom only serves to make her know
> The keen sensation of superior woe.
>
> (in Lonsdale, 1984, p. 409)

It is even more startling to find the Black poet Phyllis Wheatley apparently praising her own captivity in the poem 'On Being Brought from Africa to America' (1773):

> 'Twas mercy brought me from my pagan land,
> Taught my benighted soul to understand
> That there's a God, that there's a Saviour too:
> Once I redemption neither sought nor knew.
> Some view our sable race with scornful eye:
> 'Their colour is a diabolic dye.'
> Remember, Christians, negroes black as Cain
> May be refined and join th' angelic train.
>
> (in Lonsdale, 1984, p. 616)

The difficulties of reading this poem – is it as pious as it looks, or is it bitterly ironic? – come from the gap between the poet's experience of slavery and deracination, and her orthodox Augustan rhetoric and Christian theology which can only articulate these as 'mercy'. Even if we give the poem an orthodox reading, it would be quite wrong to assume that Phyllis Wheatley is simply assenting to the tenets of the slave trade: for a black, ex-slave woman living in a society of white slave-owners to write and publish poems at all was an act of extraordinary courage, clarity and self-assertion. Her rejection of prejudice against 'our sable race' and her use of the imperative to admonish her presumably white readers – 'Remember, Christians' – indicate her independent consciousness; and yet phrases like 'my benighted soul' and 'negroes black as Cain' also reproduce the racist associations of Africa and black skins with biblical curses which her argument disputes. But conversely, the line 'Once I redemption neither sought nor knew' has a potential double meaning, evoking her African childhood as a time when she did not need to be 'bought back' (the original meaning of 'redeem') because she had not been sold into slavery. I am not sure whether the poet intended this subversion of Christian orthodoxy, but certainly the crisp clarity of her verse throws its key words 'mercy' and 'redemption' into vivid relief, illuminating their ambiguity and duplicity. The poem can be read as an example and as a parody of 'the oppressor's language'.

All the women poets I have so far discussed attempted, with varying degrees of success, to appropriate highly formalized conventions of poetry to articulate their own concerns and experiences. The practice and theory of romantic poets, and particularly their insistence on the importance of poetry not as a learned skill but as a communicated act of perception, made possible a different relationship between women and poetic tradition in which some women could and did define poetry on their own terms. The classic definition of romantic tenets is Wordsworth's 'Preface' to the 1805 edition of the *Lyrical Ballads*, in which the poet, opposing Augustan notions of poetry as a matter of knowledge, skill and brilliant execution, emphasizes instead the poet's power of feeling, his gift for communication, his perceptions, the universality of poetry and its close connection to 'the language really spoken by men'; the poet is 'an upholder and preserver, carrying everywhere with him relationship and love' (ed. Roper, 1964, pp. 29, 35).

What is radical about this conception of the poet as transcendent subject is that its valorization of poetry is not tied to narrow forms of educational privilege. It is significant that the romantics were attacked by conservative contemporaries for the simplicity of their language and their belief that the words of 'ploughmen and market-wenches' without 'just taste and refined sentiments' (Jeffrey, 1802, quoted by Roper, 1964, pp. 410–11) could be the material of great poetry. Wordsworth's Poet, then, is something other than a classically educated gentleman.

I do not of course mean that because the romantic myth of the poet as a transcendent consciousness is inspiring and potentially democratic, it must therefore be universally valid. Deconstructive critics such as Catherine Belsey have shown how dependent this concept is on the bourgeois fantasy of the undivided, autonomous self (Belsey, 1980, p. 7); other feminist critics have pointed out how the definition of the poet as a 'man speaking to men' excludes women from this privileged domain (see Kaplan, 1986, p. 85; Montefiore, 1987, p. 10); and Margaret Homans has argued in her influential book *Women Writers and Poetic Identity* (1979) that Wordsworthian poetry, being structured on the model – or fantasy – of a masculine mind contemplating a maternal Nature, actually inhibited women by leaving them no space to define their own identities. Yet there is strong evidence that the most ambitious women poets found the idea of romantic transcendence exhilarating and enabling. For there was no inherent reason why a woman should not become a transcendent subject; it could even become a way of transcending the limits of her gender. If imaginative perception was what made a poet, why should not a woman participate in this faculty? So Emily Dickinson writes:

> I reckon – when I count at all –
> First – Poets – Then the Sun –
> Then Summer – Then the Heaven of God –
> And then – the List is done –
>
> But, looking back – the First so seems
> To Comprehend the Whole –
> The Others look a needless Show –
> So I write – Poets – All –
>
> (ed. Johnston, 1970, p. 277)

Dickinson's declaration of the poet's transcendence is even more absolute than Wordsworth's, though it is shot through, characteristically, with sceptical irony: divinity, the poem concludes, exists only in the poet's imagination. Dickinson's pioneering predecessor, Elizabeth Barrett Browning, was even more deeply engaged with the concept – or myth – of romantic transcendence, because it enabled her to define herself as a major poet, in terms of a consciousness that was independent of her woman's body. This is particularly evident in her long poem *Aurora Leigh* (1856), in which both the nature of poetry and women's relation to it are hotly debated issues. The heroine Aurora defines poetry in terms of a Shelleyan Romanticism: it is, she insists, the key link between material and spiritual realities. Against the arguments of her cousin Romney, who thinks that poetry is unimportant compared to social reform and that as Aurora is only a woman her poems are bound to be second-rate anyhow, she defends the primacy of the creative imagination and her own vocation as a poet, one of 'the only truth-tellers now left to God, /The only speakers of essential truth' (ed. Kaplan, 1978, p. 65).

But appropriating Romanticism is not easy, and cannot be accomplished by a simple act of will. The contradiction between Aurora's femininity and her ambition is spelled out in an extraordinarily powerful passage about her early, unsuccessful attempts to write the poetry of which she knows herself capable. She connects her failure directly with her femininity: her poems are stillborn:

> The heart in them was just an embryo's heart
> Which never yet had beat, that it should die;
> Just gasps of make-believe galvanic life;
> Mere tones, inorganised to any tune.
>
> And yet I felt it in me where it burnt,
> Like those hot fire-seeds of creation held
> In Jove's clenched palm before the worlds were sown, –
> But I – I was not Juno even! my hand
> Was shut in weak convulsion, woman's ill,
> And when I yearned to loose a finger – lo,
> The nerve revolted. 'Tis the same even now:
> This hand may never, haply, open large,
> Before the spark is quenched, or the palm charred,
> To prove the power not else by the pain.
>
> (ed. Kaplan, 1978, p. 122)

The opposition articulated here between women as bodies, bearers of mortality on the one hand, and divine masculine creativity on the other, may suggest that the speaker is entirely trapped in the bind of patriarchy, her investment in masculine tradition (including, of course, her knowledge of the classical canon, which is signalled in her mythological allusions) leading her to articulate a myth of creativity from which her own biology, 'woman's ill', debars her. Defining herself as one who has failed to achieve even 'Juno's' second-rate divinity, she has, it would seem, learned to speak the 'oppressor's language' of patriarchal learning only too well, and has lost her own mother tongue.

The poet's relation to the classical myths through which she articulates her own relation to language is, however, much more complicated, interesting and independent than this straightforwardly radical feminist reading of the poem allows for. Her image of Jove as a sower, scattering the worlds like sparkling grains from his palm is not to be found in either Hesiod's or Ovid's cosmogonies: as in Augustan usage, 'Jove' seems to signify God the creator. There may be a reference to Plato's *Timaeus;* if so, she has altered his story. Plato's Demiurge is a sower, but when he is planting souls on the planets, not inventing worlds (Cornford, 1937, p. 146). The immediate source of the image seems to be a passage in Browning's 'Essay on Shelley' where the poet's mind is said to share in God's contemplative powers: 'Not what man sees, but what

God sees – the *Ideas* of Plato, seeds of creation lying burningly on the Divine Hand' (ed. Berkey *et al.*, 1981, p. 138). But for the woman poet, the 'hot fire-seeds of creation' represent not things in their original Platonic essences, but her own powers, the pent-up energies which burn her from within: the image of all-powerful sight is transformed into vividly felt physical pain. The hand clenched over its own hurt, the 'palm charred', also alludes to a passage in Charlotte Brontë's novel *Shirley* (1849), itself a powerful narrative of female frustration where women are ironically exhorted to endurance: 'Close your fingers firmly upon the gift, let it sting through your palm' (Brontë, [1849] 1969, p. 82).

The myth of the poet as divine visionary has been transformed by a feminized language of bodily experience into a paradoxically powerful image of powerlessness. And the connection which Barrett Browning suggests here between 'power and pain' has been taken up, more than a hundred years later, by the feminist poet Adrienne Rich, in the poem 'Power' which meditates on the relationship between heroism, brilliance and hurt. The heroine is here not a poet but a scientist, Marie Curie:

> she must have known she suffered   from radiation sickness
> her body bombarded for years   by the element
> she had purified
> It seems she denied to the end
> the source of the cataracts on her eyes
> the cracked and suppurating skin   of her finger-ends
> till she could no longer hold   a test-tube or a pencil
>
> She died   a famous woman   denying
> her wounds
> denying
> her wounds   came   from the same source as her power
>
> (Rich, 1986b, p. 225)

The radiant energies at the heart of creation – Barrett Browning's 'hot fire-seeds' – are brilliantly (so to speak) revised into nuclear power; the burning within into 'radiation sickness' and the 'charred palm' into 'suppurating finger-ends': the metaphorical now including the literal. The effect of this intertextual transformation is not to write the heroine into a Faustian fable of the price of knowledge, but to question that myth of transcendence which divorces the visionary mind from the suffering, material body, showing up the extent to which it rests on denial.

The complex production of intertextual meanings between a poem by an American profoundly influenced by modernist poetics as well as by feminist politics, and the novel-epic of her Victorian ancestress, makes it clear that the tradition of women's poetry has by now become a reality rather than a hypothesis. But the variety and range of women's poetry in the twentieth century is such that it is now misleading to speak of anything so narrow and unitary as a single 'woman's tradition'. In the modernist mode, there are the poems of H.D. which hold their own opacity marvellously up to the light:

> and I remembered bell-notes,
> *Azrael, Gabriel, Raphael,*
>
> as when in Venice, one of the campanili
> speaks and another answers,
>
> until it seems the whole city (Venice-Venus)
> will be covered with gold pollen shaken
>
> from the bell-towers, lilies plundered
> with the weight of massive bees...
> > (H.D., [1945] 1973, p. 78)

English poets, quieter and more straightforwardly formal, have seemed more determined by canonical tradition. Some, like Stevie Smith (and her feminist successors Liz Lochhead and U. A. Fanthorpe) have transformed it by feminine irony; others have developed the formal lyric into a poetry of meditation, as when Edith Scovell meditates on the way a baby's illuminated head

> seems a field of corn by the wind liquefied
> Streaming over the arches of a round hill-side.
> Contours and skin make tender the planes of light and shadow
> The pale and darker gold of the upland meadow.
>
> Only for a moment your cavernous human brow
> Will dwell in the world of sense as naturally as now,
> Beautiful with no meaning, but that it commands
> Those to love, who hold you in their hands.
> > (Scovell, 1988, p. 73)

Finally, feminist poetry by now constitutes its own tradition with several different tributaries, including the work of lesbian-feminist and of Black poets. Always political and highly-charged, often informal in structure or even close to prose, feminist poets work to deconstruct the oppressor's language, not only with anger, but, like Grace Nichols's Fat Black Woman in her bubble bath, with humour:

> O how I long to place my foot
> on the head of anthropology
>
> to swig my breasts
> in the face of history
>
> to scrub my back
> with the dogma of theology

to put my soap
in the slimming industry's
profitsome spoke

Steatopygous sky
Steatopygous sea
Steatopygous waves
Steatopygous me
(Nichols, 1984, p. 14)

FURTHER READING

Barrell, John (1988) *Poetry, Language and Politics*, Manchester University Press, Manchester

Benstock, Shari (1986) *Women of the Left Bank, Paris, 1900–1940*, University of Texas Press, Austin

Belsey, Catherine (1980) *Critical Practice*, Methuen, London

Gilbert, Sandra and Gubar, Susan (eds) (1979) *Shakespeare's Sisters: Feminist Essays on Women Poets*, Indiana University Press, Bloomington

Homans, Margaret (1979) *Women Writers and Poetic Identity*, Princeton University Press, Princeton

Kaplan, Cora (1986) *Sea Changes: Culture and Feminism*, Verso, London

McConnell-Ginet, Sally, Borker, Ruth and Furman, Nelly (1980) *Women and Language in Literature and Society*, Praeger, New York

Miller, Nancy K. (ed.) (1986) *The Poetics of Gender*, Columbia University Press, New York

Moers, Ellen (1978) *Literary Women*, Women's Press, London

Montefiore, Jan (1987) *Feminism and Poetry: Language, Identity, Experience in Women's Writing*, Pandora, London

Ostriker, Alicia (1986) *Stealing the Language: The Emergence of Women's Poetry in America*, Women's Press, London

Rich, Adrienne (1980) *On Lies, Secrets and Silence*, Virago, London

——(1986a) *Blood, Bread and Poetry*, Virago, London

ADDITIONAL WORKS CITED

Berkey, John, Crowder, A. B., Crowl, S., Fitch, R. and Hunt, N. (eds) (1981) *The Complete Works of Robert Browning*, vol. 5, Ohio University Press and Baylor University, Texas

Brontë, Charlotte (1969) *Shirley*, Dent, London [first published 1849]

Cornford, F. (1937) *Plato's Cosmology: The 'Timaeus' of Plato, Translated with a Running Commentary*, Cambridge University Press, Cambridge

Greer, Germaine, Medoff, Jeslyn, Sansome, Melinda and Hastings, Susan (eds) (1988) *Kissing the Rod: An Anthology of Seventeenth Century Women's Verse*, Virago, London

H.D. (1973) *Trilogy*, edited by Norman Holmes Pearson, Carcanet, Manchester [first published 1945]

Johnston, Thomas H. (ed.) (1970) *Collected Poems of Emily Dickinson*, Faber & Faber, London

Kaplan, Cora (ed.) (1975) *Salt and Bitter and Good: Three Centuries of English and American Women's Poetry*, Paddington Press, London

——(ed.) (1978) *Elizabeth Barrett Browning: Aurora Leigh*, Women's Press, London [first published 1857]

Lonsdale, Roger (ed.) (1984) *The New Oxford Book of Eighteenth-Century Verse*, Oxford University Press, Oxford

——(ed.) (1989) *Eighteenth-Century Women Poets*, Oxford University Press, Oxford

Nichols, Grace (1984) *The Fat Black Woman's Poems*, Virago, London

Rich, Adrienne (1986b) *The Fact of a Doorframe*, Norton, New York

Roper, Derek (ed.) (1964) *Lyrical Ballads by W. Wordsworth and S. T. Coleridge, 1805*, Collins, London

Rowse, A. L. (ed.) (1978) *The Poems of Shakespeare's Dark Lady*, Cape, London

Scovell, E. J. (1988) *Collected Poems*, Carcanet, Manchester

Woolf, Virginia (1970) *A Room of One's Own*, Penguin, Harmondsworth [first published 1928]

15

MEDIEVAL POETRY

DEREK BREWER

The tumult and the shouting die, the corpses keep possession of the slaughter-field, but indomitable words echo down the centuries in defence of honour, comrades, country. The places of doom themselves may still be seen – the river near Maldon in Essex, Roncesvalles in the Pyrenees, the fields by Catterick in Northumberland – English, French, Celtic, and those of other peoples from Iceland to Spain, who took part in the struggles of the seventh and later centuries. We inherit their words in the languages of Europe, summed up by the greatest poet of the English language in the twentieth century:

> We have taken from the defeated
> What they had to leave us – a symbol:
> A symbol perfected in death.
> And all shall be well...
> (T. S. Eliot, *Little Gidding*, 1942)

Then an aristocratic voice arises in the twelfth century from near Poitiers to sing eleven songs of love strikingly varied from bawdy jest to passionate desire and religious devotion – that of the ninth Count William of Poitiers, soldier and lover, the first recorded troubadour. Soon the new sense of self is expressed in long stories of chivalrous adventure and love, beginning late in the twelfth century in the north of France with Chrétien de Troyes, unleashing a flood of ultimately very varied narrative poems. Along with these there burst out thousands of lyrics expressive of a huge variety of feeling, changing with the centuries. Then drama itself of very many kinds in verse. In every case music is not very far away. The early epics were probably chanted to the rhythms of a simple harp, but in the centuries from the eleventh to fifteenth music developed with song into an extraordinary richness only recently being discovered.

The accompaniment of music reminds us of the great difference of medieval poetry from modern. Although, as we shall see, the arts of reading and writing, of literacy, developed, the basis of poetry remained oral, whether spoken or sung. The poet was the voice of the social group who heard him, and by the exercise of a little imagination we can rejoin him in his world. We might find ourselves amongst Bishop Aldhelm's seventh-century English audience, reluctant to listen to sermons, but very ready to stop to hear him on the bridge chanting the English stories he was so skilful in composing. We might be in a smoky Anglo-Saxon hall to hear a nobleman renowned for his ability to compose stories and songs about past and present heroic deeds; or in the fields or on ships, to hear work-songs, or in evening groups to hear love-songs and to dance. Later, in the thirteenth and fourteenth centuries, in the colourful, dangerous courts of kings and nobles, we might hear poems of wonderful elaboration which, though now with a written base, are still read aloud by such poets as Gottfried, Dante, Froissart or Chaucer.

The presence of the group made the occasions of poetry warm and natural. The skill of the good story-teller or poet in a community was always valued, but the poet was not venerated for special moral or intellectual insight. He (rarely she) was the singer of tales, the spokesman of the tribe, who spoke or sang the language of the tribe, to be understood by the people. The occasion was itself part of the poetry. The poet did not have to create a whole context for his work, or rely on the imagination of the solitary reader poring over cold, silent print, ignorant of the author. The poet was an 'insider', whether the noble counsellor of earlier times, or the talented courtier, humble minstrel, or the pub and market-place entertainer of later days. The poet could not be the romantic 'outsider', whether his social status was high or low. He had to please an audience.

There were consequences for style and attitude. The spoken word is less firmly attached to 'things', it is less precise, more 'rhetorical' – that is, lively, colourful, evocative, extravagant. Oral poetry needs repetition with variation. It evokes the general wisdom of common experience. It deals with stories that are known, and characters drawn on large, general lines, recognizable as hero or villain. We can see this still in Shakespeare, who as a dramatist has to be an oral poet, though much modern criticism of Shakespeare, as of medieval poetry, ignores this historical social dimension.

But literacy also has its place, even in earlier poetry – or it would not have been written down for us to know. The main early source for literacy was Latin. The great inheritance of classical Latin was preserved by the church, and those few who went to school read Virgil and Ovid. Latin developed as the common language of learning and at its best medieval Latin is as vivid and powerful as classical Latin.

The first recorded medieval poetry and a continuing stream of it throughout the medieval period was in Latin. Hymns became general in the church from the fourth century and a huge number of them, naturally of very variable quality, was produced. The simplicity and power of some have a timeless quality which ensures that they are still sung today: 'Come Holy Spirit'; 'Jesu, the very thought of thee'; 'The banners of the King go forth'. They are great religious poetry. Secular Latin poetry, like the religious, is strong and direct. The lyrics are marked by a vigorous rhythm which echoes down the ages. Secular Latin poetry is announced by the delightful *Pervigilium Veneris (The Vigil of Venus)*, probably of the fifth century, which combines a hymn to Venus with a description of spring and of a festival. It strikes many of the most characteristic notes of medieval love poetry. The springtime of the year and of life is the time for love. The stanzas have the refrain 'Who never loved will love tomorrow; whoever has loved will love tomorrow'. At the end is a touch of sadness: 'The nightingale sings, we are silent. When will my spring come?'

But vernacular poetry has left a different record. Most of the early songs are lost, though they must have continued in great variety, whether of battles long ago, or trivial matters of the day. What remains of early medieval poetry is mainly the sterner stuff.

For example, the Englishmen of Essex, mostly peasants, were gathered together under the general leadership of the brave but aged Byrhtnoth, the alderman, or chief thane, of Essex, on 11 August 991 to resist a Viking raiding force encamped on an island in the River Blackwater. They exchanged shouts across the ford, as modern visitors can still. The Vikings said it would not be a fair battle if they were held back by the ford. The high-hearted Byrhtnoth allowed them passage and they fought. A coward caused the untrained English peasants to break and run. Byrhtnoth's household troop, his loyal warrior comrades, companions of his feasts, receivers of his gifts, fell with him to a man. The poem, even in translation, vividly memorializes their heroic last stand. One of them,

> Byrhtwold spoke, he raised his shield,
> He was an old companion in arms, he shook his spear,
> With great courage he cheered on the men:
> 'Courage shall be the keener, heart the braver,
> Spirit shall be the greater, as our strength weakens.'
> (*The Battle of Maldon*, ed. Gordon, 1937, ll. 309–13;
> translated here by Derek Brewer)

Art here makes of a historical event a potent symbol, always relevant. Our oldest songs are those of triumph in defeat. The earliest poem recorded in a Celtic language laments in Welsh the brave death of 300 warriors from Edinburgh who attacked the English at Catterick around 600. Separate stanzas commemorate various warriors, as this one:

> Hero of the protective shield below his grey forehead,
> In movement like a horse,

He was a tumult on the battle-slope, he was a fire,
His spears were swift, he was radiant,
He was food for ravens, he was benefit to the crow,
And before he was left at the fords
At dew-fall, the eagle of graceful movement.
Besides the wave's spray near the hillside
The poets of the world judged him to be of manly heart.
(Aneirin, *Y Gododdin*, trans. 1988, ll. 268–76)

The primitive but always contemporary fierce emotions of war, its horror, anguish, glory and pity (there would be no glory nor pity were it not for the horror and anguish), are expressed in dense imagistic phrases, in no logical order, repeated like hammer-blows. Time and event are juxtaposed, not sorted into sequence. Repetition with variation, both of word and scene; pattern not causality; these are the characteristics of this ancient oral style.

The earliest European vernacular is English (called Old English till the twelfth century, then Middle English till the end of the fifteenth). Some thirty thousand lines of Old English poetry survive, including biblical paraphrases, a heroic account of Satan in Hell whose sublimity is not matched till Milton, battle pieces, wise sayings, charms, riddles, meditations, laments. We have no doubt lost many lighter songs and work-songs which were of no interest to the monks who recorded Old English poetry. What remains is in the so-called alliterative style, with lines of four main stresses and a variable number of unstressed syllables in between. The first three stressed syllables are linked by beginning with the same letter – hence the name. Both stress and alliteration in a less formal way occur throughout later English poetry, but are peculiarly well suited to the emphatic oral style.

The outstanding heroic poem *Beowulf* was probably composed about the middle of the eighth century. Our only copy was written by monks in a book that has been at Exeter Cathedral for a thousand years. The book contains a collection of various verses and such prose as a story telling of the marvels of Alexander. *Beowulf* records the deeds of the hero of that name in his battles against monsters. We hear how men in the joy of the hall listened to, in the poem, 'the harp music, the clear song of the poet. He, who knew how to tell it, spoke of the creation of the world', from far past, how God made the beautiful land surrounded by water, the sun, the moon, trees and leaves (*Beowulf*, ll. 89–99). Poetry, like the hero, represents humanity struggling against nature and evil. The maker of such a poem may well have been himself a nobleman. The story itself is traditional: that is to say the events are versions of a widely diffused story with a recognizable core and shape. The excellence of the poet lies in his ability to repeat known themes, and vary them by adapting them to new circumstance.

Beowulf's valiant deeds in youth are crowned in age when as king he fights to defend his people against a marauding dragon and in killing it dies himself. This is the true heroic end. He is nobly mourned as the bravest and gentlest of men, the paradoxical praise of the Christian warrior throughout the medieval world, a lion in battle, a lamb in hall.

Beowulf's fights are the symbolic core of the poem but they are surrounded by genuine historic reference to events in the sixth century. A similar seed of history is found in other heroic poems which spring from a people's pride and interest in their past reinforcing their own present confidence and sense of identity (see Burrow, 1973). The hopeless but indomitable defence of a narrow place against odds is the archetypal heroic situation. It is not limited in real life to the medieval period, but the exalted celebration of heroism is peculiarly characteristic of early medieval literature.

In Old English the heroic strain is blended with a vigorous confident Christianity in such a poem as *The Dream of the Rood*, composed perhaps early in the eighth century, which presents the Crucifixion as a heroic encounter by Christ the young warrior-hero meeting Death. The Cross in its jewelled splendour speaks of itself as the unwilling accessory to the devil's battle with Christ, who accomplishes his triumph over death through his own death in true heroic style. *The Wanderer* and *The Seafarer*, both probably composed in the late ninth or early tenth century, are meditative poems each over a hundred lines long in alliterative metre put into the mouths of noble retainers who have lost their lord and are now desolate but sustained by Christian hope.

The heroic ethos in its strange but potent mixture with Christian piety and its equally potent mingling of history and legend appears in French in *The Song of Roland* (composed about 1100), the earliest and best of some seventy French *chansons de geste* (songs of deeds). A version of it was sung by William the Conqueror's bard Taillefer leading the Norman warriors into action against the English at the Battle of Hastings in 1066. The tiny historical seed of *The Song of Roland* was a rearguard cut to pieces at Roncesvalles in the Pyrenees on 15 August 778. The story developed through oral retelling into one of magnificent if foolhardy bravery and became a great poem by a great poet, whose name is unknown. The oldest manuscript dates from the twelfth century. Another great poem is the Spanish *Poema de mio Cid*, probably composed in its present form in the thirteenth century. It tells the story of the champion called El Cid who is a well-attested historical figure of the eleventh century. He came to represent in poetry Spanish pride and glory in the centuries-long struggle against the Moors.

These stern poems of bloodshed, loot, loyalty, treachery, revenge and religion have roots deep in humanity. They are vainglorious yet noble, secular, but Christian in conviction, if of a different brand of Christianity from ours. Their style is as repetitious as the Psalms. Their characters are large, solid, simple. Good and evil, though composed differently from modern standards, are clearly differentiated. The world is stark, harsh, vigorous, tragic, but never meaningless.

Though these poems are in no way allegorical, and the heroes by no means entirely without blame (for their warrior-pride is the source both of their grandeur and their defeat), the heroes may be said to represent the collective spirit of their society, its archaic unity. That is why they are kings or nobles. Individual psychology, an interest in personal characterization, are not to be sought in these grand poems. There is no domesticity, no representation of the inner life, in these broad sweeps of action and meditation on life and noble death. Women are rarely seen or heard of. The queen in *Beowulf* is a gracious brief presence in hall. The beloved of Roland is mentioned only as she dies when she hears of Roland's death. The essence is the traditional story, known before, a pattern of action indeed, but told allusively, meditatively, richly, not a speedy sequence of existing events like a boy's adventure yarn or a modern thriller. The thrills are profounder; they are echoing reverberations of great happenings.

This ancient mode was supplemented and supplanted, though the underlying collective ethos of honour and bravery persisted in European literature until the mid-twentieth century. Even now it may be found in archaic or oppressed or deprived societies. But in Europe from the twelfth century new modes of feeling evolved, centred more on the individual lives of those few who were freed from grinding daily poverty and toil by religious or social status. A sense of the self evolved through the relation of the self to another person, either to a woman or to God; in the religious sense especially to the person of Jesus. The generating force of this change was a new sense of love, rising out of sex in the secular world, but raising desire to devotion, and in religion sublimating sexual desire to a new transcendental passion. Love was personal as sex could not be. It took on some of the ancient warrior virtues of loyalty unto death, complete devotion to one's lord, or one's lady, self-sacrifice; yet in so doing it sought a fuller self-fulfilment, a satisfaction deeper than that of membership of the group, a deeper unity than that of the one with the whole, in the unity of one with one. So high a desire (which of course found only intermittent or partial expression in most life and literature) could not but be often frustrated, which is perhaps why so many of our sweetest songs are those of saddest thought.

In both religious and secular poetry, but especially the latter, medieval culture discovered and celebrated the magical potent bitter-sweetness of the glorious image of the Feminine. Of many influences perhaps the most significant, paradoxically enough, was that of the great enemy to Europe, the superior civilization of Arabia. The Arabs, or 'Moors', had spread across North Africa and far into Spain. Arabic influence was profound in the intellectual world of the early Middle Ages but it also provided an impulse towards the most delicate love-poetry. It is probable that the earliest vernacular European love-songs were written in Arabic and Hebraic scripts in Spain in the eleventh century.

Romantic love (sometimes in the twentieth century called 'courtly love') was perhaps the greatest literary invention of the Middle Ages. Sexual love, rising above promiscuous sexual lust, is of course found to some extent in many cultures and historical periods. But it was medieval European literature, with its mixture of pagan and Christian love, that established it as a major literary institution. It is usual to see the beginning of this tremendous development in southern France, with Count William IX (1071–1127), the first known troubadour. William left only eleven poems, five of which are burlesques and satires, including some which are very gross, but five are passionate love-songs. The last is a poem written in the fear of death. An anthology containing only William's poems would give a very fair cross-section of the range of typical moods of medieval poetry. The Provençal tongue became the language of poetry and some 500 troubadours are recorded, not all of them coming from Provence.

The women addressed in medieval love-songs vary from great ladies to milk-maids; the poems of frustrated desire (which is perhaps the most constant troubadour theme) are to some extent offset by those which either exalt the lady herself, or the joy of love, describing feelings with great delicacy. Others, on the other hand, indulge in derisive satire or bawdy merriment. One of the most delightful of William's poems, so fresh, springlike and gentle, reads in part:

> In the sweetness of new spring
> the woods grow leafy, little birds
> each in their own language, sing,
> rehearse new stanzas with new words,
> and it is good that man should find
> the joy that most enchants his mind...
>
> (Dronke, 1968, p. 115)

Many other poets followed. A Provençal dawn-song from the fourteenth century or earlier immortalizes the sweet sorrow of parting:

> When the nightingale beside his mate
> heralds the night and the day,
> I lie with my fair beloved
>   on the flowers
> till the watchman on the tower
> cries 'Lovers awaken!'
> I see the dawn, the bright day
>   breaking.
>
> (Dronke, 1968, pp. 173–4)

There are plenty of lesser lyrics of comic, satirical, realistic or ribald nature.

When technology and science were so weak, there was plenty of crude intract-able physical matter, plenty of pain, cruelty, bitter injustice, to make life nasty, brutish and short. Painful experience also finds lyrical expression as in the grimly humorous poem by the devout friar Jacopone da Todi, complaining about his imprisonment by the Pope:

> The prison that's been given me,
> a house below the ground.
> A privy drains off into it –
> its scent is not of musk.
>
> (Dronke, 1968, p. 215)

Along with the great efflorescence of lyric poetry went a great change and blossoming of narrative, mostly inspired by the exploration of love and adven-ture, where the supreme adventure was love itself.

The remarkable narrative poems in French of Chrétien de Troyes (*fl.* 1180) flow so easily on a clear rippling stream of octosyllabics that their mysterious depths have until recently been missed by critics. Chrétien is the flag-bearer of romance, which now prevails over the heroic poem. His heroes are not stern, mature warriors fighting for king and people, but young men who, though outstandingly brave, are often inexperienced, setting out on their own, leaving the court in search of love and adventure. They become characters capable of self-examination and remorse. Their adventures usually end in success and a happy return to court with their bride. The underlying theme is the maturing of the individual, undergoing tests, solitude, uncertainty. He leaves home to seek love, returning to society and the stability of marriage with the loved one. Symbolic stories, often fantastic in surface content, convey-ing this deep theme, of trial, success and integration within society, are aston-ishingly widespread within human societies. Society needs such imaginative models, for if we do not mature and marry and generate successors in a stable society the race will die out (see Brewer, 1980). Romance therefore is both questing and optimistic and it is irrelevant to accuse Chrétien of lacking the tragic depths of the earlier dying heroic world. Chrétien's world, no less noble, survives.

Chrétien is a self-conscious author whose name we know. He is not only literate but learned, self-consciously artistic, individualistic. In Chrétien's romances there is a greater sense than in the heroic poem of individuality and even of the inner life of the hero. Moreover, Chrétien can be detached in his attitudes. He is not indissolubly one of the collective group. He is sometimes ironical, and perhaps even slightly amused in recording the adventures and sufferings and extravagant feelings of his young heroes. This may be so even in his most influential poem, which tells of the extraordinary adventures of Lancelot, lover of Queen Guinevere, whom he seeks to rescue from an abductor. Since Lancelot owes allegiance to King Arthur, yet is in love with the king's wife, the story must (as later poets and storytellers saw) end in tragedy, and perhaps for this reason Chrétien, devoted to themes of survival and success, left the poem for another to finish.

Many other writers took up the story of Lancelot and King Arthur and there is a vast corpus of Arthurian literature, though much of it is in prose, especially in the later period. In verse the great culmination of Arthurian legend in English is the alliterative poem *Sir Gawain and the Green Knight*.

The two greatest European Arthurian poems, both German, are the *Parzival* by Wolfram von Eschenbach (*fl.* 1200–1220) and *Tristan* by Gottfried von Strassburg (*fl.* 1210) which was based on an Anglo-Norman poem by Thomas (*fl.* 1160–70), now surviving only in fragments. *Parzival* derives from a poem by Chrétien. It is a richly developed story of testing, of romantic love leading to marriage, and of mystical religion culminating in the vision of the Holy Grail. Gottfried's *Tristan* brings the climax of romantic adulterous love to a pitch of religious ecstasy in the extraordinary passage of the 'Cave of Love' which Tristan and Isolde create in the forest, but the story as a whole provides a classic case-history of love that is irredeemably tragic. The dark and destructive notes of the lovers' obsessive passion ring down the ages as far as Wagner's *Tristan and Isolde*.

Gottfried, however, is no Wagner. He tells his story not only with deep feeling but with Chaucerian wit, irony and self-consciousness. He has an amazing genius for combining the sensual, the ribald and the spiritual. Other more delicate and domestic but often equally tragic stories of love are found in the exquisite French *Lais* of Marie de France whose brief, poignant poems of usually (though not always) frustrated love have, like Chrétien's, a rich symbolism beneath their apparently simple surfaces. Unusually for medieval literature they are told from a woman's point of view.

Such romances as these and hundreds more in many European languages, full of varied adventure, love and religion, develop the self-awareness of European culture in parallel with an increasing self-awareness in the religious life. Perhaps because of their interest in love and in the feminine which they share with so many lyrics they develop some feeling for other people, a sense of sympathy, despite a continuing wildness of adventure. They are idealistic and emotionally expressive. We share the hero's and heroine's desperate sorrow in love and can appreciate their joy in its fulfilment. Though many of the adventures are fantastic there is a kind of decorative realism which enhances our sense of the richness and glamour of life. These romances are primarily courtly, especially in origin, but they are in essence folk-tales of the chivalric ethic, and their themes are common to all human nature. They soon spread down the social scale. It is characteristic of traditional literature that the stories themselves should be retold with greater or less effect, according to the ability of the teller. In the later Middle Ages, continuing to Shakespeare's time, they had an enormous vogue, and Elizabethan writers, including Shakespeare, were deeply influenced by medieval romance, even when retold at tedious length in prose. Such was the power of the essential story and theme. Eventually, after the seventeenth century, they descended into the chapbooks of the semi-literate. Yet their themes may still be found to underlie many a nineteenth- and twentieth-century novel.

The courtly romances which idealized love had, particularly in France and Germany, a complementary side. This was composed of bawdy folkloric tales in verse, equally fantastic and courtly, but set in realistic, everyday village settings and written in a much plainer style. The subject of these short poems, usually called *fabliaux*, is lust, not love. The comically ingenious plots are of seductions, tricks, beatings. The heroes (if that is the right word for the leading male agents) are often young clerics, and the victims tend to be rich bourgeois husbands, their luscious wives, and lecherous or lazy parish priests. The settings are the domestic interiors of the moderately well-to-do in towns or villages far from the forest of romance. The plots of these *fabliaux* are inter-national comic tales, repeated in most languages and centuries of the medieval period, in origin courtly, but popular no doubt with all classes. There is however only one in English, apart from Chaucer's adaptations in *The Canter-bury Tales*.

The juxtaposed pair, romance and *fabliau*, accompanied by an ever-widening range of lyric, and a huge amount of utilitarian versifying on all kinds of improbable subjects, signals our emergence into the Gothic period of high medieval literary culture, the later thirteenth and the fourteenth centuries, bright with new light. As with the Gothic art with which it may be compared, pattern is valued, not perspective. Time and space begin to emerge from the less differentiated world of epic to become significant in the conduct of the story, though still far from the controlled naturalism of the eighteenth and nineteenth centuries. Fantasy is told with realistic detail. The grotesque goes along with the delicately beautiful.

There is also an increased bookishness. Versions of biblical stories had always necessarily depended on the Bible. Now a wider range of reading sustains long learned poems in Latin which make a piquant Gothic contrast with other more popular material, such as the beast-fables used to devastating satirical effect in Nigel Longchamp's Latin *Mirror of Fools (Speculum Stultorum)* written about 1180. This pillories monks in the shape of Brunellus the Ass. Another example is the *Ysengrimus*, written about 1150, pseudo-epic of the battles between the fox and the wolf, again satirizing clerics. Both these works had widespread popularity.

Wider and deeper book-learning also encouraged the growth of allegorical writing, which used personifications of abstract qualities or of general concepts to make some exposition or argument. The most influential example was the *Complaint of Nature (De Planctu Naturae)* (about 1170) of Alan of Lille, partly in prose, partly in elaborate verse. The author represents Nature as a lovely woman, with a beautiful but torn dress, complaining about the perversions of mankind. With such works we are in the realm of moral and philosophical argument, for which poetry was still appropriate. There is no lack of passion in the polemic of learned men. The influence of literacy reveals itself in closer argument, more originality, wider vocabulary, more technical subject-matter, a more specialized audience, a more logical, specific point of view.

The laity too had a hunger and thirst after literacy in the vernacular and this was most strikingly supplied by the most popular poem of the later Middle Ages, also allegorical, the French *The Romance of the Rose (Le Roman de la Rose)*, written in the thirteenth century in octosyllabic verse by two authors. The first, William of Lorris (*c.* 1237), failed to complete his charming courtly allegory about love in just over 4,000 lines, and the second, John of Meung, massively completed it in 1275 in almost 18,000 lines more.

The first part of *The Romance of the Rose* presents the author as wandering in a charming riverside landscape in May. This is the time of youth. He enters the garden of Idleness in which such beautiful persons as courtly Mirth and Joy are dancing. In the figure of a beautiful rose which he wishes to pluck is represented his falling in love. Various 'people' argue, encourage, threaten him.

Reason, represented as a beautiful woman, and the God of Love, represented as a vigorously youthful hunter, urge him in opposite directions, and give a great deal of advice more or less useful to a young man in love in the thirteenth century and fascinating for social and historical reasons to us. We have here a psychological drama represented through the self as hero confronting various projections of his own mind, as well as real difficulties, such as the girl's reluctance, her husband or guardian, etc., in the real world.

John of Meung's continuation is a hugely varied argument carried on through personifications and their long speeches, to do with free-will, satire of clerics, advice on sex, an evocation of a sort of Earthly Paradise of sexual promiscuity. It is partly feminist, partly anti-feminist, all conducted with great gusto, including the climax of the allegorical representation of copulation. Such is the characteristic inclusiveness and mixed nature of medieval Gothic literature. The poem was reproduced in hundreds of manuscripts, sometimes sumptuously illuminated, and debate about it continued till the sixteenth century, to be resumed by twentieth-century scholars. It was the seed-bed of many another poem, including some of Dante and Chaucer.

Supreme Gothic literary works are Dante's *Divine Comedy*, Langland's *Piers Plowman* and Chaucer's *Canterbury Tales*, all structured on the pilgrimage quest but richly ornate. Dante's sublime work is the climax of the quest of romantic love, but also of the quest for knowledge, for goodness, all of which find their true home in the love of God. The poet, as so often in later medieval poetry, is the hero of his story. He tells of his pilgrimage through Hell and Purgatory, to Heaven, led first by Virgil (representing secular learning), then by Beatrice, the supreme image of the beloved Feminine, representing the higher divine inspiration. She leads him to the inexpressible divine source of all love, that 'Love that moves the sun and other stars', as the last line of Canto 101 of the vast poem calmly and sublimely states. The style of Dante's eleven-syllable, three-line stanzas with their interlinked rhyme, the *terza rima*, is wonderfully solid, powerfully energetic, rich in comparison, relatively sparse in metaphor.

Dante's huge scheme of a systematically organized religious and imaginative world is real enough within the fiction and not so remote from Dante's reality as it is from ours. Even for us, it is a grand symbol for the whole of experience. In this respect it corresponds to the general medieval view of the world as being real in itself but also significant of a deeper invisible reality. In a letter to the Count Can Grande (though its authenticity has been disputed), Dante asserts that his poem should be interpreted, like the Bible and like the world itself, on four levels. The literal, or actual; second, the allegorical; third, the moral (for the moral lessons it teaches); and fourth, the anagogical (or mystical, relating to heavenly experience). This scheme, whether or not the letter is authentic, is the scheme which had been developed by scholars for very sophisticated biblical interpretation. It can perhaps be applied to *The Divine Comedy*, but some have argued that it applies to all medieval secular vernacular literature. This is to impose an impossible uniformity on a huge variety and cannot be sustained, but it points to the inherently symbolic nature of all literature. It also reminds us that many medieval poems, too numerous to list here, directly use allegorical figures.

In English the most complex use of allegory is made by William Langland, who probably completed the first version of his poem *Piers Plowman* about 1377. The questing poet, seeking the meaning of life and the way of salvation, is again the hero of his own poem. He questions the church, presenting it as a stately lady with a sharp tongue. The problems of fair reward and corruption are presented in the dubious actions of Lady Meed. The Seven Deadly Sins are vividly shown. Piers Plowman, after whom the poem which Langland spent his life writing and re-writing is called, is as much a symbol of the quest as an allegorical figure. He represents in various ways the productive, dutiful peasant, the earnest seeker after truth, and Christ himself. He is what the poet himself is seeking. The poet's anguished yet robust and sometimes grimly humorous search for truth, his pity for the poor, his concern for social justice, strike modern notes without being untrue to that troubled century which saw the Peasant's Revolt (1381) when peasants used Piers Plowman himself as a symbol.

Langland wrote in the alliterative metre deriving from Old English but in his day mainly associated with the west and north of England, and it reflects his Englishness and the fluidity of his thought. The poem begins with a sight of the world from a very specific place, looking east from the Malvern Hills in Worcestershire. The poet sees a great plain where men work and play. On one side is a heaven-aspiring tower on a hill and on the other, in a deep dale, a castle with its dark dungeon. Our active lives are spread between hope and despair, joy and misery, and ultimately Heaven and Hell. He presents himself in the poem, as no doubt he often was in real life, as a poor and solitary wanderer. His encounters with allegorical figures represent his testing of hard experience against conventional concepts and institutions. He is vividly aware of the goodness of nature and the wickedness of men. He watches the turmoil of life. He was not a priest, and he obsessively satirizes the friars, but his poem is deeply, unsentimentally, devout, laced with Latin quotations from Bible and liturgy. He is neither a market-place nor a courtly entertainer but a writer for serious men on serious topics. We feel strongly the power of his mind turning and twisting vital problems. Poetry is the natural vehicle of his intellectual, moral and social passion, and the intensity of his concern encompasses a Gothic variety of perspective and subject-matter.

Literacy is even more evident in Chaucer. In early poems, *The Book of the Duchess* (1368) and *The Parliament of Fowls* (around 1380), he describes reading himself to sleep. He translated the fifth-century Latin philosophical work *The Consolation of Philosophy* by Boethius, and incorporated much of its themes and even words into the philosophical romances *Troilus and Criseyde* and the poem about Palamon and Arcite now known as *The Knight's Tale*. Fourteenth-century European courtly poets aimed to be learned men. Yet Chaucer also sedulously cultivates an oral style. He does not disdain entertainment. The result in his case is an ambiguity which he cherished, partly no doubt because it was in his temperament, but partly because of the nature of the culture of the Gothic period, where so many conflicting currents met. *Troilus and Criseyde*, the first great English poem to be written in the rhyme-royal stanza, celebrates a noble romantic love, yet it is a tragedy told with ambiguous subtlety, sympathy and even humour. It has remarkable realism and character portrayal, but ends with a condemnation of unstable worldly love which is contrasted with the faithful love of Christ. *The Canterbury Tales* (*c.* 1390), written in a variety of forms, has romance, a saint's life, narratives of great fascination about patient and enduring women, along with bawdy but immensely sophisticated tales not unlike the French *fabliaux*. All are among the great poems of the language. The *General Prologue* to *The Canterbury Tales* has the most famous opening to a poem in English, describing the coming of spring in traditional yet always fresh style. It sums up much that is so attractive in medieval poetry.

Chaucer is often ironical. Another contrast within the literature of the period is provided by his great contemporary who wrote the poems *Sir Gawain and the Green Knight, Patience, Cleanness* and probably *Pearl* (1375–1400). The poet is very different from Chaucer and no ironist, though he has humour. He has a creatively mythic imagination both in scenes of chivalric romance, as in *Gawain*, in the biblical narratives on which *Patience* and *Cleanness* are based, and in the moving elegy, in the form of a visionary dialogue with his dead daughter, in *Pearl*. The brilliance and variety of these poems shows the medieval tradition at its ripest. He is highly original in his use of traditional verse forms, mixing the alliterative metre with rhyme. He also (notably in *Pearl*) creates the kind of pattern which is constructed by using significant 'magic' numbers of lines (e.g. groups of five) which is called 'numerological'.

This particular feeling for numerological form is very hard for a modern to appreciate, though since it depends on line-counting it is obviously highly literate. Some European Latin poets do this, but no other English poets seem to have used this highly elaborate artistic form till Spenser.

The fourteenth century is the second major phase of European medieval poetry, the age of romance and intellect. The ideal quality is summed up in Dante's exclamation at heavenly bliss:

> Pure intellectual light, fulfilled with love,
> Love of the true God, filled with all delight,
> Transcending sweet delight, all sweets above.
> (*Paradiso*, trans. 1962, XXX, 40–2)

After the grim endurance of the heroic ethic, this is like entering a Gothic church, all bright windows and aspiring pointed arches, growing out of yet contrasting with the sturdy crouched rounded vaults, the massive walls, the ancient mysterious darkness, of the Romanesque. Yet whereas the Romanesque image of the crucified Christ is calm and even triumphant (as in *The Dream of the Rood*) the Gothic Christ, at the heart of the hope of joy, is a tormented, very human person. Suffering is now more exquisite and more significant. Suffering, love and joy are intertwined.

The unifying theme is still love, but contrasts abound. Though the great works may be called Gothic miscellanies they are not unlike a modern newspaper with their extraordinary mixtures of joy with sorrow; seriousness with satire and farce; idealizing love with bold bawdry; high aspiring devotion with gross realism. The forms match this new fullness of variety. Neither *The Canterbury Tales* nor the Spanish *The Book of True Love* by Juan Riz, Archpriest of Hita, is finished. Their authors seem to have kept working on them, as Langland kept re-working *Piers Plowman* all his life. Process is preferred to product. One must not exaggerate such fluidity. Dante's works are finished, as are those of Petrarch and Boccaccio in Italy, Dafydd ap Gwilym in Wales, and a hundred others. But in fourteenth-century poetry there is a sense of movement in both space and time, a more individual self-consciousness, leading both to deeper religious devotion and sharper scepticism.

Poetry thus developed process, hence change, variety, contrast, yet still contained all these elements within a loose unity. Poetry was the highest form of communication while remaining an important form of entertainment. Song and story were the basic elements, enjoyed by all classes. Long verse narratives, short lyrics, even if produced by someone who was a moralizing monk, were still conditioned by the art of the story-teller, the minstrel. The spoken word, even when supported and extended by literacy, as in the church liturgy, was the conditioning medium, with its need for repetition, generalization, hyperbole, word-play, conventional wisdom; there was still a communal element in the singular art. Language was primarily for telling a story, persuading hearers to feel or act, expressing personal feeling, rather than for describing with precision the physical world of cause and effect. Ultimate reality was felt to be interpersonal and invisible, rather than the materialistic solid objectivity, as attractive and as painful as it might be, of the visible physical world. The great change from this world-view to ours developed rapidly in the seventeenth century. In his world-view and attitudes Shakespeare is closer to medieval poetry than modern. Still conditioned by orality as a playwright must be, our last medieval poet might be thought of as Shakespeare.

FURTHER READING

Barron, W. J. (1987) *English Medieval Romance*, Longman, London

Brewer, Derek (1983) *English Gothic Literature*, Macmillan, London

Chaytor, H. J. (1945) *From Script to Print*, Heffer, Cambridge

Curtius, E. R. (1953) *European Literature and the Latin Middle Ages*, Routledge & Kegan Paul, London

Dronke, E. P. M. (1968) *The Medieval Lyric*, Hutchinson, London

Ford, Boris (ed.) (1982) *Medieval Literature: Chaucer and the Alliterative Tradition* (vol. 1, Part One of *The New Pelican Guide to English Literature*), Penguin, Harmondsworth

——(ed.) (1983) *Medieval Literature: The European Inheritance* (vol. 1, Part Two of *The New Pelican Guide to English Literature*), Penguin, Harmondsworth

Heer, F. J. (1962) *The Medieval World*, Weidenfeld & Nicolson, London

Ker, W. P. (1896) *Epic and Romance*, Macmillan, London

Lewis, C. S. (1964) *The Discarded Image*, Cambridge University Press, Cambridge

Loomis, R. S. (ed.) (1959) *Arthurian Literature in the Middle Ages*, Clarendon Press, Oxford

Pearsall, Derek (1977) *Old English and Middle English Poetry*, Routledge & Kegan Paul, London

Raby, F. J. (1927) *A History of Christian-Latin Poetry*, Clarendon Press, Oxford

——(1934) *A History of Secular Latin Poetry*, Clarendon Press, Oxford

ADDITIONAL WORKS CITED

Aneirin (1988) *Y Gododdin*, edited and translated by A. O. H. Jarman, The Gomer Press, Llandysul

Brewer, Derek (1980) *Symbolic Stories*, D. S. Brewer, Cambridge; 2nd edn 1988, Longman, London

Burrow, J. A. (1973) 'Bards, Minstrels and Men of Letters'. In D. Daiches and A. Thorlby (eds), *The Medieval World*, Aldus Books, London, pp. 347–70

Dante (1962) *Paradiso*, translated by Dorothy L. Sayers and Barbara Reynolds, Penguin, Harmondsworth

Eliot, T. S. (1942) *Little Gidding*, Faber & Faber, London

Gordon, E. V. (ed.) (1937) *The Battle of Maldon*, Methuen, London

16

RENAISSANCE POETRY

ALASTAIR FOWLER

Late Victorian interest in the Renaissance was keen, as for example, Tudor retrospective styles in architecture and furniture partly reflected. The enthusiasms of John Addington Symonds, the literary evolutionist, ranged from Italian Renaissance subjects to Sir Philip Sidney. But, at a time when the lyric mode dominated, Elizabethan and later song were especially valued, and Robert Herrick even, if possible, overvalued. For the poet A. C. Swinburne, Herrick was the 'the crowning star', superior even to Shakespeare: 'as a creative and inventive singer he surpasses all his rivals in quantity of good work' (1891, p. x). Still, contrasting strands of Renaissance poetry were by no means ignored – as indeed T. S. Eliot quite modestly acknowledges: 'I have sometimes been credited with starting the vogue for Donne and other metaphysical poets . . . But I did not discover any of these poets. Coleridge, and Browning in turn, admired Donne.' In particular,

> the enthusiastic tributes of Swinburne are by no means without critical merit. In our own time, John Donne has lacked no publicity: Gosse's *Life and Letters*, in two volumes, appeared in 1899. I remember being introduced to Donne's poetry when I was a Freshman at Harvard by Professor Briggs, an ardent admirer; Grierson's edition of the Poems, in two volumes, was published in 1912; and it was Grierson's *Metaphysical Poetry*, sent me to review, that gave me my first occasion to write about Donne.
>
> (Eliot, 1965, pp. 21–2)

Eliot, who had not a specially good ear, depended heavily on the taste of Swinburne, whose preferences have thus exerted a disguised influence on modern criticism. The Victorians could be good reader-critics: the sensitive academic Walter Raleigh and the journalist Edmund Gosse are examples, now neglected. But, with a few exceptions like William Courthope, W. P. Ker and the honest, insensitive Oliver Elton, their literary history cannot be called impressive. Perhaps the most readable is George Saintsbury, an omnivorous reader himself, whose *Elizabethan Literature* (1887) and *History of English Pros-*

ody (1906–10) give an internal or subjective account, and are still interesting and locally valuable.

The attractions of Metaphysical poetry were not obvious to Victorian and Edwardian readers whose taste had been formed on lyric; so that modernist critics found themselves obliged to go into more detailed explanations and recommendations than had ever been customary. But this was congenial enough to the new school. As modernists, they had an interest in difficult literature, in the complexities with which compressed language could be loaded. By favouring the Metaphysicals, Eliot and F. R. Leavis, the Cambridge critics and American New Critics were correcting real neglect; and they produced work of lasting interest. Eliot's 'The Metaphysical Poets' and 'Andrew Marvell' (*Selected Essays*, 1932), J. C. Smith's article 'On Metaphysical Poetry' (1934) and William Empson's wild, brilliant *Seven Types of Ambiguity* (1930) have the status of classics. And George Williamson (1930), followed by Leavis (1936), attempted with some success to discover a far-reaching tradition – a 'line of wit' – within which the Metaphysical school would be established as the basis of the best subsequent poetry, rather than a mere aberration. What these modernist critics were attempting – especially, perhaps, T. S. Eliot and F. R. Leavis – was to validate the contemporary poetry of witty compression, by creating for it an antecedent tradition in seventeenth-century epigram. To do this, they rearranged literary history, where necessary rewriting it, in effect, to bring out respectable precedents for obscurity, symbolist imagery and colloquial, low-style diction. And with this in view, their criticism concentrated on difficult poems, particularly ones with complex 'conceits' or far-fetched comparisons.

Advancement of the Metaphysicals in its turn went to excess. John Donne, indeed, is almost a great poet, and will surely continue to be read; although he has probably been focused on too closely (being an amateur poet he invested too little time in his craft, and does not always repay detailed study). We still await a great critical treatment that will bring to bear the Oxford English Texts editions of Donne by Helen Gardner (1957) and others, and the acute scholarly work of Barbara Lewalski (1973) and, particularly on Neoplatonic aspects, A. J. Smith (1972). George Herbert continues to attract penetrating criticism such as Vendler (1975), less and less, however, under the Metaphysical aegis. Carew, similarly, is interesting as a Jonsonian, or in connection with the visual arts, rather than as a follower of Donne. Andrew Marvell, a poet effectually discovered during this century, whose reputation has risen more dramatically than any other, was indeed at first treated as a Metaphysical (by Eliot, and later by Leavis and Empson). But much later work, some of it brilliant – by Leishman (1966), Kermode (1952b), Colie (1970) and others – has developed a more baroque or Augustan view of Marvell, as a subtle, tonal poet, relating his work much more to its social and landscape contexts. But as for the minor

Metaphysicals, they have mostly failed to make a mark, and are likely to be reconsigned to oblivion.

In any event, the limitations of the notion that seventeenth-century poets can be divided into Metaphysicals and 'Sons of Ben' have for some decades become steadily clearer. It ignores the Metaphysical element in Jonson's poetry, besides the numerous poets who belong to both groupings – as an improved literary history has pointed out. Douglas Bush's learned but critically perfunctory *English Literature in the Earlier Seventeenth Century* (1945, revised 1962) gave generous space and treatment to Jonsonian poets like Herrick, as well as to a third grouping, around Michael Drayton. Drayton's influence, it emerges, had a strong revival in the 1630s, and extended, through its own filiation, to Alexander Pope. American criticism has tended to retain a more conservative regard for the Renaissance lyricists: even Cleanth Brooks's New-Critical *The Well Wrought Urn* (1949) paired essays on Herrick and on Donne. As a consequence of these reconsiderations, there has been a return of interest in the Caroline poets, evidenced in Herrick's case, for example, by noteworthy editions (Martin, 1956; Patrick, 1963) and criticism (Deming, 1974; Rollin and Patrick, 1978). But the most striking shift of focus has been to Jonson himself, as appears not only in the monumental but often laconic edition by C. H. Herford and Percy and Evelyn M. Simpson (1925–52), and two discriminating editions by Ian Donaldson (1975 and 1985), but also in commanding critical work such as Richard S. Peterson's *Imitation and Praise in the Poetry of Ben Jonson* (1981). Peterson has an inward grasp of the Renaissance rhetoric of praise, and is often able to explain in detail what his poet has attempted. Again and again he brings to bear the subtexts of Jonson's imitations, in such a way as to restore passages to their original brilliance, and reveal their author as engaged in a process of moral assimilation.

Modernist revision of the poetic canon (by Eliot, Leavis and others) was at its most controversial in the attempt to demote Milton – for it is not at all the case that 'Milton's dislodgement, in the past decade, after his two centuries of predominance, was effected with remarkably little fuss', as Leavis optimistically put it in *Revaluation* (1936, p. 7). Ostensibly the 'dislodgement' was necessary because of the insensitive monotony of Milton's verse, and because his imagery lacked sensuous richness and 'organic' variety; although it seems obvious now that the true motive had rather more to do with the Miltonic basis of the established poetic diction that Eliot and Ezra Pound were ambitious to replace with their own. The belligerent challenge of Leavis's *Revaluation* essay, and of such others as A. J. A. Waldock's *Paradise Lost and its Critics* (1947), naturally provoked defences. C. S. Lewis's *Preface to Paradise Lost* (1942) defended its conventions on their own terms; while Christopher Ricks's *Milton's Grand Style* (1963) totally outflanked the attack by showing that the poem satisfies even Leavis's criteria. In fact, the 'fuss' continued – so much so as to call for a distinct change of front between T. S. Eliot's essays of 1935 and 1947 (see Eliot, 1957a and 1957b). A new attack by Empson in *Milton's God* (1961, revised 1965) took this time the substantive ground that the Christian God was too sadistic for Milton to sustain consistent belief throughout *Paradise Lost*. But, again, these alleged inconsistencies were argued to be only subtler beauties in Alastair Fowler's edition (1971).

More recently, sceptical reconsideration of Milton has not only pursued inconsistencies in the Empsonian manner, but dwelt deconstructively on indeterminacies. Stanley E. Fish had already done much to justify the poem's logic to such sceptics in *Surprised by Sin* (1967). In the event, the productiveness of the Milton industry (more than 300 journal articles a year, besides monographs) has made nonsense of the notion of his 'dislodging'. From this wealth of criticism it is almost invidious to select. But Barbara Lewalski's *Milton's Brief Epic* (1966) was decisive in revaluation of *Paradise Regained*; C. A. Patrides's *Milton and the Christian Tradition* (1966) learnedly supplied contexts of Reformation thought necessary to a grasp of Milton's meaning; and John M. Steadman, in such studies as *Milton and the Renaissance Hero* (1967), brought erudition in historical poetics effectively to bear on problems of interpretation. The plethora of Milton criticism has posed serious problems for editors. A. W. Verity (*Milton: Paradise Lost*, 1910) set a high benchmark for scholarly annotation. The great Columbia Milton (ed. Patterson, 1931–40) does not include commentary; but the deficiency is partly supplied by Merritt Y. Hughes (1957); Douglas Bush (1966); and John Carey and Alastair Fowler (1968, the first complete edition with both explanatory and critical notes). The Yale-Routledge Milton *Variorum Commentary* (ed. Hughes, 1970) succeeds in representing the best of the scholarly output, at least from the USA; as does W. B. Hunter's *A Milton Encyclopedia* (1978–80). On the biographical side, a solid foundation for much of the above work is offered by William R. Parker's excellent *Milton: A Biography* (1968), a worthy successor to David Masson's great *Life of Milton* (1881–96).

Currently, Milton criticism seems to be developing in two rather different directions. Some, like Barbara Lewalski, are following the path of genre criticism, identifying Milton's local modes with greatly increased precision, and often managing to show his poetry as even better than had been thought. Others are boldly exploring philosophical and theological and political implications. What philosophy of language do Milton's ambiguities imply? When exactly does the Fall in *Paradise Lost* occur? And who is responsible for it? Did Milton mean this to be problematic? And what about his historical allusions, which have been neglected for so long? This return to large issues opens the exciting prospect that just appreciation of this remarkable poet may at last be achieved.

Criticism of sixteenth-century poetry has proceeded on similar, if less spectacular, lines. Here, too, there has been modernist elevation of a colloquial poet – Wyatt – and here, too, the complementary qualities of very different poets, such as Surrey, have reasserted their claims. The attempt to dislodge a great poet, Spenser, provoked a luxuriant efflorescence of Spenser criticism, from Paul J. Alpers's *The Poetry of 'The Faerie Queene'* (1967), concentrating powerfully on the words and their immediate implications, to James Nohrnberg's deep mythographic speculations in *The Analogy of 'The Faerie Queene'* (1976). Much of this criticism finds mention in A. C. Hamilton's fine Longman edition of *The Faerie Queene* (1977), or in Thomas P. Roche's Penguin edition (1978). The result is to reveal *The Faerie Queene* as an altogether more coherent work than it used to seem. Nohrnberg, for example, brings together widely separate passages, and interprets them in the context of learnedly adduced mythographic material, in such a way as to establish complex interconnections at all points. Spenser may not obey modern narrative logic; but his poem has a highly consistent mytho-logic.

Shakespeare's poems have naturally challenged much ambitious criticism – some of it Empsonian or else structuralist, like Roman Jakobson's exhaustive inventory of formal patterning in one of the Sonnets (1970). But it is not clear how many of the possibilities Jakobson conjectures have any relevance to Shakespeare's meanings. Perhaps the most valuable fruit of much labour by critics of Shakespeare's poems has been in commentaries on the Sonnets, notably John Kerrigan's (1986), and in general accounts of the sequence, such as J. B. Leishman's (1961) and Stephen Booth's (1969, 1977). The overall structure of the Sonnets still eludes analysis, however; partly because they were originally intended for a small readership. Another reason is that their collective form is numerological (Fowler, 1970): many critics have an understandable dislike of this difficult aspect.

There has been some acute criticism of other poets: Hallett Smith's well-judged *Elizabethan Poetry* (1952) and J. W. Lever's *The Elizabethan Love Sonnet* (1956) come to mind; and recently there has been a revival of interest in Sidney's poetry. A breakthrough came with Hallett Smith's perception that Astrophil was a persona, not to be identified with Sidney himself. That in turn has led to radical rethinking of Sidney's larger intention in *Astrophil and Stella*. Thomas Roche (1986), Anne Ferry (1983) and others have shown how much satire it contains of conventional erotic attitudes; and this is complicated by self-parody and camp exaggeration. Astrophil, in fact, is a negative example. In such ways, Sidney has become a much more promising subject for criticism. Most of the strategic work on the sixteenth century, however, has related to Spenser and Shakespeare, or to the period of transition from medieval to Renaissance.

The phases of sixteenth-century poetry have been much pondered. What used to be thought of as the 'Scottish Chaucerians' are now, in large part through the work of John MacQueen (1967), 'Scottish Renaissance' poets. (These have attracted thorough editions: Kinsley's Dunbar, 1979; Fox's Henryson, 1981; and Bawcutt's Gavin Douglas, 1967.) Critical monographs illuminating the same period of transition include C. S. Lewis's *The Allegory of Love* (1936), Priscilla Bawcutt's *Gavin Douglas* (1976) and A. C. Spearing's *Medieval to Renaissance in English Poetry* (1985). We have at last an informed revaluation of Skelton, by Arthur Kinney (1987); and there is a fine edition by John Scattergood (1983). Literary history of the sixteenth century has long been dominated by C. S. Lewis's wonderfully readable *Oxford History of English Literature in the Sixteenth Century* (1954), which first labelled the phases ('drab' and 'golden') that Tudor verse is still often divided into. Attempts at radical revaluations – such as Yvor Winters's in the interest of Gascoigne and Greville – have not had much success. Apart from his dispraise of Wyatt, most accept the Lewisian canon.

Much of the most interesting Renaissance criticism of the 1950s and 1960s arose from exchange between inventive critics and corrective scholars. And the Herbert controversy between Empson (1950) and Rosemond Tuve (1952) had in addition a strategic outcome for scholarship. Empson was a pioneer of the sort of criticism concerned with what readers can make a poem mean, rather than with what its author meant. But in *A Reading of George Herbert* (1952) – intellectually superior although stylistically graceless – Tuve restored Herbert's 'The Sacrifice' to its liturgical contexts, and demonstrated beyond question that features Empson had taken as original in Herbert's poem were actually 'implicated in its past', connected rhetorically, that is, with texts familiar to every seventeenth-century churchgoer. Her demolition of Empson's argument showed decisively how essential it is for a critic of Renaissance poetry to take account of what is being done rhetorically. Similarly, the aim of her earlier *Elizabethan and Metaphysical Imagery* (1947) had been to examine how seventeenth-century imagery differed from that of the sixteenth century, and how far differences supposed due to distinctively metaphysical qualities were actually attributable to unchanged criteria like decorum of subject. That book, too, had strategic implications. If imagery was as important as the modernists claimed, it behoved the critic to know something about Renaissance rhetoric.

Studies of rhetoric put Renaissance criticism on an altogether firmer footing, by making it possible to locate more precisely the literary events intended. With this ultimate objective in view, there have been many technical studies of rhetoric, as well as editions of Renaissance rhetorics, such as Ethel Seaton's of Abraham Fraunce's *The Arcadian Rhetorike* (1950). It has proved quite another matter to make such specialist work conveniently accessible to the critic of poetry.

Perhaps the most interesting application of rhetoric has been in exploring *imitatio*, the process whereby, through a succession of thefts or borrowings or translations or rewritings, poetry grows out of previous poetry. In this direction, one of the most influential books of the century has been Ernst R. Curtius's *European Literature and the Latin Middle Ages* (1953). Curtius, correcting the romantic stress on individual genius, traced some of the topoi or commonplaces shared by works in the classical tradition; an emphasis not uncongenial to structuralists eager to dismiss poets from consideration. But the concreteness of rhetorical studies had almost as great an effect. It is striking how treatments of indebtedness have matured since Harold Ogden White's important *Plagiarism and Imitation During the English Renaissance* (1935), from mere identification of sources to a subtle assaying of intertextuality, most penetrating of all in Thomas Greene's *Light in Troy* (1982). It is largely equipment in rhetoric and language studies that enables Greene to go beyond deconstructive admiration of indeterminacy to trace the actual aetiological links with the past that keep old meanings accessible. Other brilliant successes in the history of imitation include Gordon Braden's *The Classics and English Renaissance Poetry* (1978) and Charles Martindale's *John Milton and the Transformation of Ancient Epic* (1986). Significantly, both of these resume discussion of poets' intentions. Perhaps the stress on collective intertextuality is felt to have gone far enough: after all, much to the poet is due.

Knowledge of rhetoric also quickened studies of genre, challenging them to new precision in treating intertextualities. Older studies like Dwight Durling's worthy *Georgic Tradition in English Poetry* (1935), although of lasting value for their data, were outmoded vehicles – powered, in effect, by the annalistic mule. Even W. W. Greg's formidable *Pastoral Poetry and Pastoral Drama* (1906) seldom tried to make sense of the patterns it traced. Douglas Bush's flavoursome *Mythology and the Renaissance Tradition* (1932) attained a different plane of intellectual activity, although it tended to ignore differences in genre between the poems compared. Empson's *Some Versions of Pastoral* (1935) popularized the genre approach, but showed a widening gap between 'creative' and scholarly criticism; readers familiar with Thomas G. Rosenmeyer's *The Green Cabinet* (1969), for example, cannot but think Empson's book nebulous by comparison, at least in its treatment of pastoral. There is more instruction in Frank Kermode's little essay introducing *English Pastoral Poetry* (1952a). A critical generation that cut its teeth on rhetoric has examined generic coding in far greater detail than at any time since the eighteenth century – and with less readiness to accept old labels.

A suggestive essay in this direction was Rosalie Colie's *Resources of Kind* (1973). Its influence shows clearly, for example, in Barbara Lewalski's *Paradise Lost and the Rhetoric of Literary Forms* (1985) and in Alastair Fowler's *Kinds of Literature* (1982). On the broadest view, one could say that the most ambitious scholarship of the last century has engaged with questions of genre, or taken the form of explicitly generic studies, such as James Hutton's of the epigram (1935), and Maren-Sofie Røstvig's of the retirement poem, in *The Happy Man* (1954).

The literary context is not the only one necessary to meaning: a broader intellectual environment also requires attention. As the most recent domain of assumptions obviously different from our own, the Renaissance 'world picture' has challenged many studies. Here, ground-breaking works were Hardin Craig's *The Enchanted Glass* (1935), E. M. W. Tillyard's *The Elizabethan World Picture* (1943) and Marjorie H. Nicolson's *The Breaking of the Circle* (1950). Such works, and others more recent, like S. K. Heninger's *The Cosmographical Glass* (1977) and C. A. Patrides's *Premises and Motifs in Renaissance Thought and Literature* (1982), have occasionally been brought to bear on poetic texts, but not nearly often enough. Yet recovery of older forms and schemes of thought is essential to any deep understanding of Renaissance poetry.

Recently, critics of the 'cultural materialist' school in this country (Alan Sinfield, Jonathan Dollimore and others), like the American New Historicists (Stephen Greenblatt, Louis Montrose and others), have objected that the Elizabethan world picture was merely a dominant ideology, or machinery of socio-political legitimation, and never, in any case, a consistent system. The first objection is ill-founded. Far more than propaganda was involved: poets of every political persuasion – even a republican like Chapman – used imagery of the Elizabethan world picture, and thought within its schemes. But the second objection has exposed a real weakness in Tillyard's work and that of his imitators. For the Elizabethan world picture was never continuous. It existed in many variant forms; and these have yet to be analysed adequately. Nevertheless, so far as politicizing English literature goes, none of the New Historicists has had anything like the penetration of the old historicist David Norbrook. His *Poetry and Politics in the English Renaissance* (1984), although locally in need of correction, is in the main informative and just. Useful studies of patronage, such as J. A. van Dorsten's *Poets, Patrons, and Professors* (1962) on Sidney and the Low Countries, have begun to explore biographical contexts, important in an age of manuscript circulation, and necessary to any full account of the politics of poetry.

Work on Renaissance education, notably T. W. Baldwin's *Shakspere's Small Latine and Lesse Greeke* (1944), has also played a vital part. Among the fruits of this sustained effort to recover earlier contexts have been several fine studies in the history of ideas, among them Rosalie Colie's rambling but stimulating *Paradoxia Epidemica* (1966) and James Hutton's *Themes of Peace in Renaissance Poetry* (1984), a work of cosmopolitan erudition. Currently, one of the most interesting directions of enquiry lies through Renaissance theories of language.

In recent decades, Renaissance speech itself has been minutely studied. Through the work of Eric Dobson, Fausto Cercignani and others, the original phonetic character of Renaissance poetry is now better understood. Prosodic analysis has in consequence been put on a firmer basis. Derek Attridge achieved a definitive treatment of classicizing quantitative verse in his *Well-Weighed Syllables* (1974). And the musical interface, a largely neglected subject, was effectively approached in John Stevens's *Music and Poetry at the Tudor Court* (1961) and Winifred Maynard's *Elizabethan Lyric Poetry and its Music* (1986).

In the 1960s, along a different but not unrelated line of enquiry, study of Renaissance theories of proportion threw unexpected light on poetic form. It had long been known that medieval poets practised numerical composition, whereby numbers of lines or other units were meaningfully organized. But A. Kent Hieatt (1960) and Alastair Fowler (1964, 1970), working independently, found patterns of calendrical, symmetrical and other number symbolism in Renaissance poems also. Such criticism was at first called lunatic; but Hieatt's *Short Time's Endless Monument* (1960) is now a classic, and numerology as standard an instrument of scholarly criticism as prosody. It is understood still by almost as few people; but John MacQueen's readable introduction, *Numerology* (1985), may alter that. Part of the interest of numerical composition lies in its status as an extra-syntactic bearer of meaning, not subject to exactly the same indeterminacies as words. Much exploratory work remains to be done in the field of numerology – especially, perhaps, on shorter poems. George Herbert's reputation should be still further enhanced, for example, when it is appreciated how far he organized his poetry at the minutest levels of numerology.

By treating a poem's form as an emblem of its meaning, numerological criticism is in a sense a special case of criticism that relates poetry to visual art. Here several strands need to be distinguished, of which the first, both in time and importance, connects poetry with iconography. From the beginning, systematic iconographers such as Erwin Panofsky drew examples from literature; and literary critics were quick to entertain the hope that the new approach might in turn offer skeleton keys whereby to decode obscure imagery in poetry. Here again Rosemond Tuve's work was strategic, not only in *A Reading of George Herbert* (1952) but in her more methodical *Allegorical Imagery* (1966). Others followed, notably Don Cameron Allen, whose deeply learned hermeneutic investigations are gathered in such collections as *Image and Meaning* (1960) and *Mysteriously Meant* (1970), and Roland Mushat Frye, with his invaluable survey *Milton's Imagery and the Visual Arts* (1978). Scholars now perceive that iconography is far from offering a straightforward dictionary of old meanings; nevertheless, it has become established, like rhetoric, as a necessary part of the organon.

A second strand – taken up in Jean H. Hagstrum's *The Sister Arts* (1958) – connects poetry with ecphrastic or descriptive art, focusing particularly on resemblance or on competition (*paragone*) between poetry and painting. Monographs by Farmer (1984), Gilman (1986) and Roston (1987) have shown how fruitful this line of enquiry can be. After all, it was largely because of the *paragone* that iconography came to have special importance in Renaissance poetry. The third strand, the emblematic, has tended to be a highly specialist preserve. It was opened up only to be closed off by such tantalizingly erudite works as Mario Praz's monumental *Studies in Seventeenth-Century Imagery* (1964). Only very recently has the vast emblem literature begun to be brought to bear in a more accessible way, through such journals as *Word and Image* and *Emblematica*. Yet full appreciation of a poem like Donne's 'A Valediction: Forbidding Mourning', with its conceit of the compasses, can in a sense only begin when it has been restored to its context of emblems of *constantia* and of divine perfection. This is not merely a matter of attaching abstract labels: the rhetorical details of such a passage have to be read like the descriptive enumerations in emblem book epigrams.

Consideration of the connections between poetry and visual art has led naturally on to problems of periodization – not least, problems of reconciling the chronologies of the different disciplines. Reconceiving the Scottish Chaucerians as Scottish Renaissance poets has not made it easier to locate a pure Renaissance phase. So far as England is concerned, this has proved oddly elusive. Its Renaissance was certainly later than Scotland's, and is put by some critics as late as Spenser. Others (E. M. W. Tillyard, for example) eliminate it altogether. But at least it has become clear that Surrey's poetry, formerly grouped with Wyatt's, properly belongs not only to a different generation but to a different stylistic phase. And in recent decades Elizabethan poetic form has come to be appreciated as akin to mannerist art in its self-conscious stylishness, its self-references and its bravura. Certain features of mannerist style are explored in Fowler's *Conceitful Thought* (1975) and in James V. Mirollo's *Mannerism and Renaissance Poetry* (1984); but much remains to be done along this line.

What are the ways forward in criticism of Renaissance poetry? An early objective should be to reopen the *terra* now almost *incognita* of neo-Latin poetry, where recently only a few intrepid explorers like Leicester Bradner (1940) and J. W. Binns (1974) have ventured: it goes without saying that Latin intertextualities are crucial for this period. In the same way, while French and Italian comparative studies have been given some attention, Spanish and Dutch contexts have been badly neglected. Neglected genres include seventeenth-century georgic, where Røstvig's *The Happy Man*, Kitty Scoular's *Natural Magic* (1965) and Anthony Low's *The Georgic Revolution* (1987) suggest many lines of enquiry; and formal imitation, where the publication of Harold F. Brooks and Raman Selden's long-awaited Oldham edition (1987) and Keith Walker's Rochester (1984) provide a timely stimulus. The transition from Caroline to

Augustan poetry needs much more attention: institutionalized division at 1660 has had a stultifying effect on the study of mid-century poetry.

Among earlier neglected figures, the one whose poems cry out most urgently for criticism is surely Michael Drayton, whose originality, variety and even historical importance still await recognition. Currently, the sixteenth century is attracting as much attention as the seventeenth: New Historicists, in particular, find generalization easier in the lesser-known period. But indeed, this new interest is fortunate, for in the sixteenth century almost everything remains to be done. A promising point of entry is through the sonnets, which offer an interesting subject for feminist criticism. Pioneering work by Thomas Roche (1970, 1974) and others has revolutionized thinking about the sonnet sequences: it remains to apply the new concept, of the sequence as a didactic form, to criticism of individual poets, and to larger questions of genre and individuation. Currently, there are many theoretical analyses of Renaissance psychology and logic and education, such as Patrick Grant's *Literature and the Discovery of Method in the English Renaissance* (1985). Whether they will prove to have a useful bearing on criticism of Renaissance poetry remains to be seen.

FURTHER READING

Carey, John and Fowler, Alastair D. S. (eds) (1968) *The Poems of John Milton*, Longman, London

Hamilton, A. C. (ed.) (1977) *The Faerie Queene*, Longman, London

Kermode, Frank (1952a) *English Pastoral Poetry*, Cassell, London

Lewalski, Barbara Kiefer (ed.) (1986) *Renaissance Genres*, Harvard University Press, Cambridge

Lewis, C. S. (1954) *English Literature in the Sixteenth Century*, Clarendon Press, Oxford

Martindale, Charles (1986) *John Milton and the Transformation of Ancient Epic*, Croom Helm, London

Martz, Louis L. (1954) *The Poetry of Meditation*, Yale University Press, New Haven and London

Nohrnberg, James (1976) *The Analogy of 'The Faerie Queene'*, Princeton University Press, Princeton

Norbrook, David (1984) *Poetry and Politics in the English Renaissance*, Croom Helm, London

Patrides, C. A. (1966) *Milton and the Christian Tradition*, Clarendon Press, Oxford

Peterson, Richard S. (1981) *Imitation and Praise in the Poems of Ben Jonson*, Yale University Press, New Haven

Ricks, Christopher (1963) *Milton's Grand Style*, Clarendon Press, Oxford

Tuve, Rosemond (1947) *Elizabethan and Metaphysical Imagery*, University of Chicago Press, Chicago

ADDITIONAL WORKS CITED

Bawcutt, Priscilla (1967) *The Shorter Poems of Gavin Douglas*, Scottish Texts Society, Edinburgh

Binns, J. W. (1974) *The Latin Poetry of English Poets*, Routledge & Kegan Paul, London

Booth, Stephen (1969) *An Essay on Shakespeare's Sonnets*, Yale University Press, New Haven

——(ed.) (1977) *Shakespeare's Sonnets Edited with Analytic Commentary*, Yale University Press, New Haven

Braden, Gordon (1978) *The Classics and English Renaissance Poetry*, Yale University Prerss, New Haven

Bradner, Leicester (1940) *Musae Anglicanae. A History of Anglo-Latin Poetry 1500–1925*, Modern Language Association of America, New York; Oxford University Press, London

Brooks, Harold F. and Selden, Raman (eds) (1987) *The Poems of John Oldham*, Clarendon Press, Oxford

Bush, Douglas (ed.) (1966) *Milton: Poetical Works*, Oxford University Press, London

Colie, Rosalie L. (1970) *'My Echoing Song': Marvell's Poetry of Criticism*, Princeton University Press, Princeton

Curtius, Ernst R. (1953) *European Literature and the Latin Middle Ages*, translated by Willard R. Trask, Routledge & Kegan Paul, London [first published 1948]

Deming, Robert H. (1974) *Ceremony and Art: Robert Herrick's Poetry*, Mouton, The Hague

Donaldson, Ian (ed.) (1975) *Ben Jonson: Poems*, Oxford University Press, London

——(ed.) (1985) *Ben Jonson*, Oxford University Press, Oxford

Eliot, T. S. (1957a) 'A Note on the Verse of John Milton'. In T. S. Eliot, *On Poetry and Poets*, Faber & Faber, London [essay first published 1935]

——(1957b) 'Milton'. In T. S. Eliot, *On Poetry and Poets*, Faber & Faber, London [essay first published 1947]

——(1965) *To Criticise the Critic*, Faber & Faber, London

Empson, William (1930) *Seven Types of Ambiguity*, Chatto & Windus, London

——(1950) 'George Herbert and Miss Tuve', *Kenyon Review*, 12, 735–8

Farmer, Norman K. (1984) *Poets and the Visual Arts in Renaissance England*, University of Texas, Austin

Ferry, Anne (1983) *Inward Language: The Sonnets of Wyatt, Sidney, Shakespeare and Donne*, University of Chicago Press, Chicago

Fowler, Alastair D. S. (1964) *Spenser and the Numbers of Time*, Routledge & Kegan Paul, London

——(1970) *Triumphal Forms*, Cambridge University Press, Cambridge

——(ed.) (1971) *John Milton: Paradise Lost*, Longman, London

Fox, Denton (1981) *The Poems of Robert Henryson*, Clarendon Press, Oxford

Frye, Roland Mushat (1978) *Milton's Imagery and the Visual Arts*, Princeton University Press, Princeton

Gardner, Helen (ed.) (1957) *Metaphysical Poets*, Penguin, Harmondsworth

Gilman, Ernest (1986) *Iconoclasm and Poetry in the English Reformation*, University of Chicago Press, Chicago

Greene, Thomas (1982) *Light in Troy*, Yale University Press, New Haven

Herford, C. H., Simpson, Percy and Simpson, Evelyn M. (eds) (1925–52) *Ben Jonson*, 11 vols, Clarendon Press, Oxford

Hieatt, A. Kent (1960) *Short Time's Endless Monument*, Columbia University Press, New York

Hughes, Merritt Y. (ed.) (1957) *John Milton: Complete Poems and Major Prose*, Odyssey, New York

——(ed.) (1970) *A Variorum Commentary on the Poems of John Milton*, Yale University Press, New Haven

Hutton, James (1935) *The Greek Anthology in Italy to the Year 1800*, Cornell University Press, Ithaca

Jakobson, Roman and Jones, Lawrence G. (1970) *Shakespeare's Verbal Art in 'th'Expence of Spirit'*, Mouton, The Hague

Kermode, Frank (1952b) 'The Argument of Marvell's "Garden" '. In William R. Keast (ed.) (1952), *Seventeenth Century English Poetry*, Oxford University Press, New York

Kerrigan, John (1986) *The Sonnets and 'A Lover's Complaint'*, Penguin, Harmondsworth

Kinney, Arthur (1987) *John Skelton: Priest as Poet*, University of North Carolina, Chapel Hill

Kinsley, James (ed.) (1979) *The Poems of William Dunbar*, Clarendon Press, Oxford

Leavis, F. R. (1936) *Revaluation*, Chatto & Windus, London

Leishman, J. B. (1961) *Themes and Variations in Shakespeare's Sonnets*, Hutchinson, London

——(1966) *The Art of Marvell's Poetry*, Hutchinson, London

Lewalski, Barbara Kiefer (1966) *Milton's Brief Epic: The Genre, Meaning and Art of Paradise Regained*, Methuen, London

——(1973) *Donne's 'Anniversaries'*, Princeton University Press, Princeton

MacQueen, John (1967) *Robert Henryson*, Clarendon Press, Oxford

——(1985) *Numerology*, Edinburgh University Press, Edinburgh

Martin, L. C. (ed.) (1956) *The Poetical Works of Robert Herrick*, Clarendon Press, Oxford

Parker, William R. (1968) *Milton: A Biography*, 2 vols, Clarendon Press, Oxford

Patrick, J. Max (ed.) (1963) *The Complete Poetry of Robert Herrick*, Norton, New York

Patterson, F. A. (ed.) (1931–40) *Milton: Works*, 20 vols, Columbia University Press, New York

Roche, Thomas P. (1970) 'Shakespeare and the Sonnet Sequence'. In Christopher Ricks (ed.), *English Poetry and Prose, 1540–1674* (vol. 2 of *The Sphere History of Literature in the English Language*), Barrie & Jenkins, London

——(1974) 'The Calendrical Structure of Petrarch's *Canzoniere*', *Studies in Philology*, 71, 152–72

——(1986) *Petrarch and the English Sonnet Tradition*, A. M. S. Press, New York

Rollin, R. B. and Patrick, J. Max (1978) *'Trust to Good Verses': Herrick Tercentenary Essays*, Pittsburgh University Press, Pittsburgh

Rosenmeyer, Thomas G. (1969) *The Green Cabinet*, University of California Press, Berkeley and Los Angeles

Roston, Murray (1987) *Renaissance Perspectives in Literature and the Visual Arts*, Princeton University Press, Princeton

Scattergood, John (ed.) (1983) *John Skelton: The Complete English Poems*, Penguin, Harmondsworth

Smith, A. J. (1972) 'The Dismissal of Love'. In A. J. Smith (ed.), *John Donne: Essays in Celebration*, Methuen, London

Smith, J. C. (1934) 'On Metaphysical Poetry'. In F. R. Leavis (ed.) *Determinations*, Chatto & Windus, London

Steadman, John M. (1967) *Milton and the Renaissance Hero*, Clarendon Press, Oxford

Swinburne, A. C. (1891) *Robert Herrick, the Hesperides and Noble Numbers*, edited by A. Pollard, The Muses Library, London

Tuve, Rosemond (1952) *A Reading of George Herbert*, Faber & Faber, London

Vendler, Helen (1975) *The Poetry of George Herbert*, Harvard University Press, Cambridge

Walker, Keith (1984) *The Poems of John Wilmot, Earl of Rochester*, Basil Blackwell, Oxford

Williamson, George (1930) *The Donne Tradition*, Harvard University Press, Cambridge

17

'AUGUSTAN' POETRY

A. J. SAMBROOK

In 1660 John Dryden welcomed the restoration of Charles II with a long, celebratory, heroic-couplet poem, *Astraea Redux*, where he likens the king to Augustus, who brought peace home after the agony of civil war and inaugurated a glorious era of power abroad and flourishing arts at home. Earlier in the seventeenth century James I had been similarly praised by Ben Jonson and Cromwell by Edmund Waller. Eighteenth-century poets would also compare their rulers with Augustus, but they would do so ironically as often as not. Seventeenth- and eighteenth-century references to an 'Augustan Age' of English literature are few and far between. The earliest appears to be by Francis Atterbury, who in 1690 bestowed that title upon the reign of Charles II, by virtue of the poets flourishing then; this attribution was contradicted by Jonathan Swift and David Hume, among others, but was still being made at the end of the eighteenth century. Oliver Goldsmith's opinion, published in 1759, that the 'Augustan' age of English literature was under William III and Anne, enjoyed a certain amount of contemporary support too (Erskine-Hill, 1983, pp. 236–63). In the twentieth century, though, 'Augustan' has been applied fairly indiscriminately to the period of literature from 1660 or 1700 to about 1800. The once-powerful critic George Saintsbury gave the term his authority in *The Peace of the Augustans: A Survey of Eighteenth-Century Literature as a Place of Rest and Refreshment* (1915), and, however strange he may appear as Saintsbury's bedfellow, the still-powerful critic F. R. Leavis lent it further authority twenty years later. Leavis saw the poetry of what he called 'the Augustan Tradition' as characterized by 'neatness and prose propriety', or, at its best, rising to 'a strong conventionality' (Leavis, 1936, pp. 105–6), though he excepts the varied achievement of Alexander Pope from his dismissive generalizations. After the Second World War the term became commonplace in surveys and background books: e. g. John Butt, *The Augustan Age* (1950) and A. R. Humphreys, *The Augustan World* (1954). Two more recent commentators, Pat Rogers (1974) and Margaret Doody (1985), retain 'Augustan' as a convenient piece of shorthand which inspires recognition, but both of them bend their considerable critical energies to countering certain misconceptions which it evokes in the average reader. These misconceptions, broadly, are of a literature dominated by ideas of correctness, decorum and urbanity, and enslaved by rules; they constitute an inadequate account of Restoration and eighteenth-century poetry, and, for that matter, of Virgil, Horace, Ovid and their contemporaries. While Rogers partially accepts the notion of a 'Peace of the Augustans', he draws attention to the exuberance and energy beneath an apparently untroubled surface. Doody more adventurously displays to the full the stylistic versatility, complexity, richness, excitement and strangeness of 'Augustan' poetry.

Virgil is as great a master for the English so-called Augustans as he was for Spenser and other Elizabethan poets. Dryden's most substantial poetical undertaking was his translation of Virgil, completed in 1697, though it so happens that his longest original poem, *The Hind and the Panther* (1687), is a modern, witty adaptation of the medieval and Spenserian device of beast-allegory for religious apologetics. Virgil's *Aeneid* patriotically celebrates the imperial destiny of Rome embodied in its hero and in Virgil's patron Augustus, but the major English 'Augustans' use this poem primarily as a quarry for mock-heroic. Dryden's brilliant lampoon *MacFlecknoe* (1682) rests upon the mischievous notion that there is a mock-empire of poetical nonsense ruled by a mock Augustus and his imperial successors; this notion finds its full creative expression in Pope's *The Dunciad* (1728–43), a blackly comic satirical fantasy which has something of the scale and complexity of an epic. Virgil's *Aeneid* also contributes richly to Pope's Lilliputian mock-epic *The Rape of the Lock* (1712–17). There is an English counterpart to Virgil's patriotism during the century following Dryden's *Annus Mirabilis* (1667), which is the first attempt by a great English poet to embody contemporary history in a long, seriously heroic, patriotic poem; our two national anthems, 'Rule Britannia' and 'God Save the King' appeared in the 1740s, the first being the climax of a masque commemorating that cynosure of patriotic feeling in the eighteenth century, Alfred the Great; but Englishmen did not need Virgil to teach them patriotism. Pope planned to write a serious patriotic epic in blank verse, which would, in a sense, be a sequel to the *Aeneid*, in that its hero was Brutus the legendary founder of Britain, but its British material, including Druids, acknowledges a distinctively unVirgilian tradition.

Virgil's *Eclogues* were much imitated by poets great and small in this period. Pope's highly-wrought *Pastorals* (1709) self-consciously echo Virgil and every other great pastoralist, for they are intended to summarize and complete the long tradition of classical and neo-classical pastoral; but as with the *Aeneid*, the *Eclogues* were more productively employed as a resource for parody. The most creative work of this kind is *The Shepherd's Week* (1714), where John Gay mocks the notion of an Arcadia in contemporary England, but ventures beyond parody to convey in vivid comic images his hearty enjoyment of the goings-on of ordinary rural life.

Virgil's own greatest celebration of rural life, his *Georgics*, provided a more fruitful object of serious imitation. The georgic is at once heroic and mundane; its recognition of the dignity and importance of the ordinary activities of men evidently attracted eighteenth-century poets. Its primary subject is rural labour, sports and pastimes, as in John Philips's *Cyder* (1708), Gay's *Rural Sports* (1713–20), James Thomson's *The Seasons* (1726–30), William Somerville's *The Chace* (1735) and Christopher Smart's *The Hop-Garden* (1752), but it was adapted to a wide variety of other topics: satirically to urban life in Gay's *Trivia, or the Art of Walking the Streets of London* (1716), philosophically to the mind in Mark Akenside's *The Pleasures of Imagination* and to the body in John Armstrong's *The Art of Preserving Health* (both 1744), patriotically to the wool trade in John Dyer's *The Fleece* (1757) and to seamanship in William Falconer's *The Shipwreck* (1762–9), exotically to West Indian scenes and products in James Grainger's *The Sugar-Cane* (1764). No subject is foreign to the English georgic; it embraces all moods and it testifies just as much as mock-epic does to the adventurousness with which 'Augustan' poets treated Virgil.

The georgic's celebratory, half-truthful, half-idyllic view of rural life reappears in one of the favourite home-grown literary kinds of this period, the 'local poem', of which, according to Samuel Johnson in his *Lives of the English Poets* (1779–81), 'the fundamental subject is some particular landscape, to be poetically described, with the addition of such embellishments as may be supplied by historical retrospection, or incidental meditation' (ed. Hill, 1905, vol. 1, p. 77). Such works ranged from substantial lyrics, like Dyer's *Grongar Hill* (1726), to poems on the scale of Virgil's *Georgics*, like Richard Jago's *Edge-Hill* (1767): a hill was commonly chosen for the subject of a local poem because, seemingly, it could afford a commanding viewpoint of scenery, history and moral truth. The greatest poem of this kind is Pope's *Windsor Forest* (1713), which often recalls Virgil as it moves between pastoral retreat and imperial grandeur.

Alongside the georgic and the local poem there grew up towards the end of the century a less clearly defined socially-concerned kind of poetry in which, as John Butt says, 'the sentiment of place has an important part to play' (1979, p. 133). Of this kind are Goldsmith's *The Deserted Village* (1770), John Langhorne's *The Country Justice* (1774–7), George Crabbe's *The Village* (1783) and William Cowper's *The Task* (1784); though the last of these is so inclusive as to belong, like Thomson's *Seasons*, to a genre of its own.

Second only to Virgil in the Augustan pantheon of poets stood Horace. Both were admired more for their art than their moral integrity because both flattered Augustus, whereas a common opinion among English poets, not to mention historians, in what modern critics call the 'Augustan' period was that the original Augustus was an infamous, cruel and artful tyrant, whose destruction of the republican constitution marked the beginning of Rome's irreversible decline (see Weinbrot, 1978, as qualified by Erskine-Hill, 1983). The mature Dryden, in the Preface to his translations of Juvenal and Persius (1693), calls Horace 'a Court Slave'; Joseph Warton, in his edition of Pope (1797), condemns both Virgil and Horace as servile court poets; so did many critics between those two.

Pope asserted his own moral superiority over the flatterers of Augustus in his 'Epitaph on one who would not be buried in Westminster Abbey' (1738): 'Let Horace blush, and Virgil too.' When he imitated Horace in the most personal and outspoken of his mature satires and epistles in the 1730s, he explored the contrast between Horace's situation as an imperial favourite and his own as an opponent of the Hanoverian court. The ironies of Pope's *Epistle to Augustus* (1737) comprehend the belief that its addressee, George II, is similar to the hateful Roman Augustus politically and morally, while being dissimilar to him in that he is not a patron of the modern Horace (i.e. Pope), and that Pope is like Horace in his poetic art but unlike him in not wanting patronage from Augustus. This paradox of Pope's being artistically but not politically a modern Horace is stated more clearly in the 'First Dialogue' of Pope's *Epistle to the Satires* (1738). For all that, Pope zestfully, intimately, brilliantly and creatively adopts a Horatian manner, with a ceaseless, self-conscious play of styles and a self-dramatization of virtue and friendship, in the Horatian *Moral Essays* and the specific *Imitations of Horace* published between 1731 and 1738. Here, and in Pope's letters, his house and garden at Twickenham acquire some of the moral and aesthetic value of Horace's Sabine farm.

Horace's descriptions of his farm and Virgil's apostrophe to the 'happy husbandmen' in the second book of his *Georgics* were among the most influential poetic embodiments of rural values, but praise of the countryside and country folk was an older Roman theme. In Virgil and Horace themselves there is an implicit nostalgia for pre-Augustan, republican days, when, it was believed, Rome was a nation of small, hardy, independent, busy, virtuous, patriotic farmers. These values and this nostalgia are implicit in many of the English georgics; they retain most vitality in Goldsmith's *Deserted Village* (1770), a political yet personal elegy on a community and a way of life.

Ovid (a victim of Augustus) was admired and imitated by the English 'Augustans', though not as much as by the Elizabethans. There are richly comic Ovidian metamorphoses in Jonathan Swift's *Baucis and Philemon* (1709) and Gay's *Trivia* (1716), both of which characteristically display their period's witty domestication of the Roman classics and its delight in the ordinary goings-on of life; but the most famous poem of an Ovidian kind is Pope's heroic epistle *Eloisa to Abelard* (1717), an exciting, sensational dramatization of the struggle of virtue and passion.

Among later, post-Augustan, Roman poets Juvenal (another victim of imperial tyranny) is the most strongly present to the late seventeenth and eighteenth centuries. Swift and Pope recapture his sardonic tone in their satires and Johnson transposes his work into a profoundly elegiac mode in *The Vanity of Human Wishes* (1749).

However hostile the general English opinion of Augustus was, poets under his reign provided significant models upon which many of the best English writers of the period 1660–1800 played creatively; but Englishmen looked to other important classical models too. They recognized that the Greeks excelled the Romans in most fields of intellectual endeavour and that, though the Roman republican period was rich in models of public virtue, the longer history of the various Greek states was even richer. Homer was the first epic poet and Theocritus the originator of pastoral poetry: they were Virgil's great originals.

From the beginning of the eighteenth century Homer was generally preferred to Virgil as the more simple, impassioned poet, the man of more natural genius; from the middle of the century Theocritus was generally preferred to Virgil, too, for roughly the same reasons. Pope paid lavish tributes to Homer's powerful and copious creative imagination; his translation of both the *Iliad* and the *Odyssey* (1715–26) was his own greatest poetic undertaking and was hailed by Johnson as 'that poetical wonder . . . a performance which no age or nation can pretend to equal' (ed. Hill, 1905, vol. 3, p. 236); like Dryden's Virgil, it was the classic version for the eighteenth century.

Theocritus provided an alternative to what some critics thought was the excessive refinement of Virgilian pastoral: his earthiness was best caught and his unforced art most brilliantly recreated in Gay's *The Shepherd's Week* (1714). When Joseph Warton translated Virgil in 1753 he praised the 'rural, romantic wildness of thought' in Theocritus and his 'pictures of simple unadorned nature' (Warton, 1753, vol. 2, p. 68); this conception of Theocritus gave rise to an eighteenth-century tradition of naturalized pastoral, of which Wordsworth was the most notable inheritor.

The third highly praised and much imitated Greek poet was Pindar. In the English Pindaric ode an elaborate but unconstricted verse form, daring metaphor, and an elevated, rapturous manner were applied typically to lofty historical and mythological subjects. The possibilities of the form were fully exploited by the ever-versatile Dryden in two odes to music and funerary odes on Charles II, Anne Killigrew and Henry Purcell. Ancient Greece was known as the birthplace of political freedom as well as poetry, so, appropriately, the free Pindaric form was used by William Collins, in 'Ode to Liberty' (1747), and Thomas Gray, in 'The Progress of Poesy' (1757), to celebrate the migration of liberty and the arts from Greece to Britain. Later Greek poets, especially Callimachus, provided models of simplicity for Akenside's odes, (secular) hymns and short blank-verse inscriptions, and for some of Collins's odes.

Callimachus, not to mention Pindar, Anacreon, Horace and Catullus, contributed richly to the English lyric, but a native tradition, dating from the Elizabethan period, was still strong: popular, learned and aristocratic cultures still met in the song-books and miscellanies, where amorous songs by Restoration courtiers, such as Sedley and Dorset, and by later wits, such as Congreve, Prior, Gay and Chesterfield, could be found alongside street-ballads, folk-songs, songs from plays, sea-shanties, patriotic anthems, and songs for hunting, harvest-home or maypole-dancing. A distinctive and healthy Scottish lyrical tradition, drawing much of its strength from common life, found vigorous expression in the work of Allen Ramsay in the 1720s and Robert Fergusson in the 1770s; it culminated in the *Poems, chiefly in the Scottish Dialect* (1786) of Robert Burns. The greatest, most original, and most popular achievement of lyrical art in the eighteenth century, though, was the invention and development of the church and chapel hymn in the hands of Isaac Watts, Charles Wesley, John Newton, William Cowper and a host of others. These enduring hymns still testify that the so-called Augustan period was rich in Christian poetry: so does Milton, who overshadows this period more than any Greek or Roman does.

That there is no successful serious English epic between *Paradise Lost* (1667) and William Blake's *Milton* (1804–8) would seem to indicate that Milton was a forbidding presence, but, however cautious poets were about the formal epic, they were not inhibited by him from justifying the ways of God to man in ambitious long poems. Milton's great theme is restated as a reading of the book of nature in Thomson's *Seasons* (1726–30), it is transliterated into a rationalist argument with satirical overtones in Pope's *Essay on Man* (1733–4), and it is internalized and spiced with thrilling mortuary images in Edward Young's overlong *Night Thoughts on Life, Death and Immortality* (1742–5). The most enthusiastic great religious poems of the century, Smart's rhapsodic *Jubilate Agno* (written 1759–63) and *Song to David* (1763), were, however, inspired by ancient Hebrew biblical poetry, rather than by Milton.

There is a lively re-use of Miltonic materials for unMiltonic ends in such modern, worldly, witty allegories as Dryden's *Absalom and Achitophel* (1681) and *The Hind and the Panther*, and Pope's *Rape of the Lock* and *Dunciad*. *Absalom and Achitophel*, for instance, appropriates the moral energy of Milton's great fable in a Tory argument to justify the ways of Stuart kingship against its political enemies, who were of Milton's party. Much as he distilled the essence of the whole European pastoral tradition into his little *Pastorals*, Pope compressed the entire heroic tradition from Homer to Milton into his dazzling, rococo, amoral, Lilliputian, mock-epic *Rape of the Lock*, a poem which, for all its playfulness, ends with claims as high as Milton's on behalf of the visionary power of the poet's eye. Milton's heroic similes are literalized and his Edenic ideas naturalized to the English scene in those blank-verse georgics, such as Philip's *Cyder*, Thomson's *Seasons*, Dyer's *Fleece* and Cowper's *Task*, which constitute one of the main lines of eighteenth-century poetry. His *L'Allegro* and *Il Penseroso* stimulated Gray, Collins and others to compose subjective, meditative lyrics concerned with the character of a poet.

Beyond Milton lay Spenser, whose *Faerie Queene* was more extravagantly idolized in the eighteenth century than, perhaps, at any time before or after. Spenser was praised as the romantic master of what Dryden, in the dedication to his *King Arthur* (1691), called 'the fairy way of writing', where the poet works entirely out of his own fertile imagination and creates new-fabled worlds of his own. Dryden's successors valued rich description, vivid personification and allegory; they seized upon the romantic, non-didactic elements in Spenser, and sometimes in Milton too: witness Collins's subjective and almost surreal *Ode on the Poetical Character* (1747), written in a style and mood that sets it half-way between *Il Penseroso* and 'Kubla Khan'. Others used imitation of 'the Poet's poet' as an opportunity for more deliberate and coherent self-exploration: the castle in Thomson's *The Castle of Indolence* (1748) represents the poet's own self-absorbed, amoral, creative imagination; James Beattie's *The Minstrel* (1771–4) traces the growth of a poet's mind under the influence of natural objects; the sorrows of childhood sound through William Shenstone's affectionately idyllic-parodic *The School-Mistress* (1737). Spenser had earlier provided materials for two expansive, digressive, learned, unromantic satires in octosyllabic couplets: Samuel Butler's *Hudibras* (1663–80) and Matthew Prior's *Alma* (1718), but their parodic style and quizzical interest in the goings-on of ordinary life make these poems, as they make Gay's Spenserian burlesque in *The Shepherd's Week*, the very antithesis of 'the fairy way of writing'.

Shakespeare was extolled in the so-called Augustan period at least as highly as Milton and Spenser were, but was not so frequent a model for non-dramatic poets. He was generally revered as the great poet of human nature: so too was Chaucer, whose admirers and imitators included Prior and Pope, and especially Dryden, who preferred him even to Ovid as a story-teller and demonstrated a genuine kinship with him in some spirited versions of Chaucerian tales in his *Fables* (1700). Chaucer, who, according to Dryden, was the father of English poetry, was as 'classical' a writer as Spenser and Milton, in that he consciously attached himself to a literary tradition that extended unbroken, through the poetry, rhetoric, history and myth of ancient Rome, back to ancient Greece. This continued to be the mainstream of English poetry, but in the eighteenth century poets and critics became increasingly aware of mistier, no-less-ancient northern and western literary traditions, sometimes associated with Spenserian and other romance, sometimes with the simplicity of Celtic tribes, presided over by Druidic poet-priests who worshipped nature, and sometimes with the scarcely-better-documented 'Gothic' liberties enjoyed in the northern heroic age, transplanted to Britain by the Anglo-Saxons, and ripened under Alfred the Great. (There was, indeed, something of an Alfredian cult in 'Augustan' England, where the West-Saxon constitutional monarch was idolized as much as the Roman imperial autocrat was reviled: for instance, Johnson, a Tory not given to cant, referred to 'Alfred's golden reign' in his Juvenalian satire against modern decadance, *London*, 1738; the Whig Thomson's 'Rule Britannia' was first sung in the masque *Alfred* in 1740.) Sir William Temple's essay 'Of Heroic Virtue' (1692) first brought Old Icelandic poetry to wide notice; Addison's praise of the old ballad of 'Chevy Chase' in two *Spectator* papers (1712) was influential; Allen Ramsay collected medieval Scots songs and ballads in *The Ever-Green* (1724); Gray published his free translations of two Icelandic and two Welsh poems in 1768; Thomas Warton's *History of English Poetry* (1774–81) brought to light a vast body of medieval verse; but, as Wordsworth and Coleridge testify, the greatest impact was made by Thomas Percy's *Reliques of Ancient English Poetry* (1765), which drew together edited versions of medieval Border ballads, metrical romances and Elizabethan songs.

Eighteenth-century poets sought to recreate in their own verse 'medieval' effects of many different kinds, from the emotional freedom of Pope's characteristically daring imaginative projection of a passion-crazed twelfth-century nun in his Ovidian heroic epistle, *Eloisa to Abelard*, and the extravagant sublimity and prophetic afflatus of Gray's perhaps less convincing representation of a doomed thirteenth-century Welsh bard in his Pindaric ode 'The Bard' (1757), to the simple style, simple emotions and folk superstitions of David Mallet's ballad 'William and Margaret' (1723). Imitations by Mallet, Prior, Goldsmith, Percy and others of medieval ballads are half-way towards the total impersonation practised by James Macpherson, when, in the 1760s, he wrote what purported to be translations of ancient Gaelic epics by Ossian, son of the legendary Fingal, or by Thomas Chatterton, when, between 1768 and 1770, he employed an invented 'medieval' language in writing the 'Rowley' poems, which he attributed to an imagined fifteenth-century Bristol monk. 'Gothic' settings of medieval buildings or ruins in uncultivated landscapes feature in a wide variety of lyrical poems in which the exterior scene reflects the perceiver's melancholy and which generally echo Milton's *Il Penseroso*. Milton's *Lycidas* encouraged interest in the Druids; they are hailed as the earliest native poets of Albion in Dryden's 'To My Lord Chancellor' (1662) and Swift's 'To Mr. Congreve' (1693), and as the original patriots in Pope's unwritten *Brutus*, Thomson's *Liberty* (1735–6), Collins's and Gray's odes, and Cowper's 'Boadicea' (1782); their reputation as nature poets impelled Collins to call Thomson a druid in his haunting elegiac ode upon that poet (1748); their complex image lived on to tease the imaginations of Blake and Wordsworth.

Behind the efforts of poets to link themselves to medieval English, Scandinavian or Celtic sources lay the notion that genuine poetry was to be found only in simple, primitive societies. Similar primitivist notions are implicit in the conclusion of Goldsmith's *Deserted Village*, when poetry itself flees a luxurious, sophisticated land alongside the dispossessed peasantry, and in the reference to a 'mute inglorious Milton' in Gray's *Elegy in a Country Church-Yard* (1751). Such notions also underlie the eighteenth-century cult of the noble savage abroad and a search among the lower orders at home for simple, untutored 'natural' poets, a search which turned up Stephen Duck the 'Thresher-Poet' in 1730, and the more promising figure of Robert Burns the Ayrshire ploughman in 1786. Finally, primitivism and the cult of simplicity prompted poetry for, or ostensibly by, children: such verse ranged from the absurd 'namby-pamby' rhymes of Ambrose Philips in the 1720s to Blake's *Songs of Innocence* (1789), which were modelled upon Isaac Watts's highly popular *Divine Songs for the Use of Children* (1715).

The medieval disguises assumed by Gray, Chatterton and others provided means to explore the character of the poet, but self-characterization is by no means uncommon in less exotic poetry of the 'Augustan' period. Swift, for instance, offers self-portraits in his birthday poems to Stella and *Verses on the Death of Dr. Swift* (1739); Goldsmith's *Deserted Village* alternates between the voices of the solitary man of feeling (rather like Gray in the *Elegy*) and the outraged politician. The most fully self-drawn character of the period is that of Pope, the little hermit of Twickenham and the powerful censor of manners and morals: his self-portrayal in the *Epistle to Arbuthnot* (1735), for instance, takes in the affectionate friend, the loving son and the savage libeller, each role being intended to authenticate the other.

Pope is Wordsworth's kind of poet in as much as he is 'a man speaking to men'; so were most of his contemporaries. Poetry in the 'Augustan' period was much concerned with the goings-on of the ordinary world, full of real, tangible objects. Critics may be correct in adducing the Bibles on Belinda's dressing-table as symbols of their owner's moral confusion, but the Bibles (plural) are undoubtedly heavy, physical, functional objects, their function being to keep ribbons pressed; they are part of *The Rape of the Lock*'s real, everyday world of things, like the amber snuff-box, clouded cane, sword-knots, chocolate mill and horse-hair fish lines. For all its surreal nightmare, the townscape of Pope's *Dunciad* is as recognizably and distinctively set in Hogarth's London as Swift's 'Description of a City Shower' (1709) and Gay's *Trivia*. Disorderly country-town streets are painted with a Dutch, indeed Hogarthian, realism in Butler's *Hudibras* (1663–80).

Verse satire, a more predominant genre in this than in any other period, is rooted in contemporary events and the contemporary scene. The political crisis which is the subject of Dryden's *Absalom and Achitophel* was continuing as Dryden wrote the poem; his religious poems were hardly less topical. Later satirists, from Pope, Swift and Gay to Charles Churchill, Christopher Anstey and John Wolcot, respond no less immediately to great national events or passing fashions: always conveying a sense of the variety and vitality of felt social life.

The georgic is rooted in the ordinary world; it is concerned with the way things work and how jobs are done; it can embrace all moods and no subject is foreign to it. Similarly, the local poem takes in everything under the poet's mental and corporeal eye. Johnson observed that Gay's pastorals in *The Shepherd's Week* were 'read with delight as just representations of rural manners and occupations' (ed. Hill, 1905, vol. 2, p. 269), and 'just representation' is the motive for a great mass of agreeable minor verse, some of the best of which is now readily available in Roger Lonsdale's *New Oxford Book of Eighteenth-Century Verse* (1984). Almost at random one might instance: poems about games, such as James Dance's *Cricket, an Heroic Poem* (1744) and Samuel Bowden's evocation of childhood in *The Paper-Kite* (1733); poems about occupations, such as Robert Tatersal's *The Bricklayer's Labours* (1734) and Henry Taylors's *The Country Curate* (1737); poems on new technology, such as the hot-air balloon in Henry James Pye's *Aerophorion* (1787) and steam power in Erasmus Darwin's *The Botanic Garden* (1791); poems on observed human mannerisms, whether those of a servant, as in Swift's 'Petition of Frances Harris' (1709), or of a monarch, as in Wolcot's (Peter Pindar's) description of George III's visit to Whitbread's brewery in 1787 (Lonsdale, 1984, pp. 374–5, 271–3, 278, 297–9, 725–6, 762–3, 9–11, 737–40). Drink and marriage are perhaps the commonest topics. What is the case with minor poets is even more true of established poets: 'Nothing is so common, so bizarre, so "unclean" – or so grand – that it can't be apprehended and consumed by the poetic process. Everything that has being, physical, or mental, is available to the poet' (Doody, 1985, p. 9). 'Just representation' and daring creative imagination unite to the highest effect in Pope, of whose Horatian imitations it is said: 'Under his magisterial wand, like the wrecked voyagers in *The Tempest*, lords and rich men, ministers and society-wenches, kings, courtiers, Quakers, clowns, and good Ralph Allens move through the paces of an intricate satirical ballet, which combines the features of reality and dream' (Mack, 1969, p. 236).

Pope has been regarded by many twentieth-century critics as the prime example of an English 'Augustan' poet. He was the greatest of the many eighteenth-century poets who drew from and transformed Roman models in their mock-epics, epistles, georgics, local poems, naturalized pastorals and rural-retirement verse. He and they admired the poets of Augustan Rome but detested Augustus; so it is, at least, paradoxical that they should be saddled with an epithet drawn from his name. Pope and many of his contemporaries are, in a sense, 'classical' or 'neo-classical' poets, by virtue of their admiration for Roman culture (republican as well as imperial) and their generally more unreserved admiration for all things Greek. This, however, does not make the years from 1660 to 1800 or any part of them a specifically 'classical' period, any more than admiration for Virgil makes it an 'Augustan' period. A moment's reflection ought to remind us that there is quite as much of the Greek and Roman classics in Spenser, Ben Jonson, Milton, Shelley, Tennyson, Arnold and Morris, to name but a few, as in any late seventeenth- or eighteenth-century poet.

Some features of the period, from Dryden's *Absalom and Achitophel* and *Fables* to Macpherson's impersonation of Ossian and Cowper's domestication of Milton, which are more remarkable than 'classicism' or 'Augustanism' would suggest, include a broad, unprecedented eclecticism in choice of literary models, and a creative response to the new, challenging, central presence of Milton in the tradition. Though 'Augustan' might be convenient shorthand, and is preserved in the title of this chapter for the sake of uniformity with other chapter titles, we might better avoid prejudgement of the complicated, varied and eclectic poetry of the period 1660–1800 if we used a neutral term to name the age: perhaps just calling it '1660–1800'.

FURTHER READING

Butt, John (1979) *The Mid-Eighteenth Century* (vol. 8 of *The Oxford History of English Literature*), Clarendon Press, Oxford

Buxton, John (1978) *The Grecian Taste: Literature in the Age of Neo-Classicism*, Macmillan, London

Chalker, John (1969) *The English Georgic: A Study in the Development of a Form*, Routledge, London

Dobrée, Bonamy (1959) *English Literature in the Early Eighteenth Century* (vol. 7 of *The Oxford History of English Literature*), Clarendon Press, Oxford

Doody, Margaret Ann (1985) *The Daring Muse: Augustan Poetry Reconsidered*, Cambridge University Press, Cambridge

Jack, Ian (1952) *Augustan Satire: Intention and Idiom in English Poetry, 1660–1750*, Clarendon Press, Oxford

Lonsdale, Roger (ed.) (1984) *The New Oxford Book of Eighteenth-Century Verse*, Oxford University Press, Oxford

Price, Martin (1964) *To the Palace of Wisdom: Studies in Order and Energy from Dryden to Blake*, Doubleday, New York

Rogers, Pat (1974) *The Augustan Vision*, Methuen, London

Rothstein, Eric (1981) *Restoration and Eighteenth-Century Poetry 1660–1780* (vol. 3 of *The Routledge History of English Poetry*), Routledge, London

Sutherland, James (1969) *English Literature of the Late Seventeenth Century* (vol. 6 of *The Oxford History of English Literature*), Clarendon Press, Oxford

Weinbrot, Howard D. (1978) *Augustus Caesar in 'Augustan' England: The Decline of a Classical Norm*, Princeton University Press, Princeton

ADDITIONAL WORKS CITED

Erskine-Hill, Howard (1983) *The Augustan Idea in English Literature*, Edward Arnold, London

Hill, George Birkbeck (ed.) (1905) *Lives of the English Poets, by Samuel Johnson*, Clarendon Press, Oxford

Leavis, F.R. (1936) *Revaluation*, Chatto & Windus, London

Mack, Maynard (1969) *The Garden and the City*, Toronto University Press, Toronto

Warton, Joseph (1753) *Works of Virgil*, London

18

ROMANTIC POETRY

J. H. ALEXANDER

In spite of the radical questioning of almost every aspect of English literature that has taken place during the last quarter century, the term 'Romantic poetry' still denotes very much what it did in the 1960s. It covers most poetry written between 1789 and 1832. The first of these years saw the beginning of the French revolution which dominated the period up to Waterloo in 1815, and also the engraving of Blake's *Songs of Innocence*; the second was the year of the first Reform Bill and also of the death of Sir Walter Scott (born in 1771). The dates are thus less than wholly arbitrary in demarcating the divisions between the Romantic period and the Age of Sensibility (or what used to be called pre-romanticism) on the one hand, and the Victorian period on the other. Furthermore, in spite of recent questionings of the traditional English literary canon, 'Romantic poetry' still means primarily the work of six great poets: William Blake (1757–1827), William Wordsworth (1770–1850), Samuel Taylor Coleridge (1772–1834), Lord Byron (1788–1824), Percy Bysshe Shelley (1792–1822) and John Keats (1795–1821). Small groups of enthusiasts have made more or less urgent claims for attention to be paid to George Crabbe (1754–1832) and John Clare (1793–1864), and to Scott and James Hogg (1770–1835) as poets as well as novelists, and it is probable that in periods less poetically rich than the romantic these claims would be readily recognized, but a glance at the annual bibliographies of recent years makes clear the overwhelming dominance of the great six. It may be conjectured that this situation is unlikely to change radically, on the principle enunciated by C. S. Lewis that we value most highly those authors who make the most demands of us as readers.

Whatever may be questioned, firmly attested dates seem unassailable. It will be observed that Wordsworth and Coleridge are of one generation (the 'first generation romantics'), Byron, Shelley and Keats of the next (the 'second generation'), and the change of atmosphere as the reader passes from one to the other is generally accepted as fundamental: broadly speaking it involves a shift from piety (however unorthodox) to scepticism, from the austere north to the warm south. Blake was of an older generation than Wordsworth and Coleridge, though he actually outlived Byron, Shelley and Keats and was writing major poetry several years after Wordsworth and Coleridge had stopped doing so. He was largely isolated from the other writers (the possibility of a direct influence on Shelley is one of the great unsolved mysteries of literary history); but he has come to be treated by later twentieth-century scholars as a romantic – rather than the outstanding late eighteenth-century eccentric to be classed along with (if immeasurably above) Thomas Chatterton and James Macpherson – because of his anticipation of central romantic concerns.

During the first half of the present century romantic poetry endured a period of comparatively low esteem. Reacting against late Victorian romanticism in particular, major creative figures such as T. S. Eliot and Ezra Pound preferred to take as models the metaphysical poetry of the seventeenth century, or Chinese imagists, valuing ironic objectivity and their conscious craftsmanship above what they dismissed as romantic expressionism. The anti-romantic reaction had a strong ethical as well as aesthetic motive, T. E. Hulme (1924) rejecting the romantics' 'spilt religion' (vague religious feeling without the recognition of original sin) and Irving Babbitt (1919) dismissing Rousseauistic primitivism. This general downgrading of the period was reinforced by the dominant critical schools of the mid-century. In America the New Critics found that the romantics lacked the qualities of ironic complexity that they especially valued in poetry, and in Britain F. R. Leavis (1936) mounted a fierce assault on Shelley in particular for his alleged self-regarding emotionalism and lack of respect for the object. Only Keats, with his open questioning of the validity of his own enterprise, survived the first half of the century almost wholly unscathed.

Any official history of dominant critical attitudes always involves a potentially misleading over-simplification. People did not stop reading the romantics between 1900 and 1950, and there were outstanding critical appreciations during this period. Probably the most significant was G. Wilson Knight's *The Starlit Dome* (1941), a remarkable collection of essays investigating the unique image worlds of the major poets in such a way as to suggest not only 'The Wordsworthian Profundity' of the first essay, but the psychological and imaginative depth and fascination of Coleridge, Shelley and Keats (Blake was not yet considered a romantic, and Byron was the subject of a series of separate studies). Knight taught for a while at the University of Toronto, where one of his colleagues was Northrop Frye. The English critic's delight in imaginative vision may have interacted with the Canadian's theological training to constitute one of the impulses behind Frye's massive study of Blake, *Fearful Symmetry* (1947).

Frye's remarkable book is the first in a sequence of immensely detailed,

scholarly and appreciative studies of individual poets: it was followed by Geoffrey H. Hartman's *Wordsworth's Poetry 1797–1814* (1964), Robert F. Gleckner's *Byron and the Ruins of Paradise* (1967) and Earl R. Wasserman's *Shelley:
A Critical Reading* (1971). The emphases of these three studies are all slightly
different, but they are all concerned, as Wilson Knight had been, to approach
their authors as Yeats had learned to approach Shelley: 'I only made my
pleasure in Shelley contented pleasure by massing in my imagination his
recurring images . . . till his world had grown solid underfoot and consistent
enough for the soul's habitation' (quoted in Frye, 1981, p. 49). By scrupulously
analysing the characteristic images and thought patterns of their chosen authors
these critics show how superficial and careless much New Critical reading had
been. They build up hosts of small details into massively impressive analyses,
so that one feels that the criticism has the measure of its subject. The same
approach has been applied to the thought of the romantic period as a whole
in M. H. Abrams's *The Mirror and the Lamp* (1953) and *Natural Supernaturalism*
(1971).

A term often applied to the six critics discussed in the previous two paragraphs is 'apocalyptic'. They all see the romantics as engaging with fundamental issues of life and death in a broadly religious manner – though the vision
may be dark, as it often is in Hartman's Wordsworth or as it fundamentally is
in Gleckner's Byron, and it may involve a dialectic between scepticism and
tentative assurance as in Wasserman's Shelley. Frye envisages Blake's entire
corpus as a systematic expression of a single fundamental vision, and although
his successors see more development in their authors' oeuvres the reader
leaves each of these studies with a sense of achievement: personal achievement,
of course, at having won through to the end of massive tomes, but, more
significantly, heroic imaginative endeavour on the part of the author and an
appropriately energetic and intellectually rigorous systematic response on the
part of the critic. All three participants have been involved in a significant part
of the great humanist enterprise of contributing to the Song of Humanity,
which may also be the Song of God.

The most striking critical and scholarly developments over the last quarter
of a century have in general had the effect of questioning the sense of heroic
achievement described above. The three movements that have most radically
altered ideas about romantic poetry for many readers are deconstruction, the
new historicism and textual criticism.

Very broadly speaking, the studies discussed above were concerned to take
the romantics basically on their own terms, after they had spent fifty years
being demoted on other people's terms. Deconstruction and the new historicism refuse to do this, but rather adopt a sometimes extreme scepticism,
exposing latent ideologies, seeking blindnesses and aporias, and at the limit

pulling at every loose end in sight in an ecstatic orgy of textual unravelling. Just as Wilson Knight cast his apocalyptic seeds on the apparently stony ground of the early 1940s, so one can discern proto-deconstructionists already at work in the heady 1960s. E. E. Bostetter (1963) used the 'negative Romantic' Byron to expose what he believed to be the common syntax of the other poets of the period, at whose core

> were to be found certain simple organizing principles: that the universe revealed to science was a moral universe; that a creative and benign power expressed itself in and through nature and was manifest to the imagination of man; that as an 'inmate' of this moral universe man was naturally good and perfectible, though at present corrupted by his society and education.
>
> (pp. 3–4)

From this outmoded syntax, Bostetter suggests, Byron alone fully escaped to witness to the modern world about his contemporaries' illusions concerning life and art. Read in the light of more recent post-structuralist developments, *Don Juan* (1819–24) is a virtuoso high-wire act – or a series of such acts – in verse, executed with huge panache and great delight over an abyss littered with the largely unravelled safety-nets of once plausible significances. The acrobat is at most a constructed personality, as Anne Mellor has argued (1980); or perhaps he is a device too fragmented to be called a personality at all, the product of a quasi-deconstructive denial of character and presence. This constructed personality, or deconstructed non-personality, is acutely aware of the ideological loading of traditional verse forms (*Don Juan*, VI, 59), and it expresses itself with extreme tonal instability.

In some ways not only Byron but all the second-generation romantics can be seen as adumbrating our 1970s and 1980s, to be set against the heroic period of high romantic criticism between 1947 and 1971. Shelley and Keats, as well as Byron, produce works in which self-deconstruction functions as a fundamental conceptual and structural principle. Earl Wasserman's 1971 study benefited from absorbing the seminal investigation by C. E. Pulos (1954) of Shelley's debt to the British sceptical philosophical tradition (Pulos's book was published by the then rather obscure University of Nebraska Press and it was more than a decade before it became generally known): he was able to move beyond his own earlier idealizings (Wasserman, 1953), while preserving his admirable analytical subtlety, to show Shelley sceptically and agnostically experimenting with contrasting epistemologies in different poems, or within single poems, while moving tentatively in the direction of idealism in his later work. Wasserman's approach has been subjected to a sternly deconstructive critique by Tilottama Rajan in a book which exhibits some of the dangers of the approach (1980). Rajan argues that Shelley is confused, rather than rigorously sceptical as he ought to have been: 'his encounter with skepticism leads him to postpone or relocate rather than revise his idealism, to respond to skepticism sentimentally rather than ironically or tragically' (p. 59): only in the late unfinished 'Triumph of Life' does he show signs of moving from an idealism detached from the common world to a tragic recognition of that real world's agony. It is typical of deconstructive thought to place so much weight on a fragment: Rajan does the same with Keats's 'Fall of Hyperion', and the Shelley fragment figures prominently in the set of essays edited by Bloom (1979), notably in a study of almost impenetrable complexity by the purest of American post-structuralists, Paul de Man.

One trouble with Rajan's approach is that it gives the impression that Shelley was rather stupid, which he was not, and that Rajan knows the answer, or at any rate more of it than Shelley did – the answer being that 'The radical heteronomy in the self and its enterprises disclosed by the movement beyond the sphere of illusion cannot be covered up or healed, but only mediated' (p. 141). One may also object that the concentration on unfinished poems shows a distrust of the achieved work of art. A revealing footnote asserts that 'one must distinguish ... between problems of vision and problems that are merely technical and structural' (p. 203). But Shelley and Keats were dedicated artists, for whom technique and structure could not ever be 'merely' anything. They were concerned to explore moral, philosophical and religious conundrums which are still with us, and which have not been resolved, as some deconstructionists maintain, by means of a Copernican shift in criticism (Belsey, 1980). Although accompanying the statement with a dubious negative valuation, Rajan actually puts this very point well in discussing 'Hyperion: A Fragment', where Keats

> reveals a desire both to demystify and to reconstruct the fiction of an ideal Greece. In this respect he is no different from the theorists of the period who also try to develop through the ironic and sentimental modes forms that will contain their uncertainties without renouncing the aspirations of idealism.
>
> (1980, p. 159)

As critics we must never forget that we are dealing with works of art. There is a tendency in post-structuralist criticism to neglect or fail to recognize the peculiar strategies which works of art have for arriving at, or hinting in the direction of, something that may be called a truth – not by philosophical argument, but by way of beauty. Here we are on Keats's home territory, and the point may become clear if we refer to an accomplished completed masterpiece which is at the same time a near-perfect example of a self-deconstructing poem, his 'Ode on a Grecian Urn'. The famous final aphorism spoken (probably) by the urn, is as much a question as the actual question that ends the 'Ode to a Nightingale'. One of the most sensitive post-structuralist readers, David Simpson, argues (1979) that the speaker of this poem is to be distinguished from the controlling persona, the 'poet', as much as from the sententious urn itself, and he goes on to explore the consequences of this fragmentation of personal identity impressively in the sort of close reading where post-structuralist critics are often at their best (p. 8). We the readers, along with the metacommenting 'poet', observe the speaker in the third stanza trying to make the urn represent pure happiness. Up to this point deconstruction serves the poem well. But it ignores the supreme beauty of the dejected fourth stanza. We can debate endlessly the self-reflexive complexities of this poem, but its beauty, especially the beauty of the fourth stanza, does not depend on a solution sweet, whether philosophical, moral or religious; indeed it depends on there not being a solution in the poem, because as Shelley puts it 'our sweetest songs are those which tell of saddest thought'. When Rajan (1980, pp. 16–17) says that 'to deconstruct a text is . . . to assume that it is a disunified and contradictory structure tacitly involved in contesting its own meaning' there is a failure to perceive that it is Keats's greatest strength to have found a way of producing perfect structures, in one sense rock firm, which contain recessive deconstructions of potential meaning and doubt.

The more traditionally faithful poets of the older generation have also benefited from certain deconstructive insights. By the end of the 1960s the radical ambiguity of 'The Ancient Mariner' (1798) was well established. Neither R. P. Warren's attempt to read it as a poem of imaginative redemption (1946) nor William Empson's equally ingenious dismissal of the gloss as a superficial late Christianizing of a vision of nightmare arbitrariness (1973) does justice to the work. Viewed from a post-structuralist perspective, its text and marginal gloss have come to look uncannily like a Derrida performance. It would perfectly exemplify Hillis Miller's tentative experimenting with deconstructive critical possibilities in the mid-1970s:

> Such a criticism would entertain the possibility that a work of literature, rather than having a single mind at its origin, may be dialogical. Such a work would have two or more implied generative sources; it could not, therefore, be reduced to a single, coherent, all-inclusive reading. The interpretation of such a work might reach the impasse of two incompatible readings, both arising from the text itself. Such a text would be 'undecidable', 'unreadable'.
>
> (1975, pp. xi–xii)

The same poem raises in a particularly acute form another related issue. David Simpson is much concerned with the tone of voice implied in a poem, with the imagined presence which a poem can imply to some extent (rightly rejecting the 'either it can or it can't' of extreme Gallic deconstructionist logic). Simpson (1979, p. 102) is concerned with the notoriously difficult conclusion of 'The Eolian Harp', but his insight might be applied to 'The Ancient Mariner', where the moral at the end could be read in a host of different ways, but only on different occasions in actual live performance: the post-structuralist insistence on text as against logocentric presence suggests that reading poetry aloud is more like performing music or producing plays than has often been recognized. There is no good reason for rejecting the notion of presence in a wider sense: Coleridge's poetry remains, as it has always been, recognizably the product of the man Coleridge, with all his complexities, his blindnesses and insights – not a mere junction-box of available devices, to borrow David Lodge's metaphor.

David Simpson has also written (1982) on Wordsworth, a poet who has been fortunate in his post-structuralist critics in that they have proved unusually sensitive and (dare one say) loving. There is in their work an implied sense of that wonder which some might dismiss as mystification, but which does not exclude wide-awake intelligence, and without which criticism of great art quite misses the point. The same critics actually reinforce one's sense of the peculiarly Wordsworthian nature of the poetry, those endlessly complex distinctive qualities which the *paroles* of authors of genius have, and which those of third-rate artists largely lack. Yet at the same time these critics explore the complexities of Wordsworth's self-awareness and chart the scrupulosities of his self-examination. Frances Ferguson's book (1977) and Hartman's later articles (1987) are outstanding examples, but it is Simpson who shows most clearly the illumination to be derived from a sensitive post-structuralism. He argues that in Wordsworth, as in Coleridge and Shelley, 'the more that the "real" is recognized as the "figured", the more important it becomes to keep in play as many figurings as possible' (1982, pp. 120–1). Simpson's tracing of Wordsworth's strategies for avoiding the premature closing-off of possible significance, and of his attempted solution of the problem of communication between people of different backgrounds arising from multiple conflicting figurings, is among the finest criticism of our time.

Of the six major poets, the oldest, Blake, has attracted by far the least attention from post-structuralists. Perhaps this is because, in spite of his unmatched hatred of mystification, his outlook seems at first sight so totally opposed to the premises that underlie the movement. He is intensely ironical but utterly opposed to spectral scepticism:

> If the Sun & Moon should doubt,
> They'd immediately Go out.

But Leopold Damrosch Jr. (1980) has probingly and lucidly challenged Frye's assertion of the exemplary perfect unity of Blake's corpus – already questioned, on a more modest scale and with some speculative historical and biographical material, by E. D. Hirsch Jr. (1964). Damrosch exposes the four inconsistencies – epistemological, psychological, ontological and aesthetic – that he believes to lie at the heart of Blake's work, but his study though undoubtedly deconstructive is in no sense destructive, and he makes clear his immense admiration for his subject:

> Blake was far less confused than most men. His difficulties arose from the heroic ambition with which he tackled unresolvable tensions at the heart of Western thought, exploring them more searchingly than most philosophers, let alone most poets, have been willing to do.
>
> (p. 4)

When deconstruction is sensitive, readable and not over-concerned with being novel or with drawing attention to itself it can illuminatingly expose the tensions and the weird energies that the heroic creative endeavours rightly celebrated in earlier criticism sought to bring into constructive mental fight, rather than destructive, nihilistic warfare. One does not need to be a paid-up Nietzschean to benefit from the revelation of energizing tensions and complexities almost undreamt-of in the 1960s.

Whereas deconstruction exposes unsuspected conceptual tensions and contradictions in a work, the new historicism asserts that every writer's position and attitude is determined by specific socio-economic developments. Hirsch (1964) and many other detailed historical studies, sometimes written from an avowedly Marxist or more generally materialist perspective, prepared the way for the movement whose most wide-ranging and influential romantic exponent has probably been Marilyn Butler (1981). Butler is (unexpectedly) at her most illuminating on Coleridge, where her exposure of the political motivation behind the apparently elevatedly philosophical *Biographia Literaria* is masterly. It is 'a book deliberately written for an hour of public peril', and the link between the discussion of German philosophy in the first half and the criticism of Wordsworth in the second is to be found in political ideology: 'Coleridge commends the German example, which is religious, and so exalted that it is meaningful only to a small educated élite. He criticizes Wordsworth's 1798 experiment because its simplicity and universalism are associated with the radical, levelling tendency of the pre-revolutionary Enlightenment' (pp. 62–3). Butler's study unfortunately also sometimes displays the reductivism endemic to the new historicism: she roundly asserts that the *Lyrical Ballads* were rather old-fashioned and reactionary, which was not at all the way that they struck their brilliant young admirers of the time (Hazlitt, De Quincey, John Wilson), and her presentation of Jane Austen in this book manages to make that author sound impossibly dull. New historical reductivism has been particularly unhelpful where Wordsworth is concerned. Marjorie Levinson (1986), for example, makes a point of writing about what Wordsworth does not write about, such as the beggars at Tintern Abbey, a procedure with rapidly diminishing returns, however ingeniously pursued. A much better example of how to apply new historical techniques sensitively can be found in Barrell in a study (1988) which, in spite of a virulent foreword by other hands, includes a suggestive reading of 'Lines Written a Few Miles Above Tintern Abbey' in terms of Wordsworth's culturally conditioned use of Dorothy as a necessary representative of feminine syntactic inarticulacy. Barrell is often tendentious, and on occasion he produces simplified misreadings to match the worst of the New Critics on the romantics, but most of the time he is undeniably reading the poem that Wordsworth wrote.

One of the most potentially rewarding new historicist approaches has been to consider the social and cultural implications of the way in which texts were originally published, and indeed of the different ways in which they continued to be published. Jerome J. McGann (1983) has argued that the production of a text in this period should be regarded as to some extent a co-operative enterprise. Not only author but publisher, printer, critics and of course public were involved. He has pointed out (1985, pp. 264–5) that Byron's *Don Juan* was permitted to be a more subversive poem when it changed publishers from John Murray to John Hunt after Canto V. To this insight may be added Neil Fraistat's investigation (1985) of the added significance that well-known poems acquire when they are viewed in the context of their neighbours in the original collections. Fraistat may at times fail to convince the reader that the poets were quite as calculating as he suggests; but how many readers have ever seen, let alone taken note of, the contents list of Keats's *Lamia* volume:

> Lamia
> Isabella
> The Eve of St. Agnes
> Ode to a Nightingale
> Ode on a Grecian Urn
> Ode to Psyche
> Fancy
> Ode ['Bards of Passion']
> Lines on the Mermaid Tavern
> Robin Hood
> To Autumn
> Ode on Melancholy
> Hyperion, a Fragment

Such a contents page may cast well-known poems in a new light and also encourage the reader to take Keats's minor 'rondeaux' more seriously. The study of works in their publishing context can include the significance of format and pricing, illustrations, punctuation conventions whether authorial or compositorial, and critical reception along with its possible influence on the author. This last possibility has been greatly facilitated by the assembling of all known periodical reviews of the major romantics (Reiman, 1972). Perhaps not every author is, as Hazlitt said of Scott, 'the mere amanuensis of history', but to some extent each writer is a socio-economically conditioned intelligence presiding among many such intelligences, and undeniably the creature of her or his time. It has been the achievement of the new historicism to alert readers to more radical implications of this fact than had been suspected.

The general tendency to fragment, dissolve and complicate evident in decon-structive, new historical or other critical approaches can be avoided easily enough by any reader of the romantics who chooses to do so; but the parallel textual developments of recent years have changed, and are changing, radically the actual experience of reading the poetry. The results of textual, as of archi-tectural, theory are all around us: so that changing ideas of how a text should be arrived at constitute the most important subject to be considered in this essay.

The stable orthodoxy of mid-century textual criticism asserted that it was the editor's duty to arrive at a text as close as possible to the author's final intentions. Hence de Selincourt's Oxford Wordsworth is based on the poet's final preferred text, earlier (and usually more vigorous) versions being generally relegated to notes. It is now accepted that the idea of a definitive text is a mirage. Indeed, the modern purist will be found asserting that every stage of a text has its own authority and validity, and that each stage should be separately edited and offered to the reader. The theory is immaculate, but economic reality makes this ideal difficult to achieve, and in any event most readers will want only one or at most two texts.

The problem is particularly acute in the case of Blake. The instability of Blake's texts and the unique experience offered by each hand-coloured and hand-assembled copy of his poems have greatly complicated the reading of his work. It is now generally realized that it should be experienced in colour and with the designs, even if of necessity this is achieved by means of mass-produced books providing more or less cheap approximations of the originals. Most readers will settle for one of the simplified collected works and one or two of the most easily available reproductions of individual poems, but the serious scholar and the aficionado will ideally compare all the copies in exist-ence from New York to New Zealand: some idea of what this involves may be gleaned from Erdman's invaluable (though alas monochrome) *Illuminated Blake* (1975).

The old stabilities of Wordsworth's finally approved texts have now been generally abandoned. Going to the opposite extreme, the Cornell Wordsworth offers photographs and transcripts of the manuscripts, as well as reading texts which form the basis of the new popular editions such as the Oxford Authors selection (Gill, 1984). Gill makes a point of printing the earliest, sometimes incomplete, versions of the poems, so that 'The Ruined Cottage', 'Home at Grasmere', and the skeletal early version of 'Peter Bell' take their place alongside the 1805 *Prelude*. In the now standard parallel text *Prelude* (ed. Jonathan Wordsworth, 1979) the 1850 and 1805 versions are joined by the two-book version of 1799. The result is a rougher, more provisional Wordsworth than the poet who was generally available twenty years ago. Readers then were not expected to balance with precarious heroism over voids like this in the Oxford Authors 'Home at Grasmere' (itself a new addition to the established canon):

> The darkest Pit
> Of the profoundest Hell, chaos, night,
> Nor aught of [   ] vacancy scooped out
> By help of dreams can breed such fear and awe
> As fall upon us often when we look
> Into our minds, into the mind of Man,
> My haunt, and the main region of my song.
>
> (ll. 984–90)

The favouring of primitive ur-texts is not, it may be noted, confined to poetry: the forthcoming Edinburgh Edition of the Waverley Novels will present a rough, early-text Scott rather than the homogenized and smoothed-out collected classic known to readers since 1829. Scott undoubtedly approved of that 'Magnum Opus' text at the end of his life, and throughout his career he relied on his collaborators in the printing house to make his rough manuscripts fit for a polite audience. But his more rustic and in many respects hardly less gifted compatriot James Hogg disapproved of the bowdlerizing and tidying-up of *his* texts, as did John Clare of similar treatment. The publication of Clare's poetry with its idiosyncratic spellings and non-existent punctuation (as again in the Oxford Authors series: Robinson, 1984) is among the most radical challenges to revaluation, aesthetic and social, that romantic poetry has witnessed in the last decade.

Although it has been suggested that the three developments outlined in this essay constitute the most obvious innovations in criticism of the romantic poets over the last quarter-century, three qualifications must be made in conclusion. First, as has been noted above, none of the developments is wholly unanticipated in earlier decades. Second, there have been many other fruitful and largely innovatory approaches; for example, structuralist readings of individual texts (rather than complete oeuvres); Freudian interpretations ranging from the crudely reductive to the sensitive; reader response criticism; and as yet tentative venturings-out from the Mary Shelley enclave of feminist revaluations. The last of these is (textual theory and practice always excepted) likely to be the most important development of the 1990s: indeed, between the initial drafting of this essay and its final revision several noteworthy and not at all tentative feminist studies made their mark (see Lefebure, 1986; Levin, 1987;

Mellor, 1988). And third, traditional modes of scholarship and criticism have retained their vitality: up-to-date biographies (though the weight of scholarship is such that it is becoming almost impossible for full critical biographies of major writers to be produced by individual scholars); statistical verbal analyses, with sophisticated computer techniques beginning to make their appearance; traditional studies of imagery, where much remains to be done; investigations of sources and influences; and a host of others – not least sensitive and alert readings by those determinedly innocent of radical ideological apartness from their subjects. It is still permissible to remain something of a 1960s idealist and (albeit sadder and wiser) to hold, with a degree of good faith, that not many of the myriad words dispatched in the direction of this amazing cohort of major poets will return wholly void.

FURTHER READING

Barrell, John (1988) *Poetry, Language and Politics*, Manchester University Press, Manchester

Bloom, Harold (ed.) (1979) *Deconstruction and Criticism*, Routledge, London

Butler, Marilyn (1981) *Romantics, Rebels and Reactionaries: English Literature and its Background, 1760–1830*, Oxford University Press, Oxford

Damrosch, Leopold, Jr. (1980) *Symbol and Truth in Blake's Myth*, Princeton University Press, Princeton

Ferguson, Frances (1977) *Wordsworth: Language as Counter-Spirit*, Yale University Press, New Haven

Fraistat, Neil (1985) *The Poem and the Book: Interpreting Collections of Romantic Poetry*, University of North Carolina Press, Chapel Hill

McGann, Jerome J. (1983) *A Critique of Modern Textual Criticism*, University of Chicago Press, Chicago

——(1985) *The Beauty of Inflections: Literary Investigations in Historical Method and Theory*, Clarendon Press, Oxford

Mellor, Anne K. (1980) *English Romantic Irony*, Harvard University Press, Cambridge

Rajan, Tilottama (1980) *Dark Interpreter: The Discourse of Romanticism*, Cornell University Press, Ithaca

Simpson, David (1979) *Irony and Authority in Romantic Poetry*, Macmillan, London

——(1982) *Wordsworth and the Figurings of the Real*, Macmillan, London

ADDITIONAL WORKS CITED

Abrams, M. H. (1953) *The Mirror and the Lamp: Romantic Theory and the Critical Tradition*, Oxford University Press, New York

——(1971) *Natural Supernaturalism: Tradition and Revolution in Romantic Literature*, Oxford University Press, London

Babbitt, Irving (1919) *Rousseau and Romanticism*, Houghton Mifflin, Boston

Belsey, Catherine (1980) *Critical Practice*, Methuen, London

Bostetter, Edward E. (1963) *The Romantic Ventriloquists*, University of Washington Press, Seattle

Empson, William and Pirie, David (eds) (1973) *Coleridge's Verse: A Selection*, Faber & Faber, London

Erdman, David V. (1975) *The Illuminated Blake*, Oxford University Press, London

Frye, Northrop (1947) *Fearful Symmetry: A Study of William Blake*, Princeton University Press, Princeton

——(1981) *T. S. Eliot: An Introduction*, University of Chicago Press, Chicago [first published 1963]

Gill, Stephen (ed.) (1984) *William Wordsworth*, Oxford University Press, Oxford

Gleckner, Robert F. (1967) *Byron and the Ruins of Paradise*, Johns Hopkins University Press, Baltimore

Hartman, Geoffrey H. (1964) *Wordsworth's Poetry, 1787–1814*, Yale University Press, New Haven

——(1987) *The Unremarkable Wordsworth*, University of Minnesota Press, Minneapolis

Hirsch, E. D., Jr. (1964) *Innocence and Experience: An Introduction to Blake*, University of Chicago Press, Chicago

Hulme, T. E. (1924) *Speculations: Essays on Humanism and the Philosophy of Art*, edited by Herbert Read, Kegan Paul, Trench, Trubner, London

Knight, G. Wilson (1941) *The Starlit Dome: Studies in the Poetry of Vision*, Oxford University Press, London

Leavis, F. R. (1936) *Revaluation: Tradition and Development in English Poetry*, Chatto & Windus, London

Lefebure, Molly (1986) *The Bondage of Love: A Life of Mrs Samuel Taylor Coleridge*, Gollancz, London

Levin, Susan M. (1987) *Dorothy Wordsworth and Romanticism*, Rutgers State University Press, New Brunswick

Levinson, Marjorie (1986) *Wordsworth's Great Period Poems: Four Essays*, Cambridge University Press, Cambridge

Mellor, Anne K. (ed.) (1988) *Romanticism and Feminism*, Indiana University Press, Bloomington and Indianapolis

Miller, J. Hillis (1975) *The Disappearance of God: Five Nineteenth-Century Writers*, 2nd edn, Belknap Press, Cambridge

Pulos, C. E. (1954) *The Deep Truth: A Study of Shelley's Scepticism*, University of Nebraska Press, Lincoln

Reiman, Donald (ed.) (1972) *The Romantics Reviewed*, 9 vols, Garland, New York

Robinson, Eric and Powell, David (eds) (1984) *John Clare*, (The Oxford Authors), Oxford University Press, Oxford

Warren, Robert Penn (1946) *The Rime of the Ancient Mariner*, Reynal and Hitchcock, New York

Wasserman, Earl R. (1953) *The Finer Tone: Keats's Major Poems*, Johns Hopkins University Press, Baltimore

——(1971) *Shelley: A Critical Reading*, Johns Hopkins University Press, Baltimore

Wordsworth, Jonathan, Abrams, M. H. and Gill, Stephen (eds) (1979), *William Wordsworth: 'The Prelude' 1799, 1805, 1850*, Norton, New York

19

VICTORIAN POETRY

ISOBEL ARMSTRONG

It has become customary to designate the poetry written between 1830 and approximately the year 1900 by the name 'Victorian', whereas the poetry of the previous decades, 'Romantic' poetry, is described with reference to a movement of ideas. One group of poets is anchored securely to a monarch and a nation (though that monarch came to the throne in 1837), the other to a trans-European philosophical and political project. Thus a particular way of reading these groups of poets has been perpetuated which has been both cause and effect of these groupings. The accident of death has been partly responsible for causing a chasm to open up between the groups: Keats, Shelley, Byron and Blake died within six years of one another in the 1820s. Only Wordsworth lived on, dying in 1850, when the Laureateship was handed on to Tennyson. Tennyson began publishing in 1830, Browning in 1833. The work of both becomes homogenized as they appear to dominate the century as major Victorian poets.

The work of these 'homogenized' poets tends to be read in terms of decades – the 1830s, 40s and 50s. This is encouraged by the convergence of their work in what seems a 'peak' in the 1850s. Tennyson's *In Memoriam* and *Maud* appeared in 1850 and 1855 respectively; Browning's *Men and Women* in 1855. But there are other ways of reading the work of these poets, and different relationships to be made. Even if one provisionally accepts the artificial Romantic/Victorian divide, it is possible to argue for another picture than the conventional one. But first, what is that conventional picture? What follows is a simplified presentation of a simplified picture, but it can stand as a kind of parody against which I shall set an alternative reading.

People tend to start with Tennyson's early poetry of the 1830s, though not with that of Browning, whom they pick up in the 1850s. Tennyson's early volumes, *Poems, Chiefly Lyrical* (1830) and *Poems* (1832), are accessible as symbolist poetry before its time, pre-modernist psychological poetry of the *paysage intérieur*. It is possible to make this reading because the poems seem to be in perfect consonance with the theory of his friend and reviewer, Arthur Hallam. Hallam pointed to Tennyson's capacity to 'fuse', as he self-consciously put it, the objects of perception with mind 'in a medium of strong emotion' (Hallam, [1831] 1972, p. 93). Such chemistry (and he deliberately borrowed his metaphor from science) was achieved by what he called the poetry of 'sensation' rather than the poetry of 'reflection', represented by the didactic poetry of Wordsworth as against the image-laden writing of Keats and Shelley (p. 87). So Tennyson is seen as an aesthetic poet, bound up with internal landscapes. The drugged cadences of 'The Lotos-Eaters', and the language which fuses psychological categories with the objects of perception – 'rolling a slumberous sheet of foam below' – or the neurotic intensity with which the details of landscape are experienced in 'Mariana' as discrete items of sensation – clinking latch, pear tree held with rotting nails, blackened moss – all seem to endorse this reading. From there Tennyson goes backward into the Victorian age. *In Memoriam* (1850), with its doubts, its God, its Geology, generating worries about ethics and immortality (worries about a positivist science which seem themselves positivist) engages with what are thought to be typically Victorian categories. He goes further back still into the Victorian period with the Arthurian *Idylls of the King* (the first parts of which were published in 1859). To those who see Tennyson as the poet of a national Arthurian epic and a theological poem, *Maud* (1855) seems to be a freak, an inexplicable psychodrama hard to reconcile with the work of his maturity.

It is here that Browning catches him up. Browning's early work, which is complex and arcane, does not lend itself easily to discussion (it tends to be forgotten that he wished to be a popular poet and issued *Bells and Pomegranates* in the form of cheap pamphlets on the model of Shelley's *Queen Mab* and associated with R. H. Horne, called 'the farthing poet'), but *Men and Women* (1855), the volume which first made him popular, is accessible. Since many poems in it are dramatic monologues, it is possible to see the whole of the early poetry as aspiring towards the dramatic monologue. Though a reading of these poems in terms of the psychological realism achieved by the monologue form has begun to give way, and the subtle epistemology which evolves an unstable consciousness through the dramatic form has enabled them to be read instead as deconstructive moments undermining a coherent subjectivity, it is largely in terms of the monologue that they are read – or else a glance is given to the black symbolism of 'Childe Roland to the dark Tower Came' (see Bloom, 1979). The virtuosity of monologues such as 'Fra Lippo Lippi', with its aggressively libertarian aesthetics, or the paradoxically nihilistic theological belief disclosed in 'Bishop Blougram's Apology', certainly lend themselves to a complex hermeneutics, but Browning wrote lyrics, love poems and philosophical poems which cannot all be coerced into the category of monologue.

The inordinate length of *The Ring and the Book* (1868) seems to prevent it from being tackled seriously on any terms, despite its ostensibly dramatic form.

The work of the second generation Victorian poets, Arthur Hugh Clough and Matthew Arnold, converges with the mature work of Tennyson and Browning, and it is remarkable how what is designated as 'Victorian poetry' actually falls into the narrow band of the late 1840s and the 1850s. Clough, who developed through the hexameter a multiplicity of dictions and registers to articulate a new kind of democratic poetry, is often seen through Arnold's eyes. The pastoral elegy to Clough, 'Thyrsis', describes the poetry of the anxiety state – his 'piping' took 'a troubled sound/Of storms that rage outside our happy ground' (ll. 48–9) (the happy ground of Oxford University) – and associates his work with morbid introspecton. Arnold, reacting against the modernity which he imputed to his own poetry, the introspective 'dialogue of the mind with itself', formulated an aesthetic of detachment and objectivity which made it an ethical imperative for the poet to shape his poems round 'great human actions', cleared of redundant verbal decoration and excess. The Preface to his poems of 1853, from which these quotations come, where he rejected the dialectics of his earlier *Empedocles on Etna* (1852), an analysis of estrangement and intellectual exhaustion, has come to signify a typically mid-Victorian poetics.

It is possible, after this mid-Victorian band of poetry has been encountered, to see the rest of the century as aspiring towards modernism. Swinburne and Meredith, Dante Gabriel Rossetti and William Morris, are loosely grouped as 'Pre-Raphaelite poets'. Helped by an angry reviewer who described Rossetti and Swinburne in particular as the 'fleshy school of poetry' (Buchanan, [1871] 1987), it is possible to find a common element in their work, which is associated with subversive sensuousness and the eroticizing of Christian symbol. They can be assimilated into the aesthetic of Symbolism and Pater's understanding that all art, in flight from referentiality, aspires to the condition of music. Though 'eccentrics' like Gerard Manley Hopkins and James Thomson do not really fit into this group, they can be assimilated to the modern tradition in other ways: the complexity of Hopkins's language, its highly metaphoric structure and its synchronic nature, readily entitle him to be assimilated into modernism's linguistic experiments, while the city landscapes of Thomson's *The City of Dreadful Night* (1874) suggest an anticipation of the fragmented urban world of T. S. Eliot's *The Waste Land*. It is a short step from the decadents – Dowson, Wilde, Johnson and the early Yeats – into the twentieth century. Some people would tack on to this a rural tradition, through John Clare, William Barnes and Thomas Hardy, and others would also add an urban tradition of self-taught industrial artisans – Ebenezer Elliot, for instance, or Samuel Bamford and Thomas Cooper. Yet others would remember the women poets. Emily

Brontë, Christina Rossetti and Elizabeth Barrett Browning are the poets most likely to be seen as important.

This understanding of the shape of Victorian poetry is limiting in a number of ways. It ignores, in the first place, the political events round which this poetry configures – the reform bills of 1832 and 1867, which engendered important debates about representation which implicitly or explicitly enter into the consciousness of this poetry. It ignores the European revolutions of 1848, and the Crimean war (1853–7), the beginning of which coincides with the year of Arnold's 1853 Preface. When the connection between poetics and politics is registered, a rather different reading of the poetry is possible. It is not so much that unknown texts emerge, but another reading of the existing texts can be made, and a different configuration of their work. The exception to this is the poetry of the women. There were many more women poets writing than have ever been generally discussed. The constraints of space do not allow a complete re-reading of the poetry of this period, but it is possible to dramatize its concerns by concentrating on four moments where a radical poetry clearly emerges in contradistinction to a conservative tradition. Browning in the 1830s, Morris in the 1850s, Thomson in the 1870s, and a group of women writing in the latter part of the century, will be the focus of discussion.

Browning came of a dissenting Congregationalist family. Dissenters were excluded from certain privileges and powers (unlike Tennyson, for instance, Browning could not have been admitted to one of the older universities) and they tended to form their own centres of power and thought. Browning gravitated to one of the foremost dissenting intellectuals of this time, William Johnson Fox (he called Fox his literary godfather), and it was Fox who reviewed his early poems and published two of the earliest monologues in his journal, *The Monthly Repository*, in 1836 (see Mineka, 1944). The nature of Browning's early experiments can be understood by looking at one of these poems, 'Porphyria's Lover', and the intellectual formation to which it belongs.

The Monthly Repository was a Unitarian publication, radical, utilitarian, and powerfully committed to social change. In the year of the reform bill, 1832, Fox wrote:

> The public mind has outgrown public institutions, which must soon be shattered. . . . The question of reform in the representation of the people could never have arisen in its present interest and importance but in connection with a strong and general conviction of other changes . . . The Church cannot remain as it is . . . The Law cannot remain as it is . . . Education cannot remain as it is. The poor must be educated, though at the public expense . . . The means for disseminating information cannot remain as they are . . . taxes on knowledge . . . intercept information in its passage to the people. They suppress or restrict . . .

A different principle in the distribution of wealth must gradually make its way into society.

(*The Monthly Repository*, vol. 6, new series [1832], pp. 1–4)

He might have added that the condition of women could not remain as it was, for this publication was instrumental in creating one of the first groups of organized feminists in England. The Fox group, forging a utilitarian, Benthamite aesthetic, and attempting to democratize literature, had a developed understanding of the relationship between literature, ideology and power. Celebrating Shelley as the revolutionary poet, and castigating Words-worth and Coleridge for reneging on revolutionary ideals, it was natural that Fox should turn in a subsequent article to a consideration of poetry and the poor ('The Poor and their Poetry', *The Monthly Repository*, vol. 6, new series, 1832, pp. 189–201). Adopting a cultural relativism theorized from Herder, he concluded that just as different cultures and countries would develop different forms of art, so there would be a corresponding difference between the poetry of the rich and the poetry of the poor in the same country. The problem was not only to produce a poetry which included within itself an understanding of the environments of the poor – the city, the workhouse, the prison – but one which would not be produced by the gentlemanly looker-on of the middle class, one which might be produced by the poor themselves. Browning, of course, was exactly one of these gentlemanly lookers-on, but Fox's conviction that modern poetry, experimental nineteenth-century poetry that is, must represent modern states of consciousness by utilizing the possibilities of associationist theory, projecting itself provisionally into different states of mind, provides the poet with a radical aesthetic. For such a projection becomes a drama of mental events, not a private drama but a public drama in which a dialectic of feeling and conflict is objectified. Since drama does not avail itself of a single position it enables a democratic reading, as the reader engages with the hermeneutic process and attempts to grasp the structure of relationships evolving in the poem. Such a process was for Fox not only psychologically but ideologically liberating because it lays bare the nature of conflict. Add to this a sophisticated understanding of the instability of the 'truth' of the text derived from a reading of German biblical criticism (for *The Monthly Repository* had responded to these new ideas well before they became generally known later in the century) and a powerful concern with the role and status of women, and a context for reading 'Porphyria's Lover' is available to us.

But this context is also one of intellectual debate – a quarrel. Fox had accidentally passed on to Browning John Stuart Mill's annotations to his first poem, *Pauline* (1833). These were fiercely critical of its morbid subjectivity, but quite apart from this Mill's understanding of drama was different from that of Fox: he thought of the poem as a private soliloquy, overheard by the reader, not a public event (Mill, [1859] 1950). 'Porphyria's Lover' carries Mill's 'overheard' poem satirically to its logical conclusion by presenting a private experience so solipsistic that it might be mad. The absolutely private subjectivity of feeling confessing itself to itself either imagines or enacts a sexual murder; strangling Porphyria on her illicit visit to him, the speaker confirms the moment of possession as an ownership which can only issue in murder – 'That moment she was mine, mine, fair,/Perfectly pure and good' (ll. 36–7) – for what is 'perfectly pure and good' contains no further development within itself, and a total possession of it and a total affirmation of one's ego implies the act of annihilation. Porphyria, willing the moment of subjection which calls forth masculine power, is made responsible for it and fittingly strangled with her own hair. The contradictions of the private contract outside the public sphere are remorselessly pursued. 'When no voice replied' (l. 15), 'And God has not said a word!' (l. 60): the private experience needs no answering voice and negates the dialogue of the other. The itemizing of Porphyria's body in seduction – waist, shoulder, hair – already turns her into the 'it' she becomes at the end of the poem. As her lover attempts to 'dissever' her from the 'ties' of other obligations she is literally dissevered as a dismembered body. This is a prescient poem in many ways, for later, in his essay 'On Liberty' (1859), Mill was to say that sexual relations are exempted from the public sphere. 'While I debated what to do' (l. 35), the lover says. Whatever action is in the private sphere, and what its significance and ethical standing is, becomes crucially important in the poem. At the same time it is far more than a quarrel with Mill. It is an enquiry into the standing of fantasy and its fictions and therefore implicitly an enquiry into the standing of poetry itself. It never is clear whether the murder is an accomplished fact or a fantasy. The purpose of the poem is not to keep us guessing so much as to ask how far this matters. Bentham, whose thought was of central importance to the Fox group, had developed a theory of language in terms of fictions, and for him fictions are never unimportant. Words correlate with things we can see (hence they are 'real' entities) or with things we cannot, such as the soul, in which case they are 'fictional' entities. But fictions make as decisive an intervention in the world as do real entities of language. In law, for instance, which is where Bentham first developed his ideas (and it is no accident that contract features so strongly in Browning's poem) they have to be negotiated and investigated as if they were real, or injustice and oppression will result. So the speaker's soliloquy is a substantive cultural fantasy, about possession, power, sexual property and the paradoxical nature of women's subjection – for the speaker gives to Porphyria the power of infantilizing him even as he asserts his power. A fiction constructed out of other fictions, it has entered the world. In disclosing itself as a construct the poem both declares itself to be an analysis of a condition as well as an expression of feeling, an analysis which asks for the active inspection and participation of the reader.

The critique of Mill, then, issued in a way of exploring the political and imaginative importance of poetry through the drama of objectified feeling which Browning was to develop through the rest of his writing life. One could say that he was a Benthamite poet right up to *The Ring and the Book* and beyond. It should not be forgotten that Fox published the poems of Ebenezer Elliott, sharp, gnawing poems about the plight of the poor, and also the work of R. H. Horne, whose 'Political Oratorio', for instance, was a sardonic burlesque about the position of Trade Unions (Horne, 1835). The word 'oratorio' suggests the public world excluded from Mill's theory of poetry.

The Tennyson group on the other hand, forming itself round Arthur Hallam and the Apostles at Cambridge (at that time an avant garde secret society) was a group which might be described as subversive conservatives (see Allen, 1978). They wanted social change, but change which was to be achieved not through political transformation but through the imaginative regeneration of the whole nation. They celebrated the mythopoeic aspects of Shelley's work (Hallam was instrumental in the publication of 'Adonais') rather than its revolutionary possibilities. In his review of Tennyson's early poems Hallam wrote of the split and fragmented modern mind. A nation united through the unifying continuity of its myths is no longer possible, however desirable. The poet of sensation, however, a latter day self-conscious poet, defamiliarizing fixed positions with the solvent of feeling, working from the outside of his culture by exploring disruptive states of consciousness, was the nearest thing to a mythopoeic writer. Myths, the Apostles learned from Thomas Keightley's *The Fairy Mythology* (1828), are aspects of intuitional thought, often used as forms of power, continually reinterpreted simply because they were not true (see Armstrong, 1989). One can see Tennyson exploring what it is like to be a mythological being outside human culture in poems such as the paired Mermaid and Merman poems, considering the multiple significance of the Kraken, symbol both of revolution and the apocalypse, representing the enclosed and divided world of women through Arthurian myth in 'The Lady of Shallot', and examining, through the classical myth of the Lotos-Eaters, the oppressed consciousness which is committed so deeply to labour that it can only imagine a world of half-consciousness governed by Epicurean gods remote from it, gods whose perceptions it cannot change, and who exist in a mystified relationship to those whom they oppress.

Tennyson's fellow Apostles tended to move either towards the poetry of sensation, as did Monckton Milnes, or to the poetry of reflection, as did Richard Chenevix Trench. *In Memoriam* may be seen as an attempt to combine the two. 'So careful of the Type?' Tennyson asked (section 56), appalled by the implications of geological change. Myth, evolving and comparing experiences through typologizing, enabling analogies between past and present to be made, is also careful of the type. It preserves fixed points of reference just as the classifications of science do. But these sustaining and conserving categories seem to have broken down for Tennyson as this poem was written, and *In Memoriam* is both a record of this breakdown and its philosophical and social implications and an attempt to reintegrate experience. Perhaps the rest of Tennyson's poetry can also be seen in terms of an effort to explore the breakdown of the Type: certainly Pater thought of him as the poet of the Type (Pater, [1888] 1889) and of Browning as the poet of the grotesque (Pater, [1857] 1873) and these terms were often used in the later criticism of the period to denote conservative and radical poetry.

Where did the category of the grotesque come from? During the 1840s John Ruskin was working on *Modern Painters*, developing a new aesthetic, implicitly a democratic aesthetic, by which the works of Turner could be appreciated. He broke off from these volumes to write *Stones of Venice*, and in the third and last of these volumes (1853) he elaborated the category of the grotesque, one of the characteristics of Gothic art, devoting a long chapter to it (chapter 3). Interestingly, this is the same year that Arnold was considering great human actions, typical, universal actions, as the materials of poetry. Ruskin did not believe that art was typical or universal but that it expressed different historical moments. Grotesque art, he said, manifested itself in a number of historical periods, but it took different forms according to the culture to which it belonged. One form of it appears in the art of the Gothic cathedral, where the workman gave expression to resistance against the social order by carving sculpture embodying the will to freedom. Some nineteenth-century discussions of Gothic art associated it with an integrated, organized society, but Ruskin did not. All forms of grotesque art are related to play, and play is directly related to the forms of work a society evolves and to its social hierarchy. In connecting play with forms of work and the social structure Ruskin is implicitly escaping from the idea of pure aesthetic play which had been developed in Schiller's influential *Letters on the Aesthetic Education of Man* (1795). He details many forms of play, but some societies have a structure of work so intransigent that its members cannot play at all. The nineteenth century has developed such a society through the organisation of industrial labour, and whether they participate in oppressed labour or not, all classes will produce the art which is formed by it. Mechanics and artisans express the distortions of the grotesque only in jibes, jests, facial expressions and carica-ture. For other classes the sense of distortion will be expressed through an art which he sees as a distorted form of the sublime. The rupture of understand-ing, the epistemological break created through the sublime moment, is a distortion which, in the case of the grotesque, gives rise to a sense of limit, of a painfully narrowed perspective, of non-transcendence. The movement of

Burke's sublime was a movement from the experience of dissolution and terror in the infinite to a new integration, where the sense of the breakdown of perception and relationship was surmounted in a new synthesis. The grotesque stays with the sense of a gap in experience, of incomplete synthesis and restriction, and consequently the art of the grotesque is an art of infinitely self-generated desire, an economy of perpetually expended feeling. The sense of limit finds its expression in a preoccupation with death, the ultimate limit of all experience, and with violence, the site of frustration. Above all the gap opened up by the withholding of meaning results in a fascination with the inadequacy of the sign, with the mystified symbol and with misprisioned representation, where the very correctives to distortion lead to further progressively distorted representations and misprision, the flawed mirror of perception. For Ruskin these are ideological forms, created by the conditions of labour in an oppressed society. But once it can be seen that this is so, the possibility of critique is available to us.

Morris, who knew Ruskin, takes up the challenge of making a critique of the grotesque through the very form of the grotesque itself in *The Defence of Guenevere and other Poems* (1858). This volume is often seen, as Pater saw Morris's work, as a Pre-Raphaelite retreat to the pure abstractions of feeling embodied in the medieval and the chivalric. On the contrary, it is more helpful to see the medieval world as a construction of oppressed consciousness. Medievalism will be the form the oppressed consciousness appropriates, a misprisioned form, to satisfy its fascination with death, with violence and with the inadequacy of the symbol: images of the medieval will be the projections of desire, that ever-unsatisfied desire of the alienated consciousness. The frightful intensity of discrete and unrelated detail, a phenomenon which Ruskin saw as one of the psychological discoveries of Pre-Raphaelite painting, is Morris's compositional method in this volume. But the manifestations of the grotesque also take larger forms. The title poem of the volume, 'The Defence of Guenevere', contains a distortion within it: this is the defence made by Guenevere and a defence of her by the author – and a defence is both a case that can be made and a means of shielding the truth, a misprisioned representation, a covering up. For Guenevere's defence is both an explanation and a protective shield of words which never fully represent the hidden acts motivating the defence – sexual betrayal and adultery. The more she explains the more she conceals and distorts. For distortion is intrinsic to her situation: sexuality itself is the distorting element in this volume, constituting the consuming desire Ruskin names as the characteristic grotesque experience. It is not simply that sexuality and libido are grounded in repression: taboos, obligations and contracts govern chivalric marriage, and the withholding of courtly love is predicated on marriage, forming the conditions of oppression within which both men and women live. It was bold of Morris to interpret desire in sexual terms, something Ruskin does not do. Guenevere holds up her hand to the light, and can and cannot see through it, an emblem of the obfuscations with which the characters in Morris's world exist. A fetishizing of the hand, of parts of the body but particularly of the hand, is a recurrent feature of this volume. In a concealed way Morris introduces the ground of oppressed labour in his own culture, for 'the hand' is the metonym for the industrial labourer, and thus oppression in marriage is indirectly linked with other forms of contractual power.

Desire, violence, death and the misprision of symbol come together in a short poem, 'Two Red Roses Across the Moon'. The title forms an enigmatic refrain to the poem, and represents the heraldic emblem of the knight who is described on his journey to the violent slaughter of battle in which the heraldic colours of both sides, 'scarlet and blue', are obliterated in the 'brown' of meaningless signification in battle, and of course, in the 'brown' of mud or dust to which death brings both sides. The knight returns to his lady, celebrating the pure 'gold' of chivalric love. But the distinctions made so clearly in his world are not so clear in fact. The refrain is inherently contradictory, for in it the yellow moon of chastity and the erotic intensity of the rose, which suggests also blood and violence, exist in incompatible relationship. And just as the colours of battle are blended with and to the colour of mud, so the red and the yellow gold of the courtly life become the colour brown when they are mixed. It is not possible to keep the worlds of battle and sexuality pure of one another. This haunting poem, so simple on one level that it is immediately accessible, contains at the same time all the contradictions of the grotesque vision. It is a democratic poetry because it can be read as a ballad by a wide audience, and its enigmatic contradictions can be recognized even when they cannot be explained.

Almost every poem in *The Defence of Guenevere* reminds one of the slaughter and carnage of battle, a carnage in no way aestheticized. The volume was published the year after the last year of the Crimean war, and it could quite properly be seen as a volume of war poetry, a critique of a society which habitually goes to war. The controversy over the Crimean war, the first major European war of Victoria's reign, in which the European powers reconfigured over the Eastern question, is filtered through Morris's poems. In 'The Wind' the shadowy ghosts of knights (or are they living men?) return to haunt the chamber of the speaker, who is overburdened with his own power to kill, a power which he works out in terms of the mysterious death of his lover, Margaret, but which redounds upon him in the form of the shadowy knights, with whom he shares guilt by association ('I knew him by the arms I used to paint/Upon their long thin shields: but the colours were all grown faint').

If Morris registers the shock of war by defamiliarizing it, paradoxically recording its traumas through a society which takes it for granted, Tennyson, who was far more equivocal than Morris about the violence of the war and the necessity of going to war, chose to articulate the contradictions of the war 'ethic' through the speech of a madman in *Maud: A Monodrama* (1855). His equivocation emerges in the way the poem yields two readings. A conservative reading emerges through the speaker's railing against 'the blessings of peace'. His decision to go to war, to be 'one with my kind', seeing the unity of the nation in war as the equivalent of a new-found psychological integration, is a way of re-establishing a new chivalric code inherited from a conservative aristocracy. The hero and his class, regaining a feudal solidarity in the face of the trading interests who resist war because it endangers trade, embody the romantic reactionary ideology to which, at its worst, Hallam's ideal of national unity through myth could lead. Such romantic nationalism embodies 'aestheticized politics', a term which Walter Benjamin used much later to describe the rise of Fascism. The poem, however, does have a contrary reading. The speaker is insane, or certainly becomes insane when he kills, in a duel, the brother of Maud, who is the young girl around whom his erotic fantasies and passions, inseparable from violence, gather and fester. It is not simply that his testimony is untrustworthy but that through him there is a critique of the rampant individualism which sinks its identity in the higher unity of war, a way of collectivizing individualism.

In this period one can see the poetry of the type uneasily responding to contemporary pressures. Matthew Arnold's *Sohrab and Rustum*, for instance, is such an uneasy poem. It was written to exemplify the poetry of the great human action. Published in 1853, the same year as the start of the Crimean War, it is not, as he wished, abstracted from the contemporary events he deprecated as the subject of poetry. It is set in the Caucasus, the site of conflict in the struggle of the Eastern question, and is about a heroic battle in which affiliations are uncertain and confused, for father and son are on different sides and meet in fatal single combat without knowing each other. It is as much a contemporary poem as Clough's *Amours de Voyage* (1850), set in modern Italy in 1848, when Rome was invaded by the French. Clough's work, with its exposure of conflict, belongs rather to the vein of radical satire developed round the Fox group in earlier decades. Clough's contemporary intellectual and 'hero', Claude, in *Amours de Voyage*, fascinated by sex and battle, but distanced from both by a capacity for self-undermining reflection, is obsessed by the sense of limit. He is a parody by anticipation of Arnold's ancient philosopher Empedocles, the exhausted intellectual whose alienation makes him seek reunion with the sources of vitality in suicide by throwing himself into the volcano of Etna. This death is the very type of the distorted sublime Ruskin represented by the grotesque. It is provoked by the sense of limit, of the impossibility of achieving a synthesis of experience except in the moment of death. Interestingly, this is parodied in Browning's 'Cleon', in *Men and Women* (1855), where alienation becomes literally a grotesque aestheticism. Here the intellectual labour of Browning's classical polymath is fiercely exposed as a dependence on slave labour, a dependence concealed or unrecognized by the protagonist. Browning, like Morris, uses the forms of the grotesque itself as a critique of the grotesque in the poetry of his middle period. The Benthamite fictions proffered by his speakers, whether in lyric or monologue, develop a hermeneutics of the grotesque in which the narrow aperture of ideological perception opens up progressive ideological distortions, whether it is the scientific 'objectivity' of his physician, Karshish, or the perpetual seeking of the lover in 'Love in a Life', who in seeking 'herself' meets either himself, his own projection of love, or nothing.

In the latter part of the century the distinction between conservative and radical poetry continues. It is manifested in the work of James Thomson, materialist, freethinker and republican, and in the antithetical poetry of Gerard Manley Hopkins, Catholic convert and anti-democratic conservative. In *The City of Dreadful Night* (1874) Thomson developed a rhetoric of the black sublime to explore oppression, while Hopkins's *The Wreck of the Deutschland* (1876) epitomizes the grotesque and its struggles in the intense strain of its reaching after transcendence, the violence of its desire for the embodiment of godhead in symbol and in the literal experience of the incarnation. Language breaks down in Stanza 28: 'But how shall I . . . make me room there:/Reach me a . . .'. Hopkins's elaborate aesthetics of individuation (in which each word, in its strain to be incarnate sign rather than a proxy representation of or substitute for experience), often leads to a language of torsion and distortion, as syntax is pulled towards immediacy and words are forced towards uniqueness. Compounds, often condensing temporality into simultaneity, do the work of syntax – 'How a lush-kept-plush capped sloe . . .' – and words are forced back from abstraction to their most concrete form – for instance, 'tell' instead of 'count'; 'wording it' instead of 'expressing' something. For Hopkins strives to make the word flesh as a guarantee of the relationship with godhead in the incarnation. This is the essence of the nun's saving vision at the centre of his poem and it guarantees salvation to her and to 'two hundred souls' who died in the wreck. In recognizing the uniqueness of each soul, the poem implicitly argues, the Catholic religion establishes a truer humanistic concern than any democratic politics could achieve: for democracy, abstracting and quantifying individuals through the proxy of the vote, is the antithesis of that authority, God, who in 'Mastering' His subjects grounds their individuality and grants it immortality. But the strain of celebrating the disaster of the wreck and the horror of 200 deaths is evident in the poem. It is arguable that rather than deconstructing the grotesque, as radical writers did, Hopkins expresses through it the strain and limit of his conservative vision.

For Thomson, who did not, of course, know of Hopkins's work, such reactionary understanding of a 'Mastering' God was anathema, and it may be that the grim lucidity and the curiously violent purity of his language is an attempt to dissociate himself absolutely from gothic diction which may have signified to this poet ideological consent to oppressed consciousness embodied in grotesque writing. One of the paradoxes of his poem is the Dantean limpidity and iron chastity with which its materialist universe is disclosed. *The City of Dreadful Night* (1874) is often compared with T. S. Eliot's *The Waste Land* (1922): both poems appear to explore the estrangement and anomie of the city. But nothing could be further from Eliot's poem, with its humanized quasi-mystical symbolism taken eclectically from different spiritual traditions, and its subjectivized reading of the crises of European civilization, than Thomson's poem. The estrangement of *The City of Dreadful Night* is not caused by spiritual breakdown but precisely by the oppression of theist and Christian ideology itself. Thomson, almost always described as a 'pessimist' and not the anarchist and atheist he was, is easy to misread because his project was to re-write Christian language, using its symbols against itself. The symbols of the *Inferno* become for him the symbols of a materialist universe. His association with Charles Bradlaugh, editor of the freethinking *National Reformer*, the journal in which the poem was first published, provides a context for his poem.

Bradlaugh wrote consistently against the landed and feudal class interests which organized political power in England. He pointed to the huge consolidation of landed power which, he felt, was behind industrial power because it often owned the land leased to industrialists or developed industry on its own account, and continued to exploit despite electoral reform. He was also a propagandist for atheism. He argued that change, not teleology, was the governing principle of the universe. 'Cause' is a word we use with mistaken teleological meaning, where it is simply a word which includes all that determines change. Nothing falls outside matter: we may destroy a gold coin but not the metal it is made of. The distinctions we make between 'matter', 'nature', 'substance', 'existence' are merely effects of language. If the universe is founded on change, an unchanging God is a contradiction. If man were made in the image of God he would never change or forget: 'Can God forget?' he asked (Bradlaugh, 1877, p. 13). Forgetfulness and amnesia are defining characteristics of human experience, a principle Thomson developed in the oblivion of his city, seeing that the oblivion of repression is what makes human energies possible.

In his prose work, 'A Lady of Sorrow' ([1862] 1881), Thomson portrayed a symbolic world of ceaseless material reproduction and destruction in which tragedy and creativity are dialectically dependent on each other. 'A Lady of Sorrow' is a Malthusian rhapsody which turns the incessant reproduction and blind creativity Malthusians and post-Darwinians had dreaded into fierce rejoicing and the celebration of constant change. *The City of Dreadful Night*, on the other hand, is far more sombre, and explores, with black and terrible irony, the landscape of false consciousness, adapting Dante's 'Abandon hope all ye who enter here' (section 6) and turning it into a paradox: it is precisely because people will not abandon hope in a transcendental world that the world becomes for them a place of suicidal despair. The great black effigy of Melancholia which ends the poem suggests that through negation of hope creativity in the material world is possible, but the poem concentrates on a kind of sublime deconstruction of the landscape of Christian despair. It is in no way a realistic poem: though one short section describes the hearse-like passage of oppressed labour through the streets, 'strangled by that city's curse' (section 9), its landscape is phantasmagoric and depopulated because the ideologies which have made the city landscape are individualism, a personal religion and idealism. Thus we come across a grotesque, Beckett-like, crawling figure, a geriatric infantilist, who is enacting a fantasy of the return to innocence, a return which is actually impossible in a materialist world of change. Thomson is remorseless in his materialist analysis: 'The City is of Night; perchance of Death,/But certainly of night; ... The sun has never visited that city,/For it dissolveth in the daylight fair ...' (section 1, ll. 1–7). There are ambiguities in the phrase 'it dissolveth': on the one hand it refers to the ever-cooling world postulated by physics; the city also 'dissolveth' because its inhabitants conceptualize their environment as phantasmal because of the fantasies of Christian idealism. But 'it' might refer both to the sun and to the city, and depending on which we see as subject here the words suggest either that in the true daylight of materialism the city and its horrors vanish, or that even in the daylight the sun dissolves, and thus never can penetrate the city. This is a chilling vision, and makes the nihilism of the better known 'aesthetic' or 'decadent' writers – Swinburne, Wilde, Dowson, for instance – seem both self-conscious and limited.

Finally, the women writers. It is unfair to group such distinguished poets together at the end of an essay mainly devoted to re-writing the history of politics and aesthetics in poetry by men. But at this point in time, when there are only good editions of the pre-eminent poets, Christina Rossetti and Elizabeth Barrett Browning, and when other poets do not even get into general anthologies of Victorian poetry, and cannot be found in modern editions, it is probable that sexual politics transcend other politics. Every poet I mention here deserves a modern edition of her work – Adelaide Anne Procter, Dora Greenwell, Jean Ingelow, Augusta Webster, Mathilde Blind, Amy Levy. When these have been produced, and these poets are seen as the major writers they are, it will be possible to relate sexual politics to other areas of their thought with more precision and exactness. Very often relative conservatism in social or political matters coexists with an intense understanding of the restrictions under which women lived. Charlotte Brontë's high Tory politics coexisted with her sense of limit; Elizabeth Barrett Browning's social sympathies (expressed in poems such as 'The Cry of the Children'), class prejudice and fascination with strong rulers (she and Browning disagreed about Louis Napoleon's *coup d'état*) coexisted with her sense of the oppression of the woman writer; Christina Rossetti's high church Anglicanism coexisted with an extraordinarily daring conception of her own relationship to God; Dora Greenwell's relatively conventional defence of the kinds of work women are fitted for (Greenwell, 1866) coexisted with some passionate poetry of protest and desire. One has only to contrast Adelaide Anne Procter's poems on the Crimean war with those by Tennyson or Gerald Massey to see that women entered into political debate, though very few would have argued for political means of changing their position, such as the vote. Nevertheless, whether covertly or directly, women poets all share a common interest in the limits set on women's lives.

It is not possible to do justice to the energy and power of this work here. It is only possible to point to its variety. There is the intense polemic of Elizabeth Barrett Browning's *Aurora Leigh* (1857), a verse novel about a limited and arrogant woman poet whose world is expanded and changed by her care for a raped girl, her rival in love, and her child. At one point the poem suggests that the suffering of rape entitles a woman to displace Christ as the supreme symbol of suffering on the cross (see Marion Erle's story, the last 200 lines of Book 6). 'Since when was genius found respectable?' Aurora Leigh asks, early in Book 6. Sometimes, under seemingly 'respectable' forms such as the fairy story or the folk tale, women explore subversive and radical themes. Christina Rossetti's 'Goblin Market' (1862) is a poem which begins with an enticing chorus of market cries, expressed through her characteristically self-effacing metrical virtuosity, describing the fruit for sale in the fairy market, offering a succession of sensuous and erotic experiences to the two girls who hear them. However, it is not the sensuous or the erotic in itself which is a problem – in fact the sensuous is welcomed – but the fact that this fruit is for sale, its price and conditions of sale fixed by 'Goblin men', arbitrarily withdrawn or offered for consumption as they alone think fit. Laura suffers the anguish of a sexuality seen as an object of consumption. Her sister understands how to manoeuvre in these conditions. Christina Rossetti's laconic and crystalline lyricism continued to take such risks throughout her writing life.

These poets, however, are comparatively well known; other equally gifted writers are not. As an example of the possibilities which await the exploratory reader one might cite Augusta Webster's brilliant monologue, 'The Happiest Girl in the World' (1870), spoken by a newly-engaged girl whose conventional understanding of her future role as wife gradually exposes its contradictions – wife, child, mother, mistress, friend, servant – and slowly discloses her own insecure and unwilling participation in the role, particularly the role of mother. Also through the dramatic monologue, Amy Levy deconstructs feminine roles, but more violently, in poems such as 'Medea' (1884), where Medea's fury and destructiveness questions conventional paradigms. Lastly, the ambitious Mathilde Blind, who tackled theological and evolutionary themes in her work, takes up the problem of violence. One of her most ambitious poems is *The Heather on Fire* (1886), a narrative of the clearing of the Highlands in the early 1830s, recent but forgotten history. It describes the brutalized way in which the crofters were evicted, seen as animals rather than human beings, and suggests how a simple category change alters behaviour – 'So let them een be smoked from out their holes ... help to clear away/This stinking rubbish heap'.

As our own history changes, so our need to reconsider the past changes too. Twenty years ago, Victorian poetry looked very different, seen as it was from the ground of high modernism and its preoccupations with the non-didactic, with the symbol, with the self-referential, the autonomy of art. Now, as our perception of modernism shifts, and particularly our perception of its politics and its embroilment with reactionary or fascist thinking, to look back to Victorian poetry is to see something rather different from the rather stolid moral and theological categories it appeared to deal with. It is to see a poetry of great complexity and experiment. In another twenty years, probably sooner, what is in this chapter may well be re-written in the light of changed circumstances which alter a reading of history and the meaning of the word 'Victorian'.

FURTHER READING

Armstrong, Isobel (1972) *Victorian Scrutinies: Reviews of Poetry 1830–70*, The Athlone Press, London

——(1982) *Language as Living Form in Nineteenth Century Poetry*, Harvester Press, Brighton

Ball, Patricia M. (1976) *The Heart's Events: The Victorian Poetry of Relationships*, The Athlone Press, London

Christ, Carol T. (1984) *Victorian and Modern Poetics*, University of Chicago Press, Chicago and London

Edmond, R. (1988) *Affairs of the Hearth: Victorian Poetry and Domestic Narrative*, Routledge, London

Gilbert, Sandra M. and Gubar, Susan (1979) *Shakespeare's Sisters: Feminist Essays on Women Poets*, Indiana University Press, Bloomington and London

Johnson, E. D. H. (1952) *The Alien Vision of Victorian Poetry*, Princeton University Press, Princeton

Langbaum, Robert (1957) *The Poetry of Experience: The Dramatic Monologue in Modern Literary Tradition*, Chatto & Windus, London

Machin, Richard and Norris, Christopher (eds) (1987) *Post-Structuralist Readings of English Poetry*, Cambridge University Press, Cambridge

Sinfield, Alan (1986) *Alfred Tennyson*, Blackwell, Oxford

Slinn, Warwick (1982) *Browning and the Fictions of Identity*, Macmillan, London

Tucker, Herbert F. (1980) *Browning's Beginnings: The Art of Disclosure*, University of Minnesota Press, Minneapolis

ADDITIONAL WORKS CITED

Allen, Peter (1978) *The Cambridge Apostles: The Early Years*, Cambridge University Press, London

Armstrong, Isobel (1989) 'Tennyson's "The Lady of Shallot": Victorian Mythography and the Politics of Narcissism'. In B. Bullen (ed.), *The Sun is God: Painting, Literature and Mythology in the Nineteenth Century*, Clarendon Press, Oxford, pp. 49–107

Bloom, Harold (1979) 'Browning: Good Moments and Ruined Quests'. In Harold Bloom and Adrienne Munich (eds), *Robert Browning: A Collection of Critical Essays*, Prentice Hall, New Jersey, pp. 123–47

Bradlaugh, Charles (1877) *A Plea for Atheism*, Free Thought Publishing Co., London

Buchanan, Robert (1987) 'The Fleshly School of Poetry'. In Joseph Bristow (ed.), *The Victorian Poet: Poetics and Persona*, Croom Helm, London [essay first published 1871]

Fox, William Johnson (1832) 'The Poor and their Poetry', *The Monthly Repository*, 6, 189–201

Greenwell, Dora (1866) *Essays*, Alexander Strahan, London and New York

Hallam, Arthur (1972) 'On Some of the Characteristics of Modern Poetry'. In Isobel Armstrong (ed.), *Victorian Scrutinies: Reviews of Poetry 1830–70*, The Athlone Press, London, pp. 84–101 [essay first published in 1831]

Horne, R. H. (1835) 'A Political Oratorio', *The Monthly Repository*, 9, 37–44

Mill, John Stuart (1950) 'Thoughts on Poetry and its Varieties'. In Edmund D. Jones (ed.), *English Critical Essays*, Oxford University Press, London, pp. 341–67 [the essay, a revised version of two 1833 essays, was first published in 1859]

Mineka, F. E. (1944) *The Dissidence of Dissent: The Monthly Repository, 1806–38*, University of North Carolina Press, Chapel Hill

Pater, Walter (1873) 'Winckelmann'. In Walter Pater, *The Renaissance*, Macmillan & Co., London, pp. 146–206 [essay first published 1857]

——(1889) 'Style'. In Walter Pater, *Appreciations*, Macmillan & Co., London [essay first published 1888]

Thomson, James (1881) 'A Lady of Sorrow'. In James Thomson, *Essays and Phantasies*, Reeves and Turner, London, pp. 4–50 [first published 1862]

20

THE FRENCH SYMBOLISTS

CHARLES CHADWICK

Symbolism, as a literary movement, originated in nineteenth-century France among a generation of poets who were more consciously concerned than their predecessors had been with expressing and conveying an emotional state rather than with describing and defining it. The only way of so doing, through the medium of language, is by finding a symbol, or what T. S. Eliot was to call, in his 1920 essay on *Hamlet*, an 'objective correlative . . . a set of objects, a situation, a chain of events which shall be the formula of that particular emotion' (ed. 1964, p. 61). Stéphane Mallarmé had said much the same thing thirty years before Eliot in 1891 when he had defined Symbolism, of which he was one of the chief practitioners, as the art of 'evoking an object so as to reveal a mood or, conversely, the art of choosing an object and extracting from it an "état d'âme" ' (ed. 1956, p. 869).

This creation of an emotion in the reader through the medium of its symbolic representation is, however, only one aspect of nineteenth-century French Symbolism, what may conveniently be called the personal aspect that remains on the human plane. There is a second aspect, sometimes called 'transcendental Symbolism', in which images are used as symbols not of the emotions that lie within us, but of an ideal world to which we aspire and which is attainable through the medium of poetry. 'It is through and by means of poetry', wrote Baudelaire in his 'Notes nouvelles sur Edgar Poe' in 1857, 'that the soul perceives the splendours lying beyond the grave' (ed. 1975, vol. 2, p. 334), and it was he and his successors who elevated the poet to the rank of priest or prophet or what Rimbaud, in his celebrated 'Lettre du voyant' in May 1871, called 'the poet seer', endowed with the power to see behind and beyond the objects of the real world to the essences concealed in the ideal world (ed. 1972, p. 251). The purpose of poetry became to create this world outside reality by a transformation of reality as we know it. Mallarmé defined this goal in a well-known passage in a preface he wrote in 1886 for the *Traité du Verbe* of his fellow poet René Ghil in which he claimed that he created in his poetry not any real flower but 'l'absente de tous bouquets' – the essential flower that is not to be found among any flowers of the world below.

But although the aim of the transcendental symbolist is to go beyond reality, he must obviously, like the human symbolist, use reality as his starting point and, again like the human symbolist, shift the focus from the superficial image to what lies behind it. Mallarmé's own definition of this process, the concluding words of which have already been quoted, runs as follows: 'je dis: une fleur! et, hors de l'oubli où ma voix relègue aucun contour, en tant que quelque chose d'autre que les calices sus, musicalement se lève, idée même et suave, l'absente de tous bouquets' (ed. 1956, p. 857). Mallarmé thus starts from a real flower but its actual tangible shape is consigned to oblivion and something other than a 'known calyx' rises from this oblivion, the perfect Idea (in the Platonic sense) of a flower, the 'absente de tous bouquets'.

It is significant that in the passage quoted Mallarmé uses the adverb 'musicalement', because one of the tenets of Symbolism, of both the human and the transcendental kind, which further helps to define its meaning, was the equation between poetry and music in preference to the equation between poetry and painting or poetry and sculpture that had been current in the middle of the nineteenth century in France. Music possesses just that quality of suggestiveness that the symbolists were looking for, and lacks just that element of precision which words necessarily possess and which the symbolists wished to avoid. 'De la musique avant toute chose' is the celebrated opening of the 'Art Poétique' written in 1874 by Mallarmé's contemporary Verlaine, who ended his poem with a peremptory dismissal of everything that does not possess this vague, suggestive, musical quality, as mere 'literature' (ed. 1959, p. 207). Another contemporary, Rimbaud, in his 'Lettre du voyant' three years before, had dismissed in equally peremptory fashion the whole of French poetry as nothing more than 'rhymed prose' (ed. 1972, p. 250).

It was because of this desire to attain the fluidity of music that symbolist poetry so often refused to conform to accepted conventions as regards versification. The kind and the degree of freedom practised by the symbolist poets vary, of course, as we shall see, with the individual. The earliest of them, Baudelaire, was no great innovator in this respect and Verlaine did little more than weaken rigid patterns of rhyme and rhythm. Rimbaud, on the other hand, soon went far beyond the latter's modest attempts to liberate French verse and adopted the form of the prose poem. Mallarmé too devised a startlingly original form for the work he wrote in the last months of his life in 1897, *Un Coup de Dés* (ed. 1956, pp. 457–77).

Symbolism can therefore be defined as an attempt to penetrate beyond the surface of reality in an inward direction so as to create in the reader the emotion experienced by the poet, or in an outward direction so as to convey some sense of the nature of the ideal world. In order thus to get behind reality there is often a kind of blurring of the foreground imagery so that the reader can focus more on the thing symbolized than on the symbol. Great emphasis is also laid on the musical quality of poetry and, because of the wish to attain a greater fluidity, conventional patterns of rhyme and rhythm are modified or wholly discarded.

But although all four of the major poets who have been mentioned, Baudelaire, Verlaine, Rimbaud and Mallarmé, can be described as symbolist in these general terms, each of them also makes his own individual and distinctive contribution to Symbolism.

In the case of Baudelaire the double symbolist concept that reality is no more than a façade concealing either a world of emotions within the poet or an ideal world towards which he aspires is associated with the doctrine outlined in his celebrated sonnet 'Correspondances'. Sensations, for Baudelaire, do not remain merely at the level of the senses; they can convey thoughts or feelings of, for example, corruption, wealth or triumph; and objects are not merely objects, but are symbols of ideal forms concealed behind them.

There are a number of poems in Baudelaire's one volume of poetry, *Les Fleurs du Mal*, first published in 1857 and followed four years later by a second, considerably enlarged edition, which illustrate the first of these two related concepts. 'Harmonie du Soir', for example, might appear at first reading to be simply a description of a landscape since it consists almost entirely of a series of images – the fading perfume of flowers, the dying note of a violin, the last rays of the setting sun. The final line, however, 'Ton souvenir en moi luit comme un ostensoir', standing detached from the rest of the poem, indicates that the repeated images, all of which possess as a common factor the notion of something beautiful that has passed away, are in fact objective correlatives whose purpose is to recreate in the reader the emotion experienced by the poet at the memory of a past love affair.

Precisely the same process is followed, though with the aim of recreating a very different emotion, in the first of four poems entitled 'Spleen', where all the images again have a common factor, this time of coldness and death – the rain pouring down on the cemetery; the town shrouded in mist; the starving cat; the tolling bell; the smoking fire; the wheezing clock; the dirty pack of playing cards where, significantly, the knave of hearts and the queen of spades talk of their long dead love. Again it is the final line – 'causent sinistrement de leurs amours défunts' – which provides the hint that the purpose of the preceding images is to make the reader feel the emotion experienced by the poet dragging out a relationship with his mistress long after it has ceased to have any warmth and affection.

Human Symbolism of this sort plays a considerable part in Baudelaire's poetry, but perhaps an even more important part is played by transcendental

Symbolism. To some extent the two overlap in that 'Harmonie du Soir', for example, may be said to evoke not only a feeling of total happiness, but also a picture of paradise – there are several religious terms in the poem which subtly convey the impression that Baudelaire is recounting an almost mystical experience. Similarly, 'Spleen' may be regarded as depicting a scene from Hell as well as conveying a mood of black despair. Other poems, however, lay much greater stress on the endeavour to penetrate beyond reality to another world. In 'La Chevelure', for example, it is not his negro mistress's hair that really fascinates Baudelaire, nor even the fact that its jet-black colour and wavy texture remind him of a voyage he had once made through the Indian Ocean to Mauritius. What he is really looking for is a non-existent paradise and it is this for which he finds a symbol in a past memory concealed within a present reality. Once more there is a common factor to the various images in the poem and what they transmit to the reader is a notion of eternity and infinity, conveyed by such expressions as 'tout un monde absent, lointain, presque défunt', 'un ciel pur où frémit l'éternelle chaleur', 'infinis bercements', 'l'azur du ciel immense et rond' and 'l'oasis où je rêve'.

Both human Symbolism and transcendental Symbolism in Baudelaire have been called 'correspondances verticales' involving movement, as has been said earlier, from the surface of reality either inwardly to the poet's emotions or outwardly to the ideal world, from sights and sounds and smells to the emotions or notions they inspire. But there also exist in Baudelaire's poetry what have been called 'correspondances horizontales' or movements on the same plane from one physical sensation to another. In the lines from the sonnet 'Correspondances' that have been referred to, Baudelaire not only contends that perfumes can be 'corrompus, riches et triomphants', he also claims that they can have the same quality as the soft feel of children's flesh, or as the gentle sound of oboes, or as the green colour of fields. This process of sense transference, or synaesthesia, is a frequent feature of *Les Fleurs du Mal*. Thus, in 'Harmonie du Soir', the feelings of past happiness and paradise lost are conveyed through three images appealing to the three different senses of smell, hearing and sight. Similarly, in 'Spleen' the visual images of the rain, the mist, and the starving cat are linked to the auditory images of the tolling bell and the wheezing clock as well as to the olfactory image of the pack of playing cards 'plein des sales parfums'.

It was the Baudelairian characteristic of insistently repeating the same thing in different guises, not infrequently with an actual system of refrains, as in 'Harmonie du Soir', that led certain contemporary critics to accuse him of never managing to say what he wanted to say, and it is a measure of the originality of *Les Fleurs du Mal* that such critics should have so signally failed to understand and appreciate the novelty of the symbolist approach to poetry.

Verlaine, born in 1844, a generation after Baudelaire, and just beginning his career as a poet when the latter was at the height of his fame, could not help but be influenced by *Les Fleurs du Mal*. Like 'Harmonie du Soir' and 'Spleen', many of Verlaine's poems are apparently descriptive, save for some slight indication that their true purpose is rather different. 'La lune blanche', for example, seems at first sight to paint a picture of moonlight and birdsong in a wood where the branches of a weeping willow are reflected in the still waters of a pond. But the detached lines at the end of each verse – 'O bien-aimée', 'Rêvons, c'est l'heure' and 'C'est l'heure exquise' – indicate that there are two people involved and that it is a tender love poem with the emotion transmitted via the medium of the symbolic lanscape.

Verlaine thus practises the same kind of human Symbolism as Baudelaire. But he differs from the older poet in that the transcendental aspect of Symbolism is largely absent from his work. He lacks Baudelaire's sustained imaginative power and his ability to create a compelling picture of the heaven, or hell, awaiting him. He prefers to indulge his particular and peculiar genius for conveying his feelings in a few swift strokes sketching out the objects or events which symbolize those feelings.

A second difference between Baudelaire and Verlaine is that although the latter adopts, or rather adapts, the former's technique of repetition, of circling round the feeling he is trying to put across, his accumulation of images is much less developed and much less ordered and he is no great user of 'correspondances horizontales' or of refrains. Moreover, Baudelaire's preference for the majestic, twelve-syllable alexandrine is replaced by a preference for much shorter lines, often of an uneven length of five or seven syllables and not infrequently so closely linked grammatically that they cannot be separated rhythmically, thus giving Verlaine's poetry a strangely 'uncomposed' quality, an extraordinarily casual and intimate tone. But Verlaine never went beyond these modest innovations to the use of, for example, lines of an irregular length in an irregular pattern. And although he dismissed rhyme, in his 'Art Poétique', as a cheap trinket – 'un bijou d'un sou' – he never went so far as to abandon it completely. He was still enough of a traditionalist to feel that although verse is not, of course, always poetry, poetry is, nevertheless, always verse, and it was left to his revolutionary friend Rimbaud to demonstrate that this is not in fact the case.

As early as May 1871, less than six months after he had published his first poem, the sixteen-year-old Rimbaud, in his 'Lettre du voyant', condemned the whole of French poetry as mere 'prose rimée'. What he wanted was a new form of poetry that would give freer rein to the poet's genius. 'JE est un autre', he wrote in an oft-quoted if enigmatic phrase that he did, however, clarify by adding that the poet's task is to give the initial impulse but then to stand aside, simply watching and listening to the unfolding of his thought (ed. 1972, p. 250). Pushed to its extreme, this principle of allowing the poem to develop on its own without the conscious intervention of the poet leads to Surrealism, and Rimbaud is indeed regarded as one of the fountainheads of this movement which developed in the early years of the twentieth century. But in the 'Lettre du voyant' he is not so much elaborating a fully worked out theory as expressing a vague feeling of impatience and discontent with the conventional discipline of verse. The ground was thus prepared for the influence of Verlaine to exercise the maximum effect when the latter invited Rimbaud to join him in Paris in September 1871. From that date on Rimbaud introduced revolutionary techniques at an astonishing rate, soon out-distancing the more timid older poet. He not only adopts Verlaine's favourite device of using the line with an uneven number of syllables, he goes further and mixes lines of different lengths in an irregular pattern, as in 'Bonne pensée du matin'. Rhyme too is treated in cavalier fashion, as in 'Larme', where, since he cannot hit on a proper rhyme for 'auberge' he makes do with 'perche' and decides that 'coquillages' is an adequate echo of 'vierges' and that 'noisetiers' will suffice as a very approximate rhyme for 'villageoises'. In one poem, 'Bannières de mai', he abandons even the last vestiges of rhyme and writes blank verse, which had never been a feature of French poetry because the unstressed nature of the language means that there are no strong rhythmic patterns to be exploited as in English.

It was no doubt for this reason that Rimbaud moved over to prose in his *Illuminations* which he began to write late in 1872 and in most of which all trace of rhyme and any uniform rhythm has disappeared. Rimbaud achieves his poetic effects instead by creating changing rhythmic patterns that ebb and flow with the movement of the passage and by piling brilliant and unexpected images one on top of the other, as in the following evocation of a moment of ecstatic happiness which, with its closely related rhythmic groups, is not yet too far removed from blank verse: 'J'ai tendu des cordes de clocher; des guirlandes de fenêtre à fenêtre; des chaînes d'or à étoile; et je danse' ('Phrases'). Though typically Rimbauldian in its directness and brevity, this 'poème en prose' with its accumulation of unexplained images to translate an emotion is clearly related to Baudelaire's more elaborate 'Harmonie de Soir' and to Verlaine's more conventional 'La lune blanche'.

It was not only in the domain of human Symbolism, in the realm of the emotions, that Rimbaud adopted and extended the techniques used by the two older poets. As regards transcendental Symbolism, too, where he plays a much more important role than Verlaine, who entirely lacks his intellectual strength, Rimbaud conveys to the reader a vivid impression of the nature of his ideal world without ever analysing it. This is the case even with one of his relatively early and relatively conventional poems, which is no doubt the best-known of all his works, 'Le Bateau Ivre'. This could be read simply as an account of its travels by a personified boat drifting wildly out of control, but the real meaning of the poem, like that of Baudelaire's 'La Chevelure', lies in the extraordinary accumulation of images with a common factor that insistently build up, not a description, but an impression of the paradise the poet is seeking.

Rimbaud's paradise, however, is not the quiet and peaceful refuge that Baudelaire longs for. On the contrary, it is a world of violence and tumult and above all of total freedom. The function of the image of the boat plunging rudderless through countless seas, dancing like a cork on the waves, encountering giant serpents and sea monsters, icebergs and waterspouts, is to make the reader feel the intense excitement and almost delirious happiness that Rimbaud had in fact already experienced on the two or three occasions he had run away from home some months before. Although at that date Rimbaud, unlike Baudelaire, had never even seen the sea, his world of imagination was as vivid as Baudelaire's world of memory. But this capacity to re-mould reality did not last. In the summer of 1873 Rimbaud wrote *Une Saison en Enfer*, looking back with bitterness on the previous months which he had at first conceived as a season in heaven with himself playing the role of the creator. What he had previously called 'the sacred disorder of my mind' he now describes as a delirium – 'Délires' is indeed the title of one of the central chapters of *Une Saison en Enfer*. Similarly one of the subtitles of the same chapter, 'Alchimie du Verbe', implies that his one-time belief that the power of the word could change base metal into gold was as foolish as the dream of the medieval alchemists. But if Rimbaud lacked the patience and firmness of purpose steadfastly to pursue his goal, the last of the symbolist poets, Stéphane Mallarmé, possessed those qualities to a remarkable degree and persisted throughout his life in his attempts to attain his world.

Mallarmé's theory of transcendental Symbolism sprang originally from the same sense of dissatisfaction with reality as Baudelaire and Rimbaud experienced, but he soon found that, unlike them, he could not simply take refuge in some exotic memory or vision of an ideal world. If there was an alternative to reality then it must, in Mallarmé's view, be capable of rational definition. But when he turned the cold light of reason upon the question of the existence of an ideal world he at first came to the conclusion that beyond the real world there lies nothing but an empty void, and several of his letters at this time contain allusions to 'le Néant' and 'le Rien qui est la vérité'. But he soon passed beyond this first conclusion to a second conclusion – that the ideal world lies hidden in the empty void, that 'l'infini' is contained within 'le néant'.

This is the theme of what is probably the key poem in the whole of Mallarmé's work, a sonnet he wrote in 1868 about an empty room in which there are only two objects, an onyx statuette serving as a candle holder in which someone's dreams have been burned, and a mirror near to the window facing north in which, in the final line of the sonnet, rise up the reflections of the seven stars of the constellation of the Great Bear (ed. 1956, pp. 68–9). Like the poems of Baudelaire, Verlaine and Rimbaud, this could be taken as a purely descriptive poem, but bearing in mind that its original title was 'Sonnet allégorique de lui-même' and taking account also of Mallarmé's ideas, there can be no doubt that the images are symbolic of the process of attaining the ideal world. Apart from the destructive candle-flame the only object in the room is the mirror, which has no existence in itself but merely serves to reflect and underline the total emptiness. Yet, having stressed the notion of 'le néant' throughout the first thirteen lines of the sonnet, in the very last line there is a sudden and magical change as, in the empty surface of the mirror facing north through the open window, rises the symbol of 'l'infini', the huge constellation which dominates the sky beyond.

But in this celebrated sonnet Mallarmé is not only reiterating, in poetic and symbolic form, his conviction that the ideal world can be conjured up out of the void, he is also giving some indication of the lines along which he was working in order to create his absent world. For example, the constellation of the Great Bear is never named, nor is even the word 'star' ever used, so that in a sense it is wrong to say that at the end of the poem the constellation of the Great Bear appears in the mirror; what actually appear are seven sparkling points of light created by Mallarmé, seven stars absent, one might say, from any known sky. Furthermore, not only does Mallarmé offer the visual image of seven mysterious points of light appearing in an empty room, but he conveys a similar impression by auditive means in that the rhyme scheme, which is an astonishing *tour de force*, is based exclusively on the two rhymes 'yx' and 'or', the one being the phonetic transcription in French of the letter 'x', the universally accepted symbol for the unknown, the non-existent, and the other having as its primary meaning 'gold', the generally accepted symbol for the ideal world, as in 'Eldorado' and 'the golden age'.

To create something from nothing in this extraordinarily complex way, to use all the resources of language, not to describe a reality which already exists outside the poem, but to create a new, hitherto non-existent reality, is a daunting task and one which Mallarmé never carried through to a successful conclusion. The few poems he wrote between 1868 and his death in 1898, totalling only about thirty, most of them sonnets, are incidental poems or what he himself modestly called 'preliminary studies'. Several of these poems, like the 'sonnet en yx' (as it is sometimes called), deal with his attempts to create his new reality, but others deal with one particular variation on the theme of 'l'infini du néant' – that of eternal life arising out of death. Most of the latter are elegies to well-known literary figures of the time – Poe, Gautier, Baudelaire and Verlaine – and they follow the usual elegiac pattern of proclaiming that although the poet is dead he continues to live on in his work.

There was, however, a period, between 1885 and 1890, when he temporarily turned to less intellectual pleasures, while still continuing nevertheless to write poetry, and poetry of the same kind in that he still aimed at suggesting rather than describing. Just as the first line of the 'Sonnet allégorique de lui-même' ends with the sound 'yx' and the last line with sound 'or', so one of his love sonnets (ed. 1956, p. 53) begins with the words 'la chevelure' and ends with the word 'torche', and in between these two poles Mallarmé twists and turns his syntax so as to cram into the fourteen lines of the poem an astonishing number of words evocative of light and warmth – 'flamme', 'occident', 'diadème', 'couronne', 'foyer', 'or', 'ignition', 'feu', 'joyau', 'astres', 'fulgrante', 'rubis' and 'écorche'. But what he thus manages to convey, by a process of repetition far more intensive than anything Baudelaire and Verlaine had ever used, is an inner feeling rather than an ideal form, which means that in the late 1880s he changed from being a transcendental symbolist into being a human symbolist. His purpose is to re-create in the reader, through a visual impression of the flame-like quality of his mistress's flowing red hair, the warm sense of well-being and the radiant feeling of happiness he experiences in the presence of this 'joyeuse et tutélaire torche'.

In the last few years of his life Mallarmé returned to his preoccupation with the ideal world while continuing to experiment with the form of his poetry. The tortured syntax and lack of punctuation which make his sonnets so difficult at first to understand is extended still further in an extraordinarily revolutionary work written in 1897, the year before his death. Here the main clause, 'Un coup de dés jamais n'abolira le hasard', is printed in bold capitals with the words irregularly spaced over some twenty pages which are treated as double pages so that the sentence flows across from the left-hand pages to the right-hand pages, as do a number of subordinate clauses, some in smaller capitals, some in italics and some in ordinary lettering, which are interspersed among the words of the main clause (ed. 1956, pp. 457–77). In devising this complex and intricate system Mallarmé was clearly breaking away from the restraints of conventional forms of expression even more perhaps than Rimbaud, but in a conscious and controlled fashion that was the very opposite of the method adopted by his fellow symbolist.

Although Symbolism, as it has been defined in this essay, is limited to four major French poets of the last half of the nineteenth century who, despite the differences between them, shared many of the same purposes and the same practices, certain aspects of Symbolism were taken up by other writers both inside and outside France. The technical innovations of the symbolists, for example, held a particular fascination for Gustave Kahn, the great advocate of free verse in the closing years of the nineteenth century in France, and for René Ghil, the founder of the 'école instrumentiste', who pushed to extremes the notion of musicality and the importance of the sheer sound of words. The greatest name in this respect, however, is that of Paul Valéry who, as regards the form of his poems, although not their content, is very much the heir of Baudelaire and Mallarmé. It was he who defined poetry as 'cette hésitation prolongée entre le son et le sens' (ed. 1965, vol. 2, p. 637) and the poems of *Charmes*, first published in 1922, make an audacious use of assonance, alliteration, internal rhymes and other devices which are as important as the actual meaning. Other writers were more attracted by the anti-reality side of Symbolism, either looking sardonically at human existence, like Jules Laforgue, or turning away from it in a particular direction, like Isidore Ducasse, better known under his pseudonym of Lautréamont, who, in his *Chants de Maldoror* (1868), plunged into a disturbing nightmare world.

The largest and most important category of writers, however, turned away from reality with an optimistic attitude. The theatre, in particular, seemed to lend itself to this idealist side of Symbolism. In 1865, at an early stage in his career, Mallarmé had attempted two unusual verse dramas, *L'Après-midi d'un Faune* and *Hérodiade*, both of which are entirely divorced from reality and create a strange atmosphere of mystery and hallucination. At the same time Wagner's recreation in his operas of the mysterious world of medieval legend exerted enormous influence in France in the last quarter of the nineteenth century, particularly with the founding, in 1885, of the *Revue Wagnérienne*, and did much to encourage dramatists to abandon realism in the theatre. Three of the most notable of them were Villiers de l'Isle Adam, with his plays *Elën*, *Morgane* and *Axel*, published in 1865, 1866 and 1890 respectively, whose titles alone suffice to indicate their strong Wagnerian influence; Maurice Maeterlinck, with such plays as *La Princesse Maleine* (1889), *Les Aveugles* (1890) and *Pelléas et Mélisande* (1892) in which mysterious hidden forces are at work; and Paul Claudel, whose epic dramas such as *Partage de Midi* and *Le Soulier de Satin*, written in the early years of the twentieth century although not actually staged until much later, are concerned with the great Christian issues of sin and redemption. The idealist side of Symbolism can be discerned in the novel as well as the theatre, in Villiers de l'Isle Adam's *L'Eve future* (1886), for example, looking forward, as the title implies, to a new paradise, or J. K. Huysmans's novel *A Rebours*, published in 1884, whose hero lives in an exotic, artificial world of jewels and perfumes not unrelated to the one of which Baudelaire had dreamed. The greatest novelist in whom the influence of Symbolism can no doubt be detected (although the concept of the symbolist novel is not one which has ever made any great headway among literary historians) is, however, Marcel Proust who, from 1913 to 1922, wrote his novel *A la recherche du temps perdu*. Just as Jeanne Duval's hair awakens in

Baudelaire memories of his trip to the tropics, and just as this fusion of past memory with present reality creates for him 'l'oasis où je rêve', so Proust tastes the little cake called a 'madeleine' he had tasted as a child and all the memories of his early days in Illiers, the village near Chartres which he calls Combray in the novel, come flooding back to him, purified and crystallized by the passage of time; or he steps on an uneven paving stone, similar to the one he has stepped on in Venice many years before and those forgotten and even, at the time, unnoticed days, suddenly come to life for him. 'Je dis: une fleur!' Mallarmé had said, 'et hors de l'oubli . . . se lève l'absente de tous bouquets'; similarly, from behind the vast panorama of Parisian society that Proust depicts in *A la recherche du temps perdu*, emerges a new and fascinating world situated, as the final words of the novel put it, not in space but in time.

While Symbolism was thus having its effect upon writers in France it was also making an impact in other countries. Among English writers, or to be more accurate, writers in English, the idealist side of Symbolism made a particular appeal to W. B. Yeats who, from his early twenties, was interested in the occult and in the world of Irish legend. Although his knowledge of French was slight, he acknowledged his debt to Villiers de l'Isle Adam's *Axel* and must have known of the other French symbolists through his friend Arthur Symons whose book *The Symbolist Movement in Literature* (1899) names Yeats as their principal heir. Yeats's imagery is, of course, very much his own, but 'Sailing to Byzantium', for example, can nevertheless be said to belong to the same kind of poetry as Baudelaire's 'Le Voyage', Rimbaud's 'Le Bateau Ivre' and Mallarmé's 'Un Coup de Dés' in that all these works, through an accumulation of powerful images, create an impression of the spiritual goal each poet is seeking. T. S. Eliot, on the other hand, might be described as a transcendental symbolist of a pessimistic bent, seeing life as a waste land, a 'correspondance de l'enfer' rather than a 'correspondance du ciel', a kindred spirit to Baudelaire once the latter had sunk from 'l'idéal' to 'le spleen'. He might also be described as a human Symbolist in his use of imagery not simply for the sake of making his descriptions more powerful, but so as to create a mood, again in the manner of Baudelaire.

German literature was also influenced by French Symbolism, especially as regards the work of Rainer Maria Rilke, who acknowledged the debt he owed to Paul Valéry, and Stefan George, who was deeply impressed by Mallarmé whom he met during the time he spent in Paris during the last decade of the nineteenth century. In Russia, too, a number of writers in the 1890s and in the early years of the twentieth century enthusiastically adopted the ideas of the French symbolists. Some leaned towards human Symbolism, such as Bryusov who wrote in 1894, in his introduction to *Russian Symbolists*, that 'the Symbolist tries to arouse in the reader by the melody of his verse a particular mood' (in West, 1970, p. 108), while others were transcendental symbolists, such as Volynsky who wrote in 1900, in an essay on 'Decadence and Symbolism' in *The Battle for Idealism*, that 'Symbolism is the fusion of the phenomenal and divine worlds in artistic representation' (in West, 1970, p. 108). The repercussions of French Symbolism were thus extensive. It may well be that they have not yet ceased to reverberate and that the strangely real yet unreal world of so many works of literature written at the present time, the way in which they try to create an emotional state rather than to put across an intellectual message, and the unconventional forms which they so often take will be seen, in future years, to be indebted in no small measure to the symbolist poetry of late nineteenth-century France.

FURTHER READING

Balakian, Anna (1967) *The Symbolist Movement*, Random House, New York

Bowra, C. M. (1943) *The Heritage of Symbolism*, Macmillan, London

Chadwick, Charles (1971) *Symbolism*, Methuen, London

Donchin, G. (1958) *The Influence of French Symbolism on Russian Poetry*, Mouton, The Hague

Houston, John Porter (1980) *French Symbolism and the Modernist Movement*, Louisana State University Press, Baton Rouge

Peyre, Henri (1974) *Qu'est-ce que le Symbolisme?*, Presses Universitaires de France, Paris

——(1976) *La Littérature Symboliste*, Presses Universitaires de France, Paris

Pinto, Vivian de Sola (1967) *Crisis in English Poetry 1880–1940*, Hutchinson University Library, London

Symons, Arthur (1899) *The Symbolist Movement in Literature*, Heinemann, London

Taupin, René (1985) *The Influence of French Symbolism on Modern American Poetry*, translated and introduced by William Pratt, AMS Press, New York [first published 1929]

West, J. G. (1970) *Russian Symbolism*, Methuen, London

Wilson, Edmund (1931) *Axel's Castle: A Study in the Imaginative Literature of 1870 to 1930*, Charles Scribner's Sons, New York

ADDITIONAL WORKS CITED

Baudelaire, Charles (1975) *Oeuvres complètes*, edited by Claude Pichois, Bibliothèque de la Pléiade, Gallimard, Paris

Claudel, Paul (1956) *Théâtre*, edited by Jacques Madaule, Bibliothèque de la Pléiade, Gallimard, Paris

Eliot, T. S. (1964) *Elizabethan Essays*, Haskell House, New York

Huysmans, J. K. (1977) *A Rebours*, Gallimard, Paris [first published 1884]

Lautréamont (1970) *Oeuvres complètes*, edited by P. O. Walzer, Bibliothèque de la Pléiade, Gallimard, Paris

Maeterlinck, Maurice (1903) *Théâtre*, Lacomblez & Lamm, Brussels and Paris

Mallarmé, Stéphane (1956) *Oeuvres complètes*, edited by Henri Mondor and J. G. Aubry, Bibliothèque de la Pléiade, Gallimard, Paris

Proust, Marcel (1956) *A la recherche du temps perdu*, edited by Pierre Clarac and André Ferré, Bibliothèque de la Pléiade, Gallimard, Paris

Rimbaud, Arthur (1972) *Oeuvres complètes*, edited by Antoine Adam, Bibliothèque de la Pléiade, Gallimard, Paris

Valéry, Paul (1965) *Oeuvres*, vols 1 and 2, edited by Jean Hytier, Bibliothèque de la Pléiade, Gallimard, Paris

Verlaine, Paul (1959) *Oeuvres poétiques complètes*, edited by Yves Gérard Le Dantec, Bibliothèque de la Pléiade, Gallimard, Paris

Villiers de l'Isle Adam, Auguste (1986) *Oeuvres complètes*, edited by Alan Raitt and P. G. Castex, Bibliothèque de la Pléiade, Gallimard, Paris

Yeats, W. B. (1961) *Collected Poems*, Macmillan, London

21

MODERN POETRY

JOHN LUCAS

Attempts to define modernism are necessarily contentious. Should we try to bracket it within certain dates, pin it down to place, identify it by formal and stylistic concerns, or link it to particular ideological positions? Is it an extension of earlier movements, such as Romanticism, or a repudiation of them? Merely to put the questions is to indicate that a short essay cannot hope to deal satisfactorily with the many issues they raise. Such questions do, however, make clear that the blanket term 'modern poetry' inevitably covers a number of widely divergent poets and poetic enterprises. Like the modernism of which it is a part, it is far less homogeneous than has sometimes been assumed. And as it is almost certainly better to speak of 'modernisms' rather than the abstractive 'modernism', so the all-inclusive phrase 'modern poetry' is probably less satisfactory than the more cumbersome but also more enabling term 'modern poetries'.

There is, though, one generalization which does less harm than most. It is that modernism was born at the stroke of a pen with mass commodity culture. The usefulness of this statement, when applied to poetry, is that it signals the determination of a number of writers to try to resist the incorporation of their poetry into a culture which would treat it as merely consumable matter. This is not to say that they succeeded. There is virtually nothing that cannot end up on the coffee-table. Nevertheless, the works I have in mind, and which may be said to constitute the canon of modern poetry, are made as unassimilable as possible. Hence, the 'difficulty' of such poetry. Hence, too, the accepted split between the popular and the good. This split was eloquently traced by Henry James, in an essay on 'The Art of Fiction' ([1884] 1957). Disputing what he saw to be a growing orthodoxy, one which took for granted that fiction 'should either be instructive or amusing', James insisted that the writer's ultimate responsibility must be to his art and not to its consumers. His impassioned, resourceful defence of the right of the novelist to consider only the needs of his work became one of the central dogmas of modern poets, especially Ezra

Pound and T. S. Eliot. Like James, the two poets were American *émigrés*. Both of them were intense admirers of James's art and theoretical writings. Neither, however, saw anything to admire in the poetry of pre-Great War England, which was the poetry they were introduced to as soon as they arrived here, Pound in 1908, Eliot six years later. This is not to be wondered at. English poetry at that time was for the most part dull, often technically incompetent, and the poets who produced it exuded a deep complacency which was bound to be anathema to Pound and Eliot.

For the two Americans, as for all writers who can be claimed as modernists, the true artist was to be a critic of consumerist society. He had to be, given that modern society was indifferent to art and therefore 'civilization' and 'culture'. These terms are in quotation marks because they are intended to direct attention towards a central tension in modern poetry (and therefore modernism as a whole). The poet as social critic develops in one of two, fundamentally opposed, directions. He may see himself (and it *is* nearly always a 'he') as an upholder of civilized values which lie 'rooted' in the past; or he may identify with emergent forces, the full realization of which lies in the future. As is well known, a number of modern poets were strongly attracted to the kind of reactionary politics whose most extreme form is Fascism. Others committed themselves to progressive politics: to socialism and Marxism. What they had in common was disaffection with the present, and it was this that did more than anything to define both the content and the formal considerations of what is usually thought of as modern poetry.

The place where disaffection most clearly showed itself, and where the divergences between writers most powerfully emerged, was the city. The city was to modernism what the Copernican revolution had been to the Renaissance: it changed everything. Space, time, language, human relationships and personal identity – they were all profoundly altered by the experience of the city. As Raymond Williams has argued in his seminal essay 'The Metropolis and the Emergence of Modernism', the metropolis was where new social and economic cultural relations, beyond both city and nation in their older senses, were beginning to be formed (Williams, 1985, p. 20). If in the remainder of this essay I continue to use the word 'city' rather than 'metropolis' it is not because I am unmindful of Williams's distinction, but simply because by and large modern poets did not themselves make use of the latter term. The result was that in calling this bewildering new reality by an old term they added to the bewilderment.

There had, it is true, been earlier attempts to cope with the accretion of phenomena and responses to it which produced the experience of the city. But in most cases, and in England certainly, this amounted to little more than writing the city off. This is essentially the tactic adopted by James Thomson ('B.V.') in his poem 'The City of Dreadful Night' (1870–4). Thomson sees the unnamed city (it is presumably based on London) as a phantasmagoric vision of hell, without purpose or meaning. In a typical stanza he notes:

> The world rolls round for ever like a mill;
> It grinds out death and life and good and ill;
> It has no purpose, heart or mind or will.
>
> (Thomson, 1899, p. 20)

This attitude was characteristic of many later nineteenth-century writers, and it led to the position adopted by Gerard Manley Hopkins. Writing to his friend Robert Bridges in 1878, Hopkins told him that 'My muse turned utterly sullen in the Sheffield smoke-ridden air' (ed. Abbott, 1970, p. 84). Hopkins did, however, write one poem about the city. 'Tom's Garland' (written 1887), which is subtitled 'upon the Unemployed', shows how difficult, not to say impossible, Hopkins found the task of confronting the city experience, although there is no reason to doubt that the poem testifies accurately enough to the only way he knew of finding terms for it:

> This by Despair, bred Hangdog dull; by Rage,
> Manwolf, worse; and their packs infest the age.
>
> (Hopkins, ed., 1967, p. 103)

Here, by means of a trope which was becoming a contemporary cliché, Hopkins turns the unemployed into animals. His loathing of city life is nourished by the thin gruel of crude social Darwinism. The struggle for survival in the city breeds degeneracy. The survival of the fittest means the triumph of the bestial.

I do not claim Hopkins as a modern poet. But the language of the closing lines of 'Tom's Garland' points us to a phenomenon which is undoubtedly a quasi-modern response of the individual in the city. It is of rejection, which then modulates into a sense of alienation, and which in its turn can modulate into paranoia. In the city the otherness of others becomes a threat. Because they are unknown they constitute a visible expression of what is always unknowable; the city's dark, secret places, its 'infestation' by crowds of men and women who do not have the interests of the city as a whole at heart. But then the city is not and cannot be whole. You cannot apply such terms as 'rooted' or 'organic' to it. It is the opposite of a genuine community. Hence the individual's feeling of alienation from the city crowds. Baudelaire was probably the first great poet to recognize and exploit this feeling. In his essay 'On Some Motifs in Baudelaire', Walter Benjamin quotes from a letter in which the poet refers to 'shocks of consciousness' which come to those 'who are at home in the giant cities and the web of the numberless interconnecting relationships'. He then comments that there are two insights to be derived from this letter:

> For one thing it tells us about the close connection in Baudelaire between the figure of shock and contact with the metropolitan masses. For another, it tells us what was really meant by the masses. They do not stand for classes or any

sort of collective; rather, they are nothing but the amorphous crow of passers-by, the people in the street.

(Benjamin, 1973, p. 167)

Benjamin notes that this is the new experience of the city, the experience which Engels recorded of London in his *Condition of the Working Class in England in 1844*: 'The greater the number of people that are packed into a tiny space, the more repulsive and offensive becomes the brutal indifference, the unfeeling concentration of each person on his private affairs' (Engels, [1845] 1969, p. 58).

Here, however, we must note that Engels reacts very much as the shocked, even outraged, bourgeois male. Behind his remarks there is a real sense of grievance that his social status was not registered by the crowd. But this can become a characteristic deployment of modern consciousness, although in such consciousness, and operating as a mode of definition, the recognition of one's anonymity is accompanied less by outrage than by self-deprecating irony. This is the tone which later French poets such as Corbière and Laforgue develop. Its fullest expression is to be found in the poetry of T. S. Eliot.

At this point it will be obvious that I am crossing national boundaries. This, too, may legitimately be claimed as distinctively modern. By the same token, of course, English poetry at the end of the nineteenth century is almost entirely backward-looking, and this is so whether we consider its forms, its language or its subject-matter. Thomson and Hopkins apart, the only attempts to write about the city come in the 1890s with such poets as Ernest Dowson, Arthur Symons and Richard Le Gallienne; and what they have to offer amounts to little more than milk-and-water impressionism. For the rest, the city might never have existed. England continues to be identified in terms of rural values and there is a general sense that a 'rooted' society is alive and well. This is endlessly reiterated by Alfred Austin, Poet Laureate from 1896 to 1913. It follows that the best English poets of the time, Thomas Hardy and Edward Thomas, searched out the inadequacies of this myth and registered their dissatisfactions with it.

This is why T. S. Eliot must come at the centre of any account of modern poetry. As an outsider, the immigrant in the city, Eliot was able to register its impact as no English poet of the time could do. And as a visitor to Europe he recognized that French poets had accustomed themselves to confront city experiences. This is hardly to be wondered at. After 1789 French poets were unlikely to be tied to a myth of rooted, rural values. Certainly Baudelaire's fascination with the city, and the blend of attraction and repulsion which characterizes the attitude he adopts in his city poems, became hugely influential for later nineteenth-century French poetry. In that he emigrated to the city, Eliot was typical of his period. But his particular American longing for a rooted

311

culture created within him tensions – between the old and the new, the rooted and the rootless – that are a decisive expression of modernist poetry.

Like James before him, Eliot came to Europe to escape from the 'unformed' society of America. In a famous letter to William Dean Howells, in which he defended his right to settle in Europe, James remarked that 'it is on manners, customs, usages, habits, forms, upon all things matured and established that a novelist lives' (ed. Lubbock, 1920, vol. 1, p. 72). James chose to see European culture, and English culture in particular, as virtually fixed in amber. His gradual disillusionment with this dream of fixedness led to the novels of the 1880s and 1890s, beginning with *The Princess Casamassima*, a prolonged lament for the loss of a favoured culture and its usurpation by 'new vulgarity', where the 'new' is typically associated with the city and its brash, anonymous energies. This sets the pattern for Pound and Eliot.

As a graduate student at Harvard, Eliot was taught by Josiah Royce, whose *The Problem of Christianity* (1913) he certainly knew. There, Royce remarks that

> The psychological unity of many selves in one community is bound up . . . with the consciousness of some lengthy social process which has occurred, or is at least supposed to have occurred. And the wealthier the memory of the community is, and the vaster the historical processes which it regards as belonging to its life, the richer – other things being equal – is its consciousness that it *is* a community, that its members are somehow made one in and through and with its own life.
>
> (in Gray, 1982, p. 97)

Royce inevitably focused his idea of community on Europe, and this idea was widely shared among those Americans who looked with dismay on what they regarded as the 'rootlessness' of their own society.

This is why the shock of European and English actualities produced so powerful a reaction in Eliot, as they did in Pound. And what more than anything shocked them was the Great War, that cataclysm for which, in James's grieving words, 'the treacherous years' had been preparing. The war enforced an awakening to disillusionment with the dream of culture.

In a sense, Eliot was already adjusted to the possibilities of disillusionment. The Laforguian ironies of 'The Love Song of J. Alfred Prufrock' (1917) allow him to touch on the painful, comically self-aware insufficiencies of the near-invisible *flâneur* who wanders the city streets and whose self-alienation, and alienation from the threatening others, is registered as a series of fibrillations of consciousness: 'I should have been a pair of ragged claws/Scuttling across the floors of silent seas' (Eliot, 1963, p. 15). Not even a whole crab, merely the claws. Even if we suppose that Prufrock's thoughts drift in this direction as he contemplates his feet moving through a city street (or imagines that the men leaning from hotel windows will see him in this way), the image, comic, self-disgusted, rueful, inevitably produces a sense of someone who doesn't fit, who wants only to hide, who cannot connect to a culture, a community. The tone of 'Prufrock' comes close to Arthur Symons's account of Laforgue's characteristic tone: 'The verse is alert, troubled, swaying, deliberately uncertain, hating rhetoric so piously that it prefers, and finds its piquancy in, the ridiculously obvious' (Symons, [1899] 1958, p. 56). Eliot had read Symons's *Symbolist Movement in Literature* from which that remark comes, and he would have known of Laforgue's habitual concern with a poetry of missed or deferred opportunities. That, though, was centred on individual consciousness. The war seemed to justify an extension of the concern to an entire culture.

In *Hugh Selwyn Mauberley* (1919–20) Ezra Pound spat out his disgust at a culture on whose behalf so many had died. They had been killed

> For an old bitch gone in the teeth
> For a botched civilization
> For two gross of broken statues,
> For a few thousand battered books.
> (Pound, 1952, p. 200)

Pound's idea of a civilization is an insistently literary one, not merely because he implies that a few thousand battered books can act as metonym for a civilization, but more importantly because for him Europe is a kind of cultural museum. Like James, Pound saw Europe from the standpoint of an outsider who was determined to find in it 'traditional sanctity and loveliness'. The words are in fact Yeats's, from 'Coole Park and Ballylee, 1931', but they can fairly be used to identify Pound's ideal of a fast-rooted culture which has been wantonly destroyed. In the last analysis this is as maunderingly sentimental as later lines in which Pound produces an image of 'civilized' values:

> To have, with decency, knocked
> That a Blunt should open
> To have gathered from the air a live tradition
> or from a fine old eye the unconquered flame
> This is not vanity.
> (Pound, 1964, p. 557)

It takes considerable innocence – to put it mildly – to see in that disreputable, womanizing, and exceedingly minor poet Wilfrid Scawen Blunt a live tradition, let alone a tradition that deserves to survive. These lines, which conclude Canto 81, are however to be expected from one for whom modernism means essentially resistance to the contemporary. It is therefore of the utmost importance that we understand how Pound's editorializing helped to shape *The Waste Land* as a distinctively modern poem.

Thanks to the Facsimile and Transcript edition of Eliot's poem, which

Valerie Eliot edited and published in 1971, we can now see that the version of *The Waste Land* published in 1922 is in many ways different from the poem Eliot intended. Or – since it is not quite clear what he *did* intend – we can say that the scraps and fragments he gave to Pound were turned by his friend, 'Il miglior fabbro', into one of the major texts of modernism. Eliot's sly disclaimer is well known:

> Various critics have done me the honour to interpret the poem in terms of criticism of the contemporary world, have considered it, indeed, as an important bit of social criticism. To me it was only the relief of a personal and wholly insignificant grouse against life; it is just a piece of rhythmical grumbling.
>
> (in Valerie Eliot, 1971, p. 1)

It was always a great deal more than that. Yet there can be no doubt that Pound's editorializing not only improved the poem, it gave it a focus which had previously been lacking. At Pound's suggestion, Eliot cut passages, altered others, and in a sense re-jigged the entire poem. The title he had proposed for his piece of rhythmical grumbling had been 'He Do the Police in Different Voices', a remark taken from Dickens's *Our Mutual Friend*, where it is spoken by an old woman about the brain-damaged youth she lovingly looks after. For Eliot to want to use the remark draws attention to his poem's ventriloquism, its kaleidoscopic arrangement of voices. But it also, more troublingly, hints at mental problems in the person who 'does' the voices. Eliot suffered a nervous breakdown and had spent some time recuperating at Margate ('On Margate sands./I can connect/Nothing with nothing'). The poem had originally opened with a long, semi-drunken monologue, in which a man talks of a succession of late-night gate-crashing parties, at clubs, houses. In its suggestion of febrile, joyless hedonism this rather remarkably anticipates the 1920s diaries of Evelyn Waugh. It also serves to locate the poem in terms of hysterical or viciously self-destructive behaviour, which may then turn it towards self-reflexivity, so that we may with reason anticipate that the real subject of the poem is the narrator with which it begins. By cancelling this passage, so that the poem as we have it now begins with the famous 'April is the cruellest month', Pound sees to it that *The Waste Land* feels to be more objectively about post-war society.

One explanation for Pound's decision may lie in his preference for image over argument. He had been at the centre of – some would say the inspiration for – the imagist movement of a decade earlier. The imagists had argued that poetry needed to be freed of all the inessential trappings with which Victorian poets had encumbered it and as a result of which contemporary poetry, absorbing this bad influence, was hopelessly defective: soft, woolly, padded. In his famous essay 'Romanticism and Classicism', T. E. Hulme, a leading theoretician of the imagist movement, announced that it was essential to prove 'that beauty may be in small, dry things'; and he pronounced the great aim for future poets as being the achievement of 'accurate, precise and definite description'. This led him to prophesy that 'a period of dry, hard, classical verse is coming' (Hulme, [1912] 1960, pp. 132–3). *The Waste Land* is not an imagist poem, but it may be said to owe a great deal to imagist ideas and tactics, the more so in view of Pound's editorial endeavours.

It is not difficult to see why Imagism should have appealed to Pound, nor why its influence rubbed off on Eliot. Imagism appears to offer a way out of a dilemma confronting the modern poet, who would wish to comment on the bewilderingly complex and confused world in which he finds himself – epitomized by the city – and yet for whom the bewilderment may well owe more to his own alienation than to the phenomena he experiences. He cannot know what it is that he sees, nor how to judge it, and if this is so he is denied his subject. Imagism, however, seems to resolve this problem. By providing, without comment, a series of conceivably discrete images, as though the poet's perceiving eye has the implacable objectivity of a camera, the poem, as an imagistic cluster, invites its readers to look at what it offers and judge for themselves.

The intention of the imagistic poem is, then, to offer as dispassionately as possible an account of the world 'out there'. In *The Waste Land* this dispassionate recording is the responsibility of Tiresias. It is he who witnesses the coupling of the typist and the clerk, he who listens in to the neurasthenic wife or mistress complaining of her isolation, he who hears the women in the pub. From this it is a short step to making Tiresias the wise truth-teller of the horrors of twentieth-century life, so that the poem he utters is granted its status because, in the words of Cleanth Brooks, 'the fact that men have lost the knowledge of good and evil, keeps them from being alive, and is the justification for viewing the modern waste land as a realm in which the inhabitants do not even exist' (1965, p. 138). Other critics might not press the claim with Brooks's bland confidence, but with some notable exceptions *The Waste Land* was commonly agreed to be a great, diagnostic poem about the post-war world. This is why Eliot's use of echo, quotation and allusion have been so often granted an unchallengeable authority. Delmore Schwartz, for example, could say that these features of the poem are an 'inevitable habit of mind, a habit which issues in judgement and the representation of different levels of experience, past and present' (1967, p. 279).

Yet the objectivity claimed for Imagism by its adherents is false. (The camera can deceive, and it makes a difference who chooses to point it, and how.) A glance at Eliot's *Poems 1920* raises a number of awkward questions about *The Waste Land*'s presumed objectivity, its imagistic power of diagnostic confrontation with European society, and therefore about Eliot's capacity for judgement. In the first place, it is evident from these poems that Eliot finds heterosexual relationships disgusting. In the second, it is obvious that he is rabidly anti-Semitic. There is no space here to enlarge on these statements, but the evidence abounds notably in such poems as 'Whispers of Immortality', 'Sweeney Among the Nightingales', and 'Burbank with a Baedeker: Bleistein with a Cigar'. One particular aspect of Eliot's anti-Semitism does, however, require comment. Here are some crucial lines from 'Gerontion', the poem with which the 1920 volume opens:

> My house is a decayed house,
> And the Jew squats on the window sill, the owner,
> Spawned in some estaminet of Antwerp,
> Blistered in Brussels, patched and peeled in London.
>
> (Eliot, 1963, p. 39)

Jewishness here is explicitly connected to the rootlessness of modern life. The imagery invites us to accept that the modern city is characterized by the virtual collapse of the house as a symbol of continuity. The agent of this collapse is the Jew. In other words, Eliot contrasts contemporary rootlessness – by implication at least – with the rootedness of a past culture whose dominant symbol was the Great, or country, House.

Eliot was by no means alone in identifying the breakdown of cultural vitality in terms of the loss of values associated with the Great House. We have seen Pound knocking 'with decency' at Blunt's door. Yeats repeatedly lamented the fate of Coole Park, the house in the west of Ireland where his patroness and friend Lady Augusta Gregory lived and worked. This symbol of the Great House and its 'rootedness' is at the heart of that tragic account of social history in which a cultural continuum is disrupted by forces at work within history, so those who mourn its passing insist. These forces break in upon the Great House and turn it to a 'shapeless mound'. Yeats, however, does not try to equate those forces with Jewishness. Instead, he reads into the history of his times an inevitability of breakdown, whose signs and shows are everywhere: in the fact of the Great War, the Russian Revolution, the Irish Civil War. Yeats sees all these manifestations, and more beside, as decisive evidence that Western civilization is about to enter on a new era:

> And what rough beast, its hour come round at last,
> Slouches towards Bethlehem to be born.
>
> (Yeats, 1950, p. 211)

Eliot's anti-Semitism may have been partly activated by Action Française, a reactionary group of French writers and intellectuals with whose work he was familiar. It may also owe something to Pound. But his insidious suggestion that the modern waste land is somehow caused by Jews is all his own. Not that it actually surfaces in *The Waste Land* itself (although Pound cut a passage of Popeian pastiche in which Eliot writes of a London society lady recalling her visit to 'Lady Kleinwurm's party' before she plunges into a bath where 'Odours, confected by the cunning French,/Disguise the good old hearty female stench'). The politics of *The Waste Land* are, however, very definitely of a piece with Action Française. Eliot, that is, is profoundly anti-democratic. He refuses to allow his city characters, especially the women in the pub and the typist and clerk, to escape from the insistent dehumanizing of Tiresias's disgust. (The latter pair were even more degraded in the draft version.) Like Eliot's Jew they are spawned and spawn with, at most, the ecstasy of animals. And this is why the pretence that the *The Waste Land* is a *bricolage* of imagistic objectivity will not do. The same man who wrote 'Gerontion' wrote *The Waste Land*, and a very little analysis of Tiresias's language is sufficient to show that not only is it remarkably lacking in the kind of scientific objectivity which Zola, for example, brought to such city novels as *Thérèse Raquin* (1868), but that it is actually deeply infected. At the very least we would have to say that such language betrays the very alienation it purports to identify in others. It says something about the politics of those critics who saw in *The Waste Land* a great diagnostic poem of our century that this should not have worried them.

But perhaps they, like Eliot, may be said to have been badly shaken by the events and aftermath of the Great War. It is difficult now to recapture just how traumatic the shock of those four years must have been for Western civilization. Yet we need to make the effort, for without it we will not understand the creation and the impact of modern poetry and above all of *The Waste Land*. (In passing I will note that it is not surprising that the poem caused far less of a stir among poets in the United States, for whom the war had by and large meant comparatively little. Hence, no doubt, Hart Crane's remark that *The Waste Land* was 'good, of course, but so damn dead'.) It was not that the war lasted longer than most people expected, though it did; it was that it changed things so radically. By 1919 what James called 'the record of the long, safe centuries' had been smashed. This is alluded to in some haunting lines of Section 5 of *The Waste Land*, 'What the Thunder said':

> What is that sound high in the air
> Murmur of maternal lamentation
> Who are those hooded hordes swarming
> Over endless plains, stumbling in cracked earth
> Ringed by the flat horizon only
> What is the city over the mountains
> Cracks and reforms and bursts in the violet air
> Falling towers
> Jerusalem Athens Alexandria
> Vienna London
> Unreal
>
> (Eliot, 1963, p. 77)

George Seferis, the great Greek poet who came to know Eliot at a rather later date, wrote that Eliot felt strongly 'how paper-thin, how groundless, how unreal and anarchic is, in fact, the order offered by the mechanical society of today' (1967, p. 154). Seferis's use of the word 'groundless' is, I suspect, meant to carry a good deal of metaphoric weight. There is no ground in which to root contemporary civilization – that is his meaning. 'Cracks and reforms and bursts': the crack of a rifle, of falling masonry, which may reform but because of reforms – or revolutions – will do so only in broken shapes as civilization bursts apart (from bursting shells, bursts of rhetoric): it is all there as the 'hooded hordes' swarm on. The hordes are the barbarians, and they had been anticipated in another great modern poem, C. P. Cafavy's 'Waiting for the Barbarians', although there they never arrive.

Were they to have done so, they would almost certainly have come from the East. The uncivilized rough beast, in so far as it promised energy and some form of vital renewal no matter how frightening, had been regularly associated with primitive, Dionysian energies and, as Nietzsche had pointed out, the god Dionysus came from the Middle East. The interest in primitivism at the end of the nineteenth century has connections with, or can be used by, those who focus their sense of the decadence of modern society on the city. The primitive promises renewal as an alternative to the depleted stock of city man. Cafavy's poem was written in 1898, and its ending is deliberately ambiguous:

> And now, what's to become of us without barbarians?
> These people were some sort of a solution.
>
> (trans. 1984, p. 15)

Twenty years later, it might be said that the barbarians had arrived, that Europe was, in fact, given over to them, whether 'they' were the armies of the Russian revolution, the German Spartacists, the Irish Nationalists, or, more generally, the forces which had unleashed and been unleashed by the Great War, and as a result of which the ancient ideal cities of Western culture had come crashing down, leaving only decayed houses and the faceless swarms of modern, de-individualized beings. Given this, it is not perhaps so surprising that Eliot should read the contemporary world as inscribing a message of despair:

> A crowd flowed over London Bridge, so many,
> I had not thought death had undone so many.
>
> (Eliot, 1963, p. 65)

This crowd of the unreal city may be the same as, or analogous to, the hooded hordes.

From the rubble of *The Waste Land*, Eliot begins to reconstruct the idea of order which he had come to Europe expecting, like his previous compatriots, to find. In this, too, he is central to modern poetry. Decayed houses are exchanged for aged houses: for Burnt Norton and East Coker. The final apotheosis of this is reached in the *Four Quartets* (1943) in *Little Gidding*, a country chapel where 'History is now and England'. The alternative to the amorphous synchronicity of the city, where narrative is denied by the arbitrary simultaneity of events, meetings and partings, is the diachronic reading of a nation's history as meaningful narrative. Needless to say, it is a narrative from which hordes are absent or are present only to be subdued to the patterns of reconciliation which this account of history always provides. In putting Commonwealth against monarchy, Eliot writes

> These men, and those who opposed them
> And those whom they opposed
> Accept the constitution of silence
> And are folded in a single party.
> (Eliot, 1963, p. 220)

The problem with this is that the 'constitution of silence' is simply imposed. This is linguistic manipulation, and Eliot's modernism insists on the propriety of one kind of language only, from which all departures are to be seen as desecrations of culture and social value. ('O O O O that Shakespeherian Rag.') The heterogeneity of city life is condemned as chaos just as the inherent value of other voices is denied. If you do the police in different voices it is only to prevent them from speaking for themselves. Yet at the same time you give the appearance of letting them condemn themselves out of their own mouths. Like much modern poetry, *The Waste Land* is therefore essentially caricatural. It is about the fear of others in a way Eliot could hardly have intended.

This fear is, I suggest, central to modern poetry, which wishes to impose control and authority on a world seen to be tumbling into chaos. But the mission to save civilization inevitably depends on an assumption that the poet knows what civilization is and that others do not. To consult those others would require that same poet to step out into the city streets without the predetermining fear or its concomitants which define modern poetry. That would in its turn lead to a welcoming of heterogeneous voices, and a readiness to incorporate them into poetry without caricatural intent. This is the way taken by Auden. But it leads beyond the confines of modernism and beyond the limits of this essay.

FURTHER READING

Benjamin, Walter (1973) *Illuminations*, Fontana, London
Brooks, Cleanth (1965) *Modern Poetry and the Tradition*, Galaxy Books, North Carolina
Eliot, Valerie (1971) *T. S. Eliot, The Waste Land: A Facsimile and Transcript*, Faber & Faber, London

Gray, Piers (1982) *T. S. Eliot's Intellectual and Poetical Development, 1909–1922*, Harvester Press, Brighton

Hulme, T. E. (1960) *Speculations*, Routledge & Kegan Paul, London [first published 1912]

Kenner, Hugh (1972) *The Pound Era*, Faber & Faber, London

Lucas, John (1986) *Modern English Poetry from Hardy to Hughes*, Batsford, London

McDiarmid, Lucy (1984) *Saving Civilisation*, Oxford University Press, London

Seferis, George (1967) *On the Greek Style*, Denise Harvey, Athens

Smith, Stan (1982) *Inviolable Voice, History and Twentieth-Century Poetry*, Macmillan, London

Stead, C. K. (1964) *The New Poetic*, Hutchinson, London

Symons, Arthur (1958) *The Symbolist Movement in Literature*, Dutton & Co, New York [first published 1899]

Williams, Raymond (1985) 'The Metropolis and the Emergence of Modernism'. In Edward Timms and David Kelly (eds), *Unreal City: Urban Experience in European Literature and Art*, Manchester University Press, Manchester

ADDITIONAL WORKS CITED

Abbott, C. C. (ed.) (1970) *The Letters of Gerard Manley Hopkins to Robert Bridges*, Oxford University Press, London

Cafavy, C. P. (1984) *Collected Poems*, translated by E. Keeley and P. Sherrard, The Hogarth Press, London

Eliot, T. S. (1963) *Collected Poems 1909–1962*, Faber & Faber, London

Engels, Friedrich (1969) *The Condition of the Working Class in England in 1844*, Panther, London [first published in German 1845]

Hopkins, Gerard Manley (1967) *The Poems of Gerard Manley Hopkins*, edited by W. H. Gardner and N. H. MacKenzie, Oxford University Press, London

James, Henry (1957) 'The Art of Fiction'. In Henry James, *The House of Fiction*, edited by Leon Edel, Rupert Hart-Davis, London [essay first published 1884]

Lubbock, Percy (ed.) (1920) *The Letters of Henry James*, Charles Scribner's Sons, New York

Pound, Ezra (1952) *Personae*, Faber & Faber, London

——(1964) *The Cantos of Ezra Pound*, Faber & Faber, London

Schwartz, Delmore (1967) 'T. S. Eliot as the International Hero'. In Irving Howe (ed.) *Literary Modernism*, Fawcett Premier Printing, New York

Thomson, James ('B.V.') (1899) *The City of Dreadful Night and Other Poems*, Dobell, London

Yeats, W. B. (1950) *Collected Poems of W. B. Yeats*, Macmillan, London

22

BRITISH POETRY SINCE 1945: POETRY AND THE HISTORICAL MOMENT

JOHN WILLIAMS

A poem floats adjacent to, parallel to, the historical moment. What happens to us as readers when we board the poem depends upon the kind of relation it displays toward our historical life.

(Seamus Heaney, *The Government of the Tongue*, 1988, p. 121)

Augustan literature may seem an unpromising point of reference from which to initiate a review of British poetry since the last war; if we look back to the immediate post-war years, however, there clearly did exist a conviction that the Augustan, 'Enlightenment' model of classicism should be seriously studied by contemporary poets. In *Before the Romantics*, an anthology published in 1946, Geoffrey Grigson celebrated 'the lean and active verse . . . of the Enlightenment, its active and strong habits of mind', and attacked the 'loose, ugly, detestable, liquefying drivel' of neo-romantic, surrealist poets: '. . . remember that the Babel tower of Fonthill Abbey crashed, and that St. Paul's is still there' ([1946] 1984, pp. ix-x). Wren's classicism survived the Blitz, the tower of Beckford's late eighteenth-century Gothic mansion at Fonthill collapsed almost as soon as it was finished.

Grigson's views were shared by others, among them William Empson and Donald Davie. Commenting on Empson's 'intellectualist' distaste for Romanticism, and Davie's dislike of Imagism and Symbolism, Geoffrey Thurley (1974) argues that such anxieties were misplaced. English poetry, he claims, remained firmly in the grip of an 'over-tidy sensibleness, a reliance upon rationality' (p. 2). 'Sensibleness' and 'rationality' suggest qualities generally associated with the literary tradition to which Grigson appealed, a tradition offering an appropriate discourse for a nation seeking consensus in the course of a political identity crisis, while at the same time facing economic chaos. In such conditions an emphasis on 'control' was bound to seem laudable, as was 'a language so perspicuous and so definite that it can be followed by everyone'. These qualities, Grigson claimed, were a product of 'the Enlightenment's own belief in reason and uniform nature' (p. x).

Enlightenment culture has arguably played a continuing role in shaping the evolution of poetry since the war; to appreciate why, we should first consider some of the ways in which the Augustan period marked the beginnings of modern British society. Augustan taste in literature and the arts signified the appropriation of a cultural model that could respond satisfactorily to economic and political changes which were potentially productive of greater material well-being, but at the same time tended to be worryingly divisive. A new spirit of rational, empirical enquiry helped to create an intellectual and scientific climate that subsequently fostered the industrial revolution and the political reforms of the nineteenth century. It was also a time when the accumulation of capital by significant sections of the middle classes threatened to destabilize existing social structures. Augustan writers addressed themselves in many respects to these new arbiters of taste and morality, mediating between the old and the new worlds; they were a product of the new order, and therefore had a vested interest in its success; but, in keeping with a literary tradition rooted in Roman, classical antiquity, they also cultivated the virtues of common sense and plain speaking in the face of a materialist ethos that threatened complacency and corruption.

One important function of Augustan poetry, establishing itself in the wake of the English Civil War, was the celebration of a national 'British' identity. Though the visual and literary image tended to be ideologically classicized, that identity was necessarily, determinedly English. The Jacobite rising of 1745 was followed by a brutal military campaign to subjugate the Scottish Highlands, while throughout the century the status of Ireland effectively remained that of a colonial possession. The consequence of marginalizing Scottish, Irish and Welsh poetry within emergent 'British' Augustan culture still contributes significantly to the context within which twentieth-century British poetry has evolved. In recent years the complexity of the situation has increased with the advent of racial and cultural tensions of the kind reflected in the work of poets such as James Berry, Nicki Jackowski, Grace Nicholls and Linton Kwesi Johnson.

Augustan culture was also essentially metropolitan, the consequence of which was a tendency to view with condescension (or suspicion) poetry emanating from any other source. The pastime of patronizing 'rural' poets was a familiar eighteenth-century phenomenon. Again, the emergence of 'regional' poetry in the twentieth century – Jack Clemo in Cornwall or the Liverpool poets in the 1960s, more recently the work of Tony Harrison and Douglas Dunn – has taken place within a set of assumptions about a British poetic identity initially laid down in the eighteenth century.

Augustan cultural marginalization occurred as a part of the process of promoting an expedient, rationalized creed of political control; behind it inevitably lurked the brutality of the Roman imperial model it invoked. Contemporary writers remain conscious of this inheritance precisely because Augustan cultural assumptions still tend to inform aspects of contemporary British culture and society. Given the regional, class and ethnic instabilities of Britain in the 1980s, most notably the government's failure to win support in Scotland and Wales and the continuing crisis in Northern Ireland, it is hardly surprising that Howard Brenton's play *The Romans In Britain* (1980) created the political furore it did.

In his Foreword to *The Cleaver Garden* (1986), George MacBeth locates the themes of cruelty and violence with which he deals in the context of questionable 'classical' virtues, reflected variously in warfare, education and architecture: 'Roman discipline, which has ironed Europe, echoes in the girders of St. Thomas's Hospital as menacingly as in the plastered marbles of Highgate Cemetery or along the pillared frontages of a hundred public schools':

> Thus it was always. Thus it may
> Be still. The Roman prefects, and the sway
> Of lashes make our brutal institutions pay.
> (XXI, ll. 10–12)

Augustan aesthetic vision was essentially one of class-based political and economic stability which fostered the rise of the bourgeoisie; it looked to the natural world to reflect that vision – '*Nature Methodiz'd*' as Pope put it in 1711 in the *Essay on Criticism*; in Grigson's words, 'uniform nature'.

In the late eighteenth and early nineteenth centuries the romantic movement challenged Augustan hegemony. Romanticism was in part a consequence of the prospect of increasing political instability, and the intrusion of specific and fundamental political issues into literature helped revive the concept of poetry as a vehicle for enthusiastic, revolutionary ideas rather than as a means of common-sense ironic deflation. Political enthusiasm was accompanied by a resurgence of interest in spiritual experience as a fit subject for poetry. This was signalled in part by an enthusiasm for gothic against classicism, and also by the discovery of the inadequacy of nature when '*Methodiz'd*' by man; nature became a living, mysterious source for image, symbol and myth. But though Romanticism effectively destroyed the dominance of Augustan culture in Britain, it by no means obliterated it.

Matters of style and form are symptomatic, not fundamental to this debate. British poetry after the Second World War reveals a continuing friction between an Augustan 'common-sense' tradition and its romantic counterpart, a friction seen specifically in the varying perceptions of the way in which the image functions. Grigson recommended Augustan poetry as a literary device controlled by a firm, unambiguous intent. Its images were a product of the poet's learning and intellect which could be striking either for their aptness, or indeed for their difference. In the latter case unambiguous meaning was conveyed through controlled, ironic distancing. The poetic image thus becomes admirable to the extent that it does what the poet requires of it, and no more. The writing of poetry is a highly self-conscious act, where the poet addresses, rather than identifies with, his subject.

Compared to this, the romantic image encourages the erosion of such carefully ordered distinctions, and infinitely expands the possible functions of poetry. The image may well expose and question a contrived, controlled distance between the poem, its author, the poem's subject and its readership. The image, in effect, may claim a life and reality of its own, multiplying the possible readings of the poem. It may encourage belief in a spiritual meaning of some description beyond the immediate social and political context of the poem, and the poet's rational intellect. Anne Stevenson's work (1987), for example, owes much to the tradition of romantic nature poetry, while a persistently self-analytical tendency often leads her to question Romanticism as a male-oriented construct. Questioning the structures of her own poetic discourse becomes an integral part of her exploration of gender distinction, religious experience and response to landscape.

The poetry of Seamus Heaney reflects a similar awareness of the complexities endemic to writing poetry in the twentieth century. As a self-consciously Irish poet, he has used writing as an image of the traditionally fraught relationship between the act of literary production and specific political involvement: 'The poet's double responsibility to tell a truth as well as to make a thing . . .' (1988, p. 135). The extent to which a poem, through the act of composition, establishes an existence intellectually removed from an act born of political commitment is repeatedly challenged. 'Alphabets', 'From the Frontier of Writing', 'A Daylight Art' and 'Parable Island', are four examples from *The Haw Lantern* (1987) where the titles alone suggest how the poetry is subjecting itself to a scrutiny of the nature of its otherness. Such self-scrutiny is seen in 'From the Frontier of Writing' where the estrangement created by political interrogation is conflated with the experience of the interrogating, concentratedly analytical writer:

> and everything is pure interrogation
> until a rifle motions and you move
> with guarded unconcerned acceleration
> (1987, p. 6)

The image of the pen as rifle is the opening gambit of 'Digging': 'Between my finger and my thumb/The squat pen rests; snug as a gun' (1966, p. 13). Heaney knows what it is to have to wait before the writing can begin 'with guarded unconcerned acceleration'.

In 'Casualty' he employs an image of physical work (in this case fishing) to convey the experience of the poet's craft:

> To get out early, haul
> Steadily off the bottom,
> Dispraise the catch, and smile
> As you find a rhythm
> Working you...
>
> (1979, p. 24)

The stillness, the remoteness, the otherness of the poem contains within it an intense activity. Like the pot Heaney contemplates in 'Station Island' (1984), the poem possesses a 'patient sheen and turbulent atoms' (p. 87). The imagery insists upon a reconciliation that seems impossible for his compatriot Derek Mahon who, in 'Rage for Order' (1979), sees poetry and the poet hopelessly cut off from the subject-matter of the troubles:

> Somewhere beyond the scorched gable end and the burnt-out
>   buses
> there is a poet indulging
>   his wretched rage for order
>
> (ll. 1–4)

It was a 'wretched rage for order' that many poets searched for after the war, emphasizing precision and rationality through their images, while frequently ridiculing the multi-faceted complexities of Romanticism for 'drenching with confectionery/One image, one event's hard outline' (Amis, 1956, p. 44). D. J. Enright, Roy Fuller, Donald Davie and Kingsley Amis all adopted a common-sense rhetoric, underpinning it with a formal poetic style. In 'The Interpreters' (1956), Enright ironically deflates the modern critic:

> Good lord, if a poet really meant what he said,
> we should all be out of a job – why on earth
> would he sing of the merely real?
>
> (ll. 27–9)

Enright's ironic reference to the 'merely real' is Augustan in its appeal to common-sense values. What in fact emerges is poetry dismissed by Charles Tomlinson as the product of a parochial 'middle-class muse' retreating 'behind the privet hedge' ([1961] 1963, p. 471).

If the poetry that Tomlinson criticized was the fruit of a persistent Augustanism, a more immediate inspiration was the impact that W. H. Auden had had on British poetry since the 1930s. Auden's influence was viewed uneasily by Robert Conquest in his Introduction to *New Lines* (1956), an influential anthology of post-war poetry whose contributors subsequently became known as the Movement poets. Conquest attacked poetry inspired, as was Auden's, by Freudian theories of the mind, and pointed approvingly to 'the methods of

Mr. William Empson in poetry', identifying 'eighteenth-century forms' in his verse with the admirable determination to maintain 'a rational structure and comprehensible language' (Conquest, 1956, pp. xv–xvii). By this time Auden, however, was considered a supreme craftsman, while his deflationary use of idiomatic English established precisely the tone of ironic common sense that the *New Lines* poets (Kingsley Amis, D. J. Enright, Roy Fuller, Donald Davie, Philip Larkin) were said by Conquest to share.

What distinguished Auden from the majority of the *New Lines* poets was his grasp of the nuances contained within his ironic discourse. Auden's was a genuinely disaffected, disinherited voice that reflected the social and cultural confusion of the post-war years. In 'Under Which Lyre' (1946) 'raw veterans' returning to campus life find little reassurance when reunited with the clear-sighted, intellectual, 'metaphysical' view of life that Grigson and Conquest were recommending:

> Among bewildering appliances
> For mastering the arts and sciences
>   They stroll or run,
> And nerves that never flinched at slaughter
> Are shot to pieces by the shorter
>   Poems of Donne.
>
> (Auden, 1982, p. 178)

In 'In Praise of Limestone', a poem which significantly meditates upon a classical Italian landscape, Auden maintains that there can be no single point of cultural reference 'Where something was settled once and for all' (Auden, 1982, p. 186).

Two of the most successful poets to emerge from the immediate post-war era were John Betjeman and Philip Larkin. Both poets cultivated personae that tended to belie the seriousness of their intent. Betjeman (1980) expresses his distaste for post-war England by describing it through images more properly suited to romantic poetry. Yet the limited, 'real' world of suburban lives, loves and architecture is his subject, and the imagery is constantly undercut; the irony is one of despair only superficially rescued by humour, nostalgia and technical perfection.

Similarly, Larkin's subject is the world of everyday reality; middle-class, dreary, profoundly pessimistic. 'Dockery and Son', first published in 1963, closes on a characteristically lugubrious note:

> Life is first boredom, then fear.
> Whether or not we use it, it goes,
> And leaves what something hidden from us chose,
> And age, and then the only end of age.
>
> (Larkin, 1988, p. 153)

That which is 'hidden from us' remains hidden; any tendency to dispel the gloomy prospect with mystical speculation is suppressed. In 'Church Going' (1954), which appeared in *New Lines* two years later, Larkin is as wary of intellectuals as he is of religious mystics: '... the roof looks almost new – /Cleaned, or restored? Someone would know: I don't' (ll. 11–12). His apparent recognition of the church as a 'serious house' (l. 55) is qualified by the image he uses for that seriousness, a robe, an outer garment beneath which lies as ever the one real certainty: 'If only that so many dead lie round' (Larkin, 1988, pp. 97–8).

What the *Collected Poems* (1988) of Larkin now illustrate is, by way of contrast to the anti-intellectual tone he cultivated, the seriousness with which he worked to perfect an art that encapsulated his uncompromisingly reductive response to life. The social context in which Larkin wrote was one of profound change, and with this in mind it is possible to explain his poetry partly in terms of middle-class neuroses, looking with distaste on the crude display of affluence by the working classes in 'The Whitsun Weddings' (1958), noting in 'Self's the Man' (1958) the rise of consumerism, 'the kiddies' clobber and the drier/- And the electric fire' (ll. 7–8), in every respect finding a society bent on self-deception. His poetry operated as an ironic means of control, applying a traditional leaven of common sense to what might otherwise destabilize both the individual and society. In 'Love Again' (1979), his conflation of self-knowledge with social comment is painfully revealed:

> ... but why put it into words?
> Isolate rather this element
>
> That spreads through other lives like a tree
> And sways them on in a sort of sense
> And say why it never worked for me.
>
> (ll. 11–15)

A year after Charles Tomlinson had complained that British poetry was retreating behind the privet hedges of suburbia, A. Alvarez published his essay 'The New Poetry, or Beyond the Gentility Principle'. Tomlinson's dissatisfaction with mainstream British poetry was primarily aesthetic, and his own work reflected a continuing commitment to modernism. Alvarez's objections, by contrast, registered a lack of patience with the political unreality of 'Movement' poets: '... gentility is a belief that life is always more or less orderly, people always more or less polite, their emotions and habits more or less decent and more or less controllable' ([1962] 1966, p. 25). Alvarez's plea that the poet 'should face the full range of his experience with his full intelligence' (p. 28), that he should 'face the more uncompromising forces at work in our time' (p. 26), was in effect a plea on behalf of poets largely ignored since the war. Alvarez concentrated primarily on male poets, but the list here should include

Edith Sitwell, Ruth Pitter and Stevie Smith, with George Barker, David Gascoyne, Basil Bunting, and poets representing the marginalized areas of British society – R. S. Thomas in Wales, Hugh MacDiarmid, Edwin Muir and Kathleen Raine in Scotland.

Although no friend to the new wave of popular poetry that the 1960s was producing, Alvarez was responding to symptoms of disaffection newly emerging in British society; the campaign against nuclear armaments and the phenomenon of a youth culture seemed to challenge everything that Grigson's generation stood for. Alvarez used Ted Hughes as chief protagonist for the new poetry of the 1960s. He compared Hughes's 'A Dream of Horses' with Larkin's 'At Grass' to illustrate the way in which the former poet's imagery created 'a powerful complex of emotions and sensations' (p. 31) over against Larkin's limited, provincial response. He might equally have drawn attention to 'The Horses' by Edwin Muir (1960, pp. 246–7). Alvarez's discontent, still largely controlled by an intellectually abstract response to social and political change, was, however, to be rapidly overtaken by political events, specifically in Ireland.

The group of poets who came together in Belfast under the aegis of Philip Hobsbawm in the early 1960s (Stewart Parker, Michael Longley, James Simmons, Heaney and others) initiated a dialogue between poetry and politics that stood in opposition to everything 'Movement'/*New Lines* poetry had come to represent. The specifically political context of this second renaissance in Irish poetry was in due course augmented by Medbh McGuckian, and threw into clear relief the conservatism of the English literary establishment. David Trotter (1984) argues that the latter was in fact explicitly Tory, a reactionary tradition of poetry and criticism which links F. R. Leavis, Davie, Amis, C. H. Sisson and Michael Schmidt of the Carcanet Press. In particular, Trotter specifies Schmidt's advocacy of a literature of 'authority', and Davie's comments in the late 1960s that 'good writing depends on "the drive towards authority, the authoritative note and tone" ' (p. 238). While immediate political issues do not in any precise way define antagonisms within British poetry (Heaney, McGuckian and Tom Paulin are examples of three very different Irish poets), they do reveal a continuing debate inherent in modern society since the early eighteenth century.

Augustan poets, like those who in various ways sought to emulate them in the twentieth century, were necessarily engaged in rewriting history, providing a chronology that legitimized the social order they sought to confirm. In the 1960s and 1970s poets who represented disaffected sections of British society, including the Liverpool trio of Roger McGough, Brian Patten and Adrian Henri, were in a position to insist on a hearing. In consequence the 'Augustan' establishment version of history – how things had been and how they should continue – came under attack. For George MacBeth (1986) history becomes the story of how Rome triumphed by destroying the histories of the vanquished. For Kathleen Raine, David Jones and Geoffrey Hill the present is part of a religious, cultural, political and geological continuum in which all time is immanent. Our society becomes a complex structure of human experience which – notably in Hill – tends to minimize the eighteenth century. Heaney's suggestion that the ritual murder practised by Iron Age bog people in Jutland has an archetypal relevance to contemporary killings in Northern Ireland is a further example of relocating historical significance.

Using imagery which blends physical signs of the distant past with its continuing numinous presence, Ted Hughes also explores the relationship between history and poetry. 'Pike' (1960) and 'Ghost Crabs' (1957) are well-known examples; more recently 'Saint's Island' (1986) pursues a similar theme:

> (As if our lives were lichenous rock
> Or a sleep of roots. Or a tin or sardines,
> An apple, a watch, a thermos.)
>   (Hughes, 1986, p. 30)

There is a swift movement through these lines from the suitably impressive, evocative images of existence out of time, 'lichenous rock' and 'roots', to a seemingly random list of transient objects. The watch, thermos and sardine tin are all debris indicative of a contemporary way of life designed to avoid any encounter with naked reality; fish are preferred prepacked rather than from the ocean, a comforting hot drink is kept close by, and we must always keep an eye on the time. In *Crow* (1970) Hughes challenges the received 'historical' version of the way life is ordered by concocting a subversive creation myth. R. S. Thomas (1986) has equally insisted on a subversive reading of Welsh history while accepting that there remains a ritualistic acceptance of the official line. It has become, however, a gruesome dance of death:

> There's a man still farming at Ty'n-y-Fawnog,
> Contributing grimly to the accepted pattern,
> The embryo music dead in his throat.
>   ('The Welsh Hill Country', ll. 16–18)

In the Preface to *The Anathemata* (1952), a vast, fragmentary free verse meditation which includes passages of lyrical prose, David Jones explains that he is investigating the apparent incompatibility of a world of 'myths', and a world of 'formulae' (p. 17). The poet's problem is a 'situational' one, 'born into a given historic situation' (p. 22). For Jones, political and social history are intertwined with geological change in a way which brushes aside official histories written to suit a specific time, and a specific cultural bias.

Jones writes within the context of a mystic tradition in British poetry which is traceable back to Blake and beyond, and which latterly includes poetry by Mary Casey (1981) where a rigorous control of spare free verse succeeds in liberating the numinous quality of human experience. Meaning is not achieved through rational, 'perspicuous' language, yet the vision is clear and uncompromising, and in a very specific sense physical:

> rhythm is proportion
> progress of pilgrim hours
> advance to prepared attainment
> a journey for the feet
> ('Nothing Is Without A Part In Soul', ll. 1–4)

What these poets offer is in part what Geoffrey Hill (1985) has described as 'decreation' ('Pavana Dolorosa', l. 8), a dismantling of the rational empiricism of our dominant Enlightenment cultural tradition, to reveal in its place a much older Christian tradition of thought:

> ... Poetry
> Unearths from among the speechless dead
>
> Lazarus mystified, common man
> Of death.
> ('History As Poetry', ll. 3–6)

A significant factor in deconstructing post-war, neo-Augustan orthodoxy has been the recognition of women poets, part of a much more comprehensive process of rewriting history. The variety of work here is immense. In many respects Carol Rumens (1987) has close affinities with Larkin in her ironic observations of suburban detail. But in, for example, 'Coming Home', the fact that it is a woman's voice provides a new perspective to the otherwise predictable conclusion:

> We chug towards our own front door
> anxiously, seeing as if for the first time
> how tight the plot that locks us in,
> how small our parts, how unchosen.
> (ll. 21–4)

Elizabeth Bartlett (1983) also shares something of Larkin's concern for grim reality, but she combines this with a vitality reminiscent of Sylvia Plath; she is certainly not tempted into the tone of lugubrious solemnity that Larkin could sustain so effectively. Fleur Adcock (1983) has been one of the most successful poets to write on specifically feminist themes; more recently Carol Ann Duffy (1987) has emerged as a poet capable of an impressively wide range of work, revealing the inadequacies of language where meaning is controlled by assumptions rooted in such things as gender ('Psychopath'), village life ('Model Village') and polite discourse ('Mouth, With Soap'). Feminist issues are by no means the preserve of women poets, however, and Alan Brownjohn (1988) has shown a sensitivity to issues very similar to those explored by Duffy.

Sylvia Plath (1965) exposed the hypocrisy of the classical idealization of feminine 'perfection' through her deft use of line length:

> The woman is perfected.
> Her dead
>
> Body wears the smile of accomplishment,
> The illusion of a Greek necessity...
>
> ('Edge', ll. 1–4)

Equally conscious of the consequences of a classical cultural tradition, Irene Fekete (1971) comments on the insufficiencies of a notion of beauty and fulfilment in 'Palladian Lament', where 'Containment is all' (l. 21). The interweaving of gender, class, race and political divisiveness has presented a particularly strong challenge to the tradition of 'containment'. Poets like Barbara Burford, Lindsay Macrae and Nicki Jackowski approach the issues with an often conscious effort to avoid or deflate conventional poetic devices, while Libby Houston (1986), in 'Childe Roland takes on the dark tower one more time', makes a witty reference to the male dominated literary heritage with which such poetry has to contend.

By way of contrast to these disaffected and dissenting voices, there continues a body of work which in a variety of ways bears the stamp of the Enlightenment ideal. Largely as a result of a professional marketing campaign in the late 1970s, a school of poetry formed around the work of Craig Raine and Christopher Reid, taking as its exemplar Raine's 'A Martian Sends a Postcard Home' (1979). Blake Morrison and Andrew Motion describe the distinguishing features of this 'new spirit in British poetry' in their 1982 edition of *The Penguin Book of Contemporary British Poetry*; they include 'a preference for metaphor and poetic bizarrerie to metonymy and plain speech' (p. 12). It is above all a highly intellectual poetry, generally dismissive of the numinous, describing reality with metaphysical inventiveness. Before becoming a fully-fledged 'Martian', Raine had already been dubbed the 'metaphor man' (Trotter, 1984, p. 249). While the 'Martian' phenomenon was clearly a hype, there is important and interesting work being done by the poets associated with this group. Like many Movement poets before them, most 'Martians' would prefer to be taken on their own merits. Larkin, Thom Gunn and Elizabeth Jennings resented being defined in the way they were; 'Martians' find themselves often unfairly stereotyped as practitioners of superficial metaphoric pyrotechnics.

In general, though, the appearance of Raine, Reid, James Fenton, Hugo Williams and others as influential poets (Raine is the Faber poetry editor) is symptomatic of a continuing Augustan sensibility. The 'traditional' subjects for poetry, Blake Morrison claimed in 1987, '...a lover or spouse ... a particular place ... society at large ... God', have been abandoned in favour of 'the relationship with parents' (p. 179). What this at once alerts us to, as

Alan Robinson (1988) has pointed out, is the general mistrust this group has 'of the politicisation of poetry' (p. 17), though inevitably the political world impinges on their work. In 'Travelling', Penelope Shuttle (1980) epitomizes the way these poets use their craft as a sophisticated means of evasion: 'Darkness grows up in black clusters around me/But I step back from that edge' (ll. 38–9).

It is by no means coincidental that Morrison chose to head his essay of 1987 on 'Contemporary British Poetry' with a quotation from Pope: 'I am more certain that it is a duty of nature to preserve a good parent's life and happiness, than I am of any speculative point whatever' (p. 179). Naming domesticity as a central feature of contemporary poetry effectively defines in very specific ways the poet's responsibility. In 'One Life' by Andrew Motion (1982), the news on the radio is ignored in favour of scientific study. The latter part of this poem, however, suggests that such loss of contact with the outside world can lead to an unhealthy isolation damaging to personal relationships. Michael Hoffman, Hugo Williams and James Fenton have all written impressively around the subject of isolation and loneliness, born in part from their determination to keep at bay a romantic or numinous sense of history. In Fenton's 'A Vacant Possession' (1982) we have a reenactment of Penelope Shuttle's response to the romantic lure of distant parts:

> ... Shall I go down?
> I hear my name called, peer over the bannister
> And remember something I left in my bedroom.
> (ll. 51–3)

Morrison's chosen theme of poetry as a 'filial art' enables him to incorporate Heaney, Douglas Dunn and Tony Harrison in his essay. These are certainly poets for whom family roots are important, but in seeking to 'domesticate' them in this way, Morrison minimizes the significance of their achievement. Douglas Dunn (1971) and Tony Harrison (1987) have both experienced the kind of social mobility that educational opportunities have made increasingly possible since the war. Both relentlessly question the experience. In some respects they see themselves as traitors to the working class, particularly in the light of the political climate that established itself in the 1980s. Both feel alienated from the cultural milieu in which they now work; though they believe in poetry, they do not believe in the dominant cultural context in which it still operates despite recent gestures made by anthologies of working-class, homosexual, Caribbean and feminist poetry.

Harrison's 'v' is a *tour de force* of class-based social and political frustration. The poem embraces the foul language of vandals 'pissed' on lager, and so insists on a literal, 'real' representation of a particular type, while formally it remains tightly controlled; and even while the expletives are tumbling out, the poet enters into a wholly unrealistic dialogue with a hooligan spraying graffiti on his family tombstone. We are continually being skilfully relocated, moving from the literary territory of a recognizable poem to Leeds cemetery, then to a contrived, theatrical set where it becomes possible for the vandal to match – albeit in his own terms – Harrison's demand for a reflective discourse.

Where 'Martian' poetry has undoubtedly created a stir within academic literary circles, it was the proposed televised version of '*v*' that captured the attention of the general public following protests in the House of Commons by morally outraged Members of Parliament. This in itself is of course no absolute guarantee of quality, but given that the underlying reason for the protest was probably Harrison's powerful, measured, unhysterical indictment of Thatcherite Britain, it was an illustration of the way contemporary poetry can move out into the sphere of public political debate and begin to function at the centre of society, rather than on an academic periphery:

> These Vs are all the versuses of life
> from LEEDS v. DERBY, Black/White
> and (as I've known to my cost) man v. wife,
> Communist v. Fascist, Left v. Right,
>
> class v. class as bitter as before,
> the unending violence of US and THEM,
> personified in 1984
> by Coal Board MacGregor and the NUM...
> (ll. 65–72)

Throughout the poem Harrison reveals a resonant awareness of the literary models that have contributed to his development as a poet. The effect is partly ironic, but it also suggests that the legacy of English culture has its uses, even if they are not always what we might suppose them to be. Wordsworth is present as more than a name on one of the gravestones; the line 'Will Earth run out of her "diurnal courses" ' alludes to one of his most poignantly elegiac Lyrical Ballads, while Gray's *Elegy* is recalled most specifically by Harrison's composition of his own elegy for the final stanza.

In a period now of increasing political polarization, in a society at its most divided since the war, there would seem to exist a situation where what has for long been considered the most rarefied and remote literary form is moving steadily nearer to the centre of political and social life.

FURTHER READING

Alvarez A. (1966) 'The New Poetry, or Beyond the Gentility Principle'. In A. Alvarez (ed.), *The New Poetry*, Penguin, Harmondsworth [first published 1962]

Conquest, Robert (ed.) (1956) *New Lines*, Macmillan, London

Grigson, Geoffrey (1984) *Before the Romantics*, Salamander Press, Edinburgh [first published 1946]

Heaney, Seamus (1988) *The Government of the Tongue*, Faber & Faber, London

Morrison, Blake (1987) 'The Filial Art: A Reading of Contemporary British Poetry', *The Yearbook of English Studies*, 17, 179–217

Morrison, Blake and Motion, Andrew (eds) (1982) *The Penguin Book of Contemporary British Poetry*, Penguin, Harmondsworth

Robinson, Alan (1988) *Instabilities in Contemporary British Poetry*, Macmillan, London

Thurley, Geoffrey (1974) *The Ironic Harvest*, Edward Arnold, London

Thwaite, Anthony (1985) *Poetry Today*, Longman, London

Tomlinson, Charles (1963) 'Poetry Today'. In Boris Ford (ed.), *The Pelican Guide to English Literature*, vol. 7, Penguin, Harmondsworth

Trotter, David (1984) *The Making of the Reader*, Macmillan, London

Williams, John (1987) *Twentieth Century British Poetry*, Edward Arnold, London

ADDITIONAL WORKS CITED

Adcock, Fleur (1983) *Selected Poems*, Oxford University Press, London

Amis, Kingsley (1956) 'Wrong Words'. In Robert Conquest (ed.), *New Lines*, Macmillan, London, p. 44

Auden, W. H. (1982) *Selected Poems*, edited by Edward Mendelson, John Murray, London

Bartlett, Elizabeth (1983) *Strange Territory*, Peterloo Poets, London

Betjeman, John (1980) *Collected Poems*, John Murray, London

Brownjohn, Alan (1988) *Collected Poems 1952–86*, Hutchinson, London

Casey, Mary (1981) *Christophorus*, Enitharmon, London

Duffy, Carol Ann (1987) *Selling Manhattan*, Anvil Press, London

Dunn, Douglas (1971) *Terry Street*, Faber & Faber, London

Enright, D. J. (1956) 'The Interpreters'. In Robert Conquest (ed.), *New Lines*, Macmillan, London, p. 60

Fekete, Irene (1971) *Time Elsewhere*, Chatto & Windus, London

Fenton, James (1982) *The Memory of War*, Salamander Press, Edinburgh

Harrison, Tony (1987) *Selected Poems*, Penguin, Harmondsworth

Heaney, Seamus (1966) *Death of a Naturalist*, Faber & Faber, London

——(1979) *Fieldwork*, Faber & Faber, London

——(1984) *Station Island*, Faber & Faber, London

——(1987) *The Haw Lantern*, Faber & Faber, London

Hill, Geoffrey (1985) *Collected Poems*, Penguin, Harmondsworth

Houston, Libby (1986) 'Childe Roland takes on the dark tower one more time'. In Sylvia Paskin, Jay Ramsay and Jeremy Silver (eds), *Angels of Fire*, Chatto & Windus, London, p. 119

Hughes, Ted (1986) *Flowers and Insects*, Faber & Faber, London

Jones, David (1952) *The Anathemata*, Faber & Faber, London

Larkin, Philip (1988) *Collected Poems*, Faber & Faber, London

MacBeth, George (1986) *The Cleaver Garden*, Secker & Warburg, London

Mahon, Derek (1979) *Poems 1962–78*, Oxford University Press, London

Motion, Andrew (1982) 'One Life'. In Blake Morrison and Andrew Motion (eds), *The Penguin Book of Contemporary British Poetry*, Penguin, Harmondsworth, p. 133

Muir, Edwin (1960) *Collected Poems 1921–58*, Faber & Faber, London

Plath, Sylvia (1965) *Ariel*, Faber & Faber, London

Raine, Craig (1979) *A Martian Sends a Postcard Home*, Oxford University Press, London

Rumens, Carol (1987) *Selected Poems*, Chatto & Windus, London

Shuttle, Penelope (1980) *The Orchard Upstairs*, Oxford University Press, London

Stevenson, Anne (1987) *Selected Poems 1956–86*, Oxford University Press, London

Thomas, R. S. (1986) *Selected Poems 1946–68*, Oxford University Press, London

23

CONTEMPORARY AMERICAN POETRY

THOMAS GARDNER

Any attempt at an overview of recent American poetry must begin with the fact that it follows, and defines itself in relation to, the work of Yeats, Pound, Eliot, H. D. (Hilda Doolittle), Williams and Stevens. Whether repeating, refining or revising that achievement, no contemporary poet, as Helen Vendler remarks, can 'quite take the work of the great modernists for granted. . . . When the history of the relation between the two halves of the twentieth century is written, the second half will be seen . . . to be a long critique of the first, as well as a long absorption of it' (1985, pp. 3–4). A number of solid attempts at that history have appeared in recent years, most describing a series of swerves away from and back towards the audacity of modernist attempts to link language and experience. James E. B. Breslin, for example, begins his history of contemporary poetry at mid-century, when 'The moderns were haunting figures, at once inaccessibly distant and omnipresent . . . they had pre-empted the revolutionary possibilities of their successors'. Quoting Randall Jarrell – 'How can poems be written that are more violent, more disorganized, more obscure . . . than those that have already been written?' – Breslin suggests the inheritance must have seemed both intimidating and extreme (1983, pp. 2–3).

If Pound proposed that an image 'presents an intellectual and emotional complex in an instant of time', or Eliot defined an objective correlative as 'a set of objects, a situation, a chain of events which shall be the formula of [a] particular emotion', the first generation to follow these poets, as Breslin sees it, domesticated the powerful (and generative) contradictions of such strategies by shying away from their extremes. In place of Eliot's grinding lament that despite his desire to fix emotions, 'Words strain, / Crack and sometimes break under the tension, slip, slide, perish, / Decay with imprecision, will not stay in place' (1963, p. 180), we find in the 1950s what Breslin calls an easy 'verbal conjuring, a series of light, quick, beautiful changes . . . [reminding us] that the poem, while creating the illusionary presence of "mastery", remains a fictive construct' (1983, p. 35). A release from modernist tensions was accomplished, this suggests, by swerving away from their ambitious attempts to shatter and re-present the world, settling for a carefully made 'construct'. By the late 1950s and early 1960s, Breslin continues, such a poetry seemed, in its lightness, to have deliberately reduced its engagement with the world. A second swerve followed. Attempting to 'reground art in temporal immediacy' (p. 54), such poets as Allen Ginsberg, Denise Levertov, James Wright and Frank O'Hara once again made bold claims for the reach of their art. 'Extending their medium toward a world of *independent* objects in *temporal* flux', these writers came to see poetry as a series of attempts 'to find new ways of binding form and flux so that temporality will not *seem* to have been violated' (pp. 262, 60). As the emphasis suggests, this second swerve purchased its sense of immediacy by sliding attention away from the 'binding' involved in its creation.

The next shift, predictably, occurred as the 'open poetics' of the 1960s settled into a kind of orthodoxy, inadvertently pointing out the series of issues it had attempted to set aside. Charles Altieri picks up this part of the history, describing the situation of American poets in the 1970s for whom the work of these powerful predecessors, 'seeking to make the poem a testament to new ontological or psychological frameworks', had begun to seem 'illusionistic' and 'based on elaborate adventures of immediate discovery' (Altieri, 1984, p. 36). Unavoidably aware of the evasions and duplicities within language which shape all 'terms we might apply to the self or to intimate experience', many American poets of the 1970s, according to Altieri, refused to allow themselves the illusion of seeming to bind without violating. Avoiding claims of mastery or sudden insight in favour of 'nontheatrical, personal voices recording a moment of "poetic excitement" or "heightened sensitivity" grounded in and explained by a specific event', such poets, in refusing to overreach, once again moved away from any need wholeheartedly to confront the basic tensions underlying their use of the language (p. 22).

Altieri suggests, near the end of his study and at length in a recent article, that the stronger poets of the 1970s have refused such strategies, opting instead for a poetry by which we might more fully 'engage ourselves in what the language does' (in Lazer, 1987, p. 50). 'Giving full play to the energies, tensions, and duplicities that enter into the artist's constructive acts', the work of such poets as John Ashbery, Adrienne Rich and Robert Creeley 'fully elaborates its medium' by deliberately exemplifying and allowing itself to reflect upon the full range of tensions inherent in making and shaping the world (pp. 42, 43). Taking us full circle, Altieri claims that such attention to 'the linguistic situation of a reflective, writing presence' is actually a return to 'the possible powers we now tend to overlook in Modernist poetry' (p. 31) – particularly that poetry's ability to engage larger issues by putting into play both its attempts and its acknowledged failures to grasp the world.

Responding to the larger shifts of the last four decades, Breslin and Altieri make what seem to me to be convincing histories of the period. But, I suggest in what follows, another sort of history could be written that stresses not the swerves of decade to decade but the period's continuous rediscovery and rephrasing of poetry's inevitable confrontation with its own 'materiality and opacity' (Vendler, in Lazer, 1987, p. 215). That is, acknowledging with Altieri the 'possible powers' set in tension early in the century, might we not read a series of crucially self-reflective poems and sketch a set of shared concerns and strategies by which that generative swirl has kept its full force?

Take, for example, a poem published by Elizabeth Bishop in 1955 – 'At the Fishhouses'. It begins with just the sort of careful description we are told to look for in work of that decade:

> Although it is a cold evening,
> down by one of the fishhouses
> an old man sits netting,
> his net, in the gloaming almost invisible,
> a dark purple brown,
> and his shuttle worn and polished.
> The air smells so strong of codfish
> it makes one's nose run and one's eyes water.
>
> (Bishop, 1983, p. 64)

This is description of a peculiar sort, however, for what this scene presents us with – the cold, the dark and the overpowering smell about to render the old man, his worn shuttle and his tattered net 'invisible' – is a question everywhere alive for Bishop: acknowledging the inevitable erasure of the nets we use to describe and master the world, why go on working them? That such a question prompts both the opening 'although' of the poem and its patient descriptive weave is reinforced by the next swing of her eye:

> The five fishhouses have steeply peaked roofs
> and narrow, cleated gangplanks slant up
> to storerooms in the gables
> for the wheelbarrows to be pushed up and down on.
> All is silver: the heavy surface of the sea,
> swelling slowly as if considering spilling over,
> is opaque, but the silver of the benches,
> the lobster pots, and masts, scattered
> among the wild jagged rocks,
> is of an apparent translucence
> like the small old buildings with an emerald moss
> growing on their shoreward walls.
>
> (p. 64)

What we notice first is that the domination of the dark, cold, overpowering

air has been picked up by the 'heavy surface' of the 'opaque' sea. Like the
evening, the swelling sea both displays its temporarily checked potential to
erase the things of the shore (it is 'considering spilling over') and has scattered
about it what, in this light, could be taken as traces of its previously having
done so: the benches, pots and masts rendered silver and translucent by the
apparently corrosive effects of the sea's heavier, swelling silver. The fishhouses
themselves – numbered, in focus, and, all slants and peaks, drawn as a series
of load-bearing vectors – seem opposed to the threat of dissolution. The eye
greedily lights on them, only to notice – nudged by Bishop's almost silent
revision of herself – that these same buildings, by the end of the passage
above, have become 'small old buildings' of an equally eroded translucence:
walled now with 'an emerald moss' only a fool would cleat or climb. Bishop's
initial description of the fishhouses, that is to say, suffers the same forceful
erasure predicted for the scene's fragile nets, pots and masts.

Why do that? Why would a poet committed to description begin with an
acknowledgment of limitation? Begin, more than that, by slyly miming the
breakdown of descriptive mastery? This poem, like the others we will be
examining, answers by demonstrating new ways language can move once its
fragility has been acknowledged and wholeheartedly embraced. Turning her
ordering eye toward the threatening sea, letting it follow a 'long ramp /
descending into the water', Bishop records this confrontation:

> Cold dark deep and absolutely clear,
> element bearable to no mortal,
> to fish and to seals . . . One seal particularly
> I have seen here evening after evening.
> He was curious about me. He was interested in music;
> like me a believer in total immersion,
> so I used to sing him Baptist hymns.
> I also sang 'A Mighty Fortress Is Our God.'
> He stood up in the water and regarded me
> steadily, moving his head a little.
> Then he would disappear, then suddenly emerge
> almost in the same spot, with a sort of shrug
> as if it were against his better judgment.
> Cold dark deep and absolutely clear,
> the clear gray icy water . . .

(p. 65)

Twice, Bishop attempts to edge down that ramp and describe the sea, only to
break off in ellipses. As with the torn net and the peaked fishhouses, her
words seem to shatter, rendered invisible and unstable by an 'absolute' beyond
the grasp of 'mortals'. But – here is her version of why one would insist on
acknowledging the weightlessness of words before weaving them – a new sort
of language, language that resists its own dreams of containment and seizure,

fills the gap opened by those hesitations. And fills it – we see in the joke about baptism, appropriate hymns, and a shrugging seal – with a confession (total immersion is an impossible dream) that calls attention to something else as well: that which cannot be accommodated, but which, while remaining outside and other, has been lightly and intimately involved with the words it silences. This poem – neither assenting with a wink to the illusionary nature of language nor backing away from the attempt to make contact with what is outside of it – suggests that by foregrounding the problems involved in using language one might ride its inevitable erasure toward a different sort of involvement. As Altieri would have it, such a poem elaborates possibilities within the medium.

Whereas an awareness of language's materiality leads Bishop to a study of its fragility, it involves a poet such as Theodore Roethke, absorbed with the problem of self-portraiture, with another sort of mismatch. Convinced that one shapes a self through embracing a medium, Roethke, in his strongest poem 'North American Sequence', names the sea as a possible medium to rouse the self to awareness. At the same time, and quite deliberately, he stresses the impossibility of such a desire. Although the poem begins by longing to break out of a state in which 'the spirit fails to move forward, / But shrinks into a half-life, less than itself' (Roethke, 1966, p. 187), Roethke's first attempt to enter and embrace the sea becomes, curiously, a demonstration of hesitancy. 'Meditation at Oyster River', the second poem of the sequence, begins with Roethke sitting on a rock at the edge of a bay, the mouth of a river at his back. The world around him steadily increases in activity; 'the first tide-ripples' move towards where he waits, but when 'one long undulant ripple' breaks through the barrier of small stones before him, he responds by retreating: 'I dabble my toes in the brackish foam sliding forward, / Then retire to a rock higher up on the cliff-side' (p. 190). This dramatized failure, like Bishop's erasure of her first description of the fishhouses, is a way of deliberately stressing the difficulty of such an embrace. Self and medium, for this poet, never become the same. 'The self persists like a dying star, / In sleep, afraid', he writes – afraid that in giving itself totally to the sea it would be erased and only the sea expressed. Instead, Roethke proposes, one might insist on the difference between them, then follow out the problems posed by this mismatch. And *that* contact, Roethke suggests, the self both distinguishing itself from and engaging itself with the medium, prompts a new sort of movement of the sleeping spirit.

In 'Oyster River', for example, Roethke's acknowledgement that he cannot be the same as the swirling currents drives him to create a series of images expressing that failed longing. 'I shift on my rock, and I think', he writes: first of a 'trembling ... Michigan brook in April, / Over a lip of stone, the tiny rivulet', then of a 'wrist-thick cascade tumbling from a cleft rock', and finally of the Tittebawasee River, poised 'between winter and spring, / When the ice melts along the edges in early afternoon. / And the midchannel begins cracking and heaving from the pressure beneath' (p. 191). Such images, I would suggest, work with and enter the medium indirectly, with no claim to a full embrace. And yet, writes Roethke, through that limited engagement, 'the spirit runs, intermittently, / In and out of the small waves' (p. 192). Other poems in the sequence construct what Roethke calls 'rehearsals' or 'detours' in response to the questions he raises about his ability to embrace the sea directly, those detours playing out the problems inherent in the act of using a medium and thereby constructing a richer, more tentative way of speaking. But although a kind of moving self is created, Roethke is careful to insist, in the last poem of the sequence, that he has done so only indirectly. In contrast to the sea rose which 'Stays in its true place', rooted in stone, yet also unfolds its petals, extends its tendrils, and drops down to the waves – 'Moving with the waves, the undulating driftwood' (p. 203) – Roethke notes that his constructs have kept him 'far from the crash / Of the long swell, / The oily, tar-laden walls / Of the toppling waves'. Rather than claiming that 'another man appeared out of the depth of my being, / And I stood outside myself, / Beyond becoming and perishing, / A something wholly other' (p. 205), Roethke has faced that failure and created, in his examination of the medium, something smaller and more nuanced:

> I sway outside myself
> Into the darkening currents,
> Into the *small* spillage of driftwood,
> The waters swirling past the *tiny* headlands.
> (p. 202, my italics)

Where Roethke uses the acknowledged gap between himself and the sea to push him towards ways of more fully confronting that medium, Robert Duncan uses the distance between himself and the world of human creation to generate his attempts at self-portraiture. 'There is no being heard', he writes, 'except as we hear how we sound in the community around us' (1985, p. 199). Duncan's understanding of that community is a radically inclusive one – 'We find our company in Euripides, Plato, Moses of Leon, Fauré or Freud, searching out keys to our inner being in the rites of the Aranda and in the painting processes of Cézanne' (Duncan, 1968a, p. 146) – but like Roethke he also stresses 'the tension between speaking oneself and the utter commonality of the language that must be the medium of that self' (1985, p. 22). For Duncan, that tension is generated by the unfinished nature of the world he seeks to enter: still-in-process, that world can no more be grasped and made to speak simply and directly for the self than can Roethke's distant, because overwhelming, sea. For both poets, as for Bishop, that tension becomes a place in which it is possible to dwell.

These issues are brought forward most notably in Duncan's long poem 'Passages', published between 1968 and 1987. 'Passages 2', early in the sequence, sees in Ezra Pound's re-figuring of Circe's loom in *The Cantos* the problematic starting-point for Duncan's work:

> my mind a shuttle among
>   set strings of the music
> lets a weft of dream grow in the day time,
>   an increment of associations,
>   luminous soft threads,
> the thrown glamour, crossing and recrossing,
>   the twisted sinews underlying the work.
>
> Back of the images, the few cords that bind
>   meaning in the word-flow,
>   the rivering web
>   rises among wits and senses
> gathering the wool into its full cloth.
>
> The secret!   the secret!   It's hid
> in its showing forth.
>   (Duncan, 1968b, p. 11)

The 'twisted sinews' of a tapestry form its warp, the 'set strings' of humanity's made things that the poet's mind moves in and out of, while the 'luminous soft threads' of his attention, 'crossing and recrossing' those underlying cords, work to create its weft. Through such a process, the tapestry's 'full cloth' or 'rivering web' gradually appears. But, since that totality is 'secret', its complete form 'hidden' in its gradually shown forth manifestations, the shuttling mind's work is never complete. It is always 'crossing and recrossing'; its engagement with the medium is piecemeal and never finished. What this means is that Duncan, like Roethke, must invent new ways to handle this not-fully-graspable medium. How does one sound a set of fixed strings which will have to be crossed and recrossed in order to be fully revealed? What sort of approach to language does such handling represent? 'Passages 12', a reading of Baudelaire's 'Du Vin et du Haschisch', offers one answer. Baudelaire tells the story of a Spanish guitarist in a foreign city to give a concert who, discovering and getting drunk with one of his countrymen, insists on being accompanied by his new friend when he is forced to play that evening. Duncan begins his weaving with this dancing engagement:

'*Commence,*' *dit le guitariste au marbrier.*

He draws the sounds forth from his drunken violin
Bacchus in delirium cuts from the stone with a saw.

What does be play?   What does he   attempt to play?
It makes no difference,   the first ayre comes,

and suddenly,

an energy, a melody,   suave, capricious ·

   all the time   encircles me,

stifles the cry in my mouth, stops the beat
of my heart, conceals the rage of the child squalling,

       until I lie at the edge

                (p. 34)

The first line, in French, presents Baudelaire as a fixed string, apparently complete in itself. For six lines Duncan translates accordingly, transparently rendering the powerful original. Then he breaks the text with a bullet mark and begins writing himself ('encircles me') into the place of the violinist whose clumsy notes are transformed by the master guitarist. Such a break – and there are a series of them as the poem goes on – is Duncan's acknowledgment that the medium he is working with (in this case the Baudelaire poem) is an incomplete reflector, one that, in time, will need to be crossed by a series of other texts until its full nature is revealed. Duncan's break marks the place where that re-weaving might occur – not just of Baudelaire with Duncan but, as fragments from this now-splintered piece sound across 'Passages' as a whole, Baudelaire with Whitman, the Moravian Count Zinzendorf, the Berkeley Free Speech Movement, Kipling, and the thirteenth-century Albigensian crusade. Foregrounding that limitation, Duncan shatters the world he would embrace and sparks the sequence's cascading engagements with its medium.

Though with a much different tone, John Ashbery also uses that mismatch of self and medium to launch his language in different directions. Like Duncan, he realizes that since a medium is never a complete reflector, its embrace always involves a series of splintered-off encounters. As Ashbery puts it, handling one's experience always involves a movement from 'the inner emptiness from which alone understanding can spring up, [to] the tree of contradictions, joyous and living, investing that hollow void with its complicated material self' (1972, p. 63). Ashbery's 'Self-Portrait in a Convex Mirror', an account of a series of responses to a puzzling Renaissance mirror painting, quite vividly acts out the contradictory nature of those material exfoliations and defines the process as both 'joyous and living'. Once again, limitation fully acknowledged becomes a way to work and explore the medium more richly.

As the poem begins, Ashbery, apparently considering 'lifting the pencil to his own self-portrait', finds in the peculiarities of his model a way of mastering flux. Looking at his reflection in a convex mirror and copying what appeared there on a wooden globe of similar size, Parmigianino created a portrait in which his face seemed safely preserved from the changing world:

> the right hand
> Bigger than the head, thrust at the viewer
> And swerving easily away, as though to protect
> What it advertises. A few leaded panes, old beams,
> Fur, pleated muslin, a coral ring run together
> In a movement supporting the face, which swims
> Toward and away like the hand
> Except that it is in repose. It is what is
> Sequestered.
>
> (Ashbery, 1975, p. 68)

On second thought, however, the foregrounded hand and locked-together elements of the studio background seem intent not on 'protect[ing]' or 'support-ing' the face but on holding it 'captive', at a distance. The very act of lifting the face out of its environment, the portrait now seems to insist, changes it: 'The secret is too plain. The pity of it smarts, / Makes hot tears spurt: that the soul is not a soul, / Has no secret'. The foregrounded hand, then, comes to seem a complaint against medium, pushing against the sign of 'its dimension, / What carries it' (p. 69). Like the other poets we have examined, Ashbery begins by acknowledging the insufficiency of the medium – the painting – he has embraced. Rather than finding it equivalent to himself, he backs off and stresses 'the distance between us' (p. 71). In contrast to Ashbery's inner life which seems a rich weave of voices heard and half-heard, Parmigianino's world seems fearfully over-controlled:

> Whose curved hand controls,
> Francesco, the turning seasons and the thoughts
> That peel off and fly away at breathless speeds
> Like the last stubborn leaves ripped
> From wet branches? I see in this only the chaos
> Of your round mirror which organizes everything
> Around the polestar of your eyes which are empty,
> Know nothing, dream but reveal nothing.
>
> (p. 71)

What is most interesting about this poem and, I would claim, typical of a series of post-war American poems, is that this insisted-upon distance frees Ashbery to view the painting in a more detached manner, responding to the issues raised by its peculiar manner of construction. Prompted by the painting's celebration of distortion, for example, Ashbery traces out a set of reactions that run from a defence of form (it is the only 'instrument' we have), to a lament for what it dismisses ('the vacuum of a dream'), to a realization that such a lament is perhaps characteristic of all art:

> We notice the hole they [dreams] left. Now their importance
> If not their meaning is plain. They were to nourish

A dream which includes them all, as they are
Finally reversed in the accumulating mirror.
They seemed strange because we couldn't actually see them.
And we realize this only at a point where they lapse
Like a wave breaking on a rock, giving up
Its shape in a gesture which expresses that shape.

(p. 73)

Art, in this view, in the break-up of its expressive gestures, signals the loss of power, not the promise of accessibility – testifying, nevertheless, to the importance of what has been left behind. The poem, however, is not content with this bittersweet acknowledgement. Returning to the issue of medium, Ashbery realizes that it is the very distance of the painting from his world that has prompted the lazy exfoliation from that first encounter. He realizes, moreover, that such a response is a kind of life:

Since it is a metaphor
Made to include us, we are part of it and
Can live in it as in fact we have done,
Only leaving our minds bare for questioning
We now see will not take place at random
But in an orderly way that means to menace
Nobody – the normal way things are done,
Like the concentric growing up of days
Around a life: correctly, if you think about it.

(p. 76)

Here is the final twist: the orderly, concentric spelling-out of the self that has happened here is 'normal' – normal in the sense that it is how we live our lives, go about the business of shaping and communicating ourselves. That is what Ashbery's slippery language displays: not the self, but a playful struggle with medium that helps us engage and re-experience other equally limited forms of human activity:

Is there anything
To be serious about beyond this otherness
That gets included in the most ordinary
Forms of daily activity, changing everything
Slightly and profoundly, and tearing the matter
Of creation, any creation, not just artistic creation
Out of our hands, to install it on some monstrous, near
Peak, too close to ignore, too far
For one to intervene? This otherness, this
'Not-being-us' is all there is to look at
In the mirror, though no one can say
How it came to be this way.

(pp. 80–1)

345

Turning finally to the work of a younger poet, Jorie Graham, and her struggle to enter and confront what she calls 'the long sleep of resemblance', we find ourselves circling back to some of Bishop's strategies. 'To a Friend Going Blind' (1983) offers a clear defence not only of Graham's approach to this problem but of those of the other poets we have examined here as well. Addressing a friend whose approaching blindness is a version of our language-bound separation from the world, Graham describes a detour around 'the entire inner perimeter' of a walled, medieval town taken because she 'couldn't find the shortcut through' to the world beyond its walls, flickering here and there through its cracks. Next, still not directly engaging the issue of blindness, she slides to an account of another friend's instructions in dressmaking:

> Saturdays we buy the cloth.
> She takes it in her hands
> like a good idea, feeling
> for texture, grain, the built-in
> limits.
>
> (1983, p. 27)

Such a loving acknowledgement is, of course, the crucial strategy shared by our poets: whether it is Roethke and Duncan tracing out and combining detours, Bishop erasing her descriptions, or Ashbery spinning out language's inevitable sense of 'not-being-us'. But what does that have to do with Graham's friend? Circling around to that approaching loss of sight, Graham links her wandering within confines and her work with the cloth, offering this defence of accepting limits: 'I shut my eyes and felt my way / along the stone. . . . / the walls are beautiful. They block the view. / And it feels rich to be / inside their grasp' (p. 27). Showing and knowing those limits, at ease with their necessary sense of separation, Graham, much like Bishop, comes to an over-powering experience of the world breaking through gaps in the stone. Which is to say that taking on the condition of blindness, like acknowledging the limits of description or of memory, not only forces us to put aside the desire to master the world, but also permits us to run our hands along the cracks and gaps explosively patterning our attempts at order. As all of these poets would agree, there is never a shortcut through.

Much of Graham's energy in her recent work, much of the energy of recent American poetry in general, has been put into finding ways of catching herself in such moments of blindness, then holding herself in and stroking that condition until its gaps reveal themselves. This makes for a peculiar and quite remarkable use of language. So, for example, luxuriating in a childhood memory of ironing with a maid ('Patience'), Graham catches herself over-emphasizing the neatness of that buried scene, then forces herself to acknowl-edge the inevitable inaccuracy of such tidy structures: 'The fragile stem / from here / to there is tragedy, I know, / the path we / feed it by until it cracks / open at last' (p. 44). Accepting the blindness of the blossom held in her memory, realizing its tragic distance from actual events, she goes on to 'feed' that stem with attention and puzzlement until it 'cracks' and gives her a sidelong glimpse of the scene's actual horror. My point here is that Graham has created a situation in which memory's actual status as detour surprises her and can then be exploited. So, too, her own quite ready use of 'characters and the knife / of a plot' to make sense of a backyard scene ('The Age of Reason') or her admiration for a painter's light-drenched love of surfaces ('Two Paintings by Gustav Klimt') are eventually acknowledged as blinded, then shattered into a new sort of response to the world.

All of these poets, then, would agree with Graham when she says 'I need to feel the places where the language fails, as much as one can' (1984, p. 409). Neither retreating from that inevitable failure into an ambitionless parlour activity nor ignoring it and walking blithely out on the thinnest of planks, these American poets (and others) have accepted that full tension, even courted it – exploring a series of ways both to signal that limitation and masterfully to spin out the riches that follow.

FURTHER READING

Altieri, Charles (1984) *Self and Sensibility in Contemporary American Poetry*, Cambridge University Press, Cambridge

Breslin, James E. B. (1983) *From Modern to Contemporary: American Poetry, 1945–1965*, University of Chicago Press, Chicago

Gardner, Thomas (1989) *Discovering Ourselves in Whitman: The Contemporary American Long Poem*, University of Illinois Press, Urbana

Hass, Robert (1984) *Twentieth Century Pleasures: Prose on Poetry*, Ecco, New York

Lazer, Hank (ed.) (1987) *What Is a Poet?*, University of Alabama Press, Tuscaloosa

Nelson, Cary (1981) *Our Last First Poets: Vision and History in Contemporary American Poetry*, University of Illinois Press, Urbana

Perloff, Marjorie (1985) *The Dance of the Intellect: Studies in Poetry of the Pound Tradition*, Cambridge University Press, Cambridge

Vendler, Helen (1980) *Part of Nature, Part of Us: Modern American Poets*, Harvard University Press, Cambridge

——(1988) *The Music of What Happens*, Harvard University Press, Cambridge

Von Hallberg, Robert (1985) *American Poetry and Culture, 1945–80*, Harvard University Press, Cambridge

ADDITIONAL WORKS CITED

Ashbery, John (1972) *Three Poems*, Viking, New York

——(1975) *Self-Portrait in a Convex Mirror*, Viking, New York

Bishop, Elizabeth (1983) *The Complete Poems 1927–1979*, Farrar, Straus, Giroux, New York

Duncan, Robert (1968a) 'The H. D. Book: Part I, Chapter 6', *Caterpillar*, 2, 125–54

——(1968b) *Bending the Bow*, New Directions, New York

——(1985) *Fictive Certainties*, New Directions, New York

Eliot, T. S. (1963) *Collected Poems 1909–1962*, Harcourt, New York

Graham, Jorie (1983) *Erosion*, Princeton University Press, Princeton

——(1984) 'Some Notes on Silence'. In Philip Dow (ed.), *19 New American Poets of the Golden Gate*, Harcourt, New York, pp. 409–15

Roethke, Theodore (1966) *Collected Poems*, Doubleday, Garden City

Vendler, Helen (ed.) (1985) *The Harvard Book of Contemporary American Poetry*, Harvard University Press, Cambridge

IV. DRAMA

24

STAGECRAFT

LESLIE DU S. READ

'Perfection in the theatre consists of imitating an action so exactly that the spectator, for whom the illusion of reality is never interrupted, imagines that he is present at the action itself' (Diderot, ed. 1978, p. 163). When Diderot wrote this, in the mid-eighteenth century, he was both summarizing a trend in western stagecraft and heralding its future dominance; for, during the following century, theatrical literalism began to establish an orthodoxy throughout Europe which is still prevalent in spite of the fact that much of twentieth-century theory and practice runs counter to it. It is important when considering stagecraft to recognize that this literalism is only one of a number of possibilities. To represent actions faithfully, to recreate them 'exactly' as they appear to happen, is (in terms of the history of world theatre) a specific and recent craft. It is not some inherent feature of drama.

Literalism in theatre developed out of a tradition of pictorial illusion stemming from the work of Peruzzi, Serlio and others (Kernodle, 1944; Hewitt, 1958). This tradition had its roots in Renaissance painting, in notions of perspective and frame. 'First of all, on the surface on which I am going to paint, I draw a rectangle of whatever size I want, which I regard as an open window through which the subject to be painted is to be seen' (Alberti, [1435] 1972, p. 55). An illusion of reality is organized with reference to this 'window' and, through the employment of perspective, is made present *behind* it. Inigo Jones introduced elements of this scenography to England, and his design for the Royal Cockpit in 1630 (Wickham, 1972, pp. 117–22, plates XX and XXI) is a precursor of the proscenium arch. However, it was only after the interregnum had broken the continuity of indigenous staging methods that the English theatre adopted this form of stagecraft. At first, only the scenic world was governed by a frame and a centre of projection, and the crafting of the play occurred in front of this world in a space common to both actors and audience. Players made their entrances and exits through permanent proscenium doors and moved into the playhouse to act *in front of* the frame through which the changeable scenery was to be viewed (Southern, 1952). In time, however, economic and social pressures ensured that performers were estranged from this space they shared with the audience and increasingly became part of the pictorial illusion. That this was not always comfortable is clear in the complaint attributed to the eighteenth-century actor William Dowton: 'Don't tell me of frames and pictures. If I can't be heard by the audience in the frame, I'll walk out of it' (Lawrence, 1912, p. 184). This shift into a world organized round a single viewpoint can be clearly traced in the design of London playhouses (Leacroft, 1973), in alterations which imposed both on the stage action and on the relation between actors and audience. By 1880 the Haymarket theatre had a gilded frame behind which *all* was pictorial illusion, for there was not even a vestigial stage in front of this 'open window'. Advances in technology combined with this shift to establish the orthodoxy of literalism. Gas enabled auditorium lights to be dimmed, but this was saved for special effects, used only to intensify a moment of illusion:

> Storm – a mist begins to arise, through which VANDERDECKEN is seen crossing the sea in an open boat with LESTELLE, from R. U. E. – the storm rages violently – the boat is dashed about upon the waves – it sinks with VANDERDECKEN and LESTELLE – a peal of thunder – the Phantom Ship appears (a la phantasmagorie) – the stage and audience part of the theatre in total darkness.
>
> (Fitzball, 1826, p. 36)

It was Irving, at the Lyceum in the 1880s, who began consistently to darken the auditorium throughout a performance. With the advent of electricity, this was a practice readily followed in theatre after theatre. Now a performer could seem to be unaware of either audience or auditorium, could seem to *be* where the imagined action *was*, and each individual spectator, encouraged by the darkness, could 'forget' the immediate surroundings and become a passive unseen presence at the place and time of the action itself.

In proscenium stagecraft the player works in a separate acoustic space from that of the spectator. The auditorium is one room and the stage is another. Dowton's complaint recognized the radical nature of this change. In place of an immediate encounter is a mediated encounter. This disturbed Edward Gordon Craig: 'the present theatre aims at "effectiveness" at all costs . . . it prefers what is called the fake to the genuine. The fake "tells"; the genuine falls short of theatrical "effect" ' (1921, p. 37). Of importance to this form of encounter is the stage curtain, framing time as the proscenium arch frames space. It enables playwrights to shape the action without having to concern themselves all the time with the physical exits and entrances of performers. It can govern the rhythm of words and movements as the picture-frame can govern the spatial organization of groups and figures. It can manipulate response by allowing a climax or anti-climax to be underlined, an attitude or statement to be highlighted. The convention of tableau and curtain line is used, for example, with wit and cunning by Harold Pinter at the end of Act 1 and the beginning of Act 2 of *The Caretaker* (1960). In contemporary practice, the blackout has in large measure replaced the curtain. It is important to remember, though, that lighting can serve many forms of stagecraft, but a curtain which can hide and reveal all the stage action demands an enclosed space separate from the audience. Such a curtain suggests that some things must be seen while others must be withheld. It creates mystery. That is why a half-height curtain became such a critical element in Brecht's practice. It was a reminder of what needed to be challenged, constantly. Acceptance of the 'magic' or the 'naturalness' of a sequence of events is not the prerogative of proscenium staging, but it is – without doubt – best handled by this form. (Film, after all, is heir to this picture-frame tradition.) All the elements that compose a performance on an enclosed stage can be arranged according to a hierarchy established by the single viewpoint. This encouraged Craig, for in this authority he saw a place for his 'ideal stage-manager' and a possibility of 'the reform of the Art of the Theatre' (1911, p. 177). There is no doubt that the role of the director has been a major force in the twentieth-century theatre. However, Craig's enthusiasm for a figure distinct from both playwright and actor is not without its problems in regard to stagecraft. As the proscenium arch divides actors from audience, so the authority of this figure can divide dramatists from actors. As John Arden (1977) has argued it is a matter of play-writers or playwrights. Appia is uncompromising:

> When anyone says 'Dramatist' he says 'Stage-director' in the same breath; it is a sacrilege to specialize the two activities. We may set up as a rule, then, that if the dramatist does not insist on controlling both, he will be incapable of controlling either – since it is from their mutual correlation that *living* art must be born.
>
> ([1921] 1960, p. 44)

Appia and Craig were important influences in the New Movement which was active in the theatre during the early decades of this century. Many aspects of the stagecraft advocated then are now taken for granted: the use of stage lighting as a dramatic motif, of illumination and planes to suggest locations, of steps and levels to create a constant setting for a variety of scenes (subtly transformed by light, colour and use), an emphasis on sculptural rather than pictorial form with a movement out of the picture-frame and towards the audience, a rediscovery of platform staging, of expository and rhetorical modes, of presentational rather than representational styles. What united many of the innovators was a rejection of proscenium stagecraft:

> Over some fifteen years a growing number of minds have been more or less actively seeking a way towards a new type of theater. They have been abusing

the picture-frame stage, stamping on the footlights, pulling out the front of the apron, pushing the actors into the loges, down the orchestra pit, onto the prompter's box, out upon the runways or up the aisles. They have even gone clear out of the playhouse and into circuses, open air theaters, and public parks. All to set up a new and mutual relationship between the actor and the audience.

(Macgowan and Jones, 1922, p. 157)

Appia shared this desire for an open relationship (in his work with Dalcroze he was concerned with architectural unity between stage and auditorium), but he was also aware of the tenacity of the familiar:

Our theatrical habits make it very difficult to imagine what freedom in staging could mean, and to visualize a new handling of the elements of production. We cannot conceive of a theatre, it seems, except in terms of the present-day stage – a limited space filled with cut-out paintings, in the midst of which actors pace up and down separated from us by a clear-cut line of demarcation.

([1921] 1960, p. 49)

If the crossing of this boundary was to be more than an 'effective' trick, a thorough appraisal of stagecraft was necessary. Some fundamental elements were clear – time, space and the human body. 'In space, units of time are expressed by a succession of forms, hence by movement. In time, space is expressed by a succession of words and sounds, that is to say by varying time-durations prescribing the extent of the movement' (Appia, [1921] 1960, pp. 7–8). For Craig, the corporeal was a problem; the actor's sensations, emotions, ego and bodily functions got in the way of Art; hence his concept of an 'Über-Marionette' (1911, pp. 54–94). For Appia, however, human existence was paramount: 'We must maintain the living and plastic body as our point of departure' ([1921] 1960, p. 9). The 'new and mutual relationship' had to spring from the living performance – 'the text gives over to the actor the entire responsibility for its realization in space' (p. 17) – *not* from some ideal manipulator:

Their desire to be found *alone* in front of the stage, like the painter in his workshop, has prevailed! Such a choice is perhaps excusable. But how can we imagine a living corporeal humanity content in the long run with a dramatic art that is mechanized? Would that not oblige us to be still more passive in the theatre than we already are?

(pp. 32–3)

The art, Appia maintained, lay in a *living* discipline: 'In order to proportion Space, our body needs Time! The time-duration of our movements, consequently, has determined their extent in space. Our life creates space and time, one through the other' (pp. 53–4). Though the discipline might at times be solitary the art could never be: '*Living* art implies a Collaboration. *Living* art is social; it is, unconditionally, the social art' (p. 59).

The path Appia charted in theory has been mirrored in practice a number of times this century. Each practice has been, of course, individual and distinct but the trajectories have been similar. The journey made by Grotowski's Teatr-Laboratorium from flexible staging through 'poor theatre' to para-theatrical experiments and a 'theatre of sources' is a recent and influential example (Kumiega, 1987). The Living Theatre's odyssey is perhaps the most challenging (Biner, 1972). Aspects of these journeys have at times been lifted out of context, assimilated into the familiar, and labelled. The appropriation of Brook's careful depiction of a Holy Theatre in *The Empty Space* (1968) and its transformation into a slogan and a fashion is an unfortunate example. What these explorations in stagecraft share is a sense of quest, a continual striving for 'freedom in staging', and an affirmation of 'the living body'.

In the modern theatre, this work is an extreme alternative to proscenium stagecraft. Between these extremes a range of staging methods have been advocated, explored and partially assimilated during this century. What most of these methods share is a preference for an open rather than an enclosed form of theatre. However, continued use of proscenium buildings, modified in one way or another, has often led to a compromise, an admixture of open and enclosed stagecraft. Open theatre forms 'can be characterized by their having the acting area and the auditorium in the same achitectural volume' (Joseph, 1968, p. 9). The major forms are centre stages, thrust stages, and end stages. The centre stage is the most radical (as Richard Southern has stressed, it is a primary configuration, 1962, p. 57). It requires distinct performance techniques:

> This is because whichever way the actor turns he has as many people behind him as in front of him; and he must project his performance in every direction. Let us contrast this with acting on all other forms of stage, whether open or enclosed, where a mean line can be imagined between the extreme edges of the audience, and the actor may legitimately project mainly along this line; I call it linear projection as opposed to the organic projection which is demanded by the centre stage and the transverse stage.
>
> (Joseph, 1968, p. 28)

Central staging, like transverse staging (where the audience is separated by the acting area into two parts) is not essentially a scenic form. The crafting of most of Alan Ayckbourn's plays, written initially for production in a theatre-in-the-round at Scarborough, is best understood with this in mind. Unlike the scenic mechanics of much nineteenth-century farce, which call for distance, door-frames and cupboards, his cruel humour thrives on the proximity of the entrances and exits of a hectic consumerist arena where furnishings, properties and fashions are under close scrutiny from all sides, and some embarrassing public intimacy seems the order of the day. Central stages are rarely raised, unlike the other open acting areas which usually are.

A thrust stage has the audience on three sides. Although scenery is possible, its strengths lie in motion, in gestures, in words. The rediscovery of the distinctive stagecraft which this form demands has had a major influence on European theatre, and particularly on English theatre, over the last thirty years. In spite of the fact that there are few genuine examples of a thrust stage in Britain, its techniques have been applied to extended apron stages in modified proscenium buildings to great effect, combining with the lessons learnt from Symbolism and Expressionism to create a modern form of emblematic staging. This fragmenting of scenic illusion has allowed for the flow of stage action from one scene into the next. Much of the impetus for this springs, of course, from the fact that the thrust stage is the form Shakespeare and his contemporaries crafted. Since the time of William Poel's productions with the Elizabethan Stage Society (Speaight, 1954) knowledge of this platform stage and appreciation of the vigour and flexibility of its presentational style has deepened.

End stages are the closest in form to proscenium arch theatres. Communication between actor and audience is frontal, with a single viewpoint, but there is no picture-frame and both parties share the same four walls and the same acoustic space. It is a configuration which encouraged the most persistent innovations in stagecraft during the first years of this century, innovations which have been applied and developed consistently ever since. Particularly influential was the work of Jacques Copeau. His insistence on a naked stage, on a concrete functional environment for performer and spectator, re-established a tradition of presentational performance for the twentieth-century theatre. 'Actors of *parts* are sustained by a dramatic illusion of which they are part; performers of *plays* by a nothing-to-hide, open contract with the spectator' (Rudlin, 1986, p. 60). Of particular interest and influence was his use of a wooden platform-stage placed on the end stage of the Vieux-Colombier (Rudlin, 1986, plate 18):

> The actors played both on the platform and around it. The younger actors could leap on to the platform with exuberant wildness, while the older characters were obliged to climb the steps laboriously.
> The platform, with its uneven wooden surface, was hollow, and therefore resonant and springy. This intensified, in a pleasant manner, the sounds made on it, either by the stamping, jumping feet of the younger characters or by the slow stomping of their elders accompanied by the tapping of walking-sticks. In the swiftly moving scenes of pursuit, the actors, leaping from the hard coldness of the cement floor up onto the warm, resounding wooden surface and back down again, created a kind of by-play of sound.
>
> (Saint-Denis, 1982, p. 29)

An issue which is raised by this quotation is the ubiquity of non-verbal elements in stagecraft. It is an issue which distinguishes playwright from play-writer. The crafting of these elements which engage the play between actors and audience is a proper concern of a playwright. The relation of the auditorium to the acting area is primary in understanding how they may best be shaped, although it is usual for the architectural features of a building to be a given circumstance. Not everyone has the opportunity, as did Shakespeare, of having a hand in the dismantling of a theatre and its refashioning for performance. The achievements of the decade from 1599 stem in part from this fact. 'For the first time in England, and perhaps anywhere in the world, a theatre was to be built on land leased by the actors, paid for by the actors and designed by the actors' (Thomson, 1983, p. 18). A more usual experience was Synge's in crafting and re-crafting *The Playboy of the Western World* (1907) for the minuscule dimensions of Dublin's Abbey stage. Not all such experiences are happy ones. Inappropriate or obsolete means of production have often delayed satisfactory realization of a playwright's vision: Ibsen's *Peer Gynt* (1867) and Strindberg's *A Dream Play* (1901) are well-known examples. If playwrights cannot see, revise, and share with a theatre public their vision, then their grasp of the concrete nature of their social art is diminished. The twentieth-century theatre is distinguished by a deepening understanding of this fact, but casualties abound. A sad example is that of Sean O'Casey, where a major body of work still awaits serious practical recognition: 'O'Casey's plays as social documents have not yet become out-of-date: as poetic creations they have not even begun to be realized' (Arden and D'Arcy, 1988, p. 42). This reluctance to realize is due in part to politics and in part to preconceptions concerning the use of allegory and the mingling of representational and non-representational styles. As with the late plays of Tennessee Williams, it is easy to feel superior, but this ease clings to the familiar and avoids the challenge of what is both a unique stagecraft and a feasible one. 'The theatre has changed a lot since his heyday – we have had the example of Brecht . . . to show us that the kind of emblematic precision that O'Casey required can in fact be attained on a stage' (Arden and D'Arcy, 1988, p. 42). Unfamiliar modes of stagecraft undermine habits, conventions and ideologies. If they cannot be ignored, they must be turned into a nine-day-wonder, a fashion soon to be dropped and forgotten.

Two major plays have, in the second half of this century, openly attacked prevailing ideologies through the structure and substance of their staging methods. I am thinking of Jean Genet's *The Screens* (1961) and *The Non-Stop Connolly Show* (1975) by Margaretta D'Arcy and John Arden. They are constructed round a freer actor/audience relationship than that available in most conventional theatre buildings. Genet imagined his play in the open air: 'One ought to be able to enter and leave during the performance without bothering anyone. And remain standing too, and even walk up to the stage if one feels like it, the way one approaches a painting, or steps back away from it' ([1966] 1969, p. 27). A similar freedom is implicit in D'Arcy's and Arden's work where 'the continuous struggle' is 'to be shown as one complete connected sequence' which would last twenty-four hours and 'ideally a number of stages should be used, arranged around the audience, and connected perhaps with gangways at various levels' (D'Acy and Arden, 1977, p. vi). The configuration is reminiscent of Artaud's 'single site, without partition or barrier of any kind, which will become the theatre of the action' ([1938] 1958, p. 96). Both plays spurn a single perspective for their public. Like Brecht before them, they oppose a theatre which 'shows the structure of society (represented on the stage) as incapable of being influenced by society (in the auditorium)' (Willett, 1964, p. 189). Both texts act on the perception that the spatial arrangements of a performance reflect social values and assumptions, and that these arrangements impinge on a sense of ourselves and of others, on our perception of the structures of power. In his *Letters to Roger Blin*, Genet echoes a motif, central to his play, when he considers the Italian-style theatre and the social order of its tiers and galleries (the sardonic puns are lost in translation; *poulaillers* means both 'the gods' and a 'hen roost'):

> I feel it dying together with the society which came to see itself mirrored on-stage. This fulfillment corresponded to a fundamental immorality: for the poultry of the top galleries, the 'house' – dress circle, orchestra, boxes – was an initial spectacle, which in essence formed a screen – or a prism – which their gaze had to pass through before perceiving the spectacle on-stage. The top galleries saw and heard, as it were, through the screen made up of the privileged public of the orchestra and box seats.
>
> ([1966] 1969, p. 25)

In recent years environmental and promenade productions have been mounted with increasing confidence (*1789* in 1970, *The Speakers* in 1974, *The Mysteries* in 1985 are outstanding examples), but the radical dramaturgy of *The Screens* and *The Non-Stop Connolly Show* is still a challenge and an inspiration. Each has its own particular and finely-wrought stagecraft, aiming at jolting sensibilities and unacknowleged habits of thought, notating the non-verbal resources of a heightened form with precision.

Antonin Artaud and Bertolt Brecht have been mentioned. No essay concerned with the state of stagecraft as this century draws to its close can safely ignore their perceptions, practice and influence. Artaud's path parallels Appia's thoughts on a *living* art, but – painfully – he rarely had the opportunity to 'collaborate', though his perceptions have proved a major stimulus to collaboration in theatre-making throughout the West since the 1950s. His rigorous journey was made in a public solitude traced by his writings (which at present fill twenty-four volumes in the Gallimard edition). His practice was rooted in acting (his portrayal of Brother Massieu in Carl Dreyer's film *La Passion de Jeanne d'Arc*, 1927, is a haunting record of this). His emphasis was on a 'creative' not an 'interpretative' actor, on the corporeal inscription of performance. Against the repetition of theatre he set the actuality of theatre 'where a gesture, once made, can never be made the same way twice' (Artaud, [1938]

1958, p. 75). In Derrida's words: 'This is indeed how things appear: theatrical representation is finite, and leaves behind it, behind its actual presence, no trace, no object to carry off. It is neither a book nor a work, but an energy, and in this sense it is the only art of life' ([1967] 1978, p. 247). Artaud stressed immediacy in the physical relationship of the spectator to the action, but he was not advocating the immediacy of everyday life; he felt too keenly that habits and repetitions made the present often less 'alive' than the artifice of theatre. The notion of the 'double' had its repetitions in the traces of his journey. In Artaud's works, as Derrida argued, 'Whatever can be said of the body can be said of the theatre' (p. 232). With examples from non-Western stagecraft before him, he was reaching towards a drama that

> will not be written out and fixed a priori, but will be put on the stage, created on the stage, in correlation with the requirements of attitudes, signs, movements and objects. But the whole method of feeling one's way objectively among one's materials, in which Speech will appear as a necessity... all these gropings, researches, and shocks will culminate nevertheless in a work *written down*, fixed in its least details, and recorded by new means of notation. The composition, the creation, instead of being made in the brain of an author, will be made in nature itself, in real space, and the final result will be as strict and calculated as that of any written work whatsoever, with an immense objective richness as well.
>
> (Artaud, [1938] 1958, pp. 111–12)

Interest in the staging traditions of other cultures has grown throughout the century. Yeats, Claudel, Artaud, Brecht, Brook and Grotowski have been important figures in this development. Artaud's contribution is that his testimony helped to turn *practical* attention to the techniques of a disciplined control of the sensory elements of stagecraft.

Brecht's theories on stagecraft are rich, fascinating and contradictory. They constitute a major collection of criticism, but it is his practice as a playwright and as a director that matters. Not that one can disregard the theories, for they were a constant part of his work, the 'seeing' which accompanied his 'doing' as a man of the theatre. They *are* important, but their importance lies in their outcome – in the plays and in the performances. In one sense, Brecht wanted to re-establish theory in the theatre (in the theatre, *not* in private study); theory as a 'looking at', ' a contemplation', 'a speculation'. This was the reason – as Walter Benjamin saw – for the discontinuities in epic theatre:

> Its basic form is that of the forceful impact on one another of separate, distinct situations in the play. The songs, the captions included in the stage decor, the gestural conventions of the actors, serve to separate each situation. Thus distances are created everywhere which are on the whole, detrimental to illusion among the audience. These distances are meant to make the audience adopt a critical attitude, to make it think.
>
> (Benjamin, [1938] 1977, p. 38)

Clarity in the use of space and time helps to differentiate the concrete from the causal. Concreteness in staging, especially in stage properties, was dear to Brecht. There was no pretence about the objects chosen to be used, as there was no pretence about the audience being anywhere else but in a theatre: if the 'doing' wasn't honest how could the 'seeing' be honest? *Verfremdungseffekte* served as brakes both for actor and for audience so that the ease with which we slip into 'not seeing' might be checked. 'Before familiarity can be excited into awareness, the familiar must be stripped of its inconspicuousness' (Needle and Thomson, 1981, p. 133). What we most accept as 'natural' we do not see, and when we identify with the sufferings of an individual we cannot 'see' their social operation. 'It is scarcely possible to conceive of the laws of motion if one looks at them from a tennis ball's point of view' (Brecht, in Willett, 1964, p. 275). Brecht's ideological precision in stagecraft is evident in many aspects of present-day production, and in the work of contemporary playwrights as diverse as Bond, Brenton, Hare and Barker. A major contribution is his realization of *gestic* narrative. For Brecht, there was no place for scenic background, the *stage* must narrate. 'Everything hangs on the "story"; it is the heart of the theatrical performance. For it is what happens *between* people that provides them with all the material that they can discuss, criticize, alter' (Brecht, in Willett, 1964, p. 200).

All stagecraft handles actions *done* from the point or points of view of actions *seen*. This relationship is fundamental:

> A performance has to become a meeting, a dynamic relationship between one group that has received special preparation and another group, the audience, that has not been prepared. Theatre only exists at the precise moment when these two worlds – that of the actors and that of the audience – meet: a society in miniature . . . .
>
> (Brook, 1988, p. 236)

In Britain, the last three decades have witnessed shifting attitudes to the way this 'meeting' should be organized. During the sixties, existing theatres were adapted and 'new forms' were constructed to allow for an 'open' and sizeable forum. In the seventies, the tendency to move outside existing structures and use 'other' spaces increased, and there was an emphasis on smaller but more frequent gatherings: small rooms, a small audience and a small cast, but a direct relationship. The history of the Portable Theatre company is an example of this movement and its value to new playwrights. Economic changes in the eighties have glossed the politics of the small-cast play, and some playwrights are now consciously envisioning new relationships in size and number. As I write this essay, I am pondering Howard Barker's *The Bite of the Night* (1988) where techniques learnt from small open spaces are shaped by rhythms which echo the size, spectacle and sensationalism of the nineteenth-century pictorial tradition. However, these rhythms are distorted, fragmented into a new and powerful staging method, reflecting film and video techniques, which defines a unique theatrical relationship. Stagecraft, like a performance, moves on.

FURTHER READING

Appia, Adolphe (1960) *The Work of Living Art*, translated by H. D. Albright, University of Miami Press, Florida [first published 1921]

Arden, John (1977) *To Present the Pretence*, Methuen, London

Artaud, Antonin (1958) *The Theater and its Double*, translated by M. C. Richards, Grove Press, New York [first published 1938]

Brook, Peter (1988) *The Shifting Point*, Methuen, London

Craig, Edward Gordon (1911) *On the Art of the Theatre*, Heinemann, London

——(1921) *The Theatre Advancing*, Constable, London

Genet, Jean (1969) *Letters to Roger Blin*, translated by R. Seaver, Grove Press, New York [first published 1966]

Gorelik, Mordecai (1947) *New Theatres for Old*, Dobson, London

Joseph, Stephen (1968) *New Theatre Forms*, Pitman, London

Leacroft, Richard (1973) *The Development of the English Playhouse*, Methuen, London

Willett, John (1964) *Brecht on Theatre*, Methuen, London

ADDITIONAL WORKS CITED

Alberti, Leon Battista (1972) *De Pictura*, translated by C. Grayson, Phaidon, London [first published 1435]

Arden, John and D'Arcy, Margaretta (1988) *Awkward Corners*, Methuen, London

Benjamin, Walter (1977) *Understanding Brecht*, translated by Anne Bostock, New Left Books, London [first published 1938]

Biner, Pierre (1972) *The Living Theatre*, translated by R. Meister, Avon Books, New York [first published 1970]

Brook, Peter (1968) *The Empty Space*, MacGibbon & Kee, London

D'Arcy, Margaretta and Arden, John (1977) *The Non-Stop Connolly Show*, Pluto Press, London

Derrida, Jacques (1978) *Writing and Difference*, translated by A. Bass, Routledge & Kegan Paul, London [first published 1967]

Diderot, Denis (1978) 'Les Bijoux indiscrets'. In Denis Diderot, *Oeuvres Complètes*, edited by Jean Macary, Aram Vartanian and Jean-Louis Leutrat, vol. 3, Hermann, Paris [first published 1748]

Fitzball, Edward (1826) *The Flying Dutchman*, Lacy, London

Hewitt, Barnard (1958) *The Renaissance Stage*, University of Miami Press, Florida

Kernodle, George R. (1944) *From Art to Theatre*, University of Chicago Press, Chicago

Kumiega, Jennifer (1987) *The Theatre of Grotowski*, Methuen, London

Lawrence, W. J. (1912) *The Elizabethan Playhouse and Other Studies*, Shakespeare Head Press, Stratford-upon-Avon

Macgowan, Kenneth and Jones, Robert Edmond (1922) *Continental Stagecraft*, Harcourt Brace, New York

Needle, Jan and Thomson, Peter (1981) *Brecht*, Basil Blackwell, Oxford
Rudlin, John (1986) *Jacques Copeau*, Cambridge University Press, Cambridge
Saint-Denis, Michel (1982) *Training for the Theatre*, Theatre Art Books, New York
Southern, Richard (1952) *Changeable Scenery*, Faber & Faber, London
——(1962) *The Seven Ages of the Theatre*, Faber & Faber, London
Speaight, Robert (1954) *William Poel and the Elizabethan Revival*, Heinemann, London
Thomson, Peter (1983) *Shakespeare's Theatre*, Routledge & Kegan Paul, London
Wickham, Glynne (1972) *Early English Stages: Volume Two, Part II*, Routledge & Kegan
    Paul, London

25

TRAGEDY

KENNETH MUIR

THE DIFFICULTY OF DEFINITION

In the British Academy Shakespeare Lecture for 1958 I advanced the heretical notion that there was no such thing as Shakespearian Tragedy: there were only Shakespearian tragedies. A few weeks later a distinguished classical scholar was reported to have said that there was no such thing as 'Greek Tragedy': there were only Greek tragedies. We were both arguing that the differences between plays were more significant than the resemblances, obvious though these were: and if the differences even between the plays of a single dramatist can be as great as those which separate Racine's *Bérénice* from *Phèdre*, it follows that when the whole range of tragedy is considered, from Aeschylus to Anouilh, an overall definition would seem to be impossible. A definition adequate for a single play of Sophocles would seem irrelevant to Ibsen's *Rosmersholm*. There is an additional danger: a definition may be used to disparage a masterpiece to which it does not apply. Shakespeare was so used by Stendhal when he wished to criticize Racine, and Voltaire spoke of *Hamlet* as the work of a drunken savage because it was unlike French classical tragedy.

There is another point to be borne in mind. When Aristotle in his *Poetics* considered the tragedies he knew, he was not laying down rules but merely analysing the qualities and defects of the plays under discussion. He concluded that although the action of some tragedies could proceed from woe to happiness, the more effective tragedies went in a reverse direction (Aristotle, trans. 1965, p. 42). *Alcestis*, in which the heroine agrees to die in place of her selfish husband and is brought back from the grave by Heracles, or *Iphigenia in Tauris*, in which the heroine saves the life of her brother, would be regarded as tragi-comedies by most modern critics, while Aristotle would have classified *Cymbeline* and *The Tempest* as tragedies.

THE TRAGIC HERO

Aristotle believed that tragic heroes should be neither absolutely evil nor absolutely good. Applying this to Shakespeare's plays we should rejoice in the destruction of a villain, such as Richard III, but we are able to sympathize with a character who commits as many murders, such as Macbeth, because even at the end of the play we feel that he is not irredeemably evil. Aristotle thought that audiences would be disgusted by the downfall of a perfectly good man. But audiences are not disgusted by *Saint Joan* or *Murder in the Cathedral*, perhaps because both protagonists could have saved themselves by the sacrifice of their integrity. Aristotle concluded that the tragic hero should be good, but flawed. The tragic error (*hamartia*) is well described by Hamlet in Act 1, Scene 1 (in lines later deleted from the Folio text). It may be a bad habit, such as drunkenness, or a result of birth, or due to bad luck, that 'a man has the stamp of one defect'. Despite his virtues, Hamlet continues, this minor defect spoils his reputation and, Aristotle would add, brings about his ruin.

Because the tragic hero is like ourselves, we feel that, but for the grace of God or by the luck of the draw, we might have met with a similar disaster. We might have dithered like Hamlet, believed Iago's lies, been bullied into murdering Duncan. But although the tragic hero is like ourselves, Aristotle insisted (p. 52) that he should be a person of some eminence, whom we would normally look up to, so that his fall would be more shocking and have greater repercussions on the society in which he lives. In medieval times, a fall from high estate was the defining characteristic of tragedy:

> a certeyn storie . . .
> Of hym that stood in greet prosperitee
> And is yfallen out of heigh degree
> Into myserie, and endeth wrecchedly.
> (Chaucer, *Prologue to The Monk's Tale*, ll. 1973–8)

The same view of tragedy was expressed in Tudor times in the popular *Mirror for Magistrates*, in which many historical and legendary characters bewailed their disastrous falls. In the reign of Elizabeth I it was still usual to have eminent persons as tragic heroes – a king, a prince, a general – whose ruin affected many other people. Even Tamburlaine, a shepherd, became ruler of half the world before the end of his career; Faustus, a scholar, became famous before his downfall; and only in a few plays, such as *The Yorkshire Tragedy*, did Elizabethan dramatists choose for tragic hero a man of low degree. But with the historical and social changes of the last three hundred years kingly heroes are out of fashion. One could not imagine a tragedy about the Duke of Windsor, using Dryden's title, *All for Love*. The heroes and heroines of modern tragedies are not 'eminent' in Aristotle's sense. They are mostly middle-class. Some of them are eminent only in their integrity or in their self-realization. Eddie Carbone in Arthur Miller's *A View from the Bridge* has neither quality, but 'he allowed himself to be wholly known'.

Many people feel nevertheless that Aristotle was right to require the tragic hero to be of power and eminence. It is arguable that novelists have been more successful than dramatists in creating tragic figures of comparable majesty without the advantages of birth or position. One could instance some of Dostoevsky's heroes, or Hardy's Tess and the Mayor of Casterbridge.

Another of Aristotle's beliefs was that plot, rather than character, was the prime essential of tragedy (p. 40). Both, of course, are important. When plot is all-important and characterization minimal, we have the recipe for a detective story or a thriller: and where character is the first essential and plot of minor importance, we may get the kind of play which reads better than it acts. Yet some of the best tragedies of the past four hundred years depend more on character than on plot. Shakespeare's and Racine's tragedies all have complex and exciting plots, but it is the characters involved in the plots who make the tragedies great. Hamlet is unwillingly involved in two revenge plots, in which the avenger of one becomes the victim of the other; but it is the character of the hero which transforms a thriller into great tragedy. The tragic events of *Phèdre* are brought about by the accidents of the plot – the false tidings of her husband's death, for example – but from the beginning Phèdre is dying of her suppressed passion, and the greatness of the play depends more on her character than on her deeds.

In most Greek tragedies plot is less important than Aristotle believed. It is, indeed, centrally important in *King Oedipus*, apparently his favourite tragedy. The plot is ingenious, Oedipus being caught in a trap set by the gods – caught by the actions of well-meaning people who were trying to prevent the fulfilment of a terrible prophecy. Oedipus is doomed by the gods who are like the sadistic monsters described by the blinded Gloucester in *King Lear*:

> As flies to wanton boys are we to the gods:
> They kill us for their sport.
>
> (IV. i. 36–7)

Such is the feeling aroused by the stranglehold of the plot in *King Oedipus* that the chorus in the sequel, *Oedipus at Colonus*, concludes that since life is inescapably tragic, it is best never to be born. To which one is tempted to retort that not many men kill their fathers and fewer still marry their mothers.

THE FUNCTION OF TRAGEDY

Although Aristotle was well aware that tragedy gave pleasure, in the most discussed sentence in the *Poetics* he said that tragedy by means of pity and fear brought about the purgation (*catharsis*) of such emotions (trans. 1965,

p. 39). Milton quoted these words in his preface to *Samson Agonistes* and he added the gloss, 'to temper, and reduce them to just measure'. This modifies Aristotle's meaning, for he thought that pity and terror should be expelled.

Aristotle was replying to Plato's complaint (trans. 1955, p. 383) that poetry had an unhealthy effect because it made its readers too emotional. Aristotle retorted that tragedy had a salutary effect because it purged us of pity and fear. Now most people would agree that it is desirable to rid ourselves of fear, but as many have asked, 'Who wants to purge himself of pity?' – only scoundrels. Commentators have hopefully pretended that Aristotle was referring only to the excess of such emotions and that he was merely advocating the moderation which Greeks regarded as a desirable ideal. Perhaps he was: but it is difficult to square this interpretation with the idea of purgation.

The theatre is not a clinic or a health-farm. No one goes to watch a tragedy for therapeutic reasons, but for enjoyment. There have been many attempts to adjust Aristotle's words to common sense. But at this point it will be convenient to refer to two later attempts to discuss the function of tragedy.

Hegel's theory of tragedy ([1835] trans. 1975, *passim*) is based on a dialectical principle that a tragic conflict will lead to reconciliation and harmony, despite what happens to the protagonists. His favourite play was Sophocles' *Antigone*, in which the heroine buries her brother in defiance of Creon's edict. Antigone is duly slain and as a direct result Creon's son and wife both die. The harmony of which Hegel speaks is invisible to other readers. In the *Oresteia*, however, the chain of revenges is brought to an end and the Furies become the kindly ones. There are few Greek tragedies to which Hegel's theory can be usefully applied: and it is totally inapplicable to all the masterpieces of Shakespeare and Racine.

The other critic is A. C. Bradley, whose chapter on the substance of Shakespearian tragedy provides a valuable summary of the main characteristics of the tragedies; but he concludes with the much-quoted words:

> We remain confronted with the inexplicable fact, or the no less inexplicable appearance, of a world travailing for perfection, but bringing to birth, together with glorious good, an evil which it is able to overcome only by self-torture and self-waste.
>
> (1904, p. 39)

The glorious good, Bradley later suggests, is a character such as Cordelia. 'What happens to such a being does not matter: all that matters is what she is' (p. 325). This is all very well: but if we examine the conclusions of all Shakespeare's tragedies, we find that only in *Romeo and Juliet* does good come out of evil with the reconciliation of the warring families. Fortinbras, Hamlet's choice of successor, succeeds to the throne of Denmark: he is dreadfully 'flawed'. What follows the end of all the tragedies cannot really be described as glorious good. Edgar and Malcolm become kings and Octavius becomes sole master of the world, but what comfort can we get at the end of *Othello* or *Coriolanus*?

One is tempted to suggest that the effect, though not the function, of tragedy is to increase, not diminish our pity and terror – the compassion which is essential to the survival of humanity, and the terror that is akin to awe. We are fearful of man's vulnerability, but awestruck at his ability to endure. We feel, in Wordsworth's phrase, that we are greater than we know, more able to suffer with dignity the changes and chances of this mortal life.

THE MORAL PURPOSE

When Sir Philip Sidney wrote his *Defence of Poetry*, his standard of tragic excellence was represented by Seneca. Defending poetry from attacks on the stage he sought to show that tragedy inculcated stern moral lessons. He praises *Gorboduc* for being 'full of notable morality' and argues that tragedy makes 'kings fear to be tyrants' and 'with stirring the affects of admiration and commiseration, teacheth the uncertainty of this world' ([1595] 1966, p. 45). Years later Shakespeare revealed 'the ulcers that are covered with tissue' at the court of Claudius and made Horatio comment on the woe and wonder of the final slaughter, and perhaps Hamlet's words about 'guilty creatures sitting at a play' were suggested by an anecdote of Plutarch's quoted by Sidney.

That Shakespeare had read Sidney and quoted Seneca does not necessarily mean that he agreed with his fellow-dramatists that tragedy should be didactic. He would have smiled at Rymer's attack on *Othello* that the play makes us 'repine and grumble at Providence and the government of the world' (1693, p. 138). It is not a dramatist's business to falsify his picture of life to satisfy a particular ideology. Shakespeare, committed as he was to truth-telling, was more effectively didactic than those dramatists who set out to provide comfortable words.

Most great dramatists have assumed that what they write will instruct as well as give pleasure. Racine, defending *Phèdre* against his old teachers who regarded the stage as a school of wickedness, claimed that in his play 'the very thought of a crime is regarded with as much horror as the crime itself . . . and vice is everywhere depicted in colours which make the deformity recognized and hated' ([1677] trans. 1960, p. 177). John Dennis would have approved. He declared that 'every tragedy ought to be a very solemn lecture, inculcating a particular providence, and showing it plainly protecting the good and chastising the bad' (in Lucas, 1927, p. 37). Poetic justice had come to mean that poets ought to give a deliberately false picture of the world.

Although dramatists, if only from self-protection, defended their didactic intentions, it is surely not true that moral teaching is the main function of tragedy. We do not go to the theatre to hear sermons any more than we go to be purged. We go there to experience a pleasure which cannot be had in any other way.

THE ENJOYMENT OF TRAGEDY

At first sight it may seem strange that we enjoy a performance in which people with whom we sympathize suffer mental or physical agony; enjoy a play which demonstrates that life is inescapably tragic, that the horrors we witness are by no means exceptional, and that the gods, or the fates, are malign.

Many people, indeed, fail to get pleasure from tragedy. They go to the theatre for pleasures of a different kind – to be amused, to laugh, to be sent away happy with the lovers married, the villains foiled, and the foolish taught a salutary lesson. My neighbour at a performance of *Twelfth Night* told me how much he liked it, whereas '*Hamlet* errs on the tragic side'. During the whole history of English drama, for only a period of thirty years was tragedy widely popular. Yet tragedies continue to attract an enthusiastic minority of normal citizens.

The explanations offered to account for the enjoyment we experience are varied. The crudest is that we enjoy watching the sufferings of the hero, just as hangings used to attract crowds. There is, of course, an essential difference. Audiences know that what they are witnessing is merely the imitation of an action, that the actors will emerge unscathed. Apart from this, it is difficult to believe that audiences at performances of *King Lear* are like this at all. An alternative explanation is that audiences are masochists who identify with the hero and enjoy suffering with him. As the suffering is feigned, it is always kept within bounds and ceases with the fall of the curtain. All of us, no doubt, have traces of sadism or masochism in our make-up: but unless we are self-deluded none of us enjoys tragedy for these reasons.

John Holloway in *The Story of the Night* (1962) argued that Shakespeare's tragic heroes were scapegoats who were driven out or destroyed for the benefit of society; that the members of the audience participate in the sacrifice of the hero and feel cleansed as a result; and 'The ritual sequence emerges from, and returns into the world we know' (p. 154). Many of Shakespeare's tragedies do not conform to this pattern, as Holloway admits. (Sophocles' *King Oedipus* fits it exactly; but a theory which has only a limited application cannot explain our enjoyment of tragedy.) But, as Clifford Leech (1969, p. 58) points out, tragedy is 'a rite, a celebration of a past act'. (Greek tragedies, with their use of music and chorus and their performance at festivals are more tied to ritual than the plays of Shakespeare and Racine.) The sufferings of the dead hero belong to the past; their re-enactment by a living actor goes with a consciousness that 'after life's fitful fever he sleeps well'; and the pain is alleviated by the beauty of the poet's language. The pleasure of tragedy, as Nietzsche pointed out, is essentially aesthetic (Silk and Stern, 1981, *passim*).

The fate of most tragic heroes is exceptionally terrible. Compared with the fate of Oedipus or Lear, our own, comparatively minor, misfortunes seem bearable. Moreover we realize that Cordelia could have been saved if Edmund had spoken five minutes sooner and that when Macbeth declares that Life is 'a tale, told by an idiot, signifying nothing', he has made life meaningless by his deeds, so that our reaction is to restore meaning to human existence.

We come away from the performance of a tragedy, exhausted perhaps, but uplifted rather than purged. We feel a kind of awe and reverence for the tragic victims because they have borne so much, and relief that their suffering is over. We have appreciated, consciously or unconsciously, the way in which the events have been arranged and transmuted into a work of art and the way in which the beauty of the words can provide consolation. Above all, perhaps, although the hero is 'struggling in vain with ruthless destiny', he is not merely a victim. He is often superior to the powers that destroy him. Lear hopes that the gods will learn from man to become more just; and although Hamlet because of the situation in which he finds himself speaks of man as a quintessence of dust, he knows that, more objectively considered, man is 'noble in reason, infinite in faculties', 'how like an angel in apprehension how like a god'. He is great, and greatly vulnerable. L. C. Knights concluded (1959, p. 119) that the final impression one gets of *King Lear* is 'affirmation in spite of everything'. Kitto, comparing *Hamlet* to Greek tragedies, regarded it as essentially a 'religious' play: 'The real focus is not the Tragic Hero but the divine background' (1956, p. vii). A totally different view was expressed by I. A. Richards when he said that 'Tragedy is only possible to a mind which is for the moment agnostic or Manichean' (1924, p. 246). Obviously the impact of the tragedy will be impaired if we think of Lear and Cordelia being reunited in heaven. All depends on how we interpret the words 'for the moment', for all great poets – and that is why they are great – have thoughts beyond the reaches of their souls.

RELIGIOUS OR SECULAR

Some support for Richards's view is provided by Spanish drama of the Golden Age, when both dramatists and audience were Catholic. As they believed that the world was providentially governed, the good were rewarded and the evil punished after death. The natural genre for them was therefore tragi-comedy. This can be illustrated from some of Calderón's plays. The would-be seducer in *The Wonder-Working Magician* is converted to Christianity and shares the heroine's martyrdom. The hero of *Life's a Dream*, given a second chance, learns to control his passions. Henry VIII, in *The Schism in England*, repents of his infatuation for the devilish Anne Boleyn and ensures that Mary will succeed to the throne. Anne is executed and the villain Wolsey commits suicide. The raped victim in *The Mayor of Zalamea* becomes the bride of Christ. Even the incestuous pair in *Devotion to the Cross*, despite their numerous crimes, are miraculously saved. There are, however, some tragedies. The man who murders his wife by employing a surgeon to bleed her to death, though pardoned by the king and married off to another woman, is clearly marked for damnation.

Racine, also a Christian, wrote eleven tragedies, but only one of them, *Bajazet*, is set in the Christian era, albeit in Turkey. Eight of them are set in the Graeco-Roman world, and the last two had Old Testament themes. By this means he was able to evade any conflict between Christian beliefs and the pessimism of tragedy. There is no reason to believe that he ceased to be a Christian when he wrote about a pagan world; but it is true that his choice of material made it easier for him to be absolutely tragic. In one play, *Bérénice*, Titus renounces his love for the sake of duty, thus reversing the choice of Racine's other heroes. This comes close to a religious conversion, but Racine expresses it in secular terms.

Shakespeare's case is particularly interesting. *Richard II* is steeped in biblical phraseology and the hero repents in prison. Richard III, an avowed villain, admits on the eve of Bosworth that he is damned. Hamlet is concerned with the snares of the devil and with the operations of providence. Othello sets a high value on his baptism and believes that he has damned himself. Macbeth knows that he has given his soul to the common enemy of man. None of these plays is rendered less tragic by the Christian framework. Five of the other tragedies are set in the Roman world where other considerations apply. *King Lear* is more controversial. The source play has a Christian setting. Shakespeare altered this either because he knew that Lear lived before the birth of Christ, or because the earlier playwright had omitted the sequel in which Cordelia commits suicide in prison. Whatever the motive, the change gave him an enviable freedom. He could raise awkward questions about the operations of providence in a pagan world without being accused of heresy. He could suggest that the gods did not answer prayers and even raise doubts about their very existence. Yet Shakespeare seems to imply that the Christian ethic was valid, even without the promise of heaven or the fear of hell; and, what was more important to him as a dramatist, the tragedy was left stark and unrelieved. 'For the moment' (to use Richards's phrase) he could probe the possibilities of nihilism, even though the plays which preceded and followed *King Lear* were Christian in setting and tone.

REVERSAL, REALIZATION, SURPRISE

Aristotle mentions three characteristics of a plot which are valuable, though not essential, in tragedy (trans. 1965, p. 46). *Peripeteia* (or reversal) is when the result of an action proves to be the opposite of what was intended, as when the messenger who is summoned to prove Oedipus' innocence actually proves his guilt. Macbeth, who thinks himself safe because he cannot be harmed by a man born of woman, discovers that Macduff was delivered by Caesarian section; Othello learns that the handkerchief he thought was a proof of Desdemona's guilt was in fact a proof of her innocence; Antony's marriage to Octavia, designed to strengthen his friendship with Octavius, does the opposite; Rebecca murders Beata so that she can marry Rosmer, and finds that the deed destroys any possibility of such an outcome; and, to give a last example, Nora in *A Doll's House* acts to save her husband and his behaviour shows her that she has been living in illusions.

Anagnorisis (discovery or realization) is when a character realizes a truth for the first time. Gloucester, in the scene of his blinding, realizes that Edgar is innocent; Lear realizes that he has taken too little care of the poor naked wretches; Albany realizes that his beautiful wife is fiendish. Ibsen provides many examples of realization, some sudden and some spread over years. Mrs Alving had already seen through the hypocrisy of Manders and the profligacy of her husband; but, in the two days covered by the action of *Ghosts* she comes to realize that her son is suffering from hereditary disease, and that her marriage to a man she did not love was a prime cause of Captain Alving's profligacy.

In *Ghosts* the present is haunted by past deeds and obsolete ideas; and some of the most effective tragedies are those in which the past is gradually revealed. *Rosmersholm* contains glimpses of the household while Beata was alive, of Rosmer's conversion and of Rebecca's influence on him. In her first confession Rebecca almost implies that the murder was politically motivated. Her second confession turns it into an act of wild passion, a passion that has since been purified into selfless love. Meanwhile Kroll's revelation about her illegitimacy suggests that she has unwittingly committed incest.

Middleton has two beautiful examples of realization. In *The Changeling*, Beatrice, who has incited De Flores to murder her husband, is made to realize that she is enslaved to the murder – she is 'the deed's creature'; and in *Women Beware Women*, Isabella is informed by her aunt that her relationship with Hippolito is incestuous.

Surprise, mentioned by Aristotle, became a more important element in Renaissance theory and practice. Sidney substitutes 'admiration' for fear in the Aristotelian formula. It is the 'wonder' Horatio speaks of when Fortinbras and the English ambassadors are confronted with the corpses of the Danish royal family and of Laertes, the last survivor of the Polonius family.

VERSE AND PROSE

Verse continued as the accepted medium of tragedy during the Renaissance in England and France and throughout the seventeenth century; but the attempts of even the best poets in the next centuries were poor imitations of their great predecessors. In Germany it was different because its dramatists seemed at the beginning of a tradition, rather than at the end. In Norway Ibsen, who began as a poet, decided that verse had done great injury to the art of the theatre and he devoted himself to prose drama. He started a trend that has prevailed to the present day.

Dramatists who wrote about middle-class characters could achieve verisimilitude by remaining close to colloquial speech; but Ibsen himself did not remain strictly naturalistic, and he retained some of the resources of poetry. This is suggested by the symbolic titles of his plays – *Ghosts, A Doll's House, The Wild Duck* – in characters as fantastic as the Rat-Wife, in references to superstitions, and in occasional poetic similes, as when Rebecca compares her sudden passion for Rosmer to one of the storms that sweep the northern seas, and the later placid love to 'the silence of the bird-cliffs under the midnight sun'.

Verse tragedies continued to be written for coterie audiences, but the most successful poetic plays of the last hundred years have been written in prose, such as Synge's *Riders to the Sea* and *Deirdre of the Sorrows*. Synge made splendid use of the speech of Irish peasants, which he transformed for dramatic purposes.

The abandonment of verse is not without some advantages. It is easier in prose to imitate the give and take of ordinary conversation, and to avoid the levelling effect of verse on characterization, since few poets have varied the verse to suit the speakers. The disadvantages are equally obvious. Great poetry affects us as even the best prose cannot. We ought, as good egalitarians, to feel that Mrs Alving's tragedy is as significant as that of Phèdre. She is, after all, highly intelligent, and fully conscious in the end of the tragedy of which she is a part. Yet the play lacks the grandeur provided by the mythological background of Racine's tragedy and the poetry in which it is expressed.

CHORUS AND COMIC RELIEF

Greek tragedy evolved from the Chorus and in the plays of Aeschylus and Sophocles it took part in the action as well as mediating between the poet and the audience. In Euripides, however, the choric odes give lyrical relief after the painfulness of the tragic events.

Except for the plays of the French and English Senecan dramatists, such as Jodelle and Greville, dramatists of the sixteenth century dispensed with the chorus. Nevertheless many Elizabethan dramatists felt the need of characters who could perform one of the functions of the classical chorus. Edgar, for example, is not only a well-drawn, developing character but also, after the disappearance of the Fool, he instructs the audience on how they should react to the events and characters of *King Lear*. Enobarbus similarly guides the responses of the audience to the events of *Antony and Cleopatra*, though he himself is an active participant. In the present century the introduction of choric speaking enabled poets to experiment with the use of a fully-fledged chorus, notably by T. S. Eliot in *Murder in the Cathedral*.

Comic relief was excluded from Greek tragedy, its place being taken by the satyr plays which were performed after the tragic trilogies, and avoided altogether by writers of French classical tragedies. English dramatists on the other hand, perhaps because of a tradition going back to the mystery cycles, introduced comic scenes into their tragedies. There are comic episodes in every one of Shakespeare's tragedies, but to designate them as comic relief is often misleading. The humour of the grave-digger in *Hamlet* is concerned with man's mortality and with the grave being prepared for Ophelia; the Porter in *Macbeth* identifies himself with the Porter of Hell Gate, and the audience is impatiently awaiting the discovery of the murder; the funny scene of Cassio's drunkenness is part of Iago's devilish plot; the Fool in *King Lear* reminds us, as well as the king, of his foolish behaviour. In other plays there may be some relief from tension, as torturers break down their victims' resistance by giving them intermissions. But the main function of comic relief seems to be to remind us that the isolation of tragedy from the rest of life gives only a one-sided picture. In some plays the humour becomes the last twist of the knife as when we realize that the farce of O'Casey's Paycock augments Juno's tragedy.

THE PRESENT AND THE FUTURE

In his brilliant but sombre book *The Death of Tragedy* (1961), George Steiner offers little hope for its future. Poets look back nostalgically to the masterpieces of past ages, but classical mythology can no longer be used creatively; both Christianity and Marxism are optimistic ideologies and therefore opposed to the tragic vision; and the shared conviction that life is essentially meaningless inhibits the writing of tragedy. Although some of Steiner's points are questionable, none of the dramatists who have emerged since his book was published have written viable tragedies: it is their farces that arouse pity and terror. It seems likely that, for the future, dramatists will mix their genres. We shall have tragical-comical-satirical-farcical plays in which jeers and tears will be mingled.

FURTHER READING

Bradley, A. C. (1904) *Shakespearean Tragedy*, Macmillan, London
Dixon, W. Macneile (1924) *Tragedy*, Edward Arnold, London
House, Humphry (1956) *Aristotle's Poetics*, Hart-Davis, London
Leech, Clifford (1969) *Tragedy*, Methuen, London
Lucas, F. L. (1927) *Tragedy*, Hogarth Press, London
Poole, Adrian (1987) *Tragedy: Shakespeare and the Greek Example*, Basil Blackwell, Oxford
Steiner, George (1961) *The Death of Tragedy*, Faber & Faber, London
Vickers, Brian (1973) *Towards Greek Tragedy: Drama, Myth, Society*, Longman, London

ADDITIONAL WORKS CITED

Aristotle (1965) *Aristotle Horace Longinus*, translated by T. S. Dorsch, Penguin, Harmondsworth
Hegel, G. W. F. (1975) *Aesthetics: Lectures on the Fine Arts*, 2 vols, translated by T. M. Knox, Clarendon Press, Oxford [first published 1835]
Holloway, John (1962) *The Story of the Night*, Routledge & Kegan Paul, London
Kitto, H. D. F. (1956) *Form and Meaning in Drama*, Methuen, London
Knights, L. C. (1959) *Some Shakespearean Themes*, Chatto & Windus, London
Plato (1955) *The Republic*, translated by H. D. P. Lee, Penguin Books, Harmondsworth
Racine, Jean (1960) *Five Tragedies*, translated by Kenneth Muir, Hill & Wang, New York
Richards, I. A. (1924) *Principles of Literary Criticism*, Kegan Paul, Trench, Trubner, London
Rymer, Thomas (1693) *A Short View of Tragedy*, London
Sidney, Philip (1966) *A Defence of Poetry*, edited by J. A. Van Dorsten, Oxford University Press, Oxford [first published 1595]
Silk, M. S. and Stern, J. P. (1981) *Nietzsche on Tragedy*, Cambridge University Press, Cambridge

26

COMEDY

PETER THOMSON

Common usage, in the twentieth century, permits us to call it a 'tragedy' if we scratch the paintwork of a new car and to call it a 'comedy' if we lock the keys inside it. That is to say that we may label 'comic' the events that ensue from a mishap that doesn't really matter, comes out all right in the end and costs little or nothing. Nor is this association of comedy with the fundamentally unserious confined to the banter of manifestly uncritical discourse. Ann Jellicoe, herself the author of the successful comedy *The Knack* (1961), has recently written and directed community plays, about which she has published a practical guide. The section subheaded 'Practical Demands of the Script' offers this advice to playwrights: 'The play should have lots of action. It should aim to be popular. It may be serious – people love serious things as much as they love comedy' (1987, p. 131).

Jellicoe's opposition of seriousness and comedy is slipshod, but it signifies a stage in the history of a word. Spoken in modern, middle-class comfort, 'I like a good comedy' should be interpreted as: 'If I do go to the theatre – which is a rare occurrence – I like to see a play which makes me laugh, but doesn't make me think.' The pervasive influence of television is significant here. A regular splash of laughter from a studio audience increases the fireside appeal of 'situation comedy'. There is no clear reason why this should be so, although the tendency of laughter to spread is well observed. The television series *M*A*S*H* is not more 'comic' in America, where it is accompanied by canned laughter, than it is in Britain, where it is broadcast without accompaniment. The question is of some historical importance, for although the provoking of laughter has been a characteristic effect of comedy throughout its existence, it is only in the television age that the provocation has been perceived as the single goal. A similar teleological transformation has already overtaken the kindred word 'comedian'. A Polonius, informed that the comedians are in Elsinore, would not be surprised to find them playing a tragedy. It was primarily through radio that the word became tied to the stand-up act of an Arthur

375

Askey or a George Burns. 'Comedy' is on the journey that has been completed
by 'comedian'. Its destination is a television slot, normally no longer than thirty
minutes, and eventually unprefaced by even so unspecific a specification as
'situation'. And yet criticism, whose task is to engage with the culture that
generates it, has paid little attention to television sit-com, evidently assuming
it to be, at worst, corrupting and, even at best, inferior to stage comedy. If
students are to be deflected from the television screen – and it is reasonable
to wonder whether they should be – and drawn to Aristophanes, Shakespeare,
Jonson and Molière, we should be asking what it is that distinguishes their
'comedy'. To be sure, classroom life would be easier if the greedy broadcasting
media had swallowed the word 'farce' instead. As it is, we must probably
recognize that it is too late to save the word 'comedy' and too early to abandon
it.

No reputable theorist has ever argued that comedy is trivial. Modern reconstructions of Aristotle's lost notes have plausibly proposed that he would have
claimed for the genre a purgative effect comparable with that of tragic catharsis,
a provoking of pleasure and laughter that would have the effect of curbing
harmful excesses of either. Such theorizing can be remote from practice. More
significant in the subsequent history of drama is the neo-Aristotelian distinction
between the social status of the characters appropriate to tragedy and to
comedy. By the mid-sixteenth century, the confidently opinionated Scaliger
could announce, in his *Poetices Libri Septem* (1561), that 'Comedy employs
characters from rustic or low city life' (Clark, 1947, p. 61). The distinction is
less important at its extremities than in the generally accepted belief that
comedy is about people who are not socially removed from the majority of the
audience. It was this compatibility that gave currency to Cicero's famous
dictum that comedy is 'an imitation of life, a mirror of custom, and an image
of truth' (*De Re Publica*, IV, xi). The writers' craft, that is to say, is displayed
in the quality of their imagination, the accuracy of their mirroring, the vividness
of their images, but the subject (and the object) is life, custom, truth. For
Aristotle, comedy is 'an imitation of men worse than the average; worse,
however, not as regards any and every sort of fault, but only as regards one
particular kind, the Ridiculous, which is a species of the Ugly' (trans. 1920,
p. 33). What is held up to ridicule is also held up for correction, and it was
the intention 'to mix profit with your pleasure' (Jonson, Prologue to *Volpone*,
1605) that came to distinguish high comedy from its hangers-on in Elizabethan
and post-Elizabethan Britain. There are, as we might expect, echoes of Aristotle and of Cicero in the Prologue Jonson wrote for the revival (*c.* 1612) of his
Every Man in His Humour. Determined to guide his new audience's responses,
he promises:

> ... persons such as Comedy would choose

> When she would show an image of the times,
> And sport with human follies, not with crimes.

But he warns that follies become crimes if we persist in them:

> I mean such errors, as you'll all confess
> By laughing at them, they deserve no less:
> Which when you heartily do, there's hope left, then,
> You, that have so grac'd monsters, may like men.

Jonson is the articulate advertiser of a form of critical, or corrective, comedy which provided a model, honoured in the breach as well as in the observance, for what became the dominant European tradition. Prefigured in the 'New Comedy' of Menander, it is variously reflected in the work of Molière and Beaumarchais, of Lessing, of Griboyedov, Gogol and Ostrovsky, of Wycherley and Congreve, of Bjørnson and Ibsen, as well as of countless lesser writers. It is a kind of comedy which invites us to laugh at the faults and fetishes of its chosen victims and may scold us if we fail to do so. Having exhibited their own intelligence, the authors expect intelligent responses. This, for George Meredith in his much-quoted *Essay on Comedy* (1877), is 'true comedy', whose test is that 'it shall awaken thoughtful laughter' (in Sypher, 1956, p. 88).

Meredith's essay was the expanded version of a lecture delivered in 1877, shortly after George Henry Lewes had mourned the decline of the drama, throughout Europe and America, from art to amusement (1875, p. 213), and may fairly be said to herald a dramatic revival, although Meredith was not to know that Ibsen's *Pillars of Society* was first staged in the same year. To a modern ear, Meredith is too floridly enamoured of 'the comic spirit', but he opens up a prospect for Ibsen and Shaw with the lively perception that 'any intellectual pleading of a doubtful cause contains germs of an Idea of Comedy' (Sypher, 1956, pp. 87–8). The last quarter of the nineteenth century saw comedy shaken by the ears. The prolific Dion Boucicault, triumphant in 1841, supreme by 1874, could no longer find a theatrical buyer for his comedy *Ourselves* after 1887. The old formula had lost its authority. Meanwhile, Ibsen was crowning his already substantial achievements, Wilde would soon preach, through lucid inversion, the importance of not being earnest, Chekhov be given a second chance by the founding of the Moscow Art Theatre, Shaw would begin his sabotaging of the British theatre with *The Quintessence of Ibsenism* (1891) and some 'unpleasant' plays of his own, and in Paris, on 10 December 1896, Alfred Jarry's *Ubu Roi* would scandalize a theatrical public that was going to have to learn fast. The need for a reassessment of comedy was met, at the very outset of the new century, by the French philosopher Henri Bergson. Bergson's particular subject was laughter – the title of his 1900 monograph is *Le Rire* – but he explored his theme largely through the work of Molière and later French playwrights. Whatever the limitations of *Le*

Rire – and those who look to comedy for a subtle and multi-faceted expression of human experience have been at pains to expose them – it brings expertly into focus the social effect of laughter in particular and, by association, comedy in general.

Bergson's significant contention that laughter acts as a regulator of social behaviour is sharply focused in a passage on Molière's *L'Avare*:

> If Harpagon could see us laughing at his avarice, although I do not say that he would correct it, he would show us less of it or he would show it differently. Let us say now, then, that laughter 'corrects manners' (*castigat ridendo mores*), in this sense above all. It makes us try straight away to seem what we should be, what we shall no doubt end up truly being, one day.
>
> (in Sypher, 1956, p. 71)

It is an absence of self-awareness, a spectacular rigidity, that isolates, for Bergson, the comic character. As a social gesture, laughter inspires fear and thus 'restrains eccentricity' (in Sypher, p. 73) and it is this that leads Bergson to formulate the view that comedy's prime attack is less on immorality than on unsociability. The vision, still supported by the majority of sit-coms, is of comedy as a socially conservative form, punishing/rewarding deviations from a bourgeois norm with laughter. The audience laughs at the mechanistic predictability and social inappropriateness exhibited by characters with whom it has no strong emotional ties: 'the comic, we have noted, addresses itself purely to the intelligence: laughter is incompatible with emotion' (in Sypher, p. 150). It does no justice to Bergson to represent his complex analysis by selected conclusions. Later theorists have tended to stress the shortcomings of his argument. Certainly he neglects the 'laughing *with*', which Robert Weimann (1978) finds at the heart of the popular tradition of comedy, in his concentration on 'laughing *at*'. In *The Life of the Drama* (1965), Eric Bentley taxes Bergson with 'Gallic overprecision' and with belittling comedy as 'hardly an art at all but a sort of cross between art and life' (p. 42), although these judgements should be read in the context of Bentley's chapters on farce and comedy, from which it will emerge that Bergson's stern proposals properly apply less to comedy than to the crueller world of farce.

Bergson, we should remind ourselves, undertook a study of laughter and used comedy to illustrate his thesis. Freud's investigation of *Jokes and their Relation to the Unconscious* (1904), despite an even greater distance from the theatre, has influenced the development of comic theory, not least in its recognition that jokes can override taboos, license vicarious indulgence and permit both teller and listener to express their hidden hostility towards the restrictive attitudes and practices that circumscribe their lives. The implications for comedy here are very different from those argued by Bergson. Bergsonian laughter punishes eccentricity (comedy is conservative), whereas through the

Freudian laughter that greets a joke and the anger/desire/frustration that motivates its telling, eccentricity briefly triumphs over authority (comedy is subversive). The contradiction is neatly reconciled in the formula, 'through release to clarification', which C. L. Barber uses, in his influential *Shakespeare's Festive Comedy* (1959, p. 6). Barber's subtitle is significant – 'A Study of Dramatic Form and its Relation to Social Custom'. The pattern of festive comedy, persuasively elucidated by Barber, involves an escape from hierarchical repression into holiday merrymaking, which leads in time to a new understanding and the eventual reintegration into a wiser, but still hierarchical, society. It is a reading of festivity and government which, as Michael Bristol has noted, 'necessarily favors a benevolent repression as the source of collective harmony' (1985, p. 32). It is, then, a transformation 'upward' that Barber proposes as a function of festive comedy. Bristol prefers Bakhtin's perception of carnival as the Renaissance's 'transformation downward ... of dependency, expropriation and social discipline' (p. 22), and, as Jarry's *Ubu Roi* (1896) makes manifest, there are clearly possibilities for comedy here, too. The journey from Barber through Ian Donaldson's *The World Upside Down* (1970), Robert Weimann's *Shakespeare and the Popular Tradition in the Theater* (1978) and Mikhail Bakhtin's *The Dialogic Imagination* (1981) to Bristol's *Carnival and Theater* offers new perspectives on the interaction of plebeian culture and comedy. It is the same interaction in the working world of the theatre that fuels John McGrath's arguments in *A Good Night Out* (1981).

Many of the twentieth century's most strenuous critical encounters with the strategies of comedy have centred, unsurprisingly, on the differences between Shakespeare and Jonson. We may take as exemplary a short and elegantly turned essay by Robert Ornstein (1969), which begins by offering the two writers as either twin pillars of Elizabethan comedy or its opposite poles: 'one romantic, positive and attractive; the other satiric, negative and (now and then) repelling' (p. 43). Ornstein's Jonson consciously rejects 'the earlier romantic mode of comedy' to strike out on 'a new path of satiric realistic comedy ... narrowly focused at the point where bourgeois greed meets underworld guile'. This is a man unable to conceive that 'the fumblings of a Dogberry might confound the schemings of a Borachio', a man for whom the first commandment is 'Be anything but a fool', a man whose comedies 'remind us how little Shakespeare's comedies tell us of the rise of capitalistic enterprise and of the mercenary humours of his age' (pp. 43–4). The eventual contrast is between the Shakespearian revelation of 'our common bond of humanity' and the Jonsonian uncovering of 'the commonness, the baseness and enormity of our humanity'. Ornstein's concluding paragraph spells out this opposition:

> History, I suppose, testifies to the truth of Jonson's comedies. For centuries life has been, in the main, crass, vulgar and mindless. But the value of life does not

exist 'in the main'. It exists in the rare particulars, in the special Shakespearian instances.

(p. 46)

Much that has been written on Shakespeare's comedies is similarly soft and transcendental. As Sir Walter Raleigh ambiguously observed in his 1907 monograph, 'the tradition of geniality clings to his name like a faded perfume' (p. 18). Ornstein's stance towards Jonson is almost headmasterly, towards Shakespeare humble. There is, of course, substance in the contrast – Bergson could have used Jonson to illustrate his argument, but not Shakespeare – but it is time to question the service done to critical discourse at large, and to Shakespeare in particular, by those who continue to write in 'the tradition of geniality'. After reading Ornstein, you could be forgiven for thinking it merely perverse of later writers to model themselves on Jonson, thus nurturing Bergson's conclusions on laughter's 'unavowed intention to humiliate, and . . . at least to correct the exterior'. It is certainly Jonsonian rather than Shakespearian practice that explains Bergson's immediate deduction, 'That is why comedy is so much nearer real life than the non-comic theatrical genres'. Jonson's was a major contribution to the establishment of Ciceronian realism as the norm of the comic stage. Its force and longevity can be savoured in the angry opening paragraph of an article contributed by Howard Barker to the *Guardian* on 22 August 1988:

> For some years I have been attempting to create a theatre which lent its audience rights of interpretation. To do this has involved transgressing in the two sacred groves of contemporary theatre – clarity and realism. The text or production which is lauded for its clarity is inevitably the one which allows least ambiguity, the least contradiction, and the least room for evading the smothering sense that someone is giving you a meaning to take away with you. It is a form of oppression masquerading as enlightenment.

I shall have to return to classic comedy in order to explore Northrop Frye's important ideas on comic form, but it will be useful to consider first the example of a modern playwright as uneasy as Barker with the prevailing view of comedy.

The exasperated Author who steps on to the stage at the start of Peter Barnes's *Laughter!* (1978) is met by a large custard-pie and an off-stage voice promising, 'It's going to be that kind of a show, folks!' He protests with vehemence:

> No it isn't. Gangrene has set in. Comedy itself is the enemy. Laughter only confuses and corrupts everything we try to say . . . The stupid're never truly laughed out of their stupidities, fools remain fools, the corrupt, violent and depraved remain corrupt, violent and depraved. Laughter's the ally of tyrants. It softens our hatred . . . So we must try and root out comedy, strangle mirth . . . Laughter's too feeble a weapon against the barbarities of life. A balm for battles

lost, standard equipment for the losing side; the powerful have no need of
it.

(p. 2)

And the doomed Author, urging the rooting out of laughter, ends his brief
prologue with his trousers round his ankles, revealing spangled underpants.
The tricks of the theatre conspire to divert his protest. Barnes is a learned
playwright, an admirer of Jonson, and a man who would like to wrestle the
theatre out of the benevolent control of those who have tamed it. He knows
that entrepreneurs and audiences will draw the sting of what I have loosely
called 'Ciceronian realism'. Indeed, 'realism', like 'comedy', is a word in
decline. The 'realistic', as mediated through television, is scarcely distinguishable from the 'readily recognized'. (It is in something like this sense that
Howard Barker seems to be using it.) Supported by an ideology, though,
realism is a word that can be made to work. Brecht, arguably the greatest
comic dramatist of the century, has this to say in an essay on 'The Popular
and Realistic' (*c.* 1938):

> *Realist* means: laying bare society's causal network/showing up the dominant
> viewpoint as the viewpoint of the dominators/writing from the standpoint of the
> class which has prepared the broadest solutions for the most pressing problems
> afflicting human society/emphasizing the dynamics of development/concrete and
> so as to encourage abstraction.
>
> (in Willett, 1964, p. 109)

It is this kind of programme which Barnes sets himself in *Laughter!*, not a
single play but two grotesque comedies linked by a common concern with
mass murder. Distress accumulates – and so do the jokes. In the first play,
we witness the personal cruelty of Ivan the Terrible; in the second, the
impersonal cruelty of the comedy-bureaucrats who detail gas-chamber deaths
in Nazi Germany; and for an Epilogue, Bimko and Bieberstein perform a
Jewish double-act as the Zyklon B pours over them:

> (They cough and stagger.)
> *Bieberstein.* I could be wrong but I think this act is dying.
> *Bimko.* The way to beat hydro-cyanide gas is by holding your breath for five
> minutes. It's just a question of mind over matter. They don't mind and we
> don't matter.
> (They fall to their knees.)
> *Bieberstein.* Those foul, polluted German bastardized . . .
> *Bimko.* Hymie, Hymie, please; what you want to do – cause trouble?
>
> (p. 70)

Laughter! is an attack on a comic theatre that can reprocess anything, that is
no longer shocked by Jonson, by Jarry, by Brecht, a theatre that has been
rendered powerless by the powerful. At the beginning, an Author fulminates
against Bergson and the critical apologists for comedy – and is made a fool of

– and at the end, Jewel and Warriss (or Vladimir and Estragon?) invite us to laugh while they die. It is not, I think, a successful play, but, if Barnes is right about comedy today, what difference would it make if it were?

Barnes's humanitarianism is, finally, too insecure an ideology to sustain an alternative comic realism. The sure-footed Northrop Frye treads across world literature from a home-base in Christianity: 'From the point of view of Christianity . . . tragedy is an episode in the larger scheme of redemption and resurrection to which Dante gave the name of *commedia*' (in Lerner, 1967, p. 320). He has written extensively on comedy, in *Anatomy of Criticism* (1957), with a Shakespearian focus in *A Natural Perspective* (1965), and in concise essays, of which I shall examine 'Old and New Comedy' (1969). Frye's proposed distinction between the two kinds of comedy (*the* two kinds) is primarily structural. Old Comedy, of which Aristophanes is the familiar exemplar, is based on the *agon*, or contest. Its approach is dialectical and its preferred structure processional or sequential. New Comedy, given a preliminary sketch in the *Ion* of Euripides, developed by Menander and handed on by Plautus and Terence to the playwrights of Renaissance Europe, is plot-based. Its approach is teleological and hence its structural impulse is towards satisfactory completion. Frye recognizes two forms of New Comedy, 'the romantic form of Shakespeare and the more realistic and displaced form of the Neo-Classical tradition', but in both, 'a new society is created on the stage in the last moments'. A story that begins under the constraint of irrational law, unjust obstruction or mistaken identity will find resolution, and that resolution, often signalled by marriage but representing, more profoundly, rebirth, will express itself in festivity. New Comedy, then, is readily accommodated in a Christian *schema*, where the sense is of tragedy (or near-tragedy) as the inseparable prelude to comedy. This is not true of Old Comedy, 'a more existential form in which the central theme is mockery'. A historical pincer movement has, for Frye, restored Old Comedy to the stage: 'the dramatic genius of Old Comedy is the one now established on our stage, and as we enter the age of anarchism it is likely to remain there.' New Comedy, having lost command in the theatre during the years that separate *Tom Jones* (1749) from *Little Dorrit* (1855–6), donated its structure to the domestic novel.

In very general terms – and it is couched in very general terms – Frye's argument has validity. An age that has lost faith in marriage is liable to find sentimental the joyful resolutions most typical of New Comedy. But Frye has made a dauntingly capacious handbag out of Old Comedy, dropping into it *Waiting for Godot* (1955), black comedy, absurd drama, 'Sweeney Agonistes' (1932), *Mac Bird* (1967) and unspecified plays about Churchill, the Pope and Hitler. It is asking too much of a single receptacle to carry the variety of contemporary comic forms. The common possession of eight legs, as I have heard Frye himself warn, is insufficient to excuse the confusion of an octopus with a string quartet, and his Old Comedy category is, quite simply, too inclusive. We can, however, agree that the pattern of New Comedy, starkly drawn by Scaliger – 'The beginning of a comedy presents a confused state of affairs, and this confusion is happily cleared up at the end' (in Clark, 1947, p. 61) – has faded. Even those modern comedies that end happily promise no permanence in the resolution. Schopenhauer's view of comedy, hurrying 'to lower the curtain in the moment of joy so that we do not see what comes afterwards' (1888, vol. 3, p. 500) was recorded in the last years of what might reasonably be called New Comedy. The predominant tone of twentieth-century comedy, usefully explored in J. L. Styan's *The Dark Comedy* (1968), is bleak. The playwright Christopher Fry used comedy as an escape 'not from truth but from despair' and proposes the Book of Job as 'the great reservoir of comedy' (1963, pp. 111, 113). Among Ionesco's *Notes and Counter-Notes* is, 'We are afraid of too much humour, (and humour is freedom)' (1964, p. 46). The consensus seems to be that modern comedy points, not to resolution, but to a universal loss of confidence in resolution.

In few modern comedies does anything change significantly for the better. *Waiting for Godot* is, in this context, an archetype, with Chekhov on one side of it and writers as disparate as Pinter, Ayckbourn, David Mamet and Sam Shepard on the other. The 'comedy' of such playwrights depends less on the unfolding of a plot than on the presentation of repetitive behaviour and the rejection of psychology as the provider of adequate explanations. The self-aware 'spoof' play – Holberg's *Jeppe on the Hill* (1722), Kleist's *The Broken Jug* (1806) and Gogol's *The Government Inspector* (1836) are outstanding examples – has been purveyed in the twentieth century by Pirandello and Anouilh and is still the province of Tom Stoppard; but Stoppard risks the charge of anachronistic whimsy, of Gilbertian cleverness, of fiddling while Rome burns. Even the philosophical challenge of absurdist comedy looks culpably passive from the viewpoint of Thatcherite Britain. There is, among playwrights, an urgent search for new comic forms, which sometimes, as in Caryl Churchill's *Cloud Nine* (1978) and *Serious Money* (1987), involves a new investigation of old forms. But the vested interests of stage practice continue to curb and frustrate more writers than Barnes and Barker. John Arden, one of the most original, has turned his back on the professional theatre, but not before firing off a salvo in his preface to *The Workhouse Donkey* (1964):

> The theatre must be catholic. But it never will be catholic if we do not grant pride of place to the old essential attributes of Dionysus:
> noise
> disorder
> drunkenness
> lasciviousness
> nudity

generosity
corruption
fertility
and
ease.

The Comic Theatre was formed expressly to celebrate them: and whenever they have been forgotten our art has betrayed itself and our generally accessible and agreeable god has hidden his face.

(p. 9)

It is a position understood by another playwright, who confronts the Bergsonian theme of laughter in one of the most troubling of post-war British plays. Trevor Griffiths's *Comedians* (1976) is in three acts. In the first, six trainee comedians assemble in a Manchester classroom to be briefed by their tutor, Eddie Waters, before their performance in front of a London agent. In the second, they perform their acts to us in the audience. In the third, they reassemble to hear the agent's verdict. Not only is the structure persuasively Aristophanic, but the discipline is that of Old Comedy – the debate/conflict. On the one hand is Bert Challenor, the London agent:

Don't try to be deep. Keep it simple. I'm not looking for philosophers, I'm looking for comics. I'm looking for someone who sees what the people want and knows how to give it them ... Any good comedian can lead an audience by the nose. But only in the direction they're going. And that direction is quite simply ... escape. We're not missionaries, we're suppliers of laughter.

(p. 33)

On the other is Eddie Waters, retired comedian:

A real comedian – that's a daring man. He *dares* to see what his listeners shy away from, fear to express. And what he sees is a sort of truth, about people, about their situation, about what hurts or terrifies them, about what's hard, above all, about what they *want*. A joke releases the tension, says the unsayable, any joke pretty well. But a true joke, a comedian's joke, has to do more than release tension, it has to *liberate* the will and the desire, it has to *change the situation*.

(p. 20)

The climax of the play comes with the last of the performances in Act 2, a disturbingly violent and, to Challenor, 'repulsive' working-class assault on the dominators. If it is an 'act' at all, it is an act of defiance, and its perpetrator, Gethin Price, in unrepentant:

It was all ice out there tonight. I loved it. I felt ... expressed. (Pause, lifting suddenly.) The Jews still stayed in line, even when they *knew*, Eddie! What's *that* about? (He swings his bag off the desk, ready for off.) I stand in no line. I refuse my consent.

(pp. 67–8)

The comic theatre that will reject Gethin Price is one that can tolerate only some of the truth. Perhaps Griffiths, who has largely abandoned theatre for television, shares the resolution of the character he has created: 'I go back. I wait. I'm ready.'

FURTHER READING

Bentley, Eric (1965) *The Life of the Drama*, Methuen, London
Bergson, Henri (1956) *Le Rire*. In Wylie Sypher (ed.), *Comedy*, Doubleday Anchor, New York [essay first published 1900]
Corrigan, R. W. (ed.) (1965) *Comedy: Meaning and Form*, Chandler Publishing Company, San Francisco
Frye, Northrop (1965) *A Natural Perspective*, Harcourt, Brace & World Inc., New York
Howarth, W. D. (ed.) (1978) *Comic Drama*, Methuen, London
Kerr, Walter (1967) *Tragedy and Comedy*, Simon & Schuster, New York
Lauter, Paul (ed.) (1964) *Theories of Comedy*, Doubleday Anchor, New York
Merchant, W. Moelwyn (1972) *Comedy*, Methuen, London
Meredith, George (1956) *An Essay on Comedy and the Uses of the Comic Spirit*. In Wylie Sypher (ed.), *Comedy*, Doubleday Anchor, New York [essay first published 1877]
Rodway, Allan (1975) *English Comedy*, Chatto & Windus, London
Styan, J. L. (1968) *The Dark Comedy*, Cambridge University Press, Cambridge
Sypher, Wylie (ed.) (1956) *Comedy*, Doubleday Anchor, New York
Weimann, Robert (1978) *Shakespeare and the Popular Tradition in the Theater*, Johns Hopkins University Press, Baltimore

ADDITIONAL WORKS CITED

Arden, John (1964) *The Workhouse Donkey*, Methuen, London
Aristotle (1920) *On the Art of Poetry*, translated by Ingram Bywater, Clarendon Press, Oxford
Bakhtin, M. M. (1981) *The Dialogic Imagination*, University of Texas Press, Austin
Barber, C. L. (1959) *Shakespeare's Festive Comedy*, Princeton University Press, Princeton
Barnes, Peter (1978) *Laughter!*, Heinemann, London
Bristol, Michael D. (1985) *Carnival and Theater*, Methuen, London
Clark, Barrett H. (1947) *European Theories of the Drama*, Crown Publications, New York
Donaldson, Ian (1970) *The World Upside Down*, Clarendon Press, Oxford
Freud, Sigmund (1960) *Jokes and their Relation to the Unconscious*, translated by J. Strachey, Routledge & Kegan Paul, London [first published 1904]
Fry, Christopher (1963) 'Comedy'. In R. W. Corrigan (ed.), *Theatre in the Twentieth Century*, Grove Press, New York
Frye, Northrop (1957) *Anatomy of Criticism*, Princeton University Press, Princeton
____(1969) 'Old and New Comedy', *Shakespeare Survey*, 22, 1–5
Griffiths, Trevor (1976) *Comedians*, Faber & Faber, London
Ionesco, Eugène (1964) *Notes and Counter-Notes*, John Calder, London
Jellicoe, Ann (1987) *Community Plays*, Methuen, London

Lerner, Laurence (ed.) (1967) *Shakespeare's Comedies*, Penguin, Harmondsworth

Lewes, G. H. (1875) *On Actors and the Art of Acting*, Smith, Elder & Co., London

McGrath, John (1981) *A Good Night Out*, Eyre Methuen, London

Ornstein, Robert (1969) 'Shakespearian and Jonsonian Comedy', *Shakespeare Survey*, 22, 43–6

Raleigh, Walter (1907) *Shakespeare*, Macmillan, London

Schopenhauer, Arthur (1888) *Sämmtliche Werke*, 6 vols., Leipzig

Willett, John (ed.) (1964) *Brecht on Theatre*, Methuen, London

27

SHAKESPEARE

ANDREW GURR

The fact that Shakespeare wrote close to a million words that have survived into print is one reason for the multiple uses to which his words have been put in the four centuries since he first began to make them available. His forty major works are a massive corpus of invention by any standards. Writing so many different pieces of the highest quality has meant that he can accommodate a massive body of analysis, and the widest possible variety of critical approaches. His oeuvre therefore stands not just as a quarry for every generation to dig new wonders from, but as a reflection of the widest possible range of human preoccupations.

Shakespeare is a mountain into which one tunnels. No two tunnellers find quite the same ores, and, like a magic mountain, whatever ores are extracted they are still there for the next tunneller. This is one way of conceiving the great oeuvre and its benefits. A quite different concept, also a half-truth, is of the Shakespeare canon as a kind of mirror, which reveals its readers and their preoccupations much more immediately and vividly than it shows what it really is in itself. These two ways of thinking about Shakespeare have their uses today. They illustrate some of the main turns of modern critical thinking, and they help to explain both the strengths and the weaknesses of modern approaches to Shakespeare.

The oldest critical approach of all, and the one most derided today, is the biographical. Its weaknesses, most clearly expressed in a famous essay by Barthes, 'The Death of the Author' ([1968] 1977), are chiefly that it directs attention in the wrong way and for the wrong reasons. It may be perfectly proper, for instance, to take the view that Shakespeare's choice of the name Arden for the forest in *As You Like It* ought to prompt speculations not only about the mythical significance of the Ardennes but also the possibility of more private and personal references to Shakespeare's mother Mary Arden. Any return on the second speculation is, however, likely to be unrewarding because it turns biographical speculation in on itself, in a circular argument. The Forest of Arden is a private reference of the author's for the author's own satisfaction, if it is one. Even more dubiously, when Prospero says farewell to his art (of theatrical illusion) in *The Tempest* and promises to drown his magic book (not burn it, as that other magician Faustus did), it might excite a similar sort of romantic curiosity about Shakespeare making Prospero an image for himself. Such speculation might be intensified by the knowledge that *The Tempest* was probably the last play Shakespeare wrote solo. The trouble is that such ideas are really only interpretations, conjectures, aimed at identifying the elusive author, and that every such interpretation embodies an unsupported presupposition about what the author's thinking really is. Biographical speculation of this kind is now seen as idle, and a distraction, since the author is not only long dead but completely irrecoverable. To focus on the will of the dead author is to appeal to a fixed though also rather hypothetical source of authority, an authority which inevitably restricts and reduces meaning and significance. We apply our attention instead to what the words he has left can give to readers.

This kind of evidence is found most securely in the sonnets, where the author might be thought to be speaking in his own voice, rather than in the multitude of voices in the plays. It has been suggested, for instance, that some of the sonnets were written to a 'dark lady' called Emilia Bassano, daughter of a Venetian Jewish musician at Elizabeth's court and mistress of Henry Hunsdon, the Lord Chamberlain, who became the patron of Shakespeare's playing company in 1594. The Bassano coat of arms had a silkworm moth as its crest, and three moths on a mulberry tree on the shield. The Italian for mulberry is 'moro', which also means a Moor, or black person. Thus the identification of Emilia as the mistress in the sonnets supplies a new range of connotations to the 'black' aspects of the mistress and the many uses of 'more' ('All mine was thine, before thou hadst this more', complains the poet in Sonnet 40 to the young nobleman who has stolen his mistress). It also adds nuances to the Jewish presence in *The Merchant of Venice* and the Moorish presence (and the Emilia) in *Othello*.

The question is really in what way this information should be directed. Traditionally attention has been focused on Shakespeare's biography out of curiosity about the life of the greatest wordsmith and inventor of plays. But since Barthes insisted that the author cannot be used as a unifying concept, a justification for fixing meanings immovably, this direction has been reversed. The hypothetical life or lives of the hypothetical author and the connotations supplied by that story direct our attention instead to the multiplicity of meanings inherent in the words. The modern focus is not on the fixative author, but the variable reader. The implicit criterion is a heuristic question of value. Does the reader learn more from the life of a single individual, from the immediate circumstances of his writing, the engagement of minds in discourse at that long-dead time, or should the reader rather engage himself or herself in the exercise of analysing the interaction between that dead discourse and the discourse of the present?

It has long been recognized that every age rewrites its Shakespeare. Samuel Schoenbaum prepared the way for his 'documentary' life, *William Shakespeare: A Documentary Life* (1977), which is an assemblage of the material evidence for what Shakespeare did and who he was, by writing *Shakespeare's Lives* (1970), a history of previous attempts to write biographies of the man. The 'logocentrism' that Derrida sees as the central feature of all Western thought demands a fixed identity for an author, his individuality giving him his authority. By the same need the concept of a settled culture and Fish's 'interpretive community' (1980) of readers has traditionally insisted on having the fixed set of texts which have been produced from the original editions by the labour of generations of meticulous editors. Both of these concepts are now under question. Current challenges to the biographical impulse extend far beyond the question of the dark lady.

We have a hugely rich inheritance from the logocentric tradition, though like many bequests it has also proved something of an embarrassment. The idea of 'sacred Shakespeare' as a cultural tradition and the consequent quasi-religious devotion to the Shakespeare 'canon' (a term taken from biblical studies), both stand as manifestations of that concern for the fixities of the written word and a hierarchy of settled values which Derrida's 'deconstruction' and post-structuralist thinking generally have set themselves to deny and demolish. An essay by Terence Hawkes, 'Telmah' (in *That Shakespeherian Rag: essays on a critical process*, 1986), is about the principles lying behind the edition of Shakespeare which John Dover Wilson conceived in the First World War and the early days of the Russian revolution. It gives a vivid account of the fixative logocentric impulse which critics usually now see as negative and reductive. Studies of Shakespeare today cover the entire range, from the continuing efforts of editors to 'fix' the text and the material facts about the Shakespeare oeuvre at one extreme, to the most deconstructive attempts to dismantle the hierarchy of values found in the work by centuries of traditionalists at the other. It is worth looking at both the historical spread of different approaches to Shakespeare through the centuries, and the present geographical (and political) spread.

Historically, Shakespeare's work first rose to fame on the stage. Stage performance was evidently the only form of publication that the author wanted for his plays, and if his fellow-players had not put together an edition of the surviving play-texts for the press seven years after his death, in 1623, most of them would not be available for reading now. Early in the eighteenth century the first edition designed for the reader rather than the playgoer appeared, a process which reached its height with the appearance of Dr Johnson's edition in 1768. For two centuries there were alternative Shakespeares, the versions presented by the theatres of the time, often in quite radically altered forms, and the texts for the study and the scholarly reader. Not until the twentieth century, and the firm lodgement of Shakespeare as a subject in education syllabuses, did the two alternatives begin to be reconciled.

With the rise of Romanticism and the predominance of the novel as the chief literary form in the nineteenth century, the tendency was to treat Shakespeare as a novelist. Character and plot, and the emotional forces generated by the major tragedies, were the main focus of attention. A. C. Bradley's lectures on what he called the 'central' tragedies, published as *Shakespearean Tragedy* in 1904, are the finest example of this approach. His treatment of the plays as novels led him to express qualms about such non-realistic features in *King Lear* as Edgar writing a letter to his brother when both lived in the same house, but he was finely sensitive to plot structure and emotional power. The same qualities, together with a much more theatre-orientated concern for the movement of the story in the short time of performance on stage, were demonstrated in the succeeding years by Harley Granville Barker in his *Prefaces to Shakespeare* (1927–48). These essays were strongly influenced by William Poel and his experiments in staging Shakespeare in a simulacrum of the original conditions by the Elizabethan Stage Society of the 1890s. Poel tried to 'rescue' Shakespeare from the static and scenic staging of the Victorian theatre tradition represented by Henry Irving and Beerbohm Tree. He staged the plays without sets, giving his audiences speech rather than spectacle. Poel and Granville Barker were both ruled by the assumption that Shakespeare was far greater than his successors, and that faith in his work demanded the restoration of the original conditions for which the plays had been composed.

This loyalty to the 'historical' Shakespeare lost some of its impetus in the 1930s. By then the rise of modernism had directed attention away from the realism of the nineteenth-century novel towards symbolism. Shakespeare in the theatre lost favour once again, and it came to be seen that the plays could be read as if they were poems or imagistic constructs. G. Wilson Knight's books (especially *The Wheel of Fire*, [1930] 1949) embodied this fresh approach from the beginning of the 1930s, though the classic statement of the principle was made in an essay of 1933 by L. C. Knights, satirically putting the question which might have bothered Bradley in his title, 'How Many Children Had Lady Macbeth?' (reprinted in *Explorations*, 1946). The approach to the plays as poems gained some impetus from the discoveries by Caroline Spurgeon (1935) and Wolfgang Clemen (1951) that some of the major plays made consistent use of particular clusters of images. This led to the 'holistic' analysis of plays as complex image-patterns.

The attempt to grasp the plays whole, the 'holistic' principle upheld by Wilson Knight, involves what has become known in critical theory as the

hermeneutic circle. Friedrich Schleiermacher in the nineteenth century identified the essential problem of interpretation as the need to know the parts
before the whole can be known, at the same time as we need to know the
whole in order that the parts can be understood. This circularity could, it was
thought, be overcome by a grasp of the systematic patterns of imagery evident
in Shakespeare's major tragedies. The plays were poems, and could be understood as coherent artefacts organized through their imagery.

This way of reading the plays as poems was consistent with the Russian
Formalist approach and the New Criticism which flourished especially in the
USA in the years following the Second World War. Both these approaches
were broadly structuralist. They existed at least in part as a reaction against
political readings and critical postures. The New Criticism devoted itself to
close reading of the text alone, free from any moral, political or social postures.
It saw paradox or significant ambiguity as the finest kind of poetry, a form of
expression which embodied the inherent complexity of any meaningful statement. Poetry, as W. H. Auden put it in one of his characteristically throwaway
remarks, is the exact expression of mixed feelings. The New Criticism became
a popular way of reading texts for several reasons. One was that at the height
of the Cold War literature was thought to be really accessible only if the reader
was politically and socially neutral. Another was that the moralistic values
which literature was expected to teach (and of which F. R. Leavis was the
increasingly influential exponent) were matters of sensitivity and sensibility
for which paradox and ambiguity were the best form of expression. Thus
Shakespeare's plays had to be approached as poems expressing the paradoxes
inherent in their ruling image-patterns.

The problem of the hermeneutic circle is now seen as one which extends
far beyond the confines of the written text itself. A whole text is itself only a
part of a much larger whole, one which the human consciousness can only
grasp by relating it to the whole of its own consciousness, its personal and
cultural identity, and even then only transiently and as part of an infinitely
larger whole. The structural hierarchies in which societies exist are in a state
of permanent flux. Every form of words is relative, contingent on the whole
social structure within which it is composed and inside which it is read or
heard. Thus in modern thinking the texts of Shakespeare are to be thought
of as contingent, whether they are approached as word-games by the semioticians or as hierarchical structures to be challenged by the deconstructionists.

The semiotic approach to literature is presented with its greatest test by
Shakespeare's plays. Semiotics as a study of signs and codes of communication
undergoes by far its toughest challenge when it has to deal with performance
texts in the theatre. A signifier in semiotics needs both a speaker and a hearer.
A phrase spoken by an actor to an audience intimately familiar with the actor,
his text, his author and the shared culture of the day is a contribution to a

hugely complex interchange of signs and signifiers. Subsequent analysis, restricted to working only on the printed record of the words that were spoken by the actor, cannot easily retrieve much from the original complex of communication, with its many non-verbal signifiers. This difficulty extends from the purely verbal to the whole culture in which the exchange between actor and audience is embedded. And Shakespeare's plays were all composed as performance texts, for a specific company of actors to perform in a specific theatre to a community of audiences that he knew intimately, and most of whom knew his work equally intimately. In the face of such intimate and intricate exchanges, the work of reconstructing the historical conditions in which the plays were originally performed becomes an almost impossible one. Only a continuing belief in the unique value of the magic mountain has sustained the most recent studies at this end of the present geographical expanse of different approaches to Shakespeare.

Modern work in reconstructing the original Shakespeare has been tackled in various ways, most notably by the linguistic semioticians and by the 'New Historicists'. They work at opposite ends of the spectrum, the semioticians dealing with words and the New Historicists with society. This spectrum is not in any significant way political. Marxist criticism does occupy some of the same territory as the New Historicists, and uses similar terminology. In general, and rather flippantly, it might be said that most British New Historicists are left-wing in their politics, while most of the Americans are carefully neutral or implicitly right-wing. This range is evident in, for instance, Dollimore and Sinfield (1985), Greenblatt (1980) and Goldberg (1983). But they all share similar techniques and to some extent a similar approach to historical evidence. If there is a basic division of principle it probably lies between structuralism on the one hand (or wing), associated as it is with Formalism and the old New Criticism in its pure concern with the text, and the various post-structuralist positions on the other, which prefer to concentrate on the subtext (semiotics) or the context (New Historicism and Marxism). Semioticians, by their close focus on the words themselves, often seem to operate as structuralists, although their principles, coming largely from Saussure, give them some affinities with the post-structuralists. New Historicists and post-structuralists share some principles, including the assumption that the modern reader should be the focus, rather than the original author. Both parties deplore the fixity of hierarchies and settled convictions of any sort. In some sense deconstruction can be seen as the most anti-conservative of the current theories, since it resists the idea of any sort of fixed and durable structure, though its position is in no way ostensibly political (see Miller, 1977).

It is not easy to describe in a discursive account what these tangled webs of theory look like. If we were to try to make an image for them all, it might best be conceived of as a circle across which is drawn a rather randomly disposed set of diameters, like an irregular bicycle wheel. Each of the diameters represents two opposed positions, though none corresponds neatly to the old left wing/right wing opposition, and no one diameter lines up with any of the others. The centre of the circle, the crossing-point for all the diameters and the central position where traditional British pragmatism usually likes to put its nest of twigs, is just a blackened mess of crossed lines.

The problems of modern theorizing about how to approach Shakespeare are at their clearest with deconstruction. Its firm opposition to hierarchical structures which maintain settled value-systems makes its advocates fundamentally hostile to the concept of a 'sacred Shakespeare', with a holy 'canon', and all the minutely detailed editorial labours on the text which go with that concept. This position the deconstructionists share with all the post-structuralists who focus on the responses of the modern reader rather than the original compositions themselves. It seems a little ironical that Shakespeare himself should show himself to be a perfect deconstructionist in at least one of his great plays, *Troilus and Cressida*. It is a play notable above all for the way it takes the oldest and most famous of all literary stories, Homer's *Iliad*, and undermines everything it has traditionally been taken to stand for. The play questions all the traditional value-systems by giving them a broad context which subverts what they seem to uphold. The Greeks are mercantilists, valuing Helen as a commodity, and scheming to sustain their system of authority by fighting for the rights of property. The Trojans are chivalric fools, who value Helen for romantic rather than commercial reasons, and will fight for the pleasure of fighting as readily as they steal wives for the pleasure of loving. Troilus argues for valuation according to personal pleasure ('What's aught but as 'tis valued?' he argues in the Trojan council in Act 2 Scene 2), and Hector tacitly admits the point when, after arguing that 'these moral laws / Of nature and of nations' insist that Helen should be returned to the Greeks, he tells the Trojan council that he has already sent a 'roisting challenge' to the Greeks to come out and fight. Hector values the war because he likes fighting.

The play counter-balances one set of values against another, at the cost of faith in either. Commercial Greeks think of wives as property, while romantic Trojans think of them as the basis for all other valuations. Helen is worth fighting for as a love-object, not Menelaus's possession. There is a sweet fool, Pandarus, who thinks everything is lovely, and a bitter fool, Thersites, who thinks everything is foul. The play sets up no absolute values. Time is the ultimate test of everything, including not only Cressida's durability as a value for Troilus, but all the traditional valuations of the Homeric heroes themselves, seen in this novel way across three thousand years of myth-making. Nothing is left undamaged. Words are used to reflect the different applications of value, and are themselves damaged as instruments of durable meaning. Every speech, seen in context, becomes merely an expression of the speaker's values. Every assertion is contingent. The play exemplifies all the principles of inevitable misreading, the contingent nature of every statement and the changeable values of every context, which the deconstructionists maintain is true of all speech. When Troilus despairingly says 'This is and is not Cressida' he speaks like a deconstructionist. The play provides a perfect exemplar for Derrida's ingeniously intricate concept of '*différance*'. Even the post-structuralist concern with identity, closely explored in its manifestations in *Troilus and Cressida* by Jonathan Dollimore's *Radical Tragedy* (1984), can be seen represented there at its most sensitive. Contemporary concern for critical theory can too easily lose sight of such points. It is not so much a matter of not finding the needle in the haystack as not seeing the haystack for the hay.

Post-structuralist and deconstructionist approaches to Shakespeare are by no means all negative. In particular the feminist approaches, examining gender and role-playing, have given substantial insights, particularly into *Twelfth Night* and *As You Like It*, where the possibilities of an Elizabethan boy actor playing Rosalind as a girl who then plays a boy playing a girl offer the same kind of riches for the question of identity as *Troilus and Cressida* (see Dusinberre, 1975, and Belsey, 1985). It is in the nature of drama, and above all Shakespeare's plays, that it examines identity, social and sexual, and role-playing, in the subtlest and most complex forms.

A similar use, rather more strangely, lies in the concept of reflexivity, the idea that a written construct is a wholly subjective composition, and that a writer writes chiefly about the problem of writing, reflecting himself in his work. Since plays put the writer's words into the mouths of distinctly identified characters interacting on stage, this is a concept we might think would be less readily available to the dramatist than to the poet or novelist. None the less it has been explored through the idea of 'metadrama'. The sequence of history plays from *Richard II* to *Henry V*, for instance, has been thoroughly examined in this regard by James L. Calderwood (1979) as a study of the ways in which the plays show language devalued, and how putting thoughts and actions into words alters them. A broader concept of metadrama is of course latent in Shakespeare's own frequent and various presentations of the 'All the world's a stage' idea.

The main preoccupation of the New Historicists is a broader version of the question of sexual identity which the feminist critics have taken up so well. Identity for the New Historicists, however, operates on the social rather than the individual scale. Patriarchy, for instance, is not seen as a feminist concern but as a question about authority in political life, and its manifestations in the subtext of the plays. This approach, while its ultimate interest is in the individual psyche or subconscious, is similar in many ways to that of the Marxists. Marxist historians work within an overarching programme of economic and social process, a relatively settled patterning which the deconstructionists reject for being too structured and therefore facile. The Marxist view, like many others, is subject to the problem of the hermeneutic circle, needing to understand the whole before the parts can be understood and vice versa. In a limited sense the New Historicists avoid or at least minimize this problem of circularity by limiting their concern to individual texts and individual manifestations of the questions of identity, in a world which they accept as fluid and ever-changing. The avoidance of assumptions involving fixity of any kind is now a fairly standard feature of modern critical thought.

The problem which these theoretical debates leave most obviously unresolved is the need to be comprehensive, a new version of the hermeneutic circle. For all the concern with the modern reader as the basic focus, the original text has to be known, too, if anything valid is to be obtained from it. With Shakespearian drama this returns us to the problem of the performance text. Saussure's concern for the semiotics of the interconnections between play and audience, the distinctive nature of theatrical discourse, ought to sit at the heart of any modern 'reading' of Shakespeare. The trouble is that most modern approaches to this problem are frankly inadequate. Debate has settled itself into an unresolvable choice between different kinds of modern approach, Shakespeare on the stage or Shakespeare on the page. The facile answer is that Shakespeare is much more accessible on the page, given the extra leisure for study which a reader has, and our loss of knowledge about Shakespeare's original staging conditions. That is too facile, indeed too defeatist, an answer, because it shuts off investigation into a convenient capsule, one drily sealed off (like the New Criticism approach to texts) by the loss of any fresh input.

The approach to Shakespeare as a performance text involves some obvious losses, in the opportunity to analyse the semiotic intricacies in the words and in the loss of immediate access to footnotes and similar information about the word-games, the echoes of famous phrases, reiterated images, even the use of once-familiar Elizabethan proverbs. All the editorial aids to understanding are lost, or at least put aside, when the play is seen in the theatre. Equally, though, the approach to Shakespeare as a written text involves losses. The collective experience of laughter and other emotions is not an insignificant element in the growth of a play's story. Laughter in a theatre is much more coercive than the private amusement which happens in reading. The intimate cohesion of the performance, the flow of feeling which accompanies the brief but compelling surge of the story on stage, the very substantiality of a drama enacted by living people in a theatre, are likely to evaporate when it is taken in private.

The challenge is to try to combine the assets of both approaches. Each process, seeing and reading the plays, can strengthen the other. One example may help to clarify the profits and losses. In Act 3 Scene 1 of *I Henry IV*, Prince Hal and Falstaff entertain their idle hours by acting out the confrontation where the prince is to be reproved by his father the king for associating with Falstaff.

The joke reaches its climax when Falstaff, playing the prince, pleads with the prince, who is playing the king, not to banish Falstaff: 'banish not him thy Harry's company. Banish plump Jack, and banish all the world.' The prince's reply is 'I do, I will'. The reader can contemplate a variety of ways of taking this exchange. Beneath the play-acting there is a real plea from Falstaff, which the prince answers with an equal awareness of the reality they are talking about. Falstaff paraphrases the marriage service by presenting himself as the world (implying the flesh and the devil too, which candidates for marriage are expected to renounce), and the prince's answer parodies the same service, with 'I do'. But is he firm and grimly concise or is he hesitant, deferring the positive assertion of 'I do' to some vague future with 'I will'? Why does he need two different phrases for his answer? Is he wholly and firmly serious, taking up the reality behind the comic plea, or does he pause and pull back from the brink? Is he speaking in his father's voice or his own? The reader has a variety of intriguing choices, each one of which has implications for the rest of the play and the relationship between the two speakers.

On stage the actor has to make his own choice. The prince has declared in his early soliloquy (at the end of Act 1 Scene 2) that he is only using his low companions so as to make his eventual reform look the brighter. In the event he does not banish them until the end of the sequel play, nine acts after he has said that Falstaff is only a temporary entertainer of his light moments. The length of this interval raises doubts about the prince's resolution, doubts which come to a head with the exchange in Act 3 Scene 1. The actor has to know what specific relationship he is to develop with Falstaff, and in what ways it shifts through the two plays. How Prince Hal is played will determine which of the many possible ways of speaking the four words of his reply to Falstaff's plea can be used here. The stage prince's attitude must be clear, and (one hopes) consistent with his presentation throughout the play. The poignancy of that moment when the doubts and tensions between the prince and Falstaff come to the surface is there whatever kind of reading the performance offers. The prince's answer is perhaps the most intensely revelatory moment in the play. The actor has to choose his role.

From this rough summary of the possibilities it might be thought that the reader of this moment will be the gainer because reading makes it possible to take up all the different possible interpretations and try them against one another. In the process, however, the reading will lose all the intensity and momentum which a good performance, experienced in a receptive company of playgoers, is unique in its capacity to give. The single reading of a performance draws its strength from the context of the entire play. The emotional intensity of the confrontation between these two mighty opposites, witnessed by an audience focusing its attention and responses exclusively on their struggle which comes to the surface only here, is gathered and concentrated by the sweep of the play's action into this one crucial moment. A performance carries the audience through its version by reducing all the many alternatives to one single and potent experience.

Of course if any single performance is taken to be the definitive version of the play by any playgoer it will become as reductive as any other fixed reading. That is one of the many grounds for post-structuralist hostility to the approach which conceives the plays as theatre texts. A performance invites consideration of a play as a whole, an organic unity, and semioticians, New Historicists and deconstructionists all prefer to deal with plays in or as fragments. The idea of the work of art as an organic unity carries with it the undesirable assumption that the author is an authority on his or her own work. To engage with a performance, particularly one composed as what is sometimes called 'director's theatre', where the director's interpretation reshapes every component of the performance into a particular 'reading' of the play, is little better than facing a surrogate author. Semioticians and post-structuralists are all readers, not playgoers. What they lose by that is not insubstantial.

Before structuralism began to take over British thinking about critical theory, the standard defence against the invasion was eclectic. It ignored the attempt to establish a single controlling principle, preferring to make a selection from amongst the more appetizing isolated ideas. This approach is usually known as pragmatism. Among philosophers it is sometimes also known as the British disease. To a large extent pragmatism is a defensive posture, designed for protection against the rigidly doctrinaire positions of the theorists and allowing the believer to enjoy a relatively casual and unhindered romp through the daffodils of literature. Consistent adherence to theory is distinctly strenuous by comparison. Pragmatism is the selective middle position implied by the evaluation of reader's text against performance text and the calculation of the losses entailed in the adoption of either as an exclusive position. It is not, however, a comfortable position. One of the major troubles with any attempt such as this one to grapple with conflicting theories is that each theory seems to contradict its rivals, the result being that the increasingly despairing reader is drawn more and more towards a central position and the classic posture of the pragmatist. That central position may seem like the still point in a turning world, but it might equally well turn out to be a whirlpool which will drown the reader. It is certainly a black tangle in the middle of the circle of intersecting and diametrically opposed theories, a no-man's-land where everyone on the surrounding perimeter is your enemy. In the end its difficulties become a version of the hermeneutic circle. To be a successful pragmatist you have to know all the theories, and the postures they put you in. To know all the theories properly you have to believe in them. If that seems more like Catch-22 than the hermeneutic circle, it is because they are versions of the same difficulty.

397

Every theory is in some degree reductive. A theory provides a system by which experience can be organized and made into sense, or at least into something which the hopeful student will find comprehensible. All theories are constructed against the threat of chaos, which is the absence of system or organizing principle. We need theories, organizing principles, to make sense of what comes at us, however provisional and imperfect that sense may have to be. That is the basis for all dogma, religious and political alike. What applies to experience in life also applies, in a smaller way, to Shakespeare. We need some theoretical basis for any coherent approach to the plays, but any theory is by its nature reductive, and the temptation sometimes to stray beyond the bounds of system and the coherence provided by system is unavoidable. Different people will in any case find different theories to fit their different needs, and even in a single individual the theories may change as the needs change. Critical apostasy, like religous or political apostasy, is not a rare phenomenon. The one essential is to know where you are in the circle at any given time.

Miners have worked the magic mountain for nearly four centuries now. It is riddled with tunnels, each of which has been cut into the shape of the tunneller. New miners will usually find some tunnel shaped more or less to suit their individual needs, before they start their own digging. If you know where you are in the mountain, the act of digging should at least show something about your own shape.

FURTHER READING

Bevington, David (1984) *Action is Eloquence*, Harvard University Press, Cambridge

Bradley, A. C. (1904) *Shakespearean Tragedy*, Macmillan, London

Calderwood, James L. (1979) *Metadrama in Shakespeare's Henriad: 'Richard II' to 'Henry V'*, University of California Press, Berkeley

Dollimore, Jonathan (1984) *Radical Tragedy: Religion, Ideology and Power in the Drama of Shakespeare and his Contemporaries*, Harvester, Brighton

Elam, Keir (1981) *The Semiotics of Theatre and Drama*, Methuen, London

Evans, Malcolm (1986) *Signifying Nothing: Truth's True Contents in Shakespeare's Text*, Harvester Press, Brighton

Granville Barker, Harley (1945) *Prefaces to Shakespeare*, 4th series, Macmillan, London

Greenblatt, Stephen (1980) *Renaissance Self-Fashioning: More to Shakespeare*, University of Chicago Press, Chicago

Knight, G. Wilson (1949) *The Wheel of Fire*, revised edn, Methuen, London [first published 1930]

Mahood, M. (1957) *Shakespeare's Wordplay*, Methuen, London

Schoenbaum, Samuel (1970) *Shakespeare's Lives*, Oxford University Press, London

ADDITIONAL WORKS CITED

Barthes, Roland (1977) 'The Death of the Author'. In Roland Barthes, *Image-Music-Text*, translated by Stephen Heath, Fontana, London [essay first published 1968]

Belsey, Catherine (1985) 'Disrupting sexual difference: meaning and gender in the comedies'. In John Drakakis (ed.), *Alternative Shakespeares*, Methuen, London

Clemen, W. H. (1951) *The Development of Shakespeare's Imagery*, Methuen, London

Dollimore, Jonathan and Sinfield, Alan (eds) (1985) *Political Shakespeare: New Essays in Cultural Materialism*, Manchester University Press, Manchester

Dusinberre, Juliet (1975) *Shakespeare and the Nature of Women*, Macmillan, London

Fish, Stanley (1980) *Is There a Text in This Class? The Authority of Interpretive Communities*, Harvard University Press, Cambridge

Goldberg, Jonathan (1983) *James I and the Politics of Literature*, Johns Hopkins University Press, Baltimore

Hawkes, Terence (1986) *That Shakespeherian Rag: essays on a critical process*, Routledge, London

Knights, L. C. (1946) 'How Many Children Had Lady Macbeth?' In L. C. Knights, *Explorations*, Chatto & Windus, London [essay first published 1933]

Miller, J. Hillis (1977) 'Arachne's Broken Woof', *Georgia Review*, 31, 44–60

Spurgeon, Caroline (1935) *Shakespeare's Imagery and What it Tells Us*, Cambridge University Press, Cambridge

28

MEDIEVAL DRAMA

WILLIAM TYDEMAN

Had this compilation been called for forty years ago, it is unlikely that the drama of the Middle Ages would have featured in its list of contents, so recently has its repertoire inspired positive reactions among literary critics. Even in 1987 the *Oxford Illustrated History of English Literature* allocated no more than thirty-seven lines to the medieval dramatic canon, the same number devoted to the much less varied output of Joe Orton. Fortunately, modern advocates have usually succeeded in gaining for the plays of late medieval Britain a higher status than at any period since their rediscovery. Vigorous discussion, now infused with a fuller understanding of putative origins, purposes, composition and conditions of performance, has also brought to the forefront of academic enquiry the complex relationships between dramatic creation and religious ideology, doctrinal exegesis and demotic culture, theatre and ritual, text and presentation, the stage and the community.

Although the surviving repertoire of medieval drama is not extensive, sufficient material escaped the ravages of the Reformation to warrant the appearance of a substantial corpus of criticism during the first half of the present century, had the intellectual climate been favourable. Nor can linguistic difficulties or a lack of helpfully edited texts be held responsible for the sluggishness with which commentators sought to engage with the plays. The dearth of enthusiasm must rather be attributed to the prevalent belief that medieval drama constituted one of literature's 'arid zones' which did not merit critical irrigation.

For nearly half a century this assumption sustained a near-permanent divorce between scholars inclined to regard medieval plays as philological phenomena of specialized dialectal interest but limited literary appeal, and others happy to treat performance-data as being of exclusively antiquarian, sociological, cultural or anthropological relevance. It rarely occurred to the pioneers that the way in which contextual or material circumstances condition a play's techniques is as worthy of serious scrutiny as the orthographic peculiarities of its scribe or its deployment of variable stanzaic forms, or that the information culled from archives and artefacts, traditional customs and ecclesiastical injunctions, can only achieve full pertinence when viewed in conjunction with situations embodied in existing theatre-scripts. A dramaturgy whose purpose was often obscure, and whose *mise-en-scène* was invariably disregarded, suffered particularly from the failure to perceive that medieval plays possessed not merely historical importance but intrinsic quality. Only when the *Zeitgeist* permitted a change in taste could meaningful criticism come into being.

The general wariness in getting to grips with a genre for which there were few known precedents is understandable, given the dominant literary, cultural and theatrical preoccupations of the early twentieth century. Men and women of letters, reared in the traditions of classical scholarship and inheriting some of the Augustan prejudice against anything smacking of 'Gothick' lawlessness, tended to scrutinize medieval dramatic achievements in the spirit in which John Evelyn had in his *Diary* dismissed the 'fantastical and licentious' buildings of the same period as 'congestions of heavy, dark, melancholy and monkish piles, without any just proportion, use or beauty'. Nor did the sheer face of an anonymous *massif* offer a toehold to those whose preference was to scale the peaks of literature by the biographical route: the unavoidably awkward fact that medieval playwrights were nameless men deterred those anxious to pronounce with Edward Dowden or Hippolyte Taine on the presumed correlation between life and art in the case of a Shakespeare or a Christopher Marlowe.

Critical discussion was also impeded by a failure to comprehend the nature of medieval dramatic composition. The fact that publication of the relevant texts coincided with the heyday of Ibsenite and post-Ibsenite naturalism made the skilful but alien techniques of medieval playwrights far harder to appreciate than is the case today. For example, character portrayal in cycle-play episode and morality-drama does not lack subtleties, but the absence of 'psychological interest' arising from the indirect revelation of private feelings and motives was deemed a weakness; the subordination of the 'natural' idiom of everyday speech-patterns to exigencies of rhyme and metre, and to the principles of rhetorical organization, was dismissed as stilted. Few critics of the 1890s and 1900s could appreciate what confronted them, and with Shakespeare's transformation into a psychological naturalist by A. C. Bradley and others, the denigration by comparison with their successors of plays castigated as 'primitive' in conception and 'quaint' in style was thereby facilitated.

Moreover, in 1890 appeared the first version of that Victorian monument to anthropological comparativism, Frazer's *Golden Bough*, which was to exercise such a potent influence on research in a wide variety of disciplines. Frazer's persistence in establishing what he adjudged to be universal patterns of religious worship and belief, so that heterogeneous phenomena were treated as having a common origin and all cultures construed as a single culture, encouraged early commentators to give fertility rites too prominent a role in accounting for the origins of drama in general, and to do less than justice to the Christian matrix of much medieval theatrical activity in particular. By endorsing evolutionary theories then fashionable, Frazer also helped to strengthen the dangerous notion that highly selective techniques applied to the variegated texture of dramatic compositions could legitimately accentuate such features as could be shown to have 'reached fruition' in Jonson and Shakespeare, and marginalize those which could not.

These tendencies coalesce in E. K. Chambers's *The Medieval Stage* (1903), which as a feat of synthesis still commands respect, but is disqualified as criticism by the author's admission that he had almost wholly neglected the literary aspects of his topic, reacting against such earlier writers as A. W. Ward who had 'shown themselves but little curious about the social and economic facts upon which the medieval drama rested' (vol. 1, p. v). Chambers had little faith in the intrinsic merits of the extant texts: scarcely ever does he embark upon evaluation, and medieval drama is largely respected for the way it 'made the great Shakespearean stage possible' (vol. 1, p. vi). Conditioned therefore to regard the theatre of the Middles Ages as a mere foyer to the splendours of the Elizabethan playhouse, Chambers is only too willing to incorporate medieval dramas into a continuing process which he views as stemming from the gradual infiltration of 'secular' elements into Latin music-dramas demonstrated to have evolved late in the tenth century from developments within the offices and liturgy of the Roman Catholic Church. Associating this trend with what he terms 'laicization', he sees the transfer of the plays from church interior to market-place and their translation from Latin into the European vernaculars as confirming a progressive tendency towards humanizing and rendering comedic the uncompromising presentation of Christian doctrines, and ultimately triumphing to make possible the major achievements of the theatres of the Renaissance, with Herod the prototype of the ranting tyrant, the 'uncoverted Magdalen' offering opportunities for 'scenes of wholly secular luxury and romance' (vol. 2, p. 90), and non-scriptural characters lending themselves to comic exploitation. Because Chambers cannot reconcile himself to the role of such devices in furthering the didactic purposes of the Church, he conveys a sense of perennial conflict between the free-wheeling anarchy of the medieval artist and the restraining interdictory hand of ecclesiastical authority. His affections appear chiefly engaged by wandering mimes, mock-kings, fools and boy-bishops whose activities are linked to a classic and pagan past, rather than by the clerics, saints and patriarchs whose censorious tendencies he tacitly deplores. The lusty 'medieval spirit' Chambers invokes in such contexts has too many affinities with 'Merrie England', that other outmoded myth of his era, to have long-term validity.

Few critics sought to integrate their insights with Chambers's lively relish for facts. Scholarship and appreciation did set off hand-in-hand with C. M. Gayley's *Plays of Our Forefathers* (1907), but it did not take long for them to part company again. Though Gayley urged upon literary investigators 'a more minute and sympathetic study of these monuments than has hitherto been undertaken' (pp. 211–12), more than forty years passed before the challenge was adequately met, despite G. R. Coffman's timely reassertion (1929) of Gayley's approach. The stigma conveyed in the Victorian coinage 'Pre-Shakespearian Drama' still prevailed: W. P. Ker's *English Literature, Medieval* (1912) left out plays entirely; Allardyce Nicholl's *Masks, Mimes and Miracles* (1931) re-worked Chambers but likewise avoided assessment, and Karl Young's compendious assemblage in *The Drama of the Medieval Church* (1933) of major and minor Latin music-dramas with their roots in Roman Catholic places of worship was scholarly rather than critical. By reproducing his texts out of chronological sequence, Young perpetuated the heresy that these liturgical plays observed a progression which went from simple to sophisticated, spiritual to spectacular, which neatly mirrored Chambers's assumption that this pattern was reproduced in later centuries.

In the next decade the prejudicial attitude persisted. When, in *British Dramatists* (1942), Graham Greene wrote that 'One reads these plays now for pedantry rather than for pleasure' (p. 8) he was expressing a generally uncontroversial view. Also typical was A. P. Rossiter's *English Drama from Early Times to the Elizabethans* (1950) with its emphasis on 'cultural continuities' and its almost apologetic justification for taking medieval drama into account at all. For this writer a Chambers-like search for the sources of 'certain deep-rooted themes' was maintained at the expense of such playwrights as the Wakefield Master, whose mastery manifested itself for Rossiter in 'half a dozen crabbed old plays' whose 'crudeness' of diction acted like 'a gag in the mouth', leaving one to reflect 'on how much might be made of all this, given a better tongue' (p. 81), and so presumably to confer greater distinction on his Elizabethan successors. Five years later Hardin Craig's *English Religious Drama of the Middle Ages* (1955) adopted a comparably reductive line on the quality of the plays as dramatic literature, exhibiting them as 'museum pieces'. Singularly well-informed on these works, Craig seemed immune to their theatrical vigour and artistry, stating baldly that 'the technique of the mystery and miracle plays and of the main current of English popular drama consisted merely in telling a story on a stage by means of dialogue, impersonation and action' (p. 9), a remark which begs every important question.

The revaluation of medieval drama during the past four decades was prefaced by the appearance of Harold Gardiner's *Mysteries' End* (1946), which brought the training and sympathies of a Roman Catholic cleric to bear on the genre. Although again ostensibly emphasizing the Elizabethan end of the historical spectrum, Gardiner's conclusion that the religious plays did not peter out because their inspiration was spent, but because they provoked the hostility of the Protestant reformers, not only broke the evolutionary chain but gave fresh prestige to a drama whose effectiveness even as late as the mid-sixteenth century was sufficiently potent to threaten the cause of the Reformation. Far from being antagonistic to the popular religious drama and eager to deplore its 'secular' tendencies, said Gardiner, the Catholic Church acknowledged its didactic function 'as a helpful handmaid in her preaching efforts' (p. 5), with the result that readers began to reconsider the plays' contents and techniques as governed by their role in an instructional programme of evangelization. Gardiner may have been over-influenced by his pre-determined perspective to undervalue other causes for the demise of civic religious theatre, but his book was an important step in reorienting criticism towards more relevant and less damaging standards of judgement.

Equally significant for the future was the fact that in 1951 the city of York chose to celebrate the Festival of Britain with a revival of its civic cycle in a modernized adaption directed by E. Martin Browne, so that medieval drama could again be experienced at least periodically in its proper element, as live performance. The increasing accessibility of presentations demonstrating the literary vitality and theatrical viability of the medieval repertoire was a major factor in improving its critical reputation. Certainly F. M. Salter's incisive monograph *Medieval Drama in Chester* (1955) took performance conditions as central to an understanding of the Chester Cycle. By spelling out in detail just how painstaking, elaborate and expensive an undertaking the mounting of an annual cycle sequence was, Salter demonstrated implicitly the unlikelihood that the texts themselves were cobbled together by men who lacked the education and expertise to produce anything better. Practical questions of staging also dominated Richard Southern's heroic attempt in *The Medieval Theatre in the Round* (1957) to employ textual, theatrical and pictorial analysis to provide a plausible reconstruction of the original presentation of *The Castle of Perseverance*, the most spectacular of the morality plays, and thereby enhance appreciation of medieval authors' skills in suiting play to playing-area. Some of Southern's conjectures have been challenged and refuted, but his close attention to the script enforced a new respect for the medieval dramatist's craft, as well as undermining the then current preoccupation with proscenium staging.

The main lines of contemporary critical discussion were laid down in the following decade. In 1959 came the first volume of Glynne Wickham's *Early English Stages*, an all-embracing survey of stage conditions during the late medieval and early Renaissance period, which did not fall into the trap of regarding medieval drama as a curious product created and organized by artless illiterates. The visual splendours and technical sophistication of the plays were now regarded as appropriately complementing dramatic and even literary talents of no mean order. Even if for Wickham 'the public theatres of Elizabethan London were the crowning glory of mediaeval experiment' (p. xxvii), it was no longer suggested that medieval experiment could boast no glories of its own making.

Wickham extended the relevant contexts for medieval drama to include tournaments, pageant theatres in the streets, and such forms of indoor entertainment as masks, mummings and disguisings, thus bringing both scripted and unscripted theatre into a vital relationship linked by common reliance on stagecraft and visual symbolism. Religious performances, claimed as being staged under church auspices even when the trade guilds assumed responsibility for their organization, were seen to owe a debt to the processional pageantry of civic celebrations. Decisive, too, was Wickham's rejection of the earlier belief that a line of continuous development extended from the Latin liturgical church-plays to the alfresco dramas in the European vernaculars; instead he postulated a hiatus attendant on the institution of the Feast of Corpus Christi and the missionary zeal of the friars of the Dominican and Franciscan orders, manifesting itself in a novel creative impulse:

> Let us then try to rid ourselves of the notion of a sacred drama made profane by the steady encroachment of wordly things upon it. Let us recognize instead the deliberate challenge that was issued to a secular world by the injection into it of a sacred drama ... at the insistence of friars or like-minded priests and clerks, who were determined to bring the relevance of Christ's sacrifice to bewildered mankind in the market place.
>
> (Wickham, 1959, pp. 314, 316)

Undoubtedly Wickham's insights had been strengthened by his own practical concern with dramatic production, and over the past thirty years criticism of medieval plays has been informed by at least some awareness of their stage potential. Indeed, many academics have engaged in practical experiments to investigate the nature of medieval stage performance, and devoted time and energy to solving problems of presentation, in terms of both present-day and medieval settings (e.g. Collins, 1972; Nelson, 1974; Tydeman, 1986). While there is a danger that critics may be diverted from their regular function by a fascination with technical matters of nuts and bolts, processional routes and waggon-widths, some of the greatest enthusiasts for the minutiae of plays-in-performance have also made notable contributions to our understanding of medieval English drama as literature, especially now that verbal and visual creativity are appreciated as complementary skills.

One of the most avidly explored practical questions is the notorious issue of whether or not, at certain centres at least, cycle presentations were given from pageant-waggons moving through the streets in sequence and performing at anything up to a dozen separate viewing-points or 'stations'. Liveliest debate

has focused on York, since the traditional view of day-long processional performances there has been most strongly queried by scholars who argue that
the number of individual episodes and the time available to play them render
processional production impossible, and that the only plausible solution is to
assume a parade of silent tableaux followed by a sole performance of the
complete sequence at a single site either indoors or outside. Alternative presentation modes and sites have been canvassed for York and other centres,
including Chester where the degree of reliance to be placed on Archdeacon
Rogers's sixteenth-century testimony as to the nature and use of pageant-
waggons has been eagerly discussed. Equal controversy surrounds Southern's
conjectural theatre-in-the-round setting for *The Castle of Perseverance*, which
has led such sceptics as Natalie Crohn Schmitt (1972) to doubt the predominance of this mode of staging in the Middle Ages, although Southern's conclusions have gained support from those, like Catherine Belsey (1974), convinced by the symbolic connotations of his projected stage-plan.

Visual symbolism has generally assumed a more central place in critical
discussion since 1960, now that dramatic value is perceived to reside in more
than the mere words of a play's text; scholarly exegesis has enabled readers
and spectators to recover in some measure the meaning inherent in important
iconographical objects and figurations, with the cycle-play shepherds' gifts to
the Christ-child a frequent subject of conflicting interpretations. In the pictorial
and artefactual area the seminal work was clearly M. D. Anderson's *Drama
and Imagery in English Medieval Churches* (1963) which, along with Otto Pächt's
The Rise of Pictorial Narrative in Twelfth-Century England (1962), helped to
guide critical investigation in the direction of the analogies to be discovered
between theatrical iconography and that recoverable from medieval stained-
glass, alabasters, manuscript illustrations and related material. The leading
exponent of this approach today is Clifford Davidson, who argues that drama
modelled itself on art, rather than vice versa as Anderson's enthusiasm sometimes betrayed her into suggesting. Davidson's *From Creation to Doom* (1984)
attempts to reconstruct the visual aspects of the York Cycle; far from simply
providing a set of mere speculative parallels, he demonstrates how York's
combination of iconographical and illusionistic modes of aesthetic expression
is echoed in the stylistic strategy of the text. Here traditional, somewhat
hieratic methods of characterization and expression are modified by the more
naturalistic and individualistic techniques deployed by the York authors. The
danger with any approach via graphic analogies is obviously undue dogmatism,
but drama was a major branch of medieval art, and that its rationale and
techniques should derive from a similar set of principles is not unreasonable.
Moreover, now that critics have developed an ability to handle the non-
realistic dimension in medieval aesthetics – allegorical, symbolic, typological –
commentary has rightly concentrated on recovering the ways in which our

forefathers would have interpreted what we without skilled assistance can only view one-dimensionally within a literal frame of reference. Such an approach obviously impinges on literary criticism proper: perhaps the most thoroughgoing attempt to alert modern readers and spectators to less familiar levels of meaning has been Helterman's *Symbolic Action in the Plays of the Wakefield Master* (1981), which by focusing on the interplay between differing levels of interpretation sequentially or concurrently presented, greatly enhances our appreciation of the subtlety inherent in the Master's art.

Much of the authority displayed in recent criticism of medieval drama stems from a considerably sharpened understanding of the processes of medieval Christian thought and worship; here Eleanor Prosser's *Drama and Religion in the English Mystery Plays* (1961) and O. B. Hardison's vastly influential *Christian Rite and Christian Drama in the Middle Ages* (1965) led the way. Prosser was able to demonstrate in detail how the cycle plays served the ends of both dramatic artistry and religious didacticism, but it was Hardison's magisterial revisionist account that caused the most stir. Hardison brought his scepticism to bear not only on the Chambers–Young explanation of dramatic origins and developments, but demolished the notion that one could in any meaningful sense separate the routines of ritual from those of drama, and so called in question the demarcation line former scholars had drawn between religious observance and prototype 'play':

> Although Chambers and Young both recognized that medieval drama developed out of a religious context, neither was willing to accept the implications of this fact. . . . I have attempted to show that in the ninth century the boundary that Chambers and Young posited between religious ritual (the services of the Church) and drama did not exist. Religious ritual was the drama of the early Middle Ages and had been ever since the decline of the classical theater.
>
> (Hardison, 1965, p. viii)

While the latter statement remains open to question, Hardison's reassessment certainly scotched the concept of so-called 'secularizing' tendencies in the vernacular religious drama, to the extent that Rosemary Woolf was able to demonstrate in *The English Mystery Plays* (1972), which was chiefly concerned with the background sources and homiletic analogues to the mystery play episodes, that vernacular elements were introduced as much for literary reasons as for demotic appeal. The search for a fuller understanding of medieval drama's theological sophistication has been foregrounded in a number of modern studies concentrating on the more recondite aspects of the texts, notably the presentation of the doctrine of the Atonement, and the presence of the theme of Lucifer's 'abuse of power' in the N-Town plays. Such criticism, while not always revealing much feel for the plays as theatre, strongly supports the case for their medieval authors' intellectual grasp, particularly where the doctrinal complexities and their implications required sensitive handling.

Equally concerned with doctrinal formulations but tinged with a greater sense of what makes for effective theatre, is V. A. Kolve's *The Play Called Corpus Christi* (1966). A masterly contribution to a fresher understanding of the cyclic drama, Kolve's book is excellent in revealing how the selection of incidents treated reflected hallowed patterns involving prefiguration and fulfilment as demonstrating the divine plan for the salvation of the human race. Kolve supports Wickham in relating the theme governing the cycles to the doctrinal mysteries celebrated at the Feast of Corpus Christi, and identifies a radical and distinct spirit behind the vernacular plays:

> When drama moved into the streets and the market place, into a milieu already the home of men's playing and games, it was redefined *as* game and allowed to exploit fully its nonearnest, gratuitous nature at the same time as its range of subject and its cast of sacred persons grew.
>
> (p. 48)

This conviction enables Kolve to write perceptively on the occurrence of the 'game' element as a unifying factor, even in such unlikely places as the Crucifixion pageants and the Wakefield *Buffeting*, where it fulfils an almost cathartic role. In the Wakefield *Crucifixion*, for example, Christ's executioners play out an elaborate fantasy in which their victim, as befits His royal status, is prepared for jousting in a tournament, but one where He will demonstrate to sinful Man how victory over Satan is to be won:

> Stand nere, felows, and let se
> how we can hors oure kyng so fre,
>   By any craft;
> Stand thou yonder on yond syde,
> And we shall se how he can ryde,
>   And how to weld a shaft.
>   (ed. England, 1897, p. 261)

Alan Nelson (1974) sees the doctrines underlying the Corpus Christi celebrations as having a negligible influence on the development of the cyclic plays' subject-matter, but Kolve's work and that of others has led recent critics to concentrate attention on matters of theme, structure and unity, with Chester a popular cycle for debate. The most fruitful discussion here is Peter Travis's *Dramatic Design in the Chester Cycle* (1982) which, unlike John Gardner's over-ambitious *Construction of the Wakefield Cycle* (1974), propounds no ultra-radical theory of internal organization, but explores the triple principles governing the design of the Chester sequence both helpfully and sensibly.

Nor has the influence of external factors on compositional tactics been ignored recently. Our modern understanding is now governed by a more developed awareness that a spirit of diversity and plurality lies at the heart of the literature which medieval theatrical activity engendered. Where Woolf can often give the impression that the cycle texts all display generic resemblance, others now insist on the recognition of local conditions and requirements as vital to critical assessment. The publication of complete sets of extant regional records in the *Records of Early English Drama* series (general editor Alexandra Johnston, 1979–) is of incomparable value in pursuing this exercise. One cardinal influence here has been that of Stanley Kahrl's *Traditions of Medieval English Drama* (1974) with its cautionary emphasis on establishing appropriate criteria of presentation when attempting to analyse dramatic craftsmanship in the moralities and cycles: processional production in the north of England suggests the application of different critical standards from those suited to a place-and-scaffold mounting in East Anglia. The close relationships between individual play text and local community life are immensely variable, and in a similar manner the firm line marking secular entertainment off from sacred performance has become blurred in recent years, as it becomes more apparent that religious plays not only used comparable techniques to those employed in popular diversions, but assimilated elements from communal tradition and game routines: the morality *Mankind* and the Croxton *Play of the Sacrament* have proved invaluable texts for this type of exploration, which owes much to Kolve's perceptions and Richard Axton's related analyses of earlier material in *European Drama of the Middle Ages* (1974). The interrelationship of sacred and profane has yet to be fully explored and may go deeper, though few would go as far as Benjamin Hunnigher (1961) in attributing the birth of Christian drama to the importation of secular mime-actors into monastic ceremonials of the tenth century.

These numerous lines of approach have persuaded critics to return to the texts with renewed appreciation of their strengths as literature and drama, a movement to which a spate of new improved scholarly editions has contributed a great deal. Verbal and visual symbolism, pictorial analogues, Christian thought and doctrine, community contexts, methods of staging and styles of performance, now sustain a major reappraisal of medieval dramatic strategies and literary technique, along with more conventional investigation of structural organization, narrative development, characterization, linguistic texture. Medieval characterization, now acknowledged as basically dissimilar from that in which naturalistic drama excels, has been shown to require no external justification, but its symbolic devices take on new value if viewed as governed by didactic or thematic factors; its interest currently resides in determining the precise blend of individuality and conformity to typological or homiletic demands which a writer permitted himself. In the same way a richer understanding of the verbal idiom and imagery of the plays has become evident, notably in *Mankind*, while specialized features of lexis have been explored in individual cycle texts, whose diction has sometimes been traced to oratorical strategies. In *The Rhetoric of Free Will* (1974), for example, Merle Fifield related the language of the morality protagonists to their spiritual condition; Richard J. Collier's *Poetry and Drama in the York Corpus Christi Play* (1978) demonstrated how the verse-medium in blending colloquial freedom and formal restraint has a direct relation to the overall meaning of the cycle as a whole, and similar efforts to correlate dramatic, doctrinal and linguistic purpose in other texts must complement other ways of seeing the cycles as unified totalities.

Future critical enquiry will undoubtedly concern itself with terminology: already there have been efforts to modify the old arbitrary divisions into 'cycle play', 'morality' and so forth, and to define more precisely that evasive term 'the interlude'. David Mills, in the Revels *History* (Cawley, 1983, pp. 69–91), has pointed out that our own concepts of 'drama' and 'characterization' differ profoundly from those of the Middle Ages, while others have stressed the ambiguities inherent on the very words 'play' and 'plays' in such a context. The semantic significances of terms very much taken for granted are only just beginning to provoke a response.

Rooted in the community and arising from key events in the social, spiritual and seasonal cycle, medieval plays depend for their rich intensity on that close association with the rhythms and moods of demotic life and the vigour and verve of popular speech also found in Chaucer, Langland and Skelton. Highly pictorial, relying on presentational rather than representational techniques, exhibiting a range of registers from formal hymns of adoration to satirical subversions of the temporal hierarchy, the drama of the Middle Ages is not in danger of falling out of fashion. It testifies to a firm belief that drama can render sharply and graphically abstract concept and didactic moral, and offer to reader and spectator a theatrical replication of 'God's plenty' which exalts vitality and variety.

What the twenty-first century holds is unclear: one suspects that for most people English drama will still begin with Shakespeare. Even the finest critics of today and tomorrow can probably never make the medieval drama familiar or accessible to the man in the street. Yet it cannot be denied that John R. Elliott Jr.'s words are even truer at the present time than when he wrote them in 1969:

> These plays have ceased to be mere historical curiosities and have become for us works of art, as impressive in their scope and intensity as the greatest products of medieval literature.

FURTHER READING

Bevington, David (ed.) (1975) *Medieval Drama*, Houghton Mifflin, Boston

Happé, Peter (ed.) (1975) *English Mystery Plays: A Selection*, Penguin, Harmondsworth

Hardison, O. B., Jr. (1965) *Christian Rite and Christian Drama in the Middle Ages*, Johns Hopkins University Press, Baltimore

Kahrl, Stanley J. (1974) *Traditions of English Medieval Drama*, Hutchinson, London

Kolve, V. A. (1966) *The Play Called Corpus Christi*, Edward Arnold, London

Potter, Robert (1975) *The English Morality Play: Origins, History and Influence of a Dramatic Tradition*, Routledge & Kegan Paul, London

Southern, Richard (1957) *The Medieval Theatre in the Round*, Faber & Faber, London

Taylor, Jerome and Nelson, Alan H. (eds) (1972) *Medieval English Drama: Essays Critical and Contextual*, University of Chicago Press, Chicago

Tydeman, William (1978) *The Theatre in the Middle Ages: Western European Stage Conditions c. 800–1576*, Cambridge University Press, Cambridge

Wickham, Glynne (1959) *Early English Stages 1300–1660*, vol. 1 (1300–1576), Routledge & Kegan Paul, London

——(1974) *The Medieval Theatre*, Weidenfeld & Nicholson, London

Woolf, Rosemary (1972), *The English Mystery Plays*, Routledge & Kegan Paul, London

ADDITIONAL WORKS CITED

Anderson, M. D. (1963) *Drama and Imagery in English Medieval Churches*, Cambridge University Press, Cambridge

Axton, Richard (1974) *European Drama of the Early Middle Ages*, Hutchinson, London

Belsey, Catherine (1974) 'The Stage Plan of *The Castle of Perseverance*', *Theatre Notebook*, 28, 124–32

Cawley, A. C. et al. (1983) *The Revels History of Drama in English*, vol. 1, *Medieval Drama*, Methuen, London

Chambers, E. K. (1903) *The Medieval Stage*, 2 vols, Clarendon Press, Oxford

Coffman, George R. (1929) 'A Plea for the Study of the Corpus Christi Plays as Drama', *Studies in Philology*, 26, 411–24

Collier, Richard J. (1978) *Poetry and Drama in the York Corpus Christi Play*, Shoestring Press, Hamden

Collins, Fletcher, Jr. (1972) *The Production of Medieval Church Music-Drama*, University Press of Virginia, Charlottesville

Craig, Hardin (1955) *English Religious Drama of the Middle Ages*, Clarendon Press, Oxford

Davidson, Clifford (1984) *From Creation to Doom*, AMS Press, New York

Elliott, John R., Jr. (1972) 'The Sacrifice of Isaac as Comedy and Tragedy'. In Jerome Taylor and Alan H. Nelson (eds), *Medieval English Drama: Essays Critical and Contextual*, University of Chicago Press, Chicago [essay first published 1969]

England, George (ed.) (1897) *The Towneley Plays*, Early English Text Society, vol. 71, Oxford University Press, London

Fifield, Merle (1974) *The Rhetoric of Free Will*, University of Leeds School of English, Leeds

Gardiner, Harold C. (1946) *Mysteries' End: An Investigation of the Last Days of the Medieval Religious Stage*, Yale Studies in English, 103, Yale University Press, New Haven

Gardner, John (1974) *The Construction of the Wakefield Cycle*, Southern Illinois University Press, Carbondale and Edwardsville

Gayley, C. M. (1907) *Plays of Our Forefathers*, Duffield, New York

Greene, Graham (1942) *British Dramatists*, Collins, London

Helterman, Jeffrey (1981) *Symbolic Action in the Plays of the Wakefield Master*, University of Georgia Press, Athens

Hunningher, Benjamin (1961) *The Origin of the Theater*, Hill & Wang, New York [first published 1955]

Nelson, Alan H. (1974) *The Medieval English Stage: Corpus Christi Pageants and Plays*, University of Chicago Press, Chicago

Pächt, Otto (1962) *The Rise of Pictorial Narrative in Twelfth Century England*, Oxford University Press, Oxford

Prosser, Eleanor (1961) *Drama and Religion in the English Mystery Plays*, Stanford University Press, Stanford

Rossiter, A. P. (1950) *English Drama from Early Times to the Elizabethans*, Hutchinson, London

Salter, F. M. (1955) *Medieval Drama in Chester*, University of Toronto Press, Toronto

Schmitt, Natalie Crohn (1972) 'Was There a Medieval Theatre in the Round? A Re-examination of the Evidence'. In Jerome Taylor and Alan H. Nelson (eds) *Medieval English Drama: Essays Critical and Contextual*, University of Chicago Press, Chicago [essay first published 1968–70]

Travis, Peter W. (1982) *Dramatic Design in the Chester Cycle*, University of Chicago Press, Chicago

Tydeman, William (1986) *English Medieval Theatre 1400–1500*, Routledge & Kegan Paul, London

Young, Karl (1933) *The Drama of the Medieval Church*, 2 vols, Clarendon Press, Oxford

29

RENAISSANCE DRAMA

CATHERINE BELSEY

A procession passes over the stage of the Globe Theatre. Attendants carry torches to suggest that it is night, though in the broad daylight of an afternoon performance in the open air no serious attempt can be made to simulate darkness. The actors move silently, like figures in a pageant. Standing apart from the procession, apparently invisible and inaudible to them, another figure holds a skull. He comments on the four 'excellent characters' leading the pageant across the stage:

> Duke; royal lecher; go, grey-hair'd adultery;
> And thou his son, as impious steep'd as he;
> And thou his bastard, true-begot in evil;
> And thou his duchess, that will do with devil.
> (Tourneur, *The Revenger's Tragedy*, 1605–6?, I. i. 1–5)

The four figures are 'characters' only in the seventeenth-century sense of the term. They are not idiosyncratic individuals, but representative types, like the protagonists of Sir Thomas Overbury's *Characters*, which first appeared in 1613, or like the whore defined by Monticelso in Webster's *The White Devil* (1612): 'Shall I expound whore to you? sure I shall; I'll give their perfect character' (III. ii. 78–9). The Duke and his family, the text makes clear, are emblematic figures, the lecher, the bastard, the voracious woman. The Duke's son and heir, the stage direction reveals, is called Lussurioso, lecherous in Italian; his bastard's name is Spurio, the fake. Meanwhile, two of the Duchess's sons, who have not yet appeared, are called Ambitioso and Supervacuo. The phrase 'grey-hair'd adultery' evokes a personified abstraction from the morality tradition, rather than the illusionist 'character' familiar to a modern audience from nineteenth-century novels and twentieth-century soap operas where, in the interests of an imaginary verisimilitude, lechers might be expected also to have a kindly streak, or lascivious women hearts of gold. Even when Renais-

413

sance characters change, as they do, often abruptly and inexplicably, they tend to be true to a succession of types in the course of the play.

Though *The Revenger's Tragedy* is a relatively striking instance of the emblematic Renaissance dramatic tradition, it is by no means uncharacteristic in its explicit labelling of social and moral types. De Flores deflowers the heroine of Middleton's *The Changeling* (1624): he is a vice-figure who remains unremittingly vicious. Middleton's *A Chaste Maid in Cheapside* (1613?) depicts the world of financial and sexual rapacity which exists when the decaying gentry and the rich city merchants decide they need each other. Here the dissolute Sir Walter Whorehound sets out to marry Moll Yellowhammer, the goldsmith's daughter, for her money. And the entire cast of Jonson's *Volpone* (1605) consistently live up to their animal names, from the Fox himself through to Lady Pol[l], who talks incessantly, but without much meaning, in phrases she has learnt from others.

The choric figure holding the skull at the opening of *The Revenger's Tragedy* is at the same time the tragic protagonist, Vindice: Revenge. The procession remains unconscious of his commentary. Later in the scene it will become clear that they are not in the same place, that while the parade of vices represents the court, Vindice is at this moment far away in the country, and that these distinct locations designate corruption and innocence respectively. To an audience in the second half of the twentieth century, familiar with the work of Ionesco or Beckett, the mode of *The Revenger's Tragedy* is readily intelligible: the play's way of making meaning does not depend on the construction of an illusory resemblance to a world the spectators might expect to experience outside the theatre. But for an earlier generation, brought up to suppose that all fiction aspires to the condition of the novel, much Renaissance drama seemed hopelessly alien, primitive beside the human realism of Shakespeare. More recently the success of Renaissance drama in production has paradoxically begun to make visible to modern audiences the emblematic elements in Shakespeare's plays, which had been so long ignored by a novelistic critical tradition. Vindice's closest intertextual relation is evidently Hamlet, who holds a succession of skulls in the scene with the gravediggers, an episode which appears largely unmotivated by the plot of the play, but which can be read as an emblematic turning-point, in so far as it represents Hamlet's encounter with the meaning of death.

Shakespeare, it now appears, shared with his contemporaries the opportunities offered by a theatre in transition (some would say in crisis) between emblem and illusion. The apron stage, projecting out into the audience, isolated the fictional space of the play from the real world of the spectators. But there were no backdrops, and the evidence suggests that many of the props were designed to be indicative rather than convincing. Blood, on the other hand, was often simulated with loving fidelity. Meanwhile, the human protagonists moved emblematically between 'the heavens' and 'hell', the areas above and below the stage which released supernatural figures, goddesses or demons, as the action required. After 1609, when the adult actors took over the indoor theatres like the Blackfriars, elementary lighting effects were possible. But the auditorium was not darkened. And with the audience on three sides of the stage, even this was still theatre in the round, making no attempt to simulate an illusionist scenic spectacle.

It is no surprise, then, that Vindice's opening speech slips easily from narrative to emblem and from personal anguish to general satirical denunciation. The skull he holds is both a reminder of his individual tragedy and a memento mori for the audience. The skull is, he tells us, all that remains of Gloriana; it was 'Once the bright face of my betrothed lady', poisoned for her refusal to submit to the lecherous desires of the old Duke (*The Revenger's Tragedy*, I. i. 16). But it is also a signifier of death itself, a 'terror to fat folks,/ To have their costly three-pil'd flesh worn off/ As bare as this' (ll. 45–7). Vindice is simultaneously the avenging lover of Gloriana and vengeance itself, 'murder's quit-rent', the tragic destiny of deadly crime. This slide from the specific to the general is a recurrent feature of Renaissance drama. It is particularly striking in Webster's plays, where action commonly freezes momentarily into abstraction as plot gives way to moral generalization. Bosola, for instance, on his way to report to the murderous Ferdinand that his sister has had a baby, pauses to extract a meaning for the event: 'Though lust do mask in ne'er so strange disguise,/ She's oft found witty, but is never wise' (*The Duchess of Malfi*, 1613–14, II. iii. 76–7).

The occasion of Vindice's meditation with the skull is a woman, his chaste love, poisoned by the Duke for refusing to submit to his lust. Now Lussurioso is making similar overtures to Vindice's sister, Castiza. Both women are presented as paragons of virtue, unable to be corrupted by power or money. Meanwhile, Vindice's mother, Gratiana, is an altogether more venal figure, willing under the influence of the court to persuade her daughter to see where the family's material interests lie. And the Duchess is bent on seducing Spurio, her husband's bastard son. All these women are defined in terms of their relations with men. Whereas for the men in the play sexuality is a powerful force, one motive among others, for the women sexuality is synonymous with identity. While the Duke is a husband and father *and* a ruler, while Vindice is a lover and (in consequence) a revenger, the women in the play are identified above all as lovers, wives or mothers, and their moral standing is assessed in terms of sexual morality.

This morality has its own extraordinarily stringent imperatives. Antonio's wife, raped and therefore irretrievably dishonoured, has killed herself, to the admiration of her husband and the court: 'That virtuous lady!', 'Precedent for wives' (I. iv. 6). Unchastity in women, even involuntary unchastity, is commonly punished by death in Renaissance drama. Good women, who have nevertheless lost their 'virtue', often follow the example of Lucrece and kill themselves. All that is left to Lavinia is death at the hands of her father, Titus Andronicus. In Heywood's *A Woman Killed With Kindness* (1603) Anne Frankford, who has betrayed her husband, starves herself to death. Repentance is not enough. 'Virtue' is a physical condition: for daughters virginity, and for wives exclusive possession by their husbands.

Conversely, wicked women not only behave like whores but, in extreme cases, arrange the murder of their husbands or lovers. The Duchess in *The Revenger's Tragedy* considers this course, but Vindice saves her the trouble. Alice Arden makes a complex series of contracts to be rid of her husband and marry Mosby; in *The White Devil* Vittoria induces her lover, Bracciano, to have her ageing husband killed; and Beatrice-Joanna instructs De Flores to murder the man her father has betrothed her to. In these circumstances it is tempting to see in Renaissance drama the familiar patriarchal proposition that all women can be (exhaustively) classified as either virgins or whores, chaste wives or murderesses. And there is some support for this analysis of the plays. A chaste maid is evidently a rarity in Cheapside. There is a clear contrast between the Duchess of Malfi, faithful and loving wife and mother, and Julia, the Cardinal's mistress, between the predatory Vittoria and Isabella, Bracciano's self-sacrificing wife, or between Beatrice-Joanna and another Isabella who, in the subplot of *The Changeling*, resists all masculine overtures, despite the oppression she experiences at the hands of her jealous and proprietary husband.

But although these antithetical stereotypes undoubtedly exist in Renaissance drama, there are also alternative possibilities. The Duchess of Malfi herself, for instance, explicitly disobeys the commands of her brothers when she marries Antonio. As a widow and Antonio's social superior, she does the wooing. Until recently criticism of the play, uninfluenced by feminism on the one hand, and oddly anxious to find in these plays instances of poetic justice on the other, went to some lengths to insist that the Duchess must be morally responsible for her own tragic death. This reading, however, pulls violently against the imagery of the play, which consistently identifies the Duchess with light, vitality and natural things. The text seems in practice to sympathize with a woman who acknowledges her sexual desires and displays a high degree of autonomy. And there is an even more striking instance of transgressive sympathy in *The Roaring Girl* (1607?) by Middleton and Dekker. Here Moll Frith is presented as a free spirit who repudiates all the conventions of femininity. She wears men's clothes, she 'roars' (quarrels and fights) and she has no patience with fools. At the same time, she is honest and generous, she is not a whore, and she takes the side of the young lovers against the harsh law set in motion by a repressive father. In this play it is the conventional city women who are depicted as voraciously adulterous.

Indeed, though the tragedies of the period frequently depict a woman's decline from virtue, they rarely do so without some degree of sympathy for her position. The relationship between Annabella and her brother in Ford's *'Tis Pity She's a Whore* (c. 1630?) is presented as in many ways a romantic one. Even Alice Arden has a case against her financially rapacious husband, and the audience is invited to understand her desire for sexual freedom. We see why Beatrice-Joanna wants the right to choose her own partner. In each of these cases the overall moral position of the text is clear: in each case the woman is condemned. But her actions are seen as the (wrong) response to a problem, not as the expression of an intrinsic and unmotivated wickedness.

The problem is brought into being by the new status of romantic love. The Renaissance is the historical moment when love begins to be understood as the ground of marriage based on consent. Now that the ideal of marriage is once again open to question, the crisis which occurred in the Renaissance is more readily visible to us. In Chaucer's *Troilus and Criseyde* passionate love does not necessarily lead to marriage: indeed, the question does not even arise, though we might think that it would have solved the problem of lovers separated by war. Elsewhere in Chaucer, perhaps because of the influence of the Italian Renaissance on his work, it is possible to trace a much more modern view. But even in *Antony and Cleopatra*, two centuries later, as in Sidney's *Astrophil and Stella*, romantic love is dangerous, a distraction, 'dotage'. In the course of the sixteenth and seventeenth centuries, however, desire is moralized and spiritualized, domesticated to become the basis of the nuclear family. The Duchess of Malfi stands for happy and fruitful marriage based on free choice. Most Renaissance plays sympathize with virtuous young love against paternal intervention. A great many of them proclaim the miseries of enforced marriage. But a number of plots also turn on the uncertainties, and indeed the contradictions, of romantic love. As an ideal it remains dangerous, to the extent that desire is arbitrary, subject to a succession of displacements, unstable. If love is to be the basis of a lifelong partnership it requires rigorous control. This proposition is almost explicitly allegorized in Fletcher's *The Faithful Shepherdess* (c. 1609). Here the action begins in a pastoral utopia, where desire circulates freely among men and women equally. Shepherdesses are anxious to seduce coy shepherds, who recoil from their outspoken advances. When several of the characters are wounded in the action, they are able to be magically cured by the constant Clorin, faithful to her own dead shepherd-love, but only on condition that they all learn to subject desire to the discipline of chaste fidelity to a single partner.

But if the theatre plays a part in promoting the new ideal of marriage, it is able to be critical of it too. Middleton's *Women Beware Women* (1621?) must be in some ways one of the most anti-feminist plays of the period, and yet it is in that play that the half-witted Ward is shown conducting a physical inspection of Isabella, rather as if she were a horse, in order to decide whether to take possession of her in marriage. It is very clear that the audience is not expected to sympathize with this process. Earlier in the play Isabella points out that for women marriage is a kind of slavery, even if their 'thraldom' is made happy by love (I. ii. 170–8).

But love, the same play makes clear, does not necessarily dissolve the inequalities of marriage. Bianca has, after all, eloped with Leantio: what could be more romantic? But when he neglects her for his work and confines her to the house with his old mother, romance is rapidly dissipated. Bianca becomes the mistress of the Duke. The one play of the period that we know to have been written by a woman, Elizabeth Cary's closet drama *The Tragedy of Mariam* (1603–4?), explores a wife's right to resist a tyrannical husband. Horror at Herod's murderous behaviour has put Mariam's love to flight; she believes that she could use her sexuality for her own protection; but she scorns to appease him with her body. In the end she opts for death as the price of defiance, and the play seems, however uneasily, to endorse Mariam's heroism. Meanwhile, it is probably Moll Frith who spells out with the greatest equanimity the problem of marriage in a patriarchal society:

> I have no humour to marry, I love to lie o'both sides o'th'bed myself, and again o'th'other side; a wife you know ought to be obedient, but I fear me I am too headstrong to obey, therefore I'll ne'er go about it. . . . I have the head now of myself, and am man enough for a woman; marriage is but a chopping and changing, where a maiden loses one head and has a worse i'th'place.
>
> (*The Roaring Girl*, II. ii. 35–44)

If the women in *The Revenger's Tragedy* represent the extremes of chaste virginity and rapacious lust, the male figures operate at the limits of masculine violence. In this Vindice outdoes them all. The figure who has enlisted the sympathy of the audience in the opening scene, from whose perspective we perceive the vices of the court, achieves his revenge by inducing the Duke to kiss the poisoned skull of Gloriana, disguised as a courtesan. While the Duke writhes in torment, Vindice forces him to witness the illicit embraces of his wife and his bastard son. He accompanies his actions with a series of macabre jokes, referring to Gloriana as 'the bony lady' and commenting, 'sh'has a somewhat grave look with her' (III. v. 121, 137), while Hippolito exults in Vindice's ingenuity: 'Brother, I do applaud thy constant vengeance,/ The quaintness of thy malice, above thought' (III. v. 108–9).

Again *The Revenger's Tragedy* is only an instance of the extravagance that characterizes so many Renaissance plays. This is a theatre of excess. 'As for myself', Marlowe's Jew of Malta announces gleefully, 'I walk abroad a' nights/ And kill sick people groaning under walls;/ Sometimes I go about and poison wells'. And Ithamore, asked how he has spent his life, replies, 'Faith, master,/

In setting Christian villages on fire,/ Chaining of eunuchs, binding galley slaves' (*The Jew of Malta*, *c.* 1590, II. iii. 175–7, 203–5). Hieronimo in Kyd's *The Spanish Tragedy* (*c.* 1590), having secured the real deaths of his son's murderers in a play, bites out his own tongue on the stage before stabbing himself. After arranging the Duchess's of Malfi's murder, Ferdinand comes to believe he is a wolf and takes to digging up dead bodies at midnight. In Ford's *'Tis Pity She's a Whore* Giovanni, unable to retain possession of his sister by any other means, cuts out her heart and holds it before him on a dagger at her husband's birthday party.

Renaissance drama deals in rape, incest and mutilation. Dead fingers and dead hands are exchanged on stage. And if passion is murderous, ambition is always grand in these plays. Marlowe's Tamburlaine puts kings in cages and massacres virgins in his quest to conquer the whole world, 'Measuring the limits of his empery/ By east and west, as Phoebus doth his course' (1 *Tamburlaine*, 1587, I. ii. 39–40).

Nor is the excess purely a matter of action. The grand scale of the figures on the stage is an illusion produced by the way they talk:

> Good morning to the day; and, next, my gold!
> Open the shrine, that I may see my saint.
> Hail the world's soul, and mine! More glad than is
> The teeming earth to see the longed-for sun
> Peep through the horns of the celestial Ram,
> Am I, to view thy splendour, darkening his;
> That, lying here, amongst my other hoards,
> Show'st like a flame, by night; or like the day
> Struck out of Chaos, when all darkness fled
> Unto the centre.
>
> (*Volpone*, I. i. 1–10)

Here the imagery moves in expanding circles, intensifying the scandal as it increases the dimensions of Volpone's avarice. The gold is like daylight; it is a saint (ll. 1–2). The comparisons reverse expectation: the metal comes out of underground darkness; worldly wealth and spiritual values are polar opposites. As the speech builds on the original metaphors, the gold becomes so brilliant that it darkens the spring sun (ll. 4–6). And then it comes to resemble not just daylight but light itself, the light that God struck out of chaos in the inaugural moment of his creation (ll. 8–10). The blasphemy which begins with 'saint' culminates in this allusion, which retrospectively turns Volpone's command, 'Open the shrine', into an appalling parody of the divine fiat, 'Let there be light'.

Alternatively the excesses of the society are simultaneously listed and specified in a way which implies that there is no reason why the speaker should ever stop. This rhetorical strategy constructs the illusion of a monstrous world where both speech and sexuality are only tenuously under control:

> Now 'tis full sea abed over the world;
> There's juggling of all sides. Some that were maids
> E'en at sunset are now perhaps i'th'toll-book.
> This woman in immodest thin apparel
> Lets in her friend by water; here a dame,
> Cunning, nails leather hinges to a door,
> To avoid proclamation; now cuckolds are
> A-coining, apace, apace, apace, apace.
>
> (*The Revenger's Tragedy*, II. ii. 136–43)

An earlier generation of critics found all this excess embarrassing and called it decadence. Recently, however, the preposterous has become much more familiar on the twentieth-century stage and in film (and even in some instances in soap opera), so that it is possible to read the extravagance of Renaissance drama rather differently. Until 1609, when the Blackfriars was opened as a theatre for an adult company within the city limits, the theatres were located in the margins of the city in the Liberties of London. As Steven Mullaney argues in *The Place of the Stage* (1988), the Liberties were a place where law and order was uncertain. They were beyond the control of the Crown and the sheriffs, but nominally subject to the Lord Mayor. Taverns and brothels, gaming-houses and bear-baiting arenas, as well as theatres, flourished in the Liberties. In a sense, then, we might expect this theatre, located at the edges of civilized control, to embrace what is eccentric (ex-centric) or transgressive, asserting in this respect its kinship with the circus. Like a freak show, the stage offers to satisfy curiosity, to display human violence, sexuality, rhetoric at its limits.

Differing from the novel in this respect too, Renaissance drama is in consequence not normative. Nineteenth-century novels depend for their intelligibility on the presentation of what is familiar. Dickens, of course, portrays eccentrics, but at the heart of his novels is a consciousness we feel we can recognize. The central character is, inevitably, an individual, as all nineteenth-century readers no doubt felt themselves to be, with idiosyncratic habits, weaknesses and insights. The reader is thus not necessarily invited to identify with the protagonist. But his or her feelings and reactions are traditionally recognizable, precisely to the degree that they are 'normal'. This impression is confirmed by the rhetoric of the novel, which tends to be intimate, conversational, everyday or, in other words, familiar again. The novel gives us glimpses of 'normal' ways of being, falling in love, mourning. And if the protagonist's ways of doing these things are odd, the narrative voice is there to draw attention to the eccentricity. Since many of us encounter more instances of these experiences in fiction than we should have time for in the busiest life, there is a sense in which the novel is profoundly normative, a source of information (and thus instruction) on what it is like to confront love, hatred, rejection, death. (Norms can, after all, prove coercive.)

Shakespeare's plays can be accommodated to the expectations generated by the novel: Hamlet and Rosalind may be seen as individuals who react in familiar ways, however intensely, to their circumstances. And there are other Renaissance plays which can be read novelistically: *The Duchess of Malfi*, perhaps; *Arden of Faversham*, in some ways; *'Tis Pity She's a Whore*. But in each of these cases there is an element of excess which pulls against such a reading. These are plays, it seems, which explicitly and overtly explore extremes, extravagant actions, the grotesque.

A great many Renaissance plays are based on 'fact'. In this period there is a sense in which 'fiction' has not wholly distinguished itself from 'fact', not because people did not know the difference, but because the narrative genres were not yet clearly differentiated. Thus the stories of the plays often come directly or indirectly from history. *Arden of Faversham* (*c.* 1590), like *A Warning for Fair Women* (*c.* 1590), *The Miseries of Enforced Marriage* (1607) and *A Yorkshire Tragedy* (1608), was a representation of a relatively recent and widely reported murder. And Mary Frith was alive and well in London at the time of *The Roaring Girl*, though she may have been less innocent than her bioplay suggests. A number of 'history' plays, of course, were based on English chronicle narratives. And several tragedies derived their stories ultimately from the extraordinary events which took place at a series of Italian Renaissance courts. Vittoria Accoramboni, familiar to us from *The White Devil*, was murdered in 1585. The substance of the main plot of *Women Beware Women* occurred at the court of Francesco de' Medici in late sixteenth-century Florence. *The Duchess of Malfi* is based on events which took place about a century before the play was written.

It does not follow that the plays are in any sense trying to reconstruct the characters, their motives or their feelings. Nor are they much concerned with fidelity to the 'facts': they rewrite history as it suits them. But it is possible to read them as serious attempts to make sense of the events, to assess their moral status, and to specify their implications for an understanding of what it is to be human. Implicitly they pose questions about the things that human beings do, and the actions they are capable of. What are the limits, they ask, of human behaviour? And what limits ought there to be?

At this historical moment there were no ready, obvious, 'normal' answers to such questions. In contrast to the outmoded image presented in E. M. W. Tillyard's *Elizabethan World Picture* (1943) of a harmonious, contented, docile community, it now seems that no society has ever been more divided on every imaginable issue. A declining feudal economy based on land confronted the expanding wealth and power of the city merchants. The more the monarchy laid claim to absolute sovereignty, the more fiercely Parliament resisted the claim. Recent scientific developments were hotly debated; religion was a site of struggle between Anglicans and Puritans over vestments, rites, the meaning of the scriptures and the nature of salvation. There were riots and treason trials, both telling symptoms of instability in the state. And the meaning of the family was in radical transition, often with painful consequences for living individuals. In all this what was unclear, unsettled, was what it meant to be a human being, a man or a woman. What, if any, were the limits of human capacities and human desires? At this moment of crisis the plays seem to propose that both were virtually unlimited – and terrifying. But to the extent that the plays leave the issue unresolved, they also imply that the answers might be for the audience to determine, in practice as well as in theory.

Does it follow that a drama which raises these questions is intrinsically radical? The critical debates of the 1980s centred on the question whether the Renaissance stage primarily challenged existing values, or constituted an ideological apparatus of the state, containing incipient subversion. In my view the question itself stems from mistaken assumptions. There were, I have tried to suggest, no clear norms in place to be subverted. Of course the plays are vehemently critical of many existing practices. They satirize greed and social aspiration; they condemn sensuality and cruelty. And yet there is a sense in which they celebrate them too. The audience is invited to derive pleasure from the entertainment provided by the actions and the rhetoric of Volpone and Tamburlaine, Giovanni and, of course, Vindice. And beyond this pleasure, the spectators are also, perhaps, invited to judge the events they witness, to cast their vote, without feeling that the ethics of the matter have always been decided for them in advance.

The Revenger's Tragedy, for instance, to return finally to that play, poses a political question about the nature of justice and about the role of the subject in a corrupt state. Is Vindice right to murder the Duke? Is he right to murder him horribly, so ingeniously fitting the punishment to the crime? What is the relationship between revenge and justice? There is no doubt that the court is corrupt, and that it is doing its best to spread its corruption into the country. What should the subject do when the sovereign source of justice is poisoned? This was a real political question in the Stuart period, and differences of view about the correct answer led finally to the civil war of the 1640s.

Revenge, the play seems to suggest, resides in the margins between reason and madness, justice and crime. Like the theatre itself, located in the margins of the city, Renaissance drama refuses to close off the issues it raises, in this instance to settle either for submission to an existing order or for the affirmation of anarchy. In this sense it plays a part in the construction and reconstruction of the meanings in circulation in the period, making visible their plurality and thus their uncertainty.

But if meaning is plural, and the plays can accordingly be read in different ways, what is the status of my reading of Renaissance drama? It makes no claim to absolute authority: this is not necessarily the 'correct' way to interpret these plays. But it is perhaps a way which is appropriate to the postmodern uncertainties of the late twentieth century. We too inhabit a moment of crisis, when the moral and political commonplaces of the past no longer seem pertinent. In consequence meaning, and in particular the meaning of what it is – or might be – to be a human being, a man or a woman, is once again at issue, and is perhaps open again, this time for us to determine.

FURTHER READING

Barroll, J. Leeds *et al.* (1975) *The Revels History of Drama in English*, vol. 3 (1576–1613), Methuen, London

Belsey, Catherine (1985) *The Subject of Tragedy: Identity and Difference in Renaissance Drama*, Methuen, London and New York

Dessen, Alan C. (1984) *Elizabethan Stage Conventions and Modern Interpreters*, Cambridge University Press, Cambridge

Dollimore, Jonathan (1984) *Radical Tragedy: Religion, Ideology and Power in the Drama of Shakespeare and his Contemporaries*, Harvester, Brighton

Edwards, Philip *et al.* (1981) *The Revels History of Drama in English*, vol. 4 (1613–1660), Methuen, London and New York

Lever, J. W. (1987) *The Tragedy of State: a Study of Jacobean Drama* (with a new Introduction by Jonathan Dollimore), Methuen, London [first published 1971]

Patterson, Annabel (1984) *Censorship and Interpretation: the Conditions of Writing and Reading in Early Modern England*, University of Winconsin Press, Wisconsin

Rose, Mary Beth (ed.) (1990) *Renaissance Drama as Cultural History: Essays from 'Renaissance Drama' 1975–87*, Northwestern University Press, Evanston

Shepherd, Simon (1986) *Marlowe and the Politics of the Elizabethan Theatre*, Harvester, Brighton

Wickham, Glynne (1963–72) *Early English Stages, 1300–1660*, vol. 2 (1576–1660), Routledge & Kegan Paul, London

Womack, Peter (1986) *Ben Jonson*, Basil Blackwell, Oxford

ADDITIONAL WORKS CITED

Mullaney, Steven (1988) *The Place of the Stage*, University of Chicago Press, Chicago

Tillyard, E. M. W. (1943) *The Elizabethan World Picture*, Chatto & Windus, London

30

RESTORATION THEATRE

DEREK HUGHES

Over four hundred new plays were performed in London between the re-opening of the theatres in 1660 and the end of the seventeenth century – surviving details of performances are collected in Part 1 of *The London Stage 1660–1800* (Van Lennep, 1965). Two theatrical companies, the King's and the Duke's, were authorized by royal patent in 1660, and under the guidance of Sir William Davenant the Duke's Company quickly became a trend-setter, with innovations such as the introduction of changeable scenery to the public stage. Davenant was the one pre-Restoration dramatist to produce any quantity of new work for the Restoration stage, but even his contribution consisted largely of adaptations and revisions of older plays, and the absence of an experienced corps of professional playwrights meant that the first few years were ones of tentative and often uncertain experiment, the kinds of tragedy and comedy that we most readily associate with the period only starting to appear in any quantity in the late 1660s. Thereafter, theatrical activity falls readily into two distinct phases. By 1682 the King's Company was in serious financial difficulties and merged with the better managed Duke's Company, with the result that the London stage was monopolized by a single company until a group of senior and justly discontented actors formed a breakaway company in 1695.

One immediate result of the disappearance of theatrical competition was that the demand for new plays dropped sharply, only recovering after the Glorious Revolution of 1688. But when the demand for new plays revived, most of the great figures of the previous generation – Wycherley, Etherege, Otway, Behn, Lee – had died or retired from the stage. Conversely, the leading dramatists who emerged in the 1690s – Vanbrugh, Congreve, Farquhar – were boys at the time of the first great successes of Restoration drama (Farquhar, indeed, had not been born when Wycherley's *The Country Wife*, 1675, and Etherege's *The Man of Mode*, 1676, received their first performances). While some minor dramatists, such as John Crowne and Thomas Durfey, were active

424

in both periods, only Dryden and Shadwell made substantial contributions to both, and even Shadwell died early in the nineties. The dangers of facile generalization about Restoration drama are therefore clear: we are dealing not only with a vast number of plays but, essentially, with two periods dominated by different generations of playwrights with different political ideologies. *The Country Wife* (1675) and Congreve's *The Way of the World* (1700), the two most popular 'Restoration comedies', are in many respects plays from different eras.

The most valuable scholarship on Restoration theatre during the last thirty years has been that which has avoided and challenged entrenched generalizations made on the basis of a small fraction of the available plays, and has instead documented the diversity of the drama, and the complexity and rapidity of its transformations. An especially important work is Robert D. Hume's *The Development of English Drama in the Late Seventeenth Century* (1976), which charts the rapid shifts and divergences of fashion which were as characteristic of the Restoration stage as of the modern. *The Country Wife*, for example, should not be seen as an archetypal example of comedy between 1660 and 1700 but as part of a relatively brief boom in sex comedy which did not get under way until the early 1670s. Although studies of Restoration drama based on very partial reading of the available evidence continue to appear, the growing tendency for serious scholars to base their work on total coverage of the period means that in the last two decades virtually all the received commonplaces about the subject have been discredited or questioned. The form that we know as the 'Comedy of Manners' was not the sole or even the dominant type of comedy. Nor is it true that Restoration comedy habitually glamorizes successful rakes: comedy which cheerfully portrays and endorses extra-marital sex does not appear until the early 1670s, and although such plays then continue to appear until the mid-1690s, the real boom in sex comedy was located in the years 1672–82. Even here harsh criticism of the predatory rake can easily be found (e.g. in Otway's *Friendship in Fashion*, 1678, Nathaniel Lee's *The Princess of Cleve*, ?1680, and some of Durfey's plays). Although Aphra Behn champions adultery as the refuge of the oppressed wife, she naturally condemns the predatory and domineering instincts of the male, which darken even many of her most sympathetically portrayed liaisons. Etherege's Dorimant and Wycherley's Horner are exceptional, not typical, creations.

It is also untrue that the audience of Restoration drama was predominantly a court coterie audience. The Duke's Company seems from the outset, even in the location of its theatres, to have sought the patronage of city audiences, and Harold Love (1980) has offered the rough guess that ten to fifteen percent of the available public (that is, excluding children, pregnant women, shopkeepers, etc.) may have attended the theatre in any year. The reassessment of audience composition means that we can no longer assume that a rising tide of middle-class sentiment drove sex comedy off the stage in the 1690s and ushered in a century of sentimental comedy after the pattern of Cibber's *Love's Last Shift* (1696), where the rakish protagonist experiences an effusive reform in the final act. Hume and Scouten (1980b) have shown that audiences of the late 1690s were rejecting plays of many kinds in a seemingly random fashion and that, although new plays after the mid-nineties no longer portray adultery and fornication approvingly, established sex comedies continued to be popular well into the eighteenth century. In any case, reformed rakes were not an innovation of the 1690s, and the comedy of the eighteenth century was not in fact predominantly sentimental.

Restoration drama, then, is a large and diverse field, but there are nevertheless recurrent points of reference that enable us to detect, if not uniformity, at least a coherent pattern of variety. One such point of reference is the dramatists' interpretation of the relationship between individuals and the social and cosmic realms in which they are placed. After the early years of the Restoration, we rarely encounter the idea that the individual, the state and the whole natural universe are in their ideal functioning mirror images of each other, embodiments on different scales of the same essential principles and patterns of order. In his famous speech in Act 1 of Shakespeare's *Troilus and Cressida*, Ulysses had contemplated the Ptolemaic universe and urged that the hierarchical order visible in the relationships between the sun and the lesser heavenly bodies should be the essential and natural foundation for all man's social relationships. It is now widely agreed that Shakespeare's play itself questions Ulysses' vision, but when Dryden rewrote the play in 1679 the vision had become an irrelevant archaism, no longer even worthy of question: Dryden's Ulysses delivers a simple homily on political order, stripped of the analogy between earthly and heavenly order that is the essence of the Shakespearian original. Order is necessary, but there is no sense that the orders that sustain human society may be identical in kind with the eternal patterns of order written in the stars.

We are, of course, dealing with a shift of emphasis rather than a simple and total reversal: with the further decay of an already decaying ideology. Nevertheless, a shift is perceptible, and one fact neatly illustrates the widened sense that the laws which govern human affairs are confined to the sphere of the human, and that they have no force or application outside the human sphere. A recurrent assumption in Elizabethan and Jacobean drama is that the human and celestial realms share a common language: that the words which make possible human communication and community are echoes of the ordering word of God. In *Richard III* the final restoration of order is ratified by a divine 'Amen', and the murderers of the princes have earlier been briefly deterred by the sight of a prayer-book by their victims' pillow. In *Macbeth*, King Edward has the divinely given power to speak words of prophecy and healing. In *Cymbeline*, Jupiter lays an inscribed tablet in the breast of the sleeping hero Posthumus. And in *The Tempest*, Prospero controls the spirit world with his book. All these plays were adapted for the Restoration stage, and in each case the symbols of linguistic community between the earthly and the celestial were excised. The laws that govern the political sphere are no longer direct echoes of the ordering divine word.

It has been mentioned that the earliest phase of Restoration drama was one of sometimes hesitant experiment, with inevitably inexperienced and often amateur dramatists trying out a variety of new and old forms. One early successful gentleman amateur was the Earl of Orrery (brother of the scientist Robert Boyle), who produced a sequence of remarkably similar heroic plays in the period up to 1668, when the sameness of his formula at last became intolerable to audiences. A characteristic Orrery situation is for two friends who are rivals in love selflessly to assist each other's courtship, each pleading with the loved one to marry the other (this very conventional plot device is parodied when the foolish Sparkish virtually thrusts his fiancée upon Harcourt in *The Country Wife*). Orrery's plays affirm the essential harmony between individual desire and the framework of social order and obligation in which the individual must live. Passions which conflict with prior oaths and obligations are easily eradicated, and heroic characters gain dignity and happiness through mastery of those desires that estrange the individual from the shared demands of human culture. The medium that enables an individual to participate in a shared culture is, of course, language, and whereas many later playwrights see language as a problematic and unreliable intermediary between the individual consciousness and the community, Orrery portrays the words that enshrine the imperatives of social order as being themselves things of power and authority: the hero of Orrery's *The Black Prince* finds that 'Divinity' dwells in the 'Pow'rfull Names' of father and king (III. iii), and former vows of love have the power to restore erring lovers to their first passion. Such ready conformity between individual desire and the constraints which order society is, of course, quite uncharacteristic of later comic heroes, such as Horner and Dorimant. It is equally uncharacteristic of later heroic protagonists such as the turbulent and egocentric Almanzor of Dryden's *The Conquest of Granada*.

Orrery's plays were among the earliest successful Restoration tragedies. If they represent a species quite remote from our normal ideas of Restoration drama, so does one of the earliest successful comedies, Sir Robert Howard's highly chaste *The Committee* (1662), a play set in the late Interregnum, in which two heroic cavaliers rescue their estates and their loved ones from venal and hypocritical Puritan bureaucrats. The play asserts that the traditional hierarchies of society reflect natural and permanent principles of order. In the *'topsie-turvie'* world of the Interregnum (IV. i), former servants have become the 'new Gentry' (I. i), but the intrinsic instability and transience of this inverted state of affairs is indicated even in the upstarts' surname (Day), and the natural worth of the true gentry remains unimpaired amidst the social chaos: Anne Thorowgood, a cavalier's daughter brought up by the Days since the age of two, nevertheless preserves (like Shakespeare's Perdita) the natural character infused by her ancestry. Moreover, the misdeeds of the upstart servants are contrasted with the actions of Teague, a good-natured but dim-witted Irishman who attaches himself to the cavaliers, needing the paternalistic protection of a servant–master relationship in order to survive. This natural and benevolent hierarchy of protection and dependence represents the old world which has been temporarily violated by the rapacious and self-serving reign of parvenus.

A different viewpoint can be found in the popular farce *Sir Martin Mar-all* (1667), which Dryden wrote in collaboration with the Duke of Newcastle. This juxtaposes three titled characters, all morally or intellectually vacant, with an intelligent servant, Warner, a déclassé royalist gentleman who lost his estate during the Interregnum and has not been able to recover it after the Restoration. Although Warner eventually marries the rich heiress originally designed for Sir Martin, who inadvertently marries the heroine's maid, the sense of social disarray continues, for the maid is now a Lady, and takes precedence over her former mistress. The concluding elevation of the servant institutionalizes and renders permanent what in *The Committee* had been a temporary aberration. In *Sir Martin Mar-all* the traditional terminology of social rank survives, but the effective hierarchy is one of wit coupled with aggression, and in this respect the play looks forward to later and better-known works by Etherege and Wycherley. The complex and ironic comparisons between Dorimant and the shoemaker in *The Man of Mode* are a world away from the paternalistic superiority of Howard's cavaliers to Teague, and one of Dorimant's practical jokes involves a defiant subversion of rank, when he pays a whore to sit in the most respectable area of the theatre and outrage the people of quality.

Restoration divines repeatedly lamented the popularity of non-Christian ideas among men of fashion: the libertine belief that sexual promiscuity is sanctioned by nature, and that moral codes prohibiting it are the killjoy inventions of politicians and priests; the belief, originating with the ancient Greek philosopher Epicurus, that the universe was created not by divine design but by a chance collision of atoms; and, most of all, the tenets of Hobbes, who saw man's nature and consciousness as the products of material, physiological processes in which appetite was the dominant force and reason its servant. For Hobbes, the dominance of appetite meant that men are naturally in a state of war with each other, and that societies are formed not because man is an Aristotelian political animal but for the very opposite reason: because he needs to escape from the horror of his anti-social nature. Paradoxically, society is the necessary consequence of man's unfitness for society. Although there are natural laws for the containment of chaos which are inevitably dictated by reason, many particular laws – such as those concerning the canon of the Bible – derive their validity from the arbitrary decree of the monarch. Since most men (and women) are roughly equal in power, social hierarchy, though necessary, is essentially arbitrary, unrelated to a natural and genetically transmitted scale of superiority and inferiority. And language is a creation of social convention, easily misunderstood and misused by the individual, and quite incapable of describing a supernatural sphere beyond the realm of human affairs.

Such ideas were held by only a small minority of the educated population, but they seem (though the question is a subject of keen scholarly debate) to have been deeply interesting to a number of prominent dramatists, and leading churchmen such as Tillotson, South and Stillingfleet certainly saw the stage as a worrying source of intellectual and moral unorthodoxy (see Hughes, 1986). Thomas Shadwell displays a sympathetic interest in Lucretian epicureanism, including Lucretius' denial of divine involvement in human affairs, and Etherege repeatedly stresses the role of chance (rather than Providence) in determining human affairs. Although no dramatist affirms the possiblity of total sexual freedom, the reservations can be practical rather than moral (at the end of Dryden's *Marriage à-la-Mode*, 1671, a wife-swapping arrangement is rejected because of the husbands' possessiveness), and dramatists such as Aphra Behn clearly champion adultery as an escape from an unwanted marriage. Moreover, there was a widespread, if eclectic and unsystematic, use of Hobbesian ideas. The paradox that society is the product of man's anti-social savagery, that its structure is at once dictated by and alien to his nature, proved widely fascinating. In Dryden's *The Conquest of Granada* (1670–1), the presence in the city of the valiant savage Almanzor reflects the pervasive persistence of socially unassimilable elements in man's constitution, and Almanzor struggles unsuccessfully to acquire the subordination of individualistic appetite to sociable reason that had been second nature to Orrery's heroes. In *The Country Wife*, Horner's ruse of getting access to the beds of all the outwardly respectable women by pretending to the men that he is a eunuch similarly indicates the indomitable continuance of untamed and unrestrained instincts in a society whose public rituals and conventions depend on the assumption that they have been contained. It should be noted, however, that the impulse to society is no more escapable than are the cravings of instinct: Horner, the champion of liberated appetite, ends up as the shared property of a secret community of sexually voracious women, revealing the persistence of social procedures even among those who most transgress outward social form. Man is suspended between two realms, capable neither of abandoning society for the wilderness nor of surrendering the instincts of the state of nature to live the life of a citizen.

In such plays, the coherence of individual character and social roles celebrated in *The Committee* and Orrery's plays has gone, and the disappearance of coherence is reflected in the treatment of language, the bridge between the individual consciousness and the social world. In a famous scene in *The Country Wife*, Horner and one of his mistresses redefine 'china', by a tacit and arbitrary social compact, as a synonym for copulation, and conduct a conversation which has entirely separate public and private meanings. The coexistence within the same city of the rituals of society and the instincts of the wilderness produces a coexistence within the same language of two entirely separate systems of meaning. Indeed, dramatists of this period repeatedly see sexual desire as something that cannot be accommodated in the social contrivance of language, and characters often seek to escape from the gaze and discourse of society into moments of pure and inarticulate instinct. If language can be seen as an external social convention only partially appropriate to those who use it, however, it can also be portrayed as a kind of mental prison, reflecting the impossibility of direct contact between the mind and the outside world which it seeks to apprehend. In Dryden's tragedy *Aureng-Zebe* (1675), for example, the characters repeatedly fail to distinguish between the words that express their consciousness and the external realities of which the words are signs. There is no way of proceeding from possession of a mental image to immediate knowledge of the thing itself.

But such developments did not go unchallenged. Whereas his leading contemporaries sceptically explored the limitations of language, Shadwell – more conservatively – attacked the corruption of literate communication by poor education, scientific jargon (in *The Virtuoso*, 1676) and pretentious playwrights (notably Dryden), and his classical epicureanism was quite consistent with a sustained campaign against what he saw as the social and moral subversiveness of Dryden's plays. Moreover, despite the fashion for sex comedy, there was a steady stream of minor plays (such as John Leanerd's *The Counterfeits*, 1678, and Thomas Southerne's *The Disappointment*, 1684) in which a repentant rake ultimately marries the heroine he has wronged. Thomas Durfey, a prolific dramatist of some talent and originality, scored an early success with a joyful and farcical celebration of adultery, *A Fond Husband* (1677), but many of his plays (such as *The Virtuous Wife*, 1679) emphasize the triumph of women over unscrupulous rakes or fortune-hunters.

Indeed, one feature of the diversifying interpretations of the basis of power and social order was a widespread questioning of the subordinate status of women. The rambling, unperformed dramas of the Duchess of Newcastle had made a passionate, if unimpressively communicated, claim for the rights and abilities of women (while conceding that some were happiest as submissive wives). The oppression of women was more mildly (not to say patronizingly) deplored by Sir Robert Howard's brother Edward, two of whose plays (*The Women's Conquest*, 1670, and *The Six Days' Adventure*, 1671) depicted experiments in gynocracy which fail, but which nevertheless induce men to exercise authority with greater sensitivity. The best-known feminist dramatist is Aphra Behn, whose plays subtly challenge traditional representations of sexual hier-archy (whether the male self-abasement that characterized courtly love or the male supremacy that characterized everything else) by examining the pragmatic social and psychological bases of male and female power. The mentality of courtly love, in which the mistress is queen and the lover slave, can be genuinely shared by both partners, but on the man's side the impulse to worship is a transient sacrifice of power made possible by his permanent capacity for violent domination. When the rake Willmore emerges from Angel-lica's house in Part I of *The Rover* (1677), Belvile, the most sober and principled man in the cast, asks if he has succeeded in sleeping with her by demanding whether they are 'to break her Windows, or raise up Altars to her' (III. i). There is the thinnest of boundaries between violence and worship, and the recurrent and perceptive exploration of the linked male impulses to see the woman both as goddess and object of plunder is one of Behn's greatest strengths.

But such concerns were not confined to Behn and later women dramatists. The unifying principle of J.D.'s *The Mall* (1674) is the depiction of the violence, slavery and indignity to which women are subjected, and in Shadwell's unjustly neglected *The Woman Captain* (1679) a tyrannical old husband, Gripe, suddenly finds that the customary hierarchies which sustained his tyranny have dissolved: tricked into believing that he has been impressed into the army, he finds himself subject to an officer who is in fact his wife in disguise. Here the subordinate position of women is plainly a matter of sheer convention: when the heroine asks a sergeant how a woman can acquire a macho mastery of resonant oaths, she is told that it is a mere question of practice. It is also noteworthy that the rejection of belief in female inferiority is associated with rejection of the belief – fundamental to *The Committee* – in the natural inferi-ority of servants to masters: in his spell as a soldier, Gripe is not only the subordinate of his wife but the equal of his servant, and in the parallel plot (where a group of libertine gentlemen are revealed to be not unshackled sexual conquerors but the slaves and dupes of whores) an old family servant witheringly refuses the new heir's command to start fornicating by retorting that it is beneath his dignity.

As noted above, the production of new plays fell sharply in the mid-1680s, and one notable feature of the succeeding phase of Restoration drama was the virtual collapse of tragedy as a significant dramatic form. Many new tragedies were produced, but only two – Dryden's *Don Sebastian* (1689) and Southerne's *Oroonoko* (1695) – are of real importance. In comedy, the portrayal of promis-cuity becomes more uniformly unfavourable. Even Congreve's *The Old Bachel-our* (1693), one of the raciest comedies of the period, indicates the emptiness of obsessive sexual pursuit by portraying a character so exclusively interested in conquering women that he cannot be bothered to consummate his conquests; and, though Mirabell's sexual adventures are over by the start of *The Way of the World*, the unhappy marriage of his former mistress Mrs Fainall focuses attention on the human consequences of easy-going libertinism, in that it forces us to contemplate the aftermath of the hackneyed comic ending in which the fallen woman is married off to an unsuspecting dupe. A number of lesser-known plays, such as Shadwell's *The Squire of Alsatia* (1688) and Henry Higden's *The Wary Widdow* (1693), give still more emphasis to the plight of the seduced and rejected woman.

Whereas Wycherley and Etherege portray and accept a tension between the sociable and anti-social dimensions of human nature, later comedy writers are either less complaisant or more constructive. In Southerne's *The Wives' Excuse* (1691) and *The Maid's Last Prayer* (1693) the vapid observances of public life obliterate the private self, to the point that even copulation becomes an empty social ritual. The attenuation of social and personal existence into ritualized vacancy is illustrated by yet another subversion of the master–servant relationship: the opening scene of *The Wives' Excuse* is dominated not by fashionable society but by the servants who support it, who theatrically mimic their employers and discuss their intrigues, so that the pursuits of the gentry are devalued by appearing initially as the property of their servants. By contrast, while Congreve accepts that the structures of society in no sense express or reflect the natures of its component individuals, he is much concerned with the creation of systems that provide an acceptably ordered framework for individual life. In the celebrated proviso scene in *The Way of the World*, Mirabell and Millamant propose contractual arrangements which guarantee the separateness and integrity of the individual within the institution of marriage, and a more formal species of contract (the conveyance of her estate to Mirabell) enables Mrs Fainall to live in some peace and security with a rapacious and contemptible husband, though it cannot transform the marriage into a human as well as a legal union. Both arrangements recognize that the individual cannot simply be absorbed into the institution: there is a marked difference from, say, *The Taming of the Shrew*, where Kate is finally assimilated into a hierarchical natural and social order that prescribes her proper identity.

With Congreve, too, redefinition of social order leads to redefinition of the master–servant relationship. In *Love for Love* (1695), Sir Sampson Legend recoils in ridiculous incomprehension from the discovery that the servant Jeremy has the same natural constitution and appetites as a gentleman; yet Jeremy, as well as having the same body and senses as a gentleman, has picked up more wit and verbal skill during his service at Cambridge than has Sir Sampson's favourite son during his life as a sailor, which has left him incapable of describing anything except in the language of shipping. Class structures are not in any way attacked, but their basis is pragmatic rather than natural: like wives, servants are not fully defined by the institution that prescribes their role. Nor is the condition of language an easy and precise reflection of social order, for the acquisition of language and of social position are here determined by quite separate processes of cause and effect.

Other dramatists of the 1690s, however, postulate a closer – though still sometimes imperfect – relationship between the individual and the values and language of the society which he or she inhabits. Etherege and his leading contemporaries had accepted that man had desires which need not be contained within the forms and discourse of society, but for Vanbrugh the moral relationship between the two spheres is more complex. The plight of maltreated wives like Amanda and Lady Brute (in *The Relapse*, 1696, and *The Provok'd Wife*, 1697, respectively) presents the temptation to adultery in a sympathetic and compelling light, but Vanbrugh also makes clear its moral and practical untenability as a solution. Lady Brute's flirtations with the forbidden make her vulnerable to the power of characters she could previously despise, and when her husband returns from a night of hooliganism to smear his blood and filth over her, marking her with the signs of his own lifestyle, Vanbrugh indicates that her attempts to escape a morally repugnant husband inevitably and ironically lessen the moral distance between them. On the other hand, the language that enshrines the truths of sexual morality is an ambiguous and unpersuasive medium, possessing authority but lacking power. When Lady Brute shrugs aside an inconvenient biblical text by saying that the translation may be wrong, we disapprove, but we are reminded that even the language of the Bible is mediated to us by fallible and often disagreeing humans, and our confidence in its power to guide and reflect human nature is accordingly diminished. We are a long way from the direct contact and harmony between divine utterance and human aspiration symbolized when Jupiter lays the inscribed tablet on Posthumus' breast.

In this later period, dramatists return to the popular pre-Restoration topic (favoured, for instance, by Fletcher and Shirley) of defining the moral character of the true gentleman, and in doing so they reject the identification of the gentleman and the libertine common in earlier sex comedy (Etherege, for example, had specialized in outrageously unorthodox and unmoral definitions of gentlemanly conduct). Chaste comedies featuring exemplary gentlemen become more prominent (e.g. Shadwell's *Bury Fair*, 1689, and Durfey's *Love for Money*, 1691), and, in comedies whose protagonists indulge in genteel fornication, the transition from seducer to husband is more likely than in the earlier period to be part of the maturing of a gentleman (as in, for example, *The Squire of Alsatia*). But although the gentleman continues to dominate comedy, his natural right to dominate was coming under critical examination. Sympathy for the mercantile class is not quite as rare as is generally assumed (the best-known, and most passionate, defence of mercantile wealth is that which concludes Mary Pix's *The Beau Defeated*, 1700), and the pretensions of gentle birth could be mocked: when the heroine of Crowne's *The English Frier* is told that a drunken rake has good blood in his veins, she retorts 'So has a pig. Wou'd he had some good manners, and good sense' (IV. i).

On the whole, the world picture of *The Committee*, in which hierarchy of class embodies a hierarchy of nature, is now rarely evident. In early seventeenth-century comedy, the gentleman's role in society is defined by his ancestry and also by his estate, which, with its nucleus of traditions and responsibilities, gives its owner both a moral and literal place in society. In Farquhar, however, despite a constant preoccupation with the maturing gentleman, gentlemen are defined more exclusively by their money, and can initially appear strikingly rootless. In *The Constant Couple* (1699), Sir Harry Wildair, his rank validated solely by his possession of £8,000 a year, saunters to and fro between two houses, neither of them his own and neither of them perceived in its proper character (one being literally and the other effectively mistaken for a brothel). In *The Beaux' Stratagem* (1707) the improvident gentlemen Aimwell and Archer lug from town to town the chest of money that is the prime – portable and unfixed – evidence of what remains of their status. Moreover, whereas the two impoverished gentlemen in *The Committee* maintained a natural and benevolent superiority to their Irish servant, Farquhar's gentlemen are forced by need to alternate between the roles of master and servant as they drift from town to town: social relations are shifting responses to the demands of material security. Farquhar's heroes regularly grow into amiable gentlemen, and the impoverished heroes gain estates as a reward for reform; but, as their acquisition of new estates indicates, the reformed gentlemen are not so much fulfilling the ancestral implications of their status as justifying for the first time a previously unmerited rank. Only in *The Twin-Rivals* (1702) do we find the more traditional pattern of a gentleman rescuing a threatened ancestral inheritance, but it is an interesting aspect of Farquhar's contribution to the redefinition of female status that his heroines generally have both the inherited estates and the fixed moral character that his heroes initially lack.

In one highly successful play, however, there was a return to more traditional systems of order. Colley Cibber's rake-reformed play *Love's Last Shift* (1696) not only portrays a libertine's repentance but the growth of a gentleman into conformity with the traditions of his position. The language which defines social identity here exercises total power over the individual's nature and desires, for the rakish Loveless's moral transformation is completed when he recognizes his name on the arm of his abandoned and unrecognized wife. Loveless's recovered gentility also brings a re-establishment of social gradation, in that he resumes authority over the servant who has previously been his companion in dissipation, commanding him to atone for a rape by marrying the victim. Only in much later plays did Cibber start showing sympathy for non-gentle characters, *Loves Last Shift*, often mistakenly labelled a bourgeois death-blow to the upper-class excesses of Restoration comedy, in fact displays an exceptionally rigid insistence on the value of social degree, preserving attitudes which the most exploratory Restoration drama had in manifold ways sought to modify and redefine.

FURTHER READING

Burns, Edward (1987) *Restoration Comedy: Crises of Desire and Identity*, Macmillan, London

Highfill, Philip H., Jr., Burnim, Kalman A. and Langhans, Edward A. (1973–) *A Biographical Dictionary of Actors, Actresses, Musicians, Dancers, Managers, and Other Stage Personnel in London, 1660–1800*, 16 vols in progress, Southern Illinois University Press, Carbondale and Edwardsville

Holland, Peter (1979) *The Ornament of Action: Text and Performance in Restoration Comedy*, Cambridge University Press, Cambridge

Hughes, Derek (1981) *Dryden's Heroic Plays*, Macmillan, London

——(1986) 'Providential Justice and English Comedy 1660–1700: A Review of the External Evidence', *Modern Language Review*, 81, 273–292

——(1987) 'Naming and Entitlement in Wycherley, Etherege, and Dryden', *Comparative Drama*, 21, 259–89

Hume, Robert D. (1976) *The Development of English Drama in the Late Seventeenth Century*, Clarendon Press, Oxford

——(ed.) (1980a) *The London Theatre World 1660–1800*, Southern Illinois University Press, Carbondale and Edwardsville

——(1983) *The Rakish Stage: Studies in English Drama, 1660–1800*, Southern Illinois University Press, Carbondale and Edwardsville

Hume, Robert D. and Scouten, Arthur H. (1980b) ' "Restoration Comedy" and its Audiences, 1660–1776', *Yearbook of English Studies*, 10, 45–69

Love, Harold (1980) 'Who Were the Restoration Audience?', *Yearbook of English Studies*, 10, 21–44

Staves, Susan (1979) *Players' Scepters: Fictions of Authority in the Restoration*, University of Nebraska Press, Lincoln

Van Lennep, William, Avery, Emmett, L. and Scouten, Arthur H. (1965) *The London Stage 1660–1800*, Part 1 (1660–1700), Southern Illinois University Press, Carbondale and Edwardsville

31

THE ORIGINS OF THE MODERN BRITISH STAGE

JAN McDONALD

Plus ça change, plus c'est la même chose. It is a truism that the theatre of today has its roots in primitive ritual and early religious festivals. Periodically throughout the history of the theatre, reformers – Edward Gordon Craig and Peter Brook being two notable examples – have sought to improve contemporary practice by returning to scenic and histrionic first principles. There were, however, certain developments both in drama and in theatre in Britain in the period between 1890 and 1914 which very specifically laid the foundation for much of what is now common theatrical practice.

By the 1880s, mainstream theatre in Britain had developed from a popular cultural activity for the post-industrial revolution working class to a comfortably upholstered entertainment for a middle- and upper-middle-class audience, for whom 'nice plays with nice dresses, nice drawing rooms and nice people were indispensable' (Shaw, Preface to *The Devil's Disciple*, 1901). The growth of the social respectability of the theatrical profession brought considerable advantages to its members and, in certain respects, a raising of artistic standards, but these were to some extent offset by the parallel growth of commercialism which dominated London's West End theatres. The expense involved in mounting spectacular and elegant presentations which the new audiences had come to expect necessitated the introduction of the long-run system and of full-scale provincial tours by entire companies in order that the large financial outlay on settings and costumes might be recouped. This meant the demise of the indigenous provincial companies which had hitherto provided back-up for the visiting London 'star' and which had served as training schools for aspiring performers (see Rowell and Jackson, 1984, pp. 7–13).

The need to cover costs in those pre-subsidy days also meant that there was a reluctance to experiment with innovative dramatic texts. The average repertoire was a diet of old successes, newly garnished, and contemporary pieces that followed well-tested recipes. The hierarchical actor-manager system meant that a star actor chose plays that would most effectively demonstrate his talents and selected a company of actors that would support his performance rather than become integrated into an ensemble.

The promise of the new century, however, brought to many of those involved in every sphere of artistic and social activity a desire for reform of the old order that was passing. In education, politics, social welfare, and not least in the theatre, there was an impetus towards change, coupled with growing awareness, particularly among middle-class intellectuals, of an individual's responsibility to, and for, society.

The 'new drama' movement of the 1890s drew on three major sources: first, the 'Free Theatre' movement in Europe, pioneered by André Antoine at the Théâtre Libre in Paris; second, the impact of the dramas of Henrik Ibsen; and third, the development of a style of acting and a method of production that had been evolved by T. W. Robertson and the Bancroft management at the Prince of Wales' Theatre in the 1860s.

It was the visit of Antoine's company to London in 1889, two years after its foundation, that inspired J. T. Grein to begin his campaign in *The Weekly Comedy* for a British Théâtre Libre (see Schoenderwoerd, 1963). He sought the creation of 'a theatre free from the shackles of the censor, free from the fetter of convention, unhampered by financial considerations' (*The Weekly Comedy*, 30 November 1889). In the Independent Theatre Society, established in 1891, his vision was realized. The first production was *Ghosts* by Henrik Ibsen, banned for public performance by the Lord Chamberlain's Reader of Plays. The following year the Society presented *Widowers' Houses* by the well-known music critic and novelist, George Bernard Shaw.

The I.T.S. was able to be 'free from the shackles of the censor' in that it was a private society whose members paid for their subscriptions rather than for an individual performance, and so normal licensing laws did not apply; but, in the event, *Ghosts* was the only banned piece presented, for in the wake of the public outcry precipitated by the first production of Ibsen's play theatre managers were reluctant to risk their own licences by renting their premises to the Society. The Society did, however, produce several unconventional pieces that would never have had a presentation on the commercial stage. Issues of social significance, particularly the problems confronting women who sought equal status in a male-dominated society, were tackled in the I.T.S.'s repertoire, John Todhunter's *The Black Cat*, Brieux's *Blanchette* and *Alan's Wife* by Mrs Hugh Bell and Elizabeth Robins being three notable examples.

Grein's withdrawal from the Society, which even in its heyday boasted no more than 175 members, led to its demise in 1898, but its pioneering work led to the establishment of the Stage Society, which rose from its ashes in the following year and which, harnessing the talents of Shaw and Harley Granville Barker, made a significant impact on later theatrical developments.

Grein had adopted the 'Free Theatre' idea from Antoine, but his Independent Theatre differed from the Théâtre Libre in two important respects. In the first place, Grein quite deliberately avoided the more extreme forms of Naturalism, *rosserie* as it was called, which Antoine was thought to favour. Grein wanted realism but 'realism of a healthy kind' (Grein, 1889). The 'new drama' movement in Britain was influenced far more by the plays of Henrik Ibsen than by the naturalistic theory of Zola and his disciples. Secondly, one of Antoine's primary aims in setting up his company was a desire to reform contemporary acting style. His dissatisfaction with what he saw as stilted and conventional playing, nourished in the Conservatoire and practised at the Comédie-Française, led to his choosing amateur actors for his first revolutionary company. Grein did not see acting as a problem. It was the paucity of good texts rather than the lack of good players that motivated the zeal for reform. It is also true that, thanks to the work of the Bancrofts and T. W. Robertson in the 1860s, a style of acting had evolved in the British theatre that was perfectly capable of dealing with the 'new drama'. Grein's idea to employ his actors 'from the huge crowd of the disengaged' (Grein, 1889) was not simply indifference to the histrionic art. He, probably rightly, believed that there already existed a vast pool of talent, waiting to be used in challenging work. As a rule, in even the most pilloried avant-garde play, the acting was praised. The demand which the new theatre movement in Britain made on the actors was for increased flexibility within the naturalistic mode, so that they were capable of playing more stylized roles, rather than for the creation of techniques required for playing 'real' people on stage, skills which they already possessed.

Although the Independent Theatre Society drew the bulk of the fire from conservative critics with its inaugural production of *Ghosts*, the Society was not alone in the campaign to introduce the dramas of Ibsen to the British stage. His social prose plays were particularly attractive to the women of the theatre, frustrated by a succession of vapid parts of melodramatic heroines or pert soubrettes. The production of *A Doll's House* in 1889, in which Janet Achurch played Nora, was the first serious presentation of an Ibsen piece in London. It inspired the American actress Elizabeth Robins, and her compatriot Marion Lea, to mount *Hedda Gabler* only months after the 'terrible success' of *Ghosts* in 1891. A subscription series of *The Master Builder, Rosmersholm, Hedda Gabler* and Act 4 of *Brand* followed in 1893, and in 1896 Robins appeared with Jane Achurch and Mrs Patrick Campbell in *Little Eyolf*.

The 'high-priestesses of Ibsen', as Shaw christened these pioneering actresses, met with difficulties very similar to those encountered by the I.T.S. The commercial theatre was utterly uninterested. Ibsen was a minority taste attracting only a small audience of intellectuals – 'effeminate men and male women', as one critic described them (see Egan, 1972). The pieces were thought 'provincial', in that the drawing-rooms of Chislehurst and the music-rooms of Mayfair were replaced by rain-drenched fiords and uncomfortable attics inhabited by captured wild-life. Ibsen's women were singularly 'unwomanly' and often stridently independent. The attempts of Elizabeth Robins and Marion Lea to enlist the support of the actor-managers, who saw no starring roles for themselves, met with unmitigated failure. The plays were presented by *ad hoc* companies, the actors were paid only expenses and had to expend intellectual and creative energy on parts that they might play only once at an ill-attended matinée. There was virtually no adequate scenery, technical rehearsals were non-existent as the theatres were rented for only one or two days, and the brave promoters found themselves in charge of a multitude of administrative activities, in addition to playing major roles. Yet despite all the practical difficulties, the impact of Ibsen's plays on the British theatre was immeasurable. This was partly because of a tendency among British critics to regard Ibsen primarily as a social prophet and reformer – a description which he categorically denied – rather than as a dramatist. Clement Scott's word 'Ibsenite' (for him it was a synonym for 'crank') came to mean far more than someone who enjoyed Ibsen's plays (see Egan, 1972). 'Ibsenism' – as developed in Shaw's *Quintessence of Ibsenism* in 1891 – meant a belief in a socialist political philosophy, an opposition to unthinking adherence to social convention, and a belief in a new role for women in society. The critics and audiences who praised Ibsen's work and the actors who performed in it to a greater or lesser extent adhered to this social creed. Members of the Fabian Society frequently formed the bulk of the 'nasty-minded people', as Scott chastised those who attended performances of the plays (see Egan, 1972). The prevalent view (however misguided) of Ibsen as a propagandist, had a fortunate result in that it became clear to serious writers that it was possible to discuss important issues on a stage that need not be merely a show-place for the trivial and the narcissistic.

In addition, the performances by the Ibsen pioneers, like those by the I.T.S. and the Stage Society, created a desire in the younger and more intelligent members of the acting profession for similarly challenging work. A return to the hack-work of the West End stage after tackling a complex role in the emergent 'new drama' was a dispiriting prospect. The relief from the drudgery of the long-run system and from the domination of the actor-managers opened the eyes of the performers to alternative methods of theatre administration and company organization. Increasingly, participation in these one-off performances was regarded as prestigious and, despite the financial and technical problems, as artistically rewarding work.

It was not only the contemporary drama on the British stage that required reformation at the end of the nineteenth century. Presentations of Shakespeare's plays had become over-encumbered with spectacular and historically accurate scenery, which, although often beautifully executed by carpenters and

439

scene-painters, was felt by the more discerning to be fundamentally opposed to the spirit of the works. Actor-managers and designers, fresh from research trips to Venice, Rome or Egypt, gave their audiences a travelogue rather than a play. The scenery required an army of stagehands and, even with their help, intervals were protracted, and the text had to be cut or re-organized to accommodate the splendid visual set-pieces (see Booth, 1981).

Just as the impetus towards change in playwriting came from groups outside the mainstream theatre, so the reform in the contemporary fashion of staging Shakespeare's plays came from the Elizabethan Stage Society, and its director, William Poel. Poel's fundamental belief was that a play ought to be presented in stage conditions that approximated as far as possible to those in which it had been originally performed. In the case of Shakespeare's plays, this meant an architectural set, with two levels, an alcove and, most important, a platform extending into the auditorium. The Victorian picture-frame stage and the consequent loss of the apron made nonsense of Shakespeare's dramaturgy which frequently relied for its effect on continuous playing and the sensitive juxtaposing of scenes. The long intervals, the re-ordering of the text to facilitate changes of set and the banishment of the actor behind the proscenium arch were anathema to Poel. His productions were largely mounted in halls or out-of-doors, but when he did use a conventional theatre it was reconstructed to fit his demands. His most famous presentations were the production of the First Quarto of *Hamlet* in the St George's Hall in 1881, and of the morality play, *Everyman*, in the Master's Court at Charterhouse in 1901.

Poel's passion for a reform in stage diction came second only to his desire to recreate Elizabethan stage conditions. He was convinced that Shakespeare's actors had spoken much faster than their Victorian successors. Using the First Folio, he sought to interpret the punctuation and capitalization of the text in order to determine rhythm and stress. This process, which he called 'learning the tunes', dominated the rehearsal period, actors often spending three or more weeks in the exercise before they set foot on a stage. The impact of Poel's work on voice-production was considerable, both among the younger members of the acting profession and among those who were involved in training for the stage (see Speaight, 1954).

In some respects, Poel was as much of an antiquarian as the actor-managers whose 'historically accurate' productions he sought to supplant. His detailed programme notes, citing the sources for his costumes, properties and scenery, are often as pedantic as those of Charles Kean. Yet despite his archaism, Poel paved the way for producers who had more theatrical flair and who could adapt his reforms more imaginatively for contemporary audiences. Granville Barker's season of Shakespearian productions at the Savoy Theatre in 1912 and 1914 owe much to Poel's attempt to free the theatre from spurious historicism (see Dymkowski, 1986).

By the end of the nineteenth century, then, there was evidence of a new movement in dramatic writing and in theatrical presentation. There had been 'fruitful failures' and *succès d'estime*. What was needed was a consolidation of the activities of the Societies, a permanent home, where the problems of *ad hoc* companies, haphazard administration, uncertain funding and lack of coherent planning could be eliminated. This was found in Granville Barker's management of the Royal Court Theatre between 1904 and 1907, aptly christened, 'The Promised Land of the London Stage'. Barker was quick to acknowledge the debt he owed to the pioneers, recognizing that his venture was built on the shoulders of those who had founded the I.T.S. and the Stage Society.

Barker's management of the Court broke the mould of conventional theatre practice in several ways. The choice of repertoire was atypical in that it consisted of plays which presented 'a critical dissenting attitude towards conventional codes of morality', as the critic Desmond MacCarthy put it (1907, p. 15). Most notable in this category were the plays of George Bernard Shaw, which formed the bulk of the theatre's repertoire – 701 out of 988 performances. There were also pieces by new young British authors, John Galsworthy, St John Hankin, John Masefield, and by Barker himself. The Court continued the tradition of the Societies by presenting the best of contemporary European drama, plays by Ibsen, Hauptmann, Schnitzler and Maeterlinck, and finally, there were Gilbert Murray's translations of Euripides' works, which provided a classical element to the repertoire, yet preserved the contemporary flavour of the programme.

The new playwrights were allowed the right to fail by the institution of a short-run system accompanied by experimental matinées. A new piece would be tried out at a matinée performance and, if it proved successful, it would be transferred to the evening bill for a run of three to six weeks. Shaw's *Candida, John Bull's Other Island, You Never Can Tell, Man and Superman,* Barker's *The Voysey Inheritance* and Galsworthy's *The Silver Box* were among those pieces which began as matinées and which were subsequently incorporated into the evening repertoire. While this system was very demanding on the actors, it gave them opportunities for versatility that were sadly lacking in the West End theatre. It was common practice for the same members of the company to be used in the matinée and in the evening performance. In one day, Edith Wynne Matthison played Electra in the afternoon and Mrs Baines in *Major Barbara* in the evening. Norman Page went on from being a Court Usher in *The Silver Box* at the matinée to take the role of Patsy Farrell in *John Bull's Other Island* at night. The artistic opportunities, however, were felt to outweigh the pressures, and the actors were grateful to their authors not only for 'a whole new gallery of theatrical types' but also for the chance to play a variety of roles in the one season (see McDonald, 1984).

Barker remained faithful to the short-run system throughout his management, although it almost certainly meant financial loss, for many of the productions, most especially those of Shaw's plays, could have had very respectable runs by West End standards. He was supported in this policy not only by the company but by his business manager, J. E. Vedrenne and, indeed, by Shaw himself.

Another practice of the commercial theatre, the star system, was likewise reformed at the Court. This meant greater flexibility in the choice of repertoire, as a play could be chosen on its merits, not as a showpiece for one player's talent. It also created a spirit of co-operation in the company which resulted in a standard of ensemble playing that had never been seen before on the London stage. Members of the company were able and willing to alternate leading roles with minor parts. When John Galsworthy went backstage to congratulate the extras in the police court scene in his first play, *The Silver Box*, he found that they were established members of the company and included Lewis Casson, Edmund Gwenn and Norman Page. In thanking his actors for their work over the three Court seasons at a dinner given in his honour in 1907, Barker said, 'I would rather think of them as a company than as individuals, brilliant individually as they may be, for I feel very strongly that it is the playing together of a good company which makes good performances' (Barker, 1907).

Both the critics and the audiences appreciated the change in emphasis. The real successes of the Court were achieved with modest, youthful casts, and in any event, the cult of personality acting was inappropriate for interpreting the subtleties of the new drama. As there were no stars, there were no star salaries, but the economic equity established within the company was no deterrent to the young actor in search of artistic opportunities. Lillah McCarthy, who had been earning £30 with the Wilson Barrett Company, was glad to assume the Court 'Twelve-Pound look', as she called it (see *Myself and My Friends*, 1933).

The presence of a director, or a producer as the term was then, is, of course, a *sine qua non* in the creation of an ensemble company, and the Court was the first theatre in Britain to give to the director a major role in the theatrical process. T. W. Robertson had directed his own work in association with the Bancrofts at the Prince of Wales', and the actor-managers had drilled their companies to create attractive stage pictures and to highlight their own performances, but the rise of the 'new drama' with its difficult philosophical ideas and its complex literary style meant that a single interpreter was necessary to give intellectual unity to the performance. The early efforts by the Societies in the nineties had suffered from the lack of a director, but the Stage Society encouraged its members to produce, a practice which gave Granville Barker, the first real director in the British theatre, his first opportunity in 1900.

At the Court, Shaw directed his own work and Barker undertook the rest. Both were very highly regarded by the actors, but they were very different in style. Shaw revelled in the big effect, the theatrical flair that he had admired in Barry Sullivan and which he came to love in Lillah McCarthy, whom he praised for playing his heroines exactly as she would play Belvidera in *Venice Preserv'd*. He encouraged these actors skilled in naturalism to develop a presentational style, to move from playing the individual to playing the typical. Just as Brecht saw in Shaw's plays traces of the epic quality that he was to employ later in the century, one can discern in Shaw's directorial style an attempt to achieve alienation and *gestus*.

Not only the effects which they aimed for, but the working methods of Shaw and Barker were very different. Shaw favoured a four-week rehearsal period, during which he would work every morning from 9 a.m. to noon. During the first and the last week, he would go on stage with the company giving moves and discussing interpretations, but he considered any interruption of their efforts in the middle weeks counter-productive. Instead he wrote copious notes, usually communicated to the actors by post. Analysis of these notes reveals, in the first place, a determined effort towards ensemble playing. 'Play to' a character is the most common instruction. Second, there is an impulse towards recreating on stage the musicality of the rhetoric and rhythm of the text, and third, there is a plethora of instructions regarding details of costume and setting, from notes on Prossy's blouse in *Candida* and Ann Whitefield's sash in *Man and Superman* to the position of the coat-hooks and the lamp in Mr Morrell's study. Shaw's expert handling of his actors, for which they give him very proper credit, is demonstrated in the carefully judged admixture of charm and admonition that is a feature of these missives (see Dukore, 1971).

Barker, despite the very high standards of stage diction which he demanded – an understandable preoccupation in a disciple of William Poel – was, in many respects, a less technical and a more psychological director than Shaw. For both, of course, the faithful interpretation of the text was paramount, but Barker, years before he met Stanislavsky in 1914, was employing his own techniques for creating the inner life and truth of a role. Barker's stage directions, as lengthy as Shaw's but quite different in tone, are designed to lead the actor to the character by describing aspects of his or her life that are not always directly relevant to the action. Shaw's directions give a critical authorial opinion on the character; Barker's seek to integrate the player and the role (Kennedy, 1985). So it was that the latter excelled in the direction of the more naturalistic pieces in the repertoire, and, on the rare occasions when Barker was involved in the production of a Shaw play, the author deplored the misplaced delicacy of the result. Despite the difference of their directional methods, however, the partnership which was created at the Court was one of the most artistically fruitful in the twentieth-century theatre.

The success of the Court experiment encouraged Barker to move to the

Savoy Theatre in 1907. This was a larger house, situated more centrally in London's West End and the new theatre challenge was taken closer to the heart of commercialism. Regrettably, the transfer was unsuccessful for a variety of reasons. The house was probably too large for what was still, to a certain extent, a coterie audience, and the rates and overheads were much higher. Vedrenne became increasingly preoccupied in promoting his personal interest in the newly built Queen's Theatre. Shaw, altruistically but mistakenly, thought that the Savoy ought to be viable without his work and elected to play only a small part in its management. Barker was greatly disheartened by the banning of his latest play, *Waste*, by the Lord Chamberlain. The ill-fated repertory season at the Duke of York's in 1910 financed by Charles Frohman, in which Barker and Dion (George) Boucicault were joint directors of a series of plays, including Galsworthy's *Justice*, Shaw's *Misalliance* and Barker's *The Madras House*, was as financially disastrous as it was artistically interesting. Demoralized and impoverished, the new drama impulse appeared to have returned to its nomadic and sporadic beginnings.

Yet from these endeavours emerged three major initiatives that were to have far-reaching results, namely, the fight against the censorship, the campaign for a National Theatre and the rise of the provincial repertory movement.

The law governing the censorship of plays, instigated by Robert Walpole in the Licensing Act of 1737, had been confirmed by the Theatre Regulation Act of 1843. Quite simply, this meant that it was necessary for theatre managers to submit the texts of plays which they wished to stage to the Lord Chamberlain's Reader of Plays, fourteen days prior to the first performance. In effect, few pieces were banned in the first eighty years of the nineteenth century. W. S. Gilbert's *The Happy Land* (1871), a fairly mild satire on the government of the day, became a cause célèbre, because it was an exception. Parliamentary committees of inquiry set up in 1853, 1866 and 1892 reported that the censorship was working satisfactorily, and only the lone voice of William Archer, the iconoclastic Ibsenite critic, spoke out against the existing system (see Archer, 1886, 1892). Whether or not there was a *hidden* censorship, in that dramatists tailored their subject-matter to suit the somewhat idiosyncratic rules of the Examiner of Plays, can only be a matter of conjecture.

With the advent of a socially-conscious drama, heralded by the translations of Ibsen, the attitude of the playwrights changed radically. These were no dramatic hacks, but serious men of letters, and they objected to their work being banned or mutilated by one individual whose aesthetic taste was suspect and whose moral standards were those of the hypocritical establishment which the new drama set out to disturb. The banning of, for example, Ibsen's *Ghosts*, Tolstoy's *The Power of Darkness*, Maeterlinck's *Monna Vanna*, Brieux's *Maternité*, Shaw's *Mrs Warren's Profession*, Wilde's *Salomé*, Laurence Housman's *Bethlehem*, raised the temperature of opposition to the censorship and this reached a climax with the refusal to allow the public performance of Granville Barker's *Waste* and Edward Garnett's *The Breaking Point* in 1907. Garnett's Preface to the published version of his play crystallized the new dramatists' reaction to what they regarded as an iniquitous government control of the theatre.

Seventy-one dramatists formed a deputation to the prime minister and wrote a letter to *The Times* protesting against 'An office, autocratic in procedure, opposed to the spirit of the constitution, contrary to public justice and to commonsense' (see Findlater, 1967). In 1909, the banning of two plays by Shaw, *The Shewing-up of Blanco Posnet* and *Press Cuttings*, added fuel to the fire. In the same year, a Joint Select Committee of Enquiry was set up by Parliament. Among the leading dramatists and theatre practitioners who gave evidence were Barker, Shaw, Galsworthy, W. S. Gilbert, A. W. Pinero, Beerbohm Tree, Sir Squire Bancroft and George Alexander. The objections were, first, that so much power ought not to be invested in one individual, second, that the existence of the censorship was a deterrent to serious drama in English, third, that the commercial theatre and the music-halls were allowed to perpetrate all kinds of scurrility because there the supposed indecencies were presented frivolously and dressed up in music and song. Those who supported the *status quo*, including the majority of theatre managers, maintained that objectionable plays would lower the status of the profession, and that the opinion of an impartial arbiter of public taste was essential prior to their embarking on a production, for they would lose money if a local authority were to prosecute them after the piece had been mounted. Both sides were in complete agreement that the power of the stage was greater than that of the written word (see Findlater, 1967).

The outcome of the proceedings was unsatisfactory. The Report itself was probably well-intentioned but confused, and the government took advantage of its ambivalence by doing nothing. The appointment of Charles Brookfield, a playwright and actor, to the position of Examiner of Plays in 1911 fired the new dramatists to further protest. Just before his appointment, he had published an article attacking the avant-garde playwrights for their 'morbid imagination', and it is hardly surprising that there was a concerted move to cancel his appointment (see Findlater, 1967). In June 1912, the authors sent a letter to the king, but Brookfield's death in 1913, and the beginning of the war in the next year, took the heat out of the issue. It was more than fifty years before the censorship of the stage was finally abolished, in 1968.

It was in this period, too, that the seeds of the subsidized theatre were sown. The sustained campaign against commercialism had proved to the pioneers that, in the first place, experimentation was necessary for the health of the theatre, and, second, that the repertory system with its proven advantages for authors and actors could not flourish without funding independent of box-office returns. The idea of a subsidized National Theatre, constructed perhaps on a continental model, was the basis of much of the pioneering activity in the nineties. The scheme was articulated in more detail in William Archer's and Granville Barker's *Scheme and Estimates for a National Theatre*, compiled and privately printed in 1904, and made available to the public in 1907. It was endorsed by Sir Henry Irving, Sir Squire Bancroft, J. M. Barrie, H. A. Jones and A. W. Pinero. It was not expected that government money would be forthcoming for such an enterprise. The funding was to come from private sponsorship. Today, with the introduction of incentive or enterprise schemes as part of government policy to make the theatre increasingly self-reliant, we have, perhaps regrettably, returned to the realism (or pessimism) of the early pioneers after the post-Second World War honeymoon period of state support for the arts.

It was not envisaged that the National Theatre should be élitist and appeal only to a specially cultured class. 'It must be visibly and unmistakably a popular institution, making a large appeal to the whole community' (Archer and Barker, 1904, p. xviii). The proposed repertoire for the first season includes plays by Dumas, Carton, Grundy, Gilbert, Jones and Pinero as well as Shakespeare, Sudermann, Yeats, Brieux and Maeterlinck. Barker modified the list in the second edition to include plays by Ibsen, Shaw, Hauptmann and the rest of the new dramatists. His experience at the Court had proved both the artistic and the financial viability of plays by these writers.

The ideal capacity of the National Theatre was 1550: prices were to be lower than those of the West End, because the theatre should be 'a place of habitual resort', not the venue for an expensive special outing. The company of 66 performers (42 actors and 24 actresses), of whom about 20 would be newcomers to the profession, would be employed for not less than three years, with a fixed annual salary and a certain number of guaranteed performances at a given fee for each performance. This proposal, together with the detailed pension scheme, was designed to give a hitherto unknown security to a precarious profession. A training school for actors was to be attached to the company, not only to provide it with promising new blood, but to improve the status of the actor in society by distinguishing the trained professional from the casual amateur. As well as technical training, instruction on literary and artistic subjects relevant to the actor's art was to be included. The idea of a BA degree for actors was mooted, but thought to be too 'visionary'. That vision has, of course, now come to pass.

The detailed financial plans for the proposed National Theatre require commentary by an economic historian, but one fundamental principle of the Theatre's financial policy deserves mention. *'We regard economy not merely as a necessity likely to be forced upon the Theatre for lack of lavish endowment but as the indispensable means to an artistic end'* (Archer and Barker, 1904, p. xxiii). This statement reflects not only the Fabian puritanism of the theatrical reformers of the nineties, but also their distaste for the spectacular commercially dominated mainstream theatre of their day. Today, when it is too easy to attribute lack of artistic invention solely to lack of money, the sentence provides a useful *caveat*.

Although Archer and Barker saw London, the capital city, as the proper home of a National Theatre, Barker, in particular, was greatly concerned with the revitalization of theatrical activity in the provinces. Indeed, in the revised Preface to the 1907 edition, he looks to Manchester, Birmingham and other provincial centres to spearhead the growth of the repertory movement rather than 'monstrous, inarticulate London'. His subsequent experiences at the Savoy and at the Duke of York's confirmed him in his view that the real function for the new theatre lay in the post-industrial cities, brimming with civic pride and enterprising energy. Repertory theatres were founded in Manchester in 1907, Glasgow in 1909, and Liverpool in 1911.

Barker had suggested that in the large industrial cities, civic support for a repertory theatre might well be forthcoming. So it was in Glasgow and in Liverpool, where the city corporations, the universities and the enlightened press joined together to support 'citizens' theatres'. In Manchester, the money to fund the theatre came from an individual benefactor, Miss Annie Horniman, a worthy veteran of the 'new drama' movement, who had funded a season at the Avenue Theatre in 1894 which included Shaw's *Arms and the Man*. Miss Horniman had also made a substantial contribution to the Abbey Theatre in Dublin.

The first provincial repertory theatres shared a common desire to present drama that was meaningful to their local audiences as an alternative to the undiluted fare of commercial successes exported from London (see Rowell and Jackson, 1984). Theatre societies on the pattern of the I.T.S. and the Stage Society in London had been established in all three cities and it was natural, therefore, that the Court, the summit of the alternative theatre's achievements, became the model for the provincial companies, which presented many plays by the dramatists which the Vedrenne–Barker management had nurtured. Whereas Glasgow almost adopted Shaw as its 'house dramatist', Manchester favoured Galsworthy, who wrote new pieces for the company, and took up the classical aspect of the Court's repertoire with productions of Murray's translations of *Hippolytus* and *The Trojan Women*. The Court tradition of presenting the best of European drama, most notably plays by Ibsen, was likewise continued. The first production in Britain of a play by Chekhov was the Glasgow Repertory Theatre's presentation of *The Seagull* in 1909 (see McDonald, 1980).

As far as the creation of a school of local 'new dramatists' was concerned the results were disappointing, although all three managements made valiant

447

attempts to nurture local playwrights. The only real success was Manchester's production of *Hindle Wakes* by Stanley Houghton, in which the critical, dissenting attitude to conventional moral codes that characterized the 'new drama' movement was expertly expressed.

The group of actors who worked in the provincial companies included a great many veterans of the Court, the Savoy and the repertory season at the Duke of York's. The acting style was praised for its intelligence in representing the author's meaning, its integration of all parts into a coherent whole, the excellence of the diction, and the balance between stylized and naturalistic playing. The Court actors also provided directors for the companies, most notably Lewis Casson and Madge McIntosh. Younger performers trained in the highest standard of histrionic art were fed into the London theatre, and the provinces once again provided the practical experience that theatrical novices had lacked since the demise of the stock companies.

Regrettably, only the Liverpool Repertory Theatre survived the First World War, yet the seeds sown in Manchester and Glasgow bore fruit later, so that both cities are now centres of theatrical activity, professionally and academically. The flourishing of the repertory theatres throughout Scotland and England, which are as much our National Theatre as the edifice on the South Bank, owes its origins to the artistic and civic initiatives of the early pioneers (see Rowell and Jackson, 1984).

While acknowledging the contribution which the innovators of the late nineteenth- and early twentieth-century new theatre movement made to subsequent developments on the British stage, one must remember that a great many of the practices of the commercial stage continued. The long-run, or 'Mousetrap', syndrome still dominates the West End. There are many dramas written and produced that have the function of the after-dinner mint rather than presenting a social, intellectual or aesthetic challenge to the audience. Star performers, often these days with a reputation built in television, continue to shine, sometimes against a background of indifferent supporters. Financial considerations, despite the growth of public subsidy, too often take precedence over artistic endeavour. At the other end of the spectrum, the principles on which the new theatre movement was founded are now challenged by the myriad of small touring companies leading a precarious existence, yet in many cases emerging as the s_ed-bed of imaginative ideas in playwriting and production, and providing a new alternative to the erstwhile 'alternative' theatre of the repertory movement.

Despite all the *caveats*, however, much of what is now taken for granted as common theatrical practice was initiated by the pioneers whose work has been described here – the rise of the director and the ensemble company, the provincial repertory theatres and the National Theatre, the abolition of theatrical censorship, the notion of subsidizing performances, and the creation of a body of national drama of world-wide reputation.

FURTHER READING

Egan, Michael (ed.) (1972) *Ibsen: The Critical Heritage*, Routledge & Kegan Paul, London

Elsom, John and Tomalin, Nicholas (1978) *The History of the National Theatre*, Jonathan Cape, London

Findlater, Richard (1967) *Banned*, MacGibbon & Kee, London

Howe, P. P. (1910) *The Repertory Theatre: A Record and a Criticism*, Martin Secker, London

Kennedy, Dennis (1985) *Granville Barker and the Dream of Theatre*, Cambridge University Press, Cambridge

MacCarthy, Desmond (1907) *The Court Theatre*, A. H. Bullen, London

McDonald, Jan (1986) *The 'New Drama' 1900–1914*, Macmillan, London

Rowell, George and Jackson, Anthony (1984) *The Repertory Movement: A History of Regional Theatre in Britain*, Cambridge University Press, Cambridge

Schoenderwoerd, N. (1963) *J. T. Grein: Ambassador of the Theatre 1862–1935*, Van Gorcum, Assen

Speaight, Robert (1954) *William Poel and the Elizabethan Revival*, Heinemann, London

Stokes, John (1972) *Resistible Theatres*, Paul Elek, London

Woodfield, James (1984) *English Theatre in Transition 1881–1914*, Croom Helm, London

ADDITIONAL WORKS CITED

Archer, William (1886) *About the Theatre: Essays and Studies*, T. Fisher Unwin, London

——(1892) 'The Drama: A Note on Censorship', *The New Review*, March

Archer, William and Barker, Harley Granville (1904) *A National Theatre, Scheme and Estimates*, Duckworth, London

Barker, Harley Granville (1907) Dinner in Honour of Harley Granville Barker and J. E. Vedrenne at the Criterion Restaurant, 7 July 1907, British Library MS 010325ff503

Booth, Michael, R. (1981) *Victorian Spectacular Theatre*, Routledge & Kegan Paul, London

Dukore, Bernard, F. (1971) *Bernard Shaw – Director*, George Allen & Unwin, London

Dymkowski, Christine (1986) *Harley Granville Barker: A Preface to Modern Shakespeare*, Associated University Presses, London

Grein, J. T. and Jarvis, C. W. (1889) 'A British Théâtre Libre (A Suggestion)', *The Weekly Comedy*, 30 November

McCarthy, Lillah (1933) *Myself and My Friends*, Thornton Butterworth, London

McDonald, Jan (1980) 'Productions of Chekhov's Plays in Britain before 1914', *Theatre Notebook*, 44, 25–36

——(1984) 'New Actors for the New Drama', *Themes in Drama*, 6, Cambridge University Press, Cambridge

Shaw, George Bernard (1957) *The Quintessence of Ibsenism*, Hill & Wang, New York [first published 1891]

32

THEORIES OF MODERN DRAMA

DAVID BRADBY

Theory has played a vital role in the development of modern drama. The theorists of the last hundred years have mostly been campaigners for whom the articulation of the principles of modern drama has been important in promoting its practical realization. The first of these campaigning theorists was Emile Zola, whose writings were crucial to the creation of Naturalist drama. Almost simultaneously came the symbolist reaction, which found its fullest expression in the work of Edward Gordon Craig. In the course of the twentieth century there followed a succession of schools or styles, and since each sought to define itself by opposition to its predecessor, practitioners of all persuasions took to issuing manifestos. The 'Free' theatres of Paris and Berlin (1887 and 1889), the Vieux-Colombier of Copeau (1913), the Proletarian Theatre of Piscator (1920), the 'Alfred Jarry Theatre' of Artaud (1926), the Group Theatre in America (1931) and Joan Littlewood's Theatre Workshop (1945) are just a few of the many modern theatres established by manifesto. As practice rarely matched the principles declared in advance, these manifestos would be followed by essays, articles, letters, all refining the initial pronouncements, and so a rich body of dramatic theory has built up.

This flowering of theoretical writing is closely linked to the rise of the director in the modern theatre. Both are the consequence of intellectual developments that had taken place in the course of the nineteenth century, altering the way that human beings perceived themselves and their relationship to the natural and social environment: for the first time they had begun to see themselves principally as products of that environment. This change was also accompanied by an enhanced historical awareness, making it unacceptable to show Roman heroes, for example, in European court dress, as had been the custom in the previous three centuries. In the same period the development of electric stage lighting also began to have far-reaching implications for the art of the director, implications first developed in theoretical terms by Adolphe Appia. Inevitably, these new developments were not always welcomed by those actively engaged in theatre; it was necessary to explain, illustrate, defend, challenge. This is why so many of the important theorists of modern drama have been practitioners: directors, designers, playwrights.

EMILE ZOLA AND NATURALISM

Writing in the 1870s, Zola set up truth-to-life as the sole criterion applicable to modern drama. The enemy of truth, he argued, was existing convention, especially the conventions of the romantics, despite the liberation that romantic drama had appeared to offer to the previous generation. He wrote it off as a brief lyrical outburst, fatally backward-looking and having nothing to say to the contemporary world. In a series of militant campaigning articles (grouped together in *Le Naturalisme au Théâtre*, 1881), Zola built up a picture of what modern theatre should be: an example of truth-to-life, social as much as individual; a laboratory of human responses in which the new sociological and Darwinian views of human nature could be put to the test; a representation of Man as physiological whole, not just an abstracted psychological case.

Zola chose the term Naturalism to underline the methodological similarities that he claimed between his work and experimental work in the natural sciences. He argued that writers could and should adopt the scientific method of observing the world, forming a hypothesis and then testing it in laboratory conditions. This scientific model proved attractive to many of his contemporaries and, although it had ultimately to be abandoned, it served Zola well, providing a good rhetorical framework for rejecting romantic theories of drama. His ideas were adopted by André Antoine, who set about creating a laboratory of human responses to particular conditions at his Théâtre Libre (founded 1887). Antoine's achievement was to demonstrate in practice both the strengths and the limitations of Zola's dramatic theory. To render in scenic terms the detailed descriptions of social conditions that characterize Zola's novels, Antoine would construct astonishingly detailed stage settings in order to present these conditions in a convincing way. But it was apparent to his contemporaries that the more life-like these stage sets became, the less conviction they carried. They were somehow *too* complete and failed to engage the creative imagination of audiences, who came simply to admire the settings as miracles of realism. The mistake had been to assume that the task of demonstrating the pressures of the environment could be left to the stage setting. For the descriptive passages in Zola's novels are set in a constantly shifting, dynamic relationship with the characters themselves, whereas in naturalist plays the stage setting inevitably remains static, transformed from a living environment into mere background. Zola did not see this theoretical difficulty because he was entirely taken up with his (successful) campaign to introduce on to the modern stage the real settings of modern industrial life: factories, mines, markets, railways.

KONSTANTIN STANISLAVSKI

One of the most influential theoreticians of modern drama, Stanislavski did more than anyone else to define and establish the role of the modern director. He provides an example of how the most important theoretical work may be quite inseparable from the practice out of which it springs. In the course of his life he developed a 'system' passed on by example and by word of mouth to theatre people all over the world. Its influence was particularly strong in America, where it became the basis for the 'Method' of the Actor's Studio and had a powerful impact on playwrights, actors, directors.

The purpose of Stanislavski's system was to liberate the actor, psychologically as well as physically. Zola had called for truth-to-life on the modern stage; Stanislavski's major contribution was to concentrate on the actor as much as on the setting, giving body and shape to this notion of truth by developing a theory of 'interior realism' and a system for achieving it. According to Stanislavski's theory, actors must contrive to 'live their characters' by drawing on their own inner resources, letting themselves be guided by their own subconscious, their own emotions, their own previous experience. When this psychological truthfulness is achieved, the effect on an audience combines both emotional force and intellectual conviction: 'Only such art can completely absorb the spectator and make him both understand and also inwardly experience the happenings on stage' (Stanislavski, 1937, p. 16).

The major difficulty he encountered in putting this theory into practice was that the subconscious does not function to order, and so the greater part of his system was devoted to developing ways of stimulating the actor's subconscious, activating his emotional memory and showing how this may find expression in realized action. One of his most important contributions was to show how the profoundest levels of psychic experience may manifest themselves in the simplest actions, as in the example he gave of Lady Macbeth's hand-washing. He made a crucial contribution to the understanding of Chekhovian naturalism by showing how the simplest action or statement may reveal a profoundly complex truth. His grasp of this principle allowed him to make a success of *The Seagull* in 1898, when it had already proved a flop in a less innovative production.

SYMBOLISM AND ADOLPHE APPIA

The perception that outer manifestations may be inadequate to convey the inner life led to very different conclusions on the part of the Symbolists.

Impressed by Wagner's concept of the *Gesamtkunstwerk*, the Symbolists grouped around Mallarmé in the 1880s and 1890s completely rejected the detailed realism of Naturalist drama. Yet their positive contribution to dramatic theory was limited since they saw poetry, not music or drama, as the highest form of artistic expression. Despite the vigour of the Symbolist-inspired Théâtre de L'Oeuvre, the only new French masterpiece it revealed was Alfred Jarry's *Ubu Roi* (1896). Though Jarry's play was certainly anti-Naturalist, it can be seen as equally anti-Symbolist; in fact it could be described as the first anti-play, engaging in suicidal demolition of every current theory of drama. Jarry did make a contribution to the development of Symbolist theory in his rather tongue-in-cheek essay 'On the uselessness of theatre in the theatre' ([1896] 1962), but this had little influence in comparison with the paradoxical vitality of the savage, vulgar, brutal yet strangely appealing figure of Ubu.

It was the Swiss designer Adolphe Appia who, in the 1880s and 1890s, established the basis of a new dramatic theory capable of presenting a real alternative to Naturalism. Working from the need to find practical solutions to the problems of staging Wagnerian opera, Appia developed the theory that dramatic art must be conceived in the same terms as music – that is, as a rhythmical creation depending for its realization on a precise duration of real time. Only in this way could theatre production become an art form with its own specific aesthetics, liberated from the impossible attempt to present an imitation of real life on stage. Appia's designs for Wagner's operas employed three-dimensional settings using space and volume non-figuratively, varying their effect on the audience's emotions by exploiting the resources of the new electric stage lighting just then becoming available. With the new technology, he argued, the designer could become a creative artist in the same way as the composer. Appia was not prepared to see lighting treated as a separate specialism: all aspects of the production had to be under the control of a director, 'whose influence would be as magnetic as that of an orchestral conductor of genius' (Appia, 1984, p. 73).

The relationship between music, lighting and production enshrined in Appia's theory may at first seem somewhat arbitrary, but Appia saw a necessary link between music and light in that both are non-propositional forms of expression. Both arouse feelings of emotional intensity without necessarily evoking ideas or narrative (although they may do so). Both have an emotional impact that is immediate, though both may also function as sign or symbol of something else; both can function simultaneously as signifier and signified.

EDWARD GORDON CRAIG

Craig's influence over the development of the modern stage has been enormous. Its main theoretical base was the notion of the director as composer in

Appia's sense, to which he added the idea of the director as *restorer* of the art of theatre as it had once existed. He spoke of the need for a renaissance of theatre art and the models he looked to were those of Ancient Greece or of Oriental theatre in which, as he put it, 'the father of the dramatist was the dancer' (Craig, 1911, p. 140). He looked forward to a time in the future when the director would be the theatre's main creative force, having a perfect mastery of 'action, line, colour, rhythm and words' (p. 178).

Craig was a visionary, who dreamed of an art of pure movement, in which all forms of expression on the stage would be harmonized, or rather *composed* by the work of the director. The central element in creating theatre was not acting (as for Stanislavski) but design, by which he meant not simply the settings, but the dramatic shape of the performance seen as a whole. From the actor, he expected not idiosyncratic detail, but disciplined submission to his place in this overall shape; he favoured the use of masks and developed the idea of the actor as *Übermarionette*. By coining this term he meant to distinguish an actor capable of symbolizing, indicating or demonstrating a truth from one capable only of mimicry (Craig, 1911, pp. 54–94). Craig's researches into different traditions of marionette and mask-theatre proved particularly fruitful in stimulating subsequent theatre practice, ranging from Meyerhold's biomechanics through Expressionism to Brecht's theory of 'distanced' acting (see Bablet, 1966, pp. 111–13).

JACQUES COPEAU

In the early years of this century the theatre was enjoying the biggest commercial boom it has ever known. Yet it was also, in the view of Jacques Copeau, the point at which theatre as a serious art form had sunk to its lowest point. The contemporary stage offended him not only because of its superficiality and commercialism, but also because exciting advances in stage technology were being exploited for mere spectacle. Copeau placed his central emphasis on the expressive art of the actor, envisaging what he termed a 'retheatricalization of theatre'. The excesses of both Naturalism and of grand spectacle were to be countered by placing the art of the performer once more at the centre of the dramatic experience. All that was needed was a bare stage and a company of highly trained, inventive and acrobatic actors, working as an ensemble. Copeau's theory therefore brought together aspects of both symbolist and naturalist traditions: from symbolist ideas as developed by Craig, he took the idea of the stage as a non-representational space, while, like Stanislavski, he stressed actor training and ensemble work. But the aim of his actor training was less psychological realism than acrobatic expressivity. In this he was more like the Russian director Meyerhold, who also called for theatre to be 'retheatricalized'.

455

VSEVOLOD MEYERHOLD

An admirer of Stanislavski, in whose company he had performed for four years (1898–1901), Meyerhold soon came to the conclusion that Stanislavski's emphasis on realism was fundamentally misguided. The theory developed by Meyerhold in essays and lectures over the next forty years was based on identifying the specificity of dramatic art as a medium. In 'The Fairground Booth', an essay written in 1912 (see Meyerhold, 1969, pp. 119–42), he argued that the French term *cabotinage* ('ham-acting') should not be seen as an insult, rather the opposite, since the essence of theatre was to be found in the art of the performer: the juggler or the clown just as much as the actor who speaks a text. In developing this argument, he elaborated a theory of the grotesque, in which the contrast of opposites would be deliberately sought. Not for Meyerhold the smooth, instantly recognizable quality of naturalist dramatic style. His aim was to surprise his audience, magnifying discrepancies between the commonplace and the fantastic so as to challenge and change their perceptions of reality.

This remained the theoretical basis of Meyerhold's work, even after the Russian revolution, when he became one of the strongest advocates of theatre as a means in the struggle for liberation. He was acutely conscious of the power that can be generated in a mass audience by a carefully constructed ritual or dramatic performance. In 1929 he warned of the dangers of Fascist rallies he had observed in Italy, where the Pope had encouraged the use of Catholic ritual in Mussolini's displays. But Meyerhold did not condemn the desire for mass spectacle; he argued instead that it should be recognized and harnessed 'to carry the masses forward to a world of new revolutionary creative effort' (1969, p. 270). In order to do this, he believed it was necessary to draw on the devices of popular entertainment, and he shared with Copeau the conviction that the approach and techniques of *commedia dell'arte*, if they could be rediscovered, would answer the problems facing the theatre of the twentieth century. The natural heir of Meyerhold's theory is Dario Fo, who has consistently used the devices of the popular entertainer to expose the roots of political oppression. Fo's theory of the travelling clown or *giullare* as political subversive echoes much in Meyerhold's theory and practice (see Mitchell, 1984, p. 11).

Meyerhold's theory extended to the architecture of the playing space and to methods of actor training. The best-known aspect of this, though not necessarily the most important, was his system of 'biomechanics', which has the same attraction of spurious scientificity as Zola's theory of the writer's function. Biomechanics was both a method of actor training and a theory of how to convey meaning in performance. It claimed to discover the principles of efficient movement displayed by any skilled worker: '1) an absence of superfluous, unproductive movements; 2) rhythm; 3) the correct positioning of the body's centre of gravity; 4) stability' (Meyerhold, 1969, p. 198). On this theoretical base, he constructed a system of gymnastic routines, drawing also on eurythmics, on mime and on sports, in order to give maximum suppleness to the actor's body and to introduce into the theatre a language of physical gesture: 'Every movement is a hieroglyph with its own peculiar meaning' (p. 200).

EXPRESSIONISM TO PISCATOR

The most significant movement of the early years of this century for the shaping of modern drama was German Expressionism, responsible for the term *ich-dramaturgie* (I-drama) that grew out of Strindberg's late plays. Towards the end of his life, Strindberg became convinced that nobody could ever possess a thorough knowledge of more than one life: one's own. Hence his plays presented the drama of one subjective consciousness in its struggle with itself and with the forces of the world outside. The German Expressionists developed this theory in plays where spiritual or psychological realities were often divorced from physical realities. Expressionist drama took on a more urgent, socially committed aspect during the First World War, as writers began to use the theatre to raise a protest against War in the name of Love and Brotherhood. A more violent form of protest against Western civilization in general was expressed in the theories and performances of the Dada movement. Futurist pronouncements and performances employed shock tactics to challenge the very notion of art; members of the Bauhaus group designed machine ballets and experimented with designs for totally flexible performance spaces. This ferment of conflicting theories fed into the urgent debates about political theatre that flourished in the Weimar Republic. Piscator, for example, was a member of the Berlin Dada group in 1919 at the same time as he was directing Expressionist plays and, a year later, launching the 'Proletarian Theatre', which announced as its sole aim the developing of class-consciousness. It was followed by many agit-prop (agitation and propaganda) groups, modelled on Russian theory and practice. In the course of the 1920s, Piscator developed a more complex theory of political theatre, incorporating the use of modern stage machinery as well as film and slide projection in order to make possible a drama of historical and political forces. He wrote an account of how his theory had developed in *The Political Theatre*, first published in 1929. Forced into exile during the Hitler period, Piscator returned to Germany after the war, where he contributed to the emergence of a new documentary drama in the plays of writers such as Weiss and Hochhuth.

BERTOLT BRECHT

Like Piscator, Brecht was convinced of the need to develop a new dramatic form to handle political realities. There has been much confusion and disagreement about Brechtian dramatic theory, most of it stemming from attempts to find one true Brechtian theory. Brecht himself wrote: 'A man with one theory is lost. He needs several of them, four, lots' (*Diaries 1920–22*, trans. 1979, p. 42). The term most frequently used by Brecht for his theories was 'Epic theatre', a term that can be traced back to Piscator (1980, p. 74). Brecht used it to convey dramas presenting a broad historical sweep in the manner of the Elizabethan history play. He rejected documentary theatre as Piscator developed it, substituting his own theory of *Historisierung*. This meant examining a given social system from the standpoint of a social system from another period – for example, modern Germany viewed in the light of the Thirty Years War in *Mother Courage*.

By using the word 'Epic', Brecht was also rejecting Aristotle's distinction between epic and tragic poetry, and stressing the importance of narrative in his conception of drama. 'Everything hangs on the story [*die Fabel*]', he wrote in paragraph 65 of his *Short Organum for the Theatre*. 'It is the heart of the theatrical performance' (Brecht, 1964, p. 200). Against the classical theory of drama as a brief crisis, centring on a single place and time, Brecht set the alternative theory of drama as episodic narrative, spread over a long period of time, often involving a journey.

The purpose of the narrative in epic theatre was always to reveal the conditions in which people live. But this was not to be done, as in Naturalism, by treating people as passive products of their environment. It was, on the contrary, to illustrate the Marxist dialectic: 'Social being determines thought' but 'the human being is alterable and able to alter' (1964, p. 37). The aim of his theatre was to clarify this process in which men and women are shaped by their conditions but are also able to shape them in their turn. Brecht held that Naturalist drama's emphasis on creating an illusion of reality made this aim impossible. In the words of Walter Benjamin (the major theorist of Epic theatre beside Brecht himself), 'The Naturalistic stage is in no sense a tribune; it is entirely illusionistic. Its own awareness that it is theatre cannot fertilise it; like every theatre of unfolding action, it must repress this awareness so as to pursue undistracted its aim of portraying the real. Epic theatre, by contrast, incessantly derives a lively and productive consciousness from the fact that it is theatre' (Benjamin, 1977, p. 4).

This was the theoretical basis for all of Brecht's *Verfremdungseffekte* (distancing effects). By interrupting the action, by presenting it in a strange or surprising light, by his manner of splitting scenes up and knotting them together, he could provoke an attitude of debate, restore the stage to its function as 'tribune'.

He described graphically the critical reaction that epic theatre could provoke in its audience: not 'just like me – it's only natural – it'll never change', but 'I'd never have thought it – that's not the way – that's extraordinary, hardly believable – it's got to stop' (Brecht, 1964, p. 71).

Brecht's theoretical work has had a powerful impact on Western theatre in the second half of this century, but it was not widely read until after the visits of the Berliner Ensemble to Paris and London in the mid-1950s had demonstrated it in practice. In the politicized atmosphere of the 1960s, the social function of theatre once again became a matter of urgent debate: groups in Europe and America began to build on the theories of Brecht and Meyerhold, rediscovering popular performance techniques, abandoning theatre buildings and seeking out new audiences in new spaces.

ARTAUD AND AFTER

Antonin Artaud does not fit easily into any school or tradition. His theory was set out in the form of manifestos for the two short-lived theatrical ventures which he directed, and in numerous essays or lectures. A collection of these appeared in 1938 but did not achieve a wide readership until two decades later, some years after Artaud's death. This collection, entitled *The Theatre and its Double* (*Le Théâtre et son double*), does not confine itself to the drama. The book is first and foremost a protest: 'protest against the idea of culture as set apart, as if there was culture on one side and life on the other' (Artaud, 1964, p. 13). Artaud condemns the whole of modern Western civilization for having cut its links with the sacred and the numinous. The triumph of rationalism, he argues, has led Westerners to neglect the spiritual in favour of the intellectual, with the result that our culture is impoverished and our theatre reduced to mere talk. To express the violent reversal of attitudes that was needed, Artaud had recourse to a visionary, metaphorical language: true theatre must act like the plague, an all-engulfing experience from which few emerge alive, but those who do are changed for ever.

His ideas concerning theatre were galvanized by seeing a performance of a masked Balinese dance-drama at the Paris colonial exhibition of 1931. In the Balinese performance he glimpsed a new kind of poetry, a concrete poetry of gesture and movement, a 'poetry in space'. He concluded that written texts had no place in the profoundest form of theatre; a new language was needed, based not on words but on signs, in which actors would be transformed into moving hieroglyphs and the director become a magus or master of sacred ceremonies. In the absence of a common belief system investing life with the sense of the sacred, Artaud held that the only theatre that could touch us to the quick was a 'theatre of cruelty'. By this he meant a theatre of rigour and necessity that would shock people out of their complacent materialism and remind them that 'the sky can still fall on our heads' (1964, p. 121). The subjects he suggested as suitable material included Jacobean tragedy, the story of Bluebeard, the conquest of Mexico and destruction of Aztec civilization by European adventurers. In matters of production technique his ideas echo Craig's and those of the French director and theorist Gaston Baty: lighting, sound and costume are all to become significant elements in the new scenic language deployed by the director; settings will be abstract or symbolic; masks and puppets will be used. The playing space must be flexible and capable of alteration. The only element neglected by Artaud is the question of a public for these performances; this neglect helps to explain the failure of his 'Theatre of Cruelty' in 1935.

Artaud did not attract a broad following until the late 1950s, when the 'Theatre of the Absurd' had established itself (see Esslin, 1968). The 'Absurdist' author at first most given to theorizing was Arthur Adamov, who had been a close friend of Artaud; Adamov's statement that 'theatre, as I understand it, is linked utterly and absolutely to performance' (Adamov, 1964, p. 13) showed his affinity with Artaud, as did his theory of literality. This stated that metaphysical realities, if they were to find adequate expression on the stage, must be manifest in literal, concrete and physical form. This notion of literality is helpful in explaining the dramatic appeal of plays by Beckett, Ionesco and many other modern dramatists.

Genet, whose work is often linked with Artaud, seems rather to exemplify aspects of Symbolist theory: his emphasis is always on images rather than on objects, and his play *The Screens* might have been written for a setting by Craig. He argued that the strength of theatre is in recognizing that what it presents is mere illusion. This was not a new idea: it had been given memorable dramatic shape by Pirandello in his *Six Characters in Search of an Author* (1921). But Genet took it further than most, making it into a principle. For him the stage is a *de-realizing* space. That is to say it denies the reality of everything that appears within its confines. In a Genet play, nothing is what it seems, and the drama progresses by reversals or inversions, as in mirror images. Ultimately, human beings too are de-realized and with them goes all possibility of a fixed meaning.

The 1950s and 1960s in France was one of the rare periods of modern times when the playwrights have taken the lead in the formulation of dramatic theory. Albert Camus wrote on modern tragedy (1970, pp. 192–203); Jean-Paul Sartre developed a theory of existentialist drama (1976). While Adamov digested Brecht's epic dramaturgy, Eugène Ionesco reacted against its growing influence, becoming the chief spokesman for opponents of political theatre. In a famous controversy with Kenneth Tynan, Ionesco argued that politically motivated work only serves to replace one tyranny with another, that political theatre leads straight to the concentration camp. He argued instead for abstract theatre or 'pure drama', explaining that for him the true revolutionary was the artist who could change our perception of reality (Ionesco, 1964). Here he was linking up with Surrealist theory of art as the revealer of subconscious drives and liberator of the imagination by its challenge to accepted modes of perception.

JERZY GROTOWSKI

The one man of the theatre to have made a thoroughgoing attempt to realize something like Artaud's vision is the Polish director Jerzy Grotowski. In theorizing his approach, he uses language that is close to Artaud's: 'we compose a role as a system of signs', looking for 'a moment of psychic shock, a moment of terror, of mortal danger or tremendous joy'. When this is achieved, 'the body vanishes, burns, and the spectator sees only a series of visible impulses' (Grotowski, 1968, pp. 16–17). Acknowledging Artaud's importance, he claimed that 'the paradox of Artaud lies in the fact that it is impossible to carry out his proposals' (p. 118). So Grotowski adopted a different approach: he rejected the lavish theatre of multiple means, proposing instead 'poor theatre', where everything was reduced to a naked confrontation between actor and audience. Strongly influenced by Stanislavski, he developed a theory of actor training as 'a *via negativa*' – not a collection of skills, but an eradication of blocks. In order to achieve this, he posited the idea of a 'laboratory theatre', wholly devoted to the investigation of the actor's art. Actors who worked with him had to be prepared to abandon themselves entirely, not knowing in advance where the process would lead them. In performances given to the public, Grotowski sought to confront the inherited myths of Western culture with the nightmare of the modern world, probing for the survival (or possible recreation) of the sacred dimension so central to Artaud's theory (see Kumiega, 1985).

The theories of Artaud and Grotowski were interpreted for the English-speaking world by Peter Brook, through his book *The Empty Space* (1972) and his productions of the 1960s. Brook saw this 'Holy theatre' combining with the 'Rough theatre', or popular tradition, to create a new category, the 'Immediate theatre'. This designates the experience sought after by all dramatists and practitioners, when audience and actors are united in a common celebration of truth (that quality demanded by Zola): 'When we are persuaded to believe in this truth, then the theatre and life are one' (Brook, 1972, p. 157).

In the early 1970s, Grotowski came to the conclusion that the work accomplished by the actor on himself was infinitely more vital than what happens in the theatre when a work of art is presented for the passive consumption of an audience. His work now came to be based on a theory of 'active culture', in which the creative work was to be experienced by the participants. He abandoned the laboratory theatre in order to initiate projects of a 'para-theatrical' nature containing no element of performance to an audience, but in which the central experience is participatory. Grotowski's development presents a certain similarity with the more overtly political work of Augusto Boal in South America and that of Armand Gatti in France. Gatti (see Knowles, 1989) has argued for a 'theatre without spectators', the aim of which is not a performance, but a raising of consciousness and development of articulacy for the participants. Boal's *Theatre of the Oppressed* (1979) explains the theoretical basis for his work with communities of underprivileged, often illiterate people, for when the experience of playing out the different roles involved in, say, a land dispute, develops the understanding and articulacy required for taking effective action in that situation.

This review of the theories that have done most to shape the modern drama shows how successful the director has been in establishing control of every aspect of theatre work. That rise to power has not come about in exactly the manner predicted by Craig: the director is not the sole creative force in the modern theatre. But in matters of theory it is the directors who have provided most of the original and influential ideas that condition our view of the theatre and of its role in society today.

FURTHER READING

Artaud, Antonin (1964) *Le Théâtre et son double*, Gallimard, Paris [first published 1938]

Bentley, Eric (ed.) (1968) *The Theory of the Modern Stage*, Penguin, Harmondsworth

Boal, Augusto (1979) *Theatre of the Oppressed*, translated by Charles A. and Maria Odilia Leal McBride, Pluto, London

Brecht, Bertolt (1964) *Brecht on Theatre*, translated and edited by John Willett, Hill & Wang, New York

Brook, Peter (1972) *The Empty Space*, Penguin, Harmondsworth

Carlson, Marvin (1984) *Theories of the Theatre*, Cornell University Press, Ithaca

Carter, Lawson (1963) *Zola and the Theatre*, Yale University Press, New Haven

Craig, Edward Gordon (1911) *On the Art of Theatre*, Heinemann, London

Grotowski, Jerzy (1968) *Towards a Poor Theatre*, Simon & Schuster, New York

Meyerhold, Vsevolod (1969) *Meyerhold on Theatre*, translated and edited by E. Braun, Methuen, London

Stanislavski, Konstantin (1961) *Stanislavski on the Art of the Stage*, translated and edited by David Magarshack, Hill & Wang, New York

Williams, Raymond (1968) *Drama in Performance*, Penguin, Harmondsworth

ADDITIONAL WORKS CITED

Adamov, Arthur (1964) *Ici et maintenant*, Gallimard, Paris

Appia, Adolphe (1984) *Oeuvres*, edited by Marie-Louise Bablet, L'Age d'Homme, Lausanne

Bablet, Denis (1966) *Edward Gordon Craig*, Heinemann, London

Benjamin, Walter (1977) *Understanding Brecht*, translated by Anne Bostock, New Left Books, London [first published 1938]

Brecht, Bertolt (1979) *Diaries 1920–1922*, edited by H. Ramthun, translated by John Willett, Eyre Methuen, London

Camus, Albert (1970) *Selected Essays and Notebooks*, translated by Philip Thody, Penguin, Harmondsworth

Esslin, Martin (1968) *The Theatre of the Absurd*, Penguin, Harmondsworth

Ionesco, Eugène (1964) *Notes and Counternotes*, translated by Donald Watson, Calder, London

Jarry, Alfred (1962) 'De l'inutilité du théâtre au Théâtre'. In Alfred Jarry, *Tout Ubu*, edited by Maurice Saillet, Livre de Poche, Paris [essay first published 1896]

Knowles, Dorothy (1989) *Armand Gatti in the Theatre*, Athlone Press, London

Kumiega, Jennifer (1985) *The Theatre of Grotowski*, Methuen, London

Mitchell, Tony (1984) *Dario Fo, People's Court Jester*, Methuen, London

Piscator, Erwin (1980) *The Political Theatre*, translated by Hugh Rorrison, Methuen, London [first published 1929]

Sartre, Jean-Paul (1976) *Sartre on Theatre*, Quartet, London

Stanislavski, Konstantin (1937) *An Actor Prepares*, translated by E. R. Hapgood, Bles, London

33

THE THEATRE OF THE ABSURD

CLAUDE SCHUMACHER

Theatre is the most social of art forms and, as such, requires a great many conventions so that the theatrical event, on and off the stage, can take place in an orderly fashion. We know from history that festivals in Ancient Greece were highly organized. It was also in Ancient Greece that the theoretical foundations of our western theatre were laid and, twenty-five centuries on, the name of Aristotle is still invoked, rightly or wrongly, in discussions concerning the structure of drama. Although the Anglo-Saxon world escaped the worst excesses of neo-classical formalism, mainly thanks to the influence of Shakespeare, the rules that came to govern French seventeenth-century theatre (unities of time, place and action; unity of tone; verisimilitude and decorum) aimed at creating an orderly, coherent, harmonious, rational dramatic poem. These same rules came to embody the ideal of playwriting throughout the western world after neo-classicism established itself as the dominant aesthetic norm in the seventeenth century. A good play was a play with a strong, straightforward plot moving relentlessly to its logical, tragic or comic, conclusion, with clearly drawn and highly individualized characters, with well-written, rhetorical dialogue, to be clearly and evocatively spoken by actors who convincingly portrayed their roles in a familiar setting or in some easily identifiable exotic location. Such were the ideals upheld by all dramatists hoping to have their plays performed in the theatre, from Aeschylus to Ibsen. At the risk of further oversimplification, it can be said that, before the twentieth century, the dramatic form was eminently logical and rational (even when dealing with extraordinary events) and that it aimed at providing spectators with an authentic picture of their world. When our forebears recognized that the world was in a state of chaos – and they often did – their artists aimed at constructing meaning out of that same chaos, at creating order out of disorder, at giving shape to what is shapeless. The 'New Theatre' of the 1950s, soon to be known as 'the theatre of the absurd', overturned twenty-five centuries of tradition by rejecting all rules and by facing the chaos head-on.

'The feeling of the absurd can strike anyone round the corner of any street', wrote Albert Camus in *The Myth of Sisyphus* ([1942] 1975, p. 17), thereby putting the term 'absurd' at the centre of philosophical debate and at the forefront of artistic reflection for years to come. For Camus 'the feeling of the absurdity of the world' springs from the confrontation between man's conscience, his consciousness, his thirst for rationality and the inert, irrational, unknowable world. Yet, contrary to received ideas, the realization of such an irredeemable divorce does not lead to passive despair or intellectual suicide. Convinced of the ultimate absurdity of life, man will strive towards a moral and ethical imperative for greater lucidity and for living life to the full, since life is, after all, the only human tangible reality.

Camus's most despairing play, *Cross Purpose* (*Le Malentendu*, 1944), tells of the murder of a young man by his long-lost mother and sister who fail to recognize him in the lone traveller come to spend the night in their inn. Constructed like a mathematical equation, *Cross Purpose*, has a simple, realistic set, a small cast of well-defined characters, a relentless action that lasts just a few hours, and contains not the slightest incident that could distract the spectator's attention from the subject under scrutiny. Well played, this becomes a metaphysical tragedy of the highest order, stating that 'this world we live in doesn't make any sense'. The same clarity of meaning is also the hallmark of Camus' other plays, and of the dramatic output of his fellow existentialist Jean-Paul Sartre whose *In Camera* (*Huis clos*, also 1944) presents a metaphysical tragedy set in a metaphorical hell. Camus and Sartre, both convinced of the ultimate absurdity and incoherence of life, couch their demonstration of this truth in the most lucid and coherent prose, within a solid and conventional theatrical structure. The philosophy of the absurd does not necessarily lead to the 'theatre of the absurd'.

The term 'theatre of the absurd', coined by Martin Esslin for the title of his study of post-Second World War French theatre, came into vogue in the 1960s at a time when the so-called 'absurd' dramatists had written their major works and were already experimenting in other directions. Although the theatre of the absurd was by no means confined to France, the authors identified by Esslin as being its main figures are four 'French' writers (Jean Genet, 1910–86; Arthur Adamov, 1908–70; Eugène Ionesco, b. 1909 [sic]; Samuel Beckett, 1906–89) who dominated the Parisian stage after 1945 and who became known the world over in the wake of Beckett's notoriety following the production of *En attendant Godot* (Paris, 1953; *Waiting for Godot*, London, 1955). The backgrounds of these four playwrights could not be more disparate and, if there were any logic in the world, their careers should never have coincided.

Genet was a Parisian foundling, possibly the abandoned baby of a prostitute. He spent his adolescence in penal institutions for young offenders and during his twenties he roamed across Europe, surviving on theft and homosexual prostitution. He took up writing in French jails, where he would have lingered for most of his life had it not been for the intervention of fellow writers led by Sartre and Cocteau who obtained a presidential pardon for him. His first play, *Les Bonnes*, 1947 (*The Maids*), was premièred in Paris in a production directed by Louis Jouvet.

Adamov came from a wealthy, French-speaking, Armenian family who had fled the Russian revolution. The consequences of political exile and of his father's addiction to gambling landed him penniless in Paris in the early twenties. He began to write plays at the end of the Second World War, under the influence of Strindberg's theatre to which he was to devote a very perceptive study. His first play, *La Parodie* (*The Parody*, written in the late 1940s), a series of tableaux depicting feelings and moods which reflect isolation and a breakdown in communication, was not produced by Roger Blin until 1952, although his adaptation of Büchner's *Danton's Death* was staged at the Avignon Festival in 1948.

The birth of what in France was termed 'le nouveau théâtre' ('new theatre' being a vaguer, more general term than 'theatre of the absurd' and less likely to condition audiences' responses) is linked to the production of Ionesco's *La Cantatrice chauve* (*The Bald Prima Donna*, first performed 1950), followed in 1951 by *La Leçon* (*The Lesson*). Ionesco, born in Romania, lived with his mother in her native France until the age of thirteen; then, after having completed his studies in Romania, he settled permanently in Paris just before the outbreak of the war.

This was also the time when Samuel Beckett decided to make France his home. Beckett, born in a Dublin Protestant family, first became acquainted with French literature and culture at school and later at Trinity College. His first poems and novels were written in English, but the trilogy that brought him to the attention of the world (*Molloy, Malone meurt/Malone dies*, both 1951 and *L'Innommable/The Unnamable*, 1953) was written in French as were many of his plays, including *En attendant Godot* (1953) and *Fin de partie* (1957; *Endgame*, 1958). He continued to write sometimes in French, sometimes in English, and with a few exceptions always 'translated' his own work into the other language – although 'translation' is a misleading term as it often amounted to a 're-creation'.

Ionesco's Bald Prima Donna, as conspicuous by her absence as Beckett's Mr Godot, proclaimed the advent of the 'new theatre' and Ionesco, more than any other playwright of the time, was aware of breaking with tradition as he called his play an 'anti-pièce' ('anti-play') and his theatre 'anti-théâtre'. However, even in the artistic field, spontaneous creations are very rare indeed and antecedents are easily found. If Ionesco's anti-theatre is rooted in the existentialist philosophies of Sartre and Camus, and in the pessimism of artists trying to come to terms with the atrocities of the Second World War, the theatrical antecedents of the 'new theatre' are to be found, much earlier, in the plays of Alfred Jarry (1873–1907) and Guillaume Apollinaire (1880–1918) and in the theories of Antonin Artaud (1896–1948).

When Jarry unleashed his monstrous ('absurd') characters, Pa and Ma Ubu, on the Parisian intelligentsia of 1896 he was fifty years, two world wars, a world revolution and several dictatorships ahead of his time. *Ubu roi* (*Ubu Rex*) is an 'anti-tragedy' written by an iconoclastic budding author who knew his Shakespeare, and his anti-heroes are closely modelled on Macbeth,and Lady Macbeth. But whereas the Shakespearian royals are driven by overweening ambition, and are simultaneously stricken by remorse after their initial murderous act, Pa and Ma Ubu are a pair of exaggerated comic-strip figures, gross and greedy, stupid and vulgar, savage and yellow-bellied tyrants who rejoice in all the miseries they inflict on their innocent victims. The movement of the play, as befits a Punch and Judy show, is remorseless: no sooner have the Ubus resolved to assassinate the king of Poland than he is grotesquely dispatched, followed by the nobles, the judges, the financiers and whoever is bold enough to oppose tyranny. In contrast to Shakespeare's moral ending, when the true heir succeeds in ousting the usurpers, Jarry simply has the Ubus sail away to a golden exile. In the staging of the tale, Jarry dispenses with plausibility (locations change within a single scene; dead characters spring up to fight another day; a bear is eaten alive by hungry soldiers . . .), with complex psychology (the only two motivating emotions for all characters are greed and fear), with literary propriety (the vocabulary is scatological throughout and peppered with nonsense neologisms). Pre-dating Dada and Surrealism by a quarter of a century, Jarry allows free range to his imagination and dramatizes, in *Ubu*, the frightful nightmare of Man's irrationality on the rampage.

The impact of the play was such that even its director, Lugné-Poe, disowned it and it was not 'rediscovered' until after 1945 when it was hailed as a 'seminal work'. The same fate befell Apollinaire's *Les Mamelles de Tirésias* (*The Breasts of Tiresias*, 1917) and Roger Vitrac's *Les Enfants au pouvoir* (*Victor, or Power to the Children*, 1928), two Jarryesque creations of the first order. Although *Tiresias* is seldom staged, its preface has had a profound influence on the thinking of subsequent generations of playwrights. This text, in which the neologism 'surréaliste' is coined, is an important 'anti-realist' manifesto calling for a theatre of 'pure imagination', freed from earlier dramaturgical conventions and from the rigid actor/spectator division across the footlights. Vitrac's *Victor*, first directed in 1928 by Antonin Artaud with his short-lived Théâtre Alfred Jarry and successfully revived by Jean Anouilh in 1962, is both an attack on bourgeois values (complacency, hypocrisy, nationalism, militarism . . .) and a critique of traditional dramatic devices.

A more radical onslaught on Western culture in general and Western theatre in particular was launched by Antonin Artaud in a series of programme notes, pamphlets, lectures and essays, collectively published in 1938 as *Le Théâtre et son double* (*The Theatre and its Double*). Artaud's ideas were to become the basic tenets of the 'new theatre' which, from the outset, defined itself in total opposition to tradition:

> What we want to expose is this mass of desires, dreams, illusions and beliefs which have resulted in this lie no one believes in any longer, called, probably mockingly, the theatre. We would like to manage to revive a certain number of images – obvious, palpable images that are not tainted with continual disillusionment. We are not creating a theatre so as to present plays, but to succeed in uncovering the mind's obscure, hidden and unrevealed aspects, by a sort of real, physical projection. We are not aiming to create an illusion of things which do not exist, as was done heretofore. On the contrary, we aim to make a certain number of scenes – indestructible, irrefutable images appealing directly to the mind – appear on the stage ... One can see what a terrible task we have set ourselves. We are aiming at nothing less than a return to the human or inhuman sources of the theatre, thereby to resuscitate it completely.
>
> (ed. Schumacher, 1989, pp. 32–3)

For Artaud, theatre must operate 'by every means at its disposal', but such means must be reassessed and new theatrical techniques must be invented. He states clearly that he does not 'intend to do away with dialogue, but to give words something of the significance they have in dreams' (ed. Schumacher, 1990, p. 102). But, above all, he insists on the concrete nature of the stage, on the importance of the physical presence of the actor: 'it seems to me that on stage, above all a space to be filled, somewhere something happens, word language must give way to sign language, whose objective aspect has the most immediate impact on us' (ed. Schumacher, 1990, p. 112). Like Jarry and Apollinaire, Artaud advocated a liberation of the subconscious and gave free rein to the imagination. Artaud succeeded only partially in putting his ideas into practice, with his production of Shelley's verse drama *The Cenci* (Paris, 1935), and the task of bringing such innovative ideas to fruition was left to the next generation of playwrights and directors.

The harbinger of the 'absurd' era was *The Bald Prima Donna*, first seen in Paris on 16 May 1950 at 6 p.m., and Ionesco was well aware of breaking new ground:

> *The Bald Prima Donna* which I had subtitled 'antiplay' (which frightened quite a few people) is a short burlesque comedy. Six vaguely English characters are under the delusion that you need only open your mouth to say something. In reality Mr and Mrs Smith, their guests the Martins, the fire-brigade captain and the maid have nothing to say. That's why they talk and talk. Their speech full of clichés is a parody of speech, just as the play is a parody of theatre. The world appeared to me to be improbable, the behaviour of my characters must also

appear improbable in its ordinariness. My aim is to make the commonplace look strange.

(ed. Latour, 1986, p. 57)

Elsewhere Ionesco reveals that the idea of the play came to him when he read the absurd phrases given as examples in language primers, e.g. 'the ceiling is above and the floor is below', which insidiously find their way into everyday speech. He also tells of his amazement when the 'antiplay' turned out to be a very effective comedy, since he thought he had written *the* 'tragedy of language'.

A critic of the first night's performance warned, more than a decade before Esslin's book was written, that *'The Bald Prima Donna* is exclusively for those spectators who are not frightened by the Absurd' (*Arts*, 19 May 1950) and another called it 'a deliciously poetic absurdity' (*Match*, 24 June 1950). *The Bald Prima Donna* has no plot, a deceptively naturalistic set, no consistent characters; it is based on an ever-shifting ground of nonsense dialogue, of arbitrary entrances and exits, of unexplained appearances. Chance rules supreme and everything is equally important (or unimportant). Jarry had formulated the identity of opposites and had posited that '$O=\infty$' and thus founded 'pataphysics, i.e. 'the science of imaginary solutions'. To further the aims of that 'science to end all science' the learned College of 'Pataphysics (or 'Collegium Pataphysicum') was founded in Paris in December 1949 and Ionesco became one of its foremost professorial dignitaries.

As befits a 'professor', Ionesco, not content with being a prolific playwright, has continued to publish theoretical essays and to give interviews in the press and on radio. Thus it was that the wider English-speaking public came to know his name through a controversy with Kenneth Tynan, who had originally been one of Ionesco's admirers. Having been converted to Brecht's ideas (Ionesco's favourite 'bête noire'), Tynan was moved to attack the French absurdist in the *Observer* on the occasion of a revival of *The Lesson* and *The Chairs* at the Royal Court: 'Here at last was a self-proclaimed advocate of "antitheatre": explicitly antirealist and by implication anti-reality as well. Here was a writer ready to declare that words were meaningless and that all communication between human beings was impossible' (quoted in Esslin, 1968, pp. 125ff.). Behind Tynan's attack was the belief that art, in this case theatre, has a useful, moral, social role to play and that 'every play worth serious consideration' should present a 'statement' based on objective reality. Ionesco replied that 'a playwright simply writes plays in which he can offer only a testimony, not a didactic message', that the true artist is expected to ask the right questions, not to offer ready-made solutions. 'It is now clear', wrote Ionesco in 1975, 'that all solutions offered by ideological theatre, whether Brechtian or not, were false solutions. . . . In any case there is no solution, for the moment, to offer the human condition. Socialism as well as liberalism have failed. Life is unliveable' (in Norrish, 1988, p. 2).

So it would appear that life *and* artistic expression are impossible. But, as a true 'pataphysician, not afraid of contradictions, Ionesco further states, 'A work of art is the expression of an incommunicable reality that one tries to communicate – and which sometimes can be communicated. That is its paradox and its truth'; and he concludes, 'what literature should express is precisely that which cannot be expressed' (Ionesco, 1969, p. 100). The same intriguing paradox is even more paradoxically put by Beckett, who defines art as: 'The expression that there is nothing to express, nothing with which to express, nothing from which to express, no power to express, no desire to express, together with the obligation to express' (Beckett, 1965, p. 103).

The impossibility, together with the necessity of communicating, is the subject of Ionesco's masterpiece, *Les Chaises* (*The Chairs*, 1952). At the end of their lives, a couple of retired lighthouse keepers (he 95, she 94) invite 'distinguished people' to their lonely round tower in order to pass on the old man's 'message' to the world. Husband and wife are garrulous beyond belief and there is no cliché that they do not use in the incessant jabbering between one another or to the crowd of invisible guests that, little by little, fill the stage: the people are invisible, but a chair is brought in as each guest enters. When eventually the last has arrived, the Emperor himself, no space remains for the hosts who jump into the sea secure in the belief that the professional speaker they have hired will expertly deliver *the* message. The 'Orator' is the only other real character, but he is only capable of uttering inarticulate sounds and of scribbling meaningless signs on a blackboard. In the programme note for the first production, Ionesco wrote: 'At times the world seems to me to be void of meaning, reality to be unreal. It is the feeling of unreality, the search for an essential reality, forgotten, unnamed that I am trying to express through my characters who wander aimlessly, having nothing to call their own apart from their worries, their failures, the emptiness of their lives. People drowning in meaninglessness can only be grotesque, their suffering can only appear tragic by derision.' And he adds: 'Since I am unable to understand the world, how could I understand my own play? I hope someone will explain it to me' (ed. Latour, 1986, p. 260).

The Orator's message is as grotesque, derisory and tragic as the final image of the play: an actor who has forgotten his lines tries lamentably to communicate something to an absent audience! However, something seems to emerge from the empty gibberish: 'ADIEU' or 'A DIEU' ('Goodbye' or 'To God'). Is Ionesco, *in extremis*, affirming not only the impossibility of communication, but also the impossibility of communicating in a world without God?

God was often invoked by the critics of Beckett's first play, *En attendant Godot* (Paris, 3 January 1953) as they tried to explain the meaning of the play and the symbolic significance of 'Mr Godot' whose arrival is so eagerly expected by the two tramps, Didi and Gogo, but who fails to appear. 'In Godot, there is God', asserted one bold critic, but Beckett refuses to ratify that comment and the equation must remain 'Godot = X', 'X' being the highly speculative suggestion that each spectator or reader might honestly put forward. All that Beckett is prepared to say is that his plays are 'a question of fundamental sounds': a 'new play' is not a story 'about' something, IT IS. The performance is the event and does not refer to another, pre-existing reality that is somehow recreated on stage. In *Godot*, Didi and Gogo are waiting. Beckett merely presents us with two men waiting and shows us *how* they are waiting and how they pass the time while they are waiting. He does not tell us *why* they are there. *Godot* confronts us with the theatrical image of man 'in situation', with the 'human condition' as Beckett understands it here and now – not for all times, not for all mankind, but as he and many of his contemporaries perceive the position of the individual lost in a hostile world.

The situation of the individual in the world, invariably lost and unable to comprehend the meaning of his presence on earth in the face of the hostility of every other being or manifestation, is also the problem of Beckett's other plays, as it was the subject of the early plays by Genet and Adamov, although the latter gradually abandoned the 'absurdist' approach and adopted a more 'Brechtian' or political stance.

A similar evolution can be traced in the career of many 'absurd' dramatists, in France and elsewhere. For instance, Harold Pinter (born 1930) wrote his early plays (*The Birthday Party*, 1958; *The Caretaker*, 1960) under the direct influence of Beckett and *Godot*, but gradually he turned away from telling ambiguous, mystifying and confusing tales and in *Betrayal* (1978) charts the course of an adulterous affair in a direct, hard-hitting manner, although the story is told in flashbacks. His more recent plays (*One for the Road*, 1985; *Mountain Language*, 1988) are straightforward political statements, the first dealing with state torture and the second with genocide. Like Sartre, Genet and Adamov, all in their different ways, Pinter has left behind metaphysical speculations about man's place in the universe to grapple with the more immediate problems of how to live and survive in a precarious political situation. Edward Albee (b. 1928), the chief American exponent of the theatre of the absurd, also started by starkly stating the absurdity of the world and the impossibility of human companionship (*The Zoo Story*, 1958; *Who's Afraid of Virginia Woolf?*, 1962), but has come to try and make sense of the chaos.

Two Swiss playwrights deserve to be mentioned among the masters of the absurd: Friedrich Dürrenmatt (b. 1921) and Max Frisch (b. 1911). Dürrenmatt's plays (*The Visit*, 1955; *The Physicists*, 1962) are technically dazzling, using every theatrical trick, but they present a grotesque, meaningless, nihilistic world peopled by dangerous, self-seeking lunatics. If, superficially, Frisch appears less extreme, his plays (*The Fire Raisers*, 1958; *Andorra*, 1961) are an even harsher and bleaker indictment of bourgeois complacency, racism and indifference to man's cruelty to man. Although both writers are directly inspired by problems facing Swiss society, their plays have universal significance and appeal.

Man's helplessness in the face of the absurd is made tangible, therefore, in the 'new theatre', through plays expressing feelings of political impotence, and any contradiction between 'absurd' and 'political' writing is only apparent. Sartre and Camus, the philosophical promoters of the idea of 'the absurd', are also the prime examples of 'committed' writers: Camus began his journalistic career by writing a damning series of articles about the intolerable living conditions of the majority of Arabs in French Algeria, and Sartre took to the streets of Paris in 1968 in support of the students and the most extreme revolutionary organizations. Today the foremost playwrights in the Western world combine in their work a concern for the political issues of the day and an awareness of the artistic and aesthetic problems that dramatists, directors and actors have grappled with for almost half a century. The aesthetics of the 'new theatre' or the 'theatre of the absurd' have now been integrated into mainstream dramatic writing and theatrical presentation.

But playwrights have grappled with the notion of the absurd since the beginning of our civilization. In *Oedipus*, Sophocles dramatizes the search for the ultimate meaning of life, whereas in *Herakles*, Euripides posits the ultimate absurdity: Herakles, the absent father, returns home in the nick of time to save his children from certain death, only to kill them minutes later in a fit of madness, believing them to be dangerous and monstrous enemies. Shakespeare often paints a bleak and meaningless world, and never more so than in *King Lear* ('As flies to wanton boys are we to the gods,/They kill us for their sport') or in Macbeth's 'it is a tale/Told by an idiot, full of sound and fury,/Signifying nothing'.

Jan Kott, in his influential *Shakespeare Our Contemporary* (1964), convincingly argues that Shakespeare, although belonging to the Renaissance, is the most modern playwright, 'violent, cruel and brutal; earthly and hellish; evok[ing] terror as well as dreams and poetry; most true and improbable, dramatic and passionate, rational and mad, eschatological and realistic' (p. 223). What, however, differentiates the absurdists from Shakespeare is their dramaturgy: they strive to symbolize the 'chaotic state of existence by a corresponding anarchy in the construction' of their plays. 'Play architecture as it was understood by the writer of the well-made play has given place to a seemingly abstract void in which plot, or dramatic story-telling, is almost non-existent' (Hunt, 1962, p. 155). As for Sartre, he stresses what he terms 'the three essential refusals in the contemporary theatre', namely, 'the refusal of psychology, the refusal of plot and the refusal of all realism' (Sartre, 1966, p. 67).

The refusal of psychology has meant the death of the consistent, fully 'rounded' character who, seemingly, possessed all the attributes of humanity. The new hero is an anti-hero, only partially conceived, often with no past or any discernible future. Characters in contemporary plays are often parodic, grotesque, incomplete, self-contradictory. They do not understand who they are, they do not understand the world around them, they are baffled by all the events that occur while they are on the stage. As far as the actors are concerned, the traditional Stanislavskian identification with the role is no longer possible and a greater degree of playfulness, of invention, of fantasy is the key to a satisfactory 'portrayal'.

A play without a plot seems to be a contradiction in terms, or so it seemed until *Waiting for Godot*. The 'new theatre' is not concerned with 'telling a story', with entertaining spectators with pretty little anecdotes; its purpose is 'to build a temporal object in which time, by its contradictions and by its own structure will put the theatre into relief in an especially concentrated way which then becomes the subject proper' (Sartre, 1966, p. 68). In other words 'anti-theatre' becomes 'metatheatre': the play presents itself as play (e.g. Genet's *The Maids* and *The Balcony*), or the metaphor of life as theatre is central to its theme (*Godot, Endgame*). The metatheatrical approach to theatre is to be seen most clearly in the work of contemporary directors (Planchon, Chéreau in France; Brook, Nunn in Britain; Stein, Zadek in Germany; Grotowski, Kantor in Poland; Chaikin, Wilson in the United States) who 'theatricalize' every element of their productions. Their aim is not to create the illusion of a 'slice of life', but to present an event, theatrical in its nature, which signifies by itself and not by reference to anything outside it.

Sartre's third point, the refusal of all realism, stems from the twin conviction (a) that realism/naturalism is an outmoded and reactionary aesthetic category and (b) that an artistic creation must create its own reality. In the case of 'new theatre' that reality is often fantastic, grotesque, oneiric; the action takes place in non-defined locations, within surrealist, distorted, subjective, dream-like settings; characters behave arbitrarily, without motivation, according to a principle of discontinuity; they are prone to parody themselves or one another. The dialogue follows its own logic and has recourse to interior monologues, streams of consciousness, rhythmic repetitions, flat contradictions, sudden ruptures, logorrhoea interspersed with long aphasia-like silences.

Sartre's description of the theatre of the fifties and sixties still applies to the best of today's theatre. Although strictly speaking the 'Theatre of the Absurd' already belongs to history (*Godot* and *The Bald Prima Donna* have long since acquired the status of 'classics'), it exerts a profound influence on contemporary writers and directors and has for ever shattered the illusion that dramaturgical conformity can yield a satisfactory theatrical artefact or that an orderly discourse can make sense of this world of ours.

FURTHER READING

Benedikt, Michael and Wellwarth, George E. (eds) (1964) *Modern French Theatre*, Dutton, New York

Bradby, David (1984) *Modern French Drama, 1940–1980*, Cambridge University Press, Cambridge

Brustein, Robert (1962) *The Theatre of Revolt*, Methuen, London

Esslin, Martin (1962) *The Theatre of the Absurd*, Eyre & Spottiswoode, London

——(1968) *The Theatre of the Absurd*, revised and enlarged edn, Penguin, Harmondsworth

Hinchliffe, Arnold P. (1969) *The Absurd*, Methuen, London

Innes, Christopher (1981) *Holy Theatre*, Cambridge University Press, Cambridge

Ionesco, Eugène (1964) *Notes and Counternotes*, translated by Donald Watson, Calder, London [first published 1962]

Pavis, Patrice (1987) *Dictionnaire du théâtre*, Messidor/Editions sociales, Paris

Schumacher, Claude (1984) *Alfred Jarry and Guillaume Apollinaire*, Macmillan, London

Wellwarth, George E. (1964) *The Theater of Protest and Paradox*, New York University Press, New York

ADDITIONAL WORKS CITED

Beckett, Samuel (1965) *Proust and Three Dialogues with Georges Duthuit*, Calder, London [*Proust* first published 1931; *Three Dialogues*, 1949]

Camus, Albert (1975) *The Myth of Sisyphus*, Penguin, Harmondsworth [first published in French 1942]

Hunt, Hugh (1962) *The Live Theatre*, Oxford University Press, London

Ionesco, Eugène (1969) *Découvertes*, Les Sentiers de la Création, Skira, Geneva

Kott, Jan (1964) *Shakespeare Our Contemporary*, Methuen, London [first published in Polish 1961]

Latour, Geneviève (ed.) (1986) *Petites scènes, grand théâtre. Le théâtre de création de 1944 à 1960*, Action culturelle de la Ville de Paris, Paris

Norrish, Peter (ed.) (1988) *Adamov: Le Professeur Taranne & Arrabal: Pique-nique en campagne*, Routledge, London

Sartre, Jean-Paul (1966) 'Myth and Reality in the Theatre', *Gambit*, 3, no. 9, 55–68

Schumacher, Claude (ed.) (1989) *Artaud on Theatre*, Methuen, London

34

THEATRE AND POLITICS

ALAN SINFIELD

I don't think theatre changes the world. I think it does give information, uplift and *back-up* to assumptions and beliefs – right-wing and left-wing. Living when and where we do this support is predominantly given to the right wing.

(Maggie Steed, 1984, p. 66)

You can tell theatre is political from the interest that political authorities take in it – licensing, subsidizing and censoring theatres, companies and plays. And you can tell from the strong reactions that some plays provoke. The mistake is to assume that theatre projects which attract special hostility from the state and some critics and audiences are the only political ones. Actually, the plays that are censored or highly controversial, or can only be presented in special circumstances, are the ones that are politically oppositional, whereas the rest of theatre is adequately compatible with the prevailing ideology. Both are political: the oppositional tends to unsettle the current arrangements, whereas the compatible tends to confirm them.

Theatre people sometimes imagine that members of an audience will be transformed by a really vital performance, but this is hardly likely; people set the play alongside all their other experiences. However this may be important in the forming of attitudes and beliefs. Our sense of the power relations that pertain in the social order that we inhabit, and of the possibilities for changing them, is influenced immensely by the representations of them that we experience all the time. These representations are often in contest, as the dominant arrangements come under challenge; and theatre is one of the numerous institutions where this happens. And at some points in time, for some groups of people, theatre becomes a major arena where political allegiance is formed, consolidated or disputed.

DISSIDENCE AND CLASS

The dominant mode of theatre in twentieth-century Britain has been middle-class. Until 1956, everything about an evening in a conventional theatre made this obvious: the cost of almost all the tickets, the places where most theatres were situated, their decor and the attitudes of the staff, the way the audience dressed, the products advertised in the programmes, the settings of most of the plays, and the concerns and attitudes of the characters in them. This was specially true of London's West End, but regional and local theatres usually followed the metropolitan lead.

Most play productions tended, overall, to reassure a middle-class audience about itself and its place in the world. This is not to say that plays were frivolous, 'merely entertaining'; for unless there is some broaching of dangerous themes there will be little to sustain interest. Often the West End play revolves around the threat of an intruder or a misfit. From Tom Robertson's *Caste* (1867), through Oscar Wilde's *Lady Windermere's Fan* (1892) and Somerset Maugham's *The Sacred Flame* (1928), to T. S. Eliot's *The Family Reunion* (1939), Terence Rattigan's *The Deep Blue Sea* (1952) and Enid Bagnold's *The Chalk Garden* (1956), characters have to cope with the possibility that an inappropriate person is making his or her way into 'good' society, or that one of their own number has been betraying its ethic. In detective thrillers like those of Agatha Christie, the intrusion of the deferential but ominous policeman suggests that the household is not quite immune to attack and disgrace. Normally these dangers are satisfactorily contained by the final curtain, so the audience can go home feeling that the threat has been acknowledged and dealt with.

However, not all middle-class culture was devoted to reassurance. On the contrary, as Raymond Williams points out (1965, pp. 292–5), theatre in particular has been a venue for middle-class dissidence. This term identifies a fraction of the middle class that develops affiliations partly hostile to the main ideology of that class. Middle-class dissidents may try to change the oppression of the lower classes and other subordinated groups, or they may be backward-looking and élitist – invoking a real or supposed past when things were better (mainly, when the lower orders were more deferential). But, in one way or another, they are critical of the way the dominant part of the middle class is organizing things.

Most of the more dissident plays were first produced slightly outside the West End, in 'independent' theatres founded with a view to presenting a more thoughtful kind of play. Harley Granville Barker and J. E. Vedrenne presented plays by George Bernard Shaw, Barker and Elizabeth Robins at the Royal Court Theatre in London in 1904–7, and this contributed to the idea of new national, regional and local theatres in Glasgow, Manchester, Liverpool and

Birmingham. So middle-class dissidence struggled to establish its own institutions. However, Shaw's plays soon became acceptable and profitable in the
West End; and theatres outside London found it difficult to keep afloat
financially without adopting West End playtexts and customs.

Middle-class dissidents were often concerned about the working class, but
their plays rarely gave much reality to working people, their conditions and
aspirations. The Salvation Army hostel in Shaw's *Major Barbara* (1905) is
peopled with stereotypes who are easily manipulated by the middle-class activists. Major injustices are addressed in John Galsworthy's *The Silver Box* and
Strife (both 1909) and each includes a scene in the home of poor people, but
the dialogue is more at ease in the drawing-room.

More often, dissident authors attacked what they regarded as middle-class
complacency on its own ground, suggesting that the disruptive intruder or
misfit manifests in some ways a superior ethic or wisdom. In *Lady Windermere's
Fan* the socially unacceptable Mrs Erlynne is driven from the country, but she
has allowed the audience to see that 'good society' is not just hypocritical, that
it relies for its continuation on excluding people of superior morality. Shaw
often validates the disruption at the expense of authority; in *Saint Joan* (1923),
for example. In his *Heartbreak House* (1920) the amusing, elegant and sophisticated people suffer three intrusions. Boss Mangan is a wealthy businessman,
but though they depend upon him they feel able to patronize him. They also
cope easily with the burglar (who is not unlike the businessman). However,
they have no resources adequate to the third intrusion – an aeroplane whose
bombs only just miss the house. Next time they may hit: these civilized people
act as if their world will go on for ever, but they are complacent and may be
doomed. In *An Inspector Calls* (1946) by J. B. Priestley the ominous policeman
rightly accuses the whole family, and there is a second, implicit intruder,
exposing their hypocrisy and threatening their respectability: the lower-class
woman they have abused.

Unfortunately middle-class dissidence in the theatre was limited by just
those conventional decencies that it wanted to disturb. Until 1968, 'polite'
standards of language and theme were enforced by the state censor, the Lord
Chamberlain. Shaw wrote *Mrs Warren's Profession* in 1894, but because it is
partly about prostitution (suggesting that marriage is not so different) the play
could not be performed professionally until 1924. Rattigan in *Separate Tables*
(1954) wanted to show that respectable people might tolerate an acquaintance
convicted of homosexual soliciting, but he was not allowed to refer to such a
topic.

A crucial disruption was the feminist or strong woman (Ibsen led the way);
often Shaw presents female characters who are more interesting, forceful and
intelligent than the males around them. But although such plays depended on
powerful actresses (Mrs Patrick Campbell, Ellen Terry, Sybil Thorndike), and

sometimes on the financing and entrepreneurial enthusiasm of people like Annie Horniman and Lilian Baylis, women were hardly able to break into the dominant theatre as writers or directors. However, a vigorous women's theatre developed in alternative venues, in conjunction with the suffragette movement. The Actresses' Franchise League (1908–16) sponsored numerous productions, mainly by women and on social and political issues (Holledge, 1981, prints three of these plays).

A working-class oppositional theatre developed in the 1920s and 1930s, with diverse groups around the country inspired by the Communist-promoted Workers' Theatre Movement (1926–35). They moved towards direct political themes and current issues, and an agit-prop, cartoon, episodic, revue-sketch style of presentation. Harassed by the police, such groups often performed in the streets and during strikes. The Unity Theatre developed out of the Workers' Theatre Movement in 1935, and found a base near King's Cross in London. *Waiting for Lefty* (1935), by the US playwright Clifford Odets, became its great standby. Lefty doesn't come – not, like Godot, because he represents a metaphysical absence, but because he has been murdered: the play ends with a call to strike (the audience often joined in). Unity also drew from the United States the concept of the documentary 'living newspaper', and produced a political pantomime, *Babes in the Wood* (1938), a satire on the government's appeasement of Hitler (Samuel, 1985, prints plays and documents).

SUBSIDY AND ART

By the early 1950s left-wing oppositional theatre had been virtually squeezed out by rising costs, and by the ideological mood of the Cold War (which made socialism virtually unthinkable) and the welfare state (which made it seem unnecessary). The West End also suffered from rising costs, and from a sense that the social arrangements that had sustained it were obsolete. Many middle-class writers and theatre people lamented the passing of the old order: they anticipated a reduction in their privileges and imagined it as the end of civilization. The most prominent dissident theatre was the right-wing verse drama of T. S. Eliot, Christopher Fry and Ronald Duncan. Their plays were part of a determined programme of reactionary Christian intervention in theatre, strategically mixing West End and 'poetic' styles (Browne, 1969). Middle-class audiences were attracted by the perspective of Eliot's *The Cocktail Party* (1949) – a validation of traditional decencies that gestured also towards a transcending of unpalatable reality (Pryce-Jones, 1964). Even so, the typical responses were deference and bafflement – not very encouraging for Eliot's belief in the upper middle class as the guardians of good culture. 'It is ultimately the function of art', Eliot said, 'to bring us to a condition of serenity, stillness, and reconciliation' (1957, p. 87). This sounds beyond politics, but such refusal of economic, historical and political conditions always amounts to a conservatism (as with 'theatre of the absurd').

John Osborne's *Look Back in Anger* caused a change of direction in 1956 because West End theatre had already lost confidence in itself. 'The English have lost the art of writing a bad successful play', Kenneth Tynan wrote sardonically in 1955, detailing the class assumptions and timidity of the conventional mode (Tynan, 1976, p. 150). *Look Back* was recognizably in the line of middle-class dissidence; it was presented by a new independent, the English Stage Company at the Royal Court Theatre. It attacked the notions of taste and decorum that conventional theatre was striving, futilely, to preserve in the post-war world. In effect, Osborne sets his play on the territory of the intruder (Jimmy Porter, who has married the upper-class Alison); the play was itself an intruder. Tynan welcomed this, but his predecessor on the *Observer*, Ivor Brown, complained that Osborne might have shown Jimmy Porter 'wooing his middle-class wife in the home of a Colonel', as 'Shaw would have done' (Brown, 1956, p. 12); the conservative critic could tolerate social questions but not the 'squalor' of a lower-class lifestyle.

Such ideas of class and decorum may be noticed in the attempts of many reviewers and the censor to discredit and hinder the plays that followed *Look Back in Anger*. *The Times* asserted of Wesker's *Roots* (1959): 'since all its characters are inarticulate they are not, for the most part, given anything interesting to say'; and of John Arden's *Live Like Pigs* (1958): 'the spectacle of human beings behaving as uninhibited animals is, after all, of limited interest.' The censor's notion of good taste amounted to systematic harassment of the new drama: he objected to just the things the writers wanted to get into their plays – lower-class language, explicit sexuality, current political reference. The issue was understood as decency versus liberty, but what was actually happening was a clash between an established culture and another that was seeking to displace it. Theatre was a principal place where this political change was fought out.

Look Back in Anger changed the setting, implied a leftish point of view, addressed some contemporary topics, and developed a more vigorous language and emotional engagement. All that was not inconsiderable, but the play's importance lies more in what it set going. Theatres like the Royal Court became one of the places (higher education, the Campaign for Nuclear Disarmament, folk music and jazz were others) where a youthful, left-liberal intelligentsia identified and developed itself. These people constituted, in effect, a new wave of middle-class dissidence, a rising class fraction that felt itself stifled by the 'establishment' middle-class lifestyle, and responded keenly to more challenging kinds of play. Just at this moment left-wing thought was being released from an embarrassing allegiance to the Soviet Union by admissions about Stalinism and by the suppression of the 1956 Hungarian revolution. Theatre became one place where young dissidents could explore and elaborate new-left attitudes.

Suddenly there was a lot of talk about Brecht. Joan Littlewood's Theatre Workshop team had maintained a socialist policy since before the war and therefore been largely ignored; now it was celebrated (with *The Quare Fellow*, 1956, and *The Hostage*, 1958, by Brendan Behan and *A Taste of Honey*, 1958, by Shelagh Delaney). Osborne continued his anatomy of class and power in *The Entertainer* (1957) and *A Patriot For Me* (1965), and the theme was pursued by Arden in *Live Like Pigs* and Arnold Wesker in *Chips with Everything* (1962). In *Chicken Soup With Barley* (1958) and *I'm Talking About Jerusalem* (1960) Wesker charted the difficulties of a Jewish family in sustaining its socialist commitment from the 1930s to the 1950s. *Serjeant Musgrave's Dance* (1959) by Arden and *Oh! What a Lovely War* (1963), by Charles Chilton and Theatre Workshop, explored themes of war, resistance, pacifism and retribution in the context of imperial and class exploitation. This work may now seem hesitant or confused, but it contributed to the revival of political thought at that time.

Almost all the plays just mentioned were presented at the Royal Court, and most of them depended on Arts Council subsidy. The significance of *Look Back in Anger* and the Royal Court was partly institutional: they set going the idea that the state should finance 'good' theatre – which was understood to mean the theatre of the youthful left-liberal dissidents. They asserted the right to define art, and obtained an institutional base in subsidized theatre; they got censorship abolished. Peter Hall took the Royal Shakespeare Company (the RSC – until 1960 a quite meagre enterprise) into the Aldwych Theatre in London to produce Royal Court-type work; its subsidy was doubled and redoubled through the 1960s (Sinfield, 1985). The National Theatre began work in 1963 and the South Bank complex was commissioned to house it. Fifteen theatres were built across the country between 1958 and 1970, all with public money. This was not just a new system of funding, alternative to the West End, but a different concept of theatre – as intellectually and emotionally demanding; as progressive, serious, educational; as 'art'. Such theatre was believed to need subsidy: first, because art was defined partly as work that the market fails to recognize; second, because it was perceived as 'universal' and hence for everyone; and third, because 'good' culture was one of the benefits that the social-democratic state was to secure for all. It was a powerful concept.

ALTERNATIVES

'Fringe' theatre arose in the late 1960s out of impatience that the recent changes had not gone far enough. Peter Brook and the RSC experimented with Antonin Artaud's 'theatre of cruelty' in the early 1960s (again to the scandal of some), and Arnold Wesker tried to get trade-union funding to make theatre more widely available. But much subsidized theatre was too staid for the new younger generation: to them the 1960s seemed a time for a further assault on convention. As well as Artaud, they were inspired by the Living Theatre and the La Mama Troupe (from the United States), avant-garde happenings, pop art and poetry, and the pop-music 'underground'. At the same time, the failure of the Wilson Labour governments to pursue socialist goals, set against the Vietnam War and the political disturbances of 1968 in diverse countries, seemed to require a revolutionary theatre. The half-dozen 'fringe' theatre groups active in 1968 gained another impetus in 1970–4 from resistance in the labour movement to the Heath government's attacks on trade unions and public sector workers. By 1978 there were more than a hundred fringe companies; a handful of playwrights had grown to at least 250; and there were 200 outlets for touring companies (Itzin, 1980, p. xiv). The immediacy and flexibility of fringe productions could initially be quite astounding (though perhaps subject to diminishing returns). The RSC and National Theatre soon added 'alternative' venues to the massive concrete auditoriums they had commissioned.

Some fringe efforts – for instance the Portable Theatre of David Hare and Howard Brenton, founded in 1968 – were provoked mainly by inability to get into established theatres. However, the subsidized companies made room, and through the 1970s 'serious' theatre continued the pattern deriving from 1956, enquiring into the scope for socialist commitment. Contradictions in the revolutionary programme of 1968 were investigated by David Mercer in *After Haggerty* (RSC, 1970), Bond in *Lear* (Royal Court, 1971) and *The Bundle* (RSC, 1978), Trevor Griffiths in *The Party* (National, 1973), and Brenton in *Magnificence* (Royal Court, 1973) and *Weapons of Happiness* (National, 1976). The dangers of a right-wing resurgence were invoked in Brenton's *The Churchill Play* (Nottingham Playhouse, 1974) and David Edgar's *Destiny* (RSC, 1976). The history of Britain and the left was reviewed by Hare and Brenton in *Brassneck* (Nottingham Playhouse, 1974), Hare in *Plenty* (National, 1978) and Edgar in *Maydays* (RSC, 1983). Bond explored the relations between art and power in *Bingo* (Royal Court, 1974) and *The Fool* (Royal Court, 1975), and Howard Barker did this in *No End of Blame* (Oxford Playhouse, 1981). Barker created images of the corruption of the political system and the urgent need for change in *That Good Between Us* (RSC, 1977) and *The Hang of the Gaol* (RSC, 1978). Such a list grossly misrepresents the complexity of this work, but it shows the extent to which the younger left-liberal intelligentsia was, for a while, powerful enough to feed its preoccupations through major subsidized companies; some of these plays were shown on television as well.

Many fringe workers liked being on the fringe: they wanted to do theatre and wanted wider audiences. However, despite their hostility to the aura of the classic and their desire for change, they generally started from a position not unlike that of the subsidized companies, the Arts Council, the BBC and the education system: they believed that a good, progressive culture should be available to everyone. The difference was that fringe groups were determined to do it effectively whereas the established institutions, they believed, were hampered by their conditions of operation or had sold out. Because fringe goals were still conceived, essentially, within the perspective of the dissident middle class, the outcome, especially at first, was a failure to cope with the distance between left-liberal culture and that of other people. Too often using 'popular' modes meant resurrecting music-hall and folk-songs that had few continuing roots; and 'working with the community' meant staying for a few weeks. Hence the surprise and distress when the audience at working-men's clubs evinced the sexist and racist assumptions that often informed entertainments there (Trevor Griffiths's play *Comedians*, 1975, is good on this).

Many groups (such as the CAST, Red Ladder, General Will, 7:84, Belt and Braces) played working-men's clubs, picket lines and tenants' associations, and also students' unions, folk clubs and demonstrations (Itzin, 1980, pp. 12–23, 39–50), thus straddling the divide between working-class culture and middle-class dissidence. Some groups soon realized that they had to undertake a long haul in one region (following the example of repertory theatres like Peter Cheeseman's at Stoke-on-Trent). The Combination settled in Deptford at the end of 1971, offering theatre and all kinds of cultural resources to local people. North West Spanner played mainly in and around Manchester, at workplaces, picket lines and tenants' associations. John McGrath and members of 7:84 decided to work in Scotland, and began with a notable success: *The Cheviot, the Stag and the Black, Black Oil* (1973). This targeted issues in the Highlands (how they have been exploited at the expense of local people, first for sheep, then for hunting, then for oil production), and drew upon the *ceilidh*, a local performance tradition. McGrath's *Little Red Hen* (1975) starts from a phoney-Scots entertainment and, through flashback sketches which the entertainers are persuaded to act out, relates modern nationalism to historic labour struggles.

Three principal threats to fringe work witness to its structural difficulties. The Arts Council began to fund the fringe in 1971: in 1973–4 there was £250,000, by 1978 about £1.5 million – after strenuous campaigning in the face of official disdain. Most companies believed that their artistic commitment entitled them to subsidy, but to get it they had to behave in more regular ways – preparing scripts, planning ahead, keeping records; whereas many groups had been committed to improvization, flexible responses to local situations, and collective decision-making. Those that survived became more like ordinary theatre companies.

Then there is the temptation to produce 'art' – to achieve a 'universal' poetic statement, to write the great play. Left-liberal dissidents claimed 'art' for a progressive politics but, even so, the concept commonly retains pretensions towards authority, obscurity and profundity, and these tend to interfere with accessibility and with a commitment to out-groups (who, by definition, are not universal, not 'Man'). Edward Bond seems to have been vulnerable to this temptation.

The other threat to the fringe is of its workers and product being creamed off. It is certainly understandable that writers, performers and directors should be attracted to the National, the RSC, the West End and television by the more opulent working conditions. This is sometimes represented as a triumph for fringe theatre, sometimes as a sell-out (see Goorney, 1981, on how it affected Theatre Workshop). Actually, the buying in of innovation when it proves popular or profitable is merely the way the market operates. On the one hand, it destroys the organization of the fringe and deprives it of talent; on the other, it makes room for new people. However, John Arden and John McGrath went the other way, forsaking conventional opportunities (interestingly, this meant leaving England).

Feminist or women's theatre dates from the mid-1970s. Partly it has involved fringe groups (the Women's Theatre Group and Monstrous Regiment have been prominent, but seventeen women's and gay companies were listed by *Spare Rib* in 1979), and partly authors working at conventional theatres or in radio. It has had advantages over other political theatres: the opportunity to help a left-liberal audience discover something it did not already know and believe, and relevance to women likely to attend plays anyway (as well as to others). Theatre became one distinctive place, along with books and journals, where British feminism was thought through. *Scum: Death, Destruction and Dirty Washing* (1976) by Chris Bond and Claire Luckham, *Vinegar Tom* (1976), *Cloud Nine* (1979) and *Top Girls* (1982) by Caryl Churchill, *Dusa, Fish, Stas and Vi* (1976) and *Piaf* (1978) by Pam Gems, *Care and Control* (1977) by Michelene Wandor, *Tissue* (1978) by Louise Page, *Trafford Tanzi* (1980) by Claire Luckham, *Time Pieces* (1982) by Lou Wakefield and the Women's Theatre Group and *Rose's Story* (1984) by Grace Dayley did not promote any precise embodiment of feminism (indeed the writers generally did not start from a worked-out position). But the collectivist ethos of many groups and of the women's movement encouraged audiences to regard the plays also as a collaborative exploration, and performances afforded opportunity for women to live for a little while in a challengingly female environment – in the whole purpose and ambience of the occasion, as well as in the fictional world of the play.

The very practice of feminist theatre has been controversial and thought-provoking. It was suddenly apparent that women might not see things in the same way as men, and that women's points of view have been systematically suppressed (both in that they have not been considered as a legitimate audience response, and in that plays hitherto have almost all been written from a male perspective). The whole discourse of theatre and the arts was discomposed: suddenly there was no universal human subject to be assumed, but a choice for the playwright about which group she will angle her work towards. Consequent male anxieties became vocal, almost shrill, when it was asked whether women's theatre groups should include male performers and whether men should be allowed to attend performances.

However, the restrictions upon women in conventional theatre largely remain (Wandor, 1986, pp. 88–93). By 1980 the National Theatre had produced not a single play by a woman writer, and by 1987 only one (by Lillian Hellman) (see Davies, 1987, p. 193). And as I suggested at the start, 'feminist' plays are not the only ones about gender politics. The work I have mentioned has occurred alongside a continuing, immensely larger, conservative dramatic output that represents women as confined naturally to traditional gender roles.

CONTROL AND RESISTANCE

There is a further shift to record in the political concept and organization of theatre. The post-war assumption that it is the state's responsibility to fund 'good' culture came into question after 1979, with the election of the new-right Thatcher government. This ended the hegemony of the left-liberal intelligentsia that had ratified both the subsidized companies and the fringe. Theatre, like the other good things we were promised in 1945, is henceforth to be organized through private enterprise for those who can afford it. Major subsidized companies have been forced to accept commercial sponsorship, so bearing witness in their programmes and publicity that in new-right philosophy no culture is above the market; and anxiety about displeasing the various paymasters has made their productions adventurous only in the cunning elaboration of spectacle. Fringe companies have steadily been deprived of subsidy, especially if their work was left-wing (the criteria were said to be artistic, but political discrimination has been admitted: Gooch, 1984, p. 46). At the same time, abolition of metropolitan borough councils has removed another source of fringe funding, and it has become difficult even to do theatre while managing on social security. Meanwhile, the West End carries on fairly regardless.

From 1956 to the mid-1980s the question often was: why should the state facilitate theatre that aims to overthrow it? The answer is that it did so because a consensual, social-democratic ethos required that dissenting voices be heard; and/or because the dissidents claimed to be making 'art'. The new right discourages and punishes dissent – in theatre as in the media, education, trades unions and local authorities. Explicit censorship has returned, initially in the form of a law passed in 1988 forbidding local authorities to fund work, including theatre, that might 'promote homosexuality'. The arts lobby failed in its resistance to this legislation, indicating the weakness of such a left-liberal cause in the face of new-right determination.

This change enforces a review of assumptions about the political scope of theatre. Perhaps it was all a mirage: Howard Barker, the most fertile serious author of the 1980s, declares (1986) that politics and socialism are obsolete, endorses élitism, and plunges into apparently nihilistic explorations of interior reality. Alternatively, the relations between plays, venues and audiences have to be more precisely, and strategically, considered. Trevor Griffiths's *Oi For England* (1982), about a punk band and race riots, was produced for commercial television, then performed in youth clubs, and finally shown at the Royal Court: these diverse occasions demanded different presentations and attracted different audiences and responses. Political theatre may be mounted in all sorts of venues, but the modes that speak to working people, or other subordinated groups, may well not be those of middle-class dissidence – though the latter is a perfectly valid field for political activity. You can attract working-class people if you go about it the right way; and it is pointless to debate whether popular culture is vital or not – since it is popular, much work has to begin there (McGrath, 1981).

A persistent question has been whether there is a preferred political style. As early as the 1930s fourth-wall naturalism was held to close off the idea of change and to be characteristic of middle-class theatre (Samuel, 1985, pp. 167–201). In the 1960s the issue was addressed mainly through the theories and plays of Brecht (who was actually more invoked than followed). But much of the discussion was far too abstract – endeavouring to establish formal effects without considering the expectations of actual audiences. Some fringe performers (The People Show, Welfare State, Pip Simmons, Stephen Berkoff) have been mainly anarchic, grotesque, improvisatory, multi-media, and have sometimes suggested that theatre, when presented powerfully and directly, is a political force in and of itself. John Fox (of Welfare State) says: 'It represents quite a threat to the existing order of things for twenty or thirty people playing musical instruments and wearing fantastic costumes to suddenly appear and march through the streets in an apparently anarchic fashion' (Itzin, 1980, p. 70). Well, perhaps. The belief that theatre has a special capacity to probe profound human potential is close to Artaud, who held that it should be a revolutionary experience – though without saying what kind of revolution it will be or how it should be carried forward in the world.

In fact, most people get the overwhelming portion of their drama from television, but the idea of 'the arts' has led theatre people to despise television and undervalue its scope. There have been opportunities for radical drama – sometimes even in soap operas, certainly in plays and series. David Mercer, Tony Garnett and Trevor Griffiths have produced major bodies of television work, and there have been significant interventions by Hare, McGrath and

Alan Bleasdale. A number of fringe productions have been adapted for television. Such work has been possible because television companies have been committed to the social-democratic notion of a balanced output; however, this too is being swept aside by the new right. 'Television undeniably is closing down to people like us', Griffiths observed in 1985: 'Since Thatcher, there has been a sheer panic inside most people who run TV services' (Davies, 1987, p. 205). Government deregulation of broadcasting in the 1990s, following the pattern of dismantling state responsibility for culture, seems designed to reduce further the scope for oppositional work.

The distinctive advantages of live theatre lie in immediacy, flexibility and economy: plays can be devised and presented relatively quickly and cheaply, and they can be angled towards a particular audience. In my view the important future for theatre, especially political theatre, must depend on those advantages. To be sure, if you can get a play done at the National or on television that's worth doing; but performances that respond flexibly to the needs of specific groups are likely to work far more powerfully than the latest 'great' production of *King Lear* could possibly do for its audience composed half of tourists and examination candidates.

This point could be illustrated in terms of Field Day in Ireland; or of Polish, Cypriot, Asian and Black theatre, where Naseem Khan (1976) has found many diverse initiatives, almost all with virtually no subsidy. Taking the instance of gay men, the work of Gay Sweatshop (from 1975) has afforded unprecedented public images from a gay point of view. Usually gay men watching plays, films and television have to see themselves, when they are visible at all, through the eyes of heterosexuals. *Mr X* (1975, by Drew Griffiths and Roger Baker) charted the experience and developing awareness of a gay man; *As Time Goes By* (1977) and *The Dear Love of Comrades* (1979, both written by Noel Greig and Drew Griffiths) plot a history of oppression and resistance. Here the public quality of theatre counts, for an attitude seems that bit more legitimate once it is proclaimed aloud on stage (hence the peculiar readiness of authority to censor theatre). For an audience of gay men, such productions could have specific political effects – changing self-perceptions and stimulating activism. Initially the task was for gay men to become visible; in the late 1980s they are scapegoated daily in the gutter press (unimpeded of course by censorship), and the task is to assert occasional control over one's own image.

Explicitly political theatre tends to be relevant to its moment, whereas in a book about literature one might be looking for enduring significance. However, the latter is likely, by definition, to be conservative. These plays, these histories, are worth revisiting not as universal wisdom, but as a developing experience and analysis. They help us to see how we got to the present – the hopes that have been raised and the structures of power through which they have been controlled.

FURTHER READING

Bull, John (1984) *New British Political Dramatists*, Macmillan, London

Chambers, Colin, and Prior, Mike (1987) *Playwrights' Progress: Patterns of Postwar British Drama*, Amber Lane Press, London

Craig, Sandy (1980) *Dreams and Deconstructions: Alternative Theatre in Britain*, Amber Lane Press, London

Davies, Andrew (1987) *Other Theatres: The Development of Alternative and Experimental Theatre in Britain*, Macmillan, London

Gooch, Steve (1984) *All Together Now: An Alternative View of Theatre and the Community*, Methuen, London

Holledge, Julie (1981) *Innocent Flowers: Women in the Edwardian Theatre*, Virago, London

Itzin, Catherine (1980) *Stages in the Revolution: Political Theatre in Britain since 1968*, Methuen, London

McGrath, John (1981) *A Good Night Out: Popular Theatre: Audience, Class and Form*, Methuen, London

Rabey, David Ian (1986) *British and Irish Political Drama in the Twentieth Century*, Macmillan, London

Samuel, Raphael, MacColl, Ewan and Cosgrove, Stuart (1985) *Theatres of the Left 1880–1935: Workers' Theatre Movements in Britain and America*, Routledge, London

Sinfield, Alan (1983) 'The Theatre and Its Audiences'. In Alan Sinfield (ed.), *Society and Literature 1945–1970*, Methuen, London

———(1989) *Literature, Politics and Culture in Postwar Britain*, Blackwell, Oxford

Wandor, Michelene (1986) *Carry On, Understudies*, Routledge, London

ADDITIONAL WORKS CITED

Barker, Howard (1986) '49 Asides for a Tragic Theatre', *Englisch Amerikanische Studien*, 8, 474–5

Brown, Ivor (1956) *Theatre 1955–6*, Reinhardt, London

Browne, E. Martyn (1969) *The Making of T. S. Eliot's Plays*, Cambridge University Press, Cambridge

Eliot, T. S. (1957) *On Poetry and Poets*, Faber & Faber, London

Goorney, Howard (1981) *The Theatre Workshop Story*, Methuen, London

Khan, Naseem (1976) *The Arts Britain Ignores: The Arts of Ethnic Minorities in Britain*, Arts Council, London

Pryce-Jones, David (1964) 'Towards the Cocktail Party'. In Michael Sissons and Philip French (eds), *Age of Austerity 1945–51*, Penguin, Harmondsworth

Sinfield, Alan (1985) 'Royal Shakespeare: Theatre and the Making of Ideology'. In Jonathan Dollimore and Alan Sinfield (eds), *Political Shakespeare: New Essays in Cultural Materialism*, Manchester University Press, Manchester

Steed, Maggie (1984) 'Interpretations'. In Susan Todd (ed.), *Women and Theatre*, Faber & Faber, London

Tynan, Kenneth, (1976) *A View of the English Stage*, Paladin, St Albans

Williams, Raymond (1965) *The Long Revolution*, Penguin, Harmondsworth

35

FEMINIST THEATRE

HELENE KEYSSAR

The struggle to define woman's proper place in the theatre has been going on for at least 2,500 years and shows no signs, as we approach the end of the twentieth century, of being resolved. Critics have duly noted the increased presence in the last twenty-five years of women as writers, directors and performers – but where this has been the occasion for applause, the appreciative gesture has often been embarrassingly reminiscent of the welcome extended to a few select blacks, Jews, chicanos, deaf, children and old people whose manners assure that no offence is contemplated.

None the less, beginning in the late sixties, there was substantial evidence of new approaches to issues of gender in the theatre, and this evidence suggested the emergence of a distinct drama that we might appropriately call 'feminist'. In contrast to plays by and/or about women that back date at least to Aeschylus' *Oresteia* and to Hrosvitha (a tenth-century playwright and nun whose name translates as 'loud mouth'), feminist dramas are characterized by a specified consciousness of gender, a consciousness of the idea of man and woman *as* men and women. In these works, the art of the playwright is inseparable from their condition and ideology as men and women.

The plays created in this context of a new and profound acknowledgement of the meanings of gender do not just mirror social change but assert an aesthetic based on the transformation rather than the recognition of persons. As Aristotle long ago argued, in traditional drama the recognition scene is the centrepost of dramatic structure. In plays where the recognition scene is pivotal, emphasis is on self-discovery, on the recovery of the past as a means of finding our 'true selves'. Most plays, including those by and about women, have adhered to this dramaturgical structure. Ibsen's *A Doll's House* (1879) foreshadows feminist drama and posed a genuine threat in its time (and perhaps now as well) precisely because it insists that recognition and revelation are insufficient, that major transformations of gender practices and identities must occur in order for marriage to be reclaimed as a vital institution. In contrast, despite its thematic concern with lesbianism and its female author-ship, Lillian Hellman's *The Children's Hour* (1934) is wholly consistent with traditional Western drama.

Rejecting the basic beliefs and values of the dominant form of Western theatre, and drawing upon a theatrical device that has residual elements in medieval morality plays, Elizabethan drama, and the 'new theatre' of the sixties, feminist drama creates a dramaturgy of transformation in which the process of change and not its products is at the centre of theatrical interest. The goal of this feminist theatre is not increased self-awareness but knowledge of others and of the deep structures of sexual politics as the basis for personal, political and social change. In feminist theatre, there is no fixed, true self but human beings in the constant process of becoming other.

As the dreamer is the author of the dream, so, too, it is the polis or community that makes the stories it tells itself in its dramas. In Western culture, from the ancient Greeks to the present, theatre has repeatedly presented the struggles of women to alter their personal roles and social relationships. Among the various cultural acts in Aeschylus' *Oresteia*, few are as blatant as the privileging of the authoritative discourse of the male citizen and the silencing of counter-voices, associated throughout the trilogy with the discourse of women. The voices of women are under assault from the beginning of the 'Agamemnon' trilogy, precisely because those voices admit different meanings to every situation. By the end of the trilogy, women have agreed to relegate themselves to a fixed and constrained domain, focused on reproduction, nurtur-ance and protection of their families, a domain that has no intersection with the polis. It is an uneasy agreement, confirmed in dance more than in words. It is also an agreement reached because the women wish for peace.

The memory of that agreement, and the contested terrain to which it spoke, persisted in Greek tragedy, and the conflict it ostensibly resolved has remained a residual element of theatre and Western culture. However debased or spuri-ous its subsequent reincarnations, Greek tragedy not only exercised cultural hegemony in its own historical period but has remained a potent residual element of cultural production for 2,500 years. The persistence of strategies of marginalization of women in both the production and thematics of theatre thus raises the possibility that an authentically oppositional feminist theatre might be more than a transient response to topical issues. It might create a new form of discourse that would animate both theatre and public life.

Parented by the women's movement and the 'new theatre', feminist drama had its most immediate roots in the political and aesthetic disruptions of the 1960s. By the mid-seventies, dozens of plays significantly informed by a consciousness of gender were being produced annually in the United States and Great Britain. (Publication followed much more slowly and did not occur in a deliberate way until the eighties.) The primary intent of most of these plays was to present the voices of women; consistent with the first, consciousness-raising stage of the women's movement, these on-stage women called attention to gender-related practices and attitudes through parodies of sex-based stereotypes, gender role reversals, the recuperation of the positive accomplishments of historical female figures, vivid imagings of female sexuality from the perspectives of women, and confessions of ambivalences about bodies and selves.

At the beginning, this was enough and necessary. Distinctions between 'women's drama' and 'feminist' drama were irrelevant. Networks of women playwrights and women's theatre collectives were being formed, and the desire to be there and a shared sense of oppression were the only requisites for membership; as one attempt to avoid the errors of patriarchy, almost all women and empathetic men in theatre agreed to embrace polyphony and avoid the tyranny of a single dominant theory or approach to dramaturgy or performance. As in other areas of the women's movement, there would be not one, but many feminisms in the theatre.

By the mid-seventies, some playwrights were reaching beyond consciousness-raising and the recovery of women's voices to what I have come to call 'doing dangerous history' and dangerous feminist dramaturgy (Keyssar, 1986, 1989a, 1989b). Caryl Churchill, Pam Gems and Michelene Wandor in Britain; Megan Terry, Ntozake Shange, Adrienne Kennedy, Rochelle Owens, Myrna Lamb, Martha Boesing, Tina Howe, Maria Irene Fornes and Susan Miller, among others, in the United States, challenged conventional dramatic strategies and dominant beliefs about gender and violence, rights and responsibilities, individuation and community. These playwrights often dispersed attention among several or many characters rather than focusing on one or two stars or main characters; they presented different views of situations without choosing among them; they confronted the complicity as well as the courage of women in recurrent resolutions of battles of the sexes; they dramatized the inseparability of the personal from the political; and they used transformations to challenge rigid distinctions between men and women. Companies such as the Women's Theatre Group and Monstrous Regiment in Britain and At the Foot of the Mountain and the Omaha Magic Theater in the United States created their own dramas, drawing from the performers' autobiographies and improvizational rehearsals as well as from collaborative historical research.

Among playwrights in the United States, where feminist theatre emerged several years before its counterparts in Britain and the rest of Europe, Megan Terry was the unacknowledged 'mother of it all'. From the early sixties until 1974, Terry had directed her energies toward collaborative production endeavours, primarily in New York City with the Open Theater; although not well-known, she achieved some recognition for her authorship of *Viet Rock* (1966), one of the first American productions to address critically the Vietnam War, and she was one of the few feminist playwrights to have her work from the sixties and early seventies published. When, in the 1980s, the American press discovered the 'new women playwrights', Megan Terry was ignored or over-looked. Yet evidence for my claim that Terry is the 'mother of American feminist theater' (Keyssar, 1984) abounds in Terry's more than fifty plays.

As a body of work, Terry's dramas have explored a wide range of feminist issues. Production and reproduction, the language of patriarchy, gender roles inside and outside the family, the victimization and heroism of women, and the pain and power of women in a repressive society are all essential elements of Terry's dramatic discourse. Her plays persistently criticize and subvert specific institutions and events in American society – from the war in Vietnam to the hypocritical behaviour of parents towards adolescents – but these cri-tiques are not merely casual gestures at topical issues or facile assaults on patriarchy and sexism. Rather, they are specifications of a vision that emphasizes a transformation of morality as the basis of social and political change.

Although critical of the particular instances of violence and oppression against women, Terry's plays have never insisted, as has the work of some feminists working in other media, that revolution is necessary in order to improve the status of women in society. Her objections to inequality are not usually couched in terms of an economic system that creates such situations, but rather emerge as protests against individual circumstances, institutional corruption, or verbal and conceptual distortions. Even, for example, in a play like *Babes in the Bighouse* (1979), which harshly condemns both the treatment of women prisoners and, metaphorically, the pervasive imprisonment of women in the codes and practices of modern society, the challenge is to the audience's sense of responsibility and dignity, not to the economic and political systems that support such prisons. Terry's outlook in this regard has been archetypally American and may be a strategic choice given that her audience, too, is, for the most part, assertively American. Enacting her own feminist version of American romanticism, Terry has chosen in most of her plays to highlight the positive, though incremental, change that is available: women, in her dramas, are 'alive and well' and on the way to doing even better.

This optimism is apparent throughout Terry's work. *Calm Down Mother* (1965), one of her first plays to be explicitly concerned with women as women, depicts the tensions as well as the attachments between mothers and daughters, but ends with a ritual-like chant that invokes woman's reproductive capabilities as a source of difference and almost mystical strength. *Viet Rock* (1966) con-cludes in 'deathly silence', but the intense ambience of community in the acting ensemble deliberately encouraged spectators to believe that they – we – could overcome the various oppressions represented and enacted in that war. The most memorable moment in Terry's *Approaching Simone* (1970) occurs when each member of the acting company takes on a piece of Simone's clothing, symbolically taking on her pain and her struggle for women's freedom. Simone Weil, like theatre itself in Terry's hands, is a model, but, as dramatized, her heroism can join her to others rather than separate her from them.

When Megan Terry moved to the Omaha Magic Theater in 1974, she began a new phase of the feminist discourse she had begun to shape in the experimental theatre of the sixties. In Omaha, she became more precisely focused on joint endeavours with her colleague, Jo Ann Schmidman; together they addressed the local community in Omaha. Extensive use of music, innovative sets and transformational performance techniques made productions, on topics that ranged from drinking and drugs to jogging and family relations, entertaining and provocative to a wide range of spectators.

Terry's 1983 collaboration with JoAnne Metcalf, *Mollie Bailey's Traveling Family Circus: Featuring Scenes from the Life of Mother Jones*, represented a new and increasingly politicized direction for her drama. Retaining the basic optimism of her previous work, while venturing into one of the most contested arenas of contemporary American society, Terry dares in *Mollie Bailey's Traveling Circus* to show the possibility of authentic communication and mutual support between two types of successful women who, in today's world, would appear to be unyielding foes. The central figures and the orchestrators of events in this drama are Mollie Bailey and Mother Jones, both born in the nineteenth century, the former out of Terry's imagination, the latter out of history. In Terry's staged world, Mother Jones, a political activist, socialist and organizer for the rights of women and children, is not the evil enemy but the star performer and ally of Mollie Bailey, a woman who is a traditional housewife and, ironically, the ringmistress of a travelling 'family' circus.

In this world, dramaturgically and politically, transformation and possibility are key motifs, as they have been throughout Terry's work (see Schlueter, 1987), but their explicit presence has been augmented by an increased attention to the social-political cosmos. The onstage transformations that were oppositional conventions in Terry's dramas of the sixties (and that became accepted theatrical practice in American experimental theatre before vanishing, in the seventies, from the work of most male playwrights) are revitalized in *Mollie Bailey's Traveling Circus* as circus feats. More eloquently than in Terry's previous work, these transformations are also now the feats of American women recovering and reconstructing their history.

The 'Prologue' to *Mollie Bailey's Traveling Family Circus* signals the ironic tone and mythic frame for the play. Suspended on a wide trapeze or platform held aloft by 'invisible' stagehands, two Celtic queens, who are, simultaneously, Mollie Bailey and Mother Jones, are crossing the Irish Sea on a raft in the midst of a fierce storm. Lashed to their raft are other, unconscious members of their tribe. Mother Jones's opening line – 'Did you lash down the males?'

– instantly establishes the inversion of conventional power relations between men and women; the men are not only physically subjugated to the women but are treated as sexual types, as 'males'. (A few lines later, Mother Jones confirms this conception when she reassures Mollie that they will reach land with at least one male 'in good condition'.) The Prologue also establishes a mother–daughter relationship between Mother Jones and Mollie Bailey: literally fulfilling the role suggested by her ironic, historical name, 'Mother' Jones commands, instructs and nurtures Mollie, who, in turn, proclaims her love for 'Mother' and her confidence that she will be empowered by her mother's attachment and support.

Theatrically and culturally, this prologue is at once familiar and disconcerting. The sea-storm setting and the playful echo of 'Take in the topsail' in 'lash down the males' blatantly recall Shakespeare's *The Tempest*, which, like Terry's play, is situated in both the historical context of the discovery of the new world and the mythical context of a separate space of spectacle where time and place are magically construed. The raft of the two Celtic queens is a far cry, however, from the sailing ship of *The Tempest*, and the two women steering the raft's course would have had no place, even as passengers, on Shakespeare's all-male ship. Contrary to gender stereotypes, the men of *The Tempest* quickly lose patience and surrender to fear and chaos, whereas Mother Jones concludes the prologue of the contemporary drama warmly reassuring Mollie that 'If we're not in trouble, we're not going in the right direction'.

The right direction in *Mollie Bailey's Traveling Family Circus* is rarely straight forward, or straight backward. In keeping with many contemporary feminist plays, the prologue and the two acts that follow exploit theatre's liberty with time and place to conjoin previously disconnected elements of culture and history. Not insignificantly, Britain's most prolific and noteworthy feminist playwright, Caryl Churchill, has repeatedly employed similar temporal and spatial reconfigurations in her dramas. Both Terry's and Churchill's subversions of conventional representations of chronology and history re-orient the spectator towards alternative ways of viewing the present and the past.

Churchill's public success in the eighties – with *Cloud Nine* (1979), *Top Girls* (1982), *Fen* (1983), *A Mouthful of Birds* (1986) and *Serious Money* (1987) – further illuminates the difference between plays ostensibly *about* women and feminist drama. *Serious Money*, Churchill's dramatic display of the highs and lows of wheeling and dealing at LIFFE (an acronym for the London International Financial Futures Exchange) is obviously a play about a topical issue. Heralded as a major 'hit' at the Royal Court in London, *Serious Money* shares many attributes with Churchill's previous work: it rides on the exuberant energy of the acting company, an energy which, while disturbingly manic, is appropriate to the context; it is episodic in structure, relying on dialectic activity rather than narrative sequencing to move characters and audience through time and space; it uses song to establish an ironic distance and verbal wit to surprise and sustain the audience's interest; and, most explicitly like Churchill's *Top Girls, Serious Money* situates the contemporary situation in a historical context by beginning with a scene drawn from *The Volunteers or the Stock Jobbers*, a farce written in 1692 by Thomas Shadwell. Within and between these dramaturgical devices, the spectator can discern Churchill's ongoing critique of contemporary Western capitalism and what the drama critic Mel Gussow calls her 'fervid social consciousness' (*New York Times*, 22 November 1987).

In the end, however, and almost from the beginning, *Serious Money* is not a serious play and is not a feminist drama. This is not to say that it is simply funny, which it, oddly, is not, but that it has no coherent strategy by which it attempts, at the least, to provide the audience with a new and distinctive way of seeing the world in which they live – or long to live. The sad irony of *Serious Money* is that at no point in the play is there a character or situation that suggests that there is someone or something more commanding than money.

In contrast, Churchill's *A Mouthful of Birds*, co-written with David Lan, provides convincing evidence that drama may yet have a unique role to play in shaping the future. Developed in collaboration with Joint Stock Theatre Group, with whom Churchill had previously created *Light Shining in Buckinghamshire* (1976), *Cloud Nine* and *Fen*, *A Mouthful of Birds* began with a workshop in which the entire company explored two topics that have been an ongoing concern in Churchill's work – possession and violence. The result is a drama that unmistakably carries the Churchill signature yet extends the boundaries of politics and theatre to terrains that she had previously only begun to explore.

A Mouthful of Birds, like much of Churchill's earlier work, finds its pre-text in history. Beginning with *Light Shining in Buckinghamshire*, Churchill's plays have been hauntings, her characters ghosts, whose bodies we have buried but who find a unique space in the theatre to remind us that we cannot dream new dreams until we put their souls to rest. Whether these souls are witches, as in *Vinegar Tom*, nineteenth-century British colonists in Africa, as in *Cloud Nine*, or women of distinction from previous eras, as in *Top Girls*, they threaten our understanding of past and present because they admit the resistance of both women and men to changes in their relations.

A Mouthful of Birds also presents us with ghosts, but these spirits now hail not just from one consciousness – as was the case with *Top Girls* – or one slice of the past – as occurred in *Cloud Nine* – but from a historical/mythical moment in which simultaneously the sacred confronted the profane, ecstasy confronted reason, the 'non-I' confronted the 'I', and woman confronted man. These conflicts passed from the endless repetitions of ritual time to historical time 2,500 years ago in the theatre of Greece that staged Aeschylus' *Oresteia* and Euripides' *Bacchae*, but there have been intermittent hints ever since that the elemental struggles that may have appeared to be thus resolved were only temporarily repressed.

Such hauntings, as Churchill explained in her preface to *Traps* (1978), are neither flashbacks nor fantasy; on stage, the ghosts of *A Mouthful of Birds*, much like the fictional and historical figures who materialize in the first scene of *Top Girls*, are real and solid, as present to us in the contained world of the theatre as they are invisible in our daylight meanderings. Churchill's dramaturgical strategy here, as in other of her works, is to cast the audience as Hamlet, half-aware that there is something rotten in our past and present state, but lacking 'gall/ To make oppression bitter' (*Hamlet*, II. ii, 574–5); one common goal of many of Churchill's plays is to provide the gall that will make bitter the particular oppressions of gender and class. In *A Mouthful of Birds*, the rot that she and co-author David Lan confront is violence, and the gall is a potion comprised of brief vignettes in which contemporary characters momentarily lose their self-control. Dislodged from their situations in historical time, the characters encounter incarnations of the 'unquiet dead', from the near and distant past. For the audience, already unhinged from its usual connections to time by its situation in the theatre, these spirits, unloosed from both remote and familiar worlds, threaten our complacency.

Churchill approached this play, as she recalls in her 'Authors' Notes', with an interest in 'women being violent'; from the beginning, she was sceptical of the commonly held view that 'women are more peaceful than men'. To call that assumption into question seemed to Churchill especially important in the context of the contemporary politicization of this view, most notably by women whose protests against nuclear weapons have sometimes been grounded in claims of women's peacefulness. This is not, Churchill makes clear, an anti-feminist position, but rather an attempt to counter reductive and inaccurate images of men and women that tend to set each in binary opposition to the other. 'There is a danger', she writes in the 'Notes', 'of polarizing men and women into what becomes again the traditional view that men are naturally more violent and so have no reason to change. It seems important to recognize women's capacity for violence and men's for peacefulness' (Churchill and Lan, 1986, p. 5).

The similar emphases in Terry's and Churchill's dramaturgies on unprecedented historical representations and on explicit intertextual gestures suggest that the most potent emergent element of feminist theatre may not be the recovery of women's history but what Mother Jones calls 'getting into trouble', and what I have described as doing dangerous history. Where many feminist endeavours, in the theatre and in other media, have aimed to recuperate women's history as an inspirational resource for women and men, dangerous historical explorations seek not only to recover the forgotten achievements of women but to examine the conditions under which gender conflicts have repeatedly arisen and repeatedly been resolved in such a way that women have remained subordinate to men. Plays like Michelene Wandor's *Aurora Leigh* (1979), Viveca Lindfors and Paul Austin's *I am a Woman* (1976), Eve Merriam, Paula Wagner and Jack Hoffsiss's *Out of Our Fathers' House* (1975), Pam Gems's translation of French writer Marianne Auricoste's *My Name is Rosa Luxemburg* (1976), Melissa Murray's *Ophelia* (1979) and Steve Gooch's *Female Transport* (1973) are important in admitting the points of view of some women to history. These plays refuse to see the history of gender relationships as simply the history of the victimization of women.

The re-integration of women into history in both scholarly research and theatre may be a necessary stage in a sexual revolution, but it does not suffice. Dangerous historians, and dramatists doing dangerous history, confront the illusions of the past, including those that conceal women's complicity in the recurrent subjugation of women to men. Dangerous history also refuses to ignore women's violence at key moments in that history. The processes and effects of doing dangerous history in drama are increasingly evident not only in plays by Churchill and Terry, but in other feminist dramas such as Wendy Kesselman's *My Sister in This House* (1982), Louise Page's *Salonika* (1982), Ntozake Shange's *Three Pieces* (1981) and Sharon Pollock's *Blood Relations* (1981).

Among the most perturbing of these 'dangerous' feminist dramas are those by black American women. For the black woman playwright, there is, if not a triple-consciousness, then at least a complicated double-consciousness in which she sees the world as an American *woman* and a *black* woman. From the beginnings of theatre by black women playwrights to the present, these women's dramas have tended to create stage worlds in which diverse voices and world views collide, polyphony is asserted and sometimes celebrated, and the different signifying systems of dance, music, performance transformations and visual imagery are aggressively utilized.

Vivid but unacknowledged evidence of this inclination (perhaps this necessity) occurs in an early twentieth-century play (1916) by a black teacher of English named Angelina Grimke. Entitled *Rachel*, after its central character, Grimke's drama is usually described (by both black and white critics) as a sentimental social protest drama, deliberately written as theatrical propaganda to dissuade whites from the persecution of black Americans and specifically to urge whites to bring an end to the numerous lynchings of blacks occurring during the period when the play was written.

Focused on motherhood and what it means for a black woman and for black children, throughout the play Rachel speaks variously and sometimes simultaneously as child to her own mother, as mother to her adopted son Jimmy, and as a self-constructed spinster-virgin. This is not the familiar developmental change of role and voice we anticipate in 'good' drama but is closer to a depiction of insanity or a representation of character that fits critical descriptions of 'inconsistent' writing. Both the latter may be true, yet there is an at least equal and more important truth in the text's failure to resolve Rachel's double consciousness. The scene in which Rachel tells the man she loves that she will not marry him is characteristically demonstrative of her double-consciousness of self and the world around her. Rachel's vacillation from 'no' to 'yes' to 'no' again in response to her friend John's marriage proposal is not ordinary ambivalence: her 'yes' is as impassioned as each of her 'no's' and she rejects thought both in framing her 'yes' and in finally proclaiming her 'no'. She is similarly double-voiced in the climactic end of Act 2, where she roughly tears the buds from the rose stems sent to her by John. The rosebuds, she makes clear, are her unborn children, and, as she deliberately aborts them, saying 'I kill', she also speaks with tenderness of her victims and with grief of her loss.

If we listen well, Grimke's *Rachel* teaches us to hear the dialogism in her central character's last words. Forty years later, in the next milestone of black women's drama, Lorraine Hansberry's *A Raisin in the Sun* (1959), the representation of what it means to love as a mother *and* to be a black American woman requires an even more hybrid form of discourse than in earlier years. Written in the political and cultural context of the integrationist movement, *A Raisin in the Sun*, like *Rachel*, is a social protest play intended to persuade white people that black people are not only good at heart but sufficiently like whites in their values and cultural practices for whites to allow blacks to be their neighbours. As in *Rachel*, motherhood is at the centre of this appeal, but the leaks in the argument in *A Raisin in the Sun* are at once more threatening to the success of the plea and less apparent than in Grimke's earlier work.

A man, Walter Lee, is the central figure of the Younger family in *A Raisin in the Sun* and is also the play's protagonist, but the family and the cultural conflicts of Hansberry's drama are dominated by women. The dramatic strategy of *A Raisin in the Sun* appears to support the notion, conventional in the 1950s and 1960s and subsequently challenged, that black men were the key victims of white American racism and that the image and actuality of the black woman as the source of strength and endurance in the black family sometimes undermined the struggles of black men for self-respect (see Gutman, 1977; Stack, 1975; Genovese, 1974). The play's conclusion, in which Walter regains his dignity by informing the white man that the Youngers have changed their minds and will move into their house in the white neighbourhood, reinstates the black man as the centre of family authority and as a heroic figure in American culture.

Hansberrry has constructed a dramatic world in which the wit and charm of the characters distracts the audience from the dangers and contradictions of the social world they inhabit. Among those troublesome, marginalized issues, is the pregnancy of Walter's wife, Ruth. Ruth finds no joy in the prospect of bringing another child into this grim and potentially explosive world and makes plans for an abortion. She does not, in the end, have an abortion, and her fierce declaration at the end of the play – 'I'll strap my baby on my back if I have to and scrub all the floors in America and wash all the sheets in America if I have to – but we got to move – WE got to get out of here' – serves as the dramatic resolution to her previous conflict. But Hansberry has allowed Ruth to speak enough of her misgivings about bringing another black child into the world that, in the festive ambience of the play's ending, it is Ruth whose utterances are least convincing of all the characters. Ruth's pregnant presence remains an unconcealable reminder of the double consciousness of black women – as blacks and as women – that has been articulated on separate planes throughout the play.

A third milestone in black women's drama, Ntozake Shange's *for colored girls who have considered suicide when the rainbow is enuf* (1975) confronts and sometimes transcends the contradictions and confusions in the double-consciousness of black women that Hansberry had articulated but abandoned. Described by the author as a 'choreopoem', *for colored girls* rejects the conventions of dramatic realism for a form of theatre that makes its meanings as much from dance and the rhythms of verbal language as from semantic sources of signification. A primary example of the special application of transformational devices in feminist theatre, *for colored girls* is a series of stories of the struggles, victories and defeats of more than a dozen unnamed black women, performed by seven actresses who move fluidly from choral roles as witnesses and commentators to individual narrators. Much of the hypnotic vibrancy of the production derives from the tension between the vulnerability of each woman when she stands alone to tell a particular story and the fortitude of the women when they stand and move as a community.

Shange subtly arranges the separate stories and dances of *for colored girls* to ensure that each tale or gesture interanimates others with which it is juxtaposed, a strategy comparable to that of the use of montage in film in which meanings derive from the collision of images and ideas at least as much as from each discrete image or assertion. Continuity in the drama rests primarily on the constant presence and fluid transformations of all the women, as well as on the repetition of patterns of change in performers and modes of representation. A barely discernible chronological thread that unwinds the lives of black women from girlhood to maturity is present in the score. The one knot in this thread returns us to motherhood as a specific dilemma and source of enormous pain for black women.

For Rachel in Grimke's drama and for Ruth in *A Raisin in the Sun*, the danger and burden of acknowledgement of each woman's own hybridization threaten their senses of responsibility to others and lead to acts that at least momentarily unify the self. Not unimportantly, both these characters define themselves in relation to men and to their own mother figures. In numerous other plays by black American women, including folk drama by women like Georgia Douglas Johnson, pedagogical works such as Mary Burrill's dramatized argument for birth control, *They That Sit in Darkness* (1919), and the nine realistic dramas written by Alice Childress between 1950 and the late 1970s, black women characters strain towards and against these same pillars of support and constraint.

These 'landmarks' of black feminist drama share with the work of white feminist playwrights such as Terry and Churchill a vision of a theatre – and a world – informed by what Raymond Williams has called a 'new tragic consciousness'. This theatre represents the position of 'all those who, appalled by the present, are for this reason firmly committed to a different future: to the struggle against suffering learned in suffering: a total exposure which is also a total involvement' (1966, p. 54). To fulfil this vision, feminist dramas re-create worlds past and present in terms of a redefined notion of heritage and inspire our conviction that things could, indeed, be different.

In the late eighties, the instances of black or white women sweeping to their feet on stage have been rare and isolated. Perhaps the difficulty is in the increasing knowledge of the complexity of the gesture. For while much feminist drama envisions the future as a new, international, heterogeneous society, the same body of work specifically recalls 'societies that usedta throw us away/or sell us/or play with our vaginas' (Shange, 1981, p. 135). The task, these dramas suggest, is to create a new international theatre in which being born a girl – as well as growing up to be a woman – is a cause for celebration.

One sign of hope for such celebration is the evidence of the emergence in the eighties of similar feminist theatrical strategies outside the United States and Britain. Hélène Cixous's *Portrait of Dora* (1979), for example, offers a new but related model for feminist drama; this work shares with those of Terry, Churchill, Shange, Wendy Kesselman and Louise Page an insistence on interruption and silence and on consciousness of the processes of representation and presentation. Like the dramas of black women, *Portrait of Dora* is also pessimistic about the ability to sustain an authentic new feminist theatre within the embedded, official culture and ideology of the present theatre in the West.

The risks that must be taken in theatre are being taken, but not by everyone or even by every woman playwright. Plays by women that refuse these risks are not simply plays by women who wish to be 'just writers' or plays that 'simply' avoid politics. Marsha Norman's Pulitzer Prize-winning play, *'night Mother* (1982), illuminates the difficulties that arise when all women's plays are celebrated as equal acts of liberation. *'night Mother* obscures feminist issues such as victimization, and in form and style poses no serious alternative to dominant theatre. It is, in fact, a prime example of the unthreatening kind of gendered dramas that make it into the canon of 'good' American drama.

At the same time, most of the playwrights I have mentioned here, and others such as Louise Page in Britain and Wendy Kesselman in the United States, are continuing to experiment with new practices and new relationships with an aura of conviction that a new form of theatre is, indeed, emerging. Despite the political retrenchments of the eighties, there is little possibility of a unanimous retreat to safer terrain for feminist theatre. We should recall that the Prologue to Megan Terry's *Mollie Bailey's Traveling Circus* ends with the assertion: 'if we're not in trouble, we're not going in the right direction'. In Caryl Churchill's *Fen*, the sun and moon urge women to 'turn back', but more than one woman responds, 'I won't turn back for you or anyone'. Feminist theatre knows this to be true and knows that by dramatizing the politics of the personal it can empower theatre as well as women.

FURTHER READING

Brater, Enoch (ed.) (1989) *The New Women Playwrights*, Oxford University Press, New York

Brown, Janet (1979) *Feminist Drama*, Scarecrow Press, Metuchen

Brown-Guillory, Elizabeth (1988) *Their Place on the Stage: Black Women Playwrights in America*, Greenwood Press, New York

Case, Sue-Ellen (1988) *Feminism and Theatre*, Methuen, New York

Chinoy, Helene and Jenkins, Linda Walsh (eds) (1981) *Women in American Theater*, Crown Publishers, New York

Dolan, Jill (1988) *The Feminist Spectator as Critic*, UMI Research Press, Ann Arbor

Itzin, Catherine (1980) *Stages in the Revolution: Political Theatre in Britain Since 1968*, Eyre Methuen, London

Keyssar, Helene (1984) *Feminist Theatre*, Macmillan, London; Grove Press, New York

Leavitt, Dinah Luise (1980) *Feminist Theatre Groups*, McFarland & Co., Jefferson

Todd, Susan, (ed.) (1984) *Women and Theatre*, Faber & Faber, London

Wandor, Michelene (1981) *Understudies: Theatre and Sexual Politics*, Eyre Methuen, London

——(1987) *Look Back in Gender: Sexuality and the Family in Post-War British Drama*, Methuen, London

ADDITIONAL WORKS CITED

Churchill, Caryl and Lan, David (1986) *A Mouthful of Birds*, Methuen, London

Genovese, Eugene (1974) *Roll, Jordan Roll*, Pantheon, New York

Gutman, Herbert G. (1977) *The Black Family in Slavery and Freedom*, Vintage, New York

Keyssar, Helene (1986) 'Hauntings: Gender and Drama in Contemporary English Theatre', *Englisch Amerikanische Studien*, 449–68

____(1989a) 'Dangerous History: The Plays of Caryl Churchill'. In Phyllis R. Randall (ed.), *Caryl Churchill*, Garland Press, New York, pp. 131–49

____(1989b) 'Rites and Responsibilities: The Drama of Black American Women'. In Enoch Brater (ed.), *The New Women Playwrights*, Oxford University Press, New York, 226–40

Schlueter, June (1987) 'Keep Tightly Closed in a Cool Dry Place: Megan Terry's Transformational Drama and the Possibilities of Self', *Studies in American Drama*, 2, 56–69

Shange, Ntozake (1981) *Three Pieces*, Penguin Books, New York

Stack, Carol (1975) *All Our Kin: Strategies for Survival in a Black Community*, Harper & Row, New York

Williams, Raymond (1966) *Modern Tragedy*, Stanford University Press, Stanford

V. THE NOVEL

36

MODES OF EIGHTEENTH-CENTURY FICTION

MELVYN NEW

Clearly, this novel-centered view of prose fiction is a Ptolemaic perspective which is now too complicated to be any longer workable, and some more relative and Copernican view must take its place.

(Northrop Frye, *Anatomy of Criticism*, 1957, p. 304)

Like most upheavals of an established system of organizing knowledge, the revolution called for in Frye's often-quoted sentence has led to a far better understanding of the errors of our previous way than of the shape and substance of the system that should replace them. We now understand, for example, that earlier discussions of the forms of eighteenth-century fiction centred solely on the emergence of the novel as the *sine qua non* of the enterprise are as fallacious as the equally discredited search in eighteenth-century poetry for 'pre-romantic' qualities. Similarly, we have come to the realization that such commonplace dichotomies as that between flat and round characterization, realism and fantasy, even novels and romances, are not as useful to our exploration of the vast continent of eighteenth-century fiction as we once believed.

These systems have been exploded as fictions, but what we have also been taught by the last thirty years of literary criticism is that any system we now put in their place should also be labelled a fiction, a narrative by which we attempt to organize and characterize the flux of data under observation. That is to say, to discuss the modes of fiction in the eighteenth century is to tell a story, one that we hope will provide its audience with the belief that they better comprehend the relationship between the discrete elements under examination (a plethora of eighteenth-century narratives), but a 'story', a 'fiction', none the less. The reality is thousands of texts, each created by and creating a tantalizing web of relationships with all the others, a web never to be permanently unravelled. In this regard, the story of fictional modes is no different from the modes themselves; everywhere we see the human effort to organize the diverse parts into coherent wholes and everywhere we recognize the same limitations in the face of life's resistance to coherence and fixity.

I would start my story with an ineluctable fact: the most widely read and often discussed collection of narratives in eighteenth-century England was scripture. For the literate audience, two avenues of approach were most readily available; they could read the text itself, or they could attend weekly discussions of it every Sunday (and on many other occasions as well) from the pulpit. For those who cared to go beyond this (and many, many did), the trade in scriptural commentary was by far the most thriving part of the eighteenth-century book trade; sermons heard on Sunday were often later published – or, just as likely, had been cribbed from previously published collections; in addition, large tomes of commentaries and companions, histories and dictionaries, geographies and encyclopedias were popular, often cited and consulted. The nature of this enterprise, in some respects, did not differ significantly from the Talmudic tradition of Jewish commentary, begun some 2000 years earlier. Most particularly, the commentary called '*midrash aggadah*' (from the verbal root for narrative) produced so rich a body of literature that much of subsequent Western story-telling may find its sources in these early attempts to elaborate upon the sacred text – sources now almost invisible to us because of the twin barriers of an uncommon language (Hebrew) and Christianity's usurpation of Jewish thought. Still, more than sufficient evidence exists – from the past and in present observation as well – to argue convincingly that the most salient aspect of the existence of a sacred text is the commentary it generates.

For our present purposes one example will suffice. One of the most prolific commentators of the seventeenth century was Bishop Joseph Hall, whose numerous commentaries, paraphrases (on the 'hard texts'), devotionals, polemics, sermons, examinations and studies fill twelve volumes. Hall can take any single scriptural verse and ring elaborations upon it until one's head spins. His expansion of I Kings 17:15 can quickly illustrate this point. The narrative tells of Elijah, who asks the widow of Zarephath (upon God's instructions) to share with him her last bit of food: 'And she went and did according to the saying of Elijah'; the second half of the verse records the result: 'and she, and he, and her house, did eat many days' as the barrel of meal and cruse of oil replenished themselves. We have, in short, the record of a miracle, a providential intervention in the midst of everyday life. Hall elaborates this moment in the story by means of an imagined monologue of what a different widow might have thought and done: 'Some sharp dame would have taken up the prophet; and have sent him away, with an angry repulse: "Bold Israelite; there is no reason in this request. . . . What can induce thee to think thy life, an unknown traveller, should be more dear to me than my son's, than my own?" ' (Hall, [1612–26] 1837, vol. 2, p. 35). Hall offers ten such sentences in which his widow explores the unreasonableness of the request, all hypothetical of course since he and we know that the scriptural widow served Elijah and God.

I do not mean to imply, obviously, that Joseph Hall is the father of the novel – that would simply impose a new name into a very old story, the hunt for the ur-novel. What I do want to suggest is that Hall's method was repeated by countless commentators in the following century, and forms the hard core of the countless sermons delivered and published during the eighteenth century. Most particularly, the Anglican stress upon avoiding intricate doctrinal disputes in sermons led to the foregrounding of 'primitive' and 'practical' divinity, which meant, primarily, the retelling of biblical life in a manner that could teach contemporaries 'how to live'. One significant practitioner of such sermonizing was Laurence Sterne, who used the success of *The Life and Opinions of Tristram Shandy* (1759–67) to publish four volumes of sermons. Sterne read and borrowed from Hall for his own sermon on Elijah and the widow; his account runs on for pages, but one sentence – built on a hint in Hall – is of particular interest. The hypothetical widow argues to herself: 'If this man by some secret mystery of his own, or through the power of his GOD, is able to procure so preternatural a supply for me, whence comes it to pass, that he now stands in want himself, oppressed both with hunger and thirst' (Sterne, 1760, p. 121). The biblical verse, Hall's retelling, and Sterne's further elaboration are the pegs upon which I will try to hang my own story of the modes of eighteenth-century fiction.

I will begin with the mode we know as history, a form of fiction that represents a boundary, since so many who write and read it argue that it is not an invention but a record of reality. The metaphysical difficulties of this belief are beyond our scope, but surely we can agree that only the smallest handful in the eighteenth century would have doubted that Elijah and the widow lived the story before its telling. This is, after all, the century that considered chronology a science, a science that proved the Creation began on 23 October 4004 BC, that in 2349 BC, on 7 December to be precise, the Flood started, and that the passage through the Red Sea was opened on 11 May 1491 BC, which was a Monday (Blair, 1754, Table 1). Moreover, the same audience would not have doubted the replenishing of the barrel; the shift in the scriptural verse from the event (she obeys) to the miracle (she receives) is smooth, easy and without comment. The modern instinct to deny the miracle but grant Elijah's natural existence is still rather foreign to the eighteenth century. Quite the contrary, the great proof of Elijah's reality *is* the miracle, for God is the author of both and our faith in the Teller creates full faith in the tale. And surely this is the reason why history-writing prior to the eighteenth century so often insisted upon God's hand in latter-day events, the surprise victory, the sudden death, the appropriate heir. To see these events as purposeful interventions gave an authority to the record otherwise lacking;

rather than making the event unbelievable, the attribution of miraculous intervention fostered belief among those for whom God's sustaining presence was
a reality. Less real, then, were attempts to retell events without that presence.

The age of miracles had long passed, however, despite (and because of)
attempts by Dissenters and Methodists to revive it, and the eighteenth-century
historian stood in grave danger of re-entering the realm of fiction – whether
he chronicled his own period or attempted to re-chronicle an earlier one. One
response to this danger was a new emphasis on detail and fact. In the absence
of authority, authentication became absolutely crucial and history sought more
and more the eye-witness account, the documentary evidence, the corroboration of multiple testimony, the factual data of place, time, quantity (of people,
money, goods, etc.). But of course nothing sufficed; Marlborough's career and
his wife's virtue were referable not to a God-sustained reality, but only to
political leanings, and one reader's history became another's fiction. Moreover,
in the absence of validating miracles, each historian had to tell his own story;
the greatest historical achievement of the century, Gibbon's *Decline and Fall
of the Roman Empire* (1776–88), confronts the problem with wonderful irony,
authenticating the demise of a civilization which refused the miracle that could
have sustained it. The narrative Gibbon creates, mirrored by many other
fictions in the century, establishes its truth with an onslaught of evidence and
a sly, perhaps nostalgic glance at authority, the loss of which makes both the
empire and its history – *pace* facts – a fiction.

The opposite side of the spectrum from history (at least in the story I am
telling) is romance, a narrative in which ideally we need pay no attention to
factual authenticity, total attention to the authority of the teller, into whose
hands we willingly surrender our disbelief. To return to Elijah for a moment:
before his meeting with the widow he had been fed in the desert by God-
directed ravens; and in the second episode with the widow, Elijah will bring
her dead son to life. The emphasis in these stories is in some respects the
emphasis of scripture itself, an assertion of the power of imagination (the
Word) to create and sustain a world, the people and events of which are real
only so long as the Author maintains his dominion. At any moment we might
suggest that ravens do not feed men, but in God's world they do; and in the
romancer's world, one knight can indeed slaughter armies, one heroine can
be more beautiful and virtuous than all other women, one human being can
be blessed by the care and protection of an immanent God. The heroes and
heroines were most often modelled after classical rather than biblical sources
(although Joseph and David lurk in the suburbs of many seventeenth- and
eighteenth-century romances), both to avoid the appearance of sacrilege and
to create an illusion of exoticism that the familiar Bible could not afford; none
the less, the essential story is that of Moses and the Red Sea, Joseph in the
pit, David and Goliath, Jonah and the whale, Daniel in the lion's den – the

story of the miraculous, in which the priority of the Word over the world is dramatically reinforced.

Despite this echoing of the scriptural narrative, the romance has a difficult time of it in a religious society. While it imitates the sacred text and indeed fully supports its vision, romance is in fact superfluous to it, an indulgent entertainment that easily slides into excess because its details need not be authenticated. The sense of the apocryphal haunts romance and may help explain why it so often is accompanied by assertions of moral intent. In a period of religious intensity, the romance will be bitterly assailed as pagan and libertine, an insidious corrupter of youth and innocence; it will be defended as a reinforcer of the truths of divine justice and retribution, the assertion of God's providential concern for the virtuous. Both views are essentially correct.

Romance has an equally difficult time in a secular society, as Cervantes demonstrated. It is no accident that *Don Quixote* (1605, 1615), more than any other prose work, shaped the course of eighteenth-century English fiction, for it was Cervantes who took upon himself the dismantling of stories shaped by miracles. His insistence on the Sancho-like details of life, his equation of belief with enthusiasm (zeal), are the loud footsteps of secularism; and in England the excesses of the Puritans (and later, the Methodists) would often be tarred with the label Saint-Errantry. Romance could easily outlast the onslaught of the narrowly pious because in the long run it does serve piety, and in stretching the imagination probably serves it well; it could not, however, withstand Cervantes's true assault on its underlying and sustaining premise. Romances such as La Calprenède's *Cassandra* (first translated 1652), Boyle's *Parthenissa* (1654–76), and the immensely popular *Adventures of Telemachus* by Fénelon (first translated 1699) continued to be read by the young and innocent throughout the century, primarily reprints of seventeenth-century titles, although the production never ceased (and continues today, in detective fiction, much science fiction, and the host of drugstore paperbacks about young romance). The spiritual heart of the enterprise was gone, however, and the search was under way for fictional modes more closely reflective of the experience of life in the eighteenth century.

The modes closest to romance accepted (or pretended to accept) piety's hostility to narrative and therefore insisted upon the priority of the moral. One model for such story-telling was Jesus, whose parables gave legitimacy to the use of fiction as a way of overcoming fallen man's resistance to truth; another model was the elaborate 'misreading' of the so-called *Old* Testament as a figure for the *New*. That the eighteenth century was still overwhelmingly Christian in outlook is suggested by the pervasiveness of this mode. Hence, Bunyan's *Pilgrim's Progress*, first published in 1678, was probably the most often reprinted narrative in the next century. Allegory was, from this viewpoint, the safest use of fiction in so far as each and every element of the 'untrue' narrative had reference to an idea clearly considered as embodying truth. In a similar fashion, the brief allegories and moral fables in the *Spectator* (1711–12), the *Rambler* (1750–2), and other periodicals, even those pretending to eastern or mythical settings, shared with *Pilgrim's Progress* the subordination of narrative to whatever other more serious purpose the author could attach to it. In fact, it would be difficult to find in the entire century an author who does not claim that his or her story is designed to promulgate, encourage and reinforce Christian truth, so that whatever the mode in which we finally decide an author might have written, the justifying mode of allegory or moral fable or apologue is never far from consideration. Perhaps this may help explain, if nothing else, the persistence of names like Lovelace and Allworthy in works (Richardson's *Clarissa Harlowe*, 1747–8, and Fielding's *The History of Tom Jones, A Foundling*, 1749, respectively) we have wanted to read in quite another mode.

If the century was clearly labouring under this allegorical necessity, some were beginning to resist it. It is perhaps significant that towards the end of the century Diderot, in *Jacques le Fataliste* (1773), a work that found its origin in *Tristram Shandy*, has his narrator say, 'I plunge into allegory, the refuge of sterile minds' (trans. 1984, p. 15). But for the best example of how the mode itself was being altered, one might consider Johnson's *The History of Rasselas, Prince of Abissinia* (1759). Here is a narrative clearly subordinated to its lesson, and here is an author whose purposes in life all seem directed by Christian faith. Nevertheless the lesson of *Rasselas* remains embedded in the ambiguities of its fiction, in large part because Johnson's Christianity is defined more by hope than certainty, more by limitation than miracle. *Rasselas* opens to us the possibility that at the end of a fable might be something other than the assertion of providential design; 'a conclusion in which nothing is concluded', the title and import of its final chapter, is a significant moment in the history of narrative.

It is rather convenient for my own narrative that a major character in one episode turns out to dominate another as well, for when we look to the other side of the spectrum for a parallel to apologue, we find biography – and Johnson was, of course, the subject of the century's greatest work in the mode, Boswell's *Life of Johnson* (1791). Much as apologue begins as a defensive bulwark of the romance and comes to embody a quite different world view, so biography, in its eighteenth-century development, begins as a defence of the Christian view of history, and ends by turning in a quite different direction. If we again turn to scripture we can see that as well as telling the history of the Jewish nation, it relates the discrete biographies of numerous people, most importantly for the eighteenth-century Christian imagination, Joseph, David, Job, Jesus and, perhaps, Paul. The essence of this biographical telling was, as with history, the presence of divinity within the narrative, the immanence of

God in the lives of specific human beings. Lives of the saints was one such mode, but perhaps because that had a Roman Catholic ring, eighteenth-century England seems to have preferred lives of sinners – beginning with criminals, moving on to generals, nobility and other public figures, and ending with authors. At the beginning, the defensiveness we noted about fiction remained prevalent, whether or not the biography was based upon fact or (equally possible) was a pastiche of fact and invention. Hence every criminal biography, no matter how lurid and detailed the account of crimes committed, always had reference to divine justice, a practice embraced, for example, by Defoe, who scatters pious claims throughout both the *Fortunes and Misfortunes of the famous Moll Flanders* (1722) and *Roxana, or the Fortunate Mistress* (1724) – fictions clearly originating in the mode of criminal biography. So, too, scandal-biography always begins with pious warnings to lead a better life than did the person under scrutiny – and whatever dire catastrophe might have befallen the subject was always credited to an active and concerned God.

Johnson was not only the subject of a great biography, but a great biographer himself – and, more important, a proponent of biography neither of saints nor sinners but of men. Significantly, he still shied away from narrative for its own sake; the purpose of biography was to teach us how to live our own lives. But in practice, especially in the project of his final years, the *Lives of the Poets* (1779–81), Johnson could not simply select those lives which (like a fable or allegory) might produce a clear lesson in piety or faith; and Johnson was too scrupulously honest consciously to reshape the given facts, often provided by other people, to point a moral. As with history, the emphasis shifted to information, the accumulation of evidence as a means of describing or narrating the life of any one person. Needless to say, every Johnson biography bears the imprint of its author, just as does Boswell's biography – indeed, this is precisely why we must consider biography a narrative mode, because facts, data, do not, cannot 'tell' themselves. But by stressing the event over the moral of biographical writing (the need to present both the good and the bad) Johnson led the way for a biography freeing itself from the moral imperatives of the scriptural world.

Nowhere is this more clear than in Boswell's *Life of Johnson*. Despite the piety of the subject, despite Boswell's obvious attempt to make him even more pious than he was, the *Life* emerges as an extraordinarily secular account. Johnson's long life drives toward no apocalyptic goal, no revelatory vision, no dramatic conversion; indeed, the substantial achievements are mostly behind Johnson when the *Life* gets under way in earnest, and the great bulk of Boswell's presentation is of a social (secular?) man among his acquaintances. The favourite sport of Johnsonians over the past thirty years has been to lambast Boswell for the 'falseness' of his biography – he has not presented the 'real' Johnson. A more intelligent approach would argue that the brilliance of the *Life* is precisely in its fiction, its narrative creation of a character whom numerous generations have accepted as the true image of existence, creating a belief in presence we normally reserve for scriptural accounts. As with the presentation of history under the new dispensation, biography became in Boswell's hands a carefully orchestrated accumulation of data, documentation and eye-witness accounts, all of which were rendered necessary when people could no longer be defined in relation to a divine order. To put it in terms of the story of Elijah and the widow, it is no accident that when Hall and Sterne retell the event, they pay little attention to elaborating the character of Elijah, concentrating instead on the widow and her possible motivations, attitudes, variations. Elijah exists in God and needs no other definition besides his source of miraculous power; the widow exists outside God and can therefore be defined by an infinite number of motivational and behavioural alternatives.

What is true for writing about others is also true for writing about oneself. Significantly, Boswell is a practitioner of the mode of autobiography as well – his extensive journal-keeping throughout his adult life shows us again what happens to narrative when separated from the informing scheme of a divinely arranged world. The comparison of Boswell (or of Pepys before him) to the other dominant practice of autobiography during the period, the spiritual autobiographies associated with Puritanism and later Methodism, once again reveals the difference between human beings who consider their lives subject to intervention and susceptible to miracles and those for whom such comforts (and, to be sure, trials) are no longer feasible. Boswell's *London Journal* (1762–3) provides a good illustration of the new mode of autobiographical narrative; without question, the major episodes have been shaped after the fact, and Boswell is acutely aware of the various fictions behind his own self – the notorious brigand Macheath from Gay's *Beggar's Opera* (1728) and the silent, urbane observer of the *Spectator* being only the most obvious extremes. At the same time, however, precisely because a journal depends upon the accidents of time and place, Boswell could not significantly alter the fundamental outlines of his data – he could not, for example, know when he started the *Journal* that the meeting with Johnson would come exactly when it did – and the piety that might have singled out the event as God's great intervention is overtaken in Boswell's narrative by the flow and flux of events that naturally follow the calendar. The injunction to 'Know Thyself', which Boswell assumes as his motto, is not the cry – traditional since Augustine – to know oneself in relation to God; rather, it is an effort at definition in relation to daily, mundane – and accidental – existence and Boswell seems sincerely to believe that if he records the events of his life faithfully he will somehow be able to define himself. There is an innocence here, as in Gibbon's even more painful autobiographical attempt to remember himself (*Memoirs*, 1796), that marks perhaps the true beginning of modern fiction's self-confessional, self-referential compulsions; and when we combine Boswell and Gibbon with Rousseau's *Confessions* (1764–70), we are coming very close indeed to the denouement of the story I am telling of narrative modes in the eighteenth century.

If we return once again to the romance side of our fictional spectrum, we can find a counterpart to autobiography in that narrative mode most congenial to the early part of the century: satire. The most obvious place to look for satire in scripture would be among the patriarchal voices, Isaiah and Jeremiah most particularly. I would suggest, however, that the satiric instinct of the eighteenth century comes closer to finding its origins in an exchange between Nathan and David in II Samuel 12; the plot is worth retelling because it seems to me to embody the dominant narrative of eighteenth-century satire. David had taken Bathsheba from Uriah and then had him killed. Nathan tells David the story (in Jesus-like fashion, one might add) of the rich man who kills the favourite and only lamb of his poor neighbour. David acts with indignant rage over the injustice and demands the identity of the malefactor, at which Nathan brings him up short with the simple phrase, 'Thou art the man'. Autobiography's urge toward self-knowledge is mirrored by satire's urge to make people know themselves, tempered by the ironic awareness that self-deception is the pervasive human disease.

From this perspective, sermon and satire are closely linked, perhaps more so even than sermon and apologue. Satire justifies its quite often 'antisocial' fictions solely by their capacity to change conduct for the better, and the idea of 'better' depends upon a scriptural sense of the world, a world right-side-up. The satirist is narration's version of the Preacher, and the extremes to which he is driven in describing the vices and follies of men are, as with the romance, a means of measuring the power of his authority to know the good – and to make us conform to it. Needless to say, except in some primitive societies where shame is killing, satire rarely works. It shares with autobiography (and the pulpit) the problem of being implicated in its own envisioning, of being a human voice with a divine mission. Swift's instinct to embody that mission in horses rather than human beings was a good one, but it does not resolve the dilemma of *Gulliver's Travels* (1726), the dual vision of man who can and cannot see himself in proper perspective. Nor did Swift's other great satire, *A Tale of a Tub* (1696), resolve its dilemma – that the world he was satirizing had quite usurped the Word. That the eighteenth century was the great age of satire in the English literary tradition may be explained by the fact that its service was *in extremis*, the final bulwark against the increasing failure of scripture to impose its vision upon the narrations of society. That the century also saw the rapid fading of satiric narrative after the deaths of Pope and Swift may perhaps suggest how close to victory was the brave new world of modern secularism.

It can hardly escape notice that I have yet to bring into my story the usual hero – the novel; and that I am in danger now of doing what I discredited at the beginning, namely, bringing it in at long last as the *sine qua non* of the eighteenth-century's narrative enterprise. Let me suggest a quite different track. I believe the modes I have already discussed – history, romance, apologue, biography, autobiography and satire – when combined, mingled or fused with one another, explain almost all of the fiction written during the century. Thus, we might think about *Robinson Crusoe* (1719), to begin where many 'histories' of the novel have begun, as a romance that retells the scriptural stories of Joseph, Jonah, and the prodigal son; but also as a spiritual autobiography, illustrating God's involvement with individual salvation; and as biography (history), since a 'real' shipwrecked sailor's narrative was thought to lie behind Crusoe's. We can find the same melding of modes in all of Defoe's fiction, and in that of Fielding and Richardson as well.

Each of these modes, however, was itself being modified by the age's changing relationship to scripture, as I have been suggesting; what happened to eighteenth-century fiction was not the invention of a new mode of narration but the imposition of a new world view, and each traditional mode of storytelling – or commentary upon scripture – was altered in significantly the same manner to confront this change. Without doubt, much of the change was not conscious, certainly not as a direct challenge to the old order; indeed, the century's narrative is marked far more by a sense of nostalgia than of revolution, and a good argument can be made that we have still not found a way of storytelling totally free from a longing for the past certainties of an immanent and sustaining God.

I return to Sterne's portrayal of the widow of Zarephath's question, 'If this man . . . is able to procure so preternatural a supply for me, whence comes it to pass, that he now stands in want himself' (1760, p. 121). What the question does, with all its innocent simplicity, is demythologize the Word, establishing the priority of the world. It is a question that never occurs in a 'right-side-up' world, because it is unanswerable without a self-reflexive appeal to faith. Eighteenth-century English theology was heavily engaged in just such questions of rational belief, but my point is precisely that once the question arises the process of unravelling has begun – the question, not its answer, constitutes the problem. The great twentieth-century novelist Thomas Mann explores the point brilliantly in *Joseph and his Brothers* (1933–43), a relatively unexplored mine of ideas about narrative art. Briefly put, Mann raises the question of why Joseph did not during his long separation from Jacob send a messenger over the short distance to let him know he lived and thrived. So simple a question, like the imagined widow's imagined question, is absolutely inimical to the world in which their stories take place. Joseph is living God's story, not his own, the separation is at God's behest and reconciliation will be in accord with God's plan. These are not issues of belief or possibilities subject to alteration, but the hard facts of Joseph's reality. One might as well suggest that Joseph should have telephoned his father – the sense of anachronism should be equally strong. Certain questions do not exist in scripture because reality precludes them; when, in the course of commentary, curiosity, imagination, or simply the art of elaboration and adornment leads to such questions, the Word is put into jeopardy and the world begins to define itself anew.

As narratives begin to reflect this new definition, they offer readers stories increasingly distant from the older narratives, though still closely tied to them by tradition, vestigial belief and nostalgia. The term 'novel' arises amidst enormous generic confusions during the century. At no time is it consistently distinguished either in its own right or in contradistinction to other modes. Nevertheless, it is a splendid appellation, for what it does indeed label is the revision of commentary in the face of a *new* order. That is to say, the parallel to the novel is not the romance or any other narrative mode, but the source of narrative modes, scripture in the case of much of Western fiction. The novel is not an individual story or even a way of telling a story, but the collective force of stories told under the influence of a different way of looking at the world. It too develops its own romance, its own history, its own biography, in short its own way of commenting upon the reality embodied by the central text.

We have thus far defined the 'novel' in a primarily negative way, as that which emerges in the place of the truth of scripture. A much more positive definition seems unlikely, in part because the full text of the novel has not been established, in part because our present attempts are so replete with echoes from the earlier system. We might suggest, certainly, that man's autonomy from a Creator is a distinguishing mark, but we immediately confront the difficulty of conceiving a work without an author (a subject of immense importance to both Fielding in *Tom Jones* and Sterne in *Tristram Shandy*). Or we might think that the abandonment of direction (a sense of ending) is most characteristic of our present reality, but continue unable to produce readings or writings that do not answer to satisfying closures (and again, *Tristram Shandy*, the 'most typical of all novels' according to the Russian formalist critic Viktor Shklovsky, [1921] 1968, p. 89), is deeply concerned with this problem). Or, finally, we may simply ask why the world looks so different after the widow asks her question, the undercutting of the miraculous world of scripture that underlies works as disparate (and yet alike) as *Clarissa*, in which human actions succeed in keeping the long awaited miracle at bay until it no longer matters, and *Humphry Clinker* (1771), in which the only 'miracle' worthy of serious attention is the human effort to regain physical well-being. These are the new stories that western European fiction first began to tell in the eighteenth century, stories that commented partially upon scripture, partially upon a world in which miracles had ceased, and the creating and sustaining power of the

Word had less sway than previously over the minds of authors and readers alike. We still do not know what such a world is like, perhaps will not know until commentary centuries from now frees us from belief in the authoritative world defined by that collection of fictions we call novels, but which, one day, will be called, collectively, scripture, because the chosen texts will establish the grounds of our new reality and new Word – a new orthodoxy in which history and romance, biography and apologue, autobiography and satire, will all embody the truth of the core story about men who make themselves and their reality. And as we tell story after story reflecting that 'truth' it will almost certainly happen that someone's commentary, and then another's will begin to push toward a quite *different*, quite *new* story and yet another 'novel' will slouch towards Bethlehem to be born.

FURTHER READING

Battestin, Martin C. (ed.) (1985) *British Novelists, 1660–1800* (vol. 39 of *Dictionary of Literary Biography*), Gale Research Co., Detroit

Braudy, Leo (1970) *Narrative Form in History and Fiction: Hume, Fielding, and Gibbon*, Princeton University Press, Princeton

Damrosch, Leopold (1985) *God's Plot and Man's Stories: Studies in the Fictional Imagination from Milton to Fielding*, University of Chicago Press, Chicago

Davis, Lennard J. (1983) *Factual Fictions: The Origins of the English Novel*, Columbia University Press, New York

McKeon, Michael (1987) *The Origins of the English Novel: 1660–1740*, Johns Hopkins University Press, Baltimore

New, Melvyn (1976) ' "The Grease of God": The Form of Eighteenth-Century English Fiction', *PMLA*, 91, 235–44

Paulson, Ronald (1967) *Satire and the Novel in Eighteenth-Century England*, Yale University Press, New Haven

Richetti, John J. (1969) *Popular Fiction before Richardson: Narrative Patterns, 1700–1739*, Clarendon Press, Oxford

Rothstein, Eric (1975) *Systems of Order and Inquiry in Later Eighteenth-Century Fiction*, University of California Press, Berkeley

Sacks, Sheldon (1964) *Fiction and the Shape of Belief: A Study of Henry Fielding with Glances at Swift, Johnson and Richardson*, University of California Press, Berkeley

Spacks, P. M. (1976) *Imagining a Self: Autobiography and Novel in Eighteenth-Century England*, Harvard University Press, Cambridge

Watt, Ian (1957) *The Rise of the Novel: Studies in Defoe, Richardson, and Fielding*, University of California Press, Berkeley and Los Angeles

ADDITIONAL WORKS CITED

Blair, J. (1754) *The Chronology and History of the World*, London

Diderot, Denis (1984) *Jack the Fatalist and His Master*, translated by W. D. Camp and A. G. Raymond, Peter Lang, New York [composed 1773; first published 1796]

Frye, Northrop (1957) *Anatomy of Criticism*, Princeton University Press, Princeton

Hall, Joseph (1837) 'Contemplations on the Old Testament'. In J. Hall, *Works, A New Edition*, vol. 2, D. A. Talboys, Oxford ['Contemplations' first published 1612–26]

Shklovsky, Viktor (1968) 'A Parodying Novel: Sterne's *Tristram Shandy*'. In J. Traugott (ed.), *Laurence Sterne: A Collection of Critical Essays*, Prentice Hall, Englewood Cliffs [essay first published in Russian 1921]

Sterne, Laurence (1760) *The Sermons of Mr Yorick*, vol. 1, R. and J. Dodsley, London

37

FEMININE FICTIONS

JANE SPENCER

The novel has been presented to us as *the* 'female form' (Miles, 1987); it is more accurate to say that it has always been especially associated with women. Its development in the seventeenth and eighteenth centuries coincided with a historical shift in women's position. In the middle classes women's economic power as earners and producers declined, while at the same time they were being made the centre of a growing cult of domestic life and family affections. Increasingly a woman's experience was supposed to be emotional experience and her distinguishing attribute sensibility. A major strain in the new literary form was concerned with what the Victorians were to call 'woman's sphere'. Much seventeenth- and eighteenth-century fiction – the French romance, the epistolary novel – is concerned with the presentation and analysis of feeling, especially women's feelings. Eighteenth-century comment repeatedly assumed that novels were a female concern, and the presence not only of women readers but of a rapidly growing band of women novelists added to this sense of a female-dominated genre.

The novel, in fact, has been one of the most important media of female cultural authority: indeed the novel's emergence and the emergence of female authority can be seen as part of the same event (Armstrong, 1982). A long line of eighteenth- and nineteenth-century women writers entered public life as writers of 'feminine', domestic fiction. But although the notion of the novel's femininity offered women a position from which to write it did not preclude their work from being devalued as feminine. The feminine associations of the novel have been anxiously contested by male writers. In the earliest years of the novel some of its critics opposed the feminine novel to a masculine model which they claimed would raise the form to a greater dignity, and the comparison has often been repeated in the twentieth century. A male writer's importance may be gauged by his distance from feminine concerns, as in George Orwell's remark that 'one of the surest signs of [Conrad's] genius is that women dislike his books' (in Patai, 1984, p. 18); or a male novelist may be credited with rescuing the form from female domination, as in Andrew Hook's claim that with Walter Scott 'the novel gained a new authority and prestige, and even more important perhaps, a new masculinity. . . . [it] was no longer in danger of becoming the preserve of the woman writer and the woman reader' (Hook, 1972, p. 10). As if such critical moves were not enough to protect men's stake in fiction, feminine fiction itself, when it is valued as such, is often claimed as a male writer's achievement: Samuel Richardson has been praised for his rendering of feminine sensibility, Henry James for being 'perhaps . . . the greatest feminine novelist of *any* age' (M. Geismar, quoted in Robinson, 1986, p. 128).

Women's cultural authority as producers of feminine fiction has always been problematic, both precariously held and restricted by the gender categories on which it relies. At times, some feminist theorists have denied that it has operated at all, claiming that women have been excluded from language. Xavière Gauthier (1981) offers an extreme example of this position, contending that women have been mute throughout history and kept outside the historical process; that women admitted to higher education are forced to learn a masculine language. It becomes a matter for wonder that any women speak at all. Hélène Cixous (1981) offers a less monolithic picture of the linguistic system, acknowledging the failures of patriarchal control that have let women writers slip through into history, but it is in poetry, not novels, that such exceptions occur; novelists, allies of 'representationism' are not going to fulfil Cixous' dream of a writing that inscribes femininity, but belong rather to the majority of female writers who can be discounted because their work is just like men's (1981, p. 248). From this and other theoretical accounts we can infer a completely different gendering of the domestic fiction which conventional thinking types as feminine. The novel of domestic realism is coded as masculine because it claims to represent the real world and to offer the viewpoint of an omniscient narrator, in short because it upholds a patriarchal symbolic order. The new definitions of feminine writing emerging from these accounts have opened the way for radical readings of modernist women writers, but they imply a devaluation of women's writing which is not avant-garde writing.

This devaluation follows from the Lacanian equation of 'the feminine' with everything that is excluded from discourse. Lacan claimed that the psychoanalytical subject is brought into being by entry into the 'symbolic order' of language. Because he described this order as governed by the phallus, as the primary signifier of difference, he implied that women are excluded from full participation in human language and society; in so far as real women do take up a place in discourse, the feminine in them is absent. As Mary Jacobus puts it: 'In this theoretical scheme, femininity itself – heterogeneity, Otherness – becomes the repressed term by which discourse is made possible. The feminine takes its place with the absence, silence, or incoherence that discourse represses' (Jacobus, 1979, p. 12). This scheme sounds suspiciously in line with traditional misogynist notions that women are irrational and should be silent, and there seems on the face of things little reason to adopt it. However, it has been claimed for feminism by the operation of a Derridean reversal. A deconstructive reading claims to undo the hierarchy of opposition set up in such pairs as rational/irrational, masculine/feminine, by showing the first, privileged term to be dependent on the second which it can never completely exclude. Thus the oppressive symbolic order can be seen as continually in danger of disruption by that which it excludes. For Derrida the central opposition to undo is Western culture's privileging of speech over writing: in Derridean theorizing writing is re-defined as a play of signifiers which subverts the attempt to fix meaning.

The investing of both 'writing' and 'femininity' with revolutionary potential has proved very attractive to radical women theorizing about women's writing. Large claims have been made for writing: 'precisely *the very possibility of change*, the space that can serve as a springboard for subversive thought, the precursory movement of a transformation of social and cultural structures'; and still larger ones for feminine writing: 'A feminine text cannot fail to be more than subversive. It is volcanic. . . . If she's a her-she, it's in order to smash everything, to shatter the framework of institutions, to blow up the law, to shatter the "truth" with laughter' (Cixous, 1981, pp. 249, 258; her italics). This equation of femininity with a revolutionary force can be called the first attraction of post-structuralist theory for feminists.

This valorization of the feminine can be criticized as reintroducing old representations of woman. Alice Jardine suggests that to think of a revolutionary move '– beyond the subject, the Dialectics of Representation, and Man's Truth – as a process incarnated by women is to fall back into the very anthropomorphic (or gynomorphic?) images that the thinkers of modernity are trying to disintegrate' (1982, p. 64). One theorist whose work avoids such essentialist dangers is Julia Kristeva, for whom the force which disrupts the symbolic is the 'semiotic', which has its origin in the infant's drives before its entry into language and the institution of sexual difference. Although Kristeva still uses the term 'feminine' in connection with disruptive force, 'the moment of rupture and negativity which conditions and underlies the novelty of any praxis' (Kristeva, 1981a, p. 167), she detaches femininity from the female subject; and thus her ideas have the advantage of working against fixed sexual identities, freeing 'woman' from 'femininity'. This can be called the second attraction of post-structuralist theory for feminism.

However, to the extent that this second attraction prevails, the feminist potential of the first is weakened. Women have less of a special relationship to disruption. Kristeva places women theoretically 'on the side of the explosion of social codes: with revolutionary moments', but claims that because of their social position, they actually tend to align themselves with symbolic power (1981a, p. 166). In literary-critical practice this means that men, because of their social power, become the greatest marginal-revolutionary writers. Kristeva's avant-garde writers, praised for dissolving sexual identities, are Joyce, Artaud, Mallarmé; Virginia Woolf gets an honourable mention but she does not disrupt the symbolic in such a revolutionary way as James Joyce (1981b, p. 138; 1981a, p. 166). When men are credited with being better at giving expression to a revolutionary force still theorized as 'feminine', it seems that little has changed since Samuel Richardson and Henry James were hailed as the greatest feminine writers.

If dissolving fixed sexual identities is the aim, feminists are not helped by a theory of 'feminine writing'. Terry Lovell (1983) points out that there are no grounds for continuing to use the term 'feminine', if the qualities so designated have no special connection with women; and Chris Weedon argues that 'to equate the feminine with the irrational, even if the feminine no longer has anything to do with women, is either to concede rather a lot to masculinity or to privilege the irrational, neither of which is very helpful politically' (1987, pp. 89–90). Once the poetic or 'semiotic' disruption of the symbolic order is seen to have no necessary link with women as a group, it is time to ask what its use for women is supposed to be. The appealing prospect of disrupting a patriarchal symbolic order rests on a gross exaggeration of the power of writing. This is tacitly admitted by some post-structuralist feminist critics, who portray subversion and disruption as no more than a carnivalesque moment, and exhibit a pervasive pessimism about the possibility of lasting transformation of the structures they deplore. Nelly Furman argues that 'Through disruption of the symbolic function of language . . . we are, *even if only momentarily*, in breach of the Law-of-the-Father', and that 'Although *it may be impossible, in the end, to escape the hegemony of patriarchal structures*, none the less, by unveiling the prejudices at work in our cultural artefacts, we impugn the universality of the man-made models provided to us, and allow for the possibility of *sidestepping* and *subverting* their power' (1986, p. 76; my italics). The sidestepping and subversion are doomed to remain temporary and partial triumphs if escape is theorized as impossible. Backing themselves into a corner by theorizing the symbolic order as completely under patriarchal control, feminists start to advocate such daunting tasks as 'forging a new kind of subjectivity' (Minow-Pinkney, 1987, p. 196) and 'reinvent[ing] language . . . re-learn[ing] how to speak' (Felman, 1975, p. 10).

None of this is necessary, if we attend to Adrienne Munich's arguments about the myth of male control over language (Munich, 1986). From the Genesis account onwards, the idea has been put forward that language is a male creation; and the best feminist response is not to reject existing language but to refute this absurd claim about it. Munich's work offers a challenge to

Lacanian feminists who see feminism as a (practically impossible) struggle against the symbolic order: in interpreting that order as monolithically patriarchal, predicted on the phallus as transcendental signifier, they are taking a masculinist myth for truth. A more helpful account of women's relation to language is offered by Deborah Cameron. Arguing against the 'linguistic determinism' of Lacanian psychoanalysis – according to which the subject enters language and society only by insertion into a pre-existing patriarchal symbolic order – she points to integrational accounts of language, according to which language is continually modified in the context of social interactions, rather than itself creating the social. This open-endedness implies that there can be 'no control of meaning by men, no privileging of the phallus as signifier and thus no alienation [of women from language]' (Cameron, 1985, p. 141). As Munich puts it, 'rather than invent female language, we can appropriate what is at least half ours anyway' (1986, p. 252).

This has important implications for feminist criticism of fiction. It suggests that there is no need to valorize avant-garde writing as the main or only means for women to enter and alter patriarchal discourse. The achievements of women in realistic, 'author-centred' modes of writing need not be dismissed as pseudo-masculinity. We can turn again to the study of women's writing in various historical epochs, not to find any essentially feminine qualities nor to claim it as necessarily feminist, but to examine the uses that have been made of changing feminine authorial positions. The notion of 'feminine writing' remains of crucial importance not as a revolutionary operation to be celebrated, but as a shifting historical concept to be investigated. I intend here to outline some of the changing uses of the idea of 'feminine fiction' to be found in three well-known women's novels: Austen's *Emma* (1816), Gaskell's *North and South* (1854–5), and Woolf's *Mrs Dalloway* (1925).

For the eighteenth century, feminine fiction was sentimental fiction, concerned with expressing the finer sensibilities thought natural to women, and it was fiction concerned with a heroine's progress. Its emphasis might be gothic or romantic, with a heroine's adventures and persecutions playing an important part, or it might be more mundane, concentrating on the minutiae of domestic life, but in either case the emotional life and romantic love were central. Feminine fiction might be written by men or women but its appeal was considered to be mainly to the female reader, whose supposedly insatiable appetite for fictions that lent her a spurious importance was a frequent subject of complaint for moralists. The feminine novel as the novel of domestic realism made a respectable place for itself partly by its complex reaction to the equally feminine romance of heroinely adventure: excessive idealization of the heroine, abductions and imprisonments, rapes and escapes, were rejected as being unrealistic, while the essential appeal of romance, its centring on the woman and her emotions, was retained.

By the late eighteenth century a few critics were beginning to acknowledge that domestic stories need not be tedious or trivial: one even remarked that 'The representation of domestic life is a source of moral entertainment, perhaps, the most instructive and congenial to the universal taste of mankind' (*Critical Review*, 1769, vol. 27, p. 297). Early in the next century, Jane Austen, with her focus on the daily lives of genteel women, consolidated the status of domestic life as a proper subject for fiction. In *Northanger Abbey* and *Sense and Sensibility* the parody of and dependence on more sensational forms of feminine fiction is evident, but in her more mature work the situations of romantic fiction fade into the background, and so does the Quixotic convention of a heroine ruined by romantic reading. In *Emma* they are no more than ironic traces. This is the novel in which Austen most thoroughly sticks to her famous focus on two or three families in a country village. Highbury, a rural idyll or a claustrophobic prison, depending on taste, is shut off from the outside world in a way that the same novelist's Mansfield Park or Kellynch and Uppercross cannot be. Emma, who has never seen the sea and finds her one attempt at a solitary half-mile walk to Randalls unpleasant, is the most secluded, least experienced of Austen's heroines. Her imagination compensates for the tedium of her existence, leading her to make up romantic fictions about her acquaintances, which ironically prevent her from noticing the real romance going on. She casts plump, blooming Harriet as the heroine of mysterious origins and interesting love life, failing to register Jane Fairfax's much greater suitability for the role. She accounts for the mysteries of Jane's conduct by inventing for her a guilty romance with her friend's husband, whereas Mr Knightley's imagination, more closely harnessed to observation, comes much closer to perceiving the truth.

Austen does not, like the 'Quixotic' novelists, advocate dull reality instead of false but exciting romance: she shows the real life of Highbury to be more interesting than Emma's compensatory fictions. A key figure here is Miss Bates. Epitome of the restricted life of Highbury, Miss Bates and her trivial chatter are Emma's aversion. It is through her talk that much of our picture of Highbury as a place where no one can do anything without having it endlessly talked over by the neighbours is created. Her interminable gratitude for Hartfield's hindquarter of pork or Donwell's baked apples, her discussion of how little Jane eats for breakfast, establish the solid reality of daily life, and its tedium. What she lets drop about Highbury gossip concerning Mr Elton's courtship of Emma (Austen, [1816] 1981, p. 157) is an unwelcome reminder of the embarrassing reality that has obtruded on one of Emma's fantasies. No wonder that Emma tries to avoid her conversation or to protect herself from it by parody. But she mistakes in seeing Miss Bates's preoccupations as without significance. Her chatter indirectly discloses a great deal of what Austen makes her central concern, minute discriminations of character. Mr Knightley's patient generosity, and Jane's inclination to practise small deceptions to avoid being obliged to it, show themselves in Miss Bates's ramblings about the apples. This 'great talker upon little matters' (p. 18) also unwittingly drops many hints which could have led an attentive listener to realize something of Jane's involvement with Frank Churchill. Her speech about Frank mending Mrs Bates's spectacles shows that he encouraged her to fetch Emma, thus leaving him with Jane. On one occasion she remarks that 'we often talk of Mr Frank Churchill'; and on another the reader may infer from her words that Frank's 'dream' about Mr Cole setting up his carriage can only have been picked up from gossip at the Bates's, which Jane has presumably mentioned to him in a letter (pp. 213, 290, 312). Emma, who is so concerned to read significance into the lives around her, does not hear these hints, either because she is not there or because she listens to the suggestions of her imagination rather than to her neighbour's words. The conversation of prosing Miss Bates, then, is a place where the most 'romantic' events of *Emma* are encoded. Emma's famous rudeness to Miss Bates, when she teases her for saying dull things, is an unkindness rooted in a failure of perception: to the attentive listener Miss Bates's all-revealing conversation is not dull at all.

In *Emma*, Austen reveals the narrow domestic situation of the genteel woman, dependent on 'romance' to introduce meaning and importance to her life. At the same time she criticizes the fantasies Emma uses as compensations for her small world. Real life, the plot suggests, will provide more interesting subjects for observation, and even more romance, than the conventionally romantic musings of an 'imaginist'. While one sort of feminine fiction is criticized, another is firmly established. A genteel woman's ordinary daily life, with its restrictions heightened and exaggerated, is densely charged with moral and emotional significance. Austen's famous narrow focus allows her, while keeping to a restrictive definition of femininity, to claim universality for its preoccupations.

By the Victorian age the novel held a much greater position of cultural authority than in Austen's day. Novelists did not just comment on society but were expected to influence its development. The novel's scope was wider. It might take society itself as its subject, and deal with all classes, with differences of experience in different regions, and with the large-scale problems of industrialization. This was not the move away from the personal that it might at first sight seem: the individual remained central, all the more important for being perceived as potentially the victim of the impersonal forces of history. The Victorian novel's insistence on the importance of the ordinary life is an extension of the domestic concerns of the eighteenth-century feminine novel. The novel, in taking on a wider authority, was not removed from the feminine sphere, for that too was being widened. The Victorian ideology of femininity depended on a separation between men's public and women's private sphere, and women were supposed to be amply compensated for their lack of political and economic power by their feminine influence, which was supposed to soften men's behaviour and indirectly improve public life. In fact, during the nineteenth century middle-class women were taking an increasing part in public life, but this was rationalized by an appeal to this concept of feminine influence (Basch, 1974). Rather than moving out of woman's sphere, they could be seen as carrying the nurturing values peculiar to women into the public world as nurses, teachers and philanthropists. The woman novelist, then, was a partaker in the general expansion of the domestic sphere. The novel, which celebrated feeling, praised domestic life and was meant for family reading, could still be thought of as a suitably feminine form, while its growing scope allowed the woman novelist to comment on political change, factory life, trade unionism, and other supposedly unfeminine issues.

Elizabeth Gaskell was a central figure in the creation of this Victorian version of feminine fiction. Always diffident about her ability as a woman to deal with public issues like industrial relations, she nevertheless made them a central concern in her fiction. In *North and South* she imagines a solution to the industrial unrest of Milton-Northern, a town based on Manchester, through the feminine influence of Margaret Hale. To the Hales, moving to the north from the rural south, industrialization and its problems are new. Margaret's reaction is significantly different from her father's:

> There was something dazzling to Mr Hale in the energy which conquered immense difficulties with ease; the power of the machinery of Milton, the power of the men of Milton, impressed him with a sense of grandeur, which he yielded to without caring to inquire into the details of its exercise. But Margaret went less abroad, among machinery and men; saw less of power in its public effect, and, as it happened, she was thrown with one or two of those who, in all measures affecting masses of people, must be acute sufferers for the good of many. The question always is, has everything been done to make the suffering of these exceptions as small as possible?
>
> (Gaskell, [1845–5] 1977, p. 108)

Here the woman's viewpoint, linked to her more domestic life, is much wider than the man's. Instead of being blinded by the trappings of industrial life she enquires into the essentials, its human effects. Margaret, befriending the Higginses, the novel's representative working-class family, enacts the human connection between classes which the *laissez-faire* capitalist, represented by the mill owner Mr Thornton, sees as an unnecessary interference in the laws of political economy. Her influence is to be much broader than this, however. Through her relationship with Thornton she is to encourage a change of heart which will eventually lead to his own truce with Higgins, and to his experiment of managing his workforce with some degree of consultation between master and men.

Margaret wields two kinds of influence: a general one which arises from her womanly sympathy, and the more narrowly sexual one to which Thornton in particular is susceptible. Gaskell plays the one against the other to indicate the kind of feminine influence she is advocating: a general, all-pervasive one, not confined to the influence of the beloved on her lover. Margaret is surprised by the imputation of a sexual motive to actions which she sees as part of a woman's general duty – crucially, her protection of Thornton from the rioters. Though Gaskell shows Margaret to be mistaken herself about her feelings for Thornton, she supports her heroine's contention that she acted as part of a general 'woman's work' to oppose all violence (p. 247). The extent of Margaret's influence on the relationship between Thornton and Higgins is delicately delineated. She instigates Higgins's first approach to Thornton to ask for work. She has earned the right to ask Higgins to do this by her love for his daughter Bessy, and he claims that his reluctant consent is the first time he has allowed a woman's influence to prevail (p. 383). Thornton, at this point estranged from Margaret, spurns Higgins with blunt references to women's meddling, but later thinks better of his refusal, because he is touched at the thought of Higgins's five-hour wait to see him. He then checks up on Higgins's story – that he is only asking for work for the sake of Boucher's orphaned children – before visiting him at home to offer him a job. Thus it is not to please Margaret, but in obedience to the sympathetic impulses she has helped to arouse that he changes his mind; and his new attitude to Higgins begins with a reluctant admiration for the other man's care of the Boucher children. The feminine influence Gaskell is advocating is the discovery by men of a reservoir of 'womanly' sympathy within themselves, and the consequent transformation of the public world of industry. Margaret's importance lies in her ability to call up the womanly in men.

In the novel's ending, Gaskell tries to unite Margaret's sexual and her general role in her marriage to Thornton, in which she will provide the money for him to begin to humanize capitalist industrial relations. While Margaret will only exercise power indirectly, the womanly powers she represents will be extended, through her husband's agency, to society at large. There is a striking similarity between Margaret's womanly position of indirect influence, and the position of the novelist in Victorian society: expected to influence society by rousing readers' sympathies rather than by directing the course of public events. With the novelist in this feminine position, it is not surprising that critics felt that the novel was a form especially suited to women writers. As one commentator on another of Gaskell's novels, *Ruth*, put it: 'if we consider the novel to be the picture of human life . . . as addressed to human feeling . . . there seems nothing paradoxical in the view, that women are called to the mastery of this particular field of literature . . . only through [woman] shall we learn what resources there are in it for doing God's work upon earth' (*North*

British Review, 1853, vol. 19, p. 168). Gaskell was able to make use of this nineteenth-century version of the feminine to lay claim to a central position as prophet to her culture.

Gaskell, always critical of institutional authorities, sees solutions to her society's problems in the working of a feminine form of authority, exercised by a woman with a hold over men's affections. Margaret, repeatedly described as a stately and imposing figure, exerts considerable authority at key moments: commanding Thornton to face the rioters; insisting that Higgins act as his dead daughter would have wished; and, later, persuading him to visit Thornton. Equally, as a novelist, Gaskell assumed an authoritative voice. Always warmly sympathetic – sometimes sentimental – and concerned never to judge hastily or harshly, she is still quite sure of her values, and is not above preaching them at times.

For the Victorian novelist such an authority was feminine enough, a literary extension of the mother's didactic role; but to a modernist woman like Virginia Woolf, writing some seventy years later, all forms of authority are suspect, associated, even when embodied in women, with a destructive 'masculine' dominance. In *Mrs Dalloway* those who exert their authority to do people good are represented by Sir William Bradshaw, whose persecution drives Septimus Warren Smith to suicide, and whose sinister threat is instinctively divined by Clarissa: 'capable of some indescribable outrage – forcing your soul, that was it' (Woolf, [1925] 1972, p. 204). Clarissa Dalloway herself opposes and undermines such authority. In contrast to Gaskell, who implies that society can be transformed by the way Margaret Hale brings people together, Woolf portrays Clarissa's gathering of people at her party as a fragile attempt to harmonize disparate elements. Clarissa – ill, facing age and death – can hardly hold herself together, much less command others to take on their proper identities. Yet it is this that makes her sympathetic for Woolf. She refuses to judge, even to define: 'She would not say of anyone in the world now that they were this or were that' (p. 10).

Clarissa's 'femininity' consists in a repudiation of authority: she can love life and celebrate it because she does not try to impose herself on it. *Mrs Dalloway* is among other things Woolf's defence of her version of feminine fiction. 'This is an important book, the critic assumes, because it deals with war. This is an insignificant book because it deals with the feelings of women in a drawing room', she was to write in *A Room of One's Own* (Woolf, [1929] 1977, p. 70). Her insistence that the feelings of women in a drawing-room count too can serve as a defence of the kind of feminine fiction exemplified by Austen; and equally as a part of the modernist turn to the inward and subjective as the only true reality. Woolf does not substitute drawing-room feelings for war, though. In *Mrs Dalloway* the First World War and its consequences form a crucial concern. Her point is rather that the war can be understood only with reference to the feelings which her society considers appropriate only to women. The war offered Septimus the apparently straightforward, socially valued masculine role of defending idealized womanhood by stoicism and violent action. He 'developed manliness', which involves a sureness of his identity and the worth of his experience: 'He had gone through the whole show, friendship, European War, death, had won promotion, was still under thirty and was bound to survive' (p. 96). His inability to feel, first noticed when Evans dies, persists and spreads after the war and drives him mad. People react with the lack of comprehension which historians show to have been characteristic of public attitudes to 'shell-shock' victims: why couldn't they just be men, with their feelings unaffected by their experiences? (Showalter, 1987). Septimus, abandoning manliness, turns to the war inside the self, and communication with a man like Bradshaw becomes impossible:

> 'You served with great distinction in the War?'
> The patient repeated the word 'war' interrogatively.
> He was attaching meanings to words of a symbolical kind. A serious symptom to be noted on the card.
> 'The War?' the patient asked. The European War – that little shindy of schoolboys with gunpowder? Had he served with distinction? He really forgot. In the War itself he had failed.
>
> (p. 106)

Whereas Bradshaw cannot understand, Clarissa Dalloway comes to understand something of Septimus without having met him, through sympathetic identification: 'She felt somehow very like him – the young man who had killed himself' (p. 206). The feelings of a woman in a drawing-room reach out to Septimus, destroyed by the masculinist war on feminine feeling.

Authority, questioned in the story of *Mrs Dalloway*, is undermined by Woolf's mode of writing. Like Clarissa she refuses to say 'they were this or were that'. Her narrative voice blends with the inner voice of first one character, then another, and moves between present and past tenses, so that a shifting, fluid sense of place, time and point of view is created. This perspective can be linked to both a feminist and a modernist attack on Victorian realism: 'The real bogey handed on to [Woolf] from the nineteenth century... was the masculine voice of the omniscient narrator.' By continually modulating her tone, Woolf in her novels manages 'to undermine the very idea of any centralized moral standpoint, any authoritarian idea of omniscience' (Blain, 1983, pp. 119, 126).

Feminine writing means very different things to Austen, Gaskell and Woolf. For Austen it means a domestic focus that allows her to insist on the moral significance of apparently trivial concerns: an emphasis shared by Woolf, but transformed in Gaskell to a move to give such womanly concerns more power to act in the masculine public world. For Woolf, feminine writing means a rejection of that very authority which Gaskell claimed in the name of woman, and which Austen, too, through her irony, exercised – the authority to name, define and teach a set of values. Historical changes produce different modes of femininity: rather than fiction being feminine, it is the femininity that is a fiction. But the shifting cultural definitions of femininity have been exploitable by women writers, who have used them to create fictions appropriate to their times.

FURTHER READING

Armstrong, Nancy (1987) *Desire and Domestic Fiction: A Political History of the Novel*, Oxford University Press, Oxford

Basch, Françoise (1974) *Relative Creatures: Victorian Women in Society and the Novel*, Allen Lane, London

Cameron, Deborah (1985) *Feminism and Linguistic Theory*, Macmillan, London

Greene, Gayle and Kahn, Coppélia (eds) (1986) *Making a Difference: Feminist Literary Criticism*, Methuen, London

Jardine, Alice A. (1985) *Gynesis: Configurations of Woman and Modernity*, Cornell University Press, Ithaca

Lovell, Terry (1987) *Consuming Fiction*, Verso, London

Marks, Elaine and de Courtivron, Isabelle (eds) (1981) *New French Feminisms: An Anthology*, Harvester, Brighton

Moi, Toril (1986) *Sexual/Textual Politics: Feminist Literary Theory*, Methuen, London

Spencer, Jane (1986) *The Rise of the Woman Novelist: from Aphra Behn to Jane Austen*, Basil Blackwell, Oxford

Todd, Janet (1988) *Feminist Literary History*, Polity, London

Weedon, Chris (1987) *Feminist Practice and Poststructuralist Theory*, Basil Blackwell, Oxford

ADDITIONAL WORKS CITED

Armstrong, Nancy (1982) 'The Rise of Feminine Authority in the Novel', *Novel*, 15, 127–45

Austen, Jane (1981) *Emma*, Oxford University Press, Oxford [first published 1816]

Blain, V. (1983) 'Narrative Voice and the Female Perspective in Virginia Woolf's Early Novels'. In P. Clements and I. Grundy (eds), *Virginia Woolf: New Critical Essays*, Vision Press, London, pp. 115–36

Cixous, Hélène (1981) 'The Laugh of the Medusa'. In E. Marks and I. de Courtivron (eds), *New French Feminisms: An Anthology*, Harvester, Brighton, pp. 245–64

Felman, Shoshana (1975) 'Women and Madness: The Critical Phallacy', *Diacritics*, Winter 1975, 1–10

Furman, Nelly (1986) 'The politics of language: beyond the gender principle?' In G. Greene and C. Kahn (eds), *Making a Difference: Feminist Literary Criticism*, Methuen, London, pp. 59–79

Gaskell, Elizabeth (1977) *North and South*, Penguin, Harmondsworth [first published 1854–5]

Gauthier, Xavière (1981) 'Is There Such a Thing as Women's Writing?' In E. Marks and I. de Courtviron (eds), *New French Feminisms: An Anthology*, Harvester, Brighton, pp. 161–4

Hook, Andrew (1972) 'Introduction'. In Walter Scott, *Waverley*, Penguin, Harmondsworth, pp. 9–27

Jacobus, Mary (1979) 'The Difference of View'. In Mary Jacobus (ed.), *Women Writing and Writing about Women*, Croom Helm, London, pp. 10–21

Jardine, Alice A. (1982) 'Gynesis', *Diacritics*, Summer 1982, 54–65

Kristeva, Julia (1981a) 'Oscillation between power and denial'. In E. Marks and I. de Courtviron (eds), *New French Feminisms: An Anthology*, Harvester, Brighton, pp. 165–7

——(1981b) 'Woman can never be defined'. In E. Marks and I. de Courtviron (eds), *New French Feminisms: An Anthology*, Harvester, Brighton, pp. 137–41

Lovell, Terry (1983) 'Writing like a Woman: A Question of Politics'. In F. Barker *et al.* (eds), *The Politics of Theory*, University of Essex, Colchester, pp. 15–26

Miles, Rosalind (1987) *The Female Form: Women Writers and the Conquest of the Novel*, Routledge & Kegan Paul, London

Minow-Pinkney, M. (1987) *Virginia Woolf and the Problem of the Subject*, Harvester, Brighton

Munich, Adrienne (1986) 'Notorious signs, feminist criticism and literary tradition'. In G. Greene and C. Kahn (eds), *Making a Difference: Feminist Literary Criticism*, Methuen, London, pp. 238–59

Patai, Daphne (1984) *The Orwell Mystique: A Study in Male Ideology*, University of Massachusetts Press, Amherst

Robinson, Lillian S. (1986) *Sex, Class and Culture*, Methuen, London

Showalter, Elaine (1987) *The Female Malady*, Virago, London

Woolf, Virginia (1972) *Mrs Dalloway*, Penguin, Harmondsworth [first published 1925]

——(1977) *A Room of One's Own*, Panther, St Albans [first published 1929]

38

THE HISTORICAL NOVEL

HARRY E. SHAW

DEFINITIONS

In a sense, historical fiction is as old as literature itself: the *Iliad* recounts the history of the fall of Troy, and the Bible deals with the history of the Jewish people. Similarly, works of prose fiction that might be called 'historical' were written at least as early as the seventeenth century. When we speak of 'the historical novel', however, we tend to be thinking of something more recent. The 'modern' historical novel begins in the early nineteenth century, with a major shift in the awareness of history itself and with a single author, Sir Walter Scott.

This common origin fails to provide a clear identity. The relationship of historical novels with one another may be mapped in a number of different ways, none of them entirely satisfactory. In attempting a definition of the historical novel, we may (as in the 'synchronic' approach described below) explore our own linguistic usages, asking 'What is it that makes us call certain works "historical novels"?' Answering this question is no easy task. To suggest that 'all historical novels must have at least one actual historical figure in them' is to court triviality and inaccuracy. To suggest that 'historical novels trace their descent from the formal conventions and thematic concerns of Scott's novels' is more accurate but remains vague, offering at most a first step toward understanding.

If we seek greater substance, other problems arise. The classic mode of definition attempts to isolate an essence all historical novels share, usually an insight into the workings of history. Instead of asking why we call certain works historical novels, we ask 'What is it that makes a work a historical novel?' – a question that may easily broaden into 'What is it that makes a novel truly historical?' If we answer that 'true' historical novels reveal something about the movements of historical process, we will have isolated the most interesting kind of historical novel. In so doing we will have also decided that a large number of trivial historical novels – and indeed some impressive works as well – are not really historical novels at all, because they fail to reveal historical process at work.

This century's most distinguished critical work on historical fiction, Georg Lukács's *The Historical Novel* ([1937] trans. 1962), hardly pauses for definitions. Lukács has bigger game in his sights – nothing less than the historical spirit itself, and how it becomes available to artistic representation. (Lukács shares this concern with such critics as Erich Auerbach, who like Lukács is rooted in the rich tradition of nineteenth-century philosophy and philology, and whose chapters on nineteenth-century fiction in *Mimesis* ([1946] trans. 1953) provide an illuminating comparison with Lukács's Marxist inflection of that tradition.) For a complex of reasons, some of which we will consider when we come to the New Critics, historical fiction has tended to attract critical suspicion and condescension. Lukács's stress on the importance of historical fiction not only in the development of prose fiction as a whole, but also in the emergence of a truly historical consciousness, has more than any other critical force lent respectability and intellectual interest to an easily dismissed genre. His rich sense of historicity, coupled with his insistence that we attend to historical novels as historical (and not, say, as novels that depict timeless concerns but are inexplicably set in the past), gives his criticism an authority transcending local factual inaccuracies and larger theoretical insufficiencies.

The discussion that follows will deal extensively with the criticism of Lukács, both because of its intrinsic interest, and because it repeatedly raises issues of central importance. It will then turn to an alternative approach, one that stresses the variety of historical interests possible in the genre. Finally, it will consider the extent to which a variety of modern critical perspectives might enrich our understanding of the historical novel, and it will survey certain distinctive developments in recent American historical fiction.

LUKÁCS ON THE HISTORICAL NOVEL: A DIACHRONIC VIEW

For Georg Lukács, history finds a place in European realistic fiction through the emergence of the historical novel, an emergence made inevitable by certain historical movements, especially the eruption of palpable historical processes during the French revolution and its Napoleonic aftermath. According to Lukács, all great art is realistic, but as society moves towards ever greater complexity, the reality it seeks to master becomes increasingly complex. The eighteenth-century novel had begun to achieve a successful representation of the intricacies of class society. Then, with Scott, the historical novel, branching from the realist mainstream, moved such representation into the past, where it could more easily incorporate the historical determinants of social being.

Finally, with Balzac, who self-consciously aspires to write the history of his own time, the insights thus gained re-entered the realist mainstream, enabling novels to deal with what Lukács, following Hegel, calls 'the present as history'.

How does the historical novel capture historical process? Following Engels, Lukács sees the 'typical' character as key. Typical characters concentrate within themselves the salient aspects of a historical moment. They are unlikely to be average members of society, for in average people different historical tendencies blunt one another. Typical characters instead reveal the deep structures of history, and they reveal them as structures in motion. They serve as vectors, indicating the direction of an ongoing, exceedingly complex yet ultimately coherent process. More than that, through what Goethe called 'necessary anachronism', typical characters act as tacit interpreters, mediating between past and present: in their thoughts, words and actions what is implicit in the cultural motivation of the past becomes sufficiently explicit to be comprehensible in our own present. Centred in such characters, historical fiction is able to represent not only a historical milieu, but the movement of historical process itself.

Much recent work on the historical novel aspires consciously or unconsciously, to attain the condition of the 'post-Lukácsian'. A central way of putting Lukács behind one has been to accuse him of espousing a 'naïve reflection theory', a phrase that means different things in different critical mouths. For some critics, any notion that literature can represent an external world, historical or contemporary, is *ipso facto* 'naïve': and if in truth history cannot be represented in fiction (either because there is nothing to represent or because representation is impossible), it certainly follows that his account is fatally flawed. For other critics, 'naïve' reflection theories might be paired with 'sophisticated' theories of literary representation (or perhaps even 'true' theories!). Their complaint is not that any attempt to represent history must be futile, but that Lukács imagines reflection as occurring in too direct a manner (see, for example, Porter, 1981). They tend to be particularly dismayed by Lukács's hostility towards modernist art, by the way his theories seem to valorize only the fiction of the nineteenth century, and not even all of that fiction. Lukács find it easy to chose Balzac over Flaubert or Zola, Thomas Mann over Franz Kafka. But should we accept his judgements and the theoretical grounds on which they rest?

Much of *The Historical Novel* catalogues the failures of historical fiction. Lukács demonstrates how Flaubert descends to exoticism, how Thackeray trivializes historical forces he fails to understand. Lukács explains such failures by recourse to a simple version of the critique of ideology: novels are written by bourgeois writers, and as the hegemony of bourgeois ideology becomes ever more seamless and oppressive, piercing through that ideology becomes an overwhelmingly difficult task. But his disapproval has a deeper inevitability in a critic whose subject is how the historical spirit achieves historical representation.

For Lukács, a truly historical vision sees the past as the necessary precondition of the present. Such a teleological view, natural enough in a Hegelian Marxist, finds its extension in a suspicion that the historical novel is justified only when it fulfils its own teleological mission. In the early nineteenth century, the historical novel brings history into the mainstream; Tolstoy repeats this process in his own works, recapitulating in *War and Peace* (1868–9) the discovery of history and writing in *Anna Karenina* (1874–7) a novel which views the present in historical terms. Finally and perhaps centrally, as he writes in the 1930s Lukács voices the hope that a new socialist historical novel will arise, enriching the fictional mainstream and thereby enabling authors to replace the banalities of socialist realism with a more truly historical representation of the present as history. Teleological thinking pervades Lukács's analysis on every level: to identify the deep structure of a historical moment, Lukács tells us, we must see the past as the prehistory of the present – but also and ultimately we must see both past and present as parts of a teleological process, the underlying laws of which have been elucidated by Marxism.

Lukács's strongly teleological bias is unlikely to sit well with the modern temper, for it is part of a larger rejection of an intellectual framework central to much modern literary criticism and indeed to much modern thought in general. Put (too) briefly, Lukács's career may be seen as a concerted attempt to replace epistemology by ontology at the centre of philosophical speculation. The category of the typical is a means toward this end, for the typical provides a mode in which ontological reality offers itself up as knowledge; so too is Lukács's interpretation of the Marxian concept of 'value' in his late work on the ontology of social being. Lukács is interested in the artistic representation of structures he takes to be knowable and representable. He does not subject such categories as the typical to the withering epistemological scepticism characteristic of much modern thought, but instead employs them for the purposes of historical analysis. However unfashionable, Lukács's interest in teleology and ontology may deserve more attention than it usually receives. For the critic of historical fiction, there may be worse assumptions than that history exists, embodied in patterns that are knowable or at least aesthetically representable.

Whatever we think of Lukács's fundamental philosophical allegiances, it is possible to identify certain problems and missed opportunities that accompany even his best work as a literary critic and theorist. His strongest analyses demonstrate the social and ideological determinants of everyday life: he is particularly adept at showing how great historical novels represent moments when the potentialities of individual characters are enlivened by larger historical and cultural forces. There are even moments when he suggests that certain characters in historical novels might represent history in ways that are not directly mimetic. Thus he sees the hero of Scott's *Waverley* as a means of bringing into focus and contact two opposing historical forces and making those forces intelligible to a modern reader through 'necessary anachronism'. The idea that characters might serve as devices and not as direct representations of historical forces is, however, one Lukács refuses to pursue. Not content with his brilliant analysis of the Waverley hero as a device, he also suggests that Waverley embodies a substantial and direct depiction of the way British history has in very fact occurred: his mediocrity reflects the 'middle way' English history finds in its progressive series of compromises and accommodations.

The proximate cause of this descent into what may with some justice be considered a 'simple' reflection theory may be a quarrel with the Russian formalists, whose earlier works tended to reduce all art to a series of 'devices', thereby severing artistic representation from life in history in a way Lukács would condemn. Lukács may have feared the tendency of his own analysis to make such figures as the Waverley hero seem a 'mere device', even a device that would enable the artistic structure as a whole to represent history. However that may be, Lukács too often seeks to grant every part of an artistic structure a substantial and not simply an enabling representational force with respect to historical reality. His suspicion of allowing 'mere' devices, much less expressionistic elements, any independent place in the process of artistic representation goes a long way towards explaining his inability to deal with most twentieth-century art, an inability perhaps most famously revealed in his celebrated differences with Brecht (see Adorno, Brecht, *et al.*, 1977). The example of Lukács here suggests the need for what we might call a more rhetorical view of historical fiction, a view that would allow us to imagine the historical novel as legitimately using a wide range of artistic means to engage its readers in acts of historical cognition. 'Typicality' may be a centrally important concept for the historical novel, but it hardly exhausts the artistic possibilities of the genre. Yet Lukács's suspicion of the device and of expressionism is not entirely without justification: at the very least, it is important to discriminate between works that project a mere undifferentiated *Angst* before the spectacle of history, and works that embody a representation or even an analysis of historical forces at work.

Lukács's tendency to declare that novel after novel is defective or degenerate must in the end give even his most sympathetic critic pause. The issue is not so much whether one ultimately agrees with Lukács that the richest historical fiction attempts to capture the workings of historical process itself. What is debilitating in Lukács's approach is that he appears to have no way of bringing into focus other, perhaps less important, but hardly negligible aims historical novels have set themselves.

THE GENESIS OF 'MODERN' HISTORICAL FICTION

To give perspective to this defect in Lukács's approach, and perhaps to remedy it, we may usefully recall the enriched perception of history from which the historical novel itself emerged (see, among many others, Berlin, 1976; Meinecke, [1936] trans. 1972). During the eighteenth century there arose in Europe a vision of history with two principal aspects. On the one hand, it was realized that different ages and cultures are systematic wholes obeying their own internal laws. To use a familiar Rankean tag, 'all ages are equally immediate to God': they must be understood in their own terms, not as more or less imperfect attempts to attain a single goal. On the other hand, there arose an interest in the ways in which one kind of society gives way to another. When Scott looked at the Highlands, he was interested in Highland society as a synchronic, systematic whole, but he also wished to grasp the diachronic mechanisms by which it had given way to the society of his own day – and to determine what place if any the virtues of the old society might find in the new.

In balancing allegiances to the synchronic and the diachronic, Scott was hardly unique. Though an interest in either synchronic structure or diachronic progression may predominate in a given historian or novelist, the very possibility of the historicist vision itself depends upon a mixture of both elements. An extreme version of the doctrine that all ages are immediate to God and must therefore be understood on their own terms would imply that as a result of its uniqueness, each historical moment could be understood, if at all, only by those involved in it (or by God). But to reach such a conclusion would be to jettison the very possibility of attaining the historicist insight from which one began. If there were no continuity from one historical moment to the next, we could know nothing about the different moments that constitute history; if the moments were not importantly different from one another, there would be nothing worth knowing.

Useful theories of historical fiction, like the historical vision that gave rise to the genre, must preserve both synchronic and diachronic elements, but they may respond primarily to the one or the other. As we have seen, Lukács's theory is very heavily weighted towards the diachronic and the teleological. An alternative and supplement to such a vision would stress the synchronic and structural possibilities of employing history in historical fiction. Instead of asking, with Lukács, 'how does a given historical novel reveal the progression of history', we might ask, 'what does this novel *do* with history? what effects does it employ history to achieve? in what ways does it incorporate historical structures into its own literary structure?'

A SYNCHRONIC VIEW

If we consider the actual artistic practice of Scott and his successors, we find that history plays a number of different roles in their works (see Shaw, 1983). On the simplest level, history can be drawn upon to vivify or make more poignant a story that might as easily have been set in the present: the assumption here is one the rise of historicism probably helped to encourage, namely that the past has a particular poignancy and vitality. Historical novels written solely on this principle are often (though not always) thin and superficial; in any case, a willingness to recognize that an author is employing historical materials as a source of drama can save the critic from imputing deep philosophical or historical meanings to works innocent of them.

History can also serve as a pastoral region, providing a screen onto which present personal or cultural concerns can be projected and play themselves out. Such projection can be blatant, with modern figures dressed in ancient robes; it can also be rich and subtle, providing fertile ground for the critic of ideology, who will seek to reveal the devious ways in which present interests mould seemingly objective views of the past.

Finally, historical fiction can represent a wide range of historical interests, ranging from the synchronic particularities of a given moment in the past, to (and here we rejoin Lukács) the diachronic working of historical process itself.

By asking how authors have in fact employed history in their novels, we can avoid the rush to judgement and dismissal that at times characterizes Lukács's work. Lukács leaves us in no doubt about the radically unhistorical nature of the depiction of Jacobitism in *Henry Esmond* (1852), doubtless to his credit as a critic and our benefit as readers; he has nothing to reveal about the intricate ways in which *Esmond* projects a whole range of Victorian concerns into the past. The most interesting works of historical fiction tend to intertwine various uses of history in their structures; assuming that a given historical novel is likely to employ history in different kinds of ways simultaneously can help us to unravel its full richness.

OTHER DEVELOPMENTS: ATTACKING AND REDEFINING THE HISTORICAL

The critical fortunes of historical fiction have tended to reflect the genre's close ties with the nineteenth century, in which it flowered. Scott, Dickens, Thackeray, Eliot, and even Hardy all produced at least one historical novel of some distinction, but this consistent pattern does not continue beyond them. In the twentieth century, such authors as H. F. M. Prescott have written remarkable historical novels, without departing radically from the fictional practices of Scott or George Eliot. There has also been a thriving trade in popular historical fiction based on nineteenth-century models. But the major twentieth-century writers have shown relatively little interest in the genre. For some, this was the result of a self-proclaimed wish to transcend the nightmare of history – and of traditional novelistic form. For writers like Pound and T. S. Eliot, an interest in time, tradition and historical process was real enough, but it failed to produce prose-fiction narratives. Yet despite an artistic and philosophical climate that might be seen as inimical to the creation of historical fiction, Faulkner created *Absalom! Absalom!* (1936) and Virginia Woolf *Orlando* (1928), both significant meditations on history and tradition. Such novels as these, as well as the works of such continental writers as Hermann Broch, make it unwise to identify the historical novel entirely with its 'classic', nineteenth-century form.

The various critical movements of the twentieth century have tended to place historical fiction on the periphery. Until recently, they characteristically conceived of historical representation as a backdrop for the timeless. If 'modern' historical fiction arose as part of an enriched consciousness of history, this approach would appear to be ignoring something central. Can a distinctively historical fiction be anything but superfluous, if novels should concern themselves with timeless problems or mythic concerns transcending the 'merely historical'?

The New Critics tended either to ignore or to demean historical fiction. Dorothy Van Ghent, for instance, reveals much in her passing comment that the successful fictional character should be 'an inwardly complex agent out of whose human complexity evolve the event and the destiny' ([1953] 1961, p. 124). If one accepts the notion that milieu in the novel exists to illuminate timeless human problems centred in individual characters, then much of what occurs in historical fiction will indeed seem trivial. To be sure, important issues are at stake here, among them the question of human freedom. For Lukács, one sign of genius in Scott or Tolstoy is that their narratives lead up to great historical figures like Cromwell or Napoleon, instead of beginning with them. By the time we meet such figures, we are prepared to find in them a significance based not on timeless human interiority but on history: we see them as the products of 'external' historical forces, forces which find out a Napoleon and use him for their own ends. The inward complexity of such characters is significant only in allowing them to ride for a time the crest of history. But from a perspective like Van Ghent's, to lead up to such characters in such a matter is to lead up to nothing: it is to fashion an ornate frame but then to place inside it not a portrait, but another, similar frame.

Even in the heyday of such criticism as Van Ghent's, there were always countervailing forces: indeed, we can see them in Van Ghent herself. Such critics as Edmund Wilson and especially Lionel Trilling were always interested in what the novel had to tell us about society. Still, in general only an overriding interest (like that of David Daiches in the fate of Scottish national identity) led critics to adopt a viewpoint that did not elevate the timeless and thereby reduce historical representation to mere 'local colour' (see Daiches, [1951] 1966).

More interesting attacks on the importance of historical representation have come in the wake of structuralism and post-structuralism. Where the New Critics tended to approach historical representation using a set of spectacles that transformed it into 'local colour', much recent criticism devalues historical representation as part of an attack on representation itself. The New Critics elevated, at the expense of the historical, human interiority and eternal values; many postmodern critics elevate a pervasive 'textuality', with history itself becoming one textual reality among others. In such a situation, the special claims of historical fiction tend to evaporate; and in fact, although postmodern criticism has had a very considerable influence on our general understanding of the relationship between history and both historiographical and fictional narrative, little postmodern work has been done on historical fiction *per se*.

A brilliant exception, highly instructive as to the claims and likely results of one branch of such criticism, is Jeffrey Mehlman's *Revolution and Repetition* (1977). This work ignores standard generic boundaries, analysing historical novels by Balzac and Hugo, but turning also to various historical writings by Marx. Mehlman is interested in reading the texts he has chosen in a variety of ways – in showing how remarkable and unexpected details unite them with an author's canon as a whole, in demonstrating how they tend to unravel from within, in pointing out the uncanny marks they bear of later texts by Freud or Derrida or Foucault. He is uninterested in what they might have to tell us about their ostensible historical subjects.

Other schools of contemporary criticism have a more central interest in history than does Mehlman's version of deconstruction. The interest in the critique of ideology shared by the New Historicism, by feminist theories of various kinds, and by Marxist and Foucauldian criticism, might signally illuminate the ideological dividends different societies accrue by embodying in fiction one or another vision of history. Such approaches might, in other words, enrich our understanding of what we earlier identified as the use of history as 'pastoral'. Whether they will in fact do so, and whether at the same time they will wish to take seriously the claims of some historical novels to represent at least part of the truth about the past, remain to be seen.

To take such claims seriously, it seems likely that contemporary criticism would need to re-establish a belief in reference and literary representation, to rebuild the bridge between novels and the historical world recently dismantled. Such rebuilding has already begun on the theoretical level, in the hermeneutical work of such thinkers as Hans-Georg Gadamer and Paul Ricoeur, in the social theories of Jürgen Habermas, and in studies of narrativity as a mode of knowledge historians have for some time been pursuing (see Danto, 1985; Gallie, 1964; Strout, 1981; for Gadamer and Habermas, see Jay, 1982; for Ricoeur, see White, 1987). The hermeneutical school, with its intense interest in questions of tradition and historical mediation, would seem likely to bear fruit in this area (see Holdheim, 1984). But such theoretical speculations have yet to filter down in any sustained way into the critical discourse concerning the historical novel.

AMERICAN HISTORICAL FICTION

The discussion thus far has concentrated on the historical novel viewed primarily as a British affair. Criticism of American historical fiction, though hardly severed from the trends we have mentioned, has taken a somewhat different form. There have been 'timeless' studies of Hawthorne and even Cooper; a long-standing notion that Americans write romances and not novels has made a focus on timeless concerns seem only natural. The interdisciplinary area known as American Studies, however, with its interest in placing American literature in a larger historical and cultural context, has from its beginnings viewed American historical fiction as a reflection of the culture in which it was written and sometimes as an attempt to tell the truth about history. In the case of Hawthorne, for example, Michael Davitt Bell (1971) has studied the way in which 'the matter of New England' was treated by the entire novelistic tradition surrounding Hawthorne, and Michael Colacurcio (1984) has seen in Hawthorne's works a complex meditation upon and deconstruction of political and historical myths. George Dekker's major study, *The American Historical Romance* (1987), is able to focus squarely on the historical element in American historical fiction in part because it refuses to separate American literature from European, and romance from novel. Dekker insists that American historical romances owe at least as much to the British novel as they do to one another, and he imagines a rich counterpoint between romance and novelistic elements: indeed, for Dekker, the romance as a genre appears able to incorporate not only the novelistic, but the epic and mythic as well.

Particularly fertile possibilities for criticism have been opened by the rise of 'Documentary Fiction' in twentieth-century America. By incorporating swatches of journalistic or historical reportage into their novels, authors like Dos Passos, Mailer and Doctorow raise in an acute form central questions about the relationship between history and fiction. And an interest in history has made itself felt in other modes of recent writing as well. Should we consider the Fashoda episodes in Pynchon's *V* (1963) a historical novel in miniature? It is difficult to say whether works like these have moved so far from the historical novel's nineteenth-century origins in Scott that they constitute an independent genre; it is clear that they represent a significant development.

One work on the subject, Barbara Foley's *Telling the Truth* (1986), goes so far as to see historical fiction itself as only one part of a larger grouping called 'Documentary Fiction', a putative genre extending back in history at least as far as Defoe and stretching forward to include much Afro-American literature as well.

CONCLUSION

In many of the approaches we have reviewed, the group of works we call historical novels tends to dissolve. For Lukács, the past as history merges with the present as history; for critics of twentieth-century American fiction the category of documentary fiction, which can be as easily applied to the present as to the past, can envelop the category of the historical fiction; and the list could be extended. Why should the generic identity of historical fiction be so unstable? One reason is that historical fiction lacks its own formal resources; it has always been parasitic on the forms of the novel in general. Another reason is that recent theorists both of literature and of historiography (one thinks particularly of the historian Hayden White, 1973, 1978) have eroded the boundaries between fiction and fact, in favour of a larger textuality and a heightened awareness of the rhetorical nature of language and thought.

Perhaps most important is that, like it or not, we have since the time of Scott lived in a world in which the category of history is as inevitable as that of space. When we pursue a theoretical inquiry with respect to historical fiction, we find ourselves dealing with issues that transcend generic boundaries. Questions involving the representation of historical otherness, for example, are important for any inquiry into the historical novel, yet the problem of historical otherness raises further questions – among them the question of bridging cultural differences in the present and even the question of whether we can know other minds. Similarly, the problem of how historical fiction can refer to the past quickly spreads to realist reference in general, then to fictional reference in general, then to reference itself. This suggests that one of the best reasons for studying the incipiently disreputable, generically unstable group of works called historical novels is not only that they have something to tell us about the past and our ways of imagining the past, though this would suffice. They also raise in an acute form central intellectual problems of our day.

FURTHER READING

Butterfield, Herbert (1924) *The Historical Novel*, Cambridge University Press, Cambridge

Dekker, George (1987) *The American Historical Romance*, Cambridge University Press, Cambridge

Fleishman, Avrom (1971) *The English Historical Novel*, Johns Hopkins University Press, Baltimore

Foley, Barbara (1986) *Telling the Truth: The Theory and Practice of Documentary Fiction*, Cornell University Press, Ithaca

Henderson, Harry B. III (1974) *Versions of the Past: The Historical Imagination in American Fiction*, Oxford University Press, New York

Holdheim, W. Wolfgang (1984) *The Hermeneutic Mode: Essays on Time in Literature and Literary Theory*, Cornell University Press, Ithaca

Lukács, Georg (1962) *The Historical Novel*, Merlin, London [first published 1937]

Mehlman, Jeffrey (1977) *Revolution and Repetition: Marx/Hugo/Balzac*, University of California Press, Berkeley

Rance, Nicholas (1975) *The Historical Novel and Popular Politics in Nineteenth-Century England*, Vision, London

Sanders, Andrew (1979) *The Victorian Historical Novel 1840–1880*, Macmillan, London

Shaw, Harry Edmund (1983) *The Forms of Historical Fiction: Sir Walter Scott and his Successors*, Cornell University Press, Ithaca

Strout, Cushing (1981) *The Veracious Imagination*, Wesleyan University Press, Middletown

ADDITIONAL WORKS CITED

Adorno, T. W., Brecht, Bertolt *et al.* (1977) *Aesthetics and Politics*, New Left Books, London

Auerbach, Erich (1953) *Mimesis: The Representation of Reality in Western Literature*, translated by W. Trask, Princeton University Press, Princeton [first published 1946]

Bell, Michael Davitt (1971) *Hawthorne and the Historical Romance of New England*, Princeton University Press, Princeton

Berlin, Isaiah (1976) *Vico and Herder: Two Studies in the History of Ideas*, Hogarth, London

Colacurcio, Michael (1984) *The Province of Piety: Moral History in Hawthorne's Early Tales*, Harvard University Press, Cambridge

Daiches, David (1966) 'Scott's Achievement as a Novelist'. In David Daiches, *Literary Essays*, Oliver & Boyd, Edinburgh, pp. 88–121 [essay first published 1951]

Danto, Arthur C. (1985) *Narration and Knowledge*, Columbia University Press, New York [first published in part as *Analytical Philosophy of History*, 1964]

Gallie, W. B. (1964) *Philosophy and the Historical Understanding*, Chatto & Windus, 1964

Jay, Martin (1982) 'Should Intellectual History Take a Linguistic Turn? Reflections on the Habermas-Gadamer Debate'. In Dominick LaCapra and Steven L. Kaplan (eds), *Modern European Intellectual History: Reappraisals and New Perspectives*, Cornell University Press, Ithaca

Meinecke, Friedrich (1972) *Historism: The Rise of a New Historical Outlook*, Routledge & Kegan Paul, London [first published 1936]

Porter, Carolyn (1981) *Seeing and Being*, Wesleyan University Press, Middletown

Van Ghent, Dorothy (1961) *The English Novel: Form and Function*, Rinehart, New York [first published 1953]

White, Hayden (1973) *Metahistory: The Historical Imagination in Nineteenth-Century Europe*, Johns Hopkins University Press, Baltimore

_____(1978) *Tropics of Discourse*, Johns Hopkins University Press, Baltimore

_____(1987) *The Content of the Form: Narrative Discourse and Historical Representation*, Johns Hopkins University Press, Baltimore

39

THE NINETEENTH-CENTURY SOCIAL NOVEL IN ENGLAND

LOUIS JAMES

The term 'social novel' was used by Louis Cazamian in *Le Roman social en Angleterre* ([1903] 1973) to identify a body of fiction written on urban and industrial issues, and published between 1830 and 1850. This essay shares his focus, although the definition is to some extent an arbitrary one. As Robert Colby has demonstrated in *Fiction with a Purpose* (1967), the English novel from the 1840s to the 1860s was characteristically concerned with social and moral issues. Further, the term 'social' could be applied to many later novels, through to such works as Robert Tressell's *The Ragged Trousered Philanthropists* (1918) in the twentieth century.

Cazamian's definition is, however, useful. It not only brings together a group of works with a shared concern but different emphases, including 'the condition of England', 'the industrial' and 'the social problem' novel, it also identifies the way in which they approached their subject. The 'social novel' as Cazamian explored it grew out of a profound realignment of public consciousness, brought about by the urban and industrial changes at the beginning of the nineteenth century. The genre lost its impetus as this concern merged into an acceptance of sociological forces which denied the individual capacity for moral action. For a matter of some thirty years the novel became an imaginative arena in which human issues could be argued. By the time George Gissing and Arthur Morrison wrote, characters in 'social' fiction had become helpless victims in the web of social evolution. The novel had lost its role as an area of significant debate. Further, the growing concern with 'realism' from the 1860s paradoxically limited the novel's ability to explore social issues, for the focus on accuracy of description, the emphasis on 'objective truth', emptied the subject of its symbolic and metonymic significance.

Since Cazamian wrote his study, different approaches to the subject have evolved. It is therefore useful to preface a brief account of the genre itself with some notice of the ways in which the subject has been analysed since 1903. For Cazamian, the 'social novel' was a historical fact, a group of fictional works growing from and influencing the Victorian period. In form, it combined the arts of reportage and literature, and was affected by biographical and historical factors. This approach is well illustrated in Kathleen Tillotson's *Novels of the Eighteen-Forties* (1954).

By the 1950s current criticism was being challenged by Leavis's focus on reader response to the 'life-enhancing' values of literature (his study of the novel, *The Great Tradition*, had appeared in 1948) and from the insights of Marxism. Georg Lukács's *The Historical Novel* was written as early as 1936–7, but it was published in England only in 1962. Marxist influence on British and American novel criticism has been late, indirect and generalized. Nevertheless Arnold Kettle's *Introduction to the English Novel* (1951–3) and Raymond Williams's *Culture and Society 1780–1950* (1958) brought socialist perspectives to bear on the subject as have, more recently, such works as David Craig's *The Real Foundations: Literature and Social Change* (1974) and Igor Webb's *From Custom to Capital: The English Novel and the Industrial Revolution* (1981). Although not specifically on the 'social novel', Terry Eagleton's Marxist study of the Brontës, *Myths of Power* (1975), has also been influential. It is now difficult to consider the novel without an awareness of class perspectives.

This includes considering the audience for which the fiction was written. The Victorian novel as conventionally identified was in fact read by a small minority of the Victorian public: as Gertrude Himmelfarb has noted (1984, p. 435), the 'social novels' most Victorians read were not by George Eliot or even by Dickens, but by an author few academic critics have noticed, G. W. M. Reynolds. Works read by the Victorian masses for entertainment such as Reynolds's *The Mysteries of London* (1845–8), or those read by Radical working-class readers as sampled in Y. V. Kovalev's *An Anthology of Chartist Literature* (1956), still await extended study.

As the implied reader has been given greater consideration in interpreting the text, the focus has shifted from the fiction as documentary evidence to examination of the discourse of the 'social novel' itself. Particular attention has been paid to the 'the poor', which has become recognized as a symbol rather than an objective reality. Sheila Smith's *The Other Nation: The Poor in English Novels of the 1840s and 1850s* (1980) approached the issue through a multidisciplinary approach, exploring the transformations of 'reality' that occur between fiction and the visual arts, and parliamentary reports and journalism. Gertrude Himmelfarb in her massively researched study (*The Idea of Poverty*, 1984) took a more directly historical approach. Starting her investigation with the political economy of Adam Smith and Malthus, she examined the different modes in which the poor were portrayed. These include the various images in Dickens, the 'Gothic Poor' of G. W. M. Reynolds, Mayhew's journalism, and the 'Industrial Poor'. Thus a genre which Cazamian saw as a reflection of the times, now focuses a debate concerning the way the novel shapes and refashions history. This approach is implicit in Kate Flint's anthology of source materials for use in studying the fiction, *The Victorian Novelist: Social Problems and Social Change* (1987).

Finally, contemporary theory has considered the way the rhetorics of discourse through which the novel is told themselves have social significance. Although he died in Russia in 1975, the impact of M. M. Bakhtin in the West has come largely in the 1980s. His work *The Dialogic Imagination* (trans. 1981) contains little specific criticism of the Victorian social novel, but its ideas have influenced work in the field. 'Dialogism' declares that a 'single' literary form does not exist; it is made up of a variety of forms and meanings, all of which affect each other, so that the total meaning can only be understood in terms of interaction within the greater whole.

The implications of 'dialogism' can be seen in a work such as Catharine Gallagher's *The Industrial Reformation of English Fiction, 1832–1867* (1985). This on the one hand examines the metaphysical debates that underlie social issues in the fiction, in particular those concerning individual free will, social control and historical inevitability. Is John Barton in Elizabeth Gaskell's *Mary Barton* (1848), for instance, a tragic hero responsible for his fate, or a helpless victim of the industrial situation? On the other hand Gallagher identifies the range of available rhetorics – such as realism, melodrama, tragedy, and the domestic tale – each of which implies certain attitudes to the 'reality' it represents. Thus 'realism' involves a neutral record of appearances; melodrama, an identification of opposing and absolute moral forces; while tragedy explores a conflict within the main protagonist. By identifying the often contradictory mixture of forms of fiction contained even in single novels, Gallagher convincingly points to uncertainty and confusion within the attitudes of the Victorian author. Her important study breaks new ground, but paradoxically points up the importance of the earlier historical approach. For her findings are limited by her uneven knowledge of the literary forms she examines and their social context, particularly concerning the 'popular' ones such as melodrama and cheap magazine stories. The following argument will draw on contemporary critical developments, but as far as possible will ground them in a historical social and literary context.

One can place the 'social novel' within four overlapping phases. The first, pre-Victorian, stage saw the realignment of earlier forms to express the changing urban and social consciousness of the nineteenth century. It includes such diverse writing as the Jacobin novel, the novels of Sir Walter Scott and the fictionalized journalism of Pierce Egan. The second phase can be identified with Dickens, and establishes the imaginative viability of the city. The third incorporates economic and political debate within a fictional framework – the novels of Disraeli and Gaskell. Finally, the social issues become absorbed within a focus on the social organism as a 'given' to be analysed rather than debated, while the possibility of objective realism is itself becoming questioned. This phase can be identified with the work of George Eliot, and the influence of popular Darwinism.

The first phase has been charted by Gary Kelly in *The Jacobin Novel 1780–1805* (1976). This group of novels grew from the ferment surrounding the French revolution and was related to the early romantic movement. It dramatized the human suffering caused by social institutions, in particular those of class and the legal system. In form it was rooted in the eighteenth-century novel of sentiment and manners rather than in social realism. Nevertheless in such works as Charlotte Smith's *The Romance of Real Life* (1786), Holcroft's *Anna St Ives* (1792) and, most notably, Godwin's *Caleb Williams* (1794), this fiction does explore personal and psychological aspects of social conflicts. *Caleb Williams* centres on the relationship between master (Falkland) and servant (Williams) as the shared knowledge of a crime Falkland has committed corrupts and destroys both. It looks forward to *Frankenstein* (1818) by Godwin's daughter, Mary Shelley, which also explores the complex web of identity, power and responsibility. As George Levine has demonstrated in *The Realistic Imagination* (1981), this gothic tale is grounded in an imaginative conception of social relations for which later, more literal, fiction lacked a language. Gaskell in *Mary Barton* (1848), searching for an image to describe the uneducated working classes, turned (confusedly) to 'Frankenstein, that monster of many human qualities' (ed. 1970, pp. 219–20).

The move towards a more naturalistic engagement with reality came with the work of two totally dissimilar but immensely popular writers. Sir Walter Scott dominated the English novel from 1814 to 1830. His Chaucerian sympathy with human nature regardless of class, sex or culture, and his historical sense of the way individuals are conditioned by social context, freed the genre from earlier constrictions. The weakness of his plots and conventional heroes and heroines became a strength, turning the focus, as Lukács noted, on the 'ordinary' hero and the presentation of common life. Yet at the same time Scott infused the ordinary, through his historical sense, with romantic interest. He created a paradoxical fusion of Romanticism and Realism that was to inform the mid-Victorian and distinguish it from parallel developments on the Continent.

Scott wrote centrally of the Scottish Highlands and Lowlands. The urban world came sharply into focus with Pierce Egan's *Life in London* (1820–1). Egan was a sporting journalist with a vivacious curiosity and delight in all aspects of city life. No court, street, alley or cellar, he wrote, was too obscure to have a history and an interest, and he brought London into the field of fiction through the adventures of the innocent Jerry Abershaw, under the tutelage of Corinthian Tom, man about town. Further, he took the contrast between rich and poor, the 'light' and the 'dark', and made it his organizing principle for experiencing the city, alternating scenes of high life with those of the London underworld. The work was hugely popular. Carlyle complained that it dominated the London stage in the 1820s, and Egan himself in 1830 listed more than a hundred derivative works. It made town life accessible for fiction in a new way.

Egan was a writer of limited imagination and inflexible style, and his fiction is heavily dated. From the appearance of *Sketches by Boz* (1836–7), however, his world was expanded by the hugely talented Dickens – who also began writing as a journalist. Like Egan, Dickens showed the romantic side of everyday urban life: indeed, he created an inverse romanticism out of its squalor and human degradation. Egan described the city: for Dickens it became a moral and social geography. *Oliver Twist* (1838) sensationally 'exposed' Jacob's Island and the criminal areas around Farringdon Street: but it was also the metaphysical stage on which the demonic Fagin attempted to entrap the preternaturally good Oliver into ways of evil. In Dickens's work London places and objects carry moral weight. In *Dombey and Son* (1848) the state of Dombey's soul is reflected in the various changes to his house and the state of his city office; Camden railway cutting images the cosmic crisis of England moving into the railway era. In his later work Dickens became more rather than less symbolic in his use of urban landscapes. In *Bleak House* (1853), Chancery becomes the centre of the fog of litigation enveloping Britain; in *Our Mutual Friend* (1865) the financial world becomes contracted to the filth of urban dust heaps.

Dickens is at once central and untypical in the 'social novel'. A novelist universally associated with social issues, he was attacked for allowing his imagination to come between his writing and his subject, and his underlying attitudes can be evasive. In his fiction, most characters have a job; but Dickens rarely shows them at work. His novels are centrally about social relationships, yet his model for this would seem, as Cazamian noted, a perpetual Christmas of warm feelings, and the benevolent paternalism of Fezziwig in *A Christmas Carol* (1843). Even his explicit working-out of class and industrial issues in *Hard Times* (1854), based on a hasty visit to a factory strike in Preston, identified the factory problem not with economics but with the Utilitarian denial of human imagination, and juxtaposed the factories of Coketown against the bizarre world of Sleary's travelling circus. In his later novels Dickens's sense of Victorian society becomes increasingly dark, and his heroes and heroines express the need to escape its corruption, to preserve a private integrity, as with Esther Summerson (*Bleak House*) and Amy Dorrit (*Little Dorrit*, 1857).

Yet the lack of structured social theory opened the way for imaginative explorations of moral complexity. In *Oliver Twist*, for instance, from one perspective Oliver is the obvious hero and his final prosperity is a victory for bourgeois values of honesty and decency. Yet from another, middle-class values are identified with the workhouse and the heartless magistrate, Fang. As Arnold Kettle pointed out (1951–3, vol. 1, pp. 123–38), Fagin and the Artful Dodger by expressing a human energy in the face of an exploitative and heartless society can also be seen as the heroes. The ambivalence is expressed through the mixture of styles within the novel: Oliver Twist is presented in an aura of domestic melodrama, the Artful Dodger with comic realism. Similar complexity exists in Dickens's other works, including *Hard Times* (see Gallagher, 1985, pp. 149–66). Yet this does not imply contradiction: the imaginative perspectives complement each other, reflecting the ambiguous position of the middle-class novelist in terms of Bahktin's 'dialogic imagination'. Dickens's championing of Sleary's magical circus against the schoolroom in *Hard Times* is a paradigm of his contribution to the social novel: he transformed 'facts' through the entertainment of the imagination, making the reader see social reality in a new light.

To consider our third category of social novel, other fiction confronted issues of political and economic issues within more naturalistic parameters. Appearing before Dickens began writing, Harriet Martineau's *Illustrations of Political Economy* (1832) sold 10,000 copies in serial form, and her uncompromising advocacy of Utilitarian tenets, regardless of the promptings of sympathy, was part of the social fiction against which Dickens was to react. Her novellas, *The Hill and the Valley*, *A Manchester Strike* and *Weal and Woe in Gaveloch*, portray industrial distress and political action with insight and some compassion, but can offer no remedy for falling wages and unemployment other than birth control. The economic realities of excessive labour supply have to be accepted. This stance found its implacable opponent in Thomas Carlyle, who turned from the logical basis of Utilitarianism to the moral categorical imperatives of Kant and the transcendental idealism of Goethe. Social reality was but the symbolic clothing for the Immanent, and in *Signs of the Times* (1829), he fulminated against the contemporary worship of 'Mechanics' in place of 'the mysterious springs of Love, and Fear, and Wonder, of Enthusiasm, Poetry, Religion' (ed. 1971, p. 72). Carlyle's assertion of human values in the face of cold analysis was influential in directing the social novel in idealistic directions: Dickens dedicated *Hard Times* to Carlyle, and those who followed a more directly representative strategy found in Carlyle the vindication of a humanistic approach to social fiction.

Thus while the 1840s was marked by an intense debate about the state of the nation, by parliamentary reports, blue books and journalistic investigation, it also saw a spate of imaginative activity, exploring social issues in terms of fiction, drama and the visual arts. It was an era that turned to the idealistic modes of melodrama. Frances Trollope's *Michael Armstrong the Factory Boy* (1840) and Elizabeth Stone's *William Langshawe, the Cotton Lord* (1842) resolved economic issues in terms of good overcoming evil, although Charlotte Elizabeth Tonna's *Helen Fleetwood* (1838–40) offers a less compromising focus on the underlying injustices of the factory system. The conflicting requirements of investigative fiction and its resolution in individual and human terms, put pressures on narrative form. This was answered in different ways, one of the most striking of which was that of Benjamin Disraeli.

Of his trilogy, *Coningsby* (1844) is a *roman-à-clef*, dramatizing the political movements of the 1830s; *Tancred* (1847) is a mystical work set partly in the Holy Land, where his eponymous hero searches for enlightenment; *Sybil* (1845), by contrast, focuses on the forties, and the division between the traditional south and the industrial north. The grim wastes of the industrial Mowbray are given a realistic treatment, based on parliamentary blue books; naturalistically portrayed, too, is the amoral, vital Devilsdust, the young working-class representative of the new England. Disraeli asserts his Tory belief in the need for a governing hierarchy by satirizing the effete English aristocracy, but also shows the industrial masses to be in need of political direction. The Young England vision of leadership is heightened by theatrical presentation: Charles Egremont, younger son of the oppressive Lord Marney, sees a radiant figure gliding by moonlight among the shadows of the ruined Marney Abbey. She is Sybil, significantly the daughter of the Chartist Walter Gerard; rejected because of his rank, Charles finally wins her hand after proving himself among the poor. In the novel's climax, the abbey is burned, and Lord Marney killed by the rioters. In the process he reveals papers that prove Sybil's rights to the lands of Marney. A heady mixture of blue book realism, operatic symbolism and political theory, *Sybil* remains a unique and effective social novel.

An interesting comparison to Disraeli's work is provided by G. W. M. Reynolds's *The Mysteries of London* (1846–8). Although a radically (in both senses of the word) different work, looking to Eugène Sue's sensational *Mysteries of Paris* (1842–3) rather than to Disraeli, it has its own flamboyant style and shares similar strategies. Reynolds also shows us a social world divided and opposed; both old aristocracy and the poor are rejected. Indeed, Reynolds presents a view of the poor dehumanized even below those portrayed in *Sybil*; society is held together by a web of the crime and violence created by economic exploitation. Throughout the immensely long tale, serialized week by week in penny numbers, the 'documentary' dimension is set against a struggle, heightened by melodramatic presentation, between the virtuous Richard and his unscrupulous capitalist brother Eugene. The latter is finally murdered by his French valet, leaving Richard to depart for Europe as a freedom fighter. Reynolds, for all his Chartist sympathies, offers little hope of leadership from the proletariat, and the circulation of 40,000 claimed for *The Mysteries of*

London suggests his views were acceptable to many working-class readers (James, 1974, p. 165).

If Reynolds portrayed a bestialized poor, Elizabeth Gaskell's fiction is distinguished by its sympathetic insights into the life of the Manchester workers. The opening chapters of *Mary Barton* (1848) are unrivalled in their warmth and accuracy of perception. Yet, even here, the pressures of reconciling an objective account of the social situation with analysis and evaluation splits the narrative. The murder of a millowner's son by an embittered worker is largely based on the notorious murder of Thomas Ashton by the mill-hands Joseph Mosley and James Garside in Woodley. Yet the murder had taken place in 1831, and even then was untypical: by making it central to a novel set contemporaneously in the 1840s, Gaskell was heightening the drama at the expense of objectivity, and she confuses Chartism, Communism and trade unionism as the violent underbelly of industrial despair. The shifting of authorial attitudes, as marked by changing narrative modes, has been noticed above, and the novel's double closure evades much of its early insights. It offers the dying John Barton, in a Christ-like tableau, being reconciled with his victim's father; and finally a summer scene in a country garden overseas between the married Mary, Jem and their child.

Gaskell's subsequent novel *North and South* (1854–5) juxtaposes the three carefully characterized worlds of the south (Helstone), Manchester, and, briefly, commercial London. The issues of class and regional difference are given fictional form by the hard-fought romance between the southern Margaret Hale and Henry Thornton, factory owner. The crisis precipitated by a lock-out is resolved in melodrama as Margaret faces the mob and receives a missile aimed at Thornton, and their final marriage is paralleled by a growing co-operation between millowner and the workers. It is in many ways a more accomplished and logical work, but it lacks the fresh immediacy of *Mary Barton*.

By the end of the forties, the debate over Utilitarianism was giving way to the religious controversies aroused by Evangelicalism, the Oxford Movement, and theories of evolution. Charles Kingsley's ebullient *Yeast* (1851, but first published in serial form in 1848), consists largely of dialogues between Lancelot Smith, a rich merchant representing the questing middle classes, and a series of interlocutors, notably the Cornish gamekeeper and ex-miner Tregarva. The long discourse concludes with a mystical intimation that Lancelot will work towards the regeneration of England through the tenets of the 'muscular Christianity' of Evangelical Anglicanism.

Kingsley's theories are fleshed out in *Alton Locke* (1850), based on the lives of the working-class poets Thomas Cooper and William Lovett, and exposing the appalling conditions of the sweatshops of east London. These turn Locke to Chartism, under the influence of which he riots, is imprisoned, and converted to Christian Socialism shortly before his death. This intermittently powerful work includes a detailed documentation which reflects a new style of investigative journalism. This was being forged in particular by Henry Mayhew, and was to culminate in his *London Labour and the London Poor* (1860). Kingsley has himself been inspired by Mayhew to contribute his investigation into the tailoring sweatshops, 'Cheap Clothes and Nasty', to *The Morning Chronicle*, and he introduced this reportage directly into *Alton Locke*.

Before he dies, Locke experiences an extraordinary dream of evolution, from creation to the advent of mankind. Charles Darwin was only to publish *The Origin of Species* in 1859, but as Gillian Beer has shown (1983, *passim*), evolutionary ideas were influential at least from the publication of Charles Lyell's *Principles of Geology* (1830–3) and Robert Chambers's *Vestiges of the Natural History of Creation* (1844). There is a link between Mayhew's investigative journalism, evolutionary theory, and the demise of the social novel of the forties, for each in its way is a reflection of a scientific rather than humanitarian concern, a rejection of moral and social absolutes. George Eliot, finely analysed in terms of Darwin by Gillian Beer (1983, pp. 149–67), portrays *Middlemarch* (1870) as a web of interconnection in which characters are trapped by time and kinship, from which the only escape is into the private world suggested by another image, that of the labyrinth.

This sense of closed possibilities informs the major novels on social themes in the latter part of the century. They range across George Moore's 'realist' depiction of life in the Potteries, in *The Mummer's Wife* (1885), and of the servant class, in *Esther Waters* (1894); Gissing's despairing accounts of the life of the poor in *Demos* (1886) and *The Nether World* (1889); and Arthur Morrison's accounts of London East End life, notably *A Child of the Jago* (1896). The failure of human free will in an alien universe also haunts Thomas Hardy's great rural novels (1872–95).

The 'social novel', then, was linked to its period in ways far more complex than those envisaged by Cazamian. Its inherent problems of both form and content reflected the failure of British society to resolve the issues raised by the industrial revolution. Particularly significant was the inability of the socialist movement to create fiction embodying truly radical perspectives on the class struggle. Engels praised Margaret Harkness's *A City Girl* (1887) for a positive socialist approach to urban realism, but her gifts as a writer were minor. Robert Tressell's *The Ragged Trousered Philanthropists*, the first truly socialist classic of working-class life, appeared at the end of the First World War. William Morris created a socialist view of English society in *News from Nowhere* (1891); but, long after 1952, the year in which it was set, it remains as much a utopian fantasy as when it was written in 1891.

FURTHER READING

Bakhtin, M. M. (1981) *The Dialogic Imagination*, translated by C. Emerson and M. Holquist, University of Texas Press, Austin

Beer, Gillian (1983) *Darwin's Plots: Evolutionary Narrative in Darwin, George Eliot, and Nineteenth-Century Fiction*, Routledge & Kegan Paul, London

Cazamian, Louis (1973) *Le Roman social en Angleterre*, translated by Martin Fido as *The Social Novel in England, 1830–1850*, Routledge & Kegan Paul, London, 1973 [first published 1903]

Colby, Robert (1967) *Fiction with a Purpose*, Indiana University Press, Bloomington

Flint, Kate (1987) *The Victorian Novelist: Social Problems and Social Change*, Croom Helm, London

Gallagher, Catharine (1985) *The Industrial Reformation of English Fiction, 1832–1867*, University of Chicago Press, Chicago

Himmelfarb, Gertrude (1984) *The Idea of Poverty: England in the Early Industrial Age*, Faber & Faber, London

James, Louis (1974) *Fiction for the Working Man 1830–50*, Penguin Books, Harmondsworth [first published 1963]

Kettle, Arnold (1951–3) *An Introduction to the English Novel*, 2 vols, Hutchinson, London

——(1958) 'The Early English Social-Problem Novel'. In Boris Ford (ed.), *The Pelican Guide to English Literature*, vol. 6, Penguin, Harmondsworth, pp. 169–87

Smith, Sheila (1980) *The Other Nation: The Poor in English Novels of the 1840s and 1850s*, Clarendon Press, Oxford

Tillotson, Kathleen (1954) *Novels of the Eighteen-Forties*, Oxford University Press, London

Williams, Raymond (1958) *Culture and Society, 1780–1950*, Chatto & Windus, London

ADDITIONAL WORKS CITED

Carlyle, Thomas (1971) *Selected Writings*, Penguin, Harmondsworth

Craig, David (1974) *The Real Foundations: Literature and Social Change*, Oxford University Press, London

Eagleton, Terry (1975) *Myths of Power*, Macmillan, London

Gaskell, Elizabeth (1970) *Mary Barton*, Penguin, Harmondsworth [first published 1848]

Kelly, Gary (1976) *The Jacobin Novel 1780–1805*, Oxford University Press, London

Leavis, F. R. (1948) *The Great Tradition*, Chatto & Windus, London

Levine, George (1981) *The Realistic Imagination*, University of Chicago Press, Chicago

Lukács, Georg (1962) *The Historical Novel*, Merlin, London [first published 1937]

Webb, Igor (1981) *From Custom to Capital: The English Novel and the Industrial Revolution*, Cornell University Press, Ithaca

40

THE REALIST NOVEL:
THE EUROPEAN CONTEXT

F. W. J. HEMMINGS

Realism is a term that gained currency on the continent of Europe about the middle of the nineteenth century, to denote a new mutation in the development of prose fiction which had manifested itself a couple of decades earlier, i.e. around 1830. It was not, at that stage, a recognizable movement, as Romanticism had been, and it was only by analysing the kind of writing attempted by its major proponents that critics were able to give the term a definite meaning. Since the realistic mode affected almost every aspect of prose fiction, it is difficult even today to reduce it to a simple, all-encompassing formula; the most that can be done is to suggest a number of ways in which the realist novel, in France and Russia to begin with and later on in Germany, the Iberian peninsula and Italy, developed its particular form, distinct from what was taking shape simultaneously in Anglo-Saxon cultures. Not all the major European realists adhered to every one of these guidelines, and such prescriptions as can be deduced never formed a programme to be put into operation by a group of writers. But with hindsight one can see that, broadly speaking, there were certain overriding objectives that the major European realists had set their sights on, and that these differed in many respects from what their contemporaries in Great Britain and the United States were aiming for.

What in the first place distinguished them was the keen interest they showed in the broader political and social developments of their time. It was particularly in the work of the two French writers Stendhal and Balzac, who can be regarded as the 'founding fathers' of nineteenth-century realism, that this feature first became apparent, and for sound reasons: for France, more than any other country, had since 1789 been subject to a series of political and social convulsions, the full import of which was still, in 1830, far from certain; any novelist who could offer a convincing analysis of the contemporary state of society and could discern the significant trends of its future development could be sure of a wide readership, at any rate among the more thoughtful members of the public. Stendhal, who came to the novel relatively late in life (he was 47 when he produced his first masterpiece *Le Rouge et le Noir*, 1830, translated as *Scarlet and Black*), had served an apprenticeship as a political journalist writing, from 1822 onwards, 'letters from Paris' for publication in various London periodicals; but even if one discounts this experience, he had all his life been following with the closest attention the conflicting subterranean pressures that were to burst through the thin crust of ordered society in the explosion of the 1830 revolution. Written immediately prior to this event, *Scarlet and Black* illustrates all these contemporary currents: the struggles of the old aristocracy to reassert their authority after the catastrophic events of the earlier (1789) revolution; the current reactionary religious revival spearheaded by the Jesuits; and the new danger to social stability presented by the educated, ambitious but underprivileged youth of the country incarnated in his hero, Julien Sorel.

Balzac, who belonged to a younger generation than Stendhal, embarked on his career as a novelist at about the same date, and, not surprisingly, some of the themes developed in his work are identical with Stendhal's: notably that of the ambitious young man from the provinces who comes up to the capital determined to 'do or die' – Eugène de Rastignac in *Le Père Goriot* (1835; *Old Goriot*), Lucien de Rubempré in *Illusions perdues* (1837–43; *Lost Illusions*). But Balzac, a far more prolific writer than Stendhal and with more wide-ranging aims, decided at an early stage to structure his entire fictional output in order to provide a complete contemporary history of a kind no novelist had ever attempted before. He would deal with the whole of the social spectrum of his day, with every trade and profession, in the provinces as well as in the metropolis; there would be novels illustrating the kind of problems caused by the troublesome presence of the surviving veterans of Napoleon's armies, by the laws of inheritance and by the dowry system, by marriage and adultery, by business failures and successes; only the sufferings of the emerging proletariat failed to engage Balzac's attention. The general title he settled on for the series was *La Comédie humaine* (*The Human Comedy*), modestly echoing that of Dante's epic; but he died too soon to include in it all the novels he had planned. The grand design, however, encouraged his successor, Emile Zola, to embark on his own series, *Les Rougon-Macquart*, wisely limited to twenty novels, which dealt with a later period in French history, the Second Empire (1852–70).

In between Balzac and Zola came Flaubert, whose long, difficult novel *L'Education sentimentale* (1869; *The Sentimental Education*) attempted to present the same socio-political history of contemporary times, which in his case meant the period from 1840 to 1852, with the revolution of 1848 providing the centrepiece. Flaubert confined himself to the scene in the metropolis itself, as reflected in the often uncomprehending observations of his ingenuous hero Frédéric Moreau. Frédéric, who drifts through life aimlessly, has at his side his old schoolfellow Deslauriers, in whom one can recognize a variant of the same type of pushful *arriviste* as Stendhal had created in Julien Sorel and Balzac in Eugène de Rastignac, though Deslauriers is less successful in love than the former and less successful in his career than the latter.

The second general principle evolved by realist novelists on the Continent, particularly in the second half of the century, can be enunciated as the downgrading of the plot. This does not mean that they avoided big subjects. Tolstoy's *War and Peace* (1863–9), which many claim to be the realist masterpiece *par excellence*, has the largest possible theme: what are war and peace if not the twin poles between which nations have swung from time immemorial? But, apart from the campaigns, victories and defeats for which the historical record vouches, the events that affect Tolstoy's characters have nothing out of the ordinary: old people die, young people fall in and out of love, get married and have children, the thoughtful meditate on the meaning of life, the thoughtless give themselves up to enjoyment; they all grow older, more sedate, more serious, as the years march on. In the plot of *War and Peace* there is nothing in any way exceptional; Tolstoy made of it an exceptional novel by the art with which he wove his epic story round dozens of lives, all distinct, all fascinating, because they were all, in their different ways, utterly human, truer than any biographer could make his subject.

More commonly, the realist selected a single life and made it the subject of the novel, offering the reader a humdrum story moving inexorably to a predictable ending. The first title Zola chose for his novel *L'Assommoir* (1877) was *La Simple Vie de Gervaise Macquart*. The book was a sensational success, an immediate best-seller, but there is nothing sensational in the story as such. We meet Gervaise in the beginning, a country girl newly arrived in Paris, poorly educated, knowing nothing but her original trade as a laundress. Her good-for-nothing lover has abandoned her and her two children and made off with all their money. But she finds work, regains her self-respect, and is courted by an honest workman, whom she eventually agrees to marry. For some years the little family prospers, another child is born to Gervaise, and she is in a fair way to achieving her modest ambition of running a laundry business of her own, when her husband Coupeau, a roofer, suffers a disabling injury at work. During his long period of convalescence, in which he is nursed devotedly by Gervaise, he contracts habits of idleness and starts drinking. Although Gervaise continues to prosper for a while, the drain on her resources by her now feckless and eventually hopelessly alcoholic husband drags her down to promiscuity and beggary. Coupeau succumbs finally to delirium tremens and Gervaise, abandoned by her children and spurned by her relatives, dies on the last page of hunger and destitution.

It is in every sense a 'simple life', with none of the strange twists, mysterious happenings or fateful coincidences of the kind one finds not infrequently in the Victorian novelists from Dickens to Hardy. To achieve realism, Zola decided from the start to dispense with all improbability and to maintain his hold over the reader not by surprising or intriguing him, but by drawing him into the fiction by giving him the impression of a flat, undramatized truthfulness. Zola had, of course, forerunners; he regarded Gustave Flaubert as his master here, Flaubert who, twenty years before, had written the prototype of the 'simple life' novel in *Madame Bovary* (1857). His heroine is taken from childhood through schooldays to young womanhood, spent at her father's isolated farm. To escape from a monotonous existence she accepts the first man who offers her marriage; in this new state, she promises herself she knows not what excitements and adventures. But Charles Bovary is dull, plodding, unambitiously following an unpromising career in a small Normandy village. Dissatisfied, Emma takes a lover, a local landowner for whom she is no more than one more mistress after a string of others; when he abandons her, she finds another lover, even less satisfactory, and starts compensating for the emotional poverty of her life by spending wildly, until finally her creditors foreclose. To avoid having to confess to her husband that she has reduced him and their only child to poverty, she ends her life by swallowing arsenic.

Similarly, at the other end of Europe, Tolstoy was writing his own variant on the same theme in *Anna Karenina* (1873–7). Once again we are invited to consider the fate of an attractive woman trapped in marriage to an unsympathetic husband, longing for love, imagining she has found it, experiencing the disillusionment of an irregular relationship, and finally taking the ultimate, desperate way out of her troubles (Anna throws herself under a train). It cannot be by chance that these two novels, together with Eça de Queirós's *Cousin Bazilio* (1878) in Portugal, Alas's *La Regenta* (1884–5) in Spain, and Fontane's *Effi Briest* (1895) in Germany, all centre on discontented wives guilty of some sort of 'indiscretion' and thereafter doomed to abandonment, ostracism and in extreme cases suicide. It is as though the realists, all over the continent of Europe, with one accord fastened on the predicament of the unhappily married middle-class woman as providing the obvious fulcrum of nineteenth-century tragedy. In England and America it was an almost impossible theme, as Hardy discovered when he published *Jude the Obscure* in 1895 and, discouraged by the fiercely hostile reception it was given, decided to write no more novels.

A major problem facing the realists was that of making such drab and depressing material sufficiently absorbing, while dispensing with such artificial aids as suspense, mystery and excitement which their forerunners had not scrupled to introduce. Scott's deliberate concealment of the true identity of certain major characters in his novels – such as that of the lawless rabble-rouser Robertson in *The Heart of Midlothian* (1818), who emerges finally as the respectable heir to the Staunton estates – is designed to encourage the unsophisticated reader to press on to the end so as to discover the truth; and there are other 'mysteries', to do principally with the antecedents and earlier life of this or that character, all of which are finally unwrapped after having been carefully concealed from the reader by various contrivances. Scott was one of the few nineteenth-century British novelists who was read enthusiastically and, up to a point, imitated on the Continent: primarily by the romantics, but also by such proto-realists as Balzac, whose early work contains more than one instance of conscious manipulation of the reader's sensibility by the artful withholding of vital information until the last possible moment. Thus *Old Goriot*, perhaps Balzac's best-known novel, begins with a detailed and almost hypnotically convincing description of a particular Parisian boarding-house, the Pension Vauquer, and of its various inmates about whom we are told, however, no more than might be deduced by a keen-sighted observer lacking inside information. Minor mysteries arise even at this stage: why should Goriot, who some years earlier arrived to take the best rooms in the boarding-house, and whose dress and air of self-confidence proclaimed him a man of substantial private means, have now become so impoverished that he is relegated to the smallest, shabbiest room in the house? Why has he sunk into premature dotage and why is he still occasionally visited none the less by ladies dressed in the height of fashion and displaying every sign of affluence? Questioned indiscreetly, Goriot simply replies that they are his daughters, but no one believes him, and a fellow lodger, a robust middle-aged man going under the name of Vautrin, puts forward the plausible hypothesis that Goriot is an old voluptuary who cannot resist pretty harpies and has run through all his fortune to buy their favours. This is, however, far from being the true solution of the mystery, which it is left to Rastignac, a law-student of good family also lodging in the *pension*, to discover. Goriot had in earlier years, it seems, amassed a considerable fortune through trafficking in grains, and by settling extravagant dowries on his two daughters, had succeeded in marrying one of them into the aristocracy and the other to a wealthy banker. But Anastasie and Delphine, accustomed since childhood to having their every whim gratified, have continued to extort money from their father and so have reduced him to his present pauperdom. This particular mystery is cleared up for the reader about one-third of the way through the book, but there remains the mystery surrounding Vautrin, whose past is problematic but who is discovered towards the end of the novel to be an escaped convict whom the police have been trying to track down for years.

Keeping readers in the dark in order to whet their curiosity is not part of the realist tradition; it may have originated in Balzac's reading of Scott, as suggested, or in the stage melodrama, which was still, at the time *Old Goriot* was written, in the heyday of its popularity. In his later works, Balzac resorted to this device less and less frequently, relying instead on his ability to create powerful characters in the grip of some obsessive passion. Just as Goriot is consumed by an overmastering love of his daughters to the point of sacrificing all he possesses, so Balzac's other 'monomaniacs' (as they have come to be called) are driven on, devoured, and eventually destroyed by different dominating passions: avarice, in the case of Eugénie Grandet's father; scientific research (*La Recherche de l'Absolu*, translated as *The Search for the Absolute*); the collecting of art treasures (*Le Cousin Pons*); exorbitant sexual appetite, degenerating into paedophilia (*La Cousine Bette*); or simply the will to power (*La Rabouilleuse*, translated as *The Black Sheep*). But these children of Balzac's imagination, powerful though they undoubtedly are in their impact on the reader, can scarcely be accounted the typical creations of a realistic art. Characters in the novels of Flaubert, Tolstoy, Zola and other writers of the latter part of the century are invariably 'people of our sort', which does not mean of course that we see ourselves necessarily behaving as they do, but that we can understand only too well what makes them behave as they do. They are never extraordinary (it is precisely because Dostoevsky's four great novels all embody abnormal heroes that critics hesitate to classify him among the realists), and so in general their fates are never extraordinary. Instead of Julien Sorel, who models himself on Napoleon and does indeed succeed in racing to the top, but who before the novel ends overreaches himself, fires on his ex-mistress in church and is guillotined for the deed, we are much more likely to encounter a lucky scoundrel like Georges Duroy in Maupassant's *Bel-Ami* (1885) who, profiting by his sexual attractions, works his way up in the world of journalism and ends by marrying the daughter of a wealthy newspaper proprietor. Stendhal's *Scarlet and Black*, though full of accurate observation and perceptive social comment, has a fantastic plot; Maupassant's *Bel-Ami* rings true throughout, and Duroy's progeny, under the collective name of 'yuppies', is still around a century later.

What Flaubert in the first place, and his successors subsequently, introduced as a substitute for melodrama, suspense and larger-than-life protagonists, was the equivalent in literature of what philosophers would call determinism. Every folly that Emma Bovary commits has its roots in the circumstances in which she grew up and the temperament with which nature has endowed her. Flaubert devotes the whole of the sixth chapter of *Madame Bovary* to an account of her schooldays and adolescence, emphasizing how her reading of romantic novelettes had given her the notion of a grand life and wild, exotic adventures for which, being of an imaginative disposition, she sees herself destined. Her subsequent marriage to a bumbling country doctor, devoted to her but manifestly incapable of providing her with the sexual thrills and material luxuries she craves, drives her to seek satisfaction through extramarital affairs and by adopting an extravagant lifestyle; and we have already seen how all this ends. Everything about Emma and her life is deducible from antecedent factors; the whole story seems predetermined, not however by some Aeschylean fate, like Hardy's 'President of the Immortals' who is said, on the last page of *Tess of the D'Urbervilles* (1891), to have 'ended his sport' with the tormented heroine. This is how it was bound to end, we think when Emma writhes on her deathbed; whereas there are so many turning-points in Tess's story when, if matters had chanced to fall out differently, she would never have stabbed her lover, she would surely have escaped the gallows.

Much the same could be said of Gervaise in Zola's *L'Assommoir*, who has indeed been called a working-class Emma Bovary, though in her case it is less her upbringing and neglected education that cause her downfall than the dirty, overcrowded, drink-sodden slum in which her life is spent; the vapours of cheap brandy – vitriol as the workers call it – permeate the book and explain Zola's decision to call the novel *L'Assommoir*, the word being at the time a slang term for what in English would have been called a gin palace. But whether the determining factors are environmental or educational or a mixture of the two, the formula is most convincing when applied to a fictional biography of the type exemplified in the two French novels just mentioned and in others discussed earlier. Not all realist novels are of this kind. *Germinal* (1885), which now rates probably as Zola's masterpiece, covers only a year or two in the fortunes of a coalmining community in the north of France, and is concerned with the events leading up to a strike, the suffering it causes and the violence it gives rise to before its final collapse. Determinism plays a different role here: Zola's intention was to show how social conflicts of this kind, given the industrial and economic conditions of the time, necessarily followed some such pattern as he traced. The work might have turned into a dry economic treatise, but by enlisting the reader's sympathy for individual miners, their wives and children, and by showing at any rate some understanding of the difficult position of management, caught in the crossfire between workers and owners, he succeeds in infusing his account of the strike with a degree of human interest so that, in the end, both classes are seen as victims of a system that cries out for overthrow or at the very least radical amendment.

Germinal is perhaps an extreme instance of how far a work of realism dealing with crucial socio-economic questions could be taken without the author exceeding his brief and appearing in the guise of a social reformer. The English tradition, if one thinks of Dickens in *Hard Times* (1854) or *Bleak House* (1853) for instance, never required of an author that he adopt so neutral a stance, and it must be admitted that eventually, in the late 1890s, Zola did embark on a deliberate policy of using his pen not merely to analyse the social evils of his time but also to propound remedies. In so doing, he was knowingly breaking with the realist tradition in his country, which had set its face consistently against the overt advocacy of social reform in works of the imagination. Here we come up against the fundamentally different principles that guided writers on the Continent and in England and America, in the matter of authorial intervention. In *Scarlet and Black*, what Stendhal sought to portray was what he himself called a 'plebeian in revolt'. Julien is an unabashed careerist, prepared to adopt any expedient, moral or immoral, that will allow him to break through the barriers that separate him from 'the rich', whom he hates and envies to an almost equal degree; but what the author thought about him is far from obvious (whereas what the narrator in *Vanity Fair* thought of Becky Sharp, a rather similar creation, is only too clear), and what the reader will think about Julien depends on his or her values alone. The guidance the author offers is at best ambiguous; even when Stendhal launches into an explicit condemnation of Julien's conduct, one is never sure whether such sternness is not tongue-in-cheek. Similarly in Balzac's novels: a small minority could be classed as social treatises, but the greatest of them, whatever the social or moral questions they raise, eschew all opportunities to sway the reader to the author's point of view. Privately, in fact, Balzac professed the most reactionary political opinions; the paradox is, however, that Engels and after him Lukács, both Marxists, should have considered his analysis of the society of his time to be more enlightening, however unenlightened his outlook, than that of any other writer in the nineteenth century.

The novelist who illustrates most clearly the moral neutrality common to all the French realists is undoubtedly Flaubert, whose first published novel, *Madame Bovary*, might be mistaken for a denunciation of the institution of marriage as it existed among the less successful professional classes, especially in the remoter rural districts of France. Emma marries in order to escape from her widowed father's isolated farmstead; but she finds herself in this new condition without any occupation whatsoever. The housework is done by the servant, the child born to her is a disappointment and is put out to nurse; her husband is out all day and falls asleep over his supper when he returns; diversions such as balls and theatre-going are so infrequent as to constitute unique occurrences rather than habitual entertainments. Emma is excruciatingly bored and sees her life stretching before her as a long corridor with no doors opening off to the magic garden she imagines lying beyond. Rodolphe, the local Lothario, makes her acquaintance just when her longing for an adventure has become almost desperate, and she succumbs without a qualm. Emma is not naturally vicious or corrupt; she is, it would seem, made so by the intolerable conditions to which marriage has condemned her.

Yet *Madame Bovary* has less claim to be regarded as a critique of the married state than *Anna Karenina*, where the institution is studied in three different case-histories: firstly, that of Oblonsky, perpetually faithless but whose infidelities are tolerated by his wife for the sake of appearances; then that of Anna, the adulteress, who differs from Emma in having a husband more concerned with his career than with her, and a child whom she adores (it is true that Seryozha is a bright little boy, whereas Emma's Berthe is a graceless little girl); and finally there is Konstantin Levin, who persists, in spite of rebuffs, in wooing Kitty and is eventually accepted: the marriage turns out to be as successful as perhaps a reasonable man and a sensible woman could expect. Tolstoy's disillusioned view of the institution of marriage can be pretty accurately gauged from these three examples; that of Flaubert could never be judged by anything we find in *Madame Bovary*. He shows, it is true, that Emma finds no lasting happiness in her affairs; in a famous phrase, he says of her towards the end of the second of them: 'Emma retrouvait dans l'adultère toutes les platitudes du mariage' (Pt. 3, chap. 6; 'Emma was rediscovering in adultery all the triteness of marriage'). On the other hand, he does depict her transported and transfigured by her first experience of seduction; after her return from that fateful ride in the woods with Rodolphe, we see her staring at herself in the mirror, amazed at the transformation of her appearance and repeating to herself: 'J'ai un amant! un amant!' (Pt. 2, chap. 9), and exulting at the idea as though she had entered into a second puberty; whereas Tolstoy shows Anna, after the same experience, sinking to her knees in shame, conscious only that she is now a 'fallen woman'. Which of the two scenes is the more realistic? Impossible to say, of course, since Anna is a different woman from Emma, and a novel is no reliable source for universal moral judgements.

But there is nothing to stop a novelist from allowing his own private judgements, moral or social, to peep through in the course of his narrative, either openly, as the Victorians tend to do, or slyly, with the most delicate of ironic wit, as Jane Austen does for instance in the opening sentence of *Pride and Prejudice* (1813). For most of the nineteenth century and beyond, novelists writing in the English tradition have never felt any scruples about commenting, in general or in particular, about the various scenes, characters or incidents that they evoke in their fiction. Since, as André Gide once remarked, there are no rules governing the novel, that most 'lawless' of all literary forms, one cannot rightly complain about this practice, except that when the writer's voice intrudes, the reader risks being distracted, even infuriated, if the views expressed strike him or her as wrong-headed or narrow-minded. Perhaps for this reason the continental tradition runs on the whole counter to it, especially in the Latin countries; it is possible that the tendency towards authorial intrusion is in some way connected with Protestant habits of considering fiction to be an idle pastime unless the voice of the preacher is audible every now and then.

Among the continental realists, especially after the mid-century, the only way we are made aware of the narrator is by the manner in which he writes. As Flaubert expressed it in a letter to a friend shortly after the publication of *Madame Bovary*: 'It is one of my principles that one must not write oneself into one's work. The artist must be in his work as God in creation, invisible yet all-powerful; we must sense him everywhere but never see him' (quoted in Allott, 1959, p. 271). Only very rarely does Flaubert comment directly on the behaviour of his characters, yet we can, if we read carefully, sense the judgements he is passing in the ironic twist by which he records their thoughts and feelings. Thus, at the end of a long, almost lyrical passage describing Charles Bovary's joys in the early days of married life, as he rides off to his work in the morning sunlight, he is said to be 'chewing the cud of his happiness like those who, after dinner, have still in their mouths the taste of the truffles they are digesting'. All the egoism of the thoughtless sensualist is in this unexpected simile, where sexual rapture is equated with the gratification of the gourmet, though there is no explicit condemnation of Charles. Sometimes the irony is not even directly expressed in the language used: as, later on, when Flaubert shows the couple side by side at night, Emma imagining her coming elopement with Rodolphe, Charles meditating on the years that lie ahead, thinking of his little daughter growing up and getting married in her turn, planning a future of quiet domestic felicity. Neither, of course, communicates these daydreams to the other. The narrator, being omniscient, knows what each is thinking, and by this juxtaposition of two minds filled with such divergent thoughts, he succeeds in conveying to the thoughtful reader not just the incompatibility of these two people inseparably yoked together, but also a moral judgement on each of them: Charles, good-hearted but incapable of even conceiving his wife's unhappiness, and Emma, dreaming her impossible dreams of sensual delights in exotic surroundings, caring nothing for husband and child, the indefensible egoist.

Flaubert's impersonality is, therefore, never absolute; in *Madame Bovary*, at least, he is never quite the insensate 'god in the machine' that it seems he would have wished to be. This achievement was reserved for his disciple Zola, in *L'Assommoir*, a novel which, as we have seen already, was set in a working-class district in Paris and was, in fact, the first in any language to have a cast of characters belonging entirely to the artisan class. In his opening chapters Zola presents the scene, outlining Gervaise's desperate predicament in the same dispassionate tone he had used in half-a-dozen novels already. Shortly after, Coupeau is introduced, a cheerful, perky Parisian 'cockney'. His love-talk with Gervaise is inevitably interlarded with all kinds of colloquialisms and slang phrases which Zola, as an honest realist, transcribes; and when it comes to Coupeau's private thoughts, the same special vernacular of the Parisian working man is the natural medium in which to convey them to the reader. Finally, by a strange osmosis, this vulgar, bastardized French becomes the narrator's speech too; it could be said that Zola, as novelist, adopts it, but it would be truer to say that he bows out and passes the pen over to an anonymous witness in the crowd that surrounds Gervaise, some working-class commentator admiring her for her guts, deploring her weaknesses, heartlessly chronicling her fall into promiscuity and misery, and her final death. Conditions never allowed Zola to repeat the performance, since his later novels, though like *Germinal* they sometimes include working-class characters, also have middle-class, 'respectable' people playing major parts, so that the 'uniform style' he adopted in *L'Assommoir* was no longer appropriate. But the book remains the *ne plus ultra* of realist art – a novel without a narrator, a novel which *tells itself* and so is at once totally absorbing and as impersonal as a stone idol.

FURTHER READING

Allott, Miriam (1959) *Novelists on the Novel*, Routledge & Kegan Paul, London

Becker, G. J. (1982) *Master European Realists*, Ungar, New York

Giraud, Raymond (1957) *The Unheroic Hero in the Novels of Stendhal, Balzac and Flaubert*, Rutgers University Press, New Brunswick

Gregor, I. and Nicholas, B. (1962) *The Moral and the Story*, Faber & Faber, London

Hemmings, F. W. J. (ed.) (1974) *The Age of Realism*, Penguin, Harmondsworth

Knight, Everett (1969) *A Theory of the Classical Novel*, Routledge & Kegan Paul, London

Levin, Harry (1963) *The Gates of Horn: A Study of Five French Realists*, Oxford University Press, New York

O'Connor, Frank (1957) *The Mirror in the Roadway*, Hamish Hamilton, London

Pascal, Roy (1977) *The Dual Voice: Free Indirect Speech and its Functioning in the Nineteenth-Century European Novel*, Manchester University Press, Manchester

Seymour-Smith, M. (1980) *A Reader's Guide to Fifty European Novels*, Heinemann, London

Snow, C. P. (1978) *The Realists: Portraits of Eight Novelists*, Macmillan, London

Williams, D. A. (ed.) (1978) *The Monster in the Mirror: Studies in Nineteenth-Century Realism*, Oxford University Press, London

41

REALISM AND THE ENGLISH NOVEL

ELIZABETH DEEDS ERMARTH

Critical discussions of the English novel and of its realism once tended to treat these two separate subjects as one, as if presuming that verisimilitude was somehow the condition to which all novels aspired, and that the emergence of the English novel was tantamount to the emergence of a fully-fledged narrative realism. Realism was simply taken for granted as the aesthetic norm for the novel. Such discussions implicitly identified the scope of 'realism' with the scope of 'the novel'; the term 'realism' functioned primarily as a term of praise rather than as a tool of analysis. In such a context, moreover, the term 'realism' has tended to mean widely different things, depending on what qualities a particular interpreter associated with it. For example, some of the qualities more or less casually assumed to be evidences of realism include, to name a few, particularity, circumstantiality, humble subject-matter, viewpoint, chronology, interiority, externality. While each of these qualities does have some importance in realism, none of itself explains the realist convention.

Recently, things have changed. Under the influence of novelists like James Joyce and Gertrude Stein, John Hawkes and Vladimir Nabokov, Claude Simon and Alain Robbe-Grillet, Julio Cortázar and Gabriel García Márquez, and under the influence of theoretical writing based on the work of Saussure, Heidegger, Foucault and others, discussion of English realism has adopted a more self-conscious historical and theoretical vantage point. From this perspective earlier discussions seem to take for granted the very things that most require investigation, which is to say questions concerning exactly what primary values and assumptions the realist convention entails.

A key text, one that represents both a culmination of the first kind of discussion and a turn toward the second more philosophical kind, is Ian Watt's *The Rise of the Novel: Studies in Defoe, Richardson, and Fielding* (1959). Watt continues the tradition of equating verisimilitude with emphasis on 'particulars' and on 'circumstantial' evidence, but he also considers the implications for these features of realism of Locke's philosophy and of wider social changes including new priorities of individualism and of privacy. The fact that his discussion remains valuable thirty years after its publication testifies to the quality and importance of his argument; on the other hand, the fact that his argument does not venture into a wider discursive context seriously limits the value of many of his generalizations.

A fuller estimate of English narrative realism as a cultural achievement begins with this recognition: that verisimilitude, like any other aesthetic convention, is an abstraction. The 'life-likeness' of realism depends upon a particular set of rules for the disposition of concreteness and detail, as well as of value and questions of ultimate concern. Because the realistic convention distracts attention from its artificiality it may be in fact one of the most artificial of all conventions. In any case, verisimilitude, or realism, or the illusion of lifelikeness, is no simple or natural expression; on the contrary, it is a highly artificial and highly achieved effect.

Analogies with other art forms and other modes of description help to demonstrate the profoundly abstract as well as the profoundly consequential character of realistic narrative conventions. It is demonstrable, for example, that realistic narrative belongs to the same descriptive conventions that made possible the painting and architecture of the Renaissance and the empirical science of the sixteenth and seventeenth centuries (Ivins, 1938, 1964; Edgerton, 1975; Ermarth, 1983). In other words, realism in narrative is a temporal variant of a certain cultural formulation that became evident centuries earlier in the spatial versions of painting, architecture and geometry.

A familiar and immediately accessible instance of spatial realism is the technique of single-point perspective that co-ordinated pictorial space so as to produce a common horizon for all potential perspectives. As opposed to the space of medieval painting, which was either a frankly virtual space for icons or a quasi-representational space fractured by competing vanishing points, the space of Masaccio, Piero della Francesca, and the entire company of Renaissance painters was a homogenized, neutral medium in which mutually informative measurements could be made and in which the logic of spectator awareness was absolute. All perspectives in the realistic frame agree, or in other words, achieve a consensus which is tantamount to the creation of a common horizon and a common medium. From any spectator's viewpoint – either the one arbitrarily assigned by an artist to viewers or any others potentially available in the representational space – an invariant logic of relationships could be grasped that extended to infinity and thus had the value of universal truth. This is the convention that reigned, in Western European painting at least, from the fourteenth through the nineteenth centuries.

This technical achievement in painting belonged to the shift associated with the rediscovery of classical models in the Renaissance, a shift that changed not only the content but the entire method of understanding. One could say that the most important thing about the rediscovery of classical learning was as much the act of rediscovery as it was the creation of models. The act of historical awareness ran through the era from Piero della Francesca to Erasmus like a bolt of energy and opened the horizon, both in space and in time, to exploration and conquest. From this breathtaking effort emerged the modern idea of history: the view of time as a neutral, homogenous medium like the space of pictorial realism in painting; a time where mutually informative measurements can be made between past, present and future, and where all relationships can be explained in terms of a common horizon. In realistic painting sight is rationalized by a pictorial space that extends from here to eternity without encountering any disturbing fractures. In realistic narrative a different faculty is involved and a different medium, but the same formation inheres. In realistic narrative, that is, consciousness is rationalized by a narrative time that extends from here to eternity without encountering any disturbing fractures. All temporal perspectives, however widely dispersed, 'agree' in the sense that they do not contradict; in this powerful sense they achieve a consensus that is tantamount to the creation of a common horizon in time and hence of the power to think historically.

The narrative convention of realism took considerably longer to emerge than did the similar convention for space. It took several centuries in England – from the beginning of the Reformation in the early sixteenth century to about 1800, when the scientific and mathematical implications of the new learning had finally become broadly evident. By a massive capillary action through every social institution in England, this historical awareness produced a rationalizing of consciousness which we still take for granted today and which still informs our institutions.

The nineteenth century was the era of historical genres like autobiography and history, and the period in which the new sciences of geology, biology and sociology produced their powerfully unsettling influence on religious belief through various histories of the earth, of the human species, and of social order such as those published by Lyell, Darwin and Comte. The nineteenth century was also the era of the historical novel. Just as Piero della Francesca and his contemporaries rationalized the faculty of sight by organizing space according to a common horizon, so the novelists of the nineteenth century rationalized the faculty of consciousness by organizing time according to a common horizon, a horizon maintained by the narrative process itself, with its reflex from present to past.

It is this narrative convention, and not any more local effect of lifelikeness, that makes realistic effect possible. Precision of detail in itself has no realistic qualities; as Alain Robbe-Grillet says, speaking of Kafka, 'nothing is more fantastic, ultimately, than precision' (1961, p. 165). Rather, realism belongs to the management – one might almost say the administration – of perspective in time so that a common medium of events is maintained from the beginning of a narrative to the end. Any detail or event or perspective that cannot be assimilated in this overall temporal structure – for example, a too-conspicuous pattern, a major historical improbability – compromises the realistic effect.

The key feature in this convention of narrative temporality is the much-discussed, so-called omniscient narrator or what I suggest we think of as 'the narrator as Nobody'. Although this narrator sometimes addresses readers in personal tones, more generally it remains disembodied and indistinguishable from the narrative process itself, almost like a power of the past-tense rather than anything more individualized. At this level of awareness distinctions between individual sites of consciousness, whether of author, reader or character, seem less important than the power to slide between them; realistic narrative characteristically draws reader attention to various instances of this power of transition.

Such narrative consciousness literally *constitutes* historical time in the narrative by threading together into one system and one act of attention, a whole series of moments and perspectives. Thus the continuum of time and the continuum of consciousness literally appear inseparable, functioning together as the medium of events. The shuttle back and forth between past and future along an essentially linear but not chronological temporal sequence at once homogenizes time in the way single-point perspective homogenized space, and in the same gesture that process rationalizes consciousness in the same way that single-point perspective rationalized sight, confining it to a horizon common to all perspectives and extending to infinity.

In realistic narrative and painting, in other words, a fundamental and powerful idea takes shape: the idea that the medium of creation extends from the wall or the page into our actual space and time and, potentially, to infinity or as far as our own creative courage may take us. In addition, this aesthetic invitation comes inscribed with a promise that the realistic convention gives us a power of generalization that will enable us to subsume or eradicate whatever is inexplicable or mysterious. In a convention that extends to infinity the rationalized powers of human attention, no atrocity need remain unexplained, no mystery unsolved, no mistake unrectified.

Many nineteenth-century novels comment most powerfully on the strain involved in sustaining this particular ideal of consciousness while, at the same time, they insist on the necessity and even the heroism of it. They do this primarily in two ways: first by forcing readers to cope with problems in the management of the narrative temporality itself; second, and more modestly, by thematizing in various ways this problem of sustaining a common time. The major English realists are nineteenth-century writers and their deployments of the characteristic conventions of realism vary widely. There are what might be called centrist writers like George Eliot, Anthony Trollope, Elizabeth Gaskell, George Meredith, and even Thackeray who maintain pretty consistently the historical conventions of realism. Then there are writers like the Brontës and Dickens (especially the early Dickens) who, to varying degrees, qualify realistic conventions because they emphasize the dependence of realistic agreements and of common, historical time upon a sustaining Providence that possesses the power to suspend them (Vargish, 1985).

But the potential range of variation within the realistic convention is great. Early in the nineteenth century we find Walter Scott, the under-sung father of realism, who sustains the historical continuum in considering politics and the social order at the same time as his style renders those subjects almost as epic or heroic legend; and, at the same period, we find Jane Austen, who undertakes the domestic subject-matter congenial to the consensus of realism, with its emphasis on common time and common understandings, but who at the same time often employs a narrative temporality that has more in common with Defoe and Richardson than with the historical generalizations of realism.

Late in the nineteenth century the temporal horizon of realism becomes strained. In the novels of Henry James, for example, the narrative often focuses mainly on the stress, difficulty and importance of achieving precisely that communication between one consciousness and another that realism invites us to take for granted. Thomas Hardy and Joseph Conrad further disturb the rationalizing consciousness of realism – and its associated valorization of individuality and uniqueness – with patterns that supersede individual will or with mysteries or brutalities that exceed the system of rational explanation and, in some cases, arise directly from it. In their work the values of memory and anticipation, of projection and perspective become impossible or take on a sinister tinge.

A close look at the management of narrative temporality reveals at once the crucial feature of realistic fiction, the power of consciousness to sustain, at a certain level of transcendence, a perpetual mediation. In Trollope's *Barchester Towers* (1857), for example, the narrative process shuttles back and forth between this individual and that, this place and that, overcoming the various separations created by individual, social, spatial or temporal difference, and binding together into one act of attention a collective group that hardly sees its collective identity. *Barchester Towers* is a novel about a community where individuals seem incapable of mediating their own affairs and where, consequently, opportunists and nitwits hold sway. Everyone is so discreet and so ingenuous in Barchester that they seem prepared to credit even the most preposterous rumour rather than ask a direct question or two. The ones capable of real directness in the novel are the narrator and the phenomenal Signora Neroni, both in different ways disengaged from the community.

The narrator, for example, is capable of saying things like this: 'Miss Stanhope was a clever woman, able to talk on most subjects, and quite indifferent as to what the subject was' (chap. 9); or (speaking of Signora Neroni and Obadiah Slope) 'Her hand in his looked like a rose lying among carrots' (chap. 27); or even 'Eleanor had no such self-knowledge' (chap. 24). This kind of commentary provides a site, a mediate region where reader and narrative consciousness join to supervise a particular history. In *Barchester Towers*, as in other realistic novels, the standard set by narrative consciousness is one measure of character awareness. The Signora maintains her special status in the text partly by her ability – unique in Barchester – to express herself in a spirit similar to that of the narrator's, as for example when she asks the odious Obadiah, 'Which is it to be with you, Mr Slope, love or money?' (chap. 27). The power to take this kind of perspective is tantamount almost to a form of self-consciousness, exactly what in Barchester nobody has, except, of course, the narrator who *is* nobody in the sense of having no individual or concrete embodiment in the narrative. The burden of the plot is to show how the various Grantleys, Thornes, Hardings and Quiverfuls come closer to the saving acts of mutual recognition – in short, how they come to that objective awareness of their mutual relations which the narrator and reader (and occasionally the Signora) have had all along.

In this as in any realistic novel almost any passage demonstrates the narrative consciousness at its largely invisible work. Although the so-called narrator is most conspicuous at those moments when it delivers a prejudiced comment or overt interpretation, these are not its only or even its most powerful moments. The true power of the narrator is the abstract, non-individualized, transcendent power of mediation. By incorporating in a single mnemonic sequence all the variety of particular life, especially what seems isolated or unrelated, the narrator maintains as a perpetual possibility that social communion, with all its extensions of individual power, that remains unachieved at the level of plot. This potential for communion is most obvious to readers who necessarily operate with the narrator's perspective and consequently with an awareness of the possibility and power of transition from one perspective to another. At this level of attention the narrator must be conceived not as an individual so much as a power of transition itself, something frequently indistinguishable from the power of the past tense. In this power of transition lies the implicit possibility of those connections, those meetings of minds, those reunions that so often seem lacking in the plot. The narrative consciousness shows by its very mediation that what seems unrelated in fact is not and that events or persons widely separated in time or space still have mutual relevance and their actions mutual consequences. As readers we know this simply because no event, no moment escapes the mediating awareness that, from its vantage point in the indistinct future, acts invisibly but perpetually to co-ordinate various moments into a sequence where their meaning emerges comparatively, over time. For this narrative consciousness every 'present' event is also already a past event and thus implicitly contained in a controlled pattern of significance. Although disagreement may break out here or there in Barchester, agreement reigns in the narrative process itself: agreement not about anything so trivial as church appointments or engagements, but rather about the potential for connectedness between what seems but is not separate and unrelated. It is this power of collective – or, more accurately, *collected* – perception that creates realism's common horizon in time and its rationalization of consciousness.

The historical narrator is so fully achieved an effect, so far from inadvertent an effect in realism that the values maintained by this narrative medium often receive explicit thematic statement. Dickens's novels are an especially luminous example because one of his constant themes is the saving power of mutual consciousness to overcome separation. Unlike Trollope, Dickens expands his circuit of consciousness far beyond the private understandings of narrator, occasional character, and appreciative reader to the point that he often qualifies his realism in the process. The entire *world* is galvanized by consciousness in Dickens, furniture included; the circuit of communion runs through the whole social universe. While Dickens's narrator – and this holds true even for a first-person narrator – generally remains as unpersonified as Trollope's, his characters often find themselves in a condition of social and psychic detachment that resembles the helpless lucidity of the realistic narrator; and such characters are often referred to in Dickens as 'nobody'.

Many examples spring to mind, all of them characters who have in some way reached a margin of social consciousness and who often find that trip tantamount to death (literally the end of time): in *Bleak House* (1852–3) such 'nobodies' are Inspector Bucket, or Esther, or Nemo – literally no name; in *Little Dorrit* (1855–7), Miss Wade, Pancks and Arthur Clennam are all referred to as 'nobody', and all have terrible problems of social consciousness and conscience, problems that in Clennam's case are often couched in terms of keeping track of the time. In his last complete novel, *Our Mutual Friend* (1864–5), Dickens develops most fully the theme of 'nobody'. The main figures in the double plot, Eugene Wrayburn and John Harmon, both become somebody by becoming Nobody. Harmon returns in disguise like a modern Odysseus to the place that is his but in which he remains invisible until he can come back recognized: 'I am nobody', he says to Mr Boffin, '. . . and not likely to be known' (chap. 8). Harmon, though not dead as first thought, still remains 'unrecognized' and, so far as his social identity is concerned, unrecognized is as good as dead.

Our Mutual Friend makes it painfully clear how this mysterious detachment of consciousness entailed by a loss of social identity is actually a *saving* fracture because it preserves the consciousness from untenable contradictions entailed by multiple social identity or from the hard impositions of unenlightened materialism. The price of consciousness is disembodiment because in Dickens's world embodied consciousness always, fatefully finds itself trapped in the hopeless limitations of a hierarchical class structure. The transcendence entailed by the reflex of consciousness produces prodigious strains in individual experience. In Trollope we are so glad of the power that transcends Barchester that we practically welcome the strain. In Dickens, especially late Dickens, the strain is a saving necessity, but a necessity none the less and not entirely a pleasure, conducted as it is at the margins of society and often at the margin of temporal existence.

George Eliot's narrator avoids the margins of historical march in favour of the middle. Her narrating consciousness is not holistic like Dickens's, nor does it deal with totalized structures or with absolute values. The narrative consciousness is a kind of generalized historical awareness, often hardly distinguishable from the reader's own, a power of transition between minds and moments, an implied historical awareness that makes the realistic series possible. Like Trollope's narrator, hers sometimes inches toward personification with this or that prejudiced remark and sometimes remains a totally disembodied power of putatively 'neutral' reporting; but her narrator is much more a deliberate and complex feature of the history than is Trollope's. From her earliest writing it is clear that this medium of perception itself and not any more limited representation was her primary focus. There are very few writers who make more accessible to inspection that internal conversation of consciousness whereby awareness shifts incessantly from point to point, from moment to moment bearing its filaments of shared meaning.

George Eliot's novels thematize this power in various ways. Many of her novelistic agendas and crucial plot moments turn on the difficulties and powers of making public the private dialogue. The act of confessing, for example, has tremendous power because in confession the private shuttle of consciousness goes public, enlarging its context and the scope of its rationalizations. George Eliot's narrative consciousness, unlike the one in Dickens, finds no dead ends in the world of material embodiments because for her even material embodiments are half ideas: products of human effort and tradition over time, and the essential medium of what is highest and best. Because in George Eliot's novels institutions only exist through individual enactments and choices, institutions never take on a life of their own, as they do in Dickens, or run like juggernauts over helpless individuals. Disembodied consciousness is more to be feared than institutions in George Eliot because of the powerful solipsism that can be engendered by those private rationalizations. Characters like Arthur Donnithorne, Tito Melema, Mrs Transome, Nicholas Bulstrode, Rosamond Vincy and Gwendolen Harleth create those narrative cruxes for which George

Eliot is well known: cruxes where various characters either accept or avoid that all-powerful moment when they can say, in the spirit of Jane Austen's Elizabeth Bennett, 'until this moment I never knew myself' and, with that step, begin to adjust their private rationalizations with wider ones.

That snap of recognition is less grand and permanent in George Eliot than it is in Austen. Rosamond Vincy's case differs from Elizabeth Bennett's partly because Rosamond's world contains no secure hierarchy of virtue in which to locate but presents instead a vast range of relevancies over which even the narrator's consciousness presides sceptically, hypothetically, and constantly seeking new extensions. George Eliot's egoists, like Dickens's characters, are too encumbered by flesh and blood and daily living; but unlike Dickens's more evanescent narrator, hers provides for a complex populous universe of metaphoric articulation: a kind of flexible, provoking, sustained awareness that holds together into a single medium the roll and pitch of the temporal sequence and is essentially coextensive with it.

Recognizing this narrative medium as a major signifying element provides rich opportunities for resolving some problems that have vexed interpreters of Victorian novels over decades. Examples include, first, what has appeared to be the excessive virtue of characters like Dorothea Brooke and Daniel Deronda; the allegedly gratuitous or 'intrusive' presence of the so-called 'omniscient' narrator; and what Percy Lubbock (exploiting Henry James) called the 'loose, baggy' quality of nineteenth-century novels ([1921] 1957). Over-altruistic characters like Dorothea and Deronda demonstrate – quite explicitly once the narrative medium becomes a comparative model – that too much selflessness produces paralysis or worse and that altruistic dispersal is not much more desirable than egoistic concentricity. The epigrammatical comments made by narrators seem 'intrusive' only if they are seen in isolation from the rest of the narrative medium which moves like tides between extremes of particular consciousness on the one hand and, on the other, a generalized or collected awareness without individual definition. The loose, baggy quality of Victorian novels is not a symptom of incomplete art but, on the contrary, a necessity of the logic of realism which discovers its forms not in individual cases but in a series and over time.

While we take the historical medium for granted when we read a realistic novel, what we are really doing is accepting and reinscribing the belief – and it is no more nor less than an arbitrary and breathtaking act of faith – that it is our powers of collective agreement that literally make possible historical continuity. In the realistic medium, a contradiction is merely an incompletely grasped relationship, and one that implicitly may be resolved at a higher level of understanding. The consciousness required for transcending particulars in this way is everywhere in general and nowhere in particular: linked with individual awareness at various points but always exceeding them. The power of this consciousness is nobody's power: at once human and unspecific, powerfully present but not individualized. In realistic novels our sense of a network, a system of relationships, a balance between parts of an immense and complex and always changing social entity emerges precisely in the reflex from one moment and one consciousness to another. The narrative consciousness of realism is literally engendered by the very sequence that, in its more limited personal voice, it interprets.

This flexible and composite narrative medium, one always controlled from a vantage point in the future of the events being narrated, literally maintains by this ceaseless relay the medium of time itself, just as the single-point perspective in Renaissance painting co-ordinates all angles of vision into a common horizon. In narrative, this co-ordination is distributed over a sequence and depends on a collected consciousness to maintain it, a more intangible feat perhaps than the visual co-ordinations of realistic space, but equally powerful in extending to infinity the human capabilities it thereby inscribes.

FURTHER READING

Alter, Robert (1975) *Partial Magic: The Novel as a Self-Conscious Genre*, University of California Press, Berkeley

Beer, Gillian (1983) *Darwin's Plots: Evolutionary Narrative in Darwin, George Eliot, and Nineteenth-Century Fiction*, Routledge & Kegan Paul, London

Bersani, Leo (1969) 'Realism and the Fear of Desire'. In Leo Bersani, *A Future For Astyanax: Character and Desire in Literature*, Little, Brown, & Co., Boston

Ermarth, Elizabeth Deeds (1983) *Realism and Consensus in the English Novel*, Princeton University Press, Princeton

Levine, George (1981) *The Realistic Imagination*, University of Chicago Press, Chicago

Miller, J. Hillis (1968) *The Form of Victorian Fiction*, University of Notre Dame Press, Notre Dame

Robbe-Grillet, Alain (1961) *Essays For a New Novel: Essays on Fiction* (*Pour un nouveau roman*), translated by Richard Howard, Grove Press, New York

Stern, J. P. (1973) *On Realism*, Routledge & Kegan Paul, London

Vargish, Thomas (1985) *The Providential Aesthetic in Victorian Fiction*, University of Virginia Press, Charlottesville

Watt, Ian (1959) *The Rise of the Novel: Studies in Defoe, Richardson, and Fielding*, University of California Press, Berkeley

Williams, Ioan (1975) *The Realist Novel in England*, University of Pittsburgh Press, Pittsburgh

Williams, Raymond (1961) 'Realism and the Contemporary Novel'. In Raymond Williams, *The Long Revolution*, Columbia University Press, New York; Chatto & Windus, London

ADDITIONAL WORKS CITED

Edgerton, Samuel Y., Jr. (1975) *The Renaissance Rediscovery of Linear Perspective*, Basic Books, New York

Ivins, William J., Jr. (1938) *On the Rationalization of Sight, with an Examination of Three Renaissance Texts on Perspective*, Paper no. 8, Metropolitan Museum of Art, New York

——(1964) *Art and Geometry: A Study in Space Intuitions*, Dover, New York [first published 1946]

Lubbock, Percy (1957) *The Craft of Fiction*, Viking Press, New York [first published 1921]

42

AMERICAN ROMANCE

ROBERT CLARK

In the last twenty years criticism of nineteenth-century North American fiction has undergone a profound change. In 1968 the field was still dominated by what Bruce Kuklick (1972) termed 'the myth and symbol' school, the key works of which were Richard Chase's *The American Novel and its Tradition* (1957), Henry Nash Smith's *Virgin Land* (1950), R. W. B. Lewis's *The American Adam* (1955) and Joel Porte's *The Romance in America* (1969). In 1990 the critical energy and interest lies firmly with the New Historicists who are re-establishing understanding of how literature relates to the conditions of its production and reception. The theoretical outlook that inspired the previous paradigm was most powerfully articulated by Northop Frye, whose *Anatomy of Criticism* (1953) and 'New Directions from Old' (1960) elaborated a largely ahistorical treatment of literature as deriving its forms and concerns from the realm of myth, an entity which was primary, non-derived, an absolute origin. Frye expressed a literary ideology more generally held: Richard Chase's rather neglected *Quest for Myth* (1949) had with considerable scholarship laid similar foundations, as had the work of Mircea Eliade and Joseph Campbell. However it was Frye's grandiloquent and gnomic style which was able to conceal the circular regresses of a criticism that reduced texts to manifestations of generic ahistorical categories and enabled critics to speak as if their own constructions were transcendental objects.

Myth and symbol criticism, though, was not incompatible with apparent social concern; indeed, it rather served to articulate the ethical and cultural functions of texts which New Criticism's commitment to impartial and objective description tended to leave unexplored. However, its fundamental belief was that society needed to organize itself around myths so the criticism it produced tended to describe the archetypes thought essential to human cultures, or clarify their national cultural forms, rather than examine the groups that produced mythic representations in order to obtain and maintain social control.

Leslie Fiedler (1960) was one of the more notoriously stimulating exponents, R. W. B. Lewis (1955) one of the more scholarly.

The period from the mid-forties to the mid-sixties was, as several recent critics have demonstrated, one in which materialist understanding was prevented by Cold War show trials and anti-communist propaganda, the military-industrial complex needing to justify fantastic expenditure by constructing fantastic enemies (see especially Donald Pease's brilliant essay on cultural persuasion in Cold War readings of *Moby Dick*, 1985; Jane Tompkins, 1985; Russell Reising, 1986). The period's version of American nineteenth-century writing therefore played down the political engagements of the authors and the acute social tensions with which their writing was engaged, even to the extent of presenting accounts in which the Civil War, racism, rapid industrialization and constant genocidal war hardly seemed to affect literary production (Arac, 1985). The canon was constructed by emphasizing the largely psychological dilemmas of (American) individualism, the peculiar features of the national identity, and abstract oppositions between good and evil, whether of white versus red, man versus nature, individual versus community, America versus Europe or democrat versus tyrant. These themes were always considered to be represented allegorically and at a remove from realism or everyday mimetic concern. The typical 'American' novel was seen to be concerned with a pure, innocent, Adamic self, divorced from society and confronting in nature the true promise of America. As Nina Baym (1981) has pointed out, the individual was seen as logically prior to the social, and the social (with woman as its representative) as artificial and destructive of both nature and individualism.

Only with the struggles of the late 1960s against racism and the Vietnam War was a complex historical and ethical sense once more conceivable. Twenty years later, with the maturation of this generation of critics, a body of work has begun to appear that disrupts the old paradigm. Rather than Jung and Frye the tutelary figure is Antonio Gramsci (Gramsci, 1970, often as elaborated by Raymond Williams, 1977, chap. 6), whose concept of hegemony recognizes that not all of a nation has the same relation to its dominant myths and that history is not a matter of inevitable repetition but of differentiating human choices and a struggle for control over beliefs and actions. (For a lucid materialist explanation of the relation of literature, myth and culture, which is the very antithesis of Frye's, see Richard Slotkin's chapter 'Myth and the Production of History', in his *Fatal Environment*, 1985.)

A key sign of the rupture between old and new is the current dissatisfaction with the Miller and Chase definition of the American novel as a romance (Miller, 'Romance in America', 1956; supported by Trilling, 1950; Chase, 1957; Bewley, 1959; Porte, 1969) which occupies what Poirier (1966) called 'a world elsewhere'. According to this orthodoxy the American romance is characterized by a tangential relation to social experience, is essentially non-referential, therefore better able to deal with dark and complex truths unavailable to realism, is stylistically self-conscious and tends to use mythic, allegorical and symbolist forms. The effect of the American romance's tendency towards abstract generality is to liberate it from the parochial (always the negative possibility inherent in American exceptionalism) and allow it to deal with profound truths of universal validity. Chase's *The American Novel and Its Tradition* (1957) in particular, one of the best-selling critical books of all time, severed American writing from the complex circumstances which inspired it and made it into a vehicle displaying the timeless and global relevance of American culture just at the time when the United States was consolidating its dominion over the 'free' world.

The romance hypothesis remains influential but is now more often seen to have been produced by a radical simplification of historical and textual complexity. The idea that European novels are socially engaged, realistic, substantial, and that American novels are ethical, abstract, more dominated by the imagination, appeals because it repeats reductive New World versus Old World dichotomies and mobilizes nationalist economic and political energies. True, there is a strong spirit of historical rationalism in Europe counterposed to a strong spirit of utopian transcendentalism in the United States, but close comparison of the historical romances of Scott, Cooper and Balzac, or of the work of Melville with the Brontës, or later of Zola and Norris, fails to support a general law governing the balances of fictional imagination and social reference on different sides of the Atlantic. Recent studies of Fenimore Cooper (Slotkin 1973; McWilliams, 1972; Clark, 1984, 1985), Melville (Karcher, 1980; Duban, 1983; Rogin, 1983), and Hawthorne (Arac, 1979; Benn Michaels, 1985; Desalvo, 1987; Reynolds, 1988) have shown them to have been not just tangentially involved in the social but intimately engaged in the rights and wrongs of territorial expansion, the contradictions of Democratic ideology, the status of women and the function of property in the formation of consciousness, as well as the alienating effects of the transition to market capitalism (Gilmore, 1985; Shulman, 1987). In these readings of American works one finds a better explanation for their urgent historical relevance than in the myth and symbol approaches of the past because their very peculiarity and 'Americanness' can be seen as issuing from their concern with the country's crucial transformation to economic modernity and with factors in social experience that continue to have enormous influence on the world today.

If the strong version of the romance paradigm has collapsed before such new historical understanding its interpretative power remains considerable. Michael Davitt Bell (1980) has offered one of the better commentaries on the question, beginning by admitting the problematic status of the term but intending to put the question on surer ground by investigating 'what these writers and their contemporaries meant by using it' (p. xii). He specifically dissociates himself from the idea so essential to Miller, Chase, Bewley and Poirier that 'romance' meant a lack of 'social texture' or that it meant something clearly antithetical to the 'novel', though he does accept that in the most general sense romance signified a greater freedom for the imagination and contrasted with the novel's greater referential constraint. Using this very broad and loose understanding, Bell does not reduce all American uses of the word 'romance' to the same, but rather, as George Dekker (1987) has done in the field of historical fiction, explores the differences that exist between different writers – for example between Hawthorne and James who are usually incorporated into the same tradition but who in Bell's subtle and close analysis are shown to have had very different and indeed at times opposed understandings of the term.

Through his careful discriminations Bell comes close to agreement with another of the critics to examine the foundations of the romance hypothesis, Nina Baym (1984), whose reading of critical writings in the antebellum period leads her to dismiss the entire romance paradigm as a modern critical myth. Surveying a vast range of critical writing, Baym goes further than Bell in finding no stable and agreed conventional distinction between 'novel' and 'romance', both words often being used interchangeably within the same article, both words capable of quite opposite significations in the use of different writers. In one nice example Baym quotes a reviewer who takes issue with Hawthorne's own description of *The House of the Seven Gables* (1851) as a romance because he is so impressed with Hawthorne's realistic delineation of character. Indeed, playing the game ourselves we might add that despite the obvious gothic-romantic aspects, *The House of the Seven Gables*'s intense preoccupation with Democratic ideology, the gold rush, the history of territorial expropriation, photography and the ethics of representation make it one of the least 'elsewhere' novels imaginable. Such instances invite the recognition that all distinctions of the imaginary from the referential depend on cultural codes and these codes differ from group to group and from historical moment to historical moment. It may be that Baym somewhat overstates her case and does not see that through all the fluid and contradictory significations of 'romance' and 'novel' there subsists an elementary agreed distinction such as that with which Bell is prepared to work, but she certainly succeeds in her general aim of showing that the Miller–Chase understanding of 'romance' was based upon a highly selective knowledge of the period.

Baym's work questions another dominant assumption, the idea that American writers turned to the romance because the American culture was hostile to fiction. This idea provided the Miller–Chase paradigm with a thin explanatory base, but it had its firmest support in the undoubtedly sound work of Terence Martin (1961) on the domination of American culture at the end of the eighteenth century by Scottish Common Sense philosophers who greatly privileged the probable and factual and inculcated suspicion of the possible and imaginative. Baym does not dispute the importance of Martin's work, but argues that towards the end of the period with which he is concerned, roughly around 1820, we see fiction winning public recognition. Through the 1830s and 1840s there is a huge increase in the volume of fiction published, by both native and foreign authors, and widespread and sophisticated reviewing in an impressive list of publications with national distribution. Baym does not consider the differential responses of social classes and groups to this revaluation of fiction and so does not entertain the possibly crucial objection that in those circles from which serious critical fiction was to emerge, the novel was still a suspect genre. That aside, Baym again poses a valuable question to entertain alongside Bell's retention of the idea that the American writer turned to romance because the culture as a whole was hostile to fiction. Bell's evidence, like that of previous critics, is mainly the well-known complaints of the canonized authors about their lack of financial success. His explanation is a variation of that advanced by Miller and Chase, and repeated in various forms by recent critics (Henry Nash Smith, 1978; H. Bruce Franklin, 1978): the culture is hostile to fiction and so 'To choose the role of romancer in a society that equated romance with insanity and subversion and seldom granted its authors an enduring financial reward was to embrace what sociologists call a "deviant career".' Deviancy begins where someone 'engages in a socially proscribed or peculiar action' (1980, p. 33).

Against this it could be argued that deviancy does not begin in the socially proscribed act but in whatever drives the individual to desire transgression. It is probable that the transgressions of American writers began not in the writing of romances but in what they saw in their society and themselves. The perceptions of Fenimore Cooper, Poe, Melville and Hawthorne are all so profoundly unsettling of conventional wisdom, especially about America's supposedly God-given social perfection and right to expansion, as to necessitate any amount of romancing in the representation. So whilst Bell seems on the right lines when he suggests that the best American writing must be read in terms of 'deviance', he seems to have cause and consequence reversed when he says that American writers became deviant through embracing an illicit genre. Rather, close reading of the contexts of the authorial pronouncements on which so much depends indicates that Hawthorne and Cooper were driven to call themselves romancers, against their inclinations, because their subversive perceptions required the mask of apparently irrelevant and indirect representation. To see the origin of the tendency towards romance as beginning in the struggle to find an appropriate form for heterodox perceptions has the advantage of allowing for Baym's critique: it was not all fiction that was unpopular, just fiction of a certain kind.

The successes and failures of Bell's work are evidence of the way the romance paradigm enables and limits understanding by positing a profound separation between 'classic' and 'popular' literature. In the views of many recent American critics this separation has more to do with the élitist, modernist preferences of the scholars who established the canon than with historical actuality. David Reynolds's important *Beneath the American Renaissance* (1988) shows how erroneous any such assumptions are by carefully drawing out the myriad connections between the writing of Hawthorne, Melville and Poe with their more popular contemporaries. Other critics have sought to redress the neglect accorded the enormously popular gothic and sentimental novelists such as Brockden Brown, William Gilmore Simms, Harriet Beecher Stowe, Fanny Fern and Susan Warner. Nina Baym has provided a useful feminist critique (1978, 1981), but the work which has attracted the most attention is Jane Tompkins's *Sensational Designs* (1985) which inspects how it came about that Fenimore Cooper, Poe, Hawthorne, Emerson, Thoreau and Melville were seen as the important authors whilst the much more popular writers of their day were consigned to obscurity. In her masterly essay 'Masterpiece Theatre' Tompkins explores how Hawthorne's contemporaries valued his transparency of style, his ability to invest the everyday with spiritual significance and his genial and hearty ability to combine sunshine and shadow in such sketches as 'Little Annie's Ramble', 'A Rill from the Town Pump' and 'Sunday at Home'. The stories on which critics base his reputation today, and which are taken as evidence of his psychological depth, moral subtlety and symbolic complexity were scarcely noticed by contemporaries. Few likened him to Melville whose penchant for 'true-life' adventure and abstruse allegory seemed a far cry from Hawthorne's historical themes and concern with character and sentiment; nor, of course, did they comment on his fascination with the indeterminacy of signs, the mark of Hawthorne's genius according to such postmodernist interpreters as Millicent Bell (1982) and Michael Colacurcio (1985). (For a fine critique of this way of appropriating Hawthorne see Arac, 1985.)

Tompkins's point is not that one set of readers are right, the other wrong, rather that criticism is a privileging process determined by ideology. Hawthorne's timeless genius is not proved by his ability to generate so many kinds of interpretation but constituted by 'the literary and cultural tradition that believes in the idea of a classic and perpetuates that belief by reading and rereading ... teaching and recommending for teaching, and writing books and articles about a small group of works whose durability is thereby assured' (p. 37). It follows that if we want to be truly critical we should inspect not the text but our reasons for choosing a text and talking about it in a certain way. The construction of the classic American canon around a small group of north-eastern male WASPs, and the relegation of the influential sentimental novelists to the margins, says more about who has power now than about eternal literary values. The sociological truth of this observation, supported by so many informed critiques of how the American Renaissance came to be constructed, cannot be gainsaid. A more intractable problem remains why Hawthorne not Longfellow? Why Melville not Dana? Where is the account of the neglected novelist that convinces us of what we have been missing?

To date there is only one such essay that I am aware of: this is in Philip Fisher's *Hard Facts* (1985), a superbly written book on Fenimore Cooper, Stowe and Dreiser, which sets out from the often neglected premiss that much fiction functions not as the Russian formalists would have it, to defamiliarize, but to work through the problematic and make it seem natural. The density of analysis he brings to bear on Stowe in particular reveals that rewarding criticism is a product not of the transcendent fineness of the original text but of the intensity of concern the text can mobilize in an interpretative community. Clearly the nexus formed by women's authority, domesticity and racism will reshape the canon to return to Stowe, and possibly other sentimental writers, some of the power they once had (cf. Sundquist, 1986). Similar changes at work in black–white consciousness are also bringing attention to bear on *The Narrative of Frederick Douglass* (1845) (see Baker, 1986; Reising, 1986). Contra Tompkins, however, the very successes of Fisher's book tend to evidence the value of the materialist assumption that it is the way a text engages with the dominant ideological problems of its historical moment that determines its literary value. This makes literary value not merely the arbitrary imposition of the ideology of an interpretative community, but the recognition in the original text of the ways in which historical complexity has been lived and represented, and it is for this reason that the 'classic' text becomes important as a battle-ground where history can be obscured or enlightened. Fisher's method so much consists in his insight into social, literary and political relations that, as it becomes an historical re-education, so it tends to display the need for enormous erudition in the reader in order to appreciate the text. The implication of such work is that no interpretative community – WASMP, black or feminist – could consider its uninvestigated response adequate without similarly deep engagement with a text's context. Paradoxically, in this we may see that where New Criticism's ahistoricism was in part developed to offer quick explanations of literary response in the new classrooms of mass education, New Historicism is the sign of the high specialization and remoteness from the popular of the now established critical profession.

The recent inspection of canon formation has revealed how the canon has been narrowed since the 1930s when anthologies of American literature contained many more authors and a greater diversity of 'non-literary' texts. Then populist pressures ensured that such works as ballads and political speeches were equally important aspects of the national culture and it is evident that the current ethos of equal rights and a system of higher education that embraces a large percentage of the population is creating the demand for a similarly diverse idea of the 'literary' and the 'national'. In the United States these questions have greater import than in Europe because as an evidently made culture it is always debating what counts as 'American'. American studies of American literature have frequently tended towards exceptionalism, concentrating on what is different about American experience and tending to deduce broad generalizations about the American mind or character from literary phenomena (McWilliams, 1984, is the most recent example). In doing so they have often been willing to merge historical, sociological and anthropological insights with a benign disregard of methodological considerations. Whether this is more so than with other national cultures is too large a question for this essay, but the tones and strategies must strike non-American readers quite forcibly and therefore highlight the importance of Sacvan Bercovitch's *American Jeremiad* (1978) which takes the relation of American criticism to the American nation as its subject and provides a framework for understanding all the characteristic dilemmas of American literary criticism.

Bercovitch begins from analyses of the Puritan sermons which lamented the failure of America to achieve its sacred mission at the same time as they celebrated that mission; he goes on to show how the rhetoric of the jeremiad provides the terms for all discussion, political, ethical and artistic, within the American nation, and how its rhetoric fuses within the symbol of America both national and universal values, the earthly with the sacred, and the personal with the social. Developing with remarkable force a relatively traditional argument, he explains how it was the peculiar feature of the Puritans to have a concept of America's continental destiny, and of themselves as God's agents, and it was this that distinguished them and their inheritors from the other American peoples and infused their concept of themselves with that of a sacred mission to be that singular and yet universal nation. This argument explains in part why there is a preponderance of New England Protestant writers in the canon, for as direct inheritors they obviously explored more urgently the failure of America to fulfil its mission.

Bercovitch's argument, however, goes much further than this. He contends that the rhetoric of the jeremiad 'substitutes symbolic for social analysis, and the substitution is crucial since whilst historical or social analysis is secular and ... open to a consideration of radically different systems of thought and action', symbolic analysis 'confines us to the alternatives generated by the symbol itself. Since every symbol unites opposites, or represents them as the same thing, we can understand what is being represented only by means of measuring it against its opposite, or by placing it within a series of comparable and related oppositions. Thus the search for meaning is at once endless and self-enclosed' (pp. 177–8). In effect, whether of right or left, Indian, woman or black, in America one can make oneself heard only by appearing to speak in the true voice of America, by naming one's own values 'American' and calling on others to repudiate in themselves the un-American parts. The hegemonic effect of the jeremiad is therefore 'to transform all searches for moral and social alternatives into calls for revitalization' (p. 179) and to ensure that all critique is co-opted into an extension of the American empire. The chilling importance of Bercovitch's work is that it reveals a perpetually self-containing and self-advancing world that is protected from radical change by the extraordinary ability of the 'American way' either to convert radically different ideas of human needs and organizations into versions of the itself or to deny their relevance.

Bercovitch prefaces his book by saying: 'Insofar as my argument tends to simplify social and economic conflicts, psychic tensions and regional disparities, it does so in order to stress the growth of a certain mode of rhetoric and vision. Insofar as this book supports the notion of American exceptionalism, it does so only in terms of an increasingly pervasive middle-class hegemony' (pp. xxii–xxiii). In this admission Bercovitch points to the fact that in being brief and eloquent he has left out the conflicts, tensions and disparities, the struggling voices in history whose utterance was converted into the jeremiad in order for it to have hegemony over them. In his own terms he has tended to offer a 'symbolic' rather than 'historical' analysis and by absenting history he has created a reified idea of discourse as speaking us, rather than being the product of innumerable individual and collective social acts. Whilst Lacan and Foucault have made this idea fashionable, it is none the less regrettable that what Bercovitch describes as a historical *fait accompli* becomes the more so as the reader is led to conclude that there is no outside to discourse, no elsewhere strong enough to provide a ground of real disruption. Describing the jeremiad is an important political step, but surely to prevent description becoming repetition we need to hear the other accounts that would have provided, and today could provide, other ways of constructing a United States of some of the North American Peoples.

If understanding is to move forward, it is surely the myth of 'America' that critics need to expose, building knowledge of the fundamental determinations which have formed the consciousness of all citizens of developed industrial countries, and developing understanding of how the specific conditions experienced in the United States have enabled the production and reproduction of an exceptional myth that subserves global dominion. As we have seen, the current critical paradigm tends to repeat from previous ones the perception of nineteenth-century American writers as exiled from 'America' by temperament or experience and as deeply identifying with what they say are its highest ideals. The critique of America is seen as leading to a withdrawal to another place where America is reconstructed, a world of deviant romance, literary style or a revitalized national covenant. This portrait of the past is surely as much a portrait of academics in the present (Baym, 1981, calls it 'consensus criticism of the consensus') and Bercovitch's master thesis is not just its description but its apotheosis. The jeremiad critique tends not to fracture the consensus because it does not proceed in terms of political analysis, rather it is recuperated by the typical ideology of scholarship – that it is in the end a value-free description of essential phenomena, in this case of the essential 'American way'.

One major work which does seem to me outside the paradigm, and which indeed politically situates the ideology of impartial scholarship, is that of Carolyn Porter (1981) who founds her critique in a theoretically sophisticated socio-economic understanding of what makes the nineteenth-century United States both like and unlike other industrializing nations. Taking issue with Myra Jehlen's essay 'New World Epics' (1977, further elaborated in her book of 1986) – the best previous attempt to explain how American writers were like and unlike European – she argues that the idea of America as dominated by a 'middle class consensus' from which the classic novelist is alienated uses a reified idea of hegemony and misrepresents a situation in which many more factions and interest groups are contending for power. Porter suggests instead that the writer's alienation derives from the political and economic condition of living in a society where the rights of men are implicitly defined in terms of individualistic competition. Whilst many aspects of this condition are the same in other industrializing bourgeois states, the lack of residual ideologies and structures of ownership in the United States enabled a more rapid and intense entry to industrial capitalism than elsewhere and resulted at the literary level in an earlier and more acute onset of modernism. For Porter, Emerson becomes the archetypal figure, and one very like the modern literary scholar, because in describing himself as a transparent eyeball he produces a poetry of alienation in which human agency is reduced to utter passivity and the world manifests all the contradictions of local rationality and general irrationality that Lukács described in *History and Class Consciousness* (1923). In Porter's account the American search for a world elsewhere is less an exceptional American trait than one manifestation of the tendency under capitalism for reified consciousness to resist the reification of the world, in Emerson's case by an idealized subjectivity isolated from historical action and using intuition to bridge the antinomies between elements of a world felt to be mysterious but held to be objectively rational.

Porter's account, with the work of the other new historicists cited in 'Further Reading' below, lays the basis for a historical analysis of American literature that comprehends the rhetoric of exceptionalism within political and economic conditions. Through the perspectives provided by these critics a new reading of American romance is becoming possible: rather than seeing a pure and innocent American hero escaping from an alienating society by seeking spiritual transcendence and self-identity in the bosom of regenerate nature, we see a people's struggles with actual social conditions being translated into alienated dreams of escape from alienation. We see a society convinced by national rhetoricians that it is perfect, ever more perfectible and a spiritual example to the less enlightened peoples of the world, yet where actual conditions are of intensely exploitative economic struggle, a burgeoning 'free' labour market inflected by slavery, genocidal conquest and acute class tensions, a society of urbanization and the alienation attendant upon nascent market capitalism. The romances of such a society are of so much more interest when seen as complex attempts to engage with and disengage from this experience. Understanding them in this light will provide us with a better chance of understanding our own world and our future.

FURTHER READING

Arac, Jonathan (1979) *Commissioned Spirits: the Shaping of Social Motion in Dickens, Carlyle, Melville and Hawthorne*, Rutgers University Press, New Brunswick

Bell, Michael Davitt (1980) *The Development of American Romance: The Sacrifice of Relation*, University of Chicago Press, Chicago

Benn Michaels, Walter and Pease, Donald (eds) (1985) *American Renaissance Reconsidered: Essays from the English Institute, 1983*, Johns Hopkins University Press, Baltimore

Bercovitch, Sacvan and Jehlen, Myra (eds) (1986) *Ideology and Classic American Literature*, Cambridge University Press, Cambridge

Clark, Robert (1984) *History, Ideology and Myth in American Fiction, 1823–1852*, Macmillan, London

Fisher, Philip (1985) *Hard Facts: Setting and Form in the American Novel*, Oxford University Press, New York

Gilmore, Michael (1985) *American Romanticism and the Marketplace*, Chicago University Press, Chicago

Porter, Carolyn (1981) *Seeing and Being: the Plight of the Participant Observer in Emerson, James, Adams and Faulkner*, Wesleyan University Press, Middletown

Reising, Russell (1986) *The Unusable Past: Theory and the Study of American Literature*, Methuen, New York

Reynolds, David S. (1988) *Beneath the American Renaissance: The Subversive Imagination in the Age of Emerson and Melville*, Knopf, New York

Shulman, Robert (1987) *Social Criticism and Nineteenth-Century American Fictions*, University of Missouri Press, Columbia

Tompkins, Jane (1985) *Sensational Designs: The Cultural Work of American Fiction, 1790–1860*, Oxford University Press, New York

ADDITIONAL WORKS CITED

Arac, Jonathan (1985) 'Mathiessen: Authorizing the American Renaissance'. In Walter Benn Michaels and Donald Pease (eds), *American Renaissance Reconsidered: Essays from the English Institute, 1983*, Johns Hopkins University Press, Baltimore, pp. 90–112

Baker, Houston A., Jr. (1986) 'Figurations for a New American Literary History'. In Sacvan Bercovitch and Myra Jehlen (eds), *Ideology and Classic American Literature*, Cambridge University Press, Cambridge, pp. 145–71

Baym, Nina (1978) *Woman's Fiction: A Guide to Novels by and about Women in America, 1820–1970*, Cornell University Press, Ithaca

——(1981) 'Melodramas of Beset Manhood: How Theories of American Fiction Exclude Women Authors', *American Quarterly*, 33, 123–39

——(1984) *Novels, Readers and Reviewers: Responses to Fiction in Antebellum America*, Cornell University Press, Ithaca

Bell, Millicent (1982) 'The Obliquity of Signs', *Massachussetts Review*, 23, 9–26

Benn Michaels, Walter (1985) 'Romance and Real-Estate'. In Walter Benn Michaels and Donald Pease (eds), *American Renaissance Reconsidered: Essays from the English Institute, 1983*, Johns Hopkins University Press, Baltimore, pp. 156–82

Bercovitch, Sacvan (1978) *The American Jeremiad*, University of Wisconsin Press, Madison

Bewley, Marius (1959) *The Eccentric Design: Form in the Classic American Novel*, Columbia University Press, New York

Chase, Richard (1949) *Quest for Myth*, Louisiana State University Press, Baton Rouge

——(1957) *The American Novel and its Tradition*, Anchor, New York

Clark, Robert (ed.) (1985) *James Fenimore Cooper: New Critical Essays*, Vision/Barnes & Noble, London

Colacurcio, Michael (1985) 'Introduction: The Spirit of the Sign'. In Michael Colacurcio (ed.), *New Essays on 'The Scarlet Letter'*, Cambridge University Press, Cambridge

Dekker, George (1987) *The American Historical Romance*, Cambridge University Press, Cambridge

Desalvo, Louise (1987) *Nathaniel Hawthorne*, Harvester, Brighton

Duban, James (1983) *Melville's Major Fiction: Politics, Theology and Imagination*, Northern Illinois University Press, Dekalb

Fielder, Leslie (1960) *Love and Death in the American Novel*, Stein & Day, New York

Franklin, H. Bruce (1978) *The Victim as Criminal and Artist*, Oxford University Press, New York

Frye, Northrop (1957) *Anatomy of Criticism*, Princeton University Press, Princeton

——(1960) 'New Directions from Old'. In Henry A. Murray (ed.), *Myth and Myth-Making*, Braziller, New York

Gramsci, Antonio (1970) *Selections from the Prison Notebooks*, Lawrence & Wishart, London

Jehlen, Myra (1977) 'New World Epics: The Novel and the Middle Class in America', *Salmagundi*, 36, 49–68

——(1986) *American Incarnation: the Individual, the Nation and the Continent*, Harvard University Press, Boston

Karcher, Carolyn (1980) *Shadow over the Promised Land: Slavery, Racism and Violence in Melville's America*, Louisiana State University Press, Baton Rouge

Kuklick, Bruce (1972) 'Myth and Symbol in American Studies', *American Quarterly*, 34, 435–50

Lewis, R. W. B. (1955) *The American Adam: Innocence, Tragedy and Tradition in the Nineteenth Century*, University of Chicago Press, Chicago

McWilliams, J. P. (1972) *Political Justice in a Republic: Fenimore Cooper's America*, University of California Press, Berkeley

——(1984) *Hawthorne, Melville and the American Character: A Looking-Glass Business*, Cambridge University Press, Cambridge

Martin, Terence (1961) *The Instructed Vision: Scottish Common Sense Philosophy and the Origins of American Fiction*, Kraus, New York

Miller, Perry (1956) *Errand into the Wilderness*, Harvard University Press, Cambridge

Pease, Donald (1985) '*Moby Dick* and the Cold War'. In Walter Benn Michaels and Donald Pease (eds), *American Renaissance Reconsidered: Essays from the English Institute, 1983*, Johns Hopkins University Press, Baltimore, pp. 113–55

Poirier, Richard (1966) *A World Elsewhere: The Place of Style in American Literature*, Oxford University Press, New York

Porte, Joel (1969) *The Romance in America: Studies in Cooper, Poe, Hawthorne, Melville and James*, Wesleyan University Press, Middletown

Rogin, Michael (1983) *Subversive Genealogies: The Politics and Art of Herman Melville*, Knopf, New York

Slotkin, Richard (1973) *Regeneration Through Violence: The Mythology of the American Frontier, 1600–1860*, Wesleyan University Press, Middletown

——(1985) *The Fatal Environment: the Myth of the Frontier in the Age of Industrialisation, 1800–1890*, Athenaeum, New York

Smith, Henry Nash (1950) *Virgin Land: the American West as Symbol and Myth*, Vintage, New York

——(1978) *Democracy and the Novel: Popular Resistance to Classic American Writers*, Oxford University Press, New York

Sundquist, Eric J. (ed.) (1986) *New Essays on 'Uncle Tom's Cabin'*, Cambridge University Press, Cambridge

Trilling, Lionel (1950) 'Manners, Morals, and the Novel'. In Lionel Trilling, *The Liberal Imagination*, Anchor, New York, pp. 113–55

Williams, Raymond (1977) *Marxism and Literature*, Oxford University Press, London

43

FORMALISM AND THE NOVEL: HENRY JAMES

NICOLA BRADBURY

Formalism is the name given to a school of literary theory developed in Russia around the time of the revolution by Viktor Shklovsky and a group of other scholars in St Petersburg. Their technical approach to textual processes derives from the discipline of linguistics, and can be linked with Saussure's ideas on language, but also with later critical movements including New Criticism, Structuralism, and its successors. Viktor Shklovsky's signal contribution is the notion of *ostranenie*: 'making strange', or defamiliarization. Literature, he points out, like language, works by surprise, by substituting novelty for the habitual, shifting our expectations, and hence our perceptions (see Hawkes, 1977, pp. 62–3). This dispassionate, analytical approach in criticism has, however, one remarkable precursor amongst practising novelists, a writer whose work constitutes an exploration of formalism and its limitations: Henry James.

Bridging two periods and two civilizations – the nineteenth and twentieth centuries, America and Europe – Henry James inherited a hugely popular novel form and reconceived it, both by redefining the relationship of the work with the reader, and by giving it a new scope, which prepared for the idea of the novel which we have today. James followed Scott, Dickens and George Eliot in Britain, but those who follow him include Conrad, Ford and Virginia Woolf. He venerated Balzac and Turgenev in France; he is a contemporary of Flaubert, and anticipates Proust. Hawthorne is his American predecessor. James develops from his New England heritage as a cosmopolitan 'high renaissance' novelist (a metaphor which is vividly supported by his own considerable pictorial imagery), past decadence and towards modernism. This is no mere catalogue of names and movements in relation to James, but the shortest possible sketch of what for him was a field of exciting possibilities. He was a great reader, a passionate critic and a highly conscious writer. All these qualities survive in his contribution to the novel form.

We could scan James's career in terms of three 'points', quite different in kind: his starting point, the point of view and punctuation points. He began as the second son of a distinguished, cultured, comfortable family. His father was Henry James Sr., his elder brother the philosopher William James. Moving away, establishing himself in England, Henry James nevertheless took with him the capacity for comparison and contrast, a sense of relativism and a pragmatist's flexibility. These are the foundations of his modernism. His great technical contribution to the novel form could indeed be seen as a formal expression of this philosophical stance: the development of the point of view. And pragmatism also permeates James's later works, where the elision of punctuation points marks the evolution of an increasingly fluid style, in which possibilities are held in suspension for the reader to consider, whilst the text avoids conclusion. James is a millennial writer, who turns crisis to account; he is a novelist of change, the analyst of experience, celebrating the challenge of life.

Joseph Conrad called James 'the historian of fine consciences' ([1905] 1947, p. 44). We read him as both a moralist and a cultural diagnostician; a writer of his time (which was a time of change), but distanced from it, and made available to us, by his peculiar consciousness not only of what he saw but of the process of seeing. James expressed these things through the novel form – a form whose possibilities and whose resistance to manipulation alike he valued and enjoyed. He became a master of the exercise of reader-response, encouraging imagination and critical apprehension in equal proportions.

The novels of Henry James constitute a body of work as much for the reader as the writer. He challenges interest, understanding and feeling: 'difficulty', for James, is a stimulus to 'delight'. The aim of the novel is, unequivocally, 'to represent life', but 'the process and the effect of representation' are matters of art and imagination, involving producer and audience in a way analogous to (and perhaps inseparable from) primary experience, which James called 'the very atmosphere of the mind' ([1884] 1963, p. 85). His *Notebooks* show how often the *donnée* or idea of a text came from talk over dinner, letters from friends, or the newspaper; but having recognized the germ of a story, James would close his ears to extraneous detail and cultivate the fullest possibilities of latent significance through strict economy of presentation. This procedure is formalist, yet James's curiosity and patience, his love of life, exercise in us too 'the power to guess the unseen from the seen, to trace the implications of things' ([1884] 1963, p. 85). Through the text James cultivates an ideal reader who, like Strether in *The Ambassadors*, enjoys 'the oddity of a double consciousness. There was detachment in his zeal and curiosity in his indifference' ([1903] 1986, p. 56).

Certain themes recur through James's novels, and distinctive techniques are developed. Exploitation and betrayal, recognition and appreciation, are given imaginative force through the manipulation of voice and point of view, the range of diction and figuration, and a control of structure which works dynamically with the reader's reception of the text. James is central to the evolution of the novel form, not least because form itself assumes ideological dimensions when its subject is control: the imaginative authority of the artist dramatizes and exposes in textual terms the tyrannies of financial, social, intellectual or sexual domination. James's quiet championship of the oppressed – the dull woman, the helpless child, the impoverished lover or ineffectual ambassador – thus demands in the novel precisely that self-mastery which he celebrates so triumphantly in his Preface to *The Golden Bowl* as 'a certain indirect and oblique view of my presented action – unless indeed I make up my mind to call this treatment on the contrary the very straightest and closest possible' ([1907] 1962, p. 327). Every shift and strain in formal experimentation, every extravagance of word, image, syntax, or of mode, has this further dimension: these processes are calculated to have the double effect of stimulating the reader intellectually, while also imaginatively expressing the dangers of exploitation. Amongst James's most powerful devices are the silences, elisions, suppressions of statement, gesture or action, whose significance is framed but not wholly limited by their context.

From *Roderick Hudson* (1876) to *The Golden Bowl* (1904), and even beyond, in James's unfinished and short fiction, a series of oppositions, both thematic and formal, expose and then explore the imaginative subjects: America and Europe, rich and poor, man and woman, betrayer and betrayed. They appear at first to constitute a binary system of signification – perhaps a structure of meaning deriving from New England allegory, where the aim is both to expose and to clarify the spiritual drama of the human psyche, so as to illuminate the right and damn darkness. Something of the strength of this tradition survives through James's career, but it is transformed, rather than overlaid, with the modulations of further literary examples in different kinds. Increasing complexity does not compromise clarity, but heightens and refines it.

Form and subject, structure and feeling, are inseparable for James. His *Notebooks* (eds Matthiessen and Murdock, 1961) record a passionate intensity in this. Two entries, for 1894 and 1895, shortly after James had renounced his catastrophic career as a dramatist, remind him what matters most. Imagery and rhythm, inventive and insistent, express the force of his argument. It is worth quoting at length for its poignant lucidity:

> *Plus je vais*, the more intensely it comes home to me that solidity of subject, importance, emotional capacity of subject, is the only thing on which, henceforth, it is of the lightest use for me to expend myself. Everything else breaks down, collapses, turns thin, turns poor, turns wretched – betrays one miserably. Only the fine, the large, the human, the natural, the fundamental, the passionate things.
>
> (*Notebooks*, 23 January 1894, p. 145)

What I should like to do, God willing, is to thresh out my little remainder, from this point, tabulate and clarify it, state or summarise it in such a way that I can go, very straight and sharp, to my climax, my dénouement. What I feel more and more that I must arrive at, with these things, is the adequate and regular practice of some such economy of clear summarization as will *give* me from point to point, each of my steps, stages, tints, shades, every main joint and hinge, in its sequence. I can then *take* from the table, successively, each fitted or fitting piece of my little mosaic. When I ask myself what there may have been to show for my long tribulation, my wasted years and patiences and pangs, of theatrical experiment, the answer, as I have already noted here, comes up as just possibly *this*: what I have gathered from it will perhaps have been exactly some such mastery of fundamental statement – of the art and secret of it, of expression, of the sacred mystery of structure.

(11 August, 1895, p. 208)

These adjurations, with their psalmic solemnity, bring out at this creative crisis what has in fact been James's imperative from the first: to deal clearly with matters of human value. In his early work this is best done through comic and ironic control, and the developing capacity to exploit techniques of narration as ethical indicators. *The Europeans* (1878), *Washington Square* (1881) and *Daisy Miller* (1879) provide examples of this. By *The Portrait of a Lady* (1881), James is orchestrating a greater range of issues, articulating the international and the personal through norms of culture and forms of feeling: the story tells of romance and betrayal, but the novel treats the deeper problem of the constitution of the self. In *The Bostonians* (1886) and *The Princess Casamassima* (1886) the subject-matter is overtly political, but in the shorter *Spoils of Poynton* (1897), *What Maisie Knew* (1897) and *The Awkward Age* (1899), too, we witness the workings of power. Ostensibly family and personal issues acquire further resonance as James perfects the 'mastery of fundamental statement' which uses structure itself as an instrument of tone, and thereby of value. Technical daring and acuity learned from the stage animate highly organized novelistic structures, mimetic of social oppression: thus the symmetries of plot in *What Maisie Knew* realize for us in our reading experience what for the child Maisie is the cross-fire of life in an adulterous society. At the same time the verbal brilliance of these short texts excites resistance to structural control, and celebrates the irreducible originality of the protagonists. *The Turn of the Screw*, James's best-known novella, also dates from this period (1898), and shows obsessive intensity, conveyed through the first-person narration as much as the events of the plot, raised to the power of haunting. Generations of critics have disputed the 'supernatural' and 'psychological' readings of this tale: what all have agreed on is the finesse of James's narrative suppressions which tease us with both possibilities. Extended over a whole novel, as they are in *The Sacred Fount* (1901), such formal devices become bewildering, and risk exasperating the reader. Yet without renouncing experimentalism, in his three later novels, *The Ambassadors* (1903), *The Wings of the Dove* (1902) and *The Golden*

Bowl (1904), James avoids the domination of individual devices by the expedient of generating even more variety. These great works investigate knowledge and its limitations through the movements of the novel form, and they also celebrate life, especially, though not exclusively, through art. James engages interest and creates experience through texts which offer varieties of enticement and impedance, exploiting popular art forms, banal and clichéd expression together with the esoteric, texts in which much can be said by omission, and questions are more powerful than statements.

It is not easy to convey James's achievement in brief. (He often had trouble himself with short stories which grew beyond their conception, and with the 'misplaced middle' even in the novel form.) The novel, for James, was 'all one and continuous' ([1884] 1963, p. 88), if not in structure, yet in its inter-dependent effects. Selective comment on individual texts therefore distorts precisely that quality in James's work which distinguishes it as modern, even postmodern: the strain against form. Paradoxically, this demands at once the construction and deconstruction of all that apparatus of literary order by means of which the reader is made familiar with the space of the text, given bearings and taught the due responses. Nowhere is this more apparent than in the startlingly disconcerting and yet encouraging *What Maisie Knew*, a fragmented, fantastic version of the *Bildungsroman*, where the growing child's integrity provides both a devastating critique of adult decadence and an equally powerful affirmation of what it means to grow into full humanity, to come to know.

The germ of *What Maisie Knew* was the story of a child in a divorce, first claimed, then dumped, by each parent in turn. James approached the idea in two ways: by adding a second fictional step-parent to balance the third partner of his *donnée*, and by deciding to use the child as the structural centre of his text, and to make her a little girl. Through these formal devices James clarifies the situation he perceived latent in the unhappy anecdote: he multiplies, magnifies and, most importantly, directs our view of the spectacle. All these are part of a constructive novelistic strategy. But together with these James develops deconstructive tactics, those techniques which will expose the full horror of the story, and prevent our endorsing the comforts of patterned form. Stylistic extravagance, particularly in the figurative language of the novel, has this disruptive effect. Yet this also offers its own kind of delight, and here we find an intimation of redemption in the narrative, which is not, after all, an elegy for lost innocence, so much as the chronicle of remarkable development in its protagonist.

Exploiting the paradox of formalism, as both affirming order and exposing itself to criticism, James's technique in *What Maisie Knew* is peculiarly economi-cal. This sense of formal economy allows the text a precise tonal balance of pleasure and restraint, in acknowledgement of the moral paradox that good may come out of evil, yet not without loss. Reading the novel, we are almost bewildered by the succession of pity and delight, outrage, triumph, wry humour and controlled sorrow which come upon us. Amongst these emotions it is perhaps bewilderment itself, and its counterpart, poise, that most effectively convey (however obliquely) the experience the novel purports to reveal: that of the growing Maisie.

An extraordinary sense of all this is condensed into the bare three pages of the opening chapter. The situation, the history, the moral values involved and, most importantly, Maisie's awareness of those values, are intimated in a style which combines accuracy with brevity. Every aspect of relation is made to work towards this effect of compression: the shift from the general account to the tableau, reflection to direct speech; the modulations between an outer world of doubtful credibility, and a vivid but confused inner consciousness. So the chapter is held between formality, impersonality, distance at the opening:

> The child was provided for, but the new arrangement was inevitably confounding to a young intelligence intensely aware that something had happened which must matter a good deal and looking anxiously out for the effects of so great a cause.
>
> ([1897] 1966, p. 21)

and the deliberately breathtaking assault of the close – short, direct, rude and funny:

> 'He said I was to tell you, from him,' she faithfully reported, 'that you're a nasty horrid pig!'
>
> (p. 24)

The Maisie who can deliver this message, though she soon learns to keep her own counsel, has a spark in her which calls for admiration beyond pity. James introduces her as a 'patient little girl' (p. 21), but his first image is that of 'a drummer boy in a ballad or a story' (p. 21); and the description of her implication in intrigue is both active and disarmingly ingenuous: 'She was taken into the confidence of passions on which she fixed just the stare she might have had for images bounding across the wall in the slide of a magic lantern' (p. 21). There is both violence and delight in these strange games: James uses the rhythm of his sentences, the concatenation of images, the very disruption of sequence, to convey what for Maisie is inexplicably vivid. Briefly, the adult world and the child's have changed places, and Maisie is forced by this reversal into precocious maturity – even a premature weariness – whose perversity the style itself makes real for us as we read:

> Her first term was with her father, who spared her only in not letting her have the wild letters addressed to her by her mother: he confined himself to holding them up at her and shaking them, while he showed his teeth, and then amusing her by the way he chucked them, across the room, bang into the fire. Even at that moment, however, she had a scared anticipation of fatigue, a guilty sense of not rising to the occasion, feeling the charm of the violence with which the

stiff unmarked envelopes, whose big monograms – Ida bristled with monograms – she would have liked to see, were made to whizz, like dangerous missiles, through the air.

(p. 21)

While both adults are metamorphosed into the wild animals of a circus, bared teeth and bristles, amusing themselves with dangerous toys, Maisie stands by, a non-combatant. Recording her 'scared anticipation of fatigue', James endows her with a capacity to look beyond the future into a future perfect: her initial curiosity over effects and cause will move from apprehension towards comprehension. Through such indirect, stylistic hints, we are made privy in advance (our own 'anticipation') to a truth Maisie's nurse is soon to divulge, and the author to confirm:

'You feel the strain – that's what it is; and you'll feel it still worse, you know.' Thus from the first Maisie not only felt it, but knew she felt it.

(p. 22)

James traces the growth of Maisie's 'knowledge', in its increasing articulacy, but he never loses sight of that 'feeling' which is her real distinction from those around her. The passage in Kensington Gardens when Maisie begs the Captain, her mother's latest lover, to 'Do it always!' (p. 115) is both absurd and moving. James wrote in the preface that this was the 'type-passage' for expressing the beauty of 'the passion that precedes knowledge' (p. 13): precedes and takes precedence perhaps.

We can get some idea of the subtlety and range of *What Maisie Knew* if we add to that example another scene culminating in one of Maisie's 'gaffes', when elaborate artifice is interrupted by irrepressible feeling. Maisie accidentally encounters her father (appropriately, at the Great Exhibition). He carries her off, disgracefully, to his love-nest. The scene he manoeuvres there is to be a final parting, one in which Maisie will leave him, so absolving him of guilt. But Maisie cannot bring herself to send him away, and her love exposes his tawdry self-interest for what it is. By comparison with the opening father-and-daughter scene, this closing is lengthy: fifteen pages to a single paragraph. There is action, dialogue and rich description; there is also a good deal of interpretation, some Maisie's, some narratorial (it is not always easy to distinguish them). The child's critical capacity is shown obliquely through her appreciation of the fictional qualities of the situation:

The child had been in thousands of stories – all Mrs Wix's and her own, to say nothing of the richest romances of French Elise – but she had never been in such a story as this. By the time he had helped her out of the cab, which drove away, and she heard in the door of the house the prompt little click of his key, the Arabian Nights had quite closed round her.

(p. 127)

595

We might dispute her categorization: the scene reeks of French realism, heavily spiced with decadent romance. But that it is a fiction, staged, open to reading, is quite clear. The interpretation depends on tone and stance. Maisie's innocently penetrating opening question strikes an adult reader as uncannily pertinent, and James uses this opportunity for irony in setting out the emotional and tonal dynamics of the scene:

> 'Is she very rich?' He had begun to strike her as almost embarrassed, so shy that he might have found himself with a young lady with whom he had little in common. She was literally moved by this apprehension to offer him some relief.
>
> (p. 128)

The ambiguity of 'apprehension' here alerts us to the dangers beneath the rich surface of the scene: knowledge is associated with fear. There is a particular poignancy, then, in Maisie's willingness to wonder at all she sees. Her response to material surroundings shades into emotional generosity, too. James's careful phrasing allows us to understand that this is a valuable attribute: Maisie's openness is not gullibility. Indeed the scene is watched almost in the light of an afterglow, which is the continuing attempt to read its full meaning. This is experience as 'the atmosphere of the mind':

> The whole hour of course was to remain with her, for days and weeks, ineffaceably illumined and confirmed; by the end of which she was able to read into it a hundred things that had been at the moment mere miraculous pleasantness. What they at the moment came to was simply that her companion was still in a good deal of a flutter, yet wished not to show it, and that just in proportion as he succeeded in this attempt he was able to encourage her to regard him as kind.
>
> (p. 130)

This is not the language of dazzlement, but of consideration. James does not allow us to miss 'the small strange pathos on the child's part of an innocence so saturated with knowledge and so directed to diplomacy' (p. 132). Negotiations are conducted in a tone of mutual understanding, tactful obliquity and tell-tale ellipses. But Maisie's 'absurdity' disrupts the convenient fabrication: she blurts out stiffly, 'Then I can't give you up', and is met by her father's 'strained grimace, a perfect parade of all his teeth, in which it seemed to her she could read the disgust he didn't quite like to express at this departure from the pliability she had practically promised' (p. 138). Father and daughter are held together now by embarrassment, which is ironically diagnosed as 'renewed and intimate union' (p. 138).

A third comparison with these parental interviews could be found in the final page of the book, when Maisie leaves her stepfather Sir Claude. This involves considerably more direct speech, but the spoken words take on the quality of ritual, expressing more than they say. When Sir Claude tells Mrs

Beale, his mistress, Maisie's stepmother, that he will never give her up (thus recalling for us Maisie's words to her father), Maisie's governess, Mrs Wix, seals the finality of his vow (with an even more ironic echo):

'He can't!' Mrs Wix tragically commented.

Mrs Beale, erect and alive in her defeat, jerked her handsome face about. 'He can't!' she literally mocked.

'He can't, he can't, he can't!' – Sir Claude's gay emphasis wonderfully carried it off.

(p. 248)

After this incantation, the parting of Maisie and Sir Claude is finely understated. James can now make use of that rhythmic sense which he has just inculcated. The reader's ear is ready to pick up an unusual word order, which turns the intonations of defeat into something different:

On the threshold Maisie paused; she put out her hand to her stepfather. He took it and held it a moment, and their eyes met as the eyes of those who have done for each other what they can.

(p. 248)

'What they can': this is an expression of achievement – distinct in inflection from the expression of parting in 'for each other', which we might have expected to close the sentence. It is a muted, but not a fading conclusion.

What Maisie Knew offers a brilliant critique of formalism in the novel by an author exercising his own powers and his readers' attention to the full. James both works and plays with the formal structures of language, character and plot to heighten the satirical possibilities of his story and at the same time undermines these patterns to keep faith with the child who is their victim. In Maisie's naïve (but not stupid) consciousness the blasé world of *fin-de-siècle* London is 'made strange'; we see it afresh through her, and in the process we see her too as a marvel. So James both uses technical sophistication and dislodges it; he redefines a complex relationship between aesthetic and moral values; he shifts within the confines of a deliberately tight story towards uncertainty on an epistemological scale, and he makes it both disturbing and exciting. As Joseph Conrad wrote of James, 'His books end as an episode in life ends, with the sense of life still going on' ([1905] 1947, p. 46).

This claim is both confirmed and brought into question by James's late novel *The Wings of the Dove*. As *What Maisie Knew* offers a variant on the familiar kind of *Bildungsroman*, *The Wings of the Dove* clearly derives from a Victorian (or even earlier) tradition of the suffering heroine, with a tragic climax in death; but it defies the restrictions of its genre. James's protagonist refuses to fit the stereotype: 'You won't see me suffer – don't be afraid. I shan't be a public nuisance' ([1902] 1965, p. 297). Her directness, wry phrasing and brisk rhythms express her individuality. Amongst self-seekers, Milly Theale is alone in devoting more imagination to others than herself; but she is capable of self-assessment too. James conveys this characteristic (which has a literary function as well as moral value) in various ways. She is contrasted with other characters: Kate Croy, in her ruthless desires, Merton Densher with his fallible morality, Lord Mark in his effortless indulgence. Milly's presence is dramatized through appearance, speech, gesture; she is also used structurally as a point of view, and her penetrating judgement gives us information about the others. Though she is notably 'straight' with herself, Milly can operate in a highly formalized society. There is an element of public performance in scenes, from dinner parties to simple conversations, where the imagery of masks and ritual suggests costume drama. Yet the moments of greatest artifice in the novel can also be most nakedly revealing. Here is James's furthest development of the strain against form: the intimation of a deeper truth inaccessible to statement, and which can only be imaginatively understood. On the other hand, his highly idiosyncratic style can give episodes of apparently lesser artificiality a magnified focus. *The Wings of the Dove* shows James working form as hard as he can, and making extraordinary demands of the reader. Our reward is an experience: the revolutionary comprehension of that old paradox, that it is better to give than to receive. This wisdom in defiance of worldly values is, through James's determination, firmly attached in this novel to a love of life.

We can see James subverting expectations, formal and economic alike, in three passages from *The Wings of the Dove*: the two great set-piece 'picture scenes', and a later spell in Venice. These examples also show how the tone shifts with the manipulation of form, and in keeping with the demands of subject. The first, the 'Bronzino scene', takes place about one-third of the way through the novel, and it marks the apogee of Milly's vitality. Her visit to Matcham, Lord Mark's country house, expresses all the luxuriance of privilege, 'impressions this afternoon having by a happy turn of their wheel been gathered for them into a splendid cluster, an offering like an armful of the rarest flowers' (p. 135). It is Milly herself who is the offering, however. A quasi-Keatsian apprehension of sacrifice lurks beneath this 'beautiful and interesting experience': as in the Odes, art confronts life, and we see transience as the precondition of beauty. Milly is brought to admire Lord Mark's prized Bronzino portrait, with which she shares a strange likeness. Here James's representation of class and wealth, 'the beauty and the history and the facility and the splendid midsummer glow . . . a sort of magnificent maximum' (p. 144), moves into a critique of civilization itself, offering a comparison with the Renaissance which intimates not only splendour but the underlying conditions of oppression and manipulation. There is a superb ellipsis of art and truth, in a tableau with more significance than words to state, or even to suggest its meaning. The scene is brilliantly compacted. The conjunction of spectacle and verbal suppression stands in defiance of explication:

> The lady in question, at all events, with her slightly Michaelangelesque squareness, her eyes of other days, her full lips, her long neck, her recorded jewels, her brocaded and wasted reds, was a very great personage – only unaccompanied by a joy. And she was dead, dead, dead. Milly recognized her exactly in words that had nothing to do with her.
> 'I shall never be better than this.'
>
> (p. 144)

This is more than a moment of extravagance heralded by the repeated 'dead, dead, dead'. Milly's words look limpid, and in this alone she is distinguished from the image with which she is being compared. James does not rely on this stylistic clue, however. With remarkable assurance he interrupts the narrative to interpolate a critical, perhaps metacritical, comment, in the provocative shape of a paradox: 'Milly recognized her exactly in words that had nothing to do with her.' This clear warning against identification proposes a method of reading based on both distinction and analogy: a symbolist interpretation. Yet Milly's exclamation – 'I shall never be better than this' – through the use of the comparative, insists on drawing together two subjects. The complication comes in discerning what the second subject is. This portrait? This moment? This state? The effect of this multiple choice, and of Milly's perfect poise (contrasted with the incomprehension of Lord Mark beside her) is to elevate her above the narrative moment, giving her a quasi-authorial sanction. She is not, therefore, felt to be the victim of her situation, nor is she a mere object of contemplation, like the picture, but she is in control of it, discerning and asserting its values. So James uses cultural history, symbolism, description and dialogue, together with style, to undercut readerly presumptions about the values inherent in the situation of the doomed girl confronted with an image of past greatness. The imaginative charge released by the scene as a reading experience actually accrues imaginatively to Milly's own vitality.

The 'Veronese' picture created in Venice marks the second third of the novel. Milly's apotheosis from life to art is suggested both within the scene and by the implicit comparison with the Bronzino. James constructs the novel to carry patterns and parallels, not only between scenes, episodes or characters, but even between individual words or images: he is not afraid to demand intense concentration from the reader, and to reward imagination. So we share the mesmeric experience of the characters surrounded by Milly's 'beatific mildness'. Densher

> seemed to stand in it up to his neck. He moved about in it, and it made no plash; he floated, he noiselessly swam in it; and they were all together, for that matter, like fishes in a crystal pool.
>
> (p. 334)

Yet the elaboration of this image has a wry self-ironization. Not only Milly, but her guests and dependants are both conscious performers and critics. The courtiers admire her, from the foot of the stairs, and appraise her too (mentally valuing her pearl necklace). Using their points of view, James indicates narratively what is also shown by dialogue and plot: that now Milly is not the figure of triumph that she appeared before, but a victim of her own magnificence. Her party provides the opportunity for her companions to plot against her, to make her theirs. This appropriation is mirrored in structural terms. After Milly's grand entrance, she simply fades from textual view, while we huddle with the dialogue of Kate and Densher, bargaining 'honour' against 'business'. Milly's eclipse in this scene foreshadows her imminent exclusion from the novel and from life, when she will die 'off-stage' while the narrative carries on elsewhere.

Machiavellian intrigue finds a fitting home in Venice, where this third of the novel is set, framed by the less exotic but sombre, powerful London scenes which speak of a different realism. Just as Bronzino and Veronese connote a range of values associated with their historical eras, so Venice for James is a complex symbol of personal corruption. People, buildings, decor, all express the moral sickness of exploitation. The streets of this claustrophobic city, rather like those of Dickens's London, take on the labyrinthine qualities of the conspirators' plans. They map out the wanderings and bafflements, intrigues and self-interruptions, of Merton Densher's mind. There is a poignant echo of Milly's walk in London when she learned of her fatal illness; but whereas she turned to look outwards at the children playing about her, Densher is trapped in his own disordered imagination.

In contrast to the great painting metaphors, the city surrounds its spectators. James moves between Milly's palazzo, Densher's memory-infested rooms, where he has had Kate come to him, and the streets leading to St Mark's Square, where the outside world itself is interiorized in 'the great drawing-room of Europe': a place for gossip, intrigue and chance encounters. Space for Densher, like time for Milly, grows increasingly circumscribed. As he decides to 'let himself go – go in the direction, that is to say, of staying' (p. 359), logical contradiction reflects moral compromise, and his physical movements mirror his mental contortions. At the crisis, however, James moves outward again from the solipsism of Densher's mind, to a broader stage:

> It was a Venice all of evil that had broken out for them alike, so that they were together in their anxiety, if they really could have met on it; a Venice of cold, lashing rain from a low black sky, of wicked wind raging through narrow passes, of general arrest and interruption, with the people engaged in all the water-life huddled, stranded and wageless, bored and cynical, under archways and bridges.
>
> (p. 363)

This could be read as a figurative description of Densher's own state, stranded, bored, wageless, and caught, not on, but beneath, the bridges of communication. To commute it to this, however, would run counter to the tenor of the text. Densher's deceit is symptomatic of a larger evil, and not the other way round. Hence our sense of his smallness and, conversely, of Milly's stature, as she learns to know, to forgive, and to requite his exploitation through the larger resource of her own unlimited generosity. The last words of the novel, spoken by one of the survivors, could be applied equally to the novel form itself, and its readers: 'We shall never be again as we were!'

FURTHER READING

Bayley, John (1981) 'Formalist Games and Real Life', *Essays in Criticism*, 31, 271–81

Booth, Wayne C. (1983) *The Rhetoric of Fiction*, University of Chicago Press, Chicago [first published 1969]

Bradbury, Nicola (1979) *Henry James: The Later Novels*, Oxford University Press, London

Carroll, David (1982) *The Subject in Question: The Language of Theory and the Strategies of Fiction*, University of Chicago Press, Chicago

Chatman, Seymour (1972) *The Later Style of Henry James*, Blackwell, Oxford

Culler, Jonathan (1975) *Structuralist Poetics: Structuralism, Linguistics, and the Study of Literature*, Routledge & Kegan Paul, London

Goode, John (ed.) (1973) *The Air of Reality: New Essays on Henry James*, Methuen, London

Kappeler, Susanne (1980) *Writing and Reading in Henry James*, Macmillan, London

Lodge, David (1988) *Modern Criticism and Theory: A Reader*, Longman, London

Rowe, John Carlos (1984) *The Theoretical Dimensions of Henry James*, Methuen, London

Todorov, Tzvetan (1973) 'The Structural Analysis of Literature: Henry James'. In David Robey (ed.), *Structuralism: An Introduction*, Clarendon Press, Oxford, pp. 73–101

ADDITIONAL WORKS CITED

Conrad, Joseph (1947) 'Henry James: An Appreciation'. In F. W. Dupee (ed.), *The Question of Henry James*, Allan Wingate, London, pp. 44–7 [essay first published 1905]

Hawkes, Terence (1977) *Structuralism and Semiotics*, Methuen, London

James, Henry (1962) 'Preface to *The Golden Bowl*'. In R. P. Blackmur (ed.), *The Art of the Novel: Critical Prefaces*, Scribner's, New York [Preface first published 1907]

——(1963) 'The Art of Fiction'. In Morris Shapira (ed.), *Henry James: Selected Literary Criticism*, Penguin, Harmondsworth, pp. 78–97 [essay first published 1884]

——(1965) *The Wings of the Dove*, Penguin, Harmondsworth [first published 1902]

——(1966) *What Maisie Knew*, Penguin, Harmondsworth [first published 1897]

——(1986) *The Ambassadors*, Penguin, Harmondsworth [first published 1903]

Matthiessen, F. O. and Murdock, Kenneth B. (eds) (1961) *The Notebooks of Henry James*, Galaxy, New York

44

THE NOVEL AND MODERN CRITICISM

DANIEL R. SCHWARZ

We are at an exciting time when the challenge of recent theory has stimulated us to examine the assumptions behind traditional critical methodology. At one extreme, deconstruction argues for the free play of signifiers, the polysemy of language, and the indeterminacy of meaning. At the other extreme – as if older forms of criticism lacked implicit theoretical assumptions – scholars dismiss the theoretical explosion as an unfortunate aberration. My focus will be on the central texts of Anglo-American novel criticism, with the goal of establishing a dialogue between traditional and recent theory.

We begin our study with Henry James, because James is the first figure whom we can isolate as a major source of the way we have read and taught fiction in England and America for the past fifty years. We can trace back to Henry James the dilemma of Anglo-American novel criticism: how to focus on technique without sacrificing subject-matter. Much of the novel criticism of this century has been trying to resolve these two factors into an aesthetic. Given that novels seem to create imagined worlds with distinct time, space and causality that mime that of the real world, it seems as if subject-matter ought not be ignored. But given that novels are, like other literary forms, works of art composed of words, we cannot ignore technique. As we shall see, most 'formal' critics of the novel do not neglect content in determining meaning; nevertheless, focus on form often seems to be at the expense of content and vice versa.

The stature of James's novel criticism surely depends upon James's stature as a novelist. We should remember that his discussion of method and theory is shaped by his own experience of writing novels and, in the case of the Prefaces (ed. Blackmur, 1934), in response to his memory of his own novels. While James looks forward to concern with form and technique, he provided continuity with the high seriousness of Arnold who argued for the central place of criticism and defined it as a disinterested act of mind. For the most part, James refused to embrace the position that art was an ivory tower or sacred fount. In his essay on Flaubert (1902), James wrote, 'the form is in *itself* as interesting, as active, as much of the essence of the subject as the idea, and yet so close is its fit and so inseparable its life that we catch it at no moment on any errand of its own' (in James E. Miller, 1972, p. 259). Form enables the artist to present and understand subjects. The artist's imaginative vision implies his morality. Furthermore, James argued that an artist's total work expresses a more inclusive vision than any of the parts.

James's 'The Art of Fiction' (1884), perhaps his most important single piece on novel criticism, was a response to Walter Besant's 'The Art of Fiction' (1884). Because Besant's published lecture expressed some of the critical shibboleths of the day, James chose the same title. While James became more interested in technique as his career progressed, he never abandoned the credo expressed in 'The Art of Fiction' that 'A novel is in its broadest definition a personal, a direct impression of life: that, to begin with, constitutes its value which is greater or less according to the intensity of the impression' (in Miller, 1972, p. 33). At the centre of James's criticism is an interest in life in every aspect, even if in his work we feel that the focus is on the manners and morals of the upper middle class. James directed the novel away from its traditional emphasis on plot, an emphasis derived from neo-classicism and the novel's epic and romance antecedents. James regarded character, not plot, as central to the novel. The emphasis on point of view is central in James's novel criticism as well as in his fiction where he modified the traditional omniscient narrator of Victorian fiction. His interest in point of view is related to his concern about intensity, interest and realism. His quest for realism is related to the quest for life and truth. Life was the raw material of art.

The story of modern novel criticism continues with Percy Lubbock's codification of James's practice and theory. Lubbock's book, *The Craft of Fiction* (1921), along with Joseph Warren Beach's *The Method of Henry James* (1918) and *The Twentieth Century Novel: Studies in Technique* (1932), did much to turn James's musings on his method as a novelist into an aesthetic with rigid rules. Yet it is ironic that Lubbock and Beach sought to codify James's suggestions, for James himself cautions about theorizing upon art and often thought that a characteristic of novels was their freedom from rules and categories. Lubbock's codification stresses several concepts crucial to twentieth-century novel criticism. Lubbock taught us that a novel is 'a process, a passage of experience', revealing its form – or rather, partially revealing its form, because that form is 'an ideal shape with no existence in space' and lacks 'size and shape' and therefore can only be approached imperfectly ([1921] 1957, pp. 15, 22). Lubbock realized that the reading of fiction is a linear process and that patterns take shape and then dissolve or recede, only to be replaced by new patterns which do the same. Yet he focused on James primarily as a formal and technical master and neglected his interest in truth and life. For Lubbock, more than for James, form and unity are values in themselves, distinct and separate from how they convey meaning. The shift in emphasis is one of degree, not kind, but it is obvious that content plays a much lesser role in Lubbock than in James.

The criticism of Lubbock and James emphasized three concepts: the drama-tized consciousness of the individual character – his emotional and moral life – as subject; the author's creative transformation of art into life, and under-standing the artistry involved in that process; and the importance of arousing and maintaining the reader's interest. Each of these three concepts depends upon belief in the ability of a human being to control his life and in the implicit value of one man communicating with another.

E. M. Forster's *Aspects of the Novel* (1927) is informed not merely by the living experience of Forster's having written novels throughout his adult life, although he does not articulate what we now think of as a theory, and he lacks the dialectical and polemical edge of recent criticism. The key to understanding Forster is to realize that he writes in two traditions: the humanistic tradition, with its components of positivism, nominalism and utilitarianism, and its admir-ation of realism; and the prophetic tradition, with Platonic and biblical origins, which sees art as either an alternative to, or an intensification of, this world. In this first tradition, we find Aristotle, Horace, Arnold, and usually James; in the second we find Blake, Shelley, Pater, Wilde, Yeats, Lawrence, and Stevens. In *Aspects of the Novel*, we might imagine that Forster speaks in two voices as he tries to do justice to the appeals of both these traditions. In the chapters 'Story', 'People' and 'Plot', the voice of the first tradition dominates. But in the later chapters, beginning with 'Fantasy', and becoming more pronounced in 'Prophecy', and 'Pattern and Rhythm', the voice of the second tradition becomes gradually more prominent.

Forster's book was a response to James's critical legacy and Lubbock's codification and simplification of that legacy in *The Craft of Fiction* which argued, following James, for the importance of point of view. Forster believes that critics have overstressed point of view. His most important contribution to the aesthetic of the novel is the distinction between 'flat' and 'round' characters. While flat characters can be summarized in a single phrase and hence are often caricatures, round characters are as complex and multi-faceted as real people. 'The test of a round character is whether it is capable of surprising in a convincing way. . . . It has the incalculability of life about it – life within the pages of a book' ([1927] 1954, p. 78). He demonstrates that characterization includes different kinds of mimesis in fiction, each with its own function, and that flat and round characters can coexist in the same novel. Like the other major modernists – Conrad, Lawrence, Joyce and Woolf – Forster understood that human character is a continually changing flux of experience rather than, as depicted in the traditional realistic novel of manners, relatively fixed and static; consequently, in his novels he sought to dramatize states of mind at crucial moments. Forster's emphasis on character helped to establish the respectability of the view that character (people) in fiction takes precedence over plot. By stressing the primacy of character over plot while rejecting the emphasis of James and Lubbock on point of view, Forster continued the movement away from the traditional stress on plot. The nineteenth century increasingly had become more interested in character than plot; climaxing this trend was the interest in obsessions, compulsions, and dimly acknowledged needs and motives in the works of Browning and Hardy, and, indeed, in A. C. Bradley's *Shakespearean Tragedy* (1904).

Before we turn to F. R. Leavis's *The Great Tradition* (1948), some prefatory remarks are necessary. From 1932 until its demise in 1953, the forum for his ideas was *Scrutiny*, which Leavis edited almost from the first issue and to which he made 120 contributions. He argued in an editorial in *Scrutiny* entitled 'Retrospect of a Decade' that the university should be 'a focus of humane consciousness; a centre where, faced with the specializations and distractions in which human ends lose themselves, intelligence, bringing to bear a mature sense of values, should apply itself to the problems of civilization' (in Bentley, 1964, p. 9). Leavis believed that civilization and culture, including written and spoken language, had declined. Like Arnold, he believed that the study of English literature could be a major part of discovering the necessary values for the maintenance of English civilization. Leavis insisted on the presence in literary criticism not of philosophy but of issues that the reader could recognize from his life experience and which therefore had relevance to the growth of his moral development. In his introduction to *Revaluation* (1936), he expressed a crucial principle: 'In dealing with individual poets the rule of the critic is, or should (I think) be, to work as much as possible in terms of particular analysis – analysis of poems or passages, and to say nothing that cannot be related immediately to judgments about producible texts' (pp. 3–4). Thus eschewing theory in favour of sensibility and judgement is his basic principle.

The Great Tradition, except for the introduction and the first section of the James chapter, is a reprint of essays that Leavis published in *Scrutiny*. For Leavis literature is not merely an extension of life, although its subject-matter is how and for what man lives, but the imposition of form upon the material of life. Leavis's central value is significant form. It is defined by a set of terms that have a more aesthetic emphasis: 'essential organization', 'organization of . . . vital interests', 'intensely significant [organization]' (Leavis, 1948, pp. 150–2). Form achieves significance not only when the particular is dramatized as an example of larger issues, but in combination with moral intensity and perspicacity. Leavis not only rejects the then traditional dichotomy between discussion of the art of the novel and of novels as the raw material of life; he insists that the great novelists in his tradition are concerned with 'form'. Leavis prefers the concrete to the abstract, dramatic moments, dialogue to narrators' telling, and realism to romance. First and foremost, the work must dramatize its values; realism is not a description of a genre or a mode of narrative but a value term conferred on works which are concrete and dramatic. By 'concreteness' Leavis means the dramatized particularity of a situation or response to that situation. Concreteness usually derives from a dramatic moment. Thus Leavis helped perpetuate the preference of the James–Lubbock aesthetic for showing over telling.

Dorothy Van Ghent's *The English Novel: Form and Function* (1953) had a profound impact on the teaching of the English novel. With Wayne Booth, Van Ghent is responsible for the non-contextualist approach that distinguishes courses in the English novel from courses in American fiction. While Booth focuses on what a novel does, specifically how it persuades the reader, Van Ghent treats a novel as a representation of human experience. Each novel is a discrete ontology with its own physical and moral geography. But Van Ghent's concept of the novel includes an awareness that the imagined world was created at a specific time and place and necessarily reflects them. She attempts to show how major novels mime both the external world of the time they were written and the world inhabited by the contemporary reader. Generally, however, she uses internal rather than contextual evidence to establish the world in which the novel was written. Thus Van Ghent is part of a tradition, stretching from Plato and Horace through Arnold, Leavis, Trilling and Booth (as well as the European critics Lukács and Benjamin), that is primarily concerned with the moral effects and moral values of art and which emphasizes method rather than theory. Typical of the positivistic, empiricist Anglo-American tradition, Trilling, Leavis and Arnold also emphasize method rather than theory. Van Ghent's criticism has an urgency that most Anglo-American criticism now lacks, an urgency that recalls Leavis's and Arnold's certainty that the reading of literature can affect the quality of one's moral life. We should hear a note of Arnold's 'high seriousness' and Leavis's twin standards of tangible realism and moral seriousness in Van Ghent's phrase 'the cogency and illuminative quality of the view of life that [the text] affords' (1953, p. 6).

As part of this tradition, Van Ghent refuses to separate moral and aesthetic considerations when confronting a text. For her, literary form is the moral shape imposed upon characteristic events that make up a narrative. The 'value' of a novel depends upon its 'meaningfulness – its ability to make us more aware of the meaning of our lives' (p. 7). Form, then, is the means by which an artist controls, interprets and evaluates life, and Van Ghent is unwilling to dissociate formal analysis of the text from the quality and persuasive power of the content. 'The form of the book . . . *is* the content. The form . . . is the book itself.' When she insists that 'we cannot dissociate the author's conception of life, and its "value" and "significance" from the aesthetic structure of the literary work' (p. 113), she is stressing the importance of the integral relation between form and content and insisting that neither can be ignored. To be sure, discussion of content is often disguised in formal terms. Van Ghent presupposes a strong connection between moral and aesthetic values. This connection enables her to see a novel's structure as equivalent to the author's moral attitudes and to his suggestions about how man ought to order his life. A novel's form is equivalent to its persuasive powers added to its revelations and insights. To speak of a work of art independent of its form is thus impossible. Van Ghent shows that the verbal texture does not merely reinforce theme and form, but *creates* new levels of significance.

Erich Auerbach's *Mimesis* (1953) has been an important book because it focuses on the way imaginative literature imitates and reflects reality, including the culture in which it was written. His subject is, as he puts it, 'the history of the literary treatment of reality' (p. 116). For Auerbach, art is about something other than art, the writing of novels, or the investigation into how language means. He is interested not only in how people behave and in what people believe, but in what historical forces shape behaviour and belief. Like Georg Lukács (1954), Auerbach believes that an appropriate aesthetic standard is whether the artist establishes a compelling link between individual events or relationships and a specific social and economic milieu. Like his fellow Hegelian Lukács, Auerbach judges a work's importance by its inclusiveness and its response to historical forces, and thus his concern with the work as literature is inseparable from his interest in the work as intellectual history. Auerbach is a philologist whose curiosity about language asks questions about which historical conditions produced the written words we read. *Mimesis* inquires into the style that the author uses to present his interpretation of reality. Auerbach has cited Vico as his major mentor in his effort to use cultural evidence, including literature, to 'form a lucid and coherent picture of this civilization and its unity' (1965, p. 6). Like Vico, Auerbach assumes that language is the repository of cultural history and that the study of literature, language and myth in a given period enables us to understand the other major aspects of its culture.

Auerbach begins *Mimesis* by differentiating between two major traditions of narrative presentation: the Homeric or classical which depends on 'earthly relations of place, time, and cause', and the biblical one which depends on a 'vertical connection, ascending from all that happens, converging in God' (1953, p. 65). In Homeric literature, details are 'scrupulously externalized and narrated in leisurely fashion' (p. 1). The basic impulse of the Homeric style is 'to represent phenomena in a fully externalized form, visible and palpable in all their parts, and completely fixed in their spatial and temporal relations' (p. 4). The Homeric style 'knows only a foreground, only a uniformly illuminated, uniformly objective present'; the 'descriptive adjectives and digressions' displace the reader's attention (pp. 5, 8). By contrast, the story of Abraham's sacrifice of Isaac in the Old Testament focuses completely on current events and signifies something else. Auerbach regards modern realism as the integration of two impulses – the classical one that imitates reality by crystallizing a culture and the biblical one that seeks to render historical process – into a genre whose meaning depends on a relationship to its teleology or organizing principle or radial centre. Valuing the classical standards of *prodesse* and *delectare*, he believes that art should seek to *affect* the moral, political, and practical aspects of human lives.

In a retrospective essay on his book *The Rhetoric of Fiction* (1961), Wayne Booth differentiates between a poetics ('Study of what the work *is*, what it has been made to *be*') and a rhetoric ('What the work is made to *do*'). Booth writes: '*The kinds of actions authors perform on readers* differ markedly, though subtly, from *the kinds of imitations of objects they are seen as making*, in the poetic mode' (1968, pp. 113, 115). In *The Rhetoric of Fiction* he shows that the 'autonomous' text derives from conscious or unconscious decisions made by the author to shape the reader's response. Booth insists that an author affects the reader as the author intends, and communicates human emotions and values to an audience; the reader in turn responds to the felt presence of a human voice within the text.

Booth takes the position of a man of reason defending the house of fiction which is under siege. He shows that the 'house of fiction' – the term James used to argue for the pluralism of fiction – has been appropriated by the New Critics for their own purposes; Caroline Gordon and Allen Tate had used the title *The House of Fiction* (1950) for their seminal text that applied New Criticism to fiction. For the New Critics, telling was only acceptable in fiction when it was spoken by a distinct self-dramatizing narrator; for then it most resembled the dramatic lyric and provided the irony, tension and ambiguity that were values in themselves and hence the focus of their analytic attention. They had been influenced by Henry James and T. S. Eliot, who insisted on the fusion of thought and feeling. Booth, though, shows how 'objective' general rules become the 'subjective' values by which works are measured. But, as Booth puts it, general rules derive from the 'abandonment of the notion of peculiar literary kinds, each with its unique demands that may modify the general standards' (Booth, [1961] 1983, p. 34).

To understand Booth, we must understand his intellectual tradition. While avoiding polemics, he makes clear in the Preface to *The Rhetoric of Fiction* that he is a Chicago Aristotelian who is concerned with 'the art of communicating with readers – the rhetorical resources available to the writer of epic, novel or short story as he tries, consciously or unconsciously, to impose his fictional world upon the reader'. He dislikes criticism which ignores genres and rhetoric, and which creates, in the mode of Leavis, 'great traditions' based on subjective standards disguised as objective ones. Booth believes that novels are purposeful imitations of the real world on the part of an author who desires to affect his audience in a particular way. Booth focuses on the *effects* of literary works, and he invokes the authority of Aristotle who, he says, 'clearly recognizes that one thing the poet does is to produce effects on audiences', and those effects are not static but dynamic (1983, p. 92).

If Booth finds his intellectual paradigm in Aristotle, it is not merely as a model for rhetorical criticism, but as a central figure in the Western humanistic tradition. According to this tradition, within a world whose patterns can at least partially be understood by a rational mind, man has the intellectual capacity to impose order on the world and to discover a purposeful self. Literature can be central to our knowledge of ourselves and our community. If we only read one more book, if we only think a little bit more rigorously, we will be able to solve the problems of texts – and of life. Booth wants to teach us both how to read and how to live; he believes that books can teach us to live better lives because they contain truths. If this seems naïve, let us recall that he shares this belief with Aristotle, Horace, Pope, Shelley and Arnold. For Booth, the major function of criticism is to explain literary works in terms of values and experiences that are common to author, reader and critic. By 'rhetoric' Booth means both how books communicate with readers and, specifically, how books arouse our interest about the issues and characters in the imagined world and how they affect us morally.

Booth offers a method that stresses the primacy of two questions: 'Who is speaking to whom?' and 'For what purpose?' That the author creates both a second self and an audience is central to Booth's discussion about the importance of rhetoric. The concept of the implied author is the most original part of Booth's approach: '[An author] creates not simply an ideal, impersonal "man in general" but an implied version of "himself" that is different from the implied authors we meet in other men's works' (1983, pp. 70–1). One of Booth's major legacies is his distinction between reliable and unreliable narrators: 'I have called a narrator *reliable* when he speaks for or acts in accordance with the norms of the work (which is to say, the implied author's norms), *unreliable* when he does not' (pp. 158–9). (I prefer the terms 'perceptive' and 'imperceptive', since a narrator might be reliable and yet unaware of the implications of his behaviour.) For Booth reliability is itself a *value*: 'The art of constructing reliable narrators is largely that of mastering all of oneself in order to project the *persona*, the second self, that really belongs in the book' (p. 83). The function of reliable commentary is to shape the beliefs of the reader, in part by convincing him that the material is morally significant.

Frank Kermode's *The Sense of an Ending: Studies in the Theory of Fiction* (1967) emphasizes the reader's role in giving meaning to literary texts and thus questions the New Critical and neo-Aristotelian notion that meaning inheres in the text as a result of the author's intended or unintended pattern. When he writes 'the making of a novel is partly the achievement of readers as well as writers' (p. 139), he anticipates reader-response criticism, which emphasizes the 'sense-making' of the reader. It follows that if each of us responds to fictions according to his/her needs, then each reader would produce a different text. It is important to understand the critical and historical context in which Kermode wrote because he is engaging in a dialogue with the influential critical perspectives of the post-war period. Kermode wanted to place himself in the humanist tradition, but to separate himself from the critical nominalism of the New Critics for whom close analysis was often an end not a means. At the same time, Kermode wanted to retain the ontological perspective of those who reinvigorated New Criticism for the novel – Mark Schorer, Albert Guerard and Dorothy Van Ghent; thus he saw novels as self-enclosed, imagined fictive universes with their own cosmology, geography and moral geography; as he put it, 'the book is a bibliocosm' (p. 52). But, unlike some prior ontologists, especially Van Ghent, who tended at least partially to see the world as arrested in spatial configurations (this in part because of her debt to Gestalt psychology), Kermode shows how temporal expectations are crucial to our perceptions: 'The "virtual" time of books . . . is a kind of man-centred model of world-time' (p. 52).

Part of the historical importance of Kermode's book was to contest Joseph Frank's widely accepted idea that literary structures, particularly modern ones, were conceived and experienced in spatial terms. Frank had argued that in the great modern writers, 'Past and present are seen spatially, locked in a timeless unit which, while it may accentuate surface differences, eliminates any feeling of historical sequence by the very act of juxtaposition. The objective historical imagination . . . is transformed in these writers into the mythical imagination for which historical time does not exist – the imagination that sees the actions and events of a particular time merely as the bodying forth of eternal prototypes' (Frank, 1945, p. 232). When Kermode draws a crucial distinction between fiction and myth and belittles myths as 'degenerate' fictions, he has in mind what he considers to be Frank's spatial myth and perhaps Frye's archetypes as articulated in his important study *Anatomy of Criticism* (1957).

In our review of approaches to fiction, we must mention Marxist criticism. As Marx states in *A Contribution to the Critique of Political Economy* (1859): 'The mode of production of material life conditions the general process of social, political and intellectual life. It is not the consciousness of men that determines their existence, but their social existence that determines their consciousness' (quoted in Milner, 1981, p. 4). Thus the life we live from day to day is shaped by the material facts of our existence. Since art is deterministically affected by conditions in which the artist lives, the critic needs to understand these conditions. Marxist criticism proposes a scientific study of the relationship between society and literature. In art, representation or mimesis is conceived both as an ideological process and goal. Beginning with Engels, Marxists preferred realistic literature, particularly the nineteenth-century novel, because that genre took as its goal – its aesthetic and moral and historical ideal – the most complete account of social reality. The novel, because it allows the critic to select arbitrarily paradigmatic passages, may be more amenable than lyric poetry to the kind of polemical criticism which uses evidence to support a particular political position.

Arnold Kettle's influential, vaguely Marxist two-volume study entitled *An Introduction to the English Novel* (1951–3) lacks what we now think of as a theoretical argument. Reading Kettle, we feel the influence of Leavis's critical nominalism, as well as a quite contrary generalizing impulse which seeks to formulate broad ideas about literature as a *product* of society and about the behaviour of characters within novels as *products* of historical forces. Leavis deliberately eschewed abstractions and focused on the specific passage as a realistic depiction of a scene in the fabric of life, and Kettle is intellectually comfortable with that kind of nominalism. But, unlike Leavis, he also gropes for a system of theory to account for the socio-economic factors that shape not only the author, but the behaviour and destiny of the characters.

In his *The English Novel from Dickens to Lawrence* (1970), Raymond Williams relates the Victorian novel to historical and cultural developments in England, which by the end of the 1840s was the world's first urban society. The crucial achievement of the 1847–8 period, when a new generation of novelists emerged, was 'the exploration of community: the substance and meaning of community' (Williams, 1970, p. 11). In this period, society was no longer a framework or a standard, but 'a process that entered lives, to shape or to deform' (p. 13). Williams begins *his* tradition with Dickens, whom he praises for the 'creation of consciousness – of recognitions and relationships' and for his ability 'to dramatize those social institutions and consequences which are not accessible to ordinary physical observation' (pp. 33–4). Re-reading, we understand that Williams's own critical method is to create consciousness of new relations and to dramatize social relations in the face of industrialism and the social process it creates.

Williams is interested less in the way books present and reflect society than in the way books present the culture in which they are written and in the way they express and define that society. This interest takes him beyond the narrow formalism that sometimes restricts the focus of literary critics to a search for patterns of language or narrative modes. Part of Williams's originality stems from his seeing novels as explorations of social movement: '[The] new novelists of a rapidly changing England had to create, from their own resources, forms adequate to the experience at the new and critical stage it had reached' (p. 12).

The critics I have discussed so far might all be said to belong to an essentially humanistic tradition, one that is concerned with the moral force of literature and its relation to reality. In recent years, however, a very different kind of theoretical criticism has developed; at the centre of much of this theoretical activity, particularly in its concern with the novel, has been J. Hillis Miller. Miller has become one of our most influential novel critics. His importance is not merely that he proposed the most important sustained argument for a way of reading fiction by one of the American post-structuralists, but that he entered into a serious dialogue with past criticism of fiction.

Despite Miller's denial that *Fiction and Repetition* (1982) proposes a theory, the book is Miller's version of both Van Ghent's *The English Novel: Form and Function* and Brooks and Warren's *Understanding Fiction* (1943). It contains the major premises of post-structuralist thinking about fiction and it places that thinking in the context of, and tries to integrate it with, prior criticism. Miller stresses that presence or origin is always deferred. The text continually arouses the possibility of presence, the expectation of a dominant pattern of meaning, only to postpone it. Put another way, it arouses the possibility of the first kind of repetition, based on similarity, only to substitute the second kind based on difference. But this is not so different from the Chomskian idea of a deep structure, latent beneath the surface of the sentence, that represents the supposedly more real meaning. Earlier formal criticism also understood that the network of syntax and diction in a literary work creates its own system separate and distinct from the real world and that within that system the relation between syntax and diction has its own energy and coherence.

Miller announces that *Fiction and Repetition* is a 'series of readings of important nineteenth- and twentieth-century English novels. The readings are more concerned with the relation of rhetorical form to meaning than with thematic paraphrase, though of course it is impossible in practice to separate these wholly. The focus ... [is on] "how does meaning arise from the reader's encounter with just these words on the page?" ' (1982, p. 3).

Miller proposes two kinds of repetition. One version is 'Platonic repetition [that] is grounded in a solid archetypal model which is untouched by the effects of repetition. ... The validity of the mimetic copy is established by its truth of correspondence to what it copies' (p. 6). This is the major concept underlying Western literature, including nineteenth- and twentieth-century English realistic fiction and the aesthetic standard by which critics as diverse as Aristotle, Auerbach and James measure works. The world to which the author refers may be more or less a facsimile based on the principle of recreating a perceived image of what an aspect of the external world is really like. But the world represented in the novel is always anterior to the author's imaginative vision. By contrast, 'the other, Nietzschean mode of repetition posits a world based on difference'. It assumes that 'each thing . . . is unique, intrinsically different from every other thing . . . [Repetitions] are ungrounded doublings which arise from differential interrelations among elements which are all on the same plane' (p. 6). Miller describes the artistic process of writing and the perceptual process of reading in terms of mental processes – voluntary and involuntary memory – common to all. The first kind of repetition recalls 'willed memory' which 'works logically, by way of similiarities which are seen as identities, one thing repeating another and grounded in a concept on the basis of which their likeness may be understood' (p. 8). The second recalls the 'involuntary form of memory' which replaces the world of life with that of fiction and imagination in the form of dream: 'one thing is experienced as repeating something which is quite different from it and which it strangely resembles' (p. 8). In this kind of repetition, the emphasis is more on similarity within difference than upon total resemblance.

These kinds of repetitions suggest traditional distinctions between vertical God-centred conceptions of the world and horizontal linear man-centred concepts. They have a kinship with Kermode's *kairos* and *chronos*. On the whole, the first kind of repetition is that of humanism; the second is of deconstruction; thus it is appropriate that the first finds its model in Plato and the second in Nietzsche. These forms of repetition are themselves figures for the division in Miller's mind between humanism and deconstruction, between interest in the way man is presented in novels and 'their manifest strangeness as integuments of words' (p. 18). But we realize that we cannot rely on such simple distinctions. For humanism often implies a relativistic universe without ground, and the deconstructive mode uses arguments from authority, while referring beyond the text to anterior conceptions about language and how texts behave. In contrast to the vertical perspective of most Neoplatonism, including Christian concepts of God, humanism has itself proposed a world based on differential interrelations among elements on the same plane.

For deconstruction, 'intertextuality' refers to both the relationship among literary texts and the dialogue between them and other writing. Each text takes its meaning from other texts, not merely prior texts, but other concomitant texts and expressions of culture and language. The blank and marble pages, the squiggly lines, the scrambled chapters, the skipped pages of *Tristram Shandy* are intertextual events because they respond not only to extant literary texts, but to contemporary and medieval ideas of logic, order and rationality, particularly Locke's conception of how the mind develops ideas as presented in his *Essay Concerning Human Understanding*. But the intertextual network of *Tristram Shandy* includes subsequent texts like *Ulysses* and Beckett's novels, as well as recent theories of narrativity which give the contemporary reader a different perspective from the eighteenth-century reader on Sterne's experiments with form. Miller responds to texts in terms of other texts, sometimes in ahistorical terms and sometimes in historical terms. Even if one uses the term 'intertextuality' to define discussion of authors' lives and literary convention, is this different from a traditional approach that stresses contexts and origins?

For Miller heterogeneity means attempting a traditional and a deconstructive reading, or, put another way, a grounded and an ungrounded one. This enables Miller to argue that, at the same time, fiction is and is not mimetic of an anterior world. Finally, in giving flesh to theory and method by means of nominalistic readings, Miller is in the tradition of Anglo-American humanistic criticism which eschews theory for close-reading and particular demonstrations, and whose interest is in what and how books mean. Reflecting his training, Miller frequently uses the traditional strategies of Anglo-American novel criticism: the empirical approach, the attention to details, and the confident sense that there is an interpretation to be discovered. No sooner does he take a deconstructionist tack than he shifts to a humanistic one. While the latter comes from his sense that a novel deals with relationships among people, the former comes from his perception that novels are made of words.

With its emphasis on literature as self-sufficient and not necessarily referential, literary criticism has caught up with cubism and post-impressionism. For deconstruction is emphasizing the ontological reality of the text – the sentences and words themselves as objects, units of energy, textures, sounds, visual surfaces, spaces, and even distinct letters – as well as the perceiver's role in making sense of that reality. As turn-of-the-century European painting saw colour as decorative and shapes as forms, independent of referential meaning, so current criticism sees literary texts, like musical compositions, as having an identity separate from what they represent, and studies its self-enclosed formal relationships – to use Miller's words for Woolf – its 'intrinsic, musical, architectural form' (p. 209). In his deconstructive voice, Miller is part of this movement to rescue the text from exclusive reliance upon a representational aesthetic.

While Kermode warns us in *A Sense of an Ending* (1967), that we always believe that we live in a special era of crisis and change, such a belief seems particularly crucial to the contemporary critical environment. This feeling, central for decades to modern painting and literature, was not dominant in literary criticism until recently. Even as they interpreted the complexities of modern literature, Leavis, Trilling and the New Critics, with their conservative, nostalgic set of values and authoritative confident tone, provided a counterbalance to the uncertainty of modern literature. For we now see that these critics looked for values in literature which would sustain what they regarded as essential humanistic traditions, traditions which were in danger of going astray in the modern world. They felt as Arnold put it in 'Stanzas from the Grande Chartreuse', between one world 'dead' and 'the other powerless to be born', and yet, like Arnold, they found solace in the values that repeated themselves from the past through the present. At times Derrida and his followers, including Miller, speak as if they have passed beyond the bankruptcy of metaphysics to a new era when literary texts mean in quite different ways. Even if we resist their privileging the critic's mind over the author's, we should recognize that they have added important concepts to literary criticism and have been an important catalyst for helping traditional criticism to define its own theory and method.

The differences that separate various strands of Anglo-American criticism prior to deconstruction seem less significant than they once did. Now we are able to see that the New Critics, Aristotelians, the *Partisan Review* group, contextualists and literary historians share a number of important assumptions: authors write to express their ideas and emotions; the way man lives and the values for which he lives are of fundamental interest to authors and readers; literature expresses insights about human life and responses to human situations, and that is the main reason why we read, teach, and think about literature. While the emphasis varies from critic to critic, we can identify several concepts that define this criticism:

1. The form of the novel – style, structure, narrative techniques – expresses its value system. Put another way: form discovers the meaning of content.
2. A work of literature is also a creative gesture of the author and the result of historical context. Understanding the process of imitating the external world gives us an insight into the artistry and meaning of the work.
3. A work of literature imitates a world that precedes the text, and the critic should recapture that world primarily by formal analysis of the text, although knowledge of the historical context and author are often important. Humanistic criticism believes that there is an original meaning, a centre, which can be approached, and at times reached, by perceptive reading. The goal is to discover what the author said to *his* intended audience *then* as well as what he says to us now. Acts of interpretation at their best – subtle, lucid, inclusive, perceptive – can bring that goal into sight.
4. Human behaviour is central to most works, and should be the major concern of analysis. In particular, these critics are generally interested in how and why people behave – what they do, desire, fear, doubt, need. Although modes of characterization differ, the psychology and morality of characters must be understood as if they were real people; for understanding others like ourselves helps us to understand ourselves.
5. The inclusiveness of the novel's vision in terms of depth and range is a measure of the work's quality.

Anglo-American humanistic criticism calls into question deconstruction's insistence on the arbitrariness of signs in the only sense that such a concept matters to literary criticism. It assumes that in specific circumstances readers share similar recognition of signs and thus respond in approximately similar ways. Of course, the more readers share the same cultural background as the author, the more they will share her or his experience and the less arbitrary will appear the author's signs. Readers who have been reading similar novels and critical works in the same field will share a greater recognition of the signs I have written on this page. Thus the arbitrariness of signs is not absolute but rather a function of the reader's experience, the author's intent, and, of course, historical circumstances, which render some signs far more arbitrary to a contemporary audience than they were for the original reader. For example, Conrad would have expected contemporary readers of 'The Secret Sharer' to understand the British maritime code; he would not have expected them – as many of his readers today do – to extenuate Leggatt or to be reluctant to pass judgement about the captain's providing refuge for an escaped murderer. Nor would he have expected us to be taken in by Marlow's empathetic reading of Jim's abandoning the native passengers and crew in *Lord Jim*.

Do we not need a revised humanism that – without abandoning its stress on such formal matters as rhetoric and close scrutiny of narrative codes – turns its attention to the content, meaning and significance of imaginative literature? Rather than using literature as an occasion for speculation about the *text's* implications for semiotics, Marxism or deconstruction, this new humanism would seek to understand the essential experience of the *work's* imaginative world. Certainly this has been the thrust of the best of recent feminist criticism, including the work of Showalter (1977) as well as of Gilbert and Gubar (1979). While continuing to emphasize interpretation of literary works, a revised humanistic criticism – which I would call humanistic formalism – would develop concepts about how novels behave and how readers respond. I imagine that this humanism would unembarrassedly ask, 'What happens to characters within an imagined world?'; 'What is the nature of the voice that speaks to us; specifically, what are her or his attitudes, values and feelings, and how does the artist convey them?'; 'What do we learn from the representation of human behaviour within that world?'; 'What is the relation of form – including structure (especially beginning and ending), mode of narration, patterns of language – to meaning?'; 'What does the imagined world reveal about the author and the actual historical world in which she or he lived?' Since humanistic criticism assumes that texts are by human authors for human readers about human subjects, it follows that a humanistic criticism is interested in how and why people live, think, write and act.

FURTHER READING

Culler, Jonathan (1975) *Structuralist Poetics: Structuralism, Linguistics, and the Study of Literature*, Cornell University Press, Ithaca

Eagleton, Terry (1983) *Literary Theory: An Introduction*, University of Minnesota Press, Minneapolis

Fish, Stanley (1980) *Is There a Text in this Class? The Authority of Interpretive Communities*, Harvard University Press, Cambridge

Frye, Northrop (1957) *Anatomy of Criticism*, Princeton University Press, Princeton

Gilbert, Sandra and Gubar, Susan (1979) *The Madwoman in the Attic: The Woman Writer and the Nineteenth-Century Imagination*, Yale University Press, New Haven

Iser, Wolfgang (1978) *The Act of Reading: A Theory of Aesthetic Response*, Johns Hopkins University Press, Baltimore

Lentricchia, Frank (1980) *After the New Criticism*, University of Chicago Press, Chicago

Schwarz, Daniel R. (1986) *The Humanistic Heritage: Critical Theories of the English Novel from James to Hillis Miller*, Macmillan, London

Searle, John R. (1969) *Speech Acts: An Essay in the Philosophy of Language*, Cambridge University Press, London

Showalter, Elaine (1977) *A Literature of Their Own: British Women Novelists from Brontë to Lessing*, Princeton University Press, Princeton

Trilling, Lionel (1951) *The Liberal Imagination*, Viking, New York

Watt, Ian (1957) *The Rise of the Novel: Studies in Defoe, Richardson, and Fielding*, University of California Press, Berkeley and Los Angeles

ADDITIONAL WORKS CITED

Auerbach, Erich (1953) *Mimesis: The Representation of Reality in Western Literature*, Doubleday, New York [first published 1946]

——(1965) *Literary Language and Its Public in Late Latin Antiquity and in the Middle Ages*, Princeton University Press, Princeton

Bentley, Eric (ed.) (1964) *The Importance of Scrutiny*, New York University Press, New York

Blackmur, R. P. (ed.) (1934) *The Art of the Novel: Critical Prefaces*, Scribner, New York

Booth, Wayne (1968) '*The Rhetoric of Fiction* and the Poetics of Fiction', *Novel* 1, 105–17

——(1983) *The Rhetoric of Fiction*, University of Chicago Press, Chicago [first published 1961]

Forster, E. M. (1954) *Aspects of the Novel*, Harcourt, Brace & World, New York [first published 1927]

Frank, Joseph (1945) 'Spatial Form in Modern Literature', *Sewanee Review*, 53, 221–40, 435–56, 643–53

Kermode, Frank (1967) *The Sense of an Ending: Studies in the Theory of Fiction*, Oxford University Press, New York

Leavis, F. R. (1936) *Revaluation*, Chatto & Windus, London

——(1948) *The Great Tradition*, New York University Press, New York

Lubbock, Percy (1957) *The Craft of Fiction*, Viking, New York [first published 1921]

Lukács, Georg (1954) *Studies in the European Novel*, Grosset & Dunlap, New York

Miller, James E. (ed.) (1972) *Theory of Fiction: Henry James*, University of Nebraska Press, Lincoln

Miller, J. Hillis (1982) *Fiction and Repetition: Seven English Novels*, Harvard University Press, Cambridge

Milner, Andres (1981) *John Milton and the English Revolution*, Barnes & Noble, New York

Van Ghent, Dorothy (1953) *The English Novel: Form and Function*, Rinehart & Co., New York

Williams, Raymond (1970) *The English Novel from Dickens to Lawrence*, Oxford University Press, New York

45

THE MODERNIST NOVEL IN THE TWENTIETH CENTURY

JOHN ORR

There is no such thing as the modernist novel. It is a critical artefact, largely Anglo-American in origin and use. The French normally speak of 'la modern-ité' and 'le postmoderne', the British and the Americans of their derived 'isms' which are aesthetic constructs, not cultural processes. None the less, modernism *is* a usable artefact. The concept of the 'modernist' novel cues us in to the changing relationship of society and literary form in the twentieth century, to anomic and anonymous city life, to greater freedom and fragmentation, to a felt loss of community. It is a century when the contours of space and time take on a new and bewildering meaning. Cars and planes reduce distances and make the sensation of speed a feature of everyday life. Electronic communications introduce us to the disembodied speech of those to whom we talk and the disembodied images of those we simultaneously watch in our millions on spatially separate screens. The theory of relativity in physics has its fragmented counterpart in the relativities of everyday experience. The material world is dissolved into atoms and atoms themselves can be split for the destructive purposes of military science. If God is dead, then replacements are hard to come by. On a bad day, the world becomes a handful of sand slipping slowly through the fingers.

In this intimidating context the old distinction between the Real and the Modern, realism and modernism, should be finally buried. The great feat of the twentieth-century novel is not to show that vision triumphs over fact or that experiment triumphs over experience. It is to show that the world, once flat and later round, is now a cube. It has to be seen from all 'sides', even though there are no sides. Point of view, whereby things can be seen differently by different characters but still blend into narrative perspective, becomes problematic. We can never be sure that the whole is the sum of its parts, nor that perception exhausts experience. If science shows the world to be infinite in its complexity, the modernist novel shows experience to be limitless. Narrative becomes difficult because the real itself is more elusive than materialists ever thought. Not that it can *never* be known, as Lacanians and Althusserians suggest, but that knowledge extends and changes the boundaries of our experience of the real even while its validity as knowledge is still in dispute. The real cannot be wished away simply because it is not absolute, because in finding out more we also find we know less. We find that the real has no absolute Truth. One of the profound experiences of the Real is the discovery of limits. In Henry James's *The Ambassadors* (1903), this is the painful and singular experience of Lambert Strether. Yet James's impersonal past tense narrative distances us from the central figure's painful discovery. We have still, though only just, a vantage point from which to judge. In James Joyce and William Faulkner this is largely swept away. It is the reader, not the author, who must erect the scaffolding necessary for the high-angle master shot. The post-Jamesian novel, by and large, has swept the scaffolding away.

The Real remains the predominant quest of the novel until 1950 and beyond. Because the world of modernity has become more and not less elusive, the Real has become more and not less important. Joyce, for example, confessed his wish to reinvigorate the Real, to find new ways of uncovering it in the spirit of Flaubert and Dostoevsky (see Powers, 1974). In *Ulysses* (1922) his multiple styles, which are so often disconnected from fixed point of view, are multiple uncoverings. They are not relativist variations on a fixed theme, different angles from which to view a fixed object, but changes of style to match the changing objects of a changing world. A single day in Dublin, in which *Ulysses* as novel never shifts beyond the boundaries of the city, becomes a bottomless abyss. The past as myth and as memory seeps into the presentness of all things. The individual selves of Bloom or Molly or Gerty Macdowall are little more than sieves, porous to the point of saturation. Myth, memory and desire all devour the passing instant in Bloom's eventful, uneventful day with a ferocious voracity. Reality is no longer a cast list of round characters with intersecting perspectives on the world, for the world is no longer a consensual field of vision. In Joyce and Faulkner, reality is a swiftly moving target bombarded by heteroglot styles from all angles and distances. In Virginia Woolf, there is no threshold over which consciousness must pass in the mellifluous triangle of narrator, character and reader. It suffuses all being, or rather creates a chain of being without visible boundaries. In Marcel Proust, memory bursts in like an unexpected guest on the present instant excited by a sound or a smell, a cake or a flagstone, and the mundane world is made ecstatic through resemblances.

The world as myth and history, as past, present and future, has to be contained in a bounded text which acknowledges the infinity of things. If everything is elusive, however, nothing can be neglected or repressed. In

Ulysses eating, drinking, excreting, masturbating and copulating are ceremonies of the ordinary just as much as death and birth. In Woolf's *To the Lighthouse* (1927) death is a parenthesis in the lyric flow of existence, in the numinous experience of flowing through the hour, the day, the season which underlies the various 'apparitions', as Woolf terms them, of the self. By 1929, in Faulkner's *The Sound and the Fury*, even madness has become a narrative point of view and desire its unrecognized subject. Benjy's Blakean voice has the enforced innocence of poetic fixation, the primal desire which involves naming its love-object but which cannot know, as Quentin does, that desire for Caddy entails incest and moral transgression. Yet the parodic and mercenary prose of brother Jason equally has its limitations. Each of the three brothers 'sees' what the others cannot and fails to 'see' what the others can. The movement from Benjy's madness and Quentin's incestuous melancholia to prosaic and comic fact is a movement towards the conventional real, but it also a loss, a leap from interior vision towards the mundane. Dream and memory give way to disenchantment. And while Jason's money-fetish is more obvious and material than Benjy or Quentin's fixation on Caddy, it is just as much a mystification of the ordinary. Confused, we move forward with mixed feelings, surging out of poetic darkness towards the light at the end of the tunnel. But we also feel the move to be irreversible, like the movement out of childhood Benjy can never make, the movement which even more than madness is a trope for innocence.

To read this kind of modernist text is indeed to lose one's literary innocence. It is, at first, to panic and seek out distance when one is up against the surface of the world. It is to fear the plunge into elements which might be either solid or liquid, clear or opaque. But once immersion in this fractured experience is accepted as a way of life, former innocence is largely forgotten. We adjust to the challenge of trying to make the fragment coherent, to recompose the dissolutions of style and theme, to retotalize the discontinuous. Criticism occasionally helps us to do this. But Fredric Jameson's contention that the modernist novel is now canonic, and therefore 'known' in its entirety is misleading (Jameson, 1981). It still continues to surprise us. It still fragments, shocks and uncovers. Through its fluid mixture of tenses, narrators and styles the modernist novel brings home to us the fragilities of our space-time continuum, the fragility of our uncertain selfhood, and the evil ruptures of history in a century of war and apocalypse.

In the process we stand to lose Renaissance perspective, roundness of character and clarity of plot, all crafted assiduously over two centuries. We lose the flow of time which is change over time, which must run like a river until it reaches an ocean, the flow that finally halts. We thus have to change our sense of an ending. For if experience is fragmented, it is also unending. There is neither river nor ocean. The losses run deep, but the gains can match them. We become aware of the presentness of things, their horror and their radiance, nowhere more so than in Joyce's epiphanies. Joyce's epiphanies are secular versions of the sudden revelations of religious experience. They extend the search for clarity of the nineteenth-century romantics. If they are formal and composed, like those of the aspiring artist Stephen Dedalus, they suggest a romantic ambition which remains unfulfilled. Yet Joyce's stress on the radiance that lies 'in the whatness of a thing', in 'the soul of the commonest object', is central to twentieth-century narrative. Epiphany illuminates the smallest or most immediate object of its vision. It can be the dial on the Ballast Clock in *Stephen Hero* (written 1904–7, published 1944), the girl on the strand with the 'likeness of seagull' in *A Portrait of the Artist as a Young Man* (1916), or the legends of lead-papered tea packets in *Ulysses* which Bloom sees in the shop-window in Westland Row.

Like its close sibling Imagism, epiphany celebrates the immediate power of the image. But it renders its perception ambiguous. Is it Joyce the author, Bloom the hero, or Stephen, the aesthete posturing as author, who imparts the radiance? Or is it merely the thing itself? How long does radiance last and how does it radiate over Joyce's readers? Is it a passing moment soon to be lost or an eternal recurrence in a world full of surprises? Is the singular and self-contained episode in *Ulysses* a master epiphany all to itself? Does the 'mysterious instant' arise out of a sea of becalmed reveries or a trickling stream of consciousness? To none of these questions is there a clear answer. Epiphany is a narrative texture of the uncovering of what is present in the world, to the senses, to the imagination, to memory, to desire. Its ubiquity is formidable. This is especially so as the ordered epiphanies of *Portrait of an Artist* give way to their fragmented counterparts of *Ulysses*. The sudden heightening of experience which no longer depends on the momentous event becomes a semi-structured accident, like Stephen taking a chance that night on Nighttown.

Despite such puzzles, the narrative transition in the novel becomes clearer. The epiphanous instant displaces the perspectival sequence. A new form of the Real replaces classic realism. Epiphany, not perspective, is now the key to narrative. Narrative devolves as much as it evolves, goes sideways and backwards as much as forward. In *The Sound and the Fury* Faulkner goes back eighteen years in time from the narrative of Benjy to the narrative of Quentin. But Quentin's narrative itself goes back in time obsessively, from Harvard to Jefferson, from college to childhood. In reverie he is beating up Dalton Ames, his sister's seducer. In reality he is being beaten up by Gerald Bland, the college stud. The reverie is partly parodic of Southern honour. Quentin is quixotically defending girls who don't desire his protection, yet the reverie is also the epiphanous instant of revenge for the beating Ames has originally given him. By unwittingly repeating the dose, Bland reminds us of Quentin's compulsion to repeat his earlier failure. But Quentin feels compelled because his mind is already suicidal, his sense of self disintegrated, his longing for death equally a longing to merge fact and fantasy. Faulkner prevents us from holding the past and the present in separate hands as separate tenses. As we read the shift from one to the other, we see it like a film montage of long jumps played backwards, always ending with the start of the run-up. Equally Faulkner's epiphany makes us equidistant from truth and falsehood, the fantastic and the real. For by this time Quentin is mixing memory with retrospective desire, and wishes to do so.

If narrative changes so do narrative structures of feeling. Raymond Williams (1977, chap. 6) has seen the latter as representations of historical structures of experience, the emergent and defining structures of a particular period. In the nineteenth-century English and French novel we can posit the main structures as those of compassion and fortune. Risk, success and friendship, sympathy for the endured hardships of adverse fortune, eventual love and marriage, are the shared experience of authors, heroes and readers. While the heroes are immune, but only just, they are usually surrounded by disaster and death. The inheritance and the business fortune are convenient turns in plot, well-timed endings for heroes in adversity. Historically, structures of feeling combine wish and actuality, fear and yearning. They play on structures of experience by being utopian and dystopian at the same time. Forms of feeling both represent and idealize forms of experience in the age of progress. Dickens, Balzac and Eliot show a destitution which their readers fear, but also a compassion which goes beyond the rational and calculative ideas of Comte, Bentham and Spencer.

The end of the century sees the beginnings of a transformation which really takes off with the trauma of total war in 1914. The precarious nineteenth-century idyll of progress is supplanted by militarism, by disenchantment, and by revolution. Individual fortune and social compassion seem inappropriate to the theatre of organized slaughter. The devaluation of value prophesied by Nietzsche seemed to many to have come to pass and Spengler wrote *The Decline of the West* (1918), the transient post-war bible of the German bourgeoisie which left such a powerful impression on T. S. Eliot. In the post-war world both pleasure and destruction were more explicit, more known, more talked about as fundamental human drives. In the English-language novel the new structures of feeling which emerge are those of absence, dislocation and desire. Love, compassion, success are relics of an eclipsed age of progress, now stretched on the rack by the polar opposites of revolution and Fascism. In D. H. Lawrence's *Women in Love* (1921), for example, military metaphors are introduced into the field of passion, into an Edwardian Bloomsbury tangled up in the vicissitudes of love and hate, opposites which were no longer separable. It was a retrospective insight, reading from the mid-point of slaughter of 1916 back into a falsely secure world already dominated, in Lawrence's view, by the technological machine which combined rational efficiency and a depersonalized cruelty. For Rupert Birkin and Ursula Brangwen, love is clawed into existence by mutual animosity and endless abstract argument about its true nature. It becomes an ideological monster which devours all the feeling it is meant to signify. When words have killed it off, its exhausted speakers relapse into carnal contact as if by default.

Lawrence and Woolf reject, however, the emerging ideological currents of the Edwardian world. Lawrence abhors equally the upper-middle-class effeteness of Bloomsbury and the technological efficiency of Fordism designed to judge workers in capitalist industry as optimum machines. He also gives us in the figure of Gerald Crich, an English 'blond beast of prey' whose sadism has adjusted to the machine, an embodied prophecy of the Fascism to sweep Europe in the next decade. Woolf repudiated the rationalist ethics of G. E. Moore which held Russell, Keynes and Bloomsbury in its thrall, and which elevated common-sense explanation over the metaphysical veil. Woolf, however, had no wish to return to the veil but found instead a numinous radiance and wonder in the ordinary for which there was no rational expression. The rejection of rationalism in a secular world involved for both a concern with the present-ness of things. For Lawrence feeling rushes impetuously from one moment to the next as a lived presence which does not stop for reverie. For Woolf the world is something both to be wondered at and questioned, a source of constant astonishment and probing in which nothing is obvious and nothing can be taken for granted. Fabian rationalism, as a proposed reform of the known and the obvious, is by comparison a grotesque complacency.

Lawrence briefly injects a passionate structure of feeling into the English novel in the amours of Ursula Brangwen who stridently, raggedly finds fragile love-in-exile with Birkin. But after *Women in Love* he loses this in a quagmire of mushiness, polemics and pornography. Passion as the violation of a debased social order which is so crucial to the French and the Russian novel, becomes stillborn in the Anglo-American fiction of the twentieth century. For Joyce, Woolf and Faulkner, and also for Ernest Hemingway, Djuna Barnes and Malcolm Lowry, the reality of the modern predicament is the absence of love. Community, both as communion and communication, breaks down. The new structures of feeling are more oppositional than those they succeed. They suggest an abiding lostness at the centre of things, a failure to connect, an implosive inwardness which cannot be contained within the splitting shell of the ego. The shattered ego is immersed in a world superabundant with sense-impressions, but the centre cannot hold. If it cannot define itself, it cannot equally define the objects of its needs and satisfactions. These become, as Lacan retrospectively suggests having read the great modernists, forms of objectless desire (1966, p. 28ff). Desire is cathected by figures and objects in ways which seem more arbitrary than intended. We can see this in the overdetermined chance which governs the meetings of Joe Christmas and Joanna Burden in Faulkner's *Light in August* (1932), or that of Bloom and Gerty MacDowell in *Ulysses*. It is often sexual but not necessarily so, since it resides above all in the experiential promiscuity of objects, a restless yearning shorn of romance and cast adrift in a world of commodities.

Though they reside in the styles of narrative language, in the multiple forms of wrought epiphany, the absences of the modern novel are not primarily linguistic but social. They are defined by class, by race, by gender, by cultural periphery. They are absences within community rather than absences from community. The best novels of exile are those in which characters are immersed in the life of a particular time and a particular place, only to feel simultaneously a hollowness in their own lives. This is the fate of the Divers in Scott Fitzgerald's *Tender is the Night* (1938), the Bournes in Hemingway's controversial *The Garden of Eden* (1986), of Frederick Henry in Hemingway's *A Farewell to Arms* (1929), of Nora Vote in Barnes's *Nightwood* (1936) and of Geoffrey Firmin in Lowry's *Under the Volcano* (1947). Exile here puts the protagonists on a fraught, insecure periphery of their own world. Absent from their homeland, they cannot escape its traces. Surrounding themselves with a welcome strangeness, they can never annihilate that strangeness, so that they are simultaneously decentred by what they repress and what they resist, by what they conceal and what is thrust upon them.

But there are forms of exile nearer at home, forms of interior estrangement of those in their own habitus. This is the fate of Bloom the wandering cuckolded ad-collector, of the pre-exilic Stephen Dedalus, of Quentin Compson who is in cultural exile at Harvard and spiritual exile at home in Mississippi, of the peripatetic unnamed narrator in Ralph Ellison's *The Invisible Man* (1951) whose South is a trauma from which he must escape and whose North is a New York City in which he must keep on running. The poor whites of Faulkner and Flannery O'Connor, the black protagonists of Ellison, Richard Wright and Toni Morrison, are the damned of a particular earth whose resourcefulness entails flight. In *Light in August* Faulkner's Joe Christmas, a mulatto orphan with a white Calvinist foster-father and no known parentage, is the victimizing victim of the Southern mythology of race, his splitting self an impossible splitting of colours in a skin that has the texture of parchment. In Faulkner's *Sanctuary* (1931) the white trash bootleggers change colour with every reading, from light to dark and back again as if they were the haunted ghosts of plantation slaves. But it is Joyce's Bloom, the derided Jew, 'the whiteyed kaffir' cautious and pacific to the last in Dublin's fair, colonial city whose interior absence and objectless desire is the most powerful of all. His stream-of-consciousness is in effect a stream of pre-consciousness harnessed, as Moretti (1988, p. 197) suggests, to the equivalence of commodities, a split consciousness which lies divided under the ensign of advertising, the ultimate capitalist sign. Bloom dispersed among the bric-à-brac and detritus of the world of commodities, is Bloom the excluded insider, a human vacuum filled with the cast-offs of a colonized, commodified culture and the desires it stimulates through envy and secrecy.

The splitting of the Self portends its possible doubling and repetitions. If there is no defence against the flooding of the Self's interior by exterior objects, there is equally no containment of the ego-ideal projected outwards into the world. Freud's brilliant verbal play on the uncanny in his essay of the same name (in Freud, 1985, p. 261) indicates this clearly. The strange and the remote, after initial repudiation, are often recognized as part of something familiar. That which is unfamiliar, which is far from home ('*unheimlich*'), turns out at times to be too close for comfort. The Other becomes an apparition of the astonished Self. Doubling is at the core of modernist detection narrative, asking of its readers to find the Other whom it never explicitly names. It is a product of the weakened ego which sees its desired object narcissistically as a projection of itself. As Horace Benbow bends down to drink the spring water on the opening page of *Sanctuary* his face splinters among the ripples into 'a myriad reflection'. In the reflection the hat of the watching Popeye who stands on the opposite bank appears to be sitting on his own head. The image establishes cinematically that Popeye is his lower-class double, the impotent gangster who later violates and abducts Temple Drake. Popeye's open desire for Temple echoes the concealed wishes of Benbow, the middle-class lawyer, for Judge Drake's kidnapped daughter. But Benbow also desires Temple as a feminized persona, a beautiful version of Self whose predatory actions reflect his own inept wish to be utterly promiscuous. In his cryptic desperation he desires to be both male predator and female Other, to be violator and violated. The multitude of streams and mirrors into which he gazes, tells us, mythically, who he is. If Benbow's sister is called Narcissa by her author, then Benbow is . . .

In Joyce, the effect of doubling overlaps past and present, history and myth. Buck Mulligan is Stephen's modern double, the mouthpiece of instant aphorism and gaiety who plays with language too much and too lightly. Shakespeare is his mythic double, the historical bard he tries to recreate in his own image. At the same time the Ghost in *Hamlet* who is regarded by Stephen as a version of the playwright is also Bloom's double, the bisexual cuckold of middle-age who has failed to survive the ravages of time. Stephen must avoid being Mulligan as a young man in order to avoid being Bloom in middle age and must do so by being the shadow of the Shakespeare he has invented, narcissistically awaiting the succubus (possibly Molly) who might wound him into art.

If Bloom is one version of the disintegrating middle-aged and impotent persona, then Geoffrey Firmin, in Lowry's *Under the Volcano* (1947), is another.

Firmin's doubles are his boyhood friend, Laruelle, and his brother, Hugh, both practical men who have succeeded in love and life where he has failed. But though they are both lovers of the wife of 'the Consul from Cuckold-shaven', and successes respectively in the fields of film and politics, they are not really successes at all. They have both compromised, and thus Yvonne is attracted back to the perverse purity of her ex-husband who drunkenly seeks his cabbalistic truths and finds nothing but mirrored instances of his own degradation. Firmin wastes away in the interior world of delirium tremens just as Hugh has wasted himself as an 'indoor Marxman' in cowboy dudes and Laruelle as a European expressionist becalmed in Hollywood. As in Joyce, the protagonists double with history. Laruelle, recalling his passion for Yvonne, at one point confuses the couple with Maxmilian and Carlota in the ruined chapel of the Miramar, 'lovers out of their element' who finally turn into 'ghosts'. The tragic celebrated lovers of Mexican history, the emperor and his bride, are echoed in the tragic and doomed journeys of Geoffrey and Yvonne, separately, to the Farolito. But the doom of Firmin is also the coming doom of the world. Doubling in space as well as time, the novel places Mexico as the transatlantic double of Spain. The trivial but vicious imbroglio of Firmin's murder at the hands of fascist paramilitaries echoes the devouring of Republican Spain by the rapacious rebel army of Franco. As Lowry writes the novel, Europe appears to be repeating on a grander scale the doom of Spain, while Geoffrey and Firmin repeat on a lesser scale the noble failure of Maxmilian and Carlota and the earlier failure of their marriage. Firmin attains tragic stature by sharing complicity in his own downfall and that of the civilized world.

If doubling repudiates the self as bounded certainty, the narrative of omission repudiates self as motive. In the 'Sirens' episode of *Ulysses*, Bloom's stream-of-consciousness becomes incoherent as the cuckolding hour approaches, not so much a filling-in of consciousness as a musical *evasion* of consciousness. In Hemingway's terse narrative prose we have simple statement as important often for what it does not say as what it does. The sentence is a series of balanced conjunctions. The nouns are bleak and bare. There are few adjectives in sight. In his dialogue we read statements as clear polished surfaces whose meanings remain oblique. In *A Farewell to Arms* (1929), Catherine Barkley's tense 'Keep on lying to me' undermines the aura of that romantic love she vainly seeks. Trust constantly pledges itself as an automatism which buries misgiving. Frederick Henry in turn cannot reflect on the full meaning of the war in which he is involved without encountering an abyss, without staring into its moral void as if petrified into stone. All narrative motion is a necessary urgency, skimming over the surface of things best left untouched, over the reality after 1914 that for Eliot humankind could no longer bear.

In Barnes's *Nightwood* (1936) omission is taken to perhaps its furthest point.

After Nora has lost Robin Vote to the 'squatter' Jenny Petheridge, she turns
to Matthew O'Connor, the Irish-American doctor, for consolation, catching
him in bed late one night in transvestite garb awaiting someone else. In chapter
5 of the novel, 'Watchman, what of the Night!' the doctor, tears streaming
through his mascara, fills up the void left by Nora's limp and desolate questioning. The night that has devoured Robin is buried under his torrential invocation
of the night that engulfs Paris, and finally the world. The silence that is the
absence of all understanding is filled in by the speech in which all understanding is melted down like gold into molten liquid. It runs away with itself and
signifies nothing. Nora is calmed by the flow of words which tell her nothing,
which become more and more desperate as they pour from the doctor's lips.
As he lies in bed peeping out of the covers, they try to conceal the agony
which the night holds for both of them. For Robin, the love-object of man
and woman alike, the destroyer of lives, cannot be 'known' as Jenny the 'looter'
can be 'known' and damned as a malicious intruder. Robin is the enigma
which lies beneath the commodified object of desire her lovers have made of
her, and that is precisely her main attraction.

In Hemingway's posthumous novel *The Garden of Eden* (1986), edited down
in its published form to a third of its manuscript size, he invokes the bisexual
ambience of exile we find earlier in Barnes and which he himself, through his
various myths of masculinity but also mindful of censorship, had previously
repressed. Catherine Bourne retains the Christian name of Hemingway's
earlier heroine but none of her romantic illusions. Instead she uses the context
of their recent marriage to turn identity inside out and upside down. She and
her writer husband agree through her persuasion to become physical twins,
images of each other with their bleached blond hair and dark suntanned skins,
acting out a unisexual utopia which soon turns to nightmare. Catherine longs
perversely to be both twin and brother to the husband she calls her 'girl'. Her
dialogue has the quality of a poetic voice in which the sub-text is perversity,
or forms of perversity which cannot be openly named. Her quest is lost from
the start. There can be no permanent trading of identities, no end to the sexual
difference which suffers merely transient obliteration. There is something a
little precious too in the endless honeymooning which makes Hemingway a
lesser writer of bisexual desperation than Barnes. But Catherine Bourne's
failure is still a failure on a grand scale, an attempt to reverse the cultural
order of things which exposes by implication the vast domain of male power.
David Bourne's canny instinct for survival takes him beyond the perversity
which sees Catherine take up with another woman by eventually taking over
that woman himself in the completion of the triangle. If perversity threatens
sexual identity, or creates a new identity which cannot be sustained, then the
odds are still stacked in favour of male victory. It is Catherine who finally goes
insane.

Though Hemingway's novel has a novelist as a hero who is writing a novel within the novel about game-hunting in Africa, the novel itself still belongs to the epiphanous mode. Its reflexive dimension, however, points us to the metafictional successors of epiphany in the modernist novel. Here Robert Scholes (1980) has suggested the term 'fabulation'. Fiction becomes a never-ending story. The device of storytelling is usually exposed by the author's self-insertion within the text, his or her presence as narrator consciously creating a fiction with no solid realities or clear endings. The illusion of the real is invoked only so that it had be discarded. John Fowles writes a version of Mediterranean exotica in *The Magus* (1966) where his exotic Greeks and their planted confederates finally have no tangible nature. In *The French Lieutenant's Woman* (1969) he writes a beautiful pastiche of the Victorian novel with a knowing narrative commentary and sexual licence which the 'swinging sixties' have given to him. In *Gravity's Rainbow* (1973) Thomas Pynchon plays with the idea of destructive rocketry as the predestining weapon of an invisible Calvinist God, updating the angel of destruction to resemble Werner von Braun. In *Lanark* (1981) Alistair Gray comically doubles his autographical self in the two figures of the fifties Glaswegian Duncan Thaw and the dystopian figure of Lanark in Unthank, the city of the future, only to triple that self by making a dramatic authorial entrance as himself in the Epilogue. In fabulism, often called postmodernist but for no obvious reason, the death of the author is as far away as ever.

Even if the fiction of the last twenty years may still be called modernist in the fracturing of its narratives and the openness of its endings, it is clear that it has altered course. The boundaries between reality and fantasy have, at times, clearly dissolved. The novel's illusion of reality, even when fractured in the ways we have suggested, is no longer just being examined or just being parodied. At times it is dispensed with altogether. The wish to spin our fictions which cannot be pinned down to a material world is a response, no doubt, to an age of global electronic information where more can be known and communicated than ever before. The elusiveness of fictions gives them a special pedigree in a culture which is increasingly documented and saturated by self-advertisement. It is a way in which the world of the book can resist the world of the screen. Whether it can continue to do so into the next century remains yet to be seen.

FURTHER READING

Adorno, T. W. (1984) *Aesthetic Theory*, translated by C. Lenhardt, Routledge & Kegan Paul, London [first published 1970]

Auerbach, Erich (1968) *Mimesis: The Representation of Reality in Western Literature*, translated by W. Trask, Princeton University Press, Princeton [first published 1946]

French, Marilyn (1976) *The Book as World: James Joyce's Ulysses*, Harvard University Press, Cambridge

Freud, Sigmund (1984) *On Metapsychology: The Theory of Psychoanalysis*, (vol. 11 of *The Pelican Freud Library*), Penguin, Harmondsworth

——(1985) *On Art and Literature*, (vol. 14 of *The Pelican Freud Library*), Penguin, Harmondsworth

Gates, Henry Louis, Jr. (ed.) (1984) *Black Literature and Literary Theory*, Methuen, London

Hussey, Mark (1986) *The Singing of the Real World: The Philosophy of Virginia Woolf's Fiction*, Ohio State University Press, Columbus

Irwin, John T. (1975) *Doubling and Incest: Repetition and Revenge: A Speculative Reading of Faulkner*, Johns Hopkins University Press, Baltimore

Jameson, Fredric (1981) *The Political Unconscious: Narrative as a Socially Symbolic Act*, Methuen, London

Lacan, Jacques (1966) *Ecrits*, Editions du Seuil, Paris

Moretti, Franco (1988) *Signs Taken For Wonders*, translated by S. Fischer, D. Forgas and D. Miller, Verso, London

Orr, John (1987) *The Making of the Twentieth Century Novel: Lawrence, Joyce, Faulkner and Beyond*, Macmillan, London

Powers, Arthur (1974) *Conversations with James Joyce*, edited by Clive Hart, Millington, London

Scholes, Robert (1980) *Fabulation and Metafiction*, University of Illinois Press, London

Sundquist, Eric J. (1983) *Faulkner: The House Divided*, Johns Hopkins University Press, Baltimore

Williams, Raymond (1977) *Marxism and Literature*, Oxford University Press, London

——(1979) *Politics and Letters*, New Left Books, London

46

BRITISH FICTION SINCE 1930

PETER CONRADI

[The] novel is a comic form. A novel that isn't at all comic is [in] great danger, aesthetically speaking, that is.

(Iris Murdoch, in Ziegler and Bigsby, 1982, p. 230)

Tyrants hate jokes.

(Iris Murdoch, television interview, 1987)

It was once fashionable to denigrate British fiction written since 1930, a habit that deserves sketching in some detail. After the excitements of international modernism, we were told, British fiction reverted to its ordinary state of provincial dullness, fed by a cosy and deluded aesthetic, charting only safe topics, imitating the so-called 'bad faith' and formal inertia of the Victorian novel, 'Georgian' in a limiting sense. By 1930 modernism is effectively played out. Virginia Woolf's *The Waves* (1930) is published and she is never to outdo its technical daring. Lawrence, Proust, Conrad and Kafka are all dead. Forster, after his innovative *A Passage to India* (1924), has more or less ceased work as a novelist. The banner of modernism may be kept flying by Henry Green, but the wind itself has changed direction. The next stage of 'experiment' in the novel – postmodernism, with which this essay will be little concerned – is heralded by James Joyce's *Finnegans Wake* (1939) and by Beckett's novels; both writers significantly escaped these islands to live abroad. In this view the gravitational pull of 'realism' prevents our full entry into postmodernism as it did with modernism: 'realism' is construed as an inauthentic aesthetic from which we have never escaped.

From this standpoint the history of the British novel – and to some extent of the British people too – is perceived as a catalogue of missed opportunities and of an artificially cultivated innocence. Politically we come adrift from the European mainstream through not sharing the common misfortunes of either fascist or Stalinist occupation. We do not experience the largest psychic mass trauma of the century – the Holocaust – on our own soil, and thus fail to lose our political innocence. Our good fortune means, so the argument runs, that nineteenth-century realism can continue to nourish our writers who, as one British exponent of the postmodernist, Christine Brooke-Rose, has it, rush around like decapitated chickens unaware that the axe has fallen – the axe of history. We are seen to inhabit a fool's paradise. Because our history is untransformed, our novels are untransformed too. Our history and our literature alike are thus seen as versions of pastoral, a point to which I shall return.

Brooke-Rose, like Joyce and Beckett before her, lives abroad. The case she is associated with deserves to be disputed. What is most living and most accessible in those writers termed postmodernist (Calvino, Borges, Barth, Kundera, Grass, etc.) is not their cult of readerly frustration, nor their mystique of indeterminacy, nor their subversion of 'character' and 'story', but their rediscovery of narrative *play*: a rediscovery, one might argue, both of life in comic terms, and of the intrinsic comedy of narrative convention itself, the latter owing much to a reappraisal of Sterne, Cervantes, Boccaccio, *The Thousand and One Nights*, and of a long early tradition of narrative convolution.

Comedy, indeed, which structuralist and post-structuralist criticism has found no way of addressing, links much of the writing which has followed on from modernism. Together with pastoral, it provides us with a fresh way of looking at recent fiction. From Cervantes through to Fielding, Sterne and Dickens, the novelist's muse had indeed always been partly comic. What was striking and unremarked about the classic modernist fictions is how rarely, if at all, they make us laugh out loud. The tenets of modernism, the most portentous of movements, are as hostile to comedy as they are to democracy. Of course there is bathos, especially about sexual politics, in Woolf's *To the Lighthouse* (1927). Joyce's *Ulysses* (1922) has a Homeric wit. And the faithful always claim at least *one* moment in *Women in Love* (1921) when Lawrence subjects Birkin to comic deflation. Neither Conrad's *Nostromo* (1904) nor his *Heart of Darkness* (1902) is famous for its jokes. Indeed irony, that patrician trope, rather than comedy, with its tendency towards the demotic, marks modernism throughout.

From this perspective what is remarkable about the vigorous renewal of the novel since modernism – in such excellent writers as Evelyn Waugh, Christopher Isherwood, William Cooper, Kingsley Amis, Angus Wilson, Muriel Spark and Iris Murdoch – is their allegiance to the novel as a distinctively comic form. This might be said to be a more interesting debt on their part to the nineteenth-century novel – for example to Dickens and Dostoevsky, both deeply, darkly comic – than any to 'realism'. If the debate about realism has become stale, then this is partly because it rests on unchallenged assumptions about Victorian fiction. In Robert Alter's *Partial Magic* (1975), for example, the relaxed self-reflexiveness of the Victorian novel is wholly ignored, as is the point that it was the moderns who were frequently literal-minded and puritanical about their fictional illusions. Henry James's strictures in 'The Art of Fiction' (1884) against Trollope's 'frivolous', playful undoing of the fictional conventions under which he was operating neatly makes both points.

The tradition of British fiction since 1930 (and, in this essay, among writers born before that year) is again a strong and healthy one, but we have not always found ways of honouring its strength or its health. 'Comedy' and 'pastoral' provide two useful recurring centres of discussion. I mean by pastoral that witty and sophisticated mode of 'putting the complex into the simple' identified by William Empson (1935), *faux-naïf* and not innocent at all. Pastoral and counter-pastoral, of course, make frequent bedfellows, and comedy often accompanies both. Indeed the tragi-comedy of pastoral invaded or destroyed runs through much British fiction written since 1930.

One aspect of pastoral comedy is its propensity for social *disguise* – dressing up (or down) to impersonate a simpler or more 'innocent' social order than the one you inherit. Such disguise marks the narrative stance of a number of 1930s novelists. The thirties are often claimed as a decade of 'committed' documentary realism. Yet three of its best novelists used, on the contrary, a pastoral escapism to enable their own fiction. George Orwell, a better polemicist and journalist than novelist, wrote bitter Wellsian social comedies of lower-middle-class life, stubbornly and airily aping a dullness he deliberately chose to inherit and resent. Isherwood chronicled the raffish sexual tolerance and incipient social anarchy of late Weimar Berlin in a form of 'slumming' that was both sexual and cross-cultural. And Waugh's fantasy-escape from his Golders Green background was into a simultaneous infatuation and disgust with an upper-class world in which he had no hereditary interest, but which was to define his literary persona and subject-matter. To write, for each of these, depended on an escape from the middle-class respectability to which they were born.

Evelyn Waugh's *A Handful of Dust* (1934) is both one of his best works and one of the best novels of the 1930s. Coming when it does, there are echoes of modernism. Its title and epigraph come out of T. S. Eliot's *The Waste Land*, two chapter headings ('Du côté de chez Beaver' and 'Todd') recall Proust, and its grisly finale in the South American jungle pays tribute to Conrad's *Heart of Darkness*. The strength and savagery of its pessimism might also seem modernist. But its matter is tragic and its manner comic, a dissonance marking it off decisively from the portentous apocalypses of the moderns. The levity it describes and enacts is a source of appalled delight in the reader. It charts a world fallen into irresponsibility.

Poised between the cynical frivolity of the early fiction and the romantic excess of *Brideshead Revisited* (1945), the novel is written out of Waugh's fierce pain at the collapse of his first marriage and turns personal complaint into cultural diagnosis and bitter satire. Tony and Brenda Last keep ennui at bay by a series of futile 'menus', while the London set they belong to avoids boredom by adultery. Brenda falls for London's only spare man, John Beaver, 'second-rate and a snob and as cold as a fish', and turns against her husband. The money-minded opportunist and entrepreneur Mrs Beaver and arriviste Polly Cockpurse typify the decay of this social world, a decay further figured in the numerous changes of alliance, factitious parties to sell new ideas, and an episode of fortune-telling using the sole of the foot. Mrs Beaver, with a finger in every pie, oversees the division of Belgravia houses into bed-sits for the purposes of 'base love'. The impoverished moral code of this set is displayed in the banality of its language – 'Hard Cheese on Tony'. And the tone of the book is dead-pan, not bothering to defend itself against the levity it displays until the end of chapter 3, when pain breaks through: '[Tony] had got into the habit of loving and trusting Brenda', a phrase that gets repeated lest we miss the pathos and rage that underlie it. For Tony is another of Waugh's defeated heroes, seen from outside until the second half of the book, a betrayed romantic whose pastoral dream of Hetton, the Victorian pile he inherits, proposes the only moral positive in a naughty world. The Anglican Church exemplified by the Revd Tendril embodies a bankrupt ritual. Waugh likes to figure the care of an old house as an onerous quasi-spiritual duty in itself. Brenda's horrible brother has typically sold off his house. Yet Hetton is made deliberately unreal, a 'radiant sanctuary' in Tony's hectic delirium, a Pre-Raphaelite dream of irrecoverable innocence. The pastoral hope Tony enshrines in Hetton – like John Boot's dream of an innocent nature in *Scoop* (1938) – meets a savage counter-pastoral rebuke in the South American jungle: hideous insect life, vampire bats, a crook doctor-explorer, superstitious Indians and a madman called Mr Todd (= death) who imprisons Tony in a living death, compelling him endlessly to read Dickens to him.

The comedy springs partly from the gap between Waugh as artist and as moralist. As an artist he revels gleefully in the very anarchy, vanity and folly whose black energies the moralist in him condemns. The savage and barbarous heartlessness of the late Mayfair world is matched by the author's own cold eye. The book has at its heart a picture of Tony crying from despair, and the novel is said to be written in Waugh's blood and to be his last word on the limitations of humanism. But what we take away as readers is also Waugh's own involuntary delight in the rich vein of casual lunacy his comic genius uncovers.

Christopher Isherwood's *Goodbye to Berlin* (1939) is another novel that uses a comic tone to envisage a doomed civilization. But where Waugh consecrates his private pain and makes sense of it in the impersonality of art, Isherwood's 'objective' narrative stance is ambiguous in a different way. Waugh hides the fact that his secret relation with his subject-matter is (in part) hot, while

Isherwood foregrounds his coldness ('I am a camera'). Isherwood, too, originally intended to write a modernist epic called 'The Lost' but mercifully
ended instead with a comic picaresque journey through the different worlds
of late Weimar Berlin: philanthropic Jewish millionaires (the Landauers) contrast with the petty crime, disease and despair of the slums (the Nowaks). One
attraction of Berlin to middle-class British homosexuals of the time was the
impoverished Berliners' free and easy attitude to sex, about which the novel
('On Ruegen Island') is candid. The whole is framed by 'A Berlin Diary' in
two parts, comic, tender, lyrical and sad.

Isherwood's use of comedy becomes, as we read, part of a rhetorical strategy.
Like *A Handful of Dust* the novel starts brightly and moves towards darkness.
At the start we hear of an ugly old Jewess who has advertised for a husband
and been comically maligned by her enemy, the Bavarian *Jodlerin* Frl. Mayr.
Mayr tells Glanterneck's prospective husband that Glanterneck has (a) bugs
in her bed, (b) been arrested for fraud and released on the grounds that she
was insane, (c) leased out her bedroom for immoral purposes and (d) slept in
the bed afterwards without changing the sheets. The hilarity of the row that
ensues comes to seem by the end, set in the year 1933, distinctly whiffy. Here
Jews are already being beaten up or, like Bernard Landauer, murdered. A
seventeen-year-old youth has his eye poked out by the storm-troopers while
a crowd looks on, without much emotion. So the comic anaesthesia of the
early scene looks forward to the brutalities to come. What we have laughed at
was in deadly earnest after all: Fräulein Mayr was herself a Nazi, and the
Glanternecks are now an endangered species. The book is eloquent about the
ambiguity of laughter: 'That's why [the Nazis] are so dangerous. People laugh
at them, right up to the last moment.' They are 'capable of anything' ([1939]
1962, p. 177).

But the novel is concerned with more than the spectator-sport of foreign
politics. It is eloquent on Prussian hysteria, but good, too, on the exasperations
of friendship. Herr Issyvoo quarrels with the incomparable Sally Bowles, and
it is a good book, too, about loneliness. 'You never seem to get really warm,
sleeping alone' (p. 12), complains Frl. Schroeder, in one of the book's many
fine moments of comic pathos.

To point to such matters is to suggest that *Goodbye to Berlin*, possibly Isherwood's finest novel, celebrated a resilient human diversity. It was a celebration
the more poignant in that Nazism was so brutally to punish human difference.
It showed, too, that disaster cannot be imagined apart from the individuals
who suffer it. William Cooper's seminal *Scenes from Provincial Life* (1950)
presents characters who, we are told, will go to the concentration camp should
Hitler invade, either because they are progressive or, in the case of the
narrator's friend Tom, because he is both Jewish and homosexual. It is 1939,

in an unnamed provincial city. A cult-book among writers of the 1950s, displaying many of the strengths and weaknesses of the writing of the time, *Scenes from Provincial Life* tells of two impermanent relationships, threatened (we are assured) more by their own instability than by that of the times. Indeed the book is pastoral in its deliberate refusal ever to imagine the worst, and comic too.

The narrator, Joe Lunn, does not care for T. S. Eliot, and his gay Jewish friend Tom is gently mocked for seeing himself as Proust's character Swann. Cooper champions the 'ordinary' and has some distaste for the highbrow. The novel on more than one occasion equates the tragic with the 'solemn, false, dramatic' ([1950] 1969, p. 103) while retaining intelligent sympathy for the habit of dramatization, too. Yet tragedy and intensity are held at bay. None of the characters is killed in the Second World War. Both the homosexuals marry. Ordinary life continues. 'Sometimes I want to be just ordinary ... terribly ordinary' (p. 107) says Steve, seventeen years old and being courted by Tom; the joke here being both that Steve of course is nothing but ordinary, and beyond that that everyone else is, too; and then that the novel finally nurses a vision of the ordinary that is full of surprises and finally unknowable. Tom is one of the book's major successes, a fine comic creation reminiscent of Mr Toad, competing with the narrator Joe, full of bluster and self-conceit and hiding his selfishness, like Mrs Elton in Jane Austen's *Emma*, behind a mask of high-minded sentiment, yet loved by his author also. Joe is fascinated by the gap between self-image and what underlies it, a gap wryly etched in where his girlfriend Myrtle is concerned. Myrtle sees herself as vulnerable and is shown as adaptable and resilient instead. Her late acquisition of a red setter (called Brian) and a gun procures a comic pleasure that delights by its rightness, while suggesting the degree of flight into idiosyncrasy that the book permits. Perhaps the little Englandist aspect of the new realism Cooper appeared to herald is clearest in his lyricism about the English countryside: 'Where else, except over English meadows, does beauty leap up so nearly to the verge of being palpable? Do not ask me. I do not know' (p. 101).

Scenes from Provincial Life influenced other novelists, for example Kingsley Amis in *Lucky Jim* (1954). At the time *Lucky Jim* was read as a key text in the new class-war, catalysed by the 1944 Butler Education Act, between an older social establishment, here symbolized by the Welches, and the 'angry young men' dispossessed by higher education and with an unappeased hunger for social purpose and status. It is a key text, too, in the new 'realism' that Cooper inaugurated, which could reflect such tensions. Yet it has come to seem a darker and more ambiguous comedy than it once did. The Welches are smug, pretentious, privileged and vacuous, and represent the 'home-made pottery crowd, organic husbandry crowd, the recorder-playing crowd' ([1954] 1961, p. 227) whose corrupt version of pastoral Dixon detests and finally unmasks in the great scene of his disastrous lecture on Merrie England. Dixon resembles the *chinovniks*, the oppressed small clerks of Gogol, Ostrovsky and Dostoevsky who fight for social identity within a corruptly static and sycophantic social order. The scene where Dixon finally knocks out Bertrand Welch is notable not merely as a symbolic victory within this class-war, but because in it Dixon finally speaks his own thought. Until then a merely private exposer of hypocrisy, Dixon has a repertoire of secret and manic faces that he pulls as a species of private revenge on the social world. When he fights Welch he thinks, 'The bloody old towser-faced boot-faced totem-pole on a crap reservation'; and at once hears himself also *saying*, 'The bloody old towser-faced . . . etc.' (p. 209), the social victory marked also by an emotional truth-telling.

Yet the book is more complex than this suggests. As well as social satire the novel contains surreal and nihilistic farce. As well as rage against the folly of fake or literal-minded pastoral ('Merrie England') it already shows signs of Waugh-like hostility to the modern world that the Welches deplore; there are insolent waiters, unaccommodating taxi-drivers, insubordinate college lackeys ('very bad men') throughout, and the old army-man Atkinson is admired for the wholeheartedness of his detestation of much that he sees about him. So far from endorsing a democratic access to higher education, Dixon and Beesley deplore the erosion of standards caused by lax modern marking. While the novel censors mere aestheticism, the highbrow and high-flown, Amis also sports such words as aliment, objurgatory, ventricose, glandered, syncope and ataxically (among other recondite terms), each used with precision within a style triumphantly and expertly making play with the colloquial. And though he attacks the pretentious use of music as a mere class-badge ('filthy Mozart') yet he excels in the precise use of terms such as *maestoso* and *allegro con fuoco* (chap. 8).

There are, moreover, already signs of the later more blimpish and misanthropic Amis here, who was to make the lethally detailed attack on Merrie Englandism that partly constitutes *The Alteration* (1976) and to elegize the tost pastoral of 1940s motoring in *The Old Devils* (1986). Amis from the start speaks for a no-nonsense bonhomie, a conspiratorial freemasonry of men (and a few women who secretly count as honorary men) of good sense. Yet while he attacks the juvenile Welch-like vision of the artist that ranges him with 'children, neurotics and invalids' (p. 141), Amis also presents a hero who sticks his tongue out at an old lady whom he fears may be staring at him, and who is painfully honest about the near-incapacitating child-like intensity of his feelings. The book excels at depicting guilt, terror, anxiety, pity, embarrassment, hatred and fury, and some of its best comedy comes out of the necessity of repressing such emotion. Its triumph is Margaret Peel, forerunner of later Amis villainesses, neurotic, hysterical and castrating, who uses her apparent powerlessness to manipulate the men who come her way. Fear and hatred of women – together with silence about *male* hysteria – are continuing Amis themes, and one suspects that an interested Martian might learn as much about the real pain of contemporary sexual politics from Amis's novels as from piously 'correct' feminist fiction.

If there was a 1950s British *écriture*, then *Lucky Jim* suggests how fragile its synthesis was. For all its acute social observation, its plot borrows from romance, with a Cinderella-like hero who ends up with a fairy godfather (Gore-Urquhart), a princess, a job, and London itself. Amis has since turned more openly to romance-forms, writing a ghost story (*The Green Man*, 1969), a classic detective story (*The Riverside Villas Murder*, 1973), a spy story with some added metaphysics (*The Anti-Death League*, 1966), even a James Bond spoof (*Colonel Sun*, 1968). His interest in such supposedly 'low' genres suggests one direction British writing has taken since 1960, exploring and exploiting romance, allegory and 'gothic' writing.

Lucky Jim came out in the same year as William Golding's *Lord of the Flies* (1954) which is, like so much of Golding's fiction, an allegorical enquiry into the nature of original sin. Set on an apparently idyllic tropical island, the novel takes savagely to task the naïve and fake pastoral of Ballantyne's *The Coral Island* (1857). It enquires how evil enters the world, and discovers that it happens through humanity, in this case through children, who destroy each other and, at the end, the whole natural world that they inherit. It is a work of stunning (if un-comic) power.

An interest in how evil enters the world links much recent British writing and colours the theme of invaded pastoral. In his extraordinary account of his own fiction-making processes *The Wild Garden* (1963), Angus Wilson discusses the ambiguity both of pastoral and of innocence within his work. The sanctuaries and redoubts in which innocence hides usually end up, in his fiction, by being violated or abandoned. Such themes can be found in *Late Call* (1964), one of his finest works, which, like much of his earlier fiction, charts emotional breakdown and the new life that may follow from it.

Half-way through that novel, in a small self-consciously Fielding-like interpolated romance ('The Old Woman's Story', chap. 6), Sylvia Calvert, chief character in the book, meets her European double or counterpart in the Polish Mrs Kragnitz. Kragnitz has been through half the major disasters and displacements of the century, exiled from continent to continent. Sylvia has retired from her life as a seaside hotel manageress and is displaced into Carshall, an anomic new town that stands in as microcosm for England in the brave new Macmillan years of post-war prosperity. She is quartered with her rigid, obsessive grieving son Harold, with his children who react in various ways to his neurotic domination, and with her wastrel husband. The encounter between the two old ladies is staged to yield a moral. Just as the *morceaux choisis* Mrs Kragnitz quotes from the classics of European humanism (Tolstoy, Grillparzer, Strindberg, Pushkin, Byron and so forth) are all false (made up by the author), so Mrs Kragnitz is herself untouched by the disasters she has survived, is insensitive and empty. She uses 'high culture' to insulate herself against experience, while Sylvia finds a kind of truth in struggling with the 'inferior' romances that constitute much of her reading.

Wilson has recorded his hatred for the insularity of much English writing (see Ziegler and Bigsby, 1982, p. 245) and this episode comes not from any retraction of that mistrust, but as a warning that to endure the 'dark night' as do both Sylvia and Mrs Kragnitz comes with no guarantee of any rebirth or growth whatever. *Late Call* indeed explodes a number of false pastorals. In its prologue, set in a 1911 Suffolk summer, Edwardian idyll comes to grief both in its 'progressive' urban guise (Mrs Longmore and her daughter) and also in its myth of rural content (young Sylvia). Later the 1960s New Town idyll has its own versions of utopian bad faith, and is policed by managing and bossy women. The Midlands countryside figures in Sylvia's appalled imaginings as a figure of spiritual desolation. Nor is Sylvia's rescue by the Egan family – through which she recovers a sense of value – permitted to become stale or cosy. Wilson's imagination fights off the lyricism to which it is drawn and his characters are repeatedly ejected from any 'nursery comforts' – like Meg and David at the end of *The Middle Age of Mrs Eliot* (1958) – to which they may be tempted to return, out into the dangerous world beyond. The amalgam of real pain and profound comedy in his work recalls that writer whom Wilson has called the greatest of European novelists, Dostoevsky (see McSweeney, 1983, p. 266). The further we get away from Dostoevsky, the more he seems our true contemporary. Like Dostoevsky, Wilson's comic genius has always been curiously angled to his moral passion. His tendency to lead us to laugh loudest at what he most disapproves of is explicitly investigated in *No Laughing Matter* (1967) whose title points to the British habit of using laughter to defuse situations, and thus as a more or less subtle excuse for inertia, political or emotional.

Thomas Mann once suggested that tragi-comedy was the essential form of the century. A tragi-comic strategy, certainly, is used by both Muriel Spark and Iris Murdoch. Both are fine comic writers, presenting potentially tragic matter in a manner close to comedy. Both, too (again like Dostoevsky), are unwilling to relinquish a religious soul-picture and partly employ their fiction as an attack on scientific rationalism.

Spark excels, above all, at the pleasures of what Murdoch has termed (in Bradbury, 1977, pp. 23–31) the 'crystalline'. That is to say that Spark deliberately writes minor novels (see Whittaker, 1982, p. 134) which delight by their mythic economy and cool stylishness; and also by their apparent heartlessness and polite savagery. *The Girls of Slender Means* (1963) shows her at her slender best, returning to the 1940s where her imagination has often been content to dwell. It explores – again, like many of her works – an enclosed community, here of young ladies eking out an existence between 8 May 1945 (when the Second World War ended in Europe) and 14 August that year (when it ended in the Far East), in a genteel Kensington hostel. Their means are slender in that, in the book's famous opening words, 'Long ago in 1945 all the nice people in England were poor, allowing for exceptions'; slender, too, in that some but not all can squeeze through the skylight when their house catches fire. At that central point in the book slender Selina Redwood evokes in Nicholas Farringdon a horrified vision of evil that is to lead to his conversion to Catholicism and thence to his martyrdom in Haiti. Selina has returned to rescue a Schiaparelli dress while Joanna Childe (the good fair heroine who, in the book's romance-like and dualistic imagining, is contrasted with Selina's sexual and material grasping) tries by contrast to comfort the panic-stricken girls who await rescue. Joanna dies in the burning, collapsing building, but her ethical means – we are to see – are far from slender.

Spark's 'coolness' of tone is sometimes described in terms of her attraction to a postmodernist aesthetic, which in its turn is related to her theology; so that the merely human events of her novels can be decreated by a long, formal quasi-divine perspective. What lies behind all this, however, is a palpable fear of, or embarrassment at, pathos itself: a fear that procures many readerly pleasures. A writer's weaknesses can sometimes be turned into formal strengths, though this process of transmutation is sometimes less evident in some younger writers (Ian McEwan, Martin Amis) whose style of cold behaviourism fails to hide comparable fear.

In Iris Murdoch's case the 'stylish' – which is to say, the attempt to appear better than one is – is often a cardinal sin. Yet, fed by her love of Shakespeare and her interest in creating pastiches of Shakespearian romance, and fed also by her interest in Freud and Plato, she writes stylish and over-plotted romances herself. In the early novels what she has termed the 'phenomenal *luck*' of English innocence (Murdoch, 1959, p. 252) is often invaded and exposed by alien god figures, foreign carriers of strange knowledge: Mischa Fox and the Lusiewicz twins in *The Flight from the Enchanter* (1956); Hugo Belfounder in *Under the Net* (1954); the Levkins in *The Italian Girl* (1964); Honor Klein and Palmer Anderson in *A Severed Head* (1961); Julius King in *A Fairly Honourable Defeat* (1970).

In her more recent fiction, which is stronger than the early work, the strange knowledge is already inside the English idyll. Her recent novel *The Good Apprentice* (1985) shows her at her best. Young Edward Baltram gives his friend Mark a drug sandwich and thereby kills him. Edward enters a vividly evoked private hell of guilt and remorse, the immense dark power of his unconscious made ambiguously available to him. The novel reworks the story of the prodigal son and shows Edward journeying for comfort and forgiveness, and negotiating a number of father-figures in his attempt to find them. There is his stepfather Harry, a facile and guilty rationalist; and Harry's opponent Thomas, a disenchanted psychiatrist with a quasi-Buddhist philosophy of dying-into-life that is the novel's own, who helps push Edward towards his real father Jesse Baltram. Jesse has designed and lives in an extraordinary and wonderful house near the sea called Seegard, and the book's central and longest section takes place there, in a virtuoso episode of Shakespearian comic mock-pastoral that also draws on medieval romance. Here Edward's pilgrimage away from the illusions of guilt and back towards new life is superbly and ambiguously evoked: all release of spirit in Murdoch is essentially ambiguous.

Iris Murdoch's work attests the strength and adaptability of the traditional English novel, its capacity to survive and find new forms, feeding – in her case – as widely as off Shakespeare, gothic romance and Dostoevsky. The omnivorousness of the traditional novel is a good point at which to close. It can feed happily off many different modes, and digest them – fairy-tale and romance (Angela Carter), science fiction and myth (Doris Lessing's *Canopus in Argos Archives*, 1979–83). Omnivorousness indeed – a consuming curiosity and a consuming greed – seems its best guarantee of continuance.

FURTHER READING

Bergonzi, Bernard (1970) *The Situation of the Novel*, Macmillan, London
Bradbury, Malcolm (ed.) (1977) *The Novel Today*, Fontana, Glasgow
——(1979) *The Contemporary English Novel*, Edward Arnold, London
Bradbury, Malcolm and Bigsby, C. W. E. (eds) (1982–) *Contemporary Writers* series, Methuen, London
Haffenden, John (1985) *Novelists in Interview*, Methuen, London
Halio, Jay (ed.) (1983) *British Novelists since 1960*, vol. 14, Gale Research Co., Detroit
Jackson, Rosemary (1981) *Fantasy*, Methuen, London
Lodge, David (1971) *The Novelist at the Crossroads*, Routledge & Kegan Paul, London
Page, Norman (ed.) (1988–) *Macmillan Modern Novelists* series, Macmillan, London
Sinfield, Alan (1983) *Society and Literature 1945–1970*, Methuen, London
Stevenson, Randall (1986) *The British Novel since the Thirties*, Batsford, London
Ziegler, Heide and Bigsby, C. W. E. (eds) (1982) *The Radical Imagination and the Liberal Tradition: Interviews with Novelists*, Junction Books, London

ADDITIONAL WORKS CITED

Alter, Robert, (1975) *Partial Magic: The Novel as a Self-Conscious Genre*, University of California Press, Berkeley
Amis, Kingsley (1961) *Lucky Jim*, Penguin, Harmondsworth [first published 1954]
Cooper, William (1969) *Scenes from Provincial Life*, Macmillan, London [first published 1950]

Empson, William (1935) *Some Versions of Pastoral*, Chatto & Windus, London

Isherwood, Christopher (1962) *Goodbye to Berlin*, Penguin, Harmondsworth [first published 1939]

McSweeney, Kerry (ed.) (1983) *Diversity and Depth of Fiction: Selected Critical Writings of Angus Wilson*, Secker & Warburg, London

Murdoch, Iris (1959) 'The Sublime and the Beautiful Revisited', *Yale Review*, 49, 247–71

Whittaker, Ruth (1982) *The Faith and Fiction of Muriel Spark*, Macmillan, London

Wilson, Angus (1963) *The Wild Garden or Speaking of Writing*, University of California Press, Berkeley

47

CONTEMPORARY FICTION

ELIZABETH DEEDS ERMARTH

> There are no more stories...
> (Virginia Woolf, *The Waves*)

Contemporary fiction is a subject as vast as a Borgesian library whose shelves and pages are endless. But that magnitude is the least of my difficulties in attempting to give something like a fair summary of this field; a more formidable problem arises from the fact that novelists are writing two different kinds of fiction. In one kind the historical narrative conventions that have been familiar to readers for nearly two centuries still prevail essentially unquestioned; in the other kind a new language prevails that remains unfamiliar to many, perhaps even to most, readers. In short, there is in contemporary fiction an old novel and a new novel.

Many fine writers continue for various reasons to publish old novels in the sense that they adhere to the conventions of historical thinking and of realism current in nineteenth-century narratives. Writers with particular interpretive agendas require representational conventions: for example, in representing personal and social life under a system of apartheid, or in revealing gender-bias at work in people's lives. Nadine Gordimer, for example, or Chinua Achebe, or Margaret Atwood, or Margaret Lawrence all have excellent reasons to represent a world and hence to use the conventions of the old novel. There are a number of Indian writers, many writing in English (Anita Desai, V. S. Naipaul, Salman Rushdie, to name only a few), who use older conventions to treat new material with substantially new effects. In Eastern Europe and Germany, for example in the novels of Heinrich Böll or Martin Walser or Milan Kundera, similar forms and motives can be found, although often there is a certain heightening toward allegorical significance, a warp in representational conventions that, while it would be interesting to explore, does not essentially alter those conventions. As with any generalization about such various material, the distinction here between old and new narrative should be taken with a grain of salt; in some of the writers just mentioned, for example Böll or Kundera, one can find hints of Kafka and the world of the new novel.

The new novel has appeared primarily in France and in the Americas, most volubly in Latin America. In France, the list would include (alphabetically) Michel Butor, Robert Desnos, Marguerite Duras, Robert Pinget, Raymond Roussel, Nathalie Sarraute, Claude Simon (recent Nobel Laureate), and Alain Robbe-Grillet; for the Americas such a list would include Jorge Luis Borges, Robert Coover, Julio Cortázar (even though he lived most of his life in Europe), José Donoso, Gabriel García Márquez, John Hawkes, Vladimir Nabokov (even though he lived most of his life in Europe), Juan Carlos Onetti (on José Donoso's say-so), Thomas Pynchon, Gertrude Stein, and Mario Vargas Llosa. This essay concentrates on the new novel as it appears in two rather different forms: in the French *nouveau roman* and in the more diverse but equally surprising novels of the Americas. In this last group appears everything from the spare elegance of Borges to the endlessly playful traceries of Nabokov. In order to cope with the profundity of the issues and the mass of literature involved I have concentrated in this essay on summarizing and exemplifying the problems addressed by this new narrative, referring in detail only to a few texts and indicating the names of many writers. The reader venturing for the first time into the new novel might start with Borges (1962); Butor (1963); Cortázar (1966); Duras (1965); García Márquez (1970); Hawkes (1976); Nabokov (1972); Pynchon (1973); Robbe-Grillet (1965a); and Simon (1968).

Any generalizations about what constitutes the new narrative or who is a new novelist, however, must be taken with caution. Within the category of French and American writing alone, for example, we find different degrees and variations of style, and, more elusively, different levels of importance. For example, do Mario Vargas Llosa and Nathalie Sarraute attempt anything like the same thing? Does the list of major writers include John Barth, E. L. Doctorow, Don DeLillo, Carlos Fuentes, Manuel Puig? Can anything really new be said in old conventions and, if so, how do Margaret Atwood or Margaret Lawrence do it? The very questions call for a kind of evaluation that is, at present and perhaps fortunately, impossible to make. A very few general commentaries about the major writers are listed at the end of this essay, especially including Sharon Spencer's useful book (1971), José Donoso's personal memoir of the Latin American 'boom' (1977) and Robbe-Grillet's seminal collection of essays (1965b).

Readers entering into the world of the new novel will find an exhilarating lack of agreement among literary and other critics on just about everything having to do with this new writing. In going beyond the very circumscribed list appended here, it should be noted, readers may find that the excitement takes the form of uncomprehending hostility and gets into print even from the pens of writers who, it seems, should know better; the only caveat that follows from this is that readers should take D. H. Lawrence's advice and trust the tale, which in this case means trust that actual experience of reading which becomes the focus of the new novel, and accept for the duration of reading the various suspensions of belief that the act of reading entails.

Whether the new novel is 'modern' or 'postmodern' or just 'contemporary' is a question that leads to some central issues. At its Latin root the term 'contemporary' opens interesting questions as to just what 'the time' may be; in fact, the very idea of 'the time' as a historical moment single and rationalizable in historical terms is an idea that would be at home in the fiction written in the tradition of nineteenth-century realism but distinctly without a place in the new novel. The terms 'modern' and 'postmodern' are a little more helpful taken in their fullest meanings. The term 'modern', for example, has a local and a broader meaning; in its local meaning it refers to what is conventionally called the period of modernism extending from about the 1890s to the Second World War, in which case 'postmodern' may refer to what succeeds a fairly short cultural moment; but in its more general meaning the term 'modern' refers to the period that began with the Renaissance and experienced mutation somewhere near the middle of the twentieth century. This definition puts in the category of 'postmodern' those narratives that conspicuously reject the narrative conventions that developed in 'modern' culture broadly conceived; the new novels are just such narratives.

The new ('postmodern') narrative belongs to that critique of Western discourse which has been gaining strength for a century and which, from Friedrich Nietzsche to Luce Irigaray, entails a critique of metaphysics, of transcendence, of dialectics, of identity and the subject (the 'self', 'the same' and the other), in short, a critique of the intellectual underpinnings of that cultural formation that began with (roughly) the Renaissance and its redeployment of the Greeks. This modern formation has favoured much of what people in Anglo-American culture take for granted: representational government, Western science, realistic art, technology, capitalism, to name a few. In terms of narrative conventions, this formation has favoured, and many still take for granted, certain conventions about time and consciousness and identity that appear in the realistic novels of the nineteenth century and that still appear contemporaneously in what I am calling the old novel: especially the convention of historical development which underlies plot-and-character novels and their values of mobility, individual perspective, neutrality and projection.

The critique of this formation and its conventions is not new (elements can be found in the Enlightenment) and it is not over. Whatever one thinks of the new novel, it belongs to a cultural shift that is substantial, not ephemeral, and central to those currents that define experience and knowledge in the late twentieth century. Perhaps the most spectacular changes in our assumptions have taken place in physical science and the consequent description of the physical universe; but similar changes have taken place elsewhere such as, for example, in the study of language and culture (Saussure, Lévi-Strauss and Foucault), and broadly in communications media. All these evidences represent a now broadly implicit revision of empirical traditions and the narrative conventions belonging to them, a reformation that is still under way.

In their experiments, then, the new novelists share a spirit as well as many particular issues with that larger, broadly-based discourse analysis currently abroad in many professional and academic disciplines: a discourse analysis based in linguistic philosophy since Saussure, the critique of language focused by women's writing, and the ontological critique given momentum by Nietzsche and Heidegger. Like the philosophers and theorists the new novelists seek nothing less than the renovation of those conventions that have been the very tools of thought in Western culture for centuries, particularly the conventions that assumed the neutrality of language. The new novel is the form that most fully explores the implications of that reformation in terms of time and consciousness.

Part of the excitement produced by this vast, ambitious, cultural critique stems from its refusal to accept distinctions between practice and thought, between material and transcendental 'reality'. This effort produces a profound revalorization of practice and a new focus on thinking or reflecting *as* practices, not to mention new ideas about the nature and uses of language. In keeping with these efforts, new novelists characteristically refuse to let readers assume any distinction between what is invented and what is real, on the assumption that everything, including maps or theories about what is 'real', is invented, not 'real' in the sense of 'natural' or given. What this means is only that no 'reality' is privileged, not even the empiricist one that, in the guise of relative value, reasserts in historical conventions many of the long-standing tenets of Western culture.

This exploration has wrought major changes in narrative writing, especially changes in the very definition of language and in the role of readers. The definition of language has expanded to include all systems that work by differential function, that is, by function defined relative to all the other functions of the system; in a sentence, for example, we understand what a term 'means' not only or even primarily by reference to a 'real' world beyond it but by reference to other functional terms in that sentence, so that the 'definition' of any term – its function or what it means – depends upon its not-being in some other position or function. Definition is thus always negative, not positive, which means that 'meaning' is a more complex matter than empirical or scientific rules and usages allow. Systems that work, like the sentence, in terms of such differential function can be called languages: there is, for example, a language of fashion, a language of physical gesture, a language of strategic planning. The implications of this revaluation of language are profound because there is no longer any such thing as a 'literary' language and the segregation between literary and practical language disappears into the perception that all languages are invented, arbitrary, 'literary'. Plainly such explorations in narrative necessarily will involve making the reader self-conscious about the process of reading.

My epigraph from Virginia Woolf's novel, *The Waves* (1931), provides an occasion to comment briefly on some of the issues at stake. In this novel the writer, Bernard, worries that 'there are no more stories'. What kind of writing could there be under such conditions? By 'story' Woolf clearly means the kind of sequence with which the old novel has made us familiar: an essentially rationalized sequence in which character is developed, consequences unfold, and meaning becomes at least a little clearer. A 'story' has an origin, a causality and an end. And yet in *The Waves* we get no such story; on the contrary, even the death of the group's hero, the vigorous if voiceless Percival, is accidental, unheroic and in itself meaningless. Fortunately for Bernard, the writer, he discovers that this loss of a story is itself a story.

Writers of new novels have moved a bit further than Bernard; for them the role of language itself has become an issue and remains an open question, to the point that the powers and exclusion, the vectors and entitlements of languages themselves become the field of interest and exploration. The erring, metonymic quality of narrative generally reaches extremes in new narratives like Borges's 'The Aleph' (in *Ficciones*, 1962), a story that meanders but not aimlessly, or like Italo Calvino's *If On A Winter's Night A Traveller* (1981), a novel composed of many different novel beginnings but without middles or ends. The narrative consciousness in such stories used to be called 'unreliable', which meant 'deranged' by comparison with the 'reliable' (normal) narrators who discreetly refrained from calling attention to themselves; the question of reliability being another of the ways in which the interpreters of narrative have reinforced the Cartesian fiction of the founding subject, the natural, 'individual' mind. The new novelist, however, is not interested in consciousness of a Cartesian sort, but instead focuses attention on a narrative consciousness that is not individualized, being a function of a formal enterprise that blends both reader consciousness and textual language, and that is itself engaged in a wrestle with language. The reader, refused the usual satisfactions and reassurances, is forced to attend to (borrowing from Robbe-Grillet) an 'obscure enterprise of form'. This enterprise of form takes place at the level of language itself where sentences, like overall narrative sequences, perform Möbius twists that engage a reader in new acts of attention.

Some brilliant examples of these twists arc Julio Cortázar's short stories, especially the collection from three earlier Spanish editions called *End of the Game and Other Stories* (1967; also called *Blow Up and Other Stories*). 'Continuity of Parks', for example, achieves in two pages a basic twist of reader-consciousness that appears in countless variations through the writings of new novelists. This story begins with a reader reading: a businessman taking the train home to his large country house with its library indoors and its large park outdoors. Blessed with a satisfying sense of control over his holdings and his own powers, yet enjoying a certain detachment, he settles into his green velvet armchair to read a novel, allowing himself a momentary distraction by a melodramatic story of two lovers plotting a fatal action and agreeing, now at their final meeting, that the woman's lover must venture through the woods of the great park, into the great house, upstairs to the second floor library, and, with knife poised, up behind the man in a green velvet armchair reading a novel. Even readers familiar with the story experience a *frisson* at having to endure such a violation of the sacred boundary between fiction and so-called reality. The fiction is real and implicitly deadly; put another way, the 'reality' is fictional, invented, a powerful product of imagination.

Alain Robbe-Grillet's short novel *La Jalousie* ([1957] 1965a) may be the ultimate new narrative in the sense that it scrupulously avoids all plot interest and constructs its suspense by sheer formal play. Pattern depends on varied repetitions and not on causal or developmental relationships and meanings. The most obvious feature of *La Jalousie* is the systematic repetition of details and descriptions: a balustrade with peeling grey paint, the position of a shadow, an event like the arrival or departure of a car, or the blow crushing a centipede on the wall. Each detail or event is described many times, which is to say that in this text each 'happens' many times. Furthermore the descriptions are often contradictory. At one point, for example, the novel says 'The table is set for one person' and then, only four sentences later, it says 'The table is set for three' (p. 78). Annoyed readers may mutter, 'Well? is it one or three?' but such questions are not answerable in this novel and not interesting; they are questions which insist on the world of 'same and different', 'after and before', and in *La Jalousie* there is no sequence except the reader's sequence, no identities or events except those involved in reading the writing. Instead of plot we get pattern, instead of consistency we get contradiction. This kind of thing happens so routinely that pretty soon a reader either closes the book or gives up on consistency and begins to situate his or her awareness elsewhere than on the non-existent plot-and-character. In effect the prevailing present-tense consciousness in *La Jalousie* is eerily close to our own and not attributable to some Other character or featureless 'nobody' narrator of the kind so important to the old novel.

The new narrative characteristically forces the reader into a new activity relative to the text and into a new relationship with language. Unlike the reassuring conventions of the old novel, where history materializes along with a detached, disembodied consciousness that transcends and floats free of those specific, concrete details from which it nevertheless emerges, the unsettling new conventions literally prevent consciousness from becoming disembodied. The text consequently prevents the reader from performing various familiar acts of generalization; instead the reader must be an accomplice of the text, wrestling self-consciously with the various forms, inhibitions and permissions of the writing, always forced to be aware of the freedom as well as the arbitrariness of consciousness and of language.

FURTHER READING

Cixous, Hélène (1976) 'The Laugh of the Medusa' ('Le Rire de la Méduse'), translated by Keith Cohen and Paula Cohen, *Signs*, 1, 875–93 [essay first published 1975]

Derrida, Jacques (1978) 'Structure, Sign and Play in the Discourse of the Human Sciences' ('La structure, le signe et le jeu dans le discours des sciences humaines'). In Jacques Derrida, *Writing and Difference* (*L'écriture et la différence*), translated by Alan Bass, University of Chicago Press, Chicago, pp. 278–94 [essay first published 1966; *L'écriture et la différence* first published 1967]

Foucault, Michel (1972) 'The Discourse on Language' ('L'Ordre du discours'). In Michel Foucault, *The Archaeology of Knowledge and The Discourse on Language*, translated by A. M. Sheridan Smith, Tavistock, London [essay first published 1971]

Hayles, N. Katherine (1984) *The Cosmic Web: Scientific Field Models and Literary Strategies in the Twentieth Century*, Cornell University Press, Ithaca

Hawkes, Terence (1977) *Structuralism and Semiotics*, University of California Press, Berkeley

Irigaray, Luce (1985) *This Sex Which Is Not One* (*Ce Sexe qui n'en est pas un*), translated by Catherine Porter with Carolyn Burke, Cornell University Press, Ithaca [first published 1977]

Jakobson, Roman (1971) 'Language in Relation to Other Communication Systems'. In Roman Jakobson, *Selected Writings*, vol. 2, Mouton, The Hague, pp. 697–708

Kristeva, Julia (1980) 'From One Identity to An Other' ('D'un identité l'autre'). In Julia Kristeva, *Desire in Language: A Semiotic Approach to Literature and Art*, translated by Thomas Gora, Alice Jardine and Leon S. Roudiez, Columbia University Press, New York [essay first published 1975]

Lawson, Hilary (1985) *Reflexivity: The Postmodern Predicament*, Open Court Press, La Salle

Lyotard, Jean-François (1984) *The Postmodern Condition: A Report on Knowledge* (*La Condition postmoderne: rapport sur la savoir*), translated by Geoff Bennington and Brian Massumi, University of Minnesota Press, Minneapolis [first published 1979]

McHale, Brian (1987) *Postmodernist Fiction*, Methuen, New York

Mercier, Vivian (1966) *A Reader's Guide to the New Novel: From Queneau to Pinget*, Farrar, Straus & Giroux, New York

Ortega y Gasset, José (1956) *The Dehumanization of Art* (*Deshumanizacione del arte*). In Ortega y Gasset, *The Dehumanization of Art and Other Writings*, translated by Willard Trask, Paul Snodgress and Joseph Frank, Doubleday & Co., New York [first published 1925]

Sarraute, Nathalie (1963) *The Age of Suspicion: Essays on the Novel* (*L'Ère du Soupçon:*

essais sur le roman), translated by John Calder, G. Braziller, New York [first published 1956]

Soper, Kate (1986) *Humanism and Anti-Humanism*, Open Court Press, La Salle

Wallis, Brian (ed.) (1984) *Art After Modernism: Rethinking Representation*, The New Museum of Contemporary Art, with David Godine, New York

ADDITIONAL WORKS CITED

Borges, J. L. (1962) *Ficciones*, translated by Emece Editores, Grove Press, New York [first published 1956]

Butor, Michel (1963) *Mobile: Study for a Representation of the United States* (*Mobile: étude pour une representation des Etats-Unis*), translated by Richard Howard, Simon & Schuster, New York [first published 1962]

Calvino, Italo (1981) *If On A Winter's Night A Traveller* (*Se una notte d'inverno un viaggiatore*), translated by William Weaver, Harcourt Brace, New York [first published 1979]

Cortázar, Julio (1966) *Hopscotch* (*Rayuela*), translated by Gregory Rabassa, New American Library, New York [first published 1963]

_____(1967) *End of the Game and Other Stories*, translated by Paul Blackburn, Pantheon, New York

Donoso, José (1977) *The Boom in Spanish American Literature: A Personal History* (*Historia personal del 'boom'*), translated by Gregory Kolovakos, Columbia University Press and Center for Inter-American Relations, New York [first published 1972]

Duras, Marguerite (1965) *Moderato Cantabile*. In Marguerite Duras, *Four Novels*, translated by Richard Seaver, Grove Press, New York [first published 1958]

García Márquez, Gabriel (1970) *One Hundred Years of Solitude* (*Cien Anos de Soledad*), translated by Gregory Rabassa, Harper & Row, New York [first published 1967]

Hawkes, John (1976) *Travesty*, New Directions, New York

Nabokov, Vladimir (1972) *Transparent Things*, McGraw Hill, New York

Pynchon, Thomas (1973) *Gravity's Rainbow*, Viking Press, New York

Robbe-Grillet, Alain (1965a) *Jealousy* (*La Jalousie*), translated by Richard Howard, Grove Press, New York [first published 1957]

_____(1965b) *For a New Novel* (*Pour un nouveau roman*), translated by Richard Howard, Grove Press, New York [first published 1963]

Simon, Claude (1968) *Histoire*, translated by Richard Howard, George Braziller, New York [first published 1967]

Spencer, Sharon (1971) *Space, Time and Structure in the Modern Novel*, New York University Press, New York

Woolf, Virginia (1931) *The Waves*, Harcourt Brace, New York

VI. CRITICISM

48

BIBLICAL HERMENEUTICS

STEPHEN PRICKETT

In 1840, some six years after his death, a collection of Coleridge's essays was published by his nephew, Henry Nelson Coleridge, under the title *Confessions of an Inquiring Spirit*. The very personal connotations of that word 'confessions' were quite deliberate. H. N. Coleridge was treading on dangerous ground. His uncle's original title, *Letters on the Inspiration of the Scriptures*, had been far too descriptively accurate – not to say provocative. If this manoeuvre – together with a rather defensively pious preface – was intended to deflect criticism from the nephew, it was probably successful; it did not, however, save Coleridge's own reputation, already damaged by dark rumours about opium addiction, from taking a further dive.

Significantly, he was attacked from two quite different quarters. For the early Victorian religious public, already shaken by the suggestions of geologists and paleontologists that the dating of the Book of Genesis could not be taken at face value, Coleridge's argument from textual evidence that the Bible could not be read as a historical record of the events described could only come as further evidence that he was a crypto-infidel, seeking to destroy the church from the inside. From a smaller but more knowledgeable group, however, there was a much more damaging attack. Such arguments, they said, had originated in Germany, where they were already well known under the name of 'Higher Criticism', to distinguish them from the minutiae of textual scholarship. So far from being new or outrageous, they had in fact been commonplace among theologians there since the end of the eighteenth century, and Coleridge's book was in reality little more than a patchwork of unacknowledged plagiarisms from a previous generation of German critics such as Reimarus, Lessing and Eichhorn. Indeed, so dangerous were these suggestions considered that, when a second edition was brought out in 1849, it was prefaced by a lengthy introduction defending the author from the charge of plagiarizing Lessing, and attempting to distance Coleridge from the accusations of atheism that had (correctly as it turned out) been levelled at the German.

As so often happens, the effect of such a theological furore was to divert attention from certain much more original and important aspects of Coleridge's argument. For him the Bible was to be read as one might 'any other book', and not to be subject to what he called 'bibliolatry' – the idolizing of individual texts torn loose from their context and used as if they had a free-standing universal meaning. Similarly, its importance was not secured by divine fiat, but rather something to be discovered by practical and imaginative experience by the reader. In *The Statesman's Manual* he described the scriptures as: 'The living *educts* of the imagination . . .' giving 'birth to a system of symbols, harmonious in themselves, and consubstantial with the Truths, of which they are the *conductors*. . . . Hence . . . the Sacred Book is worthily intitled *the* WORD OF GOD' (ed. 1972, pp. 28–9).

The inversion here is quite startling – and is deliberately intended to be. We are not, Coleridge is saying, to reverence the Bible as the Word of God because it is revealed to us by authority, but we accept its authority from our own experience because it carries for us a poetic and symbolic value – acting as a 'conductor' (in the newly-coined electrical sense of that word) for divine grace and truth. In a few brief sentences, Coleridge has, in effect, stood on its head the whole hermeneutic tradition which had dominated biblical criticism since the Middle Ages.

For medieval writers it was God who was the supreme author (Reeves, 1991). Indeed, the Latin word for 'author', *auctor*, had been believed by the medieval grammarians to contain among its root meanings the verbs *agere* (to perform), *augere* (to make grow), and the noun *auctoritas* (authority). God, they believed, had not merely created all things, but was the source of all words as well (Minnis, 1984, p. 10). Every human piece of writing stemmed ultimately from the divinely-inspired word, the Bible – where God had written down the whole history of the world, and, specifically, of mankind, from the first day of Creation to the Last Judgement. Scriptural history was to be understood not merely at its face value, but also, like even the works of nature themselves, as having a 'sacramental' value. Every event narrated in the Bible was held to have both a literal historical meaning, *and* also a spiritual meaning – to be interpreted by means of an ever-elaborated system of allegory and, in particular, in the form known as 'typology'.

Such systems of interpretation were, of course, much older than the Middle Ages. Indeed, there is evidence of the use of allegory in pre-biblical Babylonian and Egyptian hermeneutics. By New Testament times it had already become part of the accepted mental 'set' of the day (Prickett, 1986, p. 23) and when the early Christians were faced with the very real problem of re-interpreting the Jewish scriptures (or what we now call the Old Testament) in the light of their own experience it would have seemed a quite normal method of procedure. Thus just as Moses put a veil over his face after he had seen God, to prevent the children of Israel seeing the shining of his face (Exodus 34:33–5), so Saint Paul sees the Old Testament as containing secrets hitherto veiled from its readers: 'until this day remaineth the same vail untaken away in the reading of the old testament; which vail is done away in Christ' (2 Corinthians 14). For Tertullian, an early commentator (*c.* 160–225 AD), the fact that Moses renamed Oshea, the son of Nun, Joshua, which in Hebrew is the same word as Jesus, is a clear piece of typology. Since it was Joshua, not Moses, who led Israel into the Promised Land, this was to be seen as prefiguring Christ's leading his people, the church, out of the desert of sin into the eternal life of the land flowing with milk and honey, not through the discipline of the Law of Moses but through the grace of the gospel (Auerbach, 1959, p. 28). To use the correct terminology, Joshua was the 'type', Christ the 'antetype'. By similar typological means over the next thousand years almost every event of the Old Testament was made by innumerable commentators to prefigure its antetype in the life of Jesus or in the events surrounding it in the New Testament and the life of the early church.

Right from its beginnings, therefore, Christianity had always been a hermeneutical religion. Its initial move was one of appropriation – in taking over and re-using the existing hermeneutic tradition of the Old Testament. But in so doing it presented itself with a problem. In its literal sense much of the Old Testament bore little or no relation to the superstructure that was now being constructed upon it. In many cases, indeed, its narratives and even ethical teachings actually seemed to contradict those of the New Testament. Some method had to be found at once to harmonize the existing written tradition – which was, of course, held to be divinely inspired – with what was now claimed to be its fulfilment. The interpretation of texts was thus not an incidental activity of the new religion, but an essential part of its foundation and development. Critical theory was what Christianity was about.

The importance of this basic need for biblical interpretation on the subsequent development of European literature and criticism cannot be overestimated. Until almost the end of the eighteenth century the literal meaning of the Bible was seen as being only one among many ways of understanding it. Not merely did allegorical, figural and typological modes of reading coexist with the literal one, they were often in practice (if not in theory) accorded higher status. Since the Bible was the model for all secular literature such ways of reading naturally became the model for the way in which *all* books were to be read. The allegorical levels of *The Divine Comedy* or *The Romance of the Rose* are not in any way optional additions to the basic story, they are a normal and integral part of what literature was expected to be. To put it another way: the idea of a primary literal meaning to a given written text is an essentially modern one – dating, in effect, from the rise of the prose novel in the eighteenth century.

This is not to suggest that allegorical and typological readings of the Bible remained constant over seventeen hundred years, or that there was general agreement among commentators about the exact meaning of the texts under discussion, or even that there was agreement over the number of interpretative levels to be found. Extreme exponents argued for as many as twelve; the Alexandrine school favoured no less than seven; more common was the belief that there were four. This, for instance, was the view of Dante, who, because he assumed it of scripture, also deliberately and explicitly created four similar levels in his *Divine Comedy*, which, though it is of course a religious poem, was never thought of as having the status of anything more than ordinary secular literature. According to John Cassian (*c.* 360–435) the four levels or senses of scripture consisted of the literal or historical sense, the allegorical, the tropological (or moral) and the anagogical. He cites as an example the figure of Jerusalem (see Minnis, 1948, p. 34). Historically it is the earthly city, capital of the ancient kingdom of Israel, etc; allegorically, however, it signifies the church; tropologically it stands for the souls of all faithful Christians; while anagogically (that is, in its mystical spiritual meaning) it is the heavenly city of God. A later popular Latin rhyme summarized them thus:

> *Littera gesta docet, quid credas allegoria,*
> *Moralis quid agas, quo tendas anagogia.*

> [The letter teaches what happened, the allegorical what to believe,
> The moral what to do, the anagogical towards what to aspire.]

It is important to realize that the word 'allegory' (Greek: *allegoria*) as used by biblical exegetes did not simply convey the normal classical sense of a fictional story with an inner meaning – the sense in which Aesop's fables, for instance, are often allegorical. For early Christian and medieval commentators it is used primarily in a 'figural' sense, that is, that *because* the people and incidents described were real historical figures, what they can be made to stand for shares in that 'reality'. The one guarantees the other. Neither level is in any sense 'fictional'. As Auerbach puts it:

> *Figura* is something real and historical which announces something else that is also real and historical.... Real historical figures are to be interpreted spiritually ... but the interpretation points to a carnal, hence historical, fulfillment – for truth has become history in flesh.
>
> (1959, pp. 29, 39)

For Christian interpreters of the Bible, the Incarnation had changed not merely the medium of allegory but also the critical context in which it arose. Allegory, and its associated figural types, became a part of history itself.

Medieval and even Renaissance commentators saw their work as much more than simply a study of critical modes, however. Protestantism itself, after all, arose primarily from a dispute over the meaning of the Bible. Moreover, was its interpretation to be in the hands of an authoritative church, which permitted its divinely inspired text to be read only in Latin? or was it to be available in the vernacular? – with the uncomfortable consequence that hermeneutics might be brought into the realm of popular debate. Anglicanism, with its insecure political foundation, was scarcely more tolerant of dissent than Catholicism had been. Some, even then, declared the plain literal meaning to be the only permissible one, but for others, faced with in effect the same problem of legitimacy that had beset the early church, the traditional modes of allegorical exegesis were to provide sufficient new ammunition. In defending their case Protestant exegetes were quick to show how the Reformation was itself a 'biblical' event that was similarly implicit both in the historical events leading to it and in the prophecies of the Bible. Thus Rome became identified with prophecies in the books of Daniel and Revelation, and phrases like the 'whore of Babylon' and the 'Scarlet Woman' passed into the rhetoric of religious and political abuse. For Catholic and Protestant sides alike, the question of biblical interpretation was less an academic study than a matter of life and death. Hundreds died in England, thousands in France, millions in Germany and central Europe.

Although more modern conceptions of history and textual interpretation had begun to appear in Germany by the end of the eighteenth century, as the reception of Coleridge's *Confessions* showed, this was to have little effect on popular thought in England until later in the nineteenth century. Thus a standard biblical commentary of 1806 like Mrs Sarah Trimmer's *Help to the unlearned in the study of the Holy Scriptures* is as firmly typological as any medieval monk's. The story of Abraham and Isaac (Genesis 22:1–14), for instance, is read primarily as a type of the Crucifixion:

> Abraham spoke prophetically, *ver.* 8, and his words were verified; God *did provide himself a lamb.* Abraham's offering up his son was a type of GOD's giving his son, our LORD JESUS CHRIST, as a sacrifice for mankind. Mount Moriah, where Abraham offered up Isaac, was the place on which the house of the Lord at Jerusalem was afterwards built. We should learn from Abraham's example to be ready to submit to GOD's will in the most severe trials, and to trust always in his providence.
>
> (pp. 130–1)

Unless we are looking for it, it is easy to miss that this is actually nothing less than a standard fourfold reading. The literal sense is too clear to need comment; the allegorical concerns Isaac as the 'lamb' of God – the 'type' of Christ, who is the antetype; the identification of Mount Moriah with the site of the later Temple at Jerusalem leads us on anagogically to the idea of the church as founded on the blood of the lamb; while the moral instructs us accordingly how we should behave.

Such an example should make us on our guard against simple-minded 'periodization'. Biblical interpretation was always a pluralistic affair. Different and even incompatible modes of thinking could and often did overlap. What we think of as the nineteenth-century conception of historical criticism has roots as far back as the seventeenth. In 1678 a French Oratorian, Richard Simon, had published his *Histoire Critique du Vieux Testament*. To counter the Protestant principle that scripture alone was necessary for salvation, Simon, by applying the kind of scholarly techniques then being developed on classical writings, set out to show how complex were the origins of biblical texts and that careful guidance (from the church, naturally) was necessary to understand their meaning. He challenged the traditional view that Moses was the author of the Pentateuch (the first five books of the Bible) and suggested that they were more likely to be the composite creation of scribes and 'public writers' (Deconinck-Brossard, 1991). Ironically, such suggestions aroused the immediate wrath of the Catholic hierarchy in France, and the book was banned there, while copies smuggled to England were translated as early as 1682. It was from England that the next developments in biblical criticism were to come.

In fact England gave Simon's *Critical History of the Old Testament* a mixed reception. Edward Stillingfleet, for instance, the Dean of St Paul's and later Bishop of Worcester, attacked it as undermining the authority of scripture. Locke and Dryden, however, were both deeply impressed by it, and its influence was widespread enough in the controversies over Deism in the eighteenth century (Reventlow, 1984) to pave the way for the next major work in the history of biblical criticism: Robert Lowth's *Sacred Poetry of the Hebrews* which was first published (in Latin) in 1753, but not fully translated into English until 1778.

Lowth was elected to the Chair of Poetry at Oxford in May 1741 and found himself with the unenviable prospect of having to begin the traditional series of lectures almost at once with hardly any time to prepare by consulting the traditional academic sources. Being an able theologian and Hebrew scholar, he seems to have turned initially to his theme of biblical poetry more as a solution to his problem of time than because he intended to say anything revolutionary. Nevertheless, for an age still accustomed to typological and figural interpretations, Lowth's avowed aim in the first lecture struck a quite new note.

> He who would perceive the peculiar and interior elegancies of the Hebrew poetry, must imagine himself exactly situated as the persons for whom it was written, or even as the writers themselves; he is to feel them as a Hebrew.... nor is it enough to be acquainted with the language of this people, their manners, discipline, rites and ceremonies; we must even investigate their inmost sentiments, the manner and connexion of their thoughts; in one word, we must see

all things with their eyes, estimate all things by their opinion: we must endeavour as much as possible to read Hebrew as the Hebrews would have done it.

(vol. 1, pp. 113, 114.)

This is not, of course, the same emphasis as Simon's. Whereas the French Catholic was interested primarily in the accuracy of the texts that have come down to us, the Oxford professor was more interested in the context from which those documents arose. Nevertheless, the latter presupposes the former: from a study of the original Hebrew texts of the Old Testament a new (and essentially modern) idea of history is beginning to emerge. Instead of trying to piece together the four (seven or twelve) -fold meanings divinely encoded with the scriptures, Lowth is trying to re-create if not the intentions of the biblical writers, at least their state of mind as human beings in a social framework. The result was two major breakthroughs in critical theory, both of which were to affect the whole development of English poetry.

The first was the identification of the Old Testament concepts of prophecy and poetry. The Hebrew word 'Nabi', explains Lowth, was used to mean 'a Prophet, a Poet, or a Musician, under the influence of divine inspiration'. The prophets of ancient Israel were, he argued, a kind of professional caste, trained both 'to compose verses for the service of the church, and to declare the oracles of God'. Similarly, 'Mashal', one of the words commonly used for a poem in Hebrew, is also the word translated in the New Testament as 'parable'. In other words, the parables of Jesus, far from being an innovation, were an extension by the greatest of the biblical 'poets' of what had always been the basic mode of Hebrew thought as it had been handed down through the prophetic tradition.

From this followed a second, technical, discovery: the secret of the construction of Hebrew verse itself. Whereas all European poetry had depended upon such aural techniques as rhyme, rhythm and alliteration, no such techniques could be discovered in Hebrew verse – even in the Psalms, which were clearly intended to be songs. Even among the eighteenth-century Jews the art of Hebrew poetry had been completely lost. Lowth was now able to demonstrate in his lectures that in fact Hebrew poetry was constructed upon quite different principles from European, and depended primarily upon a feature which he called 'parallelism':

> The Correspondence of one verse, or line, with another, I call *parallelism*. When a proposition is delivered, and a second subjoined to it, or drawn under it, equivalent, or contrasted with it in sense; or similar to it in the form of gramatical construction; these I call parallel lines; and the words or phrases, answering one to another in the corresponding lines, parallel terms.

> (vol. 2, p. 32)

The origins of this form, Lowth argued, like the origins of European poetic forms, lay in the oral tradition – but in this case in the antiphonal chants and choruses we find mentioned in various places in the Old Testament. Lowth cites, for instance, I Samuel 18:7, where David returns victorious from a battle with the Philistines and the women greet him with the chant of 'Saul hath smote his thousands' and were answered by a second chorus with the parallel, 'And David his ten thousands' (vol. 2, p. 53). He distinguishes no less than eight different kinds of parallelism, ranging from simple repetition and echo to variation, comparison and contrast – as in the case given above, where the force of the contrast was not lost on Saul, who promptly tried to have David assassinated.

These discoveries inaugurated a critical revolution (Prickett, 1986, pp. 105–23). The poet now could justifiably be seen not as an illustrator or decorator of received wisdom but as a prophet, a transformer of society and mediator of divine truth. It is the difference between Blake and Wordsworth (both of whom knew and had absorbed Lowth's work) and, say, Pope. Associated with this was a change in the status of the Bible itself. By and large in 1700 the principle literary models were classical; by 1800 they were more likely to be biblical. Even as an increasing number of people were calling the literal truth of many of the biblical stories into question, the Bible had supplanted the classics as a model of both naturalness and sublimity. At the heart of Romanticism is a return to what were seen as biblical aesthetics.

Lowth's work had another, less immediately foreseeable, consequence. Because Hebrew poetry relied on parallelism rather than the traditional techniques of European verse, it was, Lowth noted, best translated into prose:

> A poem translated literally from the Hebrew into the prose of any other language, whilst the same form of the sentences remain, will still retain, even as far as relates to versification, much of its dignity, and a fair appearance of versification.
>
> (vol. 1, pp. 71–2)

As later critics were quick to observe, this meant that, whereas conventional poetry was extremely difficult to translate into another language with any real equivalence of tone and feeling, the Bible was peculiarly, if not uniquely, open to translation. In particular, the majestic prose rhythms of the English Authorized Version were, in fact, *closer* to the original than any attempt at versification would have been. This had the unforeseen effect of blurring traditional distinctions between prose and verse. To speak of a prose piece as 'poetic' could now be more than just a metaphor. The result is apparent not merely again in Blake, who was steeped in the Bible, but also (though Lowth could hardly have suspected such a consequence) in the long-term shift from verse to prose as the main creative literary medium that took place progressively during the nineteenth century with the rise of the novel (Prickett, 1982).

If the principal effect of Lowth's work in England was literary, in Germany it was more on the development of biblical criticism itself – and, in particular, on the higher critics, such as Michaelis, Reimarus, Lessing and Eichhorn. Far from being divinely inspired, for them the Bible had to be read not merely as one might 'any other book', but specifically as the record of the myths and aspirations of an ancient and primitive near-eastern tribe. The accounts of God's appearances and other miracles were to be seen as part of a particularly powerful (and, be it said) eclectic mythology. As the French Revolutionary writer C. F. Volney pointed out in his influential book *The Ruins of Empires* (1792), many of the Genesis stories were discovered to have been borrowed from older Babylonian and near-eastern mythology, and even from ancient Egypt. What meaning there was in such stories was moral and developmental rather than historical – illustrating what Lessing, in the title of one of his best-known books, called *The Education of the Human Race* (1780). If such narratives were to be given a different status from those of, say, ancient Greece or Rome, it was on account of their 'moral beauty' or the profoundly ethical nature of their teachings. Though, as we have seen, such arguments were commonplace in Germany and France by the end of the eighteenth century, their introduction into Britain was delayed both by the political backlash against the French revolution, which was inclined to see such radical criticism of the scriptures as Volney's (which was translated into English during the 1790s) as being little more than a species of revolutionary Jacobinism, and by the lack of any corresponding native school of biblical critics to pave their way.

Coleridge's position was in fact, therefore, somewhat more original – and certainly more important – than his many critics gave him credit for. His insistence on the 'symbolic' value of the biblical narratives as 'the living educts of the imagination' was less a cover for infidelity than an attempt to preserve the traditional many-layered approach to the Bible and base it on something less shaky than the literal meaning ascribed to particular doubtful and trans-lated texts. In this respect, his claim to read it as he might 'any other book' takes on a new significance. He is, in effect, applying a hermeneutic method that is as appropriate to the novel as it is to a sacred text. Indeed, it is not accidental that even as typology as a mode of biblical interpretation was under threat from more critical and historical hermeneutics, it was to undergo a revival in the form of symbolism in the new art-form of the novel. To put it another way: the rise in status of the novel and of prose fiction generally as an art-form is closely bound up with the contemporaneous shift in the status of biblical narrative. With both, it was increasingly recognized that myth, symbolic narrative, and even transparent fiction (such as, for instance, the Book of Jonah) could convey truths more important than the most scrupulously factual history.

Yet Coleridge's *Confessions* were less the beginning of a new critical era than the end of an old. For various entirely contingent reasons (more to do with

German academic administration than hermeneutics) the study of the Bible and of secular literature became separated from one another early in the nineteenth century. At the very period when literary critics were becoming increasingly sensitive to the symbolic and polysemous nature of narrative, biblical critics were dominated by the most rigid and materialistic notions of 'history' – and fiction (Prickett, 1986, pp. 1–36).

Thus for much of the 150 years since Coleridge's time biblical hermeneutics have been polarized across a spectrum between two extremes: on the one hand, the 'fundamentalist' position that the Bible is a literal and unerring historical record of events (a position that is, of course, in its univocal form a relatively recent one dating from the scientific revolution of the seventeenth century), and on the other the view that it is to be understood not as history but as something more akin to our idea of 'fiction'. In this Northrop Frye's position in *The Great Code* (1982) differs remarkably little from Matthew Arnold's in *Literature and Dogma* of 1873. Possibly the most readable exposition of the Victorian crisis of faith caused by the new developments in historical criticism is by Matthew Arnold's niece, Mrs Humphry Ward, in her best-selling novel *Robert Elsmere* (1888). Such writers have constituted a distinguished tradition, but the use of fictional analogies in the hands of some of the early twentieth-century biblical critics prompted a justifiably sharp counter-attack from C. S. Lewis:

> I read that the fourth Gospel is regarded by one school as a 'spiritual romance', 'a poem not a history', to be judged by the same canons as Nathan's parable, the book of Jonah, *Paradise Lost*, 'or, more exactly, *Pilgrim's Progress*'. After a man has said that, why need we attend to anything else he says about any book in the world? Note that he regards *Pilgrim's Progress*, a story which professes to be a dream and flaunts its allegorical nature by every single proper name it uses, as the closest parallel. Note that the whole epic panoply of Milton goes for nothing. But even if we leave out the grosser absurdities and keep to *Jonah*, the insensitiveness is crass – *Jonah*, a tale with as few even pretended historical attachments as *Job*, grotesque in incident and surely not without a distinct... vein of typically Jewish humour. Then turn to *John*. Read the dialogues: that with the Samaritan woman at the well, or that which follows the healing of the man born blind. Look at its pictures: Jesus... doodling with his fingers in the dust.... I have been reading poems, romances, vision-literature, legends, myths all my life. I know that not one of them is like this. Of this text there are only two possible views. Either this is reportage – though it may no doubt contain errors – pretty close up to the facts; nearly as close as Boswell. Or else, some unknown writer in the second century, without known predecessors or successors, suddenly anticipated the technique of modern, novelistic, realistic narrative. If it is untrue, it must be narrative of that kind. The reader who doesn't see this has simply not learned to read. I would recommend him to read Auerbach.
>
> (1975, pp. 107–8)

The problem remains, however, that though this may be true of the New Testament, many Old Testament narratives do *not* comply with such notions of 'realism'. Modern biblical criticism has yet to come to terms with the fact that it still has no adequate models to describe its material – which stubbornly refuses to correspond to modern categories either of 'fiction' or of 'history'.

Indeed, part of the problem is that those categories are themselves being problematized. Just as the Elizabethan notion of 'history' was not that of the nineteenth, so the very hard-nosed and 'objective' nineteenth-century idea of history is not that of the twentieth. 'The past', J. H. Plumb commented drily in *The Death of the Past* (1969), 'has always been the handmaid of authority' (p. 40). It is, as we have seen throughout this account, the construct of the culturally dominant ideology. That is not to say that history is anything one can be brainwashed into believing it is – it is clearly always open to falsification – but rather that a particular dominant *interpretation* of history will lead historians to select facts of one kind rather than another. The degree to which the modern English-speaking world is openly pluralistic or unconsciously dominated by particular paradigms is a matter of debate, but either way the nineteenth-century antithesis between 'fact' on the one hand and 'fiction' on the other looks increasingly unsustainable. Most would now accept, for instance, that 'history', 'myth' and 'fiction' are *all* alike human constructs by which we attempt to make sense of the past. Yet to describe the Bible in terms of any one of these alone is highly dangerous. It belongs rather to a period when the modern categories had not yet been differentiated, and in attempting to apply such models we should always be conscious of what we have *lost* in the original by so doing.

The current collapse of confidence in the traditional tools suggests that biblical hermeneutics, far from having lost their way, may be entering a new phase. The work of John Dominic Crossan (1980) in the US explores ways in which current critical theories might have a bearing on biblical studies, while in Australia, Kevin Hart, a philosopher turned literary critic, by arguing that Derrida is best understood as a negative theologian, may have opened the way for a return to older polyvalent readings (1987). Whatever the new approaches to emerge, however, Coleridge's principles are unlikely to be superseded. In an unpublished note dating from the late 1820s he jotted down the qualifications necessary for a biblical critic:

> Great and wide Erudition, with curious research; a philosophic imagination quick to seize hold of analogies; an emancipation from prejudice, and a servile subjection to the prejudices of great names; a faith that shutteth out fear; a freedom from the superstition which assumed an absolute *sui generis* in every word of the O. and N. Testaments, and is for ever craving after the supernatural; a sound and profound Psychology – these are the principle requisites.
>
> (in Prickett, 1976, p. 45)

FURTHER READING

Arnold, Matthew (1873) *Literature and Dogma*, Macmillan, London

Frei, Hans W. (1974) *The Eclipse of Biblical Narrative: A Study in Eighteenth and Nineteenth Century Hermeneutics*, Yale University Press, New Haven

Funk, Robert W. (1966) *Language, Hermeneutics, and the Word of God: The Problem of Language in the New Testament and Contemporary Theology*, Harper & Row, New York

Gunn, Giles (1979) *The Interpretation of Otherness*, Oxford University Press, New York

Hart, Kevin (1989) *The Trespass of the Sign: Deconstruction, Philosophy, Theology*, Cambridge University Press, Cambridge

Josipovici, Gabriel (1988) *The Book of God: A Response to the Bible*, Yale University Press, New Haven

Kugel, James L. (1981) *The Idea of Biblical Poetry: Parallelism and its History*, Yale University Press, New Haven

Mueller-Vollmer, Kurt (1986) *The Hermeneutics Reader*, Basil Blackwell, Oxford

Prickett, Stephen (ed.) (1991) *Reading the Text: Biblical Criticism and Literary Theory*, Basil Blackwell, Oxford

Rad, Gerhard von (1966) *Essays on Old Testament Hermeneutics*, edited by Claus Westermann, translated by James Luther Mays, John Knox Press, Richmond

Reeves, Marjorie and Gould, Warwick (1987) *Joachim of Fiore and the Myth of the Eternal Evangel in the Nineteenth Century*, Clarendon Press, Oxford

Ricoeur, Paul (1980) *Essays on Biblical Interpretation*, translated by David Pellauer, edited by Lewis S. Mudge, Fortress Press, Philadelphia

Smalley, B. (1952) *The Study of the Bible in the Middle Ages*, Basil Blackwell, Oxford

Stroup, Georg W. (1984) *The Promise of Narrative Theology*, SCM Press, London

ADDITIONAL WORKS CITED

Auerbach, Erich (1959) 'Figura'. In Erich Auerbach, *Scenes from the Drama of European Literature*, translated by R. Mannheim, Meridian Books, New York, pp. 11–76

Coleridge, Samuel Taylor (1849) *Confessions of an Inquiring Spirit*, 2nd edn, Pickering, London [first published 1840]

——(1972) 'The Statesman's Manual'. In S. T. Coleridge, *Lay Sermons*, edited by R. J. White, Routledge, London [essay first published 1817]

Crossan, John Dominic (1980) *Cliffs of Fall: Paradox and Polyvalence in the Parables of Jesus*, Seabury Press, New York

Deconinck-Brossard, Françoise (1991) 'England and France in the Eighteenth Century'. In Stephen Prickett (ed.), *Reading the Text: Biblical Criticism and Literary Theory*, Basil Blackwell, Oxford

Frye, Northrop (1982) *The Great Code: The Bible and Literature*, Routledge, London

Hart, Kevin (1987) 'Deconstruction Otherwise'. In Eric Osborn and Lawrence McIntosh (eds), *The Bible and European Literature: History and Hermeneutics*, Academia Press, Melbourne

Lewis, C. S. (1975) *Fern-Seed and Elephants, and other Essays on Christianity*, edited by Walter Hooper, Collins, London

Lowth, Robert (1778) *Lectures on the Sacred Poetry of the Hebrews*, translated by G. Gregory, London

Minnis, A. J. (1984) *Mediaeval Theory of Authorship*, Scolar Press, London

Plumb, J. H. (1969) *The Death of the Past*, Macmillan, London

Prickett, Stephen (1976) *Romanticism and Religion: The Tradition of Coleridge and Wordsworth in the Victorian Church*, Cambridge University Press, Cambridge

——(1982) 'Peacock's "Four Ages" Recycled', *British Journal of Aesthetics*, 22, 158–66

——(1986) *Words and the Word: Language, Poetics, and Biblical Interpretation*, Cambridge University Press, Cambridge

Reeves, Marjorie (1991) 'The Bible and Literary Authorship in the Middle Ages'. In Stephen Prickett (ed.) *Reading the Text: Biblical Criticism and Literary Theory*, Basil Blackwell, Oxford

Reventlow, Henning Graf (1984) *The Authority of the Bible and the Rise of the Modern World*, translated by John Bowden, SCM Press, London

49

NEO-CLASSICAL
CRITICISM

MICHAEL MEEHAN

The world is well served with surveys and overviews of British neo-classical criticism and neo-classical theory. Through the 1950s and 1960s, scholars of the stamp of R. S. Crane, René Wellek, Walter Jackson Bate and M. H. Abrams responded in kind to the systematizing tendency of the neo-classical critics themselves, with extensive analyses and classifications of the diverse and burgeoning range of aesthetic speculation and aesthetic pronouncement that the period produced – a period still commonly though now somewhat controversially framed by the major writings of Dryden and Johnson, and thus set off from the 'spotty and erratic' critical output that preceded (Greene, 1970, p. 166) and the romantic critiques that followed. These histories and classifications, now embedded in a vast fabric of supplementary scholarship, remain of fundamental importance today, the irreplaceable starting points for any review of the principles and procedures of neo-classical criticism.

Subsequent discussions of British neo-classicism have, as the legacy of such writings, less need to begin on the defensive. The old charges that were laid at the door of neo-classical criticism, of legalism, apriorism, rigidity, and wholesale neglect of the place of feeling, have, in the main, been satisfactorily answered in a closer view of the dominant subjects, critical procedures and critical decrees of the period. The age was rich in clever caricature of its own worst criticism, in Dr Johnson's 'acknowledged critic' Dick Minim, for example, with his background in brewing and a 'common course of puerile studies' (ed. Wain, 1973, pp. 127–8), and in Addison's 'judicious and formidable critic' in his *Spectator* 291, with his 'few general rules extracted out of the French authors, with a certain cant of words' (ed. Bond, 1970, p. 81). It is ironic that, in the most misleading of the nineteenth-century characterizations, the basic categories of the eighteenth-century caricature recur in soberly descriptive forms, and it has demanded a long and arduous scholarly procedure to separate the strands of what was approved and what was condemned, what was presented as true criticism, and what was merely being proposed as the negative foil in a more open-ended critical enterprise.

Two phases may be distinguished in this resuscitation of neo-classical criticism. In the first, it was R. S. Crane who most authoritatively drew attention to the fact that so many of what appeared to be doctrines in neo-classicism were in fact merely units in a critical vocabulary, defining central areas for contention rather than prescribing specific and rigid values (Crane, 1952, p. 376). The apparent formality of neo-classical criticism – its invocation of the Rules, of the Authority of the Ancients, of the Unities – could thence be seen more as evidence of communal agreement on the subject of what critical issues ought to be addressed, rather than as a wholesale submission to authority on what ought to have been written. And as Crane indicated, not only did that vocabulary, that 'common conceptual scheme', permit a wide diversity in actual critical judgement, but it also accommodated a considerable process of change, with 'even the more seemingly revolutionary changes in the latter part of the period' (p. 374) emerging more as shifts of emphasis within that scheme rather than as a wholesale overturning of neo-classical authority.

What Crane's essay offered, in effect, was an impressively steady view of what he revealed to be a highly unsteady subject. Anything corresponding to a fully orthodox neo-classicism, in the sense of providing an appropriate negative to the then much proclaimed positives of Romanticism, became increasingly difficult to locate in Britain. It is not that paeans to the example of the ancients, and affirmations of the importance of the rules did not exist, as one important aspect of current critical practice; for if poetry, John Dennis wrote in his *Grounds of Criticism in Poetry* (1704), is truly an art and not mere whimsy and fanaticism, then it must be susceptible to description in terms of means and ends, and thus to analysis in terms of rules (Elledge, 1961, vol. 1, p. 101). It is more that a clearly formulated British neo-classical orthodoxy (one, at least, that is adequate to the caricature) is rarely found in a form that is not carefully couched in critical provisos and special allowances. The quest for an orthodox neo-classicism in Britain thus has a tendency to slip back, through Dr Johnson's appeal 'from criticism to nature', through the critical indemnities scattered through Pope's *Essay on Criticism* (1711) and his decree, in his preface to the *Works of Shakespeare* (1725), that a poet should only be tried by the laws of his own country, through the conspicuously independent and adaptable critical views of John Dryden, through both Dryden and Rymer's often manifestly liberal continental sources – with Rapin's influential *Reflexions sur la Poétique d'Aristote* (1674) as one such example – towards some mythological offshore location, from which it could haunt, inspire and inform British criticism, but never quite fully impose itself. The real force of neo-classicism in Britain was most substantially registered in contention and debate, in a critical discourse which was often, from its impressive outset in Dryden, intensely preoccupied with the hard case and the status of the wayward example, with an interleaving of local instance and critical principle rather than merely with 'magisterial prescription', and even, at times, with a broad questioning of the relevance of neo-classical principles in general to modern British society.

Much of that force and that questioning has been recovered in these earlier studies. It is unfortunate, however, that the same process of expounding the critical vitality and flexibility of neo-classical criticism against its Victorian detractors brought certain new distortions in its train. English Studies, recreating the eighteenth century's excellence and indispensability in its own image, found a substantial encouragement and reassurance in the enthusiasm and vigour with which the neo-classical critics and theorists pursued activities apparently akin to its own. Literary historians noted with satisfaction the burgeoning interest in criticism and theory, the multiplication of literary 'Prefaces' and 'Essays', 'Observations' and 'Reflections', and the first demarcations of the proper realm of literary history itself. The neo-classical period was promoted not simply as marking, with Dr Johnson's authority to support the point, the very paternity and birth of English descriptive criticisms, but also as vindicating what appeared to be a specifically and exclusively literary scholarly focus: criticism, conceived in a rather narrower sense than the eighteenth century itself would permit, was seen to have emerged through these decades, as 'an important branch of learning' (Crane, 1952, p. 372), as clad in something resembling its subsequent academic disciplinary garb. Close readings of the texture of argument in neo-classical criticism began to reveal strong native countercurrents, a considerable critical diversity and a widespread questioning of the authority of the ancients. The literary historians, superimposing one critical text neatly upon another, began to reveal impressive patterns of change and development which further questioned the conventional periodizations and characterizations. And there were, in all of this, many implied compliments paid to neo-classical criticism.

Such compliments were paid, however, at a certain cost. What was really needed was not simply this closer view of the subject. What was also needed was an extended sense of what that subject, neo-classical criticism, actually was. The procedures of the literary scholar, founded on the stated or implied assumption that the frame of reference of the criticism was 'not the republic but the republic of letters' (Crane, 1952, p. 375), tended to undervalue the social and intellectual contexts of that criticism, and perhaps more importantly, the presence within that criticism of other contemporary languages, the intersections of the language of criticism with a whole range of alternative contemporary discourses. The existence of such intersections, the complex and multilevelled nature of the period's critical language, and the significant dialogue, conducted through this language, with supporting and competing forms of discourse – many of these aspects of neo-classical criticism have been over-looked or, perhaps more commonly, neutralized by the literary scholar's curious propensity to read as mere metaphor what may in fact be allusion, and to note as mere allusion what may in fact be the invocation, within the critical dis-course, of alternative modes of critical thinking, and alternative rhetorical models. In such an atmosphere, in places where critical reference beyond the boundaries of the republic of letters has finally been too assertive to be ignored, it has characteristically been read down, dwindled into metaphor and allusion, and redirected inwardly towards the primarily literary concerns of the critical enterprise.

That enterprise was, however, somewhat richer and more varied than such readings have allowed, and more recent scholarship – that second phase – has begun to explore more fully both the place of that criticism within its local context, and the place of that context within the criticism. The reconsideration of the first of these aspects, the criticism in its social context, is now well-developed, under the inspiration of the broad interdisciplinary reference in much modern research in political thought, in the writings of J. G. A. Pocock (1972, 1975), A. O. Hirschman (1977) and others, and among literary scholars, writers like John Barrell (1983, 1986) have affirmed the importance of political polemic and political theory in the shaping of eighteenth-century language theory and aesthetics. The extensive questioning, too, of the appropriateness of the conventional Augustan appellation, in the work of such scholars as H. D. Weinbrot (1978) and Howard Erskine-Hill (1983) has indicated the extent to which the activities of literary criticism and literary judgement in late seventeenth- and eighteenth-century Britain were inseparable from a far broader hermeneutic process involving exploration into complex interweavings of aesthetic tradition and political affiliation. Critical judgement was, in numer-ous instances, premissed more firmly upon local political and social sensitivities than upon the mere dictates of literary authority, and the scholarly pursuit of those wider premisses has vastly widened the field of neo-classical criticism, to include not only a wide range of translators' prefaces, ancient and modern histories, literary and political biographies, but also many works of a less conspicuously literary character, in collections of sermons, in moral and politi-cal essays, in legal writings, in treatises on ethics and on music, and in works of political polemic and political theory. In works such as these, in the political writings of Bolingbroke, the essays of David Hume, the sermons of David Fordyce, in Lord Kames's *Sketches on the History of Man* (1774) and Adam Ferguson's *Essay on the History of Civil Society* (1767), the barriers between what is and what is not literary criticism were often intentionally overridden, or even, as in Ferguson's case, expressly dismantled. Re-examination of such writings has provided many hints and indicators as to the ways in which even those more independently conceived 'Reflections' and 'Opinions' lay deeply embedded within a wider social discourse.

Consideration of the internal aspect – what I have called the place of that context *within the criticism* – has been less effectively explored, despite the rich methodological possibilities that modern theory affords for such analysis, and the peculiar linguistic density and diversity of neo-classical critical discourse. An analytical method and considerable inspiration for an undertaking of this kind can be found in the writings of Mikhail Bakhtin, many of whose proposals for the investigation of novelistic prose are of equal applicability to critical discourse, and are of particular interest, I suggest, for an analysis of neo-classical prose. This essay is not the place for an extensive exposition of Bakhtin's views – his analysis of the 'centripetal' forces in the life of a language, his elucidation of the dialogical interaction between particular discourses within novelistic texts, and the pressure of subverting utterance against the 'norm-ative-centralizing system of a unitary language' (Bakhtin, 1981, p. 272). What the broad ambit of Bakhtinian analysis does suggest, however, is the possibility for an illuminating re-reading of certain aspects of neo-classical criticism, one which elucidates the dialogical interaction within that criticism between an inherited, sometimes alien but powerfully authoritative critical discourse, and equally authoritative indigenous rhetorical forms. The native component in neo-classical criticism, such an analysis soon reveals, was not a mere question of critical subject – as in the various defences of Shakespeare, Spenser and Milton – and nor was it merely the assertion of purportedly native aesthetic values, in Dennis's passion, Addison's imagination, and the mid-century's lost, lamented 'world of fine fabling'. The indigenous impulse is most strongly felt, in British neo-classicism, within the very texture of the critical rhetoric, in the *procedural* models that underlie the critical argument, and in the impetus given to the appreciation of those native subjects, and the assertion of those values, by powerful countervailing languages intermingled with the inherited and imported language of criticism.

In 1708, Thomas Wood, in his *Some Thoughts Concerning the Study of Laws of England, Particularly in the Two Universities*, proposed the teaching of English common law within the universities not only for its 'Plainness of Expression without Affection', its 'Perspicuity of Method' and 'solid Reasoning without scholastick Niceties' (Wood, [1708] 1727, p. 16), but also for the practical reason that it 'is infinitely of more use among us, even than the Civil and Canon Laws; for it is twisted and interwoven into all manner of Discourse and Business, comprehending almost all that is valuable with us in those Laws' (p. 14). In few other fields of contemporary discourse was that twisting and interweaving more evident than in the critical prose. From the very outset, criticism forged deep links with British legal experience, with Dryden, Rymer (a lawyer by profession), Addison, Pope, Johnson and a host of lesser critical lights seeding their critical pronouncements with reference to 'pleading' and 'edict', 'prerogative' and 'prescription'. This fact, which did not go unnoticed by the earliest neo-classical dissidents, soon began to fuel those charges of neo-classical 'legalism' which continue to colour popular views of the period's criticism. Less attention was given to the point affirmed in the second arm of Wood's provocative comment – that such 'Discourse and Business' comprehends 'almost all that is valuable with us in those Laws'. And where later acknowledgements of that interweaving have erred is in their tendency to regard the legal reference as a reinforcing aspect of the dominant discourse – the legalistic, pseudo-Aristotelian, French neo-classical tradition – rather than as what it most characteristically represents in fact – a subverting rhetoric, invoked to overturn conventionally accepted authority, to suspend quick and 'mechanical' judgement on the issue until the case be properly heard and, most importantly, to import into the critical process the procedures, checks, indemnities and general equities which guided, in an increasingly prestigious native context, the processes of judgement and discrimination in the wider social world.

The adoption of adversarial models in argument and a rhetoric imbued with the tones of legal pleading was endemic to the very nature of the neo-classical critical enterprise. The better critics of the age, taking inspiration from Dryden, characteristically regarded themselves as engaged in an advocative rather than a legislative or even judicial procedure. The business of criticism was never, amid its worthier exponents, the mere application of authoritative principle to the literary text, as the early caricatures of neo-classicism would suggest, and nor was it a Procrustean procedure in which the imposition of those 'few general rules extracted out of the French authors' would suffice. Critical analysis more frequently meant the pleading of the hard case, with the critic often arguing for the native instance, not only against the inherited principle, but also against the very implications embedded within the language of approved literary discourse. The legal reference, as employed by Dryden, by Rymer, by Pope and Johnson, was characteristically a subverting strategy that, Portia-like, ran the legalism of inherited neo-classical authority against itself. Inviting and persuasive analogies between state law and literary rules were repeatedly mounted, simply to turn that analogy into a field of subverting contention, as that state law and its attendant legal procedures quickly revealed mechanisms for attaining critical justice which run directly counter to the bland implementation of conventional literary edicts. The prose texture of neo-classical criticism was thus often fractured and internally contentious in ways that were superficially disguised by the sheer aptness of the legal allusion; allusion that was disguised, in the writing, by an artful interweaving of apparently akin but in fact conflicting critical and legal linguistic registers, and in the reading, by that metaphoric dwindling noted above, by the refusal to invest such intrusions on critical rhetoric with their true subverting force.

The roots of antagonism between the legal and the literary are planted deep in our culture. Interchanges between lawyers and creative writers have rarely been amicable. Dryden himself noted, in his preface to *Troilus and Cressida* (1679), that many of his contemporaries would be 'shocked at the name of rules, as if they were a kind of magisterial prescription upon poets' (ed. Ker, 1961, vol. 1, p. 228), and waves from that initial shock have resonated through many subsequent characterizations of neo-classicism as the realm of poets 'closely wed/To musty laws lined out with wretched rule/And compass vile' (Keats, *Sleep and Poetry*, ll. 193–5). Despite the severe reservations of so many neo-classical writers about the possibilities of creation from any kind of rule-bound poetic 'Receit', the neat aesthetic polarities that appear on the legalistic surface of neo-classical criticism – freedom against the rules, spontaneity and originality against the 'fetters' of imitation – provided too ready a source of anti-classical ammunition for later polemicists to ignore. Early misreadings of neo-classical culture of the kind so heartily propagated by writers like Edward Young, in his *Conjectures on Original Composition* (1759), already played extensively upon such highly spurious but patriotically emotive oppositions. Later commentators, too, writing far beyond the heat of critical battle, continued to appropriate terms that were heated and polemical in origin as though they were merely historically descriptive, cheerfully reconstructing the period along the 'Whiggish' lines suggested by Young, and thence taken up by Coleridge, Wordsworth, Keats and others; forgetting, perhaps, that the very ideal of civil freedom, invoked to such effect in the critical rhetoric of the time against the neo-classical legalism, was itself the product of law.

What was it, then, that was 'valuable' in those laws? Despite that literary dread of 'magisterial prescription', it is clear that not all legal reference attracted such negative associations, and the English common law in particular increasingly presented itself to critics and aestheticians as a distinctively English way of thinking and judging, a form of discourse and a critical method that was indigenous, and extensively sanctioned by the national history. Increasingly legitimated by the new spirit of nationalism in late seventeenth- and early eighteenth-century England, the common law had effectively usurped, through the period we think of as neo-classical, the role of the civilian courts. This ascendancy was extensively reinforced in the legal polemic of the era, which pointed to the association of the civil law with 'foreign' legal forms, and with continental and even local tyranny (Cairns, 1984, p. 328). As such, the common law became a central element in popular conceptions of national excellence and national identity, and a frequent and persuasive point of reference in attempts to promote 'English' values in the areas of art, ethics and language (Barrell, 1983, p. 111). It was, as Sir William Blackstone proclaimed in his

Commentaries on the Laws of England (1765–9), a 'venerable edifice', which, having shuffled off all foreign influences and all such badges of servitude as that 'barbarous dialect', law French, remained to embody and express the very 'spirit' of the British people. The common law increasingly provided a prestigious image of law as an indigenous and adaptive force, rooted in custom and the voluntary consent of the people, and hailed in both the legal theory and social panegyric of the era as a major factor in 'England's historical blessedness' (Harding, 1966, p. 287).

Wood's 'twisting and interweaving' in the field of criticism appeared in many guises. To a high degree, the adoption of a legal vocabulary occurs almost with an air of inevitability, given the very nature of the neo-classical critical undertaking. The recurrent reference to poetic 'rules' or 'laws' repeatedly invited, for example, the construction of analogies between the rules of art and social rules; though the subtlety with which that analogy was actually manipulated in English criticism has been much misrepresented. It is true that the analogy could be constructed in ways that simply allied civil lawfulness and poetic submissiveness – that the French as a nation 'born to obey', in Pope's *Essay on Criticism*, would naturally find it easier to be poetically correct, on the one hand, and that 'unconquer'd and uncivilized' political behaviour and poetic intractability must go hand in hand, on the other. But even Pope's construction of the analogy in what appears, in patriotic terms, to be an uncomplimentary form, is seeded with subtleties and ironies to trap the unwary, and the reference to 'brave Britons', still defying the Romans as of old, may be as indulgent as it is reproving, with his touching upon the patriotic nerve designed to temper rather than simply reinforce his neo-classical programme.

Literary judgement, in its more judicial modes, as in Rymer's *Tragedies of the Last Age* (1677), frequently gained force through appropriating the stentorian tones of the law – all soaring of fancy above reason is thus 'all *null* and void in law' (ed. Zimansky, 1956, p. 20) – and in general, the sheer aptness of the legal phrasing, in the language of 'rule', 'precedent' and 'authority', in 'title', 'charter' and 'inheritance', means that its intrusion in critical discourse was often virtually invisible, or conspicuous only as apparent textual decoration, as mere metaphoric emphasis. The nature of such decoration is, however, in the context of traditional analysis, likely to be misunderstood. The legal reference in neo-classical criticism is not simply in the nature of venerable images, hung from the literal 'walls' of the critical text, overseeing and informing the procedures of literary judgement. Such references are more appropriately seen as open passages, allowing information and influence to pass from alternative worlds into the critical process, as well as allowing that critical activity to reach out, to embrace and inform a far wider intellectual world.

Metaphor, I. A. Richards once provocatively suggested, is a juggernaut, lugging information backwards and forwards across the perimeters of the literary text. The neo-classical critic, in summoning up aspects of the law – in invoking, as in Dryden's preface to *Fables Ancient and Modern* (1700) or Johnson's *Preface to Shakespeare* (1765), the context of a courtroom and an adversarial procedure, in their quest for 'critical justice' – was effectively repositioning the critical act, firmly taking it beyond the literary coterie and interlinking it with wider social activities of social advocacy and interpretation. Literary criticism was, by this process, repeatedly and emphatically contextualized, not just in relation to other literature – for which the standard language of rhetoric and literary judgement might have been adequate – but also in relation to wider, popular, 'English' conceptions of value and of justice. Rymer, in his disparagement of the tragedies of the last age, could thus invoke the 'just' horrors of Tyburn against the unjust horrors of Elizabethan tragedy, in his defence of poetic justice (ed. Zimansky, 1956, p. 27), and the same mode of corrective allusion appears elsewhere in more liberal critical contexts, as in the defence, by Dryden and others, of the same writer's rights, under English law, to have his case heard in an appropriate poetic jurisdiction. Legal metaphor and legal reference in British criticism, from Dryden to Johnson, is thus in many instances the means towards a careful monitoring of the values and prejudices of the 'republic', or 'commonwealth' of letters, by reference to the outward republic itself. It is, above all, an attempt to ensure an appropriate accord between the inner textual world of critical judgement, and the procedures approved and applauded in the outer world of social organization.

Much legal reference is purely pragmatic in nature, simply expounding possible points of mutual support between literature and the law, as in Dennis's conviction, for example, that the 'versifying spirit' would flourish more vigorously under legal repression, if 'we had a sort of inquisition or formal court of judicature, with grave officers and judges, erected to restrain poetical license' (Elledge, 1961, vol. 1, p. 170), or in the Earl of Shaftesbury's counter-conviction, asserted in a more serious vein throughout the *Characteristicks of Men, Manners, Opinions, Times* (1711), that the same vigour would only develop in a situation of legal freedom. Speculation on the legal preconditons for effective satire also formed an important part of contemporary theory, with both Dryden and Addison incorporating a considerable knowledge of both Roman and English law into their consideration of the history and nature of the satiric art (Nathan, 1985, p. 375). The attendant theme, of literary activity as a means of supplementing legal action, as touching, in Pope's words, those 'safe from the bar, the pulpit, and the throne' (Pope, *Epilogue to the Satires*, II, p. 210), is a standard and well-documented theme in the defence of satire throughout the period.

Legal discourse was also 'interwoven' with criticism through extensive parody, of a kind which sometimes touched wryly upon the prescriptive tendencies in neo-classical criticism. Addison's essay on modern poetry, in his

Spectator 523, is of this kind, concluding with the announcement of an elaborate edict against the invocation of classical deities in verse, an edict pronounced by virtue of 'that Spectatorial Authority with which I stand invested', complete with preamble and a proviso in favour of permitting the 'several female poets of this nation' to continue in the conventional vein (ed. Bond, 1970, pp. 56–7).

Elsewhere, the adaptation of legal terms is more pointed, running beyond parody towards the awakening of genuine English legal emotions, activating the reader's sense of justice, and of a writer's proper due. In the writing of Dryden, the most legally adept of British critics, the language of legal succession thus figures strongly in his assertion of kinship with the dramatists of the preceding age, with reference to 'birthright', 'charter' and 'inheritance' brought in to counter the proscriptions of 'modern' criticism. In his 1693 essay prefixed to the *Examen Poeticum*, in protest at the modern critic's (Rymer's) attempts to interpose his imported critical dogma between the Elizabethans and the modern dramatists, he thus described the moderns as the Elizabethans' 'lawful issue' (ed. Ker, 1961, vol. 2, pp. 4–5), couching his critical assertions in terms that, like those employed generations later by Burke in the political context, neatly interleaved the familial and the legal in a powerful affirmation of continuity and spiritual affiliation.

In many writings, mere mimicry, appropriation or parody expanded into a more sustained adoption of legal forms, with an elaborate casting of critical discourse into the forms of legal pleading. This mode, encouraged by the ease of analogical movement between a critical hearing according to poetic rules, and a criminal hearing according to those of the state, was recurrently and influentially adopted by Dryden (most extensively in his preface to *Fables Ancient and Modern*, of 1700) in a way that was to be echoed in many later critics and most resonantly by Dr Johnson. In his *Preface to Shakespeare*, Johnson thus prefaced the resignation of his subject to 'critical justice' with an 'admission' that he had violated 'those laws which have been instituted and established by the joint authority of poets and critics'. He then followed this with the formal plea that, before judgement be passed, his virtues should be 'rated with his failings' (ed. Wain, 1973, pp. 159–60).

Pleas of this kind for the suspension of conventional poetic laws were common. Sometimes, these took the form of an appeal to the royal prerogative. Virgil, as poet-monarch, was invested, in Dryden and in Joseph Trapp's critical analysis, with special powers beyond the law. He might, Dryden wrote in his dedication prefixed to the *Aeneis* (1697), transgress in details – in relation to 'cob-web laws' such as those concerned with chronology, for example – 'by superseding the mechanic rules of poetry, for the same reason that a monarch may dispense with or suspend his own laws, when he finds it necessary to do so, especially if those laws are not altogether fundamental' (ed. Ker, 1961, vol. 2, p. 194). In Trapp's *Lectures on Poetry* (1711–19), published in English in

1742, that same 'Prince of Poets' was invested with a 'Discretionary Power' for suspending the laws; a prerogative which, Trapp is careful to add, should not be too far invaded upon by lesser exponents (1742, p. 69).

Royalist aesthetics of this kind, however, do not typify the criticism; more characteristically, the legal reference accorded more closely with Whig (increasingly seen as bipartisanly 'English') political sentiments, emphasizing less the prerogatives of the crown than the rights of the subject under the law. In the neo-classical defence of local writers, of Chaucer, Shakespeare, Spenser and Milton, it was the principle of appropriate jurisdiction that emerged as the principal resource for ensuring critical equity of this kind. Dryden thus defined, in his *Author's Apology for Heroic Poetry and Poetic Licence* (1677), the proper qualifications of the critic, and the critical tribunal itself, by such a principle. The critic must 'be a lawyer before he mounts the tribunal; and the judicature of one court, too, does not qualify a man to plead in another. He may be an excellent pleader in the Chancery, who is not fit to rule in the Common Pleas'; only those, in short, with a thorough knowledge of the subject should pretend to censure the 'flights' of heroic verse (ed. Ker, 1961, vol. 1, pp. 182–3). In his Preface for *All for Love* (1678) the same critic wrote that 'for my part, I desire to be tried by the laws of my own country; for it seems unjust to me that the French should prescribe here, till they have conquered' (vol. 1, p. 195), and in his dedication to the *Aeneis*, and his Preface to *Fables Ancient and Modern* (1700), the same principle, the assertion of the writer's right to an appropriate critical jurisdiction, is again invoked in a move to temper an alien and hostile critical principle (vol. 2, p. 248). Thereafter, this strategy seems to have become something of a commonplace in the criticism, although, it should be noted, it appears as such in the writings of some uncommon critics. The same critical strategy is thus echoed in Pope's well-known dictum, from his Preface to the *Works of Shakespeare*, that 'to judge therefore of Shakespeare by Aristotle's rules, is like trying a man by the laws of one country, who acted under those of another' (Goldgar, 1965, p. 164). It is echoed, too, in Johnson's critical interminglings of literary genre and legal jurisdiction in his *Preface to Shakespeare*, where both comedy and tragedy in their conventional forms are discarded as inappropriate and inequitable jurisdictions for the hearing of his subject's case.

In all, neo-classical criticism appears to have provided, through this diverse range of 'twisting and interweaving', an instance, rare in English literary history, of the literary and legal culture functioning in complementary rather than oppositional terms. Opposition and antagonism there was, of course, but in this instance that antagonism was artfully directed by the critics against the burden of an alien literary dogma, and in support of indigenous modes; in support, in short, of English ways of doing things. Clifford Geertz notes in his stimulating interdisciplinary analysis of law, *Local Knowledge* (1983), an old

African proverb which states that 'wisdom comes out of the antheap'. Law, for Geertz, is the 'artisan task' of seeing broad principles within that antheap, within the realm of parochial facts (p. 167). Despite the later charges that the age was foreign in inspiration, French rather than truly classical in character (Chandler, 1984, p. 491), one strand that has always commanded attention in neo-classical criticism is the constant critical reference back to the antheap of fact, to the parochial facts of local artistic achievement, with that achievement not so much being measured by the law, as providing, in the better critics, a measure to the law. In pursuit of the legal reference within that criticism, our attention is also drawn to the antheap of critical *method*, in the strength and flexibility offered to British critical discourse of the period by its supporting legal culture, a culture continually invoked in the criticism of the period by allusion, choice of dramatic context, analogy, parody and deeper procedural empathies.

The resources for a fuller analysis of the place of legal culture within British neo-classicism are now richer than ever before. Cross-cultural analysis of the kind offered by Geertz has greatly extended our sense of the pervasiveness of 'legislative' and judicial activities within society, and modern hermeneutic theory offers a clearer and enriched understanding of the nature of law itself; that it is, at its best, far less the intersection of the static and the mobile, the clash of fixed rule and wayward instance, than a pragmatic interleaving of inherited principle and present activity. It is to this model that the common law, with its basis in custom and the 'spirit of the people', was seen to conform, even in the neo-classical period, offering to the public an ideal of law as an indigenous critical and interpretative tradition, as adaptive and as organic in its development. The law, with its structure of rights and responsibilities, pleas and appeals, equities and proper jurisdictions, thus appears in neo-classical criticism most frequently as inspiration and authority for a corresponding hermeneutic procedure, preaching less the application of rules to the facts, than an adaptive application of the facts to the rules. ''Tis not enough', Dryden wrote in his *Heads of an Answer to Rymer* (1677), 'that Aristotle said so, for Aristotle drew his models of tragedy from Sophocles and Euripides; and if he had seen ours, might have changed his mind' (ed. Watson, 1962, vol. 1, p. 218). The tone is one of aggressive confidence, and if that tone was preserved in many writings in the generations of neo-classical critics to follow, it had much to do with the influence on criticism of its supporting legal culture, and the authority and flexibility of that deeply 'twisted and interwoven', subverting and countervailing legal voice.

British neo-classicism remains an elusive entity. It is elusive in that it defies neat historical confinement, and yet its conventional location in the period from 1660 to the death of Pope (or, sometimes, of Johnson) is so entrenched on the accepted map of cultural history that attempts to contend with those boundaries, to assert that Shakespeare, Milton, Keats and Shelley may have been in many respects as ardently 'neo-classical' as Pope or Swift or Johnson, or alternatively to suggest that the latter might have seen themselves as observers more of the terminal than of the climactic moment in British neo-classicism, seemed doomed to remain as mere skirmishings at the perimeter, as dissenting footnotes to be left to accumulate alongside other recent and equally valiant attempts to moderate our sense of the same period as 'Augustan' or as an 'Age of Reason'. The period under consideration will continue to be presented as the neo-classical period, to be described, in the first instance at least, as 'Augustan' and even 'rational' in character, despite the fact that so much of modern scholarship has been intent on a wholesale demythologizing, stripping back the overlays of hostile polemic, the Romantic attack on 'Ignoramuses and Pope-Admirers' (Chandler, 1984, p. 485) and the disparagements and dubious historical categories manufactured in the age that followed. Were writers of this period 'for' or 'against' Augustan aesthetic values? In what ways were they 'more' neo-classical than the preceding period? Was Johnson (and it could as well be Young, or Gray, or Collins, or even Pope) a rearguard classicist, or a proto-romantic? While literary scholarship and criticism has, in the last twenty years, performed some magnificent feats in avoiding the misleading questions, the contorted answers and the intellectual blind alleys that the inherited periodizations continue to force us into, the age will probably continue to be understood and investigated along such lines, far into the new century. If the modern scholar's pursuit of the native and the subversive in British neo-classicism has, as Walter Jackson Bate once suggested, now gone a little too far (1970, p. 16), it may be because it has been impelled by the simplifications endorsed by the term 'neo-classical'.

It is, of course, disingenuous to turn upon that fatally useful term, after having made full use of it in the preceding pages. My own reading, however, affirms in some measure what Donald Greene has suggested, that the great writers of the period were 'entirely unaware that they were "neo-classicists" ' (1970, p. 160). From one point of view – that of the Renaissance scholar looking forward – the period is principally characterized by a new spirit of critical freedom (Tillyard, 1965, p. 336). Even the most ardent admirers and emulators of the ancients, it is clear, would have been ill at ease under the burden of such nomenclature. There is much testimony, in the writings of poets and critics of the era, to a feeling that the shades of the prison house of mediocrity were fast closing in, a sense of a possible glorious cultural inheritance betrayed by intractable social and political circumstances. Despite the occasional enthusiastic revelation of classical possibilities for Britain, such as in Welsted's *Dissertation Concerning the Perfection of the English Language* (1724), classical models and classical ideals appear with greater force in much of the literature of the period, and the satiric literature in particular, as the positive against which the present cultural negatives were defined. As such, viewed as it might view itself, the age might cautiously be described less as actively neo-classical than as the most self-consciously (and self-laceratingly) unclassical era in English literary history, with that sense of the classical remove, of the dying of the light, as its central inspiration. Only at the cost of considerable distortion, or within the apologetic context of a vast supplementary literature, could the term neo-classical be used to characterize such an age.

There were many others, however – increasingly the dominant group – who saw that visionary gleam as fading before new social circumstances and under local conditions which actually threw a little light of their own. The importance of writings of this kind has long been acknowledged, and the vigour and experimentalism of mid-century literary culture in Britain extensively described, largely within the broad ambit of the eighteenth-century reconsideration of the arts, the classic to romantic shift in aesthetic values. Our literary histories have charted, in detail, the growing appreciation of native writers – Shakespeare, Spenser, Milton – and the evolution not only of forms of critical discourse, but also of social theory, to the point where not only the artistic character but also the 'legislative' and socially-constitutive role of the nation's great primitives could be properly appreciated. Analysis of this kind, however, even when properly forewarned and forearmed by such essays as that of Henry Knight Miller on the distortions inherent in all 'Whig Interpretations' of literary history (1972), is almost inevitably seduced by the lure of a satisfactory historical trajectory, with the new critical discourse seen as emerging from the negative – neo-classicism – and looking towards the positive, in the 'triumph' of Romanticism. The intellectual vitality of criticism through the period, the impressively close relationship between artistic creation, criticism and theory through the neo-classical and into the romantic era, will long continue to be vindicated on the diachronic and teleological model, the vigorously conflicting voices within that period of criticism and experiment identified by being spread out across a broad and progressive historical span.

What I have suggested above, however, is that much of that same vitality, experimentalism, quest for appropriate aesthetic values and creative participation in wider forms of cultural interpretation and criticism may be gleaned from a closer study of neo-classical criticism itself, in a more synchronic reading of the works of Dryden, Addison, Pope, Johnson and others. Many central concerns that came to be written larger in the decades to follow, often with a strong patriotic reinforcement (Lipking, 1970, p. 329) and a tendency, as in Wordsworth's *Preface to the Lyrical Ballads* (1800), to cast aesthetic questions in epochal and even apocalyptic terms, can also be found half-disguised within the dialogical texture of the earlier criticism. That criticism, while principally proceeding through an inherited vocabulary that was rhetorical in origin (Crane, 1952, p. 376), found rich resources in allied linguistic fields, with which to vary and question that inheritance. The place of local as against imported values, the balancing of the burden with the inspiration of the past, the sense of a need to keep artistic values in close accord with current and local social concerns, the need to interleave the tradition with present activity rather than simply to impose it – all these issues are raised and debated within the very linguistic texture of neo-classical criticism, in ways that are more integral rather than oppositional to the mid- and late-century concerns; and this is a fact that both the 'classic to romantic' trajectories and the neo-classical periodic bracketing have tended to disguise. The criticism of the neo-classical era was more volatile, its values less well-established and less extensively dictated than has often been suggested. It was an era in which, in a special way, British literary critics took the law into their own hands.

FURTHER READING

Abrams, M. H. (1953) *The Mirror and the Lamp: Romantic Theory and the Critical Tradition*, Oxford University Press, Oxford

Barrell, John (1986) *The Political Theory of Painting from Reynolds to Hazlitt: 'The Body of the Public'*, Yale University Press, New Haven

Bate, Walter Jackson (1961) *Classic to Romantic: Premises of Taste in Eighteenth-Century England*, Harper & Row, New York

Chandler, J. (1984) 'The Pope Controversy: Romantic Poets and the English Canon', *Critical Inquiry*, 10, 481–509

Crane, R. S. (1952) 'English Neoclassical Criticism: An Outline Sketch'. In R. S. Crane (ed.), *Critics and Criticism: Ancient and Modern*, University of Chicago Press, Chicago

Erskine-Hill, Howard (1983) *The Augustan Idea in English Literature*, Edward Arnold, London

Greene, Donald (1970) *The Age of Exuberance: Backgrounds to Eighteenth-Century English Literature*, Random House, New York

Marks, E. R. (1968) *The Poetics of Reason: English Neoclassical Criticism*, Random House, New York

Meehan, Michael (1985) *Liberty and Poetics in Eighteenth-Century England*, Croom Helm, London

Miller, Henry Knight (1972) 'The "Whig Interpretation" of Literary History', *Eighteenth Century Studies*, 6, 60–84

Patey, Douglas Lane (1984) *Probability and Literary Form: Philosophic Theory and Literary Practice in the Augustan Age*, Cambridge University Press, Cambridge

Weinbrot, Howard D. (1978) *Augustus Caesar in 'Augustan' England: The Decline of a Classical Norm*, Princeton University Press, Princeton

ADDITIONAL WORKS CITED

Bakhtin, Mikhail (1981) *The Dialogic Imagination: Four Essays*, translated by Caryl Emerson and Michael Holquist, University of Texas Press, Austin

Barrell, John (1983) *English Literature in History: An Equal, Wide Survey*, Hutchinson, London

Bate, Walter Jackson (1970) *The Burden of the Past and the English Poet*, Belknap Press, Cambridge

Bond, Richmond P. (ed.) (1970) *Critical Essays from the Spectator*, Clarendon Press, Oxford

Cairns, J. W. (1984) 'Blackstone, an English Institutist: Legal Literature and the Rise of the Nation State', *Oxford Journal of Legal Studies*, 4, 318–60

Elledge, Scott (ed.) (1961) *Eighteenth-Century Critical Essays*, 2 vols, Cornell University Press, Ithaca

Geertz, Clifford (1983) *Local Knowledge: Further Essays in Interpretative Anthropology*, Basic Books, New York

Goldgar, Bertrand A. (1965) *Literary Criticism of Alexander Pope*, University of Nebraska Press, Lincoln

Harding, Alan (1966) *A Social History of English Law*, Penguin, Harmondsworth

Hirschman, Albert O. (1977) *The Passions and the Interests: Political Arguments for Capitalism before its Triumph*, Princeton University Press, Princeton

Ker, W. P. (ed.) (1961) *Essays of John Dryden*, 2 vols, Russell & Russell, New York

Lipking, Lawrence (1970) *The Ordering of the Arts in Eighteenth-Century England*, Princeton University Press, Princeton

Nathan, E. P. (1985) 'The Bench and the Pulpit: Conflicting Elements in the Augustan Apology for Satire', *English Literary History*, 52, 375–96

Pocock, J. G. A. (1972) *Politics, Language and Time: Essays on Political Thought and Language*, Methuen, London

——(1975) *The Machiavellian Moment: Political Thought and the Atlantic Republican Tradition*, Princeton University Press, Princeton

Tillyard, E. M. W. (1965) 'A Note on Dryden's Criticism'. In R. F. Jones (ed.), *The Seventeenth Century: Studies in the History of English Thought and Literature from Bacon to Pope*, Stanford University Press, Stanford

Wain, John (ed.) (1973) *Johnson as Critic*, Routledge & Kegan Paul, London

Watson, George (ed.) (1962) *John Dryden: Of Dramatic Poesy and other Critical Essays*, 2 vols, Dent, London

Wellek, René (1941) *The Rise of English Literary History*, University of North Carolina Press, Chapel Hill

——(1955) *A History of Modern Criticism: 1750–1950*, vol. 1, *The Later Eighteenth Century*, Jonathan Cape, London

Wood, Thomas (1727) *Some Thoughts Concerning the Study of the Laws of England, Particularly in the Two Universities*, London [first published 1708]

Zimansky, Curt Arno (ed.) (1956) *Critical Works of Thomas Rymer*, Yale University Press, New Haven

50

THE ROMANTIC CRITICAL
TRADITION

DONALD H. REIMAN

SOCIO-POLITICAL ORIGINS

From the perspective of its social and political dimensions, romantic literature and the critical tradition that justified and explained it arose out of economic, social and intellectual changes that had been developing slowly from the time of the Renaissance and the age of exploration, but became fully apparent to large segments of Europe's population only through the upheavals of the Enlightenment, industrial development, and the American and French revolutions. Marxist critics see in this period the break-up of the old feudal order and the refutation of superstitions that had prevented common people from understanding their true situation as an exploited majority. The romantic writers – many of them from upper-class families or dependants of upper-class families – were deeply immersed in the most violent phase of the transition from a decadent feudal to a nascent capitalist economy. Alienated or exiled from their establishment roots, they saw both the corruption and the injustice of the feudal societies into which they had been born and the fundamental inhumanity of the economic, social and political forces that were challenging the old order. Most leading romantics, while welcoming some political changes (such as the emergence of a free press and the expansion of the franchise to a larger share of the population), regretted the loss of such positive ideals as the sense of personal honour and of individual responsibility for those at other levels in the society – ideals that they identified with the classical-Christian humanism of earlier ages. For the English romantics of the early nineteenth century, these ideals were articulated and exemplified in the writings and lives of Dante and Milton, and in the intellectual and social milieu of Sidney, Spenser, Shakespeare and their contemporaries.

Like Kant, whose philosophical reaction against the implications of Enlightenment rationalism paralleled (and in Germany helped to inspire) the romantic literary reaction, the leading romantic thinkers held that human beings are always to be treated as ends, and never as means only. They denounced the tendency of rationalists – Thomas Hobbes and his fellow reactionary pessimists, as well as Adam Smith and other optimists – to treat human beings en masse as statistical units, rather than as significant moral agents. Romantic poets and writers – among whom were also the first romantic critics – point to strategies for recovering, in a more egalitarian society, the sense of community and personal worth that, they believed, was being eroded by a utilitarian spirit of calculation that tended to dehumanize people into 'hands' of production and units of consumption.

Because the romantics looked backwards for their ideals, Romanticism never developed fully in any nation's literature and criticism until the struggle between the old feudal order and emerging bourgeois values turned clearly to the advantage of the latter. Thus romantic artists and critics appeared first in Germany, Great Britain and France, where the modern commercial-industrial bourgeoisie first asserted dominance. Only later did Romanticism flourish in America, Scandinavia, Italy, Spain, Poland and Russia – and then chiefly in commercial cities, or among exiles, where the traditional values were openly challenged by a rationalist intelligentsia that (even when politically weak, as in Poland and Russia in the nineteenth century) felt assured of its ultimate triumph by the victories of its forerunners in Western Europe. In New England, Emerson and the American transcendentalists paralleled the British romantics, except that they became a *tertium quid*, not between feudal and bourgeois forces but between the old Puritan theocracy and the rising commercial spirit. For example, Hawthorne in *The Scarlet Letter* (1850), *The House of the Seven Gables* (1851), 'The Minister's Black Veil', and many of his other tales came to terms with the brooding inwardness of the old Puritan ideal out of a present dominated by commercial spirit exemplified in the Customs House; Melville epitomized the dehumanizing force of the urban commercial spirit in 'Bartleby the Scrivener'; and Emerson's critical writings point out the dangers of both Puritan narrowness and submission to the purely utilitarian, pragmatic values that threatened to fill the void created by the collapse of the old ideals.

In Russia, the conflict of values characteristic of the romantic perspective is portrayed not only in the works of Pushkin and Lermontov, who drew part of their inspiration directly from Byron and other romantics of the West, but also by Turgenev in *Fathers and Sons* (1862), where the nihilistic scientific rationalism of Bazarov competes with the inept traditional humanism of Nicholas Kirsanov and his brother for the allegiance of Kirsanov's son Arcady. The sense of tradition and the effort to conserve the cultural values of earlier ages led the romantics of late-developing countries to try to forestall or transmute the Enlightenment rationalism that had entered their countries as Western progressivism. Such leading Polish romantics as Adam Mickiewicz, Zygmunt Krasiński, and Juliusz Slowacki (as Segel, 1977, makes clear) were not only involved in the Polish nationalistic uprising in 1831 against the partitioning powers, but in exile (in France) they – like Ugo Foscolo and other romantic literary exiles from foreign domination – kept alive their national literary traditions and political hopes, refusing to dwindle into rationalistic citizens of the world.

As is clear from the belated struggles of Slavophile romantics against such Russian utilitarians as V. G. Belinsky, N. G. Chernyshevsky and N. A. Dobrolyubov, romantic criticism tended not only to be nationalistic but to defend the great poets and dramatists of their own national heritage against the advocates of classical rules, who tended to glorify Roman and, above all, 'rational' Italian and French neo-classical art as superior to the native traditions of the Spanish Golden Age, the English Elizabethans and Germanic folk literature. Part of this emphasis on the superiority of native artistic heritage arose as a reaction to French imperialism, under the expansionist policies first of Louis XIV and Louis XV and later under the Directory and Napoleon. Indeed, McClelland (1975) has treated the late eighteenth-century roots of romantic theory in Spain primarily as a defence of the native writers of the Golden Age against Francophile cultural domination. Thus the romantics of various nationalities and different decades in the nineteenth century filled a middle ground in politics between the reactionary (but internationalist) supporters of the *anciens régimes* and the Enlightenment (also internationalist) rationalism of root-and-branch reformers who sought to purge all vestiges of the past from modern bourgeois society.

THE IDEOLOGICAL RATIONALE

The ideology that the romantics erected to justify their socio-political ambivalence included, but went far beyond, a new literary theory. Wellek (1955), McFarland (1969, 1981) and Engell (1981) have emphasized the strong interrelations between British and German philosophy and literary theory throughout the seventeenth and eighteenth centuries. This affinity reflects the political and commercial ties between England and the north German states and the rising influence of the modern bourgeoisie in the two areas. Here the bourgeois challenge to the ancient feudal establishment could work itself out more freely than in France, where the suppression of the Huguenots after the Revocation of the Edict of Nantes (1685) kept the aspirations of the middle classes corked up until the meeting of the Estates General in 1789 led to a violent outburst. In Scotland, rival schools – both Hume and his friend Adam Smith and the so-called Common Sense philosophers – articulated many of the values of commercial society and the incipient industrial class. And when Hume's application of the experimental Newtonian method to psychology and epistemology overthrew the traditional supports of the hierarchical classical-Christian synthesis in metaphysics, Kant – in the easternmost and most traditional area of Prussia – woke from his dogmatic slumbers to refute the experiential Newtonian method employed analogically in Hume's 'science of mind'.

Kant's critical philosophy reconstructed traditional moral and religious perspectives on new foundations. Following Descartes' Copernican revolution by beginning with the nature of the human mind (rather than with the existence and nature of God), Kant managed to restore the basic elements of the classical-Christian view of the universe. Abrams terms this manoeuvre, which he sees as characteristic of British and German Romanticism generally, as *Natural Supernaturalism* – a 'secularization of inherited theological ideas and ways of thinking'. He continues, 'writers I call "Romantic" . . . undertook, whatever their religious creed or lack of creed, to save traditional concepts, schemes, values which had been based on the relation of the Creator to his creature and creation, but to reformulate them within the prevailing two-term system of subject and author, ego and non-ego, the human mind or consciousness and its transaction with nature' (1971, pp. 12–13). With a different emphasis, Peckham (1970) differentiates Romanticism as a *tertium quid* between the traditional classical-Christian position, which proposed objectified solutions to human anxieties about guilt and death (in either a noumenal realm or a transcendent but personal deity), and Enlightenment rationalism, which declared such anxieties irrelevant in a perfectible natural order. Romanticism, Peckham argues, placed the source of values, not in a realm of Forms, a personal God or the laws of Nature, but within the human psyche, unaided by a transcendent being or source. In the view of Reiman (1988), the philosophical key to the English romantics – particularly Lamb, Hazlitt, Shelley and Byron – is the tradition of Academic and Pyrrhonist Scepticism. These romantics emulated Cicero, William of Ockham, Montaigne, Hume and Sir William Drummond, using Sceptical analyses to undermine dogmatisms based on either sensory evidence or rationalist arguments; they did so to win a free intellectual space and to save traditional values in the face of the mechanistic materialism of both Benthamite theorists and greedy entrepreneurs, while shedding the enervated traditional*ism* of the British establishment.

To romantics in France and Germany, where the overriding ideological threat in this period came not from religious establishments but from Enlightenment rationalists backed by French armies, religious institutions seemed a bulwark to defend traditional humane values. Thus Chateaubriand, in *Atala* (1801) and *Le Génie du Christianisme* (1802), set the tone for the same Catholic bias that Madame de Staël in *De l'Allemagne* (1813) declared to be central to German Romanticism. In Germany itself, Friedrich von Schlegel (1772–1829) and 'Novalis' (1772–1801) who began as Protestants both became leading Catholic apologists, while Friedrich D. E. Schleiermacher (1768–1834), another coadjutor in the romantic centre at Jena at the turn of the century, became the seminal theologian of modern Protestant liberalism. These men and their mentor Friedrich von Schiller (1759–1805) were all literary theorists and critics influential in European Romanticism.

THE SEARCH FOR PASTORAL-AGRARIAN ROOTS

A pastoral-agrarian and, hence, reactionary and anti-rationalist bias is clearly articulated in the critical statements of the early romantics. Wordsworth, in his Preface to the second edition of *Lyrical Ballads* (1800), writes that 'a multitude of causes unknown to former times are now acting . . . to blunt the discriminating powers of the mind, and . . . to reduce it to a state of almost savage torpor', and that one of the chief causes of this degeneration is 'the encreasing accumulation of men in cities, where the uniformity of their occupations produces a craving for extraordinary incident which the rapid communication of intelligence hourly gratifies'. Turning his back on these conditions of commercial and industrial development, Wordsworth proposes to trace in 'the incidents of common life . . . the primary laws of our nature'; he, therefore, chose

> low and rustic life . . . because in that situation the essential passions of the heart find a better soil in which they can obtain their maturity . . . because in that situation our elementary feelings exist in a state of greater simplicity and consequently may be more accurately contemplated and more forcefully communicated.
>
> (1800, pp. xviii–xix, x–xi)

Similarly, August Wilhelm von Schlegel (1767–1845) begins his *Lectures on Dramatic Art and Literature* (1809–11) by appealing to the primal and universal nature of poetry:

> Poetry . . . is a universal gift of Heaven, being shared to a certain extent even by those whom we call barbarians and savages. Internal excellence is alone decisive, and where this exists, we must not allow ourselves to be repelled by the external appearance. Everything must be traced up to the root of human nature.
>
> (trans. 1904, pp. 18–19)

Still earlier, Schiller had enunciated this romantic emphasis on the childlike and the primitive in psychological terms in his essay 'Naïve and Sentimental Poetry' (1795, 1800), where he describes the 'love and tender respect' that the civilized adult feels for nature and the primitive world. This feeling is moral, not aesthetic, says Schiller, because it is mediated by an idea: 'We love in them the tacitly creative life, the serene spontaneity of their activity, existence in accordance with their own laws, the inner necessity, the eternal unity with themselves. *They are what we were;* they are what *we should once again become*'

686

(trans, 1966, p. 85). And he goes on, later in the essay, to articulate a truth implicit in most other romantic criticism:

> The feeling by which we are attached to nature is . . . closely related to the feeling with which we mourn the lost age of childhood and childish innocence. Our childhood is the only undisfigured nature that we still encounter in civilized mankind, hence it is no wonder if every trace of the nature outside us leads us back to our childhood.
>
> (p. 103)

In the creative writings of the romantics, the centrality of a connection between childhood and nature is obvious: Wordsworth illustrates it in all his major poetry, including his unfolding of his poetic development in *The Prelude* (1797, 1806, 1850). Chateaubriand in *Atala* (1801) embodies the concept of primordial unity with nature in the conflict between natural, naïve and unified (but cruel and violent) native Americans and moral and reflective but divided Christians; his plot also turns on the relations between parents or parental surrogates and their children. A similar conflict between natural, naïve goodness and the Christian drama of sin and redemption works itself out in Samuel Taylor Coleridge's 'The Rime of the Ancient Mariner' (1798). The significance of this search for an original, childlike sense of unity with nature and with the simple society of the family derives (as Reiman, 1988, argues) from the romantics' early bereavement or sense of alienation from their parents. This sense of exile and a tendency, in Shelley's words, to 'look before and after,/And pine for what is not', also mark both the creative and the critical writings of Ugo Foscolo, the leading Italian romantic critic, a political exile in London at the same time that Shelley and Byron were social exiles in Italy. Such feelings of personal alienation allowed these writers and critics to speak, in the period of intellectual and social history following the French revolution, for the larger public that felt a similar sense of loss or alienation in their relationships to the institutions of church and state.

One effect on romantic criticism of the search for a lost – perhaps never existent – ideal childhood or youth is the difficulty of separating the romantics' critical works from their imaginative autobiographies. Many major critical statements of the British romantics invoke organic critical principles that parallel the process of maturation marking their personal growth and development. The most influential work of English romantic criticism is Coleridge's *Biographia Literaria* (1817). After tracing the growth of a critic's mind in the early chapters of the work, Coleridge in his more formal critical theory builds on the work of Wordsworth, Schiller and Schlegel, among many others, to point to the close relationship between the universal power of the human mind to organize the data of experience into meaningful relationships – the power that the child uses to come to terms with the 'other' outside himself – and the power of the poet to reorganize such fundamental experience into a new and more satisfying order. Following a tradition of German and British philosophers of terming this faculty of phenomenological experience the 'primary imagination', he defines the poetic or 'secondary' imagination as

> an echo of the [primary imagination], coexisting with the conscious will, yet still as identical with the primary in the *kind* of its agency, and differing only in the *degree*, and in the *mode* of its operation. It dissolves, diffuses, dissipates, in order to re-create; or where this process is rendered impossible, yet still at all events it struggles to idealize and to unify.
>
> (ed. 1983, chap. 13)

Here the same faculty first creates the ideal phenomenal world of childhood and then, when this is lost to the stress of the degenerate modern world of 'Getting and spending', the secondary imagination has the power to re-create the lost ideal through poetry.

In *Defence of Poetry* (1821), Shelley, who had read and been influenced by several earlier romantic milestones, defines 'Poetry, in a general sense', as 'the expression of the Imagination', which makes poetry in this broad sense 'connate with the origin of man' (ed. 1977, p. 480). After paralleling Schlegel in describing how children and savages originate mimetic actions that lead toward dramatic action and poetry as sophisticated societies know it, Shelley goes on to define 'poetry in a more restricted sense' as 'those arrangements of language, and especially metrical language, which are created by that imperial faculty' (ed. 1977, p. 483); his intention, like that of his romantic peers, is not only to make the creative shaping of poetic language one specialized function of the central mental activity of every thought and action, but to give it the power to preserve inwardly the ideal sense of control that the child loses during maturation through encounters with recalcitrant external reality.

Basic to romantic literary theory are two related ideas: first, the poetic faculty is linked with the universal imaginative process central to all human endeavours (including religious expression, the law, and other aspects of social ideology); this makes it possible for poets to arouse in all human beings responses kindred to the poets' longings and ideals. Second, because the poetic imagination is so central to human nature, the joy and hopefulness of a lost childhood could be recovered through the poetic faculty (with its accompanying sense of shaping control), and from this renewed feeling of security (reproducing the child's early sense of security when cared for by a loving family), poetry's myths could reknit the tattered social fabric to its original condition during the childhood of the race – a time of simple communities before either feudal dominance betrayed or capitalist exploitation sundered the social bonds. By pointing out the links of poetic powers with the primary imaginative faculty that evokes religious feelings and societal bonding, the romantics hoped to resist the inroads of mechanistic psychologies drawn from the physical sciences. By emphasizing the inner and primary nature of the related roots of poetry and religion, they tried to discourage the elevation of sensory factual data and rational analysis at the expense of human feelings and creative impulses.

The tone of much romantic criticism is nostalgic, describing an economy of naïve childhood ideals, youthful losses and disillusionments, and reflective recoveries that vindicate but cannot recapture the first fine careless rapture. (The language of a balance-sheet of tallied losses and gains so central to Schiller and Wordsworth is an unwitting debt of metaphor that the romantics owed to their bourgeois society and utilitarian opponents.) This comparison of past and present often becomes an elegy for the adult's loss of the imaginative insight he possessed in his youth, seasoned by the consolation that the critic can now more fully understand and appreciate the feelings of his earlier self. Charles Lamb and William Hazlitt, like their mentors Wordsworth and Coleridge, begin some of their best critical essays with a retrospective glance at their youthful impressions of a play and the actors they first saw perform it, or the occasion of their first encounter with a book. The *gusto* that Hazlitt praises in criticism concerns not only rhetoric and strong expression, but also a freshness of response naïve in Schiller's sense. In Lamb's best-known excursions into literary theory, such as 'On the Tragedies of Shakespeare ... Their Fitness for Stage Representation', he begins by denying that Garrick, a mere actor exhibiting the outward effects of Shakespeare's art, was equal to the Bard himself, and declares that no actors or stage could present the full inner meaning of a play like *King Lear*. In both 'On the Artificial Comedy of the Last Century' and 'Stage Illusion', Lamb argues that comedy depends on a spirit of collusion between actors and audience, in which both remember at all times that they are involved in an illusion that is distinct from reality – that theatres present 'plays', not realities.

Here are the germs of two or more central ideas of romantic criticism: first, the physical embodiment of a great work of art always falls short of its imaginative conception in the artist's (or even the reader's) mind, an idea that we may call the doctrine of imperfect actualization; this concept, that all sublunary attempts to embody imaginative conceptions are either hostile or irrelevant to artistic creation (a view later carried to an extreme by Croce), relates to the romantics' internalization of traditional values and was developed by writers as diverse as E. T. A. Hoffmann (1776–1822) and Robert Browning into a doctrine of the imperfect, in which unperformed or uncompleted acts show the transcendent destiny of man, whose 'reach should exceed his grasp,/Or what's a heaven for?' ('Andrea del Sarto'). A second major idea in Lamb (also adumbrated by Coleridge) is that great art requires for its creation and its reception a temporary reversion to the spirit of childish play that Schiller and Shelley also recognized as a fundamental manifestation of the creative

Imagination. This emphasis on the playfulness of the artist and the 'pleasures of the text' persists in one branch of neo-romantic criticism.

INNOVATIONS IN LITERARY THEORY

Despite contentions that there was no sharp break in literary theory between eighteenth-century neo-classical critics and the romantics, there have been demonstrations of at least two shifts in perspective during the late eighteenth century about the nature of the creative process and the language of poetry that constitute the basis of a peculiarly romantic poetics. Abrams (1953) shows that the metaphors used in writing and talking about poetic creation shifted dramatically from a mimetic to an expressive mode early in the period. Even when Hayden (1979) qualifies Abrams by arguing that the mimetic Aristotelian tradition persisted through the romantic period, he merely underscores the conservative nature of the romantic 'revolution', in which the pioneers expressed novel theories by means of inherited language, while maintaining that they were merely clarifying and fulfilling earlier traditions. At a more technical level, Stone (1967) traces a shift in emphasis from rhetorical techniques in neo-classical criticism to imaginative inspiration in romantic critical theory. While valuing the inspired psyche more than a mastery of rhetorical and versifying technique, the romantics also valorized the Sublime over the Beautiful and the Picturesque. The romantic Sublime is associated with 'waste and solitary places' that the romantics, with their bias toward inwardness, preferred to 'Nature methodized' (by the commercial utility of canals and tilled fields), and as Weiskel's Freudian study (1976) argues, it grows out of the psychological shocks of childhood. (See Modiano, 1985, for another view of Coleridge's and Wordsworth's aesthetics.)

The articulation of an aesthetics and poetics featuring the expression of strong feelings is natural enough to humanists whose sense of shock, loss and isolation was of sublime proportions and who were anxious to return to traditional values that were disappearing; these individuals felt themselves to be outcasts from a society that was so scarred and distorted that to reflect through mimetic art the life around them would betray their basic values. Having internalized the lost or betrayed values of an earlier, more nearly perfect era, they sought to become, in the words of Robert Louis Stevenson's essay (1892), 'The Lantern-Bearers' who witnessed to forgotten truth in a darkened world, hoping to provide 'the true realism . . . to find out where joy resides, and give it a voice far beyond singing'. In this effort they differ from later naturalistic and even disillusioned humanists of the twentieth century (such as Kafka) who use their art to portray an actuality they hate, but are unable to escape. This conception of the poet as the guide of a society confused as to what constitutes reality appears prominently in the critical writings of Wordsworth, Coleridge and – perhaps most vividly – in Shelley's *Defence of Poetry*:

> Poets, or those who imagine and express this indestructible order, are not only the authors of language and of music, of the dance and architecture and statuary and painting: they are the institutors of laws, and the founders of civil society and the inventors of the arts of life.
>
> (ed. 1977, p. 482)

> A poem is the very image of life expressed in its eternal truth. . . . Poetry is a mirror which makes beautiful that which is distorted. . . . Poetry lifts the veil from the hidden beauty of the world, and makes familiar objects be as if they were not familiar.
>
> (pp. 485, 487)

> Poets are the hierophants of an unapprehended inspiration, the mirrors of the gigantic shadows which futurity casts upon the present, the words which express what they understand not; the trumpets which sing to battle, and feel not what they inspire: the influence which is moved not but moves. Poets are the unacknowledged legislators of the World.
>
> (p. 508)

NEO-ROMANTIC SUCCESSORS

The burden of Shelley's and Coleridge's literary theory and criticism – echoed by Stevenson and later critics in the romantic tradition – is that a saving remnant of morally sensitive individuals can, through their inspired words or inspiring examples, guide society out of the wilderness of materialism and calculation to a realm of love and morality. This view of the function of poetry and criticism alike has a messianic flavour that was lacking in the thought of both Dryden and Dr Johnson, but continues in both branches of the descendants of the romantics. In one tradition, which includes such critics as Carlyle, Arnold, Sainte-Beuve, George Eliot, T. S. Eliot, F. R. Leavis, Lionel Trilling, Northrop Frye and Geoffrey Hartman, criticism of society is chiefly by precept. The critic or artist-critic of this stamp works within the social institutions to purify society as it is by pointing out to his contemporaries the moral implications of their degenerate practices (and, sometimes, their writings) through contrasting them with those of literary masterpieces, invariably from some Great Tradition of the past. This humanistic critical tradition variously describes itself as liberal or conservative, but it wars both with the establishment and with utilitarians and Marxists, in or out of power.

Another branch of the romantic tradition, one including Leopardi, Poe, the Pre-Raphaelites, many French poets of the mid-nineteenth century, Pater, Swinburne, Wilde, and some avant-garde poets and critics of the twentieth century, believes that the romantic artist-critic improves society not by haranguing the public, but by turning away from both moralistic and pragmatic concerns to set an example of good living. Instead of berating a society that they believe to be incorrigible, these writers seek to glorify the beautifully impractical and pursue the aesthetically pleasurable, in the hope that an intelligent minority will adopt their lifestyle. These neo-romantics create various aestheticist counter-cultures that flourish and wither in each generation. Neither preaching nor aesthetic neo-romantics embody the original romantics' balanced critical stance. Because the early romantics, separated from their parents' world by the French revolution, drew their inspiration from lost Edens that were both personal and socio-political, and because the love and security of their early childhoods fed their hopes of achieving through art both psychological renewal and a rejuvenated social order, they accepted the view that art should both teach *and* delight. They were, therefore, serious about the social value of play and imagining.

Literary critics in both neo-romantic branches emphasize high points and epiphanies – emotional moments of special illumination. Their rivals for the identification and interpretation of epiphanies are religious and Marxist critics, while the enemies of all epiphanies are Freudian and deconstructionist critics, who demystify and explain away the value of such transfigurations and turning points. Yet even these competing schools have been influenced by the original romantics as well as by their two main branches of successors. The deconstructionists' undercutting or debunking of idealizations was prefigured by Schiller's concept of Romantic Irony and exemplified in the writings of various German writers and, in English literature, by Byron's later poetry. In spite of eclectic crossbreeding during the long interactions of the various modern critical traditions, critics of the two neo-romantic branches are clearly distinguishable from one another and from their chief modern rivals. Both Social Conscience and Exemplary Genius neo-romantics value imaginative artistic expression as a good in itself – perhaps as the highest good. (Marxist and utilitarian critics would consider it merely a socially useful tool; deconstructionists and Freudians as an illusory but perhaps necessary veil over reality.) For those in the Social Conscience branch, great works of art are touchstones that, by disseminating the 'best that has been thought and known', help teach society its fundamental values. For Exemplary Genius neo-romantics, the great imaginative works and their writers exemplify how the 'happiest and best minds' rise above adversity and neglect to find happiness through the exercise of their own creativity, and/or redeem a saving remnant by exposing society's limitations by the contrasting example of the artist, either existing triumphantly in a realm of freedom and love, or destroyed by the hostility and neglect of society. These ideas derive from the writings of the original romantics (as in Shelley's *Prometheus Unbound* and Vigny's *Chatterton*), but neither moralists nor aestheticists can recreate the whole romantic ideal.

Once the modern heirs to the romantic tradition are seen in their two rivalrous branches (bickering like Stalinists and Trotskyites in most departments of literature), critics in the romantic tradition are easily identified. Clearly Frye, Abrams, Peckham, and many other academic critics who have argued that the romantics faced and, to an extent, solved the most significant modern dilemma – in the words of the title of a poem by Lamb, 'Living without God in the World' – are Social Conscience neo-romantics, pointing their contemporaries toward the values of the Romantics as an antidote to the nihilism and despair that has been rife in modern intellectual and artistic circles. I. A. Richards, Leavis, Kenneth Burke, and others whose attitude toward the romantics is more ambivalent or even hostile, have nevertheless inherited through Arnold and other Victorian derivative romantics the same prescriptions for facing modern social problems – a stiff dose of tough-minded imaginative literature every morning and a True Lie or two at bedtime. Though their cases are more complex, probably Frank Kermode and Christopher Ricks have strong affinities for the Social Conscience Romantics. Ricks's analysis of *Keats and Embarrassment* (1974) teaches a social code for people moving from one social milieu to another, while his exploration of the prejudices of T. S. Eliot provides awareness of the subtle impositions of social forces on the sensitive individual in pluralistic modern society. Kermode's efforts in *Romantic Image* (1957) and *The Sense of an Ending* (1967) to refute both rationalist and eschatological divisions of history into neat epochs, and the value he accords in *The Genesis of Secrecy* (1979) to hidden inner meanings in both early Christian and modern literary traditions, link the problems of the modern world directly to those of the age of belief and of high Christian humanism (Milton, particularly, in *Romantic Image*), thereby validating traditional – even romantic – solutions to the questions moderns face. The views of such neo-romantic critics are distinguishable, on the one hand, from the less inward, materialistic analyses of Marilyn Butler, Terry Eagleton, Terence Hawkes, Fredric Jameson, and Raymond Williams, in which the external forms of the society take precedence as signs of social good health, over the inward grace of the individuals who compose it. On the other hand, the neo-romantics differ sharply from such orthodox or neo-feudal critics of the romantics' achievement as Hoxie Neale Fairchild or A. N. Wilson, who find all romantic ideals either derivative or doctrinally flawed.

Harold Bloom and his imitators – self-proclaimed 'strong critics', who attempt to ensure their survival by asserting their own individual genius at the expense of their predecessors and contemporary rivals – epitomize the Exemplary Genius branch of neo-romantic criticism. Bloom employs two complementary strategies to maintain a place in the competition of an exploding intellectual population: first, he draws traditional humanistic ideas from the whole poetic and critical tradition since Milton and declares them his own by virtue of his conquest of his intellectual fathers; second, he creates a myth of his intellectual growth and *agon* that he hopes will generate the same imaginative interest as autobiographical credos by Rousseau, Coleridge or Carlyle.

It would probably be impossible today to develop a genuinely romantic, as opposed to a neo-romantic, criticism in the West. The early romantics had the unusual, though not unique, experience of having been born, or receiving their early training, in one social and intellectual milieu and coming of age in another. Earlier periods when the old verities broke down into intellectual wars between the scions of a stable but decadent past order and a new establishment guided by *Realpolitik* included, for example, the Greek world during the time of Alexander the Great and his successors; Rome during the civil wars that led to the overthrow of the Republic; the time of Augustine, at the decline of the Roman Empire; and the religious wars of the Reformation period. Since the Second World War, writers from Eastern Europe and the Third World have exhibited literary and critical perspectives similar to those of the German and English romantics of the early nineteenth century (though they have the additional self-consciousness of knowing the work of those earlier romantics). Such writers as Boris Pasternak and Alexander Solzhenitsyn have drawn on the traditions of Russia's past to criticize developments in Soviet society. There are surely many literary figures – creative writers and critics – known to those in Third World countries for whom their nation's independence from colonial rule and the subsequent political instability of their nations must have been traumatic. Those who remember the limitations of the old feudal or colonial rulers, while finding the succeeding regimes equally inhumane, may have been drawing from romantic idealizations of earlier cultural traditions, romantic hopes for, and images of, an idealized future for their people.

FURTHER READING

Abrams, M. H. (1953) *The Mirror and the Lamp: Romantic Theory and the Critical Tradition*, Oxford University Press, New York

——(1971) *Natural Supernaturalism: Tradition and Revolution in Romantic Literature*, Norton, New York

Bloom, Harold (1973) *The Anxiety of Influence: A Theory of Poetry*, Oxford University Press, New York

Engell, James (1981) *The Creative Imagination: Enlightenment to Romanticism*, Harvard University Press, Cambridge

Frye, Northrop (1957) *Anatomy of Criticism: Four Essays*, Princeton University Press, Princeton

Hartman, Geoffrey H. (1980) *Criticism in the Wilderness: The Study of Literature Today*, Yale University Press, New Haven

Hayden, John O. (1979) *Polestar of the Ancients: The Aristotelian Tradition in Classical and English Literary Criticism*, University of Delaware Press, Newark

Lentricchia, Frank (1980) *After the New Criticism*, University of Chicago Press, Chicago

McClelland, I. L. (1975) *The Origins of the Romantic Movement in Spain: A Survey of Aesthetic Uncertainties in the Age of Reason*, 2nd edn, Barnes & Noble, New York [first published 1937]

Peckham, Morse (1970) *The Triumph of Romanticism: Collected Essays*, University of South Carolina Press, Columbia

Stone, P. W. K. (1967) *The Art of Poetry, 1750–1820: Composition and Style in the Late Neo-Classic and Early Romantic Periods*, Routledge & Kegan Paul, London

Weiskel, Thomas (1976) *The Romantic Sublime: Studies in the Structure and Psychology of Transcendence*, Johns Hopkins University Press, Baltimore

Wellek, René (1955) *A History of Modern Criticism: 1750–1950*, vol. 2, *The Romantic Age*, Jonathan Cape, London

ADDITIONAL WORKS CITED

Coleridge, S. T. (1983) *Biographia Literaria*, edited by James Engell and W. Jackson Bate, Princeton University Press, Princeton [first published 1817]

McFarland, Thomas (1969) *Coleridge and the Pantheist Tradition*, Clarendon Press, Oxford

——(1981) *Romanticism and the Forms of Ruin: Wordsworth, Coleridge, and the Modalities of Fragmentation*, Princeton University Press, Princeton

Modiano, Raimonda (1985) *Coleridge and the Concept of Nature*, Florida State University Press, Tallahassee

Reiman, Donald H. (1988) *Intervals of Inspiration: The Skeptical Tradition and the Psychology of Romanticism*, Penkevill, Greenwood

Schiller, Friedrich von (1966) *Naive and Sentimental Poetry* and *On the Sublime*, translated by Julius A. Elias, Frederick Ungar, New York [first published 1795 and 1800]

Schlegel, A. W. von (1904) *Lectures on Dramatic Art and Literature*, translated by John Black, 2nd edn, revised by A. J. W. Morrison, George Bell, London [translation first published 1815]

Segel, Harold B. (ed.) (1977) *Polish Romantic Drama: Three Plays in English Translation*, Cornell University Press, Ithaca

Shelley, Percy Bysshe (1977) *A Defence of Poetry*. In D. H. Reiman and S. B. Powers (eds), *Shelley's Poetry and Prose*, Norton, New York, pp. 480–508

Stevenson, Robert Louis (1892) 'The Lantern-Bearers'. In Robert Louis Stevenson, *Across the Plains, with Other Memories and Essays*, Scribner's, New York

Wordsworth, William (1800) *Lyrical Ballads, with Other Poems*, 2nd edn, T. N. Longman & O. Rees, London

51

GREAT TRADITIONS: THE LOGIC OF THE CANON

GEOFFREY STRICKLAND

'The great English novelists are Jane Austen, George Eliot, Henry James and Joseph Conrad – to stop for the moment at that comparatively safe point in history...' When in 1948 F. R. Leavis began his *The Great Tradition* with these words, he did so in the expectation of being misunderstood. 'Critics have found me narrow', he went on, 'and I have no doubt that my opening proposition, whatever I may say to explain and justify it, will be adduced in reinforcement of these strictures.' I shall not try to justify Leavis's choice of great novelists, if choice is the right word – it can suggest an arbitrariness of designation which he would have perhaps disputed. Nor does it particularly need defending. What are generally regarded as the great English novelists and poets are, with few exceptions, still those whom he recommended as such, and the 'map' of English literature, as he called it, still bears a close resemblance to the one that he traced. In this respect, his influence has been more decisive probably than that of any other critic in modern times. What has been called in question in recent years is not so much Leavis's 'narrowness', which George Orwell, for example, compared in his last review for the *Observer* (6 February 1949) with that of a tyrannical schoolmaster, as the assumptions concerning not only literature but the world which lay behind Leavis's attributions of major status. Much of the more recent academic writing on literature has been theoretical, and much of the theory has been concerned with the possibility of looking in literary texts for something other than what individual readers have found beautiful or inspiring; with something other, that is, than judgements of value. It is clear that if value means merely personal preference, however, widely and intensely shared, it is not a necessary feature of any reading of the novel or poem in which it is said to inhere. And though its value may tell us something about the state of mind of an individual or the evolution of taste, it is of no more concern to the serious student of literature (or the 'text' or the 'sign system') than the latest price reached by a Van Gogh painting to the serious historian of art. This goes as well for the notion of supreme value or 'greatness' (which Leavis did not invent) and which has been taken to justify the study of literature from its origins to the present time.

However, has value no other kind of reality than this? The questions that have been raised by recent critical theory turn in the end on some of the oldest in philosophy: those of what we mean by the good, the beautiful and the true. They are also, as we are often reminded, social and political questions about the ways in which, if not with public encouragement at least at public expense, influential people try to give meaning to their lives and, by implication, to the lives of the community at large. No answers to the questions have been reached which have commanded lasting or general assent and in university departments of English and modern languages there is probably less common understanding than there has ever been at any time as to the nature of literature and what its study entails. Could it be that this is because the case against the so-called 'canonical' view of literature, though often powerful, is inconclusive and because no coherent alternative to it has yet been found?

The word 'canonical' itself is obviously appropriate to an extent, though there are many kinds of canon and the history of this and other related terms can help us to understand more clearly what we mean by them. As used today, it often has a caricatural force deriving from its original scriptural associations. In the original Greek, the word 'kanón' means a rod or bar and, by metaphorical extension, a 'rule'. According to G. W. Anderson, writing in the *Cambridge History of the Bible*, it was first used in its modern sense in patristic writings of the fourth century to refer to those texts which orthodoxy had come to regard as the Old and New Testaments. The new term, needless to say, does not altogether correspond to a new concept. There are degrees of sacredness and in the Hebrew Mishnah, the scriptures, because of the unworthiness of those who hold them, are said to 'defile the hands' (ed. Ackroyd and Evans, 1970, vol. 1, pp. 114–18). They differ in this respect from the 'canon', as the term is used anachronistically today, of the Greek and Roman 'grammatikoi', which consisted always of ten poets, ten orators and ten historians and was part of the 'artes liberales' or studies appropriate to the education of 'free' men; an education which ensured the existence of a common culture among the literate classes of the Hellenic and Roman worlds, extending over many generations. The modern term which conveys most simply the general notion of the canonical is the word 'literature' itself, which (unless we are talking, say, of the literature on the subject of canal holidays) refers to a canon of works of outstanding value and possibly even interest as well. When Verlaine, in his 'Art poétique' (1884) dismissed as 'littérature' all that lacked the pure magic of poetry, he made it clear he was referring to mere masterpieces.

The words 'literature' and 'littérature' have been used in their current sense for barely two centuries (it has a completely different meaning, for example, in Dr Johnson's dictionary) and it is often pointed out that the new term corresponds to a new kind of relationship between author and reader. It is not, clearly, that the great authors of antiquity had ever ceased to be regarded as such or had been thought of as having no successors. There is the peculiarly intimate and prophetic sense in which Dante (even literally) follows Virgil; while something resembling the Roman curriculum was reconstituted as early as Charlemagne and in the schools of the medieval and, more especially, post-Renaissance Europe. The new kind of relationship is best exemplified by the career of Voltaire, who was also influential in bringing into currency the other new related concept, that of the modern literary 'classic'. 'You give me great pleasure', he writes to a correspondent in Paris, 'when you tell me that the Academy is to render France and Europe the service of publishing a collection of our classical authors. They will give some permanent form to taste and language [*fixeront la langue et le goût*], both of which lack constancy among my fickle compatriots' (1828a, p. 76). Voltaire's enthusiasm for established criteria of usage and taste was not entirely incompatible with the radical political and religious stance which obliged him to live in virtual exile on the Swiss frontier. He thought of the French Academy, of which he was a member, as the agent not of absolutist order but of enlightenment, since its members were not paid or patronized, were elected by their peers and were subservient only to what he regarded as the interests of reason; a view which was vindicated during his triumphant reception by the Academy shortly before his death, when the pious reservations of the brave ecclesiastic who welcomed him were greeted by unacademic whistles and jeers. The designation of literary classics in the vernacular coincides with the rise of the independent profession of letters on both sides of the English Channel, with the setting up of the Société des Auteurs and with the first laws of copyright. The cult of originality carried to the point of genius among the romantic writers of succeeding generations presupposes an existing and hospitable literary Pantheon.

It is, presumably, not by chance that the rise of 'literature' took place at the same time as that of modern representative government and an increasingly widespread and profound secularization of culture. When Matthew Arnold (like Voltaire, an admirer of the French Academy) introduced in 1880 T. H. Ward's edition of *The Great English Poets*, he looked forward to the day when 'mankind' would discover 'that we have to turn to poetry to interpret life for us, to console us, to sustain us', and when 'what now passes with us for religion and philosophy' would be 'replaced by poetry'. Poetry may not have replaced religion but it has come to occupy a prominent place in the lives of British schools and universities, partly as a result of Arnold's own campaigning on behalf of what is today known as 'English'. The story of this remarkable innovation is told by Margaret Mathieson in her *Preachers of Culture* (1975); and it seems clear that the justification and purpose of 'English', both for teachers and educationalists, corresponded for many years to Arnold's explicitly stated ideals. Poetry, that is the very best poetry, more than anything else for Arnold, exemplifies 'culture' and culture, like religion, transcends all other interests, especially the particular interests of any social class. 'It seeks to do away with classes; to make the best that has been thought and known in the world current everywhere; to make all men live in an atmosphere of sweetness and light, where they may use ideas as it uses them itself, freely – nourished and not bound by them. . . . The men of culture are the true apostles of equality' (Arnold, 1935a, p. 70). The belief that the study of great literature can not only ennoble and refine but also inspire social harmony and even forestall political revolution is expressed in the Newbolt Committee's report of 1921 on *The Teaching of English in England*, which also recommended extramural education for the benefit of those 'who have not so much as heard "whether there be any Holy Ghost" ' (1921, p. 259). I. A. Richards, three years later, arguing from explicitly psychological premises and in a markedly different style, is no less convinced of the spiritual and ethical value of a literary education. 'The critic is as much concerned with the health of the mind as the doctor with the health of the body. . . . Bad taste and crude responses are not mere flaws in an otherwise admirable person. They are actually a root evil from which other defects follow' (1924, p. 62).

It is unlikely today that anyone wishing to recommend the study of literature would use arguments such as these or at least as confidently and unequivocally; or that they would or could have been used at any time in France. The success of any scheme of public education owes something to its conformity with popular tradition and in Catholic France there has never been anything quite like the habits of mind, on which Arnold and Newbolt could draw, engendered by the daily reading of the Bible. In France, none the less, as in England, following the abolition in 1885 of the teaching of 'rhetoric' in all French lycées, literature came to be studied more for what was thought to be its own sake: that is, as a means to the understanding of language at its most subtle and eloquent in the classes of 'explication littéraire' and as part of history as understood by Taine and Lanson, the literary masterpiece now being seen as the specific product of *'l'homme, le moment et le milieu'*. In both countries, the educational innovations coincided with the promotion of universal literacy and in both an approach to literature was adopted which encouraged pride in the spirit exemplified in the classics of the national culture. Both British and French propaganda during the First World War drew on literary associations, the point made by Ezra Pound when in *Hugh Selwyn Mauberley* he wrote of those who had died:

> For two gross of broken statues,
> For a thousand battered books . . .

What we now call 'modernism' was partly a reaction against cultural nationalism and against the optimism that had inspired the ideals of mass education, what Pound called, in the title of an essay of 1916, 'The constant preaching to the mob' (1954, pp. 64–5). For the young F. R. Leavis, the benefits of 'English' to the community at large were never to seem as obvious, immediate or direct as they had to the authors of the Newbolt Report. He was unable also to accept I. A. Richards's theory of individual psychology and its attempted justification in practice (Leavis, 1935, pp. 382–402). Strongly influenced for a time by Pound and T. S. Eliot, he shared their conviction that, in the new conditions of mass literacy exploited by propaganda and commerce, 'the subtlest and most perishable parts of tradition' and the 'implicit standards that order the finer living of an age' could only be renewed and passed on by an educated minority bringing its influence to bear as effectively as possible in the world (1930, pp. 3–5). Like Eliot, Leavis rejected Arnold's association of poetry with religion. Yet he thought far more highly than Eliot of Arnold as a critic (1938, pp. 319–32) and there is a clear affinity between Arnold's description of poetry as a 'criticism of life' and Leavis's recommendation of those English novels which could be read as 'dramatic poems' and whose authors were distinguished by 'a vital capacity for experience, a kind of reverent openness before life and a marked moral intensity' (1948, p. 9).

It is obvious from the history of literature and its study, however summarily it is traced, that up to the time of F. R. Leavis, the claims that were made on their behalf usually presupposed their acceptability, either naïvely or otherwise. Today anyone who wishes to defend a canonical approach to literature finds that there is far less that he or she can take for granted and that this is only one of a number of approaches between which the student of literature can choose. What are these alternatives? It would be impossible to do justice to the many possible approaches that have been elaborated in recent years; and some of the most influential are discussed in other essays in this book. But three present themselves as at least mutually incompatible and commit those who adopt any one of them to a correspondingly unequivocal view of the future as well as the past.

The first, which has the attraction not only of simplicity, is that literature should not be studied at all, a view which has been shared in the past not only by Philistines but by some of their enemies, such as Stendhal. In *Racine et Shakespeare*, he suggests that the reason why so many 'sublime' novels had been written before 1823 was that 'our pedants, finding that no novels were written by the Greeks or Romans declared the entire genre unworthy of their anger' (1928, p. 302). Writing today, he might have asked whether any successors to *Don Quixote* or *La Princesse de Clèves* had been written since the pedants declared the novel worthy of their interest after all, and whether the once despised cinema ought not to be protected also from the attentions of scholars. The question whether the so-called 'teaching' of literature has been of general benefit to mankind is, however, impossible to answer, for there is no conceivable investigation which would enable us to weigh the advantages against the cost. For one example of genuine profit, such as Stendhal's own introduction to the works of Shakespeare by an enlightened schoolteacher in Grenoble, one is bound to find another where an intelligent boy or girl has been put off literature for life by witnessing its apparent effect on those who have been exposed to it for years or by enforced participation in what has amounted to an invasion of emotional privacy.

Yet it would be an illusion to believe that the eradication of literature from the school or university syllabus would guarantee individual sensibilities against further intrusions of this kind. French literature was never taught in France in the seventeenth century, but the savage competitiveness of those who aspire to taste is one of the commonest topics of comedy in Molière. The literary canons of the academy have their origin in the world of popular taste and fashion, which is itself anything but spontaneous in origin. It is only in a Utopia like Plato's republic that we can imagine the total prohibition of art and hence of the various equivalents of what pop fans today call the 'charts'.

The policy of the academy can, of course, be to refrain from interfering in any way with the market of fashion and to remain hospitable to all popular canons of taste. This is the second genuine alternative and has led to the emergence in recent years of 'media studies', a development welcomed by Terry Eagleton in his *Literary Theory* (1983). Eagleton recommends that 'departments of literature, as we know them' should cease to exist (p. 213) and makes it clear that he regards the very notion of 'literature' and the canon of classics it presupposes as a fiction masking the imposition of certain values serving the interest of the dominant social class, whose ethos is predominantly male and which exercises hegemonic power. There is no reason, he argues, why Proust and *King Lear* should not feature in the new courses of ' "discourse theory" or "cultural studies" or whatever' (p. 210), but no reason either why these should not include children's television programmes or popular romances, such as those of Barbara Cartland. All of these 'shape forms of consciousness or unconsciousness, which are closely related to the maintenance or transformation of our existing system of power' and are thus 'closely related to what it means to be a person' (p. 210). The case for a kind of canonical pluralism was made in the United States, also in 1983, by Barbara Herrnstein Smith, who argued that the value to an individual of a work of literature depends ultimately on 'the dynamics of an economic system, specifically the personal economy constituted by the subject's needs, interests and resources' (pp. 15–16), including the extent to which he or she has happened to participate in a predominantly literary culture. Discussing the many 'who are not – or are not yet, or choose not to be among the orthodoxly educated population of the West', she argued that 'other verbal artifacts and other objects and events have performed for them the various functions that Homer, Dante and Shakespeare perform for us' (p. 35). There are, that is to say, substitutes for Homer, Dante and Shakespeare.

Both Dr Eagleton and Professor Herrnstein Smith were arguing against a certain familiar notion of what we mean by a superior culture, whether that of the individual or the group; and the latter referred specifically to the inappropriateness of criteria drawn from white Anglo-American literature when discussing the work of the black American poet Langston Hughes (Smith, 1983, pp. 13–15). Whereas she herself is concerned, however, with the problems that arise from the retention or abandonment of traditional ideas of literary value and calls for further thinking on these lines, Dr Eagleton offers his own solution. What he proposes is in effect a revival of the teaching in post-Renaissance schools of the discipline of rhetoric, taking advantage of the insights of critical theorists of recent years. 'Rhetoric wanted to find out the most effective ways of pleading, persuading and debating' in order to achieve legal, political or religious ends. 'Similarly, there must be a reason why we should consider it worthwhile to develop a form of study which would look at the various sign-systems and signifying practices in our own society, all the way from *Moby Dick* to the Muppet Show' (Eagleton, 1983, pp. 206–7). Eagleton makes it clear that he speaks as a socialist and a feminist and distinguishes his own attitude to literature from that of a 'liberal humanist', such as Leavis, by arguing that while both 'wish to discuss literature in ways which will deepen, enrich and extend our lives', he himself can only conclude that 'such deepening and enriching entails the transformation of a society divided by class and gender' (p. 210). He could have added that work on these lines is already in progress and constitutes a new chapter in the history of what is still usually called 'English'. There are schools at the present in which the programme for making what he calls a 'better person' by this means is being carried out with a single-mindedness reminiscent of that of the 'missionaries' of the Newbolt Report.

Not all who favour a non-interventionist policy with regard to fashion and taste justify this in terms of immediate and predictable benefits to mankind. It can also be justified by the belief or assumption that so-called critical 'analysis' is something that can be taught, irrespective of what is analysed. To quote Terry Eagleton once again,

> If you have nothing better to do at a party you can always try on a literary critical analysis of it, speak of its styles and genres, discriminate its significant nuances or formalize its sign-systems. Such a text can prove quite as rich as one of the canonical works, and critical dissections of it quite as ingenious as those of Shakespeare.
>
> (p. 202)

It is, of course, true that concepts such as 'genre' and 'style' and 'sign-system', in so far as they can be distinguished in particular instances, need to be learned and that theorists such as Barthes, Derrida and Julia Kristeva have added several more. The terms, however, even when used appropriately are descriptive rather than analytical. It is scientists (as Barthes had put it) not critics who make 'discoveries' (Barthes, 1964, p. 256) and there is no such thing in the human, as distinct from the physical sciences (with the exception, he might have added, of the use of statistical evidence) as a 'method' to which one can attribute a 'result' (1984, p. 355). It is unlikely that Eagleton's party-goer would have given as accurate an account of an occasion like the evening at Mrs Brookenham's as Mr Longdon in Henry James's *The Awkward Age*. A non-evaluative description of what we read or hear, however ingenious, ignores what is usually the most important thing we need to know: how much it is to be trusted and taken seriously.

My third alternative is, of course, the one with which I began and some of the consequences of accepting it and some of the objections to which it is bound to give rise will have already emerged from my discussion of its two rivals. The question of what we can rely on and take seriously is one of the first with which such an approach is concerned; and this is implicit in the choice of the earliest canons that we know: most obviously in those of the Hebrew and Christian scriptures, but in those of Greek and Roman schools as well, where the authors chosen for study were also those regarded as most worthy of imitation. The treatise on *The Sublime*, once attributed to Longinus, points out, in its ninth section, the difficulty for any writer of avoiding 'falsity' or 'frigidity' and claims that true eloquence lies 'only in those whose spirit is generous and aspiring'. Even an unspoken thought may be sublime, 'like the silence of Ajax in the eleventh Odyssey'. Marc Fumaroli has pointed out, in his monumental study of European rhetoric in the Renaissance, the recurring preoccupation not only with persuasiveness but the most persuasive quality of all, 'ingenium', a word best translated as 'wit' except when it means 'naturalness' or 'authenticity' (Fumaroli, 1980, pp. 79–85). This same freedom from affectation is regarded by Voltaire, a product of the Jesuit classes of rhetoric, and by the similarly educated public to which he could appeal, as a necessary feature of great literature and 'correct' usage.

How does one identify the authentic? Any kind of definition other than the ostensive is likely to be tautological; which is why those who value this quality have tried to do so by reference to specific examples or what Arnold calls 'touchstones'. (Voltaire's belief that there were actual 'rules' to which genuine masterpieces should conform gave rise to the excessive formalism against which the romantics were to rebel and made it difficult for him to justify his genuine admiration for Shakespeare, whom he would have preferred to dismiss as a 'drunken savage', 1828b, p. 194.) What Arnold's examples of the greatest poetry have in common is 'the accent of high seriousness, born of absolute sincerity' (Arnold, 1935b, p. 34), terms which, as Leavis points out, have limiting and peculiarly Victorian connotations, though less so when read in the context of his 'Study of Poetry' as a whole. Arnold was alert also to qualities of 'movement' and 'diction', key terms in Leavis's own discussion of poetry, and he insisted, as Leavis notes:

> (in terms that would invite the charge of circularity if we were being offered a definition, as we are not) that the evaluation of poetry as 'criticism of life' is inseparable from its evaluation as poetry; that the moral judgment that concerns us as critics must be at the same time a delicately relevant response of sensibility; that, in short, we cannot separate the consideration of 'greatness' from the consideration of 'genuineness'.
>
> (Leavis, 1938, p. 327)

This could be said of Leavis's criticism too, in which appreciation, interpretation and evaluation are indistinguishable. What we judge when we read the poem or the novel is not merely its congeniality or otherwise to ourselves, what I have called in another context 'subjective judgment' (Strickland, 1981, pp. 83–103), but the kind and degree of seriousness or otherwise of a simple appeal for help.

Hitler, it can of course be pointed out, was serious and in his appalling way genuine. The approach I am outlining presupposes also the possibility of our identifying our authentic common humanity, the point of view which, for Arnold, transcended interests of class and, one would have to add today, of race and gender as well. To say 'possibility' is to acknowledge the formidable objections, both political and philosophical, to the belief that such a point of view can be found, as well as the equally formidable objections to the conclusion that we can talk only of the temporary needs and preferences of groups and individuals. What is known as the 'humanist' point of view is, in its very origins in early Renaissance Italy, antithetical to dogma. The classics of what have come to be known as 'literature' have been recommended characteristically for qualities which exclude the didactic and have focused on what unites as well as divides humanity, including the kind of comedy or tragedy which brings out the justice of conflicting interests and needs. In tragedy, Leavis writes, it is

> as if we were challenged at the profoundest level with the question, 'In what does the significance of life reside?' and found ourselves contemplating, for answer, a view of life, and of the things giving it value, that makes the valued appear unquestionably more important than the valuer.
>
> (1953, pp. 131–2)

'Life', Leavis wrote in the title of a late essay (1972, p. 11), 'is a necessary word'. It stands in his own vocabulary for ultimate significance, recognition of which, as in the case of Wordsworth or D. H. Lawrence, is 'religious'. The great English novelists share 'a reverent openness before life' (1948, p. 9). What is at issue here is not doctrine of any kind. Nor does it exclude interest in or respect for religious doctrine, though one can see why Leavis thought Arnold mistaken in believing that he could write as a lay theologian. The religious attitude to life is ultimate individual and human authenticity.

How can such an attitude be recognized? 'A judgment is personal or it is nothing; you cannot take over someone else's' (Leavis, 1972, p. 62). But the canon is prescribed by commercial publishers and by the academic authorities, both of whom are notoriously fallible. Like Voltaire's Academy, it is, at least in theory, free from political or financial pressures and has opportunities, which its members may or may not be capable of seizing, for disinterested judgement; that is, recognition of the authentic. Leavis's hostility to the academic establishments of his day arose from a sense of opportunities lost and betrayed and from the belief that what the university represented was, none the less, the only hope for the survival of what was most civilized and humane in what we were still able to salvage from the past. This was so for Leavis because of what is or ought to be the liberal and anti-authoritarian nature of the university, as well as the actual nature of literary judgement:

> The implicit form of a judgment is: This is so, isn't it? The question is an appeal for confirmation that the thing *is* so; implicitly that, though expecting, characteristically, an answer in the form, 'yes, but – ' the 'but' standing for qualifications, reserves, corrections. Here we have a diagram of the collaborative-creative process in which the poem comes to be established as something 'out there', of common access in what is in some sense a public world.
>
> (Leavis, 1972, p. 62)

Any canon is, of course, likely to be in a state of more or less constant evolution. 'That the eighteenth century, which hadn't much lively reading to choose from, but had much leisure, should have found *Tom Jones* exhilarating is not surprising. . . . Standards are formed in comparison, and what opportunities had they for that?' (Leavis, 1948, p. 4). The word 'canon' itself, which Leavis actually never used, fails to convey the growth of sophistication and moral awareness which is what we refer to when we talk of the evolution of the English novel from Richardson to Jane Austen. Leavis's interest in literature as an expression of culture – popular culture in the case of Shakespeare and Dickens, as well as literary culture, from which literature itself derives – explains his own use of the word 'tradition'; which includes what is now known as the element of 'intertextuality', something more intrinsic to the very act of writing than 'influence'. There are precise ways, which Leavis points out, in which Jane Austen made George Eliot and Henry James possible.

Leavis's own judgements were also subject to change and *The Great Tradition* represents anything but his final view or that of his wife, Q. D. Leavis, with whom he closely collaborated, on the Brontës, Dickens, Conrad and D. H. Lawrence. What, however, remained constant throughout his career was a belief, no longer always shared by those who teach it, in the supreme importance of 'literature' and a sense of the responsibilities such a belief entails and which he himself (some say quixotically) assumed.

FURTHER READING

Bénichou, Paul (1973) *Le Sacre de l'écrivain, 1750–1830*, Librairie José Corti, Paris
Fumaroli, Marc (1980) *L'Age de l'éloquence*, Droz, Geneva
Leavis, F. R. (1937) *Revaluation*, Chatto & Windus, London
——(1948) *The Great Tradition*, Chatto & Windus, London
——(1953) *The Common Pursuit*, Chatto & Windus, London
——(1972) *Nor Shall My Sword*, Chatto & Windus, London
Marrou, Henri I. (1956) *A History of Education in Antiquity*, translated by George Lamb, Sheed & Ward, London
Mathieson, Margaret (1975) *Preachers of Culture*, Allen & Unwin, London
von Hallberg, Robert (ed.) (1983) *Canons*, University of Chicago Press, Chicago

ADDITIONAL WORKS CITED

Ackroyd, P. R. and Evans, C. F. (eds) (1970) *The Cambridge History of the Bible*, vol. 1, Cambridge University Press, Cambridge
Arnold, Matthew (1935a) *Culture and Anarchy*, edited by J. Dover Wilson, Cambridge University Press, Cambridge [first published 1869]
——(1935b) *Essays in Criticism*, 2nd series, Macmillan, London [first published 1888]
Barthes, Roland (1964) *Essais critiques*, Editions du Seuil, Paris
——(1984) *Le Bruissement de la langue*, Editions du Seuil, Paris
Eagleton, Terry (1983) *Literary Theory*, Basil Blackwell, Oxford
Leavis, F. R. (1930) *Mass Civilisation and Minority Culture*, The Minority Press, Cambridge
——(1935) 'Dr Richards, Bentham and Coleridge', *Scrutiny*, 3, 382–402
——(1938) 'Arnold as Critic', *Scrutiny*, 7, 319–32
Newbolt, Henry (1921) *Report to the Board of Education on the Teaching of English in England*, HMSO, London
Pound, Ezra (1954) *Literary Essays of Ezra Pound*, Faber & Faber, London
Richards, I. A. (1924) *The Principles of Literary Criticism*, Kegan Paul, Trench, Trubner, London
Smith, Barbara Herrnstein (1983) 'Value'. In R. von Hallberg (ed.), *Canons*, University of Chicago Press, Chicago
Stendhal (1928) *Racine et Shakespeare*, edited by H. Martineau, Le Divan, Paris [first published 1823 and 1825]

Strickland, Geoffrey (1981) *Structuralism or Criticism?*, Cambridge University Press, Cambridge

Verlaine, Paul (1884) *Jadis et naguère*, Charpentier, Paris

Voltaire (1828a) *Correspondance générale*, vol. 6, Baudouin, Paris

——(1828b) *Théâtre*, vol. 4, Baudouin, Paris

52

MARXIST CRITICISM

JOHN FROW

In a posthumously published fragment on method Walter Benjamin spoke of the temptation of analysing the literary text as though it were a 'thing in itself', a self-contained entity; and he likened literary tradition to a river, fed by numerous springs (or 'sources' – the German *Quellen* means both) and flowing for as far as the eye can see between finely outlined slopes. But, he went on, a Marxist literary theory will refuse the traditional substantialist categories, the familiarity of the 'landscape', and the sublimated interests the 'river' reflects:

> It doesn't seek the image of the clouds in this river. Even less does it turn away from it, to 'drink at the source' and pursue the 'thing itself' behind men's backs. Whose mill does the river drive? Who fishes in it? – these are the questions that critical theory asks, and it alters the image of the landscape by calling not only the physical but also the social forces at work in it by their names.
>
> (Benjamin, 1969, p. 1)

The core claim of Marxist criticism is that it cannot be ranked on the same level as other critical methods. It has a different task, works to a different urgency, asks different questions. It is or should be unlike any conventional discipline in its radical discomfort with the way things are, in its insistence on redefining – to switch metaphors – the contours of its field of study and what goes on inside this field, and in thinking this field in relation to its social determinations. However theoretically sophisticated it might become, it persists in asking crude and awkward questions about power, privilege and benefit.

At the same time it must be recognized that the questions asked by Marxist criticism derive as much from the disciplinary formations of general aesthetics and literary criticism as from an autonomous Marxist theory. The prestige of the aesthetic problematic inherited from German idealist philosophy, in particular, has, from the aesthetic anthropology of Marx's *1844 Manuscripts* (trans.

1964) and the passages on Greek art in his *Grundrisse* through to the totalizing aesthetic projects of Mehring, Lukács, Adorno, Bloch, Marcuse, Della Volpe, Jameson, and the East European academic theorists of realism, represented a continuous temptation to hypostatize and universalize the categories of art and literature. The explanation that links this preoccupation to the separation of Western Marxism from revolutionary praxis is too easy, but certainly one of Western Marxism's dominant features has been the tendency to substitute aesthetic for directly political concerns.

A number of distinct problems were posed for literary criticism and what we might anachronistically call cultural studies by the theoretical and political revolutions of Marxism. They included: first, a reformulation of the status of all symbolic activity (language, law, politics, religion, moral codes, art), such that it constituted a secondary and determinate domain of the social in relation to a primary domain of economic structures, processes and relations. The precise terms of this distinction, and of the relations it sets up between the two domains, are matters of deep contention, but some form of hierarchical ranking which stresses the greater social determinacy of one area of the social than another is central to all Marxist thinking. The architectural metaphor of the foundations and the superstructure of a building, which proposes that the upper levels rest upon and so in a sense are determined by the 'base', has been an influential way of thinking the causal relations involved, but its implications have also been widely contested; questions of the dialectical mediation or interchange between the different 'levels', of multiple and uneven structures of causality, and of the 'relative autonomy' of some areas of the social, have continuously accompanied the simpler metaphor.

If Marxism insists on the methodological separation of two domains of the social, it simultaneously supposes some sort of correlation, either in the form of a correspondence between the values produced in symbolic processes and the values arising from or serving the relations of material production, or in the more mediated form of the assertion of a generalized ruling-class control over relatively disparate areas of social life. In moving from a theory of social domains to a theory of the class agents who live them, we move from a theory of the 'superstructures' to a theory of ideology. Again, the term is contentious, but broadly speaking it designates the relativity of knowledge and belief to class interest. There are two extreme responses to the implications of the concept of ideology for literary criticism: either to read literary texts as a direct expression of class interest (this position is characteristic of so-called 'vulgar' or 'mechanical' materialism), or to exempt all or some literary texts from the realm of ideology. Most Marxist criticism works with a more differentiated and dialectical conception of ideology which allows it to define the class basis of literary production (in terms both of control of the apparatus of publishing and distribution, and of the structural imposition of ideas and values), and yet to recognize the ways in which discursive complexity (which in its turn of course has definite material conditions of existence) makes possible contradiction and even contestation.

Thus Marxist criticism, beginning with Marx and Engels, has consistently and productively worked with the paradox of a non-correlation between class position and aesthetic value. The paradigm case is that of the reactionary Balzac who produces a more valid knowledge of Restoration French society than do more 'progressive' writers free of Balzac's ruling-class sympathies. On the other hand, the concepts of ideology and class interest have forced attention to the possible role of writers and intellectuals in the revolutionary process. Much of the work of practising writers and of political activists – Brecht and Trotsky are exemplary figures – centres on questions of political commitment and effect. Overlaid on this debate throughout much of the twentieth century has been a fierce struggle concerning the political status of modernism and of formal innovation. The difficult counterpart of these issues has been that of the role of writers in the established socialist states – where 'commitment' has more often meant the demand for conformity to an official aesthetic.

One cluster of problems that was present in much of Marx's own thinking but was developed only somewhat later in the twentieth century has to do with the utopian content of literature or of aesthetic creation. The early Marxist concept of alienation (the importance of which only became apparent with the publication in 1932 of the *1844 Manuscripts*) supposes an essential (but historically developed) human nature which is distorted or repressed by the conditions of capitalist production. The reification of human relations in the production of commodities, in particular, turns social life into a play of surfaces abstracted from the deep structure of the social totality. Aesthetic creation then figures as something like an archetype of repressed human powers, and thus as a promise of a future in which history and a sense of the wholeness of being will be restored to humankind. Because it performs, or at least adumbrates, this totalizing function, literature and art are seen as general human capacities rather than as specific products of class antagonism.

Let me mention a final set of themes which, although there are throwaway sentences in Marx's writings which prefigure it, was also not properly developed until the 1930s. It concerns the material conditions of literary production – that is, the fact that it is among other things an economic activity and so belongs in part to the social 'base'. Thinking of literature as a historically specific system of production makes it easier to move away from essentialist understandings of literary discourse; it also helps in the move away from a relatively passive, 'expressive' conception of the working of texts towards a sense of their active intertextual relation to other representations of the real.

The growth of the mass media in the twentieth century probably did much to encourage attention to the systemic conditions of production, and in turn these questions seem to take on a particular intensity when they are applied to the mass media.

Marxist criticism is a diverse body of writing and it gives very diverse answers to the different problems that I have schematically identified. Posada (1969) gives a useful summary of what many of these answers have in common:

> Important sectors of Marxist criticism considered art an *ideal* translation of the *real* conditions of the historical process. Its task consisted in reflecting these more or less faithfully, and hence the interpretation of art should be an *analogon* of the (hopefully previous) interpretation of the given reality. On the one hand, mechanical materialism postulated a correlation between the evolution of the base and that of art; on the other, explicit or concealed Hegelianism made it into a direct 'expression' of the 'spirit' of a class, or the integrating element of a world-vision seen as a social group's global framework of representation of reality.
>
> (p. 217)

Let me set aside the mechanical materialist tradition (Plekhanov, Caudwell, most orthodox Soviet and East European criticism), which is of little theoretical interest, and group Marxist criticism into three main traditions, which I shall call the Hegelian, structuralist, and Gramscian traditions. By far the most important and fruitful of these in the twentieth century has been the Hegelian, and its most important representative was undoubtedly Georg Lukács.

Lukács's career began with a long pre-Marxist period and passed through a number of further phases. It seems possible, nevertheless, to map out a relatively unified conceptual schema underlying all his work. Its central categories are those of form and genre; totality and mediation; and the general and the concrete. To summarize: the 'forms' that Lukács describes in *Soul and Form* ([1911] trans. 1974) are historically mutable structures of consciousness which make possible certain kinds of knowledge of the real. They reach their maximum intensity in the aesthetic genres, which correspond to different and relatively stable modes of historical experience. In *History and Class Consciousness* ([1923] 1971a) this function is ascribed, in the realm of objective spirit, to that 'imputed class consciousness' which represents the most concentrated awareness of reality and its own real interests that a social class can attain. Aesthetic creation, which is marked by its unique degree of coherence, corresponds on the level of aesthetic form to the imputed consciousness or 'life form' which, in the case of the proletariat, is realized in the Party. The two categories are structurally identical. Thus the constant model through which Lukács (and later his disciple Goldmann) imagines the integration of levels within the social totality is one of a series of homologous and increasingly more expressive and concentrated structures, moving from the economic base through group consciousness (unformed class consciousness), through the historical 'forms' – the literary genre *or* concentrated class consciousness – to individual consciousness or the individual text.

The literary genre thus stands in a privileged relation to the historical period, but it also expresses the tension between the given historical 'form' (the structure of social life) and a transcendental form laid down in the genre as an absolute possibility. Under ideal conditions (the culture of the Greek epic, the transparent social order of achieved Communism) the sum of the literary genres would give immediate access to a totalized, coherent structure of knowledge corresponding to the *continuous* nature of the real. This continuity has, however, been distorted by the reification resulting from commodity production, and the immediacy of the social totality thus remains inaccessible except under conditions of revolutionary self-consciousness. Reflecting this loss of a sense of totality, the modernist movement in art brings about a confusion of genres and so produces only a distorted representation of the real. 'Realistic' representation remains a historical possibility, but only under certain conditions: political, on the one hand (the writer's identification with the progressive rationality of history), formal on the other (the use of features corresponding to the absolute structure of the genre; in the case of 'epic' writing, this means third-person and preterite narration, the creation of 'typical' and 'living' characters, the use of identification and catharsis, and so on). The 'organically developing work of art' must function as a piece of nature:

> The more 'artless' a work of art, the more it gives the effect of life and nature, the more clearly it exemplifies an actual concentrated reflection of its times and the more clearly it demonstrates that the only function of its form is the expression of this objectivity, this reflection of life in the greatest concreteness and clarity and with all its motivating contradictions.
>
> (Lukács, 1971b, p. 52)

Since the function of form is to negate itself, to be totally transparent, any laying bare of formal structure, any disjunction between world and fictional 'world', must destroy, along with the illusion of non-fictionality, the appearance of an objectively moving historical regularity.

It will be apparent that Lukács's central concerns are above all with questions of the representation of the real. Since the relation between 'content' and 'form' is understood in a manner parallel to that between 'base' and 'super-structure', the work of art comes to be understood as a secondary phenomenon, derivative of the reality it reflects. Its formal composition is (or should be) entirely subordinated to this task, and ultimately this entails an impatience with questions of form, and a hypostatization of certain historical genres (particularly the nineteenth-century realist novel) as absolute norms. Lukács produced criticism of considerable power which has come to form the core of orthodox Marxist criticism; but his merit is perhaps to have been essentially a great nineteenth-century critic.

Lukács's criticism is Hegelian in its insistence that the work of art is expressive of a structure which precedes it. This structure is not a brute reality, but rather the Real understood as a moment of a philosophico-historical process (the rational and orderly progression of History as it is grasped by the categories of dialectical thought). The specificity of textual structures and of the structure of literary production is of importance only in so far as it permits the shining through of this content.

Theodor Adorno's criticism is in many ways, and particularly in its committed defence of modernism and its concern with the irreducibility of formal structure, diametrically opposed to that of Lukács; but Adorno shares with him much of this Hegelian conceptual framework.

Where Lukács thinks of the literary text in terms of its representational potential, Adorno tends to think of it as a closed monad whose historicity is internal and formal rather than a function of its content. The development of artistic material corresponds (as the 'answer' to a 'problem') to the necessary stages of the self-realization of spirit, and so bears a direct but concealed testimony to the historical dialectic. The immanent determination of the truth of the work through this relation to an autonomous history of forms thus demands an uncompromising rejection of extra-aesthetic considerations. Social categories cannot be externally applied but only deduced from the work's formal structure, and 'it is only in the crystallization of its own law of form, not in the passive registration of objects, that art converges with the real' (Adorno, 1961, p. 164). Through its formal structure the work negates the empirical, and *thereby* hides empirical substance in itself. The degree of its 'negation of identity' becomes the criterion for the real and paradoxical identity of the work with social being; communication takes place precisely through the denial of referentiality implicit in the work's closure. Because of this constitution of the work through difference,

> the unresolved antagonisms of reality return in the work as immanent formal problems. . . . Relations of tension in works of art are crystallized in a pure form there, and by their emancipation from the factual façade of the everyday encounter the essence of reality.
>
> (Adorno, 1984, p. 16)

It is by means of a purely immanent analysis, then, that Adorno proceeds not to a concrete socio-historical description of the text but rather to a clarification of the historical dialectic. The categories through which this dialectic realizes itself are the historically developing poles of the individual and the general, of freedom and system, and of subject and object. Around the given relationship at any time of subject to object converge all other manifestations of social being. From it the path is opened to an understanding of the social function of the individual and the balance maintained between him or her and the social order; of the mutual determination in art of form and content, which is both equivalent to and a measure of the relationship of subject/object; and of dialectical thought itself, which reflects in the process of its formation the central shifts in the movement of history.

Much of Walter Benjamin's work depends upon a similar ability to move freely from one domain of being to another, to read any one moment of the social as possessing a kind of expressive radiance such that it can be used to illuminate other moments informed by the same historical meaning. Take the theme of the experience of shock, which Benjamin elaborates in his essay 'On Some Motifs in Baudelaire' (*Illuminations*, 1969). Beginning as part of a general meditation on the quality of modern urban and capitalist experience, especially in its organization by different modes of communication (narration, information, journalistic sensation), the concept of shock is then developed in relation to Freud's account in *Beyond the Pleasure Principle* (1920) of the link between the psyche's defence against external stimuli and the formation of unconscious memory traces. In Benjamin's version (1969, pp. 160–2), the greater the degree of consciousness involved in parrying external shocks, the more these stimuli are incorporated into conscious experience, or *Erlebnis*, and the more they are therefore sterilized for poetic experience, or *Erfahrung*. Quite different modes of temporality and memory correspond to these different forms. The experience of shock is said to be central to Baudelaire's poetry, both as a formal principle of generic rupture and as a registration of the modern experience of the city, and especially of the crowd. But beyond this, the experience of shock is said to be characteristic of a large number of features of an industrial society. Technical changes like the invention of the match and the telephone lead to a mechanization of life and the building of the shock-mechanism into everyday experience. The violence of urban traffic does the same, and the technology of film, based on the succession of discrete and rapidly moving images, is said to correspond to the new, mechanical organization of stimuli. This principle corresponds, indeed, to the whole structure of modern work: 'The shock experience by the passer-by in the crowd corresponds to the "experience" of the worker at his machinery' (p. 176) for example, at the conveyor belt. Finally, gambling is said to work according to the same principle; it involves the same alienation from the continuity of tradition as does industrial work, the same submission to a mechanical process, the same irrelevance of experience (*Erfahrung*).

Now, clearly, much of this involves a purely metaphorical connection; and this is one of Adorno's reproaches against Benjamin when he writes: 'Through-out your text there is a tendency to relate the pragmatic contents of Baudelaire's work immediately to adjacent features in the social history of his time, prefer-ably economic features' ('Letters to Walter Benjamin', in Bloch *et al.*, 1977, p. 128). Adorno himself is of course hardly immune from such a criticism – think, for example, of his analyses of the twelve-tone row in modern music through an equation between its regressive and self-repressive organization and the alienation inherent in the general system of capitalist production (1973, pp. 65–7). Fredric Jameson tends similarly to set up deliberate and often provocative connections between quite disparate domains of the social – between, for example, impressionist painting, the abstraction and the rationaliz-ation of visual experience in nineteenth-century capitalism, and the reification of human relations by commodity production; or between a vast range of 'postmodern' aesthetic forms and the structures of late capitalism. Jameson indeed turns this into a methodological principle. He writes in *Marxism and Form* (1971) of dialectical thinking as being

> marked by the will to link together in a single figure two incommensurable realities, two independent codes or systems of signs, two heterogeneous and asymmetrical terms: spirit and matter, the data of individual experience and the vaster forms of institutional society, the language of existence and that of history.
>
> (pp. 6–7)

And a few pages later he adds that in the developed form of this method

> the language of causality gives way to that of analogy or homology, of parallelism. Now the construction of the microcosm, of the cultural continuum – whether it be the formal history of costume or of religious movements, the fate of stylistic conventions or the rise and fall of epistemology as a philosophical issue – will include the analogy with the socio-economic macrocosm or infrastructure as an implied comparison in its very structure, permitting us to transfer the terminology of the latter to the former in ways that are often very revealing.
>
> (p. 10)

This I think is the core of a Hegelian–Marxist mode of analysis: a conception of the social order as what Althusser calls an expressive totality, where a single central principle of meaningfulness (which in turn is a moment of a rational, end-directed historical process) infuses all the diverse, apparently hetero-geneous domains of the social with its own informing essence. In Jameson's case this conception is linked to a totalizing interpretative method which moves from the text to its encompassing horizons in a manner which is continuous and integrative (Jameson, 1981, pp. 75–6). The form of self-reflexivity which is built into this method allows on the one hand for competing theories and methodologies to be recognized as structural effects of particular horizons, and so subsumed as partial moments within the Marxist dialectic, and on the other for Marxist criticism to relate itself to a particular historical conjuncture – but in such a way that it renders this conjuncture transparent and so frees itself from its own relativity.

I spoke before of two other thematic areas which were elaborated only in the twentieth century. One is the anthropological and utopian humanism which is present in much of Marx's own writings and which was worked out most fully in Ernst Bloch's *The Principle of Hope* (1986) and in Marcuse's attempt to use the Freudian concepts of repression and sublimation within a Marxist framework. The other is the understanding of literature as a system of production. In its early stages this is developed largely by Brecht and Benjamin (with a strong influence from left-wing Soviet theorists). The central move is to theorize literary production as a production of commodities within an industry with specific relations of production, and specific technological underpinnings; the theatre, for example, is understood in terms not only of dramatic values but of institutional ownership and control, economic and technological conditions of existence, and a range of economic and social functions (the argument is then that the structure of the theatrical apparatus frames and limits the possible political effects of theatre). Benjamin's essay on new technologies of mechanical reproduction of artworks ('The Work of Art in the Age of Mechanical Reproduction', in *Illuminations*, 1969) extends this analysis to conceptualize the effects of capitalist modes of production on the system of aesthetic values and on the interrelationship between domains of value (for example, between canonical and non-canonical domains and between different media and different stages of technological development).

The concept of production is central to the second major tradition of Marxist criticism, which I have called 'structuralist'. In part this involves a resumption of work on the institutional structure of literary production, but in the work of Pierre Macherey and Terry Eagleton the tension between a potentially reductive account of institutional determinations and a conception of literary discourse as a productive practice is resolved by an emphasis on the latter, on the productive work done by texts on other discursive structures. This entails a move away from the Hegelian problematic of representation.

That problematic depends upon the assumption of an ontological split between the real and its secondary reproduction. The structuralist tradition of Althusser and Macherey, by contrast, seeks to overcome this dichotomy, on the one hand by grouping literature with other productive activities, on the other hand by refusing to think of literary representations as being different *in kind* from what they 'represent': the real is never absolutely other because it is itself semiotically organized. It is always already invested with a structure which, far from being immanent, is a historical result. You could say that a properly dialectical 'Hegelian' account of representation would reach the same conclusion, since dialectical thinking supposes that both the natural and the social worlds are the historical outcomes of human praxis, so that there can never be an absolute split between subject and object; but structuralism takes this as its starting point rather than as its conclusion.

The theoretical innovation of structuralism consists, then, in its displacement of the problematic of an expressive or representational relation between two disparate realms. The conception of literature as a production process implies that on the one hand, as a produced object, the text is seen as a component of the general system of social production, that the 'real' is not its object but its institutional conditions of existence; and on the other hand, as a productive activity, the text is seen as a distinct practice of signification which is related not to a nondiscursive truth but to other practices of signification. In both cases literary discourse is treated as a reality in its own right, a practice which cannot be subordinated to an external reality which in the last instance determines its own representation or expression in discourse. It is not just that literary discourse mediates the real through a specific and conventional structure of logical categories, for this is true of all language. The point is rather that 'the autonomy of the writer's discourse is established from its relationship with other uses of language', that it is 'a contestation of language rather than a representation of reality' (Macherey, 1978, pp. 59–61). Rather than being the transposition of a world posited as absolute and absolutely known (but which is in fact a construct of other texts), the literary text is seen as

the production of certain produced representations of the real into an imaginary object. If it distantiates history, it is not because it transmutes it to fantasy, shifting from one ontological gear to another, but because the significations it works into fiction are already representations of reality rather than reality itself. The text is a tissue of meanings, perceptions and responses which inhere in the first place in that imaginary production of the real which is ideology.

(Eagleton, 1976b, p. 75)

The access of the text to the real is always oblique, and in particular is always overdetermined by the structure of the literary system.

Since the representations worked by texts belong to the realm of ideology, literary discourse is both of the same order as the ideological and yet is capable of a reflexive, self-distancing relation to it. The crucial questions for structuralist-Marxist literary criticism are thus epistemological: what are the mechanisms of the production of literary knowledge, how and to what extent can this knowledge be differentiated from ideology, how does it relate to scientific knowledge? In exploring these questions it runs the risk of once again hypostatizing literary discourse as a distinct ontological domain; it does also, however, open up the possibility of a detailed analysis of specifically textual processes which is nevertheless connected to an analysis (via the concept of ideology) of class power.

I have called the third tradition of Marxist criticism 'Gramscian', and I shall mention it only briefly. I mean by this term, not a particular allegiance to Gramsci's thought but a more diffuse attention to the specific conditions of ruling class hegemony. This would include, for example, analyses of literature as a historical institution (much of Raymond Williams's work belongs here, as does Eagleton's *The Function of Criticism*, 1984); of the class function of intellectuals; and of the contradictory interrelationship between canonical and non-canonical cultural forms as they are used in the formation of a 'national-popular' culture (the work of Stuart Hall and the Birmingham School, much of Tony Bennett's work, and more generally the emerging tradition of cultural studies could be included here).

Let me finish by defining what I think the current force of Marxist criticism is. It resides in a four-fold problematization which in part overlaps with the questions posed by other forms of criticism but which has both a range and a political intensity that only feminist theory can match.

The first has to do with the status of theoretical concepts and with the effects of theoretical practice. The precondition of Marxist criticism is a reflection upon its own conditions of existence – that is, upon the material and discursive conditions of the 'relative autonomy' of the cultural sphere, and upon the disciplinary network (including the relation to other critical methods) within which it is grounded.

The second concerns the status of its object: instead of taking the concept of Literature for granted, Marxist criticism has attempted to theorize the historical constitution of Literature as a system of normative values with a complex relation to class power; and it has refused the obviousness of this object in order to replace it with a different one – the processes of constitution themselves, both at a systemic level and at the level of interpretative paradigms.

This then merges with the third area of problematization, which has to do with the practices of literary study. Here the question of value is crucial; the major shift operated by Marxist criticism seems to me to have been to move away from understanding value as conformity to a set of unchanging aesthetic attributes in order to define it positionally and differentially – that is, as a function of the uses of texts. This shift has implications for understanding the process of canon-formation and for the ordinary critical practices of reading, which now neither work upon a given object nor derive from it an inherent value.

The fourth area, finally, is that of the field of relations within which the object of criticism is to be situated. This is not a merely taxonomic question, since it involves the complex and changing relations of authority and legitimacy between discursive domains and the differential status of the knowledges they produce. It is, ultimately, a question about the class control of discourse, about the possibilities of discursive contestation, and about ways of changing the image of the landscape (and eventually the landscape itself).

FURTHER READING

Benjamin, Walter (1969) *Illuminations*, translated by Harry Zohn, Schocken, New York
Bennett, Tony (1979) *Formalism and Marxism*, Methuen, London
Bloch, Ernst *et al.* (1977) *Aesthetics and Politics*, New Left Books, London
Eagleton, Terry (1976a) *Marxism and Literary Criticism*, Methuen, London
——(1976b) *Criticism and Ideology*, New Left Books, London
——(1981) *Walter Benjamin, or, Towards a Revolutionary Criticism*, Verso, London
Frow, John (1986) *Marxism and Literary History*, Basil Blackwell, Oxford
Jameson, Fredric (1971) *Marxism and Form*, Princeton University Press, Princeton
——(1981) *The Political Unconscious*, Methuen, London
Moretti, Franco (1983) *Signs Taken for Wonders*, Verso, London
Sharratt, Bernard (1982) *Reading Relations: Structures of Literary Production: A Dialectical Text/Book*, Harvester, Brighton
Sprinker, Michael (1986) *Imaginary Relations: Aesthetics and Ideology in the Theory of Historical Materialism*, Verso, London
Trotsky, Leon (1960) *Literature and Revolution*, translated by Rose Strunsky, University of Michigan Press, Ann Arbor [first published 1924]

ADDITIONAL WORKS CITED

Adorno, Theodor W. (1961) *Noten zur Literatur II*, Suhrkamp, Frankfurt am Main
——(1973) *Philosophy of Modern Music*, translated by A. Mitchell and W. Bloomster, Sheed & Ward, London
——(1984) *Aesthetic Theory*, translated by C. Lenhardt, Routledge & Kegan Paul, London
Benjamin, Walter (1970) 'Fragment über Methodenfragen einer marxistischen Literatur-Analyse', *Kursbuch*, 20
Bloch, Ernst (1986) *The Principle of Hope*, 3 vols, translated by N. Plaice *et al.*, MIT Press, Cambridge
Eagleton, Terry (1984) *The Function of Criticism*, Verso, London
Lukács, Georg (1971a) *History and Class Consciousness*, translated by Rodney Livingstone, MIT Press, Cambridge [first published 1923]
——(1971b) *Writer and Critic*, translated by A. D. Kahn, Grosset & Dunlap, New York
——(1974) *Soul and Form*, translated by Anna Bostock, MIT Press, Cambridge [first published 1911]
Macherey, Pierre (1978) *A Theory of Literary Production*, translated by G. Wall, Routledge & Kegan Paul, London

Marx, Karl (1964) *Economic and Philosophic Manuscripts of 1844*, translated by M. Milligan, International Publishers, New York

Posada, F. (1969) *Lukács, Brecht y la situacion actual del realismo socialista*, Editorial Galerna, Buenos Aires

53

THE NEW CRITICISM

RICK RYLANCE

The new criticism is the name given to the major movement in American criticism this century. Its origins are to be found in the 1920s, and its developed theory was articulated by 1950. Thereafter it exerted a powerful influence on the practice of criticism and student study of literature until the late 1960s, and has remained a benchmark for subsequent developments. Recent Anglo-American post-structuralist theories, for instance, have frequently proceeded through rejection of its proposals, or those of its British equivalent, Practical Criticism.

In fact the American theory found the initial impetus for its ideas in British sources, principally the work of the Cambridge critic I. A. Richards and the American expatriate poet and critic T. S. Eliot. Moreover, several of the major New Critics were, especially in their early careers, powerfully attracted to English culture. Indeed, many leading New Critics worked at English universities and one, Cleanth Brooks, served from 1964 to 1966 as cultural attaché at the American Embassy in London. This enthusiasm for what was perceived as the English way of life was then applied to the American situation, particularly that of the deep South. In respect of general cultural analysis, as well as critical method, there were real similarities between American and British theoretical developments between the wars, and the New Critics and their British colleagues did much to establish the discipline of English literature as it is today, for it was in these years that its characteristic methods and approaches were laid down.

That said, however, it would be wrong to lose sight of the New Criticism as a specifically American phenomenon. It began with the work of a group of theorists at Vanderbilt University in Tennessee. Most prominent among these were John Crowe Ransom (1888–1974), Allen Tate (1899–1979) and Robert Penn Warren (b. 1905). All were poets of considerable reputation, and Tate and Warren were novelists also. All were academics, though Tate's career was more diverse. Initially they addressed specifically Southern concerns in their general cultural analysis, but they developed a critical method which, while influenced by their general theory, was nevertheless distinctive and flexible enough to be transferable. The name of this method of analysis was 'close-reading' or (in Britain) 'practical criticism'. Subsequently this distinctively Southern criticism became national, and other critics, whilst rejecting the broad cultural attitudes wholly or in part, nevertheless shared the critical emphases. René Wellek, a leading New Critical theorist since the forties, was born in Vienna in 1903, educated in Czechoslovakia, fled to Britain from the German and Russian threats, worked at University College London from 1935, and settled in the United States in 1939 where he taught at Yale. Wellek thus brought not only a range of cosmopolitan experience to the New Criticism, but also a different and enriching intellectual tradition. Meanwhile native New Criticism found an intellectual identity in the North also. Austin Warren – Wellek's collaborator on the influential *Theory of Literature* (1949) – was born (1899) in Massachusetts and taught in Boston, Iowa and Michigan. W. K. Wimsatt (1907–75) took his PhD at Yale in 1939 and taught there throughout his career. Cleanth Brooks (b. 1906), a Vanderbilt graduate who taught from 1932 to 1947 at Louisiana State University with R. P. Warren, also settled at Yale in 1947. Even the founders moved further afield. Warren, too, settled in the North and taught at Yale and Minnesota. Ransom left Tennessee in 1937 for Kenyon College in Ohio where he taught until retirement in 1959, and Tate pursued his career at Princeton, New York and Minnesota whilst also working as a publisher and broadcaster. The New Criticism thus became national, even international, and dominated the style and assumptions of American criticism; even its opponents – like the 'Chicago School' of the 1950s – seem in retrospect (as George Watson puts it) more a heresy than an alternative faith (1964, pp. 222–3).

What then were the developments that began regionally but led to the establishment of a national critical style? Ransom, Tate and Warren were at the centre of two formative organizations: the 'Fugitive' circle in the 1920s and then, in the 1930s, the 'Agrarian' movement. Both had important bearings on the formation of the New Criticism. The Fugitives were a Vanderbilt-based group established informally in 1915. Their journal, *The Fugitive*, published poetry and essays by the group until 1924 and formed a small part of the 'Southern Renaissance' in American literature in these years (as found, for example, in the work of William Faulkner and Tennessee Williams). It also consciously fostered a receptive attitude to the new writing coming from European modernism. (T. S. Eliot's was particularly important.) The new literary techniques and the new critical attitudes of European modernism were decisive in the development of the New Criticism, but the 'Fugitive' name also suggests disaffection and withdrawal in the manner of the romantic artist alienated from his society, and alienated pessimism can be seen also in the

Agrarian movement of the 1930s. Though in many respects still a literary movement, the Agrarians had a wider programme stemming from the political and social views of the Vanderbilt intellectuals. By the late 1920s Ransom had abandoned the writing of poetry for aesthetics and cultural criticism influenced by his perception of the cultural and political situation of the South. Tate, too, and Warren became interested in the region's distinctive cultural identity and political prospects.

The essentials of the Agrarian outlook were set out by Ransom in *God Without Thunder* (1930), though a collective volume from the same year, *I'll Take My Stand* (original title 'A Tract Against Communism') 'By Twelve Southerners' (including Ransom, Tate and Warren), was a more effective manifesto and launched the movement. The Agrarians recommended a return to a Southern culture based on the small farm and the agricultural town, and the recovery of the traditional virtues associated with the 'Old South' prior to the Civil War. This traditional culture, it was argued, had been destroyed by science, industry and big business, which were identified with the North. The culture of the South – based on the community's relationship with the land – was celebrated by Tate, in his well-known elegiac poem 'Ode to the Confederate Dead' (1928) and his biographies of major figures of the Confederacy, *Stonewall Jackson* (1928) and *Jefferson Davis* (1929). Its recovery, the Agrarians proposed, would mean that the cultivated sensibility and love of the natural world would flourish, that industrialism and its scientific 'abstractions' would wither, and social harmony would be found through a neo-feudal paternalism modelled on the old plantation life. As the arts and learning prospered, so too would rural skills and crafts and the general customs and beliefs of a people living close to the soil. It would be a society of culture, plenty and God.

There was, at first, much to appeal to Southerners in this. Not only did the emergency of the Depression, beginning to strike hard into the South, encourage reforming proposals (particularly those which blamed the North), but the Agrarian platform appealed to well-established myths and beliefs, including the idea of the 'Southern gentleman and his belle', and the chivalric aristocracy of the South, which drew on Scott and other British writers of a Romantic-Tory disposition. (Henry James portrays this, partly satirically, in the figure of the high-conservative Basil Ransom in *The Bostonians*, 1886.) But the Agrarian proposals also appealed to fundamentalist Christianity which had strong connections with the Ku Klux Klan, then numbering over six million. Ransom opportunistically defended fundamentalism in *God Without Thunder* and mixed political with literary and religious perception. The god without thunder alluded both to the lifelessness of modern faith (especially in the North) and to Eliot's grim poem *The Waste Land* (1922) which influenced pessimistic conservative perceptions of the modern world on both sides of the Atlantic. Either way, the only solution to this crisis appeared to be a revived regional culture, though the theory of this culture seemed to owe more to literature than to life. As a result Agrarianism failed. It attracted some popular attention for five or six years but it was widely perceived to be sentimental in inspiration and to have few practical policies to offer, though Ransom studied hard at economics for a year or two.

Ransom's borrowing from *The Waste Land* was not accidental, for there are similarities between Agrarian ideas and those of the literary right in Britain. Tate, for instance, had connections with 'The Distributists' founded by G. K. Chesterton and Hilaire Belloc, who also looked for the redistribution of property and a neo-feudal remodelling of society. More significant were the links between the cultural ideas articulated by Ransom and those being explored by influential literary critics in Britain, principally Eliot and F. R. and Q. D. Leavis (see Mulhern, 1979). Agrarian theories about the past, Ransom and Tate acknowledged, were drawn from English models, and their ideas of social organization were based on English ideas of the village as the focus of the good life. Hostility to industrialism, and the celebration of the village's socially-integrative, life-enhancing local culture are widespread in the literary and social analyses of Eliot and the Leavises. In the 1930s, the argument went, such communities could just be found in the memories of the living, but were best expressed in Renaissance English literature, that is, just before England's disintegration into a mercantile and then an industrial nation. Thereafter, this cultural paradigm could be found enacted in the living language and values of the best writing. These arguments were taken over pretty much wholesale by the Agrarians.

Both the Agrarians and their British counterparts, then, shared a sour perception of the modern world, and looked for solutions in a redrawing of society based upon myths of the rural past and the importance of literature. If both groups were a little hazy in their perception of the political means for such a social revolution, neither was in doubt about general aims and concepts. In a world drifting to the dogs, it was literature which best carried and represented desired cultural standards. The significance of the Agrarian movement, therefore, was its articulation of a perception of the world which created a modern role for literary study. In response to a culture increasingly scientific and industrial, literature was to act as the communicator and preserver of central human values. And if the Vanderbilt intellectuals proved ineffective in launching Agrarian politics, they did not prove so as founders of their literary programme. Here they knew what they were about. In defence of vanishing standards, the New Criticism became a populist movement which aimed at the teaching of criticism on a mass scale. Ransom, in his essay, 'Criticism, Inc' of 1937, argued for the establishment of English Departments as departments of *criticism*, not departments for the study of language or literary history or other scholarship. Criticism was to become as professional as a limited company, and was to take its wares into the world (see Ransom, 1964, pp. 327–50). Thus, leading New Critics became important in the formation and staffing of university departments (Ransom founded the Kenyon School of English for example), and several ran leading critical journals. Ransom edited the influential *Kenyon Review* from 1939 (see Ransom, 1951b), which in 1942 merged with *The Southern Review* edited since 1934 by Warren and Cleanth Brooks. Tate edited *The Sewanee Review* and *Hound and Horn*, broadcast for CBS, and, like Warren after him, was poetry consultant for the Library of Congress. But most important, perhaps, among these public activities was the influence the New Criticism had upon classroom practice through the establishment of a critical method and the preparation of textbooks.

Brooks and Warren edited the most important of these: *An Approach to Literature* (1936), *Understanding Poetry* (1938: probably the most successful classroom anthology ever), *Understanding Fiction* (1943), and (Brooks with Robert Heilman) *Understanding Drama* (1945). Each was prefaced by a 'Letter to the Teacher' setting out a regime of use and a defence of its cultural occasion which lamented the corrupting effect of popular writing on the young, and stressed the need to introduce students to quality literature to extend their experience and guard against mournful self-regard, to familiarize them with moral concepts, and to establish a secure sense of judgement and a lasting sense of worth. The anthologies included carefully set-out proposals for the conduct of literary study and advice on what teachers were to guide their students to seek. The selection of material was large (though short works or extracts were obviously favoured) and included specimen analyses at regular intervals. Often these are highly judgemental and now appear prejudiced. Shelley, for instance, a poet much disliked by the New Critics (partly for his leftist politics), emerges from *Understanding Poetry* as a slovenly and cliché-ridden writer, full of cheap effects and intellectual fancies (Brooks and Warren, 1938, pp. 463–73). Here apparent judgements about poetic worth and detail are in fact displaced (and rather dishonest) assessments of a writer's beliefs. This dislike of Shelley was part of a more general anti-romantic stance. For if the New Critics can be seen in some senses as the heirs of Romanticism – in their anti-industrialism and celebration of the unique importance of poetry and the imagination – they were also opposed to what they saw as romantic poetry's slapdash technique, rampant individualism, moral insecurity, frequent atheism (many of the leading New Critics were Christians) and political radicalism. Shelley was frequently the whipping-boy on all these accounts, while others – like Wordsworth and occasionally Keats – come out better.

The critical method on which these anthologies were based was articulated initially by Ransom, whose two books *The World's Body* (1938) and, especially, *The New Criticism* (1941) – which helped name the movement – were important early formulations. I will concentrate here on the latter. The new criticism discussed in Ransom's book is that of Richards, Eliot and Yvor Winters, an American critic who shared some New Critical views. Ransom assesses what is usable in these writers' work for American criticism, acting as a customs officer for the importation of foreign ideas, and rummaging through Eliot's and Richards's work pretty thoroughly. Richards, for instance, is too scientific in outlook, too enthusiastic for reductive psychology, and gives too much attention to the reader rather than the work. This is the first of the New Critical principles; criticism should focus on the 'poem itself' and not the reader or author. (New Critics almost always speak of lyric poetry in their generalizations.) Richards's criticism is too *affective*; that is, oriented towards the feelings the poem arouses in the reader, rather than the calm description of textual detail. Nevertheless his theories do offer:

> a dramatic setting for a furious effort towards bigger and better knowledge. I believe they suit a sort of pioneering, start-at-the-bottom Americanism, and are an excellent strategy for us, as I idealize our national temper and prospects of knowledge.
>
> (Ransom, 1941, p. 6)

The language of this quotation is noteworthy, and very typical of Ransom's style. It sounds like a political speech, and it is possible to read *The New Criticism* in this way, as a kind of displaced political rhetoric addressed through literature to a stumbling nation which is by turns idealized and lambasted.

Ransom does, however, have concrete proposals for criticism. Criticism is the study of form and structure. Literature can offer a high emotional content, but this passion is always mediated by the poem's formal structure and particular detail, and it is this that the critic studies. It is because the New Critics tended to emphasize the formal organization of poems that they are sometimes called *formalist*, in a negative sense implying that they neglect matters of content or response; and, as we shall see, the problem of content (or belief) is a tricky area for Ransom's theory and those of other New Critics. Nevertheless, the theoretical outline Ransom proposes in *The New Criticism* remained fundamental to New Critical procedures.

For Ransom a poem develops a 'dramatic situation' (p. 62), and this forms its structural principle; that is, 'the poem develops its local particularities while it progresses towards its functional completion' (p. 58). Just as a drama has a plot, but also features which detain our interest as the plot progresses (character, language, milieu), so in all significant works of literature our experience of reading is a structure of interlocking elements, some of which help the completion of the narrative or argument, while others complicate this in various ways. These may, for instance, introduce reservations about the moral status of ostensible heroes, or doubts about the direction and details of an argument, or make one or more features ironic. Thus the work is experienced as a system of tensions which may operate without ultimate solution, and this is the sign of a truly valuable work of art. Whereas inferior or popular works – the terms tend to be interchangeable in New Critical theory – offer simple solutions or messages, 'mature' works resist easy satisfactions. Nevertheless, quality literature is not messily incomplete or indecisive, for whilst it may ironize or complicate, the various components are integrated into a satisfying, 'organic' whole whereby one element balances another. The poem is thus like a complex living entity – in fact, like life itself:

> The texture of a poem is the heterogeneous character of its detail, which either fills in the logical outline or else overflows it a little. And it may be said to be imperatively a character to be looked for in anything living, such as 'living force', even if it is not a human force; life is such a prodigal kind of being, so much in excess of its own biological functioning.
>
> (Ransom, 1941, p. 163)

As in this passage, Ransom separates the structure of a poem into two features. These he calls main *structure* (or sometimes logic, or argument) and local *texture* (or sometimes density, or particularity). The critical interpretation of a poem thus consists of integrating the two components, of spotting how they balance and enable one another, and this is a significant feature of all New Critical analysis.

This balancing act is central to Ransom's account of poetic structure and, as might be expected, has an explicit political bearing:

> A poem is a democratic state, hoping not to be completely ineffective, not to fail ingloriously in the business of a state, by reason of constitutional scruple through which it restrains itself faithfully from a really imperious degree of organization. It wants its citizens to retain their personalities and enjoy their natural interests. But a scientific discourse is a totalitarian state. Its members are not regarded as citizens, and have not inalienable rights to activities of their own, but are only functions defined according as the state may need them to contribute to its effectiveness.
>
> (1941, pp. 43–4)

Ransom was fond of this topical analogy (he repeats it for instance in his 1941 essay 'Criticism as Pure Speculation'; see Ransom, 1951a, pp. 646–7) and it is also used by Tate (see Tate, 1952, p. 146). It formed a significant part of early New Critical thinking, for not only does it make clear the difference between art and science (to the latter's detriment), but it also defines the social responsibilities of art. In addition to alarm about Hitler and Stalin, there is also the anxiety of the Southern writer concerned to defend the integrity of his own locale: 'The relation of Dramatic Situation to Argument is analogous to the relation, in politics, of Local and Personal Autonomy to the Effective State' (Ransom, 1941, p. 62). In poem and State alike, texture, the apparently 'anti-structural' principle, provides the field of action and validity for the structure.

Conversely, though, the overall form of the work of art makes the individual details significant. In the essay 'Forms and Citizens' in *The World's Body* (1938), Ransom argues that literary form is the inherited component of literature just as manners are the inherited form of social behaviour, or property the inherited form of economic life. In all cases form 'mediates' the object to us and checks individualism or scatty innovation. Further, it is convention and form which create the world's desirability and the appreciation of its mystery and beauty. In Bolshevik Russia even sex is now reduced to 'its pure biological business' with the disappearance of love-taboos. Humanity is reduced merely to 'efficient animality'. Thus Ransom produces an American version of T. S. Eliot's famous declaration in the introduction to *For Lancelot Andrewes* (1928) – classicism in art, royalism in politics and Anglo-Catholicism in religion – and opts for 'a program going something like this: In manners, aristocratic; in religion, ritualistic; in art, traditional' (Ransom, [1938] 1964, p. 42). This was echoed by Tate and others. In *Reactionary Essays* (1936), Tate fulminated against the New Criticism's opponents, the 'spiritual cannibalism' of the American Literary left, at its strongest in the 1930s and best found in the work of Edmund Wilson (see Lasch, 1973), and the 'moral Fascism' of contemporary humanism and faith in science.

Despite these political convictions, however, the problem of belief remained a difficulty for New Critics. They were men of passionate conviction, and yet they proposed a critical theory which seems to advocate democratic pluralism, a balancing of argument and counter-argument. Ransom himself in *The New Criticism* is unsure of the status of beliefs and ideas in works of art. Against Richards he argues for the importance of overall logical, intellectual structure; against Eliot and Winters, however, he argues that literature should *not* contain any statement of formal belief. He claims that Dante is a better poet than Shelley because his views are better (Ransom, 1941, pp. 207–8), yet 'the moralistic critic is an impaired critic' (p. 215). These contradictions were not lost on Ransom's contemporaries. Winters, for example, in a damaging reply to Ransom's critique of his work, pointed out that Ransom's 'great embarrassment as a theorist is that he knows that the poet cannot dispense with rational statement . . . yet he does not know what to do with the rational content, how to account for it or evaluate it' ([1943] 1959, p. 95.) Ransom therefore, claims Winters, has a poor conception of morality, and continually confuses ethical positions with mere didacticism. Even his disapproval of the latter stems not from an assessment of the rightness or wrongness of any moral claim, but from an aesthete's suspicion of action. Ransom, then, despite his ambitions to make crticicism morally and humanly central, ends with a reduced, even amoral, theory. The relish for local texture is pictured by Winters as an end in itself, a cult of sensibility deaf to moral circumstance. Similarly, Lionel Trilling, in 'The Meaning of a Literary Idea' (1949), argued against Wellek and Warren's claim in *Theory of Literature* that poems can only make use of ideas when they cease to be ideas and become symbols or myths. Trilling pointed out that such a conception would surprise many artists, that as a moral claim it was dubious, and as an aesthetic claim seemed to conceal an anxiety concerning the 'legitimacy of contemplation' itself (Trilling, [1949] 1970, p. 287).

The problem of belief and context in literature dogged New Criticism throughout and was never settled satisfactorily. For Ransom and Tate the problem was primarily political, but for other critics it had different dimensions. Many New Critics were sincere Christians. Ransom and Brooks were Anglicans, Tate and Wimsatt Catholics. Wimsatt tackled the problem of religious conviction and the New Critical approach to literature in 'Poetry and Christian Thinking' (1951). He found no difficulty in the idea that poetry gloried in the 'inherently ambiguous and polysemous nature of verbal discourse' (see Wimsatt, 1970, p. 268). This was perfectly compatible with Christian revelation, because, although poetry may conflict with the truths of faith, none the less in its very being poetry was spiritual, and as such it sided with religion against their common enemy, science. As Lionel Trilling noted in 'The Meaning of a Literary Idea', this turned literature into a substitute religion, and this dualistic perception had been apparent from the start. Tate in 1940 asserted 'the belief, philosophically tenable, in a radical discontinuity between the physical and the spiritual realm', and declared that 'the higher forms of literature offer us the only complete, and thus the most responsible, version of our experience' (see Tate, 1952, p. 146). But this was a contradiction, for, as Murray Krieger pointed out, the New Criticism never settled a fundamental problem: do works of art refer to a world outside themselves, or are they self-referring and self-generating, living an independent life of their own? The difficulty for the New Critics stemmed from the contradiction of trying to maintain these two opposed positions at the same time (Krieger, [1956] 1977, pp. 135–6).

None the less, it is easy to see why the New Criticism became so successful and so popular. It articulated a political and spiritual view of the world which was in tune with the hardening attitudes of the Cold War of the 1950s when the difference between capitalism and Communism was seen to reside in the former's respect for spiritual values. Art, in New Critical theory, seemed an autonomous entity, composed and permanent in contrast to the strident demands for 'realism' made by left-wing theorists. Meanwhile at a practical-critical level the techniques of the New Criticism were equally attractive. The method was highly portable and adapted to classroom practice; it was cheap in equipment, requiring only the 'words on the page' (preferably in approved anthologies) and not the resources of scholarly libraries; it had a clear sense of purpose and a coherently worked out set of aims and objectives; it required relatively little prior training or learning by teachers or students alike; its terminology and jargon was carefully adapted from that already in use, though standard meanings were often altered (for an acknowledgement of this see Brooks and Warren, 1943, pp. xvi–xvii); it drew upon and helped develop a sense of mission and professional identity and expertise; it drew to it the glamour of the new, the topical and the innovative; it could generate a high yield of interpretation apparently very quickly and – within the protocols set – of high and verifiable quality; and its methods and results looked neutral and objective. To test this claim I close with an account of a piece of New Criticism in action.

Cleanth Brooks's *The Well Wrought Urn: Studies in the Structure of Poetry* (1947) is classic New Criticism. It consists of ten chapter-length studies of individual poems (*Macbeth* is treated as a poem), flanked by statements of theory and principle which are duly circumspect and apologetic about their 'abstraction'. The book also includes the texts of all but the two longest poems. It is thus well adapted to classroom use. The theoretical statements are exclusively literary. The 'Preface' insists on the need to treat poetry as poetry (a well-established New Critical axiom), and proposes to investigate what remains when a poem is separated from its 'cultural matrix'. Thus the book neglects historical context because otherwise criticism becomes 'cultural anthropology' (Brooks, [1947] 1968, p. vi). Further, poetry (unlike science) cannot be paraphrased: it cannot be simplified even though modern man is 'habituated . . . to an easy yes or no' (p. 7) and cannot unravel 'into "facts", biological, sociological, and economic' (p. 13). Poems cannot do so because their particular structural properties draw them into 'unity', that is, 'balancing and harmonizing connotations, attitudes and meanings' (p. 159), and the 'unification of attitudes into a hierarchy subordinated to a total and governing attitude' (p. 168). This, though, is a 'dramatic process, not a logical' one (p. 169). The choice of poems for analysis is not startling, and all are English (except Yeats) and male: Donne, Shakespeare, Milton, Herrick, Pope, Gray, Wordsworth, Keats, Tennyson and Yeats. These writers represent the 'central stream of the tradition' (p. 157). The urn of the title features in a number of them, including Keats's 'Ode on a Grecian Urn'.

As a romantic Keats had not earlier been an overly appealing writer for Brooks. His comments on Keats's poems included in *Understanding Poetry* had on the whole been dismissive. 'Ode to a Nightingale', for instance, lacks logic and structure, draws on imagery which is 'on the decorative side', and is only 'mildly ironical'; the poem sacrifices 'sharpness of perception to mere pretti-ness' (Brooks and Warren, 1938, pp. 412–14). Nevertheless, in *Modern Poetry and the Tradition* (1939), Keats's work is considered preferable to Shelley's: it has a leaven of self-irony, and its lyricism is restrained, unlike Shelley's sentimental self-indulgence (see Brooks, 1948, pp. 230–1). The problem presented by the 'Ode on a Grecian Urn', however, is different. It presents a problem of belief, not of language: how are we to respond to its final lines?

> Beauty is truth, – truth beauty, – that is all
> Ye know on earth, and all ye need to know.

These lines seem to offer a discursive proposition, and would thus seem to offend New Critical principles. Brooks, though, sets out to defend the poem.

For him these lines are a dramatic utterance, to be taken in dramatic context as part of what 'is obviously intended to be a parable on the nature of poetry, and of art in general' (Brooks, [1947] 1968, p. 125). Brooks reads the poem as organized by paradoxes and 'ironic undercurrents': a silent urn that speaks, a rigid urn that reports 'wild ecstasy', statically carved but dynamically active, an urn that is young and old, immortal but lifeless, a 'cold pastoral' (pastoral implying 'warmth, spontaneity, the natural and informal', p. 133). The Ode is thus a model of New Critical propriety, organized by self-checking ironies as it advances towards its conclusion. Brooks fastens on Keats's portrayal of the 'little town' in stanza 4, and his account of it shifts the argument towards the closing proposition. Its 'people are knit together as an organic whole' as they turn out for collective ritual on this 'pious morn'; the 'green altar' represents 'natural spontaneous living', 'something naturally related to its terrain'; the town is one of 'stability and independence without imperialistic ambition', its 'peaceful citadel' brings together peace and war in a characteristically paradoxical New Critical fusion (pp. 131–2).

It is striking, of course, that the analysis here concisely reflects the Agrarian scenarios with which New Criticism began, and the critic, far from neutrally describing the poem's structure and workings, fills its details with beliefs of his own. As the argument proceeds this becomes yet clearer, for, says Brooks, 'the town implied by the urn comes to have a richer and more important history than that of actual cities' (pp. 132–3); that is, it challenges actual history (a sad story in New Critical conception) with a reviving myth related to the message of the Ode's final lines. Brooks argues that the resolving paradoxical tension arises from the poet's attitude towards the town and eventually the urn itself:

> The poet, by pretending to take the town as real – so real that he can imagine the effect of its silent streets upon the stranger who chances to come to it – has suggested in the most powerful way possible its essential reality for him – and for us. It is a case of the doctor's taking his own medicine: the poet is prepared to stand by the illusion of his own making.
>
> (p. 133)

The argument works by making a distinction between reality and 'essential reality', and holding that the poem, like the poet (a very un-New Critical introduction of the author), encourages us to believe in the latter. This 'essential reality' is the challenging, alternative world of art which embraces town, urn, poem and critic. The urn is 'a formed thing, as an autonomous world'; it indicates a 'life beyond life', a 'history beyond time, outside time' which speaks across the mess of real history to generations of like minds (p. 133), and what it says – Brooks's gloss on the final two lines – is 'that "formed experience", imaginative insight, embodies the basic and fundamental perception of man and nature' (p. 134). It is not science and other forms of knowledge that reveal truth, but art. Art yields the 'essential reality' of 'formed experience', an oxymoronic phrase that itself is alive with tension and paradox.

So the urn utters its truth:

> the only kind we *have* to have. The names, the dates, the special circumstances, the wealth of data – these the sylvan historian quietly ignores ... [for] mere accumulations of facts – a point our own generation is only beginning to realize – are meaningless. The sylvan historian does better than that: it takes a few details and so orders them that we have not only beauty but insight into essential truth. ... It has the validity of myth – not myth as a pretty but irrelevant make-believe, an idle fancy, but myth as a valid perception into reality.
>
> (p. 134)

The conclusions are validated by their dramatic enactment, 'the maturity of attitude, the dramatic tension, the emotional *and* intellectual coherence' (p. 134) of the poem. Brooks invites the reader to celebrate the Ode's rich organization, but is actually recommending his version of its message. The interpretation, by working towards a New Critical dogma, violates New Critical practice. A theory which set itself against formal statement, which encouraged attention to the poem itself, which relished ambiguity and irony, ends (and Brooks is not singular in this respect) substituting for these things a restatement of New Critical theory, and that theory finds what it wishes. Brooks is not, for instance, alert to the multiple meanings embedded in the final lines of Keats's poem, for who is 'ye'? In one reading 'ye' could include the urn itself, and the poem in its conclusion could say exactly the opposite to Brooks's reading: ye, as an urn, can believe beauty is truth; I, as a human being, need other wisdom. The lines are a notorious interpretative crux (which is clearly set out in Allott, 1970, pp. 537–8), but the argument about them is shut out by Brooks's supposedly ironic, paradoxical reading.

This kind of closure is visible in much New Criticism which began, as its theory succeeded, to restate and repeat its premises. The very coherence, lucidity and manageability of its project began to work against it. What looked a flexible and open method began to harden into programmatic restatement. At the close of their famous essay 'The Affective Fallacy', originally published in 1949 two years after *The Well Wrought Urn*, Wimsatt and Beardsley echoed

Brooks's Keats: 'The field worker among the Zunis or the Navahos finds no informant so informative as the poet or the member of the tribe who can quote its myths. In short, though cultures have changed and will change, poems remain and explain' (see Wimsatt, 1970, p. 39). In the same year René Wellek in *Theory of Literature*, specifically with Keats's poem in mind, guarded against the 'reduction of a work of art to a doctrinal statement . . . [it] is disastrous to understanding the uniqueness of a work: it disintegrates its structure and imposes alien criteria of value' (Wellek and Warren, [1949] 1973, pp. 110–11).

Theory of Literature indicates the strengths, and some of the weaknesses, of New Criticism. It is adventurous and richly speculative, it attempts to indicate a coherent approach to literary study where, in the Anglo-American world, none had been; and, unlike his colleagues from the South, Wellek, particularly, looks to extend horizons beyond that Anglo-American world. Thus the book is informed by (among other things) Saussurean and Czech linguistics, Russian Formalism and Polish phenomenology. It has been translated into twenty languages and is still available as a popular paperback forty years later (see Wellek, 1982, p. 78). It deserves its success. Yet, while adventurous, the book also illustrates the way New Criticism fell into dogma. In his chapter on 'The Mode of Existence of a Literary Work of Art' (originally published in 1942, and recommended by Brooks in *The Well Wrought Urn*), Wellek, drawing on phenomenology and linguistics, formulates a way of understanding the structure of a poem not as balanced ambiguities and ironies, but as a determining 'structure of norms' which are realized – usually only partially – by actual readers. These norms have different levels of operation, different 'strata', from sound patterns to articulations of beliefs, and they embrace formal features such as point-of-view and tone. Wellek recommends a critical operation he calls 'perspectivism' in which the critic unfolds the rich verbal world of the poem from the perspective of one of its strata of norms. Wellek's theory follows the analytically formalist bias of New Criticism, but suggests a fuller, intellectually richer formulation of it, and the analysis closes looking to subsequent chapters to take the argument forward. The result is disappointing. Chapter 18 (by Warren) resumes, but the horizons of 'perspectivism' shrink to New Critical formulae: 'the maturity of a work of art is its inclusiveness, its awareness of complexity, its ironies and tensions' (Wellek and Warren, [1949] 1973, p. 246). It was the repetitions of these formulae, their staid moral vocabulary, their limited range of approved writers, their conservatism of outlook and approach, that led to their rejection in the 1960s and 1970s and their replacement with a new – though perhaps equally jargonized and inflexible – formalism in the post-structuralism of the 1980s.

FURTHER READING

Brooks, Cleanth (1968) *The Well Wrought Urn: Studies in the Structure of Poetry*, Methuen, London [first published 1947]

Fekete, John (1977) *The Critical Twilight: Explorations in the Ideology of Anglo-American Literary Theory from Eliot to McLuhan*, Routledge & Kegan Paul, London

Krieger, Murray (1977) *The New Apologists for Poetry*, Greenwood Press, Westport [first published 1956]

Lentricchia, Frank (1980) *After the New Criticism*, Athlone Press, London

Ransom, John Crowe (1941) *The New Criticism*, New Directions, Norfolk

——(1964) *The World's Body*, Kennikat Press, New York [first published 1938]

Robey, David (1982) 'Anglo-American New Criticism'. In Ann Jefferson and David Robey (eds), *Modern Literary Theory: A Comparative Introduction*, Batsford, London, pp. 65–83

Stewart, John L. (1965) *The Burden of Time: The Fugitives and Agrarians*, Princeton University Press, Princeton

Thompson, Ewa M. (1971) *Russian Formalism and Anglo-American New Criticism: A Comparative Study*, Mouton, The Hague

Wellek, René (1963) *Concepts of Criticism*, Yale University Press, New Haven

Wellek, René and Warren, Austin (1973) *Theory of Literature*, Penguin, Harmondsworth [first published 1949]

Wimsatt, W. K., Jr. (1970) *The Verbal Icon: Studies in the Meaning of Poetry*, Methuen, London [first published 1954]

ADDITIONAL WORKS CITED

Allot, Miriam (ed.) (1970) *The Poems of John Keats*, Longman, London

Brooks, Cleanth (1948) *Modern Poetry and the Tradition*, Editions Poetry, London [first published 1939]

Brooks, Cleanth and Warren, Robert Penn (eds) (1938) *Understanding Poetry: An Anthology for College Students*, Henry Holt, New York

——(eds) (1943) *Understanding Fiction*, Appleton-Century-Crofts, New York

Lasch, Christopher (1973) *The Agony of the American Left: One Hundred Years of Radicalism*, Pelican, Harmondsworth

Mulhern, Francis (1979) *The Moment of 'Scrutiny'*, Verso, London

Ransom, John Crowe (1951a) 'Criticism as Pure Speculation'. In Morton D. Zabel (ed.), *Literary Opinion in America*, 2nd edn, Harper, New York, pp. 639–54 [essay first published 1941]

——(ed.) (1951b) *The Kenyon Critics: Studies in Modern Literature from the 'Kenyon Review'*, Kennikat Press, New York

Tate, Allen (1936) *Reactionary Essays on Poetry and Ideas*, Charles Scribner's Sons, New York

——(1952) 'The Present Function of Criticism'. In Ray B. West (ed.), *Essays in Modern Literary Criticism*, Holt, Rinehart & Winston, New York, pp. 145–54 [essay first published 1940]

Trilling, Lionel (1970) 'The Meaning of a Literary Idea'. In Lionel Trilling, *The Liberal*

Imagination: Essays on Literature and Society, Peregrine, Harmondsworth [essay first published 1949]

Watson, George (1964) *The Literary Critics*, revised edn, Penguin, Harmondsworth

Wellek, René (1982) *The Attack on Literature and Other Essays*, Harvester, Brighton

Winters, Yvor (1959) 'John Crowe Ransom, or Thunder Without God'. In Yvor Winters, *On Modern Poets*, Meridian, Cleveland, pp. 73–120 [essay first published 1943]

54

STRUCTURALISM AND POST-STRUCTURALISM: FROM THE CENTRE TO THE MARGIN

STEVEN CONNOR

The crossings and recrossings of literary theory in the critical upheavals of the last twenty years or so seem in retrospect to have been battles as much over metaphors as over matters of belief and procedure. The most powerful organizing terms in critical-theoretical debates are all metaphors which embody concepts tactically; that is to say, they conjure up a physical or psychical geography in which one may situate one's own practice as opposed to that of one's opponents or predecessors. In fact, it is space or territory itself which provides the most extensive repertoire of critical metaphors, in terms like 'boundary', 'site', 'terrain', 'frame', or 'domain'. Metaphors like these are part of the rhetorical weaponry of criticism, but should not be dismissed as 'mere' rhetoric, for they are neither simply decoration, nor ever simply chosen. The metaphors by means of which any particular institutionally validated form of reading simultaneously understands itself and organizes its material can determine the actual ways in which such a reading functions and is recognized. Critical readings, in an important sense, *are* their metaphors.

I want to focus on what seems to me to be the single most important critical metaphor of the last twenty years. This is the metaphor of the 'centre', along with its associated and opposed spatial or geometrical co-ordinates, of framing, circumference and marginality. I want to try to read and interpret the mesmerizing power of this metaphor, or concept-metaphor (as we may call it, in acknowledgement of the way that the metaphor shapes critical thought itself), and to explore some versions of the following question. The passage from structuralism to post-structuralism can be described as a passage from centred to decentred or centreless structures: if this can be seen as breaking away from the gravitational pull of the centre, then what are we to make of the compulsive orbiting around this very concept-metaphor in post-structuralist criticism, even in its strategies of decentring?

The first announcement of the death of structuralism and inauguration of the era of post-structuralism is usually taken to be Jacques Derrida's essay 'Structure, Sign and Play in the Discourse of the Human Sciences' (1978). This essay was first delivered in October 1966 at the International Colloquium on Critical Languages and the Science of Man at Johns Hopkins University in Baltimore, Maryland, a conference designed to mark the opening of the American mind into the much-rumoured mysteries of structuralism. But it turned out that what Derrida had to say involved a rethinking and transformation of the central principles of structuralism itself. Early accounts of the structuralist revolution in literary studies, like Jonathan Culler's *Structuralist Poetics* (1975) and Terence Hawkes's *Structuralism and Semiotics* (1977) show the marks of this muddled inheritance, the sense that structuralism had already turned into something else. After 1966, the austere rigours of structuralist method were increasingly shadowed by Derrida's dark prophecy of the 'formless, mute, infant and terrifying form of monstrosity' which was to supersede it, the rough beast of post-structuralism slouching towards Yale University to be born.

All structures, Derrida says – or all concepts of what a structure is – depend upon two aspects. The first and more familiar is that of the relationship of parts. The definitions of *structure* offered by the Oxford English Dictionary bear this out: 'the mutual relation of the constituent parts or elements of a whole as determining its particular character or nature . . . the coexistence in a whole of distinct parts having a definite manner of arrangement.' Applied to a literary text, it is clear what this implies, though perhaps not yet clear what might be distinctively 'structuralist' about it. A literary text, like any other conceptual or material structure, is made up of different, co-operating parts, including such things as rhythm, imagery, figures of speech, plot, etc., and the business of all criticism is, in a sense, to separate and identify these functioning parts. Indeed, what characterizes some classic structuralist analyses is their apparent desire to name *every* functioning part of a text – as in Roman Jakobson and Claude Lévi-Strauss's painstaking study of the thematic and grammatical patternings in Baudelaire's poem 'Les Chats', or Jakobson's even more dogged dissection, morpheme by morpheme, of Shakespeare's Sonnet 129 (Jakobson and Lévi-Strauss, 1972a; Jakobson, 1970).

But Derrida points to another requirement of the concept of structure, one that the OED definitions also point up very well; a structure is a collection of parts which are related not only one-to-one in molecular fashion, but which form and derive from a single, common whole. Another way to say this is that a structure needs to be organized around a centre. The metaphor of the centre is a useful one, because it highlights the relationship between two

737

incommensurable dimensions. Every circle must have a centre, for it is the existence of this centre that allows for its very definition, but the centre can never accurately be said to be 'in' the circle that it governs, since, by definition, a centre has no mass or extension. Everything in a circle, every point on its circumference or within its area, is defined by its relationship to or distance from the sum of other such points, except the centre itself, whose position is always simply given. As Derrida puts it, 'it has always been thought that the center, which is by definition unique, constituted that very thing within a structure which while governing the structure, escapes structurality' (1978, p. 279).

So Derrida diagnoses here the seeming requirement to refer every structure or system of related parts, whether it be a book, a poem, a computer program, or a body of scientific evidence, to a central principle which defines its essential nature, allowing us to determine that it *is* a book, a poem, a computer program, or body of scientific evidence. This principle is exemplified in the influential doctrine of organic wholeness. When W. B. Yeats enquires at the end of his poem 'Among School Children', 'Oh chestnut tree, great rooted blossomer,/ Are you the leaf, the blossom, or the bole?', he is articulating the belief that a tree is a tree and not some other thing by virtue of a central principle which is not to be identified with any of its individual parts. The 'treeness' of the tree is simultaneously everywhere, irradiating and giving significance to every part of it, and nowhere, in that it cannot ever be detached for inspection. Derrida teases this duality into the following paradoxical formulation: 'The center is at the center of the totality, and yet, since the center does not belong to the totality (is not part of the totality), the totality *has its center elsewhere.* The center is not the center' (1978, p. 279).

It may seem incongruous to characterize structuralist method in such organic terms – after all, structuralism has the reputation for a hard-headed antagonism towards organic ideals like wholeness and spontaneity. And yet Derrida has identified here a common purpose and identity between Roman Jakobson on the one hand and 'organicist' critics like Coleridge and I. A. Richards on the other, for all of them envisage verbal structures as governed internally by unifying principles.

The most developed example of the fusion between structuralist practice and organic attitudes is to be found in the work of Michael Riffaterre, and especially his book *The Semiotics of Poetry* (1978). Riffaterre is concerned in this work to identify the linguistic conditions specific to poetry. In this, he follows Roman Jakobson and other structuralist writers who have defined poetry as that form of language which displays a 'set towards the message', that is to say, points to and compels awareness of its verbal and linguistic substance (shape, sound and structural patterning), rather than referring to the world in any direct or uncomplicated way. For Riffaterre, a poem comes into being in its movement away from representation ('mimesis') and towards the formation of patterns of significance, which are specific to its own verbal structures ('semiosis'). This movement comes via a series of irregularities, deviations or even ungrammaticalities which progressively jolt the reader out of the calm expectation or acceptance of mimesis. In an analysis of a poem by Théophile Gautier, 'In Deserto' (1845), Riffaterre argues that, rather than attempting to button poetic language neatly on to reality, like the dutiful editor of Gautier who goes to the Spanish sierra to check out the accuracy of the poem's climatic and geographical descriptions, the reader ought to be concerned more simply with what the poem's language *does* in itself (1978, p. 7).

So far this is fairly consistent with established structuralist procedure and theory, and, indeed, finds in poetry a model for the theoretical re-angling which typifies the structuralist enterprise itself, namely, the movement from a referential view of language to a theory of the ways in which significance is generated out of the interaction of textual elements among themselves. What characterizes Riffaterre's procedure is its stress on the discovery of unity. He argues that mimesis always brings about variety and multiplicity, since it requires every element of a text to refer separately to a different portion of external reality. Conversely, the turn away from reference means that the poetic text is free to concentrate its energies inward, and thus to form itself into an integrated whole. For Riffaterre, the verbal transformations effected through a given poetic text are always organized around a single theme, which may often be a particular key word, or 'matrix'. So, for example, Gautier's poem 'In Deserto' is construed as a series of verbal improvisations upon the theme 'desert', encompassing water, sand, aridity, solitude, etc. But this governing matrix is always absent from the poem itself; although it initiates and frames the poem's significance it is never itself openly articulated and so 'becomes visible only in its variants' (Riffaterre, 1978, p. 13).

This idea may appear unexceptionable, except that it seems to reduce the writing of poetry to something like an infant-school exercise, and, in the case of a poem which is actually called 'In Deserto', to do little more than state the obvious ('poems are about the subjects announced in their titles'). Riffaterre wants to go further than this, however, to find some centre for the poem which is not so palpably in or of its substance. He does this by inviting us to pay more careful attention to the form of the poem's title, which is not, after all 'In the desert', but 'In deserto', the second half of the familiar phrase 'vox clamans in deserto', the voice crying in the wilderness. This motto, says Riffaterre, is the hidden motor of the poem, which reveals itself suddenly not to be about the desert, but about the idea of the *voice*, or of blocked utterance, for which the desert only provides a symbolic locale. The conditional verbs which saturate the poem are 'the grammatical icon of unfulfillment', writes Riffaterre, and are the verbal traces of the 'repressed despairing voice' from

739

which 'the whole poem is derived' (p. 12). Riffaterre wants to insist that the poem is not identical with this hidden centre, since it comes into being only as a series of semiotic transformations of it. But although he says that the poem's significance really consists in 'the reader's praxis of the transformation', he nevertheless restricts its scope by representing the process of reading and understanding as 'acting out the liturgy of a ritual – the experience of a circuitous sequence, a way of speaking that keeps revolving around a key word or matrix' (p. 12).

The logical end-point of this transformation of mimesis into semiosis is a poem that has polished away the last speck of reference to a real world and left itself free to flex its own autonomous verbal substance – a poem about words alone, or a nonsense poem. Riffaterre takes such poems seriously and, like Mallarmé, is prepared to see such extreme non-referentiality as the purest kind of poetry. But even here, Riffaterre tracks down a motive principle in the nonsense poem's very denial of referentiality. In such a poem 'the mimesis is now quite spurious and illusory, realized only for the sake of the semiosis; and, conversely, the semiosis is a reference to the word *nothing*' (p. 13).

Riffaterre's work therefore conveniently demonstrates Derrida's claim that to conceive a structure is inevitably to summon up the dialectic between a system of parts and an organizing centre. For Riffaterre, as for other structuralists, the concepts of relationship and centring are inseparable. Although he cleaves to the structuralist credo that 'a sign is only a relationship to something else', this leads as it were automatically to the corollary that the sign 'will not make sense without a continuous translatability from component to component of a network' and thence to the claim that 'every signifying feature of the poem must be relatable to the system' (p. 11). Controlled by its matrix, the diffuse material of a poem becomes 'a single sign . . . wherein nothing is loose' (p. 12).

Now, the point for Derrrida is that this idea of the absent but omnipresent centre is fundamentally contradictory, and that such a contradiction can only be overcome by acts of intellectual will or wish-fulfilment. The very idea of the centre is thus for Derrida not a spontaneous confirmation of the principle of organic life, but a conceptual violence, practised not only in structuralism, but throughout the history of thought in the West, in order to contain or repress the play of pure relationship between signs. What distinguishes structuralism from previous forms of thought is that it goes so far towards discovering the truth about the decentred condition of all structures, in its affirmation that every sign derives its meaning and function only from its relationships to other signs, without actually making the break with centred thinking. Derrida's own compensating violence is to rip apart the organic bond of interdependence between structure and centre, to leave structures of pure and absolute relationship – although he coolly admits in passing that a structure without a centre is hardly thinkable, indeed may represent the unthinkable itself (Derrida, 1978, p. 279).

Structuralist thinking has ways of registering the influence of the centre which are less direct than Riffaterre's theory of buried code-words. Most famously, there is the principle of the dialectic or binary opposition. The critical strategy offered by Roman Jakobson and Claude Lévi-Strauss, for instance, suggests that a poem is likely to be organized not so much around single central principles, as around pairs of mutually-defining thematic opposites. Jakobson and Lévi-Strauss's analysis of Baudelaire's 'Les Chats' finds that the sonnet, which seems at first merely an atmospheric and rather ornate evocation of the languorous mystery of domestic cats, in fact depends on and actualizes a series of related contrasts, between the domestic and the mythological (the cats are the 'pride of the house', but also, metaphorically, 'great sphinxes stretched out in deep solitudes'), the localized and the infinite (the cats 'seem to sleep in a dream without end'), the earthly and the celestial (they stretch out like sphinxes in the desert sand, but the stars seem to twinkle in their eyes) and the funerary and the fertile (they are imagined as funeral-bearers in Hades, but have 'fecund thighs').

If this kind of analysis obviously does not depend upon the attribution of a fixed but absent centre in the same way that Riffaterre's does, the striking thing about it is the way that it frames or contains the play of these mutually-defining thematic couples. Structural centring is here achieved not around a hidden core of meaning, but by patterns of symmetry, balance and repetition, which the analysis aims to concentrate together. Jakobson and Lévi-Strauss end triumphantly with the following condensation of these patterns of equivalence through the poem: 'dilation of the cats in time and space, constriction of time and space in the person of the cats' (1972a, p. 144).

Jakobson and Lévi-Strauss's analysis resembles Lévi-Strauss's own method of interpreting a body of myths, which is to render them down into their most fundamental binary structures. He analyses the Oedipus myth, for example, as the attempt to mediate between two related sets of oppositions: first, the exaggeration of blood-relations as opposed to the denial of blood-relations (Oedipus marrying his mother but killing his father), and second, the belief in the autochthonous origin of life, or life born from earth itself, as opposed to the denial of that belief (the figure of the Sphinx, as a monster born of the earth and the defeat of the Sphinx). Lévi-Strauss cannot rest until he has found a point of contact between these two preoccupations, and he concludes that the myth is a way of brooding over or imaginatively working through the logical problem faced by a culture which believes that mankind has its origin in the earth but can see perfectly well that individual human beings are born from the meeting of the sexes. The 'bundles of relations' which Lévi-Strauss has said constitute the myth can be stripped back to the one question, 'born from one, or born from two?' (1972b, p. 180).

Such schemes of interpretation therefore substitute the principle of the resolution of opposites for the idea of the fixed centre. But, in the terms of Derrida's critique, this principle is still a centring force, in that it focuses and controls the play of relationship between elements in a structure while itself remaining immune from that play; though it governs everything in a poem or body of myths, 'resolution' itself can never be isolated from that structure or be evidenced except in its effects.

There exist other versions of Lévi-Strauss's procedure but all of them are open to Derrida's charge that they fix, filter, or otherwise centre the play of relationship within texts. An elaborated version of Lévi-Strauss's homology (i.e. the coupling of two equivalent sets of opposites) is A. J. Greimas's 'semiotic square', which complicates the simple binary logic of A versus not-A, to surround any sign with a cluster of different forms of contrast and negation. Greimas's semiotic square has been used to generate literary analyses of Conrad's *Lord Jim* by Fredric Jameson (1981, pp. 251–7) and of *Dombey and Son* by myself (Connor, 1985, pp. 20–43). But even this expanded form of oppositional analysis nevertheless reproduces the centring effect which Derrida denounces as wish-fulfilling violence on the openness and arbitrariness of relations among signs.

Derrida's claim, therefore, is that there is a multiplicity of different forms of centring. Among these he instances the following philosophical principles: origin, presence, transcendence, essence and *telos* (metaphysical end-point). These have their literary equivalents in such principles as the belief in the original intention of the author, the idea of a uniquely individual style, the power of literary texts to resolve and unify thematic conflicts, and the historical narratives of the slow growth to perfection, either in the work of individual authors, or in the development of literary traditions. But the most intriguing form of centring that Derrida isolates is the notion of the 'work' itself. Focusing on Lévi-Strauss's own work on myths, Derrida asks the methodological question, how can you be sure that you have enough variants of a particular myth to be able to analyse it properly? In other words, how can you ever be sure that you have the 'text' that you wish to analyse before you? In asking a form of the question 'how long is a piece of string?' Derrida is really speculating about the boundaries of a myth; where are these to be drawn, such that one might know what lies 'inside' and what lies 'outside' a myth in all its variant forms? Most disconcertingly of all, Derrida (along with Lévi-Strauss himself, it must be said) wonders about the relative position of the mythographer's analysis of a myth itself; is it outside the body of the myth, or is it another version of it? Ought Lévi-Strauss to include Freud's interpretation of the

Oedipus myth as one of its retellings? Ought he to include his own (Derrida, 1978, pp. 288–9)?

Derrida's question reveals the structural interdependence of centre and circumference. We determine the edges or boundaries of works, texts or other fields of enquiry, by reference to their postulated centres. Anything that is not felt to be in the gravitational field of the centre can be assumed to be extrinsic or alien to the text or structure. In order to define the edges of what is 'literature', for example, it is necessary to hypothesize a centring principle which will govern all the particular manifestations of the literary – hence 'science-fiction/women's romance/football chants are *not* literature because they do not use imaginative forms creatively to ennoble or extend the human spirit'. But since this form of reasoning must always in a sense have predetermined its grounding principles, it can lead to embarrassing tautologies, as when Lévi-Strauss says 'we define the myth as consisting of all its versions; to put it otherwise: a myth remains the same as long as it is felt as such' (1972b, p. 181). This self-validating form of thought can develop into the exercise of cultural power and exclusion, as, for example, when it involves the compacting of human history around centring concepts like (male) Man, or (European) Civilization, or even History itself.

The movement away from a structuralist mode in literary and cultural studies since the 1970s has expressed itself almost entirely in a suspicion of 'centred' thought. (Not all of this derives from Derrida, for the work of writers like Jacques Lacan, with his systematic assault on the idea of a centred and unified self, and Michel Foucault, with his abandonment of the idea of a single and continuous history of mankind, has contributed greatly in various ways.) One of the earliest critical texts produced in this climate of decentring is Roland Barthes's *S/Z* (1974), a protracted and sportively self-indulgent reading of Balzac's short story *Sarrasine*. Barthes here resists the idea that the play of relationship among elements of a text (and the other texts which it summons up by allusion and association) can or should be 'delegated to a great final ensemble, to an ultimate structure'. Reading should simply be a process of movement, among and between the signifying particles of the text. Barthes even disallows in advance the idea that his analytic procedure, which consists of chopping the text up into morsels of sense (or 'lexias') of variable length and recording the interplay between the different reading codes at work in and between them, could ever itself become a regular, repeatable procedure, since this would again be to arrest and centre on this one reading, which 'is not an (inductive) access to a Model, but entrance into a network with a thousand entrances' (Barthes, 1974, p. 12).

However, it proves difficult for Barthes to resist the centring impulse altogether, as Barbara Johnson has shown in her essay 'The Critical Difference: BartheS/BalZac' (1980, pp. 3–12). Balzac's story concerns the love of a sculptor, Sarrasine, for a castrato opera singer, La Zambinella; Sarrasine is devastated to discover that his beloved is in fact a man and ends up being killed. Barthes identifies a concern with castration throughout the text and makes it stand for the loss of every kind of wholeness and totality (of the body, but also of meaning and truth). However, where Balzac's text flirts with, but never reveals the word 'castration', Barthes turns the term into a thematic positive, making of the absence connoted by castration an organizing, invariant presence. Barbara Johnson alleges that Barthes thereby 'erects castration into *the* meaning of the text, its ultimate signified' (1980, p. 11).

A similar charge is made by Derrida in a response to Jacques Lacan's reading of 'The Purloined Letter' by Edgar Allan Poe. The story revolves around three characters, the Queen who at the beginning receives a compromising letter, presumably from her lover; the Minister, who steals and conceals the letter; and Dupin, the detective who discovers and returns the letter. But the real subject of the story, says Lacan (1972), is the letter itself and its peregrinations, not the characters who dance obediently into position around it, playing the part in turn of recipient, thief and onlooker. Lacan claims that what he is doing is to focus on the movement of the text, with its dissolving and reforming configurations of meaning, rather than trying to fix the text's meaning as such. Again, it is castration which is the key term for Lacan, who takes the letter as a sort of fetish – a symbolic substitute for a unifying organ that is feared lost. Castration is therefore for Lacan as for Barthes the sign of the absence of fixed or unified meaning. But Derrida, making the same argumentative move as Barbara Johnson, reads this as an unhealthy fixation upon a notion of absence which promotes it into a centring principle: 'that which is missing from its place has in castration a fixed, central place, freed from all substitution. Something is missing from its place, but the lack is never missing from it' (1987, p. 441).

Another example of decentring criticism is J. Hillis Miller's *Fiction and Repetition* (1982). His reading of *Wuthering Heights* demonstrates his procedure very well. Miller's argument is that the history of critical readings of the novel, Freudian, romantic, symbolic, Marxist, feminist, etc., has shown hitherto a desire to discover 'a single secret truth . . . a univocal principle of explanation which would account for everything in the novel' (p. 51). No such centring principle exists, Miller declares. But his own reading of the novel attempts, not simply to do away with the idea of a centre, but instead to show how we must tolerate the idea of texts with multiple centres. He quotes three passages from the novel, all of which, he claims, might stand as an emblem for it as a whole: the first is a passage in which the names of the central characters swirl through the mind of Lockwood, the narrator, the second a description of his journey through the snow guided by a line of painted stones, and the third, the final two paragraphs of the novel, describing the headstones of Edgar

Linton, Catherine and Heathcliff. Each of these passages 'implicitly claims to be a center around which all the other details can be organized' (Miller, 1982, p. 59), the first in terms of the permutation of names, the second in its imaging of the reader's journey towards understanding, the third in terms of the 'memorial narration' placed together by Lockwood. Miller wants to demonstrate the simultaneous interdependence and incompatibility of these organizing centres: 'Each leads to a different total design. Each such design is incompatible with the others' (p. 59).

Miller's work is, in this sense, more conservative than that of Barthes. For Miller, the absence of a centre does not mean that 'criticism is a free-for-all in which one reading is as good as another' (1982, p. 51), and he affirms, not the absolute openness of meaning in a literary text, but the presence of particular, textually-determined forms of 'undecidability'. In fact, the contrast between *S/Z* and *Fiction and Repetition* illustrates usefully the division between post-structuralism in general and the more particular strategy of reading known as deconstruction. We can say that, where post-structuralism hedonistically attempts to proclaim absolute centrelessness against the repressive creed of the centre, deconstruction attempts to think its way through and perhaps out of the very structure of centre and margin. So, in deconstruction, the point is not simply to affirm the margin against the centre; as Jonathan Culler explains, 'reversal, attributing importance to the marginal, is usually conducted in such a way that it does not lead simply to the identification of a new center . . . but to a subversion of the distinctions between essential and inessential, inside and outside. What is a center if the marginal can become central?' (1983, p. 140).

But, for all its persuasive elegance, J. Hillis Miller's work illustrates plainly enough the ways in which the incendiary implications of deconstruction can be damped down. The return of the centre in Miller's work occurs, not in the fixation upon particular forms of meaning, but upon particular forms of framing, or bounding. In the case of *Wuthering Heights*, the framing principle is centrelessness itself, so that the most authoritative critical readings are those 'which repeat in their own alogic the text's failure to satisfy the mind's desire for logical order'. This is a reading which stresses the reader's interpretative activity, but restricts him or her to an obedient conformity with the decentring operations of the text itself, which 'forces him to repeat in his own way an effort of understanding that the text expresses, and to repeat also the baffling of that effort' (Miller, 1982, p. 53).

Here, as elsewhere, the notion of the coercive power of 'the text itself' is a formula which disguises the power of criticism itself to legislate over texts, their meanings, and the ways of deciding them. Miller's very willingness to confine the implications of deconstruction to questions of the interpretation of single, canonical texts produces an instrumentalized post-structuralism, a

745

theory in the service of a series of operational goals, and harnessed by the professional and cultural protocols of the literary academy. This is not to charge Miller with cynicism or opportunism, since his work has boldly made a number of difficult and important new ideas available and comprehensible to new audiences, but it is to suggest the continuing necessity for criticism to investigate its own conventional frames or limits. The fact that Miller's deconstruction, along with many of the institutionalized forms of post-structuralist theory, has shown little interest in seriously challenging the actual forms and structures of academic life, the article, the book, the lecture, the seminar, the conference, the examination, the thesis, or in changing the social function of academic institutions, indicates the ways in which successfully institutionalized critical discourses of this kind may always be partially propelled by the need to reproduce centres of authority rather than to dissolve or question them.

At the same time, there have been other attempts to think outside or beyond the concept of the 'literary' as presently constituted, and to speak on behalf of what that concept pushes to the margins. Much contemporary feminist analysis, for example, particularly those forms energized by post-structuralist ideas, works with a paradigm of decentring as subversion. Toril Moi's work is representative in its call for a feminist analysis which will not simply reoccupy the traditional centres of male writing and male criticism, the belief in absolute truth, universal meaning and the serenely self-knowing individual (Moi, 1985). 'Woman', for Moi, is often made the privileged inhabitant of the margin; expelled from the centres of power and authority, woman can also speak from the position of discredited non-being in order to unsettle the fixed and absolute truths of patriarchy.

Other work, particularly in the area of cultural politics, aims to extend the project of articulating the margins. Such work may not identify itself obviously as post-structuralist in its vocabulary, concepts or procedures, but nevertheless is one of the most significant of the ways in which the post-structuralist decentring of traditional notions of literature and the literary is being carried through. This work is concerned with such things as the analysis and promotion of working-class culture, women's and popular culture, colonial, post-colonial and 'Third World' writing, though its aim may be to widen and pluralize the very notions of culture and value which sustain literary studies, rather than necessarily to subvert the concept of the centre. Though it continues to gnaw at the edges of literature, it is a fact that such work remains, or continues to be seen as, self-evidently marginal. For some working at these potent edges of authority, the real centring principle may be the figure of the critic 'him'-self, rather than the particular form of literary text or critical reading that 'he' espouses, and hence a widened cultural politics may depend on the discrediting of this form of authority. As Iain Chambers writes, 'the traditional chains that once tied "truth" and "meaning" to the powers of an intellectual priesthood and their exclusive institutions (the academy, the university, the scholarly journal, academic publishing) are snapping under the expansion of the contemporary world and the invasion of our experiences by the heterogeneous, the incommensurable, the diverse, the different' (Chambers, 1987, p. 20).

There is, however, a danger with this romance of the marginal, whether it be in terms of the individual literary text, or in terms of literary-cultural history in general. The danger is that the concentration upon the marginal may bring about a kind of reverse fixation upon the principle of the centre itself, so that the metaphor which began as a conceptual tactic hardens into a machine that programmes all possible interpretative moves, binding them strictly into a rhythm of exhilarated flight to the periphery and dispirited return to the centre. We have already encountered examples of this rhythm in Barbara Johnson's reading of Barthes on Balzac, and Derrida's reading of Lacan on Poe, in which one attempt to deny or evade the authority of an interpretative centre is gleefully capped by a critique that reveals the ways in which the original analysis is trapped by centred thinking. The compulsiveness of this movement is instanced by yet further moves in the game, such as Barbara Johnson's essay, 'The Frame of Reference: Poe, Lacan, Derrida', a reading of Derrida's reading of Lacan's reading of Poe, which in a similar way charges Derrida with narrowing the frame of reference too tightly in his decentring of Lacan (Johnson, 1980, pp. 110–46). To follow through this series of critiques and metacritiques (as we are doing at this moment) is to experience the force, paralysing and galvanizing at once, of the movement set up by the metaphor of controlling centre and free margin.

Oddly, it is the will to project the centre and the margin as absolute antagonists which seems to ensure their indissoluble confederacy; the epochal 'rupture' which Derrida's 'Structure, Sign, and Play' essay promised, its rending of the bond between centre and structure, may paradoxically produce a structure of hysterically fixated absolutes, in which every leap into a world of pure, decentred play is snapped back by the remorseless elastic of the centre. It may be that for criticism to attempt to speak for and occupy the place of the absolutely marginal is an illusory compensation for the larger tendencies which have been affecting the literary academy and the humanities in general over the last twenty years, an attempt to give a melancholy glamour to the fact that the humanities have indeed been progressively edged from the centres of cultural power and influence. This is a resuscitation of the avant-garde belief that there is a place to stand and mount a critique which lies innocently outside or beyond the centres in which power, tradition and authority are invested. As John Tagg has suggested, this structure of thought fails to acknowledge the complexity of situations in which one may be both 'inside' and 'outside' structures of authority at the same time (this is precisely the condition of any present 'oppositional' literary-critical practice), and inhibits the responsive analysis of complex or 'overdetermined' structures of power in language and thought (Tagg, 1985–6). Post-structuralist criticism will need now to find some more expansive way of imaginatively 'territorializing' the concept of structure than in the frozen map of centre and margin. Specifically, post-structuralist literary studies need to maintain their interrogation of the functions and limits of literature and criticism in order to resist being rationalized into mere procedural routines. Necessary to this is a renunciation of the romance of the absolute outsider, and the attendant consolations of marginality, and an acknowledgement of the complex, conjunctural forms in which language, knowledge and power always function.

FURTHER READING

Barthes, Roland (1974) *S/Z*, translated by Richard Miller, Hill & Wang, New York
Culler, Jonathan (1975) *Structuralist Poetics: Structuralism, Linguistics, and the Study of Literature*, Routledge & Kegan Paul, London
——(1983) *On Deconstruction: Theory and Criticism After Structuralism*, Routledge & Kegan Paul, London
——(1988) *The Framing the Sign*, Basil Blackwell, Oxford
de Man, Paul (1981) 'Hypogram and Inscription: Michael Riffaterre's Poetics of Reading', *Diacritics*, 11, 17–35
Foucault, Michel (1972) *The Archaeology of Knowledge*, translated by A. M. Sheridan Smith, Tavistock, London
Harari, Josué (ed.) (1980) *Textual Strategies: Perspectives in Post-Structuralist Criticism*, Methuen, London
Lacan, Jacques (1977) *Écrits: A Selection*, translated by Alan Sheridan, Tavistock, London
Lodge, David (ed.) (1988) *Modern Criticism and Theory: A Reader*, Longman, London
Miller, J. Hillis (1982) *Fiction and Repetition: Seven English Novels*, Basil Blackwell, Oxford
Spivak, Gayatri Chakravorty (1987) *In Other Worlds: Essays in Cultural Politics*, Methuen, London
Young, Robert (ed.) (1981) *Untying the Text: A Post-Structuralist Reader*, Routledge & Kegan Paul, London

ADDITIONAL WORKS CITED

Chambers, Iain (1987) 'Maps for the Metropolis: A Possible Guide to the Present', *Cultural Studies*, 1, 1–21
Connor, Steven (1985) *Charles Dickens*, Basil Blackwell, Oxford
Derrida, Jacques (1978) 'Structure, Sign and Play in the Discourse of the Human Sciences'. In Jacques Derrida, *Writing and Difference*, translated by Alan Bass, Routledge & Kegan Paul, London, pp. 278–94
——(1987) 'Le Facteur de la Verité'. In Jacques Derrida, *The Post-Card: From Socrates*

to *Freud and Beyond*, translated by Alan Bass, University of Chicago Press, Chicago, pp. 411–96

Hawkes, Terence (1977) *Structuralism and Semiotics*, Methuen, London

Jakobson, Roman (1970) *Shakespeare's Verbal Art in 'Th'Expence of Spirit'*, Mouton, The Hague

Jakobson, Roman and Lévi-Strauss, Claude (1972a) 'Charles Baudelaire's "Les Chats"'. In F. and M. de George (eds), *The Structuralists from Marx to Lévi-Strauss*, Doubleday, New York, pp. 124–46

Jameson, Fredric (1981) *The Political Unconscious: Narrative as a Socially Symbolic Act*, Methuen, London

Johnson, Barbara (1980) *The Critical Difference: Essays in the Contemporary Rhetoric of Reading*, Johns Hopkins University Press, Baltimore

Lacan, Jacques, (1972) 'Seminar on the Purloined Letter', translated by Jeffrey Mehlman, *Yale French Studies*, 48, 38–72

Lévi-Strauss, Claude (1972b) 'The Structural Study of Myth'. In F. and M. de George (eds), *The Structuralists from Marx to Lévi-Strauss*, Doubleday, New York, pp. 169–94

Moi, Toril (1985) *Sexual/Textual Politics: Feminist Literary Theory*, Methuen, London

Riffaterre, Michael (1978) *The Semiotics of Poetry*, Indiana University Press, Bloomington

Tagg, John (1985–6) 'Postmodernism and the Born-Again Avant-Garde', *Block*, 11, 3–7

55

FEMINIST LITERARY CRITICISM: 'NEW COLOURS AND SHADOWS'

CORA KAPLAN

In a 1929 essay titled 'Women and Fiction', published in the same year as *A Room of One's Own*, Virginia Woolf speculated on the 'new colours and shadows' in women's writing which would inevitably appear now that the 'English woman' was transformed 'from a nondescript influence, fluctuating and vague, to a voter, a wage-earner, a responsible citizen'. As women took up their place as full civic subjects in the public sphere, Woolf considered that their 'relations' would become 'not only emotional' but also 'intellectual' and 'political'. Their novels would become more engaged with the 'impersonal', more 'critical of society, and less analytical of individual lives'. No longer the 'dumping ground for personal emotions' women's fiction would observe men and women 'as they cohere and clash in groups and classes and races'. This political transformation of imaginative writing would, she hoped, be but a first 'short step to the practice of the sophisticated arts . . . to the writing of essays and criticism, of history and biography'. More important still, for Woolf, the 'greater impersonality of women's lives will encourage the poetic spirit' that will lead them even further, 'beyond the personal and political relationships to the wider questions which the poet tries to solve – of our destiny and the meaning of life'. Lest this hope resonate as pure idealism, Woolf reminds the reader that 'the poetic attitude is largely founded upon material things', 'upon leisure, and a little money' which provide 'the chance . . . to observe impersonally and dispassionately'. With all the advantages of middle-class men – a professional job, a vote, economic independence, leisure and a legitimate public presence – women, Woolf prophesied, 'will make a fuller and more subtle use of the instrument of writing' ([1929] 1979, pp. 50–1).

Woolf's projection of a dynamic transformation and exponential increase in women's writing turned out to be well-founded, if we accept the social boundaries of her utopian vision that the requirements of leisure, money and the novelty of wage-earning implies. Even so, it took another world war, the expansion of education in Britain and America, and the second wave of the twentieth-century woman's movement to give white middle-class women, and to some extent their less privileged sisters also, the professional base, the political platform and the reading audiences on which to build their new discursive Jerusalem. Feminist criticism as a lively and growing body of work is one aspect of that cultural revolution. Yet although Woolf's writing in every genre remains a touchstone for many feminist critics, the 'field' of feminist criticism in its anglophone formation is now some twenty years old, and no longer needs to display a distinguished lineage to legitimize its project. Indeed, feminist criticism today prefers to play down the question of its origins and to emphasize instead the present richness, diversity and intellectual influence of its product. For it is a modern phenomenon, a broad strand, wider and more dazzling than even Woolf's euphoria allowed her to imagine. Its rubric now includes the criticism of visual narrative from avant-garde cinema to pornography, interdisciplinary studies that fully integrate social and cultural material, and work in which theory is read and written through the strategies of literary analysis. Competing perspectives, theoretical and political, reflect debates within feminism, within literary and cultural studies generally and at the busy intersections of English-speaking academia where they meet and engage. Origins may be elided amidst this confusing bounty, but genealogy still has its uses in helping us to focus upon the most significant differences between discrete moments in the development of feminist criticism. In this sense genealogy may serve as historical critique, without implying either justification or progression.

As a first step we might explore the ways in which Woolf's inter-war agenda for women novelists, which included her hopes for criticism as well, is in synch or at odds with the premises which underlay feminist cultural analysis from the late 1960s onwards. A crucial distinction between the two is their characterization of the domestic and private. Woolf described this women's world of cooking and childrearing as intangible, vague, anonymous – a 'dark country' she calls it ([1929] 1979, p. 50), echoing Mary Wollstonecraft's charge, almost 150 years earlier in *A Vindication of the Rights of Woman*, that women were 'immured in their families, groping in the dark' ([1792] 1988, p. 5). Second-wave feminists, too, would repeat this analogy, locating woman's oppression initially as her imprisonment in the bourgeois household as mother and unpaid servant, a position, they argued, that was not fundamentally changed either by the franchise or by the expanded opportunities for women workers in the decades that followed it. Yet although marriage, the family, motherhood and the fetishization of domesticity were subjected to a powerful attack in post-war feminist analysis, this critique tried hard not to denigrate either the lives or the creativity of those female subjects caught and fixed in the exploitative ideologies which maintained the separate spheres. Under the banner of 'the personal is political', feminist critics reread the domestic and sensational fiction that Woolf had stigmatized as the mere 'dumping ground for the emotions' as political texts, honouring, as Woolf did not, both the autobiographical impulse, and the proto-feminist one, the desire to expose their own suffering, to plead their own cause. Woolf saw the intrusion of 'a woman's presence' in the form of woman's 'anger' – 'of someone resenting the treatment of her sex and pleading for its rights' ([1929] 1979, p. 47) – as a distortion or weakness in writing. Her analysis reduced this anger to a selfish subjectivism – 'personal discontent or grievance' (p. 47) – rather than reading it as collective or general. Post-war feminist criticism would effectively reverse this judgement, arguing instead for a revision of critical value to include an aesthetics of anger. Instead modern feminist criticism championed a politics of writing that thrived on difference and protest and did not yearn, as Woolf did, for an 'aloofness' of vision, with 'little or no foreign influence to disturb it' (p. 48). As a consequence recent feminist criticism has singled out the 'angry' fictions that Woolf used as her examples of 'flawed' texts, *Jane Eyre* and *Middlemarch*, for special praise and attention, and has reread more conventional women's fiction against the grain to find in them elements of rebellion, rage, and resistance to the hierarchies of gender.

In Woolf's repeated use of it the term 'impersonal' as an ideal for women's writing comes to signify an impossible relationship between gendered identity and artistic practice. Women's art, Woolf argued, would become both more political and more poetic if liberated from the claustrophobic intensity and self-absorption of a female subjectivity bred and confined in the domestic ghetto. In it there are no libidinally creative spaces – neither kitchen, nursery nor bedroom can serve – except perhaps, and her disgust is vivid and visceral, the lavatory or 'dumping ground' which is the only women's room available when the private sphere is all she has. There is something distressing and unreflective in the subliminal, scatalogical violence of this attack which involves a blurring of the domestic setting of women's subordination with an already degraded definition of femininity. The oppositions between the personal and impersonal become those between the grotesque and the classical body which are figured as feminine and masculine. The one is pathologically distressed, transgressively emotional, execratory, unaesthetic – the other 'aloof', imperially remote, objectively observing. Woolf's metaphor betrays among other things the naïve nativism, even racism of her inter-war nirvana for the creative imagination. She evokes a social and psychic writing space imagined as an intellectual little England – with 'no foreign influence to disturb it' ([1929] 1979, p. 48). And here her liberating visions become wholly incompatible, the aesthetic radically at odds with the political, for women writers in her new dispensation were simultaneously to remain distant from and engaged with the conflict of men and women as they 'cohere and clash in groups and classes and races' (p. 51).

These unresolved contradictions focus a particular set of cultural anxieties for Woolf and other feminist modernists of the 1920s and 1930s. However, the issues these aporias raise are part of a more general crisis of representation in the twentieth century and they continue to haunt second-wave feminist criticism, for they both define and interrogate the terms of its feminist agenda. The 'personal'/'impersonal' binary, for example, gets translated into 'experience'/'theory', 'social'/'psychic', 'humanist'/'antihumanist', 'essentialist'/ 'antiessentialist', 'psychoanalytic/materialist'. These opposed categories are, today, further divided into different post-structuralist camps, where, for example, feminist Derrideans face feminist Foucauldians. These are by no means the only or most important differences within feminist cultural analysis. The tacit cultural exclusions of Woolf's analysis, reproduced by some of the most important feminist work of the 1960s and early 1970s in America, elicited another kind of response from the groups thus marginalized – a defiant and productive fragmentation of feminist criticism into categories of identity – Black feminist criticism, lesbian feminist criticism, for instance. Work in these tendencies, as in the more heterogeneous and nominally post-modern strands of 'gender studies' and 'gay and lesbian studies', crosses and recrosses both disciplinary and theoretical divides.

Feminist criticism today is as much concerned with woman as reader as with woman as writer – what Elaine Showalter usefully defined in 'Towards a Feminist Poetics' (1979) as the twin projects of 'feminist critique' and – in a word she coined – 'gynocritics'. Showalter originally thought of 'feminist critique' as a somewhat negative enterprise, teaching us 'only what men have thought women should be', and, in its theoretical register, requiring 'a long apprenticeship to the male theoretician' (1979, p. 27). In practice, however, it has seemed more liberating and less depressive than that, generating a wide variety of work that does much more than confirm the burden of our oppression, from Kate Millett's *Sexual Politics* (1969), which made it impossible to read the sexual scenarios of modern literature as innocently liberatory, to such different kinds of studies as Alice Jardine's *Gynesis: Configurations of Woman and Modernity* (1985), Naomi Schor's *Reading in Detail: Aesthetics and the Feminine* (1987) and Tania Modleski's study of Hitchcock, *The Women Who Knew Too Much* (1988).

I have begun, however, with a discussion of the shifting terms and recurrent pitfalls of gynocriticism partly because in some sense the issues which it foregrounds include those which arise when we consider woman as reader – of men's texts and women's texts, whether literary or theoretical. Men's writing across discourses, as feminism has rightly argued, constructs a range of denigrating ideological representations of 'woman', in order to attach a virtuous masculinity to a miscellany of valorized concepts – aesthetic, philosophical, political or scientific. Decoding, in order to disarm these insidious negative inscriptions, has been one of the most important tasks of feminist critique, and belongs to a project that goes back to the origins of modern feminism, that is, to the early years of modernity itself and to the writings of Mary Wollstonecraft. But, as we have just seen in relation to Woolf, a shift of attention to the woman writer, or woman theorist/critic, does not necessarily displace these negative and projective descriptions of the feminine, though they are now seen as inscribed from a different subject position. In order to really 'dismantle the Master's house', in poet Audre Lorde's words, post-war feminist criticism has had to stand back a little from the generally celebratory register in which it had initially constructed an alternative canon of women's writing. The texts in that revised canon and the principles underlying their selection can, it is now recognized, reinstate old and instate new negative femininities at the same time as they imagine feminist utopias.

As part of its sometimes painful review of its own history, feminist criticism in the 1980s has fielded a series of questions that move across the binaries noted above and break down the distinction between woman as reader and woman as writer, as well as between imaginative writer and critic. Concerned with textuality as well as subjectivity, the first cluster of questions is simultaneously epistemological and political: 'What is woman?'; 'Where is writing?'; 'What and where are woman *and* writing when women are writing about women?'

The first question – 'What is woman?' – summarizes a long debate within feminism about its appropriation of both liberal humanism and essentialism. Immanent in all the feminist critical interventions of the 1960s and early 1970s, liberal humanism assumes the possibility of a coherent social and psychic identity, an identity endowed with individual agency. Humanism insists on a concept of self as potentially unified even where it has been fragmented by the cultural violence of oppression – that aspiration to psychic unity and social agency is the nub of women's freedom, the heart of her emancipation. Woolf's ideal combination of the rational impersonal with the poetic is a fair enough representation of its aesthetic dimension. Feminist humanism has rewritten the script of a universal human nature, redressing to a certain extent its masculinist bias, but it does not necessarily endow supposed female virtues – of nurturance, non-violence or relatedness for instance – with a biological base, or claim that sexual difference is somehow fixed as gender divided human essence. Essentialism, therefore, adds another element to humanism (though the two terms are often used interchangeably) and one which makes it easier to claim both transhistorical and transcultural unity between women, as well as to emphasize the similarity between all forms of patriarchal domination.

The positions sketched out above are necessarily abstracted outlines of a general philosophical ground from which specific works of humanist feminist criticism proceeded. In answer to the question 'What is woman?', we might argue that such criticism did not ask enough questions about the relationship between patriarchal ideologies – the dominant discourses of sexuality in Victorian England for example – and subjectivity. Was bourgeois femininity a set of prescriptions imposed on an ungendered humanity, or a female but not feminine subject; or, as a materialist feminism would argue, were sexual identity and difference constructed by and through those discourses? Most of these early feminist humanist studies do not even address these kinds of epistemological questions or their political implications. To dismiss this body of work because of this absence is, however, to miss the real contribution of the recent past to feminist theory and analysis. The major achievement of feminist criticism of the 1960s and 1970s was to rewrite the cultural history of nineteenth- and twentieth-century Britain and America, putting gender, not just women, in where it had been left out by an older liberal tradition of cultural history and criticism. The effect of this intervention was a profound disruption of the androcentric and universalizing assumptions of that tradition about culture and subjectivity. None of the work of younger critics today could have proceeded without this spirited challenge to male humanism in the interventions of Mary Ellman (*Thinking of Women*, 1968), Sandra Gilbert and Susan Gubar (*The Madwoman in the Attic*, 1979), Ellen Moers (*Literary Women*, 1976) or Elaine Showalter (*A Literature of Their Own*, 1977); nor have their studies been superseded by new cohorts of critics who write from other perspectives. Their original research, innovative interpretations and eloquent, elegant polemics provided a base and a model for others to build their critiques upon. Kate Millett – the only radical feminist in this imposing critical vanguard who might, at a stretch, be called an essentialist in that her work seems often to play into a notion of a naturally nasty masculinity, psychic and social – is also, interestingly, the critic whose post-war project most closely resembled that of Michel Foucault – to write the history of sexuality and the history of representation together by looking at the power relations immanent in the languages and practices – what Foucault calls 'discourse' – of particular historical periods. *Sexual Politics* (1969) was a stunning example of 'feminist critique' (Showalter, 1979, p. 25), a reading of male texts, which made a whole generation who came of age as *Lady Chatterley's Lover* entered the public domain, and who naïvely celebrated it as a liberating narrative, look again – and again – at the textual politics of sexual narrative.

Yet these studies were vulnerable in ways that now seem obvious, and which return us to the question 'What is woman?' Marxist-feminist criticism from Britain in the 1970s, and socialist-feminist criticism in the United States in the same period, had been quick to point to the universalizing assumptions of feminist humanism and its implication in a bourgeois aesthetics. Toril Moi's influential *Sexual/Textual Politics* (1985) initiated a sharp socialist-feminist critique from an Anglo-European point of view of the politics of American feminist humanism; her emphasis is on the unexamined 'liberal individualism' of their perspective. Another set of Anglo-American criticisms focused on the textual/authorial exclusions in this work. Where feminist humanists focused on middle-class women's writing as the marginal or suppressed writing in the public domain, they rarely looked for or at what was marginal or suppressed within that writing, at the negative class and racial identities, often gendered female, which framed the bourgeois 'heroinism' of their texts. Even less did they look at women's writing from the margins – the work of working-class, black, colonial or lesbian writers. Humanist feminists assumed that the specific concerns of white, middle-class heterosexual women writers virtually represented the narrative of all women, and read their psychic and social narratives as emblematic of the vicissitudes of gender.

Against this generalizing force, the various versions of feminist anti-humanism and anti-essentialism (but also an important strand of social humanism that lies philosophically and politically somewhere in between) have all highlighted the differences between women – differences of class, race, nationality and temporality, targeting the universal and the natural as ideological concepts that serve to reify negative definitions of women. Most feminist post-structuralism, whatever its particular critical orientation (Derridean, Foucauldian, Lacanian, New Historicist) now goes much further in directly challenging the category of 'woman' itself, focusing on the differences within any given definition of woman, or the feminine. And there are considerable differences within and between these positions. A neo-Marxist, feminist anti-humanism, or one strongly influenced by the work of Michel Foucault, might well want to stop at the rejection of the universality of the feminine or any version of identity or subjectivity that is not socially constructed. Their notion of a discourse emphatically includes both linguistic expression and social practice. For strict feminist deconstructionists, on the other hand, subjectivity itself is an effect of language, a figuration constantly undermined by the competing terms which define it. Their focus is primarily on the rhetorical operations of language, on its play, its textuality. But for feminist psychoanalytic theorists and critics such as Jacqueline Rose, the issue of 'the social' remains, though it no longer does so as a 'simple dichotomy between inside and outside' (1986, p. 23). Rather, she sees femininity as a precarious and dangerous identity, the product of a psychic process marked by its violence which establishes all gendered subjectivity as inherently unstable. This instability is not, however, reducible to a series of rhetorical devices or tropes, although the psychic in language operates through repetition, displacement, condensation, projection, metonymy and metaphor. For her, deconstruction cannot resolve the political and theoretical problem which the dichotomy between social/psychic presents for any practice, like feminism, which demands human agency for its realization. She argues that the Derridean 'dispatching of the subject and its dissolution into a writing strategy . . . leads to the political demand for its return. For the political necessity of the subject is met in part by the psychic necessity of the subject, but in a way which finds itself suspended between each of these demands, for this subject is neither pure assertion nor play' (1986, p. 26).

As a response to this same problem Barbara Johnson, a feminist deconstructionist, defends the politics of deconstruction as political, and feminist, identifying the theoretical project and its contradictions with the literary one. 'The task of the writer . . . would seem to be to narrate both the appeal and the injustice of universalization, in a voice that assumes and articulates its own, ever-differing self difference' (Johnson, 1987, p. 170). Johnson's exemplary writer is the African-American novelist and folklorist Zora Neale Hurston, who can move in the opening pages of *Their Eyes Were Watching God* (1937) 'from the seduction of a universal language through a progressive de-universalization that ends in the exclusion of the very protagonist herself' (Johnson, 1987, p. 170). In a daring appropriation of a typically 'essentialist' or 'humanist' strategy, Johnson identifies the task of a feminist deconstruction with the literally endless tasks of women's work, and these with their literary embodiments, Mrs Ramsay's knitting, 'Penelope's weaving . . . nightly re-unraveled' (Johnson, 1987, p. 171). For Johnson, it is precisely Derrida's undecidable, as it might reside rhetorically in the ambiguity of address, in an African-American woman's poem about abortion (and in the abortion issue for women generally), that points us towards the understanding that 'rhetorical, psychoanalytical, and political structures are profoundly implicated in one another' (Johnson, 1987, p. 199).

Johnson's attempt to instance the feminist politics of deconstruction as non-coherent identity, and ambivalent positionality, through the work of African-American women writers, is a complicated engagement of her own cultural and critical identity, for she is a white feminist critic. Among African-American feminist critics the debate about the uses of theory – as well as about what theory to use – has been as impassioned and productive as elsewhere within cultural/literary studies. Barbara Christian, the author of *Black Feminist Criticism* (1985), probably emerges as the most recalcitrant 'humanist' in this tendency; the 'discovery of self' is a central theme in her work. Even so, her deployment of the term 'universal' suggests her difference from white feminist humanism, for it is a universality born of the historical experience of the Black diaspora and of specific alliances between women of colour which she refers to. Among African-American feminist critics, Hortense J. Spillers ([1985] 1989) foregrounds the whole range of post-structuralist theories as part of her critical strategies, but she is not eager to turn African-American women's fiction or poetry into ideal deconstructive texts. In contrast to Johnson, she is interested in the appropriation of humanist modes in African-American writers and the limitation this imposes on their work. Deborah McDowell, another African-American feminist critic, might well be in debate with Johnson when she interprets Sherley Ann Jackson's novel *Dessa Rose* (1984) about gender and American slavery as participating 'aggressively in the critique of the subject and the critique of binary oppositions, both commonly associated with the post-structuralist project' (McDowell, 1989, p. 147). The novel, she argues, 'wrestles with questions about the politics and problematics of representation', but 'swerves away from the empty notions of radical indeterminacy' in order to ground 'the oppositions it stages – slavery and freedom, orality and literacy, fact and fiction – in an untidy network of social and material specificities' (1989, p. 147).

The need to centre historical/cultural specificity when questioning the textual politics – ideological frameworks and generic conventions – used by Black women writers from the mid-nineteenth century onwards is argued at length by a black critic from Britain, Hazel V. Carby, in her important book *Reconstructing Womanhood: The Rise of the Black Woman Novelist* (1987). Carby writes about the history of African-American women as a neo-Marxist whose theoretical perspective comes out of British cultural studies. In her essay 'The Historical Novel of Slavery', Carby sees a danger in the way in which Black male critics' use of contemporary critical theory has 'produced a discourse that romanticizes the folk roots of Afro-American culture and denies the transformative power of both historical and urban consciousness' (Carby, 1989, p. 140). In line with Carby's resistance to the political pastoral, as fiction, criticism or feminism, we might see writer Toni Morrison's argument, that what cultural critics describe as the effects of post-modernity – the fragmentation or erasure of identity, the loss of historicity – had already happened to Black people in slavery. Morrison has little romantic investment in the rural or 'folk' tradition. Her concern, like Carby's, is the uses of fiction in modernity and post-modernity. In 'Rootedness: The Ancestor as Foundation', Morrison suggests that Black fiction today functions for a widely scattered Black population across the world as a forum for debate and interpretation of their experience, replacing the forms of communication in Church and polity of those now vanished tightly-knit Black communities (Morrison, 1985, pp. 340–1). All these Black feminist critics address the third question I posed earlier, 'What and where are women *and* writing when women are writing about women?' For them, however, this issue is bound up inextricably with other political and cultural questions of modernity in an international as well as nationally specific framework.

This 'global' orientation demands that western feminist critics reflect more fully on their ambiguous and often uncomfortably privileged position *vis-à-vis* other cultures and the history of imperialism. The feminist critic and theorist who has put this view most urgently and eloquently is Gayatri Chakravorty Spivak, herself the cultural product of at least three geopolitical contexts – the Indian subcontinent of her birth, the world of European theory which she helped to bring to America as an early translator and interpreter of Derrida, and the United States where she lives and teaches. A leading deconstructionist, her answer to the 'suspension of the subject between assertion and play' that Rose describes is rather different from any of the other critics we have considered. Although her work on both First and Third World texts uses a wide range of neo-Marxist and deconstructive arguments, she now advocates a 'strategic essentialism as a way to break the stalemate between a sophisticated anti-humanist theory of gender and the political imperatives of feminism' (Spivak, *In Other Worlds*, 1987).

The 1980s have therefore been a period of renegotiation for feminist criticism of the political and conceptual nature of their project and its relation to other forms of criticism and cultural analysis. As Spivak often reminds her readers and audiences, even these less ethnocentric and more globally literate agendas are being, by and large, formulated in the First, not the Second or Third Worlds, for the Anglophone West still owns the cultural capital – the economic and institutional framework and the means of distribution of texts – through which these feminist critiques of representation are funded and disseminated. Accordingly, feminist criticism today is more aware than ever that critic and text both need to be understood in relation to their position within culture – any new reading practice, any interrogation of gender that moves between the narrative and its audiences must first locate itself, and in doing so must reflect on its limitations and possibilities for its readers.

The critical pilgrim's progress of what Spivak has called one of feminism's 'cult texts' (1985, p. 263), Charlotte Brontë's *Jane Eyre* (1847), might be a useful instance of the shifts in feminist criticism's theory and perspective, from Woolf to the present. Brontë's novel occupies a central place in Woolf's own before and after assessment of women's writing. Its Victorian author is targeted as the paradigmatic case of the angry and 'thwarted' proto-feminism of the mid-nineteenth century. Woolf's distaste for any political fictional voice which 'pleads its own cause' – women, working-class men and Negroes are her three linked examples – is intensified by her disavowal of 'feminine' emotion and sentiment. *Jane Eyre* is her example of a 'flawed text', both soppy and shrill, in which the *declassée*, eternal feminine, 'always a governess, always in love', is disastrously doubled with a soap-box feminist defending her credo of emotional equality – 'women feel just as men feel' – from the rooftops of Thornfield. This moment of polemic, Woolf's 'awkward break' in the narrative, becomes the point of entry for second-wave feminist critics to insert their sequential rewriting of the aesthetics and politics of the novel. Feminist humanism in the 1960s and 1970s read *Jane Eyre* as the triumph of female agency over patriar-

759

chal power, celebrating Jane's self-conscious 'rebellious feminism'. Less problematically, they reversed Woolf's negative view of Brontë's aesthetic. Collectively, these critics successfully argued for gendered writing and for the
focusing on issues of sexual difference as they are played out in the novel, but
this phase of criticism paid scant attention to the equally important class and
racial resonances which orchestrate the drama of heterosexuality in the narrative. It was not until the mid-1980s that the book's feminist reputation underwent a fundamental reversal at the hands of feminist criticism.

Three new interpretations by Nancy Armstrong (*Desire and Domestic Fiction*,
1987), Gayatri Chakravorty Spivak ('Three Women's Texts', 1985), and Mary
Poovey (*Uneven Developments*, 1988) stake out new political and theoretical
terrain. The first two critics situate *Jane Eyre* as an ur-text of capitalism and
empire. Armstrong's perspective is neo-Marxist and Foucauldian, and her
thesis rewrites the history of the novel in relation to the centrality of gender.
She argues that 'domestic fiction actively sought to disentangle the language
of sexual relations from the language of politics and, in so doing, to introduce
a new form of political power' (1987, p. 3). Domestic fiction, but especially
the late romanticism of the Brontës, was central in 'formulating universal forms
of subjectivity', translating 'all kinds of political information into psychological
terms. As they displaced the facts and figures of social history, the Brontës
began producing new figures of desire that detached the desiring self from
place, time and material cause' (1987, p. 187). These 'figures of desire' are,
says Armstrong, in *Jane Eyre* aligned with the imperialist ideologies of the
novel itself. Armstrong's reading credits the sentimental power of the novel,
and its conservative rather than radical force. Implicit in her analysis is the
view that a feminism so rooted in the philosophical ground of capitalism and
empire cannot be progressive. Spivak's argument runs parallel to Armstrong's
in some respects, both in her general view of nation and novel – 'It should
not be possible to read nineteenth-century British literature without remembering that imperialism, understood as England's social mission, was a crucial
part of the cultural representation of England to the English' (1985, p. 262)
– and in her specific placing of *Jane Eyre* as a fiction which vividly articulates
the 'axioms of imperialism' (1985, p. 262). Jane's achieved goal of 'companion-
ate love' and St John Rivers's martyrdom on behalf of 'social mission' (pp.
263–4) are the complementary Victorian ideologies that reinforce that imperialism.

Mary Poovey tackles 'the ideological work of gender in Mid-Victorian
England', the subtitle of her book, from a different angle. Taking the debate
about the status of governesses in the 1840s as an historical 'border case', an
issue which condensed and focused contemporary anxieties about class and
gender, Poovey reads *Jane Eyre* as a contradictory text, part of a 'complex

ideological system' which can be heard as offering both challenge and hostage to contemporary social conservatism (1988, pp. 126–63).

Each of these readings displaces the feminist humanist emphasis on female agency, decentring Jane/Brontë as a composite heroine of modern feminism's prehistory. But while Armstrong and Spivak challenge the very ground of that feminism, using *Jane Eyre* as a case study which uncovers the reactionary origins and effects of feminist individualism, Poovey offers a somewhat less negative account of the text's engagement with contemporary socio-economic questions. Each of these readings invites more detailed work on the historical articulation of the text in contemporary discourses, and asks for more complex theorizations about the interrelation of race, class and gender. Each supports the argument that the representations of sexuality and difference were crucial components in the co-ordinate constructions of nation and novel in the nineteenth century.

As feminist criticism in English moves into the 1990s it does so with a much firmer institutional base and much greater cultural legitimacy than its early second-wave practitioners could have envisioned. Its frame of reference is more comprehensive and politically sensitive to the intersections between gender and other cultural determinants, race and nationality in particular. The heterosexual melodrama, the leitmotif in so much imaginative literature and visual narrative by men and women, is being deconstructed by feminist critics and theorists alike as an ideological scenario which fixes difference through the disavowal of other sexual positions and relations. Feminist criticism has gone far beyond its initial revision of the canon, or its rereading of particular texts, to argue successfully that the histories of representation very broadly conceived are fundamentally altered when gender is located at the centre of cultural analysis. The politics of subjectivity remains at the heart of feminist criticism's concern with gender and representation. However, the political and epistemological status of the female subject herself as author, reader, character, or supposed historical actor has become a question for discussion, not an assumed referent. Feminist criticism has become increasingly concerned with historicizing and theorizing the discursive construction of the gendered subject, and understanding how that semiosis always operates under and through the signs of other social and psychic systems of meaning.

The 'new colours and shadows' that inform feminist criticism today have put feminism itself, in its earlier paradigms and definitions, into question, shaking up, and in some cases breaking up, its philosophical, epistemological and political certainties, but confirming its importance as an analytic perspective. That interrogative force may, in the end, be its greatest strength and its most enduring contribution.

FURTHER READING

Carby, Hazel V. (1987) *Reconstructing Womanhood: The Emergence of the Afro-American Woman Novelist*, Oxford University Press, New York and Oxford.

deLauretis, Teresa (ed.) (1986) *Feminist Studies/Critical Studies*, Indiana University Press, Bloomington.

Gilbert, Sandra and Gubar, Susan (1979) *The Madwoman in the Attic: The Woman Writer and the Nineteenth Century Literary Imagination*, Yale University Press, New Haven

Johnson, Barbara (1987) *A World of Difference*, Johns Hopkins University Press, Baltimore

Millett, Kate (1969) *Sexual Politics*, Virago, London

Moers, Ellen (1976) *Literary Women: The Great Writers*, Doubleday Press, New York

Moi, Toril (1985) *Sexual/Textual Politics: Feminist Literary Theory*, Methuen, London and New York

Pryse, Marjorie and Spillers, Hortense J. (1985) *Conjuring: Black Women, Fiction, and Literary Tradition*, Indiana University Press, Bloomington

Rose, Jacqueline (1986) *Sexuality in the Field of Vision*, Verso Press, London

Showalter, Elaine (1977) *A Literature of Their Own: British Women Novelists from Brontë to Lessing*, Princeton University Press, Princeton

——(ed.) (1989) *Speaking of Gender*, Routledge, New York and London

Spivak, Gayatri Chakravorty (1987) *In Other Worlds: Essays in Cultural Politics*, Routledge, New York and London

Todd, Janet (1988) *Feminist Literary History*, Polity Press, Oxford

Wall, Cheryl A. (ed.) (1989) *Changing Our Own Words: Essays on Criticism, Theory and Writing by Black Women*, Rutgers University Press, New Brunswick

Woolf, Virginia (1979) 'Women and Fiction'. In Virginia Woolf, *Women and Writing*, introduction by Michèle Barrett, The Women's Press, London [essay first published 1929]

ADDITIONAL WORKS CITED

Armstrong, Nancy (1987) *Desire and Domestic Fiction: A Political History of the Novel*, Oxford University Press, New York and Oxford

Carby, Hazel V. (1989) 'Ideologies of Black Folk: The Historical Novel of Slavery'. In Deborah E. McDowell and Arnold Rampersad (eds), *Slavery and the Literary Imagination*, Johns Hopkins University Press, Baltimore

Christian, Barbara (1985) *Black Feminist Criticism: Perspectives on Black Women Writers*, Pergamon Press, New York

Ellmann, Mary (1968) *Thinking About Women*, Harcourt, New York

Jardine, Alice (1985) *Gynesis: Configurations of Women and Modernity*, Cornell University Press, Ithaca

McDowell, Deborah E. (1989) 'Negotiating Between Tenses: Witnessing Slavery after Freedom – *Dessa Rose*'. In Deborah E. McDowell and Arnold Rampersad (eds), *Slavery and the Literary Imagination*, Johns Hopkins University Press, Baltimore

Modleski, Tania (1988) *The Women Who Knew Too Much: Hitchcock and Feminist Theory*, Methuen, New York and London

Morrison, Toni (1985) 'Rootedness: The Ancestor as Foundation'. In Mari Evans (ed.), *Black Women Writers*, Pluto Press, London

Poovey, Mary (1988) *Uneven Developments: The Ideological Work of Gender in Mid-Victorian England*, University of Chicago Press, Chicago, and Virago Press, London

Schor, Naomi (1987) *Reading in Detail: Aesthetics and the Feminine*, Methuen, New York and London

Showalter, Elaine (1979) 'Towards a Feminist Poetics'. In Mary Jacobus (ed.), *Women Writing and Writing About Women*, Croom Helm, London, and Harper & Row, New York

Spillers, Hortense J. (1989) 'Changing the Letter: The Yokes, the Jokes of Discourse, or Mrs. Stowe, Mr. Reed'. In Deborah E. McDowell and Arnold Rampersad (eds), *Slavery and the Literary Imagination*, Johns Hopkins University Press, Baltimore [essay first published 1985]

Spivak, Gayatri Chakravorty (1985) 'Three Women's Texts and a Critique of Imperialism'. In Henry Louis Gates, Jr. (ed.), *Race, Writing and Difference*, University of Chicago Press, Chicago

Wollstonecraft, Mary (1988) *A Vindication of the Rights of Woman*, W. W. Norton & Co., New York and London [first published 1792]

56

PSYCHOANALYTIC CRITICISM

ELIZABETH WRIGHT

Psychoanalysis has problems with its credentials: it is not at present falsifiable and because of this it has not been regarded as one of the physical sciences. Its data depends on the clinical evidence it has defined, and its theory is built on accepting this evidence as true. Psychoanalytic theory, whether Freudian, Jungian, Kleinian or Lacanian, rests on the assumption that sexuality is the constitutive factor in the construction of the subject. Each school has its own mythology and this is often taken by opponents of psychoanalytic theory as proof that it must be nonsense. But this is forgetting that what all the schools have in common is that they find structural images in the mind which point to the way that the present is determined by the past in terms of the subject's sexual history. The beginning of this history is seen in every case as the sense of loss the subject experiences upon its separation from the mother's body.

What, though, has psychoanalysis to do with literary criticism? Much has been made by modern critics of the analogy between mental and linguistic processes: Jakobson in linguistics pointed to the links via metaphor and metonymy, and Lacan went further with his re-interpretation of the dreamwork's mechanisms as identical with certain classical tropes. This certainly makes psychoanalysis literary. But if what we really want is to make literary criticism psychoanalytic, another answer would be as follows: if we have any knowledge of the genetic origin of language in the individual and its growth through the interchange between mother, father and child, such knowledge is essential to the understanding of the literary process. Psychoanalytic theory brings out the intentional aspect of language through its concentration on the relationship between sexuality and social role: the unconscious aspect of utterance cannot be left out, when, as clinical practice has borne out, sexuality is so much the component of intention. All such utterance is concerned with the search for representations bound up with the satisfaction of drives. The literary text is a form of persuasion whereby bodies are speaking to bodies, not merely minds speaking to minds.

A psychoanalytic reading thus crucially involves accounting for the presence of sexuality in the text. This has been done in a number of ways. Historically the process of revealing and theorizing these sexual fantasies has gone through a series of by now familiar stages, moving from the analysis of the unconscious of the author, to that of the reader, to that of the text. These stages involve a changing view of the dynamics of the unconscious, and hence provoke different kinds of readings, based on different ideological assumptions. The field has become so complicated that it is no longer possible to work within a simple tripartite scheme of criticism that is author-based (and its corollary, character-based), reader-based and text-based, because each of these is subject to further divisions which may overlap the three boundaries. Another way of doing it is to use groupings based on theories of the subject rather than on methods by which such theories are applied. The present account is accordingly compiled under the following main headings: (1) Classical Freudian criticism; (2) Post-Freudian criticism; (3) Lacanian criticism; (4) Schizo-analysis; (5) Psychoanalytic Feminist Criticism. Within each of these headings there will be some smaller sub-headings.

CLASSICAL FREUDIAN CRITICISM

Classical applied psychoanalysis has analysed the literary work as a symptom of a particular artist. This has led to certain well-known presuppositions, such as the work of literature as analogous to a fantasy, within which the literary character is treated as if he or she were a living being and all figures become symbols which are part of a given and rigid code. This approach rests on the assumption that the purpose of the work of art is what psychoanalysis has found to be the purpose of the dream: the secret gratification of an infantile and forbidden wish. Though it was never claimed that this accounted for the creative writer's genius, it nevertheless led to a constant uncovering of a predictable content. However, it is often overlooked that psychoanalysis, for all its monotonous rehearsing of a set number of themes, can lead to a better understanding of the complexities of the relation between desire and figuration. Since this relation must involve an analysis of tropes, there is even here already an area where psychoanalysis and the literary text can mutually inform each other, establishing a relation between psychoanalysis and aesthetics.

Psychopathography

The classical psychoanalytic critic sees the relationship between author and text as analogous to that between the dreamer and his 'text'. The aim is to reveal the psychology of the author in terms of his unconscious infantile wishes, the emphasis being on the role played by the drives in accordance with Freud's dynamic model of the psyche, in which the pleasure principle conflicts with the reality principle.

The earliest probings of an author's life began with questions about the sources of the artist's/writer's creativity. In the latter half of the nineteenth century there was an attempt to relate genius to madness, and the artist's work was scrutinized for symptoms of the sick and the abnormal in the hope that a particular pathology could be classified (for early examples see Fischer, 1980). This seems to be how 'pathography' began, but it soon became indistinguishable from 'psychobiography', and hence the often-used compound term 'psychopathography'. Freud himself wavered over what to call his study of Leonardo, finally settling on the original term (Freud, 1985). His study is a case in point for the critical potential of the genre, dealing as it does with the effects of the unconscious on the figures and configurations in Leonardo's paintings. Having once moved away from the purely medical interest with which it began, psychopathography became largely text-centred, although the text is always treated as a symptom, analysed to betray the artist's individual intra-psychic conflict in terms of its reappearance in disguised and distorted forms, either in a single work (Heinz Kohut, 1982, on Thomas Mann's *Death in Venice*) or throughout the artist's oeuvre (Marie Bonaparte, 1949, on Poe). When the psychic history of an artist is rigorously explored in terms of the compulsive images which structure his work these studies still make fascinating reading. Even where such readings centre on the conflict of characters in the work (Kohut, 1982), it is usually related to the author by means of the argument that in displacing his conflict on to a character he thereby manages to preserve his artistic productivity.

The reductiveness of this approach has perhaps been made much too much of and a recent book has striven to redress the balance (Spitz, 1985). While it rightly points out that the critic is also involved and that her or his selection of material is hardly value-free (being influenced by her or his unconscious response to the artist's conflict), nevertheless the analysis involves a scrutiny of both the biography of the person and of the theory implied in the clinical material, which makes it less wild than the all-too-common psychologizing of literary characters. The old prejudice which holds that psychopathography can tell the reader nothing about the work should perhaps be re-examined in the light of modern reader-theory. If the artist is to be regarded not so much as an author but as a reader in his own right, then perhaps the history of his life, which gives closer access to his reading (over and above the history of his culture) might not be such a negligible element.

POST-FREUDIAN CRITICISM

Jungian criticism

Carl Jung's 'analytical psychology' differs very substantially from Freudian psychoanalysis. First, it is a self-psychology, with the self seen as the ultimate source and centre of the psyche: with Jung it is always a question of the *re-birth* of something that is already there. Second, he rejects Freud's theory of the libido as the energy underlying the transformation of the sexual drive, positing instead a notion of libido as a flux of undifferentiated energy, required to recharge the psyche periodically by re-investing certain primordial symbols he calls 'archetypes', for which he believes there is a predisposition. Although, like Freud, he believes in a personal unconscious as a repository of repressed contents, it is the notion of a 'collective unconscious' common to all cultures and capable of revitalizing both individual and race which is the cornerstone of his theory.

The consequences for a psychoanalytic criticism are that the text is no longer seen as a site of conflict where drives and defences meet, producing at best 'compromise formations' (where the drives get through in disguise), and at worst neurotic symptoms. Instead Jung maintains that the structure and dynamics of the psyche, as he has come to know it in his clinical work with schizophrenic patients, enable him to gain access to the images, myths and symbols of past cultures. Analytical psychology traces mental problems to an imbalance in the psyche of the individual, whether normal or abnormal. Both the individual in dreams and the artist at work will produce archetypal images to compensate for any psychic impoverishment in man and society. In keeping with his belief in an innate force, Jung sees the act of creation as an 'autonomous complex', originating in the unconscious (Jung, 1972). Hence for him there can be no question of analysing the work on the basis of the artist's or reader's personal psychology. Nor does Jung avail himself of the method of 'free association', since it is not the personal unconscious of the writer or reader that is at stake. He decodes texts, be they patients or literature, by a method he calls 'amplification', whereby images of the personal unconscious are immediately extended to those of the collective. A typical narrative centres on the figure of a hero as symbol of the dynamics of the libido. The hero's experience usually takes the form of a quest, whereby he journeys through a landscape of caves, water, labyrinths, and other dangerous enclosures that represent the unconscious, as well as the symbol of the Great Mother. The hero has to regress to a state of primal conflict with this figure, who threatens to devour him: his task is to free himself and break the regressive libidinal bond, the ultimate renunciation of the mother being what Jung calls 'the sacrifice'.

In his book *Wagner's 'Ring' and its Symbols* (1974), Robert Donington has attempted a large-scale Jungian interpretation in a dark mode: the hero is betrayed by his unconscious incest pursued via mother-fantasies, which he projects on to the various women he encounters. An earlier example is *Archetypal Patterns in Poetry* (1934) where Maud Bodkin analyses English poetry, drawing upon Jung's method of amplification, thereby giving the reader a more active role.

Ego-psychology

The post-Freudian critics who stayed with Freud's libido theory were critical of the approach based on Freud's dynamic model of the psychic apparatus, showing the pleasure principle opposed to the reality principle. They developed an approach based on Freud's structural model of the psyche as having three groups of functions (id, ego and superego), and concentrated on the ego as an adaptive agency. This shifted the emphasis in three respects: (1) the ego was seen as a creative force in its own right, the emphasis initially moving from the author to the text and its formal qualities (Empson, 1930; Kris, 1964); (2) aesthetic form was seen as giving pleasure and regulating anxiety (Lesser, 1957); (3) the focus of interest gradually shifted from text to reader, leading to a psychoanalytic reader-response theory.

The criticism of Norman Holland provides a clear instance of the move from classical to post-Freudian principles of reading. Like Freud, Holland sees the source of the pleasure the reader gets from literature as the transformations of unconscious wishes and fears through the form of the work. But he moves on from this to give the reader a more active role, in what he calls 'transactive criticism': a transactive account makes plain a reader's personal involvement with the text and thus makes central the effects of his identity. The expectations the reader brings to the text are challenged by the encounter; defensive strategies come into play to transform meanings that will allow the adaptation of the reader's identity, finally confirming it in a reassuring unity. Holland conducts experiments on empirical readers to compare their different responses to the same text, finally analysing his own responses to their response (Holland, 1975). He thereby avails himself of the psychoanalytic model of transference and counter-transference, the projection and counter-projection on to persons or objects of traumatic material from the past. But whereas this was formerly seen as mainly the author's problem, Holland makes it the reader's, thus reversing the traditional reader-text relationship: it is no longer the author that is being analysed but the reader.

Object-relations theory

The classical model of creativity is based on the notion of intra-psychic conflict: it shows the literary work as the outcome of a struggle culminating in the successful transformation of the sexual drive, with a consequent therapeutic effect on the reader. Object-relations theory provides another model of creativity, with the emphasis on inter-psychic relationships, and this gives the reader a new role.

It was Melanie Klein (1977) who formulated a theory of creativity which saw sublimation no longer as a transformation of the sexual drive but as a desire to make reparation for the imaginary damage once inflicted by the infant in the throes of innate aggressive and destructive impulses on the primal good object, the mother: by means of 'projection' unconscious wishes and feelings are expelled from the self and attributed to another object; by means of 'introjection' qualities belonging to an external object are absorbed and appropriated. The creative act gratifies the need to expiate and make whole again: it involves seeing the work of art as an object in its own right, analogous to the infant's ability in time to see the mother as a whole object, instead of split into good and bad parts. D. W. Winnicott (1974) went a step further. Where Klein had made use of play to enable the child to communicate its early experience, Winnicott produced a theory of playing in which play, art and cultural experience are seen as 'potential space' between mother and child, within which the child invests its 'transitional' objects, their boundaries as yet undecided, with dream meaning and feeling. For Winnicott this is a step on the way to shared playing and cultural experience.

Object-relations theory has found its way into both literary and art criticism in a number of ways. In England Adrian Stokes (1977) and Peter Fuller (1980) have used Kleinian theory as a transhistorical mode of interpretation for selected periods of sculpture and painting, in which the relation both of the artist to his medium and of the viewer to the artist is crucial, since in each case to allow for the otherness of the object amounts to an ethical commitment. The French psychoanalyst and critic André Green (1980) has used Winnicott's notion of potential space as an analogy of what goes on between author and reader, seeing the text as a neutral ground, where the loss each feels might be assuaged by the filling of this space with the communicative act of a writing and reading self, doubles of the historical author and the individual living reader, who are each excluded from this space. The analytic space is analogous to the reading space, where the text works on the two readers (author and reader), recreating the intense relationships of the past. The reader gives the figures of the text the kind of 'free-floating attention' which the analyst gives the patient, but rather than treat the text as patient, the reader treats it as a co-analyst. Both the double de-centring and the intersubjective nature of this relation have links with the theories to be discussed under Schizoanalysis below.

Psychocriticism

Charles Mauron is the inventor of 'psychocriticism', a type of psychological criticism which, according to its own assumptions, sets out to study the subjective phenomenon of art by a scientific understanding grounded in psychoanalytic theory. The method Mauron has developed is fourfold: (1) to search out compulsive motifs – obsessive structures and metaphors – which work across an author's oeuvre; (2) to 'superimpose' one set with another, with the object of finding the dominant fantasy lurking beneath and between; (3) to chart the variation of this 'network of associations' throughout the works; (4) to scrutinize the author's life for corroboration, finally arriving at his 'personal myth' (Mauron, 1958). It is the understanding of how the fantasy operates in the author's life which leads to the personal myth; the relations between the man and the myth are thus one of the main objects of the exercise. Mauron has written on Nerval, Van Gogh, Mallarmé, but he is not interested in the latent content of the work as indicative of an author's pathology, as is the case in classical psychopathography. What interests him is the way an artist has mastered his obsession by certain psychic feats and to this end he has adapted and assimilated a variety of ego-psychologies, notably those of Klein (projection and introjection), Anna Freud (defence mechanisms), and Jung (personal myth). Another factor that distinguishes his practice from that of the classical Freudian critic is that he does not use literature to validate the findings of psychoanalysis, but reverses the hierarchy by using psychoanalysis to confirm what the critic had discovered in the artist's work. What is finally at stake for Mauron, however, is the discovery of a hidden unity, the work of the personal unconscious. The method has been of value to others, for instance, to Serge Doubrovsky (1978) in a close textual reading of a scene in Sartre's *La Nausée*.

LACANIAN CRITICISM

Central to Lacan's return to Freud is his move from Freud's concept of the wish as subjective, private, regressive, to the concept of desire as intersubjective, public, future-directed. The wish in Freud's theory is directed towards the reactivation of a memory-image associated with a past satisfaction or frustration, in which the mother's role is decisive. Lacan avoids this concentration on regression by means of a theory grounded in structural linguistics. He takes from Saussure the notion of language as a system of signs determined by their difference from each other. But where Saussure sees the sign as a bonding of signifier (sound-image) and signified (concept), Lacan sees each signifier as invested with unconscious desire. A gap opens between the inner private experience of bodily need and the outer public interpretation of it. Neither the subject nor others recognize this gap. Lacan's theory of the subject stresses this gap coming into being with the unconscious by the imposition of signifiers upon need. Through language, need is addressed to the Other (other subjects in the sign system) in the form of a demand for absolute love which the Other has not got to give. What is left over is unassuaged desire, desire for recognition of the Other's desire. The discourse of psychoanalysis is here taken as a model for any kind of speech or writing: there is no fixed meaning, either latent or manifest, to which Lacan's notorious style bears witness.

Whereas classical psychoanalytic criticism operated with a firm distinction between conscious and unconscious meaning, in Lacan's theory conscious and unconscious cannot be separated. The unconscious bears the marks of the signifiers impressed upon it. The text no longer harbours regressive wishes but engages with current desires encompassing both past and future experience. As a child once lured by its mirror-image (Lacan's 'Imaginary order'), which promised it a wholeness which it lacked, so the text lures the reader by the force of its representation. But at the same time the text is also Law (Lacan's 'Symbolic order' of language), shattering the mirror illusion and dispersing the reader. The lure of the Imaginary is a prelude to the capture of the subject in the signifying chain, as both the reading subject in the text (the characters) and the reading subject of the text (the empirical reader) are caught in a structure of repetition (Felman, 1977). The text is a trap for the unwary reader/character who chases his/her image, only to become trapped in the signifying chain. The reader can hence be seen as at the mercy of the text, since she or he will not know what referential effects will be brought into play in the course of reading; but the text is also at the mercy of the reader, because of the mediating effects of her or his own unconscious.

Language is the place where the personal and the cultural intersect, where there is a constant displacement of meaning. One of the difficulties of psycho-analytic reader-theory has been the problem of assigning an unconscious to the text: for Lacan transference is a process that goes on in language, but, because the unconscious is that residue or excess that cannot be defined, there will always be gaps that neither author nor reader will finally be able to fill in. Both author and reader are controlled by the strategies of language. In his reading of Poe's *The Purloined Letter*, Lacan (1972) offers an allegory of the displacement of the signifier: the characters in the text are determined by the position of the master-signifier, which for Lacan is the phallus. Lacan's reading of this story is not a literary interpretation, but a study of discourse in the light of psychoanalytic theory. Lacan reveals a structure of desire which assigns a set of characters their places in a predetermined power-system.

SCHIZOANALYSIS

Gilles Deleuze and Félix Guattari (1975) have argued for a more radical criticism, one grounded in Lacan's notion of a signifying chain, but one which refuses the necessity of a master-signifier, of the Father's Law as dominant. They rebel against psychoanalysis because it shows the unconscious as characterized by hunger and want. For them the Freudian unconscious is a capitalist construction, an internalized set of power relations, the result of repression produced by capitalism in the family. Psychoanalysis aids and abets this process, whereas 'schizoanalysis' sees libido as still fluid, as a flow prior to representation and production. Schizoanalysis aims to construct an unconscious. For Deleuze and Guattari desire is not rooted in lack, but is unaccountably present from the beginning: they refuse any notion of a subject in search of a lost object. The function of a productive unconscious is *not* to preserve the trace of a fundamentally lost object. Energy is not reduced to anxiety (as in Harold Bloom's theory, 1973), but to be fostered as a positive intensity, striving towards new articulations. Bodies are 'desiring machines' because machines arrange and connect flows. What these Lacanian revisionists take from Lacan is an understanding that language-systems have a built-in instability because the self is constructed out of bodily experience by means of language.

For Deleuze and Guattari unconscious desire tends to one or other of two poles, a schizophrenic one which 'deterritorializes' desire, constantly shifting boundaries, and a paranoiac one, which 'territorializes', marking out certain directions for desire. Deleuze and Guattari's 'material psychiatry' becomes a political factor in its attempt to release the libidinal flow from what they see as oppression rather than repression. They enlist literature because, like schizophrenia, it too tries to break out of the system. They find Kafka's work particularly suited to their project: Kafka's work is a 'rhizome', a fertile tuber that sprouts unexpected plants out of concealment (Deleuze and Guattari, 1975). They isolate certain sets of images, not in any tidy binary opposition (in the Freudian sense of drive against defence), but ones that constantly combine and recombine with other images. What Deleuze and Guattari are aiming for is the recapturing of pre-linguistic experience, unconscious investments of sounds and sights which stimulate resistance to repression and liberate desire. Kafka's work is revolutionary for Deleuze and Guattari because their schizoanalysis allows them to reveal the unconscious investments of desire as more powerful than those determined by family and state. Desire has to begin with a line of flight, a deterritorializing move: the revolutionary reader/ writer conducts experiments to try and find a way out of a given representation.

FEMINIST PSYCHOANALYTIC CRITICISM

To find a way out of the given representation is precisely the project of a feminist psychoanalytic criticism, though this is not where it would want to stop. Freud's several attempts to construct a narrative adequate to female sexuality (Chasseguet-Smirgel, 1981) end up with the same bleak theme: the girl is a little man until the advent of the castration complex. Feminist psychoanalysis evolved out of two different narratives, two re-readings, one made by object-relations theory in England and America, the other by Lacanian theory in France. Object-relations theory concentrates on the pre-oedipal relations between mother and child as a moment before the realization of the father's place in the social disrupts the symbiotic relation between mother and child. Whereas in England and America this attempt to re-centre the mother-child relation has tended to ignore the question of sexual difference (sexual identity is not in question), in France the pre-oedipal relation has acquired a more radical potential. This is owing to a difference in theory: while the self in object-relations theory is regarded as rudimentarily present from the beginning, for Lacan the self, constituted via an illusory mirror-image of wholeness, remains fictional throughout life, acquiring a provisional identity by giving up the (maternal) phallus. Castration is here seen as a symbolic event suffered by both sexes, irrespective of their biological sex. While some feminists accept Lacan's 'phallocentrism', arguing that he develops Freud's non-biologistic thinking to its logical conclusion by showing how men and women are constructed in a patriarchal system, others take the argument further by maintaining that Lacan does not merely lay down the phallic law, but reveals the frailty of psychic identity and the mobility of desire, both of which point to the fictionality of gender definitions (see Mitchell and Rose, 1982, who respectively hold these positions). French theorists, too, have returned to the pre-oedipal relation between mother and child and have constructed new narratives of this relation. Julia Kristeva (1984) sees the pre-oedipal as a play of bodily rhythms and pre-linguistic exchanges between infant and mother, but displaces the Lacanian Imaginary as a site of illusion with the 'Semiotic' as a zone of resistance within the margins of the symbolic, producing effects before language has introduced psychic repression and continuing to do so throughout life. The Semiotic is involved in the production of a poetic text that disrupts and subverts the conventional language system (for a comprehensive introductory survey, see Moi, 1986). Kristeva takes her examples from male avant-garde poets, which illustrates her position regarding a gender-free marginality but does not please feminists.

The problem facing a feminist psychoanalytic criticism is how to give woman access to discourse: the choice for her has been either submitting to the public language of patriarchy or of inventing a private language which keeps her marginalized and/or involves the risk of making her sound mystical. The worlds that have encoded projections of women are to be subjected to decipherment with the help of a re-reading of psychoanalysis. The feminine, like any other term, is to be regarded, not as a natural given, but as a construction. What the various books of feminist criticism show is that discourses are not merely about producing definitions but that they determine the 'nature' of the body and the mind of the subjects they govern. In the past this has been done by a process of 'hysterization', the turning of women's bodies into wombs; Freud 'discovered' psychoanalysis in the course of his researches into the bodily symptoms of hysteria. The most discussed case-history in the annals of feminism must be the case of the girl hysteric given the name of 'Dora' (Bernheimer and Kahane, 1985), who walked out on Freud because he misrecognized her desire. Feminist critics examine the relation between psychoanalysis and feminism in order to produce subversive readings of psychoanalytic theory (Gallop, 1982) or of traditional literary texts (Garner, Kahane and Sprengnether, 1985). Taking psychoanalysis as a form of narrative as well as a method of interpretation, they re-read Freud and Lacan, patriarchal texts, and texts by women writers re-writing woman. The common ground of their readings is the attempt to revise the maternal narrative, the disadvantageous way the mother has been constructed by psychoanalysts, from Freud to Klein to Winnicott, as always seen from the viewpoint of the child.

The writings and readings of feminist psychoanalytic critics are concerned with the interaction of literature, culture and sexual identity, emphasizing the way that configurations of gender are located in history (Miller, 1986). The feminist psychoanalytic enquiry has perhaps the potential for becoming the most radical form of psychoanalytic criticism, since it is crucially concerned with the very construction of subjectivity. Science is a long way from providing a theory. Meanwhile psychoanalytic criticism can confront the issue because it addresses the question of the genesis of the self as revealed in literature and the arts, and in all writing, including that of psychoanalysis itself, in all of which there is the attempt to insert the subject into the social.

FURTHER READING

Bersani, Leo (1986) *The Freudian Body: Psychoanalysis and Art*, Columbia University Press, New York

Felman, Shoshana (1987) *Jacques Lacan and the Adventure of Insight: Psychoanalysis and Contemporary Culture*, Harvard University Press, Cambridge

Freud, Sigmund (1974–86) *The Pelican Freud Library*, 15 vols, Penguin, Harmondsworth. In particular, vol. 3, *Studies in Hysteria* (1974) and vol. 14, *Art and Literature* (1985)

Freund, Elizabeth (1987) *The Return of the Reader: Reader-Response Criticism*, Methuen, London

Gallop, Jane (1985) *Reading Lacan*, Cornell University Press, Ithaca

Jung, C. G. (1972) *Two Essays on Analytical Psychology*, Princeton University Press, Princeton

Lacan, Jacques (1977) *Écrits: A Selection*, Tavistock Publications, London

Laplanche, Jean and Pontalis, Jean-Baptiste (1973) *The Language of Psychoanalysis*, Hogarth Press, London

Nägele, Rainer (1937) *Reading after Freud: Essays on Goethe, Hölderlin, Habermas, Nietzsche, Brecht, Celan, and Freud*, Columbia University Press, New York

Rimmon-Kennan, Shlomith (ed.) (1987) *Discourse, Psychoanalysis and Literature*, Methuen, London

Wright, Elizabeth (1984) *Psychoanalytic Criticism: Theory in Practice*, Methuen, London

ADDITIONAL WORKS CITED

Bernheimer, Charles and Kahane, Claire (1985) *In Dora's Case: Freud, Hysteria, Feminism*, Virago, London

Bloom, Harold (1973) *The Anxiety of Influence: A Theory of Poetry*, Oxford University Press, London

Bodkin, Maud (1934) *Archetypal Patterns in Poetry*, Oxford University Press, London

Bonaparte, Marie (1949) *The Life and Works of Edgar Allan Poe*, Imago, London

Chasseguet-Smirgel, Janine (1981) *Female Sexuality*, Virago, London

Deleuze, Gilles and Guattari, Félix (1975) *Pour une littérature mineure*, Les éditions de Minuit, Paris

Donington, Robert (1974) *Wagner's 'Ring' and its Symbols: The Music and the Myth*, Faber & Faber, London

Doubrovsky, Serge (1973) ' "The nine of hearts": fragment of a psychoreading of *La Nausée*'. In Alan Roland (ed.), *Psychoanalysis, Creativity and Literature: A French-American Inquiry*, Columbia University Press, New York, pp. 312–22

Empson, William (1930) *Seven Types of Ambiguity*, Chatto & Windus, London

Felman, Shoshana (1977) 'Turning the screw of interpretation', *Yale French Studies*, 55/56, 94–207

Fischer, Jens Malte (ed.) (1980) *Psychoanalytische Literaturinterpretation*, Max Niemeyer Verlag, Tübingen

Freud, Sigmund (1985) 'Leonardo da Vinci and a memory of his childhood'. In Sigmund Freud, *Art and Literature*, translated by James Strachey (vol. 14 of *The Pelican Freud Library*), Penguin, Harmondsworth, pp. 143–231

Fuller, Peter (1980) *Art and Psychoanalysis*, Writers and Readers Publishing Cooperative, London

Gallop, Jane (1982) *The Daughter's Seduction: Feminism and Psychoanalysis*, Cornell University Press, Ithaca

Garner, Shirley Nelson, Kahane, Claire and Sprengnether, Madeleine (eds) (1985) *The M(other) Tongue: Essays in Feminist Psychoanalytic Interpretation*, Cornell University Press, Ithaca

Green, André (1980) 'The unbinding process', *New Literary History*, 12, 17–18

Holland, Norman N. (1975) *Five Readers Reading*, Yale University Press, New Haven

Jung, C. G. (1972) 'On the relation of analytical psychology to literature'. In C. G.

Jung, *The Spirit in Man, Art and Literature*, Princeton University Press, Princeton, pp. 65–83

Klein, Melanie (1977) *Love, Guilt and Reparation and Other Works, 1921–1945*, Hogarth Press, London

Kohut, Heinz (1982) 'Thomas Manns "Tod in Venedig": Zerfall einer künstlerischen Sublimierung'. In Alexander Mitscherlich (ed.), *Psycho-Pathographien des Alltags: Schriftsteller und Psychoanalyse*, Suhrkamp, Frankfurt, pp. 137–59

Kris, Ernst (1964) *Psychoanalytic Explorations in Art*, Schocken Books, New York [first published 1952]

Kristeva, Julia (1984) *Revolution in Poetic Language*, Columbia University Press, New York

Lacan, Jacques (1972) 'Seminar on "The Purloined Letter" ', *Yale French Studies*, 48, 39–72

Lesser, Simon O. (1957) *Fiction and the Unconscious*, University of Chicago Press, Chicago

Mauron, Charles (1958) 'La psychocritique et sa méthode', *Orbis Litterarum*, supplement 2, *Théories et prolèmes: contributions à la méthologie littéraire*, Munsgaard, Copenhagen, pp. 104–16

Miller, Nancy K. (ed.) (1986) *The Poetics of Gender*, Columbia University Press, New York

Mitchell, Juliet and Rose, Jacqueline (1982) *Feminine Sexuality: Jacques Lacan and the école Frendienne*, Macmillan, London

Moi, Toril (ed.) (1986) *The Kristeva Reader*, Basil Blackwell, Oxford

Spitz, Ellen Handler (1985) *Art and Psyche: A Study in Psychoanalysis and Aesthetics*, Yale University Press, New Haven and London

Stokes, Adrian (1977) 'Form in Art'. In Melanie Klein, Paula Heimann and Roger Money-Kyrle (eds), *New Directions in Psychoanalysis*, Maresfield Reprints, London, pp. 406–20

Winnicott, D. W. (1974) *Playing and Reality*, Penguin, Harmondsworth

57

DECONSTRUCTION

NIGEL MAPP

In a typically thorny locution, Paul de Man notes approvingly of 'deconstruction' that 'no other word states so economically the impossibility to evaluate positively or negatively the inescapable evaluation it implies' (1979, p. x). How might this be, since the word conjures the painful impression of pulling something apart? And does not deconstruction leave texts looking very little as we are used to seeing them? A deconstructive reading does indeed have a target in view, but normally that target is the tradition of interpretation surrounding the work under scrutiny. And this attack is not (usually) stimulated by the desire for an exciting or original case. Deconstruction in fact springs from a respect for the text at hand, and for the terms of understanding that it lays down. It is by adhering to this principle that the deconstructive reading proves opposed to the critical tradition. Therefore, the upshot of deconstruction is not a destroyed literary or philosophical work. Barbara Johnson argues the point thus:

> *Deconstruction* is not synonymous with *destruction*. . . . It is in fact much closer to the original meaning of the word *analysis*, which etymologically means 'to undo' – a virtual synonym for 'to de-construct'. The de-construction of a text does not proceed by random doubt or arbitrary subversion, but by the careful teasing out of warring forces of signification within the text itself. If anything is destroyed in a deconstructive reading, it is not the text, but the claim to unequivocal domination of one mode of signifying over another.
>
> (1980, p. 5)

It appears that reading has just been bad before now. But care is to be taken here. In this instance, 'analysis' proves misleading, as will any attempt to provide 'a virtual synonym' for 'deconstruction'. This is because 'deconstruction' is also a name for what makes definition impossible.

Jacques Derrida, the French philosopher whose writings inspired the practice of deconstructive criticism from the late sixties, and who first employed the word 'deconstruction' in his influential *De la Grammatologie* (1967), is helpful enough to note some dictionary meanings he wanted 'deconstruction' to suggest (1983a, p. 2). These involve both linguistic and mechanical senses of dismantling. It remains the case, however, that 'deconstruction' takes on its meanings from its deployment in Derrida's work rather than from the establishment of a 'primitive meaning or some etymology sheltered from or outside of any contextual strategy' (Derrida, 1983a, p. 3). Here is Derrida on the undefinability of 'deconstruction':

> All sentences of the type 'deconstruction is X' or 'deconstruction is not X', *a priori*, miss the point . . . one of the principal things at stake in what is called in my texts, 'deconstruction', is precisely the delimiting of ontology and above all of the third person present indicative: S is P.
>
> (p. 7)

This is one context, then. Derrida notes that 'deconstruction' functions in part as a translation of Heidegger's *Destruktion* or *Abbau*, and denotes 'an operation bearing on the structure or traditional architecture of the fundamental concepts of ontology or of western metaphysics' (p. 2). In defining the term, as in reading, we rely on certain categories of metaphysical control – centre, unity, and so on – which cannot necessarily be escaped, but which language problematizes. Derrida's word lands in an exemplary if insurmountable problem: it is obligatory for the sake of its definition to 'multiply the cautionary indicators and put aside all the traditional philosophical concepts, while reaffirming the necessity of returning to them, at least under erasure' (1983a, p. 4). Since one casualty of deconstruction is the metaphysical priority of 'the unity "word" and all the privileges with which it was credited, especially in its *nominal* form', Derrida is wary of offering any definitions, especially of 'deconstruction' itself (pp. 6–7). He believes that the unity of the 'logos' cannot be maintained, that definition is impossible; deconstruction aims at 'all the predicates, all the defining concepts, all the lexical significations, and even the syntactic articulations' which need to be employed to aid its definition (p. 6). Of course, this is blatantly paradoxical, since all these determinations of a context are a means of pinning 'deconstruction' down. Deconstruction is nevertheless unimpaired in its ability to specify language's disruption of conceptual understanding, the activity of *dissemination* which cannot be fastened and controlled by a contextualization, or any appeal to an overarching meaning or signified.

This sounds rather hopeless, but we are now better able to state why 'analysis' will not do to characterize deconstruction. Again a quotation from Derrida's 'Letter to a Japanese Friend' (a lucid point of entry into what is a formidably difficult corpus): '[Deconstruction] is not an analysis in particular because the dismantling of a structure is not a regression toward a *simple element*, towards an *indissoluble origin*. These values, like that of analysis, are themselves philosophemes subject to deconstruction' (1983a, p. 4). The idea here is that the reading deconstruction opens is not oriented towards the uncovering of a structure, a pattern of meaning (or anything that would ground one). In fact such principles of textual organization are always destabilized by language itself.

The phrase 'dismantling of a structure' adverts to the ambiguous relationship of deconstruction with structuralism, another crucial context. Deconstruction is often labelled, rather misleadingly, as a form of post-structuralism. But deconstruction is a *working-over* of the structuralist project: 'it was . . . necessary to understand how an "ensemble" was constituted and to reconstruct it to this end . . . [deconstruction is] a genealogical restoration rather than a demolition' (Derrida, 1983a, p. 4). Paul de Man notes that the understanding of deconstruction in a structuralist context tends to conceive texts 'as grids, as patterns', patterns that are subsequently shown to be unsustained by the work. But the structure-deconstruction model can only be a metaphor for the reading of texts, which are not to be understood as structured entities at all (Moynihan, 1984, p. 601). Another reason against the understanding of deconstruction as a species of post-structuralism is that there are other contexts within which Derrida works – the phenomenological tradition for instance, especially the writings of Edmund Husserl (see Derrida, 1973). Derrida offers readings of Hegel, Heidegger, Husserl, Rousseau (and others), as well as the structuralist avatars Saussure and Lévi-Strauss (see Dews, 1987; Taylor, 1986).

However, it is certainly Derrida's reading of the structuralist project which informs many of the ways his work is received. All those binaries which organize language for the structuralist are unpicked by deconstruction, which shows that language works to move beyond such oppositions. In Derrida's work the oppositions thus overturned are ones that typically anchor a 'metaphysical' tradition – for example, the privileging of speech over writing. Writing, notes Derrida, has always been repressed (as a mere supplement) by a speech-oriented ('phonocentric') notion of language – one that attempts to ensure unequivocal meaning, the remainderless circulation of thought and speech, a language never falling beyond intention, pure 'presence'. By way of demonstrating that language can never be pinned down in speech, Derrida argues that writing indeed takes language beyond the grip of subjective intention, relocating its origin in its own economy rather than the intuitions of a subject, but also that this is a necessary possibility for the spoken word too. Any language – a text which raises speech above writing, for example – always eludes such simple organization of meaning, and is able to generate any number of conflictual structuring effects (Derrida, 1973, 1976). We shall see how this leads Derrida to develop a notion of writing that accounts for and subsumes all effects of presence and structure. The play of language beyond the powers of taxonomical binarism to comprehend is, naturally, an inspiring model for the many who wish to use Derridean themes to overcome any particular ideologically instituted pattern – gender binarisms for example, and the values they attempt to keep in place (see Moi, 1985). And all this is certainly congruent with the general thrust of deconstruction: to note the rhetorical powers of language and their ability to disorder conceptual knowledge. (Derrida's writing is often a good example of this activity, with its proliferating puns and etymologies.)

For Derrida, structural understanding turns out to be another craving for univocal meaning. It aims to fix signification according to a non-linguistic principle, a structure or centre – what Derrida calls a 'transcendental signified'. A reading is not to be related to anything beyond the text, especially not to some pre-textual understanding or meaning: '*There is nothing outside of the text* [there is no outside-text; *il n'y a pas de hors-texte*]' (Derrida, 1976, p. 158). All that the deconstructor has is what the text offers. Yet this is sufficient. Naturally, the work can be grasped only with the conceptual resources of a 'logocentric' discourse (that is, of Western philosophy), but within this conceptuality deconstruction discerns a point of otherness that the text cannot embrace. Writing is always the 'writing of the other' (Derrida, 1983a, p. 8). And the claim is that texts *demand* such a reading, so deconstruction is perhaps something other than exegesis. It is at least clear that 'deconstruction is not a method and cannot be transformed into one', although some have been led astray, says Derrida, by 'the technical and methodological "metaphor" that seems necessarily attached to the very word' (1983a, p. 5).

So the metaphysical assumptions upon which an argument rests may be inescapable, but they are also productive of tensions and absolute incompatibilities in the *text*. A famous example is the word *supplément* in Rousseau, whose meaning – either to supply a lack, to complete, or to add to, to provide extra, to go beyond – Rousseau himself cannot control, and the text ends up unable to contract this surplus of meaning into a coherent identity (Derrida, 1976). This is usually the upshot of Derrida's readings of the Western philosophical tradition – of Hegel, Husserl, Nietzsche or Heidegger, for example; he displaces these canonical texts, showing that their meanings issue always in unfathomable paradox (or aporia). And the *thematic* concerns of Derrida's readings are a result of this philosophical work. He deploys philosophy's concepts in ways which demonstrate these concepts' fissured and problematic function within a text.

Therefore to a great extent Derrida's results remain ungeneralizable; there is no handy nest of concepts with which the adept can set about the deconstruction of metaphysics. Deconstruction is not (merely) exegesis, then, but also a philosophical project. It elicits through close reading the necessary and universal impossibility of totalizing metaphysical schemes. The deconstructive task is to explore the *transcendental conditions of the possibility and impossibility of meaning*. Derrida is clear that this is only preliminary, however. He notes: 'all the apparatus of transcendental critique [is] one of the essential "themes" or "objects" of deconstruction' (1983a, p. 5). Both theme and object: deconstruction names what it is that renders meaning impossible, but the detailed specification of such an inquiry would by the same token be one of its casualties. The tensions that deconstruction dwells upon in its object writing are precisely problems for *reading*, not capable of being thematized into a method. By bringing this rhetorical awareness to philosophy, and a philosophical attitude to the discussion of 'literary' effects, Derrida's work raises problems for the sharp demarcation of those two disciplines. For the critic Paul de Man, Derrida 'restore[s] the complexities of reading to the dignity of a philosophical question'; and also, therefore, '[his] work is one of the places where the future possibility of literary criticism is being decided' (de Man, 1983, pp. 110–11).

In short, Derrida maintains that deconstruction is *not only* not a 'set of rules and transposable procedures', and its 'event' *not only* irreducibly singular. Not destruction, not analysis, not exegesis; says Derrida, 'it must also be made clear that deconstruction is not even an *act* or an *operation*' (1983a, p. 5). It is passive; reading has something happen to it. Derrida describes what happens thus:

> Deconstruction takes place, it is an event that does not await the deliberation, consciousness or organization of a subject, or even of modernity. *It deconstructs it-self. It can be deconstructed. (Ça se déconstruit)*. . . . And the 'se' of 'se déconstruire', which is not the reflexivity of an ego or of a consciousness, bears the whole enigma.
>
> (1983a, pp. 5–6)

We are summoned by the text to make a certain response – to deconstruct even against our desire. This is the ethical moment of reading (Critchley, 1989). The language of closure and totality contains within itself an otherness, an alterity that cannot be devoured by a homogenizing signified. To ignore this otherness in order to pursue 'truly philosophical' or 'purely thematic' matters is not an option at all, since this other is the very questioning of the possibility of that enterprise. Philosophy has concealed something it is the business of the deconstructive reading to broach, an other which resists the syncretic understanding. And – this is the important move – this other is not just an incomprehensible residue; it proves to be the constitution of logocentric thought itself. All metaphysics and understanding is implicated in a 'system' of 'traces', a general writing that exceeds the centripetal action of the concept or word. Philosophy *must* be inscribed in this system of traces. Writing, a general textuality, is the ground of possibility of logocentric discourse, but also, unfortunately, the demonstration of its impossibility. In Derrida's readings language is shown never to operate as a present, specifiable element, and this is what leads him to radicalize Saussure's notion of the differential nature of meaning. Rather than linguistic elements attaining an unproblematic identity by their merely differing from other elements (as Saussure believed), Derrida maintains that the problems reading raises for self-present unities – the terms of a binary opposition, for instance – demonstrate that language is not vouchsafed such inviolable stability. In fact, Derrida believes that all elements refer to others, and contain the traces of others, rather than just excluding them. The linguistic element cannot therefore be characterized simply in terms of presence or absence. *Différance* is Derrida's neologism that describes this spacing of terms (see Derrida, 1973, pp. 129–60). It captures Saussure's sense of differing, but also another – that of deferral. What is deferred is presence, the presence of an intuition or perception, a subject or structure, all of which are made possible by the play of *différance*, a play of past and future elements, prior to which there is no meaning, nothing that would fix signification or establish presence (see Derrida, 1976, 1981). *Différance* itself, caught between at least two definitions (and like 'deconstruction' taking on many more in various contexts), would be an example of this activity. Rodolphe Gasché (1986) has attempted to demonstrate that Derrida's quasi-concepts of *différance*, trace, *supplément*, and so on, are infrastructures which allow us to address what is in writing in general that is other to philosophy. This is the paradoxical burden of Derrida's work. It remains an admirable lesson that it is only the disseminative force of writing that 'can make up for the incapacity of the word to be equal to a "thought" ' (Derrida, 1983a, p. 7). The impeccable readings of this enabling text, not as mere book but as infrastructural matrix, are Derrida's most enduring philosophical legacy.

In North America especially, Derrida's work is the avowed inspiration for a variety of critical practices. Gasché has argued that literary deconstruction has little to do with Derrida's philosophical enterprise of the specification of 'quasi-transcendental' infrastructural play (1986, pp. 1–9). Indeed, deconstruction often appears to be just a celebration of the rich and productive paradoxicality of language, a method which finds itself in a position of compromised understanding which the text has both eluded and foreseen, and which allows for no reliable statement about anything at all. The literary work is presumed a deliciously flawed system whose secrets can be levered out by recourse to the magic term *différance*. Deconstruction becomes, in short, a thoroughgoing scepticism which, perversely, is aesthetically valorized. This is not, of course, always the case. These various forms of airy persiflage are only the extreme development of a more properly deconstructive enterprise (which still feels liberated enough to exploit the critic's more playful tendencies). Geoffrey Hartman's work, for instance, indulges an obvious talent for puns and ambiguities in an attempt to dissolve away criticism's claims to objectivity – both by making manifest the object text's radical diffuseness, and by criticism's becoming itself excitingly multiplex, part of an anti-totalitarian project (Hartman, 1981).

However, it is the work of the late Paul de Man, for many years a teacher at Yale (like Hartman), that has developed both the most sophisticated and influential mode of 'literary' deconstruction (and one arrived at independently of Derrida as well). Again, the focus is on the rhetorical dimensions of language, and how they evade the hermeneutic embrace. But, crucially, de Man is as concerned as Derrida to open a reading that will probe the conditions of possibility of textual understanding (he reads Kant and Hegel as well as Wordsworth and Baudelaire). And this reading is built on a scrupulous attention to the work, rather than on the application of Derridean themes. Or as de Man notes in an interview given in 1980, 'the humility of the critic in relation to the work is total' (Moynihan, 1984, p. 592).

We can now better grasp the import of our opening quotation from de Man. As he specifies, deconstruction avers that the question whether it is a positive or a negative process 'should not be asked' (Moynihan, 1984, p. 600). The question is one of *necessity*: 'the real theoretical question is what it is in language that necessarily produces meanings but that also undoes what it produces' (p. 587). De Man is fully aware of the difficulty of understanding a literary text. So he begins by locating the epistemological moment entailed in all reading. In one of the most important statements of deconstructive principle, he writes:

> Understanding is not a version of one single and universal Truth that would exist as an essence, a hypostasis. The truth of a text is a much more empirical and literal event. What makes a reading more or less true is simply the predictability, the necessity of its occurrence, regardless of the reader or of the author's wishes ... what takes place is a necessary understanding. What marks the truth of such an understanding is not some abstract universal but the fact that it has to occur regardless of other considerations. ... Reading is an argument (which is not necessarily the same as a polemic) because it has to go against the grain of what one would want to happen in the name of what has to happen ... understanding is an epistemological event prior to being an ethical or aesthetic value. This does not mean that there can be a true reading, but that no reading is conceivable in which the question of its truth or falsehood is not primarily involved.
>
> (de Man, 1978, p. xi)

There is no sense of critical option about this process, for 'the text imposes its own understanding and shapes the reader's evasions' (1978, p. xi).

So de Man inherits a paradigm of close-reading from the New Critics, but it is not possible to reduce his work to more New Criticism (Moynihan, 1984, pp. 589–90). For de Man's meticulous readings do not tend towards the aesthetic encomium of the literary work; he does not ignore the affront to understanding that the sophistication of language implies. It is no mere technical effect to some higher aesthetic end, wherein problems are sublated in the prized effects of 'paradox', 'ambiguity', and so on. A close reading reveals problems for any hierographic project that would prematurely synthesize meaning into a whole. The crucial question is this: is the meaning we think we find in fact compatible with the specific linguistic structures that make up the text (de Man, 1987, p. 25)? For de Man, they are certainly not compatible. Hermeneutics, or the interpretation of meaning, is dropped in favour of a poetics which seeks to specify what it is in language that can constitute so many meanings, multiple and ambiguous, and then undermine them. Literature remains the point where this interruption of interpretative mastery takes place, although the notion is now purged of any aesthetic priority (Johnson, 1980, pp. xi–xii). The heterogeneity upon which interpretation runs aground is not to be recuperated in any way.

De Man believes that the problems for understanding can often be diagnosed as a conflict between rhetorical and grammatical significations. His most famous example is the question 'What's the difference?', which grammatically asks for a difference to be specified, but rhetorically demands that it be ignored (de Man, 1979, pp. 9–10). The last line of Yeats's 'Among School Children' is another example de Man seizes upon in this connection: 'How can we know the dancer from the dance?' De Man's grammatical reading unpicks the rhetorical dimension of this image (which seems to promise the aesthetic union of part and whole, of sign and significance). The question is read by de Man thus:

> Since the two essentially different elements, sign and meaning, are so intricately intertwined in the imagined 'presence' that the poem addresses, how can we possibly make the distinctions that would shelter us from the error of identifying what cannot be identified?
>
> (de Man, 1979, p. 11)

Thus a symbolist reading and a de Manian one clash head on: 'the one reading is precisely the error denounced by the other and has to be undone by it' (p. 12). It would be naïve merely to offer the ambiguity of the question as an example of the fertile multifariousness of literary language; there is here a real threat to understanding. So what is the critic's relationship with such difficulties, and how are they characterized?

One way of tackling the problem is to take up de Man's notion of irony. This irony is one that gets out of control very fast. It is not a mere trope, a device which can always (in principle) be traced back to a specifiable intention or unified signification. This irony is the irony of understanding, and the difficulties it involves are no mere subjective quandary. Irony is the universal predicament of language. It is not a rhetorical mode characterizing one period of literary history or other; it is the very interruption language poses to such historicizing, perhaps to understanding as such. Literary history may be precisely the type of *narrative* understanding that irony problematizes (Moynihan, 1984, p. 580). Irony indicates the uncontrollability of meaning itself, and, like the figural interruptions of grammatical meanings, it cannot be conquered by an appeal to the logical or aesthetic structure of language, since these are precisely the notions at stake. Here is one of de Man's latest formulations of what is understood by irony in his texts:

> So irony doesn't stop. . . . There's irony when language starts to say things you didn't think it was saying . . . things that go against your own quest for meaning or admitted intention. So irony is so fundamental, that, for me, it is no longer a trope. Irony is generally called a trope of tropes, but actually irony is a disruption of a continued [*sic*] field of tropological meaning. . . . It's uncontrollable because it is just that: it has to do with the lack of control of meaning.
>
> (Moynihan, 1984, p. 584)

The irony, then, is the search for definitive meaning. De Man sums up his attack on the pretence of controlled meaning in a pointed idiom: 'I intend to take the divine out of reading' (Moynihan, 1984, p. 586). All readings can be ironized, but we can be specific in the demonstration that language's figurality will not yield up a simple pattern. So all readings are *not* equally good (Moynihan, 1984, pp. 585–6).

One of de Man's most famous essays is 'The Rhetoric of Temporality', first published in 1969, wherein is undertaken an immaculate deconstruction of the romantic ideology of the symbol, and which provides an early treatment of some of the themes outlined here (see de Man, 1983, pp. 187–228). The idea that language can overcome the bifurcation of subject and object by synthesizing mind and nature in a timeless union without residue, a romantic claim for the henotic powers of imagination, is undone by those aspects of language – here metonymy and allegory – into which the favoured tropes of metaphor and symbol can be seen to decompose. There is in this essay a pathos of division and distance, a self contemplating the splitting of subject and object which the power of symbolic language is unable to heal. The principal point is well made, though. There can be no recreation of authorial experience in language, and all we have is a language of temporal and allegorical falling-away from any sense of origin. Here allegory is the privileged trope, since it names the true status of language: 'allegory designates primarily a distance in relation to its own origin, and, renouncing the nostalgia and the desire to coincide, it establishes its language in the void of this temporal difference . . . it prevents the self from an illusory identification with the non-self' (de Man, 1983, p. 207). The contingent nature of language, and the arbitrary representation indicated by the very structure of allegory, marks the shift to a rhetorical critical approach. Now rhetoric is conceived as 'a transformational system', which constructs meanings as well as subjects, and the aim of criticism becomes to demonstrate how tropes 'engender systems' (Moynihan, 1984, pp. 590–1). The task is, then, to specify in the language of tropes – to which all understanding is reducible – how meaning is constituted and subverted by language, and to demonstrate that any understanding of this process is only another trope itself (or is ironic to the extent that its relation to the work is undecidable). '[The] attempt to master a system of tropes by reducing it to an actual system is itself a typical tropological fallacy', warns de Man (Moynihan, 1984, p. 591). So what trope is reading going to be? The answer, obvious enough, is allegory. Unreadability, as de Man calls it, inheres in the text, and every reading that claims to unite all the elements into a coherent narrative or paraphrase is 'always susceptible of being made to point out consistently what it was trying to conceal' (1978, p. xi). All readings, in so far as they are an orderly expression of incoherency, are just another aberrant narrative. This is the unmasterable irony. All we have is an allegory of reading, an allegory that speaks of something other than the closed economy of its own exposition. 'Allegory is sequential and narrative, yet the topic of its narration is not necessarily temporal at all', says de Man in a late text, and this condenses the de Manian notion of the relationship between understanding and language (1986, p. 1). This process was thematized in de Man's earlier work of the sixties as the necessary co-implication of critical blindness and insight (de Man, 1983).

In his later work, de Man develops the idea that there is something in language upon which the mechanical operations of tropes work, but to which this operation bears no specifiable relation. Aesthetic meanings are to be exploded by a close-reading that attends to rhetoric, and the rhetorical creation of meaning from meaningless linguistic matter. De Man calls that meaningless stratum of language its *materiality*, by which he understands, for example, the actual configuration of letters in a word. Language is shown at base to be thoroughly random; and meaning an uncalled-for imposition, since tropes do not operate according to a principle which would allow textual understanding to be integrated unproblematically with intuition. Language does not function like the world. This is what de Man means when he argues that language is a-phenomenal; all the effects that seem to secure its intelligibility and useful-ness are *just* effects; mimesis, for example, is only a pun, language imitating a non-linguistic entity (de Man, 1987, pp. 10–11). The movement from lan-guage to cognition is itself a trope. So language is opposed to understanding. The 'semantic play of the signifier' is one aspect of language that proves contrary to understanding, a semantic activity of letters, the constituent parts of words, which disrupts stable meaning and which tends to be ignored or aestheticized away – hygienically given a category of its own and therefore controlled. What is discovered in language is the aporia, 'a true opposition which blocks', a paradox which ultimately cannot be solved, and which 'cannot be . . . assimilated by a trope' (Moynihan, 1984, pp. 588–9). (This a-phenomenal interference of understanding is often found by de Man to be represented *thematically* in the text, but this can only be a provisional move.) Reading charts the struggle of materiality and phenomenalism.

On this reading, literary history proves impossible, as does any characterization of history in general. Such naïve understanding can never be more than a trope, de Man argues, and a trope that is foisted on language by the reader in an attempt at understanding. Narratives of development, of dialectical unfolding, all are just that, allegorical impositions of a temporal ordering that belong to rhetoric, not to the world. Ideology for de Man is analysable in this way – a textual mode of understanding going beyond its legitimate reach (de Man, 1987, p. 11). Language speaks only of itself. All meaning seems, therefore, to be a mere allegory of the text, an effect of the text, but one that can say two or more things at once. Deconstruction involves locating the point where the fabric which tropes are so adept at weaving is unravelled.

This critical movement is hardly vitiated by the breaking of the charm of the concept. History, for instance, is freed from conceptual grasp in this model. Is de Man really susceptible to the charge that his work is ultimately a-historical, an absolute privileging of text over politics (see Eagleton, 1984)? Perhaps it is his opponents who dissolve history into text when they elaborate what history (and the 'real world') is; such models are only allegories for de Man. De Man talks of *occurrence*, which he opposes to temporalized versions of history (de Man, 1987, pp. 73–105). These reflections on the concept and history seem congruent with a (Western Marxist) tradition of culture criticism, as does de Man's deconstruction of 'aesthetic ideology' – the tyranny of meaning, and romantic claims for the unifying potential of language (see Norris, 1988). De Man's is a heterogeneous reality which will not permit dialectical synthesis; his is a theory destructive of mystification in language. Thus one obligation of deconstruction becomes to work out the connections between de Man's work and that of others, like Theodor Adorno, whose concerns hitherto have seemed alien to deconstruction. Deconstruction is leaving far behind the charges of nihilism and hermeticism that still characterize its reception. It seems that the status of history and politics intrigued de Man all along. A criticism whose interests are in the demolition of the unwarranted assumptions that ground literary study is therefore rising to the challenge of this work.

So it is that any confusions the deconstructor unveils are those of the critical tradition, not of the text. Even Derrida, according to de Man, does not go far enough in crediting Rousseau's works with the deconstructive insights which lift them from the metaphysical tradition in which they are implicated (de Man,

1983, pp. 102–41). Therefore, deconstruction is not a nihilistic enterprise; we have already registered the ethical dimension of Derrida's work, and de Man too gives deconstruction's necessity an ethical scope:

> The point is ... whether the epistemology of understanding should be predicated by ethical or aesthetic considerations or the other way round. Is the integrity of understanding a function of the integrity of meaning, or should meaning be allowed to disintegrate under the negative impact of elements in a text, however marginal or apparently trivial, that can only be silenced by suppression?
>
> (de Man, 1978, p. x)

De Man obviously favours the epistemological integrity, for 'how could a text have its understanding depend on considerations that would not be epistemologically determined?' (1978, p. xi). His reading will be 'productive of its own ethical imperative', since it proceeds 'regardless of the consequences of the understanding ... whatever it may turn out to be – including the hard-earned conviction of its impossibility' (p. xi).

J. Hillis Miller, another member of the so-called 'Yale School' (which flourished in the 1970s and early 1980s), has been at the head of the recent trend to establish what an ethics of reading looks like in the wake of deconstruction (Miller, 1987). It seems that the ethical moment has to do with what for de Man were the discrepancies which a text throws up to thwart understanding. Relying on this de Manian insight, Miller suggests that it is at such problematical junctures that there is an ethical demand made by the text, one which must not be obviated by a desire for coherence or aesthetic effect. There is a law beyond our desires, an ascesis demanded of the reader (see Harpham, 1987, pp. 139–40). It is when understanding is scuttled by aporia that there is a properly ethical moment. Deconstruction does not serve any system of values which enshrines a certain power distribution, but indicates instead the fundamental structure of ethics, a discourse of self-resistance. This ascetic disavowal of method or values, disingenuous or not, lands deconstruction in great problems with institutional literary or philosophical study (at least in principle). Some argue that deconstruction can only betray itself in subsumption by the academy (Felperin, 1985, pp. 104–46). And much of the important work in deconstruction now addresses the problem of how it can find a place within an institution it seems its *raison d'être* to undermine. Deconstruction has to live with the fact that it is becoming absorbed. Derrida's latest work often grapples with this question of how, while adhering to rigorous protocols of argument, deconstruction can criticize the institutions which appear elastic enough to reduce it to just another critical method (see, for example, Derrida, 1983b; Salusinszky, 1987). The attempts now to elaborate the political and ethical necessity of deconstruction will prove the true test of how effortless that reduction can be.

FURTHER READING

Abrams, M. H. (1979) 'How to do Things with Texts', *Partisan Review*, 46, 566–88

Culler, Jonathan (1983) *On Deconstruction: Theory and Criticism after Structuralism*, Routledge & Kegan Paul, London

de Man, Paul (1984) *The Rhetoric of Romanticism*, Columbia University Press, New York

Derrida, Jacques (1982) *Margins of Philosophy*, translated by Alan Bass, Harvester, Brighton [first published 1972]

Hartman, Geoffrey (1985) *Easy Pieces*, Columbia University Press, New York

Llewelyn, John (1986) *Derrida on the Threshold of Sense*, Macmillan, London

Miller, J. Hillis (1982) *Fiction and Repetition: Seven English Novels*, Harvard University Press, Cambridge

Norris, Christopher (1987) *Derrida*, Fontana, London

Rorty, Richard (1982) 'Philosophy as a Kind of Writing: An Essay on Derrida'. In Richard Rorty, *Consequences of Pragmatism (Essays: 1972–1980)*, Harvester, Brighton, pp. 90–109

Ryan, Michael (1982) *Marxism and Deconstruction*, Johns Hopkins University Press, Baltimore

Silverman, Hugh J. (ed.) (1989) *Derrida and Deconstruction*, Routledge, New York

Waters, Lindsay and Godzich, Wlad (eds) (1989) *Reading de Man Reading*, University of Minnesota Press, Minneapolis

ADDITIONAL WORKS CITED

Critchley, Simon (1989) 'The Chiasmus: Levinas, Derrida and the Ethical Demand for Deconstruction', *Textual Practice*, 3, 91–106

de Man, Paul (1978) 'Foreword'. In Carol Jacobs, *The Dissimulating Harmony: The Image of Interpretation in Nietzsche, Rilke, Artaud, and Benjamin*, Johns Hopkins University Press, Baltimore, pp. vii–xiii

——(1979) *Allegories of Reading: Figural Language in Rousseau, Nietzsche, Rilke, and Proust*, Yale University Press, New Haven

——(1983) *Blindness and Insight: Essays in the Rhetoric of Contemporary Criticism*, revised 2nd edn, Methuen, London [first published 1971]

——(1986) 'Pascal's Allegory of Persuasion'. In Stephen J. Greenblatt (ed.), *Allegory and Representation*, Johns Hopkins University Press, Baltimore, pp. 1–25

——(1987) *The Resistance to Theory*, Manchester University Press, Manchester [first published 1986]

Derrida, Jacques (1973) *Speech and Phenomena: And Other Essays on Husserl's Theory of Signs*, translated by David B. Allison, Northwestern University Press, Evanston [first published 1967]

——(1976) *Of Grammatology*, translated by Gayatri Chakravorty Spivak, Johns Hopkins University Press, Baltimore [first published 1967]

——(1981) *Positions*, translated by Alan Bass, Athlone Press, London [first published 1972]

——(1983a) 'Letter to a Japanese Friend'. In David Wood and Robert Bernasconi (eds) (1985), *Derrida and Différance*, Parousia Press, University of Warwick

——(1983b) 'The Principle of Reason: The University in the Eyes of its Pupils', *Diacritics*, 13, 3–20

Dews, Peter (1987) *Logics of Disintegration: Post-Structuralist Thought and the Claims of Critical Theory*, New Left Books, London

Eagleton, Terry (1984) *The Function of Criticism: From 'The Spectator' to Post-Structuralism*, New Left Books, London

Felperin, Howard (1985) *Beyond Deconstruction: The Uses and Abuses of Literary Theory*, Clarendon Press, Oxford

Gasché, Rodolphe (1986) *The Tain of the Mirror: Derrida and the Philosophy of Reflection*, Harvard University Press, Cambridge

Harpham, Geoffrey Galt (1987) 'Language, History, and Ethics', *Raritan*, 7, 128–46

Hartman, Geoffrey H. (1981) *Saving the Text: Literature/Derrida/Philosophy*, Johns Hopkins University Press, Baltimore

Johnson, Barbara (1980) *The Critical Difference: Essays in the Contemporary Rhetoric of Reading*, Johns Hopkins University Press, Baltimore

Miller, J. Hillis (1987) *The Ethics of Reading: Kant, de Man, Eliot, Trollope, James, and Benjamin*, Columbia University Press, New York

Moi, Toril (1985) *Sexual/Textual Politics: Feminist Literary Theory*, Methuen, London

Moynihan, Robert (1984) 'Interview with Paul de Man', *The Yale Review*, 73, 576–602

Norris, Christopher (1988) *Paul de Man: Deconstruction and the Critique of Aesthetic Ideology*, Routledge, New York

Salusinszky, Imre (1987) 'Jacques Derrida', *Criticism in Society*, Methuen, New York, pp. 9–24

Taylor, Mark C. (ed.) (1986) *Deconstruction in Context: Literature and Philosophy*, University of Chicago Press, Chicago

58

NEW HISTORICISM

DON E. WAYNE

As I write, the critical movement currently designated by the term 'New Historicism' is about ten years old. The movement has produced its programmatic statements, and has already generated a growing body of commentary, and some controversy, from which the list of further reading that follows is only a brief selection. Limitations of space will not permit me to trace the earlier history of the term 'historicism', but the reader may wish to consult Maurice Mandelbaum's article in the 1967 edition of the Macmillan *Encyclopedia of Philosophy* (vol. 4, pp. 22–5). What strikes me as a necessary task in the present historical context, when experience and theory have combined effectively to undermine so many older assumptions about culture and civilization, is to give an account of the significance of this most recent trend in historical criticism not only in relation to older historicisms but in relation to other kinds of critical practices current today.

Up to now, new historicism has been a movement associated principally with scholarship in the United States. Consequently my comments will refer primarily to this context. I have written elsewhere about the differing social and political constraints that help to account for the respective differences in the kind of cultural criticism produced by new historicists in the US and cultural materialists led by Raymond Williams in the UK (Wayne, 1987). To carry this effort at historicizing new historicism a step further, I want to consider here its status in relation to deconstruction as a rival postmodern critical practice. Both new historicism and deconstruction are related as well to the broad range of criticism identified as feminist which is itself a major force in recent American criticism. But in each case the relationship with feminism is complex, involving both sympathetic and appropriative aspects, a complexity that places the question beyond the scope of the present essay (see Boose, 1987; Neely, 1988; Newton, 1988).

If asked to justify my emphasis on deconstruction and new historicism to the exclusion of other critical discourses, I would simply point to the fact that these modes of criticism (and the opposition between them) have been legitimated by scholars who are widely recognized as speaking authoritatively for the institution of literary criticism in the United States. This representation of the state of literary studies was promulgated from the top of the official edifice by J. Hillis Miller in his 1986 presidential address to the Modern Language Association. It has also appeared in the mass media. Thus, *Newsweek* concluded its report of the recent revelations concerning Paul de Man's early anti-Semitic writings for a Belgian collaborationist newspaper by conflating deconstruction and new historicism. *Newsweek* relies principally on the authority of Professor Frederick Crews who is said to contend 'that there's more than a trace of deconstruction in the new historicism – which is one reason traditional humanists hope that it, too, will self-deconstruct in the wake of the de Man disgrace' (*Newsweek*, 15 February 1988, p. 63). Professor Crews expresses an anxiety that is presumably widespread among traditional scholars. But given the deconstructionists' own anxieties about a purported 'shift from language to history' (J. Hillis Miller, 1987, p. 283), one suspects that a struggle for dominance among counter-traditions in the field of literary studies is well under way in the United States.

As D. A. Miller suggests, toward the end of a recent exchange with J. Hillis Miller, such debates tend to be 'spurious (because specular)'; that is, one critical orthodoxy will seek a revitalized image of itself by constructing a straight man of an opponent 'who then must be – for in this department one can never take too many precautions – "straightened out"' (D. A. Miller, 1987, p. 58). Apart from giving a distorted account of the opponent, polemics of this kind reduce cultural controversy to professional rivalry and, in so doing, tend to defuse more fundamental debates of wider social consequence. In effect, this polarization and reduction of new historicism and deconstruction is likely to pre-empt whatever potential *both* critical orientations may have of serving as 'counter-discourses' that can 'upset received evaluations of fundamental social operators' (Terdiman, 1989, p. 229). Moreover, such polarizing arguments, especially when engaged in by those who hold authoritative institutional positions, disseminate a representation of the entire field of literary and cultural studies that effectively marginalizes critical practices other than those named by the polemicists themselves.

Having acknowledged these dangers, I think it worth pausing to consider why deconstruction and new historicism should have come to occupy the polar positions in at least some current representations of the state of the art of literary criticism in America. No doubt professional demographies, and the genealogies of academic patronage are a significant factor. But apart from sociological explanations, one can account for the success of both deconstruction and new historicism by seeing them as different, perhaps now competing extensions of the formalist tradition that has dominated American literary studies throughout this century. Deconstruction is more easily seen in this light. Yet while the recent shift to history may constitute a reaction against post-structuralist versions of literary formalism, the work of the most influential new historicists also derives much of its authority from what Alan Liu calls, in the revealing title of a probing essay (1989) on new historicism, 'the power of formalism'.

'New' historicisms have been proclaimed before, and there are at least several versions of new historicism coexisting in the present. As far as I can tell, in most recent usage the term 'new historicism' does not pertain to a school or to a coherent theory of cultural history. Rather, it designates a fairly diverse body of scholarship with some common attributes. The range of such work includes a type of literary criticism that deals principally with the importance of local political and social contexts for the understanding of literary texts; a type of cultural history influenced by the work of symbolic anthropologists, most notably Clifford Geertz; a related type of cultural study that emphasizes 'history from below' in the manner of the *Annales* school of social historians; and several types of cultural critique that are often vaguely Marxist and feminist, but are more commonly derived from the work of Michel Foucault on the history of institutions, the history of sexuality, and the history of subjectivity. A number of methodological features can be found to characterize all these approaches: (1) a shift from ideas to power relationships as the fundamental units for analysis and interpretation in cultural history, leading to a focus on such issues as patronage, patriarchal authority and its legitimation, the role of culture in the formation of the modern nation-state, the creation of a special role for literary production and authorship within modern culture, the delineation of separate domains of public and private space, etc.; (2) a tendency to refuse hierarchies and dichotomies among texts of different kinds (canonical/non-canonical; high culture/mass culture; documents/fictions; (3) the assumption that in a given historical moment, different modes of discourse (such as law, theology, moral philosophy, literature, art, architecture, cartography, chorography, choreography, costume, stage design, science of various types, etc.) are rarely if ever autonomous, that by studying the permeable boundaries of the discourses constitutive of a given cultural field, the scholar can arrive at an understanding of the broader ideological codes that order all discourse in that particular culture; (4) the symptomatic reading of this wider cultural field by means of an attention to rhetorical devices and strategies, and a consequent revival of interest in the history of rhetoric, though from a critical, rather than a merely descriptive perspective (see, e.g., Whigham, 1984; Kahn, 1985); (5) related to all of the above, the governing assumption that discourse and representation form consciousness rather than merely reflecting or expressing it, that culture is therefore an active force in history. These represent some of the more salient features of the new historicism as I understand it.

It could be argued that many of these features were already evident in the earlier *Geistesgeschichte* tradition of intellectual history (i.e., the history of ideas or of world views as expressed in such cultural institutions as religion, law, political systems, poetry, art, etc.). But there is at least one major respect in which the latest type of historicism is distinguishable from the old. In most of the work identified as new historicist one senses an absence of a kind of conviction that governed earlier types of historicist criticism. In his book *Toward a New Historicism* (1972), which predated the most current use of the term, Wesley Morris identified four major types of traditional historicism: (1) the metaphysical, deriving from Hegel's transcendental philosophy, where a literary work was understood as the poetic expression of a moment in the unfolding narrative of history as the self-realization of the absolute; (2) the naturalistic or positivistic, where the literary text was treated as a medium through which a given historical epoch could be viewed by a scholar who imagined himself in the role of scientific observer; (3) the nationalistic, a relativist variant of the metaphysical, in which the literary work was viewed as expressing the native spirit of a given culture or race; (4) the aesthetic, which diverges from the other types in seeing the literary work not as the reflection or expression of an existing cultural domain but as a way of *making* cultural meanings and values (pp. 9–12). Regardless of their respective differences, all of these types of historicism – and, I would add, the version of a 'new historicism' that Morris himself sought to articulate – entailed the conviction that poetry either reflected or expressed the *human* subject, however various may have been conceptions of the nature of that subject. A poetic act was understood to express, to illustrate or to dramatize a stage in the history of consciousness or of human *praxis*, whether of an individual or collective kind (Jameson, 1981, pp. 26–7). In all its traditional forms, historicism adhered to one or another master narrative that governed the historical critic's interpretation of specific narrative or poetic acts. It is the apparent absence of such a narrative, or a certain embarrassment at its lingering presence, that characterizes much of the criticism currently identified under the rubric 'new historicism'.

There are, of course, notable exceptions, including critics whose work verges on a Marxist conception of *praxis*, or those whose view of the subject in history is consistent with liberal humanism. Nevertheless, if traditional historicism adheres to a grand narrative – what Roy Harvey Pearce, a most tenacious historicist, unabashedly terms in the title of his latest book (1987), the *gesta humanorum* – more recent historical scholars have shrunk from making broad claims as to the efficacy of a human subject as the agent of history. New historicists tend to eschew the eschatological or teleological connotations of the term 'history'. Rather, in a way that may be consistent with other aspects of postmodern culture, human subjects are treated by many of these scholars as functions in a structural ensemble of cultural practices at a specific moment in what is still termed 'history', though the term is now employed with a discernible reluctance to specify its referent. While perhaps less confident than earlier cultural historians as to the precise meaning of 'history', new historicists are, on the whole, more self-conscious in acknowledging that the historiographer is never simply describing or retrieving the past but is engaged in constructing *a* past. It is, I think, precisely because of post-structuralism's destabilizing effect on historiography, as on epistemology in general, that recent historical criticism has displayed an awareness of the degree to which a reading of the past is an ideological construction mediated by a desire or a drive to position oneself in the present. However, to say that history is always to a degree the construct of ideology is not to say that it is inevitably false. For, of course, that construct, however intentionalized by the historian's subjectivity, is also constrained by the materiality of the texts that the historian selects as the sources of historical data (by which I mean such immediate constraints on reading – therefore, on historical evidence – as diction, syntax, orthography, typography, mode of publication and dissemination, etc.). And these texts bear the traces of the history of subjectivity itself within a given culture – hence, the renewed interest in the history of rhetoric and in the rhetorical analysis of all modes of writing including historiography itself (White, 1978, pp. 105–6).

The principle that cultural practices often entail conflict and contradiction points to another factor distinguishing the current mode of historical criticism from its antecedents. Most earlier types of historicism emphasized the unifying function of culture. Even where pluralities were allowed to exist within a given cultural context, the historical critic would ultimately resolve the plural into the singular *Geist* of an age, a nation, a civilization or a race; or, in a more empirical, positivistic historical method, into the more narrowly defined but still unitary political or social event, action, interest group, etc.; or in the specific domain of *literature*, into such a notion as period-style. This tendency to contain plurality within a higher unity, to reinscribe difference within the representation of the same, has been especially the case in the work of American cultural historians and is no doubt an instance of the longstanding strategy within American ideology of 'staging [pluralist] interpretation as a means of co-opting dissent' (Bercovitch, 1988, p. 12). By contrast, new historicists are often most interested in how different kinds of discourse intersect, contradict, destabilize, cancel or modify each other.

True, in the work of some new historicists the analysis of such a complex structure of interrelated discourses and practices will ultimately be resolved into an ideological dominant. Historical studies of this type seek to demonstrate how a dominant ideology will give a certain rein to alternative discourses, ultimately appropriating their vitality and containing their oppositional force (most often cited in this regard are Greenblatt's essay 'Invisible Bullets', reprinted in his *Shakespearean Negotiations*, 1988b, and Goldberg's *James I and the Politics of Literature*, 1983). There has been much criticism of this tendency (e.g. Sinfield, 1985, pp. 259–61; Porter, 1988), including some from within the ranks of prominent new historicists (Helgerson, 1986, pp. 64–5). But even where contradictions are resolved and subversive energies are said to be re-contained by a dominant ideology, the emphasis in new historicism will be not on the triumph of one set of ideas and values over others, but rather on the *strategies* and *tactics* by which hierarchies are sustained and power, howsoever modified, is reasserted. This shift in emphasis is already evident in work on Renaissance court culture that anticipates the new historicism (Orgel, 1975), though not in a way that displays the impact of theory that one finds self-consciously registered – at the very least, by allusion – in much of the writing associated with the new historicism proper. To the degree that there is a theoretical basis for this kind of historiography, the obvious sources are Foucault and Althusser. But it would be a mistake, I believe, to seek a coherent theoretical basis to the new historicism or a pattern of theoretical and methodological consistency among its practitioners. In this respect, like the New Criticism before 'it, New Historicism does not name a school but rather serves to denominate a general tendency within the field of literary and cultural studies.

It is perhaps no accident that this kind of criticism was associated initially with work on the Renaissance and the seventeenth century. Revising the history of early modern Europe has become a corollary of the recent theoretical effort to define present-day culture as 'postmodern'. With the growing sense that we are in the last phase of an epoch, there has been an understandable interest in studying the development of modernism, and especially the development of modern notions of subjectivity. There is of course a long scholarly tradition going back to Jakob Burckhardt that viewed the Renaissance as the heroic, originary moment of modern individualism. But recent scholars have objected to the nostalgic and complacent lenses through which earlier historians scanned Renaissance culture in order to discover there the origins of permanent qualities, if not of human, then at least of *humanist* nature.

The emphasis in the most recent historical scholarship will thus be on difference and discontinuity, a conception of historicism which perhaps owes something to anthropology in claiming that by focusing on past cultures as *Other* we can gain a more critical perspective on our own culture and its ideological constraints. A more politically charged version of such historical distancing, derived from Brecht, is evident in the work of cultural materialists in the UK (Heinemann, 1985, pp. 215–16). If not completely Other, the past history of Western culture will nevertheless be viewed by new historicists principally in terms of its difference from the present, and this orientation produces in turn a certain suspicion with regard to all universalist claims concerning the nature of human experience. Psychoanalysis, the most powerful modern theory of subjectivity, is therefore described by Stephen Greenblatt as a 'causally belated' hermeneutic when applied to Renaissance texts because the psychological categories it invokes are themselves the after-effects of complex historical changes in the conception of the self which these categories are said to explain. For Greenblatt, 'psychoanalysis can redeem its belatedness only when it historicizes its own procedures' (Greenblatt, 1986, p. 221).

In various ways, then, the watchword 'historicize!' has become an injunction to recognize what differentiates Renaissance notions of subjectivity from modern ones, even as the culture of the earlier period is shown to have laid the groundwork for such modern notions as the Freudian psyche. Yet, while there is no question that new historicists have been more self-conscious about their methodological assumptions and about their cultural biases than earlier historical critics, one may wonder to what degree the new historicism is itself a projection of present-day concerns and present-day modes of identity-formation on to the past. So, for example, the interest of new historicists in such themes as patronage and negotiation, in cultural forms as instruments of state power and control but also as means of individual self-fashioning, may be symptomatic of the extent to which the academic world these critics inherited resembled the patron-client system and the emergent professionalism of Renaissance court societies (see Wayne, 1987, pp. 61–2) – though one would have to add that by the time new historicism became a fashion, the humanities had already moved beyond such a stage into something more like a market system with its aggressive and entrepreneurial competitive ethos. To raise the question of new historicism's role within the context of a *new professionalism* in the field of literary studies, requires analytic tools that are somewhat different from those normally employed by new historicists themselves. This is where a consideration of new historicism in relation to deconstruction, as two competing postmodern critical practices, may be helpful.

Until recently, the main institutionalized alternative to the dominant tradition in American literary criticism has been deconstruction. I say 'institutionalized' because there have been a variety of alternatives to traditional humanism struggling for recognition for some time – alternative modes of scholarship concerned with issues of gender, race, sexuality, social class and ethnicity. These have either been foreclosed by dominant cultural institutions, or they have attained a marginal, dependent status within those institutions (which is not to say that their capacities to resist, disrupt and ultimately change these institutions have been successfully contained). On the other hand, since the mid-1970s an institutionalized form of deconstruction has existed in America where it replaced New Criticism as a mode of reading that served to guarantee the integrity of the literary (which is not to say that deconstruction is inherently conservative, but rather that among the various modes of cultural critique developed in post-colonial France, deconstruction – with its emphasis on textuality and on the tropological nature of all language – was the most easily accommodated to an existing literary critical orthodoxy in the United States).

It is not surprising that the principal challenge to deconstruction as a major force in institutionalized criticism should be the return to history. I would suggest that, in fact, the project of new historicism shares with deconstruction the goal of shoring up a tired cultural tradition in which, since Matthew Arnold, literary criticism has functioned as a form of secular theology. But it also needs to be acknowledged that both movements are related, howsoever indirectly, to the oppositional politics of the 1960s and early 1970s. The sheer audacity of these movements in criticism can be viewed, I think, as an epiphenomenon of the combative, countercultural politics of the 1960s modulating into the assertive professionalism that has characterized middle-class America in the 1980s.

One model for understanding the shift in critical orthodoxy that both decon-struction and new historicism represent in the field of literary studies is the analysis which Jean-François Lyotard has given of the state of knowledge under what he calls post-industrial capitalism, whose culture we now conven-tionally term postmodernism. In *The Postmodern Condition* (1984), Lyotard identifies two metanarratives whereby knowledge and its institutions were legitimated in the modern era. The first of these is the emancipatory narrative associated with Enlightenment egalitarianism and the French revolution. The second, more specifically philosophical, is that of the German idealist tradition descending from Kant and Hegel. Lyotard discusses the decline in credibility of such grand narratives, a decline that is in direct proportion to the pre-eminence given to technology from the beginnings of industrialization to the current revolution in information technologies. In this context a mode of legitimation emerges

> in which the goal is no longer truth, but performativity – that is, the best possible input/output equation. The State and/or company must abandon the idealist and humanist narratives of legitimation in order to justify the new goal: in the discourse of today's financial backers of research, the only credible goal is power.
>
> (1984, p. 46)

The last move in Lyotard's analysis is to envision a strategy for legitimating knowledge that is appropriate to the postmodern condition, a mode of legitim-ation Lyotard terms *paralogy*. The practice of *paralogy* is not clearly defined but is derived from Wittgenstein's concept of language games. Lyotard charac-terizes postmodern discourse as a heterogeneous group of language games which diverge from all those grand narratives whether in the name of truth, justice or performativity that ground legitimacy in appeals either to a universal subject of knowledge or to consensus. As Fredric Jameson suggests, in his introduction to Lyotard's text, 'Lyotard's ultimate vision of science and knowledge today [is] as a search not for consensus, but very precisely for "instabilities" . . . in which the point is not to reach agreement but to undermine from within the very framework in which the previous "normal science" had been conducted' (Lyotard, 1984, p. xix).

Now it seems to me that in the present context of literary critical discourse in the United States, both deconstruction and new historicism fit within the historical model for the legitimation of knowledge that Lyotard presents. But the question is how do they fit? I suspect that partisans of either camp would see themselves as engaged in a sort of paralogical practice, while viewing the other movement as an instrument of ideology or of performativity in one form or another. But in the present entrepreneurial setting within which these movements compete, performativity is endemic. And performativity is inseparable from performance anxiety. They go hand in hand, as it were; and, in most instances, both hands belong to the same performer whose role – where knowledge and its legitimation are concerned – demands an imaginary relationship to others as the agent of information, but also of a gendered, classed, racially and ethnically hierarchical structure of institutional power. This is not a role from which one can escape by virtue of a personal politics or ethics, or by substituting the criterion of play for that of truth, not so long as one is engaged in the pursuit of knowledge within existing institutional frameworks. I find it difficult to imagine something like paralogy occurring in a sustained way, if at all, in any institutional setting where power is so structured. And I know of no institutionalized form of cultural practice, no *discipline* where this condition is yet radically altered.

Despite these reservations, I do think that both deconstruction and new historicism fit Lyotard's description of a postmodern form of the legitimation of knowledge. In its way, each of these current movements came into being as a kind of paralogical activity (which is why each came under attack from more traditional modes of criticism); but each also gained its notoriety by virtue of its capacity to fulfil the criterion of performativity. In claiming the latter, I realise that I am engaging in a kind of paralogical play with Lyotard's own concept and that, in fact, I diverge from his conclusions in at least one significant respect. For in his analysis, the primary agent of performativity is technology which provides a means of controlling the context we call 'reality', even if 'performance improvement [is] won at the expense of the partner or partners [nature, or human beings] constituting that context' (p. 47). Deconstructionists and new historicists alike are no doubt acutely aware of their marginal status in relation to the technological protocols for research governed by the criterion of performance. In particular, some new historicists have articulated a sense of their own powerlessness in relation to technocracy, and this perhaps accounts for the recurring theme in their writings of containment, of the short-circuiting of resistances to authority, of a dominant ideology's capacity to recuperate all modes of subversion. Still, the extraordinary reception of first deconstruction and now new historicism would suggest that there is some residual power that society invests in what we call 'the Humanities'.

In fact, it is precisely the recognition of this kind of power that leads J. Hillis Miller to worry about the resistance to theory within the profession in his 1986 presidential address to the MLA, a resistance that he views as animating the new historicism. Miller's account of what he calls the 'triumph of theory' sounds like the latest version of an old romantic epic in which America is the heroic (and phallic) agent of a westward passage from Europe to the Indies. The imperialist itinerary is roughly the same; only in its latest avatar the spirit of Euro-America is no longer mystified by a doctrine of 'progress'; it is now unabashedly identified as 'power'. Miller writes:

America has become the center of technological and economic 'power,' if I may dare to use that word. Although literary theory may have its origin in Europe, we export it in a new form, along with other American 'products,' all over the world – as we do many of our scientific and technological inventions, for example the atom bomb. Theory is exported to Japan, to Australia, to China, back again to Europe, almost everywhere. In each new environment and language it is displaced, transformed, or translated once more in an ever-proliferating hetero-geneity.

(1987, p. 287)

Despite my own sympathy for the project of new historicism, I must admit that on the question of the relative power involved in presiding over the teaching of reading and writing Miller has a point. In daring to use the word 'power' in relation to his own activity as a theorist he is refreshingly, if no more than rhetorically, honest. By contrast, new historicists, who are accustomed to using the word 'power' in writing about the past, have had relatively little to say about the power of their own critical practice in the present. Indeed, I believe it is the disavowal of power that produces in the writing of new historicists a quality that leads Walter Cohen to remark on 'the strangely quietist feel of these radical critiques' (1987, p. 37).

To assume that those of us who profess the humanities are marginal, hence powerless, hence impotent in an increasingly technologized educational system is to ignore the technologies of our own discipline. These are basically reading technologies which, beginning with the ethos of 'close-reading' advocated by the New Criticism, have been our discipline's response to the demand that knowledge be legitimated by performance, a demand that has characterized American society since the Second World War. It seems to me that what we can observe in the dialogue that is now under way between American deconstruction and new historicism is a struggle for power in the form of competition for an academic market, and in each case the main criterion for success in the market-place is performativity.

Performativity in American criticism has been and continues to be measured in terms of the effective display of some type of formalism whether in the mode of New Criticism, structuralism or deconstruction. New Historicists have also effectively appropriated the power of formalism. J. Hillis Miller is perhaps justified in viewing the turn to history as one manifestation of a resistance to theory; but he is hardly justified in claiming, as he does, that new historicism constitutes a 'resistance to reading'. On the contrary, the best of the new historicists are nothing if they are not excellent readers. And it is precisely in the readings they have produced that these critics have gained their legitimacy and their power. A major strength of the movement lies in the way it has acknowledged and elucidated the textuality of history and the intertextual relations between canonical literary texts and other kinds of cultural data. Moreover, since in the past 'good' readings entailed a certain ideal of what 'good' texts are (i.e., canonical texts), one important effect of the work of some new historicists has been to dislocate this notion of a canon and thereby to change not only *how* we read but *what* we read. Indeed, from the standpoint of a more empiricist historiography, new historicism is dubious and dangerous because its very emphasis on reading, on discourse analysis, on semiotic, hermeneutic, even deconstructive modes of exegesis casts some doubt on the validity of a historiography in which the literary is subordinated to the documentary. As Jean E. Howard suggests, 'instead of a hierarchical relationship in which literature figures as the parasitic reflector of historical fact... [the new historicist] imagines a complex textualized universe in which literature participates in historical processes and in the political management of reality' (1986, p. 25).

In this respect new historicism can lay claim along with deconstruction to having a destabilizing effect on existing modes of critical discourse, thus to being a form of that postmodern critical practice Lyotard terms *paralogy*. At the same time, as reading technologies both deconstruction and new historicism have met the criterion of performativity and in so doing have sustained certain traditions associated with what we term the 'Humanities': deconstruction has helped restore rhetoric and philology to a place of dignity in the constellation of academic discourses; and new historicism has made its own contribution to the revival of rhetoric while also renewing interest among literary scholars in the resources of the archive. However, as types of formalism that 'read' the world as a 'text', both critical practices render the world in a disturbingly abstract form. J. Hillis Miller acknowledges that American theory is a 'power' comparable to American technology. New historicists tend to be more reticent or embarrassed by the imperialism of their own textual strategies. 'To "read" the world, after all', writes Alan Liu, 'is not an ideologically neutral act. It is to appropriate the world from the masses of the less articulate and literate. It is a statement of privilege, of new Fugitivism.' Finally, then, the phenomenal impact that deconstruction and, subsequently, new historicism have had on the profession in recent years can be seen partly as a function of their respective capacities to restabilize existing institutional structures. And in the case of new historicism, despite the scrupulous concern to describe culture in terms of historical processes, the necessity of fulfilling a performativity criterion as a reading technology has sometimes generated a peculiarly static, formalistic version of those processes.

One way in which new historicism diverges from earlier types of historical criticism is that new historicists register the fragmentation of the subject if only by virtue of the fact that in their writing the subject of historiography is itself fragmented. Hence the charge of arbitrary connectedness that has been made against the movement's practitioners (Cohen, 1987, pp. 34–8). This refusal, or this sense of powerlessness, to locate the historian's own subjectivity is, incidentally, a major factor in distinguishing new historicist from feminist scholarship in the field of Renaissance studies. It is also what limits new historicism as a vehicle of an ethical and political criticism. As Judith Newton points out, many of the governing assumptions of new historicism have informed other critical practices for years. Newton mentions specifically 'cultural materialism and many strands of feminism and Afro-American criticism' (1988, p. 89). However, a distinction can still be made here, one to which Newton herself points throughout her essay – and it is a distinction that makes a major difference – i.e., that in the recent past these other critical practices have openly defined themselves as modes of what Edward W. Said calls 'oppositional criticism' (1983, pp. 29–30). And to write oppositionally means to acknowledge at least a provisional subject-position within a shared political and social practice that resists cultural domination and containment.

New historicists have belatedly tried to link their scholarly work to such politically charged subject-positions; but to date the politics and ethics of new historicism have remained highly abstract, purely textual phenomena. No doubt my invocation of politics will feed the phobias of an old-style humanism. But invoking ethics may feed the complacencies of such a humanism, and that is hardly my aim. I do think that new historicism, like most forms of postmodern discourse, is a language game played around the effect of fragmented subjectivity which has begun to displace alienation as the existential condition of intellectuals in the dominant, consumer societies of the Western world today. By means of an often ingenious and agile rhetoric new historicists have, up to now, managed to avoid articulating what I would describe as the cultural economy of their relation to the past, though there have been recent calls for precisely such an articulation of how the historical critic negotiates a place in the present through the construction of a past (Tennenhouse, 1986, pp. 7–12;

Wayne, 1987, pp. 60–2; Marcus, 1988, p. 36; Montrose, 1989, pp. 23–4). This is not an indictment, for I think too that new historicism, and postmodernism in general, constitute the prerequisites of an ethos that is struggling to emerge. And an ethos implies a relation to what we once confidently termed the 'self'. Like many of their contemporaries, new historicists have been justly resistant to notions of subjectivity in terms of *identity*. What some of these critics sense is the need for an ethics based on the acknowledgement of difference, but also on the principle of relationship. By understanding our relationship to the past as different though not disconnected, and by recognizing that our construction of the past is a function of our relation to the present, we can participate in producing alternatives to the present. But to accomplish this in our cultural roles as intellectuals, we shall have to move beyond the neo-romantic aesthetic of language games and beyond the abstractions of theory to a more specific account of our respective roles, not as originary authors and agents, but as wilful, deliberate and articulate participants in a present historical process that can disturb and disrupt (even if it cannot fully subvert) existing power structures. This means, too, acknowledging our relationship to those who are most brutalized by such power structures and who are not privileged to engage in worried meditations in search of the subject of history.

FURTHER READING

Boose, Lynda E. (1987) 'The Family in Shakespeare Studies: or – Studies in the Family of Shakespeareans: or – The Politics of Politics', *Renaissance Quarterly*, 40, 707–42

Cohen, Walter (1987) 'Political Criticism of Shakespeare'. In Jean E. Howard and Marion F. O'Connor (eds), *Shakespeare Reproduced: The Text in History and Ideology*, Methuen, New York, pp. 1–46

Dollimore, Jonathan and Sinfield, Alan (eds) (1985) *Political Shakespeare: New Essays in Cultural Materialism*, Cornell University Press, Ithaca

Greenblatt, Stephen (ed.) (1988a) *Representing the English Renaissance*, University of California Press, Berkeley

Howard, Jean E. (1986) 'The New Historicism in Renaissance Studies', *English Literary Renaissance*, 16, 13–43

Liu, Alan (1989) 'The Power of Formalism: The New Historicism', *English Literary History*, 56, 721–71

Montrose, Louis (1989) Professing the Renaissance; The Poetics of Culture. In Harold A. Veeser (ed.), *The New Historicism*, Routledge, New York, pp. 15–36

Neely, Carol Thomas (1988) 'Constructing the Subject: Feminist Practice and New Renaissance Discourses', *English Literary Renaissance*, 18, 5–18

Newton, Judith (1988) 'History as Usual? Feminism and the New Historicism', *Cultural Critique*, 9, 87–121

Porter, Carolyn (1988) 'Are We Being Historical Yet?', *South Atlantic Quarterly*, 87, 743–85

Veeser, Harold A. (ed.) (1989) *The New Historicism*, Routledge, New York
Wayne, Don E. (1987) 'Power, Politics, and the Shakespearean Text: Recent Criticism in England and the United States'. In Jean E. Howard and Marion F. O'Connor (eds), *Shakespeare Reproduced: The Text in History and Ideology*, Methuen, New York, pp. 47–67

ADDITIONAL WORKS CITED

Bercovitch, Sacvan (1988) 'Hawthorne's A-Morality of Compromise', *Representations*, 24, 1–27
Goldberg, Jonathan (1983) *James I and the Politics of Literature*, Johns Hopkins University Press, Baltimore
Greenblatt, Stephen (1986) 'Psychoanalysis and Renaissance Culture'. In Patricia Parker and David Quint (eds), *Literary Theory and Renaissance Texts*, Johns Hopkins University Press, Baltimore, pp. 210–24
——(1988b) *Shakespearean Negotiations: The Circulation of Social Energy in Renaissance England*, University of California Press, Berkeley
Heinemann, Margot (1985) 'How Brecht Read Shakespeare'. In Jonathan Dollimore and Alan Sinfield (eds), *Political Shakespeare: New Essays in Cultural Materialism*, Cornell University Press, Ithaca, pp. 202–30
Helgerson, Richard (1986) 'The Land Speaks: Cartography, Chorography, and Subversion in Renaissance England', *Representations*, 16, 50–85
Jameson, Fredric (1981) *The Political Unconscious: Narrative as a Socially Symbolic Act*, Cornell University Press, Ithaca
Kahn, Victoria (1985) *Rhetoric, Prudence, and Skepticism in the Renaissance*, Cornell University Press, Ithaca
Lyotard, Jean-François (1984) *The Postmodern Condition: A Report On Knowledge*, foreword by Fredric Jameson, University of Minnesota Press, Minneapolis
Marcus, Leah S. (1988) *Puzzling Shakespeare: Local Reading and Its Discontents*, University of California Press, Berkeley
Miller, D. A. (1987) 'The Wrong Man: A Response to J. Hillis Miller's Reply', *ADE Bulletin*, 88, 58
Miller, J. Hillis (1987) 'Presidential Address 1986: The Triumph of Theory, the Resistance to Reading, and the Question of the Material Base', *PMLA*, 102, 281–91
Morris, Wesley (1972) *Toward a New Historicism*, Princeton University Press, Princeton
Orgel, Stephen (1975) *The Illusion of Power: Political Theatre in the English Renaissance*, University of California Press, Berkeley
Pearce, Roy Harvey (1987) *Gesta Humanorum: Studies in the Historicist mode*, University of Missouri Press, Columbia
Said, Edward W. (1983) *The World, The Text, and the Critic*, Harvard University Press, Cambridge
Sinfield, Alan (1985) 'Power and Ideology: An Outline Theory and Sidney's *Arcadia*', *English Literary History*, 52, 259–77
Tennenhouse, Leonard (1986) *Power on Display: The Politics of Shakespeare's Genres*, Methuen, New York

Terdiman, Richard (1989) 'Is There Class in this Class?'. In Harold A. Veeser (ed.), *The New Historicism*, Routledge, New York, pp. 225–30

Whigham, Frank (1984) *Ambition and Privilege: The Social Tropes of Elizabethan Courtesy Literature*, University of California Press, Berkeley

White, Hayden V. (1978) 'Historicism, History, and the Figurative Imagination'. In Hayden V. White, *Tropics of Discourse: Essays in Cultural Criticism*, Johns Hopkins University Press, Baltimore, pp. 101–20

VII. PRODUCTION AND RECEPTION

59

PRODUCTION AND RECEPTION OF THE LITERARY BOOK

JOHN SUTHERLAND

All four items in the title ('Production', 'Reception', 'Literary', 'Book') pose difficulties. In what follows I fragment them, to indicate a variety of their meanings and usages over the last five hundred years.

THE LITERARY BOOK: PRELIMINARY OBSERVATIONS

For purposes of international classification, 'book' is defined as a work of printed and bound text of 49 pages or more. Rules of thumb have been devised by the book trade, librarians and statisticians to sub-categorize the 'literary book'. As racked by retail stores, it comprises an ensemble of easily identified genres – fiction, poetry, belles-lettres, criticism. For cataloguing purposes, librarians and statisticians are often guided by master 'Cataloguing in Publication' (CIP) data, supplied by the Library of Congress and the British Library.

THE LITERARY BOOK: NEW AND OLD

The book trade distinguishes sharply between 'new' and 'old' product – though not in such a way as to discard the old as unsaleable. The practice of frontlist (window) and backlist (warehouse) stockholding creates two orders of in-print (i.e. available) book (Mann, 1982, pp. 90–117). The proportion of front- to backlist items in contemporary book culture is around one to six. Another distinction between 'new' and 'old' books is in physical packaging. Newly created ('original') literary books are typically issued in an expensive form – 'hardback' in contemporary literary culture. Older items are often reprinted in inexpensive softcover form. (One side-effect is to make them spuriously 'new' again.) Commercial considerations dictate this division. The original work represents a greater financial risk, and a high per-copy return reduces that risk. ('Break-even' can be achieved on relatively small sales.) Reprint items are typically those whose previous career in more expensive form assures large sales. Longer production runs and smaller per-copy profit can thus be gambled on. The ratio of original to reprint literary books has varied over the centuries (in the sixteenth century, for instance, the vast majority of literary books were reissues or new translations). Nowadays it is about one-to-one. These alternative forms of issue are trade conventions devised in response to a perceived market demand. There is a symmetrical academic division of the literary book between the 'canonical' and the uncanonical. Canonical (the term originally applied to books approved by the church) indicates literary texts which have perennial value and thus repay study as cultural objects which transcend their immediate historical condition. They are – mystically – outside time and place. Traditionally, canonical texts are conceived to have been winnowed out by history and by exercise of the most strenuous critical scrutiny. Academies are notoriously conservative on eligibility for canonization and new candidates are admitted only very grudgingly (Graff, 1987). As identified by examination topics, a cadre of fifty to a hundred authors of literary books enjoy canonical status. Following the 'relevance', feminist, anti-racist and anti-elitist interventions of the 1960s, enlarging the canon and decanonization have become burning (sometimes literally) issues for academic curriculum-makers.

THE LITERARY BOOK: 'LITERARY' AS A CRITICAL CONCEPT

'Literature' and its derived adjective 'literary' are highly loaded and historically relativistic terms. As Raymond Williams notes in *Keywords* (1976), up to the seventeenth century, 'literary' had the same neutral sense of the present-day 'literate', and was used interchangeably. The highly evaluative use of 'literary' – to indicate a culturally superior form of book – begins in the eighteenth century (when it covered all 'belles-lettres') and culminates in the nineteenth century. Williams observes complexities in the modern application of the word:

> In relation to the past, *literature* is still a relatively general word: Carlyle and Ruskin, for example, who did not write novels or poems or plays, belong to *English Literature*. But there has been a steady distinction and separation of other kinds of writing – philosophy, essays, history and so on – which may or may not possess *literary merit* or be of *literary interest* (meaning that 'in addition to' their intrinsic interest as philosophy or history or whatever, they are 'well written') but which are not now normally described as *literature* which may be understood as well-written books but which is even more clearly understood as books of an *imaginative* or *creative* kind.
>
> (p. 152)

PRODUCTION: THE PUBLISHER AS PRODUCER

Publishers have traditionally regarded themselves as the primary 'producers' of books which are otherwise 'created' by authors and 'distributed' through various sales outlets (Mann, 1982, pp. 62–3). Within the book trade 'production' has two main conventional usages:

(1) Day-to-day it applies to the planning of books by the publisher's 'Production Department' and their (usually subcontracted) manufacture. Production involves decisions on such matters as numbers of copies to be printed, choice of paper, type and jacket design; advertising budget; promotional effort; co-publishing and subsidiary rights arrangements.

(2) Year-to-year 'production' denotes the level of activity within the book industry, as measured by output. The simplest approach to production is thus to record total book-trade statistics, and the proportion of literary books within that total. Since the fifteenth century, the ratio of literary books to all titles has varied (roughly) between 10 and 25 per cent. H. S. Bennett estimates that there were 6,000 titles produced in England between 1477 and 1557 (1952, p. 20). Current title production in the late 1980s is between 40,000 and 50,000 in Britain and in America. Edith L. Klotz (1938) estimates that between 1480 and 1640 the proportion of 'literary' titles produced was 13 per cent, although in some years, it could go as high as a quarter of all titles. In the most recently available American figures (1988–9) the proportion of literary titles within the annual output is also 13 per cent (approximately). Within this relatively stable fraction, the popularity of different literary genres has recorded one major shift. Since the early nineteenth century in Britain and America, the novel has constituted around a tenth of all annual title production, and has become by far the dominant 'literary' genre. Analysis of catalogues discovers a significant growth in fiction items to have occurred between 1773 (when novels constituted around 8 per cent of the whole output) and 1803 (when novels jumped to just under 15 per cent of the whole). This advance was at the expense of poetry and translation. According to John Feather, around half of all titles published in the eighteenth century were poetry. By 1825, poetry was level-pegging with fiction, at about 10 per cent of the whole book output. Verse lost ground throughout the nineteenth century, to become an entirely minority taste in the twentieth.

PRODUCTION: MATERIALS AND CONSTITUENTS

As a physical object the book is composed of materials, worked on by a labour force and assembled by a productive apparatus. Writing is a necessary precondition; and it seems that alphabetized script systems (such as the Roman and Cyrillic) lend themselves to book production earlier and more naturally than ideographic, logographic or pictographic systems (Harris, 1986). The root technology of printing – moveable and rearrangable blocks or type – was known in China but never developed because of the logistic problem of handling thousands of characters. Ink, paper, board – or their synthetic equivalents – are the basic physical resources necessary for constructing a book. For type founding, early presses borrowed soft metal technology from jewellers. (As a hangover, some of the jeweller's craft seems to have influenced the ultra-costly *édition de luxe* through the ages; books, especially new British books, have always been exorbitantly priced wares.) Retailing practices for the primeval book trade were borrowed from kindred commercial activities in the town market-place – especially those like the cloth trade (where Caxton was trained) which had international connections. The early book trade similarly borrowed its display, delivery and advertising techniques from other retail businesses and, at the lower end of the market, from peddling (Bennett, 1952). Caxton in the late fifteenth century centralized in himself many functions which later exfoliated into separate book-trade departments: he was commissioning agent, editor, typesetter, printer, warehouseman, wholesaler, publisher, bookseller, publicist – and, when the need arose, author and translator. But it is astonishing how modern his specific publishing activities look. His books were primarily in English and addressed a 'reading public' in a spirit of commercial invitation (they were not, that is, commissioned or vanity-published); like later general trade publishers, Caxton put together a 'mixed list'; his editions seem to have been surprisingly large and he evidently operated a primitive front- and back-list arrangement; he was in business primarily to make a commercial profit. We may also assume that Caxton intuitively assumed the crucial 'gatekeeper' role of the modern publisher: that is, not just putting some books into print but keeping infinitely more out. There is always a superfluity of manuscripts soliciting the dignity of book form; and it is the publisher's principal cultural responsibility to ensure – by the exercise of taste and judgement – that only worthy candidates succeed. Publication has always been a scarce facility, one which requires judicious rationing and firm use of the rejection slip. The publisher accepts this role not primarily out of philanthropy, but because of the financial structure of the business. It requires a high initial capital investment in equipment and sometimes the purchase of literary material. ('Sometimes' is a necessary qualifier. Caxton long predates the notion of the author as the privileged creator and legal owner of his literary 'property'. This sophisticated legal concept was not devised and implemented until the eighteenth century. The main reason for the delay was that bookselling did not generate enough surplus value to support independent authorship.) Cash returns at all periods are slow for the publisher – never more so than in the twentieth century, when most literary writers expect payment years in advance. And success is hazardous: it has always been the case that more books lose than make money.

PRODUCTION: CAPITAL VENTURE AND RISK

There are several ways of minimizing risk. Making the author insure his work by pre-publication subsidy ('vanity publishing') is one. Making readers insure the work by pre-publication subscription is an alternative which had some vogue in the eighteenth century. Another – even more venerable – is via patronage, in which some wealthy outside person or institution assumes the financial risk. Bennett estimates that 90 per cent of all English books published up to the seventeenth century were financed by patronage (1965, p. 51). Sharing the risk with other publishers (as in the eighteenth-century 'conger' or the twentieth-century pre-publication auction of subsidiary rights) is a third option. Working through closed-circuit distribution reduces risk in so far as these circuits – unlike the open market – create precisely predictable sales levels. (Typical closed circuits are the lending library, the book club and the coterie.) Cross-subsidy is a favoured modern means of reducing publishing risk – that is, putting out books which have a secure market (i.e. educational works) to generate funds for works with an insecure market (i.e. poetry). All these techniques have served at various times to offload some of the publisher's financial anxiety at producing literary books – traditionally very chancy things. But a high degree of risk remains; publishing has always been an industry with daunting rates of commercial failure. The principal safeguard which the publisher has is his professional skill in selection, production and promotion of his wares. And the consistent exercise of this skill creates the 'character' of the house and – over a period – the emergence of a distinct publishing style (Mumby and Norrie, 1974).

PRODUCTION: THE PRODUCTIVE APPARATUS

Superficially there seem to be distinct starting points and thresholds in book-trade history – but these melt when we regard them closely. There was, for instance, a book trade remarkably similar to that of the modern period in ancient Rome, employing not technology but the massed scriptorial services of literate slaves – an unusual combination (Putnam, 1894). Although we celebrate the innovation of European printing with Gutenberg as an epochal innovation, the wider-ranging book historians downplay it. Thus Febvre and Martin's *The Coming of the Book* (1976) opens with the wonderfully laconic observation – 'About the year 1450 some rather unusual manuscripts made their appearance in the northern regions of Western Europe' (p. 9). There was no revolution. The printed book was just another efficient mutation in a long process. As important as the new technology was the pre-existing manufacturing (literally 'handmaking') base of scriptorial reproduction. This had by the early fifteenth century broken out of the closed circuits of the monastery and the noble household, and set up a network of commercial and public trade. The printer merely streamlined a department of the scrivener's activity, as the publisher later enlarged a department of the early bookseller's activity and – in our own day – the computer typesetter has taken over a large part of the hot metal printer's activity. Although Caxton enjoys a folkloric fame among his countrymen his name does not loom large in European histories of the book, which remind us that there were at least fifty European presses before our first printer set up in Westminster. Nevertheless, despite its slowness off the mark and the ordinariness of the British book compared with continental achievements, Britain supplied a clement environment for the production of literature. As John Feather notes in a subsequent essay (see below, p. 848), 'From its very beginning, English publishing was vernacular and insular'. This character favoured the emergence of an English literature in the English language. (Chauvinism was given the force of law by a series of ordinances from 1484 to 1534 which effectively squeezed foreigners out of the London printing profession.) Additionally, the British book trade has over the centuries suffered remarkably little control from the state or from other institutions. Licences, privileges, prohibitions, censorship, occasionally figure – but never for long and never with any lasting impediment. Surprisingly, the most controlled phase of the British book trade's activity has been the most recent, with the setting up of interlocking professional and trade associations in the 1880s and 1890s (i.e. the Booksellers Association, the Publishers Association, the Society of Authors). This institutionalization has led in the twentieth century to the Net Book Agreement (which standardizes retail price) and the royalty agreement (which makes authors partners in their books' fortunes). These, however, are intramural regulations imposed by the book trade on itself and in the larger sense are evidence of autonomy rather than control (Barnes, 1964; Bonham-Carter, 1978).

PRODUCTION AND THE LARGER SOCIAL FORMATION

Although the British book trade appears independent (compared, say, to broadcasting or – for much of its evolution – British journalism) this autonomy is not absolute. Book trades, even relatively uncontrolled book trades like the British, conform to their host society and to current dominant conditions within the society. The English book trade has had a markedly different character and way of doing business during wartime, for instance. In the Second World War – to take a recent example – its production was distorted by 'austerity', ideological conformism and a voluntarily assumed propaganda role (see Mumby and Norrie, 1974, pp. 391–409). During periods of extreme illiberalism the book trade follows suit (e.g. the late 1880s, when the seventy-year-old publisher Henry Vizetelly was sent to prison for publishing translations of Zola). In periods of cultural liberation the book trade can play a vanguard role, as when Penguin Books published *Lady Chatterley's Lover* in 1960 (Sutherland, 1982). There is, then, a sense in which the whole social formation can be said to produce books. Terry Eagleton has devised the term 'General Mode of Production' for this and has elaborated a subtle concept of ideological mediation and causation (Eagleton, 1976a). But the degree to which books are 'national' or 'social' products remains extremely tricky; more so since at any historical moment there are seditous, blasphemous, pornographic and counter-cultural literary productions.

PRODUCTION, REPRODUCTION AND DESECRATING THE BOOK

The book is extraordinarily the same thing that it has always been. Unlike other technologies of communication, it has suffered virtually no physical or mechanical transformation over the last four hundred years. Were Caxton to be resurrected he could – given his fifteenth-century workshop – reproduce something remarkably similar to this week's best-seller (title pages, which did not appear until the 1490s, might faze him a little, as would dust-jackets – a twentieth-century innovation). This inert core of antiquity is linked to the book's aura of sacredness. Viewed profanely, books are nothing more than portable storage devices: of the same order as a computer disk or a magnetic tape. Some books (telephone directories; mail-order catalogues) aspire no higher. But typically the book – and particularly the literary book – is potentially an object of iconic dignity and authority. Writing in the 1930s (at a time when this dignity and authority had been expropriated by the Nazis), Walter Benjamin argued that a self-consciousness of its 'mechanical reproduction' was necessary to modernize the book which should thereby (like Brecht's epic theatre) be stripped of its sacred aura, the better to perform its necessary social functions (Benjamin, 1968).

'PRODUCTION' AS CRITICAL CONCEPT: PRELIMINARY OBSERVATIONS

Superficially the phrase 'writers and readers of texts' seems not very different from 'producers and consumers of books'. But if we try to operate these terms with any critical precision they make awkward misfits. For practical purposes, we get round the awkwardness by a mixture of doublethink and willed amnesia. Thus in a class the teacher will turn to chapter 21 of her text of *Middlemarch* – say a battered 1887 Blackwood's 'Cabinet' volume bought twenty years since, when she was a student herself, for 6d in a second-hand bookshop. The class meanwhile will turn to the corresponding passage in their text – say the 1989

World's Classics bought last week from a stack in the campus bookstore for £4.50. Both parties can happily assume that they are discussing 'the same book'. Indeed, while discussing Dorothea's traumatic experiences in Rome they simply will not *see* any differences in their *Middlemarches*, except as an occasional problem in 'finding the place'. But if we make the genealogical effort to see them, the wholly commercial processes which produced the 1887 cheap uniform reissue of Eliot's novel for the 'common reader' are radically different from the academic-commercial processes that produced the 'authoritatively edited' paperback primarily for the education market. Both are superstructural literary events, resting on radically different productive bases.

PRODUCTION AS A CRITICAL CONCEPT: PROBLEMS OF MATERIALIST PERSPECTIVE

The literary experience is taught in Anglo-American schools and colleges as a 'meeting of minds': something magically immediate, stripped of all contingency and circumstance. The laborious conditions which produced the literary work and even the tainted conditions in which it is currently being consumed (e.g., a teacher paid – or underpaid – to expound meaning; a literary text produced to make money for a publishing house with an annual turnover of £50 million) are dissolved in an invisible *mise-en-scène*. The material does not matter. But what happens if we make it matter, and deliberately regard the book *qua* book: a made, distributed, sold and consumed commodity? Terry Eagleton makes some relevant observations as he asks himself this question in the 'Art as Production' section of his *Marxism and Literary Criticism* (1976b):

> I have spoken so far of literature in terms of form, politics, ideology and consciousness. But all this overlooks a simple fact which is obvious to everyone and not least a Marxist. Literature may be an artefact, a product of social consciousness, a world vision; but it is also an *industry*. Books are not just structures of meaning, they are also commodities produced by publishers and sold on the market at a profit. . . . Writers are not just transposers of trans-individual mental structures, they are also workers hired by publishing houses to produce commodities that will sell. 'A writer', Marx comments, 'is a worker not in so far as he produces ideas, but insofar as he enriches the publisher, insofar as he is working for a wage'. It is a salutary reminder.
>
> (pp. 59–60)

Recalling it may be salutary, but what does one *do* with this 'obvious' but conveniently forgettable productive infrastructure? Publishing history is, after all, extraordinarily distracting stuff. What does it benefit us, while reading *Middlemarch*, to know that Eliot earned £10,000 from the copyright and that Blackwood sold almost 10,000 copies in the first three years (see Sutherland, 1976)? William Charvat, a pioneer of academic publishing history, offered an answer in 1959:

Facts and figures about sales of books and incomes of authors are interesting – but not interesting enough, unless they specifically reveal something about the ways in which writers and their writings function in a culture. Similarly the history of publishing, with which I am deeply involved, tends, like most specialties, to become an end in itself. Publishing is relevant to literary history only in so far as it can be shown to be, ultimately, a shaping influence on literature.

(p. 7)

Charvat offers two modest ways forward. The first is that 'publishing history' should subordinate itself as 'literary sociology' within the larger ensemble of 'literary history' – something which he sees as very important to preserve. The second is that publishing history should be employed as a critical underling in the service of better understanding 'literature'. Charvat's prescribed role for publishing history is essentially stabilizing. It would cement 'literature' in the honoured position it has occupied since the Renaissance. Nothing much will change with the addition of knowledge it brings. Eagleton (writing in 1976 after a turbulent decade) believes quite otherwise. For him, uncovering the productive apparatus of the literary enterprise will produce (in its turn) effects which are grossly disturbing and destabilizing. One is that literature will cease to be 'literary', in the accepted honorific sense. Deconsecrated, we shall see it as 'practice' and 'work'. And this will be 'part of our liberation from oppression'. A slightly less profoundly disturbing option is offered by Hans R. Jauss, the principal exponent with W. Iser of Reception theory. According to Jauss (1982), it is not Charvat's traditional notion of 'literature' but of 'literary history' which is at risk from a materialist perspective. Literary history, Jauss asserts, must be 'written anew' from the perspectives of productivity and reception.

PRODUCTION AS CRITICAL CONCEPT: AUTHORSHIP, PRODUCERS AND OWNERS

The differences among history's various *Middlemarches* are, for the purposes of academic discussion, ironed out by the idea of a Platonically archetypal *Middlemarch* which inhabits each materialization of the text. (In another arena of academic activity, textual scholars labour at the quixotic task of reproducing this elusive noumenon as the 'definitive edition'.) A similarly useful confusion of materiality and immateriality is central to the law of copyright. As it has emerged since 1710, the definition of literary property assumes that the author creates a bodiless 'work' which transcends any physically constituted version of itself – e.g. the book which the manufacturer makes, the merchandiser sells and the purchaser buys. What the author 'owns' is an inalienable form of words (Ploman and Hamilton, 1980). 'Immaterial property' is not the only paradox of copyright. Something extraordinary happens to authorial property when the copyright clock runs out (nowadays fifty years after the creator's death). At this point, the work enters 'the public domain' to become – like the open sea – everybody's and nobody's. No other form of private property is dealt with in this imaginative and communistic way. Legal fictions are clearly quite as inventive as literary fictions. But what is striking about the law of literary property is how, after the eighteenth century, statute and literary theory converge on the idea of the single author-owner. In a work like *The Prelude*, Wordsworth's sublime egotistic self who 'creates' the literature (as God created the world) and who is at the same time the subject of the poem is also – in a third role – the monopolistic owner of his mental production. As one of their more utopian projects, Wordsworth and Coleridge aspired to write 'ballads'. They would both merge and submerge their separate selves to create works which like their orally circulated models would have transmission but no authorship. The *Lyrical Ballads* failed in their overt intention for a number of reasons: but not least because they were published commercially as a book, under the proclaimed authorship (and ownership) of Wordsworth and Coleridge. Capitalism and Romanticism thus combined in the eighteenth and nineteenth centuries to bolster the sovereignty of the author-owner. It was not always so, nor – one apprehends – will it always be so. Much currency has been given recently to the following description by Saint Bonaventura of the emergence of the author from the thirteenth-century writing ruck:

> A man might write the works of others, adding and changing nothing, in which case he is simply called a 'scribe' (*scriptor*). Another writes the work of others with additions which are not his own; and he is called a 'compiler' (*compilator*). Another writes both others' work and his own, but with others' work in principal place, adding his own for purposes of explanation; and he is called a 'commentator' (*commentator*). . . . Another writes both his own work and others' but with his own work in principal place adding others' for purposes of confirmation; and such a man should be called an 'author' (*auctor*).
>
> (in Eisenstein, 1983, p. 84)

A version of this passage was placed prominently on the cover of the French edition of Roland Barthes' immensely influential critical tract *S/Z* (1970). This was in line with the Barthesian project of expropriating the title of 'producer' from the author and awarding it to the readers of the text. For Barthes, the essential liberation (with some conscious play, perhaps, on 'libre' and 'livre') was 'to make the reader no longer a consumer, but a producer of the text' (Barthes, [1970] 1975, p. 4). Following Barthes, other post-structuralists further diminish the author, until he or she is a mere 'effect', 'function' or 'production' among all the other productions which compose a text. Without using the term (although it is clearly denoted by 'certain discourses') Michel Foucault in 'What is an Author?' (1979) diagnoses authorship as a production peculiar to the 'literary book', itself a historically timebound production:

> In a civilization like our own there are a certain number of discourses that are

endowed with the 'author-function', while others are deprived of it. A private letter may well have a signer – it does not have an author ... An anonymous text posted on a wall probably has a writer – but not an author. The author-function is therefore characteristic of the mode of existence, circulation, and functioning of certain discourses within a society.

(p. 148)

A highly narrowed critical concept of 'production' has been given currency by Pierre Macherey's monograph *A Theory of Literary Production* ([1966] trans. 1978). Macherey starts from the position that the literary work 'is not *created* by an intention (objective or subjective) it is *produced* under determinate conditions' (p. 78). His literary criticism interrogates the inner workings of texts: their symptomatic silences, gaps, fissures and factitious ideological closures. The primary production for Macherey is the intra-textual production of meaning, or significance.

PRODUCTION AS CRITICAL CONCEPT: THE AUTHOR AS PRODUCER

Over the last twenty years the semiotic, post-structuralist and deconstructionist enterprises have generally succeeded in replacing the sovereignty of the author with that of the text and the critic. Nevertheless, a powerful cross-current has preserved the authority of author by recasting him or her not as 'creator' but 'producer'. The main critical text in support of this thesis is Walter Benjamin's essay, 'The Author as Producer' (*Der Autor als Produzent*, in Benjamin, 1979). Originally written and delivered in 1934 at the Paris Institute for the Study of Fascism, Benjamin's polemic was given new currency in the 1970s. His argument is that the author has it in his [*sic*] power to transform not just his literary statements, but his productive apparatus – literature itself. The productive author should be constantly aware of the historically conditioned nature of his literary forms, and his power to 'recast' them. In this way, he produces not just the content, but the 'means' of literature. In one of his more daring flights, Benjamin imagines a future without novels – when that form has become as antique for modern purposes as 'rhetoric' or the epic. These transformations (in Benjamin's view) will depend entirely on 'productive' authorial initiative.

RECEPTION: PRELIMINARY OBSERVATIONS

For the lay public, 'Reception' means two things: (1) Reviews; (2) Sales. These can be glossed as reaction to the literary work by the reviewing establishment (journalistic and academic) and the literary work's performance in the marketplace.

PRODUCTION AND RECEPTION: ASYMMETRIES

Not every literary book that is produced is 'received' (i.e. it is not reviewed, not bought). This has been a matter of considerable anxiety to the Anglo-American book trade since its earliest days. Typically, the literary book thrives in a condition of chronic commercial overproduction – verging on saturation. Over the whole field more titles are produced than demanded; more copies are on offer than will ever be sold – up to 50 per cent of American mass-market paperbacks are pulped (Sutherland, 1978); more copies are sold than will be actually read. This built-in discrepancy puts a premium on advertising and other mechanisms like best-seller lists designed to stimulate consumption. In the largest sense, the Anglo-American book trade is structurally and permanently distorted by its hopeless quest to balance underconsumption and overproduction.

RECEPTION: LITERACY, READING PUBLICS, MARKETS

Literacy represents general reading competence in a population using the same language resource. (This last is a fairly recent European phenomenon; Chaucer, for instance, complains of the 'great diversity in English, and in writing of our tongue'. By the late twentieth century – with Orwell's nightmare vision of 'Newspeak' – it is standardization, or lack of linguistic diversity, which is seen as the greater danger.) Within literacy – as a social domain – are reading publics: more or less homogenous formations of readers with general characteristics in common. Markets are such reading publics, considered from the point of view of their buying capacities and habits. Juveniles constitute, for example, a group part in, part outside literacy (even in advanced societies). They make up a distinct reading public, but – more carefully considered – a plurality of smaller reading groups (boys, girls, the very young, pre-teens, etc.). As a market, juveniles – even where they coincide in taste with adults (in the case, say, of older-girl and adult women readers of romance) – are different by virtue of having less economic power. They are poorer.

RECEPTION: OPEN AND CLOSED CIRCUITS

Few literary books are given away. Post-production books normally circulate in two ways. Through the 'open' commercial circuit books are made available to the general public via publisher-wholesaler-bookshop distribution networks. Closed circuits normally comprise exclusive associations of readers (e.g. the Left Book Club of the 1930s; the Book of the Month Club) and libraries. Coteries (i.e. affinity groups such as Russian émigrés in Paris in the 1930s) can also act as closed circuits.

RECEPTION: EVOLUTION OF THE RECEPTION APPARATUS

Although universal literacy was not enshrined in law until William Forster's education act of 1870, Britain evidently had a sizeable, competent reading public from its earliest days. It has not been the role of the book trade to teach its customers to read, but to exploit a literacy which was primarily created for other ends than to enjoy literary books. Book reviewing, by contrast, originates within the book trade, as a self-serving mechanism for discrimination among the surplus of production and for stimulating further production. The origin of modern reviewing is found in the carping of the 'Zoilists' in the late sixteenth century and the legislations of the neo-classicists in the seventeenth. Out of this grew the modern reviewing apparatus in the eighteenth century; an apparatus dominated by the 'man of letters' until the rise of the academic reviewer and critic in the twentieth century. Modern reviewing of creative literature has had to make an uneasy pact with mass-market advertising. A number of the main organs of review – for instance the *London Review of Books* and *New York Review of Books* – were started opportunistically during protracted newspaper strikes (of the *New York Times* and *Times* Newspaper London groups). It is quite common, in journals like the *TLS* or the *Sunday Times* literary supplement, to see a review of a book – for which the reviewer may receive around £150 – in company with an advertisement for the same book that may have cost up to five times as much. Maintaining critical neutrality in such circumstances requires great editorial firmness.

RECEPTION: THE READING PUBLIC AND THE LARGER SOCIAL FORMATION

Just as the productive apparatus of the book trade conforms to the larger social formation, so do(es) the reading public(s). In the sixteenth century, the class divisions of the reading public were clearly demarcated by the Act of 1543 which decreed that for the 'advancement of true religion' the reading of the Bible in English was forbidden to women, artificers, apprentices, yeomen and all lower orders. This strict hierarchical regimentation of readers was unmanageable with the growth of individualism, class mobility and the spread of literacy in the mid-sixteenth century. (It is estimated that four times as many titles were produced in 1550 than in 1500.) From the first emergence of a national market for reading materials, there has been a partially submerged echelon of 'lewd' or 'low' literature. The products for this segment of the reading population tend to be physically less durable than the bourgeois book. (It is estimated that there were some 2,000 broadside ballads published in the sixteenth century, of which only around 260 survive; the survival rate for 'literary' books at the same period is well over 50 per cent; see Livingston, 1981.) In succeeding centuries productions for the working-class or 'popular' market are frustratingly evanescent. Underground, pornographic and 'ephemeral' publications of the present day remain largely unknown countries.

RECEPTION AS A CRITICAL CONCEPT: PROBLEMS AND POTENTIAL

A reception-aesthetic approach, which sees the meaning in texts as primarily constituted by the reader, encounters two initial problems. The first is plurality – there are as many readings as readers, and the same gradations of (in)competence. Secondly, that texts mean different things at different historical periods. (*Uncle Tom's Cabin*, for instance, was a very different novel after the American Civil War.) Although it was first articulated in Europe (principally Germany) reception-aesthetic – or reader-response – criticism has been at the centre of Anglo-American literary critical debate since the 1970s. A number of dominant voices have emerged: Stanley Fish (who is principally interested in the dialectical interactions of text and reader); Hans R. Jauss (who has theorized the histories of texts' reception); Wolfgang Iser (who has worked principally on the aesthetics of Reception); Jane Tompkins (whose criticism reinserts texts – typically 'popular' texts – into their historical moments). The work of these reader-response critics proposes an elegant collapsing of previous separate categories. It is the consumer ('reader' or what Fish calls the 'interpretive community') who produces and reproduces the text out of the material contingency of the literary work. Critics like Jon Klancher collapse distinction still further by exploring how texts, in turn, constitute or 'produce' their readers (Fish, 1980; Klancher, 1987). Of all the critical styles in current practice, reader-response is the most strenuous, requiring as it does an extraordinarily rapid oscillation between theoretical model and the infinitely various historical instants of literary experience across time and space. Yet it is this approach which will most probably give a new and more delicate precision to the terms 'production' (with its Marxist baggage) and 'reception' (with its stultifying implication of inert passivity).

FURTHER READING

Altick, Richard D. (1957) *The English Common Reader: A Social History of the Mass Reading Public 1800–1900*, University of Chicago Press, Chicago

Belsey, Catherine (1980) *Critical Practice*, Methuen, London [see particularly chap. 6, 'Towards a Productive Critical Practice']

Bennett, H. S. (1952) *English Books & Readers: 1475 to 1557*, Cambridge University Press, Cambridge

——(1965) *English Books & Readers: 1558 to 1603*, Cambridge University Press, Cambridge

——(1970) *English Books & Readers: 1603 to 1640*, Cambridge University Press, Cambridge

Cross, Nigel (1985) *The Common Writer*, Cambridge University Press, Cambridge

Febvre, L. and Martin, H.-J. (1976) *The Coming of the Book*, translated by David Gerard, New Left Books, London [first published 1959]

Jauss, Hans R. (1982) *Toward an Aesthetic of Reception*, University of Minnesota Press, Minneapolis

Lane, Michael and Booth, Jeremy (1980) *Books and Publishers*, Lexington Books, Massachusetts

Mann, Peter H. (1982) *From Author to Reader: A Social Study of Books*, Routledge, London

Mumby, F. A. and Norrie, I. (1974) *Publishing and Bookselling*, Cape, London

Ploman, Edward W. and Hamilton, L. Clark (1980) *Copyright: Intellectual Property in the Information Age*, Routledge, London

Putnam, G. H. (1894) *Authors and their Public in Ancient Times*, Putnam, New York

Sutherland, J. A. (1978) *Fiction and the Fiction Industry*, Athlone Press, London

Tompkins, Jane P. (1980) *Reader Response Criticism*, Johns Hopkins University Press, Baltimore

Williams, Raymond (1967) *The Long Revolution*, Harper & Row, New York [first published 1961]

——(1976) *Keywords: A Vocabulary of Culture and Society*, Oxford University Press, London

ADDITIONAL WORKS CITED

Barnes, J. J. (1964) *Free Trade in Books*, Oxford University Press, Oxford

Barthes, Roland (1975) *S/Z*, translated by Richard Miller, Cape, London [first published 1970]

Benjamin, Walter (1968) *Illuminations*, Harcourt Brace Jovanovich, New York

——(1979) *Reflections*, Harcourt Brace Jovanovich, New York

Bonham-Carter, V. (1978) *Authors by Profession*, The Society of Authors, London

Charvat, William (1959) *Literary Publishing in America*, University of Pennsylvania Press, Philadelphia

Eagleton, Terry (1976a) *Criticism and Ideology*, New Left Books, London

——(1976b) *Marxism and Literary Criticism*, University of California Press, Berkeley and Los Angeles

Eisenstein, Elizabeth L. (1983) *The Printing Revolution in Early Modern Europe*, Cambridge University Press, Cambridge

Fish, Stanley (1980) *Is There a Text in this Class? The Authority of Interpretive Communities*, Harvard University Press, Cambridge

Foucault, Michel (1979) 'What is an Author?' In Josué V. Harari (ed.), *Textual Strategies: Perspectives in Post-Structuralist Criticism*, Cornell University Press, Ithaca, pp. 141–60

Graff, Gerald (1987) *Professing Literature*, University of Chicago Press, Chicago

Harris, Roy (1986) *The Origin of Writing*, Open Court, La Salle

Klancher, Jon P. (1987) *The Making of English Reading Audiences, 1790–1832*, University of Wisconsin Press, Madison

Klotz, Edith L. (1938) 'Subject Analysis of English Imprints for every tenth year from 1480 to 1640', *Huntington Library Quarterly*, 1, 417–19.

Livingston, Carole Rose (1981) *The Extant English and Scottish Broadside Ballads of the Sixteenth Century: A Catalogue and an Essay*, Dissertation, Ann Arbor

Macherey, Pierre (1978) *A Theory of Literary Production*, translated by Geoffrey Wall, Routledge, London [first published 1966]

Sutherland, J. A. (1976) *Victorian Novelists and Publishers*, Athlone Press, London

——(1982) *Offensive Literature*, Junction Books, London

60

THE PRINTED BOOK

JOHN FEATHER

The printed book is a physical object as well as a medium of communication. Indeed, it is not always wholly possible to distinguish between these two characteristics. They are most obviously merged, perhaps, in Blake's 'illuminated' books, where the poem, the illustration, the *mise-en-page* and even the techniques used for engraving and printing were part of a single artistic concept. In other, and more typical, cases, however, there is an intimate relationship between form and content. The literary structure of many Victorian novels, for example, was partly dictated by two of the forms in which much nineteenth-century English fiction was published, the serial and the three-decker (Griest, 1970, pp. 35–57; Sutherland, 1976, pp. 20–4). It follows, therefore, that the printed book itself is a matter which literary scholars cannot ignore; this is not merely true of textual critics or editors, although it is indeed of special concern to them, but of all students of literature which is extant only in its printed form, or of which the printed form is the only authoritative version.

The serious scholarly study of the printed book grew out of two related traditions, book collecting and librarianship. Within a century of the invention of printing, scholars and librarians alike had already recognized that the new technology of book production had not only increased the number of books but also the difficulty of knowing what books existed and where they were to be found. Theodore Besterman, in *The Beginnings of Systematic Bibliography* (1940), has studied the early development of what is now called bibliographic control, and shows that by the end of the sixteenth century the need for accurate and logically structured records of printed books was accepted and beginning to be practised. For the bibliophile, however, the printed book is an object which is desirable in itself. In France for a hundred years before the revolution, and in Britain and the United States since the early nineteenth century, collectors have cherished books for their printing, their bindings, their illustrations or even simply for their age or place of origin. Bibliophilic book collecting, as distinct from the more severely practical approach of some scholar-collectors and most if not all librarians, provided the impetus for a growing understanding of the nature of the printed book itself (Blum, 1969, pp. 78–134).

By the middle of the nineteenth century, the necessity of bibliography was fully recognized, but so too were some of the problems which it entailed. In particular, there was a serious problem about some of the earliest products of the printing presses of Europe which were collected both by bibliophiles and by libraries and were among the most valuable and desirable books of the age. About half of the surviving books printed in the fifteenth century contain no indication of the place and date at which they were printed. A group of bibliographers, notably Henry Bradshaw and Robert Proctor in England and M. F. A. G. Campbell in the Netherlands, set out to remedy this deficiency by seeking evidence from within the books themselves (Scholderer, 1949, pp. 32–41). They looked primarily at the types with which the books had been printed. Because fifteenth-century type designs were far less standardized than those of later centuries, the trained eye could distinguish with some certainty between one fount of type and another. From these distinctions, the early bibliographers felt able to make assumptions about the date and location of the printing of the books themselves. They based their theories on the assumption that once a particular fount could be identified with a particular printer, then all books printed in that fount could be ascribed to his press. (This is a gross oversimplification of a complex argument, but it conveys the essence of the case.) Not until Harry Carter published his *View of Early Typography* in 1969 was this premiss to be seriously challenged, and by then the basic chronology of early European printing had apparently been established by such methods and enshrined in great catalogues such as Robert Proctor's *Index to the Early Printed Books in the British Museum* (1898–1900) and the British Museum's own *Catalogue of Books Printed in the XVth Century* (1908–).

Bradshaw referred to what he was doing as 'scientific' bibliography, and wrote of his 'natural history' method, phraseology which reflected the fashionable ideas of late nineteenth-century Cambridge, where he was University Librarian. Bradshaw, however, was principally concerned with creating accurate and adequate catalogue records. He was a librarian, and in a sense the massive contribution which both he and Proctor made to the history of early printing was almost coincidental to their real objective of cataloguing books. Nevertheless, that contribution was crucial not only in terms of the specific knowledge which it yielded, but also in directing the attention of bibliographers away from the title-page and into the body of the book. The whole edifice of analytical bibliography is built upon the foundations laid by the pioneering nineteenth-century incunabulists.

The study of printing type, which lay at the heart of Bradshaw's method-ology, led inevitably to the study of printing itself, not only in terms of the dates and locations of printing houses, but also in terms of the techniques and equipment used in the printing process itself. Bibliographers began to turn for guidance to early printers' manuals, of which by far the most important in English was Joseph Moxon's *Mechanick Exercises on the Whole Art of Printing* ([1683–4]; ed. Davis and Carter, 1962). From such sources they learned of the conditions in the printing house, the skills and duties of the various employees and the tools and equipment used in typesetting and printing. Applying this knowledge to the books produced by such methods, they were able to detect characteristics on the printed page which enabled them to argue that they could reconstruct the processes through which the book had gone in reaching the form in which it was issued for sale. From there it was a comparatively short step to considering the effect of these processes on the transmission of the text which was being printed, and thus bibliography entered the mainstream of literary studies as an adjunct of textual criticism.

This work was particularly associated in its early years with two English scholars, A. W. Pollard, Proctor's successor at the British Museum, and W. W. (later Sir Walter) Greg. They shared a common interest in the text of Shakespeare, a subject to which both made seminal contributions. Pollard's *Shakespeare's Fight with the Pirates* (1920) was the first study to make the systematic distinction between the 'good' and the 'bad' quartos which is now familiar to every undergraduate (see Wilson, 1945), while Greg took the whole of Shakespeare for his province, and in dozens of articles and books, notably *The Editorial Problem in Shakespeare* (1954) and *The Shakespeare First Folio* (1955), revolutionized the study of the text of Shakespeare (Greg, 1914, 1930, 1932, 1933; see Wilson, 1970). In the next generation, the initiative passed across the Atlantic, most notably in the work of Fredson Bowers and Charlton Hinman. In their hands, bibliography was in danger of becoming simply a tool for the textual critic; certainly this is how Bowers himself presented it in his *Bibliography and Textual Criticism* (1964). In less skilled hands than those of Bowers and Hinman some of the techniques which they advocated became crude and unconvincing mechanical exercises in the 'analysis' of data of ques-tionable statistical validity. Bibliographers claimed to be able to identify individ-ual compositors from their alleged preferences for particular orthographic forms or other 'characteristics'; in Hinman's *Printing and Proof-reading of the First Folio of Shakespeare* (1963) this phase of bibliographical scholarship reached its climax. While Hinman's arguments were fundamentally sound because his evidence was ample in extent and convincing in presentation, few other books proved able to yield such a mass of data for the bibliographer.

By the 1960s, bibliography and bibliographically dependent textual criticism had become a sub-discipline within literary studies, and it received a great impetus in that decade from the proliferation of editions of texts intended both for students and for more advanced scholars. The great editions of American authors sponsored by the MLA, and bitterly criticized for their pedantry by Edmund Wilson in one of his last articles in the *New York Review of Books* (Wilson, 1968), turned editing into an industry, and not always to its advantage. The reaction was perhaps inevitable.

Ironically, the concentration on the text had turned bibliographers away from what had been their original concern: the book itself. Although both Greg and Bowers professed to believe that bibliographers treated words and letters simply as random marks on a piece of paper, both were primarily students of literature whose concern was ultimately with the text rather than the book. What had been lost was the broader context, the context of the printing house, the publisher and the bookshop which form the core of the commercial world of the book; the context of the reader and the writer who lie at the opposite ends of the chain of communication of which the book is merely an instrument; and the context of the society from which and for which books are written and in which they may even, through their readers, come to exert social, cultural and political influence. The most fruitful bibliographical scholarship of recent times has been concerned with precisely these issues.

The bibliographers of the first half of the twentieth century had made detailed studies of the processes of typesetting and printing; indeed, much of R. B. McKerrow's classic *Introduction to Bibliography* (1928) is concerned with these matters, and with such cognate subjects as papermaking and typefounding. They were, however, rather less familiar with the reality of the printing house than they themselves believed. Because they worked from the books, in isolation, they drew conclusions which, although they were certainly in accord with physical phenomena on the page, could not be reconciled with the practices forced on the printer by economic and technical imperatives. In recent years, the surviving archives of printing houses have been used to remedy this serious defect. D. F. McKenzie, in his massively detailed study of *Cambridge University Press 1696–1712* (1966), and in other work (McKenzie, 1969), showed that the neat patterns of production which were assumed by bibliographers were belied by factual records. Many different books were in simultaneous production; in the larger houses, whole teams of compositors were at work; many problems and interruptions were encountered for both technical and human reasons. These conclusions, so obvious in retrospect, seemed revolutionary in the late 1960s, but have been confirmed by work on the ledgers of the eighteenth-century printer William Bowyer (Maslen, 1971, 1972, 1975), and on the roughly contemporary ledgers of the Strahan printing house (Hernlund, 1967). Continental records, notably those of the Société

Typographique de Neuchâtel (Rychner, 1979), suggest that similar conditions were to be found in printing houses throughout Europe. The printers were concerned above all with making a profit; they achieved this by working as quickly as possible, to an acceptable but certainly not rigorous standard.

A full understanding of the circumstances in which books have been printed can only be reached if we also study the history of the printing industry. This means that the scholar of the nineteenth-century printed book is concerned not only with the great technical changes which transformed the processes of printing, but also with the consequential changes in the structure of the industry itself. Until the late eighteenth century, even large printing houses were small by the later standards of mass-production industry; they might employ fifty workmen, but even that number was the exception rather than the rule. From about 1800 onwards, however, a series of technical innovations in printing, in typesetting and in illustration processes forced the industry into a new pattern (Clair, 1965, pp. 205–38). The need for higher capital investment inevitably created larger businesses. At the same time, the growing complexity of the processes forced printers into specializations, especially in such fields as the lithographic printing of maps and music. These matters are all essential to an understanding of nineteenth-century book production, but so also is a knowledge of the economic and political context of the printing industry. Trade unions, for example, are found at a very early date, perhaps inevitably so, for printing was an industry in which almost all the workers had to be literate in order to do their work at all. Combinations among the workers led to combinations of masters, and to the negotiation both of standard rates of pay and of standard charges to customers. If some of this is closer to the domain of the economic historian than it is to that of the literary scholar, it merely emphasizes the extent to which the production, and indeed the writing, of literature is influenced by economic considerations (Child, 1967, pp. 47–152).

The printer, however, is only one part of the complex chain which leads from author to reader. The crucial figure is the publisher, the capitalist who finances and organizes the production and commercial distribution of books. Until the early seventeenth century, most printers were their own publishers, and most publishers of any importance were both printers and booksellers. From that time onwards, however, there was a gradual separation of functions. Long before 1700, the great majority of printers had withdrawn from publishing, to become, as they have remained, the paid agents of the publishers, undertaking work on their behalf. Less than a century later, the publishing and bookselling functions had also become distinct, and by 1820, and in some cases forty years earlier, we can clearly distinguish between the publisher on the one hand and the retail or wholesale bookseller on the other (Belanger, 1978). The judgement of the publisher thus became a vital element in the circulation of books, because it was he or his employees who actually selected works for publication. The selection could be subject to many different influences. The common thread through almost all publishing has been the likelihood of profit, but political and religious opinions, and reactions to real or perceived social pressures, have been almost equally potent forces. By the nineteenth century, when British publishing was already dominated by a few major houses, a handful of publishers and their readers, and even major customers such as the circulating libraries, could effectively determine what was published and what was not.

Although publishing is, in its very nature, a highly individualistic and sometimes idiosyncratic occupation, one of the strongest themes running through the history of British publishing is the very tight organizational structure within the industry itself. For over a century, the whole book trade was controlled by the Stationer's Company, which played a central role not only in its commercial regulation, but also in the enforcement of successive regimes of state control from the reign of Mary I to that of Charles II. When the Company's power was broken in the 1660s, and even more after the abolition of formal pre-publication censorship in 1695, small groups within the trade itself came to exercise a comparable commercial dominance (Blagden, 1960, pp. 47–62, 110–77). Chief among them were those booksellers who owned valuable copyrights, which they zealously defended against all potential interlopers. At a time when the law of copyright was obscure, they claimed perpetual rights in the copies which they owned, and traded them on that basis. Similar and overlapping groups controlled the mechanisms of wholesale bookselling and hence the system of distribution upon which the successful sale of printed books in large quantities ultimately depends (Feather, 1987, pp. 68–71).

In the nineteenth century the ethos of free trade broke the old cartels of the book trade, but that same ethos produced a climate in which co-operation was still necessary. Price competition between retail booksellers led to many bankruptcies in the trade, and hence to a loss of outlets for the publishers. In the 1890s, after difficult negotiations, the publishers and the booksellers, through their respective trade bodies, concluded the Net Book Agreement which still survives, although it is now under serious threat. In effect, the NBA ensures that any book published in Britain is sold at not less than a minimum retail price fixed by the publisher. This guarantees the profit margins of both the publisher and the bookseller, and, it is argued, therefore allows publishers to produce small editions of worthwhile books, such as poetry, which would not be economically viable in a wholly uncontrolled market economy (Barnes, 1964).

The history of publishing, both in general and in detail, has been a considerable growth area of scholarship in the last two decades. Even more remarkable, however, has been the parallel growth of more broadly based studies of the printed book, referred to as *l'histoire du livre*, or in the less elegant English phrases, 'the history of the book' or 'book history'. The French term is perhaps more appropriate, since the scholarly tradition from which book history derives is essentially French in origin. The detailed study of past societies, exemplified in the work of Lucien Febvre, Marc Bloch, and more recently, de Roy Ladurie and Braudel, has been applied to the study of the role of the printed word in Western societies by Henri-Jean Martin and his pupils in France and by scholars in both Britain and the USA who have been influenced by their work and their approach. It was Martin who completed Febvre's unfinished *L'apparition du livre* (1959, translated as *The Coming of the Book*, 1976) which marks the beginning of this tradition of book scholarship. It is a tradition very different from the minute analysis which has characterized the work of so many British and American bibliographers in the present century. Book historians are not uninterested in the production of books, and certainly regard the sale and distribution of books as central issues, but the ultimate concern is to assess the influence of the printed word on society at large, and the influence of society on the production and the writing of books (Birn, 1976; Kirsop, 1979).

This vastly broadens the interests of the scholar of the printed book, for it forces him to confront some very wide historical issues. Legal matters loom large in this. In almost all societies until very recently, and in many countries today, the publisher and the author are constrained by the censor. The influence of censorship, and the means of evading it, are one of the primary concerns of the book historian, and indeed of the literary scholar who is studying the texts produced under such constraints. These studies require not only a knowledge of the law, but also of the extent to which it was, or could be, enforced. The literary scholar will also question how far self-censorship influenced authors who knew that they had to write within legally acceptable limits as well as the conventions imposed by contemporary notions of morality (Thomas, 1969).

Censorship, and less formal restrictions on the expression and circulation of ideas, have never been entirely absent from the world of the printed book, even in the most liberal societies. The circulation of ideas, however, is not limited to the printed page. Indeed, it is now clear that orality survived long into the age of the printed book, especially in rural societies. Nevertheless, it can be cogently argued that printing has defined the intellectual and literary traditions of post-medieval Europe. In particular, 'folk' literature, although it may survive in an oral form, has entered the mainstream only when it has been printed, often in a modified form. Much of the ancient popular literature of the West survives today only as 'fairy' stories for children in the versions of Perrault or the Grimms, perhaps further modified to suit less earthy modern concepts of what is 'suitable' for children (Darnton, 1984, pp. 9–74). Scholars have, however, come to recognize the significance of the pre-printed versions in the creation of a common culture outside the literary élites. Some of the traditional stories found their way into print in the sixteenth and seventeenth centuries in books whose audience was envisaged as consisting of adults as well as children (Spufford, 1981). The 'peasant reader' is now the object of much scholarly interest. The existence of books for the sub-literary market has raised many questions about literacy and education which are of crucial importance to the historian of the book at all periods from the sixteenth to the nineteenth centuries (Altick, 1963; Cressy, 1980; Lacquer, 1976; Schofield, 1972–3; Webb, 1955).

It is, nevertheless, true that the oral tradition was submerged, at least among the cultural and political élites of the West, until orality was to some extent revived by broadcasting. For over four centuries, printing was the only medium of mass communication. It did, however, break down the greatest of all barriers to communication, for it enabled ideas to be transmitted not only across distance but also across time. The printed book created the conditions for the development of a multitude of competing intellectual and literary traditions, and allowed their dissemination and preservation in a permanent form. There is little 'lost' literature of the age of the printed book. A writer may be neglected or dismissed for decades or centuries, as was the case, for example, with Donne, but because his works were embodied in print, and the printed books were preserved, they awaited 'rediscovery'. Modern literary scholarship, exploring the byways of our literary heritage and discovering new connections between literature and society, is vastly indebted to the mere existence of such books, and should be equally concerned with the conditions of their production, distribution and, indeed, neglect.

Of the millions of books printed since the middle of the fifteenth century, only a handful is of direct concern to the literary scholar. On the other hand, imaginative literature has, in general, been published through the same channels as other books and has consequently been subject to the same commercial and political pressures. Moreover, the intellectual climate from which a work of literature emerges, into which it is released and whose further evolution it may influence, was, until the middle of this century, largely created by the printed word. The literary scholar, therefore, must take account of the whole world of the printed book, not least so that he can form a valid historical judgement of the place occupied in that world by the texts or authors with which he is particularly concerned. Two well-known examples will illustrate the point. The £20 which Milton received for the copyright in *Paradise Lost* (1667) was a perfectly reasonable payment by contemporary standards, and perhaps even generous for a long and obscure poem by a man whose very life might be in danger because of his personal political history. Similarly, the commercial disaster which initially attended the publication of the first edition of *Lyrical Ballads* (1798) is at least partly explained by its publication in the provinces rather than London, and certainly has to be contrasted with the general background of a buoyant and expanding book trade at the end of the eighteenth century.

The study of the printed book, in all its aspects, substantially enlarges our understanding of the interaction between a work of literature and the circumstances of its production and reception, between text and context. Equally complex, however, and equally illuminating, is the relationship between form and content. The physical history of the printed book is far more than merely the history of printing. How words are presented on the page influences the way in which we read them and how we react to them. As a general rule, most authors are content for their work to be printed in the form which is normal for their time. Deviations from the norm are therefore of some importance, and especially so when those deviations are demanded by the author himself. Jonson and Pope, for example, were both concerned not only with textual accuracy, but also with the physical appearance of the book as a whole and of the page on which the text was printed. The format, and even the very title, of Jonson's *Workes* of 1616 was a literary and cultural statement of Jonson's own conception of the literary importance of vernacular drama in general and his own contribution to it in particular. The word *Workes* deliberately invited comparison with the *Opera* of the classical authors, and the folio format imitated the conventional physical form of scholarly editions of classical texts. Jonson's innovation was imitated both by the editors of Shakespeare and by Beaumont and Fletcher. These three great examples played a key role in the establishment of the Elizabethan and Jacobean drama as something more than a transitory entertainment in the theatre.

Extreme deviations from contemporary norms of *mise-en-page*, whether by the early seventeenth-century emblemists or by e. e. cummings, are easy enough to identify. In both examples, the authors are using a visual device as part of the mechanism for conditioning and controlling the reader's response to the poem. We can similarly identify cases where the author made special technical demands on the publisher and printer, as Sterne did in *Tristram Shandy* (1759–67). It is not difficult to find examples, of whom Dickens is one, of authors exploiting technological developments in printing and graphic processes to enhance the appearance of their works. Even so, it is necessary to understand the relationship between the general and the particular, the conventional and the unusual. The generous page layout of the quarto editions of Pope's separately published poems was, like Jonson's use of the folio format, a conscious cultural statement, referring back to classical ideals of space and form. By contrast, the Shakespeare quartos merely followed economically convenient conventions derived in roughly equal measure from the printing house and the theatre.

Little systematic work has been done on the history of book design, although 'design' is too positive a word to describe what was done to most books until very recently. Historically based criticism, however, seeking to understand a work of literature as it was understood by its contemporaries, cannot ignore the form in which those readers, and indeed its author, actually saw it. The modernization of texts by editors and publishers disguises not merely the orthography of the original but its original form, and while, as a practical matter, that is perhaps inevitable, the fact must nevertheless be understood.

The printed book has been an integral part of the Western literary tradition since the end of the Middle Ages; indeed, the invention of printing itself helps to define that chronological statement. These books cannot be seen in isolation. They are a product of technical processes which can misrepresent the words of the author, and inevitably present his work in a particular physical form. They are produced by people whose objective is to sell them, and they are subject to commercial pressures which inevitably influence the author. Literary texts are a minute and commercially insignificant percentage of the whole output of the printing press. They can be fully understood only in the broader context of the whole world of print, a world of authors, readers, printers, publishers, booksellers, censors, politicians and lawyers. The close study of a literary work can perhaps disguise these essential factors. Book historians, in trying to analyse them, hope to expound and explain how social, legal, political and economic considerations influenced the creation and the understanding of literature. Such influences can often be explained in more specific terms than might be thought possible, and do nothing to diminish our appreciation of literature. Indeed, an understanding of the context of a work of literature can significantly enhance our full comprehension of its author's intentions and of his audience's reading of his work. Seen in isolation, the literary text misrepresents itself.

FURTHER READING

Bowers, Fredson (1964) *Bibliography and Textual Criticism*, Clarendon Press, Oxford
——(1975) *Essays in Bibliography, Text and Editing*, University of Virginia Press, Charlottesville
Eisenstein, Elizabeth L. (1979) *The Printing Press as an Agent of Change*, 2 vols, Cambridge University Press, Cambridge
Feather, John (1980) 'Cross-channel currents: historical bibliography and *l'histoire du livre*', *The Library*, 6th series, 2, 1–15
Febvre, L. and Martin, H.-J. (1976) *The Coming of the Book*, translated by David Gerard, New Left Books, London [first published 1959]
Gaskell, Philip (1972) *A New Introduction to Bibliography*, Clarendon Press, Oxford
Hall, D. D. (1986) 'The history of the book. New questions? New answers?' In Donald G. Davis Jr. (ed.), *Libraries, Books & Culture*, Graduate School of Library and Information Science, Austin

McKenzie, D. F. (1969) 'Printers of the mind: some notes on bibliographical theories and printing-house practices', *Studies in Bibliography*, 22, 1–75

Steinberg, S. H. (1974) *Five Hundred Years of Printing*, 3rd edn, Penguin, Harmondsworth

Tanselle, G. Thomas (1979) *Selected Studies in Bibliography*, University of Virginia Press, Charlottesville

——(1981) *The History of Books as a Field of Study*, Hanes Foundation, Chapel Hill

Wilson, F. P. (1970) *Shakespeare and the New Bibliography*, revised and edited by H. Gardner, Clarendon Press, Oxford

ADDITIONAL WORKS CITED

Altick, Richard D. (1963) *The English Common Reader: A Social History of the Mass Reading Public*, University of Chicago Press, Chicago

Barnes, James J. (1964) *Free Trade in Books: A Study of the London Book Trade Since 1800*, Clarendon Press, Oxford

Belanger, Terry (1978) 'From bookseller to publisher: changes in the London book trade, 1750–1850'. In Richard G. Landon (ed.), *Book Selling and Book Buying: Aspects of the Nineteenth-century British and North American Book Trade*, American Library Association, Chicago, pp. 7–16

Besterman, Theodore (1940) *The Beginnings of Systematic Bibliography*, 2nd edn, Oxford University Press, Oxford

Birn, R. (1976) '*Livre et société* after ten years: formation of a discipline', *Studies on Voltaire and the Eighteenth Century*, 151, 281–312

Blagden, Cyprian (1960) *The Stationers' Company: A History, 1403–1959*, Allen & Unwin, London

Blum, R. (1969) *Bibliographia: An Inquiry into its Definition and Designations*, American Library Association, Chicago

Carter, Harry (1969) *View of Early Typography*, Clarendon Press, Oxford

Child, John (1967) *Industrial Relations in the British Printing Industry*, Allen & Unwin, London

Clair, Colin (1965) *A History of Printing in Britain*, Cassell, London

Cressy, David (1980) *Literacy and the Social Order: Reading and Writing in Tudor and Stuart England*, Cambridge University Press, Cambridge

Darnton, Robert (1984) *The Great Cat Massacre and Other Episodes in French Cultural History*, Allen Lane, London

Davis, H. and Carter, H. (eds) (1962) *Mechanick Exercises on the Whole Art of Printing (1683–4) by Joseph Moxon*, 2nd edn, Oxford University Press, London

Feather, John (1987) *A History of British Publishing*, Croom Helm, London

Greg, W. W. (1914) 'What is bibliography?', *Transactions of the Bibliographical Society*, 12, 39–53

——(1930) 'The present position of bibliography', *The Library*, 4th series, 11, 241–62

——(1932) 'Bibliography – an apologia', *The Library*, 4th series, 13, 113–43

——(1933) 'The function of bibliography in literary criticism illustrated in a study of the text of *King Lear*', *Neophilologus*, 18, 241–62

——(1954) *The Editorial Problem in Shakespeare*, 3rd edn, Clarendon Press, Oxford

——(1955) *The Shakespeare First Folio*, Clarendon Press, Oxford

Griest, Guinevere L. (1970) *Mudie's Circulating Library and the Victorian Novel*, David & Charles, Newton Abbot

Hernlund, P. (1967) 'William Strahan's ledgers: standard charges for printing', *Studies in Bibliography*, 20, 89–111

Hinman, Charlton (1963) *Printing and Proof-reading of the First Folio of Shakespeare*, 2 vols, Clarendon Press, Oxford

Kirsop, W. (1979) 'Literary history and book trade history: the lessons of *L'apparition du livre*', *Australian Journal of French Studies*, 16, 488–535

Lacquer, T. (1976) 'The cultural origins of popular literacy in England 1500–1850', *Oxford Review of Education*, 2, 255–75

McKenzie, D. F. (1966) *Cambridge University Press 1696–1712*, Cambridge University Press, Cambridge

McKerrow, R. B. (1928) *Introduction to Bibliography*, Clarendon Press, Oxford

Maslen, K. I. D. (1971) 'Printing charges: inference and evidence', *Studies in Bibliography*, 24, 91–8

——(1972) 'Printing for the author: from the Bowyer printing ledgers, 1710–75', *The Library*, 5th series, 27, 302–9

——(1975) 'Masters and men', *The Library*, 5th series, 30, 81–94

Pollard, A. W. (1920) *Shakespeare's Fight with the Pirates*, 2nd edn, Cambridge University Press, Cambridge

Proctor, Robert (1898–1900) *Index to the Early Printed Books in the British Museum*, British Museum, London

Rychner, J. (1979) 'Running a printing-house in eighteenth-century Switzerland', *The Library*, 6th series, 1, 1–24

Schofield, R. S. (1972–3) 'Dimensions of illiteracy, 1750–1850', *Explorations in Economic History*, 10, 437–54

Scholderer, V. (1949) 'Early printed books'. In *The Bibliographical Society 1892–1942: Studies in Retrospect*, The Bibliographical Society, London, pp. 32–41

Spufford, Margaret (1981) *Small Books and Pleasant Histories: Popular Fiction and its Readers in Seventeenth-century England*, Methuen, London

Sutherland, J. A. (1976) *Victorian Novelists and Publishers*, Athlone Press, London

Thomas, Donald (1969) *A Long Time Burning: The History of Literary Censorship in England*, Routledge & Kegan Paul, London

Webb, R. K. (1955) *The British Working Class Reader 1790–1848*, Allen & Unwin, London

Wilson, Edmund (1968) *The Fruits of the MLA*, New York Review, New York

Wilson, J. D. (1945) 'Alfred William Pollard', *Proceedings of the British Academy*, 31, 257–306

61

LITERACY

DAVID CRESSY

'Literacy' means different things to different scholars. For some it is a matter of choice and sensibility, what people read and what they made of their reading. It touches on vocabulary and phrasing, and how people engaged with text. Literacy, for others, involves a package of skills, including the elementary ability to read and write, a matter of technique rather than taste. Many discussions of literacy focus on the social uses of writing, and the degree to which a particular culture employs print or script. Anthropologists, social psychologists, educational theorists and literary critics have converged in various ways on the topic, and have credited literacy with diverse cultural, economic or cognitive consequences, including logical thinking and heightened self-consciousness.

Social historians have been concerned with the extent and context of literacy in various historical settings. They have set out to discover what proportion of the population could read and write at different times, and how those primary skills were distributed among social and occupational groups. Questions are raised about the gradations of literacy, the margins of literacy, and how literacy levels changed. This essay, written by a social historian, is concerned with the meaning and measurement of practical literacy in early modern England. It reviews what is known about the spread of literacy from the sixteenth to the nineteenth centuries, and the purposes for which literacy was acquired. It questions, also, the value of literacy in various social contexts, and considers the interaction of oral and literate culture.

British society has made use of literacy since the time of the Romans. Anglo-Saxon scribes and Norman clerks used writing to record their history, to conduct their government and to make literature. So too did their medieval and Renaissance successors. Reading and writing have always been important skills, even though no more than a fragment of the population possessed them. Not until the sixteenth century did basic reading and writing abilities extend much beyond the clerical and gentle élite, and not before the nineteenth century were they found among the majority of the population. England, for most of her history, has been a partially literate society, in which the art of writing and record-keeping was confined to a clerical, governmental and commercial élite.

From the middle of the sixteenth century, under the three-fold pressure of Renaissance humanism, reformed Protestant religion, and a diversifying capitalist economy, a succession of writers and agitators made high claims for the advancement of literacy. Among churchmen and businessmen, leaders of the spiritual and the secular order, the belief was widespread that reading and writing were vital skills that produced a broad range of benefits. Most writers stressed the religious advantage in being able to engage directly with the written word of God, and some also drew attention to the worldly assets accruing from competence with script and print. And most writers, explicitly or implicitly, associated literacy with a variety of civic and moral benefits, as if it were the indispensable correlate of civilization. In this they founded a tradition, still followed by some scholars and policy-makers, which associates literacy with modernity, rationality and a more deeply satisfying life.

It is possible, however, that the early promoters of literacy exaggerated their case, and paid too little attention to the needs and circumstances of the general population. Literacy was by no means a necessity in early modern England, and its mystery was limited to less than a third of the population.

Elizabethan religious reformers urged 'every man to read the Bible in Latin or English, as the very word of God and the spiritual food of man's soul, whereby they may better know their duties to God, to their sovereign lord the king, and their neighbour' (Bishop John Parkhurst's *Injunctions* for the Diocese of Norwich, 1561). Seventeenth-century Puritans often repeated this theme, lamenting, 'Alas, the people perish for want of knowledge. And how can they know God's will that cannot read it?' (George Swinnock, *The Christian Man's Calling*, 1663). Richard Baxter, one of the most prolific religious writers of the later seventeenth century, admonished parents, 'By all means let children be taught to read, if you are never so poor and whatever shift you make, or else you deprive them of a singular help to their instruction and salvation'. According to Baxter, 'It is a very great mercy to be able to read the holy scriptures for themselves, and a very great misery to know nothing but what they hear from others' (*A Christian Directory*, 1673). Active literacy, in this view meaning the ability to make sense of selected printed texts, would foster religious, social and political discipline; illiteracy, on the other hand, instilled dependency, ignorance and error. Without literacy to guide them in godliness, it was feared that children might become 'idle . . . vile and abject persons, liars, thieves, evil beasts, slow bellies and good for nothing'. Those who could not read were exposed to 'rudeness, licentiousness, profaneness, superstition, and any wickedness'. Literacy could be engaged in the 'reformation of manners', as part of the moral equipment of a Christian.

Reading and writing could also be credited with securing a variety of secular benefits which were equally important for cultural cohesion. Literacy and education could combat 'misorders' and 'disobedience' and could promote 'policy and civility'. There was no shortage of authors willing to testify to 'the vast usefulness of reading', and to argue that writing was the key 'to the descrying and finding out of innumerable treasures'. Through writing, according to the schoolmaster David Brown:

> All high treasures of whatsoever nature or importance are both intended and prosecuted, secret matters are secretly kept, friends that be a thousand miles distant are conferred with and (after a sort) visited; the excellent works of godly men, the grave sentences of wise men, and the profitable arts of learned men, who died a thousand years ago, are yet extant for our daily use and imitation; all the estates, kingdoms, cities and countries of the world are governed, laws and printing maintained, justice and discipline administered, youth bred in piety, virtue, manners and learning at schools and universities, and that which is most and best, all the churches of God from the beginning established and always to this day edified.
>
> (*The Introduction to the True Understanding of the Whole Arte of Expedition in Teaching to Write*, 1638)

This was as noble and eloquent an argument for literacy as could be wished. Reading was regarded as a tool for cultural integration which could keep the literate in touch with people and ideas across space and time. By programming that reading as a corpus of godly texts, a curriculum of select classical learning, or a flow of political and administrative instruction, the leaders of society could embrace, and to some extent control, the increasingly literate population.

The practical, day-to-day benefits of literacy could be even more compelling. Those who were indifferent to godliness and civility might none the less be touched by an argument which appealed to pocket and pride. The lack of literacy, it was suggested, could be socially damaging. According to David Brown, 'not to write at all is both shame and scathe'. The embarrassment of illiteracy might prejudice one's business dealings; your scrivener or partner might take advantage of your deficiency, and so through illiteracy you might 'lose some good design'. But worse than being tricked by someone with superior technical capability was the insult to one's self-esteem and public reputation.

> It is shame both to employ a notar to subscribe for thee in any security, and to want that good token of education which perhaps thine inferior hath, for wheresoever any man of honest rank resorteth who cannot write, chiefly where he is not known, he is incontinent esteemed either to be base born or to have been basely

brought up in a base or moorland desert, that is, far from any city where there be schools of learning, discipline, policy and civility.

(Introduction to True Understanding)

This theme was recurrent in the writing of Elizabethan and Jacobean educators, who insisted that literacy provided a defence against 'the manifold deceits of this world'. Some, like the London writing-master, Martin Billingsley, even urged practical literacy for women as an insurance against the risks of penurious widowhood (*The Pens Excellencie: or the Secretaries Delighte*, 1618).

Caution is essential when reading these advertisements by professional educators (the same caution that is required when looking at religious reformers) to separate their attitudes and motivations from the reality of the world they describe. David Brown, for example, was himself newly arrived in London from Scotland and knew how to work on parvenu insecurities. The preachers were promoting godly reform. There is no direct evidence to tell us whether ordinary people in everyday circumstances felt shamed by the limitations of their literacy, or experienced frustration or complication in their designs. In both its religious and its secular strands, the rhetorical stream gave great weight to the value of literacy, but that does not prove that the population at large agreed with its sentiments or experienced the problems or delights to which it referred. Before agreeing with the historical proponents of literacy, we need to evaluate the context in which they were uttered and the world to which they belonged.

It is no doubt true that deficiencies in basic literacy constrained the audience for written work and limited participation in the political, religious and commercial culture of the past. But we must take care not to project our own high valuation of literacy on to an earlier world. In practice, the importance of literacy varied with social, cultural and historical circumstances. In seventeenth-century England, as in centuries before, a competent and contented life could be lived entirely innocent of literate skills. The English countryman, according to one observer, could perform his seasonal tasks without recourse to reading or writing. 'We can learn to plough and harrow, sow and reap, plant and prune, thresh and fan, winnow and grind, brew and bake, and all without book. These are our chief businesses in the country, except we be jurymen to hang a thief or speak truth in a man's right, which conscience and experience will teach us with a little learning' (Nicholas Breton, *The Court and Country*, 1618). Why should the husbandman send his son to school, at cost of time and money, if the skills he would bring home had no obvious immediate application? Who needed to be able to read or write if he had standing enough with his neighbours, was possessed of an adequate mind and memory, and had learned and could pass on his knowledge of animals, the land and the weather through observation and practice? One could grow prosperous, and go to heaven, without being able to write one's name, since neither wealth nor salvation was utterly dependent on literacy.

This last point, which cuts against the grain of most early modern discussions of literacy, requires amplification. Traditionalists had never conceded that Bible literacy was essential in religious devotion. Thomas More had observed during the stormy first decade of the Reformation: 'Many . . . shall with God's grace, though they never read a word of scripture, come as well to heaven' (*The Apologye*, 1533). Despite the evangelical insistence on reading, the Protestant church in England continued to stress the oral elements in liturgical worship and catechetical instruction. Psalms could be sung and sermons heard without the complications of print. The Protestant revolution notwithstanding, it was not necessary to be literate to be devout. A country preacher told his congregation after the Restoration, 'Though you cannot read a letter in the book, yet you can by true assurance read your name in the Book of Life, your scholarship will serve. . . . If you cannot write a word, yet see you transcribe a fair copy of a godly, righteous and sober life, and you have done well' (Richard Steele, *The Husbandman's Calling*, 1678).

In his other roles, too, the ordinary countryman was under no pressure to become literate. As tenant and farmer, subject and householder, the world of print and script made few inroads into his life. If he dealt with the manor court, quarter session or church courts, all courts of record with a high turnover of paper and ink, his participation was oral, interlocutory, and required no mastery of reading or writing. The officials, of course, were literate, but the people who came before the courts most often were not. If a signature was needed to authenticate a document a mark had just as good standing in law.

Illiterate and semi-literate people were not necessarily disadvantaged when they came into contact with the world of writing. Every street or village had its informal scrivener or writing man who met the needs of his illiterate neighbours. Someone could always be found to set one's affairs in the appropriate form if you needed to write a lease, a letter or a will. Illiterate lovers could correspond with each other at a distance, so long as a third party was available to pen the letters. Nor was authorship impossible. A classic Elizabethan work on horses (*The Schoole of Horsemanship*, by Christopher Clifford) is said to have been written, through dictation, by a groom who could neither read nor write.

Multiple paths and bridges linked the literate and illiterate worlds. The possession of literacy did not remove one from the culture of speech and action, nor did illiteracy necessarily bar one from the culture of script and print. In practice there was feedback and interaction. As students of theatre know well, much of the cultural life of the seventeenth century was neither strictly literate nor oral, but a combination of both. Jests and proverbs that originated in folklore appeared in printed editions. Folk-singers could broaden their repertoire by reference to printed ballads, including some collected from illiterate performers. Sermons were crafted on paper in the minister's study, then delivered live from the pulpit; a sermon that sparked discussion in the church or the tavern (having drawn, perhaps, on some parishioner's written notes) might also be polished for further circulation in print. Important documents were read out loud as well as filed for the record. Proclamations were proclaimed as well as posted. News-sheets and letters could be read to an illiterate audience at the alehouse as well as studied privately at home. Instead of a great divide between oral and literate culture, it is now generally recognized that there was substantial overlap and interaction.

Literacy contains many levels and gradations. It can be imagined as a spectrum or curve, in which even the narrow definition as 'reading and writing' shades into an extensive range of competencies. Literacy, in early modern England, involved an ascending order of accomplishments, from the simple ability to recognize the letters of the alphabet to full fluency in handling the most sophisticated texts. Fine penmanship and stylistic ease belonged to the high end of the range, and literacy in Latin and Greek marked the gilded culmination of the most rarefied scholarly élite. In between were many layers and components, all of which have historical and cultural significance, but few of which are susceptible to measurement.

At the lowest level were people who could not read or write anything. These were totally illiterate, though not necessarily totally disadvantaged. Even people for whom the alphabet was a meaningless jumble were exposed to the influence of writing by virtue of belonging to a literacy-using society. Those who had learned just to read the alphabet, to distinguish the letters, and then to make sense of their combination into simple words and phrases, hovered on the threshold of literacy. They could hardly be called 'readers', but with purpose and effort they could make direct connections to the world of print. Next came the ability to read simple passages. Some people cultivated this skill, and became the readers of popular publications. Others forgot what they knew and sank back towards illiteracy through lack of practice.

There may have been a further hierarchy of skill as readers gained mastery of writing in different forms. The easiest to understand was black-letter print, the bastard gothic form used in the elementary teaching texts, the ABC hornbook, the catechism and much popular literature. Black-letter printing continued well into the seventeenth century, especially for ballads, almanacs, and publications aimed at the less educated reader. More sophisticated publications used Roman type, the dominant form in printing today.

Familiarity with print came before the ability to read handwriting. Only the more experienced or better educated readers could penetrate the mystery of script or 'writ' as it was known. There are anecdotes describing people who could spell their way through the Bible, but were completely helpless when faced with a hand-written letter. The different kinds of hand in use – court hand, secretary, italic, etc. – may also have posed different levels of challenge.

Reading, by its nature, leaves no record, so there is no reliable guide to the extent of reading ability within the English population. It seems certain, however, that more people could read than could write. Just how many more is a matter for speculation, allowing historians to adopt optimistic or pessimistic positions. Reading and writing were separate skills, taught at different stages in the educational process and often by different specialists. If a child was fortunate enough to attend a school in Elizabethan or Jacobean England (and most did not), he would learn to read during the first few years and would only move on to writing as a secondary activity. Reading is a passive skill, involving the visual recognition of patterns; writing, by contrast, is an active skill, requiring manual dexterity, the co-ordination of hand, eye and brain, and also, before the modern era, initiation into the arts of cutting quills and preparing ink. Only the more privileged or the more determined reached this level.

A few people may have learned the trick of writing their names when they were otherwise unable to read, but there is little evidence on this score. More common were people with some modicum of reading ability who did not know how to write their names. When put into the situation of having to authenticate a document, illiterates and semi-illiterates alike often made crude scrawls with the pen, producing a line or a cross as a mark. More experience taught some of them to draw a pictogram of their occupation, like Shakespeare's father whose mark represented the shape of a glover's compasses.

It was a significant step from being able to read to being able to write. There may have been a further gradation from forming a signature to writing a sentence, but once a person had mastered the pen there was no limit to what he might express in writing. Only at this stage do we see full and free literacy, a skill that belonged to a minority of the population. Only after the crossing of this threshold do considerations of orthography, syntax, style and substance enter the discussion.

Writing, unlike reading, leaves a direct historical record. Most historians accept that one form of writing – the writing of personal signatures as opposed to marks – provides a meaningful measure of the distribution of literacy. The indicator is not without problems, nor free of controversy, but it has the advantage of being universal, standard and direct. A large body of research has produced figures comparing the literacy of men to women, gentlemen to tradesmen, Londoners to countrymen, one period to another, and so on. So robust are the statistics, so clear-cut the pattern, that most scholars now place confidence in them.

In the middle decades of the sixteenth century, about the time of the accession of Queen Elizabeth and the birth of William Shakespeare, only 20 per cent of the adult males in England possessed sufficient literacy to write their own names. Male illiteracy, measured by the making of marks rather than signatures, was close to 80 per cent. For women the figures are even worse. No more than 5 per cent of Tudor women were literate, 95 per cent or more being unable to write their names. Almost a century later, after the full course of the celebrated but overrated 'educational revolution', illiteracy among men was reduced to just 70 per cent. At the beginning of the English Civil War, more than two-thirds of all Englishmen – contemporaries of Milton and Cromwell – could not write their names. For women at this time the level of illiteracy was still as high as 90 per cent. By the end of the seventeenth century, however, literacy had become more widespread. Close to 50 per cent of the male population could write, and the figure for women was 25 per cent. The improvement was sluggish rather than spectacular, but it continued into the eighteenth century as English society became more commercial and more complex.

These figures remind us that high literary achievements could coexist with popular illiteracy on a vast scale. English society did not have to be broadly literate for its most accomplished members to make subtle and assertive use of literate forms.

All the evidence points to a popularization of literacy between the sixteenth and the nineteenth centuries. But the growth was irregular and halting, rather than steady and progressive. The summary figures mask periods of acceleration and recession, and obscure important social and geographical variations. A surge in literacy in the Elizabethan period was not matched in the century that followed; the long eighteenth century saw marginal improvements and some stagnation. In the early modern period, the improving literacy of tradesmen and craftsmen outstripped that of husbandmen and labourers. Pastoral communities were almost entirely illiterate, while weaving villages often had substantial populations who could read and write. The urban population became increasingly literate in the late seventeenth century, at a time when the rural sectors appear to have regressed.

One of the most remarkable findings of this research is the precocious literacy of women in later Stuart London. At a time when three-quarters or more of the women in provincial England could not write their own names, illiteracy in the metropolis, so measured, was reduced to 50 per cent. Affected by the quickening commercial environment, the social demands of the city, and the expanding availability of print, the women of Aphra Behn's London were as literate as men in the countryside.

Every study demonstrates that literacy in pre-industrial England was closely and consistently associated with social and economic position. The ability or inability to write followed the gradient from clean, respectable commercial pursuits, through various types of specialist craft activities, to rough, manual, outdoor occupations. A distinctive hierarchy emerges, in which illiteracy is correlated to status, occupation and wealth. This can be illustrated with figures from the seventeenth century. The percentages varied, of course, from the sixteenth century onward, but the social pattern held remarkably consistent over time. A simple table (adapted from Cressy, 1980) will summarize the evidence.

Illiteracy of selected groups in seventeenth-century England

Social group	% illiterate	
	rural	London
clergy and professions	0	0
gentlemen	2	2
grocers	5	0
merchants	10	0
bakers	27	26
yeomen	33	30
weavers	49	34
tailors	51	43
blacksmiths	56	38
carpenters	62	40
husbandmen	79	–
shepherds	82	–
labourers	85	78
miners	96	–

Particular circumstances affected the individual's acquisition of basic literacy. Educational opportunity, religious disposition, and family background all played a part, so that men and women of humble origins sometimes went on to become readers and even writers. But overriding these cultural variables was the force of economic and social structure.

The gentle, clerical and professional classes, of course, had full possession of literacy, except for a few who were decrepit or dyslexic. Members of this dominant class, who comprised no more than 5 per cent of the population, were the primary audience for most of the output of the press. Literacy was an attribute of their status and an active element in their lives. Here, and here only, was the cultivated élite. And among their wives and daughters were the principal female participants in literate culture, a minority within a minority.

Approaching the level of the gentry were city merchants and tradesmen. Country merchants and superior shopkeepers, including drapers and haberdashers, grocers and apothecaries, ranged from 5 per cent to 15 per cent illiterate. Their London counterparts were fully literate. In the seventeenth century it was still possible to smell a profit without a literate education, but the pressure of shipping news and trade regulations, commercial correspondence and memorandums, made fluency with print and script increasingly important.

Next came a variety of skilled craftsmen and tradesmen of the second rank, men like goldsmiths and clothiers, dyers and leather sellers, who lived by providing specialist services or expensively wrought products. Their literacy reflected their wealth and their social standing. Below them were clustered 'the industrious sort of people', between a third and a half of whom could not write their names. Many were involved in the textile industry, as weavers or fullers, in the processing of agricultural produce, as brewers or maltsters, or in manufacturing articles of dress, as tailors or cordwainers. Artisans and craftsmen made little use of literacy in their day-to-day employment, although those who could read became part of the audience for the popular press.

Village artisans, such as blacksmiths and carpenters, millers and butchers, belonged to a less literate cluster in which a half to three-quarters could not sign. Illiteracy was more widespread among bricklayers and thatchers, masons and miners, and all-weather outdoor workers like fishermen, shepherds and labourers. Most of their work was heavy and dirty, requiring more brawn than brain. Their employment often isolated these men from regular contact with the rest of society. Paper and writing rarely came their way, so it is not surprising that three-quarters or more were unable to sign; illiteracy among thatchers and miners topped 90 per cent.

Most yeomen could read, and only a third could not write. Literacy was not vital to them, but, as independent farmers involved with leases and land-improvements, it was often useful to be able to read and write. The yeoman's practical literacy included the reading of broadsheets and almanacs, and might extend to works on husbandry and self-improvement. Some yeomen were also part of the audience for religious chapbooks and editions of merry tales.

Husbandmen, by contrast, were mostly illiterate. These were modest tenant farmers who lacked the yeomen's resources or incentives to acquire education. Four out of five husbandmen could not write their names, and the proportion showed little reduction before the eighteenth century. Their cultural level was similar to that of shepherds and bricklayers. Elizabethan and Stuart poets who idealized the pastoral life must have known that its real practitioners were unlikely ever to read about it.

This strong social patterning persisted into the eighteenth and nineteenth centuries, as the overall level of illiteracy declined. By the accession of George III illiteracy had fallen to 40 per cent among men and 60 per cent among women. At the beginning of the Victorian era more than one in three Englishmen were illiterate, along with half the women. But the situation changed rapidly with the onset of universal schooling. Male illiteracy fell below 10 per cent for the first time in the 1880s, and reached its modern level before the First World War. Illiteracy among women was reduced to 30 per cent by 1870, and then fell rapidly as girls, too, benefited from educational reform.

Whether the industrial revolution affected the development of literacy is still a matter for debate. On balance it seems that industrial development was culturally disruptive, especially in places like Dickens's 'Coketown'. Nineteenth-century figures for the geography of literacy show the new industrial centres lagging behind the rest of the country. In 1856, for example, at a time when national figures show 26 per cent of men and 36 per cent of women unable to sign the marriage register, the boom town of Wigan, Lancashire, had illiteracy rates of 50 per cent and 71 per cent. Burgeoning literacy was to be found in the market towns and politer suburbs, and here too was the most ready readership for Victorian print. By the end of the nineteenth century mass education had flattened out most differences. The question then turns to what readers did with their literacy, rather than the distribution of skills.

FURTHER READING

Baumann, Gerd (ed.) (1986) *The Written Word: Literacy in Transition*, Oxford University Press, Oxford

Clanchy, Michael T. (1979) *From Memory to Written Record: England, 1066–1307*, Edward Arnold, London

Cressy, David (1980) *Literacy and the Social Order: Reading and Writing in Tudor and Stuart England*, Cambridge University Press, Cambridge

Graff, Harvey J. (ed.) (1981) *Literacy and Social Development in the West*, Cambridge University Press, Cambridge

Houston, R. A. (1985) *Scottish Literacy and the Scottish Identity: Illiteracy and Society in Scotland and Northern England, 1600–1800*, Cambridge University Press, Cambridge

Ong, Walter J. (1982) *Orality and Literacy: The Technologizing of the Word*, Methuen, London

Resnick, Daniel P. (ed.) (1983) *Literacy in Historical Perspective*, Library of Congress, Washington

Stephens, W. B. (1987) *Education, Literacy and Society, 1830–70: The Geography of Diversity in Provincial England*, Manchester University Press, Manchester

Street, Brian V. (1984) *Literacy in Theory and Practice*, Cambridge University Press, Cambridge

62

PUBLISHING BEFORE 1800

JOHN FEATHER

Publishing, as it is commonly understood, is the process of making printed books available for sale, by organizing the writing, editing, production and distribution of them, and by paying for these operations to be conducted. Although there were medieval stationers who performed many of these functions, it was the invention of printing in the middle of the fifteenth century which led to the development of publishing as it is now practised. Printed books could only be produced in multiple copies; to produce a single copy, as a scribe did of a manuscript, was an economic and technological nonsense. The multiplication of copies, even in the very small numbers which were common in the first century of printing, forced the printer to look for markets beyond his immediate vicinity and to find a means of reaching such markets. In the late fifteenth and early sixteenth centuries, the Latin texts of the common culture of the West were sold throughout Europe, regardless of where they were produced, and elaborate trading networks were developed to sustain this trade (Febvre and Martin, [1958] 1976, pp. 224–33). The gradual breakdown of the common culture, by the forces of nationalism, Protestantism and the wider adoption of the use of the vernacular, all of them in part attributable to the availability of the printed book, created a multitude of publishing trades in different parts of Europe, confined by linguistic, if not yet by national, boundaries. This process began in England contemporaneously with the introduction of printing itself. William Caxton had printed a few English books on the Continent before he returned to England in 1476, but they were for the English market, and, once he was installed at Westminster, he concentrated on vernacular books to an extent unparalleled elsewhere in the early history of European printing. From its very beginning, English publishing was vernacular and insular, and so it was to remain until English became an international language and British books were carried around the world.

The historian of publishing is concerned to trace the development of the trade, and recent years have seen great advances in this field of study. A century ago, the history of the book trade was seen primarily as the history of printing. Blades's pioneering study (1861–3) of Caxton is almost entirely concerned with the minutiae of typography to the exclusion of the literary, linguistic and political considerations which were to attract his later biographers (see Blake, 1976, pp. 33–54, 85–119). The history of publishing is now conceived as a broadly-based study of the economic and social conditions of the writing, production and dissemination of printed books.

In the early years of printing, the publisher and the printer were normally the same man. The printer, with his need for equipment and materials and being an employer of labour, was necessarily the capitalist of book production, but by the end of the sixteenth century profound change was beginning. In essence, these changes sprang from the creation of a capital base in the English book trade which consisted of something other than the equipment in the printing house. This capital was derived from the growing acceptance of a text as a piece of property which was quite distinct from the physical form in which it happened to exist, the concept which would come to be called 'copyright'. The distant origins of copyright can be seen in the granting of licences to print by Henry VII and Henry VIII in the early sixteenth century (Siebert, 1965, pp. 38–9). These licences, or patents, were issued largely because of a desire to regulate the output of the press for political and religious reasons, but they had the effect of creating the concept that the right to print a particular text might be uniquely conferred on a particular individual. As the book trade grew in size, and came to recognize the need for a degree of self-regulation for the general good of all of its participants, this principal became paramount in the relations between members of the trade.

In 1557, Mary I granted a charter of incorporation to the Company of Stationers of London, usually called the Stationers' Company (Blagden, 1960, pp. 19–21). Again the motive was primarily that of control. The charter effectively restricted the practice of the art of printing to London, and within London to the freemen of the Company. Later regulations, in the form of the Company's own ordinances and executive decrees from the crown and the prerogative courts, reinforced this regime. By the mid-1580s, the Stationers' Company was in *de facto* control of the censorship system; it also regulated the numbers of presses and master printers and the number of apprentices entering the trade, and had some oversight of the sale of imported books within England (Siebert, 1965, pp. 56–63, 71–4). In its most extensive form, the system based on the Stationers' Company did not survive the Civil War, but by then some of the fundamental conditions of British publishing had been established. The trade was based in London, and its leading members, although they were in competition with each other, were always ready to co-operate for mutual benefit if they were threatened with competition from outside their own small circle.

849

Part of their protection against outsiders came from the development of a second means of acquiring copyright, parallel to, but separate from, that derived from the crown patents. The effective devolution of the power of censorship to the Stationers' Company in the 1560s was achieved partly by requiring the Company to keep a register of all books which had been licensed for printing. This register seems to have been started in the early 1560s and very quickly came to be used for another purpose. In origin, the Stationers' Register was a record of licences to print, but, since such a licence was normally granted to a named individual, it came to be regarded as a record of that individual's unique right to print a named text. These licences, recorded in the Stationers' Register, are the immediate ancestor of copyright (Greg, 1956, pp. 74–7; Siebert, 1965, pp. 63–82). At the end of the sixteenth century such licences were held by many members of the trade, but there was a marked tendency for them to be concentrated in comparatively few hands. These men, the copy owners, became the pivotal figures in the trade, for without their co-operation no book could be printed or reprinted. There was, however, no reason why a copy owner should own a printing press, and gradually the balance of power within the trade began to shift. Printing capacity began to outstrip demand, and the printers became the paid agents of the copy owners, as indeed they have remained (Feather, 1987a, pp. 39–40).

By the end of the sixteenth century, there was a group of men – perhaps no more than a dozen – who could be loosely defined as publishers, although some scholars would argue that it is anachronistic to use the word at so early a date. Certainly, even allowing for the wholly different scale of the enterprise, they differed from their modern successors in one crucial respect. The copy owners were booksellers as well as publishers, and used their retail bookshops to sell their own products and perhaps those of other printers and publishers. This pattern of a trade dominated by copy-owning booksellers was to persist until almost the end of the eighteenth century. Formal developments in the law had surprisingly little effect. The Copyright Act of 1710 was the result of a lobbying by the book trade and, as they understood it, did little more than confirm existing rights. In fact this was not strictly true, but it was not until 1774 that the House of Lords authoritatively ruled that the property in a copyright expired no more than twenty-eight years after publication (Feather, 1980, 1987b). That ruling was to have important long-term consequences, for the copy owners now had to seek out new copies to publish. In the last two decades of the eighteenth century a new breed of entrepreneurial publisher began to emerge, taking risks on new books rather than reprinting existing favourites. This new kind of publishing was closer in spirit to the nineteenth century than it was to the eighteenth (Feather, 1987a, pp. 116–22).

The dominance of a small group of copy owners was to have a crucial effect on what is perhaps the most delicate relationship in the book trade, that between author and publisher. Although the demand for reading-matter grew continuously throughout the period, then as now there were always more would-be authors than there were publishers willing to issue their works. The copy owners became the essential intermediaries between writers and readers, the former unable to reach the public without them and the latter dependent upon them for what they were able to read. The copy owners, however, were in business to make money, and whatever the intrinsic literary or scholarly merits of a work, they were unlikely to be attracted to it if it did not seem likely to produce an acceptable level of profit. In the seventeenth century this proved to be a major obstacle to the development of learned publishing in England, and to circumvent that obstacle the system of private publication by subscription was developed, a system which was to be exploited on a larger scale in the eighteenth century, by literary authors as well as by scholars (Feather, 1984, pp. 22–57).

By the middle of the seventeenth century the copy owner was firmly in charge of the relationship between himself and the author. He normally paid a single fee, in return for which he was understood to be buying all the rights in the book. From there it was but a small step to the commissioning of books by publishers, and contracts which specified the subject-matter, length, time of delivery and other matters which are familiar enough to any author in the twentieth century. Examples of such contracts survive from the eighteenth century, and we can see from them that, although the publishers were not ungenerous to their authors, they were nevertheless undoubtedly the dominant partners.

By the early eighteenth century, the trade had accumulated a valuable corpus of rights in books which were in continuous demand. The commercial heirs of those who had first published Shakespeare, Milton, Bunyan and Dryden, and the equally valuable non-literary works of Locke, Burnet and the author of *The Whole Duty of Man* (1658), owned properties of great commercial value. Many of these rights were subdivided into shares owned by different members of the trade, but even that was not allowed to open up the system to outsiders. By the second decade of the eighteenth century, at the latest, there had developed the practice of selling such shares only at private auctions, known as 'trade sales', at which only invited members of the inner circles of the trade were present. It was possible, but extremely difficult, for a newcomer to establish himself in this circle; in essence, the trade sales, and the share-book publishing which they sustained, ensured that the leading copy owners were invulnerable to competition (Belanger, 1975; Blagden, 1950; Pollard, 1978, pp. 24–34).

The position of the copy owners, however, was secure only for so long as they could fulfil the public demand for books. This they were able to do by their effective control of the distribution system. From the bookseller's point of view, the problem was to obtain regular and reliable supplies of books for their customers. By the second half of the seventeenth century, this problem was becoming acute, especially for the growing number of booksellers in the provinces, and to solve it the copy owners evolved a system of wholesaling which also had the effect of relieving some of their own financial difficulties. The early wholesaling system, for which there is evidence in the 1680s, was, like the later sales of copies for which it was probably the model, based on a closed auction attended only by invited booksellers in the 'conger', as this group was colloquially called in the trade. The copy owner who had produced and paid for an edition of a book offered it for sale, in multiple copies, to his fellow members of the conger. He thus recouped a large part of his capital investment as soon as possible after he had made it, and was thus able to finance further publications. The buyers, who were themselves often copy owners, and almost always retail booksellers, would retain some copies for sale in their own shops, marking up the price to give themselves a profit, and then sell the copies on to provincial booksellers, or to smaller booksellers in London itself. Thus there developed the efficient mechanism of distribution upon which a successful publishing industry ultimately depends (Feather, 1987a, pp. 68–70).

The internal workings of the trade are only one aspect of publishing history. Of equal importance is its public history, the way in which its activities are reflected among authors and readers. Publishing, or rather the invention of printing which impelled the development of publishing, forced writers and readers alike into the market-place. The medieval monk writing for the glory of God might be compared with the modern scholar writing for his academic colleagues, but even the latter is under commercial constraints, for, whether or not he receives any direct financial rewards, his work will be produced and disseminated under commercially controlled conditions. The commercialization of literature, most often perhaps associated with the development of periodical journalism, was actually well advanced by the end of the seventeenth century.

Among the copy owners of the Restoration period, there is a handful who can, in something akin to the modern sense, be called publishers. Three in particular, Henry Herringman, Francis Kirkman and Jacob Tonson, were publishers of literary works, both of contemporary authors and of earlier writers in whose copies they had bought or inherited shares. Herringman was, in all but name, Dryden's publisher during the first part of his career (Miller, 1948), and he was succeeded in that position by Tonson (Lynch, 1971, pp. 17–36). We know something of the commercial arrangements between them, and certainly enough to know that the fashionable Dryden was a good deal better rewarded for his labours than was the distinctly unfashionable Milton. Throughout the eighteenth century there were always a few men whose publishing activities were associated with particular forms of writing, or with particular circles of writers. The Tonsons through three generations, from the last quarter of the seventeenth century to the middle of the eighteenth, published many of the major, and indeed many of the minor, new literary works. They gradually accumulated a vastly profitable collection of copies and shares in copies, which came to include not only Dryden, but Shakespeare and Milton from the seventeenth century, and Addison and Steele from the eighteenth. Robert Dodsley was another such publisher. He published many of the works of Johnson's circle although Johnson himself, once he was established, never tied himself to any particular publisher (Straus, 1910, pp. 36–57, 67–88).

If the authors were constrained by the commercial activities of the cartel which controlled the London book trade from the late seventeenth century onwards, so also, although rather less directly, were readers. There was, of course, competition between publishers, and certainly between retail booksellers. On the other hand, the customer for a particular title could only buy a copy of the edition issued by the publisher. The resentment which this sometimes aroused can be measured from the ample evidence that cheap reprints of popular books were imported illegally into Britain, in breach of copyright, and were openly sold in the bookshops, in response to public demand for cheaper books. The evidence suggests that from the Restoration, at the latest, the market for books was continuously increasing. This phenomenon was a consequence of many factors; increased literacy, a rising standard of living among the middle classes and the greater time available for leisure pursuits are only three of the most obvious. Whole new classes of literature came into being to cater for this new audience, far removed from the influence of court or of élite literary circles. The most important of these was the novel, the only literary genre to be invented after the invention of printing itself, and entirely a product of the commercial ethos of the late seventeenth- and early eighteenth-century book trade. Kirkman was indeed part-author of one of the pioneering novels, *The English Rogue* (1665), and what might be argued to be the first great English novel, *Pamela* (1740), was written by a printer, Samuel Richardson.

The other genre created for the new bourgeois audience was the periodical. Although newspapers can trace their origins to the 1620s, and were of great political importance as early as the Civil War, the general interest magazine is, like prose fiction, essentially a product of the late seventeenth and early eighteenth centuries. Early experiments were not entirely successful, but the essay periodical came of age with *The Spectator* (1711–) and the general interest journal with *The Gentleman's Magazine* (1731–), both of which were important commercial properties because of the audience, huge by contemporary standards, which they could command. The general interest magazines, and indeed the newspapers, provided a source of income for authors which was more regular, and often more lucrative, than the writing of books. Defoe, Johnson, Goldsmith and many others all derived a substantial part of their incomes from periodical journalism, and in that sense the magazines made possible both the writing and the publishing of many books. At the same time, the magazines offered to the readers a regular diet of by no means inconsequential writing, both fiction and non-fiction, which was of considerable importance in widening the mental frame of reference of the middle classes, especially in the provinces (Wiles, 1976).

A successful publishing industry, however, depends on access to the market where books are made available to potential customers. The development of the wholesaling conger at the end of the seventeenth century was one attempt to answer this commercial imperative, but it was by no means the only one. At the same time, the trade began to develop mechanisms through which booksellers and their customers alike could learn what books were available. Catalogues of various kinds had been a feature of the book trade throughout Europe since the fifteenth century, but there were few systematic catalogues of British books until after the Restoration. An attempt to compile such a catalogue in the late sixteenth century, by Andrew Maunsell, had proved to be too difficult, and despite the appearance of catalogues from a few individual booksellers and publishers, the first general catalogue of new books did not appear until 1662. This was *Mercurius Librarius*, commonly known as the *Term Catalogues*, which from 1662 to 1709 was published quarterly, and was a remarkably comprehensive list of new books and new editions of older books. Although it was intended primarily for the booksellers, it is clear from the Preface to one of the four cumulations that the publishers of the *Term Catalogues* also envisaged their use by private individuals. After the *Term Catalogues* came to an end in 1709, it was some time before a satisfactory and successful replacement was devised. For much of the eighteenth century, the main source of information about new books was the long and very comprehensive list which appeared each month in *The Gentleman's Magazine*, although from the middle of the century onwards there were serial bibliographies which filled the gap left by the death of the *Term Catalogues* (Pollard, 1934).

The book lists in the magazines (for its competitors imitated the *Gentleman's*, although never very satisfactorily) were, on the whole objective and factual. A parallel and rather later development was the evaluative book review. Until the 1750s, 'reviews' in the magazines and newspapers were little more than summaries, or even lengthy extracts, from the books under consideration. It was in two magazines founded for the purpose, *The Monthly Review* (1749–) and *The Critical Review* (1756–), that the critical review first found its place on the literary scene (Roper, 1978, pp. 20–2).

Unlike the trade bibliographies, which were primarily aimed at the booksellers themselves, the lists in the magazines and the reviews were targeted at the reading public, those who would actually buy the books. So too were advertisements for books, which had begun to appear in the newspapers in their earliest days. By the mid-eighteenth century, some London publishers were mounting sophisticated marketing campaigns which involved advertisements in the main London newspapers, which were nationally distributed, supported by more selective advertising in the vigorous provincial press which had developed since the beginning of the century. Books were advertised in papers which served regions of the country where their subject-matter was of particular interest or where the author was a local celebrity. Local booksellers from whom the book could be bought were named in many of the advertisements, and we can suspect, although we cannot prove, that the whole advertising effort was carefully co-ordinated and perhaps jointly financed by London publishers and provincial booksellers (Feather, 1985, pp. 44–53).

Widespread advertising implied the existence of bookshops through which books could be bought, and this was indeed the case. There is evidence for the availability of books, on a limited scale, in almost all major towns during the seventeenth century. By the middle of the eighteenth century there were many hundreds of bookshops, and only in the most remote rural areas was access to a bookshop of some kind impossible. Shops in the major cities were well-stocked, and had the latest publications on their shelves. An efficient system of distribution had been evolved through which it was possible for the bookseller to order books for stock, or to fulfil an order from an individual customer. By the end of the eighteenth century, the British book trade had a highly organized and highly effective machine for the profitable production, distribution and sale of its products.

It was not only, however, by buying books that readers were able to obtain them. Among the poor, both in the countryside and in the towns, the habit of reading aloud survived, so that even the illiterate were brought into some contact with metropolitan printed culture. This was especially true of the newspapers, which were available in coffee-houses and taverns as well as at the bookshops, and certainly reached a far larger number of readers, or auditors, than circulation figures of a few thousands would superficially suggest. For the literate man who could not afford to buy as many books as he wished to read, the development of the commercial circulating libraries was of great significance. Such libraries had existed in London since the second half of the seventeenth century, and within less than a century were found throughout the country. Indeed, it seems likely that there were few bookshops which did not also have a few shelves of books in a loan collection. Such libraries made a small contribution to the profits of the book trade, and a much larger contribution to the wide circulation of the printed word. Moreover, contrary to the common impression, often found among eighteenth-century writers themselves, the stock of the circulating libraries was not confined to the latest popular fiction. Surviving catalogues and loan records suggest that, except perhaps in the very smallest libraries, history, biography and accounts of voyages and travels were at least as popular as fiction among the patrons of the libraries (Kaufman, 1967).

The output of books grew almost continuously during the 350 years between Caxton's time and the end of the eighteenth century, with the possible exception of the middle decades of the seventeenth century, when the trade was disrupted by the Civil War and Interregnum. It is difficult to quantify precisely the total output of the trade, because we know that much has been lost but do not know how much. In round figures, however, perhaps 50,000 separate editions were printed between 1476 and 1640, a further 100,000 before 1700 and perhaps a million during the eighteenth century. Quantification is made more difficult by problems of definition. As early as the first half of the sixteenth century, printed documents of all kinds were in use for purposes of advertising and administration. As literacy grew, and indeed as the organization of society as a whole and of commercial activity in particular became more complex, the production of 'ephemeral' printed matter increased dramatically. By the middle of the eighteenth century, many printing houses were sustained by 'jobbing' work rather than by book printing. Although these printed documents were of great significance, and are indeed of great interest to the social and economic historian, and although they are an integral part of the history of the book trade, their production and distribution was not, in the normal sense, an aspect of publishing. For statistical purposes they should probably not be defined as 'books', and yet the lines of demarcation can be very difficult to draw convincingly. Even allowing for these reservations, it is safe to say that the output of the publishing trade was large and increasing, and that the increase far outstripped the rate of increase of the population. There were more people able to read, and more books were read by those who could do so.

It is of considerable interest to study what kind of books were actually published; for the literary scholar this is a salutary exercise which can put into context the commercial and social significance of the works of literature which he regards so highly. In fact, it was cheap popular books which sustained the publishing trade in the sixteenth, seventeenth and eighteenth centuries. Many such books have disappeared, including whole editions of which there are neither survivors nor records. Nevertheless, we know enough to know that a great deal has been lost, and to form some judgement of it.

Until the nineteenth century, by far the largest single category of printed matter was in the field of religion. Formal theology accounted for only a tiny proportion of this. The Bible was an essential possession of every Protestant household, and was certainly the most widely read, commonly owned and often printed book in pre-industrial England. Commercially, the English Bible, in its successive 'official' recensions from Coverdale to King James, was a monopoly of the King's Printer and the English universities. Indeed, it gave the King's Printer a uniquely strong economic base in the trade. Associated with the Bible, both liturgically and commercially, was the Book of Common Prayer; it too was a monopoly, and sold in millions of copies over two-and-a-half centuries.

There was also, however, a vast output of religious writing aimed not at theologians but at ordinary Christian men and women. Such books antedate the Reformation, and indeed the invention of printing. Meditations on the Virgin Mary or on the Rosary, intended for the pious layman and written in the vernacular, were printed in England in the fifteenth and early sixteenth centuries. The Reformation, with its emphasis on the personal nature of the relationship between an individual and God, greatly increased the demand for such devotional works. They poured off the presses in the form of prayers, paraphrases of parts of the Bible, simplified theology and sermons, and were to be found in every bookshop and many homes. Some of these works became the best-sellers of their day. A few are still remembered, and one, *The Pilgrim's Progress* (1678–84), genuinely survives as a popular classic. A few more, *The Whole Duty of Man* and Taylor's *Holy Living* (1650), for example, are remembered by name, but largely unread. Others have fallen into complete oblivion; Stanhope's late seventeenth-century version of the Psalms is one of these, and yet in the early eighteenth century it was one of the most commercially valuable of all copyrights. Every resurgence of popular Protestantism, from the first stirrings in the reign of Edward VI down to Methodism and the evangelical revival in the Church of England in the reign of George III, multiplied the number of such books and the audience for them. An anonymous early eighteenth-century critic of the trade wrote of its 'mammon-monopoly', but it was a monopoly firmly based on the belief in a Protestant God (Bennett, 1965, 1969, 1970).

Among secular books, the most popular were those which were to be deplored by the eighteenth-century evangelicals, the ballads, the chapbooks and the almanacs. The ballads, like much of the material in the chapbooks, derive in large part from orally transmitted folk stories, some pure fiction and others based loosely on distant historical events and characters. Robin Hood, Guy of Warwick, the Seven Champions of Christendom and many others survived in the popular imagination, and were transmuted into printed form by publishers who recognized their potential for generating profit. In *The Winter's Tale*, Shakespeare presents Autolycus as a typical seller of the printed ballads; he sang the songs and then sold the printed texts so that his audience could sing them for themselves. Although few of the ballads printed between 1550 and 1800 were genuine folk verse, for they were written for printed publication, they were based on genuine folk traditions. Millions were printed;

only a handful survives, many in unique copies, out of editions which ran into tens of thousands (Neuburg, 1977, pp. 20–39, 60; Shepard, 1973, pp. 14–21).

The chapbooks are the prose equivalents of the ballad. While the ballads were printed on single-sheet broadsides, the chapbooks were little pamphlets execrably printed in twelve pages. The old stories are found here too, but over the centuries new stories were added to the stock. Robinson Crusoe is only one of many fictional heroes whose fame reached far beyond the closed world of readers of formal literature because of his appearance in the chapbooks. Such books were already common in the seventeenth century (Spufford, 1981, pp. 129–47), and by the 1750s the production of chapbooks was a major industry within the book trade. Although the large-scale production of secular chapbooks did not survive the assaults of Hannah More and other evangelicals in the 1790s, they remain as a vivid testimony to the living popular traditions of pre-industrial England and to an increasing dependence on print as the medium of transmission for those traditions. Many chapbooks were undoubtedly read by children, and they have sometimes wrongly been regarded primarily as children's books. From the middle of the eighteenth century, books were indeed published specifically aimed at the children's market, and this too became a commercially significant part of the publishing trade.

Chapbooks and ballads were probably the largest categories of printed matter produced for the mass market before the end of the eighteenth century, but they were almost rivalled in popularity by the almanac. Almanacs, which combined the characteristics of a diary, a pocket reference book and a set of astrological predictions, were, like the ballads and chapbooks, printed in millions, and like them, have survived in mere hundreds. Almanacs by the most popular astrologers, such as Moore or Partridge, were best-sellers in successive annual editions, and retained their original names long after the deaths of their founders. The Stationers' Company claimed a monopoly of almanac printing, and used it to provide work for some of its poorer members among the printers. By the middle of the eighteenth century, however, the almanac monopoly was under challenge both from provincial pirates and from legally-minded publishers. When this monopoly was declared illegal in 1780, the Company lost the last residue of its formal role as the central organizational body in the book trade. The almanac did not, however, consist only of astrological predictions. They also contained a great deal of valuable information on everyday matters of great concern to ordinary people. Agricultural and veterinary matters loomed large in this, and the almanac played some part in spreading a wider knowledge of these subjects. Medical remedies for people as well as animals were to be found in many almanacs, and may well have been no more harmful than the attentions of a seventeenth- or eighteenth-century country physician (Capp, 1979, pp. 23–66, 238–69).

In the midst of the outpouring of popular literature and works of religion, works of learning and literature were of little commercial significance. Indeed, there was little scholarly publishing in Britain until the seventeenth century, and even then such works were issued only with great difficulty. Oxford and Cambridge both put their university presses on a sounder footing between 1660 and 1700 but, although both produced a number of significant works of scholarship, neither was commercially successful until the nineteenth century when they were able to exploit the newly created market for school textbooks. Commercial publishers did sometimes venture into learned publishing, but rarely without the support of pre-publication subscriptions collected in advance from those who wished to buy the books. The money was often used to support the author during the time when he was working on his book, as well as the costs of publication itself. In the harsh world of commercial publishing, there was little room for high-flown ideas of the service of scholarship. The same considerations applied to journals. At a time when scientific journals were already common in Germany, England had only the *Philosophical Transactions*, supported by the Royal Society from the time of its foundation in 1667. Literary publishing faced many of the same problems as learned publishing: a small market, limited interest and low profits. Certainly, a poet, dramatist or novelist had less difficulty in finding a publisher than did a scientist or a classical scholar. A few authors of undoubted literary merit became popular best-sellers, but far more did not.

Publishing is the commercial channel through which books travel from author to reader. Between the invention of printing and the industrial revolution, the book trade underwent slow transformation rather than rapid change, and indeed many of its most characteristic features were substantially unchanged. The publishers themselves – the copy-owning booksellers – were in business to make a profit, not to serve the cultural development of society. They developed mechanisms of supply and distribution which enabled them to do so. They participated in the evolution of trade practices and indeed laws which protected their investments in the rights to publish particular books. They concentrated on books which made profits, and although they would follow fashions they would rarely lead them. Few of the books they published are remembered even by name, and fewer still are read. We may treasure those few as part of our heritage, but we should never forget the many hundreds of forgotten novels, thousands of forgotten histories, tens of thousands of forgotten sermons, and as many again of books on every subject under the sun, which provided the profits which sustained the book trade.

FURTHER READING

Bennett, H. S. (1965) *English Books & Readers 1558 to 1603*, Cambridge University Press, Cambridge

——(1969) *English Books & Readers 1475 to 1603*, 2nd edn, Cambridge University Press, Cambridge

——(1970) *English Books & Readers 1603 to 1640*, Cambridge University Press, Cambridge

Blagden, Cyprian (1960) *The Stationers' Company: A History, 1403–1959*, Allen & Unwin, London

Feather, John (1987a) *A History of British Publishing*, Croom Helm, London

Greg, W. W. (1956) *Some Aspects and Problems of London Publishing Between 1550 and 1650*, Clarendon Press, Oxford

Neuburg, Victor Edward (1977) *Popular Literature: A History and Guide*, Penguin, Harmondsworth

Plant, Marjorie (1965) *The English Book Trade*, 2nd edn, Allen & Unwin, London

Pollard, Graham (1978) 'The English market for printed books', *Publishing History*, 4, 7–48

Siebert, Frederick S. (1965) *The Freedom of the Press in England 1476–1776*, University of Illinois Press, Urbana

ADDITIONAL WORKS CITED

Belanger, Terry (1975) 'Booksellers' trade sales, 1718–1768', *The Library*, 5th series, 30, 281–302

Blades, William (1861–3) *The Life and Typography of William Caxton*, 2 vols, London

Blagden, Cyprian (1950) 'Booksellers' trade sales 1718–1768', *The Library*, 5th series, 5, 243–57

Blake, Norman Francis (1976) *Caxton: England's First Publisher*, Osprey, London

Capp, Bernard (1979) *Astrology and the Popular Press: English Almanacs 1500–1800*, Faber & Faber, London

Feather, John (1980) 'The book trade in politics: the making of the Copyright Act of 1710', *Publishing History*, 8, 19–44

——(1984) *English Book Prospectuses: An Illustrated History*, Bird & Bull, Newton

——(1985) *The Provincial Book Trade in Eighteenth-Century England*, Cambridge University Press, Cambridge

——(1987b) 'The publishers and the pirates: British copyright law in theory and practice 1710–1775', *Publishing History*, 22, 5–33

Febvre, Lucien, and Martin, Henri-Jean (1976) *The Coming of the Book*, translated by David Gerard, NLB, London [first published 1958]

Kaufman, Paul (1967) 'The community library: a chapter in English social history', *Transactions of the American Antiquarian Society*, 57

Lynch, Kathleen M. (1971) *Jacob Tonson, Kit-Kat Publisher*, University of Tennessee Press, Knoxville

Miller, C. W. (1948) 'Henry Herringman, Restoration bookseller-publisher', *Papers of the Bibliographical Society of America*, 42, 292–306

Pollard, Graham (1934) 'Bibliographical aids to research. IV. General lists of books printed in England', *Bulletin of the Institute of Historical Research*, 12, 165–74

Roper, Derek (1978) *Reviewing Before the 'Edinburgh'*, Methuen, London

Shepard, Leslie (1973) *The History of Street Literature*, David & Charles, Newton Abbot

Spufford, Margaret (1981) *Small Books and Pleasant Histories: Popular Fiction and its Readers in Seventeenth-Century England*, Methuen, London

Straus, Ralph (1910) *Robert Dodsley*, John Lane, London

Wiles, R. M. (1976) 'The relish for reading in provincial England two centuries ago'. In Paul J. Korshin (ed.), *The Widening Circle*, University of Pennsylvania Press, Philadelphia, pp. 86–116

63

PUBLISHING SINCE 1800

SIMON ELIOT

THE PERIOD OF TRANSITION 1800–1830

Publishing in the nineteenth century opens with a period which displays more signs of continuity than of change: the traditional monthly pattern of publication with a peak in spring, a dip in summer and a modest rise in December remained undisturbed; the prices of books listed in trade journals remained high (further inflated by economic problems caused by the Napoleonic wars); religion was still the most popular subject in terms of numbers of titles published (see Eliot, 1990).

Yet things were beginning to stir. In 1814 *The Times* was printed by steam press for the first time, and by the 1820s books were also issuing from powered presses. Population and literacy were growing fast. In 1814 a new Act had extended copyright from twenty-eight years to the life of an author if that were longer. A string of best-sellers was emphasizing literature's enormous commercial potential. Constable (founded 1798) and Longman were publishing Walter Scott's poetry (*The Lay of the Last Minstrel*, 1805, had sold 44,000 copies by 1830). John Murray (founded 1768) published Byron and sold 10,000 copies of *The Corsair* (1814) on the first day of publication (Altick, 1963, p. 386).

Prose could be even more profitable: throughout the early years of the period publishers such as Lane (Minerva Press), J. F. Hughes and Colburn were pouring out gothic, sentimental and 'fashionable' novels. Scott, too, when squeezed out of the poetry market by Byron, published works such as *Kenilworth* (1821), whose enormous popularity helped to establish the inflated format of the Victorian middle-class novel: three volumes at 31s 6d.

Publishers were also experimenting with review periodicals which catered for a middle-class audience which was larger but less leisured than its eighteenth-century equivalent. In October 1802, Constable established the Whig *Edinburgh Review* (and insisted that all contributors be paid, an important step towards the professionalization of writers); in 1809, Murray responded with the Tory *Quarterly Review*; and in 1817, Blackwood (established 1804) set up the lighter and more maverick *Blackwood's Edinburgh Magazine*. Generally speaking, the reviews were not subject to newspaper stamp duty, which by 1800 stood at 3½d for every whole sheet. In 1815 this duty was raised to 4d, and in 1819 the definition of 'newspaper' was extended to include all periodicals which carried news less than twenty-six days old. As a result the price of newspapers rose to 7d and more, and rendered papers such as *The Times* beyond the reach even of many middle-class readers. This problem gave rise to periodical reading-rooms through which, for an annual subscription, a reader had access to hundreds of different periodicals (Wilson, 1985, p. 17), and to the hiring out of daily newspapers at a penny an hour.

Although affecting everybody, the high levels of newspaper stamp duty had been designed to curb working-class radicalism. The years 1800–20 had seen a great upwelling of publishing for the popular market, not only in traditional forms such as almanacs, broadsides and chapbooks, but also in the area of political pamphlets and radical newspapers. This was led by William Cobbett whose *Political Register* (in a stripped-down form without current news but with comment) was first issued on 2 November 1816 at 2d and within a few months was selling at least 50,000 copies a week. The 1819 Act effectively put an end to cheap news and comment by pricing newspapers out of the reach of the literate working class.

The Religious Tract Society (founded 1799) and the British and Foreign Bible Society (founded 1804), working with the long-established Society for Promoting Christian Knowledge, produced tracts and Bibles in their millions. Many of these would be sold at under cost price, or even given away free, so their significance in terms of commercial publishing was less than the numbers might suggest. Nevertheless, the sheer size of production was so great as significantly to influence the context in which reading was done. The secular version of these societies was the Society for the Diffusion of Useful Knowledge (founded 1826) whose publisher, Charles Knight, produced worthy (if sometimes dull) works of science and practical instruction such as the *Library of Useful Knowledge* (32–page pamphlets selling at 6d from 1827) and *The Penny Magazine* (from 1832).

Under the pressure of high production costs, low volume sales and punitive taxation, both educated and uneducated audiences had been trained into a relationship with text that depended to a significant extent on borrowing, hiring or segmenting into parts. The only texts generally available whole and cheaply were non-copyright materials, mostly classics of one kind or another, few of which had a wide enough appeal to be profitably mass-produced. Those penny and twopenny part-works which needed long-term commitment (such as Knight's *Penny Cyclopaedia*, 1833–44) appealed to that part of the population which recognized the value of the finished work and could always afford it. The endless, soap-opera-like penny romances, which provided undemanding escapism and required no consistent commitment, more effectively catered for a larger, poorer audience.

A general financial crisis in 1826 precipitated certain under-capitalized publishers and printers into bankruptcy. Most notable among these were Constable and the printing firm of James Ballantyne & Co. in which Sir Walter Scott was financially involved. Recent research has, however, suggested that 1826 did not witness a massive collapse, and that most publishers survived, albeit in changed conditions (Sutherland, 1987, pp. 156–60). The booksellers specializing in the sale of remainders (such as Thomas Tegg) benefited enormously from all the bankrupt stock. Otherwise publishers seem to have survived by concentrating their efforts on lower-priced books with a readier sale. In this respect, 1826 was a rehearsal for what was to come later.

INDUSTRIAL AND DISTRIBUTION REVOLUTIONS
1831–1870

The revolutionary changes in production brought about by machine-produced paper, powered book presses, stereotyping and publishers' cloth bindings inevitably had dramatic effects on publishing activity: in 1840 the *Publishers' Circular* listed 2,912 new and reprinted titles; by 1870 the figure had risen to 4,656. The price of books began to fall, and by the early 1850s trade journals were listing more books at 3s 6d or under than in any higher price category. The traditional spring publication season remained, but the Christmas season rose to challenge it and, during the 1840s, to achieve first position. The nature of what was being published in this season was distinctive: annuals, yearbooks, lavish illustrated gift books and, most important of all, children's books. By 1870 literature in all its forms had replaced religion as the most popular subject in terms of titles published (Eliot, 1990).

The 1842 Copyright Act gave protection for 42 years or the author's life plus seven years, whichever was longer. Along with this enhanced definition of literary property came the publisher's reader, normally an experienced professional writer whose part-time job it was to assess the literary quality and commercial potential of submitted manuscripts. The first really influential reader was Geraldine Jewsbury, whose reports from 1860 strongly influenced the construction of Bentley's list (Gettmann, 1960, pp. 194–230). George Meredith at Chapman & Hall and John Morley at Macmillan performed similar functions.

Publishers could not sustain low-priced books unless they could sell to a large market. From the 1840s railways provided the fast, cheap bulk transport needed. Speed was of the essence for newspapers, and it was the mastery of railway timetables which allowed W. H. Smith II to expand the wholesaling and retailing of periodicals. From 1860 Smith's also ran a circulating library which specialized in single-volume works that could be carried comfortably on a railway journey (Wilson, 1985, pp. 355–62). Station bookstalls also provided new outlets for printed goods and, unlike the shaking and dimly-lit mailcoach, the train created a new type of customer – the reading traveller. Meanwhile, book distribution was being improved by wholesalers such as Simpkin, Marshall & Co., who specialized in supplying provincial and overseas booksellers (Curwen, 1873, pp. 412–20). Wholesalers also helped publishers by providing them with bulk orders on publication, thus generating much-needed immediate income.

Another distribution system which influenced the nature of publishing was the circulating library, most importantly Mudie's Select Library. The first print-run of a three-decker novel was usually between 500 and 1250 sets, of which Mudie might buy two thirds (at a substantial discount). This order alone often guaranteed the publisher a profit. Conversely, if Mudie did not order it might be difficult not to make a loss. Whatever other inhibitions constrained a publisher of novels, the commercial necessity of selling to Mudie should not be underestimated (Griest, 1970, pp. 58–86). So universal was the three-decker that publishers occasionally forced shorter novels into this Procrustean form: in 1847 Anne Brontë's *Agnes Grey* was published with *Wuthering Heights* in order to bulk out the latter.

The distribution of information about books was also being improved by new trade journals: *The Publishers' Circular* (fortnightly from 1837) and *The Bookseller* (monthly from 1858) helped identify common interests and, incidentally, improved bibliographic control by their comprehensive listing of new and reprint publications.

In 1836 newspaper duty was reduced from 4d to 1d a copy, and in 1855 the duty was abolished altogether. The final 'tax on knowledge', paper duty, was removed in 1861. Enormous jumps in the production and sales of newspapers were recorded in 1836 and 1855, yet most dailies remained resolutely middle-class until the 1890s. Periodicals helped promote fiction by advertising, reviewing and, frequently, serializing it. Some working-class Sunday papers went even further, carrying sensational accounts of crime and serialized stories to the exclusion of almost everything else (Altick, 1963, p. 346; James, 1974, pp. 39–40).

Apart from periodicals, publishing for the working-class market consisted mostly of producing sixteen- or thirty-two-page pamphlets selling at 1d or 2d a week. Some of these would be abridgements, others would be parts of serialized longer stories, or plagiarisms of popular middle-class novels (early Dickens novels were frequently pirated). 'Penny Dreadfuls' were a predominant feature of working-class reading in the 1840s and 1850s, and publishers such as Edward Lloyd were issuing them weekly by the 100,000 from Salisbury Square and Holywell Street (James, 1974, pp. 32–9).

Holywell Street was also the centre of pornographic publishing, whose profitability or size should not be underemphasized: for instance, in 1845 just one convicted dealer had in stock 12,346 prints, 393 books and 351 copper plates (Montgomery Hyde, 1964, p. 167). The border between this and legitimate publishing was not always clear. J. C. Hotten, who issued various pornographic works in the 1860s, also published Swinburne and Mark Twain.

When the new publishing firm of Chapman & Hall commissioned Charles Dickens to provide the accompanying prose for a series of sporting prints in monthly parts at a shilling, they were taking a great risk: Dickens was virtually unknown and part-publication of fiction was regarded as essentially a working-class form. Despite poor sales of the first few parts, *Pickwick Papers* (1836–7) ended up selling some 40,000 per month. The majority of Dickens's subsequent novels were first published in twenty monthly parts (with the final two as a double number at 2s), the method proving successful both as a means of keeping in close contact with his readers, and of allowing them to buy a large novel in instalments. Both Thackeray and Trollope experimented with this newly respectable method, and Blackwood issued George Eliot's *Middlemarch* (1871–2) in eight parts at two-monthly intervals at 5s each (Sutherland, 1976, pp. 191–203). Most novels, however, continued to be first issued as three-deckers.

Although poetry could not compete with fiction sales, certain poets, most notably Tennyson, did benefit from the mass-marketing system of mid-Victorian publishing: in 1864, for instance, Moxon published *Enoch Arden* in a first edition of 60,000 copies which sold out in five months (Hagen, 1979, p. 112). A less elevated poet, Martin Tupper, sold 200,000 copies of *Proverbial Philosophy* between 1838 and 1866 (Altick, 1963, p. 387). Browning experimented with publication in parts when Moxon issued eight numbers of his *Bells and Pomegranates* between 1841 and 1846. It was not a roaring success.

Perhaps the most important development in middle-class publishing was the speed and cheapness with which fiction was reprinted. Between 1829 and 1833 Cadell & Co published the collected edition of the Waverley novels at 5s a volume: in 1831 Bentley & Colburn launched their *Standard Novels* series at 6s. Dickens's works began to come out cheaply in 1847 (prices ranged from 2s to 5s). Routledge's 'Railway Library' began in 1848 selling reprints of Bulwer-Lytton's novels and others at 2s. This gave rise to the term 'railway novels' or 'yellowbacks' (from the colour of their pictorial bindings), which by 1870 were being issued by most of the major fiction publishers. By 1870 the common publishing pattern for a novel was serialization in a magazine or newspaper followed immediately (often before the final part had been published) by a 31s 6d three-decker; reprinted a year or two later in a single volume at 5s or 6s; and then as a 'yellowback' at 2s (Eliot, 1985, pp. 38–53).

It was common for a bookseller to offer the customer a discount of anything up to 25 per cent on the notional price of a book. At least two efforts (in 1829 and 1848) had been made by London publishers and booksellers to stop this 'underselling'. Neither was successful, the second leading to arbitration by Lord Campbell who, in 1852 and in conformity with the political orthodoxy of the time, declared for free trade (Barnes, 1964, p. 66). From 1852 to 1890 there was no attempt to control the retail price of books.

MASS PRODUCTION AND PROFESSIONALIZATION
1871–1920

Further technical developments in this period – high-speed rotary printing of periodicals, hot-metal composing machines (e.g. Linotype, Monotype) – inaugurated an era of mass production of books and periodicals. In 1871 the copyright receipt registers of the British Museum recorded 23,509 items; by 1912 this figure had more than trebled to 78,012 (Eliot, 1990). The concept of copyright itself was firmly established internationally by the Berne Convention (1887) and the Chace Act (1891), which allowed non-residents to establish their US copyright. Within the UK the 1911 Act defined copyright roughly as we have it today: it was to last for the author's lifetime plus fifty years.

The period 1883–95 saw authors, booksellers and publishers organizing themselves professionally. In 1883 the Society of Authors was established to offer guidance and support to members negotiating with publishers. The formation of the Booksellers Association and the Publishers Association, both in 1895, improved the trade's organization, as did the development of the literary agent. A. P. Watt (began late 1870s), J. B. Pinker (1896) and Curtis Brown (1899) were the first to provide a professional service to any writer who was prepared to pay for it. With larger markets and securer copyright, literary property was becoming both more valuable and more extensive. By the 1890s a novel, apart from the obvious rights linked to book publication, had serial rights (including syndication in provincial and foreign newspapers), translation rights, and rights for publication in English abroad (often taken up by the Tauchnitz series). There would be reprint, dramatization and, later, film and radio rights. The intensive farming of literary property by acute agents resulted in substantial increases in the incomes of successful authors during this period.

Earlier in the century there had been two main ways an author could make money from a book: the first was to sell the copyright for a fixed sum; the second was to have a 'half-profits' arrangement whereby the publisher and author shared the profit (if any). Both were open to abuse. The later nineteenth century saw the gradual introduction of the royalties system in which the author receives a certain percentage (usually 10 per cent) of the selling price of each copy sold. Sometimes an author would receive an advance payment which anticipated royalty income. But royalties need careful monitoring, something most writers were unable or unwilling to do (an exception to this rule was Lewis Carroll who was constantly interrogating his tolerant publisher, Macmillan, on business matters). It is no coincidence that the royalty system and the literary agent emerged at the same time. To work, however, the system needed stable book prices, something the free market in books did not encourage.

In 1890, Frederick Macmillan wrote to the *Bookseller* suggesting a system of 'net' books: the publisher would issue a book at a fixed, or 'net' price below which it should not be sold. Booksellers would get a fixed discount only if they re-sold the book at the net price. Throughout the 1890s Macmillan, and gradually other publishers (among them Dent, Longman, Murray, Methuen), experimented with net books. Finally, in 1899, the Net Book Agreement (NBA) was negotiated between the Publishers Association, the Booksellers Association and the Society of Authors. Since 1 January 1900 retail price maintenance has been a feature of the British book trade (Barnes, 1964, pp. 143–6).

By the 1880s the three-decker novel was becoming a dinosaur. Although requiring about a year of undisturbed library circulation to make a profit, it frequently found itself competing with cheap reprint versions within three months of first publication. In 1894 Mudie's and Smith's, in refusing to pay more than 4s a volume for fiction, effectively killed off the three-decker, the last appearing in 1897. Henceforward a novel would first appear in one volume at 6s, a price which was held until after the First World War. This was good news for the expanding local public library system which was catering for the new, state-educated mass readership (Kelly, 1977, pp. 496–511). Initially, local library authorities represented a new market for the publishing industry, particularly for the cheap reprints and the new 6s novels, but gradually resentment built up among authors and publishers as they saw a few library copies of a new work being borrowed by scores of readers who might otherwise, so the argument went, have bought their own.

As early as the 1860s firms had begun to experiment with 6d and 7d reprints: Routledge issued 6d paperbound reprints of Dickens's novels; for the working-class audience, publishers such as John Dicks produced sensational novels (sometimes reprints of 'penny dreadfuls' of the 1840s) at 6d and 3d. But not only popular fiction was mass-marketed at 6d or below: by the 1880s the non-copyright classics of English literature were freely available from publishers such as Cassell and Routledge at 3d paperbound and 6d clothbound. By 1896 Newnes was selling 30,000–40,000-word abridgements of eighteenth- and nineteenth-century novels at 1d a volume ('The Penny

Novelists'). At the same time J. M. Dent was issuing the 'Temple Shakespeare' at 1s a volume and the 'Temple Classics' at the same price. By 1904 Dent had founded Everyman's Library which successfully combined cheapness with well-edited texts. Indeed, books on almost all subjects became cheaper. In 1875, of the titles listed in the *Publishers' Circular* in April and October, 55 per cent were priced at 3s 6d or under, 29 per cent between 3s 7d and 10s, and 16 per cent over 10s. By 1905, 64 per cent were at 3s 6d or under, 25 per cent between 3s 7d and 10s. and only 11 per cent over 10s (Eliot, 1990).

Periodicals, too, became both cheaper and more numerous: in 1870 *Mitchell's Newspaper Press Directory* listed 2,016 titles; thirty years later that number had more than doubled to 4,799. But it was not merely a quantitative change. The 1880s and 1890s saw the emergence of the 'New Journalism' – a racy mixture of exciting front pages, investigative reporting, gossip and a plethora of serialized fiction. This fiction would in turn be syndicated to provincial papers, a process encouraged by 'Fiction Bureaux' such as Tillotson's of Bolton which, from 1873 on, offered serial fiction already set up on stereotype plates.

Between the early 1880s and the coming of the cinema there was a brief golden age where the popular form of entertainment and information was the cheap publication which sold in huge quantities at home and abroad. Specialized publishing also benefited: Forster's Education Act of 1870, and subsequent reforms in secondary and higher education, had stimulated the production of both basic and advanced textbooks, but it was the enormous export market generated by the English-speaking empire which allowed firms like Longman, Macmillan, Collins and Oxford and Cambridge University Presses to sell in such large quantities. Such publishers were also responsible for a national information revolution which encompassed everything from tourist guidebooks and Post Office directories to *The Dictionary of National Biography* (Smith & Elder, 1885–1900) and the *New* [later *Oxford*] *English Dictionary* (Oxford University Press, 1884–1928).

The British publishing industry continued to expand rapidly in the first thirteen years of the new century. In 1900, *The Publishers' Circular* recorded the production of 7,149 new and reprinted titles; by 1913 it was listing 12,379 titles. Inevitably, the First World War interrupted production as costs went up, the supply of paper became restricted, and the labour force was lost to the armed services. In 1918 the *Circular* recorded just 7,716 titles. Despite this, the war had stimulated demand and created new markets, particularly cheap reprints for men on active service: Chatto & Windus's 'Khaki Library' was but one of many such series.

MARKETING AND PROMOTION 1921–1970

With almost universal literacy and fewer technical advances, the evolution of publishing became for a time dependent on the way books were marketed. The trade itself contributed by establishing the National Book Council (later League) in 1925, the Book Token scheme in 1932 and, much later, administering the Booker (from 1968) and other literary prizes. Individual publishers, however, proved to be the greatest innovators.

Jonathan Cape, for instance, issued his first list in 1921 and, with Edward Garnett as his reader, rapidly built up an adventurous list including Robert Graves, T. E. Lawrence, H. E. Bates and Ernest Hemingway. He attempted vertical integration of the business by buying a printing firm in 1929 and a bindery in 1936, and promoted his books by issuing a house magazine freely available to all on his mailing list.

Victor Gollancz, who established his own publishing firm in December 1928, heavily promoted his books through newspaper advertising, much of it pushy and exciting. With advice from the typographic reformer Stanley Morison, he quickly established a distinctive visual style for his books (typically a yellow dustwrapper with a strong black typeface). This identity extended to the contents of the books published, for Gollancz was essentially an intuitive publisher who worked best with authors with whom he could enthusiastically identify. Gollancz published much excellent detective fiction (including Dorothy L. Sayers); he experimented successfully with the publication of contemporary plays and with 'Omnibus' editions which effectively targeted particular interest groups (for instance, readers of ghost stories or of sporting tales). His 'Mundanus' paperback series (1930–1) failed, however, due to a poor selection of titles (Hodges, 1978, pp. 50–6).

His most characteristic invention was the Left Book Club (1936–48). Unlike earlier book clubs (such as the Book Society established in 1929), the LBC acted as a publisher as well as a postal bookseller and offered books at a standard low price (2s 6d). At its peak in 1939 the LBC had a membership of 57,000 (Edwards, 1987, p. 231). Despite the often doctrinaire nature of its selections (Gollancz turned down Orwell's *Homage to Catalonia* as being too heterodox), the LBC did demonstrate that there was an audience for serious non-fiction at low prices.

In 1935, Allen Lane of the ailing Bodley Head published the first Penguins, attractively paperbound books reprinting contemporary authors at 6d each. Their success depended on a confluence of factors: the series was launched in a decade when inflation had reduced the value of sixpence, so it was in real terms even cheaper than series at that price in the 1890–1914 period; much care was given to the quality and distinctiveness of the design (books were colour-coded according to subject); most importantly, they were marketed not only through bookshops but also through less conventional outlets (such as Woolworth's).

In June 1937, Lane initiated his second revolution: 'Pelican Books'. In many ways this was more radical than Penguins because many Pelicans were specially-commissioned non-fiction titles rather than reprints. Within a few months Lane's third innovation hit the publishing world: 'Penguin Specials' was a series, partly reprints, partly new works, which dealt with issues of the day. Not surprisingly, most of the early ones dealt with the European situation. Between 1937 and 1945, 153 Penguin specials were published (some selling well over 100,000 copies).

Penguins were a risky experiment: many rival publishers believed that cheap books undermined the trade, and most booksellers felt that they could not possibly survive on the low profits derived from sixpenny books. Both groups were wrong. Between August 1936 and September 1939, Lane sold over 28 million copies (Lloyd Jones, 1985, p. 28).

As 1914–18 had proved, war, in reducing other entertainments, increases the demand for books. Had sufficient paper and staff been available, the publishing industry would have boomed during the Second World War. As it was, demand outstripped supply, even after the Book Production War Economy Agreement of 1941 had reduced the quality and size of books. The war had more direct effects on publishing than this, however. The bombing of London in 1940–1 destroyed not only many publishing offices and their records, but also stockpiles of books. Perhaps the most serious blow was struck when Simpkin Marshall, the main book wholesaler and distributor, was hit. The loss of stock was bad enough, the disruption of the book-supply system was far worse and lasted much longer.

Despite these problems certain firms, particularly Penguin, continued to innovate: between 1939 and 1945 it introduced no less than 19 new series including 'King Penguins' (1939), 'Penguin New Writing' (1940), 'Puffin Picture Books' (1940), 'Penguin Poets' (1941) and 'Puffin Story Books' (1941). By 1944 Pan Books (owned jointly by Collins, Heinemann and Macmillan) had also been established. Unlike Penguin, and more like American paperback publishers, Pan and the companies which were to follow it concentrated on current titles and did not try to maintain a large backlist.

By the end of the war more than 52,000 titles were waiting to be reprinted (Unwin, 1972, p. 138) and this, coupled with continued paper rationing (not abolished until 1949), meant that it was the early 1950s before the publishing industry fully recovered. By this time, however, publishers were faced not only with competition from radio and the cinema, but also from television. Abroad, and particularly in the traditional Commonwealth markets, competition was building up from American and new home-grown imprints. Book clubs were also growing. In the 1950s they were restricted by not being allowed to produce cheap editions in the first year of publication: by 1968 these restrictions had been eased and, with the creation of Book Club Associates by W. H. Smith and Doubleday, clubs revived to such an extent that by 1980 their total membership was over a million with a turnover of £20 million (Curwen, 1981, p. 85).

In the 1950s and 1960s more and more general trade and university publishers introduced paperback series. In popular publishing firms like Mills & Boon, starved of their traditional markets by the closure of Smith's (in 1961) and Boots' (in 1966) commercial libraries, went into mass paperback marketing and exploited the same diversity of outlets as Penguin had used thirty years before.

Two legal cases set the tone for the 1960s: in 1962 the NBA was successfully defended against a charge of restrictive trade practice, and in October 1960 Penguin successfully defended *Lady Chatterley's Lover* against a charge under the new Obscene Publications Act (1959). In the subsequent seven weeks the book sold two million copies.

PUBLISHING IN THE GLOBAL VILLAGE 1971–1988

In the last twenty years British publishing has been profoundly changed by economic pressures and technical revolutions. The oil crisis of 1973–4 and the period of inflation and austerity which followed squeezed publishing: production and distribution costs soared, forcing book prices into an inflationary spiral; government spending was cut and with it the capacity of public libraries to buy new hardback books, particularly fiction (Sutherland, 1978, pp. xv–xvii). Bookshops, despite the partial protection offered by the NBA, were declining in numbers. In 1976 the British Commonwealth Market Agreement (1947) was found to contravene US anti-trust laws: this rendered British publishing, which in some years had exported 45 per cent of its production (particularly educational texts), more vulnerable to foreign competition (Norrie, 1982, pp. 170–1).

The need for stricter financial control led to a reduction of backlists, fewer and less risky new titles and a greater concern with cash flow (this in turn led to a more rapid remaindering of books and the growth of remaindered bookshops in the 1970s and 1980s). Smaller publishing firms needed more capital, larger firms needed to protect themselves from the danger of takeovers. Both motives led to an enormous increase in mergers and self-defensive alliances between British publishers. More positively, publishers increased investment in US firms as an alternative means of access to American and Commonwealth markets. Book marketing for both literary agents and publishers was now international, a fact which explained the growing importance of the annual Frankfurt Book Fair.

As an example of these changes we might look at Penguin. In July 1970 Penguin became part of the Pearson Longman Group; in 1974 its new publications were cut from a planned 800 to 540 titles; in November 1975 it acquired the American publishing house Viking. Penguin had expanded geographically in the 1970s by establishing Canadian and New Zealand branches in 1973. In the late 1970s another cut-back in new titles occurred which was accompanied by a reduction of the 5,000-title backlist (Lloyd Jones, 1985, pp. 83–91). By 1985 Penguin had acquired the publishing firms of Warne (in 1983), Michael Joseph and Hamish Hamilton (both in 1985) and was producing 1,200 new titles a year.

The 1980s have seen an even more desperate round of takeovers and amalgamations: the self-defensive group of Chatto & Windus, Bodley Head and Jonathan Cape proved not to be quite defensive enough, since it was taken over by Random House. Similarly, Paul Hamlyn absorbed Heinemann and Secker & Warburg before being in turn bought out by Reed International. Collins (UK), one of the larger independent publishers, was acquired by Rupert Murdoch's News Corporation, providing yet another example of a traditional book publisher being sucked into a multi-national media company whose primary interests are not necessarily those of book publishing. Furthermore, there has been a clear move towards vertical integration in which the original hardback publisher will also own a paperback imprint, so that the increasingly important profits from paperback rights are not lost.

The 1980s have also seen some hopeful developments. One was the emergence of small independent publishers such as Bloomsbury, Frances Pinter and Boydell & Brewer. Many survive by identifying a market niche unexploited by the general trade publisher. After the depressions of the 1970s, bookselling is once again expanding as chains such as Dillons and Waterstones experiment with new forms of retailing.

Sometimes technology challenges publishing: illicit photocopying, for instance, of textbooks and music now represents a serious drain of potential income, as does the use of modern reprinting techniques to produce unauthorized copies of British books in countries which have still to sign the Berne Convention. More importantly, however, technology changes publishing. In the last thirty years microform publishing has assumed a considerable importance, particularly in reproducing large-scale manuscript and printed works from the past, and in current reference works which need constant updating (such as Whitaker's *British Books in Print*). Even more critical in the long term is the impact of computers: in terms of sophisticated stock-control in bookshops; in terms of editorial manipulation of text (what will the literary historian do when the various drafts of a novel exist only on floppy disc and are erased when finished with?); in terms of the individual's use of a micro and a laser printer to design and print books. However, to call this 'desk-top publishing' is a misnomer for, as we have seen, the publisher's job is rather one of selection, distribution and marketing than production. When the text of a book can be transmitted directly to a reader's pocket computer and read with the ease of a cheap paperback, then the writer may have no further need of a publisher. While it remains cheaper, more convenient and pleasanter to carry a book, the publisher will remain a vital mediator between author and reader.

FURTHER READING

Altick, Richard D. (1963) *The English Common Reader: A Social History of the Mass Reading Public 1800–1900*, University of Chicago Press, Chicago [first published 1957]

Barnes, James J. (1964) *Free Trade in Books*, Clarendon Press, Oxford

Cross, Nigel (1985) *The Common Writer*, Cambridge University Press, Cambridge

Curwen, Peter J. (1981) *The UK Publishing Industry*, Pergamon Press, Oxford

Gettman, R. A. (1960) *A Victorian Publisher*, Cambridge University Press, Cambridge

Griest, Guinevere L. (1970) *Mudie's Circulating Library and the Victorian Novel*, David & Charles, Newton Abbot

Hepburn, J. (1968) *The Author's Empty Purse and the Rise of the Literary Agent*, Oxford University Press, Oxford

James, Louis (1974) *Fiction for the Working Man 1830–1850*, Penguin, Harmondsworth [first published 1963]

Keating, Peter (1989) *The Haunted Study*, Secker & Warburg, London

Norrie, Ian (1982) *Mumby's Publishing and Bookselling in the Twentieth Century*, Bell & Hyman, London

Patten, Robert Lowry (1978) *Charles Dickens and his Publishers*, Clarendon Press, Oxford

Sutherland, John (1976) *Victorian Novelists and Publishers*, Athlone Press, London

——(1978) *Fiction and the Fiction Industry*, Athlone Press, London

Wilson, Charles (1985) *First with the News: The History of W. H. Smith 1792–1972*, Jonathan Cape, London

ADDITIONAL WORKS CITED

Curwen, Henry (1873) *A History of Booksellers*, Chatto & Windus, London

Edwards, Ruth Dudley (1987) *Victor Gollancz: A Biography*, Gollancz, London

Eliot, Simon (1985) 'The Three-Decker Novel and its First Cheap Reprint', *The Library*, 6th series, 7, 38–53

——(1990) *Patterns and Trends in British Publishing 1800–1919*, Occasional Papers Series, Bibliographical Society, London

Hagen, June Steffenson (1979) *Tennyson and his Publishers*, Macmillan, London

Hodges, Sheila (1978) *Gollancz: The Story of a Publishing House 1928–1978*, Gollancz, London

Kelly, Thomas (1977) *A History of Public Libraries in Great Britain 1845–1975*, Library Association, London

Lloyd Jones, L. (1985) 'Fifty Years of Penguin Books'. In *Fifty Penguin Years*, Penguin, Harmondsworth, pp. 11–101

Montgomery Hyde, H. (1964) *A History of Pornography*, Heinemann, London
Sutherland, John (1987) 'The Book Trade Crash of 1826', *The Library*, 6th series, 9, 148–61
Unwin, Philip (1972) *The Publishing Unwins*, Heinemann, London

64

BRITISH PERIODICALS AND READING PUBLICS

JON KLANCHER

Cultural critics and historians have lately become fascinated with what until only a few years ago was still regarded as a mere backdrop to literary creation. Now we are hearing that British periodicals were crucial to the making of modern culture – to the development of the reading audiences, public languages, gender constructs, class discourses and disciplinary formations of eighteenth- and nineteenth-century England (Shevelow, 1989; Schoenfield, 1990; Klancher, 1987; Eagleton, 1984; Hohendahl, 1982; Mulhern, 1979). Some theorists of criticism are finding its history inseparable from the rise of literary criticism and its later withdrawal from public life. Once criticism moved out of the periodicals and into the universities, Terry Eagleton has argued (1984, p. 110), it effectively 'committed suicide' by abjuring the great 'public sphere' fashioned by periodical writers and readers since the moment of Addison and Steele. Doubts about the ordinariness of 'ordinary' language have led such critics to begin reading the periodicals as complex texts and active discursive contexts. Empirical and statistical methodologies have given way to interpretive and ideological inquiries spurred by new-historicist, Marxist, feminist and post-structuralist reading strategies. Once considered a simple given of cultural history, the idea of a unified 'reading public' has also been put into doubt. The new work has been showing diverse reading audiences that were as much constructed by their texts as they were defined by social structure and historical change. The abstract notion of the 'reader-in-the-text' has also been challenged as new understandings of English periodicals and audiences have helped generate fresh empirical researches that are redrawing the maps of English cultural transmission since 1688.

Both familiar and previously uncharted periodical writings are central to this project. The *Spectator, Tatler, Rambler, Gentleman's Magazine, Edinburgh Review, Quarterly Review, London Magazine, New Monthly Magazine, Blackwood's, Athenaeum, Fraser's Magazine, Chambers' Journal, Cornhill, Nineteenth Century, National Review* and *Scrutiny* are familiar enough to students of literature, but they are no longer being read within the limiting category of 'English literary periodicals'. They now share attention with journals like *The Black Dwarf, The Republican, The Gorgon,* Cobbett's *Political Register, The Athenian Mercury, The Penny Magazine, The Hive, The Mirror of Literature and Instruction, The Friend* and others that were crucial to the making of female, radical, mass and other subcultural readerships who often contested the dominant voices of 'literary' culture. 'Cultural production', not literary 'creation', forms the enabling category of the new scholarship, and it is clear that this is not an isolated development within literary study. It coincides with a more general shift towards revaluing the place of 'culture' in regard to politics, social structure and economics, visible in the disciplines of anthropology, sociology and historiography. In the complex French revolution debate among historians, for instance, the 'revisionist' challenge to the classical Marxist account of the revolution has increasingly been mounted on the cultural grounds of publishing history, the periodical press, and the reconstruction of historical readerships in eighteenth-century France (Allen, 1987; Censer and Popkin, 1987; Roche and Darnton, 1989). Few Marxist historians have yet responded to the complications this turn towards historical reading has created for historical materialism. Yet Marxist and cultural-materialist questions have often guided the new work on periodicals and historical reading (Eagleton, 1984; Klancher, 1987; Hohendahl, 1982; Mulhern, 1979). Whatever its outcome, the French revolution debate has implications for the study of British literary and political culture yet to be explored, and it suggests that the new work in British periodicals and reading publics converges on questions of history and culture well beyond the pale of a 'periodical literature' as traditionally conceived.

EARLIER WORK: THE CULTURAL CRITICS AND THE MODERNIZERS

Most work on periodicals and publics has been empirical and descriptive while keeping silent about its critical, ideological or theoretical principles. Yet it has played a crucial if unheralded role in situating literary and critical discourses among the institutions of British culture. From Alexandre Beljame's *Le public et les hommes de lettres en Angleterre au dix-huitième siècle* (1881) to Walter Graham's *English Literary Periodicals* (1930), literary historians documented the journals and audiences as part of a general literary culture focused on the 'man-of-letters'. But the assumptions behind this scholarship were not exposed to scrutiny before Q. D. Leavis sketched her polemic against *Fiction and the Reading Public* (1932). Here she performed an 'anthropological' reading of English cultural history, a compelling narrative of cultural crisis and decline which called for an organized research programme to investigate the social bearings of English print culture – its magazines, broadsides, popular fiction and reading audiences. All this was meant to bolster the Leavisite case for the embattled 'cultural minority' seeking militantly to preserve cultural standards in the midst of mass-cultural decay. Her key point was to claim that, during the reign of the man-of-letters in the nineteenth century, artists and critical intellectuals had shifted subtly but crucially from the dominant to the dominated sector of the bourgeois class: 'the people with power no longer represent intellectual authority and culture' (p. 191). This argument teased out a basic but unstated faith of the earlier scholars – a belief that social power and cultural power were the same, negotiated in a spiritual evolution of the English mind that suffused the realm of 'general literariness' displayed in the periodicals and reviews ('The periodical literature of the English people contains a living record of their esthetic and intellectual progress'; Graham, 1930, p. 4). The Leavises would cast a withering eye on the crass print products of the English middle and lower-middle classes; as Francis Mulhern points out, the *Scrutiny* group was only too aware of its own lower-middle-class origins (1979, p. 320). But despite their distaste for modern popular culture, the Leavisite cultural critics committed themselves to reading it rather than taking refuge in Graham's 'literary periodical' as a mark of class distinction.

Q. D. Leavis's ambition for a vast programme of cultural-historical research yielded few results. (Among the best were Richard Hoggart's *The Uses of Literacy*, 1957, and R. K. Webb's *The British Working Class Reader*, 1955, both on the left of the Leavisite camp.) Virtually the orthodoxy of English studies by 1958, Leavisism did produce the panoramic, integrative Penguin *Guide to English Literature*, where chapters on the great poets and novelists shared space with chapters on the 'The Reviews and Magazines' and 'The Victorian Reading Public' (Ford, 1958). Here R. G. Cox updated his earlier *Scrutiny* essay ('The Great Reviews'), where he had marked the romantic quarterly reviews as the last great moment of the British intelligentsia: 'They consistently refused to pretend that excellence was "common and abundant", and with their extraordinary influence and authority, they played the major part in creating for the writers of their age that informed, intelligent and critical public without which no literature can survive for very long, and which is so conspicuously lacking today' (Cox, [1937] 1968, p. 271). To this trope of Leavisite gloom, Cox added in 1958 a polemic against the Victorian utilitarians whose huckstering of 'cheap' reading matter and 'useful knowledge' both hastened the collapse of authoritative cultural values and prepared for the vast consciousness industry of the twentieth century.

Against this now institutionally inscribed reading of English cultural history, Raymond Williams's *The Long Revolution* (1961) came as something of a jar, with its neither-Leavis-nor-Marx prognosis of a difficult, conflicted emergence of a democratic culture founded in the access of all social classes to the realm of writing and reading. *The Long Revolution* is a crucial precursor to current cultural historiography, but its larger impact is hard to fathom without under-standing the American side of cultural-historical politics. For nothing could remind one less of Leavis's spirited polemic or Cox's dour élitism than a book like Richard Altick's *The English Common Reader 1800–1900* (1957), a landmark study of cultural history that remains a key reference for nineteenth-century literary history. Contemporary with the Penguin *Guide*, Altick's study aimed to show 'a revolutionary concept: that of the democracy of print' (1957, p. 1). This work is hardly, by current standards, informed by 'theory', but it none the less proceeds on a theory of cultural history – namely that what Altick often calls 'the reading habit' is the essence of a democratizing and moderniz-ing society. Thus the enthusiasm Altick shows for the sudden rise in quantitat-ive reading capacity – at the beginning and end of the eighteenth century, or during the Second World War (p. 366). While Beljame and Graham seemed to write from the country gentleman's house, and Q. D. Leavis from the urban flat, Altick seems to have written from the developing suburb. Obstacles to universal cultural literacy appeared to him mainly technical: 'If the audience for books and relatively serious periodicals remains dishearteningly small, it is because people still have not been sufficiently schooled to value and use good literature and because facilities for distribution still are inadequate' (1957, p. 374). The prickly ideological accents of the *Scrutiny* group vanished into Altick's enthusiastic post-war American embrace of an English cultural history 'beyond ideology'.

What Altick helped sponsor might be understood as a literary-history version of the 'modernization' scholarship then gaining a wide readership among the historians and social scientists who opposed both cultural conservatives and political radicals after the Second World War. In England the Leavises had tried to pre-empt the advance of managerial 'social-scientific' culture with their notions of 'community' and rigid cultural 'standards' (Mulhern, 1979, p. 313). But Altick and his successors read English popular writing with neither the Leavisite contempt for cultural decline nor the disabling notion of a purely 'literary' periodical that limited the earlier literary historians. Altick democratically included mass-cultural and politically radical writings in his broad survey, and thus enabled a whole field of new scholarship – the Victorian periodical and its reading publics – to come into focus. Hence the emergence of valuable reference works like the *Wellesley Index to Victorian Periodicals* (1974–87), a host of useful empirical studies, and the journal *Victorian Period-icals Review* (1968–). But the new American scholarship often failed to place its detailed studies of periodicals and publics in a compelling cultural context; strictly 'literary' critics mostly ignored it. For the *Scrutiny* critics, the view of English literature as culturally salvational required the critic to see periodicals and popular reading as a framework of cultural possibility and disappointment. But Americans tended to read their popular cultural history – Altick's democracy of print presented as a threshold of opportunity – separately from their literary meditations on subjective isolation and literary self-reference. This is why the study of periodicals and publics among the 'modernizers' has taken turns unthinkable to serious criticism, like the claim by one proponent that England's *Penny Magazine* opened important paths to human possibility, provided we think of such possibility on the scale normally attributed to Woolworth's:

> It was the commercial good judgment and daring of Charles Knight and the S[society for the] D[diffusion of] U[seful] K[knowledge], and of the other publishers who followed their example, that brought about this permanent change in the character and quality of British life.... I suspect that the emergence of mass markets should stand alongside the emergence of class-consciousness in our estimation of the new, most socially potent forces of the period.... Too often we have taken conflict and its resolution to be the sole substance of history. Mass markets develop through consensus not conflict.
>
> (Bennett, 1982, pp. 251–2)

When Bennett speaks blithely of 'the fundamental commitment to freedom in the mass reading market', he unintentionally reveals the conundrum of the 'modernization' argument. Celebrating 'the democracy of print' without a concept of ideology finally means ratifying commodity fetishism as the unspoken historical mode of the 'reading habit'. The modernizers opened new fields of cultural history with their rigorous empiricism – particularly the complex realm of Victorian reading and writing – but the cost of their achievement was to deepen the rift between an American formalist criticism of literary texts, conducted in an abstractly 'critical' mode, and a historical-sociological study of cultural history that abjured its critical function. However conservative or backward-looking the Leavisite project may now seem, it made the considerable effort to hold together those two realms as a unified if inwardly-conflicted project of cultural critique.

NEW WORK: CULTURAL PRODUCTION AND ITS CONSEQUENCES

Aspects of the Leavisite and the modernizing arguments reappeared in Raymond Williams's *The Long Revolution* (1961), but they were now arranged in the form of a historical triptych – the democratic, industrial and cultural revolutions of the last three centuries – that would later lead Williams to formulate the method of 'cultural materialism' (Williams, 1977). This theoretical framework – which has had a major impact on Renaissance cultural studies – revises classical Marxist theories of the 'superstructure' by drawing pragmatically upon the strengths of the earlier British and American cultural sociologies as well as semiotics. From 1961 to the 1980s, Williams's evolving conception of 'cultural production' came to embrace a range of forceful critical and theoretical positions while tying them to canons of empirical research and historical plausibility. While his own work added little to empirical knowledge of periodicals and reading publics, his enormously subtle synthesis of otherwise disparate realms of cultural production and reception has encouraged others to investigate and theorize those spheres of English cultural history blocked by Leavisites and modernizers alike. The 'consumptionist' cultural history of the modernizers has been an especially tempting path for scholars who resist notions of ideology or cultural production. But what strikingly distinguishes the new investigations of 'cultural production' is their fleshing out of Marx's argument that 'not only the object of consumption but also the manner of consumption is produced by [cultural] production . . . consumption is created by production not only objectively but also subjectively. . . . Production thus produces not only an object for the subject but also a subject for the object' (Marx, [1859] 1973, pp. 25–6). Drawing on Marxist, feminist and semiotic strategies, the new work on periodicals and publics has been asking how readers were produced for texts in history, how readers often resisted their representations, and what these dialogic tensions mean for literary, social and intellectual history.

Theory: from 'reader' to 'audience'

The new work has emerged amidst a conceptual crisis in the formalist category of the 'reader' of a literary text. The rise of 'reader-response' or 'reception' theory in the 1970s was a way of admitting that the interpretation of an isolated literary text had always depended on a tacitly 'ideal' reader protected from historical contingency and ideological pressure. And once made explicit, the 'implied' or 'ideal' reader of reader-response theory soon revealed his complicity in a hidden bargain: the significance being attributed to the 'response' of the reader 'in' the text was in fact being tacitly attributed to the institutional audience of literary critics who assented to such a reading 'of' the text. This contradiction was most entertainingly exposed by the American pragmatist argument of Stanley Fish, who cannily argued in *Is There a Text in this Class?* (1981) that every reading (and every ideal reader) is collectively determined by the 'interpretive community' to which the academic interpreter belongs. This key move from 'reader' to 'audience' had far-reaching implications that Fish curtailed, however, by insisting that professional socialization decisively separates academic readers from all other kinds. Hence any 'history' of collective reading would be limited to an internal institutional story around such problems as successive paradigms for interpreting *Paradise Lost* (Fish, 1986). From the viewpoint of cultural production, however, academic reading cannot be taken as a given from which to begin, but only as a mode of reading historically produced. This is why more recent work has tried to explain the making of reading audiences in history, particularly the 'middle-class', female, radical, and mass reading publics whose mutual pressures finally contributed to forming the institutional audience of academic interpreters itself.

The shift from 'reader' to 'audience' has theoretical consequences. What we call an 'audience' cannot simply be a generalized 'reader in the text' (as reception theory has had it), or a cultural inference made from the class anatomy of society (as one reading of Marx would imply), or an aggregate of empirical individuals to be identified and described (as the modernizers hoped). Rather it is a historically fluid, constructive category that was partly projected by its makers as a *concept*, partly formed by the language and textual contours of the periodical as an interpretive and ideological *field*, partly fleshed out by a combination of real social groupings as a *social formation*, and partly created as a *representation* in the texts of other audiences being formed at the same time. In other words, the 'audience in history' cannot be understood exclusively as either a purely textual, social-structural, statistical, or conceptual entity. Rather the 'audience' must be grasped from these diverse angles of view taken together. This also means that any effort to understand the audience of a single text (say, a poem, novel or non-fiction work) will fail unless it can refer to a wider scene of social reading developed by an array of interdependent yet often contradictory cultural practices.

Such ideological criticism may risk telling us that readers in history were wholly determined by what they read. While it rejects the American post-structuralist notion that readers make meanings as they please, it needs to take seriously the idea that 'reading in history' often entails *resistance* to the text, the friction between readers and texts that has now become an intensive area of research among French historians trying to understand the dynamics of pre-revolutionary culture in the *ancien régime* (Censer and Popkin, 1987; Roche and Darnton, 1989). This is a notoriously difficult kind of resistance to measure or interpret. But it is perhaps the crux of the questions we ask of historical reading, the question Baudelaire posed by confronting his 'hypocrite lecteur' and Coleridge asked in his struggles with modern print culture. 'Reader-response' theory had conceived a reader perfectly adequate to the text, but it is really by being consciously 'inadequate' to texts that readers have 'misread' and resisted the forms of cultural production by what deconstruction calls 'reading against the grain'. Such reading forms the dialectical pole of audience-making, and it compels us to avoid equating an account of cultural production with the illusion that we have thereby grasped the whole historical process at once. There are significant blanks in historical memory here. These cannot be filled by hoping to uncover a cache of historical documents telling us how this or that reader responded to particular texts (the method of Robert Darnton, 1984). Nor will it emerge if we extend the chain of individual 'reader-response' studies far enough down the historical path (the hope of some French historians; Allen, 1987, p. 275). However locally useful such studies would be, they do not offer a framework for comprehending how readers and writers have struggled over texts and, equally crucial, how readers have struggled among themselves over texts as the contentious, mutually-defining audiences of cultural history.

This is why something like the 'field' approach of Pierre Bourdieu's cultural sociology seems necessary to map out the interlocking spheres of cultural production and reception (Bourdieu, 1984). The French 'taste' cultures he reconstructs obey a 'logic of the cultural field' whereby one culture (or, in our terms, 'audience') exercises its own choices only by way of excluding or surpassing another's. Everyone operates as though he or she 'prefers' what the logical structure of the field in fact dictates, transforming 'necessity into choice' (pp. 99–168). If Bourdieu relies too deterministically upon experiential 'habit' – and too little on active cultural production – to explain the origin of these cultural choices, his method still underscores the degree to which cultural producers aim precisely to create and instil those cultural habits, particularly various forms of the 'reading habit', that will in turn give the cultural field its aura of spontaneous choice and its resistance to fundamental political and intellectual change. The cultural debates of 'middle-class' English men-of-letters, particularly from Dunton and Addison to Coleridge and Arnold, highlighted the complexities of producing the 'reading habit' that, above all, were being formed and negotiated in the British periodicals (Klancher, 1987).

Practices: literature and the periodicals

The designation 'periodical literature' emerged in the nineteenth century as a way to distinguish the local, social, transitory discursive contexts of cultural discussion from the properly and lastingly 'literary'. As Terry Eagleton has reminded us, weaning 'literature' proper from the interdiscursive realm of a 'periodical literature' was a lengthy, complicated affair. In *The Function of Criticism: From 'The Spectator' to Poststructuralism* (1984), Eagleton has adapted Jürgen Habermas's theory of an eighteenth-century 'public sphere' to the history of English criticism as it developed from the coffee-house periodicalists to the first professionals of the MLA (Habermas, 1982). Eagleton shares the view of Habermas and Peter Hohendahl that English literary and social criticism – inextricably mingled in the periodicals of Addison, Steele, Dunton or Edward Cave – originated in the bourgeois struggle against absolutism and crafted a 'public sphere' where the 'democracy' of enlightened discourse contradicted the actual social hierarchy to which its participants belonged (Hohendahl, 1982). 'The sphere of cultural discourse and the realm of social power are closely related but not homologous: the former cuts across the latter and suspends the distinctions of the latter, deconstructing and reconstituting it in a new form, temporarily transposing its "vertical" gradations on to a "horizontal" plane' (Eagleton, 1984, p. 10). This concept then serves Eagleton to plot the vicissitudes of subsequent English critical history – invaded by commodity values in the later eighteenth century, riven by party politics in the romantic age, marked off from social discourses in the nineteenth century, and finally separated from 'periodical literature' by migrating to the great universities. Plausible and polemical, Eagleton's account raises the history of periodicals and publics to a theoretical and critical level where it can be seriously pursued and debated; the contrast with the consensus-seeking work of the modernization scholars could not be more stark. But it also relies on the older cultural histories for information that makes too narrow a case for the function of periodical writing and English audiences, too simplified a view of a 'public sphere' (Klancher, 1987, pp. 18–26). The new research is providing detailed, complex readings of the public journals and an amplified sense of the 'contexts' in which English critical, literary and social discourses were carved out.

Gender and audience

The separation of male and female reading now appears to have been the earliest conflict articulated in the English public sphere. Journals like John Dunton's *Athenian Mercury* (1691–8) and Richard Steele's *Tatler* (1711–12) made the periodical what Kathryn Shevelow calls an 'early site for the production of subjectivity and its construction according to gender' (Shevelow, 1989, p. 192). Her *Women and Print Culture: The Construction of Femininity in the Early Periodical* shows us how the periodicals constructed what Shevelow, following Eagleton, calls a 'feminization of discourse' whereby ' "feminine values" increasingly assigned to the private realm were emerging as influences upon public culture' (1989, p. 4). She also makes us see how the traditionally explicit hierarchy of masculine and feminine was re-mapped in the earliest English journals so that a female audience appeared 'equal' yet 'separate', 'different in kind rather than degree from men'. This argument implies at least a revision of the Habermas/Eagleton view of the eighteenth-century 'public sphere' as a discourse among 'equals' in print. For if women appeared as 'equals' of men in the periodical public sphere, they were also essentialized as 'feminine' without differences, a seamless gendered subject (p. 197). Here women writers and readers encountered one another as cultural signs – 'the feminine' – an event Shevelow calls the making of a 'new, limiting feminine norm' that would specifically rule out the contesting of patriarchy practised outside the periodicals by Aphra Behn, Mary Wortley Montagu and Mary Wollstonecraft (p. 17). In short, the periodicals' 'feminine' language displaced the political writer's 'feminist' discourse. Shevelow's view also challenges the modernizing argument – often repeated among contemporary feminist writers themselves – that the periodicals' print culture opened paths of opportunity for female participation in culture and eventually for feminist and anti-patriarchal discourse as such. Rather, she argues persuasively, the eighteenth-century periodicals that 'were enabling, even actively promoting, women's participation in print culture were also those engaged in containing it' (p. 1).

The limiting and finally disciplinary 'feminine' discourse elaborated in the eighteenth-century periodical depended on a powerful act of making the female subject 'in her own words'. In one of the best studies of a single periodical yet written, Shevelow shows how the *Athenian Mercury* invited women to express themselves in published letters, 'speaking for themselves' in order to become the topic of discourse for others. The result was a complex interplay between the 'cultural authority granted the autobiographical subject to represent herself' – real and assertive enough – and the countervailing authority of the *Athenian Mercury*'s editors to subsume these self-representations in a larger ideological programme. Here Shevelow reproduces a striking visual image the *Athenian Mercury* used to represent its own audience as communal yet hierarchical. This woodcut portrays three tiers of cultural transmission: the 'Athenian Society' seated above a larger group of 'respectably dressed' readers and letter-writers, who in turn stand above a still larger 'crowd' beyond the pale of the 'middle-class audience'. A number of the crowd seem to be engaging in acts of violence, but as Shevelow points out, others are potential periodical correspondents, reaching expectantly toward the sites of cultural authority above. Women appear in both groups, yet only those whom the journal incorporates as correspondents or readers will embody the 'feminine', while others will remain scarred with the marks of class difference that do not allow one to speak or be heard.

Critics like Shevelow are also challenging widespread notions about reading that were predicated upon narrow conceptions of literary history. Hans Robert Jauss, for instance, once proposed influentially that literary history could be understood as changes in the 'horizon of expectations' that each audience brought to the production of new literary works (Jauss, 1982). This effort to historicize literary reception depends on a pseudo-historical premiss, namely the capacity of the individual reader to distinguish 'convention' from 'innovation'; as V. N. Volosinov objected to the Russian formalist version of this idea ('defamiliarization'), such an individual psychological distinction cannot be generalized sociologically or historically (Volosinov, [1926] 1973). But Shevelow – whose work shows the usefulness of reader-response strategies in local textual analysis – demonstrates a more complex, social sense of the female audience she reconstructs by rewriting Jauss's 'horizon of expectations' as what she calls a 'cultural consensus about the realm of the possible' (Shevelow,

1989, p. 96). Hardly a projection by the isolated self, that consensus had to be built on the kind of intra-textual as well as political and social pressures the periodicals existed to modulate and reconcile.

Class, consciousness, and audience

As with gender, the idea of 'class' in cultural history is being rethought in the new work on periodicals and audiences as well as on the novel. As an explanatory historical idea, the 'middle-class reading public' served Ian Watt's account of *The Rise of the Novel* (1957) and many other cultural histories, but like the 'English common reader' or the 'mass audience', the 'middle-class public' has been an unexplained and unverified category that admits important yet tacit ideological premises. The English periodicals arose to construct, differentiate and develop reading audiences large and small, publics that did not simply already exist passively waiting for something to read. Readers of Addison's *Spectator* did not know how to be 'middle class' without Addison showing them how. Yet nothing so firm as 'middle-class consciousness' jelled anywhere in the eighteenth century because the very category was then being struggled out in what Michael McKeon persuasively calls a conflict between the older status orientation and a new, challenging idea of class orientation being pitted against it (McKeon, 1987, p. 164). It was an intensely anxious 'status instability' that forged, over a century-and-a-half of cultural contention, the class-conscious categories familiar to the nineteenth century. Even in the nineteenth century, however, the 'middle-class' readers of *Blackwood's*, the *New Monthly* and the *London* magazines or the *Edinburgh* and *Quarterly* reviews had to learn their complex sense of social belonging by means of the pressure exerted on them by other audiences then being formed. One of those publics – the artisan and later working-class 'radical' readership first studied by R. K. Webb and E. P. Thompson – was constructed, from 1791 to the 1840s, to identify class-consciousness with audience-belonging (Webb, 1955; Thompson, 1963; Klancher, 1987). But for the so-called 'middle-class public', notions of 'class' and 'audience' gave rise to conflicting forms of collective awareness. Reading the periodicals, this audience learned to operate the interpretative strategies through which it could 'read' a social world, a symbolic universe, a textual field, in order to discover its own purpose within them. In the pages of its public journals, such an audience read the social order as a symbolically instructive text. Thus the 'middle-class' public could often edge away from any declared class identity of its own, standing apart from the order of social classes to the extent it could textualize it (Klancher, 1987, pp. 51–68). Hence, even when something like a 'middle-class consciousness' could be asserted in the English nineteenth century, it always had to define itself according to what it was not, classifying others to evade being classified itself.

As I have argued in *The Making of English Reading Audiences 1790–1832* (1987), the new awareness of social class in the nineteenth century had to be negotiated through the page-by-page manoeuvres of the periodicals that both divided audiences and represented them to one another. It was in this most confusing moment of cultural and social change that romantic writers, particularly Wordsworth, Coleridge, Shelley and Hazlitt, forged the strategies that would distinguish literary and critical authority against the pressures of the self-consciously 'middle-class', radical and nascent 'mass' audiences then being formed in the journals. Such audiences were *strategically* crucial inasmuch as their disparate ways of reading and their conflicting social locations compelled a cultural theorist like Coleridge to try to master them by concocting the most ambitious programme of cultural transmission and control in the nineteenth century. Through Coleridge's engagement with the periodical audiences and their reading protocols, we begin to see how the mastery of symbolic interpretation – later to be carried out institutionally by a professionalized 'clerisy' of literary critics – could forge a special audience whose 'readings' would adjudicate and try to contain all other modes of social and textual reading that jarred and divided the English social realm. Something like this long-range view is necessary to see how our own politics of reading is connected to the formation of shared, public reading acts that, often through the labours of periodical production and reception, constitute a major part of Anglo-American cultural history. Yet many of these connections still remain to be made.

FURTHER READING

Altick, Richard D. (1957) *The English Common Reader: A Social History of the Mass Reading Public 1800–1900*, University of Chicago Press, Chicago

Eagleton, Terry (1984) *The Function of Criticism: From 'The Spectator' to Poststructuralism*, New Left Books, London

Hohendahl, Peter (1982) *The Institution of Criticism*, Cornell University Press, Ithaca

Klancher, Jon P. (1987) *The Making of English Reading Audiences, 1790–1832*, University of Wisconsin Press, Madison

Leavis, Q. D. (1932) *Fiction and the Reading Public*, Chatto & Windus, London

Mulhern, Francis (1979) *The Moment of 'Scrutiny'*, New Left Books, London

Rawson, C. J. (ed.) (1986) 'Literary Periodicals', a special issue of *Yearbook of English Studies*, 16, 1–366

Schoenfield, Mark (1990) 'Voices Together: Hazlitt, Lamb, and the Periodicals', *Studies in Romanticism*, 29

Shevelow, Kathryn (1989) *Women and Print Culture: The Construction of Femininity in the Early Periodical*, Routledge, New York

Webb, R. K. (1955) *The British Working Class Reader 1790–1848*, Columbia University Press, New York

Williams, Raymond (1967) *The Long Revolution*, Harper & Row, New York [first published 1961]

Wolff, Michael and Shattock, Joanne (eds) (1982) *The Victorian Periodical Press: Samplings and Soundings*, Leicester University Press, Leicester

ADDITIONAL WORKS CITED

Allen, James Smith (1987) 'Toward a History of Reading in Modern France, 1800–1940', *French Historical Studies*, 15, 263–86

Bennett, Scott (1982) 'Revolutions in Thought: Serial Publication and the Mass Market for Reading'. In Michael Wolff and Joanne Shattock (eds), *The Victorian Periodical Press: Samplings and Soundings*, Leicester University Press, Leicester

Bourdieu, Pierre (1984) *Distinction: A Social Critique of the Judgment of Taste*, translated by Richard Nice, Harvard University Press, Cambridge

Censer, Jack, and Popkin, Jeremy (eds) (1987) *Press and Politics in Pre-Revolutionary France*, University of California Press, Berkeley

Cox, R. G. (1968) 'The Great Reviews'. In F. R. Leavis (ed.), *A Selection from 'Scrutiny'*, vol. 2, Cambridge University Press, Cambridge, pp. 247–71 [essay first published 1937]

Darnton, Robert (1984) *The Great Cat Massacre, and Other Essays in Cultural History*, Basic Books, New York

Fish, Stanley (1981) *Is There a Text in this Class? The Authority of Interpretive Communities*, Harvard University Press, Cambridge

——(1986) 'Transmuting the Lump: *Paradise Lost*, 1942–1982'. In Gary Saul Morson (ed.), *Literature and History*, Stanford University Press, Stanford

Ford, Boris (ed.) (1958) *The Pelican Guide to English Literature*, vol. 6, Penguin, Harmondsworth

Graham, Walter (1930) *English Literary Periodicals*, Heinemann, London

Habermas, Jürgen (1982) *Strukturwandel der Offentlichkeit*, Luchterhand, Darmstadt [first published 1962]

Jauss, Hans R. (1982) *Toward an Aesthetics of Reception*, University of Minnesota Press, Minneapolis

McKeon, Michael (1987) *The Origins of the English Novel 1600–1740*, Johns Hopkins University Press, Baltimore

Marx, Karl (1973) 'Introduction', *The Grundrisse*, translated by Martin Nicolaus, Vintage, New York [written 1859, first published 1939–41]

Roche, Daniel and Darnton, Robert (eds) (1989) *Revolutions in Print*, University of California Press, Berkeley

Thompson, E. P. (1963) *The Making of the English Working Class*, Gollancz, London

Volosinov, V. N. (1973) *Marxism and the Philosophy of Language*, translated by V. I. Titunek, Humanities Press, New York [first published 1926]

Webb, R. K. (1955) *The British Working Class Reader 1790–1848: Literary and Social Tensions*, Allen & Unwin, London

Williams, Raymond (1977) *Marxism and Literature*, Oxford University Press, New York

65

LIBRARIES AND THE READING PUBLIC

LIONEL MADDEN

Throughout their history libraries have been guardians of literature and promoters of literary study. Inevitably, though, until comparatively recently, the low level of literacy ensured that their influence was confined to a very small part of the population. The following account concentrates on the British scene and traces the development of literary provision according to the type and level of readership various groups of libraries were intended to serve.

NATIONAL LIBRARIES

Although the idea of a national collection had often been mooted, it was not until 1753 that Britain achieved a national library. In that year Parliament agreed to purchase the collection of books, manuscripts and objects of interest amassed by Sir Hans Sloane. To this was added the rich collection of literary and historical material built up by Sir Robert Cotton in the seventeenth century, the manuscript collections of the Harley family, and the Old Royal Library founded by Edward IV in 1471. The books and manuscripts acquired from these sources became the basis of the British Museum Library which opened its doors to the public in 1759.

Although the library was ostensibly intended for the use of the whole nation it was, in fact, in the eighteenth century available only to those with leisure and means. As with other libraries of its period, the lack of artificial lighting inevitably meant that it was open for limited hours during the day. The cumbersome administrative procedures for gaining admission and using the materials placed additional barriers in the way of widespread use by the public.

The early years of the nineteenth century saw a steady increase in the readership of the British Museum Library, but use was hampered by unsatisfactory accommodation, inadequate catalogues and the ineffective operation of the legal deposit law. Improvements in all these areas of the library's operations were due primarily to the efforts of Antonio Panizzi, who became Keeper of

Printed Books in 1837 and Principal Librarian in 1856. Panizzi worked hard to enforce the legal entitlement of the library to a copy of each new book published in Britain. Something of his success during the 1850s may be seen in the fact that between 1851 and 1858 the number of books acquired under legal deposit legislation rose from 9,871 to 19,578. Panizzi also laboured to produce an effective catalogue of the printed book collections and to provide adequate accommodation for readers and books. The latter efforts culminated in the magnificent circular reading-room and its surrounding stacks; the former were to bear fruit after Panizzi's death in the published *General Catalogue of Printed Books*, the first edition of which appeared between 1881 and 1900.

The first half of the twentieth century was inevitably a period of considerable disturbance for the British Museum Library as it sought to guard its treasures under the onslaught of two world wars. In the Second World War the library suffered significant damage and loss to its printed book and newspaper collections. The first part of the century was also notable for the creation of two new national libraries in Britain, the National Library of Wales in 1907 and the National Library of Scotland in 1925, the latter being based on the much older library of the Faculty of Advocates founded in 1680.

During the period since 1945 there has been a radical revaluation of the roles and functions of national libraries throughout the world. In addition to being major repositories of materials, national libraries are increasingly seen as also having a central role in the library service of the country. This change has been reflected in the transformation of the British Museum Library into part of the British Library, which was created in 1973. Although the custodial role remains important, the British Library has assumed a key role in the development of bibliographical, lending and research activities.

ACADEMIC LIBRARIES

The earliest British academic libraries were in Oxford and Cambridge. From the beginning the universities were organized as loose federations of colleges rather than as monolithic institutions and, while the colleges established their own libraries, the idea of a central university collection grew more slowly. The opening of the Bodleian Library in Oxford in 1603 and the steady if slow growth of the Cambridge University Library throughout the seventeenth century indicated their emergence as significant forces within the universities.

While Oxford and Cambridge remained the only English universities, Scotland had founded university institutions at St Andrews, Glasgow and Aberdeen in the fifteenth century and Edinburgh in the sixteenth century, all with their own libraries, while in Ireland Trinity College Dublin was founded in 1592. By 1700 the total provision of academic libraries in Britain comprised these institutions plus a few dissenting academies for Nonconformists who were not eligible for admission to the English universities. In 1709 all the universities became beneficiaries of the Copyright Act which gave them the right to receive on request one free copy of each book published in Britain. This privilege has remained with the Bodleian, Cambridge University Library and Trinity College Dublin until the present day, but was surrendered by the Scottish universities in 1837 in return for an annual payment in compensation.

By modern standards the university libraries were small until the mid-nineteenth century. As late as 1849 the Bodleian had a book stock of 220,000 volumes, while in 1837–8 Edinburgh University Library had a stock of 63,000 volumes. During the late nineteenth and early twentieth centuries, however, the libraries increased significantly in size. By 1882 the stock of the Bodleian had risen to 400,000 volumes and by 1912 it was approaching one million volumes.

While the stock of the existing academic libraries was increasing, new institutions were being founded in a development which was to change the whole face of academic library operations in Britain. The first of the new foundations was University College London in 1826 followed by King's College three years later, the University of London receiving its charter in 1836. Another collegiate university, Durham, was founded in 1832, but most other nineteenth-century foundations were civic colleges which were to receive their charters as independent universities in the twentieth century. Many of these institutions had a hard struggle to survive and their libraries often had a very precarious existence during their early years. They generally had small stocks built up largely by gift rather than by planned purchase. Where they acquired purpose-built accommodation it was usually due to a local benefactor. The libraries were run by small staffs. The first full-time librarian of Liverpool University was appointed as late as 1892. By 1916 the staff of that library was the librarian, two senior assistants and one junior assistant in the main library, with four department librarians and one library assistant acting as a class librarian.

The creation of the University Grants Committee in 1919 did much to improve the status of libraries in the universities. In its first annual report in 1921, the Committee stated unequivocally:

> The character and efficiency of a university may be gauged by its treatment of its central organ – the library. We regard the fullest provision for library mainten-ance as the primary and most vital need in the equipment of a university.

Slowly but surely standards improved. Between 1920 and 1939 library expendi-ture per student more than doubled in many university libraries. Average library expenditure per student rose from 2.2 per cent of total university expenditure in 1913–14 to 3.3 per cent in 1925–6, reaching 3.9 per cent in 1937–8 and 4.5 per cent in 1976–7.

With the granting of independent university status to Hull in 1954 and Leicester in 1957 the development of civic universities which began in the nineteenth century may be said to have come to an end. The 1960s saw the creation of a group of new universities and the elevation to university status of several colleges of advanced technology. The corresponding rise of the polytechnics and colleges of higher education, many of which incorporated the older colleges of education, led to a considerable proliferation of state and local authority funded library provision at all levels of academic study.

SUBSCRIPTION LIBRARIES

By the eighteenth century a number of factors had combined to increase the demand for libraries. The considerable growth in literacy, the increase in the number and range of books available, the development of the periodical and newspaper press, the emergence of the novel as a popular literary form, and the high price of books all encouraged the growth of libraries to serve the non-academic reader both in London and in the major provincial towns. The existing 'public' libraries – the cathedral and the endowed town and parish libraries – were often heavily theological in character and failed to satisfy the growing appetite for secular literature.

In this situation, one simple way of increasing one's access to literature was through the creation of a book club. Book clubs were essentially small societies of friends or neighbours who subscribed to a common fund from which books or magazines were purchased and circulated among the members of the club. A book club usually had a membership of between twelve and twenty-four people. When the books had been circulated among all the members they were commonly auctioned among them.

Although book clubs represented a form of co-operative acquisition, the lack of any intention to create a stock of books makes it difficult to regard them as libraries. The idea of people pooling their resources to buy books did, however, find an alternative expression in the subscription libraries which, starting with the Leadhills Library in Lanarkshire in 1741, spread widely throughout Britain during the eighteenth and early nineteenth centuries.

The subscription library, like the book club, was based on the idea of co-operative purchase of books from a fund derived from an entrance fee and annual subscriptions paid by members. In some of the subscription libraries members on joining purchased a share in the institution. These are often referred to as 'proprietary' libraries. The emphasis of the subscription libraries was usually on 'polite' literature – history, biography, travel, science and quality fiction. Books were usually chosen by a committee elected at a general meeting of the members.

By the mid-nineteenth century subscription libraries were well established in the provincial cities and smaller market towns. Some of them had amassed considerable collections. By mid-century Liverpool had some 36,000 volumes, Hull had 21,000 and Manchester had 20,000. Most libraries, however, were considerably smaller than this with perhaps 5–6,000 volumes. The libraries' clientele seems commonly to have been drawn from the gentry, the clergy, professional men, manufacturers and well-to-do tradespeople (Kelly, 1966, p. 204). Because they aimed to provide serious works they were sometimes recognized as valuable for scholars and were prepared to make special provision for scholarly visitors, even when they were not subscribers.

In the later nineteenth and throughout the twentieth century subscription libraries came under increasing pressure due to competition from circulating and rate-supported libraries and from financial problems caused by declining membership and increasing costs. Although some outstanding examples survive, most notably the London Library, the majority have now disappeared.

CIRCULATING LIBRARIES

Unlike subscription libraries, which were founded and administered out of funds paid by members, circulating libraries were commercial ventures launched by individuals for financial profit. The practice of lending books for a charge appears to have begun in the late seventeenth century and was at first adopted as a natural extension of business by some booksellers. Throughout the eighteenth century circulating libraries became widespread in the larger provincial towns and in spas and watering-places. According to the *Monthly Magazine* in 1801, there were at least 1,000 circulating libraries in Britain, including twenty-six in London.

Although it is impossible to say what proportion of the stock of circulating libraries in the eighteenth century and early nineteenth century would be devoted to fiction, it is probably no accident that the rise of the libraries coincided with the establishment of the novel as a popular literary form. Subscription libraries, seeking to establish a stock of permanent value, would naturally be reluctant to fill their shelves with large numbers of probably ephemeral novels. Circulating libraries had no such ambitions, but acquired books purely for purposes of loan and might be content to acquire a novel which would be read heavily for a short time and then discarded. The rapid development of both kinds of institution in the late eighteenth and throughout the nineteenth century is linked to the growth of a literate middle class which included significant numbers of people for whom reading provided an important means of instruction and recreation.

Most circulating libraries appear to have operated a subscription system, though the actual cost of subscriptions varied quite widely. In London towards the end of the eighteenth century subscriptions were often sixteen shillings a year, though by this time some of the London libraries were experimenting with a system of classes of subscription where readers paid a higher rate for the privilege of speedy access to recent publications or for the right to borrow several books at one time. In the spa towns, naturally, there were seasonal subscriptions and even charges by the week. Some libraries also operated a delivery service to readers within easy distance of the library and also to country readers.

From the 1820s publishers increasingly adopted the habit of producing novels in three volumes at a standard price of one-and-a-half guineas. This artificially high price served to confirm the importance of the circulating libraries as the primary source of fiction for most readers. Of the libraries which benefited from the predominance of the three-decker, none was more successful than Mudie's Select Library. Begun by Charles Edward Mudie in 1842 as a lending library operating from a London stationer's shop, Mudie's enjoyed unparalleled success which culminated in the opening of a magnificent purpose-built library in New Oxford Street in 1860.

Several features of Mudie's organization help to account for his success. He charged an annual subscription of one guinea, considerably lower than other London circulating libraries of the period. His library was a 'select' library, a collection which included the widest possible range of subjects and which deliberately excluded books which were morally unacceptable, thus encouraging family subscriptions. The library acted as a means of publicity for authors and publishers through its regular and extensively placed advertisements of 'the principal new and choice books in circulation'. Since Mudie acquired new books quickly and, where necessary, in very large quantities, subscribers could be assured of ready access to new publications.

At the height of its success in the second half of the nineteenth century, Mudie's operated a prosperous business organized in four divisions. Readers in London paid personal visits or sent their servants to Mudie's or received their orders by local delivery. Country subscribers ordered by post and received books through the book boxes which were sent to all parts of Britain as well as overseas. Surplus stock was regularly sold at reduced prices in the bookselling division. Mudie's also had a bookbinding division which undertook fine binding and decorated books for prizes and presents, repaired worn volumes and stitched the thousands of catalogues and prospectuses which were issued to assist existing readers and attract new subscribers.

The only major rival to Mudie's was the circulating library inaugurated by W. H. Smith in 1860, which operated through the network of railway stations. W. H. Smith had been providing bookstalls on railway stations from 1848. The idea of setting up a parallel system of lending libraries operating from the same stalls offered several advantages. Provincial subscribers incurred no postage charges. Travellers could borrow a book at one station and return it at another at the end of their journey. The local libraries on the stations were served from a central office in London which was responsible for the acquisition of stock and its circulation between the individual libraries. Printed catalogues allowed readers to order books which were delivered to their local station free of charge. Like Mudie, Smith was governed by strong moral convictions. Both men saw their role as the supply of wholesome books.

The sudden abandonment of the three-decker novel in 1894, although partly engineered by Mudie's, had a severe effect on the library, though it continued in business until 1937. W. H. Smith moved out of the railway stations in 1905 and established lending libraries in shops, as did Boots the chemists, whose 'Boots Booklovers Library' began in 1899. The establishment of these and also of more exclusive circulating libraries, notably the Times Book Club in 1905 and Harrod's Library in 1914, suggests that circulating libraries were doing well. In fact, for much of the twentieth century it appears that Smiths and Boots were running their library departments at a loss and could only justify them commercially on the grounds that they attracted customers to the shops and so stimulated sales of other goods.

Although the Second World War brought increased use of circulating libraries, demand subsequently fell away and by the 1960s the larger libraries were closing their doors. Their demise was attributable to the increased number of cheap books on the market, the improvement in the services and facilities offered by the rate-supported public libraries, and the development of other forms of recreation.

MECHANICS' INSTITUTE LIBRARIES

The libraries so far discussed were inevitably concerned mainly to serve readers of comfortable financial means. From time to time, however, attempts were also made to establish libraries for those of lower social and economic position. Most of the early examples were endowed parochial or town libraries. Kelly (1966, pp. 68–9) estimates that between the Reformation and the end of the eighteenth century more than 200 endowed libraries are known to have been established in England alone.

The majority of the early endowed libraries were heavily theological in character, often containing a high proportion of Latin books, and would primarily be of use to the clergy. In the eighteenth century the proportion of English-language books increased and there was a widening of the scope of the libraries, making them more accessible to the non-clerical educated readers, limited though their number would necessarily be.

The growing need for skilled workers who possessed elementary scientific knowledge and the development of popular education for the poorer sections of the community led, in the early nineteenth century, to the formation of mechanics' institutes. The origin of the institutes is usually traced to George Birkbeck's Glasgow Mechanics' Class of 1800, though the first institutes proper were not founded until the 1820s. Although often founded and assisted financially by well-to-do philanthropists, the early mechanics' institutes encouraged aspiring working men who saw knowledge as the key to skill and personal advancement at work, intellectual enjoyment and political power. Many institutes were run by their subscribing members; others were administered by a mixture of members and patrons.

There is considerable disagreement about the nature of the membership of the mechanics' institutes. There is evidence that, despite their best attempts, they did not long succeed in attempts to attract the working man. Altick (1957, pp. 191–2) paints a depressing picture of mechanics swiftly being replaced by business and professional men and their families. Kelly (1957, p. 244), however, is less gloomy, arguing that, although it is clear from the evidence that the institutes failed, after the first few years, to attract significant numbers of unskilled manual workers, they did continue to attract skilled workers.

From the beginning, the majority of mechanics' institutes aspired to have libraries, and for many the library was the focal point of their activity. At first the libraries concentrated on scientific textbooks. Under pressure from their patrons and supporters, they often excluded fiction and recreational reading, as they also excluded works of political and religious controversy, subjects forbidden in mechanics' institutes generally. Gradually, as the institutes changed direction, so the libraries changed with them. Fiction, travel and general literature provided an increasing part of the stock. A good institute library would usually have a lending stock and a reference collection of books and periodicals. It would also have a reading-room. From the 1840s most institutes also provided a newspaper reading-room or converted their reference room into a newsroom. The library stock was usually quite small, though some of the leading institutes succeeded in creating more extensive collections. By 1851, for example, Liverpool had a stock of 15,300 volumes and Manchester had 13,000, but these were exceptional. Too often the stock contained a high proportion of unsuitable gifts which lay unwanted and unused on the shelves.

Although mechanics' institutes were the most important, they were not the only bodies seeking to offer library provision to the working classes in the nineteenth century. Some rural communities had village libraries. Factory libraries, often sponsored by benevolent employers, became increasingly common towards the middle of the century. Many communities had mutual improvement societies formed by working men and most of these had small libraries. There were working-class subscription libraries, though these were never numerous. There was a considerable variety of libraries linked with religious groups, ranging from the parochial libraries to the Nonconformist libraries established by local congregations for their own use. There were also the politically radical societies such as the Hampden Clubs and the Co-operative, Owenite and Chartist societies, many of which had their own libraries and reading-rooms.

Describing the situation in the years preceding the creation of the rate-supported public library system, Kelly (1966) states:

> The simple fact is that at a time when there was a great and increasing public demand for books, and when there was no public library service, almost every political, economic, religious, social and educational group regarded it as a duty to make some library provision for its members. The resulting libraries were often pitiably inadequate, but the universality of such provision is an impressive fact.

(p. 228)

RATE-SUPPORTED PUBLIC LIBRARIES

Despite their weaknesses, mechanics' institutes and other libraries designed to serve poorer readers did at least stimulate the demand for books and highlight the need for more widespread library provision. They also demonstrated clearly that, if books were to be made freely available, libraries would have to be financed on a regular basis by local or central government.

It was this realization that lay at the heart of the movement to establish rate-supported public libraries. The passing of the Public Libraries Act in 1850 was only achieved after more than a decade of committed effort, notably by two socially conscious members of Parliament, Joseph Brotherton and William Ewart.

In 1845 Parliament passed the Museums Act which empowered councils of boroughs with a minimum population of 10,000 to levy a halfpenny rate in order to establish a museum. Three towns – Canterbury, Warrington and Salford – used the Act to establish combined museums and libraries. In 1849 the House of Commons set up a Select Committee, with Ewart as chairman, to examine the possibility of publicly funded libraries. A key witness before the committee was Edward Edwards, then a junior member of staff of the British Museum Library, whose paper comparing the provision of free public libraries in Britain with Europe and the United States had come to Ewart's notice in 1848.

Despite predictable opposition, the recommendations of the Select Committee bore fruit in the passing of the Public Libraries Act of 1850, which was amended by subsequent Acts of 1855 and 1866. By the end of the process, town or parish councils had the power to establish a public library which would be financed by the levy of a rate of up to a maximum of one penny.

The evidence suggests that the early public libraries were founded predominantly by well-intentioned business and professional people. Inevitably, the aims of the founders were mixed. The desire to offer an alternative resort to the public house, the wish to improve reading tastes, religious conviction, and the belief that public libraries would help to promote the education of the masses – these and other motives no doubt lay behind the efforts of the founders. The process of philanthropy, of course, was not without its drawbacks and could result in unsuitable stock and uncomprehending attitudes to the needs of poorer readers. In the absence of a profession of librarianship, the early libraries were too often inappropriately staffed. The foundation of the Library Association in 1877 marked the existence of a growing professional group and established a platform for future development.

The idea of a public library service took time to root itself. By 1856 only 125 authorities in Britain had established a service, but by 1918 the figure had increased to 602 authorities, with only two towns of 50,000 population lacking a library service. In the development of services the benefactions of Andrew Carnegie, the self-made American millionaire of Scottish origin, played a significant part. He offered money for buildings where the local council would provide a site and levy a penny rate. When Carnegie died in 1919 no less than 380 separate library buildings in the United Kingdom were associated with his name. Other benefactors, too, contributed to the development of libraries, often by the provision of buildings.

From the beginning public libraries regularly aimed to develop a reference library, a reading-room and a lending library. It was in the lending libraries that the greatest changes took place. From the 1890s the system of closed access, where readers had to request books from a service counter, gradually gave way to the principle of open access where readers could examine and select their books personally. The corollary of this was, of course, the need to classify and shelve books according to some comprehensible system. The Dewey Decimal Classification, which first appeared in 1876, quickly established itself as the favourite scheme for public libraries, a position which it has occupied ever since.

The system of closed access, while it lasted, necessitated the production of large numbers of printed catalogues. A significant number of these were deposited in the British Museum Library. Their potential value as a guide to the stock of public libraries during the late nineteenth and early twentieth centuries is indicated by a small investigation carried out by Simon Eliot (1986) into holdings of selected authors of fiction.

In 1913 the Carnegie United Kingdom Trust commissioned from Professor W. G. S. Adams a *Report on Library Provision and Policy*. In his report Adams estimated that 79 per cent of the urban population of Britain and Ireland had access to a public library while the corresponding figure for the rural population was only 2.4 per cent. Not surprisingly, he recommended that the Trustees should promote rural services. The experiments sponsored by the Trustees were facilitated by the Public Libraries Act of 1919 which permitted county councils to establish library services. The 'box of books era' (Munford, 1951, p. 118), characterized by the delivery of boxes of adult and junior books from a makeshift headquarters to rural centres such as schools and village halls, was gradually superseded by the development of better headquarters accommodation, increased stock, and the provision of full-time or part-time branches in the more populated areas and mobile libraries in the rural areas of the counties.

As the Second World War ended and public libraries approached the close of their first century of existence they could congratulate themselves on almost complete coverage of Britain. Nevertheless, as the McColvin Report of 1942 clearly showed, there was a great need for improved standards of service nationally. McColvin's call for larger administrative units to replace the numerous small library authorities was not to be answered until the reorganizations of local government which were to take place thirty years later. Just as significant as his recommendations, however, was McColvin's attitude to the role and significance of the public library. His philosophy of the public library as a source of enrichment and enlightenment offered equally to all sections of the community showed how far public libraries had moved from the early assumption that they were primarily designed for the underprivileged working class. Despite some opposition from those who believe that public libraries should concentrate on the needs of specific users, the story of public libraries in the twentieth century has been of an attempt to provide service to all sections of the community by offering a combination of generalist lending and reference stocks and more specialist services for particular needs and interests.

PRESENT AND FUTURE TRENDS

Two events of the 1970s have had an overwhelming influence on British libraries. The first was the reorganization of local government which established much larger units of administration for the public library service. Unfortunately, the benefits produced by this reorganization have been largely offset by subsequent cuts in public library spending. In the same way, the development of existing university libraries and the creation of libraries to meet the needs of the new universities, polytechnics and colleges which marked the 1960s and 1970s has been counterbalanced by government financial policies of the 1980s.

The second event of the 1970s which had a major influence on library development was the creation of the British Library in 1973. The centralization of national reference, lending and bibliographical services which resulted from this has had repercussions on libraries at all levels. Such a development can, of course, be beneficial only if the national library is funded to allow the concept of service to flourish.

Few would claim that the immediate future looks bright for libraries which serve scholars and students in the humanities or those readers whose interests are less formally academic. The realities of inadequate stocks, the declining purchasing power of budgets, diminishing staffs and the ever-present threat of charging for services are plain to see. Yet, if the reading and study of literature has anything valuable to contribute to individuals and society, libraries must continue to have an essential role to play in ensuring the collection, dissemination and preservation of literary materials.

FURTHER READING

Altick, Richard D. (1957) *The English Common Reader: A Social History of the Mass Reading Public 1800–1900*, University of Chicago Press, Chicago

Eliot, Simon (1986) 'Public Libraries and Popular Authors, 1883–1912', *The Library*, 6th series, 8, 322–50

Griest, Guinevere L. (1970) *Mudie's Circulating Library and the Victorian Novel*, Indiana University Press, Bloomington

Irwin, Raymond (1964) *The Heritage of the English Library*, Allen & Unwin, London

——(1966) *The English Library: Sources and History*, Allen & Unwin, London

Kaufman, Paul (1960) *Libraries and Their Users: Collected Papers in Library History*, Library Association, London

Kelly, Thomas (1966) *Early Public Libraries: A History of Public Libraries in Great Britain Before 1850*, Library Association, London

——(1977) *A History of Public Libraries in Great Britain 1845–1975*, 2nd edn, Library Association, London

Miller, Edward (1973) *That Noble Cabinet: A History of the British Museum*, Deutsch, London

Murison, W. J. (1971) *The Public Library: Its Origins, Purpose and Significance*, 2nd edn, Harrap, London

Thompson, James (ed.) (1980) *University Library History: An International Review*, Bingley, London

Whiteman, Philip (1986) *Public Libraries Since 1945: The Impact of the McColvin Report*, Bingley, London

ADDITIONAL WORKS CITED

Kelly, Thomas (1957) *George Birbeck: Pioneer of Adult Education*, Liverpool University Press, Liverpool

McColvin, Lionel (1942) *The Public Library System of Great Britain: A Report on its Present Condition with Proposals for Post-War Reorganization*, Library Association, London

Munford, William Arthur (1951) *Penny Rate: Aspects of British Public Library History 1850–1950*, Library Association, London

66

CENSORSHIP

ANNABEL PATTERSON

Literary censorship is both a centuries-old phenomenon and a fact of contemporary life, distinguishing the more or less liberal political and cultural systems of the modern world from relatively or extremely repressive ones. As a concept, censorship has broadened as it aged. The direct control over the bodies of writers exercised by men with sovereign power, like the banishment of Ovid by Augustus, or the physical mutilation by Elizabeth I and Charles I of England of some of their more troublesome writers, mutated into modern states such as the pre-*glasnost* Soviet Union, South Africa or Argentina, where writers literally disappear, though their books, paradoxically, may continue to circulate. Nobody who reads this essay within a year or two of the death sentence issued against Salman Rushdie by the Ayatollah Khomeini can fail to realize how fragile are the boundaries between that seemingly archaic and alien violence and the 'liberal' conventions of the West. Here, we assume, the operations of censorship are deflected from the author to his work (which may be seized, banned, burned, mutilated, emasculated or merely subjected to 'cosmetic surgery') and dispersed through legal and bureaucratic machinery. Libel law has increasingly shown its subtle power to inhibit journalism, the commercial and even the academic press. The concept of literary censorship has had to be extended to other media than books, with film, television, musical recordings, comics, calendars and even T-shirts becoming matter for regulation and theoretical discussion. In the India Press Act of 1910, for instance, there arose the issue of whether dhotis (long loincloths) which were stamped with patriotic poems could be considered printed matter (Barrier, 1974, p. 56). In the struggle between Israel and the Palestinians, even the colours of the Palestinian flag, when they appear in clothing or children's play, are proscribed. And we are gradually beginning to realize the role that public officials (such as customs officers), private citizens' groups or other lobbyists, and even corporations may have in controlling the public's access to thoughts and opinions, words and images.

While the chief categories of censorship still appear to be political, religious, and moral (the latter referring primarily to sexual morality), its mechanisms, motives and consequences have economic components. In 1885, for instance, George Moore complained against the practice of Mudie's Circulating Library of selecting its novels on the basis of a readership defined as young, unmarried girls and thereby controlling what fiction might enter the market (Moore, 1885). Naturally, censorship can make a book a financial success, as witness *The Satanic Verses*. Very much earlier in the history of book marketing, Sir John Hayward's *History of Henry IV*, published and suppressed at the turn of the sixteenth century, was an improbable best-seller that profited from the struggle between Elizabeth I and the Earl of Essex for control over the popular imagination. But the economics of publication has itself a political dimension, and censorship has consistently been more intolerant of cheap editions intended to reach a large audience than of specialized texts designed for an élite few. When the Book Censorship Abolition League was formed in Melbourne in 1934, one of the first questions asked was why were only *cheap* editions of Apuleius' *The Golden Ass* and Boccaccio banned? In 1857 the prosecutor of Baudelaire complained that *Les Fleurs du Mal* was not intended for connoisseurs, but for anyone who could pay two francs (Thody, 1968, p. 8); and the same concern emerged during the court case concerning *Lady Chatterley's Lover* in 1959, where Penguin Books' pricing at three shillings and sixpence was perceived as part of the challenge to received values. (There is also a story, perhaps apocryphal, of a member of the House of Lords complaining, apparently in jest, that while his daughter might read the book if she pleased, he had the strongest objection to his gamekeeper reading it – Craig, 1962, p. 169.) The paternalistic implications of this policy are manifest; less obvious is their connection with what has been seen as a great victory for liberals, the admission of the principle of 'literary value' as a defence against the charge of obscenity, and the provision for the opinion of 'experts' in these matters. If scholars alone have access to otherwise banned books, how urgently will they protest against the ban itself? And how does the provision for restricted access square with the right to educational equality and freedom of information?

Although the costs that writers and artists must face to a greater or lesser degree whenever they challenge the *status quo* remain largely objective, the voluntarist concept of freedom of thought and expression has subtly admitted qualification in terms of different kinds of self-censorship. As Anatoly Kunetsov points out, in the West self-censorship is simply self-discipline, 'but in the Soviet Union it is an ugly and unavoidable form of self-torment' (1973, p. 26). Czeslaw Milosz, who was awarded the Nobel Prize in 1980 while in elective exile in California and while all his works were still banned in his native Poland, has written in *The Captive Mind* (1951) of what he calls *Ketman*, the Eastern art of keeping silent about one's true convictions, and achieving thereby a secret conquest over one's adversary (see Milosz, 1962). But in today's Eastern Europe, he suggests, *Ketman* has acquired a whole series of nuances. There are, for instance, the various escapisms of aesthetic purity, self-justifying professionalism or metaphysical otherworldliness. Conversely, Nadine Gordimer, considering the predicament of the writer in South Africa, writes of another, equally insidious pressure exerted on the writer by political censorship:

> That other, paradoxically wider, composite freedom – the freedom of his private view of life – may be threatened by the very awareness of *what is expected of him*. And often what is expected of him is conformity to an orthodoxy of opposition.
>
> (1984, p. 135)

And Mario Vargas Llosa gives this predicament a sharply realist turn by pointing out that in Argentina, Chile and Uruguay academic departments of sociology have been closed indefinitely, thus creating a vacuum in the field of social analysis that literature has felt obliged to fill (1984, p. 163).

Censorship and its opposition has acquired its own vocabulary, technology, *causes célèbres*, tragedies, ironies and jokes – in effect, its own literature. Among its most famous victims we find: the historian Cremutius Cordus, tried in the Roman senate for an 'oblique' attack on Tiberius in his *Annals*; Galileo, a more imaginative scientist than his society could endure; William Prynne, brutally punished by the English Star Chamber in the early seventeenth century for, ironically, having published a massive attack on the English theatre; Madame de Staël, who became obnoxious to Napoleon; Franz Kafka, who died unrecognized in 1924, whose works were proscribed in Poland during the Nazi regime, and only began to be published there in 1956; Alexander Solzhenitsyn, who survived to describe the infamous Soviet Gulag of the 1950s; and Salman Rushdie, whose *Satanic Verses* challenged modern Muslim fundamentalism, and who suddenly found himself at the eye of a hurricane in international relations. Among the most notable champions of freedom of expression, whose own publications on the issue have themselves become 'texts' in the literature of censorship, were Bacon, Milton, Montesquieu, Voltaire, Chesterfield, and John Stuart Mill, whose *On Liberty* (1859), along with Milton's *Areopagitica* (1644), is almost invariably cited by subsequent polemicists. Among the *causes célèbres* over which the battles of political censorship have been fought at a theoretical level are Prynne's *Histriomastix* (1633), where the questions of authorial intention were central, and Etienne Leroux's *Magersfontein, O Magersfontein!*, a brilliant satirical work whose ban produced such conflict between the South African government and the literary establishment that in 1978 the Publications Act was emended to favour the concept of literary worth.

In the field of moral censorship, the milestones are Flaubert's *Madame Bovary* (1857), Lawrence's *Lady Chatterley's Lover* (1928), and Henry Miller's

Tropic of Cancer, published in Paris in 1934, but fought through the United States, jurisdiction by jurisdiction, between 1961 and 1965 in 60 separate legal proceedings (Hutchison, 1968). But undoubtedly the most censored book, and the one that renders the principles of censorship finally inscrutable, is Joyce's *Ulysses*. Published initially by Sylvia Beach in Paris in 1922, it was banned in England on the grounds of obscenity, and a large consignment of copies was burned under the Customs Act of 1867. In the United States, a seizure which took place in 1934 under Section 305 of the Tariff Act was ruled invalid in the famous opinions of Judge Woolsey (in the District Court) and Judge Augustus Hand (in the Court of Appeals). The grounds thereby established, and later developed in *Roth* v. *United States* in 1957, where the conviction of a distributor of pornographic magazines was upheld, and in 1959 in the case of the Postmaster-General against *Lady Chatterley's Lover*, where the judge ruled that the novel's distribution through the mail must not be interfered with, were that a work of literary merit is not obscene under the law merely because it contains explicit descriptions of sex or the sexually-orientated 'four-letter words', that parts of the text are not to be read in isolation from the whole, and that the author's intentions are to be considered. But elsewhere the fate of *Ulysses* has not hung on the definition of obscenity alone. In Australia, *Ulysses* was one of 5,000 books banned during the Depression, in response, it has been suggested, to a politics of fear, and the collapse under economic pressure of an ideal of an isolated, undefiled homogeneous society free from exploitation (Murray-Smith, 1970, pp. 79ff.). Originally banned there in 1929, *Ulysses* was released into circulation in 1937, and rebanned in 1941. It was banned in the Soviet Union, in company with Proust, as unacceptably modernist, that is to say, not socially-conscious enough, and in Nazi Germany in the bizarre company of other works whose protagonists were Jews, including Byron's *Hebrew Melodies*, Shakespeare's *The Merchant of Venice* and Marlowe's *The Jew of Malta*.

If *Ulysses* is one of the symbolic names in the history of literary censorship, others are more procedural. Both the specialized discourse of censorship and its mechanisms, for instance, are involved in *samizdat*, or unofficial, manual publishing, one of the most important forms of resistance to censorship (and to *Ketman*) in Eastern Europe. As the Czech writer Jan Vladislav points out, 'All You Need is a Typewriter', paper and carbon paper, and, even in a system where the Western conveniences of photocopying are inaccessible, you can turn out eight to ten copies of a proscribed manuscript for private distribution (1984, pp. 43–51). *Glasnost*, or cultural freedom of expression, appeared long before Gorbachev's reforms as an ideal recommended by the Soviet intellectual Aleksandr Nikitenko during his tenure as censor for the tsars in the middle of the nineteenth century (Nikitenko, trans. 1975). Its opposite is *glavlit*. Under *glavlit*, those who do not have the energies for *samizdat* may fall back on 'desk-drawer publishing' (whose opposite is the Western computerized desk-top publishing) – the act of self-silencing that consists in writing only for oneself – or conversely on Aesopian writing, the disguising of one's arguments by metaphor, fantasy, or other forms of oblique communication.

Aesopian writing links the modern history of publishing with ancient Greece, and the tradition that 'Aesop' was a hunchbacked slave of the sixth century BC, whose wit and wisdom earned him emancipation, but whose animal fables spoke to a world of terrifyingly unequal power relations. As Hegel remarked in his *Aesthetics*, the fabulist deals in animal metaphors because he 'does not dare to recite his doctrines openly but can only make them understood hidden as it were in a riddle which at the same time is always being solved' (trans. 1975, vol. 1, p. 387). Other terms also speak to the half-light of ambiguity in which censorship also inevitably operates. From eighteenth-century France comes the *permission tacite*, still useful theoretically, but then specific to a dispensation granted by the Chancellor, or a magistrate who possessed the confidence of the king, to print and sell 'partly-forbidden' works. A sign of the incoherence, arbitrariness and hypocrisy of a censorship riddled with political bias and undermined by greed, *permission tacite* flourished particularly under Malesherbes, Director of the Book Trade, who saw it as a secret weapon of tolerance (Bachman, 1934). From France also comes the concept of *l'homme moyen sensuel*, or the person of normal sexual interests, a standard invoked in evaluating cases of alleged obscenity as a reasonable (but imprecise) alternative to either prurience or virgin innocence. (It is worth noting, however, that post-Victorian societies have transferred the concept of an innocent community in need of protection from unmarried girls to children not yet in their teens.) In the opposite direction, French censorship law in 1881 established the concept of *l'outrage aux bonnes moeurs*, an impossibly vague and catholic standard for the unacceptable under which were prosecuted, both in 1857, Flaubert for *Madame Bovary* and Baudelaire for *Les Fleurs du Mal*, though Flaubert was acquitted and the verdict against Baudelaire quickly annulled (Thody, 1968, pp. 14–15). The emphasis on 'bonnes moeurs' or public standards has been typical of obscenity cases world-wide, however, and has only gradually, and not universally, given place to the recognition that such community standards are not absolute but relative, that community pressures can be extremely localized, that the climate of public opinion can change (in both directions), and that public officials (like the Postmaster-General who was put in his place in the 1959 decision in favour of *Lady Chatterley's Lover*) may be far from representative of the society for whom they claim to speak. In Russia under Nicholas 1 and in modern Australia and South Africa it has been assumed by the government that 'young' countries needed paternalistic protection from 'advanced' ideas, especially of sexual morality, that were free to circulate in Europe. The subjective aspect of all obscenity charges is probably best defined by Shelley Winters, on the subject of stage nudity: 'I think it is disgusting, shameful and damaging to all things American; but if I were twenty-two, with a great body, it would be artistic, tasteful, patriotic, and a progressive religious experience' (see Tasker, 1970, p. 37).

From the United States, the theory of censorship has acquired a set of concepts derived from the Constitution and the First Amendment, especially the notion of 'clear and present danger' to the state as the standard for invoking a political censorship; and the constitutional framework of censorship debates, with the revolutionary history behind them, has resulted in a more liberal publishing climate than in the United Kingdom. But it was also the United States that gave us the term 'Comstockery', after the nineteenth-century legislation generated by Anthony Comstock, the nadir of a fanatical moralism enforced through the Post Office; and it was also American politics of the early 1950s that permitted the development of McCarthyism, with its devastating effects on the careers of playwrights, actors and intellectuals who could be blacklisted for 'unAmerican' activities or sympathies.

Literary censorship, then, is ancient in origin, global in scope, and self-recapitulating in practice, preventing our holding any simple notions of progress. In medieval China, the rulers of the Sung Dynasty insisted on their own monopoly in the compilation and distribution of certain categories of works, including literary classics (as part of the state examination system). Almanacs and astronomical charts were controlled, both because the Chinese emperor, 'as a mediator between heaven and earth, regarded calculating the seasons and predicting fortunes as his sacred prerogative', and because it was assumed that prognosticatory texts would be used for seditious purposes (Chan, 1983, pp. 4–5). This assumption was shared by the authorities in medieval and early modern England, and explains how Spenser's *Shepheardes Calender* (1579) and Dryden's *Annus Mirabilis* (1667) operate on the hinge between temporal markers and their interpretation, the former exploiting the calendar's populist dimensions, the latter attempting to neutralize the political opposition's threatening readings of the Year of Wonders. But censorship's concern with the calendar is not restricted to supposedly more superstitious cultures. The chairman of the South African Publications Appeal Board describes a 1985 ruling on a 'Grassroots' calendar, overturning a previous ban on such productions for 'highlighting of days on which violent struggles [of black South Africans] had taken place', and replacing it with a more pragmatic judgement. While distinguishing between calls for renewed violence and a symbolic act of 'historical dedication', and while admitting that the Black community's wish to commemorate its own heroes has its own legitimacy, he observed also the 'well known fact that calendars tend to pass from notice and become part of the wall on which they are pasted. Their constant presence tends to cause them to fade from view' (Van Rooyen, 1987, p. 111). In this revealing instance, modern censorship admits its most ancient and insoluble predicament: that controls against freedom of expression are as likely to increase resistance as to weaken it, and to increase the value of works that if disregarded by the authorities would become insignificant to their audience also. 'Genius chastised grows in authority': a motto created by Tacitus out of his experience as historian under Domitian, and of Tiberius and Nero; repeated by Sir Francis Bacon, in the context of Elizabeth I's struggles with Puritan pamphleteers; and given classical status in the literature of censorship by Milton in *Areopagitica*, as he faced the irony that the English revolution of the mid-seventeenth century had merely reinstated licensing, or pre-publication censorship.

In the second half of the seventeenth century the emperor Ch'ien-Lung ordered a massive compilation of Chinese literary manuscripts, which were to be turned in from private collections to the imperial library, ostensibly for their preservation. The consequence, however, was a national censorship – that is to say, destruction of what was disapproved – on the grand scale. His motives appear primarily to have been to protect his dynasty against sedition; but the exercise may have got out of hand. Knowledge of one of the richest periods in Chinese literature, 1550 to 1750, was thereby irretrievably fragmented (Goodrich, 1935; Guy, 1987). But the damage done to seventeenth-century culture was arguably no worse than that achieved in the 1960s by the Cultural Revolution. In late nineteenth-century Russia under the tsars there was a gradual relaxation of government censorship, especially as nationalistic isolationism gave way to a more receptive attitude to European culture; but, as one commentator put it, 'incongruously, in the wake of the Revolution of November 7, 1917, the status of foreign writing in Russia gradually became reminiscent of what it had been in medieval Muskovy' (Friedberg, 1977, p. 3).

Sometimes a regime or a system will turn (or return) to censorship or its intensification when it feels vulnerable, as with the Roman Catholic Church's development of the *Index Librorum Prohibitorum* in the mid-sixteenth century (in response to the threat of the Reformation), wartime censorship of press and radio, the excessive response of the Bruce-Page government in Australia to the Depression, or the huge repressive machinery erected by the South African government to deal with its black population. As Van Rooyen put it, 'In times of war or a similar situation the law does not change, but those interests protected by the law may be regarded as being more vulnerable than usual and the likely reader as being more impressionable' (1987, p. 106). The result is not only the 4,000 books on South Africa's banned list noted in 1960 (Hepple, 1960, p. 38), but also the reintroduction of pre-censorship, along with direr emergency powers, under the Public Safety Act of 1986. The question of how political strength relates to toleration is, however, extraordinarily difficult to specify. A government's anxiety not to seem repressive frequently results in inconsistency; conversely, its anxiety not to seem weak can produce the sporadic, arbitrary penalty or cruelty, for ritual or exemplary purposes.

In England, the lapsing of licensing of the press in 1695, and its replacement by post-publication prosecution under the common law, is generally seen as a liberal advance. Yet in 1737 the Stage Licensing Act was hurried through Parliament by Robert Walpole and his supporters, and despite Lord Chesterfield's famous speech in the House of Lords – another classic text in the discourse of censorship. The motive for the Act was narrowly political – that the government was unusually harried by Henry Fielding's political satires performed in the Haymarket Theatre – though it waited for a play, *The Golden Rump*, that could plausibly be charged with obscenity. Under the Act, only two theatres in London were legally permitted to put on plays (a situation recapitulating that in Jacobean London, when it was the court that wished to control the theatre by way of monopoly and patronage). So ill-conceived was the legislation that both the Lord Chamberlain and theatre managers were forced (and able) to work around the law; as in the Elizabethan and Jacobean theatre, speeches were added after licensing and even during performance; *de facto* toleration prevailed (Conolly, 1976). But at the same time, both theatre managers and audiences exerted their own controls, so that during the Jacobite rebellion of 1745, for instance, the theatres became staunch supporters of the government, while an equally well-managed avoidance of politics marked the period of reaction in Britain that followed the French revolution (Conolly, 1976, p. 107). It is much to the point that the Stage Licensing Act was not repealed until 1968, and then only as a result of a private member's bill; the point being that at any stage a supposedly advanced democracy may find itself in political circumstances that seem to require intervention, even in media supposedly only for entertainment.

It is worth dwelling on the theatre as a special problem in the history and theory of censorship, since it crystallizes the issue of literature's *efficacy*, understood in the broadest sense, both on its immediate audience and ultimately on cultural history. From antiquity, the theatre has been recognized as the potential site of a political criticism conducted by a group, rather than a lone intellectual; and theatre censorship has over time been far more frequently political, whereas moral censorship, whose age of dominance was the nineteenth century, has focused more on poems or novels that are likely to work their seductive effects on the reader in private. While one might see an exception in the campaign against the stage waged by Puritan reformers in England from the time of Shakespeare to the Civil War, when the theatres were legally closed, even this phenomenon evinces a politics in reverse; for Puritan anti-theatrical prejudice was evidently supported by an economic critique of the Stuart court, and a class-conscious definition of decadence and social uselessness.

The surprising acquiescence of English writers in the pre-censorship of their theatre has been attributed to crowd psychology, to fears of a connection between intense group experience and social unruliness (Conolly, 1976, pp. 172ff.). The riots caused in Paris by the suppression of *Le Mariage de Figaro* in 1783 or in Poland in 1968 by the closure of Mickiewicz's classic play *Forefathers' Eve*, might seem to support a different argument, that theatre serves as a safety valve at times of social tension. But whereas some contemporary theorists have argued only a negative relationship between mass psychology, the forms of entertainment, and social good, and Adorno castigated Brecht and Sartre for their belief that theatre could change the world for the better (Adorno, 1987, pp. 300–18), for hundreds of years the legends of theatre censorship have themselves supported that belief. When Chesterfield fought the Stage Licensing Act in 1737, he cited an anecdote from republican Rome in support of a complex claim: that theatre has a significant ameliorative function in society, that this function is a product of the audience's ability to interpret a play in the light of their own immediate concerns, that the playtext itself (or its author's intentions) is only partly the cause of its effects, that the theatre is therefore incapable of effective censorship by licensing, and that good governments will rather use it as medium for the discovery of popular opinion:

> The great Pompey . . . had certainly a good Title to the Esteem of the People of Rome; yet that great Man, by some Error in his Conduct, became an Object of general Dislike; and therefore, in the Representation of an Old Play, when Diphilus the Actor, came to repeat these Words, *Nostra Miseria tu es Magnus*, the Audience immediately applied them to Pompey: who, instead of resenting it as an Injury, was so wise as to take it for a just Reproof: He examined his Conduct, he altered his Measures, he regained by degrees the Esteem of the People, and then he neither feared the Wit, nor felt the Satyr of the Stage.
>
> (Chesterfield, [1737] 1962, p. 323)

And, he continued:

> It was not the Poet that wrote, for it was an old Play, nor the Players that acted, for they only repeated the Words of the Play; it was the People who pointed the Satyr; and the Case will always be the same: When a Man has the Misfortune to incur the hatred or Contempt of the People, when Public Measures are despised, the Audience will apply what never was, what could not be designed as a Satyr on the present Times.
>
> (p. 324)

While there are elements of utopian wishful thinking in Chesterfield's theory, it can be calibrated both with historical evidence of how the theatre has been treated by censorship – as a social force that required especial delicacy of handling – and with its more or less complete displacement *as* a social force by the cinema and television, where the unpredictable aspect of the theatrical experience is controlled in the first instance by the replacement of live actors by fixed images (not to mention the more complicated effects of massive commercialization) and in the second by domestication, bringing the theatre home. Before these technological developments, even the most arbitrary rulers interested themselves in playtexts in advance of performance. In 1638 Charles I read the manuscript of Philip Massinger's *The King and the Subject* and wrote in the margin of one passage that referred to forced taxation, 'This is too insolent, and to be changed'. When James Sheridan Knowle's *Virginius; or, The Liberation of Rome* was produced unlicensed in Glasgow in 1820, with an exceptionally long two-week run, and then submitted for licensing by Covent Garden, the *Morning Herald* published a rumour that the playtext had been summoned 'for inspection in a high quarter', presumably George IV, and returned with erasures (Conolly, 1976, pp. 109–10). Tsar Nicholas I himself personally censored some of the most important nineteenth-century writers, especially Pushkin; Nikitenko reported seeing the manuscript of *Boris Godunov* full of gaps; but in 1836 he recorded the performance of Gogol's comedy *The Inspector General*, in terms that support Chesterfield's thesis:

> It is performed constantly – almost every other day. The emperor attended the first performance, applauded and laughed a great deal ... The emperor even ordered his ministers to see *The Inspector General*. ... Many people feel that the government should not approve a play in which it is so harshly censured. I saw Gogol yesterday. He wears the expression of a great man tormented by wounded pride. Gogol, however, has really performed a great service. The impression produced by his comedy adds substantially to what we are coming to realize about the existing order of things in our country.
>
> (trans. 1975, pp. 64–5)

If this anecdote illustrates the strategic tolerance sometimes practised towards the theatre by those who had the power to be intolerant if they chose (and the importance of comedy as a genre with a great capacity for self-preservation), there are others that show rather the interaction, in a complex society, of the pressures for and against tolerance. Discussing the censorship of the Australian theatre, John Tasker recorded the case of the 1936 production by the New Theatre in Sydney of Clifford Odet's *Till the Day I Die*, a famous expression of anti-Nazi sentiment. When Dr Asmis, the German consul, complained to Chief Secretary Baddeley that the play was 'unjust to a friendly power', the government banned it; but the audience threw the police out of the theatre, and the play proceeded – illegally. It was not until 1941, two years after war with Germany had been declared, that the ban was formally lifted (Tasker, 1970, p. 38). This episode echoes another famous piece of theatre history in Jacobean England, when Middleton's *A Game of Chess*, an allegorical attack on James I's pro-Spanish policies, played for two weeks in London in 1624 to packed audiences before the King finally listened to the protests of the

Spanish ambassador and closed the production down. By invoking the influence of foreign diplomacy, both episodes clearly signal the theatre's potential efficacy; the motives for governmental dilatoriness are a little harder to read.

But most of the central issues in the theory and practice of censorship and its evasion contain their own quotient of undecidability. These issues, in their complexity, go far beyond the contrast between pre-publication censorship and subsequent penalty that has tended to preoccupy liberal thinkers from Milton onwards, though even the seemingly clear concept that a work should be permitted the test of public opinion is clouded – by the problems of regulating the film industry, for instance, or by the argument that writers may sometimes prefer to know in advance what sort of trouble they may face. But there are more difficult questions, whose unanswerability grows with our knowledge of censorship's history, past and present. To what extent can and does a strict censorship succeed? To what extent does a policy of moderation, based on the safety-valve theory, prove a more powerful as well as more flexible medium of control? In repressive systems, how often are writers fired up, or rendered more ingenious, more creative, by repression, and how often are they beaten down? In liberal systems, has the legislative retreat of censorship gone too far? To what extent has the virtually complete freeing of a medium from governmental control, as in the American film industry since the 1960s, been replaced by the tyranny of the market and the virtual monopoly of a type of film, whether banal or unnecessarily violent, that a large proportion of the public would perhaps not choose to see if other options were available? To what extent should literature and its extensions into other media bear the responsibility for leading public opinion, and to what extent should it merely reflect community standards? The answers to these questions will tend to be given only in terms of personal testimony, and are rarely quantifiable. Periods of extraordinary literary productivity are sometimes coincident with, rather than intermittent between, periods of heavy censorship. This would seem to have been true of the late sixteenth and early seventeenth century in England, and of Russia under Nicholas I, where, as Nikitenko's editor remarked:

> For thirty years until this despot's death in 1855 literature managed to sneak through the seemingly impossible barriers which at any moment threatened to extinguish it altogether. The fact that this period marked the beginning of the era known as the golden age of Russian literature makes it appear all the more remarkable. . . . Was the stifling atmosphere itself responsible for such an apparently contradictory phenomenon? . . . Some historians and critics offer the theory that literature in Russia took the place of free institutions.
>
> (Nikitenko, 1975, p. xxii)

Similar guesses might be hazarded about the brilliance of Latin-American fiction today; and whereas André Brink was compelled to note that South African censorship of Afrikaans writers since the 1960s seemed to have been successful, the same period had seen in Black writing, disseminated before or despite its almost inevitable banning, 'an eruption of talent and vitality unrivalled in South African literary history' (1984, p. 145).

Finally, what should we say of the censors themselves? Are we better off when they are stupid, as Milton imagined the parliamentary licencers must be; ideological or psychological obsessives, like Sir Roger L'Estrange, who hounded the English press in the Restoration, or Mrs Mary Whitehouse, an equally self-appointed guardian of British morality who tried to invoke the charge of blasphemous libel against Monty Python's *Life of Brian*; cheerful professionals like the young Polish ex-censor who consented to be interviewed, and who saw his work as an intellectual game of chess (Anon., 1983, pp. 102–12); or urbane and humane members of the intelligentsia like Malesherbes and Nikitenko, who believed that their mediatorial role might preserve their most valuable writers from greater evils? It was Nikitenko, mindful of the fact that Nicholas I had a policy of imprisoning the censors, rather than the writers, for awkward lapses, who complained, 'What am I going to do with those petty minds that screen out mosquitoes and swallow camels whole?' (trans. 1975, p. 197), a brilliant aphorism defining (by its converse) the pragmatics of interpretation that he himself promoted; and elsewhere he reflected: 'What is meant by the literary idea? In the main it means to arouse in the hearts of people a respect for intellectual and educational achievements' (pp. 82–3).

It is arguable that this respect is most truly won when literature and the other arts stand for something important and endangered, promoted only at great and sometimes unbearable cost to the writer. If many literary conventions have been born as strategies for evading censorship, literature itself survives in the most repressive conditions in perhaps its purest form. As Mario Vargas Llosa put it, in Latin American 'the printed word, the written word, the book, have a privileged position, deserve respect and encourage hope. They enjoy total credibility. The pressures put on the pen presuppose that it is capable of telling the truth' (1984, pp. 168–9).

FURTHER READING

Balmuth, Daniel (1979) *Censorship in Russia, 1865–1905*, University Press of America, Washington

Chafee, Zechariah (1941) *Free Speech in the United States*, Harvard University Press, Cambridge

Gillett, Charles Ripley (1932) *Burned Books: Neglected Chapters in British History and Literature*, 2 vols, Columbia University Press, New York

Hanson, L. (1967) *Government and the Press, 1695–1763*, Clarendon Press, Oxford

Hewison, Robert (1981) *Monty Python, the Case Against Irreverence, Scurrility, Profanity, Vilification and Licentious Abuse*, Grove Press, New York

Jansen, Sue Curry (1988) *Censorship: The Knot that Binds Power and Knowledge*, Oxford University Press, New York

Patterson, Annabel (1984) *Censorship and Interpretation: The Conditions of Writing and Reading in Early Modern England*, University of Wisconsin Press, Madison

Randall, Richard S. (1988) *Censorship of the Movies: The Social and Political Control of a Mass Medium*, University of Wisconsin Press, Madison

Siebert, Frederick Seaton (1951) *Freedom of the Press in England, 1476–1776: The Rise and Decline of Government Controls*, University of Illinois Press, Urbana

Soman, A. (1976) 'Press, Pulpit, and Censorship in France before Richelieu', *Proceedings of the American Philosophical Society*, 120, 439–63

Strothman, D. (1960) *Nationalsozialistische Literaturpolitik; ein Beitrag zur Publizistik im Drittenreich*, H. Bouvier, Bonn.

Thomas, Donald (1969) *A Long Time Burning: The History of Literary Censorship in England*, Frederick Praeger, New York

ADDITIONAL WORKS CITED

Adorno, Theodor W. (1987) 'Commitment'. In Andrew Arato and Eike Gebhart (eds), *The Essential Frankfurt School Reader*, Continuum Publishing, New York, pp. 300–18

Anon. (1983) 'I, the Censor'. In G. Schoplin (ed.), *Censorship and Political Communication in Eastern Europe*, Frances Pinter, London, pp. 102–12

Bachman, Albert (1934) *Censorship in France from 1715 to 1750: Voltaire's Opposition*, Columbia University Press, New York

Barrier, N. Gerald (1974) *Banned: Controversial Literature and Political Control in British India, 1907–1947*, University of Missouri, Columbia

Brink, André (1984) 'The Failure of Censorship'. In George Theiner (ed.), *They Shoot Writers, Don't They?*, Faber & Faber, London, pp. 142–9 [essay first published 1980]

Chan, H. (1983) *Control of Publishing in China: Past and Present*, Research School of Pacific Studies, Contemporary China Centre, Australian National University, Canberra

Chesterfield, Earl of (1962) 'Speech Against Licensing the Stage'. In J. McCormick and M. MacInnes (eds), *Versions of Censorship*, Aldine Publishing Company, Chicago, pp. 319–32 [first published 1737]

Conolly, Leonard W. (1976) *The Censorship of English Drama, 1737–1824*, Huntington Library, San Marino

Craig, A. (1962) *The Banned Books of England and Other Countries*, Allen & Unwin, London

Friedberg, Maurice (1977) *A Decade of Euphoria: Western Literature in Post-Stalin Russia, 1954–64*, Indiana University Press, Bloomington

Goodrich, Luther Carrington (1935) *The Literary Inquisition of Ch'ien-lung*, Johns Hopkins University Press, Baltimore

Gordimer, Nadine (1984) 'A Writer's Freedom'. In George Theiner (ed.) *They Shoot Writers, Don't They?*, Faber & Faber, London [essay first published 1975]

Guy, R. Kent (1987) *The Emperor's Four Treasuries: Scholars and the State in the late Chien-lung Era*, Harvard University Press, Cambridge

Hegel, Georg Wilhelm Friedrich (1975) *Aesthetics*, 2 vols, translated by T. M. Knox, Clarendon Press, Oxford [first published 1835]

Hepple, A. (1960) *Censorship and Press Control in South Africa*, published by the author, Johannesburg

Hutchison, E. R. (1968) *Tropic of Cancer on Trial: A Case History of Censorship*, Grove Press, New York

Kunetsov, Anatoly (1973) 'Self-Censorship'. In M. Dewhirst and R. Farrell (eds), *The Soviet Censorship*, Scarecrow Press, Metuchen, pp. 26–49

Llosa, Mario Vargas (1984) 'The Writer in Latin America'. In George Theiner (ed.), *They Shoot Writers, Don't They?*, Faber & Faber, London, pp. 161–71 [essay first published 1978]

Milosz, Czeslaw (1962) 'Ketman'. In J. McCormick and M. MacInnes (eds), *Versions of Censorship*, Aldine Publishing Company, Chicago, pp. 253–75 [essay first published 1951]

Moore, George (1885) *Literature at Nurse, or Circulating Morals: A Polemic on Victorian Censorship*, Vizetelly, London

Murray-Smith, S. (1970) 'Censorship and Literary Studies'. In G. Dutton and M. Harris (eds), *Australia's Censorship Crisis*, Sun Books, Melbourne

Nikitenko, Aleksandr (1975) *The Diary of a Russian Censor*, edited and translated by H. Jacobsen, University of Massachusetts Press, Amherst

Tasker, John (1970) 'Censorship in the Theatre'. In G. Dutton and M. Harris (eds), *Australia's Censorship Crisis*, Sun Books, Melbourne

Thody, P. M. W. (1968) *Four Cases of Literary Censorship*, Leeds University Press, Leeds

Van Rooyen, J. C. W. (1987) *Censorship in South Africa: Being a Commentary on the Application of the Publications Act*, Juta, Cape Town

Vladislav, Jan (1984) 'All You Need is a Typewriter'. In George Theiner (ed.), *They Shoot Writers, Don't They?*, Faber & Faber, London, pp. 43–51 [essay first published 1983]

67

THE BIBLIOGRAPHIC
RECORD

LIONEL MADDEN

GENERAL BIBLIOGRAPHIES

Any body of literary works or studies of literature requires some form of bibliographical record if it is to be used effectively. Theodore Besterman (1936, pp. 2–6) has shown that bibliographies of manuscripts were compiled long before the invention of printing. However, there is no doubt that the vast increase in the number of books produced and the ability to disseminate them in large numbers of copies, which was the result of the introduction of printing from moveable type, greatly stimulated the production of bibliographies. This resulted in the production of both retrospective bibliographies, attempting to record earlier publications, and current bibliographies which sought to record new publications as they appeared.

The first serious attempt at a retrospective bibliography of English-language books was Andrew Maunsell's *Catalogue of English Printed Books* (1595). New books were recorded from 1554 by the Stationers' Company, whose registers have been published. The first serious attempt at a contemporary published current bibliography was William London's *A Catalogue of the Most Vendible Books in England* (1657–60). The attempt at a current record was continued in the *Term Catalogues* (1668–1711) and during the early eighteenth century in the *Monthly Catalogue of Books* and in listings in the *Gentleman's Magazine* and the *London Magazine*. The monthly reviewing periodicals, which began with the *Monthly Review* in 1749, offered extensive current bibliographical coverage of new books during the latter part of the eighteenth and early nineteenth centuries.

The successive revolutions in printing techniques and paper production which took place from 1800 were matched by ever greater attempts by bibliographers in the nineteenth and twentieth centuries to produce comprehensive records. The lure of a single comprehensive national retrospective bibliography continued to attract men like Robert Watt, whose *Bibliotheca Britannica* was published in 1824. In the twentieth century, however, the problems of general retrospective bibliography have been more realistically tackled by period. A. W. Pollard and G. R. Redgrave's *Short-Title Catalogue of Books Printed in England, Scotland, and Ireland and of English Books Printed Abroad 1475–1640 (STC)* (1926, revised 1976–) established a model for other attempts at retrospective bibliographies covering specific periods. The aim of *STC* was to give basic information about all books printed in the period with a note of representative locations in British and American libraries. This aim has been followed in successive short-title catalogues, beginning with Donald Wing's *Short-Title Catalogue of Books Printed in England, Scotland, Ireland, Wales and British America, and of English Books Printed in Other Countries 1641–1700* (1945–51, revised 1972–). *The Eighteenth Century Short Title Catalogue (ESTC)*, begun in 1976 under the editorship of R. C. Alston, from the beginning harnessed the new technology to produce a machine-readable record. Although the catalogue of the British Library's collections of eighteenth-century material which forms the bedrock of *ESTC* has been published on microfiche, the most up-to-date record, including the collections of other libraries, and the most flexible searching will be obtained by using *ESTC* online through the British Library's Blaise-Line service.

By contrast to *ESTC*, the *Nineteenth Century Short Title Catalogue (NSTC)*, begun in 1983 under the editorship of Gwen Averley, adopted publication in book form. *NSTC* is planned in three series covering 1801–15, 1816–70 and 1871–1918. So far, Series 1 has been completed in five volumes and Series 2 in fifty volumes is under way. In his review of the first volume of the *NSTC* (*TLS*, 6 April 1984, pp. 381–2), Robin Alston attempted to assess the eventual size of the project and estimated that the total number of items in the completed *NSTC* might well come to around three million.

The urge to compile an effective current bibliography of new publications led to the commencement in 1864 of the *English Catalogue of Books*, though coverage was also extended retrospectively to 1801. The *English Catalogue of Books* continued to be published as a current bibliography until 1967, by which time it was in unsuccessful competition with *Whitaker's Cumulative Book List*, begun in 1924, and the *British National Bibliography*, begun in 1950, as well as the *Cumulative Book Index*, begun by the H. W. Wilson Co. of New York in 1898, which seeks to record all books published in English throughout the world.

The vast increase in periodical publication in the nineteenth century inspired William Frederick Poole's *Index to Periodical Literature*, a retrospective subject index to the contents of 479 British and American periodicals between 1802 and 1906. The identification of authors of articles in the major nineteenth-century quarterly and monthly periodicals has been carried out by the *Wellesley Index to Victorian Periodicals 1824–1900* (1966–89). The twentieth century has also seen the development of general current indexes such as the *Subject Index to Periodicals* (1916–61), the *British Humanities Index* (1962–) and the American *Humanities Index* (1974–).

All these general bibliographies are of enormous value to students of English as of other subjects. However, English studies is also richly served by an array of bibliographies which cater more specifically for the subject. It is helpful to consider these under two headings according to whether their primary purpose is to produce a retrospective record of work published in the past or a current record of newly published work.

RETROSPECTIVE BIBLIOGRAPHIES OF ENGLISH STUDIES

Proposals for a 'General Catalogue of English Literature' were floated at the time of the foundation of the Library Association in 1877 and the Bibliographical Society in 1892. In fact, though, the title is misleading. What was envisaged appears to have been a retrospective bibliography of all books published in the English language. The idea of a single retrospective bibliography devoted to English literature in its modern sense had to wait until English studies emerged as a recognized university discipline with its own growing band of scholars and aspiring research students.

One sign of the emergence of English literary study as a separate discipline was the publication during 1907–16 of the *Cambridge History of English Literature*, edited by A. W. Ward and A. R. Waller. Each chapter of the work had a bibliography appended to it. There was apparently a proposal at the time that these bibliographies should be gathered together to form a bibliography of English literature. This suggestion is referred to in the introduction to the general retrospective bibliography which did finally emerge in four volumes in 1941, the *Cambridge Bibliography of English Literature* (*CBEL*), edited by F. W. Bateson. According to the editor, the *CBEL* was 'a descendant – though not such a direct descendant as was originally contemplated' of the *Cambridge History*:

> To each of the chapters of the *C.H.E.L.* there was appended a bibliography; and while the usefulness of the text has been but little impaired by the passage of time, the bibliographies have become in varying degrees out-of-date and misleading. The *C.B.E.L.* is at once a recognition of the fact and an attempt to rectify it by supplying a modern equivalent of the *C.H.E.L.* bibliographies – a modern equivalent, not a modern edition.
>
> (vol. 1, p. v)

CBEL represented a labour of some ten years by a large number of contributing scholars. According to its introduction, it set out 'to record, as far as possible in chronological order, the authors, titles and editions, with relevant critical matter, of all writings in book-form (whether in English or Latin) that can still be said to possess some literary interest by natives of what is now the British Empire up to the year 1900'. It was, that is to say, a record of both primary and secondary materials for the study of English literature, covering authors and writings of literary significance, beginning at 600 and ending with writers who were considered to have established their reputations by 1900.

It is impossible to exaggerate the importance of *CBEL* for English studies. It immediately established itself as the vade-mecum of literary scholars. In 1957 a one-volume *Supplement*, edited by George Watson, was published recording new editions and criticism. The supplement confined its attention to authors included in the first edition and did not seek to move into the field of twentieth-century literature. That was left to the *New Cambridge Bibliography of English Literature* (*NCBEL*), edited by George Watson and published in five volumes between 1969 and 1977. *NCBEL* brings the coverage of English literature down to authors whose reputation was established by 1950. The great increase in writing about literature during the thirty years since *CBEL* compelled the editor of *NCBEL* to adopt a much stricter definition of English literature and omit sections devoted to such topics as philosophy, history and education which found a place in the original work. Despite inevitable changes in definition and method it is, as George Watson notes in his Introduction, a tribute to the work of F. W. Bateson that the new work is able to follow quite closely the basic principles which were devised for *CBEL*.

It should be emphasized that *CBEL* and *NCBEL* are selective bibliographies of English literature. They certainly do not attempt to record everything written about the subject. Even so, their considerable bulk has encouraged the publication of many shorter bibliographical guides. One notable example was the unannotated *Concise Cambridge Bibliography of English Literature*, edited by George Watson in 1958. There have been many attempts to produce annotated bibliographies or bibliographies in narrative form. One outstanding example of the latter is F. W. Bateson and H. T. Meserole, *A Guide to English and American Literature* (3rd edn, 1976). This work, though now in need of further revision, constitutes an invaluable basic guide to the best editions of authors and the major biographical and critical writings about them, as well as to more general historical and critical works on English literature. Other narrative bibliographies are often devoted to specific periods or specific literary forms.

The development of analytical and descriptive bibliography in the twentieth century under such leading figures as W. W. Greg in Britain and Fredson Bowers in the United States has encouraged the production of fine descriptive bibliographies of individual authors. The excellent series of 'Soho Bibliographies', launched in 1951 by Rupert Hart-Davis and later taken over by Oxford University Press, has published detailed bibliographies of the works of several authors. Other notable examples of descriptive bibliographies of specific authors include R. L. Purdy's *Thomas Hardy* (Oxford University Press, London,

1954), Donald Gallup's *T. S. Eliot* (Faber & Faber, London, 1969) and B. C. Bloomfield's *Philip Larkin* (Faber & Faber, London, 1979).

The compilers of the Soho bibliography of Henry James expressed the function of a descriptive bibliography:

> This bibliography tells the story of what happened to the writings of Henry James after they left his busy work-table to be set up in type and published in magazine and book.
>
> (Edel and Laurence, 1957, p. 12)

There is, of course, also a need for retrospective secondary bibliographies of specific authors. Ideally these should list books, articles and theses relating to the author. Although they may also include a checklist of the author's own writings, their primary function is to record biographical and critical discussions. Nowhere is the effect of the vast increase in publication more apparent than in the constant flow of new bibliographies seeking to document for scholars the flood of writings about literary figures of all periods. That these bibliographies find a ready sale to libraries indicates a recognition of the problems encountered by scholars in carrying out effective large-scale searches. A few works, such as David Gilson's *A Bibliography of Jane Austen* (Clarendon, Oxford, 1982) effectively combine the functions of both primary and secondary bibliographies.

CURRENT BIBLIOGRAPHIES OF ENGLISH STUDIES

If the development of large-scale retrospective bibliographies was linked to the growth of English studies as a recognized university discipline, so too was the development of adequate current bibliographies. The first very modest current bibliography of English studies was launched by the English Association. Founded in 1906, the English Association launched a *Bulletin* which from February 1908 began to include 'a short Bibliography of recent books on English literature and language'. The list expanded steadily, noting new books and periodical articles. Although items were predominantly English-language, it was not confined exclusively to English-language works but included French and German works also. The bibliography continued to be published as a current awareness tool until 1934.

Soon after the launching of the bibliography in its *Bulletin* the English Association began to plan a more ambitious venture to record systematically work done in English studies during the last year. The idea was first mooted in 1913 but the outbreak of war deferred publication until 1921. In that year the first volume of *Year's Work in English Studies*, covering November 1919– November 1920, was published. The *Year's Work* was planned as 'a comprehensive report of pertinent English work which has been done at home and abroad during the year'. In fact, the aim of producing a comprehensive record, in the sense of including references to everything in the field of English studies, has never been seriously pursued by *Year's Work*. An early review in the *Times Literary Supplement* for 1924 acknowledged with gratitude that 'the torrent of American academic publications, which contains so much that is extremely good and bad, is discreetly filtered'. The reviewer perceived the proper aim of *Year's Work* as enabling the student to 'discover year by year almost everything of value which has been written by an Englishman or a foreigner in a given period'. This essentially selective and evaluative function has continued to the present day and still distinguishes *Year's Work* from other general current bibliographies of English studies.

The task of preparing a comprehensive current record was undertaken by another bibliography which commenced in the period immediately following the First World War. In 1918 the Modern Humanities Research Association was founded to 'promote the cause of research in Modern Languages' and three years later it launched the *Annual Bibliography of English Language and Literature* with the clear aim of producing a full listing of recent writing in its subject area. The first volume of the *Annual Bibliography* covered the publications of 1920. In contrast to the narrative-critical style of *Year's Work*, the *Annual Bibliography* aimed at a systematic, unevaluative listing of items. Its purpose from the beginning was to produce a single, comprehensive, unannotated bibliography which would simply record for the benefit of scholars everything of potential interest which had been published during a given year.

Thus in those heady days of bibliographical endeavour and aspiration immediately following the First World War did the two British giants of literary bibliography emerge, to be joined and challenged later by other bibliographies which sought to carry out more efficiently the whole or part of their appointed tasks.

The most obvious challenger was the annual bibliography produced by the Modern Language Association of America. The *MLA Bibliography* was first produced for the year 1921. Until 1955, however, it was simply an annotated listing of American publications relating to the modern languages and literatures. In 1956 it became the *MLA International Bibliography* and its scope widened to include writings from all countries. With this development its relevant sections have emerged as direct competitors to the *Annual Bibliography*. To a large extent both bibliographies now seek to perform the task of listing everything produced in a given year, in any country and any language, about the English language and about literature in English world-wide.

It is a measure of the difficulties inherent in recording all writing in such a varied and voluminous field of study that both the *Annual Bibliography* and the equivalent sections of the *MLA International Bibliography* have remained in existence as competitors for more than thirty years. Such studies as have been carried out indicate that the scholar needs to check both of them in order to keep fully informed about the output of new work.

The 'internationalization' of the *MLA* in 1956 was closely followed in 1958 by the launching of a new current bibliographical service, *Abstracts of English Studies* (*AES*). Originally founded by members of the University of Colorado Department of English as a monthly service, *AES* passed in 1981 as a quarterly to the University of Calgary and in 1989 to Basil Blackwell. From the beginning it has sought to provide non-evaluative abstracts of periodical articles and monographs, though in fact the overwhelming majority of items listed are articles. Although it is presumably intended as a current tool, issues have not concentrated so clearly as have the volumes of the other current bibliographies on the publications of a given year but have indicated a rather less precise chronological focus.

A major problem faced by all these bibliographies, of course, has always been the currency of their information. The twin aims of producing a current guide to the literature of the subject and a permanent record of achievement, while not necessarily exclusive, have in practice often become so for a number of reasons which are closely related to the vast increase in publication which has taken place during the twentieth century. The enormous output in all fields of scholarly activity and its scatter through a large number of periodicals, books and theses has inevitably meant that the production of a really up-to-date listing of new materials has become an extremely costly operation. Clearly, funding for the production of such up-to-date bibliographies will generally be most readily available in those subject areas which promise recognizable benefits to government or business interests, and least readily in areas such as the humanities which do not enjoy financial favour at such a level. Furthermore, information in scientific, technical and medical subjects is known to have only a short life-span and needs to be disseminated quickly, with a corresponding necessity for the swift production of bibliographies. By contrast, writings in English studies do not for the most part date quickly and it is difficult to advance the argument that the progress of knowledge will be significantly retarded by a delay in the bibliographic record.

For these kinds of reasons compilers of the bibliographies have to decide whether their primary aim is to keep readers abreast of the latest writings on their subject or to produce – if necessary a few years after publication – a record of achievement. In fact, there seems little doubt that the *Annual Bibliography* and *Year's Work*, as at present constituted, are emphasizing the latter function and accepting, though no doubt reluctantly, that this may involve a time-lag of several years between publication of the scholarship and its bibliographic record.

Of the major general bibliographies it is at present the *MLA International Bibliography* which comes nearest to the ideal of combining currency and permanent record. With the 1981 volume this work was strikingly remodelled as a result of the decision to computerize the bibliography. This immediately resulted in a considerable increase in the promptness with which the bibliography appeared in print and a corresponding reduction in the time-lag between publication of the scholarship and the relevant volume of the bibliography. It also enabled the production of a much more detailed annual printed subject index to facilitate and enhance scholars' use of the bibliography and to break the stranglehold of the traditional author-based approach to literary bibliographies. As the introduction to recent volumes states:

> The subject index provides access to names of persons, languages, groups, genres, stylistic and structural features, themes, sources, influences, processes, theories, and other related topics.

In addition to bringing benefits to the user of the printed index, the computerization of the record allowed the MLA to market its bibliography online. This has three potential advantages for the user. First, it offers the possibility of making information about recent publications available very quickly. It is the declared policy of MLA that its online bibliography will be updated 'every month from December through June and again in October'. Second, as coverage is gradually extended further back the online file should become increasingly useful for retrospective searching, allowing the searcher to avoid the rather cumbersome procedure of successively checking a series of printed annual volumes. Third, online searching should allow more complex subject searches than are possible using the printed subject volumes. Searches involving, for example, a number of subjects, literary techniques and scholarly approaches can be carried out using the descriptors provided by MLA, enhanced, if the searcher desires, by the additional flexibility of free-text searching.

An alternative method of providing very current information about periodical articles only has been offered since 1979 by *New Contents English Language and Literature* (published every two months by the Niedersächsische Staats- und Universitätsbibliothek Göttingen). As with current contents services in other subject fields it offers copies of contents pages of periodicals, supported by indexes of authors of articles and writers who form the subject of articles. Like the other major general bibliographies, *New Contents* defines English literature as literature in English throughout the world. This is a useful quick-reference service for the scholar wishing to keep abreast of new publications. Its very limited indexes and its restriction to periodical articles do not, however, make it a particularly useful tool for retrospective searching.

The general current bibliographies are supported by a considerable array of more specialized bibliographies designed to alert the scholar to new writings. Many of these are devoted to the study of a specific period. Some, such as the annual checklist of Victorian scholarship in *Victorian Studies*, appear as annual bibliographies within appropriate periodicals. Some periodicals carry regular narrative surveys of recent work. *Victorian Poetry*, for example, includes an annual 'Guide to the Year's Work in Victorian Poetry'. *Studies in English Literature* includes regular survey articles covering new writing on the Renaissance, Elizabethan and Jacobean drama, the Restoration and the eighteenth century, and the nineteenth century. Other period bibliographies appear as separate publications. *The Eighteenth Century: A Current Bibliography*, formerly published in *Philological Quarterly*, is now published as a separate work, as is *The Romantic Movement: A Selective and Critical Bibliography*. Periodicals devoted to specific authors, such as the *Tennyson Research Bulletin*, frequently record new work about the author.

FUTURE DEVELOPMENTS

The most evident change which has taken place in the provision of bibliographic information during the 1970s and 1980s has been the development of online databases. Although the number of online databases in the humanities is still relatively small, some notable bibliographies of value to English studies are available in this format. Among retrospective bibliographies mention has been made of the *Eighteenth Century Short Title Catalogue* which is available through Blaise-Line. Blaise-Line also markets another online database, the *Incunable Short Title Catalogue* which records items printed before 1501 from all countries and in all languages. This is an international project with the British Library as a major contributor. Records of works received by the Library of Congress since 1897 are available online as the REMARC database on Dialog. In addition, an increasing number of library catalogues are becoming available to researchers using, for example, the JANET network in Britain and similar networks in other countries.

Among current bibliographies online the outstanding example for literature and language studies is the *MLA International Bibliography* available through the Dialog service. Other online databases of value to humanities as to other scholars include, through Dialog, *Dissertation Abstracts International* and *Humanities Index* and, through BRS, *Arts and Humanities Search*, the online version of the *Arts and Humanities Citation Index*.

The advantages claimed for online databases include the fact that they can be readily updated, that they can be conveniently searched retrospectively without the need to consult long runs of printed volumes, and that they allow more flexible subject searching than is generally offered by the printed equivalents. However, the fact that each search can be separately costed has led some academic institutions to insist that payment is made by the department or individual rather than from the general library fund. Such a development has inevitably had an inhibiting effect on humanities staff wishing to search the databases.

The advent of CD-ROM (Compact Disc – Read Only Memory) technology offers a possible way forward. The basic principle of CD-ROM is that large amounts of information – the equivalent, it is claimed, of approximately 250,000 pages of print – can be stored on a single disc and searched using a compatible microcomputer. The main benefit for bibliographies produced in this way is that they can be held by libraries in the same way as books or microforms and users can search freely without the somewhat cumbersome constraints which operate when searching online from a remote host. A rapidly increasing number of bibliographies is now available on disc, including the British Library *General Catalogue of Printed Books*, the *British National Bibliography* and *Dissertation Abstracts International*.

The drawback of CD-ROM discs is that the information they contain cannot be added to or erased. For this reason a bibliography produced in this format can only be updated by producing a new disc. While this may possibly prove a disadvantage for bibliographies in some fields it is not necessarily so in the humanities where the major bibliographies are generally revised annually. In such cases libraries could subscribe to a new disc each year which would contain a cumulation of the present and previous years of the bibliography. It is possible that some such development as CD-ROM will provide an appropriate medium for the production and searching of the *MLA International Bibliography* and the *Annual Bibliography* in future years.

FURTHER READING

Altick, Richard D. (1981) *The Art of Literary Research*, 3rd edn, revised by John J. Fenstermaker, Norton, New York

Bateson, F. W. (1972) *The Scholar-Critic: An Introduction to Literary Research*, Routledge, London

Besterman, Theodore (1936) *The Beginnings of Systematic Bibliography*, 2nd edn, Oxford University Press, London

Cowell, Penelope M. (1981) 'The Provision of Current Bibliographical Information in the Field of English Literature', unpublished M.Lib. thesis, University of Wales, Aberystwyth

Linder, Leroy H. (1959) *The Rise of Current Complete National Bibliography*, revised edn, Scarecrow Press, New York

Loomis, Abigail A. (1986) 'Dickens Duplication: A Study of Overlap in Serial Bibliographies in Literature', *RQ*, 25, 348–55

Madden, Lionel (1986) 'Printed and Online Bibliographies for English Literary Studies: A Decade of Change', *Library Review*, 35, 248–54

Salvaggio, Ruth (1983) 'Interpreting the *MLA Bibliography*', *Scholarly Publishing*, 14, 363–8

Schwartz, Candy (1988) 'Humanities'. In C. J. Armstrong and J. A. Large (eds), *A Manual of Online Search Strategies*, Gower, Aldershot, pp. 623–78

Stokes, Roy (1982) *The Function of Bibliography*, 2nd edn, Gower, Aldershot

Tollers, Vincent L. and Stroud, Carole (1973) 'Is the *MLA* or *MHRA* Better?', *RQ,* 13, 126–8

ADDITIONAL WORKS CITED

Bateson, F. W. and Meserole, Harrison T. (1976) *A Guide to English and American Literature*, 3rd edn, Longman, London

Edel, Leon and Laurence, Dan H. (1957) *A Bibliography of Henry James*, Hart-Davis, London

68

THE
INSTITUTIONALIZATION
OF LITERATURE:
THE UNIVERSITY

TERENCE HAWKES

To study a subject called 'English literature' seems the most natural thing in the world. Its materials, highly valued novels, plays, poems, apparently lie to hand in abundance. Collectively, they appear to constitute a stable and clearly defined area, the basis of a ready-made, well-balanced syllabus. Yet nothing could be further from the truth. The subject has no claim to any 'natural' or objective standing. Its material does not really exist in the ready-made form we presuppose. There is no stable, clearly defined area. There is no well-balanced set of works of guaranteed, immutable value, sharing distinctive and inherent properties, which inhabit it. And to study novels, plays or poems in the way that we do is, in historical terms, a very recent and a rather unusual pursuit.

Of course, a sense of the educational potential of literature has existed for a long time and in Britain it stretches back at least to the sixteenth century. Roger Ascham (1515–68), Queen Elizabeth's private tutor, recommended the study of languages and philosophy as a suitable discipline for young minds in his *The Scholemaster* (1570). In 1598, Thomas Speght's edition of and commentary on Chaucer treated the poet as a 'classic' author in the English tongue. But it was not until the nineteenth century that these two notions, that the study of literature was an improving activity for the young and that the English language itself offered a body of material worthy of prolonged scrutiny, were brought together in an institutional context.

The reasons for the conjunction were complex. Industrialization, the rise of trade unions, the impact of dissenting religious movements which stressed private communion with the Bible, had all systematically fuelled the expansion of literacy. Romanticism, particularly the poetry of Wordsworth and Coleridge, had for some time disseminated the idea that the poetic imagination offered access to a deeper level of truth and a more complex engagement with morality than the operations of mundane reasoning. But perhaps most compelling was the fact that a number of political developments seemed poised to threaten the coherence and integrity of the British state.

To say that a new academic subject results from specific political and social pressures is to ground it in a concrete historical moment and to propose it as the product of particular material conditions. If this seems inappropriate in the case of something as apparently private, personal and non-material as literature, we should remember that our concern here is not with specific novels, plays and poems (though a strong case can be made that these are not as personal, private or immaterial in origin as we like to believe), but with the means by which they are deployed and encountered in society. A study of the process of institutionalization will focus not on single works of art but on the operations that mediate them and group them in relation to each other and to society at large: in this case the process by which individual writings are made part of a larger entity known variously as 'English literature', 'English Studies' or, simply, 'English'.

The process is not a passive, classifying and descriptive one. It is actively creative and prescriptive, moulding the very nature of whatever it deals with and changing it into something different. *Hamlet* must obviously at one time have been an interesting play written by a promising Elizabethan playwright, in English. However, as a part of 'English literature', issuing from one of the key components of that institution, the creature 'Shakespeare', it inescapably takes on a huge and complex symbolizing function, particularly when that institution is located within a system of mass education linking Britain, North America and the Commonwealth countries.

In that role, *Hamlet* becomes far more than a mere play. It is traditionally presented to us, after all, as the work of an authentic 'genius', a poet-philosopher replete with wisdom about the way things are, always have been, and presumably always will be. Accordingly, it enters our way of life as one of the resources through which that way of life generates meaning. It helps to form large categories of thought, particularly those which inform political and moral stances, modes and types of relationship, our ideas of how men and women, fathers and mothers, husbands and wives, uncles and nephews, sons and daughters ought respectively to behave and interact. It becomes part of a means of first formulating and then validating important power relationships, say between politicians and intellectuals, soldiers and students, the world of action and that of contemplation. Perhaps its probing of the relation between art and social life, role-playing on stage and role-playing in society, appears so powerfully to offer an adequate account of important aspects of our own experience that it ends by constructing them. In short, *Hamlet* crucially helps to determine how we perceive and respond to the world we live in.

Given this, it must seem appropriate that, like a number of other texts, *Hamlet* acquires a central role in a complex programme of educational classification and social advancement. The more competence examination candidates show in discussing the Prince's lack of that quality, the greater their reward. The play ultimately functions as a universal cultural reference point, a piece of social shorthand. Bits of its language embed themselves in everyday speech until it starts itself to seem like a web of quotations. You can even name a cigar after it. It ends, in short, as part of our ideology. And in so far as it is the institution of 'English' which assigns, emphasizes and confirms that role, then that institution must rank as an important and necessary object of study.

We can begin with the dimension of itself that the institution apparently most wants to conceal: its history. If the rise of what we now call 'English' is contemplated at all in the later twentieth century, it appears an effortless, inevitable process. For most students of the subject, however, the notion of its 'rise' is virtually unthinkable. So complete has the triumph of 'English' been in the last fifty years, that it appears to have no history. It seems always to have existed, a natural, permanent and 'given' feature of the academic landscape, hugely popular throughout the educational system, with its centrality guaranteed at the lower levels by legislation making the study of 'English' – the language usually presented and perceived through some form of 'literary' usage – compulsory throughout the English-speaking world.

Yet like all things manufactured by human beings, 'English' has material roots. The first professorships in the subject in England were instituted in two colleges of what subsequently became London University: University College (founded in 1826) and King's College (founded in 1831). At University College, the teaching showed a practical bent appropriate to the utilitarian spirit which informed that college's ethos. Students were instructed in composition and language studies, and the Chair had the title of 'English Language and Literature'. At King's College the emphasis was rather on moral matters, as befitted the Evangelicalism inspiring the college's founders. Students were directed towards the study of literature as an ethical and intellectual force and the Chair had the title of 'English Literature and History'. There is a sense in which these two approaches, the utilitarian and the evangelical, compete throughout its history in Britain as the opposed modes in which the subject is conceived. Their function as two sides of a common British coin is suggested by the fact that both chairs were initially occupied in turn by the same man, the Reverend Thomas Dale. Appointed at University College in 1828 and then at King's College in 1835, Dale thus has the distinction of being the first Professor of English in the history of England.

The University of Oxford founded an English school in 1894 only after a good deal of dithering, much of it occasioned by a commitment to the study of language in the form of philology (a chair of Anglo-Saxon had existed since

1849) and a fear of what the Regius Professor of History, E. A. Freeman, called the 'chatter about Shelley' that mere literary criticism was presumed to involve. Indeed, its involvement with the practical, almost utilitarian dimension of language persisted even after the establishment in 1885 of the Merton Professorship of English Language and Literature, to which a philologist, Arthur Sampson Napier, was first appointed. It took vigorous propaganda on the part of a number of those convinced of the importance of English literature in the education of English men, notable amongst them John Churton Collins, an unsuccessful candidate for the Merton chair, before the School was finally established. Even then, its concerns were dominated by the issue of language and the school was permitted only one teacher on the 'literature' side, Ernest de Selincourt. Not until 1904 did the university appoint its first real Professor of English Literature. This was Walter (later Sir Walter) Raleigh, under whose rule the contemporary shape of the subject in the early twentieth century (including its fundamentally historical approach to literature as well as its still persisting commitment to 'language' or philology) was gradually established (see Palmer, 1965).

However, a full-blown institutional commitment to the study of English literature without any anchor in 'language', and in a form which encouraged the broad development of its evangelical and moral dimensions, did not occur until near the end of the First World War. We can be quite precise about the date. English in the shape in which most contemporary students of the subject now encounter it, the form in which the subject was, until recently, most usually studied in the English-speaking world, was invented in 1917.

The date is a significant one. In the spring of that year the United States declared war on Germany, allied itself with Britain, and began an involvement in European affairs and those of the rest of the world that persists to the present day. In the autumn of the same year a successful Bolshevik coup in Russia completed a process of revolution in that country and founded the regime that still challenges the West throughout the globe. The context could hardly have been more compelling. The entry of America into the war guaranteed the dominance of English as a world language. Its chief competitor, German – hitherto the language of international science, of philosophy, of theology – found itself fatally weakened in terms of status and influence by the defeat of the subsequent year. The events of the Second World War inevitably confirmed that decline. Meanwhile, the Bolshevik action in Russia generated a palpable fear of revolution throughout the West and an urgent need for a bulwark against its spread. The promotion of a sense of national cultural coherence and involvement seemed an admirable stratagem, and the study of 'English' an appropriate instrument for the purpose. The subject had frequently been seen as conducive to and expressive of Englishness. But the times demanded a bolder, more assertive role for writings in what was now the world's leading language. It was left to the University of Cambridge to rise most powerfully to the occasion. As F. L. Lucas puts it, in March 1917, 'while Russia was tottering into revolution and America preparing for war ... at Cambridge members of the Senate met to debate the formation of an English tripos' (Mulhern, 1979, pp. 3–4; cf. Tillyard, 1958, *passim*).

Of course, it would be misleading to impute to the founders of Cambridge 'English' at any conscious level the sort of motives outlined above. They were in part the unwitting instruments of their time, responsive as we all are to the groundswell of history. But what seemed to them the transparently obvious way to proceed, freely arrived at and independent of ideological constraint, must seem no less clearly to us, when we reinsert their programmes as far as we can into their own historical context, to reflect that context's form and pressure. For instance, the decision taken at Cambridge to prise the study of literature away from the study of language was not perhaps overtly conceived as an act of liberation, freeing something quintessentially English from a degrading servitude to a Teutonic tyrant. But it is difficult, placing such developments in the context of 1917, to ignore the possibility of that dimension's existence. In any event, the absence of the 'language' component from the Cambridge syllabus, and indeed the turning away from literature written before 1350, had positive results. It gave space for papers on areas such as 'Life, Literature and Thought' which were certainly, at the time, distinctive. Cambridge's version of 'English', particularly as developed by one of its central founding figures, I. A. Richards, was thus able from the first to be more psychologically and sociologically inclined than Oxford's, more concerned with the relation between literature and the experiences from which it sprang, of which it was expressive and to which it was addressed.

It also retained, and developed in certain of its manifestations, something of that 'evangelical' fervour imprinted on the subject as institutionalized at King's College, London. This sees English Literature very much in the light in which Matthew Arnold saw it, as one of the opposed polarities of his *Culture and Anarchy* (1869): as a sacred crucible in which was mixed the redeeming essence of a national culture whose moral principles may be set against an encroaching barbarism.

The almost religious role this assigns both to literature and to its teachers, who become priests administering the sacrament of culture to the converted, or even missionaries preaching the true gospel to the heathen, was not in fact a new development. The romantic movement, as has been said, had proposed a humanizing role for poetry, just as it had claimed a capacity for trenchant insight for its language. Coleridge in particular had advocated direct social action on its behalf, in the form of a group of followers to be called the *Clerisy* who would be charged with spreading the good word. Arnold's notion of an élite corps of 'aliens' ('persons who are mainly led, not by their class spirit, but by a general *humane* spirit, by the love of human perfection' – Arnold, [1869] 1931, p. 70) had a similar, no less chilling, purpose (cf. Williams, 1958).

In 1919, just two years after the decision to establish an English school at Cambridge had been taken, a further impulse to institutionalize the teaching of literature along lines of this sort occurred when the Board of Education appointed a departmental committee to investigate what was termed 'The Teaching of English in England'. The Committee's chairman was Sir Henry Newbolt and two years later, in 1921, it produced what has become known as the Newbolt Report.

The Newbolt Report was widely influential and circulated, as one of the Committee's members later put it, like a best-selling novel. Its chief recommendation, that English should be thoroughly institutionalized and taught throughout the British educational system from primary school to university level, was by and large adopted. Indeed, the report can be said effectively to have shaped the nature of 'English' in the form in which it still predominantly exists today. Its spiritual fathers are Coleridge and Arnold, and its two central concerns are related: the promotion of social cohesion in the face of potential political upheaval, and the encouragement of pride in an English national culture. The romantic and religious roots of the project are instantly recognizable, and the shadow of its political context (the Easter Rising in Dublin, 1916; the Bolshevik Revolution in Russia, 1917; unrest and mutinies in the armed forces in France, Germany and Britain, 1917–18) falls darkly across its pages:

> The situation, as it was presented to us, is gloomy, though not entirely without the elements of hope. We were told that the working classes, especially those belonging to organised labour movements, were antagonistic to, and contemptuous of, literature, that they regarded it 'merely as an ornament, a polite accomplishment, a subject to be despised by really virile men'. Literature . . . as a subject of instruction, is suspect as an attempt 'to side-track the working-class movement'.

But literature's promise of redemption remains an offer difficult to refuse:

> For if literature be, as we believe, an embodiment of the best thoughts of the best minds, the most direct and lasting communication of experience by man to men, a fellowship which 'binds together by passion and knowledge the vast empire of human society, as it is spread over the whole earth and over all time', then the nation of which a considerable portion rejects this means of grace, and despises this great spiritual influence, must assuredly be heading for disaster.

– and the evangelical mission of its teachers, particularly those involved in higher education is clear:

> We have called the University the apex of the educational edifice. From another

point of view it may be called the inner shrine. . . . The Professor of Literature in a University should be – and sometimes is, as we gladly recognise – a missionary in a more real and active sense than any of his colleagues. He has obligations not merely to the students who come to him to read for a degree, but still more towards the teeming population outside the University walls, most of whom have not so much as 'heard whether there be any Holy Ghost'. The fulfilment of these obligations means propaganda work, organisation, and the building up of a staff of assistant missionaries. But first, and above all, it means a right attitude of mind, a conviction that literature and life are in fact inseparable, that literature is not just a subject for academic study, but one of the chief temples of the human spirit in which all should worship.

(Newbolt, 1921, pp. 252–60)

In Cambridge, this notion of literature and its social role fell on fertile ground. The 1920s had after all produced a further voice that could be added to the pleas made by Coleridge, by Arnold and by Newbolt for defensive redemptive action in the face of a culture dangerously near collapse as a result of subversion from without and within. Perhaps surprisingly, the voice hailed from St Louis, Missouri, although its accents were carefully modulated to sound perfectly (perhaps a little too perfectly) English. Nevertheless, with T. S. Eliot's *The Waste Land*, anticipated in 1920 by a volume of essays called *The Sacred Wood*, an apocalyptic vision of decay seemed to rest on a judicious critical style and method able at once to contain and express it. Certainly, Eliot's general stance, his unemotional commitment to the close, cool analysis of texts and a carefully tempered, ironic probing of their nuances, found itself taken up by the Cambridge English school with an enthusiasm matching – even, covertly, mimicking – that surrounding the Anglo-American alliance of the war.

In broad terms, and over the years, Eliot's mode and manner of critical writing can be said to have contributed decisively to the procedures which collectively came to be known as 'practical criticism', the name given to them by their chief exponent at Cambridge, I. A. Richards. Fundamentally, 'practical criticism' involved the intense, but emotionally disengaged and formal analysis of passages of prose or verse, abstracted from their historical contexts, presented starkly on single sheets of paper, considered objectively, or 'practically' as 'words on the page' and subjected in the classroom to close scrutiny and evaluation in terms of the Newbolt Report's 'conviction that literature and life are in fact inseparable' (see Richards, 1929).

As both a critical and a teaching programme 'practical criticism' had much in common with what came to be called the New Criticism in America (thus reinforcing the Anglo-American nature of the entire project). Developing before and during the Second World War, but booming massively after it, New Criticism's concern with the detached but attentive analysis of rhetorical features, usually of single poems, was obviously suited to mass programmes of higher education in America deliberately aimed at students of limited literary background. It also offered their teachers the kind of 'objective' analytic role which their growing sense of professionalism welcomed. After the war, when universities on both sides of the Atlantic were filled to overflowing with returning soldiers who had had little time for literature in the immediate past and for whom books were in any case in short supply, the poem on a single sheet of paper made a virtue of necessity. However, the method persisted as those taught in this way began to teach others, the new profession expanded, and classroom procedures of this sort came to dominate teaching methods and presuppositions about literature in the English-speaking world and beyond until at least the early 1970s – a span in British terms of roughly fifty years. I. A. Richards also maintained an abiding interest in the psychology of communication, and he can be said to have taken up the formal, almost clinically analytic mode established by Eliot and added to it the sort of interest in the psychological aspect of literary creation that animated the romantic writer he most admired, Coleridge. Meanwhile the teacher at Cambridge who responded most forcefully to the moral commitment of Arnold and the cool irony of Eliot, but who added to both the evangelical fervour of the Newbolt Report, was F. R. Leavis.

Leavis's impact on the institutionalization of literature in Britain was and remains considerable. It manifests itself most decisively in terms of a powerful programme of reform directed at the 'English' syllabus. Sketched out in his book *Education and the University* (1943), reiterated and expanded in numerous other books and articles by himself, his wife Q. D. Leavis and his followers in the influential journal *Scrutiny* (1932–53), his proposals involved nothing less than a wholesale realignment both of the material that an English student ought to be studying and the way in which that study should proceed.

Primarily, Leavis argued, the student's aim should be to engage with the 'great tradition' that gives English literature its characteristic texture, and he or she should learn about, and presumably endorse, the moral standards and positions which that tradition is supposed to embody. It was of the essence of Leavis's position to point to specific texts. Thus, in the novel, he proposed a canon consisting of the works of Jane Austen, George Eliot, Henry James and Joseph Conrad, which was said to present and transmit a series of moral positions recognizably central to English culture (the fact that two of the four were not English by birth remained unexamined) (Leavis, 1948). In general terms, these positions advocated an 'openness' in the face of life, with intimate personal experience as the guarantee of truth and worth, a commitment to the value of traditional folk ways and a mistrust of post-industrial society and of 'modern' or 'metropolitan' culture, approval of a rooted, provincial, 'organic' way of life, a faith in the ethical capacities of 'ordinary' language, and a moral imperative to 'discrimination' in all things.

Perhaps such a project derives from or reflects to some extent the minatory, judgemental stance of a professional teacher of English. If so, it offers an appropriate example of the way in which institutionalization covertly shapes its raw material to fit its own presuppositions. Leavis was certainly one of the first academics in Britain to have been fully trained in the new subject of 'English' and then to have taught it in a career at university level. His approach to the material to be studied in his programme is essentially that of the pedagogue: it evaluates, it 'places', it excludes. It aims rigorously to separate that which has worth, and is therefore to be encouraged in the face of the imminent moral breakdown of society, from that which is worthless and therefore colludes with that breakdown. At its most magisterial, it operates a principle of censorship whose authority admits of no challenge. 'Openness' hardly remains an option when even to read the worthless is felt, as Leavis once said, to condone it.

The success or otherwise of the 'Leavisite' project remains a matter of dispute. Certainly the commitment of post-Second World War governments to massive expansion in education, which meant massive expansion in the numbers of those studying English, could only be counted by Leavis and his fellow teachers as a failure. Their programme was designed for the few, those who in the modern world would inherit, in academic guise, the mantles of Coleridge's Clerisy or of Arnold's Aliens. As Leavis himself claimed:

> In any period it is upon a very small minority that the discerning appreciation of art and literature depends: it is (apart from cases of the simple and familiar) only a few who are capable of unprompted, first-hand judgement. . . . The minority capable not only of appreciating Dante, Shakespeare, Donne, Baudelaire, Hardy (to take major instances) but of recognizing their latest successors constitute the consciousness of the race (or of a branch of it) at a given time.
>
> (Leavis, 1930, pp. 3–5)

But there were other factors which made for change. That the study of 'English' burgeoned after the First World War and expanded dramatically after the Second meant in effect that its major periods of growth occurred at times when European philosophers and thinkers, inhabitants of defeated or devastated countries, were either silent or not easily accessible. The result was, hindsight confirms, that 'English' flowered in Britain and North America as an isolated and insulated hot-house plant, knowing and wishing to know little but itself, and in any case, as we have seen, covertly charged with a limited, inwardly-directed purpose: the fostering of English-speaking culture, Englishness, or that version of Americanness whose roots could still – although with diminishing credibility – be located in England. The peace of 1945 may have ushered in the Cold War. But it also brought – perhaps as an unrecognized aspect of or weapon in that war – twenty-five years of relatively untroubled expansion in 'English' on both sides of the Atlantic. It was an age which saw the unparalleled growth of university departments devoted to the subject and the further rise of a class of professional teachers and scholars to service them. Some commentators have called it the Age of Criticism.

However, by the 1970s the certainties of that age were seriously in doubt. American involvement in the world beyond its own shores had become more demanding, more complex, more questionable both at home and abroad. The questioners were often students and teachers, bred in the humanities, all too familiar with the presuppositions of 'English', and anxious to seek answers, or reformulated questions, elsewhere. Meanwhile, the decline of British influence as a colonial power, the impact within Britain of the culture of former colonies, a growing alienation from America as a result of the conflicts in Vietnam on the one hand, Northern Ireland on the other, plus an expanding and involving relationship with Europe through the Common Market, all had their effects. In short, political, economic and cultural forces from beyond the English-speaking borders now began to impinge upon the rather narrow notions of literature in play in British and American institutions.

Yet, paradoxically, one of the most important impulses for change also came from closer to home. In fact, a substantial revision of the notion of 'English', one that was quite differently aligned, prepared to confront and reassess its own relation to post-war mass culture as well as to influences from abroad, came from another Cambridge critic. Leavis always thought of himself as an alien (not only in the Arnoldian sense) in Cambridge: yet he was born in that city and spent most of his life there. Raymond Williams, on the other hand, although a product of the university's English school, had a more obvious claim to be alienated from it and from the 'Englishness' which it covertly fostered. He was not English.

Williams's personal situation at, and his lifelong concern with, the periphery of mainstream 'English' culture provides an insight into some of the more recent developments in the institutionalization of literature. As a Welshman, and the title of his best novel *Border Country* (1960) confirms it, he was aware of and able to exploit the full symbolic significance of estranging cultural boundaries. That he felt impelled to do so from a position within the British mainland indicates the narrowness with which the frontiers of an exclusive English culture had been drawn between the wars. And if Williams can in this revealing way be said to have impinged upon the centre of English culture from 'abroad', his work proved 'outlandish' in another sense for, in the latter part of his career, he was also a committed Marxist. The spirit of that commitment is perhaps most strongly felt in an approach to literature which derives centrally from his work and has come to be known as 'cultural materialism'.

Literature, it has been realized, is certainly one of the major means by which a society generates cultural meaning: defines to itself, that is to say, crucial areas whose status is otherwise indeterminate. What, for instance, do we mean by 'man', by 'woman', by 'duty', by 'justice', by 'nation', by 'honour', by

935

'marriage', by 'love'? These are far from simple questions and human blood has frequently been shed in the face of conflicting answers to them. To study *Hamlet*, for example, is to be invited to question or to reinforce inherited meanings for such terms that our society depends upon and that fundamentally make it what it is. But, as cultural materialism points out, literature is not the only means by which those meanings are generated, contested, reinforced or transmitted. Its institutionalized study has tended to prise it out of the material social context it shares with other activities to which it contributes and from which it receives contributions. These other areas – they might involve music, song, domestic architecture, political pamphlets, records of parliamentary debates, letters, legal documents, maps, the whole range of what people actually get up to in the world in which they live – would now also claim to be able to provide *texts*, the close reading of which matches in fruitfulness that formerly accorded to novels, plays and poems. In short, elements excluded from the centre by the institution of literature and banished to the border, or the periphery, begin at last to assert their relevance and demand to be heard.

The most obvious effect of this materialist challenge to the institution in Britain and America has been to make it self-conscious. What before had seemed natural, normal and 'given' now emerges, as we have seen, as something manufactured in response to specific historical, political and social pressures; hardly 'natural', but certainly 'cultural', with a built-in political dimension and – as perhaps is now clear – a discernible past that is part of the history of the ideologies of Europe and North America. Not unreasonably, some account of the institution of 'English' begins to seem worthy of a place on the 'English' syllabus itself.

But perhaps the most far-reaching effects are those which impinge upon the notion of the subject's raw material, the individual 'text'. Throughout the 1970s, the work of writers such as Roland Barthes, Gerard Genette, Wolfgang Iser, Mikhail Bakhtin, Jacques Derrida, Michel Foucault and others was regularly translated into English, and terms such as 'literary theory', 'Russian formalism', 'structuralism', 'semiotics', 'post-structuralism', 'reception theory' were heard in the land. One of the major effects of structuralist and post-structuralist thinking has been to undermine our central ideological commitment to the idea of the individual, sovereign self, the human 'subject' as the fundamental unit of existence and meaning. As a result, the notion of the text as the direct expression of that subject's innermost thoughts and feelings has also been undermined. And the chief casualty of that development is the 'authenticity' of the text as a document which supposedly offers a direct and unmediated access to its author's feelings, thoughts, emotions.

In short, the text's 'authority' has been fundamentally questioned. *Hamlet* can no longer claim to offer authoritative revelations about what Shakespeare 'thought' and 'felt' with regard to the events and characters the play seems to deploy, any more than we can assume that the 'meaning' of the play is limited by what Shakespeare intended to say 'through' it. Hence much of the evaluative scrutiny of a whole era of English studies becomes redundant. The student is invited to see the text as offering no final, determinable set of 'meanings'. Instead, it can be perceived as the *occasion* of a number of meanings which have been attributed to it at various moments in the past, and thus as an index of the variety of ideological forces historically in play. In our own time, the text can be perceived as an arena, or site of struggle, in which different and opposed readings, urged from different and opposed political positions, compete for ideological power: the power to determine cultural meaning – to say what the world is and should be.

The situation is not without its ironies. 'English' or 'Literature' has never been more powerfully placed within the higher education institutions of Europe and North America than it is today. But against this we have to set the fact that our understanding of its own history, and of the implications of its institutionalization, have undermined the very certainties that its instigators sought to reinforce. 'English' itself seems to have become a site of struggle, an arena, a text. If so, nothing is here for tears. There are few more important roles in any society.

FURTHER READING

Baldick, Chris (1983) *The Social Mission of English Criticism, 1848–1932*, Clarendon Press, Oxford

Batsleer, Janet, Davies, Tony, O'Rourke, Rebecca and Weedon, Chris (eds) (1985) *Rewriting English: Cultural Politics of Gender and Class*, Routledge, London

Eagleton, Terry (1983) *Literary Theory: an Introduction*, Basil Blackwell, Oxford

Graff, Gerald (1987) *Professing Literature: an Institutional History*, University of Chicago Press, Chicago

Hawkes, Terence (1986) *That Shakespeherian Rag*, Routledge, London

Knights, Ben (1978) *The Idea of the Clerisy in the Nineteenth Century*, Cambridge University Press, Cambridge

Mathieson, Margaret (1975) *The Preachers of Culture: a Study of English and its Teachers*, Unwin, London

Mulhern, Francis (1979) *The Moment of 'Scrutiny'*, New Left Books, London

Potter, Stephen (1937) *The Muse In Chains*, Cape, London

Tillyard, E. M. W. (1958) *The Muse Unchained*, Bowes & Bowes, London

Widdowson, Peter (ed.) (1982) *Re-reading English*, Routledge, London

Williams, Raymond (1958) *Culture and Society, 1780–1950*, Chatto & Windus, London

——(1960) *Border Country*, Chatto & Windus, London

ADDITIONAL WORKS CITED

Arnold, Matthew (1931) *Culture and Anarchy*, edited by J. Dover Wilson, Cambridge University Press, Cambridge [first published 1869]

Eliot, T. S. (1920) *The Sacred Wood: Essays on Poetry and Criticism*, Methuen, London

Leavis, F. R. (1930) *Mass Civilisation and Minority Culture*, Gordon Fraser, Cambridge

——(1943) *Education and the University: a Sketch for an English School*, Chatto & Windus, London

——(1948) *The Great Tradition*, Chatto & Windus, London

Newbolt, Henry (1921) *Report to the Board of Education on the Teaching of English in England*, HMSO, London

Palmer, D. J. (1965) *The Rise of English Studies*, Oxford University Press, Oxford, and Hull University Press, Hull

Richards, I. A. (1929) *Practical Criticism*, Routledge, London

VIII. CONTEXTS

69

LITERATURE AND THE HISTORY OF IDEAS

ISABEL RIVERS

Viewed from some perspectives, the history of ideas is a form of enquiry that has had its day; viewed from others, it is thriving as never before. As so often, this discrepancy partly depends on the question of definition. At one extreme the history of ideas is taken to refer to philosophical thought considered separately from its social context; at the other, since almost all human activities involve thinking to some extent, the history of ideas is seen as a necessary part of any historical enterprise. Sometimes it is treated as a separate entity from intellectual history or cultural history, and regarded as having been superseded by them; at others it is perceived as synonymous with them. The broad and optimistic view is the right one: the history of ideas remains both important and flourishing, and, as this essay will show, the relationship between literature and the history of ideas, properly interpreted, has never been closer.

Some differences and changes in the ways in which the subject has been treated can be illustrated by a brief comparison of the methods of two very influential scholars, Arthur O. Lovejoy (1873–1962), an American philosopher who worked at Johns Hopkins University, Baltimore, and Quentin Skinner, an English historian of political thought who works at Cambridge. Lovejoy was very largely responsible for the currency of the label 'history of ideas' and for establishing the subject as an academic discipline. He explained his position in a number of essays published between 1936 and 1940, for example in the Introduction to *The Great Chain of Being* (1936), 'The Study of the History of Ideas'. In 1940 he founded *The Journal of the History of Ideas*, which continues as an essential source and forum for students of the subject, and his method was the driving force behind the *Dictionary of the History of Ideas* (1968), edited by one of his collaborators, Philip Wiener. Lovejoy's account of the subject includes the following emphases, some of which have proved more useful and influential than others. The historian of ideas is concerned not with large philosophical systems but with the unit-ideas that recur in different patterns and combinations throughout history. In tracing these unit-ideas the historian looks in particular at the ways in which they recur 'in very diverse provinces of thought [for example science, politics, religion, literature] and different periods'. He is primarily interested in ideas which were widely diffused, not in those of an élite minority. He observes the unargued assumptions that underlie the acceptance of certain ideas at certain times, and the frequent contradictions that arise in the thought of a particular writer or in an individual work as a result of the attempt to combine conflicting ideas. He is aware that ideas sometimes prevail for psychological and aesthetic reasons. He documents the ambiguities and shifts in the meaning of terms ('philosophical semantics') and the resulting confusions caused by these changes (Lovejoy, 1936, pp. 7, 14; and 1948, pp. xiv–xvi). From about the 1920s to the 1960s Lovejoy's definition of the history of ideas spread in American universities, as his colleagues and followers took up aspects of his method and applied it in different fields. A notable example in English literature was his one-time pupil Marjorie Hope Nicolson, who wrote a useful account of Lovejoy's influence as a teacher (1948): her interest was in the relationship between science and literature in the seventeenth and eighteenth centuries (e.g. 1960, 1962), and she herself stimulated much valuable work in this area.

Quentin Skinner developed his method out of a profound dissatisfaction with the way in which the history of political thought was being practised, and published his conclusions between 1966 and 1975 in a series of essays which have been much commented on and criticized, but which have also generated a great deal of new work in the history of ideas. (The most useful of these essays for the literary student are those of 1972 and 1975.) Skinner owes a frequently acknowledged debt to the Oxford philosopher and historian R. G. Collingwood (1889–1943), who argued in his *Autobiography* that a reader cannot understand the meaning of a philosophical writer until he understands what the question is to which a particular philosophical text is intended as an answer (1939, chap. 5). Collingwood illustrated this argument very effectively with a story about his recurrent puzzlement over twenty years earlier at the apparent ugliness of the Albert Memorial; he came to the conclusion that he could not possibly see it properly until he looked at it on its own terms and understood the question that it was intended to answer. Skinner was convinced that historians of political thought were reading the classic texts of political theory as answers to quite the wrong questions, questions significant for the twentieth-century reader but irrelevant or meaningless for the ancient Greek or Renaissance writer. In addition, these texts were being read in isolation from their social and intellectual contexts and as part of a tradition of great texts which apparently referred only to each other, not to any immediate contemporary debate. Against this anachronistic practice, Skinner has urged that historians of political (or any other kind) of thought should not concentrate on the study of specific ideas (Lovejoy's method) or isolated texts, but should endeavour to establish the meaning of a particular text by recovering the intentions of the author and the context in which he wrote. The historian of ideas will therefore be concerned with understanding the questions to which the text was intended to provide the answer, and he will do this by exploring the conventions, assumptions and vocabularies of contemporary debate, and the ways in which an individual writer endorses or repudiates these. Only through this process of recovering intention and context will understanding of the meaning of a text be achieved. 'For to understand what questions a writer is addressing, and what he is doing with the concepts available to him, is equivalently to understand some of his basic intentions in writing, and is thus to elicit what exactly he may have meant by what he said – or failed to say' (1978, vol. 1, pp. xiii–xiv). Skinner has in effect modified the label 'history of ideas' to read 'ideas in context' (the title of a series of histories of which he is joint editor).

Skinner's position has much in common with that of the American literary theorist E. D. Hirsch. In *Validity in Interpretation* (1967), an attack on academic scepticism, particularly the kind that argues that we can only understand a text in our own terms, Hirsch makes an important distinction between meaning and significance. The *meaning* of a text does not change with time; it is the proper object of understanding and interpretation, validated by consideration of all the relevant evidence. The *significance* of a text does change according to its readers and the age in which it is read. Verbal meaning is determinate, significance is boundless (p. 57). It is the first which is the proper object of historical study. (Hirsch does not depreciate the second, which is the province of the critic.) The historian is engaged in the act of 're-cognitive interpretation', the cognition of what the author meant (p. 24). This is 'the only kind of interpretation with a determinate object, and thus the only kind that can lay claim to validity' (p. 27). Both Skinner and Hirsch have been attacked for identifying meaning with the author's intention and for asserting that the reader can recover it. Sceptics find Hirsch's distinction between meaning and significance untenable and regard the recovery of meaning on these terms as impossible. The distinction can perhaps be clarified by a story popularized by Marshall McLuhan in *The Gutenberg Galaxy* (1962), which shows dramatically that meaning and significance are not the same thing and that for valid interpretation to be possible understanding of meaning must come first. McLuhan quotes at length from an account of an attempt made to use film as a medium for teaching non-literate Africans about sanitation (pp. 36–7). It was a carefully made film showing a man disposing of rubbish, but when the original audience were asked what they had seen, they said they had seen a chicken. The men showing the film did not even know that there was a chicken in it, and had to search frame by frame before they found it, but it was this that the audience had seen and found significant; they had not seen the man disposing of rubbish and had not understood the meaning of the film. McLuhan's point is about the difference between oral and technologically based cultures, and how the conventions of reading film must be learnt. More generally it can be taken as a parable about the interpretation of meaning. The historian of ideas must learn to read the conventions that will enable him to recover the meaning of the text so that he will see the man disposing of rubbish and not the chicken.

Skinner's stress on understanding the text through the recovery of intention and context can be seen as part of what has been described as a movement 'From History of Ideas to History of Meaning' (Bouwsma, 1981). Where earlier historians were concerned with describing the climate of opinion, the mind of an age, or a world picture, without worrying too much about the process whereby this description was to be achieved, recent historians have concentrated on the problem of interpretation and as a result have paid much more attention to the 'languages' in which ideas are expressed. (This is a different matter from Lovejoy's 'philosophical semantics', which deals with the changes in meaning of specific terms in different periods.) J. G. A. Pocock, a political historian and colleague of Skinner who has spent thirty years in England and the US studying the languages of political ideas in the seventeenth and eighteenth centuries, regards himself as a historian not of thought or ideas but of discourse. Pocock has described and defended his method in a number of essays from 1971 to the present (indeed it scarcely seems necessary for him to keep restating his position). In 'The State of the Art', for example, he posits that 'It is a large part of our historian's practice to learn to read and recognize the diverse idioms of political discourse as they were available in the culture and at the time he is studying: to identify them as they appear in the linguistic texture of any one text, and to know what they would ordinarily have enabled that text's author to propound or "say" ' (1985, p. 9). By language or idiom Pocock means both subject-matter and characteristic arguments and vocabulary (thus the seventeenth-century author using the languages of natural law or biblical prophecy will have at his disposal different assumptions, arguments and terms). A single text may be compounded of several such languages, and one of the tasks of the historian of discourse is to identify and separate the different layers. This is a necessary preliminary to discovering what the author is doing with these languages. The historian cannot see whether an author is using a language in a new way, or indeed creating a new kind of language, until he has this knowledge. He will be concerned not only with the languages of a particular text but with the ways in which the languages of one text respond to and in turn modify the languages of others. Thus Pocock has been shifting the historical study of political literature away from philosophy and towards rhetoric.

Two observations are worth making about these changes in the last twenty-

944

five years in the definition of the history of ideas. The first is a word of caution. Many (but by no means all) practising historians of ideas are extremely self-conscious about what they are doing. There is a danger of methodology becoming an obsession. Not only essays and articles but whole books are now devoted to scrutinizing and comparing (and frequently trouncing) the views of particular historians, who then reply in more essays and articles. It is now fashionable for collections of essays or monographs in the history of ideas to begin with elaborate methodological introductions in which the author hoists his flag and shows his credentials by situating himself in the contemporary methodological debate. It is an obvious temptation for new authors. It may well be that such books have two kinds of reader: those who skip the introductions in order to get on to the historical specifics, and those who relish the methodological statements and skip the rest. But the justification of recent methodological inquiry is surely not that it is a branch of knowledge in its own right, but that it has made the practice of the history of ideas better.

The second observation takes us on to the second part of this essay, the relationship between literature and the history of ideas. In terms of method the running has been made largely by historians of political ideas. But there is no reason why this should be so in terms of practice. Indeed, as shown above, the stress in the study of the history of ideas is increasingly on languages, conventions, vocabularies, idioms and rhetoric, which are as much the province of the literary historian as of the historian of ideas. Bouwsma has predicted that 'rhetoric is . . . likely to become a major tool of the new intellectual history' (1981, p. 290). Who better to wield this tool than the literary historian?

It will be helpful now to consider some of the ways in which literary historians have practised the history of ideas before turning to ways in which the subject may develop in the future (my examples are taken largely from the seventeenth and eighteenth centuries, partly because so much excellent work has been done in these periods, partly because these are periods in which I work myself). But first it is necessary to find a definition of literature that is appropriate to the history of ideas. We suffer in the twentieth century from an attenuated sense of the term, which has its origin in the development of the concept of belles-lettres in the late eighteenth century: by literature we mean imaginative literature, categorized generically as poems, plays and novels, and we assume that it requires specific kinds of aesthetic preconceptions and responses which are different from those we bring to other kinds of writing (political, religious, historical, philosophical, etc.). But the eighteenth-century definition is much broader: literature, and the parallel term letters, meant something much more like humane learning; they derive from the classical and Renaissance concepts of *humanitas* and *literae humaniores*, liberal education and the humanities. A 'man of letters' in the eighteenth century was as likely to be a historian or philosopher as a poet. The twentieth-century concentration on genre makes it very difficult to read the eighteenth-century novel properly (since it is closely related to religious and philosophical writing, which in the twentieth-century view is not literature), and almost impossible to read eighteenth-century discursive prose: Samuel Johnson's *Rambler* essays (1750–2), for example, are neither literature nor philosophy in the modern sense. Unless the literary historian can recover the meaning of literature and its function in the eighteenth century he is very ill placed to read it in the twentieth. The literary historian of ideas must become a reader of many kinds of writing which do not now seem literary.

This broadening of the definition of literature is one reason why an earlier view of the history of ideas as a background against which literature in the narrower sense is read has become redundant. This view is implicit in E. M. W. Tillyard's over-schematic *The Elizabethan World Picture* (1943), and explicit in the titles of Basil Willey's still widely read studies, *The Seventeenth Century Background* (1934) and *The Eighteenth Century Background* (1940). (In Willey's case the titles are misleading, since he interpreted the history of ideas in a more complex way than they suggest.) Three main approaches to the literary history of ideas can be identified, though these are not hard and fast categories. The first concentrates on an individual author, exploring both the intellectual context of his work and the ideas he expresses in it. Good examples of this approach are Rosemond Tuve's *A Reading of George Herbert* (1952), which stresses biblical exegesis; Phillip Harth's *Swift and Anglican Rationalism: The Religious Background of 'A Tale of Tub'* (1961) and *Contexts of Dryden's Thought* (1968) (the shift in terms is illuminating); Maximillian E. Novak's studies of Defoe's economic and moral ideas, *Economics and the Fiction of Daniel Defoe* (1962) and *Defoe and the Nature of Man* (1963); R. S. Crane's brilliant essay on *Gulliver's Travels*, 'The Houyhnhnms, the Yahoos, and the History of Ideas' ([1962] 1967); and the very informative introductions to the monumental Yale edition of Milton's *Complete Prose Works* (1953–82), which themselves constitute an intellectual history of the mid-seventeenth century.

The second approach concentrates on particular intellectual movements (whether religious, political, philosophical or scientific) in order to illuminate the work of particular authors or the development of particular literary movements (in the narrow sense). Good examples of this approach are William Haller's *The Rise of Puritanism 1570–1643* (1938), which is invaluable for early Milton; R. F. Jones's studies of the relation between science, religion, and late seventeenth-century prose style, collected in *The Seventeenth Century* (1951); Barbara Lewalski's *Protestant Poetics and the Seventeenth-Century Religious Lyric* (1979); and Douglas Lane Patey's *Probability and Literary Form: Philosophic Theory and Literary Practice in the Augustan Age* (1984). An example of this approach directed at undergraduates is my handbook *Classical and Christian Ideas in English Renaissance Poetry* (1979).

The third approach concentrates on intellectual movements as important in themselves, incorporating the work of literary writers as evidence and/or using literary methods of analysis. The classic example of this approach is Leslie Stephen's *History of English Thought in the Eighteenth Century* (1876), which explores the context of controversy in which philosophical and religious ideas developed. Good recent examples are D. C. Allen's *Doubt's Boundless Sea: Skepticism and Faith in the Renaissance* (1964), which looks at the vexed question of atheism; Norman Fiering's *Moral Philosophy at Seventeenth-Century Harvard* (1981), which, despite its specialist-sounding title, is an important study of the shift from Puritan to sentimental ethics in England and America; and Neil Keeble's *The Literary Culture of Nonconformity in Later Seventeenth-Century England* (1987). My *Reason, Grace and Sentiment: A Study of the Language of Religion and Ethics in England 1660–1780* (vol. 1, 1991) is a further example of this approach.

It is worth pointing out in passing that the greater part of this work has been carried out at American universities. The most successful work in the history of ideas in Britain has been done in the fields of political thought and art history. There may be a number of reasons for this situation, which it is inappropriate to go into here. However, it seems likely that in the future the study of the history of ideas will become more complex and more demanding and that the research will be undertaken at institutions of higher education that are able to run graduate degree courses. There will be fewer of these in Britain in the future. This observation is not intended to discourage undergraduate study of the literary history of ideas – on the contrary, it can be undertaken successfully at this level. Nor is it inconsistent with optimism about the future development of the subject.

In what ways can the literary historian of ideas take advantage of the current methodological emphasis on context, languages, conventions and rhetoric? What questions should the student (at whatever level) be asking? The suggestions that follow are based on my own practice. In reading a work of literature (in the broad sense) in the service of one of the approaches outlined above, he should try to answer these questions: what form does the author employ (for example philosophical treatise, popular handbook, essay, dialogue)? What are the implications of this choice of form? What is his purpose in writing? What does he take the function of books to be? What are his characteristic terms and arguments? Who else is using them in the same or different ways? What are his attitudes to language, style and literary devices? Are they consistent with his practice? What is the intended audience of the work? Is there more than one (for example his intimates, his allics, those who already share his views, those whom he is attempting to influence or persuade, his opponents, those whom he regards as dangerous, those whose views he intends to refute rationally or demolish polemically)? How does he treat his audiences? How does he respond to others? Do his ideas, arguments, terms or style differ depending on the form he chooses or the audience he addresses? If they do, what is the significance of these differences? Who are the authorities to whom he defers, or whom he recommends? Who are the rival authorities whom he attempts to dislodge? With what group does he identify himself? What label does he attach to himself? What is the origin of the label (his opponents, his allies, himself)? What use does he make of literary sources (the Bible, the classics, contemporary religious, political, philosophical, scientific literature)? Is the language he uses peculiar to himself, that of a group to which he belongs, or the transmutation of the language of another group?

The assumptions underlying these questions are the Renaissance humanist ones that the function of rhetoric is persuasion and the function of literature communication. The questions do not divorce form from content: they suppose that ideas are part of human life, and that they do not exist in isolation from the forms in which they are expressed, propagated and challenged by their authors and readers. The twentieth-century reader has his own reasons for being interested in particular ideas, or groups, or authors, or works, and he is bound by the limitations to which all acts of human observation and analysis are subject. But this does not mean that his questions are unanswerable, or that the answers are his own invention. The main obstacles to the successful answering of such questions by literary readers, or indeed to the putting of them at all, are the traditional separation of literature from other forms of writing and the emphasis in current literary theory on problems of epistemology. The first restricts the works which can be read and the questions which can be put; the second makes all works unreadable in the ways in which I have suggested they should be read.

It may be helpful to give an example of an important work which has been misread as a result of both these tendencies: Bunyan's *Pilgrim's Progress* (1678, 1684). George Watson in *The New Cambridge Bibliography of English Literature*, vol. 2 (1971), which is an invaluable source for historians of ideas, ludicrously lists Bunyan not among Nonconformist religious writers of the Restoration period, such as Joseph Alleine or Benjamin Keach, which is where he belongs, but as the first of 'The Principal Novelists', followed by Defoe, Richardson and Fielding. Innocent users of the bibliography must have been bewildered by the long list of sermons and tracts written by this supposed novelist. Recent literary historians and critics have been interested in *The Pilgrim's Progress* primarily as an analysis of the problems of fiction – and thus a forerunner of the eighteenth-century novel – and an example of the self-defeating nature of didactic literature (e.g. Fish, 1972). Now Bunyan certainly was interested in the problems of fiction, and in validating his allegorical method by appeal to biblical precedent, and he took very seriously the question of the ways in which didactic literature functions in relation to different kinds of audience. In reading Bunyan the literary historian of ideas will ask questions about these matters. But they are subordinate questions. If the historian asks the whole range of questions I have suggested, he will come up with very different answers from the ones supplied by historians of the novel or reader-response theorists. He will find that *The Pilgrim's Progress* is on one level a polemical work written to defend, unsuccessfully, the decline of the religion of grace in the later seventeenth century, the Reformation doctrine of justification by faith alone, against a new kind of moral Christianity which stressed ethics at the expense of doctrine, and which was dominant until the Evangelical Revival in the eighteenth century. He will find himself confronting the irony of the work's extraordinary popularity and influence despite the fact that it was written as a defence of a religious position that was in retreat. The reader who is not interested in religious and moral ideas, and who does not consider Bunyan's context, is not reading the book that Bunyan wrote.

The development of the literary history of ideas along these lines would have three main consequences for academic study in the humanities. It would help to free readers from the stranglehold of linguistic scepticism. It would enable a much wider range of literature to be read under the auspices of literary study. And it would, through the application of the methods of literary and rhetorical analysis, bring closer together the historical study of religion, philosophy, politics, science and literature.

FURTHER READING

Bouwsma, William J. (1981) 'Intellectual History in the 1980s: From History of Ideas to History of Meaning', *Journal of Interdisciplinary History*, 12, 279–91

Collini, Stefan, *et al.* (1985) 'What is Intellectual History?' *History Today*, 35, 46–54

Darnton, Robert (1980) 'Intellectual and Cultural History'. In Michael Kammen (ed.), *The Past Before Us: Contemporary Historical Writing in the United States*, Cornell University Press, Ithaca, pp. 327–54

Kelley, Donald R. (1987) 'Horizons of Intellectual History: Retrospect, Circumspect, Prospect', *Journal of the History of Ideas*, 48, 143–69

Lovejoy, Arthur O. (1936) *The Great Chain of Being: A Study of the History of an Idea*, Harvard University Press, Cambridge

——(1948) *Essays in the History of Ideas*, Johns Hopkins University Press, Baltimore

Pocock, J. G. A. (1985) *Virtue, Commerce, and History: Essays on Political Thought and History, Chiefly in the Eighteenth Century*, Cambridge University Press, Cambridge

Skinner, Quentin (1972) 'Motives, Intentions, and the Interpretation of Texts', *New Literary History*, 3, 393–408

——(1975) 'Hermeneutics and the Role of History', *New Literary History*, 7, 209–32

Tobey, Jeremy L. (1977) *The History of Ideas: A Bibliographical Introduction*, vol. 2, *Medieval and Early Modern Europe*, Clio Books, Santa Barbara

Wiener, Philip P. (ed.) (1968) *Dictionary of the History of Ideas*, 5 vols, Charles Scribner's Sons, New York

Wiener, Philip P. and Noland, Aaron (eds) (1962) *Ideas in Cultural Perspective*, Rutgers University Press, New Brunswick

ADDITIONAL WORKS CITED

Collingwood, R. G. (1939) *An Autobiography*, Clarendon Press, Oxford

Crane, R. S. (1967) 'The Houyhnhnms, the Yahoos, and the History of Ideas'. In R. S. Crane, *The Idea of the Humanities and Other Essays Critical and Historical*, vol. 2, University of Chicago Press, Chicago, pp. 261–82 [essay first published 1962]

Fish, Stanley E. (1972) *Self-consuming Artifacts: The Experience of Seventeenth-Century Literature*, University of California Press, Berkeley and Los Angeles, chap. 4

Hirsch, E. D., Jr. (1967) *Validity in Interpretation*, Yale University Press, New Haven

McLuhan, Marshall (1962) *The Gutenberg Galaxy: The Making of Typographic Man*, Routledge & Kegan Paul, London

Nicolson, Marjorie (1948) 'A. O. Lovejoy as Teacher', *Journal of the History of Ideas*, 9, 428–38

——(1960) *The Breaking of the Circle: Studies in the Effect of the 'New Science' upon Seventeenth-Century Poetry*, Columbia University Press, New York; Oxford University Press, London [first published 1950]

——(1962) *Science and Imagination*, Cornell University Press, Ithaca [first published 1956]

Pocock, J. G. A. (1971) *Politics, Language and Time: Essays on Political Thought and History*, Methuen, London

Skinner, Quentin (1978) *The Foundation of Modern Political Thought*, 2 vols, Cambridge University Press, Cambridge

70

LITERATURE AND THE BIBLE

STEPHEN PRICKETT

A book's use and influence may not always be quite what they seem. Samuel Butler, the Victorian novelist and freethinker, used to remark that the book he used most was Frost's *Lives of Eminent Christians* – to prop up the other books he was reading in the British Museum. To assume that the principal use or even influence of the Bible has been devotional runs a similar risk of identifying a book's apparent purpose with its actual historic function. Though it has often been argued that the two most influential works of English literature are Shakespeare and the Authorized Version of the Bible, we need to consider the possibility that the Bible's obvious thematic and stylistic literary reverberations over the past 380 years, important as these have been, may in fact be less fundamental than the way in which it has unconsciously come to shape our very idea of a book and our notions of how to read and interpret any written work.

Our word 'Bible' comes to us via the French *bible* from the Latin *biblia*, a feminine singular noun meaning simply 'the book'. In its earlier Latin form, however, *biblia* was not taken to be the feminine singular, but the neuter plural form, which, following the Greek, *ta biblia*, meant 'the (little) books'. Right from the start, therefore, however accidentally, our sense of the Bible has contained within it a tension between singularity and pluralism, between unity and diversity. The Bible was seen as 'the Book of Books': an ambiguous phrase that implied that it could be seen both as a collection of many different works somehow forming a unity greater than the sum of its parts, and, at the same time, *the* pre-eminent and superlative *book* – what one might call the 'class-definer', the book from which all other books might be recognized as books. The importance of this dual origin for the development of European literature cannot be over-estimated.

The Judaeo-Christian foundations of our Western civilization have conditioned us to thinking of books – all books – in certain very distinctive ways. First, we expect to discover in a story narrative rather than chronicle; instead of a mere succession of events, we expect to find in their progression an implicit sense of meaning in relation to each other and to the whole. Second, and following from this, we are accustomed to the idea that a book is, of its very nature, hermeneutic and interpretative. Just because Christianity began with a special sense that it differed from the world that preceded it, and that its own heritage of what we now call the Old Testament had now to be understood differently from the way in which its own compilers had presumably understood it, the *interpretative* function of narrative was central to the Christian Bible in a unique way. That need for interpretation begins with the sense of the difference of the past.

When the ancient Greek historian Herodotus visited Thebes in Egypt, he gazed with awe at the list of High Priests of the temple inscribed on its walls as he realized that the three hundred generations represented there took him back thousands of years before the dawn of Greek history and civilization. In *The Death of the Past* (1969, p. 111) J. H. Plumb contrasts this disturbing experience that began to give meaning and shape to the Greek sense of history with the Chinese chroniclers, for whom the succession of one emperor after another for over five thousand years, however violent the dynastic clashes, was essentially unproblematic in that it was a record of a single continuous society. Like Herodotus, and unlike the Chinese, the compilers of the New Testament saw the past not so much in terms of continuity as of discontinuity – a problem with a meaning to be explained. Moreover, with the assimilation of Christianity into the Roman world there arose a new hermeneutic problem: the relationship between the biblical and classical cultures. It was one that worried both Augustine and Jerome. From it were to stem many of the great questions of Western philosophy, and not least our peculiar sense of history. To quote Plumb again:

> History began because scholars perceived a problem which faced no other civilization – the problem of the duality of Europe's past, its conflicting ideologies and of their different interpretations of human destiny.
>
> (p. 136)

This sense of the past as a problem that needed interpretation was compounded by the events of the first few centuries of the Christian era. One reason, perhaps, why Christianity, unlike so many of its rival religions, was able to ride out the destruction of the Roman Empire was that it already contained within its own literature models not merely for the destruction of empires, but for finding a *meaningful* pattern in their rise and fall. And this brings us to our third point: the idea of a 'book' (and consequently any written or spoken work) is not something that comes to us innocent or empty-handed. Not merely does it involve assumptions of narrative rather than chronicle, of interpretation and of the imposition of meaning: those assumptions are essentially interdependent. Europe's past is a narrative past, and it is taken for granted that the creation of narrative is a hermeneutic activity.

One example must stand for hundreds. As is well known, the raw material of Shakespeare's history plays comes mostly from Hall, Holinshed and Stow. Yet, for any Elizabethan, 'History' was much more than simply a recital of facts. Secular history was a branch of that universal and divine history revealed by God through the Bible. It was, therefore, charged with implicit meaning – meaning which it was the task of the historian to bring out and clarify. History was, in effect, a series of moral *exempla* to illustrate in practice the great unchanging truths of God's judgement. Even in pre-Reformation times such matters could clearly be controversial. But with the Reformation and subsequent wars of religion the interpretation of history acquired a new urgency. If, even before Shakespeare, most Englishmen were in no doubt that their victory at Agincourt reflected divine approval for Henry's (somewhat tortuous) claim to the French throne, the defeat of the Spanish Armada – more by the weather than by English ships – was much clearer proof that God, if not an Englishman, was at least an Anglican. In Elizabeth's reign biblical hermeneutics were also front-line politics.

Though apparently a conforming Protestant, Shakespeare (like many of his contemporaries) had strong Catholic connections. Much has been written on the question of his possible Catholic or Protestant sympathies without any decisive result; much less on the indisputable fact that anyone in his position would be deeply familiar with the modes of biblical exegesis around which the debate revolved. Not merely was the representation of history an essentially hermeneutic and in this case polemical activity, such representation was always assumed to be on many levels. It was of the nature of narrative. As has been mentioned above in the essay on Biblical Hermeneutics, medieval systems of exegesis, however much they may have disagreed with each other as to whether there were four, seven, or twelve levels to be found in the Bible, were united in their conviction that the written word was essentially polysemous. Such systems of interpretation were part of the normal habit of mind of most people, even (as we shall see) as late as the beginning of the nineteenth century, in a way that has been almost entirely lost today. Thus when, for instance, critics have noted elements of the medieval morality play in the plot of *Henry IV* – especially in the relationship of Hal and Falstaff – they have been less quick to add that this is, in effect, classic *figural* typology. A real moral truth is demonstrated from the lives of real historical people. At the same time, a much wider truth about the nature of order and power is also being disclosed.

Yet in secular literature, and even in history, the boundaries between 'fact' and 'fiction' were not those that a modern audience would necessarily take for granted. Hotspur, for example, was in reality a good twenty-five years older than Hal, yet in *Henry IV*, Shakespeare, for reasons of dramatic contrast, makes them the same age. Which is 'history' in the Elizabethan sense? the fact or the interpretation? There is a good case for saying that, for Shakespeare and his contemporaries, *Henry IV* is the 'history', and that the chroniclers merely provided appropriate raw material to be given significance by the dramatist. Once we start to think of 'history' in this way, we can see how relatively modern is our apparently self-evident distinction between 'fact' and 'fiction'. It is worth remembering that the origin of the word 'fact' lies not in any notion of objectivity but in the Latin *factum*: 'a thing done or performed'. For the seventeenth century a historical narrative is as much something *created* as any work of art. As such, it was just as bound by the polysemous conventions of narrative as any 'fictional' work.

Similarly, though the eighteenth-century novel is rooted in the convention that it tells a real story about real people, it nevertheless also shared current assumptions about figural typology. Defoe is at pains to stress the factual basis of *Robinson Crusoe* (1719). Much more flamboyant and problematical is Fielding in *Tom Jones* (1749). In the course of a whole series of comparisons of himself, as author, with a cook, a judge, a dramatist and a governor, Fielding explicitly compares himself with the Author of the book of nature: like the Almighty, the novelist creates his own universe with its peculiar inhabitants, laws, and events. The reader is thus warned:

> Not too hastily to condemn any of the Incidents in this our history, as impertinent and foreign to our main design, because thou dost not immediately conceive in what manner such incident may conduce to that design. This work may, indeed, be considered as a great creation of our own.
>
> (ed. 1966, p. 467)

This is the novelist not as exegete but as a Calvinistic God. Because the reader, like fallen man, cannot appreciate the whole mysterious outworkings of the plot, he cannot judge it. At one level, of course, this is theological parody, but there is also a serious point about textual interpretation here that a medieval writer such as Dante would have understood and appreciated.

Perhaps even more revealing is an example from a slightly later novelist whose stories appear at first sight to be entirely naturalistic and secular in construction: Jane Austen. A number of recent critics have drawn attention to the so-called 'symbolism' created by the visit to Mr Rushworth's Sotherton estate in *Mansfield Park* (1814). It is not an accident of spiritual geography that Mary Crawford has a long discussion with Edmund, the hero, who is about to be ordained, on the role of a clergyman while the party is strolling in the part of the garden technically known as 'the wilderness'. Nor is it accidental that when they come to the little iron gate that leads from the wilderness to the main park each member of the party acts in such a way as to foreshadow their eventual approach to marriage. (We recall, as doubtless did the author, the sexually-charged couplet from Marvell's 'Coy Mistress' urging the lovers to 'tear' their 'pleasures with rough strife/Thorough the iron gates of life . . .') Thus, in chapter 10, on finding the way to further pleasure barred by the iron gate, Rushworth, who is to marry Maria Bertram, goes to get the key; meanwhile, Henry Crawford, who later seduces her, persuades Maria to squeeze *round* the gate with these words:

> And for the world you would not get on without the key and without Mr Rushworth's authority and protection, as I think you might with little difficulty pass round the edge of the gate, here, with my assistance; I think it might be done if you really wish to be more at large, and could allow yourself to think it is not prohibited.
>
> (ed. 1966, p. 127)

Julia Bertram, who later elopes with Mr Yeats, simply scrambles across in their wake, while Fanny, the repressed heroine, remains on the right side, waits for Edmund – and complains of a headache.

All this has been often noted – as 'symbolism'. But, of course, it is not. It is, however ironic in its employment, old-fashioned biblical typology of the sort that Parson Austen's daughter was accustomed to hearing every Sunday from the pulpit, and doubtless reading in her biblical commentaries on weekdays too. The fourfold senses of the text are as present here as they might be in any commentary on Genesis. The literal sense of the narrative is complemented by the typological, as each character foreshadows their own antetype in their future sexual behaviour. Morally we see that waiting for legal marriage, as the 'key' to future happiness, though it takes more time and denies immediate gratification, is the correct course. Anagogically, what is being decided here is who is eventually to inherit the 'estate' itself – and the double meaning, now archaic, of both 'land' and 'position' is significant. Maria forfeits possession of Sotherton; Fanny gains not just Edmund's love, but also (spiritually, as the wife of the incumbent) Mansfield Park itself, which in the novel has clearly idealized and even paradisal associations.

If confirmation were needed of the way the Bible had penetrated the whole fabric of early nineteenth-century society we need look no further than an extraordinary passage in Coleridge's *Confessions of an Inquiring Spirit*, written in 1830 and published ten years later. What he has to say is as much cultural as theological in its implications. He begins with a recognition of the way in which the Bible has come to colour not just conscious assumptions on particular topics but the whole framework of perceptions which, by definition, lie *below* the threshold of consciousness. In the first Letter he defines his approach to the Bible in these words:

> I take up this work with the purpose to read it for the first time as I should any other work, – as far at least as I can or dare. For I neither can, nor dare, throw

955

off a strong and awful prepossession in its favour – certain as I am that a large part of the light and life, in and by which I see, love, and embrace the truths and strengths co-organized into a living body of faith and knowledge ... has been directly or indirectly derived to me from this sacred volume, – and unable to determine what I do not owe to its influences.

(1849, p. 9)

He is overwhelmingly conscious of writing within a culture so steeped in biblical assumptions and patterns of thought that it is no longer possible for someone *within* that system fully to grasp the extent of that influence or the ways in which it has come to condition his perspectives on the world. Not merely ways of perceiving but also the language in which those perceptions are given shape is permeated by the Bible. It was a theme that Coleridge was to return to over and over again in his life. In his *Table Talk* for 24 June 1827, for instance, among a welter of observations ranging from Shakespeare to craniology, we find this comment:

Our version of the Bible is to be loved and prized for this, as for a thousand other things, – that it has preserved a purity of meaning to many terms of natural objects. Without this holdfast, our vitiated imaginations would refine away language to mere abstractions. Hence the French have lost their poetical language; and Mr Blanco White says the same thing has happened to the Spanish.

(ed. 1852, p. 43)

The charge that French and Spanish had entirely lost their 'poetical language' through over-refinement is at first glance a puzzling one, but Coleridge's apparent anti-Latin prejudices in fact do no more than echo a view that had already been expressed in France by no less an authority than the *philosophe* Diderot, who had argued in his *Letter on the Deaf-Mutes* (1751) that French had indeed lost its 'warmth, eloquence, and energy' and become a language of prose best fitted for science and philosophy. Diderot does not, however, try to connect this with biblical translations. Nevertheless, Coleridge is certainly right in indirectly pointing to the very real fact that the Authorized Version of the Bible *had* played an incomparably bigger part in the development of English literature than any corresponding French or Spanish versions, and that it had influenced the development of the English language and its literature in certain quite fundamental ways. In particular, according to Coleridge, it had preserved a certain concreteness of expression in English that he clearly associates with the language's poetic vitality and which stands in sharp contrast with the spare and classical elegance of (say) Louis Segond's famous French version of the Bible.

Whatever his later disagreements with Wordsworth over the exact nature of poetic diction, Coleridge had been in 1798 a co-author of the *Lyrical Ballads*, and as passionate a believer as his friend and fellow-poet in the primitive sublimity of the language of ordinary men. For him, writing forty years later, it is still self-evident that the 'language of natural objects' is the proper medium of poetry. What is perhaps less obvious to the modern reader is why this romantic theory of diction is to be associated so closely with the Bible – and specifically with the Authorized Version of 1611.

To understand this we need to turn back to the middle of the eighteenth century to the work of Robert Lowth (1753). Whereas most critics of the day, reared on neo-classical rules, would have followed Jerome and Augustine in assuming that the Bible eschewed fine rhetoric and poetic grandeur in order to make its message more plain, Lowth argued that, on the contrary, the 'simple and unadorned' language of Hebrew verse produced an 'almost ineffable sublimity' not through elevated diction, but by the depth and universal appeal of its subject-matter. In the New Testament, Jesus, in his humble origins and in the simplicity and directness of his speech, is the direct heir of the Hebrew poetic tradition. Moreover, unlike the modern poets, the Hebrew ones had never been part of a courtly circle at the centre of power; more often than not they were opposed to the luxury and refinement of the court and city. Because they came from a rural and pastoral background they naturally tended to speak and write in the language of ordinary people with the metaphors of agriculture and everyday life. Though Lowth writes as a conservative and establishment figure, and seems quite unaware of the possible revolutionary implications of what he is saying, they were not lost on the succeeding generations who found in his scholarly reconstruction of the biblical world clear justification not merely for egalitarian politics but also for making naturalness and simplicity essential elements of the new critical vogue for the 'sublime'. His stress on naturalness as against artifice, the irregular as against the regular, the mysterious as against the comprehensible, anticipates Burke's famous *Enquiry into the Sublime and the Beautiful* (1756) by several years. For him, as for Burke, it is the ultimate criterion by which the greatness of any work must be judged. Foreshadowing Wordsworth and the Preface to the *Lyrical Ballads* even in details, Lowth insists that poetry is the product of 'enthusiasm' 'springing from mental emotion' (Prickett, 1986, pp. 108–9). Not surprisingly, therefore, it was the concrete and domestic metaphors of biblical language, mediated through the Authorized Version, that became the dominant model in the romantic revulsion against the abstract and classicized diction of the eighteenth-century Enlightenment.

Even before we turn to the influence of specific biblical themes on English literature, therefore, we find that the whole *idea* of literature, its interpretation, its evaluation, and even its diction and metaphorical structure, is shot through with assumptions and patterns of thought taken from the Bible. Such underlying patterns help to explain the way in which the major biblical themes fell on ground so fertile in English literature that its whole development can sometimes seem like little more than an extended commentary on the one Book –

a point of which Fielding was, of course, ironically aware. Even that proverbial metaphor, of seed falling on fertile ground, is itself biblical in origin – taken from the parable of the sower. Yet the transmutation of biblical themes into secular literature is not just simply a process of either re-telling or commentary. Take, for instance, the story of the Fall.

We have no reason to believe that Milton, in writing *Paradise Lost*, did not believe in the absolute literal truth of the story he was relating. But, as we have seen, that literal truth signified for him something different from what it would have for, say, a nineteenth-century fundamentalist if only because the literal was just one, and possibly the least important one, of many levels of meaning encoded in the narrative. Nevertheless, there was no possibility of tampering with the basic events in the way that Shakespeare might with Holinshed. This, after all, was Holy Writ. Yet, as a succession of critics from Blake onwards have pointed out, something rather strange has happened to the fundamental nature of the story as it appears in that monumental poem. The original biblical narrative is spare and stark in the extreme. It is told in a third-person voice which is neither that of God, Man nor Satan. In other words, it is already transmitted in a literary – or, to be more exact, mythical form. Milton's narrative in contrast is polyphonous. God, Adam and Eve, and, most important of all, Satan, have all acquired distinctive voices, with characters and motives to match. In consequence, not merely has the Fall been dramatized but it has also been inescapably *internalized*. No longer can the stress be laid upon the *act* of eating the forbidden fruit; we must take into account the motives for that action. Satan's is patently revenge – not a motive even hinted at in the Bible narrative. Eve's are more complicated. She desires the 'deity' that she seems to be being offered, but not just for its own sake: she wants to share it with Adam – partly, it is true, to impress him, but partly too out of desire to 'give' something to the man who, literally, has everything. Adam's motives are less complex, but in their own way, even less reprehensible. He loves Eve. He weighs the consequences carefully. He even goes so far as to consider that if he rejects her now God might simply blot her out and give him a new and better model woman. That decides him. He will stand by her, come what may. But by this time something catastrophic has happened to the original myth of the Fall. So far from being deliberate disobedience it has turned into something suspiciously like an exercise in love and loyalty (Waldock, 1949).

Nor is this all. The moment we start to consider *motive* rather than just deed, it is clear that in order to contemplate disobeying God the Fall *must already* have taken place. For Eve simply to contemplate trying to alter her status in the order of creation, she is already guilty of Pride; Adam, weighing his loyalty to God against his loyalty to Eve, though he may well be technically guilty of the same sin, is already into the much more complex world of moral choice between different but incompatible values – a dilemma that anyone who had lived in mid-seventeenth century England and the Civil War would have known with peculiar poignancy. Either way, the original myth has been inescapably changed in a manner that we must presume could not have been anticipated either by Milton or his seventeenth-century audience.

Yet we must be wary of taking this as evidence that the literary process of 'internalization' that we have noted above in some way invalidates the myth itself. On the contrary, the internalizing or psychologizing of the myth was actually to give it new and unpredictable resonances. William Golding, for instance, writing three hundred years after Milton in the mid-twentieth century, sees that process of internalizing that we associate with the later development of literature as a crucial aspect of the Fall itself. In his novel *The Inheritors* (1955) he portrays a species of *un*-fallen man who have no sense of themselves as differentiated from their natural environment. Though they can use a few simple words, they prefer to communicate telepathically by means of direct 'pictures' in the mind. One of this group encounters a stranger:

> The man turned sideways in the bushes and looked at Lok along his shoulder. A stick rose upright and there was a lump of bone in the middle. Lok peered at the stick and the lump of bone. . . . Suddenly Lok understood that the man was holding the stick out to him but neither he nor Lok could reach across the river. He would have laughed if it were not for the echo of the screaming in his head. The stick began to grow shorter at both ends. Then it shot out to its full length again.
> The dead tree by Lok's ear acquired a voice.
> 'Clop!'
> His ears twitched and he turned to the tree. By his face there had grown a twig: a twig that smelt of other, and of goose, and of the bitter berries that Lok's stomach told him he must not eat. This twig had a white bone at the end. There were hooks in the bone and sticky brown stuff hung in the crooks. His nose examined the stuff and did not like it. He smelled along the shaft of the twig. The leaves of the twig were red feathers and reminded him of goose. He was lost in a generalized astonishment and excitement.
>
> (p. 106)

Lok's encounter with this enemy is told through his own mode of consciousness. Its essential feature, of course, is that there is no concealment. There is, as it were, no space, no privacy for self-consciousness in our sense – and therefore no possibility of either lies or deception. Such a 'space', Golding suggests, is the creation of language. Thus Lok's 'stomach' tells him that the juice of the bitter berries is not to be eaten; his 'nose' reinforces this warning that stuff smeared on the barbs of bone is bad for him; but nothing immediately enables him to connect the man across the river, whose stick grows short and then long again, with the new and dangerous branch on the tree by his ear which smells mysteriously of both deadly berries and of goose. He cannot

959

conceptualize sufficiently to realize (as *we* eventually do) that the man on the other side of the river is shooting at him with a bow and poisoned arrows. Being totally unaggressive himself, he cannot imagine what it might mean to be attacked with the malice aforethought necessary to manufacture arrows with poisoned barbs. Such technology belongs to language alone – and with language goes loss of innocence. Neanderthal man has encountered homo sapiens, and is on his way to extinction.

The language is as visually flat and two-dimensional as the pictures by which the Neanderthals habitually communicated. The bow is not something menacing that requires evasive action; it is simply a stick that shortens at both ends. Just as Lok himself was decentralized into a stomach, a nose, etc., so the words are studiedly empty of implications of cause, effect and time. Things just are. Unfortunately, such pictures and their appropriate vocabulary are not equipped to encounter change. It is the end of the Ice Age; the landscape is thawing and great lakes and rivers are appearing – and on the water come the new people armed with bows and arrows – and one doesn't use poisoned arrows for food one is intending to eat.

The careful defamiliarization of events and deliberate elimination of the normal flow of cause and effect contrasts sharply with the opening of the final chapter, when, for the first time, the narration shifts to the perspective of the true homo sapiens.

> Tuami sat in the stern of the dug-out, the steering paddle under his left arm . . . the walls of rock folding back until this lake became so broad that he had been able to find no transits for judging their motion but had sat, guessing, with the mountains looming over the flat water and his eyes red with the tears of strain. Now he stirred a little for the rounded bilge was hard and the pad of leather that many steersmen had moulded to a comfortable seat was lost on the slope up from the forest. He could feel the slight pressure transmitted to his forearm along the loom of the paddle and knew that if he were to trail his hand over the side the water would tinkle against the palm and heap up over his wrist. The two dark lines spreading on either bow were not laid back at a sharp angle but led out almost at right angles to the line of the boat. If the breeze changed or faltered those lines would creep ahead and fade and the pressure in the paddle would slacken and they would begin to slide astern towards the mountains.
>
> (pp. 223–4)

What one might in another context think of as a very conventional piece of description of a dug-out canoe sailing up a lake against the current becomes here a startling reminder of how much of what we normally think of as 'description' in fact involves the vocabulary of precisely such explanation – implying cause, effect and time. Not merely is Tuami constantly judging the conflicting powers of wind and current, monitoring their water-speed, and attempting to cross-check his estimates by the relative movement of objects on the shore, he is going back in his mind to his calculations of the previous night to compare the actual experience with the anticipated one. The language is casually technical: he is seated in the 'bilge', and finds it hard; he looks for 'transits' on the shore, and feels the subtle pressure of the paddle's 'loom' on his forearm. And – as we learn in the following pages – as he skilfully guides the boat he is meditating murder and adultery. Post-fall, articulate and technological humanity has arrived.

So, of course, has the novel. Language has not only created space between thought and action, it has also enabled us to reflect on the phenomenon – and to distinguish between them. As Julian Jaynes (1976) observes, the true test of consciousness is in the ability to lie. He might have added more justly that it is in the ability to create fictions. Certainly for Golding the origins of narrative are rooted in the very myth of the Fall itself – and it is no accident that at the centre of the spiritual geography of *The Inheritors* is a huge frozen ice-age waterfall that blocks the path of both Neanderthals and homo sapiens on their journey inland to escape the rising waters. In the end it is the innocent but unreflecting Neanderthals who are defeated by it, for they fear water; as the ice melts, breaks up and turns into a raging torrent, it is the humans who successfully scale the fall and launch themselves on to the hitherto uncharted waters of the inland sea. The symbolism is obvious enough; what is perhaps less obvious, but in the light of his later work is equally important, is the fact that the fable relates not merely to the origins of evil, but also, reflexively, to the origins of the artist's own medium in the use of words.

If we have apparently come a long way from the biblical myth of the Fall it is only to rediscover it in a new form – one which links the origins of evil with the creation of the word itself. Though Golding's fictional form provides a peculiarly powerful version of it, such a conclusion is by no means confined to him: a recent article by a respected literary critic argues a very similar case from quite different premises (Edwards, 1984). My point, once again, is simply that the idea of a 'book' is not something that comes to us innocent or empty-handed. On the contrary, it has been culturally conditioned by the historical presence of the Bible, and its relationship to subsequent thought in very particular and highly complex ways. So central were these to our own culture that for long periods it was only by a very self-conscious effort that it was possible to focus on them at all. So long as narrative could simply be seen as a literary concomitant of the notion of historical progress, the fact that it was born of a need to reinterpret a problematic and threatening past could conveniently be forgotten. With the ending of the Second World War and the revelations of the full extent of Nazi atrocities (not to mention Allied responses), the question of human nature and history became a problem of a kind not seen in England at any rate since the end of the Civil War. The revelations contained by that chapter meant that nineteenth-century meliorist interpretations of history and liberal assumptions of progress were open to question in a quite new way. Prominent among those ideas had been the easy optimism of the kind of socio-biological developmental theories promulgated by such works as Wells's *Outline of History* (1920) – which Golding quotes as a preface to his fable. Golding's stark and disturbing story, however, holds the mirror up to a very different world from that of Wells's late nineteenth-century England. For Golding, the entire text of human history has to be re-read and re-interpreted in the light of its most recent ending. But such a re-reading is never a one-way process: in so far as that re-reading modifies our idea of humanity, it also modifies our idea of language and of books. The mode of interpretation has changed between Milton and Golding, but the referential strength of the underlying biblical myth and its sense of polysemous meaning is as creative as ever. Just as each generation has understood the Bible in its own ways, so each has in its literature reflected or refracted that understanding according to its particular needs and problems in the perennial quest to discover the world through the book.

FURTHER READING

Abrams, M. H. (1973) *Natural Supernaturalism*, Norton, New York

Charity, A. C. (1966) *Events and their Afterlife: The Dialectics of Christian Typology in the Bible and Dante*, Cambridge University Press, Cambridge

Frye, Northrop (1982) *The Great Code: The Bible and Literature*, Routledge, London

Jasper, David (ed.) (1984) *Images of Belief in Literature*, Macmillan, London

——(ed.) (1986) *The Interpretation of Belief: Coleridge, Schleiermacher and Romanticism*, Macmillan, London

Kermode, Frank (1979) *The Genesis of Secrecy*, Harvard University Press, Cambridge

Nuttall, A. D. (1981) *Overheard by God*, Methuen, London

Prickett, Stephen (ed.) (1991) *Reading the Text: Biblical Criticism and Literary Theory*, Basil Blackwell, Oxford

Smith, Eric (1973) *Some Versions of the Fall*, Croom Helm, London

Tannenbaum, Leslie (1982) *Biblical Tradition in Blake's Early Prophecies: the Great Code of Art*, Princeton University Press, Princeton

Wright, T. R. (1988) *Theology and Literature*, Basil Blackwell, Oxford

Zim, Rivkah (1987) *English Metrical Psalms: Poetry as Praise and Prayer 1535–1601*, Cambridge University Press, Cambridge

ADDITIONAL WORKS CITED

Austen, Jane (1966) *Mansfield Park*, edited by Tony Tanner, Penguin, Harmondsworth [first published 1814]

Coleridge, Samuel Taylor (1849) *Confessions of an Inquiring Spirit*, 2nd edn, Pickering, London [first published 1840]

——(1852) *Table Talk*, edited by H. N. Coleridge, Murray, London

Edwards, Michael (1984) 'Story: Towards a Christian Theory of Narrative'. In David Jasper (ed.), *Images of Belief in Literature*, Macmillan, London

Fielding, Henry (1966) *Tom Jones*, edited by R. P. C. Mutter, Penguin, Harmondsworth [first published 1749]

Golding, William, (1955) *The Inheritors*, Faber & Faber, London

Jaynes, Julian (1976) *The Origins of Consciousness in the Breakdown of the Bicameral Mind*, Houghton Mifflin, Boston

Lowth, Robert (1753) *Lectures on the Sacred Poetry of the Hebrews*, translated by G. Gregory, London (1778)

Plumb, J. H. (1969) *The Death of the Past*, Macmillan, London

Prickett, Stephen (1986) *Words and the Word: Language, Poetics, and Biblical Interpretation*, Cambridge University Press, Cambridge

Waldock, A. J. A. (1949) *Paradise Lost and Its Critics*, Cambridge University Press, Cambridge

71

LITERATURE AND THE CLASSICS

THOMAS HEALY

When I was an undergraduate studying Greek I bought a second-hand copy of Aristotle's *Nicomachean Ethics*. Inside the front cover was a note explaining that the book had belonged to:

> G. R. L. Anderson, Etonian, who came up Michaelmas Term 1908 as Scholar (Classical) of Trinity College Oxford; Fellow of All Souls; Olympic Hurdler. Killed in action near Hooge 9 November 1914 as 2/lt. 3rd Cheshire Regt.

This example serves vividly to present an important aspect of twentieth-century Britain's relation with the classics (which I shall take to mean the literary remains of Greece and Rome). The classics for more than three hundred years had helped to define a certain type of civilization: rational, stable, ordered. To be possessed of a classical education bespoke breeding, maturity of judgement, composure of body and mind. A familiarity with the classics implied not just a knowledge of antiquity, but acquaintance with a certain ideal moral outlook. Henry Nettleship, Corpus Professor of Latin, wrote of Gilbert Murray in 1889:

> He is devoted to the study of literature, but if I am not mistaken this devotion is the expression not merely of his taste and pleasure and reading but of his whole moral nature. Classical education in his hands will not be a mere engine of literary culture but a general training of the character and affections.
>
> (in Lloyd-Jones, 1982, p. 199)

The carnage of the First World War helped destroy the myth of civilization as ordered and eminently sane. The Second World War completed this loss of faith so that, as André Malraux noted in 1949: 'Western civilization has begun to doubt its own credentials' (in Dodds, 1951, p. 252). These credentials were perceived to be founded on classical antiquity, and one consequence of the historical experience of this century has been a questioning of the benefits of classical civilization. The fruits of a classically founded culture, with its patrician ease and cultivation, appeared to many to have been destroyed on the battlefields of Western France. The experience of the First World War convinced Gilbert Murray – who emerged as one of this century's finest classicists – of the 'thinness of the crust' which separated civilization from savagery (see Stevenson, 1988, pp. 19–20). Further, in discovering its own savagery, the twentieth century began to find the classical world itself primitive and irrational.

Drawing generalizations about as vast a subject as the classics and their relation with the study of literature over a century inevitably invites over-simplifications. Ample evidence exists to create a case for a variety of developments. To take three examples: first, the success of the Penguin Classics in stimulating a large readership to explore Greek and Roman literature – in the case of Rieu's translation of *The Odyssey* over a million copies sold. Second, in contrast, there is the decline in university Classics departments, the increasing absence of Latin and Greek on school curricula, as well as the claims of a critic such as George Steiner (1961) that twentieth-century civilization has reached a point where classical values have ceased to apply to the modern situation. Third, in a different manner again, there is the portrait of the slow but steady endeavours of classical scholarship, only occasionally inconvenienced by historical exigencies of no lasting consequence, which emerges from a book such as Hugh Lloyd-Jones's *Blood from the Ghosts: Classical Influences in the Nineteenth and Twentieth Centuries* (1982). The potential exists to argue about the state of the classics in tones optimistic, pessimistic, or even sublimely indifferent.

My own view of the classical tradition's effect on this century's literary and critical thought is of two dominant trends, each different but running parallel to one another. The first envisages civilization on the wane, with the classics offering a bastion from which to defend proper literary, educated and moral values. Depending on the writer's degree of optimism, the classics either lead a renewal of such values, or provide solace and an escape route to the past for the few cultivated souls remaining. The second employs the classics to revitalize a literature perceived as lifeless and affected. The classics become a means to understand the present and to indicate new literary and cultural directions. Both of these trends develop out of the shock to civilization engendered by the First World War, though there are glimpses of earlier origins. Both attitudes, however, assume the classics' continuing relevance and importance to modern life and its literary experience. One thing which can be firmly stated about this century's relation with antiquity is that it continues to perceive the writing of Greece and Rome to be important.

In his 1944 essay 'What is a Classic', T. S. Eliot proposed Virgil as providing the criterion of the classical standard (Eliot, 1957, pp. 52–74). The *Aeneid* offered a modern readership a norm which demonstrated our own literature's defectiveness and provided a standard through which to defend freedom against chaos. The cultivation of the classics was central if civilization was to survive. Eliot's is the voice of high culture and in this essay we have a forceful expression of belief in a civilized future amidst the storm of the Second World War. 'If we cease to believe in the future', Eliot wrote, 'the past would cease to be fully *our* past: it would become the past of a dead civilization' (p. 67).

The classics as a literary measuring-stick designed to gauge cultural excellence is a use they have long been accustomed to from the Renaissance onward, but the argument of Eliot's essay also offers us a good indication of why many in the twentieth century have been reluctant to embrace this traditional defence of a continuing high classical culture. Eliot considers, for instance, the meeting of the ghost of Dido and Aeneas in book VI of the *Aeneid*:

> I have always thought the meeting . . . one of the most civilized passages in poetry. . . . Dido's behaviour appears almost as a projection of Aeneas' own conscience: this we feel, is the way in which Aeneas' own conscience would *expect* Dido to behave to him. The point . . . is that Aeneas does not forgive himself. . . . Here, what I chose as an instance of civilized manners, proceeds to testify to civilized consciousness and conscience.
>
> (pp. 63–4)

Eliot accepts the depiction of Aeneas as an example of desirable civilized values: Aeneas puts national destiny before his own wishes, he selects an active martial life, he accepts responsibility for actions which he knows he is not technically culpable for. Further, Aeneas complies with his destiny without understanding the reasoning behind it, and Eliot obviously applauds such obedience and devotion. Eliot assumes a world of male order against female disorder (and one where the female becomes no more than the mental projection of the male). This may be a justifiable reading of the *Aeneid*, but it is one likely to cause us to be suspicious of this classic's cultural authority. Aeneas' treatment of Dido, and the values this represents, does not automatically define civilized living.

Eliot's essay, constantly emphasizing the 'maturity' a civilization requires both to produce and to appreciate a classic, proposes a highly élitist view of a classically inspired culture:

> To define *maturity* without assuming that the hearer already knows what it means, is almost impossible . . . if we are properly mature, as well as educated persons, we can recognize maturity in a civilization and in a literature. . . . To make the meaning of maturity really apprehensible – indeed even to make it acceptable – to the immature, is perhaps impossible.
>
> (p. 54)

This argument about the appreciation of the classics is vapidly circular. Not to agree that Aeneas defines civilized manners is a sign of immaturity, a cultural failing, not a critical disagreement. Disputing the classical criterion is dangerous and must be suppressed by those betters who do appreciate the standard. In this view you are either among the narrowly defined civilized elect or with the barbarians seeking to throw the great and the good into chaos.

Few would probably attempt similar arguments about the worth of the classics in the 1980s. Yet the assumptions of Eliot's essay are, regrettably, ones still perceived by many current students of literature as underlying the defences made for Greek and Latin. The classics are frequently associated with an élite whose pronouncements of cultural superiority have been severely questioned by the century's historical experience. Eliot's notion of the classic, with its imperial and male-centred attitudes, is one unlikely to be embraced by a large current readership. Indeed, part of this century's literary and larger cultural experience has been one of 'goodbye to all that', with the classics (or rather traditional approaches to them) often being included in the list of suspect artefacts of high cultural affectations. Tony Harrison's poem 'Classics Society', recalling Leeds Grammar School in the early 1950s, for instance, exposes the identification of Latin eloquence with the social inclinations of a ruling élite which some institutions still project: 'We boys can take old Hansards and translate/the British Empire into SPQR' (Harrison, 1984, p. 120). Harrison's poem concludes by noting the rewards offered to the student whose work incorporates a specifically conservative viewpoint: 'And so the lad who gets the alphas works/The hardest in his class at his translation/And finds good Ciceronian for Burke's/A dreadful schism in the British Nation.'

An obvious recent example of this confrontation between an older 'conserving' tradition and an iconoclastic challenge may be discovered in the arguments held in various American institutions over which texts constitute the 'core' of western civilization. The most notable of these has been the debate held at Stanford University in California which led to the resignation of the American Secretary for Education William Bennett in 1988. Stanford, like other American universities, became concerned about a student population unacquainted with both ancient and modern classics and proposed a required foundation course. This occasioned a protest among those who felt the selection of texts reflected a traditional European culture (DWEMS: Dead White European Males), ignoring the cultural inheritance of other continents, other races, and women. The Education Secretary denounced this protest as an example of a desired civilized inheritance under threat. In his view Western civilization was founded on the inheritance of Greece and Rome and later developments within this classical tradition. For many intellectually conservative thinkers the subsequent admission of works by Asiatic, American Indian, Black, and women writers to the Stanford foundation course was evidence of the decline of high cultural values which have their source in Greece and Rome.

This sense of cultural collapse is an extreme view. The Stanford debate more correctly revealed a readjustment of the role of the classics within the late twentieth century, not their eradication. At no point were writers such as Plato, Aristotle, Homer and Virgil being dismissed. Yet the Stanford controversy demonstrated that the classics, rather than providing the criterion for civilization, have become only one element in a much broader and plural conception of what constitutes the century's important cultural heritage. It also reveals the way the classics have been caught up in larger social, political and cultural debates about the construction of modern civilization.

The wariness of the conservative backlash to the DWEMS issue is not a recent development and reflects the view of many who, like Eliot, felt the classics represent a particular maturity of civilized values. It is an instance, though, of how many have felt modern civilization unable to retain a devotion to the classical standard. The classics' heritage has often been portrayed in the twentieth-century as divorced from a reorganized, much declined 'civilization'.

Ford Madox Ford's novel on the consequences of the First World War, *Parade's End* (1924–8), offers numerous examples of the disoriented, classically educated, élite whose world dissolved between 1914 and 1918. In one scene the central character, Christopher Tietjens, and another young officer, McKechnie ('a Vice-Chancellor's Latin Prize man') have a literary contest during a battle. Tietjens asks for the end-rhymes of a sonnet and writes the lines in under two minutes. McKechnie then claims he will turn the sonnet into Latin hexameters in under three minutes (Ford, 1950, p. 315). Both these characters represent the apparently effortless patrician brilliance of the pre-1914 generations. Both possess high notions of responsibility and public duty. The following exchange is characteristic. Note the way in which a self-denying commitment to the troops becomes instantly equated with a certain cultural and educational inheritance. Tietjens inquires why McKechnie did not leave his front-line battalion and go into Intelligence:

> 'I don't know. I was with the battalion. I wanted to stop with the battalion. I was intended for the Foreign Office. My miserable uncle got me hoofed out of that. I was with the battalion. The C.O. wasn't up to much. *Someone* had to stay with the battalion. I was not going to do the dirty on it, taking any soft job.'
> 'I suppose you speak seven languages and all?', Tietjens asked.
> 'Five,' the other said patiently, 'and read two more. And Latin and Greek, of course.'

> (p. 307)

As the novel demonstrates, though, these characters' accomplishments are not compatible with the modern world and they find it impossible to thrive. McKechnie, constantly on the brink of mental collapse, is unable to translate the sonnet and keeps it sealed in an envelope. Tietjens becomes increasingly victimized for trying to act according to a code of behaviour unfathomable and intolerable to the post-war scene. Despite birth, breeding and patrician dignity (all attributes portrayed as desirable within the pre-war civilization), characters such as Tietjens and McKechnie apparently have no place in the twentieth century.

Ford's view of a century inhospitable to a classically inspired high culture is commonly found in this century's literary expression. Ezra Pound's *Hugh Selwyn Mauberley* (1920) also portrays a world which: 'demanded an image/ Of its accelerated grimace', instead of an 'Attic grace' (Pound, 1968, p. 206). In the mid-century Roy Fuller's poem 'Translation' adopted a Latin pose to bewail a world now: 'Fit only for barbarians' (1985, p. 138). His list of the forces which contribute to civilization's decline include twelve-tone music, the lower classes, 'progressive organizations', and quarterlies devoted to 'dreary verse'. He suggests his role can only be one of retreat. More recently, the American novelist Gore Vidal (1987) has compared the contemporary United States with the late Roman Empire slipping into the dark ages.

One use, therefore, of the classics this century has been to continue the battle of the ancients and moderns. Greece and Rome are used to exemplify all that is best about human endeavours. Modern life, in contrast, is petty and ugly. The classics have been aligned with a high culture that attempts to preserve values increasingly remote to a new order of barbarians. There is no doubt that this viewpoint has produced some excellent writing, but it is not really a sustainable defence for keeping classical texts at the centre of our cultural experience. As we see, this century with its much widened cultural franchise has questioned the claims made for the classics' superiority and the civilization they apparently engender. Certainly, many from this newly enlarged franchise (former colonial peoples, women, the working classes) have rejected claims for a 'high culture' made by a conservative élite, who evoke the classics to defend values perceived as unenlightened and repressive.

Fortunately, the classics in this century have also been involved in transforming literary values, not only in conserving them. Changing literary styles and a rethinking of literature's larger role in the world has not significantly diminished the influence of the classics on modern writing. The finest example of this is readily observed in the importance accorded Homer's *Odyssey* by two of the century's most influential and innovative works, James Joyce's *Ulysses* (1922) and Ezra Pound's *Cantos*. Odysseus has, indeed, emerged as the classical character this century most clearly identifies with: the much knocked-about survivor determined to return to his home. A hero, subtle, scheming, even lying, who achieves his ends through energy of mind, technical skill and self-reliance. Joyce believed the *Odyssey* possessed the most beautiful and all-embracing of human themes (Ellmann, 1959, p. 430). Joyce's reading of Homer, though, is extremely selective. He perceived Odysseus as a prototype of his own life: the wanderer, father, musician, story-teller, even pacifist because Odysseus had been reluctant to go to war. Whereas the eighteenth and nineteenth centuries had expressed a preference for the *Iliad*, with its espousal of martial heroism and life-and-death confrontation on the battlefield, the twentieth has favoured the hero as wandering victim seeking a domestic peace. Joyce believed he discovered in the *Odyssey* a source for the 'pacificist' epic he was constructing during the First World War.

Ezra Pound's *Cantos*, written from the 1920s through until the 1960s, similarly celebrate Odysseus as a *persona*, a mask for the poet's own voice. Pound's poetic sequence begins with a partial version of *Odyssey* Book XI, the visit to the underworld, with Pound, too, conceiving of Odysseus as exile and story-teller – the man who goes to speak among ghosts. Like Joyce, Pound discovered in Homer a paradigm for his own artistic life. With both these writers, though, the association with the classics is not through reference to a system of ordered civilized values embraced by a dominant high culture. Rather, the classics provide an impetus for confrontation with that group. Pound viewed the verse of contemporary educated gentlemen, represented by the Georgian movement, as effete and artificially rhetorical. For both writers a return to Homeric epic was to a terser, more direct and immediate (even colloquial) manner. Civilized literary refinement as reflected by overly ornamented and mannered writing was seen as unauthentic and lacking engagement. Both writers, for instance, employ successive 'interruptions' within their work to imply the existence of other voices crowding in. The voice of Odysseus which opens Pound's *Cantos* is interrupted by Andreas Divius, whose Latin/Greek parallel edition of the *Odyssey* Pound is using. Pound's adopted Homeric *persona* is broken as the poet brings attention to himself as a wearer of masks, the putter-on of disguises. This is distinctly Pound's own selective employment of the *Odyssey*. Both Pound and Joyce forge a unique association with the classical world. Neither senses an obligation to participate in a classical tradition defined by the previous age.

The result has been that much modern writing creates links with the classics which are fragmented and protean in manner. Rather than adopt a view of the classics as indicating a unified cultural order, the twentieth-century writer frequently employs them in a selective and transmuted fashion. Associations with a high cultural classical tradition are often difficult to observe. Many readers of *Ulysses*, for instance, know the connections Joyce wished to make with the *Odyssey* but find it hard to perceive them. This is not surprising given Joyce's selective, individual view of Homer's epic (pacifism is not a much shared idea of Odysseus). The transformed scene from the ancient Mediterranean to early twentieth-century Dublin evokes more differences than similarities. *Ulysses* is not really a version of the *Odyssey*. Yet for the reader who turns to Homer after reading Joyce, there is a sense both of discovery and of familiarity. Leopold Bloom's journeying around Dublin in search of a son provides one structural similarity with Homer, allowing the *Odyssey*'s organization to suggest a way of patterning out Joyce's novel into a narrative sequence. But the relation between the two works can also be employed in the opposite direction – Joyce's unreliable narrators, for instance, offer us another perspective on how to read the stories Odysseus tells. Our awareness of the variety and types of narrative voices (and their undependability) in *Ulysses* informs our understanding of the *Odyssey*'s narratives. One of the exciting aspects of twentieth-century writing's exploitation of the classics is that the classical texts often become uncannily illuminated in new and striking ways. Rather than appearing as exhaustively repeated cultural formulations, classical texts announce themselves as possessing a new literary vigour in both style and content.

An illustration of this is provided by an imitation of the Diana and Actaeon story drawn from Book III of Ovid's *Metamorphoses*. (Actaeon out hunting accidentally stumbles on the goddess Diana bathing naked. Since the goddess cannot accept that a mortal be given this sight, Actaeon is transformed into a stag and then devoured by his own hounds.) The story has been endlessly repeated, but the example I wish to consider is a 1960s short story by the American writer John Cheever.

Cheever's story, 'Metamorphoses', is set in New York (Cheever, 1982, pp. 536–40). It recounts how a friendly if slightly uncontrolled innocent named Larry Actaeon, enthusiastically possessed of a new idea, rushes unannounced into his chairman's office. He discovers the widow of a company director standing there naked. Embarrassed, he withdraws. Slowly his world transforms. His identity is constantly mistaken, he is assumed by a porter to be a delivery boy, not an executive. As the story concludes he approaches home and hears the sound of his dogs rushing, he thinks, to greet him. One of the successes of Cheever's piece is the manner in which the assumptions about what the Diana and Actaeon story is designed to express are left suggestively open. Is the story about human beings who, despite different times and circumstances, are forced to play in some form of universal game? What are the implications of seeing the sudden demise of a corporate executive in terms of the classical myth's structure? Cheever's story directs us to Ovid, not with a set of preconceptions, but with a new curiosity. What is apparent is that the whole treatment of Actaeon is somehow dubious, an action being punished which it is difficult to regard as a serious crime. Cheever, though, is an excellent reader of Ovid. He manages to catch the scepticism which does not lose humour, pathos which does not become sentimentality. Both propose the world as essentially irrational, but with a certain delight in the rather harsh terms humanity is forced to live by. What is interesting about Cheever, and exemplary of this century's relation with the classics, is that his story accommodates the Ovidian without merely replicating it. Preconceptions about what type of cultural standards classical works ostensibly reflect are left unanswered through a highly selective yet successful reading of the *Metamorphoses*. The reader is constantly surprised to find the similarities; Cheever's portrait of New York is not distorted or made unconvincing by the story's adherence to Ovid. Ovid is reassessed from Cheever's perspective. He informs the original, just as it informs his story.

The ability of twentieth-century readers to discover in many classical texts aspects of twentieth-century experience has helped to inspire new generations to turn to these works in order to aid an understanding of contemporary experience. While some readers continue to evoke the classics as standards of enlightened, sane, human activities, others have found a darker, more disturbing side to the classical world. This view of antiquity as anti-rational began in the nineteenth century. Nietzsche's division of Greek culture into Apollonian (ordered) and Dionysian (frenzied), and his awareness of the classical world's fear of terrible and unnatural forces provided a philosophic background to this perspective. At the beginning of this century, Sir James Frazer's *Golden Bough* (1922), demonstrating the close links between classical myths and early folkloric rituals, offered a type of anthropological justification to this perception of a more mysterious side to classical culture. Critically, though, the most important book to elucidate this new perspective was E. R. Dodds's *The Greeks and the Irrational* (1951), while the effect on literature has been most noticeable in styles of translation as the century has progressed. Certainly, one of the great literary achievements of the classics in recent times has been to generate a wealth of exciting translations.

Dodds's portrait of Greek intellectual culture is a complex one. He abandons the notion of a continuously developing rationalism which reaches a peak in Periclean Athens, noting how haunted and oppressive the atmosphere of Aeschylus' drama appears in contrast to earlier Homeric attitudes. Greek cultural experience emerges as a confrontation between developing rational values and regressive irrational ones. There is no point where one replaces the other. The need for ritual to purge public and private guilt, Dodds demonstrates, was always present in Greek society, where even the shamanistic cultures of the north were sought out in order to provide needed aspects of religious experience. Rather than enlightened, rarefied individuals seeking ordered sanity, the Greeks emerge as a people frightened by the mystery of evil which is part of their own being, and seeking rituals to relieve their pent-up anxieties. Even Plato, Dodds notices, considered rationalism the prerogative of only a few philosophers. For most people in Plato's ideal kingdom depicted in *The Laws*, intelligent hedonism and magic were the guides to life.

The best classical literary response to the insecurity and fear manifested by this outlook is found in Greek tragedy, where the intensity of the emotional experience is presented in a stark, if ritualized, manner. It is interesting to note the way in which Greek verse drama finds a sympathetic audience among twentieth-century theatregoers. Tony Harrison's version of Aeschylus' *Oresteia* (which attempts to capture the 'archaic' flavour and formalized manner of the original) was an outstanding success at the National Theatre. The Grene and Lattimore edition of *The Complete Greek Tragedies* (1954–9) produced translations of the existent Greek plays which revealed their lyrically charged, rhetorically unaffected manner (sought by much modern poetry), demonstrating fully the ability of lyric tragedy to participate in contemporary literary experience. Take this example of a section of a chorus from *Agamemnon* in Richmond Lattimore's version:

> Zeus, who guided men to think,
> who has laid it down that wisdom
> comes alone through suffering.
> Still there drips in sleep against the heart
> grief of memory; against
> our pleasure we are temperate.
> From the gods who sit in grandeur
> grace comes somehow violent.
>
> (Lattimore, 1953, p. 40)

It seems clear that twenty-first century readers will continue to investigate the literary remains of Greek and Rome, that the classics will survive. But they will survive in a very different form. As this century opened all students coming up to university would have been able to discover something of Latin culture unmediated through translation. Most would have been able to do so in a moderate way with Greek. The decline in languages in schools and beyond will change our relation with the classics. Rather than be exposed to them at early formative stages in our educational experience, we are likely to come to them curious to discover the identity of works which shaped books by modern writers we admire. Our relation with the classics is likely to be achieved through the mediation of other writers. It is true, too, that many translations look to popularize classics by utterly transforming them: the mutation of the epic into proto-novels through the efforts of the populist Penguin classics series will no doubt continue. For every reader who seeks out the excellence of Lattimore's *Iliad* (1951), Robert Fitzgerald's *Odyssey* (1961) or *Aeneid* (1984), there will be a dozen reading a grey-suited Homer or Virgil in prose. The experience of classical culture is likely to become even more fragmented and idiosyncratic than at present. Such a condition may be depressing in many respects, but this position does offer the reader who pursues the classics the opportunity to come into contact with their riches without wading through the culturally cluttered, dusty responses acquired through generations of gazing at classical civilization resting securely on a pedestal. Our own century's experience has shown Greece and Rome's ability to maintain a pre-eminence in our cultural heritage despite a less receptive critical climate.

The century opened with a generation of cultivated, refined students of classics being doomed by the débâcle of the First World War. It closes with a less easy to define constituency of readers, pursuing the classics for many different ends. The most dedicated classical student of recent literary experience is the schizophrenic Phaedrus of Robert Pirsig's novel *Zen and the Art of Motorcycle Maintenance* (1974). Pirsig captures the way the classics have become the vehicle for the institutional teaching of 'culture'; but his mad Phaedrus does not accept this high cultural codified role for classical civilization. He is determined to restore rhetoric to a central place, to diminish the power of Plato and Aristotle. We are in a very different world from the one that produced the generation of 1914:

> The main struggle of the University Great Books program was against the modern belief that the classics had nothing of any real importance to say to a twentieth-century society. To be sure, the majority of students taking the courses must have played the game of nice manners with their teachers, and accepted, for purposes of understanding, the prerequisite belief that the ancients had something meaningful to say. But Phaedrus, playing no games at all, didn't just *accept* this idea. He passionately and fanatically knew it. He came to *hate* them vehemently, and to assail them with every kind of invective he could think of, not because they were irrelevant but for exactly the opposite reason. The more he studied, the more convinced he became that no one had yet told the damage to this world that had resulted from our unconscious acceptance of their thought.
>
> (pp. 342–3)

FURTHER READING

Brooks, Otis (1963) *Virgil: A Study in Civilized Poetry*, Oxford University Press, Oxford
——(1970) *Ovid as Epic Poet*, Cambridge University Press, Cambridge
Dodds, E. R. (1951) *The Greeks and the Irrational*, University of California Press, Berkeley and Los Angeles
Fitzgerald, Robert (trans.) (1961) *The Odyssey*, Doubleday, New York
——(trans.) (1984) *The Aeneid*, Harvill Press, London
Grene, David and Lattimore, Richmond (trans.) (1954–9) *The Complete Greek Tragedies*, University of Chicago Press, Chicago
Jones, John (1962) *On Aristotle and Greek Tragedy*, Chatto & Windus, London
Kirk, G. S. (1970) *Myth: Its Meaning and Function in Ancient and Other Cultures*, Cambridge University Press, Cambridge
Lattimore, Richmond (trans.) (1951) *The Iliad*, University of Chicago Press, Chicago
Murdoch, Iris (1977) *The Fire and the Sun: Why Plato Banished the Artists*, Clarendon Press, Oxford
Thomson, George (1973) *Aeschylus and Athens*, Lawrence & Wishart, London [first published 1941]

ADDITIONAL WORKS CITED

Cheever, John (1982) *The Stories of John Cheever*, Penguin, Harmondsworth

Eliot, T. S. (1957) *On Poetry and Poets*, Farrar, Straus & Cudahy, New York

Ellmann, Richard (1959) *James Joyce*, Oxford University Press, London

Ford, Ford Madox (1950) *Parade's End*, Alfred A. Knopf, New York [first published 1924–8]

Frazer, J. G. (1922) *The Golden Bough: A Study in Magic and Religion*, Macmillan, London

Fuller, Roy (1985) *New and Collected Poems 1934–84*, Secker & Warburg, London

Harrison, Tony (1984) *Selected Poems*, Viking, Harmondsworth

Lattimore, Richmond (trans.) (1953) *Aeschylus I: Oresteia*, University of Chicago Press, Chicago

Lloyd-Jones, Hugh (1982) *Blood for the Ghosts: Classical Influences in the Nineteenth and Twentieth Centuries*, Duckworth, London

Pirsig, Robert (1974) *Zen and the Art of Motorcycle Maintenance*, William Morrow & Co., New York

Pound, Ezra (1968) *Collected Shorter Poems*, Faber & Faber, London

Steiner, George (1961) *The Death of Tragedy*, Faber & Faber, London

Stevenson, John (1988) Review of Duncan Wilson, *Gilbert Murray OM, 1866–1957*, *The Times Higher Education Supplement*, 22 July, pp. 19–20

Vidal, Gore (1987) *Armageddon?: Essays 1983–1987*, Deutsch, London

72

FOLK LITERATURE

DAVID BUCHAN

From the viewpoint of cultural history, there exist three kinds of literature: the literatures of high culture, of popular culture, and of folk culture. Although interacting, they are broadly distinguishable by their different means of transmission and sometimes composition, by the nature of the material transmitted, and by different though overlapping audiences.

Popular culture provides a topic elsewhere, but the bulk of this volume deals with high literature, referred to simply as 'Literature'. The customary arrogation of the unqualified term 'Literature' to one kind of literature has produced certain unfortunate results: it has, for example, eclipsed the sobering fact that for many centuries, until literacy became general, the literature of 90–95 per cent of the population was folk literature; it has led to the application of inappropriate critical assumptions and methods to folk literature, and it has created the tacit premise that what is not 'Literature' must lack high seriousness and artistic sophistication. These terms, 'folk' and 'high' literature, though not without drawbacks because of their inherent connotations, correspond to the established usage in German of *Volksliteratur* and *Hochliteratur* (Lüthi, 1970).

The conceptions of folk literature by 'Literature' scholars have generally been impressionistic and condescending – based on notions of simpleness and earthiness and expectations of romping peasants – or dismissive, as in Loomis's repudiation of 'the fancies of plowmen, goose-girls, blacksmiths, midwives, or yokels of any kind' (1958, p. 2). How, then, does one define precisely folk literature? Folk culture is that area or, in Nicolaisen's (1980, p. 139) happy term, 'register of culture' maintained and transmitted primarily by word of mouth and customary practice. It follows, therefore, that folk literature, the literature of folk culture, is the literature maintained and transmitted primarily by word of mouth, that is, by verbal means rather than by manuscript or print. That of course is not to say that it never reaches manuscript or print; naturally it does, but that does not diminish its status as folk literature; it does not suddenly metamorphose into high literature, for the material still continues being transmitted by the traditional verbal processes.

MEDIUM

Folk literature has its own medium, genres, conventions, aesthetics, and hence its own critical methodology. Its medium is tradition. Where high literature relies primarily though not exclusively on a visual medium, that of print, folk literature relies primarily on an aural medium. Where high literature relies primarily on the written word, folk literature relies primarily on the performed word. The aural medium, tradition, acts as channel for the performance of the word and means of transmission; it also constitutes the matrix of the processes engendered by the dynamics of performance and transmission. As the medium of folk literature, then, tradition may be most briefly defined as a set of processes central to which is word-of-mouth transmission. From the chronological viewpoint, tradition has two stages, what one might call the preliterate and the postliterate or the preindustrial and postindustrial. In the first stage, the time of prevalent nonliteracy before the industrial revolution, word-of-mouth tradition pervaded the life of all the people who could not read and write: it was, in a quite encompassing sense, their means of both 'instruction and delight'. In the second stage, the time of general literacy after the industrial revolution, word-of-mouth tradition had many of its functions gradually taken over by print, writing and 'official' education, but it continued adaptively within its contracted range, retaining older material and creating new, and becoming increasingly the carrier of unofficial culture. Earlier antiquarians tended to search exclusively for relics of the preliterate stage as evidence of folk tradition, but modern students of folk literature take both stages as their province, considering both historical and contemporary phenomena. Folk literature, then, consists of the literary and linguistic products of both preliterate and postliterate tradition.

In the wake of widespread education, the nineteenth century saw tradition undergo quite substantial alteration, and a major feature of this process was the devolution of traditional material and practice from adults to children. Folk drama customs, for example, moved down from men to youths to children; the traditional rhymes that once gave colour and fibre to discourse in the adult community came, after a similar shift, to be known as 'nursery rhymes'. The most complex of the narrative genres, the *Zaubermärchen* or wonder tales, became relegated to 'nursery tales' or, outside tradition, were prettified and rewritten into children's fairy-tales. All of this led to the still not uncommon view that much traditional material belongs in some absolute sense to the juveniles, a misconception that ignores the devolutions from adults to younger generations in the nineteenth century. The value of historical perspective in this instance underscores the usefulness of seeing tradition in its two stages, the preindustrial and postindustrial. The oral tradition of the preindustrial nonliterate culture performed a different range of functions from the verbal tradition of postindustrial literate culture, when competing media and new channels of transmission materialized, and folk culture interacted more extensively with popular and high culture. Whatever the period, however, tradition remains a cultural mechanism that exists in a state of continual evolution, retaining and discarding, conserving and innovating, in response to social and cultural change.

GENRES

The major genres of folk literature exhibit a remarkable international currency. On the general level, folk-songs, folk-tales and proverbs appear in every culture in some form; on the more particular generic level, certain expressive forms occur world-wide: the *Märchen* or wonder tale, for example, did flourish from, quite literally, China to Peru. Generic diversification also obtains, so that the precise generic repertoire of a culture will vary, slightly for adjacent cultural districts, such as Yorkshire and Lancashire, more evidently for culture areas, such as Scandinavia and the Balkans, and considerably for continents, such as Europe and Africa. The discussion that follows presents the generic repertoire of most of the British Isles, which is reasonably representative of western Europe, though not of the Celtic-language regions.

Folk literature divides into four large generic areas: *folk narrative, folk poetry and song, folksay,* and *folk drama.* The first of these, *folk narrative,* bisects into the fictional and the non-fictional genres, the former – folk-tales – corresponding more or less to the sections in the basic reference work of Antti Aarne and Stith Thompson, *The Types of the Folktale* (1961). This book lists in their normal generic categories the known story-types throughout the world (more effectively for Europe than for such areas as Africa, however), so that a scholar in commenting on any given story-version will first of all assign it to its story-type as, say, a version of AT 303 ('The Twins or Blood-Brothers'). Originally produced in 1910 as *Verzeichnis der Märchentypen* by Antti Aarne, it was revised and translated by Stith Thompson in 1928 and revised again in 1961, and has been supplemented by regional type-indexes, such as the *Type and Motif Index of the Folktales of England and North America* (Baughman, 1966) and *The Types of the Irish Folktale* (Ó Súilleabháin and Christiansen, 1963). Aarne-Thompson provides for each type an encapsulation of the story's norm and standard variations, a listing of known versions in print or archive, and a bibliography of the commentary involving the type.

The section numbered AT 300–749 contains the types of the most complex of the genres, the wonder tale, known also by a variety of aliases (the magic tale or, confusingly, the folk-tale, or, inappropriately because fairies rarely appear, the fairy-tale). This genre was popularized for the nineteenth-century reading public by the polished texts of the Grimms, and the even more polished texts of their translators. In the normative type of this genre a young individual, either male or female, leaves his or her native environment, engages in various tests and tasks in an imaginative story-landscape peopled with marvellous creatures and strange beings, successfully overcomes all vicissitudes, and at the end achieves property and marriage (half the kingdom and the princess/prince), thereby attaining adult status. Centrally the genre is concerned with the maturation of the individual, and its normative story-types enact narratively a kind of rite-of-passage. Especially through the depicted conduct of the hero and heroine in the tests and trials, but also through that of other characters, the traditional tale-performer exemplifies admirable and unadmirable social behaviour, and communicates both a sense of life's grained texture and, more concretely, the values of the group to which he or she and the audience belong (Lüthi, 1982, 1976, 1984; Propp, 1968; Degh, 1969, 1972).

Among the other folk-tale genres are the realistic tale, the religious tale, the animal tale and the formula tale (Thompson, 1946). Though not without its marvels the *Novella* or realistic tale is located in a socially defined environment and its story-types concern themselves primarily with cleverness, trickery, and the operations of a keen mind. The religious tale (the term is self-explanatory) merges with the religious legend, and the animal tale when told with a moral purpose becomes also a fable. The formula tale usually contains a single idea or situation developed repetitively, in such varieties as the cumulative tale, the endless tale, and the catch tale. Another, larger, narrative division, the jocular tale, includes among its forms the *Schwank* or merry tale, the joke, and the tall tale. The *Schwank* – the frequency of German terms reflects the predominance for many decades of German as the language of folk narrative, and indeed most folk literature, scholarship – is a relatively lengthy, sometimes complex, humorous story where the humour resides in the action and the cultural appropriateness of the stereotypical actors. Compression and reliance on the punchline characterize the joke, a form which in tradition often derives its humour from the typifying attitude revealed by the climactic line. If succinctness characterizes the joke, exaggeration, together with a deadpan manner of telling, characterize the tall tale.

Where the folk-tale genres are fictional, the legend genres are ostensibly non-fictional (Christiansen, 1958; Hand, 1971). The legend is most conveniently defined as a prose narrative not told as direct fiction; or, to modify an older formulation, the legend purports to be an account of an unusual happening believed, by some people at some time, to have occurred. One cannot nowadays simply say the legend is a story told as true, as scholars once did, for it can also be told within a frame of only partial belief or disbelief ('well, that is what the old folks said, anyway . . .') though the teller feels some compulsion to repeat it. The legend proper has six, often overlapping, categories: aetiological, religious, supernatural, historical, personal, and place. The modern legend is a story told as true that circulates in contemporary society and exhibits traditional variation. The memorat or proto-legend, once defined as a first-person account of a supernatural experience, is now viewed as a category of personal experience narrative, a generic area that has only recently received serious study. Research, in fact, is still delineating the narrative forms within contemporary tradition, forms such as the group saga.

In the wider perspective, the generic division of *folk poetry and song* includes oral epic, recorded from ancient Babylonia to contemporary Africa. In the narrower British perspective, ballad and folk-song comprise in practice the major genres, though the latter theoretically subsumes the former, whose basic short definition is 'a folk-song that tells a story'. There are three kinds of ballad: the classical ballad, the broadside ballad, and the local (or modern) ballad. The first form, the classical ballad, has an extensive spread in European and European-derived cultures, and it was on the basis of its international characteristics that Gerould evolved his descriptive definition: a classical ballad 'is a folk-song that tells a story with stress on the crucial situation, tells it by letting the action unfold itself in event and speech, and tells it objectively with little comment or intrusion of personal bias' (1932, p. 11). This is the only genre of folk literature to appear regularly on 'Literature' syllabuses, attaining thereby a singularity of status whose genesis might provide an interesting sidelight on the history of cultural studies. The genre contains as its major subgenres the romantic and tragic, the supernatural, and the historical ballads, and as its minor subgenres the comic, religious, witcombat, and minstrel ballads. It was the first Professor of English at Harvard University, Francis James Child, who assembled in one of the monuments of nineteenth-century scholarship, *The English and Scottish Popular Ballads* (1882–98), the 305 ballad-types of British tradition in all their then known versions. And it was Professor Bertrand Bronson of Berkeley who, after establishing the inseparability of text and melody, supplemented and extended Child's work with *The Traditional Tunes of the Child Ballads* (1959–72). The versions of the ballad-types range in date from the manuscript text of *c.* 1450 to the tape-recorded texts of the present day.

Since tradition responds to social change, it has employed over the centuries different methods of composition and reproduction, and hence has transmitted narrative songs that vary both in the kind of story and in the treatment accorded the story. Where the classical ballad owes its genesis and stylistic hallmarks to the prevailing nonliteracy of preindustrial tradition, the broadside ballad originates in the popular culture of urbanized society with its newly literate markets. The classical ballad is a narrative song composed and re-composed by a traditional oral method; the broadside ballad is a narrative song composed or re-worked in subliterary style by commercial entrepreneurs expressly for traditional singers; and the local or modern ballad, largely a nineteenth- and twentieth-century phenomenon, is a non-commercial narrative song composed in subliterary style generally by singers within the tradition (Buchan, 1972). In North America, descriptive type-catalogues treat thoroughly the three kinds of ballad: *The British Traditional Ballad in North America* (Coffin, 1977), *American Balladry from British Broadsides* (Laws, 1957), and *Native American Balladry* (Laws, 1964); no comparable coverage exists for British balladry.

The area termed folk-song also includes different kinds of song taken into tradition at different times. Whereas 'folk-song' to such collectors as Cecil Sharp meant exclusively the songs of older tradition, to modern scholars the term encompasses also the songs of later tradition which include a variety of kinds from such 'untraditional' sources as music-hall. The distinguishing criterion for determining whether a particular text is a folk-song is not the source of the song-type but whether the song-version has been subjected to the processes of traditional transmission. It is the work of the scholar to examine why particular songs from varying sources have entered singers' repertoires in order to investigate their cultural functioning. For earlier tradition the major subdivisions would include lyric, humorous lyric, comic songs, worksongs, and songs of custom, while the later tradition would include broadside songs, sentimental songs, and occupational songs.

Although almost all language might be considered traditional in the sense that it is in habitual spoken usage, for the generic division of *folksay* one conventionally demarcates certain crystallizations of language in traditional currency that for the most part fall into some easily recognizable genres: proverbs and proverb-related forms; rhymes; and riddles. Archer Taylor provides the definitions of the forms in the first category: a proverb is 'a terse didactic statement that is current in tradition'; a proverbial phrase 'permits variation in person, number, and tense'; a proverbial comparison 'has a fixed traditional form, but contains no moral advice'; a wellerism is a 'quotation proverb' designed 'to produce a humorous effect'; conventional phrases are locutions 'conventionally used in particular situations or . . . accepted as traditional ways of expressing an idea' (1972, pp. 902, 905). Rhymes in the traditional adult community have not received the attention their pervasiveness deserves, but a survey of the Scottish material shows that there one group fulfils as its primary function the transmission of cultural knowledge where another group serves a range of social functions in varying contexts, and through no fewer than twenty-eight subgenres (Buchan, 1984, pp. 192–202). For the riddle form (Taylor, 1951) as for many other literary forms, Aristotle was the first critic, proposing a definition which, like many others since, has never quite achieved general acceptance. A reasonably convenient way of viewing the riddle, however, is to see it as a statement, often with metaphorical and contradictory elements, describing a referent which has to be puzzled out by processes of correlation. Individual riddles frequently possess a metaphoric strength and allusiveness that create a small poem, a status often accorded them by editors of Anglo-Saxon literature. The practice of riddling provided both intellectual stimulation and complete evenings of entertainment within traditional communities.

Folk drama, the final generic division, contains three main kinds of folk play: the hero-combat play, the sword dance play, and the wooing play. The latter two are localized in the English East Midlands and north-eastern England respectively, but the first occurs over a wide area in the British Isles. In all three kinds of play the core of the action is the death and resurrection of one of the characters (Cawte *et al.*, 1967).

This survey of the genres of folk literature provides merely a static outline of the major forms through the centuries; it cannot represent the dynamics of tradition and the fluidity of the genres. Some genres intermix, and some types are adapted by performers from one genre to another, there to accord with different conventions and to serve different functions. As tradition evolves and adapts in response to social change, so its generic configuration alters: some genres die out or diminish, some new generic forms emerge, and some genres carry on, hardly adapting to changing times.

CHARACTERISTICS

Under the rubric of folk literature's characteristics come conventions and aesthetics and the specific features of multiformity and adaptation. The conventions were first adumbrated many years ago by the Danish scholar Axel Olrik ([1908] 1965), who in the fashion of the times presented many of them as 'laws'; these can be more usefully regarded as sets of unitary, binary, and trinary characteristics. The first set includes concentration on the single plot strand, on the leading character, and on one or more striking scenes. The second set includes various manifestations of opposition and parallelism: the laws of contrast, of twins, of two-to-a-scene, of opening and closing; and of initial position and final position. The third set consists of folk literature's most evident form of patterning, its pervasive tendency to marshal its material – characters, ideas, events, plots – in threes. The general characteristics of the folk literature text include an internal logic, much patterning and repetition, and a unity of plot derived in large measure from particular kinds of patterning and repetition. In fact, the major aesthetic feature of folk literature is its stylization, which permeates the portrayal of character, the presentation of the action, and the nature of the language employed. In contrast, literate culture and print literature place a high aesthetic value on originality, whether in verbal expression or narrative incident or character depiction; for a piece of writing to be termed 'repetitious' is for it to receive severe dispraise. Folk literature, however, does not place the same high aesthetic value on that kind of originality, preferring instead the benefits of repetitive stylization. That, of course, has its own aesthetic attractiveness and conceptual usefulness. To stress the repetitive stylization is not to impute grey dullness, however, for folk literature possesses its own artistic individuation, since the best performers, working within their own conventions, display an impressive command of language, an acute understanding of human nature and an imaginative grasp of the relevant performance mode. In short, the works of folk literature require to be judged by the conventions of their own medium and genres, not the inappropriate aesthetic of a different cultural register.

Multiformity involves consideration of type and version. 'Version' denotes any one specific recording of a piece of folk literature (story, song, proverb, play, etc.); we might refer, for example, to the version of 'The Dress of Gold, of Silver, and of Stars' (AT 510B) recorded from Taimi Boswell in 1915 (Briggs, 1970–1, vol. A1, pp. 416–24). A 'type' constitutes, on the theoretical level, the aggregate of all the versions of a single story, song, play, etc., and, on the practical level of classification, the constants which inform the versions and identify their genetic relationship. The type 'The Dress of Gold, of Silver, and of Stars', achieves a multitude of textual realizations, of which Taimi Boswell's version ('Mossycoat') is just one, displaying in standard fashion both constants and inconstants. The types of folk literature, in short, achieve multiformity, with the individual versions being the contextually and culturally determined multiforms of the typic essence. It is as if, in high literature, one had an infinite number of texts of 'Westminster Bridge' created by different composers in different languages.

Multiformity leads on to the other highlighted feature of folk literature, adaptation. Performers adapt their versions to suit differing social, cultural and performance contexts, and to accord with the performer's own values. They also adapt material from one medium to another, from one genre to another, and from one type to another. The adaptation fulfils a variety of functions – social, cultural, artistic – and results in one half of the duality that is such a marked feature of folk literature: its blending of the innovative and the conservative. Folk literature in general is conventionally held to serve four main functions: to entertain, to educate, to validate culture, and to maintain conformity to accepted patterns of behaviour, with the individual genres all carrying their own sets of functions in addition (Bascom, 1965). The potential range of folk literature's functions becomes apparent, however, when one bears in mind how performers habitually engage in the conscious and necessarily creative adaptation of the material to serve particular purposes in particular contexts.

CRITICAL METHODOLOGY

Folk literature – the literature maintained and transmitted primarily by word of mouth – is, then, differentiable by its means of transmission, its audience, and the nature of the material. Of necessity, it possesses its own critical methodology. This methodology involves essentially the multilevel consideration of the five factors – medium, genre, type, version, and context and function – discussed above. The nature of the medium requires that the critic in adjusting from high literature abjure the use of 'writer' or 'writing' when 'composer' or 'composition' is meant, discard the concept of 'author' when traditional performer is meant, jettison the concept of 'authoritative text' when dealing with tradition's types and versions, and alter the standard conception of literary chronology from one where a work is normally datable to a particular year and classed of a particular period to one where, though versions can be dated, the type and the genre may have flourished for centuries before. The genres demand a recognition of, in general, their difference and, in specific, their conventions, functions, and on occasion inbuilt meaning. The multiformity that governs types and versions means that in order to make useful generalizations about, say, 'Sir Patrick Spens' one cannot simply treat a single text, one abstracted version, but must treat the type, comprehending all the versions, their constants and their variabilities. In analysing the versions, the researcher must again work on both macro and micro levels simultaneously; when dealing with motifeme and allomotif (at the level of narrative episode), with talerole and character (at the level of dramatic agent), and with formulaic system and formula (at the level of language). The adaptation that derives from a performer's functional adjustment to context dictates that one cannot posit a mythical golden 'ur-text' which inevitably degenerates in the process of word-of-mouth transmission. More than that, however, the importance of context determines that the student of folk literature considers not simply the text *qua* text but the text as it functions in culture.

Beyond these are two more factors: the dimensions of time and space. Folk literature has existed over many centuries. So of course has high literature, but in the case of folk literature not only genres but also individual types have existed for as long as two-and-a-half to three millennia. The earliest *Halslösungs rätsel*, neck riddle, that involving Samson (Judges 14:8–18), has been dated to the eleventh century BC; narrative material found in the *Odyssey*, of *c.* 700 BC, has been recorded in recent decades in the field, as have songs habitually classed as 'medieval lyrics' (Buchan, 1989; Green, 1972). The spread in time parallels the spread in space, for much of the material of folk literature exists in many cultures. This fact dominated the thinking of early scholars who in a post-Darwinian climate concentrated on origin and diffusion studies. The corollary of the spatial spread for critical method is that one assumes a monocultural significance for the material only at one's peril. The analyst of folk literature, in sum, must deal with a constellation of variable factors, which demand sets of textually applicable knowledge, responsiveness to contextual correlations, and a sensible flexibility to the dimensions of time and space.

If ethnocentricism is the sin of being bound by the preconceptions of one's own culture, then literacentricism is the sin of being bound by the preconceptions of one's own literacy. The two major literacentric responses which have precluded a clear understanding of the nature and processes of folk literature are the theory of *gesunkenes Kulturgut* and the theory of memorial transmission. The first theory holds that nonliterate people had no creative literature of their own but depended solely on crumbs from the tables of high literature. The second theory holds essentially that word-of-mouth transmission normally involves rote memorization of a fixed text; that is, the process is conceived of in terms of the known practices of a literate society. Neither of these theories manages to address effectively the three questions which act as a touchstone for literacentric generalizations. How does one explain the pervasive evidence in folk literature of creative adaptation? How does one explain precisely the pronounced differences in concerns and characteristics between folk and high literatures? How does one explain why the distinctive concerns and characteristics of the folk literature of one culture area, such as England, are those which inform the folk literatures of, *mutatis mutandis*, all western Europe; or, to put it another way, why English folk literature has more in common with other European folk literatures than with English high literature?

CRITICAL HISTORY

It is customary to bypass the preceding antiquarians and mark the beginning of folk literature criticism with the Brothers Grimm, whose writings not only inspired people in many countries to engage in field-collection but also provoked others into writing in refutation, support or extension of their theories. The nineteenth century saw a number of sweepingly general theories like those of the nature mythologists (such as Max Müller) who perceived mythic symbols of the natural environment everywhere, or the Indianists (such as Theodor Benfey) who held that all folk-tales derived from India. Largely in reaction to the grandiose theories there developed the first rigorous approach to folk literature, the historic-geographic method, which concentrated on origin and diffusion studies of specific types, exemplified by the works of such scholars as Antti Aarne, Walter Anderson and Kurt Ranke. The major critical approaches of the later decades of the twentieth century have been the structuralist, with Vladimir Propp ([1928] 1968) its most influential proponent, the oral-cultural which, as in the writings of Albert Lord (1960), studies the oral literature composed by the performers of a nonliterate cultural group, and the contextualist, a term that subsumes a number of related approaches influenced initially by the work of such anthropologists as Malinowski and latterly by performance and communication theory. In brief summation, then, the movement has been from grandiose theory to origin and diffusion study to an emphasis on the performer, context and function, and communicative processes. A basic knowledge of folk literature is, to put it no higher, very useful for all students of 'Literature', and essential for students of particular periods and areas, but the teaching of it is normally left to that discipline which treats traditional culture. Unfortunately the position of that discipline in Britain (and in France) remains tenuous compared to its established presence elsewhere in Europe. (Britain and France both preferred to establish the discipline of Anthropology with which to study the 'primitive cultures' of the empires rather than a discipline designed for the study of the indigenous traditional cultures.) In Britain university programmes exist only at Sheffield, in Cultural Tradition courses presented by Professor John Widdowson, and at Edinburgh, in the Scottish Ethnology degree offered by the School of Scottish Studies, the Folklife Studies programmes at Leeds and Stirling having succumbed to university retrenchment. Sheffield is linked by IFSBAC (Institute for Folklore Studies in Britain and Canada) to Memorial University of Newfoundland, the main centre in the Commonwealth for the study of traditional culture.

FOLK LITERATURE AND HIGH LITERATURE

One of the major literary findings of this century was the discovery that although we habitually equate composition with writing another method of composition has also existed: oral composition. Employed by nonliterate people for literary creation it presumably antedated and certainly paralleled the method of written composition. Milman Parry and Albert Lord (1960) of Harvard demonstrated through their field research with a living oral epic tradition in Yugoslavia how people who could not read and write were able to create and perform poems of length and complexity, and their findings have for many literatures implications that are still being investigated. It appears probable, however, that the *Odyssey* and parts of the Bible were orally composed. The nonliterate composer-performer learns not a fixed text but story outlines and a technique for re-creation of the story in performance. The technique involves the deployment of formulaic language and formulaic narrative elements within basic structural patterns. The use of the oral-compositional technique results in certain textual characteristics, especially kinds of repetition in language and narrative structuring, which have a close correspondence to the characteristics of folk literature described by Olrik (1965). It is a reasonable probability, in fact, that before the days of mass literacy most folk literature was transmitted by an oral-compositional method. Those considered the earliest works in a country's literature are also likely to have been affected, either extensively or partially, by the oral-compositional method. *Beowulf*, for example, exhibits a number of textual characteristics of oral composition, but debate exists as to whether the poem was itself orally composed or was written within an emergent written-literary tradition that had taken over many of the artistic conventions and features of the oral-compositional tradition. In the medieval period writers such as those of the Arthurian literature made ample use of folk tradition. In the Renaissance, Shakespeare drew for some of his plots on international folk-tale types from the novella genre: AT 882 ('The Wager on the Wife's Chastity') for *Cymbeline;* AT 890 ('A Pound of Flesh') for *The Merchant of Venice;* AT 901 ('Taming of the Shrew') for *The Taming of the Shrew;* and AT 923 ('Love like Salt') for *King Lear.* In the present century the high literature of emergent nations frequently contains a transformation of indigenous folk literature. Throughout the centuries, however, the interaction has been a two-way process, with high literature drawing on folk literature and, complementarily, folk literature absorbing material from high literature. Critical methodology for dealing with the interrelations of high and folk literature has lagged behind in its development, but two valuable recent works by scholars trained in both disciplinary approaches, Mary Ellen Brown's *Burns and Tradition* (1984) and Carl Lindahl's *Earnest Games: Folkloric Patterns in the Canterbury Tales* (1987), provide both demonstrations of the subject's potential and models for future research.

Folk literature and high literature belong to a triad, the third member being popular literature. It was when the spread of education and literacy created new markets for urban entrepreneurs that there came into being, at different times in different places, popular literature, a literature produced by mass media for mass consumption. In its early stages it took the form of broadsides and chapbooks which often included much traditional material. Here too, however, a two-way interaction obtained, for people used the broadsides and chapbooks as sources and incorporated the new material into their repertoires for traditional performance along with the old.

CONCLUSION

The best folk literature, like the best Literature, is both universal and local in significance. Where, however, with written literature the term 'universal significance' normally acts as a correlative for strong critical approbation, with folk literature the term has a very concrete force, in that a given story-type, for example, may have been serving human, social and cultural functions among widely diverse peoples for centuries, even millennia. Folk literature's universality, in short, is a demonstrable fact of cultural history. Folk literature is also intensely local, for the multiform versions of the types embody the conceptions, attitudes, and values of the many cultural contexts in which their performers have re-created them. It is an area of literature which deserves rather more serious attention than it has been accorded. One small attempt to move in that direction is *Scottish Tradition: A Collection of Scottish Folk Literature* (Buchan, 1984) which tries to epitomize in a critical anthology the folk literature of one culture, and which both exemplifies and expands the matter touched on in this rather rapid survey.

FURTHER READING

Bauman, Richard (1984) *Verbal Art as Performance*, Waveland, Prospect Heights

Bausinger, Hermann (1968) *Formen der Volkspoesie*, Erich Schmidt Verlag, Berlin

Burke, Peter (1978) *Popular Culture in Early Modern Europe*, Temple Smith, London

Cocchiara, Giuseppe (1981) *The History of Folklore in Europe*, translated by John N. McDaniel, Institute for the Study of Human Issues, Philadelphia [first published 1952]

Honko, Lauri and Laaksonen, Pekka (eds) (1983) *Trends in Nordic Tradition Research*, Studia Fennica 27, Suomalaisen Kirjallisuuden Seura, Helsinki

Jason, Heda (1977) *Ethnopoetry*, Linguistica Biblica, Bonn

Ong, Walter J. (1981) *Orality and Literacy: The Technologizing of the Word*, Methuen, London

Renwick, Roger de V. (1980) *English Folk Poetry: Structure and Meaning*, University of Pennsylvania Press, Philadelphia

Thompson, Stith (1955–8) *Motif-Index of Folk Literature*, revised edn, 6 vols, Rosenkilde & Bagger, Copenhagen

Toelken, Barre (1979) *The Dynamics of Folklore*, Houghton Mifflin, Boston

ADDITIONAL WORKS CITED

Aarne, Antti and Thompson, Stith (1961) *The Types of the Folktale*, 2nd revised edn, Suomalainen Tiedeakatemia Academia Scientiarum Fennica, Helsinki [first published in German 1910]

Bascom, William R. (1965) 'Four Functions of Folklore'. In Alan Dundes (ed.), *The Study of Folklore*, Prentice-Hall, Englewood Cliffs, pp. 279–98 [essay first published 1954]

Baughman, Ernest W. (1966) *Type and Motif Index of the Folktales of England and North America*, Mouton, The Hague

Briggs, Katherine M. (1970–1) *A Dictionary of British Folk-tales*, Part A, 2 vols; Part B, 2 vols, Routledge & Kegan Paul, London

Bronson, Bertrand H. (1959–72) *The Traditional Tunes of the Child Ballads*, 4 vols, Princeton University Press, Princeton

Brown, Mary Ellen (1984) *Burns and Tradition*, Macmillan, London

Buchan, David (1972) *The Ballad and the Folk*, Routledge & Kegan Paul, London

——(1984) *Scottish Tradition: A Collection of Scottish Folk Literature*, Routledge & Kegan Paul, London

——(1989) 'Folk Tradition and Literature till 1603'. In J. D. McClure and M. R. G. Spiller (eds), *Bryght Lanternis. Essays on the Language and Literature of Medieval and Renaissance Scotland*, Aberdeen University Press, Aberdeen

Cawte, E. C., Helm, A. and Peacock, N. (1967) *English Ritual Drama: A Geographical Index*, The Folk-Lore Society, London

Child, Francis James (1882–98) *The English and Scottish Popular Ballads*, 5 vols, Houghton Mifflin, Boston

Christiansen, Reidar T. (1958) *The Migratory Legends*, Suomalainen Tiedeakatemia Academia Scientiarum Fennica, Helsinki

Coffin, Tristram P. (1977) *The British Traditional Ballad in North America*, revised edn with a supplement by Roger de V. Renwick, University of Texas Press, Austin [first published 1950]

Degh, Linda (1969) *Folktales and Society: Story-telling in a Hungarian Peasant Community*, Indiana University Press, Bloomington [first published in German 1962]

——(1972) 'Folk Narrative'. In Richard M. Dorson (ed.), *Folklore and Folklife: An Introduction*, University of Chicago Press, Chicago, pp. 53–83

Gerould, Gordon H. (1932) *The Ballad of Tradition*, Oxford University Press, Oxford

Green, A. E. (1972) 'Folk-song and Dialect', *Transactions of the Yorkshire Dialect Society*, 72, 13, 20–46

Hand, Wayland D. (ed.) (1971) *American Folk Legend: A Symposium*, University of California Press, Berkeley

Laws, G. Malcolm (1957) *American Balladry from British Broadsides*, American Folklore Society, Philadelphia

——(1964) *Native American Balladry*, revised edn, American Folklore Society, Philadelphia [first published 1950]

Lindahl, Carl (1987) *Earnest Games: Folkloric Patterns in the Canterbury Tales*, Indiana University Press, Bloomington

Loomis, R. S. (1958) 'Arthurian Tradition and Folklore', *Folklore*, 59, 1–25

Lord, Albert B. (1960) *The Singer of Tales*, Harvard University Press, Cambridge

Lüthi, Max (1970) *Volksliteratur und Hochliteratur*, Francke, A. Verlag, Bern

——(1976) *Once Upon a Time: On the Nature of Fairy Tales*, Indiana University Press, Bloomington [first published in German 1962]

——(1982) *The European Folktale: Form and Nature*, Institute for the Study of Human Issues, Philadelphia [first published in German 1947]

——(1984) *The Fairytale as Art Form and Portrait of Man*, Indiana University Press, Bloomington [first published in German 1975]

Nicolaisen, W. F. H. (1980) 'Variant, Dialect, and Region: an Exploration in the Geography of Tradition', *New York Folklore*, 6, 137–49

Olrik, Axel (1965) 'Epic Laws of Folk Narrative'. In A. Dundes (ed.), *The Study of Folklore*, Prentice-Hall, Englewood Cliffs, pp. 131–41 [essay first published in Danish 1908]

Ó Súilleabháin, Sean and Christiansen, Reidar T. (1963) *The Types of the Irish Folktale*, Suomalainen Tiedeakatemia Academia Scientiarum Fennica, Helsinki

Propp, Vladimir (1968) *Morphology of the Folktale*, University of Texas Press, Austin [first published in Russian 1928]

Taylor, Archer (1951) *English Riddles from Oral Tradition*, University of California Press, Berkeley

——(1972) 'Proverb'. In Maria Leach (ed.) *Standard Dictionary of Folklore Mythology and Legend*, new edn, Funk & Wagnalls, New York, pp. 902–5 [article first published 1949]

Thompson, Stith (1946) *The Folktale*, Holt, Rinehart & Winston, New York

73

LITERATURE AND THE VISUAL ARTS

DOMINIC BAKER-SMITH

Every picture tells a story: such at least was the general supposition until the advent of a deliberately abstract ideal of painting in modern times. It is important to emphasize at the outset that the relationship between the visual and the verbal arts has been founded for the greater part of its history on a common concern with communicating: that is, with providing a socially based set of conventions for conveying ideas or images. One could go further and suggest that a great deal of the activity which the arts shared in common might be summarized under the heading of narration, of telling a story and telling it vividly. These claims will be examined in detail in a moment; for the present it will be useful to stick with the issue of representation in the arts. It is a safe generalization that the history of formal techniques in verbal and in visual art can be given in three stages: innovation, popularization, rejection. Those artists and writers who turned away in the early years of the twentieth century from conventional modes of expression in favour of 'modernism' or experiment frequently claimed to be motivated by a concern for the freedom and creative independence of their art. They viewed the conventional expectations popularized during the previous century by growing literacy and by the development of the lithograph as a threat to creative originality.

Early illustrated periodicals which aimed at a wide public, such as *The Graphic* founded by William Luson Thomas in 1869, made a serious effort to combine new graphic techniques with the best talent available, and Thomas's patronage of artists like Luke Fildes (1844–1927) and Hubert von Herkomer (1849–1914) was an important factor in the acceptance of social realism as a valid mode for artistic endeavour. Early critics complained of the introduction of ugliness and deformity into a zone that should be consecrated to images of the sublime, but the immense success of Fildes's *Applicants for Admission to a Casual Ward* at the Royal Academy exhibition in 1874 demonstrated the public's willingness to contemplate social misery if well painted. Fildes had been a protégé of Dickens, who invited him to illustrate *Edwin Drood*, and

Dickens's melodramatic handling of social problems in his novels is reflected in the engravings published by *The Graphic*. Fildes's *Casual Ward* had been worked up from a sketch, *Houseless and Hungry*, which was originally reproduced in *The Graphic*, and one impressionable reader struck by Fildes's work was the young Vincent Van Gogh. The 'Dickensian' concerns of such art emerge very clearly in a contemporary comment, by the art critic of *The Athenaeum*, on Herkomer's *Eventide* (1878), a scene of old women in the Westminster workhouse: 'Should Mr. Herkomer's beautiful work draw out more strongly our sympathies for our less fortunate fellow beings, [it] will in its more important object have fulfilled the intention of its author' (Edwards, 1987, p. 95). A number of things call for comment here. In the first place it is assumed that a work of art can qualify the attitudes and, possibly, the conduct of its perceiver – in short that it may have a propaganda aspect. Second, there is no anxiety about what we have learned to call the 'intentional fallacy': since the painting is seen as a narrative with a moral and not as an object for purely aesthetic contemplation it is assumed that this social communication can be taken as what the artist intends. Further, the very use of the term 'author' reinforces the highly literary way in which the artefact is regarded.

It may be that there is no such thing as a painting devised for purely aesthetic contemplation; there is always an irresistible tendency, at least among art critics, to verbalize response. But if one goes to extremes and juxtaposes Fildes's *Casual Ward* with, say, an abstract composition by Mark Rothko (1903–70), we can arrive at a sharp realization of what the twentieth-century revolution in the arts amounts to. Rothko's paintings in their later phase, from 1948 onwards, rely almost solely on the interaction of pulsating colours laid out in bands or oblongs, and his resistance to any hint of representation is carried further by the fact that most are untitled. Where Fildes exploits the rhetoric latent in melodrama, Rothko places the picture before the viewer as a fact in its own right: the transaction may be compared to Archibald Mac-Leish's New Critical dictum in his poem 'Ars Poetica', 'A poem should not mean/But be' (1935, p. 123). A feature of modernity in art or literature has been this recognition of the work as its own point of reference; in contrast Fildes's picture leads us beyond the canvas to an extraneous scheme of reference, it proffers a meaning. The abstract artist has shed the conventions which have underpinned most Western art since the Renaissance; in a sense this is an act of iconoclasm which in its quest to release the spirit moves painting closer to music than to verbal expression. We are, after all, prepared to accept a musical composition on its own merits without any enquiries about what it might *mean*. Yet the fact remains that the most persistent bond between literature and the visual arts has been their joint dedication to illusion, to the creation within what we revealingly call the mind's eye of an imagined reality.

Since antiquity their techniques and devices, their schemes and their strategies have attempted to lure their public into fictional worlds. The medium is strictly a means to an end.

This sense of transparency, of seeing beyond the formal surface of the work, is conveyed by Cicero in his praise of the blind Homer who describes events and actions so vividly that we see things he could not: 'it is his painting not his poetry that we see' (*Tusculan Disputations*, V, xxxix, 14). Cicero may well be alluding here to the famous dictum of Simonides of Ceos that painting is wordless poetry and poetry is verbal painting. This idea of the affinity between the arts, which was to prove fundamental to classical conceptions, found its most influential formulation in Horace's *Art of Poetry* (*Ars Poetica*) where he coined the catch-phrase which is echoed through the Renaissance and beyond: *ut pictura poesis* ('as painting so is poetry', l. 361 – trans. 1977, p. 480). The remarkable thing about Horace's verse essay is the strongly rhetorical character he gives to the arts; he regards them as persuasive, even compelling, ways of presenting information. Public eloquence was the Roman art *par excellence*, brilliantly summarized in the theoretical works of Cicero and notably in the *De Oratore*. His ideal of the orator as a man of wide learning and irresistible eloquence, able to lead his audience in whatever direction he chose, became in a surreptitious way the pattern for the writer and ultimately for the artist, and its influence in the Renaissance is to be found everywhere. Something of its effect can be sensed in Horace's linking of pleasure and profit, another formula destined for a long career in Western discussion of the arts (*Ars Poetica*, l. 343ff. – trans. 1977, p. 478).

It is not enough for poems to have beauty, Horace argues, they must possess a 'sweet delight' which will lead the mind of the reader in a desired direction (ll. 99–100 – trans. 1977, p. 458). This didactic view of the arts, alien to modern assumptions, becomes more comprehensible if seen within the limits of a society still predominantly oral in its workings, where knowledge is seen as a social possession to be handed down from generation to generation. The importance of literature lies in its effectiveness as a means to social coherence and the transmission of received wisdom. In the classical tradition quality of transmission is of greater concern than novelty of content: Pope's 'What oft was *Thought*, but ne'er so well *Exprest*' (l. 298) in his *Essay on Criticism* (1711) summarizes an entire culture. Horace's remarks about the visual arts are of interest more for their suggestive value than their explicit content: as a prelude to his treatment of dramatic illusion he notes that the mind is more responsive to whatever enters it through the eyes than through the ears, and the *ut pictura poesis* tag slips in as part of a general comparison between the arts. Yet, though Horace did not press the point, the cumulative effect of classical discussion gave a prominent role to the pictorial, whether it was achieved by the pen or the brush.

This tendency is well illustrated in the *Institutio Oratoria* by the first-century rhetorician Quintilian which gives close attention to the part played by mental images in the persuasive arts. Rhetoric was essentially an applied art devised for the politician or the lawyer and Quintilian recognizes the value of vivid narrative in winning the emotional sympathy of an audience. The issue is one of imaginative involvement: not only must the speaker feel the emotional force of his case, just like an actor, but he must convey the same feelings to his audience by effective word-painting. What is envisaged is something very close to the player's 'dream of passion' which so stings Hamlet (II. ii. 546). This capacity to make past or even fictional events seem present to the eyes of the mind by means of vivid detail in turn works to give the orator control of his hearers' emotions. The consequent effect of vividness is given the Greek name *enargia*: it is this which makes us seem not so much to narrate as to exhibit the actual scene, while our emotions will be no less actively stirred than if we were present at 'the actual occurrence' (*Institutio*, VI, 2, 29–36 – trans. 1920, vol. 2, pp. 433–9). The key to such word painting is attention to detail and in particular to those accidental details which may not be strictly relevant to the action but add greatly to the concrete realization of a scene. Quintilian provides several literary examples, including his own fictional account of a sacked city (VIII, 3, 67–70 – trans. 1920, vol. 2, p. 249), which convey a powerful sense of personal involvement. Clearly such a deliberately subjective approach to narrative will not promote understatement and to modern taste the results may border on melodrama. This is true even of the passages he takes from such an impeccably classical source as the *Aeneid*.

Quintilian provides the most specific account of the rhetorical character of the arts until the theme is taken up again in the Renaissance by theorists like Alberti in the *De Pictura* (1435) and Erasmus in his *De Copia* (1512). But Quintilian's emphasis on telling detail as an ingredient of successful description was a commonplace of the literary exercise of word-painting or *ekphrasis*. In its later stages classical rhetoric was more concerned with academic exercises than with practical oratory and the construction of elaborate verbal descriptions became an important school exercise or virtuoso display. While this was a feature of Byzantine rhetoric (Baxandall, 1971, pp. 85–8), it also influenced medieval Latin and in due course found expression in vernacular authors like Chaucer. In *The Knight's Tale* the opposed values of love and war are given concrete form in the temples of Venus and Mars (*Canterbury Tales*, ll. 1893–2088). Chaucer obviously treats this section as a demonstration of *ekphrasis*, deliberately drawing our attention to 'the noble kerving and the portreitures,/The shap, the contenaunce, and the figures'; part of the device is his use of words to give us the experience of visual artefacts, and the reiterated references to the scenes as paintings, the quiet asides on the artist's skill, his 'soutil pencel' and the expensive colours, all contrive to heighten the reader's involvement. Such a performance reveals the kind of aesthetic expectation that would match such a contemporary descriptive painting as Ambrogio Lorenzetti's *Good and Bad Government* in the council chamber at Siena. In each case the function of words or pigment is to draw the reader or viewer into imagined space.

Medieval painting and sculpture were inevitably linked to a didactic function, above all to illustration of the biblical text. In the earlier phase of Romanesque art the awesome figure of Christ as judge on the tympanum at Vézelay (*c.* 1130) can be taken as wholly characteristic with its stress on the transcendent character of Christian truth. The figure is cosmic and terrible, the act of judgement annuls all familiar experience of the natural order. As a result the inevitable mode for such art is symbolic: it uses the material world only to point to a theological reality which rises above time and space. The use of biblical typology, both in decorative schemes and in such learned hymns as those of Adam of St Victor (*c.* 1110–80), is an aspect of this transcendence of time, providing a synchronic overview of the plot of history. There is very little room here for subjective participation; the sacral world and the normal world stay firmly apart. But the development in the later Middle Ages of very different devotional attitudes based on the humanity of Christ was to play a significant part in preparing public taste for the Renaissance recovery of pictorial space.

The Franciscan order was a major force in the dissemination of these new attitudes, accommodating religious practice to the experience of a lay urban culture. The preferred topics for meditation were the Nativity and Christ's Passion, precisely those which most powerfully invited the imaginative response of the believer. Thus from the fourteenth century there is an increased emphasis in religious painting and literature on the human joys and suffering of Christ and of Mary. Whether these themes are elaborated in murals, in sermons, in the religious drama, or in texts for private meditation, it is clear that they are exploited in a rhetorical manner: the aim is the creation of powerful images in the mind which will touch the emotions and influence the will (Meiss, 1973, p. 131). The most widely disseminated of such texts, the *Meditationes Vitae Christi* (*c.* 1300) now attributed to Giovanni di San Gimignano, gave rise to numerous verse and vernacular adaptations; the English version by Nicolas Love (*c.* 1410) left its mark on the contemporary mystery plays and was among the texts printed by Caxton. It is significant that Giovanni di San Gimignano was also the author of a treatise on the memory and the aim of the *Meditationes* was to stamp powerful emotional images on the mind. As a result they skirt around the miraculous and concentrate instead on the human episodes in which the reader can identify readily with the feelings of Mary and the Apostles, the original spectators. Love's English version, designed for a lay audience, repeatedly urges the reader to apply imagination to the scenes and give them a specific material form, 'as if thou were present'.

To assist this process his text is very precise on measurements and distance, and additions are made to the gospel narrative to give it contemporary immediacy: the Christ child solicits sewing work for his mother, the disciples remove the nails from his dead body surreptitiously to avoid adding to Mary's sorrow. The kind of meditative activity promoted by such works offers a common programme for the arts aimed at striking the memory with notable images. Not only did it stimulate an accurate representation of the natural world in order to support imaginative participation, but it helped to overcome a religious distrust of visual stimuli which could have inhibited artistic activity.

As it turned out, the most remarkable response to this effort to relate the believer more intimately with divine images was the conquest of pictorial space initiated by Giotto (*c.* 1267–1337). Strictly speaking Giotto did not initiate the tendency but his achievement in the Arena Chapel at Padua (*c.* 1305) amounted to 'an entirely new stage in the development of empirical perspective' (White, 1957, p. 57). Here the exploitation of a central perspective, the box-like assertion of pictorial depth and the statuesque solidity of the figures are used as means to intensify the emotional force of the scenes from Christ's life. The figures themselves register powerful feelings which become contagious to the viewer. At the inception of a characteristically Renaissance mode of painting it is clear that the dominant conception is a rhetorical one which can rival the persuasive eloquence of the preacher. This intimate link of the arts is acknowledged by the humanist Aeneas Sylvius Piccolomini (1403–64) in his eulogy of the two men who restored them to a lost excellence:

> These arts [eloquence and painting] love one another with mutual affection. A mental gift, and not a low but a high or supreme one, is required by eloquence as well as painting. Wonderful to tell, as long as eloquence flourished, painting flourished, as can be learned from the times of Demosthenes and Cicero. When the former revived, the latter also raised its head.... After Petrarch, letters reemerged; after Giotto the hands of the painters were raised once more. Now we can see that both these arts have reached perfection.
>
> (in Panofsky, 1970, pp. 15–16)

One need not subscribe to Piccolomini's restricted view of perfection to see that the revival of antiquity is closely allied to the cultural assumptions of Cicero's orator. The early fifteenth century witnessed the recovery of several lost works by Cicero, among them the complete *De Oratore* (1421), so it is not surprising to find that the first full apology for the naturalistic mode in painting is deeply influenced by him. This was the *De Pictura* (*On Painting*, 1435) by Leon Battista Alberti.

Alberti's treatise is both a store of advice for the painter and, implicitly, an attempt to elevate the status of the art from that of a manual craft. This he achieves by adapting Cicero's model of the persuasive speaker to the visual arts and, in effect, giving particular emphasis to the 'literary' role of the artist.

Thus he insists that the hallmark of excellence in a painter is the capacity to create an effective *historia*. By *historia* Alberti means the theme or narrative subject of a picture and it is revealing that he uses this distinctly literary term which can be translated as 'narrative' or even 'fiction'. What makes an artist outstanding is not skill in drawing or in handling paint – though such skill is taken for granted – but excellence in devising scenes which impress and move the beholder. For this activity he adopts the rhetorical term *inventio*, normally applied to the finding of appropriate arguments. In fact Alberti's most original step is to make this choice and organization of a subject the key element in a picture, even to the extent of asserting that a good *historia* can give pleasure without pictorial representation. What he means by this is exactly the kind of verbal description already met under the title of *ekphrasis*, and as an illustration he quotes Lucian's description of the *Calumny* by Apelles (fourth century BC). This must constitute one of the most extraordinary themes in the history of interart relations since Lucian's detailed account of the picture, composed during the second century AD, was translated into Latin by Guarino of Verona at Constantinople early in the fifteenth century and this provided the source for Alberti's account thirty years later. In due course the Florentine artist Botticelli made an attempt to realize the *historia* in his *Calumny of Apelles* now in the National Gallery in London. Underlying the whole transaction is the belief that the essence of an invention can be preserved in words like a fly in amber, to be released by the skills of the painter.

It is therefore understandable that Alberti recommends the artist to study the poets and the orators as well as cultivating literary people who can assist him in the devising of a composition. The role of the humanist-collaborator in the *inventio* of major decorative projects such as Raphael's *stanze* in the Vatican or Rubens's apotheosis of James I on the ceiling of Whitehall banqueting chamber is an important feature of Renaissance art. In Alberti's view the arts are bonded by a common concern with arousal and control of the emotions; whether the medium is pigment or words, the goal is to involve the audience in an idealized scene by devices which range from the telling rendering of physical detail to the imitation of powerful feelings. One effective device he recommends is the use of a mediating figure in a painting, one who bridges the gap between pictorial and actual space by gazing out into our plane and by expression or gesture draws us into the action or emotional tone (Alberti, [1435] 1972, p. 83). Within a picture such a figure plays a role analogous to that of the chorus or narrator in the contemporary religious drama.

To summarize: insofar as Alberti is representative of early Renaissance discussion about the sister arts, he highlights two key features. In the first place we have the adoption of a rhetorical model with all that flows from that for the conceptualizing of the artistic process; then there is the attention he gives to the preconception of a painting as it is envisaged even prior to its realization in paint. As we shall see, this latter point has some importance for the way the Renaissance formulated its idea of imagination. If Alberti does claim a new status for the artist it is as a variant on the old ideal of the orator; as a consequence the visual arts are elevated from the manual status of decoration to become a form of discourse. Moreover, if this humanist aesthetic appears to stress the illusory powers of a naturalistic style of painting, nevertheless such realism is directed at a psychological response, that is at the active participation of the beholder. It is meant to mirror an ideal conception (Lee, 1967).

The continuity of this rhetorical appraisal of painting is demonstrated in a much later work, *The Painting of the Ancients* by Francis Junius, the Dutch secretary to the Earl of Arundel, which was published in Latin in 1637 but appeared in Junius's English translation a year later. Arundel was the first great English collector, patron of Inigo Jones, a friend of Rubens and artistic adviser to Charles I, so Junius might be said to represent the advent of neo-classical values in England. But his book strongly reinforces Alberti's rhetorical preoccupations, holding that painting and poetry 'doe hold the raines of our hearts, leading and guiding our Passions, by that beguiling power they have, whithersoever they list' (p. 55). In a sense, *The Painting of the Ancients* can be read as a manifesto for Arundel's rich collection of paintings, statuary and drawings, a collection which was designed to stimulate native talent. So Junius urges the importance of models in breaking out of 'a blameworthie consuetude'; but originality of conception is also essential. Here the argument runs close to Alberti's discussion of the *historia*, since it stresses the imaginative projection by which the mind 'fore-seeth and fore-casteth the whole worke' (p. 20). In fact Junius's account of the contagious effects of art conveniently summarizes the Renaissance basis for linking literary with visual images:

> for as the Artificers that doe goe about their workes filled with an imagination of the presence of things, leave in their workes a certaine spirit, drawn and derived out of the contemplation of things present; so is it not possible but that same spirit transfused into their workes, should likewise prevaile with the spectatours, working in them the same impression of the presence of things that was in the Artificers themselves.
>
> (1638, p. 64)

So it is this transaction, in which images are conveyed by a physical medium (paint or print) from one mind to another, which provides the common ground.

Junius's English reading evidently included Sidney's *Arcadia* (1590–93) since he cites this in the course of his book; and it is a relevant question whether he knew *An Apology for Poetry* (1595), in which Sidney approaches the literary text with a similar preoccupation about images. Certainly Sidney's pioneering defence of verbal fictions – for that is what his sense of 'poetry' conveys –

shows a distinctly visual bias. During his 'grand tour' in 1573–4 Sidney sat to Veronese and he knew the work of Titian; he was one of the first Englishmen to have a knowledge of Renaissance painting and his *Apology* is an oration on the power of images. As an apology it was aimed against the radical zeal released by the Reformation which condemned image-making as idolatry: his strategy is to establish the social utility of images as a means of instruction in private and social virtues. Again it is the contagious effect of fictions, their capacity to make ideal scenes imaginatively available, which gives them superiority over history or philosophy. In the terms of Spenser's 'October' eclogue from *The Shepheardes Calender* (1579) the poet's honour is,

> to restraine
> The hurt of lawlesse youth with good advice:
> Or pricke them forth with pleasaunce of thy vaine,
> Whereto thou list their trayned willes entice.
>
> (ll. 21–4)

Sidney adopts the identical verb to describe the poet who 'doth not only show the way, but so sweet a prospect into the way, as will *entice* any man to enter into it' ([1595] 1965, p. 113); this sense of art as a tender (and improving) trap is the classic justification of feigned images and it is exactly in the spirit of Alberti's stress on the *historia* that Sidney can claim 'the skill of the artificer standeth in that *Idea* or fore-conceit of the work, and not in the work itself' (p. 101). This may fairly be described as the first serious attempt in English to justify the role of the creative imagination, since it is precisely this ability to reach beyond the flawed limits of experience and project ideal – and compelling – forms which marks the true poet and makes him a reflection of God's creative activity. In essence, then, Sidney's understanding of fiction is the 'feigning of notable images of virtues, vices, or what else' which will delight and instruct. His argument that such speaking pictures will illuminate 'the imaginative and judging power' means that where philosophy provides abstract notions art can bridge the gulf between idea and moral action (pp. 103, 107). If there is one recurrent concern in the arts of the Renaissance it is to reach across this divide: when John Milton in his *Areopagitica* (1644) contrasts Spenser with Scotus and Aquinas it is because Sir Guyon's journey through the Cave of Mammon gives more effective instruction in the practice of temperance than any abstract analysis could do.

In general, therefore, earlier theories about the relationship of the arts have an idealistic character. They emphasize the transfer of ideas or mental images without paying too much attention to the physical medium by which the transfer is achieved. Sidney's '*Idea* or fore-conceit', the mental notion which precedes the concrete work of art, can be recreated in the mind of the reader by a process of interpretation. Mind speaks to mind in such a way that the material form of the work is seen just as a means to an end. The term 'reader' can really be applied to the visual arts as well since the observer confronted by an allegorical or mythological scene, not to say the curiously symbolic portraits which are a feature of the period, is engaged in the unravelling of a 'text'. This undoubtedly reflects, in England at least, that distrust of physical images which was a consequence of the Reformation; verbalized images, less dependent on the senses, were less open to objection. The contemporary taste for emblem books and *imprese* is a further demonstration of this wish to treat visual experience as a step towards a mental encounter, using in this case a hieroglyph or conceit which could be interpreted with the aid of the accompanying verses. However, there was an undercurrent of rivalry between the sister arts. Leonardo da Vinci had argued for the superiority of painting on the grounds that sight was a nobler sense than hearing. Just over a century later Ben Jonson echoed humanistic preference for the pen over the pencil, 'for that can speak to the understanding, the other but to the sense' (ed. 1947, p. 610). It is surprising how little of substance is said about the difference between the arts until the eighteenth century when Lessing attempted in his *Laokoon* (1766) to distinguish them in terms of their respective engagement with time and space.

The Renaissance pairing of poetry and painting was to have a lasting effect on Western art. To return to our opening contrast, Rothko and Fildes exemplify extreme tendencies in the visual arts. The abstract canvases of the former compel us to focus on the work itself and allow no escape into external reference; the latter's *Casual Ward*, to take one example, directs us away from the canvas to speculate on the private agonies that lie behind the scene. In this respect Fildes's painting, in spite of its nineteenth-century style, is operating exactly along the lines of Alberti's *historia*; in essence it is a visual parable, suggestive of past actions and future consequences. This is a characteristic of all 'realist' art and literature: to render the medium as transparent as possible so that the awareness of artifice does not intrude and we move through the medium to the possible worlds offered. The most important consequence of the rhetorical model of painting developed in the Renaissance was the subordination of the visual arts to discourse – they had to tell a story. The textual character of humanist culture promoted an art full of literary reference which presupposed an informed audience familiar with myth, history and iconographic codes. While this is modified during the course of the eighteenth century in favour of more general notions founded on 'nature' and 'feeling', the importance of the narrative theme does not slacken. Rather, the popularity of anecdotal painting in the period between Hogarth and Millais (a development linked to the rise of book illustration) points to an audience that viewed pictures with expectations little different from those gratified by the serial exposition of the novel. It is in this context that Lessing's rejection of the *ut pictura poesis* argument should be seen; his aim was to reassert the character of painting and sculpture as sources of aesthetic delight free from the restrictions of narrative. In fact, though, his real quarrel was with the way in which the rhetorical model had hijacked discussion of the arts.

If one ground for analogy between the arts has been a common drive towards the reproduction of observed reality, the creation of 'presence', the other has been the stimulus of aesthetic emotion by such means as form or pattern. The romantic use of the sublime to produce awe can be seen as a move in the direction of the second. But it is most clearly seen in that preoccupation with the creative process that has been a feature of modern activity in the arts. In painting, Impressionism – insofar as it can be called a unified movement – directs attention to the act of perception. With modernism there is a deliberate focus on the character and even the recalcitrance of the medium, be it words or paint. Not only does this draw our attention to the artificiality of art but it makes our experience of the medium a major part of the aesthetic response. The Imagist movement in the early years of the twentieth century marks in both its name and its practice a poetic attempt to take on something of the essential solidity and repose of objects, frozen in the moment of perception like a snapshot. Lessing's separation of the arts had been based on the assumption that they were both concerned with the imitation of the available world, but in a situation where they were no longer preoccupied with the reproduction of 'reality' it is no longer clear that his distinction holds. Sometime around 1906 Ernest Fenollosa, captivated by the idea of the Chinese ideogram as a speaking picture, noted that:

> A true noun, an isolated thing, does not exist in nature. Things are only the terminal points, or rather the meeting points, of actions, cross-sections cut through actions, snapshots. Neither can a pure verb, an abstract motion, be possible in nature. The eye sees noun and verb as one: things in motion, motion in things.
>
> (1969, p. 10)

All the processes in nature, he went on to conclude, are interrelated and as a result there could be no such thing as a complete or self-contained sentence, 'save one which it would take all time to pronounce'. One may be wryly tempted to think of Ezra Pound's *Cantos* (1917–70) in this connection, where each canto offers a frozen episode from the unbroken process of human culture. This instinct for synchronicity, for the simultaneous presence of differing perspectives, is as much a feature of the modernist poem – *The Waste Land* (1922) provides an eminent example – as it is of cubist painting. Gertrude Stein throws some light on this quest for epiphany in her remark that the writing of her *The Making of Americans*

> was a struggle to do this thing, to make a whole present of something that it had

taken a great deal of time to find out, but it was a whole there then within me and as such it had to be said.

(1971, p. 91)

The struggle to which she refers is that to transform temporal sequence into a spatial extension, just as cubism endeavoured to render the object in its integrity and not as it appeared at a particular moment and place. Fenollosa had already made that telling reference to the snapshot, but the fullest response to Lessing's separation of the arts of time and space would be found in the revolutionary medium of film. Not only does film reconcile the apparent opposition between action and vision but its characteristic reliance on the technique of montage – the production of a composite overview by means of selected cuttings – is already a familiar device in the modernist text.

It would be difficult to overestimate the fertility of film for interart analogies and its repercussions on the functioning of the other arts has yet to be exhaustively charted. One thing that seems clear is that the blurring of frontiers between word and image in Quintilian and in Alberti was just one expression of a perennial urge within the arts to reconcile the distinct preoccupations of vision and language, to arrive at some magical fusion such as that faintly shadowed in concrete poetry. In that case *ut pictura poesis* is as valid now as it was for the age of the Renaissance: both arts remain essentially distinct but both aspire to a condition which implicitly includes the other. By the nature of things there can be no final consensus as to their relationship, but the revival of interest in the issue in recent years owes a great deal to the comprehensive analysis of cultural systems provoked by structuralism. We may no longer think in terms of 'silent poems' and 'speaking pictures', but the old equation is still a potent influence in the practice of the arts and promises to be of central importance for the critical interpretation of our age.

FURTHER READING

Baxandall, Michael (1971) *Giotto and the Orators*, Clarendon Press, Oxford

Bender, J. B. (1972) *Spenser and Literary Pictorialism*, Princeton University Press, Princeton

Bryson, Norman (1981) *Word and Image: French Painting of the Ancien Régime*, Cambridge University Press, Cambridge

Fowler, Norman K. (1984) *Poets and Visual Arts in Renaissance England*, University of Texas Press, Austin

Gent, Lucy (1981) *Picture and Poetry 1560–1620*, James Hall, Leamington

Gombrich, E. H. (1960) *Art and Illusion*, Phaidon, London

——(1972) *Symbolic Images*, Phaidon, London

Hagstrum, J. H. (1958) *The Sister Arts*, Chicago University Press, Chicago

Leslie, Michael (1985) 'The dialogues between bodies and souls: pictures and poesy in the English Renaissance', *Word and Image*, I, 16–30

Pickering, F. P. (1970) *Literature and Art in the Middle Ages*, Macmillan, London

Steiner, Wendy (1982) *The Colors of Rhetoric*, Chicago University Press, Chicago

Sypher, Wylie (1963) *From Rococo to Cubism in Art and Literature*, Vintage Books, New York

ADDITIONAL WORKS CITED

Alberti, Leon Battista (1972) *On Painting and Sculpture*, translated by C. Grayson, Phaidon, London [written 1435]

Edwards, Lee M. (1987) 'Hubert von Herkomer'. In Julian Treuherz (ed.), *Hard Times: Social Realism in Victorian Painting*, Lund Humphries, London

Fenollosa, Ernest (1969) *The Chinese Written Character as a Medium for Poetry*, edited by Ezra Pound, City Light Books, San Francisco [first published 1920]

Horace (1977) *Satires, Epistles and Ars Poetica*, translated by H. Rushton Fairclough, Loeb Classical Library, Cambridge

Jonson, Ben (1947) *Discoveries*, vol. 8 of the complete works of *Ben Jonson*, edited by C. H. Herford and P. and E. Simpson, Clarendon Press, Oxford

Junius, Franciscus (1638) *The Painting of the Ancients*, R. Hodgkinsonne, London

Lee, R. W. (1967) *Ut Pictura Poesis: the Humanistic Theory of Painting*, Norton, New York

MacLeish, Archibald (1935) *Poems*, Borriswood, London

Meiss, Millard (1973) *Painting in Florence and Siena After the Black Death*, Harper & Row, New York [first published 1951]

Panofsky, Erwin (1970) *Renaissance and Renascences in Western Art*, Paladin, London [first published 1965]

Quintilian (1920–2) *Institutio Oratoria*, translated by H. E. Butler, 4 vols, Loeb Classical Library, Cambridge

Sidney, Sir Philip (1965) *An Apology for Poetry*, edited by G. Shepherd, Nelson, London [first published 1595]

Stein, Gertrude (1971) *Look at Me Now and Here I Am*, edited by Patricia Meyerowitz, Penguin, Harmondsworth

White, John (1957) *The Birth and Rebirth of Pictorial Space*, Faber & Faber, London

74

LITERATURE AND MUSIC

DAVID LINDLEY

That some kind of relationship exists between the arts of music and literature is a proposition unquestioned since classical times. The nature of that relationship, however, has been a matter of considerable controversy throughout history. If music and poetry are, in Milton's famous phrase, 'Sphere borne, harmonious sisters', then sibling rivalry has been as constant a feature of their relationship as sororial amity. The debate has been conducted at a number of different levels, from the abstractions of aesthetic theory to the practicalities of writing and setting song lyrics. The fascination of the topic, and the many problems that attend it, are in no small measure the product of the wide range of critical questions which can be raised through it. The history of changing attitudes is a valuable symptomatic study of fundamental shifts in the understanding of the nature of artistic production, whilst the questions raised by attention to the practicalities of writing for music may guide us to a better appreciation of poetic craft and in particular to a richer understanding of the nature and function of rhythm in poetry. The problem is often to keep a clear eye on the differences between the various kinds of interest the topic may have. Somewhat artificially, this essay divides into a preliminary consideration of larger theoretical problems, followed by some discussion of more detailed questions of the influences exerted by music on poetical practice.

Music and poetry are both arts which unfold through time. It is chiefly this property which distinguishes them both from painting or architecture. But once one attempts to go beyond this most general statement then problems arise. In the first place music is an art which always resists verbal commentary upon it. If all criticism in some measure is a 'translation' of the object under consideration, then the translation of music into words about it is peculiarly problematic. It is often suggested that music is like a language, a system which relies upon the relationships between pitch, harmony and rhythm to produce its effects and 'meanings'. But, unlike language, its system has no direct reference to the objective world outside itself. Though much recent thinking about language has sought to overturn ideas of a straightforward relationship between words and things, and might therefore seem to make it possible to bring the analysis of music and language closer together, it still remains true that one cannot go into a bar and order a drink by singing a musical phrase. This might seem so self-evident a statement as to be utterly trivial, yet it can be argued that it is precisely the paradox that music works upon the mind and feelings, but cannot be contained by meanings except those bestowed upon it by its association with particular words, ideas or visual images, which fuels much of the debate about music and poetry throughout the centuries.

At some time in the fifth century Saint John Chrysostom wrote:

> To such an extent, indeed, is our nature delighted by chants and songs that even infants at the breast, if they be weeping or afflicted, are by reason of it lulled to sleep. Nurses, carrying them in their arms, walking to and fro and singing certain childish songs to them, often cause them to close their eyes.
>
> (in Strunk, 1952, pp. 67–8)

Any contemporary parent responds to this comment, which reveals the way in which pleasure in music is pre-cognitive, pre-linguistic. But Saint John continues by expressing the nature of the anxiety that this breeds:

> Inasmuch as this kind of pleasure is thoroughly innate to our mind, and lest demons introducing lascivious songs should overthrow everything, God established the psalms, in order that singing might be both a pleasure and a help.
>
> (p. 68)

Here is clearly demonstrated the unease that the immediacy of pleasure in music generates. The history of aesthetic theory has been in part a succession of attempts to find a way of validating, directing and controlling the dangerous power of music.

One way of securing this end is to attempt to explain the source of music's power in an acceptable fashion. Until the Renaissance the commonest procedure was to derive music's power to charm from its reflection of celestial harmony. Earthly music was held to work upon us through its imitation of the patterns of the divine musician. Partaking of the harmony which bound the whole universe, it brought down the unheard music which the moving planets made and could thereby charm and heal. This theory makes possible the music which cures the distraught Lear, raises Thaisa from the dead in *Pericles*, or animates the statue of Hermione in *The Winter's Tale*. Shakespeare, indeed, provides one of the most memorable articulations of this view of music's power in the exchange between Lorenzo and Jessica in Act 5 of *The Merchant of Venice*. As this model became unsustainable in a post-Copernican world, the source of music's power was located in its rhetorical efficacy (an early attempt to work out correspondences between music and language), and later in its capacity to rouse and imitate the affections. The emptying out of music's cosmic analogy has been charted by John Hollander in his book *The Untuning of the Sky* (1961). In the last two hundred years or so a radical shift of perception has validated music precisely by its transcendence, its escape from signification. This shift has had an important effect upon the history of music's relationship to poetry in aesthetic theory.

In the late Renaissance and early Baroque it was generally assumed that music with words was superior to mere instrumental music. Monteverdi asserted roundly that it was his intention 'to make the words the mistress of the harmony and not the servant', and that musical works without words 'would be left bodies without soul if they were left without this most important and principal part of music' (in Strunk, 1952, pp. 406–7). Words control and direct their accompanying harmony, and in so doing guarantee the moral direction and value of the music. This view of the relative importance of words and music persisted into the eighteenth century and beyond. James Harris, writing in 1744, concluded:

> It is evident that these two arts can never be so powerful singly as when they are properly united. For poetry, when alone, must be necessarily forced to waste many of its richest ideas in the mere raising of affections. . . . And music, when alone, can only raise affections, which soon languish and decay if not maintained and fed by the nutritive images of poetry. Yet must it be remembered in this union, that poetry ever have the precedence, its utility as well as dignity being by far the more considerable.
>
> (in le Huray and Day, 1981, p. 39)

It was during the eighteenth century that the desire to direct and control music's power through the words it sets began to be overturned. Instrumental music gained in prestige, and so it became possible to see the indeterminacy of music not as something to be feared, but as precisely the source of its usefulness for a poetry that sought more and more to express the intangible processes of feeling and emotion. Kevin Barry, in his book *Language, Music and the Sign* (1987), traces the gradual transference from a model of poetry based on picture, to one based on music in the later part of the century. During the nineteenth century the reversal of the priority given to words in earlier periods is completed. Walter Pater's statement sums up the new attitude:

> Art, then, is thus always striving to be independent of the mere intelligence, to become a matter of pure perception, to get rid of its responsibilities to its subject or material. . . . It is the art of music which most completely realises this artistic ideal, this perfect identification of form and matter. In its ideal, consummate moments, the end is not distinct from the expression; they inhere in and completely saturate each other, and to it, therefore, to the condition of its perfect moments, all the arts may be supposed constantly to tend and aspire.
>
> ([1873] 1980, p. 109)

This belief that music is the ideal art in its transcendence of mere signification is one which animated the symbolists, and finds echo in the poetry of Eliot and Wallace Stevens. W. H. Auden gives memorable expression to the idea in his poem 'The Composer':

> All the others translate: the painter sketches
> A visible world to love or reject;
> Rummaging into his living, the poet fetches
> The images out that hurt and connect,
>
> From Life to Art by painstaking adaption,
> Relying on us to cover the rift;
> Only your notes are pure contraption,
> Only your song is an absolute gift.
>
> (1976, p. 148)

But though there is continuity between the romantic elevation of music and the expression of envy of the musician's art that can be seen in the work of a number of recent poets, it needs to be emphasized that there are important differences. To the romantics it was often the 'wild' music of nature, the wind in the Aeolian harp perhaps, which served as image for the turbulent movement of feeling. But for the moderns it has more often been the formal qualities of music which have been celebrated. Something of the difference of emphasis is brought out in a comparison of Wordsworth's 'Solitary Reaper' and Wallace Stevens's 'Idea of Order at Key West'. To Wordsworth the distant figure sings a song which reverberates in his heart; whereas Stevens's singer figures the 'rage for order'. Both romantic and modernist valorizations of music, however, are bought in part by circumventing the problems of music's doubleness. Neither contends directly with the association of music with less desirable emotion or the disorder of revel.

For if the history of music and poetry is approached from a different direction, through the ways in which the arts have figured in cultural politics, then it is precisely the opposition between the transcendent power of music on the one side and its association with popular revel on the other which has led to anxiety. Music appeals to our non-rational faculties, and may therefore be associated either with divine ecstasy or with indulgence of sensual appetite. Politically music may celebrate the power of the state, or focus the discontent of rebellion (revealingly enough, the songs of successful revolutionaries tend to become national anthems). Music, then, can either be summoned to the service of the state, or express the feeling of the dispossessed. Jacques Attali writes:

> A subversive strain of music has always managed to survive, subterranean and pursued, the inverse image of this political channelization: popular music, an instrument of the ecstatic cult, and outburst of uncensored violence. . . . Music,

the quintessential mass activity, like the crowd, is simultaneously a threat and a necessary source of legitimacy; trying to channel it is a risk that every system of power must run.

(1985, pp. 13–14)

The political significance of music should not be underestimated. In the romantic period, for example, the revolutionary energy of music was a frequent topos. In our own time the protest song, or the music of black communities, has a similar subversive charge. In literary history, the use of music in drama has always tended to deploy its potential for a political signification. Shakespeare's *The Tempest* exemplifies this possibility. The play presents us with the way that music may express the desires of slaves to be free (both Caliban and Ariel sing songs of freedom), but at the same time Prospero uses music to lead characters about the enchanted island and subject their understanding and will to his power. Music here is precisely a metaphor for political coercion even though the ends to which Prospero puts his power might be judged beneficial. The ballad-opera of Gay or the use of music by Brecht are other obvious instances of music employed in the theatre with significant political effect.

There is one area of the cultural demarcation and control of music which deserves further notice. Since music is both sub-rational and supra-rational, patriarchal discourse has often identified its capacity to stir the emotions with the effect of the female upon the male. Because woman was either idealized as an inspiration to virtue or castigated as the cause of lust, the homology between music and the female could easily be asserted. So it was in the Renaissance, when Puritan opponents of music claimed that its effect was to make men effeminate, luring them from proper manly pursuits. (It is no coincidence that few males in Renaissance drama sing unless they are in one way or another professional singers, nor that it is female characters such as Ophelia and Desdemona who most directly express their feeling through music.) In the eighteenth century music was seen as a particularly appropriate accomplishment for women (though not without its dangers in exciting unruly passions) and, indeed, there is still in our society a feeling that music is something women do (as any choirmaster desperate for tenors and basses to balance the numbers of women in his choral society will testify). The place of music in the politics of gender has not, to my knowledge, been much explored. It seems to me likely that it could be a productive field, with interesting implications for the way music is employed as a symbol and effect in drama and the novel. Be that as it may, the attempt to marginalize music by identifying it with the marginalized gender is another symptom of the way discussion of music always confronts the unease begotten by its apparently innate power to move. This is what troubled Saint John Chrysostom; it is still what troubles absolutist states. The successive attempts to describe music are, from one perspective, always attempts to circumscribe it.

Some of the large-scale shifts in theoretical perspective can be used to account for shifts in practice throughout the centuries. So, for example, as Renaissance turns into early Baroque an insistence that words must control the direction of the harmony produces the declamatory musical style of early opera. At the same time, however, the musical style which results is capable of setting prose or continuous verse, and does not demand the production of formally controlled stanzaic lyrics. It might then be argued that the lyrics of John Donne, often taken to have departed from the musical origins of poetry in pursuit of a more natural speech, can be seen as demanding, perhaps even provoking, a different kind of music for their setting. In the eighteenth century, as Barry (1987) argues, the increasingly positive view of music's indeterminacy may have played a part in affecting the attitude to language, image and poetic craft of the early romantics. For the symbolists a sense of the primacy of music led to a concentration upon sound. As Winn observes:

> The Symbolist movement reenacts and extends the Romantic tendency to celebrate and emulate the supposed vagueness of music.... In Mallarmé's mature work, subtle patterns of organisation by sound are more important than syntax. These patterns are not complex and orderly constructions ... but unique and particular creations in whose mysterious power to suggest and evoke Mallarmé believed intensely.
>
> (1981, pp. 326–7)

In the last two hundred years, as music has freed itself from subordination to words, some writers have taken music as a model for the larger construction of their works. De Quincey's 'Dream Fugue', Thomas Mann's *Dr Faustus* and Eliot's *Four Quartets* are all examples of this kind. But here one is aware that though musical structures offered a stimulus to ways of organizing language, the works are not themselves therefore 'musical' in any straightforward way. Pursuit of an analogy has a liberating effect upon writers, but the connection with music remains, for the reader, an indirect and intellectual one.

When one turns to a more specific consideration of the ways in which music might be held to influence poetry in its execution at a practical level, then a different set of questions comes into focus. These questions overlap with more general matters of theory, but they are not coterminous with them. For though the symbolists and others strove to make their poetry 'like' music, this is rather different from the problems faced by the poet who 'cometh to you with words accompanied with, or prepared for, the well-enchanting skill of music', to quote Sir Philip Sidney ([1595] 1965, p. 113). The association of lyric verse with music has a continuous history from classical to modern times. Whatever the historical truth of the matching of music and verse in ancient history or

popular culture, the authority of the myth has had a potent effect in conditioning critical understanding of lyric. In particular, it is often argued that the poet
writing lyrics for musical setting has two considerations in mind. First, that
the words must be presented in a form which makes them settable, secondly
that the words should deal with feelings or attitudes that music might be able
to express. These criteria of form and content, though they seem to have a
simple, functional basis, are conditioned by two sets of assumptions, neither
of them unproblematic.

The first set of assumptions concerns what is thought to happen when music
is added to poetry. The myth of Orpheus, of some kind of perfect fusion of
the two arts into a new, balanced whole, has had a long life. It is a notion
fiercely challenged by aestheticians like Susanne K. Langer. She writes:

> When words and music come together in song, music swallows words; not only
> mere words and literal sentences, but even literary word-structures, poetry. Song
> is not a compromise between poetry and music, though the text taken by itself
> be a great poem; song is music.
>
> (1953, p. 152)

Some obvious support for such a view might come from the fact that a poor
poem can yet form the basis of a fine song, whereas a fine lyric cannot stand
out against an inadequate setting. It suggests that in the end the words do not
matter except as props for the composer. Nicholas Ruwet (1972), however,
suggests that this is too extreme an attitude. In his argument there is always
a dialectical relationship between words and music, in which neither completely
loses itself. What both these views tend to overlook is the simple fact that
different kinds of musical setting predicate very different relationships between
words and music. The musical accompaniment of narrative in early periods
required a set of simple tones, acting perhaps as a mnemonic aid rather than
an expressive device. In the ballad, for example, the repetition of a single tune
from stanza to stanza means that the expressive function of music is minimized,
as the words dominate the listener's attention. Even in the strophic song of
two or three stanzas the relationship of word and tune is very different from
that operating in a continuous, through-composed setting, and the writer of
strophic lyric for music will exercise his art in formal control, in the repetition
of a metrical schema which will enable each stanza to be sung to the same
tune. The writer of words for a baroque aria, or for the opera house, will have
different priorities, since the words may often be little more than the pegs
upon which the musician hangs elaboration. Strong emotional cues are all that
is necessary. There can, therefore, be no simple statement of what constitutes
an appropriate form of lyric destined for musical setting. The criteria will
always be determined by the very different demands of different kinds of
music.

The second major assumption is that song is to be judged by the way it appears to the auditor on a single performance. Words have to be simple, it is argued, because listeners cannot take in complexity. This criterion is, however, misleading, since the relationship between words and their setting may be something that only fully declares itself after repeated hearings of a song, and the lyricist or the composer can surely assume that their work might merit that kind of attention. So too, the richness of the relationship between word and setting may be the source of pleasure to the performer – particularly perhaps in genres like the madrigal, intended for private rather than public perform-ance, where the complexity of the musical texture masks detail from a listening audience. Furthermore, whatever poets or critics might think song lyrics 'ought' to be, composers have always had an irritating habit of choosing to set words that disobey the criteria that such critics establish. It is often assumed, for example, that song lyrics should be 'simple, sensuous and passionate'. Thomas Weelkes seems not to have taken much notice of this rule when he chose to set a lyric which begins 'Thule, the period of cosmography/Doth vaunt of Hecla' in his 1600 set of madrigals. Indeed, composers in the late sixteenth and early seventeenth centuries seem to have delighted in the challenge of setting difficult and complex texts.

What we are led to is the realization that a distinction must be made between different objects of study, objects that are often confused with one another. Consideration of achieved matches of word and music, in chant, song or opera, has its own interest. In this context one can trace the historical variation that derives from different theoretical attitudes, different compositional practices and so on. James Winn (1981) is particularly helpful here, as he explores the ways in which the demands of formal correspondence and expressive effect have produced varying results across the centuries. It is under this heading that one might want to consider the peculiar phenomenon of opera, a battle-ground where competing theories of the right relationship of words and music have clashed, from the humanist theory of Monteverdi to Wagner's ambition to fuse the elements in the perfect music drama. Revealingly, perhaps, opera is the only earlier nineteenth-century drama regularly performed in the twentieth century. Music's capacity to transform and exalt the mundane here reaches its apogee – it seems the right dramatic vehicle for Romanticism. W. H. Auden has written of the appeal of opera for the modern poet: 'Opera is the last refuge of the High style, the only art to which a poet with nostalgia for those times past when poets could write in the grand manner all by themselves can still contribute' (1968, p. 116). But discussing such musico-poetical events is a rather different task from considering the ways in which music has served as stimulus, inspiration or model for individual poets. In this context prescrip-tive criteria for what constitutes the ideal song lyric are important primarily as notions which condition what poets might write if they want to compose a poem which seems 'song-like'. The stimulus of music, and the controls implied by writing for a specific kind of musical setting, may be significant for poets in a number of ways, but what they do is ultimately determined by the rules of language, and not of music. There is always a gap, always an analogy at work, and it is the distance between words and music which is the very thing that makes music a valuable suggestive resource for poets. Where then are we to look for that fruitful influence? Perhaps the most obvious point of connection has been the possibility of finding a relationship between musical and poetic form.

Musical form is founded upon repetition. The poet may respond to that repetition in a number of ways. In some medieval dance-song forms, for example, whole lines are repeated in strict patterns, and poets might use that kind of repetition in forms like rondeau or villanelle, whether or not their work is destined for musical setting. So, too, the straightforward refrain, one of the most obvious signals of a 'song-like' lyric, is an expressive resource which many poets have found valuable. In music it is the unit of the phrase which is fundamental, and to the listener it is the correspondence of rhyme with phrase ending which is aurally most prominent. Rhyme-schemes may derive directly from patterns of musical repetition (and the frequency with which *aabccb* patterns turn up in song lyrics may owe something to characteristic musical phrase-structures). But in another way it is the play of sounds, fore-grounded in elaborate rhyming patterns, which seems to bring poetry close to music – and from the troubadours to Cole Porter lyricists have demonstrated their linguistic virtuosity in the production of ingenious rhyme-schemes. But poets not writing directly for musical setting have also been influenced by the way in which line-lengths may be varied and the ear charmed by the tune of rhyme. Elaborate stanza forms, from Pindar, through the madrigal stanza of the sixteenth century, to the romantic odes, draw upon this resource.

But it is perhaps at the level of the rhythmic organization of language that musical influence is at one and the same time most important, and most problematic. For the rhythms of language are crudely defined compared with those of music; they are imprecise where music is exact. That this is the case is obvious if one considers words written to fit existing music, or the words produced in conjunction with music in the recording studio. From Renaissance contrafacta to the sprawling words of pop songs in *Smash Hits* it is the rhythmic irregularity of the words on the page which is often most striking, an irregularity which cannot be recovered into system unless one knows the tune. But yet, as Northrop Frye observed (1957, pp. 251–8), we use the term 'musical' to describe poems of regular movement. He contests this view strongly, claiming instead that it is poetry which obeys the rules of pulse rather than regular alternation of stressed and unstressed syllables which is most like music. In so doing he draws attention to important points, especially the significance of the 'beat' in our reading of verse, but at the same time he runs the risk of simplifying the notion of the relationship of music and verse from an opposite direction. For the 'music' of poetry, and the possible usefulness of music as a stimulus to the poet, do not derive from rhythm alone. In music what is important is the tense and variable relationship between rhythm and music's other parameters of melody and harmony, and it is precisely the same sort of complex relationship between poetic rhythm and other parameters, of rhyme, line-length, meaning and syntax, which produces our pleasure in a poem's formal control. What is at issue, then, is not simply a matter of metrics considered separately, but the relationships between rhythm and other things. Frye, for example, classes Herbert as a non-musical poet, compared with Donne – but misses therefore the claim that one might make for Herbert's wonderfully varied stanza structures and their command of rhythm in relation to patterns of sense and rhyme as being the profoundest music.

None the less, in claiming poets like Donne and Browning as 'musical', Frye performs the notable service of breaking down the all-too-common distinction which is offered between 'musical' poetry and poetry based on 'the rhythms of speech'. All speech is potentially musical, and, as Eliot observed, 'the music of poetry, then, must be a music latent in the common speech of its time' (1957, p. 31). Poetry simply has the potential to organize and foreground that music. Even free verse can be claimed for music, since the reader must search for the pulse which will allow it to be articulated. (Though there can be little doubt that much contemporary verse is written for the eye, written to offer images to readers with tin ears.) It is only when poetry calls upon the resources of rhythm to play against its other systems of organization that it establishes its link with music. But this link is not, in the end, to do with what actually happens when a particular poem is set to music, for though the arts may co-operate in particular instances, they remain always essentially distinct.

Throughout history music's doubleness has made it attractive and problematic. The sirens sing, but so do the angels in heaven. Music is at one and the same time the most disciplined of arts, and yet that least susceptible to control of its effects. It shares properties with language, but is essentially different from it. It is these paradoxes which give it such appeal to writers – and which ultimately defeat them. As Geoffrey Hill writes:

> Music survives, composing her own sphere,
> Angel of Tones, Medusa, Queen of the Air,
> and when we would accost her with real cries
> silver on silver thrills itself to ice.
>
> (1978, p. 44)

FURTHER READING

Barry, Kevin (1987) *Language, Music and the Sign*, Cambridge University Press, Cambridge

Booth, Mark W. (1981) *The Experience of Songs*, Yale University Press, New Haven

Doughtie, Edward (1986) *English Renaissance Song*, Twayne Publishers, Boston

Hollander, John (1961) *The Untuning of the Sky*, Princeton University Press, Princeton

Johnson, Paula (1972) *Form and Transformation in Music and Poetry of the English Renaissance*, Yale University Press, New Haven

Jorgens, Elise Bickford (1982) *The Well-Tun'd Word: Musical Interpretation of English Poetry 1597–1651*, University of Minnesota Press, Minneapolis

Kramer, Lawrence (1984) *Music and Poetry in the Nineteenth Century and After*, University of California Press, Berkeley and Los Angeles

le Huray, Peter and Day, James (eds) (1981) *Music and Aesthetics in the Eighteenth and Early-Nineteenth Centuries*, Cambridge University Press, Cambridge

Lindley, David (1986) *Thomas Campion*, E. J. Brill, Leiden

Stevens, John (1961) *Music and Poetry in the Early Tudor Court*, Methuen, London

——(1986) *Words and Music in the Middle Ages*, Cambridge University Press, Cambridge

Strunk, Oliver (ed.) (1952) *Source Readings in Music History*, Faber & Faber, London

Winn, James Anderson (1981) *Unsuspected Eloquence*, Yale University Press, New Haven

ADDITIONAL WORKS CITED

Attali, Jacques (1985) *Noise: The Political Economy of Music*, translated by Brian Massumi, Manchester University Press, Manchester

Auden, W. H. (1968) *Secondary Worlds*, Faber & Faber, London

——(1976) *Collected Poems*, edited by Edward Mendelson, Faber & Faber, London

Eliot, T. S. (1957) *On Poetry and Poets*, Faber & Faber, London

Frye, Northrop (1957) *Anatomy of Criticism*, Princeton University Press, Princeton

Hill, Geoffrey (1978) *Tenebrae*, André Deutsch, London

Langer, Susanne K. (1953) *Feeling and Form*, Routledge & Kegan Paul, London

Pater, Walter (1980) *The Renaissance*, edited by Donald L. Hill, University of California Press, Berkeley and Los Angeles [first published 1873]

Ruwet, Nicolas (1972) *Langage, musique, poésie*, Editions du Seuil, Paris

Sidney, Sir Philip (1965) *An Apology for Poetry*, edited by Geoffrey Shepherd, Nelson, London [first published 1595]

75

LITERATURE AND LANDSCAPE

ALISTAIR M. DUCKWORTH

In a series of brilliant chapters in volume 3 of *Modern Painters* (1856), John Ruskin showed how landscape, an ancillary feature of European literature and art in the classical and medieval periods, took on a central aesthetic and moral role only in the modern period. Dropping Ruskin's moral criticism, early twentieth-century scholars began to trace the stages by which landscape rose in the once firmly established neo-classical hierarchy of genres, variously achieving a salient place in the poetry of Thomson, Gray and Wordsworth; in the gothic novels of Mrs Radcliffe and 'Monk' Lewis and the historical novels of Scott; in the neo-Claudian landscapes of Richard Wilson and the rural paintings of Gainsborough and Constable; and, particularly, in the rise and progress of the English landscape garden, from its supposed beginnings in Kent's practice, through the triumphant reign of Capability Brown, into the era of the picturesque reaction at the turn of the nineteenth century (Allen, 1937; Hussey, 1927; Manwaring, 1925).

The eighteenth century provided a perfect stage for these scholars, as it did for some of the most influential literary historians of the 1940s, 1950s and 1960s. Arguing that a crucial aesthetic and intellectual shift occurred in the period – a shift usually assigned as a consequence of the sensationalist epistemology of Locke and his followers – mid-twentieth-century scholars variously described the shift as one from classic to romantic, or from the (mimetic) mirror to the (expressive) lamp, or (using Ruskin's distinction) from Mountain Gloom to Mountain Glory. A common assumption was that an aesthetics of the infinite or the sublime arose in the course of the century. With its beginnings in Addison's 'Pleasures of the Imagination' papers in the *Spectator* (Nos 411–21, 1712), this aesthetic found its empiricist mid-point in Burke's *Philosophical Enquiry into the Origin of Our Ideas of the Sublime and Beautiful* (1757) and its transcendental end-point in Kant's *Critique of Judgement* (1790). Though such intellectual history sometimes committed the teleological fallacy of seeing all earlier aesthetic manifestations as steps on the way to a full romantic appreciation of nature and celebration of the autonomous imagination, its basic terms of discrimination held up well.

Thus, in Ronald Paulson's *Emblem and Expression* (1975) and John Dixon Hunt's *The Figure in the Landscape* (1976), for example, one finds a common argument that distinguishes earlier from later kinds of eighteenth-century landscape art and gardening according to whether the object viewed has an 'emblematic' or an 'expressive' character. These terms, used by Thomas Whately in his *Observations on Modern Gardening* (1770), refer respectively to an art that can be 'read' through reference to a body of shared iconographical knowledge and to an art whose meanings are no longer public but arise from a private encounter between the viewer and the work or scene. The difference is exemplified in the contrast between the Elysian Fields at Stowe (dating from the 1730s) and a typical Capability Brown landscape. In the Elysian Fields, the Temple of Ancient Virtue and the Temple of British Worthies, together with their statues, busts and accompanying inscriptions, participate in a legible programme that constitutes a Country Whig criticism of Walpolean corruption. In a typical Brownian park of the 1760s or 1770s, by contrast, the appeal of the scene is less intellectual, less – if at all – dependent on classical allusion. Brown eliminated from most of his landscapes the temples, statues and inscriptions found in gardens such as Stowe and Stourhead and instead created, with an art that concealed art, a landscape of smoothly undulating lawns and serpentine lakes or streams that invited an affective response from a largely private sensibility.

Influential as it has remained, however, history-of-ideas scholarship has not gone unchallenged. In his revisionist *Garden and Grove* (1986), Hunt has taken issue with the 'Whig' histories of the English garden, which often repeat the teleological arguments of Horace Walpole's *History of the Modern Taste in Gardening* (1780). Hunt questions the 'English' origin of the English garden. Though the latter would be imitated throughout Europe as the *jardin anglais*, or the *englische Garten*, or the *giardino inglese*, it is wrong to see it as springing fully formed from the writings of Shaftesbury, Addison and Pope, and false to argue, as Walpole argued, that Milton's description of Paradise in Book IV of his epic prepared the way for landscapes like those at Stourhead and Hagley. The English garden was not called into being by English writers. Rather Kent, along with such other Palladian gardeners as Burlington and Pope, translated older Italianate modes of gardening – involving a division into garden and grove and the use of terraces, arches and grottoes – into an English idiom.

More radical challenges to traditional literary history have also appeared. Indeed, like other humanistic topics, literature and landscape has become a focus in recent decades for 'extrinsic' modes of interpretation, including those of a biological or psychological or political sort. Appleton (1975) has applied prospect-refuge and habitat theories to landscapes, analysing the formal feature of the framing *coulisse* in terms of our need (which we share with animals) to see without being seen, and accounting for our pleasure in landscapes by postulating our subliminal recognition of the scene's availability for sexual, oral, nurturing and eliminative purposes. Paulson (1982, pp. 168–72) has employed Freud's analysis of the dream work in his interpretation of Constable's landscapes, viewing them as representations and symbolic displacements of desire that are subject in subsequent revisions, or through spoken or written commentary, to the artist's 'secondary elaboration'. And Fabricant (1979) has brought a feminist perspective to bear on the topic by discovering in the figurative language of eighteenth-century writings on landscape a masculine will-to-power that parallels other modes of social and sexual domination in the period.

The most vigorous challenge to older modes of literary history has come from critics who have insisted on the ideological dimensions of landscapes in literature, art and fact (Barrell, 1972, 1980; Bermingham, 1986; Fabricant, 1982, 1985; Turner, 1979). These critics acknowledge the influence of Raymond Williams's *The Country and the City* (1973), a key study that opposed the emphasis on stylistic conventions by 'internal' literary historians and, instead, evaluated literary representations of the country according to a criterion of realism in which aesthetic achievement was tied to the achievement of a degree of progressive political consciousness. Given the extent to which writers wrote within pastoral conventions and alluded to myths of paradise and the golden age, it is not surprising that Williams should have found many of them guilty of nostalgia and of mystifying historical reality in the interests of established structures of power.

Others besides Williams, however, have influenced the work of those analysing the politics of landscape. When Barrell (1980) evaluates the depiction of the rural poor in the paintings of Gainsborough, Morland and Constable, his perspective owes much to the revisionist historiography of E. P. Thompson, which looks at the eighteenth-century shift from a 'moral' to a market economy with a viewpoint that might have been adopted by the poor themselves. Likewise, when Ann Bermingham (1986) looks suspiciously at the 'natural' claims of the English landscape garden, her argument owes something to Williams (and something to Thompson also); but the main guides to her ideological critique are Roland Barthes and Louis Althusser. To the former she owes her semiological analyses of the ways in which bourgeois society naturalizes its cultural codes; to the latter a concept of ideology, which enables her to interpret landscapes as illusory accounts of reality that nevertheless allude, through a process of 'internal distanciation', to actual conditions (1986, pp. 3–4).

Unlike earlier scholars, who assumed formal unity, thematic resolution and closure to be criteria of aesthetic worth, recent critics have often seemed to prefer the discovery of fissures and discontinuities in landscape poems and paintings. For what this might mean in a particular instance, one may refer to Bermingham's fine reading of Gainsborough's conversation piece *Mr. and Mrs. Robert Andrews* (*c.* 1748–9). The divisions in that 'eccentric masterpiece' between field and park, culture and nature, industry and idleness, georgic and pastoral, and the ways in which these divisions are imperfectly contained within 'the myth of the independent producer', allow the interpreter to value the work, not for its ability to transcend ideology or reconcile contradictions in some version of a *concordia discors*, but rather for its failure to do these things, which is also its ability to present (if not to 'know') the fact that prosperity and luxury are consequences of an economic system dependent on the labour of those excluded from the scene (pp. 28–33).

Adopting a materialist rather than an idealist stance towards literary and art history, 'suspicious' or 'ideological' criticism has reconceived the social role of art and of interpretation. In *Swift's Landscape* (1982), for example, Fabricant distinguishes between Pope and Swift in terms of their relation to the tradition of the *beatus vir*. Swift's garden in Dublin, pointedly named Naboth's Vineyard, is viewed as an anti-Twickenham, unsuited to the role of an Earthly Paradise modelled on classical and biblical precedents and incapable of sustaining a political programme based on the Horatian virtues of 'use' and 'sense' and the neo-feudal virtues of hospitality and good housekeeping. Fabricant's study not only points to significant differences of attitude in Pope and Swift, however; it also takes a cool look at the ideology of the country house, both as this found expression in Pope's poetry (following its presence in the essays of Cowley and the poems of Jonson, Carew and others in the seventeenth century) and as it was perhaps too uncritically received and explained in the studies of such scholars as Røstvig (1962–71) and Mack (1969).

To the student of literature and landscape today the differences between older and newer kinds of literary history call out for recognition but also for mediation. In fact the best ideological criticism, while remaining alert to the ways in which landscape as a genre is particularly susceptible to the elision of facts of oppression and exploitation, makes extensive use of intellectual history. It places the latter's findings in new frames – as when Barrell (1972) endorses Manwaring's proposals concerning the stylistic influence of Claude's paintings on Thomson's poetry, but then goes on to argue that the syntax of the prospect view in both paintings and poetry was particularly suited to a historical period in which improving landowners were seeking to tame and control nature.

What is clear is that literary landscapes are increasingly being appraised for their ideological as well as their aesthetic properties. The rise and progress of landscape in the eighteenth century, seem, in fact, to be intimately related in both positive and negative ways to political and economic developments. Two historical moments may be identified, corresponding to two 'revolutions': the financial revolution of the 1690s, which introduced the national debt, moneyed corporations and stock-jobbing into English history; and the agricultural revolution of the mid- and late eighteenth century, which effected a shift from a system of neo-feudal paternalism to one of employer-employee relations based on the cash nexus. At both moments writers used landscapes for political purposes, favouring or criticizing the 'revolutions' in question by extolling or reprobating their effects in the rural scene.

In the context of the financial revolution, Addison's 'Pleasures of the Imagination' papers, for example, traditionally viewed as an important stage in the rise of the 'English' landscape garden, are more appropriately seen as a Whig promotion of commercial expansionism – 'Why may not a whole Estate be thrown into a kind of Garden by frequent Plantations, that may turn as much to the Profit, as the Pleasure of the Owner?' (*Spectator*, No. 414, 1712). With this celebrated question Addison brought to the 'garden' an attitude that differed from that of seventeenth-century writers, who had tended to view the garden as a site of retirement in which to conduct spiritual or contemplative exercises or as a place in which to pursue the pleasures of country life, as these had been described in the works of Horace and the Roman poets (Røstvig, 1962–71). Addison's attitude was of a more politically active kind: he sought to contest Tory attempts to base an ideology of social virtue in a landed and pre-commercial past (Duckworth, 1989). Thus, in the *Spectator* papers (Nos. 106–31), Addison gently satirizes the loveable but anachronistic Tory squire, Sir Roger de Coverley, while in *Spectator*, No. 549, 1712, he approves of the city merchant Sir Andrew Freeport's decision to retire to the country, not for spiritual or contemplative purposes, but in order to conduct a vigorous programme of agrarian improvement ('plowing . . . fencing . . . planting Woods and draining Marshes'). By such means Sir Andrew intends to put his poor neighbours to work.

Following Addison, other writers favoring a Whig programme of improvement and promoting an ideology of 'industry' used landscapes for political purposes. Defoe, for example, in his *Tour through the Whole Island of Great Britain* (3 vols, 1724–6), is an enthusiast for rich, populous and fertile landscapes (Duckworth, 1983). Opposed to waste moors and 'horrid' mountains, Defoe is even more opposed to potentially productive landscapes that lie fallow for want of industry and investment. To Defoe the Highlands of Scotland are a 'frightful country', but their forests, even in the absence of water carriage, could, if properly exploited, provide vast and profitable 'quantities of pitch, tar, rosin, turpentine' (1974, vol. 2, p. 416). From Defoe's *Tour* it is a short step to Thomson's Spenserian imitation, *The Castle of Indolence* (1748), in which the Knight of Industry – like Sir Andrew Freeport – sees retirement as an occasion for active work and, as a result, 'New scenes arise, new landskips strike the eye,/And all the enlivened country beautify' (II, xxvii). And the ideology of this poem is continuous with that found in Young's *A Six Weeks Tour through the Southern Counties of England and Wales* (1768), which praises the Norfolk countryside between Holkham and Houghton (both celebrated Whig estates); once 'boundless wilds' and 'uncultivated wastes', the now improved country is 'all cut into inclosures, cultivated in a most husband-like manner, richly manured, well peopled, and yielding an hundred times the produce that it did in its former state' (p. 19).

Because they combine the *utile* and the *dulce*, the Whig landscapes of Addison, Defoe and Thomson were to an extent proof against Tory (or Country Whig) criticism in the early decades of the century (Duckworth, 1989). True, in Book 3 of *Gulliver's Travels* (1726), Swift reveals his suspicions of the effects of agrarian experiments on the community, when Gulliver, travelling to Lord Munodi's house, finds poorly cultivated soil, ill-contrived houses and miserable people in spite of the widespread appearance of 'industry' in the fields (chap. 4). Pope also could envisage alternative 'Tory' settings that looked back towards the values of a neo-feudal community. He does this in his letters when he fondly describes old 'irregular' houses like Sherborne and Stanton Harcourt; and in the *Epistle to Bathurst* (1732) he reveals his detestation of the moneyed men as he describes the loss of hospitality and good housekeeping in the 'good old hall' under Cotta's tenure (ll. 179–98). But Pope could favour progress also, when progress was sanctioned by traditional moral criteria. In the *Epistle to Burlington* (1731) – a poem, after all, addressed to a Whig magnate – he lauds the classical virtues of 'use' and 'sense' and, in the peroration (ll. 191–204), shows himself an advocate of improvement on an imperial scale, even as he seeks the sanctions of Vitruvius and Palladio for the schemes he urges on Lord Burlington.

The famous description of Timon's Villa in the same poem (ll. 99–168), said to be modelled, variously, on such grand Whig houses as Houghton, Blenheim and Chatsworth, is a scathing indictment of the corruption of Walpole's Court Whig regime. Pope assumes that taste in the furnishing of a house and in the design of a garden is a sign of moral and political virtue; thus the absence of taste among the moneyed men, together with their vanity and ostentation, marks them as unfit to govern the country. Pope's Platonic alignment of taste and morality was not new (it had been argued earlier in the third earl of Shaftesbury's *Characteristics*, 1711); but it had a powerful effect on many later writers, who took care not to convict their heroes of a lack of virtue by leaving them open to the charge of false taste in the disposition of their house and grounds. Samuel Richardson, for example, surely remembered Timon's Villa in *Sir Charles Grandison* (1753–4), in which he is careful to demonstrate his exemplary hero's virtue by revealing the excellence of his taste in landscaping at Grandison Hall. And Smollett, closer to Pope ideologically, chose to illustrate the subversion of traditional values in *Humphry Clinker*

(1771) by describing the vain and extravagant improvements that Mrs Baynard makes to her husband's estate after their marriage.

Mrs Baynard is, not coincidentally, the daughter of a 'citizen', a fact that places Smollett among a number of eighteenth-century writers who satirically oppose the aspirations of the *nouveau riche* by exposing their false taste in landscapes and gardens. Beginning perhaps with Pope's satire on topiary gardens in *Guardian*, No. 173 (1713), this anti-bourgeois literature continues in a conservative paper like *Common Sense* (1739–43), in a periodical like *The World* (1753–6), in poems like Robert Lloyd's 'The Cit's Country Box' (1756), in plays like Garrick and Colman's *The Clandestine Marriage* (1766), and in novels like Richard Graves's *Columella* (1779). Garden settings are used in these works to satirize citizens – the Squire Mushrooms and Mr Nonsuches – who set up 'Little Marybons' in the country and ape, in ridiculously small compass, the landscape fashions of their betters.

Distinct from frivolous 'anti-cit' satire of this kind are the implied or direct criticisms of improved landscapes that appear from the mid-century onwards. In a broad sense the dramatic shift in landscape preference that separates the early from the late eighteenth century may be seen – like Romanticism itself in many of its phases – as a protest against Enlightenment progressivism, utilitarian thinking and the agrarian revolution. The flight from the garden to the mountains has been well described by intellectual historians (Hunt, 1976; Hussey, 1927; Manwaring, 1925). Among other things, it involved a new preference for sublime mountainous scenery – in the Alps or, closer to home, in Wales, the Lake District or Scotland – over beautiful landscapes or improved agricultural scenes; for Dutch landscape painting over the landscapes of Claude and Poussin; and for native British monuments and localities over the antiquities and campagna of Rome. The change in taste is variously manifested in the work of the 'Graveyard' poets, the letters and poems of Gray, the poetry of Collins, and Macpherson's *Fragments of Ancient Poetry Collected in the Highlands of Scotland* (1760). In the *Tours* of Gilpin to Wales, the Lake District and the Highlands of Scotland, the new aesthetic was defined both verbally and visually. In Knight's poem *The Landscape* (1794) and Price's *Essay on the Picturesque* (1794), the repudiation of Brown's landscapes, now considered tame and formulaic, was accompanied by an advocacy of picturesque scenes, valued not (as in Defoe and Thomson) for their evidence of the hand of man but rather for their unimproved or even ruinous and neglected condition.

As political protest, the works in which the new sensibility to landscape appears are often problematic. Partly this is because of the writers' retreat from a political role. Unlike Pope and Thomson, who act as public poets urging programmes of improvement conducive to the nation's benefit, poets like Gray and Collins seek out what is remote in nature, discovering there occasions for the expression of private melancholy, solitary reflection or extra-social passion. No longer the expression of civilized values, poetic landscapes become – in Gray's *The Bard* (1757) or Collins's posthumously published *Ode on the Popular Superstitions of the Highlands of Scotland* (written 1749–50) – sublime alternatives to society or consolatory substitutes for what society can no longer provide. Thus, for some readers, their political worth is diminished. Gray's *Elegy Written in a Country Churchyard* (1751) may be the most celebrated landscape poem in English literary history, and it has, as Empson noted in *Some Versions of Pastoral* (1935), a message of latent political protest; but this is compromised through a naturalization of rural obscurity and a thoroughly conventional universalization of death.

Of more political force are those writings that react critically to the effects of the agricultural revolution. Viewed by Whig historians as the successful transformation of a reactionary and communal rural society, the agricultural revolution also elicited protests over the human and social costs entailed in the move from a paternalist or 'moral' economy to a free market one. Among these protests were those directed against the landscape garden. For while Walpole, in his *History of the Modern Taste in Gardening*, was praising the natural style of Capability Brown's landscapes as an emblem of English freedom in contrast to the despotism of the formal gardens of France, others were seeing the Brownian landscape more critically. In Goldsmith's *The Deserted Village* (1770) the cause of the depopulation is the extensive landscape improvements of 'the man of wealth and pride', who

> Takes up a space that many poor supplied;
> Space for his lake, his park's extended bounds,
> Space for his horses, equipage and hounds.
>
> (ll. 275–8)

Modern research has shown that dozens of old villages were in fact removed to make way for Georgian pleasure grounds (Sambrook, 1967), and it is not always a strong argument that, in some instances, they were replaced by 'model' communities. Moreover, even if, as critics claimed, Goldsmith's charges of depopulation were excessive, and his criticism of luxury disputable on the eve of the publication of Adam Smith's *The Wealth of Nations* (1776), his opposition to what he saw as the destructive effects of economic individualism in the country was sincere and long-standing. In *The Traveller* (1764) he connects landscape gardening with the depopulation of the countryside (ll. 393–412) and deplores the changes he sees:

> As nature's ties decay,
> As duty, love and honour fail to sway,
> Fictitious bonds, the bonds of wealth and law,
> Still gather strength and force unwilling awe.
>
> (ll. 349–52)

And in the early chapters of *The Vicar of Wakefield* (1766) he evokes a vision of a pre-capitalistic world observing immemorial customs and holidays and as yet unaffected by enclosures, new habits of work-discipline, or an improved agriculture. Doubtless, Goldsmith's Tory yearnings for an older 'moral' economy are open to suspicion, and his tendency to project a sense of personal desolation – stemming from his marginal role as a poet – into the external scene brings him close to what Ruskin termed the 'pathetic fallacy' and Williams 'negative identification' (1973, p. 78). On the other hand, the strain of Tory radical protest in his works may be read as a commentary on the aggressive and competitive character of a free market economy.

That landscape improvements – a concern obviously subordinate to agricultural improvements in estate economy – should become the means of more general social criticism need occasion no surprise. For not only were landscape improvements associated with the great Whig landowners (e.g. at Holkham and Chatsworth), but they were readily assimilable by conservative writers to a traditional literary distrust of improvements (Malins, 1966, chap. 5). Goldsmith was not alone in his protest. Long before Cobbett took his rural rides in the 1820s, a poet like Cowper (in Book 3 of *The Task*, 1786) could find social and moral reasons for a disapproval of the new landscapes; and the 'modern system of gardening', as it came to be called following the lead of Walpole and Whateley, was also subject to the criticism of Wordsworth and Scott. In a long letter (17 October 1805) to Sir George Beaumont, who was then engaged in improving his estate at Coleorton, Wordsworth deplored Capability Brown's improvements of the 1760s at Alnwick, and urged his correspondent to keep himself as much out of sight as possible in the 'park and pleasure ground', reserving his improvements for agriculture and his tenants' welfare. And in an informed essay on landscape gardening in the *Quarterly Review* (vol. 37, no. 74) in 1828, Scott's animus against the 'spade and mattock' school of gardening doubtless stemmed from his sense of the destructive effects of improvements on historical landscapes. In this essay, Scott in effect inverted the emphases of Walpole's history, while also defending his own picturesque practice at Abbotsford.

In appraising the literary reactions to improvements in the landscape, one needs to consider the politics of the picturesque. As a cult, the picturesque of Gilpin, Knight and Price soon invited criticism, parody and satire – in Book 12 of Wordsworth's *Prelude*, for example, in Combe's *Tour of Dr Syntax in the Search of the Picturesque* (1812) – coarsely illustrated by Rowlandson – and in Peacock's *Headlong Hall* (1816). For all its promotion of real nature over idealized academic landscapes, the picturesque had produced its own clichés and formulas. But more than its openness to ridicule, the picturesque's moral and political ambiguity has proved troublesome to scholars from Ruskin onwards (Barrell, 1972, pp. 78–84; Bermingham, 1986, pp. 63–83; Price,

1965). The paradox of the picturesque is that landscapes which are pleasing and productive in an agricultural sense are 'barren' in a picturesque sense, and vice versa. Preferring what was wild, rude and ruinous in the external scene to the improved landscapes of Brown or the farmers, picturesque poets and painters depicted landscapes featuring cottages by the edge of the wood, old mills, decaying hovels, and they populated these landscapes with beggars, gypsies and the poor. In all this they were looking back nostalgically to an older 'moral' world which existed (or so they thought) before the period of enclosures and agrarian reform. But they were also looking down on rural life from the viewpoint of agrarian paternalism – Uvedale Price, chief theorist of the picturesque, was himself a landowner who contributed to Young's *Annals of Agriculture* (Bermingham, 1986, p. 66). Moreover, by sentimentalizing rural poverty, they were deflecting attention from its historical cause; the effect of time, accident and fate, and not the agency of political change, was held to account for picturesque landscapes. For these reasons, Bermingham has argued that the politics of the picturesque, like the contemporary politics of the poor law, muted rather than exposed the problems attendant on the agricultural revolution (p. 81).

Not all writers were blind to the social and moral ambiguity of the picturesque. Jane Austen and Scott, for example, were alert to its deficiencies, as is evident, respectively, in the conversation between Edward Ferrars and Marianne Dashwood in chapter 18 of *Sense and Sensibility* (1811), and in the description of the picturesque but economically depressed hamlet of Tully Veolan in chapter 8 of *Waverley* (1814). Jane Austen and Scott, in fact, serve as an appropriate conclusion to the eighteenth-century tradition of literature and landscape; both were deeply versed in eighteenth-century literature, and, both, at a time when the French revolution had brought a new urgency to political and constitutional questions, used landscapes and settings to mediate their social and political vision.

In her novels Austen makes sparing but effective use of landscapes. John Dashwood in *Sense and Sensibility*, who encloses Norland common, engrosses a neighbouring farm and, to his sister Elinor's dismay, cuts down old walnut trees to make way for his wife's greenhouse, is exposed as a viciously materialistic improver, who has subordinated his obligations as a landowner to greed and a love of display. Henry Crawford in *Mansfield Park* (1814) is described as a 'capital improver'; but his plans to improve Edmund Bertram's parsonage at Thornton Lacey, by removing the farmyard, screening the blacksmith's shop, and reorienting the house are a threat to a worthy rural community. Jane Austen was no enemy to tasteful landscape improvements, as she shows in *Pride and Prejudice* (1813) through the heroine's delighted response to Darcy's grounds at Pemberley. Elizabeth Bennet 'had never seen a place for which nature had done more, or where natural beauty had been so little counteracted by an awkward taste' (ed. 1932, p. 245). Darcy has clearly attended to Pope's advice in the *Epistle to Burlington* to follow nature and 'consult the genius of the place in all'. But in *Emma* (1816), Austen chooses to honour a different kind of hero – significantly named Mr Knightley – who, like Wordsworth's ideal landowner, reserves his improvements for his farm and his tenants. During the absurd alfresco strawberry party organized by the *arriviste* Mrs Elton, Emma Woodhouse admires the house and grounds at Donwell Abbey. She notes the house's low and sheltered situation and its 'rambling and irregular' appearance, and she observes the 'ample gardens stretching down to meadows washed by a stream, of which the Abbey, with all the old neglect of prospect, had scarcely a sight' (ed. 1933, p. 358). All the signifiers here point to Austen's endorsement of the values of a traditional community, and what is Tory and traditional in her outlook is confirmed when Emma looks down from the Abbey grounds to the Abbey-Mill farm, 'favourably placed and sheltered' (p. 360). The home of Mr Knightley's tenant farmer, the Abbey-Mill farm provides a 'sweet view ... English verdure, English culture, English comfort' (p. 360).

The chauvinism of the description is patent, and to many readers, Jane Austen's promotion of the virtues of a paternalist economy is problematic. She was, after all, the sister of a great gentry landlord, who owned prosperous estates in Hampshire and Kent, and no more than Scott could she deplore the rural prosperity that resulted from the agrarian revolution. *Emma* indeed testifies to this prosperity in the descriptions of the upwardly mobile Martin and Cole families. Observing a prosperous and changing rural world, however, Austen invoked traditional and communal obligations as a curb on selfishness and materialism. But whether she succeeded in this is a matter of debate. Donwell Abbey as a metonym is not to every reader's taste, and Mr Knightley's gentry version of *noblesse oblige* may be read as, at best, a limited answer to the problem at the heart of the book: the predicament of the single and portionless woman.

On a much larger and more ambitious scale, Scott also used landscapes and settings in his novels to mediate an ambivalence respecting the social and political consequences of progress. A pupil of the Scottish 'philosophical' historians, who argued that history had moved through the stages of hunting, pasturage, agriculture and commerce, Scott realized that the shift from a paternalist to a market economy (or in his terms from 'arms' to 'law') was diachronic and irreversible; but like Adam Ferguson and Adam Smith he seems to have believed that the oppositions between past and present – between a system based on land and a system based on credit – could be managed. In the Scottish novels he covers a period from the late seventeenth to the late eighteenth century – a period taking in the financial, agricultural and French revolutions. And through what may be termed a rhetoric of landscape he often appears as a progressive thinker (Duckworth, 1989). In *The Heart of Midlothian* (1818), for example, Jeanie Deans, on her barefoot journey to London to save her sister from execution, walks through landscapes that unfold historically as well as geographically. When the Duke of Argyle displays to her the landscape of the Thames near Richmond, Scott displays to the reader the landscape that was dear to Defoe and Thomson, and all the notations in his description – flocks of sheep, herds of cattle, rich pastures, prosperous villas – signify a celebration of civilization and progress. Thus it is appropriate that Jeanie should be transferred to the improving duke's experimental farm in the west of Scotland and that, together with her father and husband, she should survive the dangers to her happiness there that come from the Highlands, Scott's metonym for a primitive stage of culture.

Other novels also suggest that Scott believed the opposition between traditional ideals and a commercial civilization could be reconciled. In *Rob Roy* (1818), for example, the primitive past is embodied in the figure of Rob Roy himself, the Highland outlaw, while the commercial present and future are personified in the calculating Glasgow merchant Bailie Jarvie. Scott satirizes the utterly utilitarian outlook of the latter (Jarvie proposes draining Loch Lomond to increase the availability of arable acreage), but he sees him and not Rob Roy as the figure of the future. Like Addison before him, however, Scott works in an assimilationist way. Frank Osbaldistone, the hero, marries the Roman Catholic Diana Vernon and then improves Osbaldistone Hall, the ancestral estate, turning a home of drunken foxhunters into a place of culture and progress. Like Sir Halbert Glendinning in *The Abbot* (1820), who praises the agrarian improvements in the Low Countries while deploring the barren landscapes of his native Scotland, Frank characterizes Scott's progressive intentions.

In other novels, however, Scott hardly welcomes the supersession of arms by law or of virtue by commerce. Among the characters he views most negatively are Godfrey Bertram in *Guy Mannering* (1815), Sir William Ashton in the *The Bride of Lammermoor* (1819), and King Louis XI in *Quentin Durward* (1823); all are associated with financial speculation, agrarian or landscape improvements, and the neglect or destruction of traditional customs. Thus while Scott seems genuinely to have sought in the Scottish novels for a political compromise that would marry the values of the past with the facts of the present, his fiction often fails to enact such a resolution. Honour and credit, virtue and commerce remain apart. Yet even when the landscape seems to prevent rather than promote progressive optimism – as in the fatal feudal gloom that invests Wolf's Crag, the fortress home of the doomed Edgar Ravenswood in *The Bride of Lammermoor* – it remains a significant indication of Scott's political dilemma. At a time when the constitutional proposals of the radical Whigs were threatening his sense of social stability, his view of what was permissible in the way of 'improvement' narrowed. If Scott's novels are sometimes disappointing to formal critics in search of resolution, their landscapes provide fertile fields for those interested in 'ideological' analysis.

FURTHER READING

Barrell, John (1972) *The Idea of Landscape and the Sense of Place: 1730–1840*, Cambridge University Press, Cambridge

——(1980) *The Dark Side of the Landscape: The Rural Poor in English Painting 1730–1840*, Cambridge University Press, Cambridge

Bermingham, Ann (1986) *Landscape and Ideology: The English Rustic Tradition, 1740–1860*, University of California Press, Berkeley and Los Angeles

Duckworth, Alistair M. (1989) 'Gardens, Houses and the Rhetoric of Description in the English Novel'. In Gervase Jackson-Stops, Elisabeth B. MacDougall, Gordon J. Schochet and Lena Cowen Orlin (eds), *The Fashioning and Functioning of The British Country House*, (vol. 25 of *Studies in the History of Art*), National Gallery of Art, Washington

Fabricant, Carole (1985) 'The Aesthetics and Politics of Landscape in the Eighteenth Century'. In Ralph Cohen (ed.), *Studies in Eighteenth-Century British Art and Aesthetics*, University of California Press, Berkeley and Los Angeles, pp. 49–81

Hunt, John Dixon (1976) *The Figure in the Landscape: Poetry, Painting and Gardening during the Eighteenth Century*, Johns Hopkins University Press, Baltimore

——(1986) *Garden and Grove: The Italian Renaissance Garden in the English Imagination: 1600–1750*, Princeton University Press, Princeton

Hunt, John Dixon and Willis, Peter (eds) (1975) *The Genius of the Place: The English Landscape Garden, 1620–1820*, Harper & Row, London

Malins, Edward (1966) *English Landscaping and Literature, 1660–1840*, Oxford University Press, London

Price, Martin (1965) 'The Picturesque Moment'. In Frederick W. Hilles and Harold Bloom (eds), *From Sensibility to Romanticism*, Oxford University Press, London, pp. 259–92

Turner, James (1979) *The Politics of Landscape: Rural Scenery and Society in English Poetry, 1630–1660*, Harvard University Press, Cambridge

Williams, Raymond (1973) *The Country and the City*, Oxford University Press, New York

ADDITIONAL WORKS CITED

Allen, B. Sprague (1937) *Tides in English Taste, 1619–1800*, 2 vols, Harvard University Press, Cambridge

Appleton, Jay (1975) *The Experience of Landscape*, John Wiley & Sons, London

Austen, Jane (1932) *Pride and Prejudice*, Oxford University Press, London [first published 1813]

——(1933) *Emma*, Oxford University Press, London [first published 1816]

Defoe, Daniel (1974) *Tour through the Whole Island of Great Britain*, 3 vols, Dent, London [first published 1724–6]

Duckworth, Alistair M. (1983) ' "Whig" Landscapes in Defoe's *Tour*', *Philogical Quarterly*, 61, 453–65

Fabricant, Carole (1979) 'Binding and Dressing Nature's Loose Tresses: The Ideology of Augustan Landscape Design'. In R. Runte (ed.), *Studies in Eighteenth-Century Culture*, vol. 8, University of Wisconsin Press, Madison, pp. 100–35

——(1982) *Swift's Landscape*, Johns Hopkins University Press, Baltimore

Hussey, Christopher (1927) *The Picturesque*, G. P. Putnam's Sons, London

Mack, Maynard (1969) *The Garden and the City: Retirement and Politics in the Later Poetry of Pope, 1731–1743*, University of Toronto Press, Toronto

Manwaring, E. M. (1925) *Italian Landscape in Eighteenth Century England*, Oxford University Press, London

Paulson, Ronald (1975) *Emblem and Expression*, Thames & Hudson, London

——(1982) *Literary Landscape: Turner and Constable*, Yale University Press, New Haven

Røstvig, Maren-Sofie (1962–71) *The Happy Man: Studies in the Metamorphoses of a Classical Ideal*, 2 vols, 2nd edn, Norwegian Universities Press, Oslo

Sambrook, A. J. (1967) 'The English Lord and the Happy Husbandman', *Studies on Voltaire and the Eighteenth Century*, 57, 1357–75

76

THE SENTIMENTAL ETHIC

JOHN DWYER

'Tis a quiet journey of the heart in pursuit of NATURE, and those affections which rise out of her, which make us love each other – and the world, better than we do.

Laurence Sterne, *A Sentimental Journey* (1768)

The eighteenth-century sentimental movement has been dismissed as a vapid and insipid genre, significant only as the prelude to a more highly charged and piquant Romanticism. When compared with the passionate individualism of the romantics, the polite products of the sentimental school appear cloying or dull. At best, sentiment is emotion shackled; at worst, sentiment is a sickly sweet substitute for a flesh-and-blood reality. The pathetic addresses and gently pulsating arteries which characterize the pages of Laurence Sterne's *A Sentimental Journey* are meagre fare for those who have tasted the shrieking lovers and grief-filled chasms of William Blake. Sterne's plea for a more gentle and courteous international intercourse similarly pales beside Blake's exultation in a virile and glorious Albion.

It is all too easy to sit in judgement upon the sentimental movement; it is much more difficult to understand it. There are good reasons, however, to make the attempt. The sentimental authors were the legitimate heirs of Fielding and Richardson. As novelists, they imitated the former's skill at characterization while further developing the latter's ability to delineate the complex human emotions. In their capacity as literary critics, the members of the sentimental school deserve far more attention from scholars of late eighteenth- and early nineteenth-century culture than they usually receive. For they were among the most ardent defenders of the novel during a period when many literary observers associated the genre with the spread of artificial values and unrefined taste. In journals such as *Blackwood's*, *The Lounger* and the *English Review*, members of the sentimental school assiduously instructed their readers in the skills needed to appreciate a well-written novel and astutely distinguished between superior works of literature and the more insignificant products of 'little genius' whose plots ran away with their protagonists or whose tragic situations and kailyard excesses elicited a crude and unrealistic emotional response (*The Lounger*, 1785–7, No. 20). The purpose of this 'species of composition', asserted Henry Mackenzie, one of the most influential of the sentimental authors and critics, was the realistic exploration of human nature. He consistently singled out the novels of Richardson for presenting this nature 'in its native garb, without the ornaments in which fancy or refinement delights to dress it' (*Blackwood's Edinburgh Magazine*, vol. 9, No. 50, 1821, p. 203; see also *The Mirror*, 1779–80, No. 31).

It is useful to remind ourselves of the sentimental contribution to the rise of the novel if only to counter the commonplace tendency to reject the movement as a mawkish curiosity or literary aberration. At the same time, we should beware of excessively teleological approaches to the genesis of that genre. Such approaches retrace an increasingly tedious literary pilgrimage towards one of our two modern icons – an irrational and psychological 'self' or a realistic and scientific 'society' – a pilgrimage which tends to obscure much that is distinctive and interesting in the sentimental movement (see, for example, Watt, 1972). The sentimental genre was, first and foremost, a characteristic literary product of the European Enlightenment. As such it touched and was touched by such luminaries as Francis Hutcheson, Lord Shaftesbury, Adam Smith, Diderot and, of course, the great Rousseau himself. More than any other mode of discourse, it initiated the demise of the traditional public vocabulary with its stress upon military prowess, manly independence and the idealization of man as citizen (Pocock, 1975, pp. 361ff.). In place of the paradigm of aggressive political purpose, it substituted a world view in which private friendships, the domestic hearth and specifically feminine feeling not only had a respected place but became essential characteristics of the moral community. Never again would it be possible to define a man solely by his political or professional position; never again would it be possible to ignore the place of women in the ethical equation.

The apparently short-lived and constantly defensive sentimental movement thereby achieved something that classical ethics was failing to do and which Romanticism had no intention of doing – the emotional and intellectual foundation for recognizably modern social relationships. By the mid-eighteenth century, it was apparent to many that these relationships could no longer realistically be based upon patriarchal hegemony or traditional communal sanctions, but few were as yet prepared to entertain the concept of a social system founded upon the acquisitive individual ego – a veritable market-place of desires and values. The ethic of sensibility bridged the paradigmatic gap by advocating more flexible, humane and polite kinds of human interaction. While allowing the individual heart a greater share in the governance of behaviour, the garden of sentiment attempted to cultivate that balance between personal emotion and the social conscience which could reinforce group harmony and the stability of an increasingly complex and differentiated modern society.

That the language of commerce and interest, commonplace as it had become by the age of Walpole, was neither personally satisfying nor an acceptable foundation for a new ethics, is attested by the continual stream of attacks upon luxury, credit and speculation in virtually all the late eighteenth-century journals. At a deeper level, writers as diverse in their attitude towards modernity as Diderot and Rousseau pointed to the personal and ethical alienation felt in an increasingly specialized society made up of cunning and mercenary role-players. In a 'bloody awful' differentiated economy, argued the penetrating nephew of Rameau, the 'necessitous man' often wasted 'his life taking up positions and carrying them out' (Diderot, trans. 1966, p. 120). Artificiality, argued Rousseau, became a way of life in a world in which it 'became the interest of men to appear what they really were not' (trans. 1968, p. 202). Of course, virtually all enlightened and sentimental thinkers accepted the fact that commerce and specialization were necessary factors in national strength and development. Moreover, economic 'improvement' and the extension of trade brought in their train many of the same values that sentimental authors were wont to champion – tolerance, civility, humanity and an increasingly international community. The problem was that of constructing a viable ethic which could at once compensate for the loss of personal independence and integrity while it combated the indifference, selfishness and deceit endemic to a specialized commercial society. It was precisely for this end that the sentimental movement was born. As Sterne put it in discussing his novel *A Sentimental Journey*, the work which familiarized the term 'sentimental' in the English language, his aim was 'to teach us to love the world and our fellow-creatures better than we do' (in Curtis, 1935, p. 401).

The ethic of sentiment deliberately eschewed a mechanical approach to social ethics in favour of a more organic one. 'In the earlier periods of society', argued Henry Mackenzie, a simple code of morality was all that was needed. 'In a state of society so advanced as ours', he continued, 'every one will see the necessity of a nicer and more refined system of morality.' In modern life, he concluded, the 'social virtues' had been transformed into a 'numerous list of collateral duties, many of which it needs an acute discernment to trace' (*Lounger*, No. 2). If the economy had been literally transformed in the eighteenth century, however, ethics had lagged far behind, leaving men and women increasingly confused in a world wherein the moral personality and social progress appeared to be moving in opposite directions. The particularly pressing nature of the problem can be seen in the blurred distinction which sentimental authors made between ethics, considered as an abstract science, and practical morality as a guide and exhortation to behaviour in everyday life. Thus, while Mackenzie often affirmed the 'science' or 'system' of sentimental morality, his primary aim was the more immediate one of manipulating emotion in the cause of virtue. Practice invariably took precedence over theory.

It would be misleading, however, if we were to assume that the more abstract investigation of human nature and ethics played no part in the sentimental movement. Many of the genre's practitioners demonstrated an easy familiarity with philosophers such as Shaftesbury and Hume. Others, including Rousseau and Diderot, combined the roles of philosopher and sentimental author. Henry Mackenzie claimed to be profoundly influenced by his friend Adam Smith, whose *The Theory of Moral Sentiments* (1759; major revision 1790) represented the most scientific treatment of the relationship between sentiment and ethics during the eighteenth century. Overshadowed by its influential sister, *The Wealth of Nations* (1776), the text has only recently received the attention that it deserves and rewards. Moreover, the complex relationship between Smith's ethical philosophy and the sentimental movement has either been ignored or trivialized (see, for example, Thompson, 1931, pp. 92ff.). This is a pity, because a close examination of the *Theory of Moral Sentiments* highlights the fundamental errors which many literary commentators have made in assessing the sentimental genre. One of these is that the sentimental movement stressed the ethical power of empathy (Brissenden, 1974, pp. 38–9, 68). Another is that the sentimental school inevitably regarded the 'sway of emotion' as 'superior to what one could do when judging intellectually the wisdom of an action' (Wright, 1937, pp. 32ff.). It would be difficult to describe social interaction in terms less empathetic or more logical than Adam Smith's.

Smith's original insight was that morality is a socially constructed phenomenon, ultimately founded upon the permutations of human sensibility in the typical face-to-face encounter. *The Theory of Moral Sentiments* adopts the term 'sensibility' to describe the individual's natural tendency to respond to the feelings of others (Smith, ed. 1976, p. 34). Such a relationship also implied a spectatorial ability to discriminate carefully between emotional stimuli and an unwillingness to extend one's feelings too far. While Smith underlined the critical significance of 'sympathy' in moral formation, therefore, he typically condemned 'those whining moralists' who attempted to stretch men's sensibility to the misfortunes of others 'beyond the just standard of nature and propriety' (p. 139).

For Smith, sensibility was at its most effective in the everyday face-to-face exchange. In such small-scale groupings, the 'propensity to sympathize' was at its strongest and the 'free communication of sentiments and opinions' could conceivably result in the 'most delightful harmony' possible in human society (p. 337). But even here, Smith insisted that the sympathetic pleasure and the harmony which ensued had a firm basis in the polite civility and self-control of group members. In a similar vein, Smith also maintained that inter-personal harmony in the most intimate social groups – in private friendships or the nuclear family – invariably involved 'habitual accommodation' (pp. 220–1). The man of feeling's sensitivity to the joys and sorrows of his closest associates was not only perfectly consistent with the 'manhood of self-command', argued Smith, but was the 'very principle upon which that manhood is founded' (p. 151).

Smithean sympathy, therefore, was a far cry from empathy. Indeed, for the enlightened Scottish philosopher, empathy represented a primitive and irrational emotional capacity, one that had contributed mightily to those factions and fanaticisms which had stained history's pages red with human blood. The 'man of the most exquisite humanity', on the other hand, was a finely tuned and sharply discriminating ethical instrument. Smith's man of the 'most perfect virtue' never indulged in emotion for its own sake or relinquished his self-control in a crude outpouring of emotion. Even among intimates, he retained that combination of gentleness and self-command which characterizes true politeness. Indeed, the perfectly virtuous man preferred to refer his actions to an ideal and impartial spectator or 'stranger' rather than to an excessively indulgent friend, family or clan.

If we turn from the philosopher of the moral sentiments to the most characteristic sentimental novelists, we find some remarkable similarities. Henry Mackenzie and his colleagues in Edinburgh's *Mirror* Club, for example, described the ideal family circle as a delicate mix of 'something of the stranger with the acknowledgement of our dearest friend, somewhat of the form of courtesy with the substance of affection' (Mackenzie, ed. 1927, p. 224). Clearly, for Mackenzie, the relationship delineated was sympathetic rather than empathetic and involved the acquisition of that 'delicate complacency of mind' which simultaneously led the individual to consult the feelings of others and to control his own (*Mirror*, No. 33). Harry, the young hero of Henry Brooke's *The Fool of Quality* (1766), early acquires both a discerning attention to the emotions of others and a manly firmness; even so, his moral cultivation requires an informed 'stranger' who practises all the subtle arts of pedagogy (vol. 1, pp. 54–5). Rousseau's more complex *La Nouvelle Héloïse* (1761) consists primarily of intimate exchanges between the principal characters, the lovers Julie and St Preux and their friend Lord Bomston. Despite the occasional Rousseauesque emotional outburst, what the book really delineates is the containment, modification and ultimate transcendence of passion through the civilizing art of conversation. While Julie and St Preux learn self-control the hard way, that admirable and far from insensible Englishman, Lord Bomston, practises it as a philosophical principle.

Lord Bomston is a professed devotee of the Stoic philosophers. Similarly, young Harry, Earl of Moreland, 'bore all with the firmness and resignation of a stoic philosopher' (*The Fool of Quality*, vol. 1, p. 73). Billy Annesly, in Mackenzie's second novel, belatedly learns the significance of self-control when he is captured by stoic savages, an American Cherokee tribe which scorned both suffering and emotionalism (*The Man of the World*, 1773, vol. 2, p. 177). While such characterizations do not represent the fully realized ideal type in sentimental literature – the polite man or woman of feeling – the positive attention devoted to them should warn the careful reader against the facile assumption that the discourse of sensibility pre-empted a traditional emphasis upon reason and self-command. The development of Adam Smith's moral philosophy provides a particularly graphic illustration of this point, for, in the final edition of the *Theory*, Adam Smith moved even closer to the Stoics and went so far as to include a lengthy section on those favoured ancient philosophers (ed. 1976, pp. 267–300).

The language and literature of sensibility differed, and differed sharply, from that of the romantic tradition inasmuch as it warned against an undue obsession with the self or its emotions. Its purpose was to delineate and cultivate the operations of human sympathy so as to reinforce sociability and communal virtue – not to dethrone reason or self-control. The sentimental author's avowed purpose was to increase genuine civility and humanity as far as possible. To this end, literary purveyors of sentiment effectively utilized pathos in order to enlarge the socially sensitive consciousness. While their pathetic descriptions may seem insipid and unconvincing to scholars concerned with social realism and the individualism which characterizes modern culture, they were constructed with great care and attention to moral effect. Henry Mackenzie, for example, forced his readers to participate actively in a 'symphony of sympathy', making them play the role of impartial spectators in melancholy scenarios. But Mackenzie never sought to extract from his readers an extreme emotion that could be temporary or narcissistic; instead, he teased out that 'gentle tear' which was conducive to moral reformation and active virtue. His ethical message was predicated upon sociability. Thus, *The Man of Feeling* (1771) does not end with any hatred or withdrawal from a corrupt world: 'No: there is such an air of gentleness around that I can hate nothing: but, as to the world – I pity the men of it' (Mackenzie, ed. 1974, p. 133).

Sentimental heroes, such as Yorick, Harley, or Richard Annesly may seem lethargic or inactive beings to modern readers. In large part, this is because their literary function is as much didactic as it is mimetic. They function as impartial but feeling spectators through whose eyes the reader sees the world afresh. Their misfortunes are deliberately devised to heighten the sympathetic response of readers accustomed to being let off the emotional hook by such devices as poetic justice or what Mackenzie scorned as the 'sunshiny denouement' (*Blackwood's Edinburgh Magazine*, vol. 3, No. 17, p. 571). At the same time, sentimental authors wanted to suggest that their protagonists' inability to play an active part in life was equally the result of a corrupt society's incapacity for recognizing and rewarding their exceptional sentimental talents.

Harley, for example, is demonstrably neither the passive nor one-dimensional character that he is often caricatured as being. He can give stern moral lectures; he is tempted by prostitutes; he gets jealous; he falls in love; and he provides for the sick and homeless in his neighbourhood. While it remains the case that Harley is an ideal and, by definition, an unrealistic type, his creator certainly was not suggesting that anyone attempt to ape his character. Mackenzie merely wanted to stimulate that Harley whom he believed was in every man. Or, to cite Henry Brooke, such authors tried to wake sleeping virtue by drawing characters who were relatively 'lost to every care and sensation of SELF' (*The Fool of Quality*, vol. 1, p. xxiv).

The appropriate moral question was, how could an escape from the selfishness of an increasingly competitive and luxurious world be best achieved? Moreover, how could such an escape be effected without resulting in individual disgust and concomitant withdrawal? Sentimental authors advocated various mental techniques and educational practices for weaning the mind from what Brooke and Mackenzie termed the 'bustle of the world' and from the social life of 'great cities' whose inhabitants were 'so divided and dissipated by the multitudes of soliciting objects and acquaintance, that they are rendered incapable of a particular attachment' (*The Fool of Quality*, vol. 2, p. 170). Sterne's approach often resembled that of a benign Zen master inviting his pupils to annihilate self and to unite with the 'great SENSORIUM of the world! which vibrates, if a hair of our heads but falls upon the ground in the remotest desert of thy creation' (*A Sentimental Journey*, 1768, p. 278). He exhorted them to 'fasten' their minds upon a natural object, to 'connect' with 'some sweet myrtle' or 'melancholy cypress' (p. 116). By doing so, Sterne argued, men could distance themselves from 'spleen' and 'miserable feelings'. Mackenzie similarly advocated an 'attachment to inanimate objects'; and even a 'withered stump' humanized by generations of 'school companions' could become a symbol of affection and sentiment, a contrast to the artificiality and temporizing of the modern age (*Mirror*, No. 61). In addition, he was one of the first to emphasize the 'idea of Home' which, even exclusive of its relation to persons, represented a silent and consoling friend in the midst of a 'tumultuous' world. Animals provided even more appropriate objects for identification because of their uncanny resemblance to one's fellow human beings. Thus, the character Yorick rehearsed appropriate emotional responses towards a caged canary and a dead donkey.

Sentimental writers in general condoned a nurturing attitude towards animals, especially on the part of children who were in the process of cultivating their sensibility. Brooke's young hero first learns the value of 'particular attachment' and heartfelt benevolence from his pet cock, which he nobly rescues from unenlightened and insensitive village ruffians. Mackenzie, whose treatment of such issues was far more subtle, albeit less ironic and good humoured than either that of Sterne or Brooke, brought the family dog into the social equation and the living-room parlour in such essays as the one on the Benevolus family, wherein the pet is 'so humanized by the children' that he 'bears his faculties meek' (*Lounger*, No. 96). Still, he was careful to remind his readers that the ultimate aim of such sentimental description was not kindness towards animals but heightened fellow-feeling. Mackenzie castigated those 'Lady Love Puppies' and 'Mrs Sensitives' who lavished their affection on dogs and kittens while ignoring the plight of their tenants and servants (*Lounger*, No. 90).

The primary technique for arousing latent fellow-feeling, however, was original, complex and derived from a concept which had a long cultural history in Britain. That concept was melancholy – the so-called British 'disease' (Moore, 1953, pp. 179–235). The belief in a particularly British melancholic temperament had well-established roots. The Dutch physician Bernard Mandeville made it the subject of a medical treatise on nervous disorders in 1711; his Scottish counterpart, Dr George Cheyne, studied it in his *The English Malady* of 1733; and, in *La Nouvelle Héloïse*, Rousseau added his own inimitable touch by giving his stoical Englishman, Lord Bomston, an inclination towards melancholic introspection (*Eloisa*, London, 1776, letters 45, 65, 67). The literary significance was further reinforced in the pages of *The Spectator* (1711–14), where melancholy was particularly associated with death and mourning. Addison's nocturnal peregrinations among the tombs in Westminster Abbey (No. 26) and Steele's pathetic account of the death of his father (No. 181) accustomed the British reader to indulge this problematic but strangely sympathetic mood. Young's *Night Thoughts* (1742), highly regarded by Henry Mackenzie and other sentimental authors, also favoured 'Il Penseroso' over 'L'Allegro'. In particular, Laurence Sterne's *The Sermons of Mr. Yorick* (1760) defined and circumscribed melancholy reflection in such a way as to make it integral to the sentimental movement.

In one of the most influential of these sermons, entitled 'The House of Feasting and the House of Mourning Described', Sterne argued that the common clerical discourse on death was a 'nonsensical piece of saint errantry', suitable only 'for a crack'd-brain'd order of Carthusian monks' (ed. 1927, vol. 1, sermon 3). At the same time, he suggested that a certain kind of reflection upon affliction was a useful antidote to the 'hurry and bustle of the world'. The wise, he suggested, would be well advised occasionally to turn aside from the 'gay scene' and to enter the 'house of mourning'. Neither an abode of terror nor of lamentation, Sterne's 'house of mourning' was made so by the common disasters of everyday life. It was peopled by: aged parents lamenting the death of a foolish child; a virtuous family pinched with starvation; a widow mourning her only son. Such pathetic scenes, which Sterne had already begun to explore in the story of Le Fever in *Tristram Shandy* (1759–67) but curiously failed to develop in *A Sentimental Journey* proper, checked all 'levity and dissipation', called home all 'scattered thoughts', and made us more sympathetic towards our brethren. In these situations, a man was rendered 'pensive', 'soft' and 'susceptible'; he was 'smitten with sense and with a love of virtue'.

In the decades that followed, many sermons, addresses and ethical essays bore the imprint of Sterne's original insight. In particular, the *Sermons* (1777–94) of Hugh Blair, second only in eighteenth-century sales to *The Spectator*, elaborated upon the social significance of a particular perspective on death. Blair constantly advised his readers 'On the Benefits to be derived from the House of Mourning' (*Sermons*, 1817, vol. 2, sermon 13). He encouraged his young audience, especially, to accustom themselves to consider 'the distresses of everyday life: of the solitary cottage, the dying parent, and the weeping orphan' (vol. 1, sermon 11). He also urged that by 'voluntarily going into the house of mourning: by yielding to the sentiments which it excites, and mingling our tears with those of the afflicted, we shall acquire that humane sensibility which is one of the highest ornaments of the nature of man'. In a sermon appropriately titled 'On Death', Blair further advised his readers to indulge a taste for that 'funeral melancholy' which warmed the heart with the 'glow of humanity' (vol. 3, sermon 5).

Sterne's and Blair's sermons were nothing if not influential, and the sentimental as opposed to the Calvinist or gothic house of mourning became a staple of moralizing literature during the second half of the eighteenth century. In the final edition of *The Theory* of *Moral Sentiments* (1790), Smith recommended to his readers a 'melancholy and affectionate remembrance of our departed friends' (ed. 1976, p. 143). The Rev. John Logan, a popular London preacher, editor of the *English Review* and intimate of Henry Mackenzie, suggested that there was a 'string in the heart' tuned to the 'voice of sorrow'; impressions of grief gave rise to precisely that 'virtuous sensibility' from which all the sympathetic sentiments arose (*Sermons*, 1826, vol. 1, sermon 5). James Fordyce, whose *Sermons to Young Women* (1766) provided the basis of élite female moral education during the second half of the century, advised his sensitive young readers to attend the house of mourning because there was 'attendent on virtuous sadness' a sensation which was both pleasant and ethical (vol. 1, sermon 5). British preachers and moralists, including Vicesimus Knox, John Bennett, John Drysdale, Thomas Somerville and Samuel Charters, further developed the sentimental reappraisal of death and suffering. 'Afflictions', suggested Drysdale, an intimate of Adam Smith, 'tend to soften our hearts into tender sympathy and kind affection towards our fellow creatures' (*Sermons*, 1793, vol. 2, sermon 11). 'Scenes of sorrow humanize the heart', echoed another of Smith's favourite preachers, the melancholy Samuel Charters, and 'the heart is moulded into a pure serious benevolent frame' (*Sermons*, 1786, sermon 14).

The ethical and religious appropriation of what Blair alternately referred to as 'gentle melancholy' and 'the tender melancholy of sympathy' illuminates the clearly didactic character of the sentimental movement. That didacticism was also characteristic of the best sentimental novels and essays. Brooke explored the educational-cum-ethical properties of 'pleasure in grief' in such episodes as the death of Harry Clinton's wife Matty (*The Fool of Quality*, vol. 3, pp. 71ff.). But Harry Clinton's reason is totally usurped by the poignancy of his feelings and he becomes temporarily deranged. Moreover, his attitude towards his wife's corpse has a distinctly necrophilic quality which distracts from the ethical message. It was left to Henry Mackenzie to construct episodes which most carefully elicited the appropriate sentimental response to death. In an essay entitled 'Advantages to be drawn from scenes of sorrow' (*Mirror*, No. 72), Mackenzie followed Sterne and Blair in suggesting that it was sometimes appropriate to 'go to the house of mourning'. The real or imaginary contemplation of the death of a virtuous young lady, for example, gave rise to a 'sympathetic enjoyment' conducive to virtue. Such a melancholy indulgence, he suggested, was a far cry from the 'death's head' and the 'bones' of monkish religion. Characterized by the 'warmth of social affection and social sympathy', Mackenzie maintained, 'the heart will feel the weakness, and the duties of humanity'. 'Pity', not 'horror', was the appropriate response to the final resting of the coffin in the grave.

Mackenzie emphasized the power of fictitious scenes of 'private and domestic distress' to enlarge the heart. Moreover, he established the conditions under which such representations would be most effective. Deathbed scenes were not to be 'complicated beyond the simplicity of pity', but tightly focused upon the tragedies incumbent upon everyday life. All distracting detail was to be eliminated; so too were such classical notions as 'poetic justice', whenever they interfered with spectatorial sympathy. The protagonist needed to be sufficiently gentle, modest and virtuous not to arouse that 'rivalry' or 'envy' which could interfere with the flow of sorrow. The author's words, too often tools of deceit and confusion, were to be kept to a minimum, as were the reader's responses. The language of tears, liquid virtue, was the proper acknowledgement of the author's ability. Even the narrative plot was to be pared down so as not to 'destroy sentiment' (*Julia de Roubigné*, vol. 1, p. x; *Mirror*, No. 31). Mackenzie believed that he had achieved the perfect product in *The Man of Feeling*, which he proudly described as less a romance than 'recitals of little adventures, in which the dispositions of a man, sensible to judge, and still more warm to feel, had room to unfold themselves' (ed. 1974, p. 125).

Neither *The Man of Feeling* nor, for that matter, any of Mackenzie's other novels, ever placed feeling at variance with reason. Nor, as some have suggested, did they indulge in pathos for its own sake (see, for example, Barker, 1975, p. 54). Instead, they attempted to illuminate the development of genuine and sympathetic characters from everyday life, whose misfortunes and death could elicit spectatorial sympathy. Deliberately fragmentary, each chapter of *The Man of Feeling* illustrated an isolated and essentially private scene in which moral truth and feeling were exhibited. The fragments also acted as novellas of feeling which left little to the judgement of the naïve young reader. As Mackenzie suggested in the *Mirror* (No. 16), he sought to cultivate a very precise kind of gentle melancholy in his readers, one which would stimulate active virtue. Melancholy, 'too much indulged, or allowed to become habitual', he maintained, was dangerous; it made men unfit for the enjoyment of ordinary life. But the 'gentle and not unpleasing melancholy' that Mackenzie wanted to advocate filled the soul with a 'sweet benevolence' and prompted the individual to eschew selfishness, malevolence and envy. Moreover, it encouraged the imaginary spectator to 'alleviate and assuage' the sufferings of his fellows.

Active benevolence, not passive sympathy, was the desired result of that 'pensive tenderness' which characterized superior sentimental sermons, essays and novels of the eighteenth century. Sentimental writers and preachers constantly advocated a benevolence derived from feeling rather than a mere sense of honour, duty or largesse. When he is not measuring his arterial pulsations, Sterne's hero and alter ego, Yorick, digs deep in his pockets in order to perform private acts of charity in the dark and narrow streets of France. The protagonist of *The Fool of Quality* is carefully instructed by his foster-father on the giving of alms and, indeed, spends his days not merely giving to the poor and unfortunate but meticulously researching the case histories of those who might be too proud or shy to admit need. Mackenzie's much misunderstood hero, Harley – the archetypical man of feeling – has far less financial means than Henry, Earl of Moreland. Yet Harley does much more than induce and shed tears. He provides a virtuous old soldier and his family with a home; he acts *in loco parentis* for orphaned children; and he dies tending a neighbour in distress. While he practises a heartfelt benevolence, the land around him is bought up by 'merchants' and 'stewards' whose crude sensitivity is expressed only in the language of money.

To whom was the gospel of humanity and benevolence directed? Harley comes from an ancient but now reduced family; his lifestyle and income of £250 a year places him firmly among the lower gentry. The central characters in Mackenzie's other novels, *The Man of the World* and *Julia de Roubigné*, are members of the upper gentry and aristocracy. Brooke's young Earl of Moreland, who began life as a younger son in a noble household, eventually succeeds to a large inheritance. His mentor is also a younger son who, forced to go out and earn a living as a merchant, eventually returns to landed status. The protagonists of the most egalitarian writer in the sentimental tradition, the Rousseau of *La Nouvelle Héloïse*, are also from landed families or have been classically educated at the university. Similarly, Sterne's Yorick is a classically cultivated cleric who mingles comfortably with the British gentry and French aristocracy. Moreover, the sermons of both Sterne and Hugh Blair were addressed to those who had studied Greek and Latin from tutors; who shared the polite conversation of 'men of rank and letters'; whose children made the Grand Tour of Europe and whose social duty it was to provide for widows, orphans and impoverished tenants. It is the giving, not the making of money, which characterizes these men of sentiment.

Those literary scholars and social historians who view the sentimental tradition as a mirror reflection of the individualism of a rising bourgeoisie (see, for example, Watt, 1972, pp. 197–201; and Stone, 1977, pp. 258–68) have greatly misrepresented a complex movement and its aims. In particular they have obscured the serious cultural reservations that classically trained moralists felt when confronted with an increasingly individualistic commercial empire which made selfishness and the pursuit of luxury ruling principles of social behaviour. Sentimental authors believed that economic improvement needed to be balanced not only by an abstract humanity, but by a well-cultivated appreciation of the communal bond. When Mackenzie suggested that his man of feeling would be regarded as an enigma in a world increasingly characterized by utility, expediency and self-interest, he was condemning explicitly bourgeois characteristics of the modern age.

The sentimental authors typically looked to a reformed and enlightened landed society to assume their proper role on their estates and in the nation's senate. It is the ownership of land, with its attendant leisure for self-cultivation, reflection and benevolence, which qualifies an individual to perform his 'naturalistic function' (Todd, 1986, pp. 96–7). To be sure, most of the sentimental authors were decided 'moderns' who appreciated both the importance of commerce and the role of the merchant as one whose efforts 'knits into one family and weaves into one web the affinity and brotherhood of all mankind' (*The Fool of Quality*, vol. 1, p. 104). But neither the merchant nor the manufacturer were appropriate guardians of the morals and manners of the national community. Such a task could only be carried out by those whose leisure, education and means suited them for the benevolent role. Sentimental writers such as Sterne, Drysdale, Blair, Fordyce and Mackenzie consistently urged the prerogatives of social rank. Fordyce's influential sermons not only advised sentimental young ladies to dress appropriate to their station in life (*Sermons to Young Women*, vol. 1, sermon 2) but also young men to choose their friends from the same social order (*Addresses to Young Men*, 1782, vol. 2, p. 185). His programme of sentimental education, consisting as it did of close parental supervision and classically trained tutors, made it prohibitive to all but the most wealthy members of an emerging middle class. For his part, Henry Mackenzie reluctantly agreed that those who were destined for the 'drudgery of business' could benefit from classical and sentimental values, but he deplored the 'sudden accumulation of wealth in vulgar hands'. In one of his last essays, Mackenzie suggested that only those 'high-born names' who combined 'elegance of manners', 'dignity of deportment' and the 'pride of virtue' had sufficient delicacy to profit fully from a sentimental education (*Lounger*, No. 100). And finally, Brooke, who has been caricatured as a leading exponent of 'bourgeois ascendency' and 'capitalist ideology' (Skilton, 1985, p. 55), devoted much of his novel to defining the term 'gentleman' (*The Fool of Quality*, vol. 2, pp. 135ff., 196ff.). He combines a spartan courage with condescending manners towards inferiors; he is a quixotic knight-errant of sentiment; and he abhors the bustle of city life, preferring the company of friends in the more virtuous countryside. Far from being an egoistic individual, the gentleman Brooke enshrines breaks out of the 'dark and narrow womb of SELF' while his antithesis – the selfish man – is described in terms more appropriate to the capitalist ethic. 'SELF is wholly a MISER', wrote Brooke in a later volume, 'it contracts what it possesses, and at the same time attracts all that it does not possess' (vol. 4, p. 88).

None the less, it remains the case that sentimental literature and the sentimental ethic were rapidly assimilated by bourgeois elements in society. By the time that the sentimental movement had ceased to be an 'elevated' literary and cultural force, it had made deep inroads into a slowly emerging and insecure bourgeois consciousness. Such motifs as the sentiment of home, the dying child, the cult of discrete, natural objects and the hoarding of personal mementoes all became stock characteristics of Victorian life, literature and popular consumption. Of even greater significance, the sentimental emphasis on the intimate family circle, the cultivation of the adolescent and, especially, the emerging role for women as those Victorian domestic deities whose unenviable task it became to soften the harshness of an aggressive and insensitive world (Gorham, 1982), made a contribution of enormous significance to modern culture. That such a contribution was not initiated by some theoretically dynamic middle class is less important, perhaps, than the fact that it was the nineteenth-century bourgeoisie who most fully exploited its psychological, ethical and sexual potential (Foucault, 1986). For good or evil, we still live with the results.

FURTHER READING

Atkinson, Geoffrey (1965) *The Sentimental Revolution: French Writers of 1690–1740*, University of Washington, Seattle

Bell, Michael (1983) *The Sentiment of Reality: Truth of Feeling in The European Novel*, Allen & Unwin, London

Doody, Margaret Anne (1974) *A Natural Passion: A Study of the Novels of Samuel Richardson*, Clarendon Press, Oxford

Dwyer, John (1987) *Virtuous Discourse: Sensibility and Community in Late Eighteenth-Century Scotland*, John Donald, Edinburgh

Jones, Peter (1982) *Hume's Sentiments: Their Ciceronian and French Context*, Edinburgh University Press, Edinburgh

Lindgren, J. Ralph (1973) *The Social Philosophy of Adam Smith*, Martinus Nijhoff, The Hague

McGuirk, Carol (1985) *Robert Burns and the Sentimental Era*, University of Georgia Press, Athens

Mackenzie, Henry (1967) *Letters to Elizabeth Rose of Kilravock*, edited by Horst Drescher, Oliver & Boyd, London

Mayo, Robert D. (1962) *The English Novel in the Magazines, 1740–1815*, Northwestern University Press, Evanston

Preston, Thomas R. (1975) *Not in Timon's Manner: Feeling, Misanthropy, and Satire in Eighteenth-Century England*, Alabama University Press, Alabama

Richetti, John (1969) *Popular Fiction before Richardson: Narrative Patterns, 1700–39*, Oxford University Press, London

Trahard, Pierre (1931–3) *Les Maîtres de la sensibilité française au XVIIIe siècle*, Boivin, Paris

ADDITIONAL WORKS CITED

Barker, Gerard A. (1975) *Henry Mackenzie*, Twayne, Boston

Brissenden, R. F. (1974) *Virtue in Distress: Studies in the Novel of Sentiment from Richardson to Sade*, Barnes & Noble, London

Curtis, L. P. (ed.) (1935) *Letters of Laurence Sterne*, Clarendon Press, Oxford

Diderot, Denis (1966) *Rameau's Nephew and D'Alembert's Dream*, translated by L. W. Tancock, Penguin, Harmondsworth [first published 1823]

Foucault, Michel (1986) *The Use of Pleasure*, Random House, New York

Gorham, Deborah (1982) *The Victorian Girl and the Feminine Ideal*, Croom Helm, London

Mackenzie, Henry (1927) *Anecdotes and Egotisms, 1745–1831*, edited by H. W. Thompson, Oxford University Press, London

——(1974) *The Man of Feeling*, edited by Brian Vickers, Oxford University Press, London [first published 1771]

Moore, C. A. (1953) 'The English Malady'. In C. A. Moore (ed.), *Backgrounds of English Literature*, University of Minnesota Press, Minneapolis, pp. 179–238

Pocock, J. G. A. (1975) *The Machiavellian Moment: Florentine Political Thought and the Atlantic Republican Tradition*, Princeton, University Press, Princeton

Rousseau, Jean Jacques (1968) *The Social Contract and Discourses*, translated by G. D. H. Cole, Dent, London [first published 1762]

Skilton, David (1985) *Defoe to the Victorians: Two Centuries of the English Novel*, Penguin, Harmondsworth

Smith, Adam (1976) *The Theory of Moral Sentiments*, edited by D. D. Raphael and A. L. Macfie, Oxford University Press, Oxford [first published 1759]

Sterne, Laurence (1927) *The Sermons of Mr. Yorick*, Basil Blackwell, Oxford [first published 1760]

Stone, Lawrence (1977) *The Family, Sex and Marriage in England, 1500–1800*, Weidenfeld & Nicolson, London

Thompson, Harold William (1931) *A Scottish Man of Feeling*, Oxford University Press, London

Todd, Janet (1986) *Sensibility: An Introduction*, Methuen, London

Watt, Ian (1972) *The Rise of the Novel: Studies in Defoe, Richardson and Fielding*, Penguin, Harmondsworth

Wright, Walter Francis (1937) *Sensibility in English Prose Fiction, 1760–1814: A Reinterpretation*, Russell & Russell, New York

77

THE GOTHIC

ROBERT D. SPECTOR

Not even the most myopic scholar ever believed that the gothic novel came naked into the world in 1764, prancing forth fully grown from Horace Walpole's imagination and unattended by handmaidens from the muses of the sister arts. At the very least it was recognized that Walpole's *Castle of Otranto*, gothic fiction in its infancy, wore the swaddling clothes fabricated from the architectural interests expressed in his building at Strawberry Hill and the antiquarian experiences evident in his historical works on English authors and painters. The kinship to the sister arts was apparent in the resemblances of *Otranto* to Walpole's taste in landscape gardening, interests in history and penchant for collecting.

From a broader view the emergence of Walpole's gothic novel may be seen as part of a widespread general interest in a relaxation of artistic restraints and an increased desire for imaginative freedom. Starting early in the eighteenth century, an expanding interest in the emotional experiences associated with the sublime was apparent, whether in Joseph Addison's attempt to account for his response to the awesome character of mountains or Alexander Pope's fascination with the mysteries of a grotto. In poetry the 'Graveyard School' of Thomas Parnell, Robert Blair and ultimately Thomas Gray created an emotional atmosphere whose chill became the natural climate of the gothic novel. In Christopher Smart's 'A Song to David', a sublime sentiment such as 'earth heard in dread,/And, smitten to the heart' (stanza 40) in response to Jehovah's words mustered the same fear as a terrifying scene in a gothic novel. The lure of the Middle Ages, the traditional setting of the gothic, extended from the uninhibited curiosity of antiquarians to the sophisticated critical writing of Bishop Richard Hurd's *Letters on Chivalry and Romance* (1762), the seeking out of medieval ballads, and the revised reputation of Spenser's *Faerie Queene*.

Looking to the sister arts of painting, landscape gardening and architecture, one finds the same subversion of chaste classical standards as those that characterized the gothic challenges to critical authority and established values. To be sure, the prevailing taste for historical painting, formal portraiture and idealized landscape art endured throughout the eighteenth century. However, the untamed landscape art of such seventeenth-century continental painters as Claude Lorrain, Salvator Rosa and Gaspard Dughet, offering the same emotional appeal and celebration of the triumph of nature over the works of man that marked the attraction of gothic fiction, threatened the dominance of classical art and finally wrought a change in English aesthetic values. Similarly, a new kind of landscape gardening, giving nature a freer rein and unburdened by concerns for regularity, could not immediately usurp the kind of authoritative control of man over nature exemplified by the formal gardens of Versailles, but like the gothic novel it had a profound effect in altering taste and ultimately uprooted the traditional authority. With architecture the ties to the gothic novel appear even closer. The works of Christopher Wren, Nicholas Hawksmoor and Vanbrugh, and existing gothic structures in churches and public buildings, provided steady competition for classical Palladian architecture and had achieved a respectability that enhanced that of the gothic fiction for which it suggested credible settings and offered essential local colour.

Everywhere in the eighteenth-century aesthetic climate, there were atmospheric signals of a changing barometer in public taste that forecast a welcome relief from the more stifling conditions of the controlled emotional pressures of neo-classicism. Like the gothic, chinoiserie appealed to the desire for escape. Its use of geographic remoteness to stir the imagination distanced readers and spectators from the customary domestic values and standards. Literary and artistic conventions that applied to home-bred creations had no place in the domain of a fictionalized orient. Equally escapist was the attraction of the sentimental novel, whose open declaration of the right to free emotional expression was a principle shared by the gothic novelists. The audience response to Samuel Richardson and French authors like Prévost and Marivaux proved a demand that led a more traditional novelist like Tobias Smollett to employ scenes of terror in *Ferdinand Count Fathom* (1753) that, whatever their satiric intent, played strongly upon the emotional appeal evident in the sentimental and gothic novels. Not even the political scene was secure from the climatic changes attendant upon the arrival of the gothic novel. To be sure, the term *Gothic* initially bore a derogatory meaning when it was applied to the Whig party in the century, but it also conveyed the notion of political freedom, an unwillingness to remain subservient to established authority – a significance perfectly compatible with the subversive character inherent in gothic fiction. Finally, the changing climate is attested to in one of the most important philosophical texts on aesthetics in the period, Edmund Burke's examination of the attractiveness of the emotion of terror in *A Philosophical Enquiry into the Origins of the Sublime and Beautiful* (1759). In its serious attention to the topic and its attempt to describe an emotional appeal apparent in a public that had been conditioned to admire an art predicated on principles of order, regularity and control, Burke's essay, although not mentioning the gothic, demonstrated the attractiveness of the genre even before the first gothic novel had been published.

For all that, the official reception of Walpole's *Otranto* reflected the conventional literary values of the period. In the *Critical Review* (vol. 19, 1765, pp. 50–1) and even the more liberal *Monthly Review* (vol. 32, 1765, p. 394) notices savagely condemned the 'absurdities' of the novel, its 're-establishing the barbarous superstitions of Gothic devilism', the 'monstrosities of [its] story'. Walpole himself displayed small faith in his creation that in the next two centuries would appear in more than 150 editions. Not until popular approval propped his courage did he drop his mask of anonymity and shed the pretence that *Otranto* derived from a work 'found in the library of an ancient Catholic family in the North of England' and 'printed at Naples . . . in the year 1529' (Walpole, [1765] 1964, p. 3).

Whatever Walpole's own trepidations, whatever his need to bolster his achievement with appeals to such accepted principles as arguing that his purpose had been scholarly, or that his technique was the conventional imitation of nature, or that his structure was Aristotelian, or that his goal was poetic justice, he had fashioned a form of fiction that possessed all the elements of a new genre. *Otranto* contained all the essential material that the gothic required. Like any genre it would undergo enormous changes in works that sought to create greater probability, or aimed to convey more serious social or political messages, or attempted to achieve a poetic style with picturesque description, or tried to assimilate new scientific and philosophical developments. Still, *Otranto* offered the staples of the genre. Its castle with its secret passages and mysterious occurrences; its villainous usurper and suffering heroines; its dispossessed hero; its play upon sadistic and masochistic emotions; its unbridled sexuality and sensuality – all these became the stock-in-trade of the genre. They might be altered and disguised; they might be expanded upon; and they might be used for a variety of purposes; but in their appeal to terror and their exposure of the underside of human nature, they remained the fundamental material of the gothic novel. They might offend the guardians of society and literature, but they had an enduring popular appeal.

Yet, despite Walpole's obvious attraction for the reading public and a general aesthetic atmosphere seemingly favourable to the development of the genre, *Otranto* yielded no immediate progeny. Enterprising publishers – so eager to meet the demands for the trashiest sentimental novels that reviewers accused them of turning loose the pens of their printer's devils – virtually ignored the gothic. Perhaps the fact that novels themselves had not achieved the status of respectability made publishers wary of venturing forth into even more outlandish fictional territory. Whatever the reasons, the only evidence of interest in gothic fiction between Walpole's work and Clara Reeve's *The Champion of Virtue, a Gothic Tale* (1777), subsequently entitled *The Old English Baron* (1778), was in such minor efforts as represented by Anna Laetitia Barbauld's story 'Sir Bertrand, A Fragment', published together with her essay on gothic fiction (1773).

Although acknowledging that her novel was *Otranto*'s 'literary offspring' (Reeve, [1777] 1967, p. 3), the conservative Clara Reeve manoeuvred to distance herself in every way possible from what she regarded as the gothic absurdities of Walpole's excesses. Her title change was designed to identify her work with the historical novel, to place it in the line of Thomas Leland's *Longsword, Earl of Salisbury* (1762), an attempt to increase its respectability. By dedicating the work to Samuel Richardson's daughter, Reeve sought the cachet of the more fashionable novel of sentiment. Nevertheless, she still hesitated to place her name on *The Old English Baron*. Its first edition was anonymous, and even after the title change had shifted the focus away from the gothic, she had to be 'prevailed upon, though with extreme reluctance, to suffer [her] name to appear in the title page' (Reeve, [1777] 1967, p. 6).

The novel itself indicated the incremental manner of generic change. Playing down Walpole's appeal to the marvellous, Reeve used gothic terror sparingly to 'excite attention', legitimizing it only when it had divine origins. Wherever possible, she presented rational explanations for her mysterious occurrences. Her tone and purpose were in the best traditions of neo-classical didacticism. Her characterization, like that of the novel of sentiment, offered sharp distinctions between good and evil. With obvious deliberation, she framed her historical romance as a commentary on the decay of modern morals and manners, displaying a clear preference for a time when chivalry and nobility reigned and servants behaved deferentially to their social superiors. While the very strength of the gothic novel depends on its ability to convey suspense through to its final pages, Reeve chose to settle accounts between her usurper and legitimate heir early in her story and provided a lengthy legalistic dénouement as unsettling as her rational explanations of the bizarre events in her castle. Only her introduction of the vacant wing of the castle contributed to the specific gothic elements of fiction. Important as a document of generic change, significant in its influence on Ann Radcliffe's use of the techniques of the novel of sentiment and her resort to rational explanations, *The Old English Baron* as a novel is best described in Walpole's words: 'stripped of the marvellous . . . it is the most insipid nothing' (Summers, 1938, p. 187).

Not even Reeve's cautious gothic produced an outpouring of works in the genre. Contemporary reviewers abjured her tepid gothicism, and the rising tide of gothic fiction in the magazines went unnoticed by establishment critics. The next significant work relating to the genre, when it appeared in 1786, came disguised in oriental garb. William Beckford's Asian gothic *Vathek* received praise for the erudition of its notes, its imitation of the oriental tale and its didacticism, but critics ignored its affinities with the gothic and modern scholarship has generally disregarded or rejected the connection. Yet its tone of suspense and air of mystery, its demonic possession and its depiction of horror, as Devendra Varma (1957) has noted, bind it to the gothic tradition. Varma properly points out that its final scene both mirrors the German Schauer-Romantik and foreshadows the use of terror by Matthew Gregory Lewis in *The Monk* (1795). Whether in its English or French version, *Vathek* demonstrated again the manner in which the gothic, like any genre, underwent incremental change in its development. Combining the characteristics of gothicism and the more acceptable form of chinoiserie, Beckford provided an early example of the mutations that would permit the gothic to adapt and change according to circumstances and thus endure throughout the following centuries.

In part the success of *Vathek* depended upon the ever-increasing acceptability of Romanticism. By the 1790s the new aesthetic was approaching critical dominance, and Ann Radcliffe, who took full advantage of the change in sensibility, emerged as the Queen of the Gothic. Yet neither the rise of Romanticism nor the enormous popularity of Radcliffe created critical acceptability for the genre. Throughout its history the gothic has appealed to readers, but has been scorned by the custodians of literature. In order to achieve critical acceptance, Radcliffe pretended that *The Romance of the Forest* (1791) was based on a seventeenth-century source. Both *The Mysteries of Udolpho* (1794) and *The Italian* (1797) used Clara Reeve's technique of rationally explaining their mysterious occurrences as a means of averting criticism of their gothic excesses. Still the critics objected to the specifically gothic elements in her work. For the woman known as the 'Shakespeare of the Romance Writers' and praised by Coleridge, Shelley, Byron, and the extremely demanding Jane Austen, her gothicism was in itself insufficient. What impressed the literary élite were her poetic abilities and her portrayal of landscapes in a prose that rivalled the painting of Claude, Rosa and Reni. Not until the twentieth century and the advent of psychological and feminist criticism were the depths of Radcliffe's achievement explored and the relationship of the gothic to suppressed emotions thoroughly examined. Feminist criticism especially has suggested how Radcliffe and the host of women writers in the genre used its devices to respond to the condition of women in the period, to confront the tyranny of a patriarchal society, and to challenge or subvert its values. In the fiction of major and minor female gothicists, plots, settings, characterization and supernatural machinery were the material for dealing with questions of a woman's identity in a male-dominated society.

With the success of Radcliffe's novels, including *The Castles of Athlin and*

Dunbayne (1789) and *A Sicilian Romance* (1790), the gothic became a phenomenon of popular culture. Amateurs and professionals filled the magazines with gothic short stories, tales, fragments, romances, and novellas, many written by enthusiastic readers and some pilfered from works by superior writers. 'Shilling shockers' and 'blue-books' offered an avid public an assortment of abridgements, imitations and redactions. While critics deplored the efforts of Radcliffe's offspring with their tales of haunted castles and horror and their ghosts and murderers, one-third of the English novels between 1796 and 1806 were gothic (Mayo, 1962, p. 349). Through cheap editions and circulating libraries, loyal readers, patronizingly dismissed by reviewers as 'misses', eagerly gratified their taste for what a weary sophisticated critic called 'horrid ideas of supernatural agency' (*Monthly Review*, vol. 14, 1794, pp. 464–5).

While most of this fiction remained deservedly forgotten after initial publication, modern scholarship, particularly in its concern for the literature of women, has rescued some of the more significant work. Beginning with Ellen Moers's 1963 essay on *Frankenstein* through Juliann Fleenor's 1983 anthology of sixteen wider-ranging essays, the feminist revolutionary reassessment of gothic literature has demonstrated that women played a major role in its production and that their contributions to the development of the genre were considerable: Sophia Lee's *The Recess* (1785) and Harriet Lee's 'Kruitzner, or the German's Tale' (1798) to the historical gothic; Regina Maria Roche's to the sentimental gothic in *Children of the Abbey* (1796); and Eliza Parsons's to the German Schauer-Romantik in *The Castle of Wolfenbach* (1793) and *The Mysterious Warning* (1796) deserve acknowledgement. Whatever the merits of their individual works, such women as Charlotte Dacre, Elizabeth Helme, Isabella Kelly, Mary Meeke and Eleanor Sleath, along with such men as T. J. Horsley Curties, Francis Lathom, George Moore and William Henry Ireland, entertained their readers and kept alive the gothic tradition as a popular form of art. When Jane Austen satirized their 'horrid novels' in *Northanger Abbey*, she demonstrated the tenacity of the gothic appeal, and her detailed familiarity with the genre suggests her own addiction to it.

Two other writers of the period, whose relationship to the gothic has been perceived as tenuous, display the manner in which the genre was adaptable to other forms and consequently extended. In novels like *Emmeline* (1788) and *The Old Manor House* (1793), Charlotte Smith, a very competent professional writer, properly gauged the attractiveness of the novel of sentiment and the gothic and melded the two in order to appeal to her readers. Conscious of a growing awareness of social matters and personally involved in the problems of providing for her large family, Smith brought a new social consciousness to bear on the genre, placing her seriousness behind the enticing façade of the entertainment of the genre and deliberately holding its excesses in check by a rationalism intended to keep her focus on the real world.

As Smith offered the gothic as a vehicle for social commentary, William Godwin, England's foremost philosopher of his time and the father of Mary Shelley, used it for political purposes in *St. Leon* (1800), *Fleetwood* (1806), and especially *Caleb Williams* (1794). Godwin himself declared that *Caleb Williams* fictionalized the philosophical ideas in his *Political Justice* and used the gothic for political argument. In *Fleetwood*, Godwin combined the novel of terror and the novel of sentiment; in *St. Leon* his use of terror and the marvellous dominated and his scenes of the Inquisition recalled Radcliffe's techniques, while he contributed to the gothic by combining it with the devices of detective fiction. Although modern criticism, like that in his own period, has chosen to emphasize the political philosophy of *Caleb Williams*, the kinship between his treatment of Falkland and the gothic villain, the extensive connections with the conventions of the horror novel, and the ties of its characterization to the sado-masochistic characteristics of the genre undeniably linked the novel to the gothic. Godwin helped to transform the traditional form into a psychological gothicism whose intention was to convey a political message.

Unlike Smith and Godwin, Matthew Gregory Lewis belongs unquestionably and solely within the gothic tradition in his novel, poetry, tales, translations and drama. Bringing a new dimension to the gothic through his use of German sources, liberating it from all restraints, reflecting the spirit of the French revolution and its aftermath in the Reign of Terror, and challenging the conventional values of the bourgeoisie, Lewis explored freely the horrors of murder, rape and incest in *The Monk* (1795). Unfettered by any concern for ordinary standards, his novel moved through uncharted areas of the supernatural and diabolism. In Lewis's hands the German Schauer-Romantik emerged as the English novel of terror. While even such an uninhibited critic as Byron deplored its excesses, the public savoured its unbridled passion and sensuality. Its popularity led Radcliffe, whose work had influenced Lewis, to adapt his technique in *The Italian*, and the Germans, to whom he was indebted, redeemed his obligations to them by borrowing heavily from the voluptuous sensuality of his novel. In itself *The Monk* is a masterpiece, perhaps the finest achievement in the genre. Lewis was altogether comfortable with the gothic. It expressed his own personality, his character as an outsider in his own society. He felt no need to explain away the supernatural agencies in his novel, to account for the devil's entrapment of the monk Ambrosio, or to dissipate the effectiveness of his horror by rational explanations of his character's being hurtled to his death by the Fiend. Instead Lewis managed his sense of realism and created his necessary verisimilitude by his intense depiction of Ambrosio. Beginning with a description of the monk's restraint of his natural emotions and strong desires, Lewis went on to detail the gradual deterioration in the character as he inevitably yielded to temptation and finally lost all control of his suppressed libido. Lewis's study of the deterioration of Ambrosio presented a psychological analysis that, along with *Caleb Williams*, moved the gothic in a new direction. Although Montague Summers has often been criticized for devoting so much space to Lewis in *The Gothic Quest* (1938), his treatment was appropriate, for Lewis, no less than Radcliffe, created work deserving of critical as well as popular acclaim.

The influence of Lewis and gothicism generally was not restricted to fiction in the period nor for the next few decades. Not surprisingly to anyone familiar with the symbiosis of gothic novels and cinema in the twentieth century, gothicism in the theatre, as in fiction, flourished in popular appeal, even as criticism denounced it. After some initial opposition, gothic drama progressed from comic treatment to respectable melodrama as it took advantage of the increasing acceptability of Romanticism, to which, in turn, it contributed. Adaptations of Walpole's and Radcliffe's novels met with audience approval, and, despite critical disdain, Lewis's own drama, *Castle Spectre* (1797), enjoyed a remarkable run. Equally obvious is the connection between gothicism and romanticism in poetry. The evidence is apparent not only in the general imaginative qualities of romantic criticism, aesthetic theory and creativity, but in the direct influence of Radcliffe on Wordsworth, Coleridge, Keats and Byron. Shelley as a young writer produced two gothic romances, *Zastrossi* (1810) and *St. Irvyne, or the Rosicrucian* (1811), and the theory of the genre clearly influenced his philosophy. Even in art the effect of gothicism is inescapably apparent in both the writing and painting of William Blake, John Flaxman and Henry Fuseli. In its subject-matter and sensibility, Fuseli's *Nightmare* expressed the very ethos of gothic fiction.

Out of this romantic and gothic union Mary Shelley's *Frankenstein* (1818) was born. Critics have stressed the novel's mythic qualities, its Faustian characteristics, its Miltonic inversion, its feminist recreation of the birth myth, and its role in the development of science fiction. Without denying any or all of these, the fact remains that Shelley's work extended the parameters of the gothic. Its very composition purportedly resulted from a ghost-story contest that yielded Byron's gothic 'A Fragment' and John Polidori's 'The Vampyre: A Fragment'. Her romantic companions were gothic *aficionados*, and her own short fiction demonstrates her appreciation of the genre despite the rationalism that she shared with her parents, William Godwin and Mary Wollstonecraft. In her elopement with Shelley, she defied convention and exhibited a romantic nature worthy of a gothic heroine.

Had *Frankenstein* merely repeated the old formula, it could not have attracted an audience that had become inured to re-workings of Radcliffe and Lewis. Shelley modernized her setting, but introduced the medieval through Victor Frankenstein's study of alchemy. Her scientific laboratories replaced Walpole's and Radcliffe's castles, but retained their air of mystery through remote and awesome mountain locations. Graveyard depredations to gather the material for the creation of a monster who then stalks villages and terrorizes innocent inhabitants – these were the very soul of gothic horror. Describing her aim as to find a story that would 'curdle the blood and quicken the beatings of the heart' (Shelley, [1818] 1967, pp. xiii–xiv), Shelley epitomized the qualities of the gothic. By bringing to the genre recent scientific interests displayed in Erasmus Darwin's theories of galvanism with the dangers its scientific hubris posed, and by using a framing device to intensify the immediacy of its terror, she gave life to a seemingly dying genre even as Frankenstein had given it to his monster.

With the work of Charles Robert Maturin, Shelley's Irish contemporary, what might appropriately be termed the High Gothic came to a close, although James Hogg's *Confessions of a Justified Sinner* (1824), with its emphasis on man's darkest nature and most savage instincts, also explored the psychological aspects of the gothic. Maturin began early on with a clumsy effort in *The Fatal Revenge, or the Family of Montorio* (1807), but his masterwork *Melmoth the Wanderer* (1820) presented his fullest expression in the genre. An odd combination of Radcliffe and Lewis, *Melmoth* followed the former in its treatment of horror and yet managed to evoke the latter's power in conveying the sense of fear attendant upon it. For Maturin the main interest in horror was the origins of fear, its manner of inflicting pain. Through six tales of terror presented in a frame that combined elements of the legends of Faust and the Wandering Jew, his novel employed the tools of psychological investigation more effectively than any earlier gothic in order to examine the emotions and sensations possible in the genre. For his contemporaries Maturin was an author whose imagination ran riot and whose novel was a 'phantasmagoric exhibition' (*Edinburgh Review*, vol. 35, 1881, p. 353), but in the twentieth century he has been called 'the greatest as well as the last of the Goths' (Birkhead, 1921, p. 93).

Hardly the greatest of the gothic novelists, Maturin certainly was not the last as the genre continued as both a popular form of minor fiction and a significant element in major novels throughout the nineteenth century. In America, although the climate welcomed romance, publishing conditions stunted its growth in the eighteenth century, limiting it largely to magazines where original fiction did not have to compete with English novels unprotected by copyright. The sole American example of importance in the period was Charles Brockden Brown's *Wieland, or the Transformation* (1798), a political novel inspired by Godwin. But gothic success in magazine fiction, drama and poetry had a major impact on nineteenth-century American authors. Concerned chiefly with effect, Edgar Allan Poe used gothic material – ghastly settings, Byronic characters, atmosphere and mood – to create the emotional response characteristic of the genre from its inception. His *Tales of the Grotesque and Arabesque* (1840), in which 'The Fall of the House of Usher' appeared, stands as the classic example of American gothic fiction. If the genre appears less immediately apparent in Herman Melville's novels, it nevertheless substantially influenced his writing. References to Radcliffe indicated his indebtedness, and Walpole provided the source for his *Pierre* (1852) and other novels. The profusion of gothic devices in Nathaniel Hawthorne's *Twice Told Tales* (1842), *The Scarlet Letter* (1850) and *The Marble Faun* (1860) suggests the role played by the genre throughout the career of a writer whose vision transposed it to a New England landscape. From Ambrose Bierce's minor fiction to Henry James's *The Turn of the Screw* (1898), the gothic adapted to nineteenth-century American surroundings and writers.

The gothic influence pervaded the English novel and shorter fiction throughout the same period. Sir Walter Scott gave it respectability by linking it to Scottish folk backgrounds and offering it a home in the fashionable neighbourhood of the historical novel. It stimulated the work of the Brontë sisters as it shaped the characterization of the heroes of *Wuthering Heights* (1848), *Jane Eyre* (1847) and *Villette* (1853) and haunted the novels' settings. In Joseph Sheridan Le Fanu's occult and mysterious tales, exemplified by 'Carmilla' (1871), as well as in a host of his gothic novels and his masterpiece *Uncle Silas* (1864), the novel of terror, either in itself or combined with the vampire and ghost story, provided the dominant tone and contributed to the challenge to social taboos. Charles Dickens made no secret of his debt to the genre. From such early books as *Oliver Twist* (1837–8) and *The Old Curiosity Shop* (1840–1) to his uncompleted final novel *The Mystery of Edwin Drood* (1870), gothicism saturated his fiction. Both Radcliffe and Lewis left their imprint on his novels, and the atmosphere and characterization of even his gravest and darkest fiction – *Bleak House* (1852–3), *Little Dorrit* (1855–7), and *Our Mutual Friend* (1864–5) – drew inspiration from gothic fantasies. Indeed, the list of nineteenth-century English novelists influenced by the gothic appears endless and includes such contemporaries of Dickens as Bulwer-Lytton and Wilkie Collins and such later writers as Oscar Wilde and Robert Louis Stevenson. In major works and in combination with vampire stories, science fiction and detective novels, the gothic continued, adapting to changing circumstances and reshaping itself to meet the demands of popular culture.

Nor did its presence end in the twentieth century. Whether in the fiction of D. H. Lawrence and Iris Murdoch and such Americans as William Faulkner, Flannery O'Connor and Joyce Carol Oates, or in such cultist attractions as H. P. Lovecraft and Stephen King, the genre remained very much alive in literature. But its life has been extended in other media. First on radio, then in the cinema, and now on television, gothic mystery has proved a powerful and moving force. While most critics continue to grumble at modern re-creations of the genre, readers and audiences respond, as earlier followers of the gothic did, to an art form that ignores authority, challenges convention and provides emotional thrill.

FURTHER READING

Birkhead, Edith (1921) *The Tale of Terror: A Study of the Gothic*, Constable, London

Day, William Patrick (1985) *In the Circles of Fear and Desire: A Study of Gothic Fantasy*, University of Chicago Press, Chicago

Fleenor, Juliann E. (ed.) (1983) *The Female Gothic*, Eden Press, Montreal

Frank, Frederick S. (1984) *Guide to the Gothic*, Scarecrow Press, Metuchen

Howells, Cora Ann (1978) *Love, Misery, and Mystery*, Athlone Press, London

McAndrew, Elizabeth (1979) *The Gothic Tradition in Fiction*, Columbia University Press, New York

Punter, David (1980) *The Literature of Terror: A History of Gothic Fictions from 1765 to the Present Day*, Longman, New York

Spector, Robert Donald (1983) *The English Gothic: A Bibliographical Guide to Writers from Horace Walpole to Mary Shelley*, Greenwood, Westport

Summers, Montague (1938) *The Gothic Quest*, Fortune Press, London

Tracy, Ann B. (1981) *The Gothic Novel 1790–1830: Plot Summaries and Index to Motifs*, University Press of Kentucky, Lexington

Varma, Devendra P. (1957) *The Gothic Flame*, Barker, London

Wilt, Judith (1980) *Ghosts of the Gothic*, Princeton University Press, Princeton

ADDITIONAL WORKS CITED

Mayo, Robert D. (1962) *The English Novel in the Magazines, 1740–1815*, Northwestern University Press, Evanston

Moers, Ellen (1963) *Literary Women*, Doubleday, New York

Reeve, Clara (1967) *The Old English Baron: A Gothic Story*, edited by James Trainer, Oxford University Press, London [first published 1777]

Shelley, Mary (1967) *Frankenstein or the Modern Prometheus*, edited by R. D. Spector, Bantam, New York [first published 1818]

Walpole, Horace (1964) *The Castle of Otranto*, edited by W. S. Lewis, Oxford University Press, London [first published 1765]

78

AESTHETICISM

JOHN STOKES

Aesthetics are at least as old as Plato, but 'Aestheticism' originates from the early nineteenth century. This is because Aestheticism is neither a theory, nor a philosophy, nor even a field of enquiry, but a set of priorities, born of historical circumstance: the demise of religious certainty and the growth of scientific method. Later in the century it was joined to a lifestyle – 'The Aesthetic Movement' – which involved a taste for Liberty furnishings, Whistlerian painting, *japonaiserie*, and a certain flexibility in sexual conduct. It was entirely possible to pursue the intellectual interests of Aestheticism along with the transient tastes of the 'Movement' (both Oscar Wilde and William Morris did so, in their different ways), but Aestheticism proper is a critical attitude that has survived, with modifications, from the nineteenth to the twentieth century.

That, in many ways, is a surprising fact. When we now read nineteenth-century criticism, of whatever period or school though particularly when it is aesthetic, we are likely to find ourselves alienated by the assumption that achievement of an ideal 'Beauty' is the aim of all art, especially when this is accompanied by agonizing over the relation of 'Beauty' to 'Nature'. The difference between Aestheticism and the other nineteenth-century approaches is not that it concentrated upon beauty to the exclusion of everything else, but that it made *feelings*, admittedly the feelings engendered by art in particular, the means by which mankind could discover and explore its true identity. It is often forgotten that, as Raymond Williams pointed out in *Keywords*, the precise opposite of aesthetic is not 'unaesthetic' but 'anaesthetic' (Williams, 1976, pp. 27–8).

Aestheticism even went so far as to suggest that through the contemplation of art man might find greater satisfactions than were offered by either conventional religion or mechanistic science. And it made that subversive claim in spite of, or rather because of, the failure of Romanticism to provide a lasting replacement for the first or a serious rival to the second.

For the romantics the enemy 'science' (Blake's 'Idiot Questioner') had been an eighteenth-century practice, deistic and Newtonian, to be opposed to the imagination itself (Blake's 'sweet science'), which had to rediscover its own determining place within the human perspective. The romantic attitude to science was ambivalent, however. Shelley, as we now know, made great use of scientific ideas, and it is often pointed out that Wordsworth extended Lockean associationism even as he denied it. For the post-romantic writer, especially if he was acquainted with Darwinism, science was even more seductive and even more insidious, much more like philosophy itself. Nevertheless it had been the strength of the romantic imagination, as its poets continually reminded themselves, to create a unity where there was none before. If the imagination was to continue to reign supreme then art alone must make up the kingdom. Or, in what was to become familiar phrasing: 'art for art's sake', '*l'art pour l'art*'.

The French phrase makes its formal debut in English aesthetic discourse through one English poet's revaluation of another. In his pioneering book on Blake of 1868, Algernon Charles Swinburne chose to endorse Blake's vision of the 'Idiot Questioner' by equating science with scepticism, and scepticism with restraint. This helped him to dismiss as absurd the contemporary tendency to merge art with science. Such attempts, he claimed, rested upon a blatant confusion of categories:

> Poetry or art based on loyalty to science is exactly as absurd (and no more) as science guided by art or poetry. Neither in effect can coalesce with the other and retain a right to exist. Neither can or (while in its sober senses) need wish to destroy the other; but they must go on their separate ways, and in this life their ways can by no possibility cross. Neither can or (unless in some fit of fugitive insanity) need wish to become valuable or respectable to the other: each must remain, on its ground and to its own followers, a thing of value and deserving respect. To art, that is best which is most beautiful; to science, that is best which is most accurate; to mortality that is best which is most virtuous.
>
> (1868, p. 98)

Swinburne's assertions are a sign of romantic principle stretched to a point beyond that envisaged by its originators. They herald the birth of Aestheticism proper, which emerges when the nature of art is finally separated from all other objects of intellectual enquiry, and the search continues to establish art's own unique laws. Swinburne was not to pursue that road to its end, though he did indicate a direction for others to take – among them Walter Pater and Oscar Wilde. Swinburne's account of Blake moves rapidly from defence against philistine cavil to elevation as an exemplary man. Blake's absolute dedication to uncompromised expression and his hostility to all external authority, which had first claimed Swinburne's admiration, tie in remarkably well with a portrait of Charles Baudelaire, framed in a footnote, as the poet of 'a music of emotion' and 'a unison of sense and spirit', who 'loved all fair and felt all strange things' (Swinburne, 1868, p. 91). These twin mentors inspire the apophthegms that were to become the basis for Swinburne's own creed: 'Save the shape and art will take care of the soul for you' (pp. 87–8) and 'Art for art's sake first of all, and afterwards we may suppose all the rest may be added to her' (p. 91). Scientific proof and moral purpose: both belong with Baudelaire's *l'hérésie de l'enseignement* and Blake's Urizen.

Much as Blake became in Swinburne's eyes a proto-aesthete so, in the view of Walter Pater, Coleridge appeared as a salutary failure, whose pursuit of 'the absolute' confirmed his remoteness from the present. 'Modern thought', Pater insisted in an essay on Coleridge first published in 1866, 'is distinguished from ancient by its cultivation of the "relative" spirit in place of the "absolute" ' (ed. Uglow, 1973, p. 1). This 'relative spirit' infuses Pater's attitudes and, indeed, his prose style. For all the accusations that have been and continue to be levelled against it, Pater's aesthetic style is in fact highly analytic. When he writes for example that, comprehended under modern conditions, 'Character emerges into temperament: the nervous system refines itself into intellect' (p. 2), the very balance of the sentence expresses the idea of division through antithetical exchange. An established word, 'character', becomes a newer (we would say 'psychological') term: 'temperament'; just as the more recent physiological concept, 'nervous system', can be identified, but in a new way, with an established term for 'mind'. The relativity of mind/body distinctions is actually increased by the discoveries produced by the relative method, resulting in increasingly subtle depths of understanding – even though, syntactically, 'temperament' remains balanced against 'intellect'. Thus complex differences are shown as they emerge, and become intelligible through the workings of an intellectual praxis which demonstrates how recognition of new distinctions is built upon traces of the old ones that they have replaced; and, conversely, how a new way of seeing reveals the latent meanings within the old. Confronting the pathos of such moments of change presents a challenge to the 'fine mind': that is to say, the aesthetic mind, which is itself 'refined', not merely fastidious and elegant, but purged, as in a metallurgical process.

It is important to stress the emotional accompaniment of intellectual change, because it underlies Pater's aesthetic perspective on Romanticism, which is simultaneously 'a lost cause' and a continuing, though endlessly changing way of realizing experience. Living in and for the moment, the modern intellectual ambition involves a break from a past still inhabited by father-figures whose strivings are now seen in a new light. The rational way to channel these emotions is a humorous apparent 'unconcern' in the handling of ideas. Of the species 'man' Pater will only say that it seems as if the most opposite statements about him are true: 'he is so receptive, all the influences of the world and society ceaselessly playing upon him, so that every hour in his life is unique, changed altogether by a stray word, or glance, or touch' (ed. Uglow, 1973, p. 2). But this aesthetic acceptance of the unpredictableness of life is not quite as sceptical as it might look, because it is underwritten by empiricism: re-defined (or 'refined') by their context, words such as 'receptive' and 'influence' now belong to a neo-Darwinist vocabulary.

As Pater reminds us, when he embarks on a consideration of Coleridge's notion of 'organic form', to the romantic imagination the type of the natural genius was Shakespeare. Given his own doubts about the deployment of 'genius', it is not surprising that Pater's questioning of 'organic form' should be derived from his distrust of all phenomena that are left unexplained. To compare a work of art with a work of nature is primarily, in Pater's view, to run the risk of denying the productive role of the artist. Yet characteristically Pater refutes organicism by 'refining' it. The unity of nature that allowed Coleridge's analogy was, although sometimes beyond comprehension, always present in essence, whereas for Pater nature itself is erratic, subject to unfore-seen change. Consequently Pater appears to allow that artistic innovation can sometimes present the same kind of experience as shifts in nature:

> In imaginative genius, ideas become effective; the intelligence of nature, with all its elements connected and justified, is clearly reflected; and the interpretation of its latent purposes is fixed in art.
>
> (ed. Uglow, 1973, p. 4)

But this is an effect produced upon the perceiver as much as it is part of the creative process itself, and Pater is undisguisedly hostile to the implication within the doctrine of organic form that the artist is merely a vehicle, his connection with his creation unmediated. He rejects the self-surrender which would make the artist 'something almost mechanical'.

Pater's point is that the doctrine of organic form, like that of spontaneous 'genius', would actually deny nature while presuming to invoke it. Perhaps the most important aspect of Pater's aesthetic attack lies in his fine understanding that 'organicism' reduces men to the 'mechanical', and we do well to remember that these two words, though seemingly opposites, were in fact dialectically interchangeable in much nineteenth-century theory. Although organic form may originally have denoted unity without the concomitant growth which can strictly speaking apply only to an organism and not to an artefact, in the nineteenth century that vital distinction continued to be obscured as evolution-ism proved that the whole universe was constantly changing – growing and, at the same time perhaps, decaying. The inorganic was thus at least theoretically subsumed within the organic, and art could be seen as yet another changing product of the processes of change. Evolution had provided some positive new metaphors for art.

Consequently when Pater came to write about William Wordsworth in 1874, he began his essay by transposing Coleridge's terms 'Fancy' and 'Imagination' from a metaphysical context to something like perceptual psychology. 'Fancy' becomes the name for a dull perception producing the kind of automatic prosy moralism that sometimes invades Wordsworth's work. 'Imagination', vivid perception coupled with expressive energy, concentrates meaning into significant moments. The route by which Pater chooses to investigate this higher faculty resists mystical explanations to engage with utilitarian ethics, perhaps Pater's truest adversary, and it develops Aestheticism yet further. He emphasizes Wordworth's involvement with the natural world and the poet's consequent tendency to let figures merge with landscape – a necessary preparation for Pater's own interpretation of Wordsworth, whose wisdom he wishes to reinstate, without the concomitant risks of megalomania or loss of responsibility. Since 'the office of the poet is not that of the moralist, and the first aim of Wordsworth's poetry is to give the reader a peculiar kind of pleasure' (ed. Uglow, 1973, pp. 113–614), Pater deems the utilitarian principle which judges poetic means by moral ends to be 'mechanical', because it would substitute an intellectual system for experience and feeling. Then, in a startling verbal coup, he identifies ends with means and both with art:

> To treat life in the spirit of art, is to make life a thing in which means and ends are identified: to encourage such treatment, the true moral significance of art and poetry.
>
> (p. 115)

A brilliant transformation of values, means as meanings, releases at length Pater's own evaluation of Wordsworth which, in a wide circular movement, borrows from the preface to the *Lyrical Ballads*, and yet aligns Wordsworth with the aesthetic principle that art is never didactic. The work of the poets is

> not to teach lessons, or enforce rules, or even to stimulate us to noble ends; but to withdraw the thoughts for a little while from the mere machinery of life, to fix them, with appropriate emotions on the spectacle of these great facts in man's existence which no machinery affects, 'on the great and universal passions of men, the most general and interesting of their occupations, and the entire world of nature'.
>
> (p. 115)

At the end of Pater's essay Wordsworthian calm has been justified, paradoxically, as a form of passion, but on Wordsworth's own terms, while Pater's aesthetic unease with the pantheistic concept of 'oneness', and his own strong ethical bias, have, once again, been both challenged and confirmed by current scientific theory. His remarkable essay does much more than merely wrestle with the animism that he knew to be at the core of Wordsworth's poetry, and which he felt to possess all the undoubted aura of an ancient philosophical quest. Its gruelling task is to profess the fullest emotional appreciation of that historical sanctity without at any time compromising Pater's own modern 'scepticism'. The poetic vision must be 'historicized' but the proof of the placing will lie in the emotional power with which Wordsworth's peculiar, but now distant 'charm' is evoked.

Aestheticism was never far from becoming a theory of historical consciousness, almost despite itself. Part of the problem (by no means unique to Pater), arose out of the contrast between those 'timeless moments' which are celebrated in Wordsworthian poetry and a modern recognition (partly reinforced by Hegel) that philosophical truths are discovered *within* time: the 'development' of ideas. In the nineteenth century the locus for the former was normally the prefatory testament to *The Excursion*:

> while my voice proclaims
> How exquisitely the individual Mind
> (And the progressive powers perhaps no less
> Of the whole species) to the external World
> Is fitted – and how exquisitely, too –
> Theme this but little heard of among men –
> The external World is fitted to the Mind.
> (Preface to the Edition of 1814, ll. 62–8)

In Pater's *Gaston De Latour* (1896), though, we find this subtly but significantly modified into 'that intimate fitness to the mind of its own time' (p. 72). In other words our perception of the external world is itself historically controlled.

Significantly, when Pater's devoted admirer Oscar Wilde was writing *De Profundis* in Reading Gaol in 1897 he seems to have made the mistake, in a discussion of Pater's *Marius the Epicurean* (1885), of attributing to Wordsworth a statement not in fact made by the poet but rather by Pater in his essay about him. Wilde wrote:

> But Marius is little more than a spectator: an ideal spectator indeed, and one to whom it is given 'to contemplate the spectacle of life with appropriate emotions', which Wordsworth defines as the poet's true aim.
> (ed. Hart-Davis, 1962, p. 476)

Wilde's confusion is quite understandable. In Pater's original essay there is continual equivocation in his references to a 'spectacle' which is permanent (because the objects of contemplation are cyclic, hence eternal), yet mutable (because the absorbing mind brings its own reciprocal resources: 'the appropriate emotions'). Perhaps Wilde's slip came about because the very purpose of his own essentially aesthetic project was to interrelate a number of artistic creeds, identifying the historical engagements that one writer makes from another – in the case of Pater and Wordsworth, a poetic ambition to perceive the universal, and a partly distanced critical estimation of how that ambition might latterly be understood. Moreover Pater's poise was not entirely suppressed in Wilde's act of assimilation because since it was the critic, Pater, who unwittingly stood in for the poet, Wordsworth, the poet had effectively been kept in view through the successive reinterpretations which strove to maintain his work as a significant monument for his descendants to respond to.

Ironically, it was because new scientific ideas had changed previous assumptions about the relationship between man and his surroundings that Wordsworth was such an important touchstone in the business of defining the aesthetic 'spectacle'. For instance, if evolutionism was correct in presuming universal continuous development, however erratic, then it followed that at some stage there must be a passage from inorganic to organic life. Comprehending that development provided a peculiarly intransigent crux – a literal justification for Wordsworth's 'transfusion', scientific and yet for an aesthete often profoundly troubling.

What if the speaker could be shown to be at one with the spectacle, but only at some level entirely below his own awareness? That possibility infuses one of the most celebrated of all aesthetic declarations, the 'Conclusion' to Pater's *Studies in the History of the Renaissance* (1873). Here Pater brings together an approach to art and an approach to life as coterminous means of emotional and moral survival in the face of the undoubtedly material conditions of existence. Having first extolled the 'exquisite intervals' of experience as the pattern of our consciousness, he posed the problem of the organic and the inorganic in the form of a rhetorical question:

> What is the whole physical life in that moment but a combination of natural elements to which science gives their names?
>
> (Pater, ed. 1980, p. 186)

Taking up the implications of his own rhetorical question, he then alluded to a major scientific discovery:

> But those elements, phosphorous and lime and delicate fibres, are present not in the human body alone: we detect them in places most remote from it.
>
> (p. 186)

Consciousness, in short, is a material fact; death a terminus. Pater's famous inference – sometimes criticized as 'hedonism' – is that the best we can do is strive to fill the brief interval of our life with passionate feelings.

> Great passions may give us this quickened sense of life, ecstasy and sorrow of love, the various forms of enthusiastic activity, disinterested or otherwise, which come naturally to many of us. Only be sure it is passion – that it does yield you this fruit of a quickened, multiplied consciousness. Of this wisdom, the poetic passion, the desire of beauty, the love of art for art's sake, has most. For art

comes to you professing frankly to give nothing but the highest quality to your moments as they pass, and simply for those moments' sake.

(p. 190)

The links between human experience and material process continued to haunt the aesthetic sensibility. When Wilde's fictional Dorian Gray (1891), a hedonist if ever there was one, considers his plight he speculates:

Might there not be some curious scientific reason for it all? If thought could exercise its influence upon a living organism, might not thought exercise an influence upon dead and inorganic things? Nay, without thought or conscious desire, might not things external to ourselves vibrate in unison with our moods and passions, atom calling to atom in secret love or strange affinity?

(ed. 1974, p. 106)

When we are told, some time later, that he 'inclined to materialistic doctrines of the *Darwinismus* movement in Germany', though 'no theory of life seemed to him to be of any importance compared with life itself' (p. 133), Dorian's ambivalence is once again symptomatic of aesthetic enquiry.

The founder of the *Darwinismus* movement, Ernst Haeckel, had indeed pronounced in his *History of Creation* (English translation 1876, with its epitaph from Wordsworth: 'a sense sublime/Of something far more deeply interfused . . . rolls through all things') the fervent claim that mental activity and corporeal substance were inseparable, and that 'the idea of the *unity of organic and inorganic matter* is now firmly established'. But Dorian Gray, following Pater, attempts for a time to delay final dissolution into matter by cultivating emotional experience for its own sake. His attitude is both a continuation of romantic ideas of imagination and a refutation of their tendency towards loss of identity: a continuation because the romantics themselves had made use of organic analogies to express the workings of the imagination; but also a refutation because late nineteenth-century Aestheticism is the attempt of the creative imagination to resist incorporation, an effort to maintain independence by insisting upon the visible, tangible otherness of the world and its products. Yet, paradoxically, Dorian is finally driven to destroy his portrait, the work of art, the inorganic thing that he has inevitably become, given his initial decision to renounce development and avoid death. He thereby destroys himself.

Two other great romantic poets made their contribution to Aestheticism and were in turn preserved by it. Both Keats and Shelley had come to provide images of the artistic life, and the publication of Keats's letters to Fanny Brawne in 1878 and the continuing disclosures about Shelley's domestic ménages, fixed these images to questions of morality. For Matthew Arnold, writing in 1880, Keats's achievement was 'partial and incomplete' (ed. Super, 1960–74, vol. 9, p. 214), the exact quality that made him so attractive first to the Pre-Raphaelites and later to admirers such as Wilde who thought of him 'as of a priest of Beauty slain before his time' (in Ellmann, 1970, p. 5).

A further clue to Keats's appeal to aesthetes lies in the cult of 'sensation'. 'O for a life of sensations rather than of thoughts!', wrote Keats, and in the late nineteenth century 'sensations', sometimes reduced to the merely sensual, could be the very stuff of poetry. And this quest for sensations takes us directly back to Arthur Hallam's influential essay on Tennyson (1831, reprinted in 1893), where an original distinction had been upheld between Shelley and Keats, 'poets of sensation', and Wordsworth, 'the poet of reflection':

> Susceptible of the slightest impulse from external nature, their fine organs trembled into emotion at colours, and sounds and movements, unperceived or unregarded by duller temperaments. Rich and clear were their perceptions of visible forms, full and deep their feelings of music.... Other poets *seek* for images to illustrate their conceptions; these men had no need to seek; they lived in a world of images; for the most important and extensive portion of their life consisted in those emotions, which are immediately conversant with sensation.
>
> (in Warner and Hough, 1983, vol. 1, p. 139)

Keats's devotion to 'beauty' became a talisman in the development of Aestheticism, serving many functions. A clear line runs from the 'Ode on a Grecian Urn' to Rossetti's 'For a Venetian Pastoral' or even to his 'The Burden of Nineveh': poems which include the contemplation of an art work on the painfully ironic grounds that it preserves a vision of animated life at some untraversable distance to the living spectator.

Reliance upon Keatsian testaments such as 'beauty is truth, truth beauty', 'a thing of beauty is a joy for ever' (which became the title of a work by Ruskin) went beyond mere incantation. Radical critics such as E. P. Thompson (1977) and John Goode (1971) have each shown how the revolutionary socialist William Morris turned romantic emotion back on itself to validate his dissatisfaction with the present. In 1894 Morris's Kelmscott Press devotedly published an edition of Keats's *Poems*.

For Morris, Keats remained supremely the poet of human experience, and the 'dream' structure common to many of Keats's poems became Morris's way of dramatizing his own radical alienation. Similarly for W. B. Yeats, a need to place Keats's precocity accompanied his later enquiry into 'unity of being'.

Reference has already been made to Wilde's continuation of the aesthetic bid to rival science by replicating its claims. That interest goes back to his time at Oxford in the late 1870s and has been underestimated. Wilde's extension of the basic principles of *l'art pour l'art* is better known. In a handful of critical essays, (supremely 'The Decay of Lying' and 'The Critic as Artist', both collected in *Intentions*, 1891), and in the many epigrams with which all his works are lavishly studded, Wilde set about elevating art by insisting upon its superiority to all other demands upon human attention. 'There is no such thing as an immoral book', he wrote in the Preface to *The Picture of Dorian Gray*, defying the Victorian public, 'books are either well-written or they are not', daring its critical élite to refute the principle. The question could hardly be anything less than crucial since, as Wilde also pronounced, it was nature that imitated art and not, as in commonplace versions of mimetic theory, vice versa. Aesthetic judgement was advanced even further when Wilde replaced Pater's principle that the primary aim of criticism is 'to see the object as in itself it really is' (Pater, 1980, p. xix), itself a direct echo of Matthew Arnold's edict in 1861 on the function of criticism (ed. Super, 1960–74, vol. 1, p. 140), with the devilishly paradoxical proposition that 'the primary aim of criticism is to see the object as in itself it really is not' (in Ellmann, 1970, p. 369). The critic is as free as the artist to indulge his own vision, freer in fact because he is not constrained by convention, only by natural endowments of temperament or imagination. He is in other words an aesthete: once again Aestheticism becomes a weapon against the pressures of institutionalized taste and values.

Wilde was the last nineteenth-century writer to see Aestheticism as quite such a powerful moral force as that. Among the modern poets W. B. Yeats was the most obviously aesthetic: so conscious of his historical status as someone who had actually known the great Victorians that he paid them the tribute of allotting them roles in the drama of his own career. Yet although he was implacably hostile to science, Yeats was too susceptible to deterministic systems to remain a consistent follower of the aesthetic trust in the continually wavering personality.

And while Eliot and Pound were undoubtedly more responsive to Pater and Wilde than they were usually prepared to admit, their interest in the autonomy of art was recuperative rather than subversive. Elsewhere the trappings of aesthetic style were borrowed and trivialized by the likes of Ronald Firbank and certain aristocratic poetasters. Among the 'Children of the Sun' Aestheticism became a preeningly minor predilection.

It re-emerged, quite unexpectedly, but in its full strength, in the wake of the structuralist revolution of the 1960s, a resurgence marked quite clearly by a plethora of admiring references to Wilde himself, particularly in the essays of the American critic Susan Sontag. One of these, 'Against Interpretation' (1967), carries an epitaph from Wilde: 'It is only shallow people who do not judge by appearances. The mystery of the world is the visible, not the invisible' (p. 3). Another, the famous 'Notes on Camp', is actually dedicated to Wilde, while 'On Style' and 'One culture and the new sensibility' are clearly infused by his example. Sontag's essays are true statements of Aestheticism because, although she never resorts to dangerously abstract concepts of 'beauty', the priority of feeling is preserved in her emphasis upon sensuality. There has, though, been a modification of feeling which is no longer quasi-religious so much as sexual. Art loves the libido. In what was for the time a startling gesture Sontag actually asked for 'an erotics of art'. She did so because her enemy was no longer scientific method and calculation so much as 'interpretation', a form of aggression practised upon art by academic critics. 'Interpretation' is encouraged by the ineradicable heresy that art is content smothered by style. Sontag was drawn to those modes of 'enjoyment, of appreciation, not judgement' which accept the indivisibility of style and content – or sometimes even a surplus of style. Yet her essays are, like all critical statements, very much of their time, with an optimistic trust in the liberating power of sexuality, and an enthusiasm for the newer media of cinema, popular music, photography. Sontag's demand that criticism should be seen as multiple interpretation certainly looks a little faded in the light of deconstruction; her distinctions between art and pornography (art gratifies the desire it stimulates, pornography betrays its true nature by leading thoughts of the spectator away from the image – see Sontag, 1969), are distinctly shaky judged by current feminist criteria. The growth of feminism, along with the experience of the Vietnam war and the discovery of deconstruction, has taken American criticism far beyond the impulsive radicalism of the sixties, and Sontag has herself moved on to engage with Walter Benjamin and to write about modern critical discourse, with notable results. Nevertheless the aesthetic bedrock – art is more than a mere codified message – remains fundamental to her criticism.

A converse movement would at first seem to be present in the development of the French critic Sontag always revered, Roland Barthes, who in the 1970s set about booby-trapping his own career (and perhaps evading his too clinging disciples), with a number of works most remarkable for their old-fashioned commitment to the pleasures of art. And like Sontag he found sexual feelings to be the best analogy for aesthetic experience: Richard Howard's introduction to the English-language edition of *The Pleasure of the Text* (1976) refers to an 'erotics of art', surely a direct reference to Sontag. Barthes's later works present another characteristic of Aestheticism: its fondness for the disrupted text: for separated paragraphs, epigrams, aphorisms, for dialogues and masks rather than the tyranny of continuous, systematic, expository prose. Barthes uses the French word *jouissance* with its specific sexual meaning to identify the kind of feelings engendered by art. Pleasure originates in the sway of language. The paradox that deep meaning lies on the surface obviously takes us back to Wilde, but in Barthes's Saussurean terminology that thought becomes: 'what pleasure suspends is the *signified* value: the (good) cause.... That is the pleasure of the text: value shifted to the sumptuous rank of the signifier' (1976, p. 65). According to Barthes neither the left nor the right adequately respects this pleasure. The left rejects pleasure in favour of progressive knowledge, the right welcomes pleasure but denies it any intellectual power:

On both sides, this peculiar idea that pleasure is *simple*, which is why it is championed or disdained. Pleasure, however, is not an *element* of the text, it is not a naïve residue; it does not depend on a logic of understanding and on sensation; it is drift, something both revolutionary and asocial, and it cannot be taken over by any collectivity, any mentality, any ideolect. Something *neuter*? It is obvious that the pleasure of the text is scandalous: not because it is immoral but because it is *atopic*.

(p. 23)

'Atopic' means beyond discussion. Even in the post-structuralist 1990s Aestheticism remains what it has always been: a yearning for a realm beyond discourse – for a sweet silence born of burgeoning feelings – beyond ideology: for bliss. It is that above all which makes Aestheticism, as always, such a scandalous practice.

FURTHER READING

Beckson, Karl (1966) *Aesthetics and Decadents of the 1890s*, Random House, New York

Chamberlin, J. E. (1977) *Ripe was the Drowsy Hour*, Seabury Press, New York

Clements, Patricia (1985) *Baudelaire and the English Tradition*, Princeton University Press, Princeton

Dowling, Linda C. (1977) *Aestheticism and Decadence: A Selective Annotated Bibliography*, Garland Publishing, New York

——(1986) *Language and Decadence in the Victorian Fin-de-siècle*, Princeton University Press, Princeton

Ellmann, Richard (1987) *Oscar Wilde*, Hamish Hamilton, London

Fletcher, Ian (ed.) (1979) *Decadence and the 1890s*, (vol. 17 of *Stratford-upon-Avon Studies*), Edward Arnold, London

——(1987) *W. B. Yeats and His Contemporaries*, Harvester, Brighton

Gaunt, William (1975) *The Aesthetic Adventure*, Jonathan Cape, London [first published 1945]

Hunt, John Dixon (1968) *The Pre-Raphaelite Imagination 1848–1900*, Routledge & Kegan Paul, London

Johnson, R. W. (1969) *Aestheticism*, Methuen, London

Kermode, Frank (1957) *Romantic Image*, Routledge & Kegan Paul, London

Small, Ian (ed.) (1979) *The Aesthetes: A Sourcebook*, Routledge & Kegan Paul, London

Warner, Eric and Hough, Graham (eds) (1983) *Strangeness and Beauty: An Anthology of Aesthetic Criticism 1840–1910*, 2 vols, Cambridge University Press, Cambridge

ADDITIONAL WORKS CITED

Barthes, Roland (1976) *The Pleasure of the Text*, translated by Richard Miller, Cape, London

Ellmann, Richard (1970) *The Artist as Critic: Critical Writings of Oscar Wilde*, W. H. Allen, London

Goode, John (1971) 'William Morris and the Dream of Revolution'. In John Lucas (ed.), *Literature and Politics in the Nineteenth Century*, Methuen, London

Hart-Davis, Rupert (ed.) (1962) *The Letters of Oscar Wilde*, Hart-Davis, London

Pater, Walter (1896) *Gaston De Latour*, Macmillan, London

___(1980) *The Renaissance. Studies in Art and Poetry*, edited by Donald L. Hill, University of California Press, Berkeley and Los Angeles [first published 1873]

Sontag, Susan (1967) *Against Interpretation*, Eyre & Spottiswoode, London

___(1969) *Styles of Radical Will*, Secker & Warburg, London

Super, Robert H. (ed.) (1960–74) *The Complete Prose Works of Matthew Arnold*, 10 vols, University of Michigan Press, Ann Arbor

Swinburne, Algernon C. (1868) *William Blake*, John Camden Hotten, London

Thompson, E. P. (1977) *William Morris: Romantic to Revolutionary*, Merlin Press, London [first published 1955]

Uglow, Jennifer (ed.) (1973) *Walter Pater: Essays on Literature and Art*, Dent, London

Wilde, Oscar (1974) *The Picture of Dorian Gray*, edited by Isobel Murray, Oxford University Press, London [first published 1891]

Williams, Raymond (1976) *Keywords*, Fontana, Glasgow

79

LITERATURE AND SCIENCE

N. KATHERINE HAYLES

Unlike many of the topics in this volume, literature and science is not a self-evident category for literary study. Its obvious constructedness calls out for explanation – a call that is both a curse and a blessing. On the one hand, scholars who work in literature and science feel obliged to explain what literature and science 'is', a venture that has led to many fruitless discussions of what science is, what literature is and what the the two together signify. On the other hand, precisely because it cannot take the constitution of its subject for granted, literature and science is (or should be) keenly aware of the material and cultural conditions that have led to its existence as an emerging subdiscipline. Rather than defining the field through essentialist definitions of literature and science, I prefer to regard its history as a barometer registering shifts in the culture's views of disciplinary inquiry, and indeed of the organization and constitution of knowledge in general.

Literature and science are not correlative terms. The creation and interpretation of literary texts takes place in many languages, forms, cultures and periods; nevertheless, all literary texts and theories share a concern with written language. Science, by contrast, is divided into fields so diverse it is difficult to think of any common factors they share. If the signifier 'science' did not exist, who would think to connect activities as different as calibrating telescopes and studying dripping taps, correlating stock market data and observing the mating behaviours of silver gorillas? The scientific method, once considered the common glue sticking all the sciences together, has been dissolved by the new philosophy of science into conflicting methodologies or, as Paul Feyerabend would have it in *Against Method* (1975), no method at all. How did literature and science come to be cojoined, if they are not a self-evident category and moreover not of equal weight and homogeneity?

The origin of the 'two cultures' formulation antedated C. P. Snow by more than a century. His reinscription of it in the Cambridge Rede Lecture in 1959 testifies to how enduring are the institutional patterns that make yoking the two a necessary or thinkable thought (Snow, 1969). In Snow's conception, literature stood not just for literary studies, but for an educational philosophy that believed truth could be found by introspection guided by logical reasoning and informed by wide cultural knowledge. Literature rather than, say, philosophy was the marker for this belief because during the nineteenth century in European and American higher education, literature and language formed the basis for college curricula in liberal studies. Science was the necessary other, standing for the opposite philosophy that truth could best be found by empirical investigation of narrowly defined questions about measurable phenomena. Literature and science as a category was thus constituted as and through a debate about whether university education should be based upon scientific specialization or upon a broadly conceived liberal arts curriculum. In this sense literature and science is the secular equivalent of religion and science, with its battleground located within academe rather than within cathedral and laboratory.

The outcome of the historic debate between religion and science is too well known to need rehearsing here. Once religion had been constituted as the opposite of science, it was virtually inevitable that the hegemonic power of science would continue to grow. The constitution of literature and science had a different outcome, because it arrived at a moment when post-structuralist critiques were making it possible to understand how such constructions work. Snow's argument exemplifies what Derrida in *Of Grammatology* has identified as the structure of supplementarity (1976, pp. 141–64). Consider how it proceeds. Snow observes that the scientists he knows live in a culture very different from literary scholars of his acquaintance. Almost immediately, these differences are ranked hierarchically. Literary folk are quick to dismiss scientists as philistines, Snow says, but in fact they are much more illiterate about science than scientists are about literature. The argument sets up a dichotomy between literature and science, privileges science over literature, then suggests that literary people need to know more about science. The immediate implication is that science rather than literature should form the core of college curriculums.

More fundamental is the presupposition that science possesses an originary status that places it closer to truth than does the supplementary nature of literature. Scientists read the book of nature; literary scholars read books about nature. Science comes first and is complete in itself; literature comes after and is supplementary to the truth of scientific discoveries. When F. R. Leavis (1962) attacked Snow, he denied the validity of Snow's generalizations about scientists and literary scholars, calling them an intellectual embarrassment. But because he remained within the circle of assumptions Snow set up, his response did not have the constitutive force of Snow's formulation. Only when the presuppositions that made literature into science's supplement are challenged is it possible to articulate different kinds of questions, for example what it implies to construct a debate about education in this dichotomous way.

Snow's 'two cultures' concept has remained the touchstone for literature and science not because it was profound, but because it was (and still is) representative of a way of thinking. It set the terms of debate by constructing a series of oppositions in which literature is defined as what science is not. Science is objective, literature is subjective; science is quantitative, literature qualitative; science is concerned with truths about the physical world, literature with human values. The progress of literature and science as a field can be charted by tracking the extent to which its discourse has remained within or broken free from the area inscribed by these polarities.

The essential realization is to see that in 'two cultures' constructions, literature functions as a repository for the attributes that one wants to deny to science. If literature is taken out of the equation, it becomes much more difficult to claim that science is not qualitative as well as quantitative, subjective and objective, concerned with truth and infused with values. In fact it is difficult to arrive at any construction of science at all, for without its constitutive difference from literature, 'science' is apt to degenerate into a catalogue that rivals Borges's fabled Chinese encyclopaedia in the vertiginous heterogeneity of its categories (1981, pp. 141–2). Positing literature as the supplement of science made science into a more unified signifier than it otherwise could have been. Perhaps this explains why, when the critique of positivistic science was already well under way within the philosophy and history of science, literature and science continued the quest for essentialist definitions of science.

In the early days of the field, literature was accepted as unproblematically different from science. If this difference also meant that literature was derivatory whereas science was originary, no one seemed to notice. Typical of this period were Marjorie Hope Nicolson's studies from the 1940s–1960s analysing the influence of scientific theories and inventions upon literature (see Nicolson, 1950, 1976). As Nicolson construed it, influence always flowed one way – from literature to science. In less careful hands than hers, the presupposition that science was the source of truth to which literature responded led to readings of literary texts in which authors who departed from their putative scientific sources were seen as ill-informed, scientifically illiterate, or just plain wrong. These early influence studies did not ask *why* a writer found a scientific theory or discovery compelling. Had they done so, they might have realized that to explain why a writer was influenced by one theory over others, it was necessary to suppose that he or she had already been sensitized to the issue by previous experiences, which in turn required reference to still earlier ones ... These studies also did not ask about connections between scientific theories and cultural formations. Rather, science's power to influence literature was implicitly understood to derive from the truth of the scientific theories under discussion.

For several years after Thomas Kuhn rewrote the history of science (1962), influence studies continued to dominate literature and science. It was not until 1978, when George Rousseau's review article 'Literature and Science: The State of the Field' appeared in *Isis*, that problems associated with influence models were clearly identified. Even then it was by no means obvious what should take their place. Rousseau argued for the potential importance of structuralist criticism for literature and science, but at the same time he also suggested that literature and science needed a theory of its own. There followed a series of sessions organized by Rousseau at the Modern Language Association Convention on 'Is a Theory of Literature and Science Possible?' The phrasing was unfortunate, for it led to papers that debated the difference between literature and science in terms with which Snow would have felt entirely comfortable, while ignoring the deeper implications of positing literature and science as a binary construction. Gradually, however, as the work of such important post-structuralist theorists as Foucault and Derrida became better known, the ground shifted.

A convenient date marking this shift is October 1987, when the first full-scale convention of the recently formed Society for Literature and Science was held. As a group, the conference papers were characterized by their tendency to construct the sciences as cultural and discursive practices rather than as sources of truth. With science a pluralistic enterprise rather than a monolithic given, the copula linking literature and science no longer signified supplementarity. Instead there emerged three distinct approaches for connecting literature and science. In the first approach, the connecting link is rhetoric; in the second, conceptual structures; in the third, cultural institutions. Of course rhetoric, concept and culture are interdependent, so that in practice the three approaches blend. Nevertheless, for the purposes of this discussion it is useful to distinguish between them, for each has advantages and limitations that collectively pose the major challenges that literature and science as a field will face in the coming years.

LITERATURE AND SCIENCE AS RHETORIC

The rhetorical approach comes closest to being the heir of traditional influence studies, but its premises differ significantly from its predecessor. Its range and power is exemplified in Gillian Beer's *Darwin's Plots* (1983), a fine study of Darwin's rhetoric and its influence on Victorian literature. Beer's work differs from earlier influence studies in her awareness that Darwin was a part of his culture, as much influenced by literature and other narrative forms as influencing it. Beer is at her best when demonstrating how metaphor works as a conduit for multidirectional flows between a writer and his culture. She points out that a metaphor implies both similarity and difference. Tracing the play between congruence and divergence in Darwin's metaphors, she reveals their extraordinary richness as they sometimes open new possibilities through subterranean connections, and sometimes occlude them through constraints imposed by analogical reasoning.

Beer's sensitivity to metaphoric play is amply demonstrated in her discussion of the perceived 'three blows' to an anthropocentric universe – Copernicus, Darwin, Freud (pp. 12–16). She observes that three is a magic number, suggesting closure. In this series Darwin is bracketed, the second brother who has neither the honour of being first nor the finality of being last. Her project is to extract Darwin's work from the brackets that enclose it, unfolding through Darwin's central metaphors a vision of plenitude, lateral growth, diversity. It is no accident that her own metaphors consistently image the liberation of Darwin from interpretative bonds. On one level, these images of liberation make plausible the analogy between Darwin's work and the exfoliating plots of such entangled novels as *Middlemarch* and *Daniel Deronda*. On a deeper level, the complex nuances that she locates in Darwin's language make him into a writer at least as interesting as the literary authors she discusses. In Beer's hands, Darwin *becomes* literature.

Consider, for example, her treatment of facticity in Darwin. She suggests that fact for Darwin did not have the flat-footedness it has in 'Just the facts, ma'am'. Rather it had an aura of being at once mysterious and actual, like the Heideggerian *Dasein*. In liberating facts from their putative opposite, imagination, Beer also deconstructs the literature/science dichotomy. There is no substantive difference between how she reads Darwin's texts and how she reads literary texts. In her interpretation, Darwin's scientific treatises and Victorian realistic novels both seek a balance between a rich diversity of precisely observed detail, valued for its actuality and refractory resistance to universal truths, and analogical patterns that correlate details into larger wholes without repressing their individual differences. In fact this is also Beer's project for literature and science, as she weaves between the details that support her readings and the analytical patterns that are the mark of Darwin's influence upon literature and of its influence upon him. Her analysis of how metaphor works in Darwin and Victorian fiction thus becomes a kind of meta-metaphor for her own text.

The limitations of this method are of a piece with its strengths. The capaciousness of Beer's writing is bound up with her desire to demonstrate the openness of Darwin's rhetoric, the fullness of vision and expression that it enables. Her meta-metaphor bespeaks plenitude, diversity, possibility. But just as metaphors can also restrict possibilities, so Beer's meta-metaphor keeps her from fully acknowledging moments when Darwin's metaphors function to induce blindness rather than insight, as they frequently do when they refer to race and gender. At such moments, for example in Darwin's discussion of sexual selection in the *Origin of Species*, Beer's analysis often fails to grapple with the ideological issues at stake. Similarly, her analysis of Darwin's language moves easily into concept – as long as the concepts are consistent with her vision of Darwin's language. These limitations imply that the rhetorical figure which functions as a meta-metaphor determines, at least in part, the rhetoric that will be found to be characteristic of the subject texts. Of course the meta-metaphor is presumably not chosen randomly but because it reflects metaphors that appear frequently in the subject text. Nevertheless the implication remains that rhetorical analysis, like the language it analyses, constitutes its objects even as it describes them.

Other limitations appear in Beer's assumptions about culture. She emphasizes that Darwin wrote not just for other scientists but for a general educated public. Moreover, she limits her analysis to literary authors who are known to have read Darwin. She acknowledges that in a sense all educated Victorians read Darwin, whether or not they ever picked up a book Darwin wrote. But it is important to her argument to demonstrate direct influence because she is concerned with the specific and complex ways rhetorical figures work within the context of Darwin's language. For Beer the experience of actually reading Darwin is crucial, for only so is the reader marked by the resistances, subversions and ambivalences embodied in the polysemous play of the text. More than presenting this argument, she enacts it. Moving easily between Darwin's texts and literary works, informed by wide reading and broad cultural knowledge, she creates a voice that embodies the generally educated reader she posits as the connecting link between literature and science.

The area delineated by Beer's assumptions is brilliantly lit. It is also narrow in circumference. As she practises it, the rhetorical method requires a homogeneous culture, a scientist-writer who uses the language of that culture rather than specialized discourse, and literary authors who are known to have read the scientific text in question. One could argue whether all these conditions (especially a homogeneous culture) are met for Darwin and his contemporaries. Certainly they have not generally obtained in the twentieth century. Henry Adams, welcoming and shrinking from the new century in *The Education of Henry Adams* (1914), may have been the last major literary author to assume that he could read and comprehend the scientific treatises of his day. If the rhetorical method were limited to these assumptions, it would have little or nothing to say about most of modern science and literature.

Other practitioners of the rhetorical method have pushed against these limits by broadening the sense of rhetoric. Donald McCloskey in *The Rhetoric of Economics* (1985) has demonstrated that statistical arguments have rhetorical components and can be persuasively analysed from a rhetorical viewpoint. Similarly, Charles Stoltzenburg (1978) has argued that mathematical theorems are underlaid by unrecognized assumptions shaped by language use. Calling these assumptions 'acts of acceptance of language as such', Stolzenburg suggests that mathematics is not an objective symbol system but a culturally determined code with deep linguistic roots. From these broadened perspectives, it is not necessary to assume that a writer has actually read a scientific text for there to be deep parallels between a scientific and a literary work, for the immersion of scientist and writer in the common language of the culture is sufficient to establish rhetorical parallels between them. Of course this kind of work imposes its own limitations, for one must be expert in the scientific languages and conventions to argue persuasively for their rhetorical content. Nevertheless, the suggestion that scientific symbol systems are always already linguistic opens promising new territories for the rhetorical approach. As scientific discourses are increasingly understood to be themselves forms of rhetoric, the scope and potential of this approach should continue to increase.

LITERATURE AND SCIENCE AS CONCEPT

In the conceptual approach, literature and science are linked through ideas or perspectives they share. Whereas the rhetorical approach is the heir of influence models, the conceptual approach is the descendant of *Zeitgeist* models. World-view arguments have been attacked in recent years for their broad generalizations and unconcern with material conditions, as well as for their implicit collaboration with repressive ideologies. As 'human nature' is increasingly understood not as fact but as ideological construction, assertions that posit culture as a uniform belief system have come under suspicion for being not merely unsound but pernicious as well. In the work of Michel Serres the defects of traditional *Zeitgeist* arguments are not so much corrected as exaggerated until they become (as Samuel Johnson observed of *Cymbeline*) faults too gross for detection. Yet the exaggeration is also paradoxically a refinement, for it is achieved by a paratactic style that allows rifts and discontinuities to emerge, conveying a more complex vision of the relation between literature and science than traditional conceptual approaches allow.

The mercurial essays in the *Hermes* volumes demonstrate how Serres's paratactic style works. In 'Turner Translates Carnot', Serres juxtaposes Turner's artistic vision with Carnot's discovery that the amount of heat exchanged between two heat reservoirs depends only on the initial and final temperatures, not on the heat transfer path (1982, pp. 54–64). Carnot's theorem made it possible to formulate general thermodynamic laws and led to the rapid development of steam engines. Turner saw in the steam engine the creation of a force radically different from that conveyed by mechanical devices such as levers and pulleys. Serres argues that in his paintings, Turner sought to convey the essence of this new force. Driven by fire and water, the steam engine was for Turner as paradoxical as it was powerful, manifesting itself as flux rather than as levered forces operating upon stable objects. Typically, Serres does not seek to establish a direct line of influence between Turner and Carnot, for example by demonstrating that the painter had read the scientist or had heard of his work. Rather his essay juxtaposes a warehouse sign depicting mechanical forces with Turner's paintings, suggesting by implication that Carnot's discovery intervened to move the style from A to B. In this respect Serres's writing itself resembles Carnot's theorem, for it implies that the important result is the difference between the initial and final states, independent of the particular path traced between them.

The correspondence is not accidental. Serres's work is deeply informed by paradigms that emerged from the confluence of thermodynamics with information theory, which he interprets as a shift from stasis to flow, from linear order to turbulent chaos. This conceptual shift is re-enacted in his writing, constructed to resemble turbulent flows rather than linear sequences. Evidence is not so much presented as swept along by the flow of the language, with facts bobbing up here and there in apparently random patterns that nevertheless cohere into larger swirls of meaning. From these swirls two different kinds of projects emerge. In the first Serres returns to originary moments in the Western tradition to understand why reality should have been identified with ideal forms rather than empirical variations. In the second he traces a new trajectory for Western culture now that these hierarchies are being reversed, with noise considered more innovative than information, empirical variations more real than ideal forms, chaos more fecund than order.

One way to make this argument would be to say that a shift in world view had taken place within some time period – for turbulent flow, say from 1960 on – and to claim that literature and science of the period were both affected by the shift. This is not Serres's strategy. He rather implies that there were numerous historical sites where battles between stasis and flow were fought, and that the literature and science of many periods bear the marks of tactical victories or defeats. For example he reads Lucretius' poem *De rerum natura* as a profound treatise on physical reality, verified by Ilya Prigogine's Nobel Prize-winning work on irreversible thermodynamics in the 1960s and 1970s (Serres, 1982a, 'Lucretius: Science and Religion', pp. 98–125). Molière's *Dom Juan* is read as juxtaposing an economy based on goods with an economy based on noise, and hence as an exploration into the implications of contemporary information theory (Serres, 1982a, '*Dom Juan*: The Apparition of Hermes', pp. 3–14). La Fontaine's fables illustrate how the eruption of a 'third man' into a dialogue can either threaten the stability of a system or raise it to a higher level of complexity, a result consistent with theories of self-organizing systems that date from the 1960s (Serres, 1982b, *The Parasite*). History thus becomes a kind of alphabet soup in turbulent motion, with letters randomly thrown up against one another in momentary configurations that soon dissolve and give way to different patterns.

In my view Serres is more successful when he returns to such originary sites as the founding of geometry and the forging of the dialectical method to understand why Western culture evolved as it did. Here his paratactic style works upon a historical record that is fragmentary. Often all that remains are the starting and final points, with little or no indication of the actual paths taken to decide the issues, so that Serres's speculative style works with rather than against historical evidence. Moreover, at these moments fundamental concepts like the law of the excluded middle were hotly debated issues rather than truisms. Serres's paratactic style animates these issues, conveying a sense of crisis and of order precariously achieved. As the apparent seamlessness of classical concepts yields to the torque put on them by Serres's writing, fault lines and rifts are exposed, revealing them as complex historical constructions rather than as factual givens.

By contrast, when Serres proclaims the triumph of flow over stasis by juxtaposing Lucretius with Prigogine, La Fontaine with Claude Shannon, Molière with information theory, his argument presupposes that the contemporary scientific theories he espouses are in harmony with his paratactic style. But the disciplines from which these results come remain committed to rational argument, linear sequence, causal connection and formulaic writing. Serres's allegiance to the new paradigms leads him to treat the scientific theories as if they were the same as his arguments, and to treat his arguments as if they were a re-presentation of the scientific results. However, I doubt that the scientists Serres cites would endorse his conclusions, for his appropriation of their work goes far beyond what the scientific evidence would support. Indeed, in some cases it goes against the evidence. Thus the very parataxis that allows Serres to open up classical concepts also works to conflate contemporary scientific discourse with his speculative style, obscuring or repressing the very substantial differences between them.

At nearly every conference on literature and science I attend, I hear papers that do what Serres does, only not as iconoclastically or brilliantly. Typical titles are 'Alexander Pope and Relativity Theory' or '*Tristram Shandy* and the Heisenberg Uncertainty Principle'. These papers are beset with problems that are rarely recognized, and even more rarely addressed. An important issue is what differences are suppressed to make the correspondences appear. Very often the discursive modes being compared are so different in audience, rules of argument, legitimation criteria and discovery procedures that the disparities amount to a difference in content, even if the ideas sound the same when they are summarized out of context. Another important issue is what the alleged correspondences signify. Do they reveal something about the creative process that transcends history, culture and discipline? Do they uncover underground currents of thought that surfaced sporadically in different times and writers? Or do they simply confirm that there is nothing new under the sun? Among the challenges that the conceptual approach faces is to articulate much more precisely and thoughtfully than has been done in the past the implications of extracting ideas from their discursive contexts, and to clarify the significance it claims for the correspondences it detects.

Despite these problems, the conceptual approach remains perhaps the most popular way to link literature and science. Why? Because of the fragmentation of knowledge that it seeks to overcome. The power of the conceptual approach lies in its ability to reveal similarities between theories and practices that appear on the surface to have little or nothing to do with one another. The correspondences it uncovers are compelling because on some level we believe that the divisions between disciplines which so deeply affect material practices and discursive traditions remain marks on maps. We continue to dream of a territory toward which these maps gesture, indivisible and fully present to itself.

LITERATURE AND SCIENCE AS CULTURE

In the cultural approach, literature and science are understood to produce and be produced by cultural formations. Whereas the conceptual approach puts an apple and an orange side by side to show how they are alike, the cultural approach shows how two oranges are different. More interested in fault lines than convergences, it is committed to a relativist reading of science, interpreting differences between scientific theories as ideological issues rather than as competing truth claims. Similarly, literature ceases to have the special status granted to it by literariness and becomes one kind of cultural document among many.

The strengths of the cultural approach are displayed in Mary Poovey's article ' "Scenes of an Indelicate Character": The Medical "Treatment" of Victorian Women' (1986). The article centres on a debate within the British medical community from 1846 to 1856 about the relative merits of chloroform and ether as the anaesthesia of choice during childbirth. One of the concerns about ether (and to a lesser extent chloroform) was that women who were anaesthesized by it moved and uttered sounds which were interpreted by male doctors as meaning that the women were sexually excited, perhaps even experiencing orgasm on the operating table. Poovey argues that the body of the silenced woman functioned as a blank text on to which medical practitioners projected their fears and anxieties. Silenced and alienated from her own voice, the woman's body became contested ground for representation. The different claims made for it reveal the play of power within the medical community, as medical consultants (the élite group who controlled the Royal College of Physicians) struggled to maintain their hegemony against general practitioners who engaged in obstetrics, and both groups united against female midwives. In each case the representation of woman's body served to consolidate control for the group representing it; at stake was the increasingly lucrative practice associated with medical intervention in the birth process.

Although Poovey does not discuss literature as such in this article, her representation of woman's body as a text implicitly puts literary texts on an equal footing with material practices and scientific claims about physical reality. All are staged within the theatre of representation; all are subject to interpretative acts of reading, writing and re-vision. Poovey's re-visioning stresses that the multivocality of the silenced female body is potentially liberating, for it always already contains an excess of meaning that eludes control even as it is taken to demonstrate the need for control. Identifying fault lines in dominant ideologies is for Poovey a way to defeat hegemony, to reveal and activate possibilities for resistance. Her methodology is like Beer's, in that it grants literariness to documents not usually considered literature. It differs from Beer's approach in not being particularly interested in language as such. Cultural practices become like literature not because they are linguistic, but because they are representational.

Poovey takes care to point out that truth claims are irrelevant to the medical literature she discusses, since virtually none of it would pass muster by contemporary standards. This begs the question of whether scientific debates based on research that *would* qualify as 'good science' are equally susceptible to cultural interpretation. Donna Haraway (1978) would answer emphatically 'yes', arguing in her studies of primatology that cultural assumptions permeate scientific inquiry at every level, shaping scientific hypotheses, determining research designs and dictating the interpretation of results. The emerging field known as the sociology of science, associated with the work of H. M. Collins, Barry Barnes and others would also answer affirmatively, although for different reasons (Collins, 1985; Barnes, 1985; Knorr-Cetina and Mulkay, 1983). Dealing with the complex questions raised by these challenges to scientific objectivity is beyond the scope of my purpose here. However, in my view it is undeniable that the sciences *are* cultural and material practices. The interesting question is whether the rules under which these practices are conducted also lend validity to their truth claims.

In one sense, the cultural approach to literature and science has been catalysed by the social study of science. In another sense, it has been disabled by it. It is significant that few of the writers identified with the cultural approach concentrate specifically on literature. Indeed there is no reason why they should, for with literature and science both regarded as cultural practices, there is no more compelling rationale to link these two disciplines than to connect any other two points in the cultural matrix. When a writer like Poovey does connect them, it is often for obvious institutional reasons; Poovey is trained in literature and continues to be based in an English department. The irony is that in eradicating the distinctions between literature and science, the cultural approach also removes the necessity for a field called literature and science. Since the cultural approach is rapidly gaining adherents in the field, it is worthwhile thinking about what this portends for literature and science as a subdiscipline. Conceivably, literature and science could be an interim category marking the transition from the scientism of the first part of the century to the cultural and ideological approaches that dominate the intellectual terrain of academia as the century draws to a close. This line of thought suggests that the disciplinary barriers literature and science has dedicated itself to overcome may in fact be necessary for its existence. The situation becomes even more complicated as literature and science begins to be institutionalized, for it then in effect operates as a discipline, even as it presupposes the necessity to cross disciplinary lines. Although it is too soon to say how these issues will be worked out, their effects have not been negative. Literature and science may be more turbulent and perhaps precarious than ever before; but it is also more vital and interesting.

POSSIBILITIES FOR SYNTHESIS: INCLUSIONS AND EXCLUSIONS

As indicated above, the rhetorical, conceptual and cultural approaches, have distinctive strengths and limitations. The heightened perception in each approach of a certain kind of connection between literature and science is achieved not in spite of but because of its limitations. The approaches act like polarized lenses that filter out some frequencies while sharpening others. Patterns created by these polarizations are summarized in the table below. In practice many scholars working in literature and science combine approaches, so that the schema presented in the table rarely apply exactly. Nevertheless, the patterns suggest that whereas a secondary emphasis allowing partial integration of two approaches is entirely possible, an exclusion principle operates to retard or prohibit a synthesis that would fully integrate all three approaches. If one adopts a perspective that represents literature and science as rhetoric, language is emphasized and the importance of material practices is played down. Similarly, if one focuses on material practices, cultural institutions and ideologies are foregrounded, but the conceptual coherence of a succession of developments is obscured. If one concentrates on conceptual problems, the different discursive modes within which ideas are expressed tend to diminish in importance or disappear altogether.

Table: Summary of the Three Approaches

	Rhetoric	*Concept*	*Culture*
Exemplar	Beer	Serres	Poovey
Orientation	language	idea	ideology
Style	metaphoric	paratactic	archaeological
Mode	lyric	metaphysical	detective
Primary metaphor	exfoliation	vortex	fault lines
Movement	opening out	swirling around	going deeper
Scientific change	continuous	revolutionary	political
Secondary emphasis	concept	culture	rhetoric
Suppressed element	culture	rhetoric	concept
Locus for controversy	diversity	traditions	truth claims

Are these limitations inherent, or do they merely reflect the shape of the field as it has evolved? I believe it can be demonstrated that they are the result of the historical evolution of disciplinary knowledge. If that evolution had been different, the focuses which determine what will be included and what excluded would change. Regardless of which patterns evolved, however, some exclusion is inescapable. One must always have a standpoint from which to observe, and this standpoint limits even as it enables. Although literature and science thus has limits within itself, it also points to the more fundamental limits of disciplinary knowledge. This is perhaps a contribution as important as the discoveries that its interdisciplinary approaches enable.

FURTHER READING

Anderson, W. C. (1984) *Between the Library and the Laboratory: The Language of Chemistry in Eighteenth-Century France*, Johns Hopkins University Press, Baltimore

Beer, Gillian (1983) *Darwin's Plots: Evolutionary Narrative in Darwin, George Eliot and Nineteenth Century Fiction*, Methuen, London

Hayles, N. Katherine (1984) *The Cosmic Web: Literary Strategies and Scientific Field Models in the Twentieth Century*, Cornell University Press, Ithaca

Jordanova, Ludmilla (1986) *Languages of Nature: Critical Essays on Literature and Science*, Rutgers University Press, New Brunswick

Levine, George (1987) *One Culture: Essays on Literature and Science*, Wisconsin University Press, Madison

Nicolson, Marjorie Hope (1976) *Science and Imagination*, Great Seal, Ithaca

Paulson, W. (1988) *The Noise of Culture: Literary Texts in a World of Information*, Cornell University Press, Ithaca

Poovey, Mary (1986) ' "Scenes of an Indelicate Character": The Medical "Treatment" of Victorian Women', *Representations*, 14, 137–68

Rousseau, George (1978) 'Literature and Science: The State of the Field', *Isis*, 69, 583–91

Serres, Michel (1982a) *Hermes: Literature, Science, Philosophy*, edited by J. V. Harari and D. F. Bell, Johns Hopkins University Press, Baltimore

Snow, C. P. (1969) *The Two Cultures: and a Second Look*, Cambridge University Press, Cambridge

Vickers, Brian (ed.) (1984) *Occult and Scientific Mentalities in the Renaissance*, Cambridge University Press, Cambridge

ADDITIONAL WORKS CITED

Barnes, Barry (1985) *About Science*, Blackwell, Oxford

Borges, Jorge Luis (1981) 'The Analytical Language of John Wilkins'. In E. R. Monegal and A. Reid (eds), *Borges: A Reader*, E. P. Dutton, New York, pp. 141–2

Collins, H. M. (1985) *Changing Order: Replication and Induction in Scientific Practice*, Sage, London

Derrida, Jacques (1976) *Of Grammatology*, translated by G. C. Spivak, Johns Hopkins University Press, Baltimore [first published 1967]

Haraway, Donna (1978) 'Animal Sociology and a Natural Economy of the Body Politic, Parts I and II', *Signs*, 4, 20–36

Feyerabend, Paul (1975) *Against Method*, Verso, London

Knorr-Cetina, Karin D. and Mulkay, Michael (eds) (1983) *Science Observed: Perspectives on the Social Study of Science*, Sage, London

Kuhn, Thomas S. (1962) *The Structure of Scientific Revolutions*, University of Chicago Press, Chicago

Leavis, F. R. (1962) *Two Cultures?: The Significance of C. P. Snow*, Chatto & Windus, London

McCloskey, Donald N. (1985) *The Rhetoric of Economics*, University of Wisconsin Press, Madison

Nicolson, Marjorie Hope (1950) *The Breaking of the Circle: Studies of the Effect of the 'New Science' on Seventeenth-Century Poetry*, Northwestern University Press, Evanston

Serres, Michel (1982b) *The Parasite*, translated by L. R. Schehr, Johns Hopkins University Press, Baltimore [first published 1980]

Stoltzenburg, Charles (1978) 'Can an inquiry into the foundations of mathematics tell us anything interesting about mind?' In G. A. Miller and E. Lennenburg (eds), *Psychology and Biology of Language and Thought: Essays in Honor of Eric Lennenberg*, Academic Press, New York

80

LITERATURE AND LANGUAGE

MICK SHORT

INTRODUCTION

In 1967–8 a rather unedifying, but at times humorous debate between the linguist Roger Fowler and the critic F. W. Bateson took place in the pages of *Essays in Criticism* (the exchange is reproduced in full in Fowler, 1971). The debate concerned whether or not linguistics could be of use to the literary critic. Fowler suggested various ways in which the linguist might be of help, and Bateson systematically rejected his overtures. The high point (low point?) of the *debate* occurred when Bateson stated his objections to what he called 'the mating of the language of description [linguistics] and the language of evaluation [literary criticism]'. In some exasperation, Fowler accused Bateson of resorting to a 'kind of sexual-xenophobic insult' which he then characterized by the sentence: 'Linguists have their good points – but would you let your sister marry one?' Bateson, in turn, pretended that this question was directed at him in particular, and answered it with 'and I suppose, if I am honest, I must admit that I would much prefer *not* to have a linguist in the family'. Much linguistic/critical sludge has moved under the literary bridge since Fowler and Bateson's territorial dispute, and as the amount of linguistic criticism grows, more critics and students are coming to see its value. A majority, however, still remain to be convinced of its worth. In this essay I will briefly address some general issues in the debate, provide a brief history of stylistic analysis and provide analyses from each of the three major literary genres as a partial exemplification of the approach.

GENERAL MATTERS

It is self-evident that literature is written in language and so, in order to discuss literary texts and our understanding of them, we must concentrate on the language of those texts, at least to some extent. The real issue is 'to what extent?' First, we can notice that there are two other heavyweight contenders in the competition for the 'Object of Criticism' crown, the author and the reader. Different schools of criticism have emphasized one or other of these three elements. Intentionalist and reader-response theories have concentrated on the author and reader respectively, whilst Formalism and New Criticism have emphasized the text itself. My preference for a concentration on the linguistic properties of texts is largely motivated by the wish for literary criticism to be a well-founded and coherent discipline.

A criticism which concentrates on authors and their intentions cannot be coherent unless it restricts itself unreasonably, if only because many texts which we want to examine have been written by anonymous authors or those long dead. Concentration on individual reader responses, on the other hand, leads to critical incoherence because two different readers never respond to a literary work in exactly the same way, precisely because they are different people with different histories of experience. If every engagement with a text produces different results there would appear to be no point in arguing over whether one interpretation is more valid than another, let alone trying to establish ground rules for reasonable argumentative behaviour within the sphere of criticism. The language of the text is the only candidate for 'critical object' status which is both common to all literary works and is invariant enough to allow shared investigation by more than one person. For reasons of space, this argument is extremely truncated, but I believe it in general terms to be correct.

The second aspect of the 'to what extent?' question has to do with how detailed and rigorous the examination of the language of a text needs to be. For many critics, it is enough to show that the text says what they think it says by quoting it. Intuition and the act of reading does the rest. So, if I tell you that the following newspaper headline is a joke because it is ambiguous, you only have to read it carefully to see the point:

PUBLIC BORROWING DOWN

For critics like myself, this 'pointing' strategy, with its reliance on intuitive agreement, would not be sufficient because we would also want to demonstrate *how* it becomes ambiguous. This criterion can be met by providing two alternative analyses of the grammar and vocabulary of the headline. We can understand it to mean 'public borrowing is down', in which case *public borrowing* is a noun phrase acting as subject to the 'understood' *be* verb, and *down* is a directional adverb, the whole sentence being an example of a dead metaphor. The alternative understanding can be characterized as 'public are borrowing down', in which case *public* is the subject, *borrowing* is the main verb, and *down* is its object, and refers to the soft feathers of birds. The ambiguity comes about because of the truncated syntax typical of newspaper headlines, and, given the right contextual circumstances, the reader will probably not even notice the ambiguity.

I have considered this rather trivial example at some length, because the issue behind it is one of the most important in the debate over whether or not the linguistic study of literature (usually called stylistics, or sometimes linguistic criticism) has a rightful place in literary studies. I believe that two of the most important academic questions to be addressed in the study of literature are why and how particular meanings and effects are present in particular literary works. And I cannot see how such questions can be answered without recourse to detailed linguistic analysis. The 'how' and the 'why' are important because:

1. as critics we are duty bound to give detailed support for our interpretative conclusions;
2. we need a way of checking whether the understandings we intuitively arrive at are reasonable, and careful stylistic analysis provides a large part of what is required for such a check;
3. if we are faced with someone who does not see our interpretation or who disagrees with it, we need some way, other than merely 'pointing', to help demonstrate that meaning or effect.

I do *not* believe, by any means, that this linguistic-critical activity is the only one critics should be engaged in. Far from it. But I do believe that the detailed answering of 'why?' and 'how?' cannot be ignored by critics and that recourse to careful linguistic description linked to interpretation provides much (but not all) of what is required.

The point may be made clearer by a diagram showing what I would consider to be the the essential core of critical activity:

Evaluation

↑

Interpretation

↑

Description of textual structure

Critics usually say that the prime objective of their enterprise is the evaluation of literary works. This evaluative activity presupposes interpretation, as it makes no sense to say how good a text is unless one understands it. In criticism, intuitive understanding has to be made explicit in the form of an interpretation. However, textual interpretation itself presupposes reaction to the structure of the text. This structure turns out to be largely, but not entirely (cf. plot), linguistic, as the discussion of the headline example above shows. In spite of the fact that evaluation is the goal of criticism, most of the effort in twentieth-century literary studies has been directed at interpretative matters. Stylistics has a slightly different focus in that it is centrally interested in making explicit the detailed relationship between textual structure and interpretation, and how the reader gets from the former to the latter. If criticism is to be a well-founded discipline, this explicit demonstration of the grounds for interpretation is as important as the need to state clearly the interpretations themselves.

A BRIEF HISTORY OF STYLISTICS

Stylistics as a discipline within Anglo-American literary studies is convention-ally assumed to have begun in 1966 with the publication of *Essays on Style and Language*, edited by Roger Fowler. It can be seen as a logical extension of New Criticism, with its emphasis on the text, but it was also a reaction against that school in the sense that stylistics demands a much more detailed and systematic treatment of the language of texts. However, early stylistics gained much of its impetus and insight from Russian Formalism and Czech Structural-ism. These movements in Eastern Europe early in this century had already achieved significant results in the linguistic analysis of poetry in particular, but their work only became known in the West in the 1960s.

Most of the early work in stylistics was on poetry because (1) short texts were most amenable to the detailed treatment demanded, (2) the formalist and structuralist work on poetry was relatively easy to build on, and (3) the emphasis in linguistics at that time was on phonetic and grammatical structure, the results of which were relatively easy to apply to poetry. Given its emphasis on the language of the text, it is hardly surprising that early stylistics was formalist in orientation, and this label, in spite of later reader-oriented developments, is unfortunately still applied to the discipline by those outside it.

Stylistics is obviously dependent to a large extent on work in linguistics, and the wish to develop techniques applicable to the novel in the late 1970s and early 1980s happily coincided with a growing interest on the part of linguists in textual, as opposed to sentential, structure. Work on the novel is now well established, and currently publications on drama, which had been largely neglected, are appearing at a growing rate (see Carter and Simpson, 1989). The present interest in drama is enabled by the development over the last ten years of linguistic techniques to cope with the analysis of conversational interaction. The two main areas of interest are discourse analysis, which deals predominantly with the structure of spoken discourse and relations between speakers and hearers, and pragmatics, which explores the mechanisms by which language is interpreted in context. This latter area of study concentrates on how hearers infer meanings which are not directly present in the sentences uttered (e.g. how 'grandad is tired now' can be understood to mean 'leave grandad alone'), and so is particularly suited to the interpretation of conver-sations on stage and in the novel. The attempt to provide insightful descriptions of spoken interaction has led many linguists to be interested in informal processes of understanding such as the role of informal inference, an emphasis paralleled in literary theory by recent interest in the reader. As a consequence, the stylistic analysis of the last ten years has become considerably less formalist in orientation, though it is still careful to base inferential work on a solid foundation of textual analysis.

Although most stylisticians would see recent developments in post-structuralism and deconstructionism as unreasonable excesses, there has been a development called critical linguistics, which aims through the linguistic analysis of literary and non-literary texts to lay bare the ideological assumptions and biases underlying texts. Another relatively recent development has been an interest in the teaching of language and literature, both to native and non-native speakers of English, and the role that stylistics can play in the pedagogical process.

STYLISTICS AT WORK

Given the scope of this essay, it is not possible to give extended examples of stylistic analysis at work. Instead, I will provide exemplificatory discussions of three short texts, one from each of the three major literary genres, and also suggest readings for investigation. Before I discuss the texts I have chosen, however, it may be helpful if we examine some more small-scale examples to get a feel for stylistic analysis and its assumptions.

Stylistics assumes that linguistic behaviour is rule-governed, and that this rule-governed behaviour allows readers to infer aspects of meaning not explicitly stated, especially if linguistic rules are broken. Grice (1975) has pointed out that when people talk or write to one another they usually agree tacitly to co-operate through a series of unwritten 'conversational' rules: for example, be polite, say things which are relevant to the matter in hand, and tell the truth. If a speaker breaks these rules, others are prompted to interpret this as non-conventional behaviour. Hence, if you ask me what I thought of the play I saw last night and I reply 'I thought the costumes were very good', you will infer that I am saying in an indirect way that I did not think much of it. The basis for the inference would go something like this: (1) the utterance praises the play, but only a rather minor aspect; (2) hence it does not answer the question in a maximally relevant way; (3) the lack of relevance is probably because of an overriding wish to be polite and truthful; (4) therefore in praising the costumes, the speaker is probably praising as much as he feels able to; (5) hence, by implication, he is saying that he does not think highly of the play.

There are, of course, many rules of behaviour in language, and many opportunities for inferring meaning. Another example, which does not involve rule-breaking, is what might be called the parallelism rule. If two stretches of text are parallel in terms of linguistic form (e.g. grammar or sound structure), readers tend to interpret them as having *roughly the same* or *roughly opposite* meaning. We can see this process at work in the following excerpt from the first of T. S. Eliot's 'Preludes':

> And now a gusty shower wraps
> The grimy scraps
> Of withered leaves about your feet
> And newspapers from vacant lots.

'The grimy scraps/Of withered leaves' and 'newspapers from vacant lots' are parallel in that they are both objects to the verb 'wraps'. As a consequence we apply the parallelism rule, and the easiest way of relating the two phrases together is to see them as being roughly the same in meaning. Both the leaves and the newspapers are being blown by the wind. Hence we tend to take associations from one phrase and apply them to the other. The leaves are described as grimy, withered and torn, and so, by inference, the newspapers take on the same qualities. When asked about the colour of the newspapers, a large majority of my students say they are yellow or grey, which can be explained by the associative parallel with 'withered' and 'grimy' respectively.

The effect of parallelism also helps to explain:

1. how intersubjective agreement comes about – grey or yellow are much more likely here than the white or pink normally associated with British newspapers;
2. how more than one interpretation of a text or part of a text might be equally valid – both yellow and grey have associations which cohere equally well with the associations of dirt and decay which pervade Eliot's description of the town;
3. the fact that texts open up and close down associations at the same time – grey and yellow are non-prototypical associations which have been opened up by the parallelism, and the other, prototypical, colour possibilities have been closed down; and
4. part of what is meant by the true but vague claim that meaning is to some extent determined by context.

My final small-scale example is one where a poet breaks the graphological rules of English writing:

> I caught this morning morning's minion, king –
> dom of daylight's dauphin . . .

Gerard Manley Hopkins, in these lines from 'The Windhover', extraordinarily breaks the word 'kingdom' across a line boundary. This deviation is highly noticeable and leads to the inevitable question 'why has he done it?' The first answer is that it preserves the poem's rhyme scheme. But if the poem is to be worthwhile, we will also expect interest at other levels. And indeed there is. 'The Windhover' is a paean of praise to Christ and so it is appropriate to associate Christ with the bird. Breaking the word across the line boundary emphasizes (foregrounds) both halves of it and helps to remind us of the fact that 'kingdom', which we now think of as a word containing only one building block of meaning (morpheme), was originally a two-morpheme word. The meaning of 'king' is obvious enough, but '-dom' derives from 'doom' or judgement. The concepts of kingliness and judgement normally associated with Christ are thus being raised to the reader's attention in the description of the bird.

From these small-scale examples we can see that language is rule-governed at all sorts of levels, and that on the basis of these rules new meaning can be inferred. In particular, when linguistic rules are broken, the associated stretches of text become foregrounded, or perceptually prominent. These foregroundings also become highly interpretable, and a crucial aspect of overall textual interpretation is the relating together of the foregrounded parts in a coherent way.

'The Red Wheelbarrow' by William Carlos Williams

so much depends
upon

a red wheel
barrow

glazed with rain
water

beside the white
chickens.

(Williams, [1923] 1986)

Most of the commentators on this poem concentrate on it as an example of Williams's Imagism, his attempt to make readers dwell on what Winifred Nowottny (1962, p. 119) has called 'properties of ordinary objects usually passed over in our ordinary dealing with such things'. Nowottny apart, however, few commentators have tried to explain how the poem achieves this effect. One of the central aspects of this strategy of getting us to 're-see' ordinary things is a semantic deviation, which, to my knowledge, no one has commented on. The poem consists of one sentence, with 'so much' as subject, 'depends' as the main verb and a prepositional phrase beginning with the preposition 'upon'. The noun phrase acting as complement to 'upon', which has 'wheel-barrow' as its head, comprises the last three stanzas of the poem. The second stanza has the head and the premodifying material of the noun phrase, and stanzas 3 and 4 consist, respectively, of a relative clause and a prepositional phrase, both of which postmodify the head noun. The central deviation concerns the relationship between 'wheelbarrow' and the modifying material of the final stanza, 'beside the white chickens'. It is normal semantically for us to code smaller things in terms of larger, impermanent in terms of permanent, mobile in terms of immobile, and so on. Thus the following noun phrases are normal:

(a) the house beside the factory (smaller in terms of larger)
(b) the hut beside the garage (less permanent in terms of more permanent)
(c) the horse beside the wall (mobile in terms of immobile)
(d) the horse beside the motorcycle (mobile in terms of moveable)

The following are abnormal, however, and would need, at the very least, preliminary contextualization to 'normalize' them:

(a) the factory beside the house
(b) the garage beside the hut
(c) the wall beside the horse
(d) the motorcycle beside the horse

What happens in 'The Red Wheelbarrow' is that the wheelbarrow (large, relatively permanent and moveable) is described in terms of the chickens, which are smaller, relatively impermanent and mobile. This deviant relationship leads us to see that an ordinary scene is being described in an unusual, 'one-off' way. The image thus becomes memorable, and begins to display the characteristics of a word-painting (Nowottny suggests that 'the poem attempts to make words do what a painting can do'; p. 120). Other textual details which support this 'painting' interpretation are:

1. the material modifying 'wheelbarrow' involves the sense of sight and no other sense;
2. the verb 'glazed' in 'glazed with rain water' is most often found in transitive constructions with human agents (e.g. 'he glazed the cake'); and
3. glazing is a technical process in painting and pottery.

Thomas R. Whitaker says of the poem:

> The opening assertion of importance is free of gratifying reference to the speaker as poet or self. The poem's vitality is no one's possession but a possibility for any mind that traces the line. Line units, stress, quantity, echoing sounds – are all adjusted to render the delicate movement of apprehending a 'new world'.
>
> (1968, p. 63)

James E. Breslin makes similar remarks:

> With the disappearance of the poet comes a close focus upon the object: short, jagged lines and long vowels slow down our movement through the poem,

breaking off each part of the scene for exact observation. Any symbolic reading of the scene, a possible imposition by the observer, is carefully resisted; its hard, literal, objective reality is insisted upon.

(1970, pp. 54–5)

We can use detailed analysis of the poem's language to help check the validity of these critical statements. The point concerning the absence of references to a perceiver is reasonable enough. However, the implication that the poem is mere objectified description is more difficult to sustain because of stanza one. To say 'so much depends upon a red wheelbarrow . . .' is not merely to produce objective description, precisely because the poet breaks one of the fundamental tenets of good communicative behaviour in not providing his reader with enough information (Grice, 1975). Hence the reader is invited to ask the question 'why?', and infer some reason based upon the evidence available. We are thus led to the conclusion that it is this detailed particularity that shapes the observer's views and reactions.

The two quotations above can also be used to point up the difference of emphasis between stylistics and more traditional criticism. Both of the commentaries refer to the manner in which the reader is made to move through the description of the wheelbarrow. Whitaker's description of how this is achieved ('Line units, stress, quantity, echoing sounds – are all adjusted to render the delicate movement . . .') is so vague that it provides almost no justification for his assertion. Breslin is a little more precise ('short, jagged lines and long vowels slow down our movement through the poem . . .'), but one of the pieces of evidence adduced is plainly incorrect. A transcription of the poem in standard British English reveals the text to contain 14 short vowels and 8 long (including diphthongs). Even allowing for the fact that vowel lengthening is more common in American than British English varieties, it is difficult to get the incidence of long vowels to as much as half the total. Stylistic analysis would demand more careful argumentation than these critical accounts allow.

A more productive source of the movement Breslin refers to is pointed out by Nowottny. Her account is the closest to stylistic analysis of the three I have concentrated on, and is in my view by far the most sensitive and accurate. She concentrates on 'the eccentric placing of line-endings', and points out (p. 120) (1) that stanza divisions are used to separate qualifying phrases from what they qualify, and (2) that line endings break up what would normally be compound words into their constituent parts. The former point applies to stanzas 3 and 4, where 3 is a relative clause and 4 a prepositional phrase both postmodifying 'wheelbarrow' and providing extra description which is unnecessary grammatically to complete the sentence. Sinclair (1972) calls this kind of effect 'extension'. Significantly, however, what Nowottny says about the stanza breaks does not apply to that between stanzas 1 and 2. When we get to the end of stanza

1 we do not have a potentially complete grammatical structure, and hence the enjambment produces an effect which Sinclair (1966) describes as 'arrest'. The material which I have singled out above for special interpretative comment is thus marked off from the rest of the poem in terms of the relationship between grammar and stanzaic divisions.

Nowottny's second point concerns the relationship between line endings and grammar. She points out that 'wheelbarrow' and 'rainwater' are broken across line boundaries. This produces another extension effect and fore-grounds these parts of the text. The result is to force a modifier-head parallel-ism among 'wheelbarrow', 'rainwater' and 'white chickens', pushing us to explore connections, presumably of similarity, between the phrases. This may be what Breslin is reacting to when he talks of 'breaking off each part of the scene for exact observation'. Nowottny, expanding her 'painting' interpretation, suggests (p. 120) that 'we are meant to treat the poem as though it were a picture, by moving about inside it and seeing different groupings in turn . . .' What we have noted above appears to be one aspect of the 'moving about'. Other relevant groupings are the stanzaic units 2, 3 and 4, and the two colour adjectives in stanzas 2 and 4, which we are likely to connect with 'glazed', which can be seen as a participial adjective referring, like 'red' and 'white', to visual properties of the object described.

Of the critical discussions of the poem I have alluded to I much prefer that of Nowottny. Besides bringing out the 'painting' aspect of the text, for which we have now collected quite a lot of evidence, she also describes much more accurately those textual properties which lead her to her conclusions. The other two critics, on the other hand, do not appear to know very much about the linguistic bases upon which their intuitions are founded. My analysis, though it is still technically incomplete, brings extra detailed evidence to support Nowottny's view of the poem. It is in this sense that I believe stylistic analysis to be an indispensable part of criticism. It is not enough merely to arrive at acceptable conclusions. We must also be able to give adequate reasons for them, which in turn provides a much-needed check on the conclusions themselves.

Point of View in 'Fanny and Annie'

With short texts it is possible to do reasonably complete stylistic analyses. For fiction and drama, however, most texts are too long for this sort of treatment. Instead, stylistic analysis tends to concentrate on important passages, the analysis of which can then be related to the whole, or on particular stylistic features which run through the text in a significant way. The most common strategy is to state one's interpretative stance for the text as a whole and then show in detail how the passage chosen relates to the interpretative hypothesis.

There is no assumption, as there often is for Practical Criticism, that the text analysed will be a microcosmic reflection of the themes of the text as a whole.

For reasons of space, I will restrict myself to how D. H. Lawrence uses terms of address and reference, and definite versus indefinite reference to control point of view in a portion of his short story 'Fanny and Annie' (in Dolley, 1967, pp. 208–23). The linguistic features described here are only a small part of what is involved in a complete account of the linguistic basis for point of view (for further description, see Leech and Short, 1981, pp. 173–85, 257–87, 318–50; Fowler, 1986, pp. 127–46).

'Fanny and Annie' is about Fanny, a lady's maid who returns after a number of years to her village to marry a foundry-worker called Harry. The story is told mainly from Fanny's point of view, and it appears for some time that she may well back out of the marriage, because she sees Harry as uncouth and unambitious. The story ends, however, with the surprise affirmation that Fanny will marry Harry after all. The effect of surprise is achieved because Lawrence withdraws from showing us Fanny's inner reactions for the last part of the story. It is apparent, however, that her change of heart is prompted by Mrs Nixon's denunciation of Harry in church for making her daughter Annie pregnant. The exact motivation for Fanny's change of heart (is it the result of an obstinate wish to close ranks or because Fanny now sees Harry as being more of a prize?) is never divulged.

Below, I look briefly at point-of-view features in the passage where Harry is denounced. First, however, it will be useful to examine how viewpoint and sympathy relations are indicated through the address terms (vocatives) which the characters use to one another and the terms which the narrator uses to refer to them. The naming system is one of the most straightforward ways we have of indicating relationships between ourselves and others. The narrator always refers to Fanny and Harry by using their first names. This suggests a relatively close relationship between the narrator (and hence the reader) and the characters. The use of 'Fanny' in the title of the story confirms this. The evidence of the title would also lead us to assume that Annie Nixon, the pregnant girl, will be another major protagonist. However, Annie never appears in the story, is never referred to by the narrator, and is only twice mentioned by other characters. Her first-name reference in the title helps us to infer the importance of her pregnancy in prompting Fanny's final decision.

The narrator refers to Harry's mother by using the more remote 'title-plus-last-name' formula, 'Mrs Goodall', or some distanced descriptive expression, e.g. 'the old woman'. There are various indications that Fanny does not think much of her intended mother-in-law, and when Fanny talks to her she never uses an address term. But at the end of the story Fanny's change of attitude is marked by her sudden use of 'mother' which presupposes closeness, respect and her marriage to Harry.

Now let us turn to Mrs Nixon's denunciation of Harry:

But at the moment when Harry's voice sank carelessly down to his close, and the choir, standing behind him, were opening their mouths for the final triumphant outburst, a shouting female voice rose up from the body of the congregation. The organ gave one startled trump, and went silent; the choir stood transfixed.

'You look well standing there, singing in God's holy house,' came the loud, angry female shout. Everybody turned electrified. A stoutish, red-faced woman in a black bonnet was standing up denouncing the soloist. Almost fainting with shock, the congregation realized it. 'You look well, don't you, standing there singing solos in God's holy house, you, Goodall. But I said I'd shame you. You look well, bringing your young woman here with you, don't you? I'll let her know who she's dealing with. A scamp as won't take the consequences of what he's done.' The hard-faced, frenzied woman turned in the direction of Fanny. 'That's what Harry Goodall is, if you want to know.'

And she sat down again in her seat. Fanny, startled like all the rest, had turned to look. She had gone white, and then a burning red, under the attack. She knew the woman: a Mrs Nixon, a devil of a woman, who beat her pathetic, drunken, red-nosed second husband, Bob, and her two lanky daughters, grown-up as they were. A notorious character. Fanny turned round again, and sat motionless as eternity in her seat.

(pp. 217–18)

Mrs Nixon's attitude to Harry is obvious enough, and her use of last name only, 'Goodall', is consistent with this. However, I want to concentrate on how her outburst is portrayed in terms of viewpoint. The first indication is '*a* shouting female voice rose up from the body of the congregation' (my italics). We use the definite article to refer to things already known to speaker and hearer. This use of the indefinite helps to indicate that the congregation is surprised and cannot, at first, identify the source of the voice. Note also the use of 'a shouting female voice' as subject to the verb 'rose' instead of the more normal animate subject; this helps us to feel that, from the viewpoint of the congregation, the voice is disembodied, appearing of its own volition. This disembodied aspect is continued in the next paragraph with ' "You look well standing there, singing in God's holy house," came the loud, angry shout.' 'Shout' now has definite reference because the voice is no longer new information for the congregation, but Mrs Nixon's speech is fronted before the introductory clause of saying, helping to mirror the congregation's surprise.

Given the concentration on Fanny's viewpoint for most of the story, we might be tempted to think that the viewpoint here is hers, not that of the congregation as a whole. But Lawrence uses 'the soloist' to refer to Harry, instead of 'Harry', which is used throughout by both narrator and Fanny. In the last paragraph, the relation between Fanny and Mrs Nixon is again marked by the way in which Mrs Nixon is referred to: 'She knew the woman: a Mrs

Nixon . . .', where title plus last name and the indefinite article together convey that Fanny recognizes Mrs Nixon, but does not actually know her.

A full analysis of the story would entail many other dimensions of analysis; but even knowledge of such a simple linguistic system as that for addressing and referring to others can be seen to be extremely useful in explaining what happens.

Discourse Analysis and the Beginning of Shaw's *Major Barbara*

In my discussion of the passage from Shaw's *Major Barbara* (1905) I will build on the terms of address analysis used above and supplement it by other analytical techniques used by linguists in examining conversation. Again, the account will be by no means complete. However, it should give some flavour of how discourse analysis can be used to help display what goes on in dramatic texts.

(At the beginning of the play, Stephen enters. His mother, Lady Britomart is writing at her writing table.)

Stephen: What's the matter?

Lady Britomart: Presently, Stephen.

(Stephen submissively walks to the settee and sits down. He takes up a Liberal weekly called The Speaker.)

Lady Britomart: Don't begin to read, Stephen. I shall require all your attention.

Stephen: It was only while I was waiting –

Lady Britomart: Don't make excuses, Stephen. (He puts down The Speaker.) Now! (She finishes her writing; rises; and comes to the settee.) I have not kept you waiting very long, I think.

Stephen: Not at all, mother.

Lady Britomart: Bring me my cushion. (He takes the cushion from the chair at the desk and arranges it for her as she sits down on the settee.) Sit down. (He sits down and fingers his tie nervously.) Don't fiddle with your tie, Stephen: there is nothing the matter with it.

Stephen: I beg your pardon. (He fiddles with his watch chain instead.)

Lady Britomart: Now are you attending to me, Stephen?

Stephen: Of course, mother.

Lady Britomart: No: it's not of course. I want something much more than your everyday matter-of-course attention. I am going to speak to you very seriously, Stephen. I wish you would let that chain alone.

Stephen: (hastily relinquishing the chain) Have I done anything to annoy you, mother? If so, it was quite unintentional.

Lady Britomart: (astonished) Nonsense! (With some remorse) My poor boy, did you think I was angry with you?

Stephen: What is it, then, mother? You are making me very uneasy.

Lady Britomart: (squaring herself at him rather aggressively) Stephen: may I ask how soon you intend to realize that you are a grown-up man, and that I am only a woman?

Stephen: (amazed) Only a –

Lady Britomart: Don't repeat my words, please: it is a most aggravating habit. You must learn to face life seriously, Stephen. I really cannot bear the whole burden of our family affairs any longer. You must advise me: you must assume the responsibility.

Stephen: I!

Lady Britomart: Yes, you, of course. You were 24 last June. You've been at Harrow and Cambridge. You've been to India and Japan. You must know a lot of things, now; unless you have wasted your time most scandalously. Well, advise me.

(Shaw, 1960, pp. 51–3)

Lady Britomart is portrayed here as a domineering woman who exercises almost complete control over her son. That she treats a man as if he were a small boy is itself a source of humour, but a significant addition to the fun occurs when it appears that Lady Britomart believes she is the weak participant in the conversation. What I have said so far is not particularly difficult to see. As always with Shaw, the stage directions give explicit instructions to the actors on how to play the scene. But how does Shaw achieve the effects mentioned above through the conversational behaviour of the characters?

The use of vocatives is very marked in the extract. Lady Britomart uses 'Stephen' eight times in ten utterances, and Stephen uses 'mother' four times in nine utterances. This all indicates a relatively distant mother-son relationship in keeping with our stereotypes of behaviour in English upper-class families early this century. The establishment of this formal and asymmetrical power relationship is comically interrupted after Lady Britomart's sixth 'Stephen' when she responds to his asking if he has annoyed her with 'My poor boy'.

The power structure of the dialogue can also be demonstrated by looking at the control of conversational turns and topics. As the conversation is dyadic, we would not expect to see an asymmetrical distribution of turns. However, it will be instructive to examine other mechanisms by which conversational power is indicated in naturally occurring conversation: who speaks longest? what kind of turns do each of the speakers have? who speaks first? who interrupts whom? who controls when others are allowed to speak? and who controls the conversational topic?

Stephen has 51 words, an average of 5.4 words per utterance; Lady Britomart has 213 words, an average of 21.3. Lady Britomart controls Stephen's behaviour by commanding him to do things. Stephen has no commands, but she has eight, four of which are negative ('Don't begin to read...', 'Don't make excuses...', 'Don't fiddle with your tie...', 'Don't repeat my words...'). These negative commands, designed to stop him doing things that he is already doing, give the interaction its 'mother-to-child' flavour. Adult-to-adult commands are usually positive and (because of the need to be polite) indirect. Adult-to-child commands are usually much more direct (exhibiting a marked power relationship) and negative, because adults spend much of their time preventing children from doing things which are harmful or anti-social.

Lady Britomart interrupts Stephen twice. He never interrupts her. Her interruptions effectively prevent him from changing the topic of the conversation. Besides controlling the topic, Lady Britomart initiates the conversational exchanges and Stephen merely responds. Even though Stephen utters the play's first words, it is evident that those words, via the presupposition behind them and the surrounding stage directions, are actually a response to an earlier summons by his mother. Stephen's utterance is in turn ruled out of court by Lady Britomart, who wants to finish what she is writing. Thus she controls when Stephen is allowed to speak as well as what he can speak about.

It is against this background of her extreme dominance over Stephen that Lady Britomart tells him he must take control of the family affairs. Stephen, like the audience, is amazed, something which is indicated not only by the stage directions but also by his last two utterances, which merely echo what his mother has already said. The clash between what Lady Britomart wants and what she does is perhaps most obviously realized in 'You must advise me: you must assume the responsibility', where she orders him to dominate her. A further indication of her unreasonable assumptions can be seen when she asks '. . . may I ask you how soon you intend to realize that you are a grown-up man, and that I am only a woman?' The term 'grown-up' smacks of adult-child talk, and the presupposition behind 'only a woman' is at odds with the rest of her conversational behaviour. In addition, her utterance's syntactic structure, which has an unintentional verb 'realize' dominated by an intentional verb 'intend', produces another absurd clash between pairs of presuppositions which she apparently holds.

There are many other things which could be said about the linguistic structure of this text and how it gives rise to the comedy we can all see in the scene. And the linguistic analysis I have presented is by no means as detailed as I would like. However, along with the other discussions, it will at least have suggested how stylistic analysis can be used to help explain the effects of texts, and why literary critics cannot afford to neglect the findings of modern linguistics.

FURTHER READING

Brumfit, C. J. and Carter, R. A. (eds) (1986) *Literature and Language Teaching*, Oxford University Press, Oxford

Burton, D. (1980) *Dialogue and Discourse: A Sociolinguistic Approach to Modern Drama Dialogue and Naturally Occurring Conversation*, Routledge & Kegan Paul, London
Carter, Ronald (ed.) (1982) *Language and Literature: An Introductory Reader in Stylistics*, George Allen & Unwin, London
Carter, Ronald and Simpson, Paul (eds) (1989) *Language, Discourse and Literature: An Introductory Reader in Discourse Stylistics*, Unwin Hyman, London
Cluysenaar, A. (1976) *Introduction to Literary Stylistics*, Batsford, London
Fowler, Roger (1977) *Linguistics and the Novel*, Methuen, London
——(1986) *Linguistic Criticism*, Oxford University Press, Oxford
Leech, G. N. (1969) *A Linguistic Guide to English Poetry*, Longman, London
Leech, G. N. and Short, M. H. (1981) *Style in Fiction*, Longman, London
Short, Mick (ed.) (1988) *Reading, Analysing and Teaching Literature*, Longman, London

ADDITIONAL WORKS CITED

Breslin, James E. (1970) *William Carlos Williams*, Oxford University Press, New York
Dolley, C. J. (ed.) (1967) *The Penguin Book of English Short Stories*, Penguin, Harmondsworth
Fowler, Roger (ed.) (1966) *Essays on Style and Language*, Routledge & Kegan Paul, London
——(ed.) (1971) *The Languages of Literature: Some Linguistic Contributions to Criticism*, Routledge & Kegan Paul, London
Grice, H. P. (1975) 'Logic and Conversation'. In P. Cole and J. L. Morgan (eds), *Syntax and Semantics III: Speech Acts*, Academic Press, New York, pp. 41–58
Nowottny, Winifred (1962) *The Language Poets Use*, Athlone Press, London
Shaw, George Bernard (1960) *Major Barbara*, Penguin, Harmondsworth [first published 1905]
Sinclair, J. McH. (1966) 'Taking a Poem to Pieces'. In Roger Fowler, *Essays on Style and Language*, Routledge & Kegan Paul, London, pp. 68–81
——(1972) 'Lines about "Lines" '. In Braj. B. Kachru and Herbert Stahlke (eds), *Current Trends in Stylistics*, Linguistic Research Inc., Edmonton and Champaign, pp. 251–61
Whitaker, Thomas R. (1968) *William Carlos Williams*, Twayne Publishers, Boston
Williams, William Carlos (1986) 'The Red Wheelbarrow'. In Walton A. Litz and Christopher MacGowan (eds), *William Carlos Williams: The Collected Poems: Volume One 1909–1939*, Carcanet Press, London, p. 224 [poem first published 1923]

81

CULTURE AND POPULAR CULTURE: THE POLITICS OF PHOTOPOETRY

JOHN HARTLEY

ON PHOTOPOETRY

This book is largely about graphical matters; the domain of alphabetically printed literary writing. However, I begin instead with the concept of vision. Vision, the faculty of sight, has long been used as a metaphor for its opposite, for seeing that which is not here. The seer, the visionary, is the traditional bearer of truths, or at least knowledges, which serve to inspire, discipline or even countermand the truths and knowledges of the material world. In the twentieth century such vision has escaped the confines of mere metaphor; we have the technology for seeing that which is not here. Television and video, and their popular predecessor cinema, are the means by which matter can be taken and turned into an image.

Television (= 'far-sight'), video (= 'I see'), cinema (= 'movement') are the making or creation (in Greek, 'poem') of imagination. The matter that they take is of course light – photography (= 'light-writing').

These things – light-writing, vision, poetry, imagination, image – are the stuff of what? Not necessarily of 'learning', nor of 'judgement, decisiveness', even though those concepts came into English from the classical languages, respectively, as 'literature' and 'criticism' (the stuff of this book). The contemporary visual media are literally 'I-see-far-movement', and they produce what I will call 'photopoetry' (making, creation with light). The imaginative poetics of visionary far movement is the domain of popular culture.

MEANS OF PRODUCTION, MEANS OF VISION

I want to start mid-century, with a distinction that Humphrey Jennings made between the 'Means of Production' and the 'Means of Vision' in *Pandaemonium*

(1987). Jennings is best remembered as the wartime film-maker (and co-founder of Mass Observation) whose propaganda films – *London Can Take It* (1940), *Listen to Britain* (1941), *The Silent Village* (1943), *Fires Were Started* (1943) and *Diary for Timothy* (1944) – mark a high point of British cinema poetics. His book, *Pandaemonium*, is 'the imaginative history of the Industrial Revolution'. It comprises several hundred short quotations ('images') from writings dated between 1660 and 1886, from John Milton to William Morris, on the coming of the machine.

In his introduction Jennings argues that the function of the poet has, historically, been subjected to a division of labour, such that poetry becomes more specialized, until at last it has no subject but itself. Meanwhile, the function originally performed by poet-sages like Homer, Hesiod, Moses, Lao-Tze, namely to deal with '*all* problems of life – religious, scientific, social and personal', did survive, but outside poetry. Furthermore, the industrial revolution wrenched the Means of Production and the Means of Vision apart from one another. Under 'Magical systems', says Jennings, there was no distinction between ploughing and praying, eating and blessing, hunting and magic, building and glory.

For him the industrial revolution (capital, free trade, invention, machines, materialism, science) raises a question that is urgent:

> In what sense have the Means of Vision kept pace with these alterations? I am referring not to the Arts as a commodity for Bond Street, or as a piece of snobbery in Mayfair, or as a means of propaganda in Bloomsbury, or as a method of escapism in Hampstead . . . but to the Means of Vision by which the 'emotional side of our nature' (Darwin's phrase) is kept alive and satisfied and fed – our nature as Human Beings in the anthracite drifts of South Wales, in the cotton belt of Lancashire, in the forges of Motherwell.
>
> (p. xxxviii)

The distinction Jennings makes between the means of production and the means of vision is interesting, not only because it is crucial to an understanding of the life of the imagination in industrialized countries (which it is), but also because Jennings does not take sides; he argues for imagination and for industry, not for the primacy of one over the other. His own work as a film-maker, in both its means of production and its imaginative vision, is photo-poetry; our nature as Human Beings, if you like, in the drifts, belts and forges of industrial culture.

Unlike the cultural criticism whose hegemony is being forged in Bond Street, Mayfair, Bloomsbury and Hampstead even as he writes, Jennings does not seek to rubbish civilization in the name of culture. He assumes that 'the poet's vision does exist, that the imagination is part of life, that the exercise of the imagination is an indispensable function' of humanity, 'like work, eating, sleeping, loving'. In the intellectual climate of mid-century England, this integrated theory of poetry and industry is counter-hegemonic.

ON MELANESIANS (AND PUNKS)

T. S. Eliot will serve to illustrate what Jennings was up against. Regretting the death in 1923 of the popular music-hall artist Marie Lloyd, 'the expressive figure of the lower classes', Eliot proceeds to regret also the technological successor to music-hall, and the future promised by the industrial means of production. 'With the encroachment of the cheap and rapidly breeding cinema', he writes, 'the lower classes will tend to drop into the same state of protoplasm as the bourgeoisie.' And this tendency, for Eliot, is lethal. He invokes the Melanesians, whose 'natives . . . are dying out principally for the reason that the "Civilization" forced on them has deprived them of all interest in life. They are dying from pure boredom' (1932, pp. 458–9). Eliot's vision of the future is this:

> When every theatre has been replaced by 100 cinemas, when every musical instrument has been replaced by 100 gramophones, when every horse has been replaced by 100 cheap motor cars, when electrical ingenuity has made it possible for every child to hear its bedtime stories from a loud-speaker, when applied science has done everything possible with the materials on this earth to make life as interesting as possible, it will not be surprising if the population of the entire civilized world rapidly follows the fate of the Melanesians.
>
> (p. 459)

I suppose this must be the 1923 equivalent of the Sex Pistols' 'No Future'. It is tempting to re-read Eliot's rhetoric as a fastidious version of punk graffiti, just as Matthew Arnold's Victorian vision of culture might be read as no more than an early version of 'Anarchy in the UK'. It is hard to resist the image of Eliot as culture-punk, pogoing furiously in his own *Waste Land* and gobbing contemptuously on his own audience. It is tempting to make fun of an adversarial ideology that lines up theatres, musical instruments, the horse and bedtime stories (presumably because they're all 'live', including the horse) against the 'entire civilized world'. But I refrain, because what is important, to Eliot and to this discussion, is not the content of the ideology but its adversarial structure.

For Eliot, Arnold and their loyal fans, the hope of poetry lies in pitting it against civilization; distancing the means of vision still further from the means of production. Culture is anti-technological, anti-modern, anti-popular. Popular culture is thus *structurally* the opposite of 'live' culture, i.e. death. Its content does not matter.

THE HOPE OF POETRY

For Jennings, on the other hand, the hope of poetry lies in 'the "emotional side of our nature" (Darwin's phrase)'. However, on looking up Darwin's phrase near the end of *Pandaemonium*, it is clear that the hope of poetry *qua* poetry is not what it used to be. Charles Darwin is actually quoted as finding no solace in it. Quite the reverse:

> But now for many years I cannot endure to read a line of poetry: I have tried lately to read Shakespeare, and found it so intolerably dull that it nauseated me.... The loss of these tastes is a loss of happiness, and may possibly be injurious to the intellect, and more probably to the moral character, by enfeebling the emotional part of our nature.
>
> (cited in Jennings, 1987, pp. 343–4)

The hope of poetry, it would seem, lies outside poetry; even Shakespeare is inadequate. Darwin himself makes much of the interest he retains in any writing other than poetry: history, biography, travel, essays and novels:

> Novels which are works of the imagination, though not of a very high order, have been for years a wonderful relief and pleasure to me, and I often bless all novelists.... I like all if moderately good, and if they do not end unhappily – against which a law ought to be passed. A novel according to my taste, does not come into the first class unless it contains some person whom one can thoroughly love, and if a pretty woman all the better.
>
> (p. 344)

The solace of popular culture is ever thus, but there is more at stake here than the origin of speciousness. The debate I have tracked through *Pandaemonium* is on the evolution of the politics of culture.

THE POLITICS OF POPULAR CULTURE

Pandaemonium is engaged in a politics of memory. Jennings's book is *anamnesic*, bringing to mind a history that is in touch with, but radically different from, the history of F. R. Leavis's 'great tradition' or the 'selective tradition' of Raymond Williams. It is a constructed history whose politics are post-Marxist, and this in the 1940s, long before such a term was current in cultural theory.

Jennings's history is Marxist in two fundamental ways. It is based on an acceptance of the determining force of the means of production, the form of ownership and the division of labour; and it is committed to a political socialism corresponding to the interests of the industrial productive classes (South Wales, Lancashire, Motherwell). But it is *post*-Marxist because its central focus is on images, imagination, the poetic function of humanity and the politics of culture ('animism' versus 'materialism'). That is, Jennings does not make culture superstructural but basic. His book is an attempt to trace the archaeology of a discourse. It brings to the reader's attention not just a reminder of thoughts expressed in the past, but also, in its principles of selection and in the specific items selected, an implicit theory of ideology.

More importantly, this theory and this archaeology are not designed for the community of professional intellectuals to whom Eliot and other theorists of culture normally address their remarks. It is not *intra*-class communication, but *inter*-class alliance-building. Jennings wanted *Pandaemonium* to appear in popular form (i.e. as a mass-circulation paperback). To find out why, it will be useful to turn to a film.

ON PROPAGANDA

Picture this eye-riveting scene. A South Wales miner, face blacked like a coal-commando, eyes shining with the intention to kill, crawls towards his oppressor with a rifle. In answer to Lenin's famous question 'What is to be done?' a voice intones instructions from the communist newspaper *Lais y Werin* (Voice of the People): 'Work slow. Sabotage your machines. Put water in the oil.' Meanwhile, the Welsh hymn 'Ar hyd y nos' (All through the night) renders this revolutionary programme at once nostalgic and patriotic. All through the night, Welsh miners deal out death.

Is this a scene from a nightmare vision dreamed by the Home Secretary of the day, Winston Churchill, during the Tonypandy riots early in the century, when soviets were formed by the miners, and, on Churchill's order, troops were sent into the streets of mining villages to pacify the insurrectionist Welsh? No. It is a scene from a film made by the Crown Film Unit; propaganda for the wartime government led by Winston Churchill. It is a scene from Humphrey Jennings's *The Silent Village*.

For those who have eyes to see, the film's closing speech, delivered by a representative of 'the Fed' (the miners' union), about the 'power, the knowledge and the understanding' of miners to oppose oppression wherever it occurs, is as much a statement of counter-hegemonic class consciousness as it is an idealization of popular British war aims. Such is the power, the knowledge, the understanding of Humphrey Jennings's film that it can posit the war as a people's conflict against Fascism, conducted by those who had less reason than most to support British governments; in Jennings's hands it is a socialist war, and a war for socialism.

Jennings was committed to a class alliance between intellectuals and workers, between – if you like – poetry and industry. He took the opportunity to lecture to the miners themselves on this topic while in Wales to make *The Silent Village* (and these lectures were one of the main spurs to get on with *Pandaemonium*). But more than this, his film-making practice, and his films, represent and promote an alliance between the photopoet and the people. The alliance is not merely metaphorical; the community filmed in *The Silent Village* is in fact a mining community, and the characters play themselves – schoolteacher, collier, union official, mother, shopkeeper and so on. During his stay Jennings wrote:

> I feel we have really begun to get close to the men – not just as individuals – but also as a class – with an understanding between us: so they don't feel we are just photographing them as curios or wild animals or 'just for propaganda'.
>
> (1987, p. xi)

Or as Melanesians, we might be tempted to add.

PHOTOPOETIC POPULAR CULTURE

The relationship between film-maker (or any other text-maker) and audience is always founded on actual or potential alliance. The possibility of a radical result requires not only radical intentions and practice on the part of the producer, but radical potential among the audience constituency; an 'understanding', as Jennings puts it, between the two parties, via the textual apparatus. Jennings's films are radical in the sense that they depend for their success on that understanding.

There's always a disconnection between the imaginative and the productive domain as well as a connection. Jennings's vision of the people is precisely that, not a mere reflection of some pre-existing lumpenreality. If, as a result of seeing such visions as *The Silent Village* and *Listen to Britain*, or of reading *Pandaemonium*, certain ways of making sense of the domain of production begin to circulate among the productive classes as a means whereby they can grow in 'power, knowledge and understanding' of their situation, then the credit for that belongs to them, not to Jennings. The power of a text to mobilize specific responses, whether of action or imagination, is not in the gift of the text.

However, what makes Jennings unusual is that he recognizes the possibility or potential of a relationship between the aesthetic and the industrial domains, between colliers and himself – a 'thoroughly intelligent tough aesthete . . . way above the ordinary run' as one of his collaborator-subjects called him (Jennings, 1987, p. xi). That is why he wanted his work in popular editions and in popular media.

The Silent Village is ostensibly about a Nazi atrocity in the Czech mining village of Lidice, dramatized for greater impact as if it takes place in Cwmgeidd, South Wales. So it is a true story, but a visionary drama. It is a documentary, but poetic. The figures on screen play fictionalized roles, but they play themselves. It is government propaganda, but it celebrates the power of those whose interests oppose the government; patriotic but socialist. It is a celebration of a popular culture that is not based on entertainment at all; popular without being populist.

And it is not alone. Down the years, there has been a great tradition of popular films and television productions committed to the politics of the popular imagination. The intellectual heirs to Jennings in Britain include some obvious names, but also others whose work is less obviously politicized. From the 1960s there are director Ken Loach and producer Tony Garnett's *Cathy Come Home*, Loach and James McTaggart's *Up the Junction*, director Peter Watkins's *Culloden* and *The War Game*, writer Johnny Speight's *Till Death Us Do Part*, writers Dick Clement and Ian La Frenais's *The Likely Lads*, the early *Coronation Street* (from December 1960), *Z Cars* and *Monty Python's Flying Circus*. From the 1970s there are writer Trevor Griffiths's work including the series *Bill Brand*, Loach, Garnett and writer Jim Allen's *The Big Flame* and *Days of Hope* (see Bennett, *et al.*, 1981, part 4 *passim*), Colin Welland's *Roll on Four O'Clock* and *Leeds United!*, Philip Martin's *Gangsters*, Ian Kennedy Martin's *The Sweeney*, Clement and La Frenais's *Whatever Happened to the Likely Lads* and *Porridge*. From the 1980s there are Alan Bleasdale's *Boys from the Blackstuff*, Troy Kennedy Martin's *Edge of Darkness* (which I will come back to later) and its producer Michael Wearing's *Blind Justice*, the BBC's serial *EastEnders*, and a whole swag of imaginative output from the minority commercial Channel Four, perhaps even – given its highly successful interpretation of its statutory mandate for innovation and experimentation in form and content – Channel Four as a whole.

I invoke these names – and there are plenty of others, including those from America, where the context of Network TV makes cultural radicalism look quite different – in order to show that popular culture has an intellectual and aesthetic history that is all too often lost in the perennial arguments about high and low culture. The 'money, snobbery, propaganda or escapism' of high culture has resulted in a general view that there is not much in common between them. But the two domains are in much closer touch than Eliotic rhetoric would suggest.

MEDIA + EDUCATION = MEDICATION?

There is indeed something in common between high and popular culture. High culture is a product of popular culture. High culture as a concept, as a discourse and as a body of texts, is a product of two social institutions (institutions of memory): education and the media. Its imaginative hold upon the public, if any, is created and sustained by teaching, and by constant reminder.

Education was established in the nineteenth century as universal and free, that is, mass communicated and compulsory, but that does not mean that it was democratic. On the contrary, one of its original purposes was to inoculate the people against their own unhealthy tendencies; to infect them with a controlled dose of culture in order to forestall the outbreak of more dangerous contagions like moral decline and civil commotion: culture versus anarchy. In the twentieth century, the arts are still seen by their propagandists as a shot in the arm (see Borzello, 1987); while for the people at large the injection of culture into the curriculum produces only antibodies – the natural responses of rejection and development of resistance.

The scholasticization of Shakespeare means among other things that a division of labour has occurred between the pedagogic professionals who profess his art, and the public at large, for whom Shakespeare means nothing other than Schooling – compulsion, tedium, arbitrary power, capricious morals and a collective wearing of the dunce's cap. Shakespeare's art is lost on generations of groaning students (including Darwin), for whom it is as universal and liberating as a well-swung sock full of sand.

A ROSE-TINTED SPECTACLE

The media comprise the second of the social institutions of the art of memory in contemporary culture. They are the 'bardic' remembrancers (Fiske and Hartley, 1978; Hartley, 1982, pp. 102–6) who spin into narrative and spectacular stories the doings and sayings of cultural heroes and villains.

On 12 March 1989 a news story appeared in the largest circulation newspaper in Western Australia, the (Perth) *Sunday Times*. Here is part of it:

LONDON: Actor Ian McKellen climbed down into a large muddy hole and cried out: 'To think that the voice of William Shakespeare echoed from these stones'.

Around him, archaeologists scraped at the foundations of the newly discovered Rose Theatre on Bankside, where the Bard made his London debut as an actor in 1592....

Traffic crossing the Thames River thunders along Southwark Bridge, where passers-by idle to stare at the diggers below.

McKellen was joined by 17 other Shakespearean actors and actresses supporting efforts to preserve the remains of the Rose.

... The dig has found thousands of hazelnut shells – the Elizabethans' popcorn – and clay pipes, one with a bowl as small as an acorn.

... Museum of London experts who uncovered the remains after an office building was torn down two months ago, originally had only until this weekend to dig before quitting the site to allow a new office building to go up.

But after meeting with developers Imry Merchant Securities, Harvey Sheldon, the museum's archaeological officer for Greater London, said time had been gained.

The image of an actor ten thousand miles away crying out in a hole in the ground, trampling over 400-year-old hazelnut husks and upmarket dog-ends, surrounded by collapsed walls and building sites, voice muffled by thundering traffic, playing to an audience of journalists, attracting the idle gaze of the accidentally passing public, to marvel at London's 'first commercial theatre', is perhaps a suitably complex and perplexing metaphor for the relations between high culture and popular culture in the twentieth century.

On the other side of the planet someone thinks this is newsworthy, albeit only on page 52, squashed up against a display advertisement for another kind of culture, requiring another kind of muddy hole in the ground – ready-to-install prefabricated swimming-pools. It is in this unlikely context that the contours of culture are drawn.

The story is one of celebrity conflated with culture. It narrates some contemporary oppositions: heritage versus development, art versus commerce, performers versus spectators, even echoes versus hazelnuts. Meanwhile, the story meditates on death and immortality – preserving the remains of the Rose. These are not unimportant matters, but they are not innocent either. The Manichaean oppositions characteristic of journalistic discourse (Hartley and Montgomery, 1985) serve to separate and oppose the Means of Production (development, commerce, spectators, hazelnuts) from the Means of Vision (heritage, art, performers, echoes), or, Civilization from Culture. In this version, the opposition makes heroes out of Shakespeare (and McKellen), so it tends also to make villains out of the rest, which includes the world that both the news media and their audiences actually inhabit.

Shakespeare is invoked to represent values that reproach the contemporary world. That's pretty much the only role left to him nowadays. His name supplies the necessary element of conflict around which the latter-day bards can weave anamnesic fictions, barely conscious of the contempt they show to themselves and their readers.

INVESTIGATIVE DRAMA

Troy Kennedy Martin's first television success was the long-running BBC-TV police series *Z Cars* (1962 to the mid-1970s). Acclaimed at the time for its realism, its apparently honest depiction of the bureaucratic and routine side of police work (see Geoffrey Hurd's essay in Bennett, *et al.*, 1981, pp. 53–70), it was nevertheless as much about television as about policing, with strongly identifiable characters, action, location and genre, in stories written for prime-time popular entertainment. *Z Cars* did what good television can do, using the police series as a vehicle for pursuing investigative drama into the symbolic side-streets of its own times and culture. It provided the popular audience with a shock, not of the new, but of recognition.

Much later in his career, Troy Kennedy Martin wrote the best police drama series ever made for television. *Edge of Darkness* (BBC, 1985) tests its genre to destruction. Its photopoetic vision sheds not light but darkness on the familiar landmarks of the generic and social landscape.

Its structure, the investigation of a murder by a policeman working on the edge of the law, is familiar. As he discovers just how wrong his initial assumptions are, Inspector Craven's investigation disrupts and exceeds its conventions. Generically, the drama moves from the centre of a popular entertainment form to the edges of experimental innovation. Diegetically, it moves from the concerns of an ordinary man to a heart of darkness. It's a dangerous journey to the rotten core of global power games, from the familiarity of home to an undiscovered country where understanding and death are coterminous.

TO HAVE GREAT POETS

What sets *Edge of Darkness* apart is the relationship between the text, its makers and its audience; a relationship of trust, both textual and social. Textually, it relies on the viewer to enter its imaginative space without constantly labelling the landmarks, without doing the work of understanding on behalf of the audience; both parties are on the edge of darkness. Socially, it trusts its audience to desire understanding; the shock of recognition triggered by the device of defamiliarization. The rewards are tangible; *Edge of Darkness* can get away with visions that under other circumstances (e.g. documentary or current affairs) would not make it to the screen, and its method of investigative drama can unravel some of the complexities of public life more truthfully than investigative journalism.

Unlike Humphrey Jennings, Troy Kennedy Martin displays nothing more than a dramatic vision in this work; his photopoetry is not founded on an explicit theory of ideology, but, like Jennings's films, it does build alliances with a popular audience it knows and trusts. The Means of Vision do keep pace with the Means of Production; *Edge of Darkness* offers the contemporary viewer an image of – and a sense of personal responsibility for – our nature as Human Beings (Jennings's phrase) in the era of nuclear power and environmental destruction.

The result is not just good drama, but good politics. Todd Gitlin closes his definitive study of American television, *Inside Prime Time* (1983), with these words of Walt Whitman: 'To have great poets there must be great audiences, too' (p. 335). Like Shakespeare and Humphrey Jennings, Troy Kennedy Martin is a great poet, and his greatness is founded upon that of his audience – the culture of pop culture.

THE POLITICS OF MEMORY

But to have great audiences, critics must take photopoetry seriously, too. Gitlin's invocation of Whitman is actually a pessimistic response to his conclusion that American network TV is fawning and condescending. The networks 'are not *trying* to stimulate us to thought, or inspire us to belief, or remind us of what it is to be human and live on the earth late in the twentieth century; what they are trying to do is "hook" us' (p. 334). If the commercial entertainment of consumerist popular culture has no other purpose than to act as a hooker, it may be because the alternative is too awful to contemplate. It's a long time since the BBC used the brute force of its monopoly to broadcast Bach cantatas at prime time, believing it could cultivate the people against their will and better judgement, but the cold war that has been waged between popular and high culture in the domain of criticism and cultural policy throughout this century is just as responsible for the perceived inadequacies of popular culture as it is for the preservation of the perceived qualities of high culture. The contribution of cultural criticism to popular culture cannot successfully take the form of tarting up Shakespeare for popular consumption while despising the people and what they consume. It does not work.

Criticism – the stuff of this book – is historically a failure in its attempt to preserve in literate memory a vision of culture divorced from production and opposed to it. The vision is there, right enough, but it has not succeeded in disciplining popular culture.

However, within that domain there is another history, some memories of which I have touched on in this essay. In other words, popular culture is not and never was as banal as high culture's wilfully ignorant and disdainful view of it. Instead of cold-shouldering popular entertainment, a strategy that lets it off the hook of critical self-reflexivity, cultural criticism needs to remind popular culture of its past and its potential.

Fortunately the cultural cold war is giving way slowly to a period of détente and even Gorbachevian goodwill in recent times. This is just as well, because discourses organize practices, and the practices of popular culture can only be organized through discourses that are widely circulated and themselves part of cultural memory. The means of vision in the late twentieth century are too important to be squandered in forgetfulness, while the function of criticism is too important to be squandered on Shakespeare.

FURTHER READING

Bennett, Tony, Boyd-Bowman, Susan, Mercer, Colin and Woollacott, Janet (eds) (1981) *Popular Television and Film*, British Film Institute/Open University, London
Borzello, Frances (1987) *Civilizing Caliban: The Misuse of Art 1880–1985*, Routledge, London

Chambers, Iain (1986) *Popular Culture: The Metropolitan Experience*, Methuen, London

Collins, Richard, Garnham, Nicholas, Scannell, Paddy, Schlesinger, Philip and Sparks, Colin (eds) (1986) *Media, Culture and Society: A Critical Reader*, Sage, London

Fiske, John and Hartley, John (1978) *Reading Television*, Methuen, London

Gitlin, Todd (1983) *Inside Prime Time*, Pantheon, New York

Gurevitch, Michael, Bennett, Tony, Curran, James and Woollacott, Janet (eds) (1982) *Culture, Society and the Media*, Methuen, London

Hartley, John (1982) *Understanding News*, Methuen, London

Hebdige, Dick (1988) *Hiding in the Light: On Images and Things*, Routledge, London

Jennings, Humphrey (1987) *Pandaemonium: The Coming of the Machine as seen by Contemporary Observers*, edited by Mary-Lou Jennings and Charles Madge from materials compiled by Jennings *c.* 1937–50, Picador, London

Modleski, Tania (ed.) (1986) *Studies in Entertainment: Critical Approaches to Mass Culture*, Indianapolis University Press, Bloomington and Indianapolis

Nelson, Cary and Grossberg, Lawrence (eds) (1988) *Marxism and the Interpretation of Culture*, University of Illinois Press, Urbana and Chicago

ADDITIONAL WORKS CITED

Eliot, T. S. (1932) *Selected Essays*, Faber & Faber, London

Hartley, John and Montgomery, Martin (1985) 'Representations and Relations: Ideology and Power in Press and TV News'. In T. van Dijk (ed.), *Discourse and Communication*, Walter de Gruyter, Berlin, pp. 233–69

IX. PERSPECTIVES

82

NEW ENGLISH LITERATURES

BRUCE KING

The rapid expansion of the new literatures since 1947, and particularly since 1960, is a result of the political and economic changes after the Second World War when decolonization was followed by the cultural and political assertion and economic development of many former colonies, the increase in trade and communications throughout the world and an increase in higher and mass education, especially the creation of new universities. While, viewed historically, international English literature began soon after the first English colonizers settled in Ireland and North America, both Ireland and the United States have long literary traditions and are not thought of as among the new literatures. The new English literatures fall into two groups. The older former British colonies and dominions started to produce a literature in the nineteenth, or in Canada in the eighteenth, century and before 1947 already had a history of English-language writing. This group includes Australia, New Zealand, India, the West Indies and South Africa. Then there are the much newer national states of black Africa, the South Pacific islands, Singapore, Malta, Sri Lanka and Pakistan, where worthwhile creative writing in English is a recent phenomenon.

While Canada, Australia, India and New Zealand had long histories of literature in English before the present interest in post-colonial literatures, their writers were formerly considered minor, trivial or provincial. Lacking the prestige of important nations, the dominions and colonies were believed to be without a vital culture. There were also economic reasons for the lack of sustained creativity. Already before the Second World War the colonies and dominions had produced such well-known authors as Katherine Mansfield, Jean Rhys and Claude McKay, but because it was impossible for writers to earn a living at home they became exiles, travelled and mostly wrote about abroad. As the writers did not seem part of their national literature, few critics had any context in which to place them. But once new national literatures are recognized, as began to happen in the 1960s, and their conventions and authors given more attention, they are usually found to be stronger than they previously appeared; the colonial periods are now starting to look much richer than before. Such early Australians as Joseph Furphy and Henry Lawson are now considered major writers. Canada similarly has Sarah Duncan and Stephen Leacock among its rediscovered early treasures.

One reason for the rapid development of the new literatures is the changed political and economic scene since the 1950s; another is that with modern communications, the spread of higher education and the affluence of recent decades, the new nations can now support an élite contemporary culture where formerly where was only sad colonial out-of-dateness. From the mid-1930s onwards the gap between metropolitan and colonial literary fashions decreased, a gap which had to be closed before authors from the new nations could be regarded as equals to their contemporaries elsewhere. Only after mastering modernism and giving it a local significance could the new literatures have joined the modern world.

The award of the Nobel Prize for Literature to Patrick White (in 1973) showed that the new literatures were no longer provincial or merely imitative of international movements. As Randolph Stow would soon do, White created a form of modernism – ironic, sceptical, technically advanced (using mythic and classical analogies) – which was Australian in subject-matter, characters and location. A similar adaptation of modernism is noticeable in writing by Frank Sargeson and Janet Frame in New Zealand or in Raja Rao's *Kanthapura* (1938) and G. V. Desani's *All About H. Hatterr* (1948, revised 1972) in India. This late modernist phase lasted into the 1960s when such African writers as Wole Soyinka (the second Commonwealth writer to be awarded the Nobel Prize for Literature, 1986), J. P. Clark, Gabriel Okara, Ayi Kwei Armah and Kofi Awoonor mastered European modernism to create an African literature in English. In doing so they moved beyond simple cultural and political assertion to more complex treatments of the problems of newly independent Africa. During the 1960s they were joined by a new wave of nationalism, or neo-nationalism, represented, for example, in Canada by Margaret Atwood's *Surfacing* (1972), which took Africa and the Third World as a model.

Writers in the past had to go abroad to establish a reputation, and to find other comparable writers and a market for serious literature. The history of Commonwealth literature is filled with stories similar to that of the turn-of-the-century Australian symbolist poet Christopher Brennan who, unable to sell his privately published poems, dumped them in Sydney Harbour. Where could a Nigerian or West Indian writer publish in the 1930s? As late as the 1950s Derek Walcott of St Lucia still had to print and sell his first book privately. As a result of the assertive national political and cultural movements that developed during the Second World War the situation began to change; with decolonization and national independence local cultural, literary and educational markets developed in most of the Commonwealth. The independence movements were followed by vigorous support of local arts, university courses in the national literature, the establishment of publishing houses and the study of the national literature in the schools. Soon besides the creation of a local market for serious writing there was an international market as the Commonwealth and Third World found common concerns in their literatures and histories. As the plays of Soyinka and J. P. Clark began to appear alongside those of Shakespeare and Shaw on African school and university syllabuses, and as the novels of Trinidadian V. S. Naipaul and Nigerian Chinua Achebe were introduced into secondary school courses in Australia and New Zealand, writers from the new nations established international reputations that did not depend on being published in London or New York. Indeed, by comparison the British and especially the American critical establishment in the universities seemed increasingly out of touch with some of the main cultural developments of the contemporary world.

The new literatures have a long and continuing relationship to nationalism and nationalist movements. The Australian *Bulletin* writers of the 1890s, the start of the modern Indian novel in the 1930s, the rapid development of Caribbean writing in the 1950s and the emergence of African writing in the 1960s can be directly traced to the cultural assertion, social changes and political debate that accompany nationalist movements. In each case representative subject-matter, local language usage, local history, racial or national pride, political independence and demands for social justice are among the characteristics, as are concern with national mythology, with documenting local ways, usually in a realistic literary style, and the rejection of middle-class colonial values. To write in Australian English about the outback is a challenge to the status quo, a challenge analogous to the depiction of a traditional African society with its customs being destroyed by colonialism. Such works reject the cultural values imported with colonialism (standard English, the significance of European lives and history) and assert the importance of the local and the underdog. Instead of culture being Shakespeare, Alexander Pope or the latest novel from England, culture is what is produced in Lagos or Sydney about local people in a style that says 'this is made here'.

Nationalism is both political and a state of mind. It begins in the pre-independence period as a means of organizing the masses behind native political groups that want to eject the colonizer or those felt to be alien. To organize others and to distinguish the national from the foreign, a typical, representative native culture and past must be discovered and asserted. The creation of a usable past or a cultural tradition accompanies the social and political demand for equality and independence, since people with a history, a language, customs and myths of their own deserve to govern themselves.

Nationalism involves both modernization and traditionalism. Modernization includes the creation of the modern state and learning the rules and professions necessary to run it. Modernization brings together the various tribes, clans, regions, the peasants and urban workers into a nation. Modernization includes developing transportation and communication networks, urbanization, industrialization and the mastering of modern rational and scientific thought. Such modernization is necessary if there is to be the education, technology and capabilities to produce the increased standards of living, the social justice, the sense of belonging to the modern world that independence movements promise. Few nationalists would argue against technological and scientific progress; the problems come with the cultural side of nationalism.

The imagining of a national community with shared standards and history is progressive before independence and likely to be of use to a writer as well as to a politician. Cultural nationalism offers a vision of and vitalizes society. Achebe's *Things Fall Apart* (1958) and *Arrow of God* (1964) portray a dignified, active, interesting African society, which is corrupted by the intrusion of Europe and colonialism. Similar to the Négritude movement in francophone Africa, the early novels of Achebe show that those who supposedly created nothing had in fact a rich culture and could govern themselves. After independence, however, cultural nationalism too often demands that artists repeat or stay within the conventions of an artificial nationalist folk culture. Such critics want either folk art or politically motivated works that praise the folk, thus continuing anti-colonial protest into the independence period.

After national independence the government expects the intellectuals to continue to support the older nationalists and mobilize the masses for government policies, but the writer usually moves away from the political and military leaders. Significantly many Third World professors, whose salaries are paid by the government, continue anti-colonial rhetoric long after the writers have moved into opposition. A similar conflict between creative writers and nationalists is noticeable in Australia, where the modernist, symbolic novels of Patrick White or Thomas Keneally initially met with disapproval from those committed to a supposedly 'realist' literature with its representational types, social issues and national myths. The celebration of Australia in the works of White or A. D. Hope is too ironic, too much concerned with individual will, too concerned with the unique and eccentric, too negative in its conclusions about national progress, too likely to mock slogans, to be acceptable to nationalists.

Nationalism is not, however, an outdated emotion after independence. Another generation of nationalist criticism begins because those who took over from the colonizer cannot live up to ideals of social justice and economic and cultural progress. The very modernization sought by new nations, and preached by intellectuals, brings alien influences. As new alien influences (American in place of British) appear, a neo-nationalism opposes a neo-colonialism. Neonationalist writing, such as Margaret Atwood's *Surfacing* or Frank Moorhouse's

The Americans Baby (1972), is part of what it criticizes. Its attractiveness is a contemporary version of modernization. While America has stood for modernization (individualism, anti-authoritarianism, economic progress, egalitarianism), and provided an alternative model to the existing British traditions in the colonies, American influences have usually been ambiguous. The American expansion of its sphere of political, economic and cultural influence beginning with the Second World War until the Vietnam War became a main concern of neo-nationalism as, for example, in Thomas Keneally's *The Cut-Rate-Kingdom* (1980) or C. K. Stead's *Smith's Dream* (1971).

How American literature helps modernize and provides an alternative tradition can be seen from the role of American poetry in the Commonwealth. In the 1950s the examples of T. S. Eliot and Ezra Pound helped poets to get rid of lingering colonial Victorian diction, romantic attitudes and outmoded literary forms. Through modernist influences the new literatures joined the world of contemporary poetry. In the 1960s William Carlos Williams and Allen Ginsberg showed how verse could be written about personal experience, reflect a particular society and region, and use a national English instead of following British speech or international literary models. Such poetry was democratic, in contrast to the controlled, reflective, more distanced social and moral tones of the British tradition. The new American influence was an aspect of American neo-colonialism (the indirect economic domination of others characteristic of liberal capitalism). In Canada, New Zealand and Australia, however, the Whitman-Williams-Ginsberg tradition was seen as a way to express oneself in an authentic, direct, personal manner, in contrast to the formalized, distanced, less spontaneous, traditional ways of British poetry. Irving Layton and the Montreal poets and the *Tish* group in British Columbia created a new Canadian poetry from American models. American publications, such as *Evergreen Review*, replaced British journals as the disseminators of European culture, especially the culture of contemporary modernism. Anticipating the ahistorical mixture of styles typical of post-modernism, the American counter-culture, beginning with the Beats, simultaneously discovered various phases of modernism. Suddenly Apollinaire, Baudelaire, Blake, de Sade, D. H. Lawrence, Henry Miller, Alain Robbe-Grillet and Octavio Paz were all contemporary, treated with equal respect and assumed to share similar attitudes. The new freedom felt throughout the Commonwealth after the 1960s resulted from this widespread democratic, somewhat chaotic diffusion of a modernist counter-culture.

The Canadian novelist Jack Hodgins, from British Columbia, expresses the intensity with which the colonial-nationalist need to define oneself and society continues into post-colonial literature and indeed is heightened by the withdrawal of the empire, with the resulting refocusing of 'reality' on the local:

I have always been aware of the need to 'invent' a literature which can reflect life in this place, to use the English language in the particular way it is used here, to find ways of 'unlearning' the forms which were imposed upon us as inferior colonials who were expected to imitate the language and literature of the Old World and to create something new that says: 'This is us. This is how we are. This is how we name things and how we use the language and make it ours.'

('Interview', *Kunapipi*, vol. 9, no. 2, 1987, p. 87)

While Hodgins's comments are part of the new regionalism in Australia, Canada and New Zealand, which has evolved from, and as a consequence of, nationalism, such views are now international and themselves reflect a larger historical movement of decolonization. The centre no longer holds reality. Even to speak of Hodgins and others as post-colonial is to posit an international historical movement with social, political and economic causes, as one would with Modernism, Romanticism or Classicism. The centrifugal movement is perhaps the new centre. Significantly, describing how in *Honorary Patron* (1987) he tried to find new forms to express his post-colonial perspective, Hodgins contrasts what he considers European conventional form with the deconstructive and metafictional associated in his mind with the disorder and future possibilities of local life:

> It begins in a European conventional style that gradually breaks as the protagonist becomes more and more involved in Vancouver Island life, that is, in the chaos and disorder of life itself. Towards the end it becomes metafictional when the third-person narration is interrupted by a conversation off stage. . . . They comment on the book's events while these events continue to unfold so that the reader may ask himself whether everything did not take place in the professor's head. It also leaves the future open.

(pp. 88–9)

This illustrates ways in which nationalism, or post-colonialism, is a modernizing movement which rejects the alien and attempts to bring the local up to date and remake it as significant to the contemporary world.

Culture requires a concentration of talents; universities provide such groups of talent, including painters, dramatists, actors, critics, musicians and other supporters of the arts. The new universities created after the Second World War played a significant role in the new literatures. The take-off of Nigerian literature in English can be traced directly to the universities of Ibadan and Nssuka, to such journals as *The Horn* and *Black Orpheus*, and to the Mbari Press. Wole Soyinka, J. P. Clark, Christopher Okigbo, Gabriel Okara were early associated with the two overlapping university circles. In Canada the *Tish* group, of George Bowering, Frank Davey and Fred Wah, was centred at the University of British Columbia in Vancouver.

Many writers from the new nations are part of significant cultural and artistic communities and have interests in the other arts. The Nigerian dramatist Wole

Soyinka is poet, novelist, actor, director, film-maker and critic, as well as university professor of English and Drama. The Indian poet Nissim Ezekiel is dramatist, art critic, editor, university professor of English and active in liberal-left political causes. Derek Walcott is the West Indies' best-known poet, dramatist, director of theatre and founder of a theatre group in Trinidad. The Nigerian poet J. P. Clark is translator, dramatist, literary critic, theatre director, and professor of English. Groups active in the creation of the new literatures share aesthetic and ideological concerns. The Nigerian Mbari Club, the modern Indian poets, and Walcott in the West Indies value individual freedom, freedom to write about what they want; their attitudes are more pro-western, more favourable to European culture than are nationalist or militant left politicians and intellectuals.

Kinds of language distinguish people and differentiate the local from the colonizer and alien. The conscious revival of Erse in Ireland and of Hebrew in Israel is typical of nationalist attempts to forge an identity through language. Many intellectuals in Africa and India argue that a national literature must be written in a language of local origin if the literature is to be authentic and an expression of national aspirations. English, or some other European language is, however, the language of modernization, of science, of technology and of the modern state; English holds the various tribes, clans, language groups or immigrants together as a nation. English links various communities, especially among the professional and governing classes. Since English is the language of the governing class, the kind of English used in literature has a political symbolism. In the pre-independence period advancement requires mastering the language of the colonizer or of an alien ruling class. A nationalist literature, in contrast, asserts the importance of dialect, of lower-class speech, of Australian, West Indian or Nigerian English. The writers of the Australian *Bulletin*, E. K. Brathwaite and V. S. Reid in the West Indies, Achebe in Nigeria, foreground local forms of English. Achebe's *Things Fall Apart* is a classic example in its use of Igbo proverbs, transliterations from Igbo to English, and other methods of creating a serious, dignified Nigerian English, unlike the comic associations and limitations of dialect and pidgin English.

Such self-conscious assertion is a necessary revolutionary phase against those who dismiss local writing, subject-matter and customs as inferior; but replacing the stiffness of approved standard English with more natural, personal forms of speech also fulfils a literary need. This is especially true in poetry, drama and the dialogues of novels. Part of Derek Walcott's greatness lies in the way he keeps expanding the linguistic range of his poetry; it runs through a spectrum of kinds of English from standard to dialect and even patois. The poetry of Kamala Das gains from the vigour of its Indian English. The long, apparently free lines of Jayanta Mahapatra are read by many Indians as chants. Les Murray's poetry seems to require an Australian voice. The accurate notation of local speech can be found in New Zealand writing starting with Frank Sargeson's capturing of the laconic to Keri Hulme's surprising ear for the variety of nuances, including aggression, within the laconic.

If all narrative, all history, is fiction, this is true of the past as imagined by nationalists, especially in literature where material drawn from anthropology, sociology, mythology and history is idealized. It is a selective view of culture using, as in *Things Fall Apart*, songs, legends, oral tales, rituals, oral history, games; it assumes a closeness between the nation, the rural and the past (in implied contrast to the foreign, the urban and the present). Such a view of history ignores many of the problems and evils of former native societies, such as slavery or the treatment of women, although it is probable that the writer will acknowledge some faults that led people to prefer, and convert to, Western or foreign ways. In Achebe's historical novels the killing of twins and the presence of outcasts lead to conversions, as do the economic advantages that go with a European education and Christianity. The 'past' created by such fictions soon becomes the common vision of reality, a false but accepted way of regarding the history of one's people.

The nationalist literary creation of a past needs to be treated with some scepticism because such history is moulded by current pressures. Achebe's depiction of the intrusion of the white man into Africa, the collapse of traditional society, the creation of a new corrupt class of intermediaries between rural Africa and the British, is a way of explaining Nigeria at the time of independence, when different tribes, with their own languages and cultures, suddenly found themselves needing to live together and govern themselves without a common enemy such as the British. V. S. Reid's *New Day* (1948) similarly uses the past as a warning to a modern Jamaica which has regained the right to vote and govern itself.

The continuation of anti-colonial slogans and symbols long after colonialism can be understood as an attempt to keep the people united and energized in a mass struggle. It is easier for politicians or parties to assume the mantle of protest than to handle the problems that come with independence. There is an implicit struggle over the past between those nostalgic for its supposed perfection and those sceptical of it. The latter group is more likely to be concerned with individual freedom and the continuing inequalities after independence. An E. K. Brathwaite sees an ideal Africa from which the West Indian black is exiled into a fallen world; a Derek Walcott claims all races are equally victims and masters and therefore in need of the same compassion and understanding. Because they are concerned with creating the values that will govern society in its process of modernization, the new literatures are pulled between these two opposites. Is the Caribbean to be understood as a black community governed for the benefit of blacks and with African survivals honoured (Brathwaite in Jamaica), or is it to be seen as a multiracial community with its various historical strands honoured (Walcott in Trinidad)? For the former, art will celebrate dialect, folk-dances and blackness, while remaining part of a protest tradition. For the latter, art must master European conventions before it can articulate local realities and the artist's personal life.

Some of the complexities of nationalism can be seen in the novels of Nadine Gordimer and V. S. Naipaul. In Gordimer's novels, although her views are strongly anti-apartheid, there is sympathy with the white Afrikaaner who is seen as also a victim of British colonialism and snobbery, as closer to the land and as authentic in the way later immigrants are not. Both the Afrikaaners and the black Africans are associated with romantic notions of organic, rural societies. Increasingly Gordimer's central characters (as in the *The Conserv-ationist*, 1975, or *Burger's Daughter*, 1979) are Afrikaaners, as if she wanted to show that the racial situation creates a crisis within the Afrikaaner consciousness, to which the well-meaning British liberal is peripheral. V. S. and Shiva Naipaul make us aware that the Asian Indian has as much right to be considered the voice of Trinidad or Guyana as do the blacks. They have written of the injustices done to Indians in black Africa. Both have been regarded as anti-black, or even neo-colonialist, since they offer an alternative to the widely accepted view of the West Indies as a place where the blacks are victims.

A paradox of the new literatures is that in their very specificity their texts give a sense of the expanding modern world. While the works of Soyinka or Ngugi wa Thiong'o concern the problems of Africa, those problems belong to all societies. In the alienation of V. S. Naipaul we recognize modern rootlessness, mobility and insecurity; the more personal he is, the more he speaks of our time. In fact he increasingly, as in *Finding the Centre* (1984) and *An Enigma of Arrival* (1987), offers himself as an example of the great social changes, the mass movements of people, that followed the Second World War.

Protest seems built into the new literatures. They reflect such contemporary concerns as feminism, social change, social injustice, alternative societies, alienation, exile and decolonization. The new literatures have a built-in opposition to the bourgeois as a form of colonialism. One liberation leads to another. Where in the work of Margaret Atwood does nationalism end and feminism begin? Nadine Gordimer raises interesting issues when black liberation and the liberation of women come into conflict. The new literatures, especially of Australia, South Africa, Canada, India and New Zealand, have long, rich traditions of good, often neglected women writers. And this in turn reflects long traditions of women's movements, which have often been sacrificed to nationalist concerns, or which have come in conflict with the outdoormanship and matesmanship claimed as uniquely nationalist. In the new literatures the conflicts and contradictions of liberation, individual and group freedom, can be seen with unusual clarity.

Is the form of the new literatures inherited from European models or does it become indigenized and based on local models? Is the form of African poetry an offshoot of European poetry or is the increased use of conventions from oral literature in the later works of Soyinka, Clark and Okigbo evidence that African poetry is changing from the élitism of European modernism to a neo-folk poetry? Is the dialect verse of Louise Bennett in Jamaica, or even the 'dub' poets, the central Caribbean tradition, in contrast to the more European-ized verse of Derek Walcott? Maybe it is useful to follow the anthropologists in referring to a little tradition of culture based on folk elements in contrast to the high culture normally associated with art. Achebe's *Things Fall Apart*, Ngugi's *Petals of Blood* (1978), Wilson Harris's *The Palace of the Peacock* (1960), White's *Voss* (1957) and even V. S. Naipaul's *A House for Mr Biswas* (1961) might be described as national epics rather than European novels treating of the relationships between an individual's manners and morals and society. Because of politics and the nature of new societies such novels are concerned with group and national history rather than individual identity and will. If the long lines of Jayanta Mahapatra's poetry may well be indebted to Indian chanting, the obliqueness, difficulty and the way the mind reflects upon an external reality of which it is not part owe much to modern literature from Samuel Beckett onwards.

Many Indian and African poets are ill at ease with English and American verse rhythms and insecure in using them. They therefore either stick rigidly to traditional metrics or use a very free verse, based on their own intonational and stress patterns. But American, Canadian and New Zealand poets have also had to discover their own English and rhythms. The Canadian Al Purdy and Australian Les Murray are as indigenous as the Nigerians or West Indians. The relationship of the written to the spoken word remains a controversial area of the new literatures, as it must for all literatures. The particular ques-tions raised by the relationship between their society and European literary conventions and traditions make writers of the new literature more conscious of universal problems.

As English is now firmly established as a world language, the new English literatures can be expected to become even more important in the future. Whereas in 1960 it was predicted that English would disappear in Pakistan, Sri Lanka, East Africa and perhaps India, English literature is stronger in such places and has started in Singapore, the South Pacific islands, the Philippines and Malta. Albert Wendt of Samoa is a major novelist and poet; Francis Ebejer of Malta is an interesting dramatist and novelist, deserving of attention. African literature in English is no longer a product only of Nigeria, South Africa, Ghana, Sierra Leone and Kenya. Uganda, Zambia and Malawi have their own literatures. As more and more of the governing élites, professional classes and citizens of the modern world are educated in English, they will express them-selves in English and English literature will continue its expansion as a world literature regardless of what governments or nationalist intellectuals may desire.

There has been an immense movement in the world's population since the mid-1940s. A surprising number of writers have changed their nationality or have become internationals. In the past it was assumed that immigrants would acculturate and try to become natives of their new land; but that is less likely to be the case now that the dominance of Anglo-Saxon, northern European culture and power has been challenged in Australia, the United States, Canada and elsewhere. The parallel between multi-ethnicity and the development of new nations is obvious and traceable to the same political, economic and social causes. Just as the 'Eng. Lit.' canon is opening to writers from Africa, Australia and the West Indies, so American, British, Canadian and Australian literatures are now seen as including such formerly under-represented cultural groups as women, blacks, Indians, Asians, Pakistanis and various indigenous people. The new English literatures often have overseas branches. With the appearance of such writers as Timothy Mo, Salman Rushdie and Buchi Emecheta in England, or Vikram Seth and Agha Shadid Ali in the United States, we might wonder whether the older national literatures of England and the United States are not being changed from within by the new English literatures.

FURTHER READING

Durix, Jean-Pierre (1987) *The Writer Written: The Artist and Creation in the New Literatures in English*, Greenwood Press, Westport

Gérard, Albert (ed.) (1986) *European Language Writing in Sub-Saharan Africa*, Akademici Kiado, Budapest

Griffiths, Gareth (1978) *A Double Exile: African and West Indian Writing Between Two Cultures*, Marion Boyars, London

Gurr, Andrew (1981) *Writers in Exile: The Creative Use of Home in Modern Literature*, Harvester, Brighton

King, Bruce (ed.) (1974, 1985) *Literatures of the World in English*, Routledge & Kegan Paul, London

——(1980) *The New English Literatures: Cultural Nationalism in a Changing World*, Macmillan, London

——(ed.) (1990) *The Commonwealth Novel Since 1960*, Macmillan, London

Matthews, John (1962) *Tradition in Exile: A Comparative Study of the Social Influences on the Development of Australian and Canadian Poetry in the Nineteenth Century*, University of Toronto Press, Toronto

Moore, Gerald (1969) *The Chosen Tongue: English Writing in the Tropical World*, Longman, London

New, William (1975) *Among Worlds: An Introduction to Modern Commonwealth and South African Fiction*, Press Porcepic, Erin

___(1987) *Dreams of Speech and Violence: The Art of the Short Story in Canada and New Zealand*, University of Toronto Press, Toronto

Walsh, William (ed.) (1973) *Readings in Commonwealth Literature*, Clarendon Press, Oxford

83

AFRICAN LITERATURE IN ENGLISH

C. L. INNES

'Baa, baa, black sheep,
Have you any wool?'
'Yes, sir, yes, sir, three bags full.'
(Epigraph used by Chinua Achebe for his collection of critical
essays, *Morning Yet on Creation Day*)

The award of the 1986 Nobel Prize for Literature to the Nigerian writer Wole
Soyinka has perhaps diminished the number of readers of English literature
who would question the very existence of African literature. Nevertheless,
critics who write about this area have long become accustomed to that question
from colleagues and general readers. In a number of ways, criticism of African
literature has been influenced by that all too prevalent and dismissive remark,
'I didn't know there was any'. One result has been that by far the majority of
critical texts and anthologies published over the past forty years have been
designed as introductions to African literature and its context or to particular
authors, and that it is only in the past decade that a body of criticism has
developed which assumes some previous knowledge and has not been mainly
descriptive in nature.

The assumption that the terms 'African' and 'literature' (or culture) do not
belong together has also strongly influenced African creative writers. Chinua
Achebe, regarded by many as the father of the contemporary African novel in
English, was spurred to write in part by his desire 'to teach my readers that
their past – with all its imperfections – was not one long night of savagery
from which the Europeans acting on God's behalf delivered them' (Achebe,
1975, p. 72). In particular the depiction by British novelists of Africa as the
epitome of the irrational and primitive (and as the stage for heroic white
adventurers) has angered African writers, with the result that some of their
best-known works of fiction can be read as critiques of English novels, and
specifically of English novels set in Africa. Achebe has spoken of his dismay

at the way Nigeria and the Nigerian character were portrayed by Joyce Cary in *Mister Johnson* (1939). In a 1964 interview he declared:

> I know around '51, '52, I was quite certain that I was going to try my hand at writing, and one of the things that set me thinking was Joyce Cary's novel, set in Nigeria, *Mister Johnson*, which was praised so much, and it was clear to me that it was a most superficial picture of – not only of the country – but even of the Nigerian character, and so I thought if this was famous, then perhaps someone ought to try and look at it from the inside.
>
> (in Pieterse and Duerden, 1972, p. 4)

Achebe's first two novels, *Things Fall Apart* (1958) and *No Longer at Ease* (1960), retell Cary's story 'from the inside', and in so doing create a new kind of novel which implicitly questions the form and technique of Cary's novel, as well as the content. For Achebe, Cary was an all too representative colonialist novelist, foremost among those who portrayed the African as inherently primitive and irrational, and whose work reinforced the racist assumptions upon which the British Empire had been built and maintained.

The explicit and implicit critique of Conrad's *Heart of Darkness* (1899) has also been a strong current in writing by Africans. Achebe parodies sections of the novel in his own *Arrow of God* (1964), and attacks it as fundamentally racist in its depiction of Africans in his 1975 lecture 'An Image of Africa' (Achebe, 1988). Among his objections to the novel is Conrad's silencing of Africans themselves, so that human expression is given to the white woman, but withheld from the African one, while the African men make only 'a violent babble of uncouth sounds' or 'exchange short grunting phrases'. The Kenyan novelist Ngugi wa Thiong'o set aside a dissertation he was writing on Conrad at Leeds University in order to work on his third novel, *A Grain of Wheat* (1967), where the kind of figure represented by Kurtz and the psychology of missionary imperialism are explored more fully from an African point of view in the character of Thompson. Ngugi has also written critical essays on Conrad, Karen Blixen and other European writers about Africa (1982). And in South Africa, the dialogue between Conrad and African-based writers has continued with, for example, Nadine Gordimer's story of a trip up the Congo and a European encounter with black Africa, 'The African Magician' (1965).

In discussing their own writing and that of their countrymen, one strong concern on the part of African writers has been to distinguish it from writing about Africa by non-Africans, to show how their work differs from such novelists as Cary and Conrad. Their emphasis has been on differences in both form and content, but also on the writer's relationship to his readership and his society. In the 1940s, the terms for a distinction between African and European culture were asserted by a group of francophone African and Caribbean writers led by Aimé Césaire (from Martinique) and the future President of Senegal, Léopold Sédar Senghor, who articulated the concept of Négritude. Négritude, according to Senghor, was the sum total of the qualities embodied in African civilization, chief among these qualities being 'emotion, rhythm and humour', all of which would typify the literature of Africans, Afro-Americans and Afro-Caribbeans. 'Emotion is Negro as reason is Greek', Senghor declared, and went on to describe African culture as intuitive, based on sense and feeling, in contrast to European culture which was scientific, objective and technological. Senghor drew upon the literature of the Afro-American Harlem Renaissance writers Jean Toomer, Langston Hughes and Claude McKay to illustrate his thesis. He also argued that for Africans art was always 'functional, collective and committed' and that the concept of art created for private and purely aesthetic enjoyment belonged to Europe (Senghor, 1956 pp. 51–2).

Senghor's theory of Négritude was particularly influential among Afro-American critics who explored and affirmed the notion of a 'Black Aesthetic' as a corollary of the Black Power Movement in the 1960s and early 1970s. It was also taken as gospel by one of the first critics to attempt an overall survey of African literature, Jahnheinz Jahn, in his books *Muntu: An Outline of the New African Culture* (1961) and *Neo-African Literature: a History of Black Writing* (1968), both of which were widely used as texts in Black Studies courses in the United States. Jahn's *Neo-African Literature* affirmed two of the assumptions which were to become prevalent in early critical works on African literature: the unity of African culture, no matter what part of the African continent or the African diaspora it emanated from or who had been responsible for colonizing it; and the distinctiveness of that culture from what was seen to be an equally homogenous European one. While *Muntu* expounded the conceptual framework of Négritude and the quality of African civilization, *Neo-African Literature*, which included substantial bibliographies and lists, sought to establish the quantity of literary works that civilization had produced (in African as well as European languages), and uncovered and listed a wide variety of works. In so doing, it formed the basis for later scholars who edited and/or described such seventeenth- and eighteenth-century writers as Juan Latino, Phyllis Wheatley and Oloudah Equiano, and saw contemporary writers such as Achebe and Okigbo as the descendants of a long tradition which included the Négritude writers.

There are some analogies between these early critical enterprises with regard to African literature and the history of feminist criticism. Both Africanists and feminists begin by rejecting the representation of themselves as 'other' in the literary works of their 'oppressors'. Both seek to affirm a distinctively different ethos, sometimes in remarkably similar terms, asserting the value of intuition and feeling against European/male reason and 'objectivity', and a culture which is oral and communal rather than literary and hierarchical. Both see as an important part of their enterprise the uncovering of forgotten writers and works, not only as a basis for exploring the nature of a distinctively female or African tradition, but also in order to establish, in the face of denial, that a substantial quantity of writing exists. In its post-colonial phase, the paths of African literature and its criticism diverge rather more from the increasing variety of feminist critical routes, a divergence which has much to do with the gaining of at least nominal independence and self-rule on the part of African states in the 1960s. During the past decade, a number of feminist critics have begun to turn to the work of Black women writers, although the implications of the analogies suggested above have rarely been explored (see Adams and Boyce-Davies, 1986; Jones, Palmer and Jones, 1987).

The emphasis on Négritude had its strongest influence on criticism emanating from America in the 1960s and 1970s, and particularly the work of African-American critics such as Mercer Cook and Stephen Henderson (see, for example, their joint book, *The Militant Black Writer in Africa and the United States*, 1970). And although many of the younger critics in the eighties might be only dimly aware of Négritude as a term, the emphasis on establishing the existence of an international 'Black' literature, and on comparative studies seeking continuities rather than contrasts between Afro-American, Afro-Caribbean and African authors, remains one of the most prevalent forms of critical enterprise, particularly in the United States.

Anglophone Africans and British critics have been somewhat more sceptical about Négritude as a basis for either literary or critical production, although paradoxically it is another francophone critic, psychoanalyst and philosopher Frantz Fanon, who has helped provide them with some of the tools for restructuring (rather than demolishing entirely) the building erected by Senghor. In his first book, *Black Skins, White Masks* (1959), Fanon examined and satirized the psychology of Négritude, and endorsed Jean-Paul Sartre's description of it (in 'Orphée Noir', 1948) as an 'anti-racist racism', but a psychologically necessary phase in the rebuilding of the damaged black psyche. Fanon's second and very influential work, translated as *The Wretched of the Earth* (1961), was more politically radical in its orientation. While still seeing the usefulness of the cultural nationalist phase with its concern for rehabilitating the past and validating African culture, this book emphasized the desirability of moving beyond it to a literature which sought to arouse political consciousness and which reflected the economic and cultural world of the peasantry and the proletariat.

Like Fanon, Chinua Achebe, Wole Soyinka and the South African novelist and critic Ezekiel Mphahlele have dissociated themselves from what they see as the propensity of the Négritude school to idealize the past, to see it as 'one glorious technicolour idyll', as Achebe put it in his 1964 essay 'The Role of the Writer in the New Nation', or to claim that African people are not capable of violence too. These anglophone writers share with many British critics a general distrust of theory, a distrust which is also typified in Soyinka's witty dismissal of structuralist and Marxist dogmas in his lecture, 'The Critic and Society: Barthes, Leftocracy and other Mythologies' (in Gates, 1984). However, both Soyinka and Achebe have acknowledged Senghor as an important predecessor, whose work must be seen in its historical context. Soyinka's *Myth, Literature and the African World* (1976) recognizes the early achievements of Négritude but also offers a further critique of what he sees as its static essentialism, caught in Western terms and premises. Nevertheless, Soyinka shares the Négritude school's assumption that there is a discernibly 'African' culture which is differentiated from European culture by its profound acceptance of the spiritual and mythic, and by an understanding of the world which relies on ritual rather than technology.

However, Achebe and most other African writers and critics are at one with Senghor in their critical emphasis on a literature which is not divorced from its community, which speaks to it and for it, and is committed to promoting the good of the community. As Achebe put it in 1973, in a lecture called 'Africa and her Writers':

> I will insist that art is, and was always, in the service of man. Our ancestors created their myths and legends and told their stories for a human purpose (including, no doubt, the excitation of wonder and pure delight); they made their sculptures in wood and terra cotta, stone and bronze to serve the needs of their times. Their artists lived and moved and had their being in society and created their works for the good of that society.
>
> (1975, p. 19)

In this same lecture he goes on to lament the tendency of African writers, typified in his view by the Ghanaian novelist Ayi Kwei Armah in *The Beautyful Ones Are Not Yet Born* (1968) to reach toward the illusion of 'universalism', writing about 'the human condition' in a Ghana which had been distorted by Armah's descriptions into 'some modern, existential no-man's land'.

Achebe's denunciation of Armah has been answered by a number of African and European critics who find his distinctions too simple and prescriptive and also based on a misreading of Armah's novels. His view has remained influential, however, and has set the stage for a school of criticism which rejects the works of Soyinka, Armah and the poet Christopher Okigbo as 'élitist' and 'obscure', straining too much to be a part of the 'European modernist' tradition. The most widely-read work to come from this school is *Towards the Decolonisation of African Literature* (1983) by Chinweizu, Onwuchekwa Jemie and Ihechukwu Madabuike, who first published sections of this polemic as a series of articles in 1974–5 in *Okike, A Journal of African Literature*, edited by Chinua Achebe. Dedicated to an all-male list of 33 writers and leaders, including Kwame Nkrumah, Amiri Baraka, Malcolm X and Frederick Douglass (Achebe and Senghor being the only living African writers in the list), the book attacked what the authors saw as the Eurocentric orientation of much African creative and critical writing. As the authors wrote in their Preface, their concern for 'the health of African culture' led them to undertake the 'task of probing the ways and means whereby Western imperialism has maintained its hegemony over African literature, and the effect of that hegemony upon the literary arts of contemporary Africa' (p. xi). They point out the ways in which European critics have ignored and devalued African literary and oral traditions which preceded colonization, have misnamed African literary creations by applying European-based categories, such as epic, romance, novel, etc., and then have castigated African authors for not meeting the criteria they themselves have established for such categories. They see the influence of F. R. Leavis as being particularly strong in the evaluations not only of British critics such as Gerald Moore but also of Nigerian critics such as Michael Echeruo and Donatus Nwoga, in their approval on the one hand of the clarity of prose in the works of novelists such as Chinua Achebe and Camara Laye, and on the other of the obscurity of Christopher Okigbo's poetry. Charles Larson's *The Emergence of African Fiction* (1972) is seen as typical of Eurocentric criticism in its assumption that African fiction 'emerges' only after European intervention in Africa, that it is to be judged in terms of the bourgeois European novel, and that it will develop along the same lines. Chinweizu and his co-authors gleefully adopt Ayi Kwei Armah's suggestion that Larson's 'name become synonymous with the style of scholarly criticism of which he is such an inimitably brilliant exponent, that style which consists of the judicious distortion of African truths to fit Western prejudices, the art of using fiction as criticism of fiction. I suggest we call it "larsony" ' (Armah, 1977, p. 55).

While most African writers and critics would find common cause with this denunciation of a critical stance which complacently assumes the 'universality' of European criteria and models, many have sharply questioned the 'African' criteria which *Towards the Decolonisation of African Literature* wished to set up in their place. Chief among those criteria were lucidity, accessibility and a return to an African tradition which embodied both of these qualities, rather than a 'Euro-modernist obscuranticism' which demanded 'the discovery of layers of meaning below the surface'. Soyinka, whose fiction and poetry was cited as an advanced case of this 'Euro-modernist obscuranticism', replied in the pages of *Transition* with an essay whose title conveys the spirit and content of his response, 'Neo-Tarzanism: The Poetics of Pseudo-Tradition' (1975). Just as his novels, plays and poetry often draw upon both Yoruba and European myth and use metaphors from modern technology like a modern metaphysical poet, Soyinka is at pains here to stress the complexity of Yoruba and other traditions, as well as their complex interaction with contemporary technology and other cultures, and he abjures the whole notion of a pure and simple past and stereotypical simple natives.

Chinweizu, Jemie and Madabuike focus their discussion on West and South African writers and critics, paying remarkably little attention to a writer whose fiction, drama and essays have come to stand in recent years for one of the main lines in the debate over the criteria for evaluation and future direction of African literature, Ngugi wa Thiong'o. Despite their preliminary claim to embrace the whole African continent, only one other East African writer is mentioned, the Ugandan poet Okot p'Bitek. The Somali novelist Nuruddin Farah, regarded by many as the most significant African novelist apart from Achebe, Soyinka, LaGuma and Ngugi, does not appear at all. In the 1980s, Ngugi has taken the forefront in two aspects of this debate, the language issue and the role of ideology. Ngugi's first three novels, *Weep Not Child* (1964), *The River Between* (1965) and *A Grain of Wheat* (1967), might be seen as cultural nationalist in orientation, influenced by Jomo Kenyatta's *Facing Mount Kenya* (1937) in their determination to establish the worth of Kikuyu culture and customs, and they share with Achebe's fiction a concern for even-handedness in portraying the colonial encounter. The essays in *Homecoming* (1972) reveal the growing influence of Frantz Fanon, but it is in his later novel, *Petals of Blood* and the play, co-authored with Micere Mugo, *The Trial of Dedan Kimathi*, that the form and content of his work most clearly show his commitment to a Marxist analysis of his society, combined with a Fanonian emphasis on the peasantry and the land as the source of cultural strength and political change. Ngugi's later collections of essays, *Writers in Politics* (1982) and *Decolonising the Mind* (1986), argue for a literature firmly and clearly committed to political change, and like his later fiction and drama are grounded in his conviction that international capitalism and its attendant neo-colonialism are the primary causes of the poverty of the masses and the corruption of values and culture in Kenya. This analysis of the causes, and advocacy of a worker/peasant alliance to remove the capitalist structure of society, has strongly influenced a number of younger writers and critics in Africa, including the Nigerian creative writers and critics Festus Iyayi, Kole Omotoso, Omafume Onoge and Biodun Jeyifo (see Jeyifo, 1980; Gugelberger, 1985).

After completing *Petals of Blood* (1977), Ngugi ceased writing in English, except for critical essays, and turned to Gikuyu, his mother tongue, as the medium for drama and a new prose form developed from oral story-telling. His reasons for rejecting English and taking up Gikuyu are set out in the series of essays gathered in *Decolonising the Mind*. He rejects the language of the colonizer as 'the most powerful vehicle through which [the colonizer's] power fascinated and held the soul prisoner. The bullet was the means of physical subjugation. Language was the means of spiritual subjugation' (1986, p. 9). It carried with it the cultural assumptions of the imperial power, and also encouraged a total rupture between the domestic and agrarian world of the African child and his school environment, eventually divorcing the English-educated African writer from his own roots and from the majority of his countrymen. Moreover, Ngugi argued, it is the duty of the African writer to contribute to the development of his own indigenous language and to its enrichment, rather than to its decline. As a committed Marxist writer, the strongest argument for Ngugi has to do with his desire to reach and influence the group most likely to bring about change, the workers and peasants, for whom the English language and the form of the English novel are alien.

The debate over the use of English by African writers is a long-standing one. A letter (in English) to *Transition* in 1963 from Obi Wali advocated a return to indigenous languages by African writers, since the continued use of English could only lead to sterility. In his reply to this letter and in essays and interviews, Achebe has argued that English provides Nigerian writers with a *national* language, a means of communicating with the nation as a whole, and also a means of communicating with other readers and writers on the African continent. Moreover, he insisted, it was a language that Africans had used with remarkable creativity and which they had made their own to 'carry the weight of their African experience' (Achebe, 1975, p. 30).

The use of English as a medium for writers takes on a different significance in South Africa, where Afrikaans is the official language of the ruling power, and where the insistence on the use of 'native' languages can sometimes be seen as too closely tied to the apartheid bantustan policy. Here, English is often seen as the language of resistance, and for many South Africans, whether classified black, white or coloured, it is their first language. Relatively few writers or critics from South Africa have resisted the assumption that writing cannot be divorced from its political context, although there has been much debate about the degree to which aesthetic concerns should temper political ones and Lewis Nkosi, himself a novelist and playwright, has lamented the overwhelming emphasis on realism as the form and protest as the subject of fiction by black South African writers. 'What we get from South Africa', he declares, 'is the journalistic fact parading outrageously as imaginative literature. We find a type of fiction which exploits the ready-made plots of racial violence, social apartheid, interracial love affairs which are doomed from the beginning, without any attempt to transcend or transform these "given social facts" into artistically persuasive works of fiction' (Nkosi, 1983, p. 132). As a remedy he calls for experiments with the techniques of traditional African story-telling, citing Amos Tutuola's *Palmwine Drinkard* (1952), combined with a greater consciousness of the innovations introduced by European modernist writers. In a later essay on 'Literature and Liberation', Nkosi regrets that South Africa's black community has produced no writers who can match 'the passion and precision of Nadine Gordimer or a Doris Lessing' (Nkosi, 1983, p. 163), and he ascribes this failure to a crudely reductionist view of literature as propaganda, which he sees as a misunderstanding of Marx, quoting Terry Eagleton's assertion that 'art is so ideologically powerful precisely because it isn't just propaganda' (pp. 163–4).

In general, African literary criticism has been concerned with placing the works of African writers in a cultural and social context, and with examining the writer's contribution to that context. European critics, as much from inability or unwillingness to overcome their lack of acquaintance with that context as from their adherence to the practices of the 'new critics' or the Leavis school, have been more inclined to concentrate on close textual study, comparisons with European works, and establishing genre, although there have been notable exceptions such as Claude Wauthier's wide-ranging study, *The Literature and Thought of Modern Africa* (1978). In the past decade, the influences of Foucault, Said, Spivak, Bakhtin, and other post-structuralist critics have begun to make a contribution both inside and outside the African continent. Abdul JanMohamed's *Manichean Aesthetics: The Politics of Literature in Colonial Africa* (1983) draws on Fanon and Fredric Jameson to establish a framework for exploring the literary productions of six writers, three white and three black. Biodun Jeyifo and other younger critics such as Osofisan and Amuta have been critical of what they see as a tendency in earlier critics such as Chinweizu and his school to anti-intellectualism and a nostalgic search for an authentic 'folk' Africa which obscures contemporary political, economic and cultural realities. These younger critics have also begun to question the canon which was very quickly established with regard to African literature.

Within that canon, Chinua Achebe, Ngugi wa Thiong'o and Wole Soyinka have received and continue to receive by far the greatest amount of critical attention; their works (except where they are banned) provide the staple diet for students of African literature in Africa, the United States and Europe. The Ugandan poet Okot p'Bitek and the Ghanaian novelist Ayi Kwei Armah may also be included. In the 1980s some women writers have been added, Buchi Emecheta in particular, but also the South African Bessie Head and the Ghanaian Ama Ata Aidoo. These and other female authors are more likely to appear in courses or anthologies of literary criticism concerned with 'Black Women Writers', which seek to establish or simply assume links between the situations and cultural productions of Afro-American, Afro-Caribbean and African women. Younger African writers, such as Festus Iyayi, Ben Okri and Kole Omotoso, are still generally ignored, as are those, like the Somalian Nuruddin Farah, whose works do not fit easily into the already established concept of the African novel nor into the better-known contexts of Nigeria and Kenya. Changes in the publishing world have also had their effect: in response to economic difficulties in Nigeria, Ghana and many other African countries, and also as a consequence of takeovers by multinational companies, publishers such as Heinemann and Longman have cut down considerably on the publication of new authors and their attempts to market books on the African continent. Some local publishers have begun to take their place in Africa, but distribution is not always good even within the countries themselves, and few publications are circulated, let alone reviewed, outside Africa.

FURTHER READING

Achebe, Chinua (1988) *Hopes and Impediments, Selected Essays, 1965–87*, Heinemann International, Oxford

Ashcroft, Bill, Griffiths, Gareth and Tiffin, Helen (1989) *The Empire Writes Back: Theory and Practice in Post-Colonial Literatures*, Routledge, London

Awoonor, Kofi (1975) *The Breast of the Earth*, Doubleday, Garden City

Barnett, Ursula (1983) *A Vision of Order: A Study of Black South African Literature in English*, University of Massachusetts Press, Amherst

Brown, Lloyd (1981) *Women Writers in Black Africa*, Greenwood Press, Westport

Chinweizu; Jemie, Onwuchekwa and Madabuike, Ihechukwu (1983) *Towards the Decolonisation of African Literature*, Howard University Press, Washington

Cook, David (1977) *African Literature: A Critical View*, Longman, London

Gikandi, Simon (1987) *Reading the African Novel*, James Currey, London

Gray, Stephen (1979) *Southern African Literature: An Introduction*, Rex Collings, London

Irele, Abiola (1981) *The African Experience in Literature and Ideology*, Heinemann, London

JanMohamed, Abdul R. (1983) *Manichean Aesthetics: The Politics of Literature in Colonial Africa*, University of Massachusetts Press, Amherst

Moore, Gerald (1966) *Seven African Writers*, Oxford University Press, Oxford

Ngugi wa Thiong'o (1986) *Decolonising the Mind*, James Currey, London

Obiechina, Emmanuel (1975) *Culture, Tradition and Society in the West African Novel*, Cambridge University Press, Cambridge

Soyinka, Wole (1976) *Myth, Literature and the African World*, Cambridge University Press, Cambridge

ADDITIONAL WORKS CITED

Achebe, Chinua (1964) 'The Role of the Writer in a New Nation', *Nigeria Magazine*, 81, 157–60

——(1975) *Morning Yet on Creation Day*, Heinemann, London

Adams, Ann and Boyce-Davies, Carole (eds) (1986) *Nyambika*, Africa World Press, Trenton

Armah, Ayi Kwei (1977) 'Larsony: Fiction as Criticism of Fiction', *First World*, 1, 2, 50–5

Fanon, Frantz (1961) *The Wretched of the Earth*, Penguin, Harmondsworth

——(1967) *Black Skins, White Masks*, Grove Press, New York [first published 1959]

Gates, Henry Louis, Jr. (ed.) (1984) *Black Literature and Literary Theory*, Methuen, London

Gugelberger, Georg M. (ed.) (1985) *Marxism and African Literature*, James Currey, London

Jahn, Jahnheinz (1961) *Muntu: An Outline of the New African Culture*, Faber & Faber, London

——(1968) *Neo-African Literatures: A History of Black Writing*, Faber & Faber, London

Jeyifo, Biodun (1980) *The Truthful Lie: Towards a Radical Sociology of African Literature*, New Beacon, London

Jones, Eldred D., Palmer, Eustace and Jones, Marjorie (eds) (1987) *Women in African Literature Today*, James Currey, London

Larson, Charles (1972) *The Emergence of African Fiction*, University of Indiana Press, Bloomington

Ngugi wa Thiong'o (1972) *Homecoming*, Heinemann, London

——(1982) *Writers in Politics*, Heinemann, London

Nkosi, Lewis (1983) *Home and Exile*, Longman, London

Pieterse, Cosmo and Duerden, Denis (eds) (1972) *African Writers Talking: A Collection of Radio Interviews*, Heinemann, London

Senghor, Léopold Sédar (1956) 'The Spirit of Civilization', *Présence Africaine*, Special Issue (English Edition), pp. 50–63

Soyinka Wole (1975) 'Neo-Tarzanism: The Poetics of Pseudo-tradition', *Transition*, 48, 38–44

Wauthier, Claude (1978) *The Literature and Thought of Modern Africa*, Heinemann, London

84

THE AFRICAN-AMERICAN LITERARY TRADITION

BERNARD W. BELL

'Anyone who analyses black literature', writes literary critic Henry Louis Gates, Jr., 'must do so as a comparativist . . . because our canonical texts have complex double formal antecedents, the Western and the black' (1988, p. xxiv). This has long been the considered judgment and is now the prevailing wisdom of most African-Americanists. Because of the distinctive history and acculturation of Africans in the British colonies in North America, the literary tradition of African Americans is most meaningfully assessed in the context of the tension between their attitudes toward their dual African and European cultural heritages on one hand, and their oral and literary heritages on the other. Every American writer of African descent works within and against the dual tradition – oral and literary, African and European, male and female – that each inherits as part of his or her North American cultural legacy and in which, however marginally, each participates in the elusive quest for status, power and identity. Each writer's contribution and significance are therefore influenced by his or her relationship to past and present writers, as well as by the relationship of his or her texts to others in the tradition, both in the narrow Eurocentric sense of literary formalism and in the broader Afrocentric cultural sense.

While a Eurocentric world view privileges Greece, Rome and Europe as the birthplace of civilization and the universal standard of cultural excellence, an Afrocentric world view, as the neo-Hoodoo aesthetician Ishmael Reed's novel *Mumbo Jumbo* (1972) brilliantly illustrates, stresses ancient Africa, including Egypt, as the more historically and archaeologically valid cradle of humankind and cultural diversity. It is generally accepted by scientists that human beings evolved at least 2 million years ago in East Africa, moved into Europe and Asia about 1 million years ago, and finally came to the Americas, over the Bering Strait, some 12,000 years ago. Pulitzer Prize-winning novelist Alice Walker employs magical realism in *The Temple of My Familiar* (1989) to recreate the primordial sub-Saharan African mother of us all, whether, like paleontologists or fundamentalists, we call her Lucy or Eve.

According to T. S. Eliot's Eurocentric perspective in 'Tradition and the Individual Talent', 'the historical sense compels a man to write not merely with his own generation in his bones, but with a feeling that the whole of the literature of Europe from Homer and within it the whole of the literature of his own country has a simultaneous existence and composes a simultaneous order' ([1920] 1964, p. 49). From a dual African and European perspective, as Richard Wright states in 'Blueprint for Negro Writing',

> Eliot, Stein, Joyce, Proust, Hemingway, and Anderson; Gorky, Barbusse, Nexo, and Jack London no less than the folklore of the Negro himself should form the heritage of the Negro writer. Every iota of gain in human thought and sensibility should be ready grist for his mill, no matter how far-fetched they may seem in their immediate implications.
>
> (1937, p. 60)

The point here is not that black literary texts are self-reflexive, self-sufficient intertextual sign systems. Nor is it that all black writers choose to invoke African muses and to employ exclusively black sources in creating their texts. But that black literary texts are sign systems whose referents are nonliterary as well as literary texts that illumine the meaning of the shared experience of black Americans and the complex double consciousness which, as turn-of-the-century aesthete and social scientist W. E. B. Du Bois explains in *The Souls of Black Folk* ([1903] 1961), a landmark collection of essays, is the special burden and blessing of our African-American identity.

In clarification of the group's historical determination to define and name themselves, 'Negro', first capitalized in 1930, is a socio-economic term that was popular from about 1880 to 1960 for designating the American descendants of African peoples. During the Black Power and Black Arts Movements of the 1960s, 'black', previously considered a badge of inferiority, became popular as a more prideful assertion of racial and ethnic identity that affirmed both political and cultural distinctiveness. 'Afro-American' and 'African American', the most accurate of the terms, were also popular in the 1960s in affirming the common legacy of people of African descent in the American diaspora, associating them with a specific place and past. Until 1831, when the first convention of 'People of Color' was held in Philadelphia to protest against the revival of organized efforts by the American Colonisation Society to send free blacks back to Africa, the most popular formal self-conscious group identity of free blacks was African: the Free African Society (1787), New York African Free School (1787), African Mason Lodge (1787), and African Methodist Episcopal Church (1794).

'Language', René Wellek and Austin Warren remind us, 'is the material of literature as stone or bronze is of sculpture, paints of pictures, or sounds of music. But one should realize that language is not mere inert matter like stone but is itself a creation of men and is thus charged with the cultural heritage of a linguistic group' ([1948] 1962, p. 22). Afro-American culture is the symbolic and material expression by black Americans of our relationship to Nature, to our ethnic community, and to whites as we seek to adapt to our environment in order to survive and thrive, both individually and collectively. We find the roots of this culture in the Deep South in the syncretism of residual Africanisms with elements of European and native American culture, and in the dynamics of sexual, class and ethnic differences. Culture thus signifies the constitutive social process by which people create specific, different ways of life as they adapt to environmental conditions and historical circumstances. For black Americans this process of acculturation has been shaped by a distinctive history: Africa, slavery, the Middle Passage, the Southern plantation, Emancipation, Reconstruction, post-Reconstruction, Northern migration and urbanization, and, most importantly, racism. The unique configuration of these historical experiences generated the interrelated processes of double consciousness, socialized ambivalence, and double vision that best explain the complex, creative dynamics of African-American ethnic culture and character.

Du Bois defined the African-American experience of double consciousness as the complex socio-cultural and socio-psychological duality of Americans of African descent whose humanity and culture were institutionally devalued and marginalized by people of European descent (1961, pp. 16–17). Socialized ambivalence signifies a shifting identification between the values of the superordinate white and subordinate black cultural systems as a result of institutionalized racism. Double vision refers to a tragi-comic, wry perspective toward life as expressed in the use of irony and parody in Afro-American folklore and formal art.

Some literary historians identify the beginning of the African-American literary tradition as the teenage New England slave Lucy Terry's 'Bar's Fight', a 1746 verse account of an Indian raid in Deerfield, Massachusetts, which was not published until 1855. A more meaningful and appropriate typology of valued writing by and about Afro-Americans divides the tradition into documentary, autobiography/biography, and imaginative genres (novels, poems, and plays). The early petitions of slaves for permission to purchase their freedom and to return to Africa invoke the same principle that the white colonists invoked in laying the philosophical foundation for their separation from England. Perhaps the most historically revealing was dated May 25 1774 – less than a week before the British blockaded the Port of Boston in retaliation for the Boston Tea Party of December 1773. It reads: 'That your Petitioners apprehind we have in common with all other men a natural right to our freedoms without Being depriv'd of them by our fellow men we are a freeborn Pepel and have never forfeited this Blessing by aney compact or agreement whatever' (in Aptheker, 1965, pp. 7–9). The irony of this moving document speaks volumes about the priority given by blacks, who were defined by law as commodities rather than subjects, to forging personal identities on the basis of their common condition and the evolving consciousness of a people in transition from an oral to a literate culture.

Many letters, speeches, essays, and tracts are also valued literary documents. These include astronomer and poet Benjamin Banneker's 1791 letter demonstrating his artistic and scientific attainments to Thomas Jefferson; clothier and abolitionist David Walker's 1829 revolutionary pamphlet calling for blacks to end slavery by any means necessary; abolitionist orator and journalist Frederick Douglass's eloquent speech, delivered to the Rochester Antislavery Sewing Society on July 5 1852, on the hypocrisy of the celebration of American independence; and doctor, journalist, and novelist Martin Delany's 1852 *The Condition, Elevation, and Destiny of the Colored People of the United States, Politically Considered*, which promoted the emigration of African Americans to non-white nations.

Beginning in 1760 with Briton Hammon's *A Narrative of the Uncommon Sufferings, and Surprizing Deliverance of Briton Hammon, A Negro Man*, and ending in 1901 with Booker T. Washington's *Up From Slavery*, slave narratives and black autobiographies provided dramatic, often messianic, first-person testimonies of the discovery of racism in the secondary acculturative process of interacting with whites. Slave narratives, most of which were published between 1830 and 1865, are the personal accounts of physical and psychological bondage and freedom. Some, like *Narratives of the Sufferings of Lewis and Milton Clarke* (1846) and *The Life of Josiah Henson* (1849), were dictated to white amanuenses and editors who controlled how the facts would be recorded and interpreted. But most were written by the escaped slaves themselves, some of whom had already told their stories dozens of times from an antislavery platform. The most celebrated are Olaudah Equiano's *The Interesting Narrative of the Life of Olaudah Equiano, or Gustavus Vassa, the African* (1789), Frederick Douglass's *Narrative of the Life of Frederick Douglass* (1845), and Harriet Jacobs's (Linda Brent) *Incidents in the Life of a Slave Girl* (1861), whose factual details and authorship were authenticated in 1985.

The general pattern of narratives by Frederick Douglass, William W. Brown, J. W. C. Pennington, Solomon Northrop, William and Ellen Craft, and Harriet Jacobs begins with the slave's realization of the evils of the institution, first attempts at resistance and flight, cunning victories over oppression, and detailed descriptions of different phases of bondage. The narratives end with a successful flight North and an activist role in the 'true' religion, rather than the religion that the master class used to justify slavery, and in abolitionist politics. Many read like moral and political allegories. And though the narrators' appeals are mainly to the moral conscience of whites, they clearly express a resolute faith in the humanity of blacks and the righteousness of their struggle for freedom, literacy, and wholeness, both as individuals and as an ethnic group.

Institutionalized racism and sexism, as most intriguingly illustrated in the narratives by Douglass and Jacobs, at some point frustrated the individual's efforts to realize his or her potential wholeness or balance as an American citizen of African descent. Impelled by the resiliency of African cultural survivals and by personal resistance to class, racial, or sexual domination, these individuals turned primarily to their kinship network or ethnic community for survival strategies. Within the ethnic group the individual was disciplined to internalize these socio-psychological tensions and to transform the aborted social energy into cultural energy and expression. Over a long period of time this process of acculturation has settled in the deep consciousness of the individuals who directly experienced it as both self-protective and compensatory cultural behaviour, the double consciousness that African-American writers, sometimes self-consciously but often unconsciously, illumine for readers. As this experience is expressed symbolically in the spoken and written word, both black dialect and standard English, it becomes accessible and, perhaps, strongly meaningful to a double audience: individuals within and outside of the primary speech community and ethnic groups who have never gone through it.

While it has long been known to most Afro-Americanists that William Wells Brown became the father of the Afro-American novel with the London publication in 1853 of *Clotel*, it was not until 1982 that Harriet E. Wilson was discovered to have become the mother of the Afro-American novel with the Boston publication in 1859 of *Our Nig*. Rather than the 'great American novel' or a popular romance of the 'Feminine Fifties', like Emma Southworth's multi-million-selling *The Hidden Hand, Our Nig*, as its ironic and parodic title suggests, is an intriguing synthesis of the Euro-American sentimental novel and the Afro-American slave narrative, of fiction and fact, of romance and autobiography that is addressed primarily to a black audience. Based on the author's life as an indentured servant in New England, its ironic and parodic style is derived from its ethnic double consciousness.

Like its mixed Euro-American step-brother, the Afro-American novel is a hybrid form. Rather than the culmination of an evolutionary process in the narrative tradition, it is the product of social and cultural forces that shape the author's attitude toward life and that fuel the dialectical process between romantic and mimetic narrative impulses. In contrast to the Euro-American novel, however, the Afro-American novel has its roots in the combined oral and literary traditions of Afro-American culture. It is one of the symbolic literary forms of discourse that black Americans have borrowed from Western culture and adapted in their quest for status, power, and identity in a racist, white, patriarchal North American social arena. The Afro-American novel, in other words, is not a solipsistic, self-referential linguistic system, but a symbolic socio-cultural act. 'Precisely because successive Western cultures have privileged written art over oral or musical forms', Gates reminds us, 'the writing of black people in Western language has, at all points, remained political, implicitly or explicitly, regardless of its intent or its subject' (1988, p. 132). In this sense, the nineteenth-century romances and novels of William Wells Brown, Martin Delany, Francis E. W. Harper, Harriet Wilson, and Sutton Griggs were both private and public linguistic enactments of human relationships reflecting ethical as well as aesthetic decisions inside and outside of the text. They were weapons in the struggle for freedom, literacy, and integrity.

Twentieth-century novelists like Richard Wright, Zora Neale Hurston, Ralph Ellison, James Baldwin, John A. Williams, William Melvin Kelley, Ernest Gaines, Toni Morrison, Alice Walker, John Edgar Wideman and Ishmael Reed also employ the novel and romance as symbolic acts to explore the disparity between Euro-American myths and Afro-American reality. But they do not approach the narrative tradition from the same ideological perspective as their white contemporaries, black predecessors, or each other. Among other things, radical social and cultural change has encouraged the movement towards more individualism in the novelists and their aesthetics. Most modern and postmodern Afro-American novelists nevertheless share in a common tradition. This is mainly because, as members of the largest non-white ethnic group in the United States, Afro-American novelists – except those who have been estranged by birth or acculturation, by circumstances or choice from African-American communities and culture – develop their personal and national identities within and against the distinctive pattern of values, orientations to life, and shared ancestral memories they acquired from and contribute to African-American culture.

As much as, if not more than, their white contemporaries, nineteenth-century black novelists tapped the roots of their indigenous ethnic culture for matter and method. But the world view of the politically and economically oppressed was and is hardly the same as that of their oppressors. Because the distinctiveness of each group's historical experience creates a different cultural frame of reference within which it views and interprets reality, there will inevitably be corresponding differences in the meaning of the archetypal patterns they employ to reconstruct their individual and collective experiences. Both white and black novelists of the nineteenth and twentieth centuries, for example, draw on aspects of the Judeo-Christian tradition – especially messianic and jeremiadic themes, symbols, and rituals – for terms to order their experiences. But since, more often than not, the white man's Heaven is the black man's Hell, black writers generally express strong ambivalence toward its values, whether by symbolic acts of silence or speech, submission or rebellion. Also, in contrast to the search for innocence and the Adamic vision that inform the Euro-American novel, we usually find the Manichean drama of white versus black, an apocalyptic vision of a new world order, and the quest to reconcile the double consciousness of Afro-American identity embedded in the texts of nineteenth- and twentieth-century African-American novels.

Brown, for instance, was certainly aware of his debt to the abolitionist tradition, oral and written, as his antislavery allusions in the first chapter, epigraphs, and conclusion of *Clotel* reveal. But his reconstruction of the legend of Thomas Jefferson's mulatto mistress and illegitimate interracial children is different from the use of the tragic mulatto and quest-for-freedom motifs by his white contemporaries. Similarly, Dunbar and Chesnutt continue some of the conventions of the local colour tradition while simultaneously changing others, like the power and authority of the blues in *The Sport of the Gods* (1902) and a transplanted African belief system in *The Conjure Woman* (1899), to provide more complex truths about nineteenth-century black culture and character. In the twentieth century, Hurston's rewriting of the sentimental romance in *Their Eyes Were Watching God* (1937) celebrates the liberating possibilities of love, storytelling, and autonomy for black women. Wright's rewriting of the myths of the 'bad nigger' and the American Dream in *Native Son* (1940) continues to overwhelm readers with the power of its naturalistic truth. Reed's rediscovery and revitalization of such traditional narrative forms as the Western in *Yellow Back Radio Broke-Down* (1969), the detective novel in *Mumbo Jumbo* (1972), and the slave narrative in *Flight to Canada* (1976), intrigue us by their bold experimentation with and celebration of an Afrocentric aesthetic. We are also intrigued by Alice Walker's adaptation of the epistolary method in the Pulitzer Prize-winning *The Color Purple* (1982), whose theme is a rewriting of Janie Crawford's dreams in Hurston's romance of what a black woman ought to be. And we are left spellbound by Toni Morrison's Pulitzer Prize-winning *Beloved* (1987): a Gothic neo-slave narrative and postmodern romance that speaks in many compelling voices of the historical rape of black women and of the concord of sensibilities that African-American people share.

Thematically and structurally, therefore, from Brown and Wilson to Reed and Morrison, the tradition of the Afro-American novel is dominated by the struggle for freedom from all forms of oppression and by the personal odyssey to realize the full potential of one's complex bicultural identity as an Afro-American. This prototypical journey – deriving its sociocultural consciousness from the group experience of black Americans and its mythopoeic force from the interplay of Eurocentric and Afrocentric symbolic systems – begins in physical or psychological bondage and ends in some ambiguous form of deliverance or vision of a new world of mutual respect and justice for peoples of colour. In short, the Afro-American canonical story is the quest, frequently with apocalyptic undertones, for freedom, literacy, and wholeness – personal and communal – grounded in social reality and ritualized in symbolic acts of African-American speech, music, and religion.

Like the poetry of all national and ethnic groups, Afro-American poetry has its roots in the historical experience of the group's relationship to nature and society. As I illustrate in *The Folk Roots of Contemporary Afro-American Poetry* (1974), it is to the unknown black bards of the spirituals and folk songs – a unique fusion of an ancient African cosmic sensibility and an inchoate Prot-estant American culture – that North America is indebted for its most priceless music, those sorrowful and joyous songs whose encoded message subtly yet forcefully decried oppression and celebrated the possibilities of the human spirit. And whatever is racial or ethnic in the poetry of black poets is attributable to the power and wisdom of early black music and the double consciousness that it expresses.

The colonial period was the Age of Phillis Wheatley, the first slave and second woman in American to publish a book of poems. The Senegambian-born Boston slave's heroic couplets and Christian piety reflect the preoccu-pation of the few 'privileged' black poets of the eighteenth century with neo-classical conventions and biblical symbolism refracted through the prism of an evolving double consciousness. Although Thomas Jefferson considered her poetry beneath the dignity of criticism, many of her contemporaries interpreted *Poems on Various Subjects, Religious and Moral* (1773) as indisputable evidence of the mental equality of blacks. While her neo-classicism nearly stifles her personal voice and ethnic identity, pride in her African heritage is apparent in her self-image in several poems as 'Ethiop', 'Afric's Muse' and 'vent'rous Afric'.

The most popular antebellum black poet was Francis Ellen Watkins Harper. Her first book, *Poems on Miscellaneous Subjects* (1854), clearly illustrates that her purpose and passion are one: to promote the causes of abolition, Christianity, feminism, and temperance. Her use of abolitionist conventions and standard English reflects the tension between her ethnic and national consciousness as she sought to explore the burning social issues of the nation and reconcile her personal double consciousness. The postbellum and post-Reconstruction period was the Age of Paul Laurence Dunbar, the Ohio-born poet whose ambiguous use of black speech and music is the culmination of the identity crisis of many late nineteenth-century black poets. His dilemma of being torn between the impulse to explore and expand the forms of Afro-American folklore and the desire to master Euro-American conventions is equally rep-resentative. If the antebellum popularity of the slave narratives marks the first flowering of Afro-American literature, then Dunbar's publication of *Oak and Ivy* (1893) and *Majors and Minors* (1895) marks the second renaissance. The muted cry of anguish we hear and sense beneath Dunbar's mask of humour, which is the theme of 'We Wear the Mask', is due in part to white critics' unjustly ignoring the majority of his poems in standard English and only praising the pathos and humour of what he refers to in 'The Poet' as 'a jingle in a broken tongue', a literary dialect established by the conventions of minstrelsy and the plantation tradition.

The third awakening of Afro-American art and letters during the 1920s was dominated by the prolific, versatile Langston Hughes, who is popularly considered the poet laureate of black America. This period is also known as the Negro Renaissance, Harlem Renaissance, and New Negro movement. It was the period in which Harlem was the national stage for the meteoric rise of such artists as Claude McKay, Jean Toomer, Countee Cullen, Bill Robinson, Florence Mills, Josephine Baker, Ethel Waters, Paul Robeson, Roland Hayes, Aaron Douglass, Louis Armstrong, Bessie Smith, Duke Ellington and Hughes. Many artists of the decade, like Hughes, turned to Africa and Afro-American folklore for a sense of tradition. Hughes's first book of verse, *The Weary Blues* (1926), focuses on the night life of the Harlem cabarets and captures the sights and sounds of the Jazz Age. Besides introducing jazz and blues rhythms into poetry, Hughes took the world for his audience, but, for the most part, his subject was the black urban working class. His music was the sound of Lenox Avenue in New York, Seventh Street in the District of Columbia, and South State Street in Chicago. And his language has been aptly called Harlemese: vibrant, rhythmic, direct, racy urban black speech.

In contrast to the rebellious spirit of the poetry of the 1920s and 1930s, the verse of the 1940s by Robert Hayden, Margaret Walker, Melvin Tolson, Gwendolyn Brooks and Owen Dodson seems sedate. This is not to suggest that racial themes, social protest, and experiments in prosody are absent in their work, especially Walker's 'For My People', Hayden's 'Runagate Runagate', and Brooks's *Annie Allen* (1949), for which she was awarded the Pulitzer Prize in 1950. Products of an era of American criticism that repudiated didacticism in literature and advocated the concept of art for art's sake, the black poets of the forties laboured diligently and in many cases successfully to perfect their craftsmanship.

The black poets of the 1950s were nomadic, bohemian bards whose audiences were the predominantly white patrons of Greenwich Village coffee houses and San Francisco bistros. Amiri Baraka (Le Roi Jones), Bob Kaufman and Ted Joans were among the most prominent of this black beat generation. Their chief themes were alienation, jazz, war, and death; their language was iconoclastic; and their style surrealistic. Too avant-garde for the traditional literary establishment, they gave public readings and appeared in underground magazines like *Beatitude*, *Big Table* and *Evergreen Review*.

Rising like a phoenix out of the ashes of Watts, New York, Newark, Chicago and Atlanta came the poets of the Black Arts movement of the sixties, including

Haki Madhubuti (Don Lee), Nikki Giovanni, Sonia Sanchez, Etheridge Knight, Askia Toure, Clarence Major and Larry Neal. Because the Black Arts and Black Power concepts both relate broadly to the Afro-American's desire for self-determination and nationhood, both are nationalistic. With Baraka, the multi-talented writer, as the drum major of the movement, this generation of poets – most of them under thirty-five years old – set out to create a new black aesthetic and nation. Their credo was art for people's sake, and their goal was black unity and liberation. The movement was toward Islam rather than Christianity, pan-Africanism rather than Americanism, and a black aesthetic – especially a revitalizing use of Africa, the blues, and the urban black vernacular – rather than a white.

Black poetry of the 1970s and 1980s – as illustrated by Alice Walker, Sterling Plumpp, Carolyn Rodgers, June Jordan, Michael Harper, Maya Angelou, Jayne Cortez, Rita Dove, Eugene Redmond, Ishmael Reed and Al Young – continues to illumine the tension between Eurocentric and Afrocentric aesthetic values. Regardless of the socio-political convictions of individual contemporary African-American poets, many of their poems reveal a romantic interest in and realistic evaluation of black folk values, a celebration of the black masses and of musicians as heroes, and a validation of the poetic qualities of black speech and music. The diverse styles, structures, and themes of their poems, in short, attest to the complexity of their bicultural identity as African-Americans.

Like documentary, autobiographical, fictive, and poetic African-American literature, black theatre literature, especially after the realism of Lorraine Hansberry's *A Raisin in the Sun* (1959) and beginning with the expressionism of Amiri Baraka's *Dutchman* (1964), dramatizes the tension between Eurocentric and Afrocentric sensibilities and conventions. 'In an effort to locate a specific culturally derived voice', playwright and director Paul Carter Harrison writes,

> Afro-Americans began to shape an aesthetic that reflected both the African legacy and their cumulative experience in a highly technological society. The aesthetic formulations seemed crude in the beginning, song-dance-drum – those civilizing forces of ritual – appearing quaint and exotic next to the formal canons of Western dramaturgy. However, after the discovery of oral and literary traditions among the Yoruba and the Akan, and of the ontological system of the Dogon, the rudimentary apprehension of drum as iconographic reference – the rhythmical analogue to the human voice – was elaborated into a more sophisticated aesthetic principle.
>
> (1989, p. xliv)

Baraka's *Dutchman* and *Slave Ship*, Joseph Walker's *River Niger*, James Baldwin's *Blues for Mister Charlie*, Ron Milner's *What the Wine Sellers Buy*, Paul Carter Harrison's *The Great Mac Daddy*, and Ntozake Shange's *for colored girls who have considered suicide/when the rainbow's enuf* are among the major plays that chart this development by Douglas Turner Ward's Negro Ensemble Company and Woodie King's New Federal Theatre as well as by traditional American theatre institutions, both on and off Broadway. Among the coveted awards received by African-Americans are the Pulitzer Prize-winning plays *No Place to be Somebody* (1970) by Charles Gordone, *A Soldier's Play* (1982) by Charlie Fuller, and *Fences* (1987) by August Wilson.

The consensus of contemporary specialists in the fields of African-American literary history and criticism is that the Afro-American literary tradition is best understood and appreciated by interpreting its merits within the context of its own indigenous nature and function. In addition to my *The Afro-American Novel and Its Tradition* (1987), with its theory of the novel as a socially symbolic act that formally encodes and wryly illumines the biracial, bicultural, residually oral tradition of African Americans, useful recent studies include: Robert Stepto's *From Behind the Veil* (1979), with its emphasis on the intertextuality of call-and-response in canonical black texts; Barbara Christian's *Black Woman Novelists* (1980), which traces the impact of stereotypic images on the narrative tradition of black women; Houston Baker's *Blues, Ideology and Afro-American Literature* (1984), with its focus on the blues as the key black vernacular trope; Keith Beyerman's *Fingering the Jagged Grain* (1986), which focuses on the use of black folk materials in recent black fiction; Melvin Dixon's *Ride Out the Wilderness* (1987), with its emphasis on spatial ethnic tropes as the distinctive feature of Afro-American literature; Hazel Carby's *Reconstructing Womanhood* (1987), which examines the influence of black feminist discourse on the literary conventions of early black American women; William Andrew's *To Tell a Free Story* (1988), with its emphasis on the uniquely self-liberating and empowering rhetorical strategies of black autobiography; and Henry Gates's *The Signifying Monkey* (1988), which privileges signifying and pastiche as the prototypical black vernacular and literary tropes. Best interpreted on its own bicultural terms, African-American literature revitalizes the language and challenges people to realize their human potential.

FURTHER READING

Andrews, William L. (1988) *To Tell a Free Story: The First Century of Afro-American Autobiography, 1760–1865*, University of Illinois Press, Urbana

Baker, Houston A., Jr. (1980) *The Journey Back: Issues in Black Literature and Criticism*, University of Chicago Press, Chicago

——(1984) *Blues, Ideology, and Afro-American Literature: A Vernacular Theory*, University of Chicago Press, Chicago

Bell, Bernard W. (1987) *The Afro-American Novel and Its Tradition*, University of Massachusetts Press, Amherst

Bell, Roseann P., Parker, Bettye J. and Guy-Sheftall, Beverly (eds) (1979) *Sturdy Black Bridges: Visions of Black Women in Literature*, Anchor Books, Garden City

Bone, Robert A. (1975) *Down Home: A History of Afro-American Short Fiction from the Beginnings to the End of the Harlem Renaissance*, G. P. Putnam's Sons, New York

Christian, Barbara (1980) *Black Women Novelists: The Development of a Tradition, 1892–1976*, Greenwood Press, Westport

Gates, Henry Louis, Jr. (1987) *Figures in Black: Words, Signs, and the 'Racial' Self*, Oxford University Press, New York

——(1988) *The Signifying Monkey: A Theory of Afro-American Literary Criticism*, Oxford University Press, New York

Gayle, Addison, Jr. (ed.) (1969) *Black Expression*, Weybright & Talley, New York

—— (ed.) (1971) *The Black Aesthetic*, Doubleday & Company, Garden City

Harrison, Paul Carter (1972) *The Drama of Nommo*, Grove Press, New York

Huggins, Nathan Irvin (1971) *Harlem Renaissance*, Oxford University Press, New York

Levine, Lawrence W. (1977) *Black Culture and Black Consciousness: Afro-American Folk Thought from Slavery to Freedom*, Oxford University Press, New York

Loggins, Vernon (1964) *The Negro Author: His Development in America to 1900*, Kennikat Press, Port Washington [first published 1931]

Redmond, Eugene B. (1976) *Drumvoices: The Mission of Afro-American Poetry*, Anchor Books, Garden City

Shockley, Ann Allen (1988) *Afro-American Women Writers, 1746–1933: An Anthology and Critical Guide*, G. K. Hall & Company, Boston

ADDITIONAL WORKS CITED

Aptheker, Herbert (ed.) (1965) *A Documentary History of the Negro People in the United States*, Citadel Press, New York [first published 1951]

Bell, Bernard W. (1974) *The Folk Roots of Contemporary Afro-American Poetry*, Broadside Press, Detroit

Beyerman, Keith (1986) *Fingering the Jagged Grain*, University of Georgia Press, Athens

Carby, Hazel (1987) *Reconstructing Womanhood*, Oxford University Press, New York

Dixon, Melvin (1987) *Ride Out the Wilderness*, University of Illinois Press, Champaign

Du Bois, W. E. B. (1961) *The Souls of Black Folk: Essays and Sketches*, Fawcett Publications, Greenwich [first published 1903]

Eliot, T. S. (1964) *The Sacred Wood: Essays on Poetry and Criticism*, Barnes & Noble, New York [first published 1920]

Harrison, Paul Carter (ed.) (1989) *Totem Voices: Plays from the Black World Repertory*, Grove Press, New York

Stepto, Robert B. (1979) *From Behind the Veil*, University of Illinois Press, Champaign

Wellek, René and Warren, Austin (1962) *Theory of Literature*, Harcourt, Brace & World, New York [first published 1948]

Wright, Richard (1937) 'Blueprint for Negro Writing', *New Challenge*, 2, 53–65

85

AUSTRALIAN LITERATURE AND THE BRITISH TRADITION

HELEN TIFFIN

No attempt at characterizing the national literary tradition of Australia, or indeed of any other post-colonial territory, can ignore its genesis in Anglo-European colonialism. But to describe that post-colonial literature in filiastic terms – to invoke, implicitly or explicitly, such metaphors as 'parent and child', 'stream and tributary', 'trunk and branches' – is to misconceive the relationship of the literatures and to collude in a continuing colonialism. Such metaphors not only imply a chronological and qualitative pre-eminence for the products of European culture, but also that its epistemology is normative and universally valid. Post-colonial literature comprehended, defined and evaluated by Anglo-European expectations and criteria remains a passive and subjected discourse.

Nationalist literary critics and historians rightly reject this approach and attempt to describe the characteristics of the literature in terms of its genesis in local history, sociology and landscape. For such historians, distinctiveness is a prized quality in the literature, identity a constant preoccupation, and England and English values targets for repudiation. The literature thus mapped is able to generate its own standards of criticism and evaluation, but it does so at the cost of a certain ostrich-like refusal to acknowledge its relationships with other literatures. As Peter Pierce has remarked, 'nationalist interpretation' has been seen as both the hero and the villain in the 'melodrama' of Australian literary debate, the plot of which has been refuelled by 'fears of dispossession', 'fears of losing . . . the tenuous culture which has developed in this continent or coming adrift from the parent European culture' (in Hergenhan, 1988, p. 88).

But post-colonial literatures are neither passive nor isolated, and they cannot be adequately accounted for without considering carefully their textual relations. I want to argue that Australian literature is not a reduced descendant of British literature drawing its thematic parameters and evaluative criteria from an older tradition to which it remains eternally subject, nor a self-contained phenomenon whose innate excellence is measured by the alleged distinctness it manifests. Rather, it is a cultural formation actively engaged with British literary culture which is important to it not for reasons of chronological antecedence or superior value, but as enabling material and cultural forces which continue to act upon, and partially to determine, its own circumstances and processes. First, though, it is necessary to consider the agency in colonialism of textuality.

In the process of colonization, texts and textuality play a major part. Even before explorers, pirates, slavers, administrators and settlers moved into 'other worlds' their knowledge of these worlds had been structured by European texts which had dealt, in fantastic or apparently realistic accounts of voyages, crusades, overland travels, with the non-European (Hulme, 1986). Paradoxically, however, the cumulative evocation of *difference* failed to articulate the Other. The European genesis of the accounts ensured that the Other was simply appropriated to the European archive, and rendered in terms of European epistemology.

But textuality not only formed the preconceptions of adventurers and colonial administrators, it assisted the material practices of domination and control. Historical accounts, travel narratives and fictional works not only 'captured' the African or the Oriental to a pre-scripted (European) 'otherness', they also naturalized the relationship between that 'otherness' and Europe. Hakluyt's *Voyages*, Shakespeare's *The Tempest*, Defoe's *Robinson Crusoe*, the classic formulations of Europe's (or specifically England's) encounters with other peoples, were accepted, and then presented through education to colonized subjects, not as the culturally-specific and time-and-place-bound documents they were, but as embodying supra-national, supra-political accounts of the questing human spirit overcoming obstacles on an inevitable path of progress. Specific (and often sordid) imperial perspectives were thus glorified as human destiny, and the accounts told the colonized that their subjectification was a natural element of the course of history.

A concomitant of this normative greatness of the imperial power is the inferiority, deviance and irrelevance of the colonial, an ideological pattern which could be reinforced in the mind of the colonial through the imperial power's control of the education process. Symptomatic of this is the colony's immediate availability as the butt of imperial humour:

> *Cecily:* I don't think you will require neckties. Uncle Jack is sending you to Australia.
> *Algernon:* Australia? I'd sooner die.
> (Wilde, *The Importance of Being Earnest*, Act 1)

Such apparently innocent jokes are in fact part of a sinister spectrum of denigration and educational interpellation, the effects of which have been described by many post-colonial writers. Ivan Southall, writing of his childhood in the 1930s, notes that

> Good things, which parents would buy for you, came from England. . . . Australia rarely earned a mention except as the wilderness to which profligate cousins were sent and out of which lost uncles came.
>
> (in Hergenhan, 1988, p. 547)

The Australian environment, then, was a world that lacked the reality of the Anglo-written world. White Australians were condemned to a life of shadows. As Christopher Koch has noted,

> The society that had produced us, so far away from what it saw as the centre of civilization, made us rather like the prisoners in Plato's cave. To guess what the centre was like, that centre 12,000 miles away for which we yearned, we must study shadows on the wall, as our parents and grandparents had done . . . shadows, clues to the real world we would someday discover in the northern hemisphere.
>
> (1980, p. 2)

The importance of texts and textuality in this colonization and continuing subjectification has been recognized by post-colonial writers throughout the English-speaking world. Consequently the project of much post-colonial writing has been the investigation of this European capture-by-text and the unmasking and dismantling of its strategies of containment.

The post-colonial text, whether Caribbean or Australian, is best seen, then, not in terms of its simple descent from or affiliation with an Anglo-European tradition, nor as a unique product of the national culture or place, but as a site of resistance to the interpellations effected by textuality, 'tradition' and education across the whole of that discursive field within which texts were and are situated. What makes Australian literature 'different' from British is thus revealed not within essentialist nationalist terms – terms which all too often replicate the modes, methods and frames of the imperialist culture – but in terms of its counter-discursive impetus.

Such counter-discursive resistance, as Richard Terdiman has noted in a rather different context, cannot 'be conceived as an essentialist genre or institution which could be framed *a priori*' since its manifestations are necessarily 'disparate'. 'They are more than simple antinomic formations dependent upon their antagonist in the manner of some perverse mirror image. We cannot reduce their tactics or their contents by mechanically negating elements of the dominant discourse' (1985, p. 77).

Initial Australian literary reaction against English determination was limited to the occasional complaint such as John Dunmore Lang's that all the Aboriginal place-names were being replaced by those of English governors, or Henry

Kendall's that no Australian writer could gain local acceptance without first achieving acceptance in England. By the end of the century, however, there is evidence that Australian writers were assessing their subjected position in a more coherent way. Victor Daley's rather lurid allegory sees the English market as a destructive siren:

> The story-teller from the isles
>   Upon the Empire's rim,
> With smiles she welcomes – and her smiles
>   Are death to him.
>
> For her, whose pleasure is her law
>   In vain the shy heart bleeds,
> The genius with the iron jaw
>   Alone succeeds.
>
> And when the poet's lays grow bland
>   And urbanised, and prim –
> She stretches forth a jewelled hand
>   And strangles him.
>   ('When London Calls', Daley, 1898)

Writing more than half a century later, Elizabeth Jolley figures this relationship in not very different terms in her story, 'The Well-bred Thief' (1980). Here a manuscript sent to an English pen-friend by an Australian writer is purloined by the friend who works for a publisher. She tells the Australian it has little merit, and then claims to have lost it, but publishes it under her own name. Again the English literary establishment is figured as an unscrupulous user/ abuser of colonial talent, appropriating and destroying from a position of superiority. Works like these are quite blunt in their depictions of the market morality, but exemplify only the simplest level of exploration of Anglo-Australian textual relations.

Both these examples thematize England as the acquisitive exploiter of colonial literary resources (and even in recent years there has been controversy over complaints that Australian publishers nurture Australian writers only to have them poached by English publishers once they achieve popularity). Far more important, though, is the impact of the texts England has exported. Such texts operate as semi-covert carriers of ideological baggage, their interpellative power being greatly enhanced by their privileged position in the English-controlled education system. But despite this, the transfer of the English text to Australian circumstances can energize surprisingly subversive potentials.

Thomas Keneally wrote his novel *The Playmaker* (1987) about the first production of an English play on Australian soil. *The Playmaker* interrogates the imperial conception of English literature as a 'civilizing' influence in the colonies, and demonstrates the ways in which the play's production under 'foreign' circumstances inevitably opens the ground to subversive possibility.

Governor Phillip is keen to support Ralph Clark's convict-acted production of Farquhar's *The Recruiting Officer* because he hopes the play will exert a civilizing influence on them. Ironically, the play does have an effect on those who take part in its production, not because the example of a fashionable London play 'lifts' the convicts above their moral degradation, as Phillip hoped, but because the processes of production energize a transformation in the attitudes to them of Ralph and his more sympathetic supporters. During rehearsals, the very class divisions which were ultimately responsible for the crimes many committed (and hence their transportation to Australia) are broken down. Through its production on Australian soil, then, the play undermines one of the bases of British privilege and social order.

Moreover, the meanings of the text itself change with its context. Wisehammer's new epilogue and his delivery of Farquhar's prologue which allow him a play on the word 'transported' – an emphasis thoroughly appreciated by the convict audience – make *The Recruiting Officer* a different work for this audience, again revising the 'civilizing' values which Phillip hoped to propagate.

But if Keneally's version of the first Australian production of an English play demonstrates the subversive potential of 'transportation' and 'transformation', it also attests to the destructive effects of colonialism and its cultural arsenal. It is the white convict population which Governor Phillip hopes will be 'civilized' by the play, as British administrators in India and Africa looked to literature as a valuable inculcator of English (middle-class) values – a major weapon in the colonial armoury. But as in India and Africa, colonialism – the introduction and imposition of the values and beliefs of another culture – also signalled the destruction of native cultures:

> Seen from the immensity of time, Ralph's play might appear a mere sputter of the European humour on the edge of a continent which, then, still did not have a name. This flicker of theatrical intent would consume in the end the different and serious theatre of the tribes of the hinterland. In the applause at the end of the evening... Arabanoo – had he still lived – might have heard the threat.
>
> (p. 347)

Keneally's novel is dedicated to 'Arabanoo and his brethren, still dispossessed'. His text serves as a reminder that a literary tradition like the Australian one, even as it operates counter-discursively in one direction, can serve as an excluding or oppressive agency in another. Thus, while a view of Anglo-Australian literary relations shows the Australian discourse as a subversive one, it is a complex tradition which contains its own patterns of dissidence which may be expressed through inter-textual allusion or parody. Two examples of such intertextuality by Aboriginal writers are examined later in this essay.

Keneally's novel used a specific historical incident involving a transported English text to generate its subversion. Other texts investigate the processes of colonial interpellation using English works whose provenance in Australia was at once less specific and more pervasive. Jessica Anderson's *Tirra Lirra by the River* (1978) employs a nineteenth-century English poem which featured prominently in school readers and in university curriculums throughout the Empire. In Tennyson's 'The Lady of Shalott', the Lady is, in an imagistic parallel to Christopher Koch's notion of the colonial in Plato's cave, condemned to see life only in reflection, in the mirror, never able to look directly at it without invoking the curse of death. For Nora Roche, growing up in the Brisbane she regards as 'a backward and unworldly place' (p. 11), Tennyson's poem and the other English books she reads supply a better world, one she feels she can actually glimpse by looking at her backyard through a deforming glass, converting it to Camelot. Escaping to Sydney which stood 'proxy for Camelot' (p. 18) for a time, Nora emerges from an unhappy and constraining marriage to leave for London. The colonized's profound sense of exile from the place which reading and upbringing have conditioned her to think of as the centre is evident in her account of the instinctive 'decision' she takes to leave Australia. A 'sense of exile' is not necessarily a conscious preoccupation of the colonial, but it is often absorbed as an inevitable consequence of being educated to metropolitan texts:

> I didn't really have a firm intention of going anywhere, but I said London because it was the first place I thought of. And to myself I said that I could go, too, if I pleased. Nobody could stop me.
>
> (p. 69)

Nora's actual narration of her life story begins on her return to Brisbane from London as an elderly woman, and it is then she begins to discover and recover her Australian past. *Tirra Lirra by the River* is generally concerned with different kinds of recuperation consequent upon the removal of authoritative repressions – marital and familial as well as cultural ones. Anderson's novel can be read, then, as an exploration of the development of a post-colonial consciousness in which the colonial syndrome of 'always-elsewhere' is eventually replaced by the acceptance, indeed the celebration, of the here and now. Nora's quest is not a conscious one, since the kind of false colonial consciousness she carries is cryptic. But as with the removal of the constraint of Colin, the removal of what has become a sort of state of suspension in London comes to her as a kind of gift or grace. It is thus appropriately linked with Nora's increasing understanding of and reconciliation with the values of her now-dead sister Grace, who had always accepted home, in the here and now. Nora, in taking over her family's old house, begins to assume Grace's role – reoccupying particular rooms, protecting Grace's cherished mango tree from the depredations of a neighbour, and appreciating Grace's investment in composting – in putting something back into her own soil.

Nora's return to Brisbane has occurred as a kind of blessing. Although she had made plans to return many times it is only the eventual incarceration of the paranoid Fred which releases the three women into other lives. And after Nora's return home, it becomes increasingly clear that it has been her life in London – particularly at 'Number Six' – and not, as she had once interpreted it, her childhood in Brisbane, which has represented the world of illusions and imprisonment. The gap between the London world of 'Number Six', of Hilda, Liza and Fred, and her present and past life in Australia (as she now begins to learn in old age to re-inhabit it) is drawn, amongst other ways, by the contrast between the tone of her narration and the falsely 'literary' voice she assumes when writing or talking to her London friends:

> *My dears, I am sick, and have an enormous glum doctor on the model of Frankenstein's monster . . .*
>
> (p. 31)

and

> *My dears, there are telegraph poles on one side of this street, and from those poles long black wires extend to the houses, two or three to each pole, for all the world like a small pack of dogs tethered to a post. When I first arrived, the visual impression made by all these black wires was horrible, but now . . .*
>
> (p. 89)

Significantly, Nora falls ill on her arrival in Brisbane (her illness is a sort of *rite de passage*) and during that illness and for a while after, a postal strike prevents letters from passing between Brisbane and England.

Nora is thus forced to look out at the real world of the Brisbane she had earlier preferred to see through a distorting glass, and the result is not death, as it was for the Lady of Shalott, but physical and psychic recovery. The 'disidentification' (Pêcheux, [1975] 1982) of this colonially interpellated self also enables her to confront the repressed memory of her father's death. Her later image of Lancelot, and her love of Tennyson's poem, have been conflated with her memory of the plumed and curbed horses at her father's funeral. As the culmination of her memory-retrieval, this decoding of the conflated images has particular importance, since it suggests the connection between the English world of textuality – epitomized in the romantic figure of Lancelot – and death; death not occasioned by the colonized's leaving the mirror or the cave to look at the real world, but rather the death of not accepting that world.

At the end of the novel Nora is still writing to Hilda and Liza. But though the postal strike is over, and their contact resumed, the world of London has become remote; she now recognizes it as a world of story-telling, of fictions insidious in their concealment of the real frustrations, tensions and power-relations of which that life was composed.

Tennyson's poem allegorized the difficulty for the artist of balancing aesthetic and humanist impulses. Anderson reoriented the allegory to depict the dangerous seductions of England to the colonial, and the subsequent process of disidentification of post-colonial consciousness. Her reorienting of the allegory is not directed against the values of the original work; she simply takes and redeploys a convenient motif from it. Nevertheless, *Tirra Lirra by the River* does comment upon the institutional and social deployment of the 'great' works of English literature (like 'The Lady of Shalott') throughout the English-speaking world in terms of their capture of the colonial imagination and consequent castration of local creativity. Other writers, however, engage more directly with the ideological values of the works to which they write back.

In his version of the story of Mrs Eliza Fraser in *A Fringe of Leaves* (1976), Patrick White rewrites the terms of *The Tempest* and more particularly of *Robinson Crusoe* and *Heart of Darkness*. Like *Robinson Crusoe*, *A Fringe of Leaves* deals with a sea voyage out of England, with shipwreck, isolation, exile, social origins, and with the carving out by transported/transplanted Europeans of the new world 'plantation garden' from 'virgin' land. In doing so it interrogates Anglo-European assumptions about new world 'beginnings' – about exploration and pioneering, and specifically about relations between indigenes and European interlopers – relations which Defoe's text, like Shakespeare's before, had helped to 'naturalize', to declare ordained. In Defoe's text, Friday is considered the innate inferior of Crusoe and so naturally becomes his grateful slave. Unlike the actual circumstances of European practice, Crusoe is lucky enough to land on an island only sporadically visited by local populations part of whose socio-cultural territory it undoubtedly is. But these visits are equivocated in Crusoe's eyes by their 'unspeakable' purpose. The potential claims of prior ownership are nullified by the vilification of the potential claimants' morals, an 'othering' effected, as in *Heart of Darkness*, through the charged field of cannibalism. *Robinson Crusoe*, as Neil Heims has noted, is the 'justifying fantasy' of Europeans 'for their brutal consumption of human lives'. European savagery is admitted, 'but only after it has been effectively projected onto the cannibals. Then the narrator can accuse the Europeans of acting *like* the savages. But the fundamental savagery itself has been alienated from them' (1983, p. 192). In the process of naturalizing relations between Europe and its others, cannibalism serves a very useful purpose. Like Defoe, Patrick White places a scene of cannibalism at the heart of his narrative, but does so to question the terms of its earlier usage in the European texts.

White's Ellen Roxburgh is shipwrecked off the Queensland coast while on a return journey to England. After drifting for several days in the ship's longboat, she, her husband and some of the crew are cast ashore on Fraser

Island off the Queensland coast. Unlike Robinson Crusoe, however, some, including Ellen Roxburgh's husband, are killed by the Aborigines who then capture her. Treated by the Aborigines as both fetish and slave, Ellen Roxburgh is forced to live for a matter of months with 'her' tribe, as, like Friday's people, they roam across their territory in accordance with the natural ecology. Conrad's Kurtz who also lived with 'his' African tribe, was, in the most popularly taught interpretation of the novel, 'maddened' by his contact with African 'savagery', his European veneer of civilization eroded down to its savage 'heart' to the degree of participating in their 'unspeakable' cannibalistic 'rites'. Mrs Roxburgh is an unwelcome participant in similar rites, though in White's rewriting of this deeply-charged topos of European 'othering' the terms are very different from those assumed in *Robinson Crusoe* or elaborated to a nineteenth-century ideology in *Heart of Darkness*.

Ellen Roxburgh's intrusion upon this scene of Aboriginal cannibalism is described by White through Christian sacramental analogy. As she unwittingly approaches the group, Ellen feels she is being prepared for initiation or confirmation into what she has formerly regarded as a generally hostile environment. There is something fresh and crisp about the morning; fronds stroke her. These beguiling moments cease when she suddenly comes upon her tribe and the remnants of their feast. As they abruptly depart – their ritual having been profaned by her intrusion – a thigh-bone falls from one of the overflowing dillies and Ellen Roxburgh suddenly finds that she has picked it up and gnawed the meat. Hunger has in part dictated her behaviour – in every way the scene eschews the horrified mystifications of Kurtz's acts – but her own perceptions of the incident in White's rendering suggest that beyond its simple and explicable grounding in hunger, an act of some sacramental significance has been performed:

> She flung the bone away only after it was cleaned, and followed slowly in the wake of her cannibal mentors. She was less disgusted in retrospect by what she had done, than awed by the fact that she had been moved to do it. The exquisite innocence of this forest morning, its quiet broken by a single flute-note endlessly repeated, tempted her to believe that she had partaken of a sacrament. But there remained what amounted to an abomination of human behaviour, a headache, and the first signs of indigestion. In the light of Christian morality she must never think of the incident again.
>
> (p. 244)

Defoe and Conrad saw cannibalism as symbolic of the irretrievable difference between a moral, Christian, civilized Europe and an unregenerate, savage Other, whose conquest and subjection were therefore justified. White explodes this antithesis, first by attaching Christian imagery to Ellen's cannibalistic act, and then suggesting that the Christian conscience is inadequate to comprehend what has been both a necessitous and a deeply spiritual act. The incident has, however, signalled a fleeting if uneasy moment of communion between Ellen Roxburgh and an (until then) unfamiliar land and her Aboriginal captors/ mentors.

Not only does *A Fringe of Leaves* question those paradigms of settlement and colonization enshrined in and by the English canon, it also interrogates the nationalist narrative (which overlaps with the imperialist one) of convictism, exploration, pioneering and settlement. Just as the European fringe-dwellers, adhering to a law of rigid divisions, consigned the original inhabitants of the land to a zone of convenient amnesia, so the distinctions between free and 'convicted' upon which the fledgling settlements were based break down when Ellen Roxburgh, now attuned to the falsity of any such distinction, questions their premises.

White is, of course, not alone in interrogating and dismantling the imperialist and nationalist myths of heroic exploration, pioneering and administration. In Randolph Stow's *To the Islands* (1958) and *Visitants* (1979), and in Peter Carey's *Oscar and Lucinda* (1988), the once-heroic figure of the explorer is re-cast in a very different light. The psychopathic Mr Jeffris records in his journals a very different exploration from the one given in the third person account in Carey's novel. But Jeffris, who has modelled himself on the explorer Thomas Mitchell, knows that what you write down is what counts. He forbids anyone else to keep a journal:

> Mr Jeffris was content. He had not made a great exploration – you could not have a great exploration with seven wagons in mountainous country – but he had done sound work, which would serve as evidence of his ability to lead other expeditions.
>
> (p. 472)

This 'sound work' actually consists in the egomaniacal destruction of the landscape and in savagely murderous attacks on its original inhabitants:

> He had put names to several largish creeks. He had set the heights of many mountains which had previously been wildly misdescribed. He had established a reputation for courage, having led his party through places inhabited by desperate blacks. His journals recorded that he had 'given better than we took' from the 'Spitting Tribe'. Also '6 treacherous knaves' from the Yarra-Happini had been 'despatched' by their guns.... He recorded all this in a neat and flowing hand which gave no indication of the peculiarities of his personality. His sketches of the countryside, the long ridges of mountains etc, were as good as anything in Mitchell's journals.
>
> (p. 472)

This also stands, of course, in savagely ironic relation to Carey's rendering of the Aboriginal account of these massacres.

Oscar and Lucinda gently debunks writing of another kind, and suggests its cultural limitations. Lucinda's mother has been a friend of George Eliot and so when Lucinda goes to London she calls on the novelist. But it is a disillusioning experience in every way. 'Lucinda had come to London thinking of it as "Home". It was soon clear that this great sooty machine was not home at all' (p. 203). And 'George Eliot was forty-six years old and bad-tempered with kidney stones and she had misunderstood the girl completely. . . . Lucinda thought George Eliot was a snob' (pp. 202–3). This capacity for misunderstanding, rendered in detail a page or so later, contrasts with the way in which George Eliot's works were read and taught throughout the English-speaking world as literature which dealt with the 'universally human', and attests instead to her ethnocentric prejudices – she is simply unable to understand the 'colonial' Lucinda whose manners and aspirations lie outside her own particular socio-cultural circumstances.

The rewriting of the texts of empire, the re-reading and re-interpreting of those educationally enshrined greats, and the claims of their proponents to a 'literary universality' outside cultural specificity or political hegemony, have not been the preserve solely of white Australian writers. And texts like White's *A Fringe of Leaves* have been attacked by Australian Aboriginal writers for their re-inscription of racist attitudes in spite of their otherwise reformist agendas. Colin Johnson's (Mudrooroo Narogin) *Doctor Wooreddy's Prescription for Enduring the Ending of the World* considers the place of text in the European conquest of oral Australian cultures. It also rewrites the terms of *Robinson Crusoe*, dismantles authoritative white accounts of the invasion and settlement of Tasmania, and specifically investigates the ambiguous position in this history of the man known as 'the great conciliator' – George Robinson.

Like Crusoe, Robinson (eventually) re-names his Aboriginal charges, but unlike Crusoe his dominance of them is constantly equivocated. In his 'progress' through the Tasmanian scrub he is bumbling, dependent upon his Aboriginal guides, and subject to their orchestration of events. In the novel's view he achieved neither the exploration nor the conciliation with which history credits him. In fact, the 'conciliation' was really the near annihilation of the Tasmanian Aborigine.

Johnson's rewriting of Tasmanian history, centred on Robinson, deliberately appropriates the forms of imperialist culture, filling these forms with indigenous non-European content. The perspective in Johnson's novel is not that of the administrator, explorer or settler, but that of the Aborigines. Just as Europeans annexed for themselves the notion of 'the human', relegating others to orders outside this, so Johnson places Aboriginal peoples at the centre of consciousness from where the whites are regarded as non-human *num* or ghost people. 'Where the ghosts ruled, human life was constantly under threat' (p. 97). Although the Aborigines learn some English, 'Meeter Rob-bin-un's' attempts at their languages, like his efforts at conciliation, are the subject of subversive parody. Ummarrah's parodies of 'Meeter Rob-bin-un's' hymn-singing and praying 'lift the spirits' of a people who perceive their imminent destruction and that of their environment with which their lives are so intimately bound. A contemporary subversive restitution is also achieved, not in the narrative of annihilation itself, but in Johnson's re-casting of its terms.

Although *Dr Wooreddy* is written in English, Aboriginal words and phrases and mispronunciations of English act as constant reminders of *difference* within the text. The great conciliator's 'humanitarian' motives are recast as a combination of Christian ecstasy, martyrdom and naked self-interest. Robinson, who cannot begin to comprehend the indissoluble connection between Aboriginal peoples, the land, ritual and orality, attempts to employ and then impose a destructive textuality. And writing within the *num* culture is shown to be less a form of genuine communication than an efficient technology of deceit. Not only do the *num* use their documents to deceive the *humans*, they use them to deceive each other.

If Johnson's novel reinterprets a well-known 'incident' in white Australian history, Sally Morgan's *My Place* (1987) addresses another popular white Australian conception of origins and the national character – the (male) battler, the pioneer, the genuine outback bloke, the ANZAC. A. B. Facey's *A Fortunate Life* (1983), one of the most popular of contemporary Australian works, has been frequently hailed as a classic in this tradition. As Joan Newman has noted, the book has become 'required reading for high school students and the gift of choice for elderly aunts at Christmas' (1988, p. 376), and its values have been 'read by most of its readers in terms of the Great Australian Legend' (p. 381). Morgan's *My Place*, published by the same press as Facey's book, can be read as standing in direct counter-discursive relationship to *A Fortunate Life*, even though, as Stephen Muecke (1988) has noted, the success of Facey's autobiography 'enabled' (in the sense of both production and reception) *My Place*.

My Place details Morgan's rediscovery of her Aboriginality, and her tracing of the history of her Aboriginal ancestors through the tangled interpellations of white oppression. (This ancestry was deliberately hidden from Morgan by her mother and grandmother.) In the white male Australian bush ethos (mythos in its later manifestations), Aborigines and women are noticeably absent – kept in their place – and their 'place' was not in the core cultural mythology. In this autobiography, which deliberately employs tropes from that white male tradition counter-discursively, Morgan reclaims her place from a white male usurpation and repression. Although much of the reinscribed oral accounts of her mother and grandmother tell the untold female Aboriginal story, *My Place* also includes an account by her grandmother's brother. As Newman has noted,

> The most striking effect of Arthur Corunna's narration is that the structure and emphasis of his story enable the reader to see him within the mainstream tradition

of outback Australian life. Arthur is a bush hero – tough, canny, laconic and humorous. Indeed he fits the pattern even better that does Facey.

(p. 386)

But once the reader places Arthur in this tradition, the anomaly of his Aboriginality itself begins to interrogate and dismantle the cultural assumptions on which such a myth was based, and which its power within the nationalist mythology promulgated and continues to sponsor. The notion of independent Aussie battler, the settler, the pioneer, the explorer, and the glorification of their activities, rests on a perpetuated amnesia in relation to a prior Aboriginal habitation; it depends on the concept of conquest (or survival) in virgin lands – on those European myths which empowered conquest and colonization and which were given particular forms in nationalist mythologies like the Australian. Morgan's *My Place*, then, implicitly and explicitly retraces this textual journey, recapturing some of that ground for Aboriginality and orality.

Increasingly within the Australian literary tradition other groups excluded from the white male ethos – women, Asian and later European migrants – are writing counter-discursively against its consolidating essentialisms, producing a literature which is complexly intertextual and counter-discursive; one in which an increasing hybridity and a distrust of the traditional empower a scrutiny of the textual past. The result is not a vapid neo-internationalism which occults real power relations pertaining between races or nations (or within nations), but a vigilance about social ordering and the role played by text in maintaining hegemony.

The literatures in English throughout the world can no longer be considered simply as imitative appendages of British literature, but neither can their relationship with British literature be glossed over. Just as textuality fulfilled an essential role in the implementation and maintenance of colonial power structures, so it is enabling post-colonial writers to expose and subvert those impulses to colonial control wherever they seek to perpetuate or reintroduce themselves.

FURTHER READING

Ashcroft, Bill, Griffiths, Gareth and Tiffin, Helen (1989) *The Empire Writes Back: Theory and Practice in Post-Colonial Literatures*, Routledge, London

Ferrier, Carole (ed.) (1985) *Gender, Politics and Fiction: Twentieth-Century Australian Women's Novels*, University of Queensland Press, St Lucia

Goodwin, Ken (1986) *A History of Australian Literature*, Macmillan, London

Hergenhan, Laurie (ed.) (1988) *The Penguin New Literary History of Australia*, Penguin, Ringwood

Schaffer, Kay (1988) *Women and the Bush: Forces of Desire in the Australian Cultural Tradition*, Cambridge University Press, Cambridge

Shoemaker, Adam (1989) *Black Words White Page: Aboriginal Literature 1929–1988*, University of Queensland Press, St Lucia

Turner, Graeme (1986) *National Fictions: Literature, Film, and the Construction of Australian Narrative*, Allen & Unwin, Sydney

Wilde, William H., Hooton, Joy and Andrews, Barry (1985) *The Oxford Companion to Australian Literature*, Oxford University Press, Melbourne

Wilkes, G. A. (1981) *The Stockyard and the Croquet Lawn: Literary Evidence for Australia's Cultural Development*, Edward Arnold, Port Melbourne

ADDITIONAL WORKS CITED

Anderson, Jessica (1978) *Tirra Lirra by the River*, Macmillan, Sydney

Carey, Peter (1988) *Oscar and Lucinda*, University of Queensland Press, St Lucia

Daley, Victor (1898) 'When London Calls'. In Rodney Hall (ed.), *The Collins Book of Australian Poetry*, Collins, Sydney (1981)

Facey, A. B. (1983) *A Fortunate Life*, Fremantle Arts Centre Press, Fremantle

Heims, Neil (1983) 'Robinson Crusoe and the Fear of Being Eaten', *Colby Library Quarterly*, 19, 190–5

Hulme, Peter (1986) *Colonial Encounters: Europe and the Native Caribbean 1492–1797*, Methuen, London

Johnson, Colin (1983) *Doctor Wooreddy's Prescription for Enduring the Ending of the World*, Hyland House, South Yarra

Jolley, Elizabeth (1980) 'The Well-bred Thief'. In Chris and Helen Tiffin (eds.), *South Pacific Stories*, SPACLALS, St Lucia, pp. 122–31

Keneally, Thomas (1987) *The Playmaker*, Simon & Schuster, New York

Koch, Christopher (1980) 'Literature and Cultural Identity', *Tasmanian Review*, 4, 2–3

Morgan, Sally (1987) *My Place*, Fremantle Arts Centre Press, Fremantle

Muecke, Stephen (1988) 'Aboriginal Literature and the Repressive Hypothesis', *Southerly*, 48, 405–18

Newman, Joan (1988) 'Reader-Response to Transcribed Oral Narrative: *A Fortunate Life* and *My Place*', *Southerly*, 48, 376–89

Pêcheux, Michel (1982) *Language, Semantics and Ideology*, translated by Harbans Nagpal, St Martin's Press, New York [first published 1975]

Terdiman, Richard (1985) *Discourse/Counter-Discourse: The Theory and Practice of Symbolic Resistance in Nineteenth-Century France*, Cornell University Press, Ithaca

White, Patrick (1976) *A Fringe of Leaves*, Jonathan Cape, London

86

CANADIAN LITERATURE

W. H. NEW

To suggest some of the contexts of modern Canadian writing, my strategy here is to start with three novels and two short stories: Jack Hodgins's *The Invention of the World* (1977), Rudy Wiebe's 'Where Is the Voice Coming From?' (1971, revised 1982), Joy Kogawa's *Obasan* (1981), Mavis Gallant's 'The Latehomecomer' (1979), and Margaret Atwood's *The Handmaid's Tale* (1985). From them I generalize, designing a critical narrative about place, voice, margin, memory and power – and about ways in which these various concerns have in the last two decades been challenging the received canon of Canadian literature. Yet to generalize about 'Canadian literature' is problematic. The term describes a body of writing that includes thousands of titles, mostly written in English or French, but by no means limited to these two official national languages (there are more than fifty languages spoken by the native Indian and Inuit population alone). The term 'Canadian literature' also describes an activity, one that has been underway since at least the early sixteenth century, even though Canada did not become an independent nation until 1867. Further, it describes the cultural presumptions that underlie a shifting set of social values. That the received anglophone canon in Canada should in 1968 have given priority to representational, rural, Anglo-Protestant, androcentric novels, to adventurous romance, and to nature-centred lyric poetry suggests the patterns of cultural dominance then in position. (They had essentially been in place since the 1890s, though there were recurrent challenges to realist and romantic orthodoxies.) Between 1968 and 1988, however, these patterns significantly (though not entirely) altered. The process of change resulted in lively debate. The politics of change found a congenial medium in literature. And the changes themselves became apparent in the paradigms of contemporary writing, in the increased number of experiments with oral composition and stylistic discontinuity, and in the increased popularity of alternative literary forms: drama, fantasy, parody, short fiction and long poems.

Through them, writers and readers alike began actively to question received definitions of tradition and value.

HODGINS/PLACE

Jack Hodgins's *The Invention of the World* combines several tales, ostensibly to disclose the true history of one part of Vancouver Island, but in effect to reveal two contrary powers of story-telling: creative myth-making and restrictive invention. One tale begins in Ireland, tracing the origins of the fictional 'Revelations Colony of Truth' that an Irish giant has in times past founded in British Columbia; others examine the ordinary people who now dwell on the colony property and who live out their extraordinary relationships – never far from heroism, never far from parody – in the shadow of their inheritance. The narrator, identifying empirical documentary with truth, seeks to record facts, to solve the mystery of the past. Other characters embroider reality, as they distort history, with gossip, fantasy and deliberate lies, producing 'truths' that rival the narrative exaggerations of the 'Revelations Colony' itself. The paradigms of trickster myth provide a background, while the landscape serves as setting and metaphor. The place where the characters act, the landscape, is also one of their actions – variously 'colony' and 'property' (both artificially bounded by willed walls), 'land' and 'space' (both structures shaped by the politics of defining 'nature'), and a free territory of the imagination, open to dreams of transformation, transfiguration and renewal.

Like many other Canadian literary works, this novel allows perfection to exist, but places it somewhere else ('heaven', perhaps) – being happier with the imperfect present even when this imperfection increases the difficulties of interpreting life. Arguing for plural solutions to common problems, the novel's concern for place reiterates this sensibility. Hodgins's local setting does not simply depict empirical externals (usually analysed as a 'regional difference' from a presumptive norm); rather, it encodes an alternative view of the ostensible truths of social convention. The two islands of the book – Ireland, off the west coast of Britain, and Vancouver Island, off the west coast of Canada – epitomize this offshore perspective. They suggest how a closed community can open up, at least to itself, through its own story-making abilities. The island, to extend the metaphor, finds *in story* that it no longer has to live *as colony*. Within the community, comedy therefore exaggerates the idiosyncrasies of the local, but also parodies the presumptiveness of others' notions of normality. Terms such as 'giant' and 'ordinary' come to be seen for the social constructs they are. Hence Hodgins's fiction – influenced by Faulkner and García Márquez – argues by virtue of its setting and technique the invalidity of any convention that excludes regional truths in the name of a normative 'Truth'.

Yet in so doing, Hodgins's fiction also re-enacts a process for which in Canada there have been several precedents. Margaret Laurence's 'Manawaka Cycle', for example – beginning with *The Stone Angel* (1964) – articulates the history of Canada in terms that forego the conventional dichotomy between English and French. Laurence focuses instead on the Manitoba West, the presence of the native peoples, and the shifting (aesthetic, social, intellectual) grounds of multi-culturalism. Like several other Canadian writers (Dave Godfrey, Dorothy Livesay, Audrey Thomas among them), she learned about the viability of an alternative ancestry, a cultural voice, from her experience of living in Africa. In writings such as Godfrey's *The New Ancestors* (1970) and Thomas's *Mrs. Blood* (1970), Africa is a powerful sign of political and psychological unfamiliarity. But, like Laurence, Hodgins attempted not so much to defamiliarize the foreign as to reclaim the particularity of home.

Just as Laurence, therefore, also learned from the generation of prairie writers before her – Sinclair Ross, W. O. Mitchell, Frederick Philip Grove – who had attempted to validate their place in literature, so did Hodgins learn from other British Columbia writers, especially Emily Carr and Ethel Wilson. Wilson's passionate vision of landscape as a fluid process animates the feminist argument of her novel *Swamp Angel* (1954). Carr, the expressionist painter and writer, asserted the power of a mobile universe over a static acceptance of custom in *Klee Wyck* (1941) and other verbal and visual portraits of native image and belief. In so far as the distinction between property and process encapsulates the opposition between received and reform systems, then regional writing in Canada repeatedly functions as the site of change. Place, in such a context, is implicitly political.

The West is not the only Canadian region to give rise to such opposition. Quebec can be read as the most obvious example of the regional siting of difference. Atlantic Canada – through such writings as Alden Nowlan's poetry or the fiction of Ernest Buckler and Janice Kulyk Keefer – situates another ground of tension. Even Ontario has given rise to regional alternatives – although works such as Ralph Connor's adventure *The Man from Glengarry* (1901) and (New Brunswick-born) Sir Charles G. D. Roberts's animal stories, *The Kindred of the Wild* (1902), are usually taken to typify the canonical norm. Connor and Roberts express the conventional androcentric power structure, and a triumphal version of man's Christian command over nature (rather than a collaborative participation in it, as in indigenous religious belief). The rural vignettes of Raymond Knister, however, and the feminist landscapes of Alice Munro's Northern Ontario short stories – as in *The Moons of Jupiter* (1982) – argue for the power of voice over the power of convention. The short story form itself thus challenges establishment order – as do Quebec *contes* and the oral forms of drama. Their emphasis on voice further demonstrates the sociocultural function of narrative.

WIEBE/VOICE

The remodelling of establishment norms began in Canada at least as early as the 1830s, when the Nova Scotia judge Thomas Chandler Haliburton was crafting his sketches about 'Sam Slick the Clockmaker', anecdotes which used an invented Yankee dialect to goad conservative Maritimers into economic progress. And in the 1920s, Morley Callaghan's short stories contributed to the urban rebellion against the 'Roberts/Nature' establishment, a rebellion reiterated in the poetry of F. R. Scott, P. K. Page, and Ralph Gustafson, and in the autobiographical fictions of John Glassco's *Memoirs of Montparnasse*. Determined to avoid plot and ornamentation, Callaghan made stories out of the nuances of vernacular speech forms, taking the American Sherwood Anderson as his model.

In responding to the United States, Callaghan and Haliburton both expressed their resistance to imperial Britain as the single controlling element in Canadian culture. For both, however, demonstrating the distinctiveness of a Canadian voice proved more problematic than using an American model to suggest alternatives to the status quo. While Haliburton and Callaghan used voice to address social problems, the regional writers – Laurence, Michel Tremblay (in his *joual* plays) – more clearly demonstrated the variety of Canadian speech sounds and the aesthetic force of idiom. Rudy Wiebe's 'Where Is the Voice Coming From?' was one of the earliest of contemporary writings not only to use an oral technique but also to make voice a literary subject. Responsive to the oral dimensions of immigrant and native peoples, Wiebe probes the cultural significance of oral *form*.

'Where Is the Voice Coming From?' begins as a first-person enquiry into the historical identity of Chief Almighty Voice, the Cree warrior who fought in the 1885 Riel rebellion and was later shot by the North West Mounted Police. But it abandons evidential notions of historicity as the narrator discovers limits to each of the empirical answers he gets. Historical records prove incomplete; RCMP files are contradictory; figures and names design slanted versions of events and individuals; actual fragments of hair and bone, held behind glass in a museum case, are inadequate definitions of *person*. The search for the reality behind history – couched in a passive syntax – gradually reveals that 'history' is a subjectively constructed fiction, not an empirical truth at all. Paradoxically, as the story's syntax becomes active, a live Almighty Voice begins to speak through the narrator's imagination and in words that lift off the page. Art, that is, creates living illusions that transcend the powers of historical logic, even as Wiebe's own art demonstrates the degree to which all illusions are fictions. A story can never be anything other than an approximation, a 'translation', says this story: for however powerfully a version of

Almighty Voice speaks *on* these pages, he speaks *in English*. This narrator, set apart from the culture he is probing, cannot himself understand Cree.

Such irony not only frames the numerous literary expressions of contemporary indigenous writers – the myths and satires of Basil Johnston, the social critiques of Beatrice Culleton – it also shapes the parodies and self-referential narratives of many others. George Bowering, for example – whose *Burning Water* (1980) at once reinvents the exploration journals of Captains Vancouver and Quadra, and questions the validity of all history-written-as-narrative – designs texts that foreground the conscious filter of the author's mind, the extension of subjectivity into subject or theme. Eli Mandel's phenomenological travel poetry and Michael Ondaatje's discontinuous enquiries into the subjectivity of history – the poem sequence *The Collected Works of Billy the Kid* (1970) or the muralistic novel *In the Skin of a Lion* (1987) – offer related examples, as does bp Nichol's multi-volume, unfinished, poetic record of himself-as-language, *The Martyrology* (1972–88). Bowering places himself (and comparable contemporary figures) in a line of descent from Ezra Pound and William Carlos Williams, or, in Canadian terms, not from the realists but from Howard O'Hagan, Wilfred Watson and Sheila Watson. O'Hagan's *Tay John* (1939) is a mythic account of the emergence of a new language for a new world. But Sheila Watson's *The Double Hook* (1959) is the more usually cited example of the modernist resistance to social realism. In this story of murder and slow repentance, over which broods the figure of Coyote-the-trickster, events take place less in syntactical assertions than in syntactical obliquities, less on the page than in the reader's interpretation of the fragmented language, the isolated participles and standing images, of which the text consists. From Watson, the step to the postmodern was a matter of degree.

Exaggeration, one of the features that recurs in various forms of postmodernism, sometimes intensifies the incongruities of ordinary life, as in Hodgins; sometimes it stresses the artifice of narrative or any other arbitrary design of experience, as in Bowering; in other cases – notably with Jacques Ferron, Antonine Maillet and Robert Kroetsch – the fabular or anecdotal form of the exaggeration is itself intrinsically part of the communication taking place. Ferron adapted the fable of traditional rural Quebec to attack what he saw as a political complicity between Establishment Quebec and English Canada. Maillet's Prix Goncourt-winning novel *Pélagie-la-charrette* (1979) recounts the return of the Acadians (whom the British had expelled from New Brunswick to Louisiana in 1755) as a series of Rabelaisian tales. The people survive, says Maillet, in their accretive story, making her literary form deliberately political.

Kroetsch's stories use the bawdy anecdotes of Alberta ranch life to reveal the difference between the way the current culture behaves and the inherited models that it persists in using to judge art and estimate reality (and by which it is usually judged). *The Studhorse Man* (1969) re-enacts the stages of the

Odyssey, but does so in order to tell the unlikely sexual adventures of a cowboy and his horse. But the cowboy, not the Greek classic, is what is most real here. Kroetsch thus manages to tell a local anecdote – use the local voice – while in the process parodying the traditional quest form, demonstrating its limitations as a guide to the new world. Similarly, his *Badlands* (1975) re-enacts the form of an explorer's journal, telling of a woman who seeks her father through his field-notes; but in the process she frees herself both from him and from the limits of the journal form that (by naming and claiming) has charted and enclosed the landscape and turned it into others' territory. In Canada, the written journal (those of Jacques Cartier, Samuel de Champlain, David Thompson, George Vancouver, Alexander Mackenzie, Sir John Franklin and Samuel Hearne provide examples) had presumed in its own documentary validity. It had also historically claimed place and people for Britain and France. Using the oral forms of folk and indigenous cultures implicitly rejects this particular power of possession – and the uniform and often unquestioned determination of cultural value that goes with it – in order to render culturally viable the forms of expression that are *in place*. That the West should be one site of this formal challenge to authority is partly due to its ethnic diversity; Wiebe and Kroetsch find a voice in English, while drawing on cultural roots other than the British and French roots of the ostensibly cultural norm in Canada. But the substantive nature of class and ethnicity draws attention to another set of margins, which affect yet further the shape of aesthetic expression and historical judgement.

KOGAWA/MARGIN

Framing Joy Kogawa's *Obasan* are two historical events which intensify the novel's sense of dislocation: the forced internment during the Second World War of Canadians of Japanese ancestry, and the atomic bombing of Nagasaki in 1945. With autobiographical force, Kogawa's main character, Naomi Nakasane, tries as an adult to come to terms with the impact of these events in her childhood, to find answers to her questions about her place in the world. *Nisei* (Canadian-born), she has been moved away from her home and officially denied a voice. How should she live? Her aunt Emily (her mother's vocal, politically articulate sister) provides one model; her brother Stephen (who denies the relevance of history and his Japanese roots) provides another. Naomi's desire for a third option is complicated, for a mystery seems to surround her mother's absence, and Naomi is increasingly burdened by silence until she can explain it. Paradoxically, understanding comes through a different kind of silence – the elliptical speech, the 'other-language' of her mother's second sister, Obasan. The mother has died, it transpires, at Nagasaki, where she had been visiting at the outbreak of war, and where the circumstances of history therefore differently interned her. Naomi (and the reader) gradually acquires a limited knowledge of 'facts' and an equally limited understanding of what these imply about history. They also learn something of what it means to live on the margins of understanding, with an absent voice, in the silences of the periphery of power. Seeking language (this book, in effect, will speak her elegy for her mother), Naomi also seeks recognition: a desire to speak, a desire to be heard.

Works such as Kogawa's aim to distinguish among forms of absence, not just to ratify additional forms of speech. Naomi's brother's mimic mainstream identity declares a cultural absence as surely as the mainstream society does when it uses a taxonomic vocabulary to exclude minorities. (The very category 'immigrant' implicitly denies participation in the mainstream, which is the point of some of A. M. Klein's satiric poetry about the restrictions embedded even in conventional liberal attitudes to Jews.) Naomi's own absence contains an identity which is yet to be comprehended. This sense of deferred understanding explains one of the functions of the other language in the narrative: here, Japanese. In related examples, Rudy Wiebe's *The Blue Mountains of China* (1970) recurrently uses Low German to underline the distinction Mennonite communities have made between private values and the public language of the surrounding society. Irving Layton's poetry separates Jewish passion from a costive 'Xian' world of hypocrisy and constraint. Austin Clarke's stories use Barbadian dialect to distinguish political authenticity from political imitation. In *Tales from Firozsha Baag* (1987), Rohinton Mistry shows how familiarity and foreignness are functions of perspective. Silence can be illusory – masking an identity especially to those who have defined it as silence *rather than speech* because it represents an experience beyond the reach of their own terms of reference. To be silenced nevertheless remains debilitating.

In *Obasan*, as in other writing about women's social roles, the silence of the margins of power at least in part conveys a resistance to using a received language (and hence to taking on, at some remove, its forms and values). In narratives rooted in an analysis of the margins of class, however, silence sometimes conveys deprivation more than covert speech, even though the margin will always find a way to encode its own system of operative values. The difference between the language of Ethel Wilson's 'Tuesday and Wednesday' (*The Equations of Love*, 1952) and David Adams Richards's *Nights Below Station Street* (1988) is relevant here. Wilson's work, sympathetic to the pressures that social disparities cause, is undeniably told from without, its language plain but organized according to received standards of semantic elegance and grace. Richards understands the inside workings of class-defined discourse. His deliberate use of fragmentary sentences, obscenities and solecisms represents the economic poverty of a group through a perceived impoverishment of speech. Richards's protagonists, reaching to express their sensitivity and desire, repeatedly lack the language to articulate what it is they feel; consequently they lapse into violent acts and violent words – a routine of deprivation which is a destructively accessible model of expression.

Rick Salutin's play *1837* (collectively created with the Toronto performance group Théâtre Passe Muraille in 1976) applies these notions to yet another subject, locating margins not at the periphery but at the heart of received Canadian culture. Distinguishing between official and revisionist history, Salutin tries here to reclaim the past from the contraints of an authorized version. Canadian textbooks describe 1837 as a year of rebellions: rebellions that failed, but that led to the achievement of Responsible Government. Salutin disputes both the term 'rebellion' and the presumptions of the word 'achievement', arguing that (1) these 'rebels' were ordinary farmers (the term in use in French is *patriotes*) justifiably opposing the corrupt, entrenched powers of British nepotism and class distinction, and (2) a truly responsible system has not yet come into effect. Using pitchforks against guns, the untrained against the trained, a populist rhetoric against the condescension and legalese of the ruling class, the farmers are routed. But one of them, before he is hanged as a traitor, intones the final line of the play, insisting that they have not lost, just not yet won. The litotes, or reversed negative – an important trope in Canadian letters – reiterates the cultural resistance to binary social structures. (In other contexts, the poets Phyllis Webb, Dennis Lee and Gaston Miron have all argued that structures of loss are not intrinsically negative, and that they are, respectively, characteristic of female, Loyalist, and Quebecois experience; Quebec nationalism has even turned the poet Emile Nelligan's mad isolation and the novelist Hubert Aquin's suicide into creative cultural emblems.) In fact *1837* is a contemporary as much as a historical drama, its militancy heightened by its technique. Salutin shapes a history out of fragmented symbolic scenes, in which the voices of the people are more persuasive than the speeches of the system. The discontinuity argues that the margins have the power to disrupt the centre, and that the official version of history – a narrative of linear progress – needs to be challenged for its arrangement of facts and its undeclared hierarchy of values. It urges, moreover, that such a challenge continue, against the self-interested falsifications of current social options.

GALLANT/MEMORY

The opponents of revisionist history argue that the rewriting of events distorts them, and that it thereby hands to the authoritarian few all control over the public memory (and consequently control over the people). The proponents counter that revisionism is necessary when the official versions of history are already fictions, being used by an existing authority to market a set of values not consonant with the real culture. This distinction between memory and history – and the shifting subjectivity of both – is a recurrent motif in the work of Mavis Gallant, as in 'The Latehomecomer' (*From the Fifteenth District*, 1979). Set in post-war Germany, when just enough time has lapsed for people to choose not to remember the Nazi past, it records the arrival home of a young German, a victim of a bureaucratic mix-up who has been released late from a French prisoner-of-war camp. Through a series of modal changes, the story details a moment-by-moment shift from expectation to despair. What the ex-soldier returns to he does not recognize: his brother has disappeared in action, his mother remarried, his home changed. The community does not wish to remember why he had ever been a soldier, and his mother lives with still another fiction, dreaming of retrieving the pre-war stability in which her family is together and happy. The 'latehomecomer' can only anguish at such a selective memory, such a rewritten version of history. And he, who has lived out the war in anticipation, now ironically yearns for the moment just before his return, when his own fiction was secure, when the possible had not yet been defined by the inexact.

Gallant's interest in the process by which recognition comes about also illuminates several reasons why both history and memory are open to distortion. Among them are ignorance, passivity, the fear of chaos, the equation of peace with order, the elevation of order over freedom, and the misapprehension of a cultural system that sometimes accompanies exile. Herself a Quebec expatriate living in France, Gallant repeatedly anatomizes the uncertainties of the stranger in a strange land, a theme adopted by the multitude of writers who at different times, and for different lengths of time, have taken up exile in Canada: Malcolm Lowry, Brian Moore, Marilú Mallet, Josef Skvorecky, Clark Blaise, Bharati Mukherjee, John Metcalf, Naim Kattan. Gallant's fiction also draws attention to the dominant position that linear narrative has occupied in Canadian literature and its long unquestioned progressive assumptions.

For example, Major John Richardson's historical fictions – influenced by Scott and Cooper – romanticized in the 1830s the wilderness and the native Indian, transforming both into territory to be claimed for narrative (European) resolutions. Writers such as William Kirby, with *The Golden Dog* (1877), and Sir Gilbert Parker, with *The Seats of the Mighty* (1896), applied similar techniques to the interpretation of Quebec. Anglo-Protestant presumptions about nature, man's control over nature, and the logical and ethical order of the universe (promulgated by the socially influential Canada First Movement in the latter years of the nineteenth century) read the anglicization of Canadian history as itself a natural progress. By this view, Quebec's destiny, like that of the native peoples, was inevitably to be taken over; hence Kirby's and Parker's romantic historical fictions about the fall of Quebec located what were deemed to be reasons for this development: the absolutism of Catholicism and the corruption of the French court. To be habitant (and therefore subject to the rule of these tyrannical systems) was to be exempt from this caveat – but it was also to be dismissed as backward and quaint. Plainly, to be progressive (and so to deserve the new power, by this view) was to be English. This many-levelled form of political and aesthetic closure was to be challenged both within Quebec and without, but it survived for some time not only in direct ways (political organizations, textbook excerpts, imperial attitudes, linguistic practices) but also indirectly in those literary structures that emphasized the linear forward march of history, mastery over nature, and the climactic resolution of conflict.

The emergence of a *formal* challenge (though it was not initially read as such) began to show in such works as Duncan Campbell Scott's *In the Village of Viger* (1896), which designed a book-length unit out of an interrupted series of sketches and tales – a form not new with Scott but for which in Canada there have been many subsequent practitioners. Linear fictions designed time as a line (the structure of Lucy Maud Montgomery's classic children's novel *Anne of Green Gables*, 1908, and Gabrielle Roy's analysis of women and poverty *The Tin Flute*, 1945). Subsequent writers (Elizabeth Smart, Margaret Avison, Hugh Hood) represented time as a pulse. The interrupted linear form challenged the very linearity of the tradition that history was meant to embody.

In *A Bird in the House* (1970), a broken story sequence that forms part of her Manawaka series, Margaret Laurence isolates moments from her narrator's childhood, moments perceived at once by the child and by the adult narrator remembering and reconstructing, until the process of the sequence leads the narrator from a rigid patriarchal history to a fluid, oral, matriarchal inheritance. On a larger scale, Hugh Hood's ongoing 'The New Age' sequence (beginning with *The Swing in the Garden*, 1975), projects a series of twelve non-contiguous volumes which visualizes twentieth-century history as image and listens to time as rhythm. Each of Hood's books organizes historical events around a prevailing motif – automobiles, piano keys – until history can be re-understood as an aural and tactile process rather than a phenomenon beyond human touch. Laurence and Hood do not abjure traditions; but in seeking ways to reconsider how history works, they interpret it as a function of memory, as a process that can sometimes reclaim one's own story from others' language and intellectual and ethical designs.

By contrast, Hugh MacLennan's writings read history in large part as a function of the failure of memory. While his early works, such as *Barometer Rising* (1941), provided acceptable models for mainstream Canada (they envisioned national progress, celebrated the land, cast reality in romantic terms, anticipated resolutions to internal political tensions, and essentially ignored the native peoples), his later books recognized how an unthinking acceptance of a progressivist system could lead to constraint instead of freedom. A generation uneducated to history, and unmindful of it, living for the moment only, could surrender power to Fascist forces, he argued, which do exist in Canada as a powerful minority – seeking greater power – in the 1970s and 1980s. MacLennan's novel *Voices in Time* (1980), therefore, though cast in the science fiction future, reads as a mordant history of the present, a warning about what happens to people when tradition is too easily rewritten, when it is sacrificed *even in the name of freedom* to systems of overt order and covert control. Power thus proves an ambivalent commodity – the result of both an active intelligent memory and a passive uninformed memory: but acting separately in these two different cases as an agent of conservation and an agent of authority or ownership.

ATWOOD/POWER

That power engenders violence is one of the premises of much other contemporary writing. David Gurr, John Krizanc, Brian Fawcett, Keath Fraser, and Paulette Jiles are among the many who have probed the dimensions of violence as a current (or constant) social fact, as metaphor and as a stylistic device. Stylistic violence (expressed in discontinuity and parody) is a sign of writers' continuing need to question authority – in order to celebrate as much as to condemn: that is, *in order to be able to celebrate*. For example, Timothy Findley's fiction analyses the maleness, the Fascism, of violence, in the process exposing the fictionality of political systems. *Famous Last Words* (1981) re-reads the political history of the Second World War; *Not Wanted on the Voyage* (1984) retells the story of Noah's Ark, creating an ironic parable of the tensions between authoritarian forms of patriarchal power and the more flexible and (constantly under pressure of attack and dismissal) more liberating powers of the imagination.

That the voice of 'system' is dominantly patriarchal is one of the basic tenets of feminist commentary. That science fiction, dystopia and fantasy recur in contemporary feminist writing demonstrates an approach to dismantling the structure of fixed cultural systems. It perhaps also challenges those for whom nihilism and despair seem the only likely consequences of existing social history. Among writers who have designed such speculative works are Gabrielle Roy, Anne Hébert, Nicole Brossard, and Louky Bersianik. Bersianik's *L'Eugélionne* (1976) envisions its title character as a photographic negative, a visitor from another planet seeking a place of her own kind; but on analysing Canadian society she finds only the familiar forms of male bias in religion, law, education and language. Cast as a classical parody, the book also subverts the received forms of literary tradition (like Brossard's and other feminist writing, it resists conventional definitions of genre). Quebec feminist writing has, moreover, markedly influenced anglophone feminist writing – as the work of Daphne Marlatt, Lola Lemire Tostevin, Claire Harris and Smaro Kamboureli shows.

Feminist, speculative and knowledgeable about Quebec, Margaret Atwood's work, however, derives more directly from an Ontario tradition.

Atwood's essays, poems, and fiction argue developmentally against the playing of 'circle games', mistaking mere activity for a challenge to power. Satirically, they expose the dynamics of systems of enclosure, whether the hierarchies of property, marriage, politics and business or the evaluative principles of literary history that give automatic precedence to arcane over popular forms of expression. In some sense, Atwood can thus be read as a challenge to conservative historians such as Donald Creighton (1956), whose 'Laurentian Thesis' of economic and cultural centralization influenced MacLennan; as a challenge to conservative critics such as Northrop Frye (1957, 1971), whose cyclical theories of genre and myth marked the literary designs of James Reaney and Jay Macpherson (though Macpherson's poem sequence *Welcoming Disaster*, 1974, is a powerful feminist critique of the limits of myth); and as a challenge to Catholic philosophers such as Marshall McLuhan (1964), whose versions of technology and media were to shape Earle Birney's late visual poems and much of an entire generation's understanding of language. As a cultural nationalist, however – a position shared with Dennis Lee, George Grant, Al Purdy and Dave Godfrey, though it is mocked by Mordecai Richler in one part of the country and W. P. Kinsella in another – Atwood emerges out of, even though sometimes in reaction against, the Ontario literary milieu. This is the milieu that tried initially to shape Alice Munro's short stories as simple realism, though their stylistic sophistication was not to be so contained. It is also the milieu that celebrates the wilderness romantic John Richardson, the Methodist pioneer essayist Susanna Moodie, the ironic social mannerist Sara Jeannette Duncan, the didactic apostle of 'muscular Christianity' Ralph Connor, the conservative humorist Stephen Leacock, the family-saga imperialist Mazo de la Roche, the Jungian psychological mystery-writer Robertson Davies, the popular historian Pierre Berton, and the Newfoundland-born poet E. J. Pratt, whose romantic epic poems of giant railways, giant whales, giant ships and giant battles derive from a Newfoundland tall-tale tradition but celebrate an Ontario-centred version of nationhood.

In this context – 'translating' Moodie's 1852 autobiography *Roughing It in the Bush* into her own non-linear poem sequence *The Journals of Susanna Moodie* (1970) – Atwood makes of Mrs Moodie not the attitudinally limited pioneer that convention would have her (who learned realism and became Canadian), but an emblem of division. Atwood's Moodie is a woman divided against herself, a woman whose language precludes her from adequate self-expression, a figure who (in other words) is a representative modern woman, subject to the forms of technology and convention but struggling to live at once outside them and in concert with herself and others of like mind. That this is not a new experience is part of the feminist message. Indeed, one of the earliest of English-Canadian fictions, Frances Brooke's *The History of Emily Montague* (1769), also analyses the divisive attractions – of independence and social position – that result in the oblique politics of womanhood. Mrs Brooke's context involves the English military garrison in Quebec and an eighteenth-century English delight in pastoral, but here the author's ironic, post-Voltairean wit tempers what looks like a simple emulation of conservative tradition. Like Brooke, conscious of the aesthetic and ethical appeals that pastoral makes through the pleasures of orderly design, Atwood is resolutely anti-pastoral, a position she extended in her dystopian novel *The Handmaid's Tale* (1985).

The Handmaid's Tale is cast in the not-distant future, when the USA has been taken over by Fascist religious fundamentalists and turned into the Republic of Gilead. In the name of order and stability, the cabal in control denies to ordinary people their freedom of expression in language, dress and behaviour. In particular, it allows women a limited number of options: women can be 'Aunts', 'Wives', 'Handmaids', or nuclear waste-dump cleaners, with few prospects and fewer choices. These titles are themselves part of Atwood's cautionary intent. The positive terms of language have been co-opted by the system to neutralize any opposition: the 'Aunts' are really the system's peda-gogical brainwashers, the male 'Angels' and 'Eyes' its hired thugs and spies. And 'Handmaids' are merely licensed mistresses: they lie (in Atwood's graphic image) literally between the legs of the infertile 'Wives' of the Commanders, passively servicing the (mostly infertile) men. Pointedly, women are part of the system that keeps this hierarchy in place. Nothing is in the book, Atwood claims, that is not simply an extension of attitudes currently permeating tele-vision advertising, fundamentalist politics, and other features of North Amer-ican culture. A much earlier book – James De Mille's *A Strange Manuscript Found in a Copper Cylinder* (1888) – argues that neither utopias nor anti-utopias can be conceived except in the biased and discredited terms of present politics. Atwood turns this principle to her book's own purposes.

An epilogue – cast in the further future – extends her critique into academia. This entire tale, somehow recorded by a renegade handmaid whom the system has possessively named Offred, is reconstructed in the epilogue by critics and historians, who seek not to condemn but to understand the now-departed theocracy. The sardonic point that Atwood underlines is that no reconstruction (including Offred's, including her own), and no refusal to judge, is politically neutral. And no writers, if they warrant the name, can consequently pretend to be divorced from their own society and time. Atwood has a political plea. Like many other Canadian writers at a time of acute social change, she calls for a national culture that fosters creative dissent, one that remains stubbornly resistant to definition.

FURTHER READING

Blodgett, E. D. (1982) *Configuration: Essays on the Canadian Literatures*, ECW, Toronto
Egoff, Sheila (1975) *The Republic of Childhood: A Critical Guide to Canadian Children's Literature in English*, 2nd edn, Oxford University Press, Toronto
Jones, D. G. (1970) *Butterfly on Rock*, University of Toronto Press, Toronto
Klinck, Carl F. (ed.) (1976) *Literary History of Canada*, 2nd edn, University of Toronto Press, Toronto
Lee, Dennis (1973) 'Cadence, Country, Silence: Writing in Colonial Space', *Open Letter*, 2nd series, no. 6, 34–53
——(1977) *Savage Fields: An Essay in Literature and Cosmology*, Anansi, Toronto
Mandel, Eli (ed.) (1971) *Contexts of Canadian Criticism*, University of Toronto Press, Toronto
Moss, John (ed.) (1987) *Future Indicative: Literary Theory and Canadian Literature*, University of Ottawa Press, Ottawa
Neuman, Shirley and Kamboureli, Smaro (eds) (1986) *A Mazing Space*, NeWest/Longspoon, Edmonton
New, W. H. (1987) *Dreams of Speech and Violence: The Art of the Short Story in Canada and New Zealand*, University of Toronto Press, Toronto
——(1989) *A History of Canadian Literature*, Macmillan, London
Ricou, Laurie (1987) *Everyday Magic: Child Languages in Canadian Literature*, University of British Columbia Press, Vancouver
Stratford, Philip (1986) *All the Polarities: Comparative Studies in Contemporary Canadian Novels in French and English*, ECW, Toronto
Woodcock, George (1980) *The World of Canadian Writing*, Douglas & McIntyre, Vancouver; University of Washington Press, Seattle

ADDITIONAL WORKS CITED

Atwood, Margaret (1970) *The Journals of Susanna Moodie*, Oxford University Press, Toronto
——(1985) *The Handmaid's Tale*, McClelland & Stewart, Toronto
Creighton, Donald (1956) *The Empire of the St. Lawrence*, Macmillan, Toronto
Frye, Northrop (1957) *Anatomy of Criticism*, Princeton University Press, Princeton
——(1971) *The Bush Garden: Essays on the Canadian Imagination*, Anansi, Toronto
Gallant, Mavis (1979) 'The Latehomecomer'. In Mavis Gallant, *From the Fifteenth District*, Macmillan, Toronto [story first published 1974]
Hodgins, Jack (1977) *The Invention of the World*, Macmillan, Toronto
Kogawa, Joy (1981) *Obasan*, Lester & Orpen Dennys, Toronto
McLuhan, Marshall (1964) *Understanding Media*, McGraw-Hill, New York
Wiebe, Rudy (1982) 'Where Is the Voice Coming From?' In Rudy Wiebe, *The Angel of the Tar Stands and Other Stories*, McClelland & Stewart, Toronto

87

INDIAN LITERATURE IN ENGLISH

SHIRLEY CHEW

... from the Sanskrit alphabet we passed on directly to the first lesson in the glossy primer which began with 'A was an Apple Pie'... and went on to explain, 'B bit it' and 'C cut it'. The activities of B and C were understandable, but the opening line itself was mystifying. What was an Apple Pie?

(Narayan, 1965, p. 120)

R. K. Narayan's account of his school days in Mysore is informed with a comic irony which conveys the alienating effects in general of a colonial education as well as the long-standing attachment which, in his particular case, grew out of his early encounter with the language of the colonizers. 'English in India' was a paper delivered at a conference on Commonwealth literature at the University of Leeds, but may be regarded also as a significant contribution by a notable novelist to a crucial debate which was going on in India in the years following Independence. This debate was concerned with the legitimacy of English as a medium of literary expression and, a related issue, the status and authenticity of Indian writing in English.

As a label applied to literature written in English by Indians, 'Indo-Anglian' was given general currency by the pioneering critic K. R. Srinivasa Iyengar when his volume of essays appeared in 1943 under the title *Indo-Anglian Literature* (see Iyengar, 1984, pp. 2–6). No longer fashionable, the term served at the time to draw attention to a body of creative work, limited though it was, which had emerged since the last quarter of the nineteenth century. Indian poetry in English had, among its early exponents, well-known figures such as Toru Dutt (1856–77), Sarojini Naidu (1879–1940), Rabindranath Tagore (1861–1941), and Sri Aurobindo (1872–1950). The Indian novel in English came on the scene later – the first significant achievement being K. S. Venkatramani's *Murugan the Tiller* (1927) – but quickly established itself in the 1930s with works by Mulk Raj Anand (*Untouchable*, 1935), R. K. Narayan (*The Bachelor of Arts*, 1937) and Raja Rao (*Kanthapura*, 1938). However, after 1947, and despite the fact that literary experimentation was livelier than ever, the question arose as to whether an alien language, the roots of which lay thousands of miles away and which was learnt mainly from books, could ever be tuned accurately and sensitively to the task of representing Indian experience.

Drawing upon Yeats's dictum that 'no man can think or write with music and vigour except in his mother tongue', the Bengali poet and critic Buddhadeva Bose observed in 1963 that 'to the great majority of Indians this admonition was unnecessary, but the intrepid few who left it unheeded do not yet realize that "Indo-Anglian" poetry is a blind alley, lined with curio shops, leading nowhere' (in Lal, 1971, p. 5). Bose's pessimism, it could be argued, was not entirely unjustified at that point in time. As Bruce King (1987, pp. 12–18) has painstakingly noted, the literary scene in the 1950s and early 1960s was marked by fermenting activity, with its two centres of influence in Bombay and Calcutta, its literary magazines and journals, such as *Quest* and *Miscellany*, its anthologies, and poetry readings. But apart from Dom Moraes, who was awarded the Hawthornden Prize in England for *A Beginning* (1957), and Nissim Ezekiel, whose *The Unfinished Man* (1960) has been described as 'the first volume of poetry produced in India of consistently high quality' (King, 1987, p. 18), the poets who are regarded as outstanding today had not as yet published their first books. Not until the middle of the 1960s, with the appearance of Ezekiel's *The Exact Name* (1965), Moraes's *John Nobody* (1965), Kamala Das's *Summer in Calcutta* (1965), Gieve Patel's *Poems* (1966), A. K. Ramanujan's *The Striders* (1966), could it truly be said that 'One of the most exciting periods of modern Indian verse' had begun (King, 1987, p. 20). After 1965, moreover, it became feasible for P. Lal, founder of the Writers' Workshop in Calcutta, to put together a strong rebuttal to Bose in the form of *Modern Indian Poetry in English* ([1969] 1971), a substantial volume which, running to 600 pages, included Lal's manifesto as editor of the anthology and the views of the poets themselves on Bose's objections. Lal's compilation of poems has been criticized for being unselective. Nevertheless, the volume still makes interesting and informative reading today. Among the points which he raised in his Introduction are, first, while Indian poetry in English might possibly claim as its antecedents the works of Dutt, Naidu, and Aurobindo, it took a new direction after 1947, ushering in 'two decades of revolt, experimentation, and consolidation by the younger poets' (Lal, 1971, p. iii); and second, the resulting evidence, to judge from the anthology, not only proclaims that English is a fitting vehicle for poetic expression by Indians, but that Indo-Anglian poetry is 'a part of the Indian literary spectrum' (Lal, 1971, p. xxxi). The response of the poets themselves to questions relating to their own writing was generally governed by their practical good sense and served in the main to reinforce Lal's argument. Many, like Nissim Ezekiel and Kamala Das, claimed to write in English because it is the language in which they function most happily or the only one to which, for historical reasons, they have access. Others, like A. K. Ramanujan, were inclined to be more blunt, insisting that the question was not whether Indians should or should not write in English but 'whether they can. And if they can, they will' (Lal, 1971, p. 444). Among numerous and convincing examples of what *can* be done is Ramanujan's own 'Small-scale Reflections on a Great House':

> And ideas behave like rumours
> once casually mentioned somewhere
> they come back to the door as prodigies
>
> born to prodigal fathers, with eyes
> that vaguely look like our own,
> like what Uncle said the other day:
>
> that every Plotinus we read
> is what some Alexander looted
> between the malarial rivers.
> (*Relations*, 1971, p. 42)

Here the poet's imagination is sustained upon the idea of cross-cultural transformations and, in the course of the poem, a borrowed language is elegantly worked and turned until it becomes capable of bodying forth in the image of the family house – rich in tradition, cluttered in local minutiae, and capacious in its history – an inclusive vision of Indian reality.

Along with Keki Daruwallah, Jayanta Mahapatra may be regarded as the most interesting among the poets who started to publish in the 1970s. In contrast to the plenitude of 'Small-scale Reflections on a Great House' within which decay, discord, and menace are readily accommodated, Mahapatra's poems are fractured and stricken compositions, grappling with questions concerning history and the possible claims upon the past which are open to the westernized, post-colonial poet. The impulse behind 'Grandfather' sprang from an account in Chintamani Mahapatra's tattered diary of the famine which ravaged Orissa in 1866 and drove him, a starving boy of seventeen, to embrace Christianity in exchange for food. Chintamani wrote in the vernacular and, to his descendants, 'the Oriya alphabet on the page was difficult to read; the letters were in a script mostly used by rural, unlettered folk' (Mahapatra, 1989, p. 141), but there was no mistaking the tragic note which emerged from the text, a witness to the exacting price of colonialism's so-called civilizing mission:

> The separate life let you survive, while perhaps
> the one you left wept in the blur of your heart.
> (Mahapatra, *Selected Poems*, 1987, p. 67)

The indictment of imperialism which Chintamani's document enables is implicit in Mahapatra's poem but, as the above lines make clear, inseparable from this, and more crucial for the personal history, are the rivening consequences of Chintamani's action. As the 'perhaps' indicates, the basis of 'Grand-father' consists of questions to which there will never be satisfactory answers. Was it cowardice springing from the weakness of the flesh that made him betray his own gods, roots, and self? Or was it, on the other hand, a hero's defiance 'against dying,/to know the dignity/that had to be earned dangerous-ly,/your last chance that was blindly terrifying, so unfair' (Mahapatra, 1987, p. 68). In the face of the despairing cry from the past, all that seems possible for Chintamani's descendants is to attempt to recover, from the estranging burden of history, an awareness of the flesh's commonality and a brief space in which vernacular and English, past generations and future ones, can meet.

Among more recent talents, mention must be made of Vikram Seth and Sujata Bhatt. To read Seth's *The Golden Gate* (1986), a novel in the form of a dazzling sequence of 582 sonnets, or Bhatt's *Brunizem* (1988), a versatile and fluent first collection, is to find young Indian poets laying claim with confidence to their right to the English language:

> Which language
> has not been the oppressor's tongue?
> Which language
> truly meant to murder someone?
> And how does it happen
> that after the torture,
> after the soul has been cropped
> With a long scythe swooping out
> of the conqueror's face –
> the unborn grandchildren
> grow to love that strange language.
> (Bhatt, 1988, p. 37)

Needless to say, the poise of the above lines depends as much upon a sense of the poetic tradition in English, which has been forged in India in the last 30 years, as upon a belief in the capacity of younger poets to extend that tradition.

Meenakshi Mukherjee's important critical work *The Twice Born Fiction*, which appeared in 1971, attempted to achieve for the Indo-Anglian novel what Lal's anthology did for Indian poetry in English. In it she argues that the genre, as it developed between 1930 and 1969, is 'a part of truly Indian fiction and not a tenuous extension of English fiction' (p. 206). The force of her thesis depends to a large extent upon her firm knowledge of the Indo-Anglian novel as well as the novel written in Indian languages, such as Bengali, Marathi, Kannada, Hindi, and which she has read either in the original or in translation. She is in a position, for example, to demonstrate that the Indo-Anglian novel, though a latecomer on the Indian scene compared with a nineteenth-century product like the novel in Bengali, shares similar concerns and themes with the literature written in the regional languages, and similar trends in its development. Generally speaking, there is a shift in emphasis from historical romance in the initial stages to social or political realism during the years of national revolt against British rule, to psychological analysis after 1947 when an individual's search for identity in a changing India became an urgent concern.

In the Indo-Anglian novel of the 1950s and 1960s, this sense of alienation is often articulated through a conscious engagement with problems of form and technique. As early as 1938, in his now famous Foreword to *Kanthapura*, Raja Rao pin-points the dilemma: 'We cannot write like the English. We should not. We cannot write only as Indians. We have grown to look at the large world as part of us.' The consequence is that the Indo-Anglian text becomes the site of collisions or negotiations between the conventions of a borrowed fictional form and of the indigenous art of story-telling, between history and myth. *Kanthapura* itself is one such example. Another is Narayan's *The Guide* (1958).

Simply to read this work along the lines of a traditional novel that has, as its central theme, an individual's quest for identity is to miss the layers of Hindu thought which underpin the surface. It may strike the reader that, within the novel's two-tiered structure, Raju's first-person narrative, like the railways 'which got into [his] blood very early in life' (Narayan, [1958] 1970, p. 10), is linear and progressive and aims at determining meaning. Trapped by his own cunning and the simplicity of the villagers into undertaking a fast as a penance to end the drought, Raju seeks to extricate himself by confessing to a long series of masquerades, the latest of which is posing as a swami. Whatever Raju's initial reasons for making the confession, the course his narrative takes, like that of the nineteenth-century autobiographical novel, corresponds to his growth from ignorance and self-deception to knowledge and self-realization. The reader's expectations are thwarted, however, when what should have been a climactic moment had *The Guide* been constructed strictly upon the lines of the traditional novel form, turns out to be curiously flat. Instead of being moved to sympathy or outrage at the close of Raju's story, Velan his disciple has to be pressed for an opinion and then declares: 'I don't know why you tell me all this, Swami. It's very kind of you to address, at such length, your humble servant' (p. 208). Velan's acceptance at this point signals the re-absorption of Raju's history into the timelessness of myth. What one has read (heard) as a unique tale told by an individual is only another version of the fable of con-man turned swami.

Two discourses run through *The Guide* – one of Hinduism, the other of individual romance – and the uneasy negotiations between them are registered in the third-person narrative which intersperses Raju's confession and is mainly concerned with his conduct as a fraudulent holy man and his feelings of entrapment: 'He realised that he had no alternative: he must play the role

Velan had given him' (p. 33). Raju's mask is continually slipping. At the same time, a phrase like 'he must play' has a strange resonance, gesturing beyond the man's immediate discomfiture and intimating a sense of larger designs at work.

From one point of view, the exchange between Raju and Velan seems an anti-climax; from another, it is crucial in restoring to the text the narrative patterns which have their sources in Hindu religion and thought. As elsewhere in Narayan's work, ironies abound, but it may be said broadly that, first, in the light of the ethical concept of *ashrama*, 'Raju must play' because his individual life has moved through the four stages of life as formulated by Hindu thought, leading from 'apprenticeship' (stall-keeper and tourist guide), to 'householder' (living with Marco's wife, Rosie), 'recluse' (prisoner), and 'ascetic' (swami). Second, if Raju can be denounced as a confidence trickster, he can also be said to be fulfilling his *dharma* since his duty in life is clearly to guide – whether tourists or the spiritually helpless. Finally, Raju may have presented an ordered account of his life to Velan but, outside the authority of his own narrative, he is only one participant in *lila*, the 'sport' of the World Soul. Thus it is Raju who, disliking Marco, the historian and Rosie's husband, nevertheless leads the man to the cave-paintings that will feature substantially in his reconstruction of the cultural history of southern India; and it is Raju who, exploiting Rosie's talents as a dancer, helps to establish her as a renowned interpreter of the classical dance form, *Bharat Natyam*. Raju 'must play' because Narayan's narrative operates within a cultural tradition in which inherited wisdom is passed from generation to generation and re-affirmed in the process. It is Raju after all who, recalling a Tamil poem his mother used to quote, consoles the villagers thus: 'If there is one good man anywhere, the rains would descend for his sake and benefit the world' (p. 110). And one villager, at least, has no trouble in accommodating their holy man within the mythology of recent events: 'When Mahatma Gandhi went without food, how many things happened in India. This is a man like that. If he fasts there will be rain' (p. 102).

The last chapter of *The Guide* projects an image of multitudinousness at the centre of which is the quiet figure of the swami. On the final day of the fast,

> It was difficult to hold Raju on his feet, as if he were a baby. Raju opened his eyes, looked about, and said, 'Velan, it's raining in the hills. I can feel it coming up under my feet, up my legs – ' and with that he sagged down.
>
> (p. 247)

Like the parables Raju used to relate, the novel is open-ended. The reader is not told if in fact it does rain and the narrative continues to tease the mind with questions. Is the fast a supreme piece of play-acting to the last? Or a selfless sacrifice? What is important is that a reading of *The Guide* which pursues it as individual romance, along the lines of the novel form borrowed from the West, produces Raju either as a sinner redeemed or as a supreme fraud. Locating the novel within Hindu tradition, however, produces a reading which can entertain Raju as both trickster and swami, tourist guide and spiritual guide, mimic man and a holy man of integrity, and the concluding scene as mere illusion and yet also a vision.

If the early history of the Indo-Anglian novel up to 1969, Mukherjee's cut-off date, was dominated by the 'big three', as Anand, Narayan and Rao are sometimes familiarly termed, then the last two decades have seen the rise to prominence of a number of women novelists. Kamala Markandaya and Ruth Prawer Jhabvala are already well-known, but newer reputations include Nayantara Sahgal, Anita Desai, and, even more recently, Bapsi Sidhwa and Shashi Deshpande. One common characteristic in the otherwise distinctively different work of the last four writers is a powerful compulsion to retrieve the past through the self-conscious act of revisioning history and myth. Always the spur to memory is a crisis, whether domestic and private – as with the arrival of Bims's sister Tara back at the family house in Desai's *Clear Light of Day* (1980) and the husband's alleged business malpractice in Deshpande's *That Long Silence* (1988) – or national in magnitude as with the emergency of 1975–77 in Sahgal's *Rich Like Us* (1983) and communal killings in the Punjab on a scale unknown since 1947 in Sidhwa's *The Ice-Candy-Man* (1988). And always there is discovered, as the basis of the experience of interrogating the past, a bedrock of suffering and silence.

Perhaps nowhere is the search among women writers for a voice and identity undertaken with greater sensitivity and complexity than in Anita Desai's *Clear Light of Day*. At the close of the novel, after the disruptions caused by Tara's visit, after the shared memories, Bim for a brief moment catches sight of an overall meaning and shape to her life:

> Listening to him [Mulk's Guru], Bim was suddenly overcome with the memory of reading, in Raja's well-thumbed copy of Eliot's *Four Quartets*, the line:
> *Time the destroyer is time the preserver.*
> Its meaning seemed to fall out of the dark sky and settle upon her like a cloak, or like a great pair of feathered wings. She huddled in its comfort, its solace. She saw before her eyes how one ancient school of music contained both Mulk, still an immature disciple, and his aged, exhausted guru with all the disillusionments and defeats of his long experience. With her inner eye she saw how her own house and its particular history linked and contained her as well as her whole family with all their separate histories and experiences . . .
>
> (p. 182)

Personal history is recreated here in transcendental terms, presided over by the aesthetic symbols of Eliot's poetic sequence, Mulk's song and his guru's, and the dancing figure of Shiva-Nataraja. It is a fitting climax to a novel in which the process of preserving, destroying, and creating is a lived reality throughout. It had seemed to Bim in the summer of 1947, as the fires burned every night in Delhi, and the streets beneath the city walls became choked with millions of refugees, that the city would never get over the shattering experience. Back at home, the family unit disintegrated leaving behind Baba, locked forever in his silent world, and Bim herself growing more grey, eccentric, and bitter. But as the narrative moves in intricate manner towards that concluding moment of synthesis, so the transforming power of memory and time is enacted. The sisters return again and again (as Mulk and his guru do, reworking their musical motifs) to crucial moments in their lives in the old house, remaking them by mutual reflection (in the two senses of mirroring and thoughts shared) into patterns different yet complementary; and remaking themselves, too, in ways that extricate them from some of the ghosts of the past, and leave revealed their multi-faceted identities.

Why then does the phrase with which the sisters take leave of each other – 'Nothing's over, ever' (p. 174) – sound so forlorn as well as consoling? Is it because, for all the lyrical quality of Desai's prose, there is no way of transmuting altogether the harshness of the life she is representing? Is it that the visionary ending of the novel can only encompass, not resolve, the violence which lies unredeemed at its core and which is embodied in the tragic figure of Aunt Mira? Where in the totalizing systems of Indian and European culture does she fit? Married at twelve, widowed at fifteen, a household drudge, a thing to be cast off, a nursemaid to the Das children, their old aunt, an alcoholic – had she not aged prematurely, 'her brothers-in-law would have put the widow to a different use' (p. 108); had they been permitted to do so, she would have been forced to burn at her husband's funeral pyre. That is Aunt Mira's history, neatly epitomized in the one good sari she possessed, and wore once as a bridal garment and then as a shroud. Within a narrative centring on identity and self-realization, she is throughout an object constructed and used by others. She has no voice to sing, as the guru does, like one 'who had come, at the end of his journey, within sighting distance of death' (p. 182). For her there was no redemption possible or 'new rest'. Only madness, oblivion, and regression into the childishness for which time was never allotted her.

The issue of identity, history and tradition is one that has also concerned Salman Rushdie. 'My view is that the Indian tradition has always been, and still is, a mixed tradition. The idea that there is such a thing as a pure Indian tradition is a kind of fallacy, the nature of Indian culture has always been multiplicity and plurality and mingling' (Rushdie, 1985, p. 10). Apply the statement to the Indian novel in English, which straddles two cultures at least, and the genre, once doubly marginalized, assumes a paradoxical centrality. Rushdie's statement is also applicable to his own imagination which, being peculiar to 'an emigrant from one country (India) and a newcomer in two (England, where I live, and Pakistan, to which my family moved against my will)' (*Shame*, 1983, p. 85), spawns stories as well as ingenious ways of recounting them. Not surprisingly, in a novel like *Midnight's Children* (1981), plot and character are of secondary interest when placed beside the action and excitement generated by the narrator's attempts to shape and order his irrepressible material. From the first, several choices are open to Saleem – to write autobiography or history; to use the once-upon-a-time formula and exploit the 'fantastic heart' (p. 195) of the tale or to pursue it in realistic fashion; to recite his story to Padma, his devoted companion, or to write it out for the shadowy reader waiting behind her. But, repeatedly, no sooner is a narrative genre or convention fixed upon than it is subverted, so that the *Bildungsroman* uncovers a baby swop which is the property of melodrama; science fiction shares the same space as the language of comic strips and American English; and a realistic account of the events surrounding the murder of a politician spills over into horror story and the romance of the Bombay-talkie. Like India, Rushdie's novel contains a wealth of words and competing languages which Saleem manipulates with flair and gusto even while they continually threaten to overwhelm him.

The idea of multiplicity is also foregrounded in the uneasy relationship between fiction and history depicted in the novel. The period it covers – from the First World War to the end of Indira Gandhi's emergency in 1977 – is one of momentous events, the earliest of which are still recoverable by living memory. And 'memory's truth' is the argument which Saleem uses to quell Padma's scepticism regarding his narrative. Yet ironically, for someone whose life is meant to mirror India's, his own memory is often unreliable. On two occasions, its fallibility astounds even Saleem himself. He dates wrongly Gandhi's assassination in 1948 and the elections of 1957. But to correct his mistakes would be to destroy the meaning and purpose he has given to his life and to deny the centrality of his role. By highlighting the arbitrary and distorting nature of Saleem's history, the novelist draws attention to the possibility of other versions of the same events. Even if Saleem is right in thinking that 420 of the 1001 children born between midnight and 1 a.m. of August 15 1947, the first hour of India's independence, fail to survive, that leaves another 580 stories to be told. Indeed, to be mindful of multiplicity is the means by which one extricates oneself from the imperialist view of history according to which the West 'discovered' India, and eludes also the absolutism of the Widow 'who was not only Prime Minister of India but also aspired to be Devi, the Mother-goddess in her most terrible aspect' (p. 438).

In *Shame* (1983), the narrative strategy is again an insistence upon multiplicity, this time for purposes of unearthing the concealed layers of Indian history and Indian centuries which 'lay just beneath the surface of Pakistan Standard Time' (p. 87). To tell stories is, first, a ploy the migrant who returns to his country intermittently must adopt, for it is a country which he can only know 'in slices' (p. 69); and second, it represents a political act, tantamount to resisting the authority of a one-man government and a one-book religion. The precariousness of the migrant's predicament has been aptly pinpointed by Rushdie himself – 'When individuals come unstuck from their native land, they are called migrants' (p. 86) – where the double sense of the phrase 'come unstuck', that is 'break free' and 'suffer disaster', seems especially bitter in view of the consequences which attended the publication of *The Satanic Verses* (1988). It may be that how to distinguish a satanic revelation from an angelic one is a question central to Islam but, tragically, engaging with it has brought Rushdie too close to the quick of Islamic national and religious sensibilities.

To trace the course which Indian writing in English has taken from 1947 to the present time is to note the solidity, consistency, and richness of its achievement. It is to share, if not wholly then surely to a large extent, the confidence of the authors of *The Empire Writes Back* that 'The frame remains but what is empowered within it can now be the product of an active choice' (Ashcroft *et al.*, 1989, p. 112).

FURTHER READING

Ashcroft, Bill, Griffiths, Gareth, and Tiffin, Helen (1989) *The Empire Writes Back: Theory and Practice in Post-Colonial Literatures*, Routledge, London

Iyengar, Srinivasa K. R. (1984) *Indian Writing in English*, Sterling, New Delhi [first published 1962]

King, Bruce (1987) *Modern Indian Poetry in English*, Oxford University Press, Delhi

Lal, P. (ed.) (1971) *Modern Indian Poetry in English: An Anthology & a Credo*, Writers Workshop, Calcutta [first published 1969]

Mahapatra, Jayanta (1989) 'Jayanta Mahapatra: 1928– '. In Mark Zadrozny (ed.), *Contemporary Authors: Autobiography Series*, Gale Research, Detroit

Mukherjee, Meenakshi (1971) *The Twice Born Fiction: Themes and Techniques of the Indian Novel in English*, Heinemann, New Delhi

Narasimhaiah, C. D. (ed.) (1965) *Literary Criticism: European and Indian Traditions*, University of Mysore, Mysore

Narayan, R. K. (1965) 'English in India'. In John Press (ed.), *Commonwealth Literature: Unity and Diversity in a Common Culture*, Heinemann, London

Rushdie, Salman (1985) '*Midnight's Children* and *Shame*', *Kunapipi*, 7, 1–19

Walsh, William (1990) *Indian Literature in English*, Longman, London

ADDITIONAL WORKS CITED

Bhatt, Sujata (1988) *Brunizem*, Carcanet Press, Manchester

Desai, Anita (1980) *Clear Light of Day*, Heinemann, London

Mahapatra, Jayanta (1987) *Selected Poems*, Oxford University Press, Delhi

Narayan, R. K. (1970) *The Guide*, Bodley Head, London [first published 1958]

Ramanujan, A. K. (1971) *Relations*, Oxford University Press, London

Rao, Raja (1938) *Kanthapura*, Allen & Unwin, London

Rushdie, Salman (1981) *Midnight's Children*, Cape, London

——(1983) *Shame*, Cape, London

88

NEW ZEALAND AND
PACIFIC LITERATURE

ROD EDMOND

Everybody comes from the other side of the world.
(Janet Frame, *The Edge of the Alphabet*, 1962)

When Katherine Mansfield was first thrown to the Woolfs, Virginia reported:

We could both wish one's first impression of K.M. was not that she stinks like
a – well, civet cat that had taken to street walking. In truth I'm a little shocked
at her commonness at first sight; lines so hard and cheap. However, when this
diminishes, she is so intelligent and inscrutable that she repays friendship . . .
we discussed Henry James and K.M. was illuminating I thought.

(Bell, 1982, p. 45)

The sequence of Virginia Woolf's responses – recoil, insult, condescending
acknowledgement – is in many ways typical of contact between metropolitan
and colonial cultures, one stiff-necked, the other presumptuously unbuttoned.
But Europe's habit of regarding itself as the centre and the rest of the world
as peripheral is often absorbed by the colonial culture itself. Allen Curnow,
in his much discussed Introduction to *The Penguin Book of New Zealand Verse*
(1960), accused Katherine Mansfield of 'something like shame for her country'
(p. 40). He was referring to the line, 'I, a woman, with the taint of the pioneer
in my blood', from her poem 'To Stanislaw Wyspianski'. But these lines 'From
the other side of the world' (the poem's opening) to the dramatist-patriot of
a colonized and suffering nation, are proud, not shameful:

I, a woman, with the taint of the pioneer in my blood,
Full of a youthful strength that wars with itself and is lawless,
I sing your praises, magnificent warrior; I proclaim your
triumphant battle.

(in Curnow, 1960, p. 27)

Although the poem goes on to develop a belittling contrast between New
Zealand and Poland ('My people have had nought to contend with . . . What
would they know of ghosts and unseen presences'), the speaker is able to
identify with Wyspianski because of her otherness as a colonial and as a

woman. 'Taint' is a mark of distinction, the source of youthful strength and lawlessness (as well as cheap perfume). The shame sensed by Curnow ('A New Zealand critic must not try to gloss over its implications', p. 40) is in the eye of a beholder less inured than Mansfield to the condescension of the mother culture. That a late twentieth-century reading can substitute pride for shame, recovering, I believe, Mansfield's original meaning, is an indication of the shifts that have occurred within New Zealand literature and criticism over the last thirty years which it will be the purpose of this essay to describe.

Literary critical debate in New Zealand has focused on poetry rather than on prose fiction or drama. One reason for this is that poetry is easily gathered into anthologies, and the publication of a poetry anthology in New Zealand has always been a major cultural event, a national monument requiring a ceremonial unveiling in the form of an editor's introduction. Allen Curnow's 1960 Penguin Introduction has probably been more read and discussed than the poetry it introduced. More recently there has been serious debate over Ian Wedde's Introduction to the 1985 *Penguin Book of New Zealand Verse*, an essay which takes most of its cues, however critically, from Curnow's. Crucially, both Introductions discuss the fundamental question of language; not 'what do we say?' but 'how do we say it?' Identity, that central issue for post-colonial writing, must ultimately be found in language.

Curnow's Introduction has often been read differently from this as the culmination of an attempt to create a distinctive national culture which had begun in the 1930s with the writing of Curnow himself, A. R. D. Fairburn, Denis Glover and their contemporaries. Its concluding invitation to younger New Zealand poets 'to name those "nameless native hills"' (Curnow, 1960, p. 66) has been taken as a call to complete the task of defining a national consciousness left unfinished by Curnow's own generation. C. K. Stead ([1979] 1981) has criticized this tradition for its obsession with 'the New Zealand referent', and for its anti-Modernist distinction between a poem's subject and its language. A decade after Curnow's Introduction one of those younger poets, Murray Edmond, had refused Curnow's invitation, declaring instead that it was time 'to construct a poetic rather than to name them hills and define a national consciousness' (*Freed*, 3).

The view from the present day, however, looks a little different. Curnow's nationalism seems an uneasy, shifting construction. Although his essay is undeniably obsessed with 'the New Zealand referent', it seems equally obsessed with the need to escape this ('it is not by harping on what is native, indigenous, insular that any of these songs are news', p. 18). The argument twists and turns until he comes to 'semantic problems', to what makes these songs new rather than news. This part of the argument is under-developed, but it is central to Curnow's then controversial preference of Kendrick Smithyman to James K. Baxter, and to the passage in which he suggests that a national distrust of personal speech has had a constraining effect on the development of a poetic voice in New Zealand. The famous call to 'name them hills' is, then, as much a call for a poetic as for a self-conscious national literature defined within the terms of a colonial relationship.

C. K. Stead's essay (1981) jettisons Curnow's concern with national and cultural identity altogether, and develops the argument about language. Stead's preference for a modernist poetic which sees the poem as imaginative act rather than as a vehicle, and poetic language as the material of an art rather than the servant of an idea, followed a decade in which modern American influences had been dominant among a new generation of poets. He refers to the poets who set up the journal *Freed* in 1969 (Alan Brunton, Murray Edmond, Russell Haley, David Mitchell, Ian Wedde) and suggests they helped their seniors, Curnow and Baxter for example, to develop the more open forms and natural speech patterns characteristic of the later work of these two major figures.

For Ian Wedde (1985a) the language of poetry in the 1960s and 1970s has shifted from the hieratic to the demotic. By hieratic he means 'language that is received . . . encoded *elect*, with a "high" social threshold emphasizing cultural and historical continuity'. Demotic, on the other hand, 'describes language with a spoken base, adaptable and exploratory codes . . . a "lower" . . . more inclusive social threshold emphasizing cultural mobility and immediacy (p. 25)'. By the time of this second *Penguin Book of New Zealand Verse* indigeneity is taken pretty much for granted: 'there has come to be little residual missionary sense of poets operating at a frontier where you have to carry a life-supporting canteen from some distantly-located spring' (p. 25). For Wedde the language of New Zealand poetry has finally become acclimatized. It can now relax, free at last of cultural goals and the mimic influence of 'good' English (1985b, pp. 348–9). In going beyond nationalism and cultural alienation, the language of poetry in New Zealand has established a relation with the world which is 'internally familiar' rather than 'willed'. Wedde terms this 'consummation in location' (p. 346). It not only brings language and world into taut relation with each other, but is a precondition for a confident, open culture able to give and receive on equal terms (1985a, *passim*).

Stead's 'open form' and Wedde's 'demotic' have helped remove the limescale and allow other traditions to flow, other voices to be heard. Although Curnow's anthology included a representative sample of women's writing, some of his comments about individual women poets betrayed his own limiting commitment to a particular kind of voice and were offensively patronizing. Of Robin Hyde he remarked: 'Her writing was near hysteria, more often than not, and she was incurably exhibitionistic'. (1960, p. 57) Wedde, however, notes 'a code of alert irony' in twentieth-century women's poetry running from Ursula Bethell and Robin Hyde, through Janet Frame and Fleur Adcock, to

Elizabeth Smither. By contrast with this, he thinks, 'we may feel the celebrated humour of A. R. D. Fairburn and Denis Glover . . . to be more confident than witty' (p. 36). This revaluation questions the widely accepted great tradition of twentieth-century New Zealand poetry, even if the terms on which it is established – 'alert irony' – are needlessly limiting.

Curnow's anthology was mono-lingual, although he included translations of Maori songs (*waiata*), laments (*tangi*) and ritual chants (*reo tao*), as well as a translation of the Maori creation myth. There was no suggestion that poetry in Maori was being written in the twentieth century. His introduction made passing reference to the way in which Maori culture had enriched European (*Pakeha*) New Zealand traditions but his selection gave no evidence of this. Wedde's anthology opens with a selection of nineteenth-century songs and chants in Maori and translation, and includes poems in Maori, with translations by their authors, scattered throughout the twentieth-century section. In this way Arapera Blank's 'He koingo', C. K. Stead's 'April Notebook', Fleur Adcock's 'Note on Propertius' and Muru Walters's 'Haka: he huruhuru toroa' appear within a few pages of each other.

The bilingualism of Wedde's anthology has been criticized both for being fashionable and for being tokenist. This reflects deeper divisions within New Zealand society about the spread of bilingualism and the high valuation currently accorded to Maoritanga (Maori culture). Although the Maori language is undergoing a revival, it is Maori poets writing in English who are most widely read and who are influencing the language of poetry. Foremost among these is Hone Tuwhare, who has best expressed the experience of biculturalism from the Maori point of view. In his poem 'Ron Mason' (Mason was an important poet of the 1920s and 1930s) Tuwhare sees his challenge as being 'to tilt/a broken taiaha inexpertly' (a *taiaha* is a small carved hand-spear). He tells his dead friend:

> Easy for you now, man. You've joined your literary
> ancestors, whilst I have problems still in finding
> mine, lost somewhere
>
> (in Wedde, 1985a, p. 282)

There is, however, nothing broken or inexpert in Tuwhare's best poetry which combines a communal and rhetorical Maori style with the personal intensity of the European lyric tradition. Keri Hulme is another poet, better known as a novelist, whose work draws fluently on both Maori and European traditions while writing almost exclusively in English.

Prose fiction was slower to develop in New Zealand than poetry. The quantity of published prose fiction remained very small until well into the 1960s. Between 1940 and 1951, for example, only thirteen novels and six collections of short stories were published, and three authors – Frank Sargeson, Roderick Finlayson and Dan Davin – alone wrote nine of these volumes (Chapman, [1953] 1973, pp. 71–2).

Even more striking than the relative scarcity of titles was the unusual dominance of the short story in New Zealand writing. This dominance has often been read as a literary failure, the short story being regarded as an inferior substitute for the great novels that remained unwritten. Lurking behind this has been the fear that New Zealand culture lacked the maturity to produce great novels; in this sad light the short story becomes a symptom of retarded cultural growth. This was the implied position of an influential essay by Robert Chapman, 'Fiction and the Social Pattern' ([1953] 1973). Chapman emphasized the homogeneity of New Zealand society and the consequent lack of social variation for New Zealand writers to observe. There simply was not the social breadth and complexity to sustain a native *Middlemarch*. New Zealand's George Eliot was therefore Frank Sargeson.

There is, however, nothing intrinsically inferior about the short story as a literary form. It has, after all, a central place in many European literatures. In a recent comparative study of the short story in Canada and New Zealand, W. H. New has argued that the main tradition of short story writing in both literatures is a highly sophisticated one involving narrative indirection and a commitment to open and broken forms. The main bearers of this tradition in New Zealand writing, he argues, are Mansfield, Sargeson and Maurice Duggan, and among contemporary writers, Vincent O'Sullivan, Witi Ihimaera and Patricia Grace (New, 1987).

A further point should be made about the centrality of the short story in New Zealand literature. As a literary form it is in many ways as close to poetry as to the novel. The constraints of brevity encourage self-consciousness about form and language. In a good short story the experience has somehow to be implicit in the form; remember Conrad's dictum – 'the whole of the truth is to lie in the presentation'. Whereas the social density of realist fiction demands a settling of accounts and judging of issues, short stories, because of their brevity, are likely to open out into areas of experience which remain unspoken. The New Zealand short story tradition, then, is not one of novels which failed to grow but of a self-conscious genre whose preoccupation with form and language as central to the question of identity brings it as close to poetry as to a mainstream tradition of realist fiction.

Chapman emphasized the dominance of realism in New Zealand prose fiction and seems not to have expected this to be challenged. This was based on a belief in New Zealand's social homogeneity, until very recently one of the sustaining myths of national culture. As late as 1973 Wystan Curnow described New Zealand as 'a relatively classless, homogeneous, welfare state, a democracy zealously egalitarian' (1973, p. 157). Realism was assumed to be the literary mode best suited to represent this near-organic society. This putative homogeneity was illusory. As Steven Eldred-Grigg has remarked, throughout this century it would have been more accurate to describe New Zealand as 'a profoundly unequal, divided, hierarchical nation state which has a history of aggression and is dominated by an oligarchy of wealthy white men' (1987, p. 308). Nevertheless, for many decades writers and critics propagated the myth and created the literary expectation, awaiting, like Old Testament prophets, the coming of the great New Zealand novel. Alan Mulgan's *Man Alone* (1939) seemed like a harbinger, Bill Pearson's *Coal Flat* (1963) excited interest, and Maurice Gee's *Plumb* (1978) was thought by some to be the real thing. But these and other titles fed rather than satisfied the hope for a totalizing account of New Zealand's history and culture. Now it seems clear that the gazers were looking in the wrong direction. Much of the best fiction of the last thirty years (and this is not to denigrate the achievement of Maurice Gee) is in no very obvious sense realist. Janet Frame, pre-eminent among New Zealand novelists, is unclassifiable. She certainly uses realist conventions in her fiction, but only to expose their inadequacy. Other recent major novels such as Keri Hulme's *The Bone People* (1983) and Ian Wedde's *Symmes Hole* (1986) break decisively with realist convention without relinquishing their grip on New Zealand's past and present. Indeed, the open and dissonant forms used by these novelists are better able to express the psychic and social ruptures of contemporary New Zealand than the harmonies and closure of realism.

The myth of social homogeneity has also been exploded in recent years by the widespread publication of Maori writing. Until the publication of Witi Ihimaera's *Tangi* (1973), the first novel by a Maori writer, Maori writing in English had mainly been confined to the journal *Te Ao Hau*. Ihimaera's novel was an important event and a challenge to a readership accustomed to European New Zealand literary and cultural traditions. *Tangi* mixes traditional oral features of Maori culture with the conventions of the novel form, and early reviewers approached it with caution, alert to its difference and uncertain how to place it. As more novels and short stories have followed from Ihimaera and other Maori writers, notably Patricia Grace, the problem of reception has lessened.

Grace has been publishing short stories and novels since the mid-1970s and, like Ihimaera, she dramatizes a strongly Maori way of seeing and experiencing the world. Particularly interesting is her construction of a prose style based on the speech structures of Maori English. This is so much a feature of her writing that it is difficult to quote selectively, but the opening sentences of 'The Wall', from her short story collection *Electric City* (1987), is an example of what I mean:

> The old man was the only one liked our wall, or the only one said. Our wall got in the papers.

> We saw the woman there with her camera, and a guy was with her having a
> look, writing stuff on a pad. That's good, us and our wall's going in the paper.
>
> (p. 33)

Grace is doing for Maori English what Sargeson did for Pakeha English fifty
years ago. Language is freed, new tones and registers are released, and new
points of view become visible. Grace's work is marked by restraint, suggestion
and under-statement. But in a story like 'Going for the Bread' in which a
young Maori girl is set upon by two Pakeha girls, the calm is deceptive. At
the end of the story the girl's mother decides not to send her children to the
shop again:

> They didn't have to have bread every day. Once a week she'd get a taxi and the
> three of them would go to the shops and get what they needed.
> And one day the war would end.
>
> (Grace, 1987, p. 51)

Quietly, decisively, that concluding sentence dismantles the myth of homogeneity and that 'steady development towards a cordial inter-cultural adjustment'
predicted by Bill Pearson in his essay 'The Maori and Literature' ([1969]
1973).

The most spectacular literary event in New Zealand in the last decade was
the publication of Keri Hulme's *The Bone People*. Rejected by several established publishers, it was brought out by a woman's collective, Spiral, was a
huge success in New Zealand and went on to win the Booker Prize in Britain
in 1985. This success has also produced a critical reaction. C. K. Stead has
raised the question of the author's racial identity and has argued there is
something spurious and opportunistic in its Maoriness (Stead, 1985a, b).
There has also been a wider cultural backlash against the novel's sympathetic
identification with Maoritanga. Its title has become a term of abuse for Pakeha
'fellow-travellers'. Hulme's novel has become a political event rather than a
mere literary text. Why should this be so?

As we have seen, until recently New Zealand writing was overwhelmingly
the product of a white settler society defined initially by its complex relations
with the imperial centre. It was within the terms of this relationship that
Pakeha New Zealand's literary and other identities were constructed. As this
essay has attempted to show, slowly and unevenly the differences between the
imperial culture and its distant off-shoot became less a cause of alienation,
anxiety, or even shame, and increasingly a source of strength and freedom, of
a post-colonial identity. This independence, however, has also become the
source of new anxiety and unease. The writer in a white settler society is both
colonized and colonizer. Within such a society indigenous populations are
doubly marginalized, first by the culture of the colonizing power, and then by
the new and dominant settler culture. Indigenous writing, when it finally

emerges, would seem at risk of being incorporated by the national literature of the settler colony (see Ashcroft *et al.*, 1989, pp. 144–5). Clearly this has not happened in New Zealand during the last twenty years. Socially and economically the Maoris remain an under-class, but in cultural politics the relative strength of Maori and Pakeha communities has been, if anything, reversed. Simon During has suggested that this is because in a post-colonial world white settlers are left without ethical or ideological support of their own. This 'emptiness of post-coloni*zing* discourses' within settler society creates space for post-coloni*zed* voices, needs and self-images, permitting new and vital discursive formations to emerge (During, 1985, pp. 370–1).

During's argument is over-schematic, but it offers a theoretical perspective from which to understand the complex, many-sided debate over *The Bone People*. Stead's case against Keri Hulme has been thoroughly examined and answered by Margery Fee, but she acknowledges that his scrutiny of Hulme's claim to write as a Maori raises important questions about how minority group membership is determined, and whether majority group members can speak as minority members (Fee, 1989). There is, after all, a long literary tradition of facile romantic exploitation of indigenous material by white writers. Other critics have objected not so much to Hulme's right to speak as a Maori, but to the ideological role of Maoriness within *The Bone People*. Ruth Brown has argued that the novel's Maori spirituality is a Pakeha construct which has more to do with the Pakeha need for metaphysical palliatives than with Maoritanga (1989). Simon During also sees *The Bone People* as offering an urgently needed new myth of race relations, and explains its success in terms of the need to reconcile post-colonizing and post-colonized discourses (During, 1985, p. 374).

Hulme is of mixed Pakeha and Maori ancestry and she addresses both a Maori and Pakeha readership. In *The Bone People* the central male character is mainly Maori but part-European, the leading female character is mainly European but part-Maori, and the child, Simon/Haimona, is the son of ship-wrecked European parents. The novel uses this configuration of hybridity to explore tensions in New Zealand's mixed culture in a more complex manner than these generalizations about its ideological role allow. Reconciliation, if that is the appropriate word, is incomplete and on Maori terms, reversing the historical assimilation of Maori by Pakeha culture. It is reductive to assume that because of the novel's commercial success the myths it incorporates are inevitably comforting. And with more space I believe I could show that the novel's valorization of Maoritanga is not based on a backward-looking senti-mentalized representation of some essential cultural purity.

The Bone People accepts that New Zealand, the largest Polynesian country in the world, is inescapably multi-cultural, and explores many implications of this. It does not accept that only Maoris can speak about Maoritanga, nor does it accept that Pakeha representations of multi-culturalness are bound to be either oppressive or romanticized. As someone of English, Maori and Orkney Scots descent, Hulme writes out of the heart of New Zealand's contemporary condition. This is one in which the historic dominance of Pakeha over Maori cultural discourse is being challenged and revised. For this, among other reasons, *The Bone People* is likely to remain a central document in New Zealand's literary and cultural redefinition.

New Zealand was not just a colony but also a colonial power in the South Pacific. Like other colonial powers, many of those it colonized now live in the metropolitan centre. At least 100,000 South Pacific Islanders live in New Zealand (population 3½ million.). Auckland is the largest Samoan city, and a clear majority of the population of several smaller South Pacific islands now lives in New Zealand. Indeed, New Zealand is now much more importantly the metropolitan centre for the South Pacific than Britain is for New Zealand. By South Pacific, I mean those island states formerly under the United Kingdom's Western Pacific High Commission – Fiji, Vanuatu (formerly New Hebrides), Solomon Islands, Nauru, Kiribati and Tuvalu (formerly Gilbert and Ellice Islands) and Tonga; and those related to New Zealand – Western Samoa (independent since 1962), and the Cook Islands, Niue and Tokelau (associated states with New Zealand) (see Subramani, 1985, pp. xi–xii). Importantly for literature, these are the eleven countries served by the University of the South Pacific, based in Fiji.

There is a long tradition of European written and pictorial representation of the South Pacific. This began with the later eighteenth-century explorers and continued through the next century in the work of Melville, Ballantyne, Loti, Stephenson and Gauguin, and into the early twentieth century in the writing of Jack London and Somerset Maugham. These and others tended to see the South Pacific Islander either as noble savage, whether the sentimentalized hero of natural life or victim of European corruption, or as ignoble, totally without natural virtue. This latter view was more common in missionary and administrative than in literary and pictorial discourse. But whether overvalued as an alternative to European habits of mind, or condemned as backward and barbaric, what always mattered was the significance of the South Pacific *for Europe*.

Indigenous South Pacific literature in English is of recent origin. It was not until 1968, when the University of the South Pacific was established, that a handful of writers who had published in New Zealand and Australia during the 1960s came together and initiated the conscious promotion of creative writing in the area (Subramani, 1985, pp. 17–18). In the first issue of *Mana Review*, the region's only literary periodical, Subramani noted that the South Pacific writer, even more than other third world writers, lacked a literary tradition and an audience (Subramani, 1976). In the last twenty years the writing of Albert Wendt, Epeli Hau'ofa, Konai Thaman and Subramani himself, to name but a few, has begun to establish diverse indigenous literary traditions, but the problem of audience remains acute. There is hardly a reading public beyond the walls of the two regional universities, the University of the South Pacific and the University of Papua New Guinea. Most South Pacific writers look first towards New Zealand and Australia.

Another problem shared with third world writers, particularly African ones, is that of language. There are more than 1200 indigenous languages in the region and most writers are, at least, bilingual, divided between a vernacular peculiar to their country or group, and English, which is the common language of the region. This can, however, also be a source of strength. Albert Wendt, for example, has used varieties of dialect in several stories. In doing so he is practising his own dictum that 'self-expression is a pre-requisite of self-respect'. This appeared in his seminal essay 'Towards a New Oceania', which was a call to the region 'for the creation of new cultures which are free of the taint of colonialism and based firmly on our own pasts. The quest should be for a new Oceania' (Wendt, 1976, p. 53).

Wendt himself has responded most vitally to his own call, in novels, short story collections, poetry and essays. The region's other most distinctive voice is the Tongan short story writer and novelist Epeli Hau'ofa. In very different ways – Wendt's writing is serious, often pessimistic, whereas Hau'ofa's mode is the comic-grotesque – both writers explore the transitional nature of contemporary South Pacific society, caught between traditional and modernizing forces. Both register the complexity of this process. Hau'ofa, for example, is a trenchant critic of 'the Pacific Way', an influential pan-Pacific ideology which looks back to a supposedly homogeneous, enclosed world of pre-contact Oceania. Both writers are closely in touch with the oral story-telling traditions of their own cultures. The narrative styles of Wendt's writing draw widely and fluently on these traditions, and Hau'ofa makes clever use of the Tongan tradition of the tall tale. In doing this both writers are helping create a literary language for the South Pacific.

At the end of 'Towards a New Oceania' Albert Wendt looked towards the creation of a South Pacific literature which would include New Zealand writing. In many ways Wendt himself embodies this idea. Samoan born, with a German grandfather, New Zealand educated, a former Principal of Samoa College and Professor at the University of the South Pacific, he is currently Professor of English at the University of Auckland. The New Zealand writers he then wished to bring into his category of South Pacific literature included Tuwhare, Ihimaera and Grace. In the future, however, it is likely that South Pacific literature will extend beyond Wendt's essentially Polynesian definition to include Pakeha writing – Wedde's *Symme's Hole* is a Pakeha South Pacific novel – Indo-Fijian, and other new literatures as they emerge from this complex multi-cultural region.

FURTHER READING

Davin, D. M. (ed.) (1953) *New Zealand Short Stories*, 1st series, Oxford University Press, London

Edmond, Murray and Paul, Mary (eds) (1987) *The New Poets*, Allen & Unwin/Port Nicholson Press, Wellington

Evans, Miriama, McQueen, Harvey and Wedde, Ian (eds) (1989) *The Penguin Book of Contemporary New Zealand Poetry*, Penguin, Auckland

Frame, Janet (1982) *To the Island*, (vol. 1 of autobiography), Hutchinson, Auckland

——(1984) *An Angel at My Table*, (vol. 2 of autobiography), Hutchinson, Auckland

——(1985) *The Envoy from Mirror City*, (vol. 3 of autobiography), Hutchinson, Auckland

Hankin, Cherry (ed.) (1982) *Critical Essays on the New Zealand Short Story*, Heinemann, Auckland

Ihimaera, Witi and Long, D. S. (eds) (1982) *Into the World of Light: An Anthology of Maori Writing*, Heinemann, Auckland

Jones, Lawrence (1987) *Barbed Wire and Mirrors: Essays on New Zealand Prose*, University of Otago Press, Dunedin

O'Sullivan, Vincent (ed.) (1975) *New Zealand Short Stories*, 3rd series, Oxford University Press, Auckland

Pearson, Bill (1974) *Fretful Sleepers and Other Essays*, Heinemann, Auckland

Stead, C. K. (ed.) (1966) *New Zealand Short Stories*, 2nd series, Oxford University Press, London

Wendt, Albert (ed.) (1980) *Lali: A Pacific Anthology*, Longman Paul, Auckland

Wevers, Lydia (ed.) (1984) *New Zealand Short Stories*, 4th series, Oxford University Press, Auckland

ADDITIONAL WORKS CITED

Ashcroft, Bill, Griffiths, Gareth and Tiffin, Helen (1989) *The Empire Writes Back: Theory and Practice in Post-Colonial Literatures*, Routledge, London

Bell, Quentin (1982) *Virginia Woolf*, vol. 2, Hogarth Press, London

Brown, Ruth (1989) 'Maori Spirituality as Pakeha Construct', *Meanjin*, 2, 252–8

Chapman, Robert (1973) 'Fiction and the Social Pattern'. In Wystan Curnow (ed.), *Essays on New Zealand Literature*, Heinemann, Auckland, pp. 71–98 [essay first published 1953]

Curnow, Allen (1960) *The Penguin Book of New Zealand Verse*, Penguin, Harmondsworth

Curnow, Wystan (1973) 'High Culture in a Small Province'. In W. Curnow (ed.), *Essays on New Zealand Literature*, Heinemann, Auckland, pp. 151–71

During, Simon (1985) 'Postmodernism or Postcolonialism', *Landfall*, 39, 366–80

Eldred-Grigg, Steven (1987) 'A Bourgeois Blue? Nationalism and Letters from the 1920s to the 1950s', *Landfall*, 41, 292–311

Fee, Margery (1989) 'Why C. K. Stead didn't like Keri Hulme's *The Bone People*: Who can write as Other?' *Australian and New Zealand Studies in Canada*, 1, 11–32

Grace, Patricia (1987) *Electric City and Other Stories*, Penguin, Auckland

New, W. H. (1987) *Dreams of Speech and Violence: The Art of the Short Story in Canada and New Zealand*, University of Toronto Press, Toronto

Pearson, Bill (1973) 'The Maori and Literature 1938–1965'. In Wystan Curnow (ed.), *Essays on New Zealand Literature*, Heinemann, Auckland, pp. 99–138 [essay first published 1969]

Stead, C. K. (1981) 'Preliminary: From Wystan to Carlos – Modern and Modernism in Recent New Zealand Poetry'. In C. K. Stead, *In the Glass Case: Essays on New Zealand Literature*, Auckland University Press/Oxford University Press, Auckland, pp. 139–159, [essay first published 1979]

——(1985a) 'Keri Hulme's *The Bone People* and the Pegasus Award for Maori Literature', *Ariel*, 16, 101–8

——(1985b) Letter to *London Review of Books*, 5 December

Subramani (1976) 'Editorial', *Mana Review*, 1, 1

——(1985) *South Pacific Literature: From Myth to Fabulation*, Institute of Pacific Studies, Suva

Wedde, Ian and McQueen, Harvey (1985a) *The Penguin Book of New Zealand Verse*, Penguin, Auckland

Wedde, Ian (1985b) 'Checking Out the Foundations: Editing the *Penguin Book of New Zealand Verse*', *Meanjin*, 3, 341–51

Wendt, Albert (1976) 'Towards a New Oceania', *Mana Review*, 1, 50–9

89

WEST INDIAN LITERATURE

DAVID RICHARDS

West Indian history begins in colonialism with the migrations of the Ciboney people from South America, their conquest and expulsion by the Arawaks who, in their turn, were displaced by the Caribs. The 'discovery' of the New World by European powers transformed this history of mundane, domestic violence into something of global significance as, successively, Spanish, French, British and Dutch colonialists threw themselves into the Caribbean cockpit in competition for possession of the islands and the Central and South American seaboard. For the sake of imperial ambition, vast populations from Africa and the Indian sub-continent were enslaved, enticed or tricked into mass migrations on a colossal scale. Estimates of numbers vary, but something of the order of twenty million Africans were taken by force from West Africa alone. Not all were bound for the Caribbean, of course, but the importance of the West Indies for the European powers should not be underestimated. As Louis James points out, 'the island of French Guadeloupe was once considered more important than the whole of Canada, and the Dutch gladly exchanged what is now New York State for a strip of Guiana' (James, 1968, p. x). The intensity of the struggle between the imperial powers for possession of the islands is best illustrated by the example of St Lucia which changed colonial ownership fourteen times during its history. As a source of profit, as a site of imperial aspirations or as a remote outpost of European political rivalries, the West Indies profoundly influenced the European orientation to the rest of the world and determined the development of eighteenth- and nineteenth-century empires. When the trade in slaves became unpalatable and uneconomic in the first decades of the nineteenth century, new sources of labour for the West Indies were exploited in India. The indentured labour schemes drew large numbers of Indian peasants from the subcontinent to the plantations of Guyana and Trinidad. Just as the last ship carrying the Indian labourers left for the Caribbean in the early 1950s, a further migration began, this time from the

West Indies to Britain to supply black labour to a post-war British economy suffering from a depleted manpower.

The West Indies are a historical and cultural microcosm of Empire and its decline. The imperial ideologies of racial superiority and economic exploitation bred violence, poverty and despair. Yet it is precisely out of this bloody and dislocated history that the Caribbean has produced some of the most remarkable writings in the English language. In spite of the deprivations of an imperial history and in spite of relocation to often small and remote islands, the West Indian writer is anything but insular or impoverished. The very fact that the modern Caribbean is an imperial invention means that the processes of recent history, in all their terrible actuality, are often clearly evident in the people and landscape. West Indian societies reflect a wider global population within the confines of a small geographical area, and Amerindian, African, Indian and European cultures have all contributed to the West Indian identity. This essay is about how that sense of a problematic identity is painfully and fitfully reproduced by West Indian writers.

Given the context of West Indian history, it is difficult to offer a date as the point of origin, the genesis, of West Indian writing. Faced with a dislocated history, the West Indian writer has a choice, either to view the past as a vista of the disabling theft of language, culture and ethnicity which has culminated in the radical historylessness of the Caribbean, or as a 'liberation' from history, a freedom from the constraints of tradition whereby West Indian history has uniquely enabled the writer to draw upon any and all forms of literary tradition and expression. In the broadest terms, this choice between denial and abundance of tradition typifies all West Indian literature. For instance, C. L. R. James, the Trinidadian novelist, historian and writer on cricket, chooses a French novelist as his primogenitor. Yet Alexandre Dumas never went to the Caribbean, and James's claim is based on Dumas's grandfather who owned a plantation in Haiti and kept a black mistress (James, 1972, p. 23). James is only partly serious in claiming Dumas for the West Indies, but he underlines an important element in much West Indian writing: the willingness to lay claim to much of the 'metropolitan' literary tradition and thereby offer radical reorientations of many key texts of those traditions. This rewriting of the literary tradition reads Shakespeare's *The Tempest*, for example, as a play about the West Indies, and combines early writings by West Indians, such as the eighteenth-century Latin Odes composed by Francis Williams, a Cambridge-educated Jamaican freeman, with works written by plantation owners, such as James Grainger (*The Sugar Cane*, 1764) or the gothic novelist 'Monk' Lewis (*Journal of a West Indian Proprietor*, 1834).

The problems of history and identity in the West Indies give rise to many other related issues, not least the problem of tradition. The issue is superbly and repeatedly confronted by Derek Walcott, the St Lucian poet. His poem

'Ruins of a Great House' (first published in *In a Green Night*, 1962) crystallizes the West Indian dilemma most obviously in the matter of form. The poem lies in the long tradition, from Jonson and Marvell to Yeats, of the country house poem, whereby an idyll of social and political harmony is nostalgically evoked. This minor genre of English literature is redefined within the Caribbean context since the country house can have only one meaning in the West Indies – plantation ownership and, therefore, slavery. Simultaneously the 'metropolitan' tradition is evoked and questioned; the poetic voice is enabled by a tradition which it challenges. Similarly, the poem is, Eliot-like, crowded with quotations from that tradition: Browne, Donne, Shakespeare, Milton, Faulkner, Kipling, Blake. An alternative, West Indian voice is mute, mutilated, murdered: 'I thought/Some slave is rotting in this manorial lake.' Again, the voice of the tradition is evoked in all its plenitude to indicate the silence of its victims. The tension builds to this finely balanced double ambiguity:

> I thought next
> Of men like Hawkins, Walter Raleigh, Drake,
> Ancestral murderers and poets . . .
> (Walcott, 1981, p. 5)

One ambiguity resides in the fact of a poetic culture which is also a murderous imperial regime, but even more problematic is the application of the word 'ancestral'. Are these the poet's ancestors who are both murderers and poets, or are they poets and murderers who have killed his ancestors, the slaves rotting in the manorial lake? Walcott's mixed race only serves to underline the status of the Caribbean writer's profound ambivalence, between a voiceless, denied non-tradition and a vocal, victorious culture. In *Midsummer* (1984), Walcott returns to the theme in a poem which describes a West Indian town:

> By the pitch of noon, the one thing wanting
> is a paddle-wheeler with its rusty parrot's scream,
> whistling in to be warped, and Mr Kurtz on the landing.
> Stay on the right bank in the imperial dream –
> the Thames, not the Congo.
>
> (p 14)

The reference to Conrad's *Heart of Darkness* (1902) is not accidental. In 'Ruins of a Great House', too, the tension is resolved in a way which is resonant of the opening of Conrad's novel: 'That Albion too, was once/A colony like ours . . .' This shared colonial history enables the poet to force an act of forgiveness from seemingly unpromising circumstance: 'All in compassion ends/So differently from what the heart arranged.'

Walcott's poem confronts the fundamental issue of post-colonial writing, which is that if the poet is to speak, what language and what tradition can s/he speak in and through? The issue is further complicated in the West

Indies by the convergence of so many fragments: African, Asian, Amerindian, European. Should the writer adopt one, some, all or none?

Yet however the literary past is constructed, West Indian literature is essentially a modern literature. The 'father of West Indian literature' is generally recognised as 'Tom Redcam' (Thomas Henry MacDermot, 1870–1933), whose project to give a growing Jamaican readership material written by and for Jamaicans created the climate in which the delineation of a Caribbean identity could be attempted by others. His two novels, *Becka's Buckra Baby* (1903) and *One Brown Girl And . . .* (1909), began to describe a culture not entirely deracinated and cut adrift from either a sense of community or an inherited culture. Herbert de Lisser (1878–1944), a Jamaican of mixed descent (Portuguese/Jewish/African), wrote nine novels, each showing a different phase of Caribbean history, from *Revenge* (1918), which dealt with the Morant Bay uprising of 1865, to the gothic horror story *The White Witch of Rose Hall* (1929). His most remarkable novel was his first, however, because *Jane's Career* (1913) not only has a broadly Fabian Socialist outlook but it is the first novel in the West Indies to have a central character who is both black and a peasant.

De Lisser invented a narrative form (which can be traced through successive novels) for the discovery and elucidation of the West Indian past, but in ways which attempted to observe and offer a voice to the supposedly dehistoricized and depoliticised black peasant and urban poor. Claude McKay's *Banana Bottom* (1933) deals with the return to a small mountain village of a girl brought up and educated in England. The novel explores and is a celebration of the complexity of a seemingly 'simple' rural community. V. S. Reid's *New Day* (1949) takes a more overtly historical perspective in that it is the recorded memories of an old man who, on the eve of the new Jamaican Constitution, remembers the Morant Bay Rebellion.

It would, of course, be inconceivable to discuss the reconstruction of the West Indian past without also alluding to the use made of those historical identities in framing a literature of commitment. The West Indian novel is, above all, a political literature, although this is neither dogmatic nor forced. For example, C. L. R. James's only novel, *Minty Alley* (1936), adopts a starkly realist description of life among the urban poor of Trinidad. James's political intelligence is, however, given a further twist by the brilliant invention of Haynes, a middle-class black fallen on hard times who must lodge with the poor family. This faintly bemused and uncomprehending figure is gradually involved in the family's affairs until the novel develops an uneasy attitude to its own narration, as if questioning its own voyeuristic intentions. Roger Mais's *The Hills Were Joyful Together* (1953) is more overt in its broad political sympathies. This novel is set, like James's, in the 'yard', an important site of novels concerned with social and political affairs, but here the targets are more identifiably those of corrupt and unequal laws, a repressive penal code and a smug and unconcerned middle class. As Kenneth Ramchand (1976, p. 17) has indicated, Mais's prose style 'shows strong Biblical influences' and this is a recurring feature of much West Indian fiction. Earl Lovelace's *The Wine of Astonishment* (1982) magnificently combines a sense of the history of the dispossessed with social and sociological comment in a language which blends a version of Caribbean creole with the texture of the King James Bible. His narrator is a poor black woman in a remote Trinidadian village in the 1940s, whose husband is a pastor of the banned Spiritual Baptist Church. The community's struggle against the Shouters Prohibition Ordnance (a law passed in 1917 proscribing the Spiritual Baptist Church in Trinidad and Tobago), brings them into conflict not only with the colonial powers but also with those in their own community who betray or despise their attempts to express their cultural autonomy. The text gradually promotes the idea that the spirit of the community only really exists in adversity and that 'breaking the law' becomes the truly creative action of an oppressed minority.

This brief and highly selective survey of some of the major West Indian novels has shown, I hope, two fundamental currents in Caribbean literary culture: the compelling desire to describe and comment upon the real conditions of oppressive poverty and political inequality which has none the less given rise to a vital and significant collective identity; and the need to locate that identity within an historical continuum.

Frantz Fanon, the Martiniquan psychologist and writer against colonialism, identifies three successive stages in post-colonial writing and its relationship with a dominant colonial tradition. After an initial desire to assimilate or 'mimic' the colonial culture, an alternative mode of cultural discovery brings the writer to an attempt to conjure a lost culture, in Africa or India or in American Indian culture. The 'third phase' is the 'fighting phase' (Fanon, 1961, pp. 178–9). Although this prescription is, in every way, far too formulaic, it does help to identify some of the various strategies adopted by West Indian writers in dealing with the vexed problem of 'Language [which] never fits geography' (Walcott, [1974] 1979, p. 40).

Jean Rhys, a white writer born in Dominica, has written the novel which most notably confronts the English narrative tradition. *Wide Sargasso Sea* (1966) attempts little less than a radical rewriting of one of the seminal texts of the literary canon. Rhys's novel is both embedded within and extends beyond Charlotte Brontë's *Jane Eyre*, which is its fictional skeleton. *Wide Sargasso Sea* is the story of the first Mrs Rochester, Antoinette Cosway, a Creole heiress married by Rochester for her money, discarded and driven mad by him, and who, incarcerated in the attic of his English country house, finally burns down her prison, so freeing Rochester to marry Jane. Rhys respectfully breaks open the nineteenth-century text to expose the sexual obsessions and fears, the colonial adventurism and racist dogma, and the gender and class struggles which underpin the foundations of an emerging imperial culture. The text is a dark and bitter reflection of Brontë's novel and stalks a complacent cultural tradition.

Rhys's grim vision of the dark underside of imperial culture attempts to break with a tradition, yet that very act of breaking none the less reasserts the potency of that tradition. As Walcott has written, 'those who break tradition first hold it in awe' ([1974] 1979, p. 38). Yet implicit in Walcott's statement is the assumption that the West Indian writer is engaged in a dialogue or argument with the erstwhile colonial or 'metropolitan' power. In a sense this view of the West Indian writer engaged in dialogue is itself a kind of imperial model. For very many of these writers the world is infinitely more complex given that lines of descent are drawn from Africa and the Indian sub-continent as well as the Caribbean and England.

The Barbadian poet Edward Brathwaite in his *The Arrivants: A New World Trilogy* (1973) offers just such a complex redrawing of influences and most closely resembles that strand identified by Fanon as 'cultural discoverer', particularly in the second volume of his trilogy *Masks* (1968). *Masks* is a poetic journey of discovery through Africa undertaken by a West Indian of African origins. The poems focus upon the history and cultural traditions of the Akan people of Ghana in a way which is both poetic and polemical. The texts advance the proposition that an African tradition is both a viable and desirable alternative to a European model which insists upon the inferiority of West Indian culture. Moreover, the Akan *asafo* (warrior) songs and *Ananse* (trickster) stories are very much present in the cultural life of the Caribbean and represent a more significant element in West Indian expression than the colonialists' rival productions. Brathwaite's strategy is to combine the African material with an English language medium, but the 'combination' is neither neutral nor placid: it is not simply the substitution of one structure or system of metaphors for another. The texture of the poem is perpetually disrupted by the African materials:

> White
> salt crackles at root lips, bursts like a fist
> and beats out this
> prayer:
>
> Nana Firimpong
> once you were here
> hoed the earth
> and left it for me
> green rich ready
> with yam shoots, the
> tuberous smooth cassava:

take the blood of the fowl
drink
take the *eto*, mashed plantain
that my women have cooked
eat
and be happy
drink
may you rest
for the year has come round
again.
            (Brathwaite, 1973, p. 91)

The Akan words cause the reader to stumble and the rhythm to be broken. They are there to call attention to themselves as intruders from a different tradition. They call for exegesis as 'traditional ancestors' or 'foodstuffs' in a way which simultaneously disrupts the rhythmical certainties of the English verse, indicates an alternative set of poetic traditions and gestures at the plangency of a world all but lost, though recoverable, to the West Indian. Brathwaite's task was to bend and extend the range of an English language poetic tradition in the West Indies, to embrace other material laden with symbolic significance and to make language fit a geography which includes Africa.

The importance of Africa in West Indian writing cannot be overestimated, either as providing alternative metaphors of cultural difference or as a fully developed Négritude. The discourse between African and Caribbean writers has been a vitally important element in the rise of black consciousness and its related political forms since the Francophone poet Aimé Césaire published his manifesto of négritude in the shape of the long poem *Return to my Native Land* in 1938. Césaire's influence in shaping a poetic diction and a poetic rhythm and in the overtly polemical stance he adopted has been widespread and fruitful, but there are important qualifications to be made as regards the Caribbean form of Négritude which he formulated. Certainly Africa and its traditions should, for Césaire, be a constant source of pride and strength for all the people of the diaspora, acting as a counterbalance to the history of racism which has blighted Europe and Africa. But there is also a sense in which Césaire reaches beyond that image of 'minimized blood' to a vision which embraces all oppressed peoples, black and white:

But what strange pride illuminates me suddenly?

O friendly light!
O fresh source of light!
Those who invented neither gunpowder nor compass
Those who never knew how to conquer steam or electricity
Those who explored neither seas nor sky

But those without whom the earth would not be the earth . . .
My negritude is not a stone, its deafness hurled
against the clamor of the day;
My negritude is not a speck of dead water on the
earth's dead eye,
My negritude is neither tower nor cathedral.

(Césaire, [1938] 1989, pp. 75–6)

Césaire's surrealistic epic ends in a hymn to human potential, a potential which is to be realized out of all the Caribbean's cultural possessions. Yet for many writers the very plurality of the West Indies constitutes the essential problem. To adapt a statement of Salman Rushdie's, 'the problem is that he comes from too many places, he suffers from excess rather than absence. Cross-pollination is everywhere' (Rushdie, 1982, p. 19). Against this must be placed the contrary view taken by V. S. Naipaul that 'history is built around achievement and creation; and nothing was created in the West Indies' (Naipaul, 1962, p. 29). On the matter of tradition, West Indian writers fluctuate widely between the twin poles of excess and denudation, between superabundance and impoverishment.

I asked earlier which cultural tradition West Indian writers should adopt. There is, of course, the option that they can make a literature out of the denial of those kinds of allegiances, as V. S. Naipaul seems to have done. From early novels (*The Mystic Masseur*, 1957, and *Miguel Street* 1959), which viewed the Caribbean as a marvellous if gently anarchic medley of cultural presences producing a lively human comedy, the vision has darkened. In *The Mimic Men* (1967) and *Guerrillas* (1975), and his later travel writings, the comedy has turned sour, the emerging island states have become sites of random and meaningless violence populated by deracinated and vicious individuals. Naipaul's later novels are a thorough denial of the project initiated by Tom Redcam and De Lisser to represent the communal strengths of the West Indian community. Indeed, there would seem to be grounds for seeing Naipaul's much cited Swiftian disgust as a more radical form of mysanthropy. It is this element in Naipaul which has led George Lamming to expel him from those he would call 'West Indian writers' and Walcott to rename him 'V. S. Nightfall'. But few would deny that Naipaul possesses 'an independent and fastidious talent which treats with an extraordinary understanding and detachment a violated, colonial society' (Walsh, 1973, p. 60). Yet despite Naipaul's extraordinary achievement and prolific output, his influence has been slight. Only his nephew, Neil Bissoondath, who was born in Trinidad but who lives in Canada, seems to have replicated his uncle's vision, in his short stories (*Digging Up The Mountains*, 1987) and novel (*A Casual Brutality*, 1988), of a dislocated postcolonial psychology whereby, in a mixture of pathos and disgust, 'a man moved is like a piece of meat passing through intestine' (Bissoondath, 1987, p. 178).

The West Indian world viewed through the eyes of women writers is, by contrast, the complete obverse of Naipaul's detached and sour view. Janice Shinebourne's *Timepiece* (1986) hardly blunts the effects of racial and political inequalities felt by her young Guyanese protagonist as she attempts to make her way in a male-dominated world, but the novel finds a kind of strength in the communal solidarities of a difficult but consoling matriarchy which sustains Caribbean society. Narratives of the history of the formation of the self, a West Indian *Bildungsroman*, are found also in works by Zee Edgell (*Beka Lamb*, 1982) and Olive Senior (*Summer Lightning*, 1986), and in some important respects Caribbean women writers have taken up and developed the earlier project of West Indian male writers in attempting to construct a worthwhile sense of identity, but this time out of a female experience.

An undoubted model for many of these novels about childhood, male or female, is the highly influential *In the Castle of my Skin* (1958) by George Lamming. This was Lamming's first novel, a kind of fictional autobiography, which tells the story of G.'s life in primary and secondary school and, in sensitive and moving detail, takes the reader to the point of his departure from the island where he was born. In its stress upon education, however, the novel strikes at the heart of much, if not all, West Indian writing in its emphasis upon the power of language:

> We wouldn't dare tell anybody what we had talked about. People who were sure of what they were saying and who had the right words to use could do that. They could talk to others. And even if they didn't feel what they were saying, it didn't matter. They had the right words. Language was a kind of passport. You could go where you like if you had a clean record ... And if you were really educated, and you could command the language like a captain on a ship, if you could make the language do what you wanted it to do, say what you wanted it to say, then you didn't have to feel at all. You could do away with feeling. That's why everyone wanted to be educated. You didn't have to feel. ... Language was all you needed. It was like a knife. It knifed your feelings clean and proper, and put an end to any pop, pop, pop in your head.
>
> (Lamming, 1953, pp. 153–4)

No other postcolonial writing has used and developed the issue of language to the same extent as West Indian literature. As Lamming powerfully conveys, language is the cause of both a savage denudation of the soul, the replication of a profound sense of inadequacy, and at the same time the means of liberation from that condition, even though it carries with it dangers of 'excess' and superficial fluency.

Language has been used as a kind of revolutionary device, turned against itself to conduct an assault upon what Shiva Naipaul has called 'the god-given aristocracy of skin'. As stated earlier, the English Language contains within its symbolic and metaphoric encodings those relationships of prejudice which the revolutionary poet must confront. To produce a committed poetics the poet must, in Bongo Jerry's phrase, 'cramp all double meaning/an' all that hiding behind language bar . . .' For Linton Kwesi Johnson, this involves not only a rededication of language to specific goals of liberation and action ('But love is/jus a word;/give it MEANIN/thru HACKSHAN'), but an assault upon metaphor itself ('wreckin thin-shelled words/movin always forwud' – Johnson, 1975, pp. 69, 21). The English language, for Johnson, must be subjected to violence, for:

> There is no love no more
> in emotive words . . .
> only fire.
> (Johnson, 1983, p. 3)

Yet, for other poets, this revolutionary response to the trials of language takes far too restricted a view of what it is possible to make the language do. For Louise Bennett and others, English has a broad spectrum of different forms and registers which encompasses non-standard forms, oral performances, dialects, pidgins and creoles and the rhythmical dynamism of Calypso. In the poem 'Votin' Lis' ', Bennett combines the individual voice of the oral performer with Calypsonian irony and Jamaican dialect on the subject of adult suffrage:

> Ah gwine mek dem tan deh beg me,
> Ah gwine mek dem tan deh pine,
> Ah gwine rag me haul an pull dem
> So till ah mek up me mine.
> (Bennett, 1966, p. 133)

Hers is also a powerful female voice since the personae she adopts in her poems are often women of firm and militant convictions. More significantly, however, she locates this vastly extended linguistic register within a female sphere, a sphere which comprises also the whole range of oral art from gossip to folktales (see Brown, 1978, pp. 106–17). The extent and continued importance of this linguistic and narrative resource for women's writing in the Caribbean cannot be overemphasized. For example, Michelle Cliff's *No Telephone to Heaven* (1989) is a complex novel about two characters, one male one female, and the effects upon them of a modern West Indian environment of poverty, exploitation and incipient violence. It combines fictional biography and detailed descriptions of West Indian society with a full range of postmodernist techniques including circling and converging stories, and fragmentary episodes. Its subject matter is revolutionary violence, dispossession and corruption conveyed through plural and transgressive narratives in which standard English gives way to dialect and Afro-Caribbean metaphors of spirits and spirit possession. It is hardly surprising that such a heteroglossic and cosmopolitan text should occasionally miss its mark but it is, none the less, a remarkable *tour de force*, almost a summary of many of the themes and devices of West Indian writing.

If the above reads like a conclusion then it is premature because there is much – too much – still undiscussed. But I have left until last the most individual of all West Indian writers not simply because his works cannot be pigeon-holed, but because his works represent the most 'radical experiment in post-colonial culture' (Ashcroft, 1989, p. 153). Although Wilson Harris has lived in England since 1959, his novels constantly return to the West Indies, and his native Guyana in particular, to evoke a sense of the convergence of cultures in a mythical landscape. In *The Guyana Quartet* (1985), the epic scale of the Amazonian forests gradually dissolves the distinctions between national histories and individual identities, just as the reader's expectations of narrative are also dissolved in a novel which attempts to present, to adapt a phrase of Frantz Fanon's, 'the zone of occult instability where the people dwell' (Fanon, 1961, p. 183). Harris's intention is to present 'a diversity of associations' which brings us back to where this essay began, in the rich plurality of West Indian writing and its desire to illuminate 'dark energies where images crumble, shift, dissolve and coalesce in strange combinations and paradoxical juxtapositions reflecting a Universe in the process of becoming' (see Shaw, 1985, p. 125). Harris's remarkable syncretic evocations attempt to give the lie to those who view the West Indies as, at best, an aberration or, at worst, a disaster, since for him regeneration is only possible after the cataclysm. The strength and vitality of West Indian literature is an indication that he is correct.

FURTHER READING

Anthony, Michael (1965) *The Year in San Fernando*, André Deutsch, London

Brown, L. W. (1978) *West Indian Poetry*, Twayne, Boston

De Lisser, Herbert G. (1915) *Susan Proudleigh*, Methuen, London

Hearne, John (1961) *The Land of the Living*, Faber & Faber, London

Khan, Ismith (1961) *The Jumbie Bird*, MacGibbon & Kee, London

Lamming, George (1960) *Season of Adventure*, Michael Joseph, London

Lovelace, Earl (1984) *Jestina's Calypso and Other Plays*, Heinemann, London

Mittelholzer, Edgar (1941) *Corentyne Thunder*, Heinemann, London

Naipaul, V. S. (1961) *A House for Mr Biswas*, André Deutsch, London

Ramchand, Kenneth (1976) *An Introduction to the Study of West Indian Literature*, Nelson, Sunbury-on-Thames

Reid, V. S. (1958) *The Leopard*, Heinemann, London

Selvon, Samuel (1958) *Turn Again Tiger*, MacGibbon & Kee, London

Walcott, Derek (1981) *Selected Poetry*, Heinemann, London

ADDITIONAL WORKS CITED

Ashcroft, Bill, Griffiths, Gareth and Tiffin, Helen (1989) *The Empire Writes Back*, Routledge, London

Bennett, Louise (1966) *Jamaica Labrish*, Sangster's Bookstores, Jamaica

Bissoondath, Neil (1987) *Digging Up the Mountains*, Penguin, Harmondsworth

Brathwaite, Edward (1973) *The Arrivants: A New World Trilogy*, Oxford University Press, Oxford

Césaire, Aimé (1989) *Notes on a Return to My Native Land*. In *The Négritude Poets*, edited by Ellen Conroy Kennedy, Thunder Mouth Press, New York [first published 1938]

Fanon, Frantz (1961) *The Wretched of the Earth*, Penguin, Harmondsworth

James, C. L. R. (1972) Interview in *Kas-Kas*, edited by I. Munro and R. Saunders, University of Austin Press, Austin

James, Louis (ed.) (1968) *The Islands In Between*, Oxford University Press, Oxford

Johnson, Linton Kwesi (1975) *Dread, Beat and Blood*, Villiers, London

——(1983) *Voices of the Living and the Dead*, Race Today Publications, London

Lamming, George (1953) *In the Castle of My Skin*, Michael Joseph, London

Naipaul, V. S. (1962) *The Middle Passage*, Penguin, Harmondsworth

Rushdie, Salman (1982) 'Imaginary Homelands', *London Review of Books*, October 7–20, pp. 18–19

Shaw, Gregory (1985) 'Art and Dialectic in the Work of Wilson Harris', *New Left Review*, 153

Walcott, Derek (1979) 'The Muse of History'. In Edward Baugh (ed.), *Critics on Caribbean Literature*, St. Martin's Press, New York [first published 1974]

——(1984) *Midsummer*, Faber & Faber, London

Walsh, William (1973) *Commonwealth Literature*, Oxford University Press, Oxford

90

WESTERN LITERATURE IN MODERN CHINA

YING-HSIUNG CHOU AND CHEN SIHE

In most Third World countries, as a traditional society advances into the twentieth century, its modernization process invariably involves reactions to Western influences. China is no exception, and nowhere is this transcultural dimension of modernization more visible than in the genesis of its modern literature and criticism. The history of modern Chinese literature can, in fact, be described as a complex reception process of Western literary and critical concepts.

The watershed year between the old and the new was 1898, when Yan Fu translated Darwin into Chinese. The immediate success of Lin Shu's translation of Alexandre Dumas *fils' Camille* in the following years offers a clear testament to the impact of foreign influences. Before that, Western literature had been translated only in a rather random manner. These scattered translations included part of *Gulliver's Travels* (1872), 'Rip Van Winkle' (1872), *Aesop's Fables* (1888). However, China's defeat at the hands of Japan in 1894 prompted intellectuals to call for China's modernization on a more extensive scale. The most noteworthy, and in a sense the most surprising, development was the advocacy of *xin xiao-shuo* (new fiction) by Liang Qichao. In his 'Lun xiao-shuo yu qun-chi zhi quan-xi' ('On the relationships between fiction and the rule of the masses', 1902), Liang elaborated on various pragmatic functions of novels and concluded that novels were indeed capable of renovating the entire nation as well as its citizenry.

The influx of Western literature during this period, between 1898 and 1916, aroused great interest among writers and resulted in a flurry of creative activity – more than four hundred novels were published in the first decade of this century. Some of these writers employed Western narrative techniques in treating traditional themes and were referred to as the Mandarin Ducks and Butterflies School – partly because of the frivolous nature of these novels. But in an even more significant sense, foreign influences also forced indigenous writers to search for their new national identities, which they tried very hard to achieve in the second phase, 1917–27. In 1917 there appeared a radical publication called *Xin Qingnian* (*New Youth*), which advocated, among other things, vernacular instead of classical Chinese as a medium of writing. Significant as it was, the literary movement did not really attract public attention until the May Fourth Movement in 1919.

The May Fourth Movement was triggered off by a political event – Japan's plan to incorporate the German interest in Qingdao, Shandong. Students took to the streets and demanded the resignation of corrupt government officials. But what was really significant about the movement was its attempt at cultural renovation, which culminated in a literary revolution advocated by Hu Shi and his associates. This bifurcated development of Chinese modernization – political and economic reform on the one hand and cultural enlightenment on the other – has persisted down to this day.

What is particularly intriguing is the way Western ideas were incorporated into the native tradition. Owing to some self-perpetuating tendencies in their native tradition, the Chinese were inclined to hold on to some essential concepts which have all along been assumed to be intrinsically Chinese. Consequently, foreign concepts, systems, technologies, down to simple contraptions, were often employed from a utilitarian point of view. In a similar manner, this philosophy underlay the Chinese tendency to exclude that which was regarded as likely to threaten the integrity of their native tradition, be it Confucianism or Socialism – the current campaign in China against bourgeois liberalism being part of the effort to shape a socialism with Chinese characteristics.

In the literary field, the reception of foreign ideas was generally more positive. Apart from importing Western concepts as they were – for instance, science and democracy which were seriously lacking in China – writers and critics would also introduce foreign models as a way of asserting their individual identities. And, in the process of doing so, they were also likely to re-evaluate their traditional roles. Lu Xun, for instance, studied capitalist societies and advocated self-invigoration as a way of bringing about the rejuvenation of the nation. The rebellious spirit of Byron was for that reason singled out as a model. Like Byron, Shelley came to China via Japan. And at this initial stage, Western writers were paired off with their Chinese counterparts. Shu Manshu, for instance, compared Byron to Li Bo and Qu Yuan, and Shelley to Li He and Li Shangyin. The overall emphasis in the reception process was on individualism, which had never played a major role in the life of the Chinese people. (It was, nevertheless, replaced by collectivism later, as the leftist school of literary thinking came into being in the early 1930s and dominated the entire cultural scene after 1942.)

Given this pragmatic orientation, Chinese writers tended to adopt imported forms to give voice to their individual sentiments. Epistles and autobiographies were, for instance, employed to delve into the dark recesses of the human psyche. Lu Xun's 'Kuangren riji' ('A Madman's Diary', 1918), thought to be the first short story in China in a Western sense, was written in diary form, detailing the protagonist's paranoid fear of persecution and his perception of the Chinese tradition as cannibalistic. Some distortions were, however, inevitable. In the transplantation of romantic writings, for example, Lu Xun seemed to be more interested in the satanic aspects of Byron. Self-exultation and social defiance were often pursued at the expense of the transcendental dimension in the original. Understandably, traditional Chinese literature tends to be oriented toward the real world rather than what lies beyond. On account of this general outlook, the importation of Western writers was rather selective, including such authors as Byron, Shelley, Goethe, Whitman, but excluding, among others, Wordsworth.

This does not mean that Romanticism was always taken as a monolithic entity. In some cases, finer discriminations were made, resulting eventually in a fairly diversified importation from the West. Mao Dun, for example, was very much aware of Byron's corrupt life while praising him for his heroic gestures of resistance. Lu Xun went one step further and made a comparative study of Byron and Shelley. By contrast, in 1926, under the influence of Babbit, Liang Shiqiu advocated the use of reason as a guiding principle for literary creation. Liang gave it the name of 'neo-classicism'. The Creationist Society, founded in 1921 by Guo Moruo, Yu Dafu, Cheng Fangwu and others, first adopted a fairly symbolist approach and subsequently made an about-face turn to a revolutionary position. The switch of allegiance was characteristic of the entire literary evolution in the first two decades of the century as writers' interest changed from literary revolution to revolutionary literature.

The romantic influence was, comparatively speaking, limited in its impact. By contrast, the modernist outlook on life was probably more to do with how writers viewed their world and specific strategies adopted to deal with the absurdities of life. Again, Lu Xun must be credited with the introduction of such writers as Kierkegaard, Schopenhauer, Nietzsche and Ibsen. Wang Guowei's commentary on the much studied *The Dream of the Red Chamber* in 1904 departed from the critical tradition, which saw the novel as either a *roman à clef* or an autobiography. Wang saw the universalistic qualities of the novel in terms of Schopenhauer's voluntaristic philosophy and interpreted the work as advocating renunciation of worldly values. In a similar vein, Bergson was also introduced in 1914. Other thinkers as well as writers such as Wilde, Andreev, Strindberg, Dostoevsky, Tolstoy and Turgenev were extensively introduced in *Xin Qingnian*, which served as the chief organ for the literary revolution at that time. As a result, a modernist consciousness was injected into the literary mind of China.

Equally worthy of mention are the influence of Freud and Baudelaire. Mainly through the mediation of a Japanese critic – Kuriyagawa Hakuson, author of *Symbols of Agony*, translated into Chinese by Lu Xun – the Chinese writers came under the influence not only of Bergson (and his ideas on the creativity of the life force) but also of Freud (and his works on the unconscious). The former made a comeback in the forties as Hu Feng called for the injection of humanism into realist writings. As for the latter, through further elaborations by Lu Xun, Guo Moruo (*The Story of the Western Chamber*, 1921) and Pan Guangdan (*On Sex and Psychology*, 1927), psychoanalysis became so deeply rooted that there came into being a corpus of creative writings in Shanghai sometimes referred to as the 'Psychoanalytical School'. In reality, however, writers in this category – including Tu Heng, Liu Naou, Mu Shiying, Shi Zhicun, etc. – more often than not employed narrative techniques of fragmentation in their attempts to delve into the unconscious minds of their urban characters. They are thus psychoanalytical only in a fairly imprecise sense of the term. It is probably more correct to attribute their rejection of the empirical to the French Symbolists. Dai Wangshu, a well-known symbolist poet in the thirties, was, for example, influenced by Verlaine.

This modernist camp, like their romanticist counterpart, eventually gave way to the realistic trend which was under Russian and Japanese influences and essentially Marxist-oriented. In fact, one of the most noteworthy events in the development of modern Chinese literature must be the founding of the League of Left-Wing Writers in 1930 in Shanghai, devoted to the promotion of literature at the service of the common people.

The idea was not exactly new, for as early as 1915 one of the pioneers of the May Fourth Movement, Chen Duxiu, had already proclaimed that the time was right for realism. It must also be said that some of the ideas of realism had already been included in various manifestos. The Literary Research Society, founded in 1921 in Beijing by Zheng Zhenduo, Mao Dun, Ye Shaojun and others, had already introduced foreign writers to support their platform that literature should be written for the sake of life. Mao Dun furthermore borrowed on the one hand from Taine the concept of literature as conditioned by race, milieu, age and author, and on the other from Zola the method of fieldwork observation.

Initially realism was borrowed from a utilitarian point of view, too, and, for that reason, a member of the Creationist Society, Cheng Fangwu, was rather critical of the Literary Research Society's indiscriminate use of realism and naturalism. He expressed apprehensions that realism might even lead to some form of vulgarism. In fact, initially no distinctions were made between realism and naturalism. Mu Mutian was one of the earlier critics to voice his rejection of naturalism in favour of realism – a choice which paved the way for the future development of realism in the 1930s. But in terms of literary movements, we have to wait until the second phase of the Creationist Society for the idea of realism to be better articulated. (The initial tenet of the Creationist Society was that of art for art's sake.) In 1926, another founding member, Guo Moruo, started to talk about socialist realism at the service of the proletariat. And in 1928, Cheng Fangwu, in his discussion of Chinese literary development in the twentieth century, came up with the well-known adage, 'from literary revolution to revolutionary literature'. We can now see that realism demanded that literature should not only be at the service of life but also provide a critique of life.

The official merging of realism with Marxism dated from 1930 with the establishment of the League of Left-Wing Writers. Among its members, Lu Xun, Ju Qiubai and Feng Xuefeng were from the start devoted to the translation of theoretical discussions of Marxism. The Union was also known for its political fight against various schools which were labelled collectively as capitalist literature. As a political force, the League was successful not only in silencing its opponents but also in its promotion of literature as a tool for uniting the oppressed classes in their political struggles. The League was suspended in 1936, presumably in the interest of the nation's united effort to ward off the Japanese invasion. Be that as it may, it did succeed in leaving behind a cornerstone of the Communist Chinese literary policy as set down by Chairman Mao in the Yen'an Conference on Literature and Art in 1942. It must be pointed out, though, that realism was as a result often reduced to crude mechanical reflectionism. This reflectionism later further degenerated in the 1950s into dogmas which were described idealistically as revolutionary romanticism and revolutionary realism.

With the eruption of the Sino-Japanese war in 1937, literary polemics came to a halt. But in view of the political and military necessities, the position of intellectuals was often called into question, as is fully illustrated in the writings of Ding Ling in 1941. Increasingly the intellectuals were regarded as secondary in importance and it was felt that literature should cater for the peasants and workers. In choosing as their medium folk expressions, most writers and critics were made to suspend their earlier experimentation. In their place came a literature exclusively at the service of specific political causes. In this particular sense, it was actually a far cry from realism in its original sense as writers and critics were made to conform to certain prescribed guidelines. Even Chao Su-li, who had earlier been held up as a good example of native Chinese writing with folk dimensions, was criticized for not being able to live up to the ideals of romantic realism. The purging of Hu Feng in the 1950s also stemmed from his wish to inject some humanistic elements into socialist realism. In the history of modern Chinese literature, the purge ushered in two decades of literary sterility, and the revival did not take place until 1976 after the fall of the Gang of Four.

The post-1976 literary scene was undoubtedly one of the most exuberant periods in the development of modern Chinese literature. Different schools of writing, rather imprecisely referred to respectively as scar literature, obscure poetry, retrospection literature, intelligentsia youth literature, reportage and, above all, literature in search of roots, appeared on the literary scene at different times, providing us with a wide variety of original, individualized expressions. It is true that some of these different literary expressions were inherited from the tradition initiated in the May Fourth era. It must be added, however, that new waves of foreign influences also made their way into China as it reopened itself to the outside world after almost four decades of total isolation. Particularly worth mentioning was the influx of magic realism to the Chinese soil. Somehow it lent itself conveniently to the rendering of modern conditions in a Third World context. The traditional emphasis on the socially real in China was now reinforced by what was psychologically liberating. Works by Mo Yan, Han Shaogong, Jia Pingau and Can Xue, to mention only a few, are good examples of such successful blendings.

In terms of critical activities, the work on mainland China was initially not as interesting as it was in Taiwan. On mainland China, the issue of subjectivity as a way of countering the alienating tendencies of bureaucratization was proposed by Liu Zaifu and immediately met with fierce criticism from such ideologues as Chen Yong in the 1980s. However, the defeat of the Nationalists in 1949 and their move to Taiwan forcibly severed the literary world from its immediate predecessors. In their search for a new outlook on literature, the Nationalists banned literature of the 1930s and 1940s from the mainland for being subversive. In line with its open-door policy towards the West, however, the government allowed Western literary ideas to be imported. The influx of Western critical schools was equally, if not more, exciting when compared with its creative counterpart. While experimentalism in creative writing thrived in the 1960s, e.g. existentialism, many Western-trained intellectuals also introduced critical thinking from the West. The critical activities seemed to have preoccupied people's minds as different schools of thought and analysis such as existentialism, New Criticism, myth criticism, structuralism, phenomenology and lately deconstructionism each had its field day, as it were.

In a truly Chinese tradition not unrelated to the earlier utilitarian borrowing of Western models, one question has been raised more often than anything else: how does a foreign model lend itself to application in a transcultural context? New Criticism was, for example, welcomed for its close reading of the text. Many interesting interpretations of traditional Chinese works were produced in this mode of reading. There were, however, reservations about the imposition of certain *a priori* concepts, such as tension, on a Chinese quatrain, for example. Structuralism as a methodology was also borrowed, resulting in some fairly enlightening analyses of regulated verse and folk narratives. But, again, bipolarity as a basic epistemological outlook on cultural facts was questioned. Phenomenology, with its emphasis on the subject's consciousness of the world, was promoted as one of the most likely approaches in the study of man's relationship with nature. It was quite promising, but unfortunately there seemed to be a lack in follow-up efforts. Deconstructionism seemed to have also found fertile soil in the native Taoist tradition and yielded some handsome fruits in spite of the apprehension that it would lead to some sort of critical nihilism which runs against the grain of the humanistic tradition in Chinese literature. All in all, the awareness of paradigm change in a synchronic rather than diachronic sense can be said to be a hallmark of the literary relationships between China and the West in the 1970s and 1980s as Comparative Literature took root in Taiwan and China.

In brief, the history of modern Chinese literature can well be called a history of native growth amidst foreign influences. The result is a literary tradition which has not only departed from its precedents but is also fully aware of its own epistemological crisis. To borrow a now familiar figure of speech from the much criticized TV series, *He shang* (*River Sacrifice*, 1988), it was reiterated that for China to avoid being left behind by the rest of the world, it had to turn its back on the yellow earth and head for the blue ocean. Literature and criticism of the late eighties were faced with a global modernism, with all its potential as well as limitations. It remains to be seen how contemporary Chinese literature will develop on the basis of its earlier romanticist, modernist and realist models as it tries to establish a voice of its own, as well as to conduct a meaningful dialogue with the rest of the world.

FURTHER READING

Chow, T. (1960) *May Fourth Movement: Intellectual Movement in Modern China*, Harvard University Press, Cambridge

Galik, M. (1969) *Mao Tun and Modern Chinese Literary Criticism*, Franz Steiner, Wiesbaden

Goldman, M. (ed.) (1977) *Modern Chinese Literature in the May Fourth Era*, Harvard University Press, Cambridge

Hsia, C. T. (1971) *A History of Modern Chinese Fiction, 1917–1957*, Yale University Press, New Haven

Hsia, T. (1968) *The Gate of Darkness: Studies on the Leftist Literary Movement in China*, University of Washington Press, Seattle

Kinkley, J. C. (1985) *After Mao: Chinese Literature and Society, 1978–1981*, Harvard University Press, Cambridge

Lee, L. O. (1973) *The Romantic Generation of Modern Chinese Writers*, Harvard University Press, Cambridge

Link, P., Jr. (1981) *Mandarin Ducks and Butterflies: Popular Fiction in Early Twentieth-Century Chinese Cities*, University of California Press, Berkeley

McDougall, B. S. (1977) *The Introduction of Western Literary Theories into Modern China*, Centre for East Asian Cultural Studies, Tokyo [first published 1971]

——(1980) *Mao Zedong's 'Talks at the Yen'an Conference on Literature and Art': A Translation of the 1943 Text with Commentary*, Michigan Papers in Chinese Studies, Ann Arbor

X. AFTERWORD

W(H)ITHER 'ENGLISH'?

PETER WIDDOWSON

The appropriately postmodern unease of my title is signalled by its self-conscious punning and formal mannerism: *sous rature*, inverted commas, question mark. But why that 'appropriately'? Surely this suggests a fixed point of reference even in the unstable value-systems of a period rushing towards *fin de siècle*, millennium, the high-tech/IT(ech) twenty-first century? Coming as it does, however, at the end of a monumental compendium on the state of the art in Literature and Criticism – itself a work intended to be an encyclopaedic guide and clear witness to the diversity and dissension which characterize its field – this essay can only claim that the one certainty is uncertainty. The last two decades have seen an unprecedented melt-down at the core of an academic discipline which by the mid-twentieth century had achieved a status and a popularity in secondary and tertiary education second to none. That status and popularity may well remain even now, but the field of 'English' (I will return to names) can only retain such a position if it is constantly and self-reflexively conscious of just how problematical it is. Its energy and vitality, in other words (if they are no more than the frenetic twitchings of death throes), derive from the very instability of the reaction it is undergoing.

The original title proposed for this essay by the volume's editors was 'Against English'. Leaving aside a private fear of being typecast as the subject's hit-man, that title struck me as being, in the late 1980s, *too* unequivocal, *too* hostile, too *easy*. I might be 'against' the *name* (although even here simple solutions are chimerical), but 'against' the general field of study . . . ? Whatever 'English' is or might be, I happen to be a professor of it, in a department devoted to it, within a huge modular degree scheme in which it is the single most popular (and therefore crucial) subject. It pays my wages, and those of tens of thousands of colleagues in school and higher education across the world – for, let us be clear, 'English' is a *global* phenomenon. Despite government cut-backs, in the UK at least, it attracts students like a honeypot (government, indeed, would find it had problems with its own constituency if 'English' went to the wall); and world-wide, hundreds of thousands of people study it – and *choose* to study it – every year. Who am I, then, to simply be 'against' it, as though – having read its books, learnt its skills, participated in its intellectual debates, reaped its rewards – I now wish to renege on it and deny it to others. At the very least, such a position would be cripplingly schizophrenic.

But then it is. I *am* 'against English' in many of its manifestations, but I am also sharply conscious that the 'field', the 'site', the space in the curriculum, if nothing else, is not one to be readily vacated in a late twentieth-century environment determined by those other features of the 'postmodern condition' too easily ignored in the focus on postmodernist style and manner: consumerism, managerialism, anti-communalism, mass-media leisurism – in short, international capitalism. If, reader, you hear echoes here of F. R. Leavis in the 1930s and beyond promoting 'English' as part of a 'minority culture' to challenge and rebut a 'mass civilization', then that, too, is part of the schizophrenia. Leavis has been, since the late 1960s, the symbolic stalking-horse of the 'new left' in literary studies (myself included); his 'English' – élitist, untheorized and canonic – the very model against which the new theory and practice had to do battle. They were, and are, right to attack: Leavis's 'English', conflictual and anti-establishment though it may have appeared, effectively naturalized and sustained, in its canon, practice and general project, the dominant liberal-bourgeois ideology by promoting as quintessential truth the supremacy of the free individual human subject. It is this myth which has legitimized, in our own period, that very postmodern egocentricism which is the paradoxical inverse of liberal-humanism's altruism, and which Leavis would have loathed as much as anything he observed in the thirties. Nevertheless, if Leavis saw 'English' as a location from which to subvert cultural orthodoxies, we should not necessarily reject it as irrecoverably contaminated just because he (and others) reinforced the ideology they seemed to challenge.

It all depends, of course, on what one means by 'English'. Perhaps it is a tic of my own postmodern mannerism and lack of conviction that this essay is (and will be) obsessed with *titles*: with naming and names as central to identity – a kind of neo-Shandyism which holds that names are integral to character. Be that as it may, it is clear to me that *a*, if not *the*, crucial problematic in the field under consideration is the name 'English'. In other words, if it were simply called something else (even 'Literary Studies' – but see below), there would be less of a problem about living with it. But its name – so widely naturalized as a recognized academic subject across the world (but recognized as what?) – is at once potently *present* and untenably inaccurate as a description of what it may consist of. As Peter Brooker has recently written:

Often, even while 'English' is employed as the public description of many

University and Polytechnic departments, it stands above their doors, with all its ideological freight, as the false title to courses in literary and cultural theory, literature and society, American and European literature, popular literature and women's writing.

(1987, p. 26)

Deriving as it did from late-Victorian development of the 'English subjects' (Doyle, 1982, p. 24) which ironically, in their purview of language, literature, history and geography, are closer to contemporary notions of cultural history than most intervening inflexions of 'English' have been, the subject rapidly refined itself into being principally concerned with the English language and literature. A bifurcation gradually occurred here, too, so that in many twentieth-century universities there are separate Chairs for both and undergraduate courses which are effectively discrete (as indeed have been the two GCE O-level papers in English Language and English Literature). During and after the inter-war years a further transformation took place: if one is 'reading'/'taking'/'doing'/'teaching' English in secondary or tertiary education, the assumption generally is that one is studying *Literature* ('English' or not; see below). But even here – and an essential prerequisite for any discussion of the nature of 'English' is to read the recent literature on the history of the subject's development (Doyle, 1982, 1986a, 1986b; Baldick, 1983; Eagleton, 1983) – there has been no firm consensus as to what it comprises. From the end of the First World War through to the mid-1960s, there may perhaps have been a common expectation of wide familiarity with the major figures and movements of the national literature, but critical and professional disagreements nevertheless produced widely differing syllabuses – becoming more and more idiosyncratic the nearer they approached the contemporary period. Even more to the point, for how long and how widely was the notion of exposure to 'the national literature' a guiding principle of 'English' courses; indeed – far more crucial than the question of common content – was there ever any consensus as to what studying 'English' was *for*? And if there were radical disagreements here (always supposing the question was substantively put), major differences of critical approach and focus were endemic to them, which further spawned heterogeneity. For example, if questions of form were paramount, then texts from literatures other than English might be just as appropriate; if 'Literature, Life and Thought' were the axiom, then English cultural history might be the goal of the exercise, producing a diminished central concern with the literary texts 'in themselves'. But from the 1960s onwards, with the development of cross-disciplinary studies in the 'new universities' and the Open University, of interdisciplinary courses ('Humanities') in the CNAA-approved polytechnics and colleges, of radical European (and then native) literary theory, of linguistics, semiotics, comparative literature, of cultural studies, communications and media studies, women's and Third World studies, the absurdity of trying to mean or understand anything by the name 'English' is incontrovertible.

In what institution does 'English' ever imply the sole study of the main tradition of English literary texts and literary history? And even if there are such cases, should it not at least be called 'English Literature', or rather, given the presence of Dunbar and Henryson, Dylan Thomas and Seamus Heaney, 'British Literature'? But what happens if we study Joyce, T. S. Eliot, Pound or Faulkner in Modernism courses, or Balzac and Tolstoy (in translation) in Nineteenth-Century Novel syllabuses, or V. S. Naipaul, Wole Soyinka, Margaret Atwood or Patrick White in Modern Fiction classes? Should it not then be 'Literature in English'? But again what happens if we study the journalism of Addison and Steele, literary theory, or fictional forms like TV and film as part of our courses? Is Derrida or Julia Kristeva 'literature' or 'English'? Is Polanski's *Tess*? What happens if we operate with a strong concept of historical placing for literature, or of literature in relation to a history of ideas, or of literature as an articulation of philosophical positions? If we recommend Burke and Paine with Blake, or suggest that the French revolution is a necessary context for Wordsworth or Jane Austen, or point out that David Hartley lies behind the *Lyrical Ballads*, what precisely are we studying: literature, history, history of ideas, culture? Is it the text or the context which is our real focus of attention? Crucially, on what principles of selection is the constitution of an 'English' syllabus founded: do the Chartist poets or Robert Tressell and Elizabeth Robins or Frederick Forsyth and Jackie Collins or Linton Kwesi Johnson find their expected place naturally and ubiquitously in 'English Literature'? Or are they neither 'English' nor 'Literature'? In other words, what notions of *value* is 'English' predicated on? Shouldn't we be able to explain? At the very least 'Literary Studies' is a more accurate title, always supposing we still wish to privilege the sphere of 'the literary' as a specific discourse which needs to be considered in relative autonomy, and if we also wish to expunge from it the traces of the ideological inscriptions which traverse 'English': at once and contradictorily, the supreme *national* literature and the receptacle of *universal* human values.

Here again, however, we meet problems. If we interpret 'Literary Studies' formalistically (the study of 'the literary') we may find ourselves (or our students) asking: 'but what then are we studying it *for*?' If we interpret the title historically (Literature – or indeed Literary Studies – located in history) we may well ask: 'but what *is* our focus of study, what *is* our object of knowledge?' If we think history explains the text better, then the same question occurs – 'but what *for*?'; if we read through the text to enhance our historical understanding are we really studying 'the literary'? The paradoxes and contradictions involved in naming so diverse and unstable a field multiply in geometric progression. One of the most intelligent and penetrating recent discussions of what 'English' has been and might become, of the cultural politics of its place in education, and of the function of literature in the community at large, is still entitled *Rewriting English* (Batsleer, 1985). I could have quoted it *in extenso* in support of points made here, and its concluding paragraph – at once retaining 'English' as a term and simultaneously dismantling it as a subject – is a good example of the problem. For the purposes of the remainder of this essay, however, and for reasons which will, I hope, become clear, I intend to use the term 'English' for conventional existing representations of the subject and 'Literary Studies' (with reservations) for those revamped activities which are replacing it.

As a contemporary exemplum of the paradoxes at the heart of 'English' in the late 1980s, let me adduce the Standing Conference on English in Public Sector Higher Education (SCEPSHE) and the first publication it has produced: *English in the Public Sector: The Current Debate* (ed. Daniels, 1988). SCEPSHE was inaugurated in the spring of 1986, and now has members from many of the polytechnics and colleges in England and Wales. Conceived as a pressure group/lobbying agent/information exchange, its primary constitutional aim is to 'promote and strengthen English Studies within the public sector'. (This would include assisting the academic development of English; raising public consciousness of English in public sector higher education; lobbying bodies like NAB, CNAA and HMI; collecting and exchanging information, statistical and otherwise, about the place and circumstances of English in public sector colleges.) SCEPSHE is a necessary development in the present cultural/political climate, but its effectivity remains to be seen. (A similar group has since been started by the English Association for English in the Universities. Sadly, and perhaps predictably, the two groups appear as yet to have little common interest.) What concerns me here, however, is that in the mid-to-late 1980s, and despite all the developments over the past fifteen years in CNAA Humanities courses (there are, in fact, very few single-honours English degrees validated by the Council), '*English*' as a name, a subject, and presumably a concept, has re-emerged with a high profile in an educational sector which has done so much to break down the traditional discipline boundaries. I do not mean to criticize SCEPSHE – as we shall see in a moment, there are powerful political determinants for its incidence now – but there is something bizarre about 'promoting and strengthening' a subject which has undergone such radical deconstruction over the last two decades that defining its identity at all makes the mind boggle.

Right from the start there were problems: at an early meeting of SCEPSHE the main aim, quoted above, was amended from 'English' to 'English Studies' (what did we mean by that amendment? The minutes give no record of the discussion which led to it, so perhaps we were all tacitly agreed that we knew what we meant). Further, it was quickly recognized that the institutional *locus* of 'English' (often only a small subject group contributing to a large multi- or inter-disciplinary degree) would variously shape the nature of 'the subject', so that policy formation by SCEPSHE, or even 'promoting and strengthening' it by way of the other ancillary aims, became deeply problematical. If we didn't know what our commodity was, or whether we had any common conception of it, then promoting it could be tricky.

The result of this identity crisis was that each member was asked to contribute a paragraph which s/he felt defined 'English' as s/he understood it. (This, of course, could constitute either a personal view of what it should mean, or a description of an existing institutional variant. These might not be compatible.) A seminar discussed the contributions, and the pamphlet mentioned above has brought them together in published form. It is an invaluable document because we have, for once, a compendium of brief statements by practising academics of what it is they think they profess: of what they understood by 'English' in 1988. What becomes clear is that despite many contributors' continued acceptance of 'English' (or more usually 'English Studies') as a label, their courses or conceptions are not well described by it; and that despite the diversity of presentation and emphasis, it is possible to construct a more or less common hybrid from an amalgam of repeated components. Public sector 'English Studies' in the next century, then, would comprise:

1. a study of language/linguistics/poetics/rhetoric/discourse analysis, to enable students to become highly articulate and 'culturally self-aware, by exposing the philosophical, ethical and political assumptions and implications in language and culture' (Peter Weston, p. 10);

2. a study of a wide range of texts (literary and non-literary, English and non-English, canonic and non-canonic) which would 'reflect the multi-racial nature of our society and the international role of the English Language' (Brian Hollingsworth, p. 4.), and enable the student to recognize

> literature as both a created product and a social activity, in which meaning is generated through the use, adaptation and subversion of particular conventions or codes. To this end, [it] would promote the development of competence in the analysis of literary strategies and the rhetoric of texts. It would also offer an opportunity to examine the social conditions and cultural assumptions which underpin production and interpretation of texts.
>
> (Maureen Moran, p. 12);

3. a study of literary theory and criticism, and other associated 'metacritical' discourses, in order that students should be able to participate in 'current literary critical debate' and 'form a critical understanding of the institution

of literature and literary criticism and its relationship to wider social organisation' (Stephen Glynn, p. 4);

4. study in the practice of writing ('verbal arts', 'rhetoric', 'functional and
   creative writing'), in order that students should develop 'transferable skills'
   ('written and oral competence as communicators') which may make them
   'attractive to potential employers' (Sandra Harris, p. 11), and improve their
   own 'practical skills in modes other than the discursive' (Mavis Ainsworth,
   p. 19);

5. the possibility of collaborative study with Drama, History, History of Ideas,
   Sociology, Modern Languages, Mathematics, Law, Computing, Philosophy,
   Psychology, Art, Politics and Religious Studies, amongst others.

At the core of all this – as its *raison d'être* or guiding principle – is a (variously
expressed and emphasized) belief that English Studies should 'raise questions'
(Tony Stevens, pp. 6–7); 'challenge rather than confirm' both itself as a
discursive practice (Jeff Walsh, p. 8) and the 'discourses used in our society
to structure and define human experience' (Maureen Moran, p. 12). In other
words, it is to make students aware of 'the politics of the written and spoken
word' (Jeff Wallace, p. 7); 'as part of a process of empowerment and
enabling . . . [to] give them access to the languages of power' (Stephen Glynn,
p. 3); or, to put it another way, to bring them *inside politics*: 'to think their way
out of the fairy tales and prejudice that constitute the dominant culture in
1988' (Paul O'Flinn, based on an idea by Lenin, p. 9).

So this, then, is 'English', in the public sector's eyes, in the late 1980s
(would it be true, too, of the universities?). Is it recognizable as 'English'
– this politicized, theorized, self-reflexive, cultural-historical, trans-national,
discourse analysis? If this *is* English, then I am quite happy to drop the erasure
in the 'W(h)ither' of my title: why should I wish such a praxis to 'wither', why
be 'against' it? Rather, I would want to assert the interrogative 'whither?'
For surely *this* subject cannot continue to be held within so inaccurate and
ideologically inscribed a frame of reference as that set up by the term 'English'?
One further contribution from the pamphlet ransacked above brings the problem into sharp relief. Tony Stevens asks:

> What are the relationships between texts and contexts; between the production
> and consumption of texts; between Literature and other forms of writing; between
> Literature as conventionally constituted and mass or popular culture? Further,
> if the concept of literature may be dissolved in the concept of culture, to what
> extent should culture, in turn, be conceived more broadly than as constellations
> of 'texts' (songs, novels, films, etc.), that is, as embracing an 'anthropological'
> dimension, and to what extent is it necessary to set culture in the wider context
> of the social formation in order to understand it?
>
> (p. 6)

Not for nothing is a recent book about 'English and Cultural Studies' entitled *Broadening the Context* (ed. Green and Hoggart, 1987); clearly the proper study of literature is – everything else. But what Stevens is implying above, quite rightly in my view, is that while the study of 'the literary' as a specific activity may have a place and a rationale, it can only have one within a much broader conception of politicized knowledge-seeking, perhaps called 'cultural studies' or, better to my mind, 'cultural history' (I return to this below). Only by abandoning the exclusive boundaries of 'the discipline' or 'the subject' will we ever be able to make any sense of studying 'the literary' – one cultural discourse amongst many in the historical conjunctures where it is produced and consumed.

And so we bid farewell to 'English', both as misnomer and as discrete subject. Or do we? In his Introduction to the SCEPSHE pamplet, John Daniels reminds us that there are 'two main fronts on which it is necessary for English to define itself at the present time'. One is the 'inward' redefinition of the subject discussed above, the other is: 'outwards towards a model of society in which government proposals appear to take an ever more reductive view of the Arts and Humanities'. And Daniels adds an additional twist for the public sector: 'there is the government's declaration in its Green paper that the Arts subjects should generally be concentrated in universities. The "usefulness" or "relevance" of English is of more than academic interest' (p. i). 'English' is not autonomously free to put its own house in order (if that is what one thinks the above account has been describing), but exists in a world of supply and demand, an 'enterprise culture' where individual initiative and centralized control slip in and out of focus as government defines the terms in its own interest. Another complex set of paradoxes and contradictions emerges here.

On the one hand, we know that 'English' (as a sign and as a subject) represents a huge and influential presence in the education curriculum; that it remains extremely popular with students – for many, as perceived in its traditional guise, for some, precisely because of its radical reconstitution; that in its conventional inflexion 'English' will appeal to a government committed to 'values', 'culture' and notions of national heritage and identity; that many of the government's prime constituents will have children who wish to 'read English' somewhere. On the other hand, we know that Arts and Humanities are generally threatened by the government; that the politicized cultural history and the radically critical tenor of the 'new' English will find no favour with it; that, in fact, in many institutions much of the English taught is not new at all but still, in Paul O'Flinn's phrase, 'a refuge from a nasty world' sustained by staff and students who for a variety of reasons do not wish to jettison the 'appreciation' of 'great writers' (Daniels, 1988, p. 9); that, where possible, the government only wishes to retain Arts and Humanities in the universities (the notion of 'centres of excellence' resonates with conformity and tradition), and to propel the public sector towards 'vocational' training, servicing and public accountability in terms of market forces directing demand. Pragmatically, in the circumstances, to vacate voluntarily the site 'English' offers, or to demolish it in order to erect something else even more overtly subversive, would be a perilous enterprise. But, equally, cynically to reinvent the past would be neither acceptable nor effective. Whither 'English' indeed?

For reasons outlined above, then, English cannot be simply recast as 'Cultural Studies', 'Cultural History', 'Rhetoric' or 'Discourse Analysis': it would not get approval, or it would be closed down, or it would not be allocated sufficient student numbers, or it would not recruit. And in any event, 'English' in the old guises would continue to fill that curriculum space with its protean and amorphous bulk. As I implied earlier, 'English' remains a site, even under threat, from which challenges can be launched against the prevailing mystifications and naturalizations of our social culture. So 'English' – or at best, 'Literary Studies' – it may have to remain; although, Jesuit-like, our strength will lie in our equivocation: there is comfort, even power, in knowing that what we profess to profess is spurious and that what we really do is quite *un*-'English'. This wolf in sheep's clothing, however, this militant tendency, will have several characteristics and features which identify its dynamism and functional purchase on the contemporary world.

First, perhaps, is to recognize the potential of engaging with the demands of the 'New Vocationalism'. The market wants 'transferable' and 'flexible' *skills*, but these need not merely represent a recuperated 'functional literacy' which serves the capitalist economy (being able to 'communicate' for commerce and industry): they may also constitute what the authors of *Rewriting English* call 'powerful literacy' (Batsleer, 1985, pp. 165–6). Several SCEPSHE members, as we saw above, drew attention both to the pragmatics of making English 'relevant' by the visible enhancement of skills, and to the 'empowerment' which literacy and articulateness confer. An interesting essay in *Broadening the Context*, 'Different Starting Points: A View of "English etc" from Further Education', offers higher education some salutary insights about working with the 'New Vocationalism' and how to turn it to advantage. Noting that the 'enormous range of courses' which comprises 'English etc' signals no 'one standard "literary" culture' (Edwards, 1987, p. 75), the essay considers the place of the English teacher in a world of MSC and DES 'Enterprise' initiatives. It recognizes the crude demand (to provide 'a *medium*, as in teaching people to write reports, letters or memos, make video programmes or produce brochures', p. 78) and identifies the danger, especially, of turning out competent but *unreflective* operatives for the market. But it also points out the gains to be made: in terms of 'decision-making, collective action and responsibility', issues of work, race and gender, and of enabling students to move from the personal-experiential perception of social relations to 'a more "global" view of women's/men's positions in society' (pp. 78–9). What the authors of the essay are implying – within a properly realistic perspective on the 'real' social motivation behind these new courses – is that 'functional literacy' can be 'turned' to provide understanding and control well beyond the social engineering the 'New Vocationalism' intends. We remember once more Paul O'Flinn's citing of Lenin: 'A person who can neither read nor write is outside politics; he or she must first learn the ABC, without which there is no such thing as politics but merely gossip, rumour, fairy tales and prejudice' (see Daniels, 1988, p. 9). And we may also recall the profound anxieties of nineteenth-century 'educators' who required a literate workforce to enhance profit but were terrified of what literacy would enable the working class to *learn*.

The second feature of a militant new Literary Studies derives from Cultural Studies. Precisely not, however, in terms simply of expanded *content* (introducing 'popular culture', for example – although it might usefully do that); rather, in the very terms by which Cultural Studies conceives itself: not as a new 'discipline', not as a 'field' of hitherto largely ignored materials, not as a new source of substantive knowledges, but as a *process*, a *critique*, 'a radicalizing mentality, both intellectual and political, which is applicable to all texts'. That last definition, drawing on Richard Johnson of the Centre for Contemporary Cultural Studies at Birmingham University, is from Peter Brooker's important essay 'Why Brecht, or, Is There English After Cultural Studies?' (1987, p. 27). Brooker offers a succinct and penetrating account of the siege and sack of 'Fortress English' subjected to the 'burning waves of knowledge' (p. 23) which have assaulted it since 1968, most particularly by way of Cultural Studies and especially as practised at the Birmingham Centre over the last two decades. 'English', in attempting to accommodate the enemy, effectively destroys itself: 'This process of self-extension, real and potential, has comprised a series of self-critiques which have unstitched the intellectual, institutional, and ideological identity of the subject. The three cherished autonomies of the text, the discipline, and the free individual have tumbled and cracked' (p. 25). What is now offered in many 'English' departments (as I have indicated by way of SCEPSHE earlier) would be better described, says Brooker, 'as discourse analysis, or text analysis, or again, cultural studies'; indeed, 'cultural studies has . . . appropriated English (along with other disciplines and traditions)' (pp. 26–7). But it has only 'appropriated' them because it is a 'critique', a 'radicalising mentality', not because it is an imperialist and encyclopaedic *discipline*. Cultural Studies, in this view, does not own, belong to, or side with, any specific interest; it is a 'process' which mobilizes a 'constructive quarrel' with all existing traditions and discourses, rejecting the dross and appropriating the gold. For this reason, although Cultural Studies has appropriated 'English', there is still, Brooker proposes, the possibility of 'a transformed literary studies' so long as it avails itself of 'the method of critique' (p. 27). In particular, this might mean 'a critique of dominant "interpretations" [or what we might prefer to call ideological constructions or representations]' (p. 28) because, oblique and indefinite though these may be, they do have power in the world – most especially in naturalizing ideologically constructed social relations. The cultural politics of a new 'Literary Studies' would lie, then, in deconstructing existing 'interpretations' and putting alternative ones into circulation. For Brooker, this is the relevance of Bertolt Brecht, both in terms of Brecht's 'collective' artistic practice as writer and director, and of his *Verfremdungseffekt*, the 'making strange', the *critique*, of both conventional art and orthodox, familiar, commonsense 'reality'. More generally, it seems to me, a 'radicalising mentality', sustained by this notion of 'critique', should be the primary aim of Literary Studies, not so much in the form of specific 're-readings' of texts, but as the development in students of that cast of mind. Everything, at all times, should be able to be subjected to the 'critical attitude'.

And not least, in the particular case of Literary Studies, the nature and practice of 'the subject' itself. This would be a further feature of the new critical discourse: a continual self-reflexivity; 'the subject' always under review; its history always visible; its canons and traditions ('great' or 'little') always under scrutiny as they ceaselessly form and reform; literary criticism and critical theory always subject to critical analysis – no longer seen as 'meta-discourses', but as primary constituents of the 'Literature' or the practices they promote. All Literary Studies courses, in other words, should present for their students some defamiliarizing account of the activity they are commonly engaged in, some representation of how artificially constructed 'the subject' is, how problematical is its identity, and what its aims and objectives might be: what it is *for*. If it is to be imbued with 'the method of critique', it must be scrupulously self-sceptical from the start.

Fourth, in order at once to answer the question 'What is Literary Studies *for?*' (which is impossible solely within its own terms of reference), and to recognize its 'appropriation' by Cultural Studies, the field has to regard itself as just one contributory discourse in the larger project of 'cultural history'. By cultural history I mean the hypothetical but necessary notion of a totalizing comprehension of the world we inhabit and its past determinants. That is to say that we need, theoretically, a vertical section of every historical moment up to the present. Thomas Carlyle (clearly the Ur-Foucault) writes in his 1830 essay 'On History' of the 'everliving, everworking Chaos of Being' in which 'every single event is the offspring not of one, but of all other events, prior or contemporaneous, and will in turn combine with all others to give birth to new'. This 'simultaneous' 'solid Action' comprises each lived moment of historical time, but of which, says Carlyle, the one-dimensional 'linear narrative' of written history, able only to operate with events in 'series' or 'succession', can give but a hopelessly inadequate account (ed. Shelston, 1971, p. 55). Cultural history would attempt to write the multiplex history of the moment, while also tracing the trajectory of historical processes over time insofar as they are components of the present. In a sense, this notional 'total history' is no more than an *aide-mémoire* to locate any specific study of any subject in a larger context, conscious of its complex interaction with many other social and cultural discourses. In the case of Literary Studies, more specifically, it helps to obviate the problematic focus on texts as autonomous objects, and simultaneously dispenses with the problem of 'literary value', inasmuch as any text selected for special attention has to be justified in terms of its sets of relations rather than its intrinsic merit or innate value. This is not merely to construct a history of the moment of production of a text in order to 'explain' it, rather it is to locate it as an active participant in its social and cultural relations: it is, as it were, to *sociologize* a text in the pursuit of a sociology of a historical conjuncture. But further, cultural history would require an account of the transmission of that text (if it remains current and active) through the processes of its reproduction in history. The text as we have it will be inscribed and encrusted with the accretions of these processes, which will indeed have become a constituent part of it; so that to assess the text's place and function as a cultural object in our present (the principal aim of *this* cultural history) would also require what I have elsewhere called a 'critiography' (Widdowson, 1989, chap. 1): an account of the historical production and reproduction which constitute the cultural force and meaning of a text in 1990. The point to emphasize here is that such a cultural history is not to privilege the text nor painstakingly to study it 'for itself'; it is to recognize that *Hamlet*, say, constitutes a link between the 1590s and the 1990s which we need to understand in all its complex ramifications if we are to understand our own cultural locus and the forces which shape our lives in the present. The justification for studying *Hamlet*, then, is readily explicable without having to erect a metaphysical model either of 'human nature' or of 'literary value'.

Indeed, a crucial effect of treating Literary Studies as a contributory discourse within cultural history, and as a further aspect of its self-reflexive scepticism, is to foreground the question of the selection of material deployed in syllabuses and courses. The nature of traditional 'English' meant: *either*, that it must include certain writers and texts because they *were* 'English Literature', and if that was what one was studying then one had to study *them* – no question; *or*, that certain authors and texts were 'representative', and these, too, became pre-ordained. Course-planning in the post-'English' era exposes just how artificial, how 'made-up', any course actually is; how precisely the justification for what is included has to be made; and how the reasons for inclusion point, not to the necessity of the presence of the text itself, but to the *issues* it is there to introduce or focus. While recently preparing two new courses – one a 'survey' of post-war British writing, the other a more overtly 'constructed' course on twentieth-century British 'War Literature' – I was struck by the fact, because there was so much accessible potential material and so much would have to be left out, that my questions about inclusion (why *that* text? to what end?) became centrally important, were, in effect, *the syllabus*, and would have to be publicly rehearsed if students were to make any sense of the course. For the eclectic result (but probably no more eclectic than a conventional course composed of 'unarguable' inclusions: naturalization works by presenting the partial as incontrovertible) represented not so much a selection of texts but a set of social, cultural and literary issues that it had seemed to me any student studying modern cultural history should engage with. There was indeed a selection of texts, but not because they were 'incontrovertibly' great or 'naturally' representative; and the selection of texts and issues was manifestly partial and tendentious – as all courses must always be. But there was *also* a substantive explanation for the presence of every text in terms of its allusion to a cultural history of our times, and it was this that made the course and the text teachable.

A fifth and central feature of the new Literary Studies which paradoxically follows from hypothesizing its rationale only within cultural history, is the retention of a working notion of 'the literary' as a specific category. Much of the thrust, quite rightly, of cultural and literary theory over the past twenty years has been against the literary-critical discrimination and elevation of selected writings as 'Literature', which then become the object of study in conventional 'English'. The firing of the canon, and consequently the serious consideration of 'popular writing' and many other forms of non-canonic cultural production, has effectively illustrated the factitiousness of the privileged concept 'Literature', and the term may be so contaminated as to be virtually unusable at the present time. However, to collapse it back into meaning 'all writing', and to propose a modern 'Rhetoric', as Terry Eagleton has done (1981, 1983, 1984), which would cover all the symbolic systems of the social order and regard everything as 'text', is at once logically persuasive and pragmatically unviable – on many of the same grounds, adduced earlier, for not totally abandoning 'English'. More importantly, certain aspects of the cultural history outlined above cannot be comprehended without some concept of 'the literary'. Although there may be no special value in literary texts, and non-literary texts may well be as or more appropriately studied in many contexts, it is potentially reductive to ignore the perception of difference between *kinds* of writing, not only that which readers have by way of their 'literary competence' (cf. Culler, 1975, chap. 6) but also that which texts, so to speak, self-consciously have of themselves. A novel (at least since the mid-eighteenth century) has conceived of itself *as a novel* (just as the BBC news conceives of itself as 'real' and 'factual' even though it may be generically similar to any other TV fiction), and this self-perception is part of the text's identity.

This is not just a matter of self-consciousness in deploying genre, convention, form or tradition – although these are also important aspects of a sense of being 'literary' – it is more how a text positions itself in its social relations, both as regards its anticipated effects (how it expects to be read) and its cultural status (how it hopes to be received). A sonnet 'expects' to be read as such, and to conflate it with another text, such as a beer-mat, is to ignore its self-consciousness as an active component of its textuality. (It doesn't help a reading of the beer-mat, either.) Such a sense of their own artifice suggests that there may be some point in considering literary texts as a separate category within cultural production, and that there may be specific skills and modes of analysis appropriate to the study of them. This is not necessarily to claim, *à la* Althusser, that literary works have a 'relative autonomy' because they offer unique perceptions on ideology, nor, like the formalists, that their status resides in the fact that they 'defamiliarize', or 'make strange'. Indeed, it is not to claim anything for them intrinsically, merely to propose that a material cultural history should not undervalue 'the literary' either as a specific discourse deploying particular rhetorical forms for strategic effects or as one which still has an immense public audience itself socially and culturally constructed by notions of 'the literary'. *Hamlet* functions in these discourses in a way which differentiates it from other kinds of texts which do not; it does not make *Hamlet* superior to them, but it does demand a familiarity with the discourses which hold that to be the case.

A further asset from retaining 'the literary' as a specific category is that it helps to encourage a second set of ('transferable') skills in addition to those of literacy and articulateness. This is the capacity for complex reading. Literary texts may themselves be no more complex in their deployment of language, stylistic tropes and formal devices than other written texts, but again their self-consciousness as artefacts makes them exemplary cases for studying the rhetoric of signifying practices. This is not, once more, to privilege them in terms of evaluative hierarchies of complexity, it is to mobilize them socially. To be attuned to various levels of linguistic play, to be familiar with rhetorical devices, to expect a text to be multivocal, to be attentive to ambiguity, parapraxis, paradox, irony, are skills which enable one to demystify cultural discourses by knowing something of what is being done to one in their presence; and they are skills which are not then restricted to the analysis of *literary* discourse alone. I make this point, simplistically and crudely, because in the assault on 'English' there has been, quite rightly, a rejection of the naturalized theories and practice of New Criticism, of the ultimate authority of 'the words on the page', of 'Practical Criticism' or 'Close Reading' courses as the *sine qua non* of literary study. But in the dismissal of such essentialism and formalism, there lies the danger of losing the ability to analyse texts closely. Socially-oriented literary study, on the one hand, tends to prioritize message over medium; 'Deconstruction', on the other, has not rectified this situation because it has been unwilling to admit that textual analysis may have a substantive function beyond itself. Many students, therefore, in the backlash against 'Prac. Crit.', are no longer trained in the techniques of close formal and linguistic analysis. This does nothing to equip them satisfactorily with that 'powerful literacy' which may help to decode and so rebut the pervasive subliminal messages of our society's sign-systems.

My final point relates both to this contemporary cultural 'empowerment' and to the place of 'the literary' within contemporary cultural history. I take it as axiomatic that the primary aim of education is to understand the present and shape the future. This may require us to know as much as possible about the past in as exact detail as possible, but unless we are merely scholastic or antiquarian our aim in knowing it will be determined by and for the present. It seems to me, therefore, that there should be a pronounced emphasis in Literary Studies on the *contemporary* significance of what we do. This may mean simply explaining more exactly *why* one should be studying Spenser or Dryden, Mrs Gaskell or the Chartist poets; it may mean, as I have suggested earlier, engaging critiographically with the history of a writer's reproduction; it may mean considering the place and function of a past writer in the present (what is Shakespeare doing today?). Or it may mean, as I think it should, that Literary Studies turns its attention extensively and seriously to the writing of the contemporary period itself. We need to know what is being read all around us, especially outside the academy; we need to know *how to read* all kinds of modern texts with the sophistication and penetration we lavish on past writing; we need to know how such texts function – both in shaping our lives at the personal level and in the texts' wider social relations. In other words, Literary Studies should take on a *reviewing* role in terms of contemporary written production – not, of course, 'reviewing' in the mass-media sense of puffing this and rubbishing that – but in attempting to give a serious account of 'the literary' in present society. Here, one might have a genuine cultural history in its literary inflexion: a sociology of readerships; the publishing industry; state patronage; literary prizes; school syllabuses; media coverage; the Poet Laureateship; literary magazines; the criticism industry in higher education; 'bestsellers'; 'serious' fiction; 'alternative' theatre; amateur dramatics; radio, film and TV drama, adaptations and documentaries; minority presses and community publishers; current debates in literary theory (text for study: *Literature and Criticism*). I wouldn't mind betting that anyone who had studied something of all this for the period, say, 1968–88 would know as much about 'the literary', let alone anything else, as someone who had 'read English' from *c.* 1550. We shall see . . .

FURTHER READING

Baldick, Chris (1983) *The Social Mission of English Criticism, 1848–1932*, Clarendon Press, Oxford

Batsleer, Janet, Davies, Tony, O'Rourke, Rebecca and Weedon, Chris (1985) *Rewriting English*, Methuen, London

Brooker, Peter (1987) 'Why Brecht, or, Is There English After Cultural Studies?' In Michael Green and Richard Hoggart (eds), *English and Cultural Studies: Broadening the Context (Essays and Studies, 1987)*, The English Association, John Murray, London, pp. 20–31

Culler, Jonathan (1975) *Structuralist Poetics: Structuralism, Linguistics, and the Study of Literature*, Routledge & Kegan Paul, London

Daniels, John (ed.) (1988) *English in the Public Sector: The Current Debate* (A pamphlet for the Standing Conference on English in Public Sector Higher Education. Copies obtainable from Dr D. R. Lamont, Lancashire Polytechnic, Preston.)

Doyle, Brian (1982) 'The Hidden History of English studies'. In Peter Widdowson (ed.), *Re-Reading English*, Methuen, London, pp. 17–31

——(1986a) 'The Invention of English'. In Robert Colls and Philip Dodd (eds), *Englishness: Politics and Culture 1880–1920*, Croom Helm, London, pp. 89–115

——(1986b) 'English and Englishness: A Cultural History of English Studies in British Higher Education', PhD thesis, CNAA/Thames Polytechnic, London

Eagleton, Terry (1981) *Walter Benjamin, or Towards a Revolutionary Criticism*, Verso, London

——(1983) *Literary Theory: An Introduction*, Basil Blackwell, Oxford

——(1984) *The Function of Criticism: From 'The Spectator' to Post-Structuralism*, New Left Books, London

Edwards, Dee, Maund, David and Maynard, John (1987) 'Different Starting-Points: A View of Teaching "English Etc" from Further Education'. In Michael Green and Richard Hoggart (eds), *English and Cultural Studies: Broadening the Context (Essays and Studies, 1987)*, The English Association, John Murray, London, pp. 75–90

Green, Michael and Hoggart, Richard (eds) (1987) *English and Cultural Studies: Broadening the Context (Essays and Studies, 1987)*, The English Association, John Murray, London

Literature and History (1987) 'Education Issue', vol. 13, no. 1, Thames Polytechnic, London

Literature Teaching Politics (1987) 'Changing the Subject', no. 6, LTP, Bristol

Shelston, Alan (ed.) (1971) *Thomas Carlyle: Selected Writings*, Penguin, Harmondsworth

Widdowson, Peter (1989) *Hardy in History: A Study in Sociology*, Routledge, London

THE CONTRIBUTORS

J. H. Alexander, University of Aberdeen
Isobel Armstrong, Birkbeck College, London
Dominic Baker-Smith, University of Amsterdam
Bernard W. Bell, University of Massachusetts
Catherine Belsey, University of Wales, Cardiff
Nicola Bradbury, University of Reading
David Bradby, Royal Holloway and Bedford New College, London
Derek Brewer, Emmanuel College, Cambridge
Joseph Bristow, Sheffield City Polytechnic
David Brooks, Australian National University, Canberra
David Buchan, Memorial University of Newfoundland
Charles Chadwick, University of Aberdeen
Shirley Chew, University of Leeds
Ying-hsiung Chou, The Chinese University of Hong Kong
Robert Clark, University of East Anglia
Steven Connor, Birkbeck College, London
Peter Conradi, Kingston Polytechnic
David Cressy, California State University, Long Beach
Alistair M. Duckworth, University of Florida
John Dwyer, York University, Ontario
Rod Edmond, University of Leeds
Simon Eliot, Open University
Elizabeth Deeds Ermath, University of Maryland
John Feather, University of Loughborough
Alastair Fowler, University of Edinburgh
Roger Fowler, University of East Anglia
John Frow, University of Queensland
Thomas Gardner, Virginia Polytechnic Institute and State University
Douglas Gray, Lady Margaret Hall, Oxford
Andrew Gurr, University of Reading
John Hartley, University of Western Australia
Terence Hawkes, University of Wales, Cardiff
N. Katherine Hayles, University of Iowa

Thomas Healy, Birkbeck College, London
F. W. J. Hemmings, University of Leicester
Derek Hughes, University of Warwick
Lyn Innes, University of Kent
Louis James, University of Kent
Cora Kaplan, Rutgers University
Helene Keyssar, University of California, San Diego
Bruce King, Ball State University, Indiana
Jon Klancher, Boston University
David Lindley, University of Leeds
John Lucas, University of Loughborough
Jan McDonald, University of Glasgow
Lionel Madden, National Library of Wales, Aberystwyth
Nigel Mapp, University of Wales, Cardiff
Michael Meehan, Flinders University of South Australia
Jan Montefiore, University of Kent
Kenneth Muir, University of Liverpool
Melvyn New, University of Florida
W. H. New, University of British Columbia
David Nokes, King's College, London
Christopher Norris, University of Wales, Cardiff
Michael O'Connell, University of California, Santa Barbara
John Orr, University of Edinburgh
George Parfitt, University of Nottingham
Annabel Patterson, Duke University, North Carolina
Stephen Prickett, University of Glasgow
David Punter, University of Stirling
Robert B. Ray, University of Florida
Leslie du S. Read, University of Exeter
Donald H. Reiman, New York Public Library
David Richards, University of Leeds
Isabel Rivers, St Hugh's College, Oxford
Rick Rylance, Anglia Higher Education College
A. J. Sambrook, University of Southampton
Claude Schumacher, University of Glasgow
Daniel R. Schwarz, Cornell University
Harry E. Shaw, Cornell University
Mick Short, Lancaster University
Chen Sihe, Fudan University
Alan Sinfield, University of Sussex
Robert D. Spector, Long Island University
Jane Spencer, University of Exeter

C. K. Stead, University of Auckland
John Stokes, University of Warwick
Geoffrey Strickland, University of Reading
John Sutherland, California Institute of Technology
Peter Thomson, University of Exeter
Helen Tiffin, University of Queensland
William Tydeman, University College of North Wales, Bangor
Don E. Wayne, University of California, San Diego
Peter Widdowson, Middlesex Polytechnic
John Williams, Thames Polytechnic
Elizabeth Wright, Girton College, Cambridge

INDEX

(An asterisk indicates the listing of a work under Further Reading.)

folk 831, 976–88
national 5–6, 9, 1223
periodical 883
popular/low 581, 727, 821–2, 856, 987
'literature', concept of 3–24, 697–8, 701, 810, 976, 1233
literature and science 1068–80
literature of censorship 903
Little Dorrit see Dickens, Charles
Little Red Hen see McGrath, John
Littlewood, Joan 480
Liu, Alan 793, 801, 803*
Liverpool repertory theatre 447–8, 476
Liverpool University 891
Lives of the English Poets see Johnson, Samuel
Livingstone, Carole Rose 822
Llewelyn, John 789*
Llosa, Mario Vargas 903, 912
Lloyd, Robert 1021
Lloyd-Jones, Hugh 964, 965
Lloyd Jones, L. 873
Loach, Ken 1104
local ballads 981
local poem 255, 262, 601
Locke, John 613, 1015
Lodge, David 24*, 271, 601*, 641*, 748*
Logan, John 1037
Loggins, Vernon 1147
logocentrism 47, 389, 520, 780
London, William 915
London Journal 512
London Library 893
London Magazine 876, 886, 915
London Review of Books 821
London University 891
    chairs of English 928, 930
Long, D.S. 1196
Long Revolution, The see Williams, Raymond
Longchamp, Nigel: Mirror of Fools (Speculum Stultorum) 232
Longfellow, Henry Wadsworth 203
Longman publishing company 862
Lonsdale, Roger: The New Oxford Book of Eighteenth Century Verse 103, 104*, 208–9, 210, 215, 262, 263*
Look Back in Anger see Osborne, John
Loomis, Abigail A. 924*
Loomis, R.S. 237*, 976
Lord, Albert 986
Lord Jim see Conrad, Joseph
Lord of the Flies see Golding, William
Lorenzetti, Ambrogio: Good and Bad Government 995
'Lotos-Eaters, The' see Tennyson, Alfred, Lord
Lounger, The 1030, 1031, 1036, 1041
love 236, 624
    courtly 229, 286, 431

romantic 229, 417, 522
Love, Harold 425, 435*
Love, Nicholas 995–6
Love for Love see Congreve, William
'Love Song of J. Alfred Prufrock, The' see Eliot, T.S.
Lovejoy, Arthur O. 941–2, 949*
Lovelace, Earl 1208*
    The Wine of Astonishment 1202
Lovell, Terry 521, 529*
Love's Last Shift see Cibber, Colley
Low, Anthony 153, 248
Low, Donald 112
Lowry, Malcolm: Under the Volcano 626–7
Lowth, Robert: Sacred Poetry of the Hebrews 658–60, 957
Lu Xun 1211, 1212, 1213
    'Kuangren riji' ('A Madman's Diary') 1212
Lubbock, Percy 312, 573
    The Craft of Fiction 603–5
Lucas, F.L. 367, 374*, 930
Lucas, John 308–19, 320*
Lucian 997
Luckham, Claire 483
Lucky Jim see Amis, Kingsley
Lucretius: De Rerum Natura 1075, 1076
Lukács, Georg 128, 129*, 542*, 561, 607, 711–13
    historical novel 532–7, 538
    The Historical Novel 532, 533, 545
    History and Class Consciousness 585, 711
    Soul and Form 711
'Lune blanche, La' see Verlaine, Paul
Lusiadas, Os see Camöens, Luis de
Lüthi, Max 976, 979
Lyell, Charles 552
Lynch, Kathleen M. 852
Lyotard, Jean-François: The Postmodern Condition 145*, 649*, 798–9, 801
lyric 86, 152, 188–97, 200, 232, 258
lyric verse, and music 189, 191, 1009, 1010, 1011
Lyrical Ballads see Coleridge, Samuel Taylor & Wordsworth, William
Lytle, G. 91*

MacBeth, George 328–9
    The Cleaver Garden 323
MacCabe, Colin 11
MacCarthy, Desmond 441, 449*
MacColl, Ewan 487*
MacDermot, Thomas Henry (Tom Redcam) 1201, 1205
MacFlecknoe see Dryden, John
MacGonagall, William 202
Macgowan, Kenneth 354
Macherey, Pierre 46, 48–9, 50, 56, 716, 717
    A Theory of Literary Production 819